Garage Sale & Flea Market

ANNUAL

ELEVENTH EDITION
CASHING IN ON TODAY'S LUCRATIVE COLLECTIBLES MARKET

COLLECTOR BOOKS

A Division of Schroeder Publishing Co., Inc.

CURRENT VALUES ON: **TODAY'S COLLECTIBLES**
TOMORROW'S ANTIQUES

Front cover:
Mary Poppins head vase, Enesco, 1950s, $450.00.
Little Black Sambo salt & pepper, Ceramic Arts Studio, 1950s, $495.00 – 525.00.
Horse Brooch, Trifari, white enamel, $60.00 – 80.00.
Picanette perfume bottle, Karoff/Stuart Prod., glass and fabric, $85.00.
Roy Rogers lunch box and thermos, metal, $175.00.
Green juicer, Ade-O-Matic, porcelain, $150.00.
Panther planter, gold ceramic, $35.00 – 45.00.

Cover design by Beth Summers
Book design by Karen Smith and Beth Ray

COLLECTOR BOOKS
P.O. Box 3009
Paducah, Kentucky 42002-3009
www.collectorbooks.com

Copyright © 2003 Schroeder Publishing Co.

The current values in this book should be used only as a guide. They are not
intended to set prices, which vary from one section of the country to another.
Auction prices as well as dealer prices vary greatly and are affected by condition
as well as demand. Neither the editors nor the publisher assumes responsibility
for any losses that might be incurred as a result of consulting this guide.

Searching For A Publisher?

We are always looking for people knowledgeable within their fields. If you
feel that there is a real need for a book on your collectible subject and have a
large comprehensive collection, contact Collector Books.

A Word From the Editor

When you think about it, it's life's simple pleasures that are the most enduring. Regardless of what goes on around us, no matter what comes our way, we can still watch the sun rise every morning, hear the music of the first-awake songbird, whiff the fragrance of a rose or a fresh-baked apple pie, or marvel at the sweetness of a new-born baby. These things are unchangeable. If the year since 9/11 has been full of Enron scandal, terrorist warnings, stock market casualties, and economic downturns, it has also prompted us to grab onto basics — to be as we should always be, even when we prosper materialistically and fear and emotional complications don't exist: thanking God for small favors and everyday blessings!

Yes, our country has been through some very tough times, and many major hurdles lie ahead. But in the field of antiques and collectibles, at least, things are at last looking up! Many collectors who lost money in the stock market are getting back into their hobbies. Now their feelings seem to be: 'I can do just as well with something I know about.' They buy for pleasure and investment. I think all will agree, it is a buyer's market. Many things have slipped in value, but this has only allowed the less affluent, usually younger generation to become interested in collecting, and obviously, new collectors are necessary to sustain the viability of the antiques and collectibles hobby. Rare and hard-to-find items have shown a steady increase in value. Even though they sometimes appear online with a bit more frequency than they ever did at shows or in the malls, the ratio of supply to demand has widened, since now they are being viewed by many more collectors who are financially able to pay top dollar for the privilege of ownership.

Even as highly advanced as today's technology is, changes continue. A year or so back, it seemed that the Internet might be the downfall of the industry. Prices realized on eBay were soft, and the percentage of items that didn't sell was up. Now it appears that dealers are learning to better cope. Fewer throw themselves on the mercy of online auctions and instead opt for the more secure environment of Internet malls, several of which have become very well established marketplaces. Right now, at least, this avenue of buying and selling is drawing more attention than flea markets or even the best shows. And though disenchanted participants are becoming more and more vocal on the subject, most agree it's a permanent fixture, like it or not.

If online selling has become 'top rung of the ladder' merchandising, then I suppose garage sales are the very bottom rung. That's OK. I love 'em. Like the simplest of life's pleasures, they're what they are — basic, no pretenses. It would probably be a staggeringly high figure, if we could determine what percentage of the collectibles being bought and sold today has been picked up at garage sales and ends up on eBay or some online mall. Finding the family budget strained, many people have been able to augment their income in this way; others have found more success in their Internet venture than they ever dreamed possible. But whether they're involved on a small scale or a much larger one, to a very great extent, their successes depend on what they know and how much of their time they're willing to devote to learn even more. Since garage-sale bargains come in many guises, being familiar with a wide range of antiques and collectibles is absolutely necessary.

No one can deny it, you learn as you go. Assuming you're interested in buying to sell, garage sale shopping calls for preparation. Say you've already read a book such as this one from cover to cover. Even if you buy strictly for yourself, you will have been introduced to a scope of collectibles you might not otherwise have noticed. Now you can spot items with resale potential, even if they hold no appeal for you personally. Once you get them home, the first thing you'll probably do is research them even more — whereby becoming even more familiar with the subject — and before long, you'll be a confident, knowledgeable shopper.

Some of my better garage sale finds were things I would never have looked at twice for myself, but I knew they held potential — the Indian vase that sold for $900.00 on eBay, the Griswold high dome skillet lid that made $265.00, the Wallace Rodeo dinnerware that totaled out at almost $1,000.00, or the Peek a Boo shakers I sold for $300.00. It pays to prepare. Most of the time, my 'finds' will sell in the $25.00 to $50.00 range, but considering I seldom pay more than $5.00 for anything, I feel that's a good return for my time and money. This year's finds include Van Tellingen's Mary and her lamb shakers, a Watt creamer in the Rooster pattern, an absolutely mint Fiesta egg cup, Shawnee's Muggsy salt and pepper shakers, a Hopalong Cassidy air rifle still in the box, two F&F Mammy syrup pitchers in mint condition, and a stack of Franciscan Desert Rose dinner plates. I found assorted dinnerware, teapots, Fire King, Kentucky Derby glasses, Marshall studio items, Budweiser steins, vintage purses, figurines, and jewelry — all items I know will sell. So we invite you to use this book as a tool to educate yourself toward becoming a wise garage sale shopper. Your investment of time and effort can be very rewarding.

Every year we include several new topics. If you're already into garage sale shopping, you know that competition is fierce. You'll have a definite advantage over the average shopper if you'll first take the time to become familiar with new areas of activity.

The key is knowledge. We'll suggest references for in-depth study, all written by today's leading experts. We're going to zero in on items from the 1940s on, since that's where the market's activity is strongest today. We'll list websites, clubs, tradepapers, and newsletters related to many specific areas; we recommend all of them very highly. There is much knowledge to be gleaned by networking through clubs with collectors whose interests are similar to yours.

An exclusive feature of this book is the section called Special Interests. It contains the addresses of authors, collectors, and dealers sorted by specific collectible categories. Not only are these people potential buyers, but under most circumstances, they'll be willing to help you with questions that remain after you've made an honest attempt at your own research. Just remember if you do write one of our people, you will have to include an SASE if you want a response. And if you call, please consider the differences in time zones. But first, please, read the text. Then go to your library; you should be able to find most of the books we reference. Check them out for study — they're all wonderful. Buy the ones you find particularly helpful or interesting; good books pay for themselves many times over.

If you'd like to collect some nice pieces to decorate your home, as more and more people are doing, or if you're interested in becoming a dealer but find there's no room in the budget for extra spending, we'll show you how to earn extra money by holding your own garage sale. And we'll give you some timely pointers on how to set up at your first flea market.

Remember that our prices in no way reflect what you will be paying at garage sales. Our values are well established and generally accepted by seasoned collectors and authorities; they have been checked over before publication by people well versed in their particular fields.

How to Hold Your Own Garage Sale

Just as we promised we would, here are our suggestions for holding your own garage sale. If you're toying with the idea of getting involved in the business of buying and selling antiques and collectibles but find yourself short of any extra cash to back your venture, this is the way we always recommend you get started. Everyone has items they no longer use; get rid of them! Use them to your advantage. Here's how.

Get Organized. Gather up your merchandise. Though there's not a lot of money in selling clothing, this is the perfect time to unload things you're not using. Kids' clothing does best, since it's usually outgrown before it's worn out, and there's a lot of budget-minded parents who realize this and think it makes good sense to invest as little as possible in their own children's wardrobes. Everything should of course be clean and relatively unwrinkled to sell at all, and try to get the better items on hangers.

Leave no stone unturned. Clean out the attic, the basement, the garage — then your parent's attic, basement, and garage. If you're really into it, bake cookies, make some crafts. Divide your house plants; pot the starts in attractive little containers — ladies love 'em. Discarded and outgrown toys sell well. Framed prints and silk flower arrangements you no longer use, recipe books and paperbacks, tapes, records, and that kitchen appliance that's more trouble to store than it's worth can be turned into cash to get you off and running!

After you've gathered up your merchandise, you'll need to price it. Realistically, clothing will bring at the most about 15% to 25% of what you had to pay for it, if it's still in excellent, ready-to-wear shape and basically still in style. There's tons of used clothing out there, and no one is going to buy much of anything with buttons missing or otherwise showing signs of wear. If you have good brand-name clothing that has been worn very little, you would probably do better by taking it to a resale or consignment shop. They normally price things at about one-third of retail, with their cut being 30% of that. Not much difference money-wise, but the garage-sale shopper that passes up that $150.00 suit you're asking $25.00 for will probably give $50.00 for it at the consignment shop, simply because like department stores, many have dressing rooms with mirrors so you can try things on and check them for fit before you buy. Even at $25.00, the suit is no bargain if it doesn't fit when you get it home.

Remember that garage-sale buyers expect to find low prices. Depending on how long you plan on staying open, you'll have one day, possibly two to move everything. If you start out too high, you'll probably be stuck with a lot of leftover merchandise, most of which you've already decided is worthless to you. The majority of your better buyers will hit early on; make prices attractive to them and you'll do all right. If you come up with some 'low-end' collectibles — fast-food toys, character glasses, played-with action figures, etc. — don't expect to get much out of them at a garage sale. Your competition down the block may underprice you. But if you have a few things you think have good resale potential, offer them at about half of 'book' price. If they don't sell at your garage sale, take them to a flea market or a consignment shop. You'll probably find they sell better on that level, since people expect to find prices higher there than at garage sales.

You can use pressure-sensitive labels or masking tape for price tags on many items. But *please* do not use either of these on things where damage is likely to occur when they are removed. For instance (as one reader pointed out), on boxes containing toys, board games, puzzles, etc.; on record labels or album covers; or on ceramics or glass with gold trim or unfired, painted decoration. Unless a friend or a neighbor is going in on the sale with you, price tags won't have to be removed; the profit will all be yours. Of course, you'll have to keep tabs if others are involved. You can use a sheet of paper divided into columns, one for each of you, and write the amount of each sale down under the appropriate person's name, or remove the tags and restick them on a piece of poster board, one for each seller. I've even seen people use straight pins to attach small paper price tags which they remove and separate into plastic butter tubs. When several go together to have a sale, the extra help is nice, but don't let things get out of hand. Your sale can get *too* big. Things become too congested, and it's hard to display so much merchandise to good advantage.

Advertise. Place your ad in your local paper or on your town's cable TV information channel. It's important to make your ad interesting and upbeat. Though most sales usually start early on Friday or Saturday mornings, some people are now holding their sales in the early evening, and they seem to be having good crowds. This gives people with day jobs an opportunity to attend. You *might* want to hold your sale for two days, but you'll do 90% of your selling during the first two or three hours, and a two-day sale

can really drag on. Make signs — smaller ones for street corners near your home to help direct passers-by, and a large one for your yard. You might even want to make another saying 'Clothing ½-Price after 12:00.' (It'll cut way down on leftovers that you'll otherwise have to dispose of yourself.) Be sure that you use a wide-tipped felt marker and print in letters big enough that the signs can be read from the street. Put the smaller signs up a few days in advance unless you're expecting rain. (If you are, you might want to include a rain date in your advertising unless your sale will be held under roof.) Make sure you have a lot of boxes and bags and plenty of change. If you price your items in increments of 25¢, you won't need anything but a few rolls of quarters, maybe ten or fifteen ones, and a few five-dollar bills. Then on the day of the sale, put the large sign up in a prominent place out front with some balloons to attract the crowd. Take a deep breath, brace yourself, and raise the garage door!

What to Do With What's Left. After the sale, pack up any good collectibles that didn't sell. Think about that consignment shop or setting up at a flea market. (We'll talk about that later on.) Sort out the better items of clothing for Goodwill or a similar charity, unless your city has someone who will take your leftovers and sell them on consignment. This is a fairly new concept, but some of the larger cities have such 'bargain centers.'

Learning to Become a Successful Bargain Hunter

Let me assure you, anyone who takes the time to become an informed, experienced bargain hunter will be successful. There is enough good merchandise out there to make it worthwhile, at all levels. Once you learn what to look for, what has good resale potential, and what price these items will probably bring for you, you'll be equipped and ready for any hunting trip. You'll be the one to find treasures. They are out there!

Garage sales are absolutely wonderful for finding bargains. But you'll have to get up early! Even non-collectors can spot quality merchandise, and at those low garage sale prices (low unless of course held by an owner who's done his homework) those items will be the first to move.

In order for you to be a successful garage sale shopper, you have to learn how to get yourself organized. It's important to conserve your time. The sales you hit during the first early-morning hour will prove to be the best nine times out of ten, so you must have a plan before you ever leave home. Plot your course. Your local paper will have a section on garage sale ads, and local cable TV channels may also carry

garage sale advertising. Most people hold their sales on the weekend, but some may start earlier in the week, so be sure to turn to the 'Garage Sales' ads daily. Write them down and try to organize them by areas — northwest, northeast, etc. At first, you'll probably need your city map, but you'll be surprised at how quickly the streets will become familiar to you. Upper middle-class neighborhoods generally have the best sales and the best merchandise, so concentrate on those areas, though sales in older areas may offer older items. (Here's where you have to interpret those sale ads.) When you've decided where you want to start, go early! If the ad says 8:00, be there at 7:00. This may seem rude and pushy, but if you can bring yourself to do it, it will pay off. And chances are when you get there an hour early, you'll not be their first customer. If they're obviously not ready for business, just politely inquire if you may look. If you're charming and their nerves aren't completely frayed from trying to get things ready, chances are they won't mind.

Competition can be fierce during those important early-morning hours. Learn to scan the tables quickly, then move to the area that looks the most promising. Don't be afraid to ask for a better price if you feel it's too high, but most people have already priced garage sale merchandise so that it will sell. Keep a notebook to jot down items you didn't buy the first time around but think you might be interested in if the price were reduced later on. After going through dozens of sales (I've done as many as thirty or so in one morning), you won't remember where you saw what! Often by noon, at least by mid-afternoon, veteran garage sale buyers are finished with their rounds and attendance becomes very thin. Owners are usually much more receptive to the idea of lowering their prices, so it may pay you to make a second pass. In fact, some people find it advantageous to go to the better sales on the last day as well as the first. They'll make an offer for everything that's left, and since most of the time the owner is about ready to *pay* someone to take it at that point, they can usually name their price. Although most of the collectibles will normally be gone at this point, there are nearly always some useable household items and several pieces of good, serviceable clothing left. The household items will sell at flea markets or consignment shops, and if there are worthwhile clothing items, take them to a resale boutique. They'll either charge the 30% commission fee or buy the items outright for about half of the amount they feel they can ask, a new practice some resale shops are beginning to follow. Because they want only clothing that is in style, in season, and like new, their prices may be a little higher than others shops, so half of that asking price is a good deal.

Tag sales are common in the larger cities. They are normally held in lieu of an auction, when estates are being dispersed, or when families are moving. Sometimes only a few buyers are admitted at one time, and as one leaves another is allowed to take his place. So just as is true with garage sales, the early bird gets the goodies. Really serious shoppers begin to arrive as much as an hour or two before the scheduled opening time. I know of one who will spend the night in his van and camp on the 'doorstep' if he thinks the sale is especially promising. And he can tell you fantastic success stories! But since it's customary to have tag sale items appraised before values are set, be prepared to pay higher prices. That's not to say, though, that you won't find bargains here. If you think an item is overpriced, leave a bid. Just don't forget to follow through on it, since if it doesn't sell at their asking price, they may end up holding it for you. It's a good idea to check back on the last day of the sale. Often the prices on unsold items may have been drastically reduced.

Auctions can go either way. Depending on the crowd and what items are for sale, you can sometimes spend all day and never be able to buy anything any-

where near 'book' price. Better items often go high. On the other hand, there are often 'sleepers' that can be bought cheaply enough to resell at a good profit. Toys, dolls, Hummels, Royal Doultons, banks, cut glass, and other 'high-profile' collectibles usually sell well, but white ironstone, dinnerware sets from the '20s through the '50s, silver-plated hollow ware, books, records, and linens, for instance, often pass relatively unnoticed by the majority of the buyers.

If there is a consignment auction house in your area, check it out. These are usually operated by local auctioneers, and the sales they hold in-house often involve low-income estates. You won't find something every time, so try to investigate the merchandise ahead of schedule to see if it's going to be worth your time to attend. Competition is probably less at one of these than in any of the other types of sales we've mentioned, and wonderful buys have been made from time to time.

Flea markets are often wonderful places to find bargains. I don't like the small ones — not that I don't find anything there, but I've learned to move through them so fast (to get ahead of the crowd), I don't get my 'fix'; I just leave wanting more. If you've never been to a large flea market, you don't know what you're missing. Even if you're not a born-again collector, I guarantee you will love it. And they're excellent places to study the market. You'll be able to see where the buying activity is; you can check and compare prices, talk with dealers and collectors, and do hands-on inspections. I've found that if I first study a particular subject by reading a book or a magazine article, this type of exposure to that collectible really 'locks in' what I have learned.

Because there are many types of flea market dealers, there are plenty of bargains. The casual, once-in-a-while dealer may not always keep up with changing market values. Some of them simply price their items by what they themselves had to pay for it. Just as being early at garage sales is important, here it's a must. If you've ever been in line waiting for a flea market to open, you know that cars are often backed up for several blocks, and people will be standing in line waiting to be admitted hours before the gate opens. Browsers? Window shoppers? Not likely. Competition! So if you're going to have a chance at all, you'd better be in line yourself. Take a partner and split up on the first pass so that you can cover the grounds more quickly. It's a common sight to see the serious buyers conversing with their partners via walkie-talkies, and if you like to discuss possible purchases with each other before you actually buy, this is a good way to do it.

Learn to bargain with dealers. Their prices are usually negotiable, and most will come down by 10% to 20%. Be polite and fair, and you can expect the same treatment in return. Unpriced items are harder to deal for. I have no problem offering to give $8.00 if an item is marked $10.00, but it's difficult for me to have to ask the price and then make a counter offer. So I'll just say 'This isn't marked. Will you take...?' I'm not an aggressive barterer, so this works for me.

There are so many reproductions on the flea market level (and at malls and co-ops), that you need to be suspicious of anything that looks too new! Some fields of collecting have been especially hard hit. Whenever a collectible becomes so much in demand that prices are high, reproductions are bound to make an appearance. For instance, Black Americana, Nippon, Roseville, banks, toys of all types, teddy bears, lamps, glassware, doorstops, cookie jars, prints, advertising items, and many other fields have been especially vulnerable. Learn to check for telltale signs — paint that is too bright, joints that don't fit, variations in sizes or colors, creases in paper that you can see but not feel, and so on. Remember that zip codes have been used only since 1963, and this can sometimes help you date an item in question. Check glassware for areas of wavy irregularities often seen in new glass. A publication we would highly recommend to you is called *Antique and Collector Reproduction News*, a monthly report of 'Fakes, Frauds, and Facts.' To subscribe, call 1-800-227-5531. You can find them on the web at repronews.com. Rates are very reasonable compared to the money you may save by learning to recognize reproductions.

Antique malls and co-ops should be visited on a regular basis. Many mall dealers restock day after day, and traffic and buying competition is usually fierce. As a rule, you won't often find great bargains here; what you do save on is time. And if time is what you're short of, you'll be able to see a lot of good merchandise under one roof, on display by people who've already done the leg work and invested *their* time, hence the higher prices. But there are always underpriced items as well, and if you've taken the time to do your homework, you'll be able to spot them right away.

Unless the dealer who rents the booth happens to be there, though, mall and co-op prices are usually firm. But often times they'll run sales — '20% off everything in booth #101.' If you have a dealer's license, and you really should get one, most will give you a courtesy 10% discount on items over $10.00, unless you want to pay with a credit card.

Antique shows are exciting to visit, but obviously if a dealer is paying several hundred dollars to set up for a three-day show, he's going to be asking top price to offset expenses. So even though bargains will be few, the merchandise is usually superior, and you may be able to find that special item you've been looking for.

Mail order buying is not only very easy, but most of the time economical as well. Many people will place an ad in 'For Sale' sections of tradepapers. Some will describe and price their merchandise in their ad, while others offer lists of items they have in exchange for an SASE (stamped, self-addressed envelope). You're out no gas or food expenses, their overhead is minimal so their prices are usually very reasonable, so it works out great for both buyer and seller. I've made a lot of good buys this way, and I've always been fairly and honestly dealt with. You may want to send a money order or cashier's check to save time, otherwise (especially on transactions involving larger sums of money) the seller might want to wait until your personal check clears.

Goodwill stores and re-sale shops are usually listed in the telephone book. When you travel, it will pay you to check them out. If there's one in your area, visit it often. You never know what may turn up there.

Internet shopping is still at the hub of most of the buying/selling activity today. Set-price online malls are expanding as many dealers find that auction prices are very often too soft to accept, and scores of long-time antiques and collectibles dealers now have wonderful websites. Buyers often voice the opinion that they are more confident when trading with these well-established sellers than they are some of the part-time vendors more often encountered on eBay and similar sites. Still, there is no doubt that there are many bargains to be had on eBay, and it will continue to be a big factor in the marketplace. But where you could basically sell anything via eBay a couple of years ago, now to attract a buyer, you may very often have to relist your item with a lower reserve, and you'll find some things won't sell at all.

What's Hot on Today's Market

In many areas, today's market is slow. I'm curious to see what the next several months will bring. Hopefully we'll see a turnaround in the economy and, as a result, a stronger antiques and collectibles market.

Most affected in the toy market are action figures, He Man, Beanie Babies, and Star Wars; our advisors tell us there is very little activity there. Soft but moving slowly are Pez containers, lunch boxes, board games, and Fisher-Price toys. The toys that are hot include Care Bears (make sure they're the originals), Strawberry Shortcake toys and dolls, Transformers (the originals), Hot Wheels redlines, 3¾" G.I. Joe figures, Matchbox cars, Rainbow Brite, and anything Smurf! Vintage toy soldiers have had a resurgence in popularity; good wind-up and battery-op toys are always going to sell well; and robots from the '50s and '60s bring astronomical prices at auction. Cap guns and holsters are hot, especially those that are representative of the old western heroes. Many cast-iron vehicles crossed the auction block as well this year, some bringing record book prices. Vintage Barbie dolls are still extremely popular, though the more recent versions have fallen out of favor to some extent. Pre-Barbie (1950s dolls, i.e. Miss Revlon) are doing well.

There is a considerable amount of interest in mid-century collectibles — funky molded plywood chairs, starburst wall clocks, and table lamps with stepped fiberglass shades can bring hundreds of dollars, especially when made by notable '50s designers such as Eames, Nelson, Wormely, and Robsjohn-Gibbings. Italian glassware from this period as well as ceramic sculptures and vases are sought out to enhance the vintage '50s collection.

Printed fabrics from the '40s and '50s interest the younger crowd who appreciate their wonderful graphics and range of color. Pillows, runners, tablecloths, and draperies can sometimes be found still in amazingly useable condition. Vintage aprons are hot right now, so in this edition we've included information and listings to help you get the feel for which types to watch for and basically what values the market will bear.

Dinnerware sells well — sometimes to replace missing pieces from a vintage service. Franciscan Starburst as well as similar 'designer' lines from other makers are hot, especially 1950s vintage. Blue Ridge remains very popular, while Fiesta, we're sorry to report, is down for now, though rare pieces do well. Pyrex dishes and Depression glass continue to sell very well, we're told. They're still in good supply, so prices have remained moderate over the years (except for the rare items), making them easily affordable among the newer, perhaps less-affluent collectors.

Barring catastrophic events, quality American-made pottery will never loose its place in the market.

Good examples made by Roseville, Rookwood, Weller, and Hull always find a willing buyer. Though down from their high of a few years ago, the wares of California potteries/studios such as Brad Keeler, Kay Finch, Brayton Laguna, Will-George, Florence Ceramics, Sascha Brastoff, Matthew Adams, and Howard Pierce continue strong. If you find items marked Royal Haeger (especially if they have a good glaze or interesting modeling — florist vases and pots are another matter), you'll want to pick them up. The same is true for pieces by Red Wing, Shawnee, McCoy, and Abingdon. Even run-of-the-mill pottery by any we've mentioned may be worth picking up at garage sale prices.

Lefton and Holt Howard seem to have recovered some of their popularity after a cooling-off period and are again doing well. Kreiss, sadly for those collectors who paid dearly, has plummeted, though at its peak, prices were extremely inflated. Salt and pepper shakers remain good sellers, especially advertising, Black Americana, souvenirs, and character-related examples. Those made by companies that include Rosemead, Ceramic Arts Studios, Shawnee, and the miniatures produced by Arcadia often go for $50.00 and up. Good head vases, string holders, reamers, wall pockets, and clothes sprinkler bottles hold their values, while the more common examples in each field have fallen off.

Other areas where you'll see considerable interest right now include old photos; Christmas items; real photo and linen postcards; LP records with great or interesting covers, including jazz; paintings and prints; fountain pens; Zippo lighters; men's watches; fishing lures, poles, etc.; political campaign buttons from the 1940s; Halloween collectibles; vintage musical instruments; patriotic and homefront collectibles, especially sweetheart jewelry; vintage children's books, especially Little Golden Books; 8mm boxed films with great graphics on the boxes, especially horror films; and Singer featherweight sewing machines.

For right now, at least, these areas are sluggish: Norman Rockwell items, Jim Beam bottles, Avon bottles, collector plates, unsigned rhinestone jewelry, and typewriters. There are always exceptions, however. In every field, there are rarities that are always desirable, and we all need to be aware of them, if we're going to take full advantage of all the opportunities garage sale and flea market shopping have to offer. Remember, the most important factor to consider when buying any of these items for resale is condition. If they show more than just a little wear or are damaged more than a minimal amount, don't waste you're time on them at any price. Today's collectors are more discerning than ever, thanks again to the Internet and the preponderance of supply over demand. Condition is all-important.

How to Evaluate Your Holdings

When viewed in its entirety, granted, the antiques and collectibles market can be overwhelming. But in each line of glassware, any type of pottery or toy, or any other field I could mention, there are examples that are more desirable than others, and these are the ones you need to be able to recognize. If you're a novice, it will probably be best at first to choose a few areas that you find most interesting and learn just what particular examples or types of items are most in demand within that field. Concentrate on the top 25%. This is where you'll do 75% of your business. Do your homework. Quality sells. Obviously no one can be an expert in everything, but gradually you can begin to broaden your knowledge. As an added feature of our guide, information on clubs and newsletters, always a wonderful source of up-to-date information on any subject, is contained in each category when available. (Advisor's names are listed as well. We highly recommend that you exhaust all other resources before you contact them with your inquiries. Their roll is simply to check over our data before we go to press to make sure it is as accurate as we and they can possibly make it for you; they do not agree to answer reader's questions, though some may. If you do write, you must send them an SASE. If you call, please take the time zones into consideration. Some of our advisors are professionals and may charge an appraisal fee, so be sure to ask. Please, do *not* be offended if they do not respond to your contacts, they are under no obligation to do so.)

There are many fields other than those we've already mentioned that are strong and have been for a long time. It's impossible to list them all. But we've left very little out of this book; at least we've tried to represent each category to some extent and where at all possible to refer you to a source of further information. It's up to you to read, observe the market, and become acquainted with it to the point that you feel confident enough to become a part of today's antiques and collectibles industry.

The thousands of current values found in this book will increase your awareness of today's wonderful world of buying, selling, and collecting antiques and collectibles. Use it to educate yourself to the point that you'll be the one with the foresight to know what and how to buy as well as where and how to turn those sleepers into cold, hard cash.

In addition to this one, there are several other very fine price guides on the market. One of the best is *Schroeder's Antiques Price Guide*; another is *The Flea Market Trader*. Both are published by Collector Books. *The Antique Trader Antiques and Collectibles Price Guide*, *Warman's Antiques and Their Prices*, and *Kovel's Antiques and Collectibles Price List* are others. You may want to invest in a copy of each. Where you decide to sell will have a direct bearing on how you price your merchandise, and nothing will affect an item's worth more than condition.

If you're not familiar with using a price guide, here's a few tips that may help you. When convenient and reasonable, antiques will be sorted by manufacturer. This is especially true of pottery and most glassware. If you don't find the item you're looking for under manufacturer, look under a broader heading, for instance, cat collectibles, napkin dolls, cookie jars, etc. And don't forget to use the index. Most guides of this type have very comprehensive indexes — a real boon to the novice collector. If you don't find the exact item you're trying to price, look for something similar. For instance, if it's a McCoy rabbit planter you're researching, go through the McCoy section and see what price range other animal planters are in. (There are exceptions, however, and if an item is especially rare and desirable, this will not apply. Here's where you need a comprehensive McCoy book.) Or if you have a frame-tray puzzle with Snow White and the Seven Dwarfs, see what other Disney frame-trays are priced at. Just be careful not to compare apples to oranges. Dates are important as well. You can judge the value of a 7" Roseville Magnolia vase that's not listed in any of your guides; just look at the price given for one a little larger or smaller and adjust it up or down. Pricing collectibles is certainly not a science; the bottom line is simply where the buyer and the seller finally agree to do business. Circumstances dictate sale price, and we can only make suggestions, which we base on current sales, market observations, and the expert opinions of our advisors.

Once you've found 'book' price, decide how much less you can take for it. 'Book' price represents a high average retail. A collectible will often change hands many times, and obviously it will not always be sold at book price. How quickly do you want to realize a profit? Will you be patient enough to hold out for top dollar, or would you rather price your merchandise lower so it will turn over more quickly? Just as there are both types of dealers, there are two types of collectors. Many are bargain hunters. They shop around — do the legwork themselves. On the other hand, there are those who are willing to pay whatever the asking price is to avoid spending precious time searching out pieces they especially want, but they represent the minority. You'll often see tradepaper ads listing good merchandise (from that top 25% we mentioned before) at prices well above book value. This is a good example of a dealer who knows that his merchandise is good enough to entice the buyer who is able to pay a little more and doesn't mind waiting for him (or her) to come along, and that's his prerogative.

Don't neglect to access the condition of the item you want to sell. This is especially important in online and mail order selling. Most people, especially inexperienced buyers and sellers, have a tendency to overlook some flaws and to overrate merchandise. Mint condition means that an item is complete and undamaged — in effect, just as it looked the day it was made. Glassware, china, and pottery may often be found today in wonderful mint condition. Check for signs of wear, though, since even wear will downgrade value. (Looking 'good considering its age' is like coming close in horseshoes — it doesn't really count!) Remember that when a buyer doesn't have the option of seeing for himself, your written description is all he has to go by. Save yourself the hassle of costly and time-consuming returns by making sure the condition of your merchandise is accurately and completely described. Unless a toy is still in its original box and has never been played with, you seldom see one in mint condition. Paper collectibles are almost never found without some deterioration or damage. Most price guides will list values that apply to glass and ceramics that are mint (unless another condition is specifically indicated within some descriptions). Other items are usually evaluated on the assumption that they are in the best as-found condition common to that area of collecting, for instance magazines are simply never found in mint condition. Grade your merchandise as though you were the buyer, not the seller. You'll be building a reputation that will go a long way toward contributing to your success. If it's glassware or pottery you're assessing, an item in less than excellent condition will be mighty hard to sell at any price. Just as a guideline (a basis to begin your evaluation, though other things will factor in), use a scale of one to five with good being a one, excellent being a three, and mint being a five. As an example, a beer tray worth $250.00 in mint condition would then be worth $150.00 if excellent and $50.00 if only good. Remember, the first rule of buying (for resale or investment) is 'Don't put your money in damaged goods.' And the second rule should be be, 'If you do sell damaged items, indicate 'as is' on the price tag, and don't price the item as though it were mint.' The Golden Rule applies just as well to us as antique dealers as it does to any other interaction. Some shops and co-ops have poor lighting, and damage can be easily missed by a perspective buyer — your honesty will be greatly appreciated. If you include identification on your tags as well, be sure it's accurate. If you're not positive, say so. Better yet, let the buyer decide.

Deciding Where to Best Sell Your Merchandise

Personal transactions are just one of many options. Overhead and expenses will vary with each and must be factored into your final pricing. If you have some especially nice items and can contact a collector willing to pay top dollar, that's obviously the best of the lot. Or you may decide to sell to a dealer who may be willing to pay you only half of book. Either way, your expenses won't amount to much more than a little gas or a phone call.

Internet auctions may be your preferred venue. Look at completed auctions for sales results of similar items to decide. Factor in the cost of photography (sales of items with no photograph suffer), image hosting, and listing fees. Remember that the cost of boxes and bubble wrap must also be considered, not to mention the time spent actually listing the item, answering e-mail questions, contacting the buyer with the winning bid, leaving feedback, etc.

Internet selling works. In fact, I know some dealers who have quit doing shows and simply work out of their home. No more unpacking, travel expenses, or inconvenience of any kind to endure. You may sell through a set-price online mall or an auction. If you choose the auction (eBay is the most widely used right now), you can put a 'reserve' on everything you sell, a safeguard that protects the seller and prevents an item from going at an unreasonably low figure should there be few bidders.

Classified ads are another way to get a good price for your more valuable merchandise without investing much money or time. Place a 'For Sale' ad or run a mail bid in one of the collector magazines or newsletters, several of which are listed in the back of this book. Many people have had excellent results this way. One of the best to reach collectors in general is *The Antique Trader Weekly* (P.O. Box 1050, Dubuque, Iowa 52004). It covers virtually every type of antiques and collectibles and has a large circulation. If you have several items and the cost of listing them all is prohibitive, simply place an ad saying (for instance) 'Several pieces of Royal Copley (or whatever) for sale, send SASE for list. Be sure to give your correct address and phone number.

When you're making out your list or talking with a prospective buyer by phone, try to draw a picture with words. Describe any damage in full; it's much better than having a disgruntled customer to deal with later, and you'll be on your way to establishing yourself as a reputable dealer. Sometimes it's wise to send out photographs. Seeing the item exactly as it is will often help the prospective buyer make up his or her mind. Send an SASE along and ask that your photos be returned to you, so that you can send them out again, if need be. A less expensive alternative is to have your item photocopied. This works great for many smaller items, not just flat shapes but things with some dimension as well. It's wonderful for hard-to-describe dinnerware patterns or for showing their trademarks.

If you've made that 'buy of a lifetime' or an item you've hung onto for a few years has turned out to be a scarce, highly sought collectible, you have two good options: eBay and mail bids. Either way, you should be able to get top dollar for your prize. You'll want to start your online auction with a high but reasonable reserve. Should the item fail to meet reserve, relist it with one that is lower than the original. The final bid the first time around will give you a good idea of where it may go the second time.

If you do a mail bid, this is how you'll want your ad to read. 'Mail Bid. Popeye cookie jar by American Bisque, slight wear (or 'mint' — briefly indicate condition), closing 6/31/95, right to refuse' (standard self-protection clause meaning you will refuse ridiculously low bids), and give your phone number. Don't commit the sale to any bidder until after the closing date, since some may wait until the last minute to try to place the winning bid.

Be sure to let your buyer know what form of payment you prefer. Some dealers will not ship merchandise until personal checks have cleared. This delay may make the buyer a bit unhappy. So you may want to request a money order or a cashier's check. Nowadays there are several hassle-free ways to make transactions online, for instance, through Pay Pal or Billpoint.

Be very careful about how you pack your merchandise for shipment. Breakables need to be well protected. There are several things you can use. Plastic bubble wrap is excellent and adds very little weight to your packages. Or use scraps of foam rubber such as carpet padding (check with a carpet-laying service or confiscate some from family and friends who are getting new carpet installed). I've received items wrapped in pieces of egg-crate type mattress pads (watch for these at garage sales!). If there is a computer business near you, check their dumpsters for discarded foam wrapping and other protective packaging. It's best not to let newspaper come in direct contact with your merchandise, since the newsprint may stain certain surfaces. After you've wrapped them well, you'll need boxes. Find smaller boxes (one or several, whatever best fits your needs) that you can fit into a larger one with several inches of space between them. First pack your well-wrapped items snugly into the smaller box, using crushed newspaper to keep them from shifting. Place it into the larger box, using more crushed paper underneath and along the sides, so that it will not move during transit. Remember, if it arrives broken, it's still your merchandise, even though you have received payment. You may want to insure the shipment; check with your carrier. Some have automatic insurance up to a specified amount.

After you've mailed your box, it's good to follow it up with a phone call or an e-mail after a few days. Make sure it arrived in good condition and that your customer is pleased with the merchandise. Most people who sell by mail or the Internet allow a 10-day return privilege, providing their original price tag is still intact. For this purpose, you can simply initial a gummed label or use one of those pre-printed return address labels that most of us have around the house.

For very large or heavy items such as furniture or slot machines, ask your buyer for his preferred method of shipment. If the distance involved is not too great, he may even want to pick it up himself.

Flea market selling can either be a lot of fun, or it can turn out to be one of the worst experiences of your life. Obviously you will have to deal with whatever weather conditions prevail, so be sure to listen to weather reports so that you can dress accordingly. You'll see some inventive shelters you might want to copy. Even a simple patio umbrella will offer respite from the blazing sun or a sudden downpour. I've recently been seeing stands catering just to the needs of the flea market dealer — how's that for being enterprising! Not only do they carry specific items the dealers might want, but they've even had framework and tarpaulins, and they'll erect shelters right on the spot!

Be sure to have plastic table covering in case of rain and some large clips to hold it down if there's much wind. The type of clip you'll need depends on how your table is made, so be sure to try them out before you actually get caught in a storm. Glass can blow over, paper items can be ruined, and very quickly your career as a flea market dealer may be cut short for lack of merchandise!

Price your things, allowing yourself a little bargaining room. Unless you want to collect tax separately on each sale (for this you'd need a lot of small change), mentally calculate the amount and add this on as well. Sell the item 'tax included.' Everybody does.

Take snacks, drinks, paper bags, plenty of change, and somebody who can relieve you occasionally. Collectors are some of the nicest people around. I guarantee that you'll enjoy this chance to meet and talk them, and often you can make valuable contacts that may help you locate items you're especially looking for yourself.

Auction houses are listed in the back of this book. If you have an item you feel might be worth selling at auction, be sure to contact one of them. Many have appraisal services; some are free while others charge a fee, dependent on number of items and time spent. We suggest you first make a telephone inquiry before you send in a formal request.

In Summation

The 'battle' since 9/11 has been a slow, uphill struggle, laced with the poison of continued terrorism and threats of war. But uphill it has been and so it continues, and with God's help it will always be uphill. Because we're who we are — Americans, strong and resilient. We fight best when we have to. We're strongest when we need to be. Our heritage is important to us, and we draw comfort from it. Safer, more sane times, simpler lifestyles, higher morals, and happy days harken back to childhood. In some ways, we yearn for that. Memories of eating Grandma's cowboy-hat pancakes, knowing each story she'd read us by heart, making Tinkertoy machines with Dad, and building ramps in the dirt for our cars and trucks are priceless. Some of us collect items that strengthen and refresh those memories — books, toys, kitchen gadgets, even an apron like Grandma's.

And there are other reasons for collecting things — all are positive. I personally enjoy American mid-century glassware and ceramics. I'm thrilled that someone could take an ordinary lump of clay from the earth and turn it into a thing of beauty, or heat simple grains of sand and make a wonderful piece of glass. Those are skills that Americans have developed over years of experimentation and to me mirrors the evolution of our country, which is, I think, constantly becoming better, always improving. And I'm proud of that. I have every confidence that America will prosper again, and so will the antiques and collectibles industry.

Abbreviations

dia – diameter	**NM** – near mint
ea – each	**oz** – ounce
EX – excellent	**pc** – piece
G – good condition	**pr** – pair
gal – gallon	**pt** – pint
L – long, length	**qt** – quart
lg – large	**sm** – small
M – mint condition	**sq** – square
med – medium	**VG** – very good
MIB – mint in (original) box	**W** – wide
MIP – mint in package	**w/** – with
MOC – mint on card	**(+)** – has been reproduced

Note: When no condition is noted within our description lines, assume that the value we give is for mint-condition items.

Abingdon

You may find smaller pieces of Abingdon around, but it's not common to find many larger items. This company operated in Abingdon, Illinois, from 1934 until 1950, making not only nice vases and figural pieces but some kitchen items as well. Their cookie jars are very well done and popular with collectors. They sometimes used floral decals and gold to decorate their wares, and a highly decorated item is worth a minimum of 25% more than the same shape with no decoration. Some of their glazes also add extra value. If you find a piece in black, bronze, or red, you can add 25% to those as well. Note that if you talk by phone about Abingdon to a collector, be sure to mention the mold number on the base.

For more information we recommend *Abingdon Pottery Artware, 1934 – 50, Stepchild of the Great Depression,* by Joe Paradis (Schiffer).

See also Cookie Jars.

Advisor: Louise Dumont (See Directory, Abingdon)

Club: Abingdon Pottery Collectors Club
Elaine Westover, Membership and Treasurer
210 Knox Hwy. 5, Abingdon, IL 61410; 309-462-3267

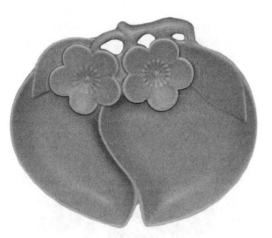

Plate, Wild Rose, #344, 12", from $125.00 to $145.00.

Ashtray, New Mode, #456, 5¾"	$28.00
Bookends, Colts, #363, 6", pr	$300.00
Bowl, Asters, #454, 6½"	$62.50
Bowl, Classic, #125, 6½x11"	$35.00
Bowl, La Fleur, #153, 6" dia	$12.00
Bowl, Pineapple, #700D, 14¾" L	$88.00
Bowl, Ribbed, #658, 10"	$24.00
Bowl, Scroll, #532, 14½" L	$20.00
Candle holders, Hurricane, w/glass, #336A, 11", pr	$40.00
Candle holders, Victory Boat, #578, pr	$95.00
Cornucopia, double, #482, 11" L	$24.00
Figurine, head, #2801, 11½"	$200.00
Flowerpot, #149, La Fleur, 3"	$12.50
Flowerpot, #397, 5¾" sq	$22.50

Jar, Chang, #310, 10½"	$125.00
Jardiniere, La Fleur, #P4, 3"	$14.00
Planter, Gourd, #667, 5½"	$18.00
Refrigerator dish, 4" dia	$25.00
Urn, Wreath, #538, 9"	$24.00

Vase, Delta, #104, 10", from $45.00 to $55.00.

Vase, Draped, #557, 11"	$46.00
Vase, Gamma, #111, 6"	$32.00
Vase, Iris, #628D, 8"	$55.00
Vase, Laurel, #443, 5¾"	$38.00
Vase, Lung, #302, 11"	$200.00
Vase (floor), Grecian, #603, 15"	$125.00
Wall masks, male or female, #378M/#378F, pr	$385.00
Wall pocket, Butterfly, #601D, 8½"	$115.00

Adams, Matthew

In the 1950s a trading post located in Alaska contacted Sascha Brastoff to design a line of decorative ceramics with depictions of Eskimos, Alaskan scenes, or with animals indigenous to that area. These items were intended to target the tourist trade.

Brastoff selected Matthew Adams as the designer. These earlier examples have the Sascha B mark on the front, and the pattern number often appears on the back.

After the Alaska series became successful, Matthew Adams left Brastoff's studio and opened his own. (In all, Mr. Adams was employed by Brastoff for three years.) Pieces made in his studio are all signed Matthew Adams in script on the front. Some carry the word Alaska as well.

Mr. Adams was born in 1915. Presently his studio is located in Los Angeles, but he is no longer working.

Advisor: Marty Webster (See Directory, Adams, Matthew)

Bowl, Eskimo child w/doll on blue, round, 7x7½"	$60.00
Coffeepot, lg moose standing in water, pine trees beyond, yellow background, 12"	$175.00
Compote, log-built cache, yellow sky background w/black-outlined mountains, 3-footed, 3x8¾x6¾"	$80.00

Cookie jar, cabin on stilts in snow, elliptical.............**$100.00**

Dish, cabin on stilts, evergreen trees & yellow sky backgroun, sq, shallow, 8"...**$65.00**

Dish, Eskimo child in maroon parka, free-form, #140, 6½" L...**$50.00**

Mug, walrus on dark blue...**$40.00**

Pitcher, 2 igloos on med blue, 5".............................**$45.00**

Smoker's set, cabin on stilts on brown, sq ashtray, match holder & lighter, 3 pcs...**$85.00**

Sugar bowl, Eskimo girl on blue, w/lid.....................**$60.00**

Vase, moose, yellow sky in background, 10"...........**$125.00**

Advertising Character Collectibles

The advertising field holds a special fascination for many of today's collectors. It's vast and varied, so its appeal is universal; but the characters of the ad world are its stars right now. Nearly every fast-food restaurant and manufacturer of a consumer product has a character logo. Keep your eyes open on your garage sale outings; it's not at all uncommon to find the cloth and plush dolls, plastic banks and mugs, bendies, etc., such as we've listed here. There are several books on the market that are geared specifically toward these types of collectibles. Some you'll enjoy reading are *Collectible Aunt Jemima* by Jean Williams Turner (Schiffer); *Cereal Boxes and Prizes, The 1960s,* (Flake World Publishing) by Scott Bruce; and *Hake's Guide to Advertising Collectibles* by Ted Hake (Wallace-Homestead). *Schroeder's Collectible Toys, Antique to Modern,* is another source. (It's published by Collector Books.)

See also Advertising Watches; Breweriana; Bubble Bath Containers; Character Clocks and Watches; Character and Promotional Drinking Glasses; Coca-Cola Collectibles; Fast-Food Collectibles; Novelty Radios; Novelty Telephones; Pez Candy Containers; Pin-Back Buttons; Salt and Pepper Shakers; Soda Pop Memorabilia.

Aunt Jemima

One of the most widely recognized ad characters of them all, Aunt Jemima has decorated bags and boxes of pancake flour for more than ninety years. In fact, the original milling company carried her name, but by 1926 it had become part of the Quaker Oats Company. She and Uncle Mose were produced in plastic by the F&F Mold and Die Works in the 1950s, and the salt and pepper shakers, syrup pitchers, cookie jars, etc., they made are perhaps the most sought-after of the hundreds of items available today. (Watch for reproductions.) Age is a big worth-assessing factor for memorabilia such as we've listed below, of course, but so is condition. Watch for very chipped or worn paint on the F&F products, and avoid buying soiled cloth dolls.

Advisor: Judy Posner (See Directory, Advertising)

Advertising card, Aunt Jemima in die-cut cardboard, w/ string for tying to flour bag, RT Davis Mills, 4¼x2¾", EX **$65.00**

Booklet, Life of Aunt Jemima, 14 pages, mail-in from RT Davis Mill Co, EX...**$110.00**

Coin purse, red w/girl's face, chain for handle, 2¾x3".**$24.00**

Container, Aunt Jemima Pancake Batter, red & white, 4-cup bottom w/2-cup lid, EX...**$50.00**

Cookie jar, Aunt Jemima figure, plastic, F&F Mold & Die Co, 1948, 11½", M/NM, from $550 to **$600.00**

Creamer & sugar bowl, Aunt Jemima & Uncle Mose, yellow w/red figures on sides, F&F Mold & Die Co, w/sugar lid, NM **$175.00**

Doll, Breakfast Bear, blue plush, in chef's hat, apron & bandana, Aunt Jemima premium, 13", M.................**$125.00**

Frying pan, Aunt Jemima Corn Meal embossed on back, cast iron, 8½" dia, EX **$165.00**

Junior Chef Pancake Set, Argo Industries, 1949, EX.**$150.00**

Magazine ad, 4-Flour Flavor of Aunt Jemima Pancakes, Southern scene above illustration of pancake on spatula, 1959, EX..**$20.00**

Measuring cup, Aunt Jemima Mixes, clear w/red, marked Fire King #498, 2-cup, EX..**$105.00**

Note pad, F&F Mold & Die Co, 1950s **$95.00**

Pancake shaker, clear glass marked Ball, 'Perfect Pancakes in 10 Shakes' on lid, mixing directions inside lid, EX **$85.00**

Paperweight, etched glass, 1978, M **$45.00**

Place mat, Aunt Jemima at Disneyland Park, paper, ca 1955, 10¼x14", EX...**$30.00**

Pot holder, red graphics on white, 1970s, M...............**$35.00**

Puzzle, jigsaw; All Aboard, Jaymar Mfg, 28 pcs, 1986, VG.**$25.00**

Recipe book, Cake Mix Miracles, 1950s, EX...............**$35.00**

Recipe cards, 17 cards w/colored scenes on back, Dear Friend note, original mailing envelope, EX........**$110.00**

Salt & pepper shakers, Aunt Jemima & Uncle Mose, F&F Mold & Die Co, 3½", pr **$55.00**

Salt and pepper shakers, F&F Mold & Die Works, 5", MIB (with rare original flyer dated 1957), from $100.00 to $125.00. (Shakers only, $70.00.)

Spice jar, Aunt Jemima, plastic, F&F Mold & Die Co, from set of 6, ea **$50.00**

Spice rack, letters across front, red lustreware, F&F Mold & Die Co, no spice jars, EX.....................................**$125.00**

Syrup pitcher, Aunt Jemima figural, F&F Mold & Die Co, 5½",
EX..**$75.00**
Thermometer, Aunt Jemima picture on top, Aunt Jemima
Mills Co on bottom, painted metal, slight rust other-
wise EX..**$35.00**
Toaster cover, Aunt Jemima, resin body w/white cotton skirt,
Youngs Co, EX..**$50.00**

Big Boy and Friends

Bob's Big Boy, home of the nationally famous Big
Boy, the original double-deck hamburger, was founded by
Robert C. 'Bob' Wian in Glendale, California, in 1938. He'd
just graduated from high school, and he had a dream. With
the $300.00 realized from the sale of the car he so trea-
sured, he bought a run-down building and enough basic
equipment to open his business. Through much hard
work and ingenuity, Bob turned his little restaurant into a
multimillion-dollar empire. Not only does he have the
double-deck two-patty burger to his credit, but car hops
and drive-in restaurants were his creation as well.

With business beginning to flourish, Bob felt he needed a symbol — something that people would recognize.
One day in walked a chubby lad of six, his sagging
trousers held up by reluctant suspenders. Bob took one
look at him and named him Big Boy, and that was it! It
was a natural name for his double-deck hamburger —
descriptive, catchy, and easy to remember. An artist
worked out the drawings, and Bob's Pantry was renamed
Boy's Big Boy.

The enterprise grew fast, and Bob added location after
location. In 1969 when he sold out to the Marriott
Corporation, he had 185 restaurants in California, with
franchises such as Elias Big Boy, Frisch's Big Boy, and
Shoney's Big Boy in other states. The Big Boy burger and
logo were recognized by virtually every man, woman, and
child in America, and Bob retired knowing he had made
a significant contribution to millions of people everywhere.

Since Big Boy has been in business for over sixty
years, you'll find many items and numerous variations.
Some, such as the large statues, china, and some menus,
have been reproduced. If you're in doubt, consult an
experienced collector for help. Many items of jewelry,
clothing, and kids promotions were put out over the years,
too numerous to itemize separately. Values range from
$5.00 up to $1,000.00.

Advisor: Steve Soelberg (See Directory, Advertising)

Ashtray, sq glass dish w/Frisch's logo & America's Favorite
Hamburger in round center, 3½", EX...............**$20.00**
Ashtray, white w/figure on edge, 1950s, M.............**$350.00**
Bank, figure holding hamburger, ceramic..................**$500.00**
Bank, figure w/ or w/out hamburger, vinyl, M, ea.....**$25.00**
Bank, figure wearing red & white checkered overalls, plastic,
1973, 9"..**$20.00**

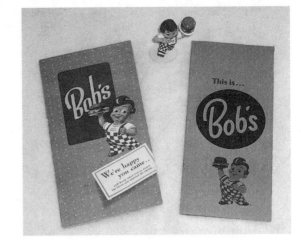

**Bob's Dinner Menu, four pages, 1956, M, $150.00; Bob's
Big Boy Restaurant Brochure (gives brief story of Bob's
and location of restaurants), 1970s, M, $50.00. (Photo
courtesy Steve Soelberg)**

Box, lunch/pencil; red plastic.....................................**$25.00**
Comic book, Adventures of Big Boy, #1...................**$250.00**
Comic book, Adventures of Big Boy, #2-#5, ea........**$100.00**
Comic book, Adventures of Big Boy, #6-#10, ea......**$100.00**
Comic book, Adventures of Big Boy, #11-#100, ea....**$50.00**
Comic book, Adventures of Big Boy, #101-#250,
ea...**$20.00**
Counter display, papier-mache figure, w/hamburger,
1960s..**$500.00**
Cup, coffee; robin-egg blue w/Bob serving burger graphics,
maroon inside, Walker China, 3"..................**$50.00**
Decal, Big Boy for President, M...............................**$10.00**
Doll, Dakin, complete w/hamburger & shoes..........**$150.00**
Doll, Dolly (Big Boy's girlfrind), pink dress w/white apron
& chef's hat, w/strawberry pie, ceramic, Wolfe Studio,
EX...**$110.00**
Food bag, Frisch's Big Boy Burger, 1950s, M..............**$25.00**
Goblet, silver, for milk shakes.................................**$50.00**
Handbook, employee, 1956......................................**$100.00**
Key chain, flat silver-tone figure, M..........................**$25.00**
Kit, paper, child's, M...**$250.00**
Lighter, Bob's in red circle on 1 side, Big Boy logo
on other side, Wellington Junior, dated 5-20-55,
1¼x2"..**$100.00**
Matchbook, Bob's logo & Big Boy w/hamburger on front
w/Bob's Seasoning Salt on back, gold background,
unused, EX..**$20.00**
Menu, Bob's original #1 location...............................**$350.00**
Menu, dated 1965, EX...**$55.00**
Menu, Frisch's Big Boy Restaurant, 1974, EX.............**$45.00**
Mug, Big Boy China, Canoga Park drive-in................**$25.00**
Neon clock, Big Boy logo, working.............................**$100.00**
Nodder, papier-mache figure, 1965...........................**$1,000.00**
Ornament, Happy Holidays.......................................**$20.00**
Pennant, felt, Big Boy Club, 1950s, 2 versions, ea.....**$50.00**
Pin, 5-Year, gold metal w/Big Boy, oval, MIB...........**$30.00**
Playing cards, red, unopened, M................................**$25.00**

Plates, Elias Brothers, dinner, $50.00; salad, $20.00.
(Photo courtesy Steve Soelberg)

Sign, entrance; orange plastic, gold letters **$250.00**
Store display, PVC w/4 figures **$50.00**
Transistor radio, can w/Big Boy logo, working **$500.00**
Tumbler, turquoise logo, 1956, tall..............................**$75.00**
Watch, Windert, man's gold quartz, MIB **$150.00**
Yo-yo, wood, blue or red, 1956 ....**$50.00**

Campbell Kids

The introduction of the world's first canned soup was announced in 1897. Later improvements in the manufacturing process created a revolutionary condensed soup. The Campbell's® Soup Company is now the primary beneficiary of this early entrepreneurial achievement. Easily identified by their red and white advertising, the company has been built on a tradition of skillful product marketing through five generations of consumers. Now a household name for all ages, Campbell's Soups have grown to dominate 80% of the canned soup market.

The first Campbell's licensed advertising products were character collectibles offered in 1910 — composition dolls with heads made from a combination of glue and sawdust. They were made by the E.I. Horsman Company and sold for $1.00 each. They were the result of a gifted illustrator, their creator, Grace Drayton, who in 1904 gave life to the chubby-faced cherub 'Campbell's Kids.'

In 1994 the Campbell's Soup Kids celebrated their 90th birthday. They have been revised a number of times to maintain a likeness to modern-day children. Over the years hundreds of licensees have been commissioned to produce collectibles and novelty items with the Campbell's logo in a red and white theme.

Licensed advertising reached a peak from 1954 through 1956 with thirty-four licensed manufacturers. Unusual items included baby carriages, toy vacuums, games, and apparel. Many of the more valuable Campbell's advertising collectibles were made during this period. In 1956 a Campbell's Kid doll was produced from latex rubber. Called 'Magic Skin,' it proved to be the most popular mail-in premium ever produced. Campbell's received more than 560,000 requests for this special girl chef doll.

For more information, we recommend *Campbell's Soup Collectibles, A Price and Identification Guide*, by David and Micki Young (Krause Publications). The book may be ordered through The Soup Collector Club.

Advisor: David Young (See Directory, Advertising)

Club: The Soup Collector Club
414 Country Lane Ct.
Wauconda, IL 60084, Fax/phone: 847-487-4917;
e-mail: soupclub@yahoo.com

Website: www.soupcollector.com or club site:
clubs.yahoo.com/clubs/campbellssoupcollectorclub

Bell, Campbell Kids fishing off bridge on white satin, Fenton, 1984, 6½", EXIB **$30.00**
Canister, Chicken Noodle Soup can shape, red & white, porcelain, Teleflora, 1998, 5½x5½" **$12.00**
Christmas ornament, Santa hands little girl a doll, 1988, MIB...**$18.00**
Cup, ceramic, Campbell Kids graphics, Westwood, M..**$5.00**
Cup, plastic, M'm! M'm! Good!, M **$5.00**
Dish, Campbells Kids ABCs, gold trim, GG Drayton, Buffalo Pottery, 1⅜x7¾"..**$65.00**
Doll, Campbell girl, Ideal, 1955, rubber & vinyl w/cloth outfit, 8", EX, minimum value **$125.00**
Doll, Campbell girl as cheerleader, 1967, vinyl, 8", EX..**$75.00**
Doll, Home Shopper, 1995, in pirate clothes, comes in lg soup-can box, 10", EX...**$79.00**
Doll kit, Boy & Girl Scottish Dolls, Douglas Co, 1979, ea...**$35.00**

Doll, thin vinyl with molded-on shoes and socks, marked 1984 Campbell Soup on head, 7", EX, $25.00.
(Photo courtesy Patsy Moyer)

Dolls, Campbell Kids, ca 1972, vinyl, (soup label premium), unmarked, 10", ea from $30 to **$45.00**
Dolls, Campbell Kids, vinyl, 1970s, 9", MIB, pr **$125.00**
Dolls, Campbell Kids, 1970s, rag-type, MIB, pr **$75.00**
Dolls, Colonial boy & girl (Paul Revere & Betsy Ross replicas), 1976 premium, 10", M, ea from $45 to **$65.00**
Figurine, Did You Hear?, china, Leeber, 1998 ....**$25.00**
Figurine, Downhill Racer, china, Leeber, 1999 ....**$25.00**
Figurine, Forever Yours, china, Leeber, 1998 ....**$30.00**
Figurine, Hole in One, china, Leeber, 1998................**$20.00**

Figurine, School Days, china, Leeber, 1998 ....$20.00
Figurine, Shall We Dance, china, Leeber, 1999 ....$30.00
Figurine, Time of Innocence, china, Leeber, 1998......$30.00
Fork & spoon, silver-plated, marked Wm Rogers Oneida Ltd, EX..$30.00
Game, Campbell Kids Shopping; board game, Parker Bros, 1955, NMIB..$70.00
Lunchbox, Campbell Kids on side, metal, red & white, miniature filled w/candy, 1998, 4½" sq $18.00
Mug, Cambpell Kids & M-M-M Good etched in copper-finished metal, stamped Wm Rogers, EX $35.00
Note pad, red & white soup can shape, bound on 1 side, Westab, 7x4¼" $4.00
Ornament, Chicken Noodle in raised letters on soup can, red & white, 1999, 3½x2½" $12.00
Ornament, figural, girl in green dress w/bowl of soup, Kurt Alder, 1998, 3¾" $5.00
Ornament, 2 Campbell Kids in cockpit of red & white plane, 1998, 4" L...$15.00

Salt and pepper shakers, plastic, F&F Mold & Die Works, 4½", $40.00 for the pair.

Shirt, black cotton w/red & white soup can $10.00
Sponge/paint set, 26 colored alphabet sponge letters & 3 tubes colored ink, Xenox, 1998, 7x5½" $12.00
String holder, Campbell Kid's head, chalkware, Copyright Campbell incised under chin, 6¾", EX, from $250 to $350.00
Toy airplane, 1938 Grumman Goose, w/bank slot, red & white, limited edition, Gearbox, 1997, 11x9" $55.00
Toy truck, 1912 Ford Model T, Campbell Soup theme, Gearbox, 1998, NM..$75.00

Cap'n Crunch

Cap'n Crunch was the creation of Jay Ward, whom you will no doubt remember was also the creator of the Rocky and Bullwinkle show. The Cap'n hails from the '60s and was one of the first heroes of the presweetened cereal crowd. Jean LaFoote was the villain always scheming to steal the Cap'n's cereal.

Bank, figural, painted plastic, 1973, VG $65.00
Beanie, Tiger Shark Meanie, in original printed bag, M, from $16 to..$20.00

Big Slick Gyro Car, blue plastic, 1972, MIP $15.00
Binoculars, blue plastic, 1972, MIP $15.00
Board game, Cap'n Crunch Island Adventure; Warren, complete, EXIB..$15.00
Boson whistle, blue & white w/Cap'n & Sea Dog, ca 1964, EX...$10.00
Cap'n Crunch Cruiser, plastic, 1987, EX $10.00
Cap'n Rescue Kit, paper, 1986, MIP $10.00
Coloring book, Whitman, 1968, VG $20.00
Comic book, Center of the Earth, 1987, 8-page, EX...$10.00
Figure, Cap'n Crunch, blue plastic, 1986, 1½", VG.....$10.00
Figure, Cap'n Crunch, vinyl, 1970s, EX, from $40 to....$50.00
Figure, Smog Master, silver plastic robot, 1986, 1½", NM..$5.00
Figure, Soggy, nearly clear plastic, 1986, 1½", EX........$5.00
Frisbee, blue plastic w/Cap'n in center, MIP, 1970s, EX....$50.00
Hand puppet, Cap'n, Dave or Sea Dog, vinyl, 9", M, ea.....$35.00
Handkerchief, white w/4 colorful scenes, 8x8", EX....$50.00
Membership kit, Quaker Oats, 1965, M (EX mailer), from $200 to..$300.00
Puzzle, 8 figures, wooden, Fisher-Price, 8½x12" $38.00
Ring, plastic figure, NM...$100.00

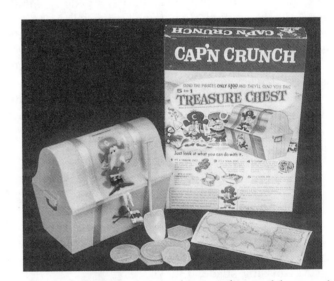

Treasure Chest bank, M, from $5.00 to $10.00 (shown with the cereal box that introduced it). (Photo courtesy Scott Bruce)

Tumbler, Ship Shape, plastic, 1963, 6", NM.................$25.00
Wiggle figures, 3 different, 1969, EX, ea.....................$50.00

Charlie Tuna

Poor Charlie, never quite good enough for the Star-Kist folks to can, though he yearns for them to catch him; but since the early 1970s he's done a terrific job working for them as the company logo. A dapper blue-fin tuna in sunglasses and a beret, he's appeared in magazines, done TV commercials, modeled for items as diverse as lamps and banks, but still they deny him his dream. 'Sorry, Charlie.'

Alarm clock, image of Charlie & Sorry Charlie sign on round face, 2 bells, footed, 1969, 4" dia, M....................$65.00

Bank, marked 1988 Star Kist Foods Inc, 10", from $50.00 to $60.00. (Photo courtesy Beverly and Jim Mangus)

Bathroom scale, Charlie & Sorry Charlie sign, oval, 1972, EX **$50.00**
Bracelet, embossed figure on gold-tone disk, M.........**$10.00**
Camera, figural, 110 film, dated 1971, EX **$50.00**
Clock, wall; Charlie w/fish friend, quartz, 8½" dia.....**$36.00**
Figure, Charlie, stuffed cloth w/pull-string talker, says 11 phrases, 14", NM...**$85.00**
Figure, Charlie, vinyl, arms up (rare version), 1973, 7½", (M $125), MIB...**$200.00**
Figurine, Charlie, vinyl, 2-tone blue w/pink hat & glass, marked, 7" **$65.00**
Key ring, raised design on gold-tone disk, M **$10.00**

Lamp, composition, copyright 1970 Star Kist, missing shade, 13", VG, $85.00. (Photo courtesy Collectors Auction Service)

Patch, Charlie embroidered on green background w/yellow coral & orange starfish, Sorry Charlie sign, 1975, 3", NM **$12.00**
Pendant, Charlie on anchor, M **$10.00**
Playing cards, Party With Charlie II, complete, EX (VG box)...**$12.50**
Radio, mounts on bicycle handlebars, 1973, MIB.......**$30.00**
Tape dispenser, black & ivory plastic, battery-operated, dated 1974, 6x4x3", NM...**$60.00**

Telephone, Charlie stands on rock w/starfish at side, eyes light up when phone rings, 1987, EX, from $35 to **$45.00**
Wristwatch, Charlie facing right, 1973, M **$40.00**
Wristwatch, employee giveaway, shows Charlie on fishhook w/Sorry Charlie sign, 1977, EX.............................**$60.00**

Colonel Sanders

There's nothing fictional about the Colonel — he was a very real guy, who built an empire on the strength of his fried chicken recipe with 'eleven herbs and spices.' In the 1930s, the Colonel operated a small cafe in Corbin, Kentucky. As the years went by, he developed a chain of restaurants which he sold in the mid-'60s. But even after the sale, the new company continued to use the image of the handsome southern gentlemen as their logo. The Colonel died in 1980.

Bank, plastic, figure, dated 1977, 7½" **$12.50**
Bank, plastic figure, holding bucket of chicken, no base, 1970s, 8", NM, from $20 to **$30.00**
Bank, plastic figure w/arm around restaurant building & holding bucket of chicken, white w/red & black trim, 6", EX **$125.00**
Bank, vinyl, figure, marked Margardt Corp 1972 Canada, 9½", from $30 to...**$40.00**
Camera, figural, Japan premium, 3x4", MIB **$35.00**
Coaster, Original Pancake & Chicken House, Tacoma Washington, paper, 1960s, EX...............................**$18.50**
Coin, Visit the Colonel at Mardi Gras, M.....................**$10.00**
Coloring book, Favorite Chicken Stories, 1960s, EX...**$25.00**

Cookie jar, ceramic (called 'lamp shade' by collectors), from $75.00 to $85.00. (Photo courtesy Joyce and Fred Roerig)

Cookie jar, glass painted as fried chicken bucket, from $275 to...**$325.00**
Hand puppet, in white suit, plastic, 1960s, EX **$20.00**
Lamp shade, glass, painted as fried chicken bucket, unmarked, from $275 to **$325.00**
Mask, multicolored plastic, 1960s, M...........................**$38.00**
Nodder, figural, bisque, marked Charlsprod Japan, 1960s, 7½", M, from $100 to **$125.00**
Nodder, figural, painted composition, 1960s, 7½", MIB..**$75.00**

Nodder, figural, plastic, holds red bucket of chicken, on white base, 1960s, 7", EX...**$85.00**

Pin, lapel; Colonel's head, metal, EX **$6.50**

Playset, Let's Play at KY Fried Chicken, Child Guidance, 1970s, EX (EX box) **$140.00**

Poker chip, plastic, w/portrait, 1960s, M **$17.50**

Postcard, Colonel's original motel on linen, EX............**$8.00**

Printer block, Kentucky Fried Chicken, smiling face, metal mounted on hardwood, 1960s, 2⅜x1½", EX.........**$9.50**

Record album, Christmas Day w/Colonel Sanders, LP, RCA, 1968, EX...**$25.00**

Salt & pepper shakers, plastic figures w/white or black base, Starling Plastics, 4⅜", pr, from $40 to **$60.00**

Sign, two-sided metal figure with pipe in center to mount on base, 55½", VG, from $150.00 to $250.00. (Photo courtesy Collectors Auction Service)

Tie tac, gold-tone molded head w/diamond chip, M.**$65.00**

Wind-up toy figure, walks w/moving arms & nodding head, 3¼", NM...**$15.00**

Elsie the Cow and Family

She's the most widely recognized cow in the world; everyone knows Elsie, Borden's mascot. Since the mid-1930s, she's been seen on booklets and posters; modeled for mugs, creamers, dolls, etc.; and appeared on TV, in magazines, and at grocery stores to promote their products. Her husband is Elmer (who once sold Elmer's Glue for the same company), and her twins are best known as Beulah and Beauregard, though they've been renamed in recent years (now they're Bea and Beaumister). Elsie was retired in the 1960s, but due to public demand was soon reinstated to her rightful position and continues today to promote the company's dairy products.

Advisor: Lee Garmon (See Directory, Advertising)

Book, My Story, Elsie on cover, Borden Co Ltd, 32 pages, 1942, 7x9", EX...**$25.00**

Bust, Elsie, resin, impressed Borden & Co, 1940s, 9½".**$210.00**

Butter mold, Elsie or Beulah, M, ea **$28.00**

Clock, milk carton shape, letter on back from Elsie, battery-operated, EX...**$30.00**

Coaster set, 4 4" punch-out coasters w/recipes on back, cardboard, 1950s, premium, on 10½x9" folder, unused, EX **$20.00**

Coloring book, From Moo to You With Love, Borden giveaway, 7x4½", EX...**$28.00**

Creamer, Elsie figural, ceramic, EX **$110.00**

Creamer, Elsie's head w/polka-dot bow at neck, 4½"..**$130.00**

Cup, Elsie head w/metal bell hanging from neck, ceramic, Borden Co, Japan, 3½".....................................**$45.00**

Doll, Dutch Elsie, cloth with vinyl head, ca mid-1950s, maker unknown, missing cap, 18", NM, $65.00. (Photo courtesy Pat Smith)

Figure, Elsie, PVC, 1993, 3½", M, from $10 to **$20.00**

Gameboard, Elsie & her Family, Get Them in the Barn, Selchow & Righter, 1941, board only, EX.............**$75.00**

Measuring glass, red Elsie head on yellow sunflower, red lettering on clear, 8-oz, EX..**$70.00**

Milk bottle, clear w/orange lettering & Elsie's head, ½-gal, M..**$20.00**

Milk bottle, clear w/red lettering, ½-pt, M **$15.00**

Mug, child's; Elsie dancing, ceramic, Elsie Enterprises, Borden Comp, 3x4"...**$115.00**

Needle book, Elsie head on sunflower in yellow on red, 5¼"..**$40.00**

Refrigerator magnet, Elsie & Beauregard fishing, 1950s, EX...**$10.00**

Salt & pepper shakers, Elsie bust, head separates at shoulders, unmarked, 4½" **$130.00**

Sign, painted metal, 24x15", $300.00. (Photo courtesy BJ Summers)

Tie clip, multicolored enameled Elsie in daisy, M **$40.00**

Toy, Elsie bendee, marked, Borden/China, 3½", EX ..**$12.50**

Green Giant

The Jolly Green Giant has been a well-known ad fixture since the 1950s (some research indicates an earlier date); he was originally devised to represent a strain of European peas much larger than the average-size peas Americans had been accustomed to. At any rate, when Minnesota Valley Canning changed its name to Green Giant, he was their obvious choice. Rather a terse individual himself, by 1974 he was joined by Little Green Sprout, with the lively eyes and more talkative personality.

In addition to a variety of toys and other memorabilia already on the market, in 1988 Benjamin Medwin put out a line of Little Green Sprout items. These are listed below.

Bank, Little Sprout, ceramic, 8¼", $50.00. (Photo courtesy Beverly and Jim Mangus)

Brush holder, Little Sprout, w/4 brushes, Benjamin Medwin, MIB **$40.00**

Clock, Little Sprout holding round dial in front of base, w/talking alarm, 1986, 10½", EX **$25.00**

Dinnerware set, w/plate, cup, knife & fork, 1991, MIB..**$10.00**

Doll, Green Giant, cloth, 1966, 16", M (in original mailer), from $25 to..**$35.00**

Doll, Green Giant, vinyl, ca 1975, 9", EX **$85.00**

Doll, Little Sprout, stuffed cloth, 1974, 10½", NM.......**$15.00**

Doll, Little Sprout, talker, MIP **$55.00**

Fabric, Green Giant & Little Sprout, heavy material, 48x45"...**$20.00**

Farm Factory, w/Little Sprout finger puppet & all accessories, MIB **$20.00**

Flashlight, Little Sprout, MIB..**$45.00**

Jump rope, Little Sprout, MIB..**$20.00**

Kite, plastic, mail-in premium, late 1960s, 42x48", unused, M **$30.00**

Lapel pin, Green Giant...**$7.00**

Magazine ad, can of Green Giant Peas in baby crib, 1948, 10½x13", EX...**$20.00**

Magnet, Little Sprout, Benjamin Medwin, 1988, 2-pc, MIB **$10.00**

Mannequin, Green Giant, fabric body w/green felt leaves on head & over body, squeeze thumb & he says Ho Ho Ho, 54", EX...**$60.00**

Napkin holder, Little Sprout, Benjamin Medwin, MIB ..**$10.00**

Planter, Little Sprout, Benjamin Medwin, 1988, MIB...**$35.00**

Puzzle, Green Giant, Planting Time in the Valley, 1,000 pcs in can, 1981, EX...**$15.00**

Puzzle, Little Sprout's Bedtime, 40 pcs in can, 1981...**$15.00**

Radio, Green Giant Niblets Corn box shape, battery-operated, 1970s, Ross Electronics, EX............................**$40.00**

Record, Green Giant 20th Birthday, 78 rpm, red wax, 7", VG **$10.00**

Salt & pepper shakers, Little Sprout, Benjamin Medwin, 1990-92, MIB, pr **$25.00**

Scouring pad holder w/pad, Little Sprout, Benjamin Medwin, 1988, MIP..**$15.00**

Soap pad holder, Little Sprout stands beside basket, ceramic, marked Pillsbury Co, 1988, Taiwan, EX...............**$15.00**

Spoon rest, Little Sprout, Benjamin Medwin, 1988, MIB..**$30.00**

Toy truck, Nylint, Green Giant tractor-trailer, w/engine noise & horn, MIB **$50.00**

Toy truck, Tonka, Green Giant Peas stake truck, 1953, EX **$300.00**

Toy truck, Tonka, Green Giant tractor-trailer, 1951, M, from $150 to..**$200.00**

Lamp, Little Sprout holding balloons, touch-on, 14½", M, $45.00. (Photo courtesy Martin and Carolyn Barnes)

Joe Camel

Joe Camel, the ultimate 'cool character,' was only on the scene for a few years as a comic character. The all-around Renaissance beast, he dated beautiful women, drove fast motorcycles and cars, lazed on the beach, played pool, hung around with his pals (the Hard Pack), and dressed formally for dinner and the theatre. He was 'done in' by the anti-cigarette lobby because he smoked. Now reduced to a real camel, his comic strip human persona is avidly collected by both women and men, most of whom don't smoke. Prices have been steadily rising as more and more people come to appreciate him as the great icon he is.

Advisors: C.J. Russell and Pamela E. Apkarian-Russell (See Directory, Halloween)

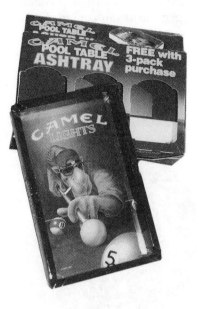

Ashtray, Pool Table, Camel Lights, plastic, MIB, $25.00 (no box, $15.00). (Photo courtesy Pamela E. Apkarian-Russell)

Ashtray set, Joe playing pool, plastic, set of 8, 7⅜x4⅝", EX **$45.00**
Banner, 50th Anniversity of Sturgis Bike Rally, 1990, 36x96", NM **$60.00**
Beach towel, Joe & the Hard Pack Band, M **$20.00**
Chair, director's; canvas back & seat w/wooden frame, Joe in seat, EX **$60.00**
Charm bracelet, 11 charms, .900 silver, 7", M **$50.00**
Coin/medallion, Joe bust, .999 silver, RJ Reynolds, M (in plastic holder in velvet case) **$35.00**
Dart board, Joe's Place on front, bristle board, MIB...**$200.00**
Doll, Joe, tux & black tie w/lg rhinestone tie pin, stuffed, Best Toy Mfg, 1993, EX **$20.00**
Golf ball set, 1st Annual Camel Classic, set of 3, Spaulding, 1994, M (in tube) **$40.00**
Knife, Joe fishing out of canoe, MIP **$20.00**
Mirror, Joe on motorcycle, 19½x19½", EX **$25.00**
Necktie, Joe w/pack of Camel Lights in hand, Savvy brand, EX **$35.00**
Pilsners, Joe's Lounge in clear glass, set of 4, MIB.....**$15.00**
Pin, campaign; Veterans For Dole, Joe in army hat w/flag in background, 3" dia, EX **$25.00**
Plate, Joe playing pool, 14k gold rim, limited edition, MIB...**$50.00**
Poker set, 150 clay chips, 2 decks of cards, chip rack, 1996, M (in collector tin) **$65.00**
Pool cue, The Miz, Steve Mizerak faux signature, Joe shooting pool on stick, M (in case) **$90.00**
Poster, 75 Birthday, motorcycle racing in background, M (sealed) **$45.00**
Radio/cassette player, jukebox shape, AM-FM radio, 13½x12x6", NM **$45.00**
Salt & pepper shakers, Joe figural, 1 in black, 1 in white, plastic, pr **$25.00**
Salt & pepper shakers, Joe figural, 1 in black, 1 in white, ceramic, pr **$50.00**

Seat cushion, tan w/purple camel w/checked neck scarf, Camel Powered, EX **$25.00**
Shot glass set, Joe Camel's Band, 1 member on ea, etched cobalt glass, set of 5, M **$70.00**

Stand-up, cardboard Joe Camel 75th Birthday, $150.00. (Photo courtesy C.J. Russell and Pamela E. Apkarian-Russell)

Stand-up, Joe w/arms crossed, cardboard cutout, 72", NM..**$60.00**
Stein, 1994 Oktoberfest, Joe playing golf, limited edition, MIB **$50.00**
T-shirt, Joe in Camel hammock, 3-pack giveaway, (no box, $15), MIB **$35.00**
Thermometer, Camel Lights, Joe holding thermometer, RJ Reynolds 1993, M...**$35.00**
Tin, Joe & the Gang playing musical instruments, came w/carton of cigarettes, 12¼x4½", EX **$35.00**
Vest, Joe's Fish & Game Club embroidered, MIP........**$20.00**
Wall clock, Joe in bomber jacket, quartz movement, 6-sided burgundy frame, 11", EX **$45.00**
Wall clock, Kick Back Joe, Joe leaning against clock, 20x24", EX...**$30.00**

M & M Candy Men

Toppers for M&M packaging first appeared about 1988; since then other M&M items have been introduced that portray the clever antics of these colorful characters. Toppers have been issued for seasonal holidays as well as Olympic events.

Advisors: Bill and Pat Poe (See Directory, Fast-Food Collectibles)

Candy tube, M&M figure waving w/Easter baskets at feet, 2" on 7" tube, EX...**$40.00**
Candy tube, M&M figures in various winter Olympic sports scenes, 2" on 7" tube, M, ea **$40.00**
Clock, M&Ms Racing Team, quartz, battery-operated, MIB..**$30.00**
Clock, Red as cuckoo, Yellow hanging by ankle from pendulum, animated/talking, demo button, M&Ms, battery-operated, MIB **$55.00**
Cookie jar, Cool Blue, sitting on black base w/white M&Ms lettered, ceramic, Mars/Benjamin & Medwin, 2000, MIB .**$35.00**

Desk lamp, Red stands on yellow base w/Yellow on his shoulders & Blue on his shoulders holding spotlight, 19", MIB **$35.00**

Dispenser, spaceship shape w/M symbol, press button to dispense candy, battery-op, red, yellow or blue, MOC, ea **$8.00**

Dispenser, 1991, M&M shape, brown, sm....................**$5.00**

Dispenser, 1991, M&M shape, holding bouquet of flowers, yellow, sm **$2.00**

Dispenser, 1991, M&M shape, red, lg **$10.00**

Dispenser, 1991, peanut shape, brown, sm................**$10.00**

Dispenser, 1991, peanut shape, orange, green or yellow, sm, ea...**$2.00**

Dispenser, 1992, peanut shape, red, lg.....................**$15.00**

Dispenser, 1995, M&M Fun Machine, shaped like a gumball machine **$12.00**

Dispenser, 1995, peanut shape, football player, yellow, lg **$20.00**

Dispenser, 1997, peanut shape, basketball player, $15.00.

Dispenser, 1999, Blues Cafe Sax Player, M&M figure playing sax, NMIB **$35.00**

Doll, M&M shape, plush, 4½"...**$5.00**

Doll, M&M shape, plush, 8"...**$5.00**

Doll, M&M shape, plush, red, 12"................................**$10.00**

Easy Bake Set, w/M&M stencil & spoon, MIB **$12.00**

Figure, M&M shape, bendable arms & legs, red, 5½" .**$20.00**

Figure, peanut shape, bendable arms & legs, blue or yellow, 7", ea **$15.00**

Figurines, Red (plain, 3"), Blue (peanut, 3½"), both waving, red w/flowers, plastic, EX.....................................**$85.00**

Tin, Christmas 1991, 7x4¼" dia, M (sealed) **$17.50**

Tin, Christmas 1992, dark green w/winter scene........**$12.00**

Tin, 1988, blue w/stars & M&Ms, sm **$10.00**

Tin, 1990, 50th Birthday, lg...**$15.00**

Trading cards, Olympic Heros, for 1980 LA Olympic Committee by Mars, 44 cards, EXIB.....................**$55.00**

Michelin Man (Bibendum or Mr. Bib)

Perhaps one of the oldest character logos around today, Mr. Bib actually originated in the late 1800s, inspired by a stack of tires that one of the company founders thought suggested the figure of a man. Over the years his image has changed considerably, but the Michelin Tire Man continues today to represent his company in many countries around the world.

Ashtray, molded plastic, ca 1940s, 4¾x6", from $75.00 to $90.00. (Photo courtesy BJ Summers and Wayne Priddy)

Costume, nylon & metal w/yellow sash, EX.............**$900.00**

Cuff links, gold-tone w/white Mr Bib on blue ground, 7⅛" dia, pr **$50.00**

Cup, plastic, Mr Bib on side, EX **$5.00**

Figure, plastic Mr Bib on motorcycle, EX..................**$110.00**

Figurine, plastic, Mr Bib standing w/hands on hips, banner across chest, 13⅞", EX...**$65.00**

Pen holder, Mr Bib figural, ceramic, marked Bibendum C Michelin, Japan, 6", EX...**$30.00**

Pendant, Mr Bib figural, metal, 2", EX **$15.00**

Pin, Mr Bib on motorcycle, enameled, Canadian, 1" L, EX **$25.00**

Puppet, push-button; Mr Bib, white on yellow base, wooden, marked Made in China, 5", EX.......................**$60.00**

Stand-up display, die-cut cardboard, 71½", VG+, from $90.00 to $120.00. (Photo courtesy Collectors Auction Service)

Mr. Peanut

The trademark character for the Planters Peanuts Company, Mr. Peanut, has been around since 1916. His appearance has changed a little from the original version, becoming more stylized in 1961. Today he's still a common sight on Planters' advertising and product containers.

Mr. Peanut has been modeled as banks, salt and pepper shakers, whistles, and many other novelty items. His image has decorated T-shirts, beach towels, playing cards, sports equipment, etc.

Today Mr. Peanut has his own fan club, Peanut Pals, the collector's organization for those who especially enjoy the Planters Peanuts area of advertising.

Advisors: Judith and Robert Walthall (See Directory, Advertising)

Club: Peanut Pals
Judith Walthall, Founder
P.O. Box 4465, Huntsville, AL 35815; 256-881-9198. Website: www.peanutpals.org. Dues: Primary member, $20 per year; Associate member (16 years old and over), $10 per year; Under 16 years old, $3 per year. Bi-monthly newsletter, annual directory and convention news sent to members. Sample newsletter: $2. For membership, write to PO Box 113, Nesquehoning, PA 18240-0113

Cookie jar, Nabisco Classics Collection, marked Made in China Distributed by Block China, 10", from $35.00 to $50.00. (Photo courtesy Joyce and Fred Roerig)

Apron, Gold Measure, blue, 1991, M **$6.00**
Bank, vending machine style, Mr Peanut stands in front of machine, Products Plus, 1996, MIB **$25.00**
Baseball, image of Mr Peanut, 1992, EX **$4.00**
Basketball, 1999 NCAA Final Four Tampa Bay, Relax Go Nuts & logo, Rawlings, M (unused) **$70.00**
Box, Planters Salt Water Taffy, multicolor, 1970s, EX .**$50.00**
Bracelet, 6 plastic charms on brass-colored chain, 1941, VG **$40.00**
Cook booklet, Planter's Oil, 1948, EX **$25.00**
Cookie jar, Mr Peanut head, hand holding monocle, Mr Peanut on hat, repro of 1966 Nabisco Classics **$25.00**

Cookie jar, seated figure, Planters, Benjamin & Medwin, 1990, MIB **$100.00**
Cruets, oil & vinegar; ceramic, figural, 7", pr, from $125 to **$175.00**
Dish set, child's; Melmac, 3 pcs, 1970s, MIB..............**$20.00**
Doll, stuffed cloth, Chase Bag Co, 1967, 21", EX........**$40.00**
Doll, stuffed cloth, Chase Bag Co, 1970, 18", NM......**$25.00**
Figure, papier-mache, hat comes off, 12½", VG **$175.00**

Figure, wooden, jointed, 12", EX, from $150.00 to $250.00. (Photo courtesy Dunbar Gallery)

Mug, tan plastic Mr Peanut head, M **$10.00**
Nodder, papier-mache, Lego, NM **$150.00**
Nut dish, Mr Peanut sits on top of peanut, Planters Livesavers Co, 1992, 7½x5½", EX...**$150.00**
Nut tray, 3 sections w/Mr Peanut on top, red plastic, 4x5" dia, EX, from $45 to..**$65.00**
Peanut butter maker, Picam, 1970s, 12", MIB.............**$50.00**
Pin, Mr Peanut Santa Claus, wooden, 1930s giveaway, 1¾", EX **$160.00**
Plate, Super Bowl XIII/Planters Snacks, pewter, Wilton, 1978, 11½" dia, MIP..**$60.00**
Radio, transistor; white w/yellow Mr Peanut & Planters, 13", MIB **$40.00**
Radio backpack, Munch 'N Go, 1991, EX, from $35 to ..**$40.00**

Salt and pepper shakers, ceramic, 4½", EX, $75.00.

Standee, cardboard Mr Peanut figure, 12", M.............**$10.00**

Store display, wooden, figural, on round base, German import, fantasy, 25", EX.........................**$95.00**

Tankard, metal pewter type, Wilton, 1983, 4¾".........**$10.00**

Tin, Planter Pennant Salted Peanuts, 10-lb size, 9x8¼", EX..**$60.00**

Toy, wind-up walker, decorated plastic, legs & arms move, 1984, 3", MIP..............................**$15.00**

Toy, wind-up walker, green plastic, 1950s-60s, 8½", NM..**$375.00**

Toy top, Persian Whip-It Top, Planters, 1947 premium, EX...**$265.00**

Toy train set, battery-op, 1988, MIB............................**$50.00**

Whistle, plastic, figural w/metal insert, 3½", EX.........**$42.50**

Old Crow

Old Crow collectors have learned to date this character by the cut of his vest and the tilt of his head along with other characteristics of his stance and attire. Advertising Kentucky whiskey, he appears as an elegant gent in his tuxedo and top hat.

Ashtray, black glass, 1¼x3½", EX **$30.00**

Bottle pourer, plastic figure **$35.00**

Cuff links, gold-tone w/black enamel around crow, EX, pr...**$35.00**

Decanter, light red vest, yellow cane, Royal Doulton, 12½"...**$125.00**

Figure, brass (hollow) crow stands on wooden top hat, 1950s, 11¾", EX...**$130.00**

Figure, brass w/We Pour It brass plaque on black base, 13", VG..**$75.00**

Figure, coated composition, 16", EX, $175.00.

Figure, composition, paint flaking, 9" **$95.00**

Figure, Outstanding Achievement Old Crow Month September 1955, brass on wooden sq base, 13", EX.................**$55.00**

Figure, painted plastic, 1950s, 4", EX **$30.00**

Glass, bourbon; crow & lettering in black on clear, 5".**$12.50**

Glasses, crow-shaped stem, crystal, Libbey, 5¾", set of 6..**$75.00**

Jigger, clear glass w/black lettering, no crow.............**$5.00**

Key chain, figural Old Crow **$5.00**

Key chain, vari-vue flasher, 1⅛x1¾"............................**$15.00**

Lamp, porcelain; red vest w/gold buttons, 1960s, 14", from $175 to...**$195.00**

Pitcher, brown w/embossed crow, marked Old Crow Distillery, 7"...**$25.00**

Pitcher, glass w/metal ring & handle, 5".......................**$25.00**

Plaque, ceramic, with applied 4¾" character crow, 8", NM, $125.00. (Photo courtesy Judith and Robert Walthall)

Roly-poly, plastic, leaded rocker, 9"............................**$95.00**

Stand for bottle, 9" crow in birdcage (on side).........**$125.00**

Standee, cardboard, 8"..**$30.00**

Thermometer, Taste the Greatness of Historic Old Crow, red, white & black, 13½".................................**$100.00**

Poppin' Fresh (Pillsbury Doughboy) and Family

Who could be more lovable than the chubby blue-eyed Doughboy with the infectious giggle introduced by the Pillsbury Company in 1965. Wearing nothing but a neck scarf and a chef's hat, he single-handedly promoted the company's famous biscuits in a tube until about 1969. It was then that the company changed his name to 'Poppin' Fresh' and soon after presented him with a sweet-faced, bonnet-attired mate named Poppie. Before long, they had created a whole family for him. Many premiums such as dolls, salt and pepper shakers, and cookie jars have been produced over the years. In 1988 the Benjamin Medwin Co. made several items for Pillsbury; all of these white ceramic Doughboy items are listed below. Also offered in 1988, the Poppin' Fresh Line featured the plump little fellow holding a plate of cookies; trim colors were mauve pink and blue. The Funfetti line was produced in 1992, again featuring Poppin' Fresh, this time alongside a cupcake topped with Funfetti icing (at that time a fairly new Pillsbury product), and again the producer was Benjamin Medwin.

Bank, gumball style, clear glass w/embossed Poppin' Fresh, cast-iron base, MIB **$45.00**

Bank, Poppin' Fresh, ceramic, marked 1988 Pillsbury Co, M **$50.00**

Beanie, Poppin' Fresh, 2 different styles, ea from $10 to..**$20.00**

Blanket, Snuggle With the Doughboy, Poppin' Fresh on blue, 76x46", EX-..$45.00

Candle holders, Poppin' Fresh, 1 holds fork, 1 holds spoon, Danbury Mint, pr $80.00

Canister, glass, clamp-on lid, from $18 to....................$25.00

Canisters, Poppin' Fresh in different cooking scenes, hand-painted, Danbury Mint, set of 4, M....................$210.00

Clock, Poppin' Fresh w/hands raised above clock w/kitchen scene, Danbury Mint, M.......................$175.00

Cookie jar, Funfetti Line, Benjamin Medwin, 1991, from $50 to..$60.00

Cookie jar, Poppin' Fresh, ceramic, Cookie embossed across chest, 1973, 11", EX, from $40 to $60.00

Cookie jar, Poppin' Fresh, white w/red details, black eyes, ceramic, McCoy, 10", NM $60.00

Doll, Poppin' Fresh, plush, MIP $40.00

Doll, Poppin' Fresh, stuffed cloth, pull-string talker, Mattel, 16", NM...$100.00

Doll, Poppin' Fresh, stuffed cloth, 1970s, 14", VG......$15.00

Doll, Poppin' Fresh, stuffed cloth, 1972, 11", EX, from $15 to..$20.00

Figure, Grandmommer, vinyl, 1974, 5", M, from $75 to...$95.00

Figure, Grandpopper, vinyl, 1974, 5¼", M, from $75 to..$95.00

Figure, Popover Place, Danbury Mint, MIB..............$100.00

Figure, Poppie Fresh, vinyl, 1972, 6", NM, from $15 to..$20.00

Figure, Poppin' Fresh, plush, 1980s, 48", NM..............$70.00

Figure, Poppin' Fresh, vinyl, 1971, w/stand, 7", M (NM box)...$60.00

Figure, Poppin' Fresh, vinyl, 1971, 7", NM $15.00

Finger puppets, Poppie Fresh & her Pals, Poppie, Bun Bun & Biscuit, EX (VG box), from $75 to $100.00

Goodies jar, Poppin' Fresh w/spoon in hand & Goodies (on blue & white label) on clear glass, w/lid, M........$50.00

Gumball machine, Poppin' Fresh, w/5 lbs of gum, MIB .$125.00

Key chain, Poppin' Fresh figure, soft vinyl, MOC.........$6.00

Mold, Poppin' Fresh, Pillsbury Co, Korea, 1975, 7½x3½x1½", EX..$50.00

Mug, ceramic, ca 1985, $15.00. (Photo courtesy Lil West)

Mug, plastic Doughboy figure, 1979, 4½", from $10 to ..$15.00

Pez, Doughboy head, limited edition, hand-painted by The Picaso of Pez, EX..$85.00

Pop-up can, Poppin' Fresh, blue version, EX $300.00

Pop-up can, Poppin' Fresh, orange version, M.........$200.00

Salt & pepper shakers, Poppin' Fresh, ceramic, white w/blue details, 1970s, MIB, from $45 to $60.00

Timer, plastic, digital, 1992, M.....................................$10.00

Tool holder, Funfetti Line, 1992, with tools, MIB, from $20.00 to $25.00. (Photo courtesy Lil West)

Water snow globe, Poppin' Fresh standing on top of the world, glass w/plastic base, 1997, MIB...............$115.00

Water snow globe, Poppin' Fresh w/2 snowmen, glass w/plastic base, MIB $110.00

Reddy Kilowatt

Reddy was developed during the late 1920s and became very well known during the 1950s. His job was to promote electric power companies all over the United States, which he did with aplomb! Reddy memorabilia is highly collectible today, with the small-head plastic figures sometimes selling for $200.00 or more. On Reddy's 65th birthday (1992), a special 'one-time-only' line of commemoratives was issued. This line consisted of approximately thirty different items issued in crystal, gold, pewter, silver, etc. All items were limited editions and quite costly. Because of high collector demand, new merchandise is flooding the market. Watch for items such as a round mirror, a small hand-held game with movable squares, and a ring-toss game, marked 'Made in China.'

Advisor: Lee Garmon (See Directory, Advertising)

Ashtray, clear w/Reddy Kilowatt & figure in red, 6-sided, 1x4½", EX..$15.00

Bus token, brass, Next Time Take the Bus, St Joseph Light & Power Co, ⅝" dia, EX..$8.00

Card holder, Reddy stands on outlet, glow-in-the-dark, 1961, w/gift box, 5½", M (on 9x4¾" card w/advertising)..$185.00

Cookbook, Empire District 'Electric' Baking Contest, Empire District Electric Co, 1951, 288 recipes, 143 pages, VG+ $60.00

Cup & saucer, Reddy w/maroon ribbon around border, Syracuse China, ca 1960, EX..................**$55.00**

Earrings, Reddy figural, screw-back style, 1955, 1", NM (on original card), pr......................................**$25.00**

Hard hat, yellow w/Reddy in black doorway & The Illuminating Co. below in black, full size, EX................................**$30.00**

Lapel pin, Reddy figural, red & gold-tone, 1955, MOC (w/original presentation folder)...........................**$30.00**

Lighter, etched Reddy/Central Maine Power in red, Zippo, some paint missing otherwise EX........................**$40.00**

Nodder, Wacky Wobbler, Reddy figural, Funko, 7½", MIB **$35.00**

Oven mitt, $15.00. (Photo courtesy Lee Garmon)

Patch, red & gold Reddy figural sewn on white, 1950s, 2¼x1¼", M...**$13.50**

Pot holder, There's No Match for Flameless Electric & figure, 1960s, 5½x5½", EX.....................................**$15.00**

Rain gauge, Let 'er Rain, red & black on white, plastic, Oklahoma Gas & Electric Co, 1970s, NM **$45.00**

Sign, Flameless Electric Kitchen, yellow w/black & red letters, star shape, 33x31", EX................................**$180.00**

Sign, Kentucky Power Co., porcelain, 36x48", G, $230.00.

Sign, Reddy Kilowatt under figure in red on white, enameled metal, 5x7", EX..............................**$145.00**

Statue, figural, holding lighting bolt, brass & pewter, wooden base, Northern State Power, 6"......................**$210.00**

Tie clip bar, Reddy figural, 1x1¾", EX (original 1955 card)..**$25.00**

Window decal, Reddy figurals (2), 1960s, 3¼x2¼", EX..**$15.00**

Smokey Bear

The fiftieth anniversary of Smokey Bear, the fire-prevention spokesbear for the State Foresters, Ad Council, and US Forest Service, was celebrated in 1994. After ruling out other mascots (including Bambi), by 1944 it had been decided that a bear was best suited for the job, and Smokey was born. When a little cub was rescued from a fire in a New Mexico national forest in 1950, Smokey's role intensified. Over the years his appearance has evolved from one a little more menacing to the lovable bear we know today.

The original act to protect the Smokey Bear image was enacted in 1974. The character name in the 'Smokey Bear Act' is Smokey Bear. Until the early 1960s, when his name appeared on items such as sheet music and Little Golden Books, it was 'Smokey *the* Bear.' Generally, from that time on, he became known as simply Smokey Bear.

Advisor: Glen Brady (See Directory, Advertising)

Ashtray, figural bust, Prevent Forest Fires Smokey Says Snuff It on hat rim, Hollywood Accessories, NM..........**$30.00**

Bank, ceramic, Smokey with shovel or bucket, unmarked, 6¼", either style: from $125.00 to $135.00. (Photo courtesy Jim and Beverly Mangus)

Bell, ceramic, Prevent Forest Fires on Smokey's sign, EX **$65.00**

Belt buckle, cast metal, 2½x1¾" **$18.00**

Blotter, I Will Be Careful, 1955, unused, EX.................**$8.00**

Bookmark, paper, Smokey & 8" ruler, dated 1961........**$8.00**

Comic, Dell #818, VG+...**$30.00**

Doll, Ideal, plush, complete w/hat, badge & buckle, 1960s, 13", NM $55.00

Doll, Knickerbocker, complete w/all accessories, 17", EX ..$35.00

Doll, 1997 Coca-Cola Collectors Convention Colorado Springs, 2,000 made, 13", NM (VG box)...............$45.00

Figurine, Smokey w/bird in hand & bunny at side, w/Norcrest sticker, 3¾x2¾", EX $35.00

Game, Smokey Bear, board game, Milton Bradley, 1968, M (VG+ box) $30.00

Hand puppet, Ideal, 1969, M..$35.00

Hankerchief, Smokey w/forest creatures on white w/pink border, License US Dept of Agriculture, 21½" sq, EX...$25.00

Poster, desk-top; highway scene w/2 wood-like signs, 1 w/Smokey's face, 1 says Only You...Fires, cardboard, EX $80.00

Poster, Smokey w/hat at chest w/Please...Help People Be More Careful, NY State Conservation, 1952, 13x18½", NM $60.00

Poster, US government, 12½x18", $100.00. (Photo courtesy BJ Summers)

Salt & pepper shakers, Smokey, figural, 1 w/bucket, 1 w/shovel, Made in Japan, 1960s, M (in #H-830 box), pr, from $60 to...$75.00

Sign, Another 30 Million Acres Will Burn...Remember, Only You ...Fires, cardboard, 1948, 11x21", EX.............$45.00

Sign, fire gauge; Smokey Says The Fire Danger Is..., pointer w/Low, Moderate to Extreme, US Forest Service, EX $45.00

Thermos, w/original cap & lid, 1960s, NM..................$55.00

Toy truck, 1926 Seagrave Fire Truck, US Forest Service, w/bank slot, white w/green running boards, Ertl #7638, MIB.$35.00

Toy truck, 1949 Dodge Power Wagon, Smokey Bear decals on doors, First Gear #19-2490, MIB $160.00

Tony the Tiger

Kellogg's introduced Tony the Tiger in 1953, and since then he's appeared on every box of their Frosted Flakes. In his deep, rich voice, he's convinced us all that they are indeed 'Gr-r-r-reat'!

Book, Coloring Fun, w/4 crayons, 1989, MIP $3.00

Doll, Bean Bag Bunch, w/tag, Kellogg's, MIP..............$9.00

Doll, plush, Esso tag on chest, 11", EX.......................$18.00

Doll, plush w/printed cloth face, ca 1960s, 13", EX ...$30.00

Doll, plush, 1991, 10", from $12.00 to $15.00; cereal bowl, plastic, 1995, from $4.00 to $6.00. (Photo courtesy Lee Garmon)

Doll, squeeze vinyl, Product People, 1970s, 9", NM+..$100.00

Duffle bag, cream, picture on front & back, drawstring closure, 17", EX...$10.00

License plate for bicycle, orange plastic, 1973, 3x5", EX+..$12.00

Mug, Tony's face, hard plastic, F&F Mold & Die, EX .$12.00

Place mat, vinyl, characters on both sides, 1981, EX..$10.00

Postcard, Hi! It's Gr-r-reat Here at Camp, Tony w/sleeping bag by sign, unused, 1960s, NM...........................$10.00

Poster, Meet Tony on Tour, paper, 1989, 14x18", NM...$5.00

Radio, figural, AM only, 1980, MIB, from $30 to $40.00

Spoon, figure on handle tip & Tony the Tiger along shaft, 1965, 6", VG+ $18.00

Stopwatch, Tony & Kellogg's Frosted Flakes on black, premium, 1992, EX...$18.00

Valentine cards, set of 30, 1986, MIB $10.00

Miscellaneous

AC Spark Plugs, doll, Sparky the Horse, inflatable vinyl w/logo, Ideal, 1960s, 25x15" L, EX.....................$100.00

Alka-Seltzer, doll, Speedy, vinyl, 1960, 8", EX, from $500 to $700.00

Bazooka Bubble Gum, foil wrapper, 5¢, Topps #42, 1953, EX $25.00

Bosco Chocolate, doll, Bosco the Clown, vinyl, NM ..$45.00

Bosco Chocolate, jar, Bosco the Clown head on glass, marked Bosco, 7½", EX..$14.00

Buster Brown Shoes, clock, Buster & Tige on white ground, Pam Clock Co, 1958, 15" dia, EX $290.00

Buster Brown Shoes, doll, Buster Brown, bisque, jointed arms, marked Japan/Buster Brown Shoes, 4", EX...........$70.00

Buster Brown Shoes, doll, Buster Brown, porcelain, Japan, 2½", EX-..$50.00

Buster Brown Shoes, kite, 1940s, NM $40.00

Cheer Detergent, doll, Cheer Girl, plastic w/cloth clothes, Proctor & Gamble, 1960s, 10", NM......................**$20.00**

Cheetos, doll, Chester Cheetah, plush, 21", MIP **$20.00**

Chicken of the Sea, mermaid doll, Mattel, 1974, 14", MIB, $50.00; Acone Premium, 1991, 12", $50.00. (Photo courtesy Pat Smith)

Chiquita Bananas, salt & pepper shakers, ceramic, unmarked, 3", pr...**$10.00**

Crayola Crayons, doll, Crayola Baby boy, blue w/multi-colored beach ball, plush, Binney & Smith, 1992, 14", EX..**$15.00**

Crayola Crayons, doll, Crayola Baby girl, pink w/yellow bow on dress, Binney & Smith, 1992, 14", EX..............**$15.00**

Crayola Crayons, doll, Crayola Bear, stuffed plush, various colors, Graphics International, 1986, 6", NM, ea..**$10.00**

Dairy Queen, ring, Mr Softee, premium, 1960s, VG+ .**$15.00**

Dairy Queen, salt & pepper shakers, figural, Dairy Queen Maids, Japan, 3⅞", EX, pr **$100.00**

Del Monte, bank, Big Top Bonanza Clown, plastic, 1985, 7", M, from $10 to **$15.00**

Del Monte, doll, Shoo Shoo Scarecrow, 1983, stuffed plush, NM **$15.00**

Energizer Batteries, baseball bat, hot pink w/Energizer Bunny, MIB **$15.00**

Energizer Batteries, figure, Energizer Bunny, plastic resin, 3¼", EX...**$10.00**

Energizer Batteries, squeeze light, Energizer Bunny figure, MIP (sealed) **$8.00**

Eskimo Pie, doll, Eskimo Pie boy, stuffed cloth, 1970s, 15", EX..**$15.00**

Florida Oranges, bank, Orange Bird, vinyl, 1974, MIP ..**$40.00**

Hamburger Helper, doll, Helping Hand, plush glove-like figure w/facial features on palm, 14", M..................**$10.00**

Hamburger Helper, soap bar, Helping Hand figural, 1980s, set of 6, NM...**$15.00**

Hawaiian Punch, doll, Punchy, talking, Fun-4-All, 15", MIB **$15.00**

Hawaiian Punch, drink dispenser, Punchy Punch, plastic, 1970s, 14", NM **$300.00**

Icee, bank, Icee bear w/drink in front of him, rubber, 7", EX...**$30.00**

Jell-O, puppet, Mr Wiggle, red vinyl, 1966, M **$150.00**

Jordache, doll, Jeans Man, Mego, 12", MIB **$30.00**

Kellogg's, bathtub toy, Diving Tony, premium, 1987, EX (w/instructions)...**$14.00**

Kleenex, paper doll counter display, Little Lulu Majorette, International Cellucotton, 1956, 10½", unused, NM..**$15.00**

Kodak, doll, Colorkins, stuffed, ca 1990, 8" to 10", ea..**$20.00**

Kool Cigarettes, figure, Dr Kool, chalk, 4½", VG........**$95.00**

Kool Cigarettes, ramp walker, Kool penguin, wooden w/leather tail & wings, 4¼", VG+ **$45.00**

Levi's, rag doll, Knickerbocker, 1984, 24", EX...........**$120.00**

Little Caesar's, doll, Pizza Pizza Man, plush, holding pizza slice, 1990, EX...**$5.00**

Magic Chef, bank, molded vinyl, 1980s, 7", $20.00.

McGregor Happy Foot, display, EX, from $500.00 to $750.00.

Meow Mix, figure, vinyl cat, EX **$35.00**

Mr Goodbar, pillow, shaped like candy bar, 4x6", NM...**$8.00**

Nestle Chocolate, doll, Chocolate Man, stuffed cloth, Chase Bag Co, 1970, 15", EX **$20.00**

Oscar Meyer, bank, Wienermobile, plastic, 1988, 10", M..**$25.00**

Reese's, doll, Reese's Bear, in Reese's T-shirt, 1989, NM+.**$10.00**

Sinclair Oil, soap, Dino the Dinosaur figure, MIB **$10.00**

Sprite, doll, Lucky Lymon, vinyl talker, 1990s, 7½", M .**$25.00**

Swiss Miss Chocolate, doll, Swiss Miss, stuffed cloth w/vinyl face & yellow yarn hair, EX, minimum value.......**$25.00**

Tony's Frozen Pizza, Mr Tony figural, vinyl, 8½", EX...**$25.00**

Tropicana Orange Juice, doll, Tropic-Ana, stuffed cloth, 1977, 17", NM......**$35.00**

Tyson Chicken, doll, Chicken Quick, stuffed cloth, 13", VG......**$15.00**

Advertising Tins

One of the hottest areas of tin collecting today is spice tins, but if those don't appeal to you, consider automotive products, cleaners, cosmetics, guns, medical, fishing, sewing, or sample sizes. Besides the esthetics factor, condition and age also help determine price. The values suggested below represent what you might pay in an antique store for tins in mint condition. But what makes this sort of collecting so much fun is that you'll find them much cheaper at garage sales, Goodwill Stores, and flea markets.

For good information and wonderful color photos, we recommend *Encyclopedia of Advertising Tins* by David Zimmerman and *Antique Tins, Books I – III,* by Fred Dodge (both by Collector Books).

AK Special Mainsprings, Albert Kleiser, Toronto, factory scene, black & yellow, ¾x2¾" sq......**$35.00**

American Brand Typewriter Ribbon, HM Storms, Indian chief, ¾x2½" sq......**$95.00**

Armand Bouquet Complexion Powder, sample size, ¼x1⅝" dia......**$25.00**

Arnica Tooth Soap, HF Miller, Baltimore, ½x2x3⅛" ...**$55.00**

Arrows Condoms, Continental Can Co, ¼x1¼x1¾" ...**$75.00**

Ben-Hur Pure Curry Powder, man in chariot driving horses on red, 1¼x2¼x3¼"......**$20.00**

Carter's Little Liver Pills $.10, ½x1⅜"......**$18.00**

Colgan's Violet Chips, The Gum That's Round, red & cream, ¾x1½" dia......**$35.00**

Colgate's Rapid Shave Powder, Colgate & Co, New York USA, 1¼x2¼"......**$20.00**

Columbia Ideal Soft Tone Needles, tan & brown, ¼x1⅝x1⅞"......**$35.00**

Comet Auto Fuses, 3-color, ⅜x1¼x1¾"......**$15.00**

Dr Charles Face Powder For the Complexion, American Stopper, 1¼x2¾" dia......**$45.00**

Dr JO Aldrich Lung Salve, Am Can Co 70-A, yellow & black, 1⅜x3½" dia......**$18.00**

Dr Lyon's Tooth Powder, green & black w/gold cap, 3x½x⅞"......**$30.00**

Dr Schoop's Lax-ets a Bowel Laxative 5¢, red, yellow & black, ⅜x1⅛x2½"......**$45.00**

Edison Bell Chromic Needles 100, Made in England, ⅜x1¼x1¾"......**$35.00**

Emergency Adhesive Plaster, Aseptic Products Co, New York USA, black & white, ¼x1⅛x2¼"......**$35.00**

Fine Service Brand (typewriter ribbons), airplane reserve, cream & black, ⅞x2½" dia......**$10.00**

Ford's Free Sample Hair Pomade, ⅜x1¼" dia......**$15.00**

Frederick Stearns & Co Aromatic Tooth Soap, Chicago Stamping Co, ½x2x3⅛"......**$75.00**

Fulton Stamp Pad No XX, ⅜x1¼x2¼"......**$8.00**

Genuine Aspirin, 12 Tablest 5 Grains Each, yellow, white, green & black, ⅜x1¼x1¾"......**$10.00**

Golden Sheaf Brande Pure Spices Ginger, 1½-oz, 3x2¼x1¼", minimum value......**$35.00**

Home Remedy Hazine Healing Ointment, yellow & black, 1x2⅜" dia......**$30.00**

Kelly's Slide Shoe Polish, TINDECO, 1x2⅞"......**$150.00**

Klein's Japanese Cough Drops 15¢, dragon logo, gold & black, ⅞x3x3"......**$40.00**

Kutnow's Anti-Asthmatic Powder, New York NY, 2-oz, 1⅜x2¼x3⅛"......**$30.00**

Lecroy's Poultry Seasoning, red, yellow & black, American Can 27-A, 3x2¼x1¼", minimum value......**$15.00**

Lexoid Reumatic Balm, Cleveland O, black & white, ⅝x1½"......**$18.00**

McGregor Ribbons, Scotsman playing bagpipes, red & black, ⅞x2½" dia......**$12.00**

Nash's Toasted Coffee, red, gold, black & white, American Can 10-A, sample size, 2¾x3⅜" dia......**$80.00**

New Brunswick Tire Repair Kit, ½x2x3⅛"......**$80.00**

Opal Red Pepper, red, yellow & black, 3¼x2¼x1¼", minimum value......**$25.00**

Otto Cold Cream, 3-color, ¾x1¾" dia......**$12.00**

Palmer's Skin Success Ointment, sample size, ¼x⅞" dia.**$25.00**

Pinex Cold Tablets 15¢, Ft Wayne Ind, black & gold, ¼x1¼x1¾"......**$16.00**

Pompeian Day Cream (Vanishing), flower, ⅜x1⅜" dia.**$5.00**

Premier Golden Snuff, Spelling & Morris, man's portrait, England, ½x1¾x2⅜"......**$20.00**

Princess Pat Lip Rouge, Chicago USA, ¼x1⅛" dia......**$10.00**

Rose-Vel The Great Healer 25 Cents, 1½-oz, 1x2½" dia..**$10.00**

Scott Vegetable Tablets, The Owl Drug Company, owl logo, red, white & black, ½x1⅝x2½"......**$40.00**

Tholene Salve 25¢, Rosebud Perfume Co, red, white & black, ⅞x2⅛"......**$20.00**

Tiger Brand Russet Shoe Polish, tiger logo, ¾x1¾" dia......**$30.00**

Tod Co Pocket Size Superior Quality Waxed Dental Floss, ¼x1¼" dia......**$25.00**

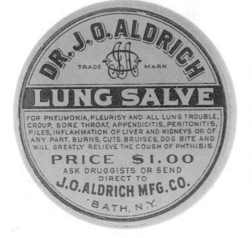

Dr. Aldrich, Lung Salve, American Can Co. 3½" diameter, $18.00. (Photo courtesy David Zimmerman)

Turkey Red Red Pepper, gobbler on front, 3x2⅛x1¼", minimum value..**$45.00**

Viking Line Typewriter Ribbon, Eriksen Ribbon & Carbon Co, sailing ship, 2¼x2½" sq...................................**$25.00**

Williams' English Lilac Talc Powder, flower, JB Williams Co, ¾x1⅜x2¼" **$65.00**

Yeast Bouillon Cubes, Harris Laboratories, black, white & yellow, ⅝x1⅞x2⅝" **$10.00**

Advertising Watches

The concept of the advertising watch is strictly twentieth century. Some were produced through the 1960s, but it wasn't until the early 1970s that watches were increasingly used for advertising. Now, many themes, subjects, and types are available. Collectible ad watches include mechanical/battery-operated pocket watches; mechanical/battery-operated wristwatches; digital/analog (with hands) watches; dress/sports watches; company logo/character watches; corporate/in-house watches; catalog/store retail watches; and giveaway/premium watches.

Condition, originality, cleanliness, scarcity, completeness, cross-collectibility, and buyer demand all affect value. The more recently issued the watch, the better its condition must be. Original mint packaging (including any paperwork) can triple value. Look for original watch offers and order forms on old packaging and magazines; they are desirable for documentation and are collectible in their own right. Look through 'parts boxes'; an old, nonworking ad pocket or wristwatch, even without a strap, may have value. A higher degree of wear is acceptable on an older watch.

A popular character/event will add value. Currently, demand is good for some '70s characters such as Mr. Peanut and Charlie the Tuna, the '80s – '90s M&M watches, and the '90s Pillsbury Doughboy. Demand for a watch that features a forgotten or less popular character may be limited, even if it is an older one, and value could be affected.

Great numbers of watches exist for Coca-Cola, Pepsi, various automobiles, Camel, and other tobacco products. These are usually of most interest to collectors who specialize in those fields. A 'reverse attitude' may exist — the more watches produced for a theme or character, the less desirable it is to the typical ad watch collector.

Copyright dates can lead to confusion about the age of a watch. The date may refer to the publishing date of the character or logo, not the year the watch was made. Date watches by style and features. Generally, analog watches are more collectible than digital. A watch need not be working; most are not of high quality. Examine watches displayed in glass cases at outdoor shows for signs of moisture buildup and sun fading. Remove dead batteries only if you can do so without damaging the watch or packaging.

Common watches that currently have little value are the 1984 Ronald McDonald House — Coca-Cola carded watches, the 1995 Kodak Lion King, Life Cereals Mask and Where's Waldo watches, and all the Burger King, McDonald's, and Taco Bell watches for various movies.

Buyer Beware: Some fantasy pocket watches are being produced using old watch cases. A pocket watch with detailed full-color artwork on a paper face is suspect, even if the case looks old or has an older date on it. These paper watch faces are easily made on a color copy machine.

Advisor: Sharon Iranpour (See Directory, Advertising Watches)

Newsletter: *The Premium Watch Watch©*
Sharon Iranpour, Editor
24 San Rafael Dr.
Rochester, NY 14618-3702; 585-381-9467 or Fax: 585-383-9248; e-mail: watcher1@rochester.rr.com Specialized newsletter on premium - advertisement - logo watches; $16 per year, black and white, bimonthly. Details on latest watch offers, news, free ads for subscribers. Send LSASE for sample copy.

Pre-1970s

Many mechanical pocket and wristwatches are known; most appeal to 'masculine' interests and professions such as automobiles and related products. As early as the 1920s, Chevrolet gave wristwatches to top-performing salesmen; the watch case was in the shape of a car radiator front. Many commemorative watches were issued for special events like world's fairs.

McLenin, 1960s (fantasy), $50.00. (Photo courtesy Sharon Iranpour)

Buster Brown Pocket Watch, 1960s, VG **$75.00**

Chevrolet Salesman's Award Wristwatch, 1927, EX...**$350.00**

FS Fertilizer Pocket Watch, G **$35.00**

Mr Peanut Wristwatch, yellow face w/date window, 1967, EX **$50.00**

Mr Peanut Wristwatch, yellow face 1966, EX **$50.00**
New York World's Fair Ingraham Pocket Watch, 1939, EX .**$400.00**
Punchy, mechanical, digital, red strap, 1960s, VG **$50.00**
Red Goose Shoes Wristwatch, 1960s, G..................**$130.00**
Reddy Kilowatt Pocket Watch, 1940s, VG **$150.00**
Rexall Ingersoll Pocket Watch, 1908, EX **$150.00**
Shell Oil Girard-Perregaux Pocket Watch, 1940s, EX..**$200.00**
St Louis World's Fair Ingersoll Pocket Watch, 1904, EX ..**$200.00**
Toppie Elephant, 1950s, G.................................**$100.00**
Twinkie the Brown Shoe Elf, 1920s, G....................**$100.00**
Westinghouse Refrigerator Pocket Watch, 1940s, MIB ..**$75.00**

The 1970s

The most common were mechanicals with a heavy metal case, often marked 'Swiss Made.' Some had wide straps with snaps or straps with holes. Mechanical digital watches and revolving disks appeared. As a general rule, special packaging did not exist. Wristwatches from the '70s are appearing at Internet auction sites and at shows in greater frequency due to growing interest. They are generally valued from $30.00 to $300.00 in very good to mint condition. Watches listed in this section are all mechanical wristwatches.

Big Boy, watch hands are arms, 1970, MIB **$50.00**
Buster Brown, red costume, VG...................................**$75.00**
Charlie Tuna, faces left, 1971, MIB **$40.00**
Charlie Tuna, faces right, 1973, M..............................**$40.00**
Count Chocula, Booberry & Frankenberry, Lafayette Watch Co, MIB **$300.00**
Ernie Keebler, 1970s, M..**$30.00**
Goodyear Tires, revolving disk, G **$50.00**
Goofy Grape, 1976, G **$200.00**
Mr Peanut, blue face, mechanical, digital, 1975, EX ...**$50.00**
Punchy, red strap, 1971, VG **$25.00**
Raid Bug Spray, revolving disk, EX...........................**$75.00**
Ritz Crackers, 1971, MIB **$25.00**
Ronald McDonald, various, MIB................................**$25.00**
Scrubbing Bubbles, M **$25.00**
Tony the Tiger, 1976, MIB **$75.00**

The 1980s

Digital and analog battery-operated watches became the norm; mechanicals all but disappeared early in the decade. Watches became slim and lightweight with plastic commonly used for both the case and the strap. Electronic hands (visible only when the battery is good), clam shell and pop-up digital watches appeared; revolving disks were frequently used. Toward the end of the decade, printing on straps began. Specially designed packaging became more commonplace. Hanger cards added design to otherwise plain digital watches. These are most desirable in excellent, unopened condition. Watches from the 1980s are generally valued from $10.00 to $50.00 in mint condition. Watches listed in this section are battery operated unless noted otherwise.

Brach's Peppermint, 1988, MIB **$15.00**
Campbell Kids windup, 4 different, 1982, MIB w/slip cover, ea **$35.00**
Captain Midnight by Ovaltine, 1988, M **$30.00**
Charlie the Tuna 25th Anniversary, 1986, MIB...........**$15.00**
Kellogg's Atlantis Do & Learn Set, 1983, MIB **$15.00**
Knoxville World's Fair, windup pocket & wristwatches, 1982, MIB, ea **$25.00**
Kraft Cheese & Macaroni Club, M **$10.00**
M&Ms, various, MIB **$15.00**
Max Headroom by Coca-Cola, man's or lady's, 1987, M, ea...**$10.00**
Stanley Powerlock, M..**$30.00**
Swiss Miss, mechanical windup, 1981, MIB **$40.00**
Welch's Grape Juice, 1989, M **$20.00**
7-Up, windup, Jerry Lewis tie-in, 4 different, MIB, ea ...**$10.00**

The 1990s

Case and strap design became innovative. New features were holograms on the watch face, revolving subdials, 'talking' features, water watches (liquid within case/straps), stopwatches and timers, game watches, giga pets, and clip-on clocks. Classic and retro styling became popular. Very well designed packaging including special boxes and printed tins became more common as did printed plastic straps. Clear printed resin straps (Swatch type) and diecut rubber straps emerged. Companies created their own retail catalogs and websites to sell logo merchandise. Licensing agreements produced many tie-ins with movies, TV, and sports events. Most plastic watches currently sell in the $5.00 to $15.00 range; there is little market for the most common. Quality, hard-to-find gold- and silver-tone watches rarely sell beyond $25.00 at the present.

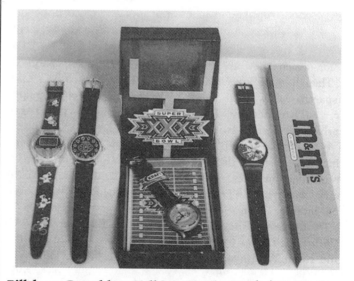

Pillsbury Doughboy Talking Watch, 1996, $15.00; Oreo Cookie Watch, 1996, $25.00; Kraft Super Bowl XXX Watch in goal post box, 1996, $20.00; New Blue M&M's Watch, 1996, $15.00. (Photo courtesy Sharon Iranpour)

Bart Simpson, Butterfingers Candy, 1990, M **$15.00**
Campbell Soup Alphabet, 1994, M **$35.00**
Cheerios Gumby & Pokey, 1997, MIB **$25.00**
Dunkin' Donuts, 1999, M **$10.00**
Eggo Waffles Eggosaurus, 1990, M **$10.00**
Kool Aid Hologram, 1991, M **$10.00**
Mars Snicker's Anniversary, 1990, M **$25.00**
Mr Magoo by Nutrasweet, 1995, M **$20.00**
Quaker Chewy Granola Bars Wildlife Hologram Watch, 1993,
      M **$5.00**

Oscar Meyer Wienermobile, 1994, $5.00. (Photo courtesy Sharon Iranpour)

The 2000s

Few true premium watches requiring a product purchase are being offered, either on specially marked packages or with store forms. More offers and retail watches are appearing on Internet websites. Online auction sites, primarily eBay.com, make it easier to find older watches, regional pieces, and corporate watches from special projects or events.

EBay has become a reliable indicator of prices and availability. Watches such as the 1970s Ritz Cracker and Tony the Tiger, once thought to be scarce MIB and valued at hundreds of dollars, are commonly available and worth $75.00. In the last two years, many watches have lost book value as their true issue numbers appear. Chances are that the availability of mint older pieces will diminish over time, so now is a good time to buy.

Take care when buying new watches related to newsworthy people or events. The price may have an early surge but drop back once the initial interest abates. At the turn of the twenty-first century, Millennium ad watches were eagerly sought by collectors. They are no longer appearing on eBay. Popular character watches continue to have a strong following.

Enron Field LE 500, MIB **$45.00**
Kellogg's Canada, Snap, Crackle & Pop, set of 3, MIP, ea ..**$3.00**
M&Ms Vending, 2002, M **$35.00**
Sears Buddy Lee, 2000, M **$15.00**
Tic Tac Incredible Stuff, 2000, MIB **$20.00**

Airline Memorabilia

Even before the Wright brothers' historic flight prior to the turn of the century, people have been fascinated with flying. What better way to enjoy the evolution and history of this amazing transportation industry than to collect its memorabilia. Today just about any item ever used or made for a commercial (non-military) airline is collectible, especially dishes, glasswares, silver serving pieces and flatware, wings and badges worn by the crew, playing cards, and junior wings given to passengers. Advertising items such as timetables and large travel agency plane models are also widely collected. The earlier, the better! Anything pre-war is good; items from before the 1930s are rare and often very valuable.

See also Restaurant China.

Advisor: Dick Wallin (See Directory, Airline)

Clubs and Newsletters: World Airline Historical Society P.O. Box 660583, Miami Springs, FL 33266

Website: www.airlinecollectibles.com

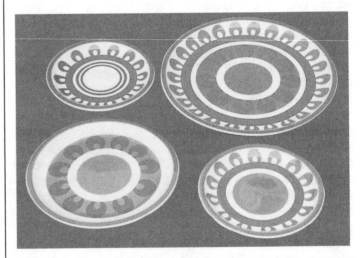

Dinnerware, Western Airlines 'Fiesta' Mexico DC10 flight, made by Block of Portugal, 1960s, from $25.00 to $35.00 per piece. (Photo courtesy Dick Wallin)

Ashtray, Pan American, blue glass, triangular w/logo ea
      side **$18.00**
Bowl, soup; Delta, widget logo, Mayer China, 1974.....**$5.00**
Bowl, soup/cereal; Western, 60th Anniversary logo, ABCO,
      1986 ....**$10.00**
Bowl, United, Connosseur, Noritake, 1994, 4½", NM .**$12.00**
Brochure, Northwest Orient, Going Our Way, 4-color, 1984,
      8x11", EX **$12.50**
Brochure, United Airlines, Yosemite, 1951, trifold, opens to
      8½x11", EX **$10.00**
Butter pat, Air France, green, bisque, 1970, NM **$5.00**
Butter pat, Lufthansa, Frankfurt pattern, gray on white, 1960,
      EX..**$20.00**
Card, Western Airlines, Seat Occupied (4 languages), red lettering on white card stock, NM **$9.00**

Casserole, National, Sun King Logo, oval, Hall China, EX ..**$12.00**

Cordial, Eastern, Rosenthal, 1970 ....**$12.00**

Cup & saucer, American, American Traveler, cobalt rim stripe, 1970s..**$10.00**

Cup & saucer, Delta, Signature Ivory, Mayer China....**$10.00**

Cup & saucer, TWA, Ambassador, Rego **$18.00**

Cup & saucer, TWA, Royal Ambassador, Rosenthal **$20.00**

Flatware, National Airlines, silver-plated fork, knife & spoon, stamped National, 1970, EX **$18.00**

Glassware, Eastern Airlines souvenirs, 1950s, each $20.00. (Photo courtesy Dick Wallin)

Handkerchief, souvenir; Lufthansa, bright print on linen, 11½" sq, M..**$8.00**

Map, American Airlines International System, multicolored, 1949, 8x9", EX..**$20.00**

Mug, coffee; Braniff, black & white, Hall China **$5.00**

Mug, coffee; Eastern, Platinum Line, REGO **$7.00**

Place card, TWA, lamimated, EX **$10.00**

Place card, Western, logo w/Occupied (smaller Occupado) on cloudy sky blue ground, 1978, EX..................**$12.00**

Plate, American, Baumgardner, Mayer China, 1973, 8"..**$12.00**

Plate, bread & butter; Delta, blue & red widget logo, Mayer China..**$5.00**

Plate, dinner; Air France, Premiere, Limoges..............**$25.00**

Salt and pepper shakers on tray, Malaysian Airlines System, by Noritake China Co., $35.00. (Photo courtesy Dick Wallin)

Spoon, souvenir; JAL, crane logo on handle, 1965, EX ..**$5.00**

Swizzle stick, Aeromexico, orange logo, 1978 ....**$2.00**

Swizzle stick, Continental, Continental to Denver, 1980 ...**$2.00**

Ticket cover, TWA Twin Globe, heavy paper stock, 1966, opens to 16x3¾" w/reservation info **$5.00**

Tumbler, Pan American, Clipper Club, Libbey, ca 1965, w/Clipper Club membership certificate **$25.00**

Tumbler, United, shield logo in oval, weighted base, 1970s **$16.00**

Wine, Air Canada, maple leaf logo, 1970 ....**$10.00**

Wings, Kiddie; Continental, red logo & gold finish **$5.00**

Wings, Kiddie; Eastern, adhesive back..........................**$2.00**

Akro Agate

The Akro Agate Company operated in West Virginia from 1914 until 1951, and in addition to their famous marbles they made children's dishes as well as many types of novelties — flowerpots, powder jars with Scottie dogs on top, candlesticks, and ashtrays, for instance — in many colors and patterns. Though some of their glassware was made in solid colors, their most popular products were made of the same swirled colors as their marbles. Though many pieces are not marked, you will find some that are marked with their distinctive logo: a crow flying through the letter 'A' holding an Aggie in its beak and one in each claw. Some novelty items may instead carry one of these trademarks: 'JV Co, Inc,' 'Braun & Corwin,' 'NYC Vogue Merc Co USA,' 'Hamilton Match Co,' and 'Mexicali Pickwick Cosmetic Corp.'

Color is a very important worth-assessing factor. Some pieces may be common in one color but rare in others. Occasionally an item will have exceptionally good multiple colors, and this would make it more valuable than an example with only average color.

Recently boxed sets of marbles have increased dramatically. When buying either marbles or juvenile tea sets in original boxes, be sure the box contains its original contents. For more information we recommend *The Complete Line of the Akro Agate Co.* by our advisors, Roger and Claudia Hardy.

Club: Akro Agate Collectors Club
Clarksburg Crow newsletter
Claudia and Roger Hardy
10 Bailey St., Clarksburg, WV 26301-2524; 304-624-4523

Concentric Rib, boxed set, opaque colors other than green or white, 21-pc **$150.00**

Concentric Rib, creamer, opaque green or white..........**$4.50**

Concentric Rib, saucer, opaque colors other than green or white **$2.50**

Concentric Rib, teapot & lid, opaque green or white...**$9.00**

Concentric Ring, lg, cereal, marbleized/blue...............**$50.00**

Concentric Ring, lg, teapot & lid, solid colors.............**$45.00**

Concentric Ring, sm, boxed set, solid colors, 16-pc.**$250.00**

Concentric Ring, sm, plate, cobalt...............................**$12.50**

Interior Panel, lg, boxed set, azure blue & yellow, 17-pc.**$325.00**

Interior Panel, lg, creamer, transparent topaz & green **$18.00**

Interior Panel, lg, sugar bowl & lid, lemonade & oxblood.**$55.00**

Interior Panel, sm, boxed set, blue & white, 8-pc **$190.00**
Interior Panel, sm, creamer, maroon & white **$20.00**
Interior Panel, sm, saucer, green & white.....................**$6.00**
Miss America, boxed set, transparent green, 11-pc .**$1,200.00**
Miss America, cup, transparent green, from $60 to ..**$100.00**
Miss America, saucer, marbleized, from $20 to **$25.00**
Miss America, teapot (open), white, from $50 to........**$60.00**
Octagonal, lg, boxed set, lemonade & oxblood, 20-pc.**$1,000.00**
Octagonal, lg, cereal, solid colors **$6.00**
Octagonal, lg, tumbler, solid colors **$10.00**

Octagonal, mixed colors, large, open handle, Play Time seven-piece water set, various colors, MIB, $245.00. (Photo courtesy Margaret and Kenn Whitmyer)

Octagonal, sm, plate, yellow/orange.............................**$8.50**
Octagonal, sm, sugar bowl, solid colors, open handles ..**$10.00**
Raised Daisy, cup, blue..**$75.00**
Raised Daisy, teapot, green...**$40.00**
Raised Daisy, tumbler, yellow & beige **$25.00**
Stacked Disc & Interior Panel, boxed water set, transparent green, 7-pc **$75.00**
Stacked Disc & Interior Panel, lg, cup, marbleized blue .**$40.00**
Stacked Disc & Interior Panel, lg, teapot & lid, solid opaque color...**$50.00**
Stacked Disc & Interior Panel, sm, cup, transparent green...**$40.00**
Stacked Disc & Interior Panel, sm, tumbler, cobalt.....**$20.00**
Stippled Band, lg, boxed set, transparent topaz, 17-pc (black box) **$275.00**
Stippled Band, lg, cup, transparent blue (azure or cobalt)...**$22.00**
Stippled Band, sm, cup, transparent topaz..................**$16.00**
Stippled Band, sm, sugar bowl, transparent green **$15.00**

Marbles

Brick (Oxblood swirled w/black or white), usually found in ⅝" to 1", from $40 to.............................**$150.00**
Carnelian (translucent orange, white & oxblood), usually found in ⅝" to ¾", from $15 to............................**$75.00**

Colored Glass Translucent Spiral (corkscrew), usually found in ⅝" to ¾", from $6 to...**$18.00**
Double Twist Opaque Spiral (corkscrew), usually found in ⅝" to ¾", from $5 to **$20.00**
Lemonade Oxblood, usually found in ⅝" to ¾", from $40 to **$125.00**
Lemonade Spiral (yellow & white opaque, corked/translucent base), usually found in ⅝" to ¾", from $8 to........**$25.00**

Opals, fifty #6s, MIB, $1,000.00. (Photo courtesy Roger and Claudia Hardy)

Opaque Oxblood Swirl, usually found in ⅝" to ¾", from $8 to...**$25.00**
Opaque 2-Color Oxblood Spiral (corkscrew), usually found in ⅝" to ¾", from $15 to.....................................**$40.00**
Royal Blue Onyx, usually found in ⅝" to ¾", from $75 to...**$300.00**
Sky Blue Onyx, scarce, most are ⅝", if M, minimum value **$100.00**

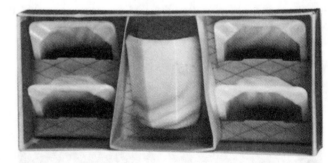

Smoker's set, MIB, green: $100.00; oxblood, $145.00; blue, $110.00. (Photo courtesy Roger and Claudia Hardy)

Tri-Onyx (Popeye, 3-color corkscrew on crystal base), navy, yellow & white), usually found in ⅝" to ¾", $15 to **$35.00**

Miscellaneous

Ashtray, black, sq...**$45.00**

Ashtray, Diamond Tire $60.00
Ashtray, marbleized, 5" sq, from $60 to......$90.00
Ashtray, shallow, no rest, from $100 to $125.00
Basket, 1-handled, blue marbleized.................$375.00
Basket, 1-handled, orange marbleized................$250.00
Basket, 2-handled, any color, ea from $40 to $50.00
Bell, crystal $30.00
Bell, ivory $75.00
Bell, white $60.00
Bowl, any color except black or marbleized, footed, 8"..$400.00
Bowl, Stacked Disc, solid color, 5"..............$35.00
Candlestick, inkwell type, blue.................$30.00
Candlestick, inkwell type, green $25.00
Candlestick, inkwell type, marbleized.............$20.00
Candlestick, Tall Ribbed, green marbleized $250.00
Flowerpot, Banded Dart, any color, #302, 5½", from $65
   to $70.00
Flowerpot, Graduated Dart, marbleized, #308, from $200
   to $250.00
Flowerpot, Graduated Dart, solid color, from $150 to..$175.00
Flowerpot, ribbed top, #291 ....$8.00
Flowerpot, ribbed wide top, from $40 to $50.00
Flowerpot, Ribs & Flutes, marbleized, #307, from $30 to ..$40.00
Flowerpot, Ribs & Flutes, solid color, #307, from $20 to ...$25.00
Flowerpot, Stacked Disc, any color, 5½"....................$25.00
Jardiniere, Graduated Dart, sq mouth, solid color, 5".$50.00
Jardiniere, Ribs & Flutes, sq mouth, solid color, 5" $35.00
Mexicali Jar w/Hat, from $45 to $60.00
Planter, Japanese, solid color, 11¼", from $400 to ...$450.00
Powder jar, Concentric Ring, marbleized, from $35 to .$40.00
Powder jar, Ivy, marbleized $75.00

Powder jar, Scottie Dog, light blue, 6½", $110.00. (Photo courtesy Candace Sten Davis and Patricaia J. Baugh)

Puff box, Apple, orange................................$250.00
Puff box, Colonial Lady, dark green $450.00
Puff box, Colonial Lady, pink.................................$80.00
Puff box, Colonial Lady, royal blue $225.00
Puff box, Scotty Dog, light green...........................$225.00
Puff box, Scotty Dog, med blue...............................$125.00
Vase, Ribs & Flutes, marbleized, from $225 to..........$250.00
Vase, Tab-Handled, black, from $90 to.......................$100.00

Aluminum

The aluminum items which have become today's collectibles range from early brite-cut giftware and old kitchen wares to furniture and hammered aluminum cooking pans. But the most collectible, right now, at least, is the giftware of the 1930s through the 1950s.

There were probably several hundred makers of aluminum accessories and giftware with each developing their preferred method of manufacturing. Some pieces were cast; other products were hammered with patterns created by either an intaglio method or repousse. Machine embossing was utilized by some makers; many used faux hammering, and lightweight items were often decorated with pressed designs.

As early as the 1940s, collectors began to seek out aluminum, sometimes to add to the few pieces received as wedding gifts. By the late 1970s and early 1980s, aluminum giftware was found in abundance at almost any flea market, and prices of $1.00 or less were normal. As more shoppers became enthralled with the appearance of this lustrous metal and its patterns, prices began to rise. A few highly prized pieces have brought prices of four or five hundred dollars and occasionally even more.

One of the first to manufacture this type of ware was Wendell August Forge, when during the late 1920s they expanded their line of decorative wrought iron and began to use aluminum, at first making small items as gifts for their customers. Very soon they were involved in a growing industry estimated at one point to be comprised of several hundred companies, among them Arthur Armour, the Continental Silver Company, Everlast, Buenilum, Rodney Kent, and Palmer-Smith. Few of the many original companies survived the WWII scarcity of aluminum.

During the '60s, anodized (colored) aluminum became very popular. It's being bought up today by the younger generations who are attracted to its neon colors and clean lines. Watch for items with strong color and little if any sign of wear — very important factors to consider when assessing value. Because it was prone to scratching and denting, mint condition examples are few and far between.

Prices differ greatly from one region to another, sometimes without regard to quality or condition, so be sure to examine each item carefully before you buy. There are two good books on the subject: *Hammered Aluminum, Hand Wrought Collectibles,* by Dannie Woodard; and *Collectible Aluminum, An Identification and Value Guide*, by Everett Grist (Collector Books).

See also Kitchen.

Advisor: Dannie Woodard (See Directory, Aluminum)

Ashtray, Bruce Fox, bass jumping in center, EX details, 6"
   sq $45.00
Ashtray, Wendell August Forge, Pine Cone, 6" dia $25.00
Basket, Continental Silver, Chrysanthemum, saddlebag shape
   w/strap handle, 3x11x7".................................$25.00

Basket, Everlast, Apple, double handle meets in center in sq knot, 6x11" dia..................**$10.00**

Basket, Hand Finished, fruit & flowers, open ends, double inside loop handle, 9x14x9".....................**$10.00**

Basket, Japan, floral pattern, hammered rim, serrated edge, hammered handle w/2 inside loops, 7x10x8" **$5.00**

Basket, unmarked, Rose pattern, 3-part divided glass insert, single loop handle w/molded twist pattern, 4x7" dia ..**$10.00**

Bowl, Continental Silver, Chrysanthemum, footed, bracket handles w/applied leaves & embossed foliage, 4½x10"....................**$25.00**

Bowl, Rodney Kent, Tulips, earred handles, serrated rim, 2x10".....................**$35.00**

Bowl, Warranted, mixed flowers & foliage, scalloped & fluted rim, 2½x11".....................**$5.00**

Bowl, Wendell August Forge, Dogwood, fluted & crimped rim, 2x7" dia.....................**$20.00**

Box, cigarette; Wendell August Forge, Bittersweet, 1½x3x5".....................**$75.00**

Cake stand, Wilson Metal, band of shields, serrated edge, 8x12".....................**$15.00**

Candelabra, Langbein, hammered, Art Nouveau influence, 13x6" sq base, pr.....................**$125.00**

Candlesticks, Everlast, hammered, scalloped base, fluted boboche, 3x4", pr.....................**$20.00**

Candy dish, Buenilum, 2 leaves w/looping stems joining & forming handle, 6x5".....................**$10.00**

Candy dish, Cromwell, fruit & flowers decor in bottom only, double bowls w/center handle, 13" L.....................**$10.00**

Casserole, Arthur Armour, Dogwood & Butterfly, glass insert, ring finial, lipped handles, 4x10".....................**$65.00**

Casserole, Everlast, Apple, flower finial, 5x9".....................**$5.00**

Casserole, Everlast, Bamboo, bamboo-like handles & finial, lid cut to accomodate glass insert, 5x7".....................**$18.00**

Coaster, Alpha Swiss, Capitol Building in Washington DC, 4½" dia.....................**$3.00**

Coaster, unmarked, hammered effect, glass center w/embossed flower, 4½" dia.....................**$3.00**

Compote, unmarked, allover hammered effect, tulip & ribbon finial, hammered base, w/lid.....................**$15.00**

Crumber & tray, Everlast, leaf design.....................**$18.00**

Double boiler, Buenilum, highly polished, wood handle & finial, Pyrex liner, 7" dia.....................**$10.00**

Fish dish, Royal Hickman, EX detail, 18¾x8⅛".....................**$85.00**

Ice bucket, Everlast, intaglio flowers, 3x7" dia.....................**$20.00**

Ice bucket, Kromex, hammered effect, black handles & finial, 12x8" dia.....................**$10.00**

Lazy Susan, unmarked, acorn, open flower & leaf decor on 2 sides of plate, 18" dia.....................**$15.00**

Mint dish, unmarked, Chrysanthemum, pansy shape w/3 compartments, 10".....................**$20.00**

Pitcher, Buenilum, hammered effect, 8x6" dia.....................**$25.00**

Pitcher, Continental, Chrysanthemum, applied leaf at base of handle, ice lip, 9".....................**$35.00**

Plaque, hobbyist; unmarked, Pine Cone, scalloped & fluted edge, 11" dia.....................**$2.00**

Plate, Wendell August Forge, Dogwood, 9".....................**$18.00**

Salad fork & spoon, unmarked, 12", pr.....................**$45.00**

Silent butler, Everlast, Rose, 6" dia.....................**$10.00**

Table, Wendell August Forge, twisted cable X-brace & legs w/stanchion finial, Pine Cone & Needles, 19x21" dia.....................**$450.00**

Tray, bar; Everlast, rope & sea gulls, applied handles, 15x9".....................**$30.00**

Tray, bar; Wendell August Forge, flying geese scene, 17x9".....................**$50.00**

Tray, bread; unmarked, Apple Blossom, fluted sides, 13x9".....................**$5.00**

Tray, cheese & cracker; Continental, Acorn & Leaf, 15" dia.....................**$15.00**

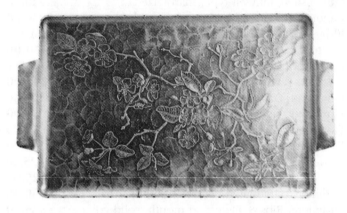

Tray, Cherries, Wendell August Forge, 16" long, $45.00.

Tray, Everlast, Bamboo, 2-tier, bamboo finial, 9x10" dia...**$15.00**

Tray, sandwich; Hand Forged, Crested Crane & Bamboo, applied handles, 9" dia.....................**$10.00**

Tray, sandwich; unmarked, Acorn & Leaf, fluted edge, applied handles, 11" dia.....................**$15.00**

Tray, serving; Cromwell, Fruit Band, wire loop handles, oblong, 19x13".....................**$10.00**

Tray, serving; Everlast, horses, handles, 12x16".....................**$15.00**

Tray, serving; unmarked, intaglio flying duck scene, 15x9".....................**$5.00**

Tray, serving; Wendell August Forge, Larkspur, 13x20"..**$75.00**

Tray, snack; unmarked, fruit, lipped, self handles, 10x6".**$2.00**

Trivet, Continental, Acorn, serrated edge, 10" dia.......**$12.00**

Water set, hammered, no mark: pitcher, 7", $15.00; tumblers, 5", set of six, $18.00; tray, $7.00.

Anodized (Colored)

Ashtrays, crown-like shape, cigarettes held in notches, Parkit Safe, 3x1", set of 4, MIB....................**$24.00**

Bowl, ruby red, textured w/embossed grapes on border, West Bend, 14" dia, EX....................**$17.50**

Bowl, serving; 10" dia, w/4 6½" dia matching bowls, unmarked, EX **$12.00**

Bowl, 6", Bascal, set of 8, EX **$26.00**

Cake salver, hot pink w/black handle on cover, Regal, 13" plate, EX **$30.00**

Candle holders, leaf-&-grape embossed pattern in bowl-like bottom, Kraft, 4½", EX, pr **$20.00**

Canister set, ginger, allspice, cinnamon, cloves & nutmeg, w/lids, Chef Kitchen Ware w/chef's head logo, 4x3¾" **$45.00**

Coasters, set of 8, strong colors, M **$25.00**

Coasters, set of 8, pastel colors, flying duck scene, 3¼", M....................**$20.00**

Coffee maker, blue w/ivory Bakelite handles, West Bend Flav-O-Matic, complete & working, EX....................**$25.00**

Creamer & sugar bowl on tray, gold w/black Bakelite handles, Neocraft, EX **$40.00**

Cups, Heller Hostess Ware, set of 8, MIP **$45.00**

Cups, 4½", in black rack, 16x8", w/white handles & rubber ball feet, Anohue, EX+ **$25.00**

Cups, 5½", set of 6, M....................**$30.00**

Dessert bowls, w/glass inserts, 3½", set of 8, NM **$50.00**

Dessert cups, footed, set of 8 ....**$50.00**

Goblets, marked Stokes Australasia Limited Melbourne, footed, 4¼x2¾", set of 6, 1960s, EX....................**$38.00**

Ice bucket, red apple shape, 7", NM....................**$25.00**

Measuring scoops, ½-cup, ⅓-cup & ¼-cup, set of 3, NM..**$20.00**

Measuring spoon set, Tallscoops, M in package, from $25 to....................**$35.00**

Napkin rings, narrow, set of 8, MIB....................**$28.00**

Napkin rings, wide, set of 4, M (in original plastic box)...**$50.00**

Pitcher, gold, w/ice lip, unmarked, NM....................**$28.00**

Pitcher, green, w/8 5" tumblers, Colorcraft, Indpls Ind, NM....................**$60.00**

Popcorn set, 11" bowl & 4 5" individuals, M **$30.00**

Refrigerator boxes, 5¼x4⅜", set of 4, NM, from $40 to...**$50.00**

Rolling pin, w/stand, EX....................**$30.00**

Salad set, Bascal, lg bowl & 8 footed individuals, EX+ ..**$50.00**

Shot glasses, 1¾", 6 in metal holder w/handle, Germany, MIB, from $25 to....................**$35.00**

Shot glasses, 6 on tray, NM....................**$30.00**

Soda/seltzer bottle, bright blue, Soda King, 11½", MIB..**$65.00**

Spoons, iced tea; 8", NM, set of 6 ....**$25.00**

Straw/stirrer, set of 12, M, from $25 to **$30.00**

Straws, rose, silver, gold, turquoise, magenta & dark blue (2 ea color), Bascal, set of 12, 9", M....................**$45.00**

Teapot, gold w/red plastic knob on lid, rattan-wrapped handle, Japan, 6½", EX....................**$35.00**

Tray, copper, handles, Colortrym Co, Seattle Wash, 22x14", MIB **$15.00**

Tray, serving; purple, 14" dia....................**$15.00**

Tray, serving; ruby red w/gold rim & handles, no-skid pattern on top w/4 rubber feet on bottom, Woodmet, 12¼x20½"....................**$30.00**

Tree ornaments, Christmas bells, 2x2", set of 5 ....**$18.00**

Tree ornaments, twisted icicles, 15 in box, NM..........**$25.00**

Tumblers, Rainbow Colors, Alpine Brand Tops Them All on plastic container, M (VG+ package) **$60.00**

Tumblers, set of 8, straight-sided, Perma Hues, 5½x2½", NMIB....................**$25.00**

Tumblers, 5", set of 8 in chrome carrying rack, Perma Hues, M....................**$45.00**

Tumblers, 5", w/matching 9" straws, set of 6, NM......**$45.00**

Tumblers, 5½", horizontal embossed rings, West Bend, set of 8, M....................**$35.00**

Vase, red with silver-tone base, 6", $10.00.

Anchor Hocking/Fire-King

From the 1930s until the 1970s, Anchor Hocking (Lancaster, Ohio) produced a wide and varied assortment of glassware including kitchen, restaurant ware, and tableware for the home. Fire-King was their trade name for glassware capable of withstanding high oven temperatures without breakage. So confident were they in the durability of this glassware that they guaranteed it for two years against breakage caused by heat.

Many colors were produced over the years. Blues are always popular with collectors, and Anchor Hocking made two, Turquoise Blue and Azurite (light sky blue). They also made pink, Forest Green, Ruby Red, gold-trimmed lines, and some with fired-on colors. Jade-ite was a soft opaque green glass that was very popular from the 1940s until well into the 1960s. (See the Jade-ite category for more information.) During the late '60s they made Soreno in Avocado Green to tie in with home-decorating trends.

Bubble (made from the '30s through the '60s) was produced in just about every color Anchor Hocking ever made. It is especially collectible in Ruby Red. You may also hear this pattern referred to as Provencial or Bullseye.

Alice was a mid-'40s to '50s line. It was made in Jade-ite as well as white that was sometimes trimmed with blue or red. Cups and saucers were given away in boxes of Mother's Oats, but plates had to be purchased (so they're scarce today).

In the early '50s they produced a 'laurel leaf' design in peach and 'Gray Laurel' lustres (the gray is scarce), followed later in the decade and into the '60s with several lines of white glass decorated with decals — Honeysuckle, Fleurette, Primrose, and Game Bird, to name only a few.

One of their most expensive lines of dinnerware today is Philbe in Sapphire Blue, clear glass with a blue tint. It was made during the late 1930s. Values range from about $50.00 for a 6" plate to $1,500.00 for the cookie jar.

Early American Presscut was made from about 1960 through the mid-1970s. Few homes were without at least a piece or two. It was standard dime-store fare, inexpensive and accessible. It looks wonderful for serving a special buffet, and you'll find it often on your garage sale rounds, at prices that are a fraction of 'book.'

If you'd like to learn more about this type of very collectible glassware, we recommend *Anchor Hocking's Fire-King and More, Second Edition,* by Gene Florence (Collector Books). See also Jade-ite.

Alice, cup & saucer, Vitrock...............................**$5.00**
Alice, cup & saucer, Vitrock w/red trim **$45.00**
Alice, plate, Vitrock, 9½"...................................**$20.00**
Anniversary Rose, bowl, dessert; white w/decals, 4⅝".**$8.00**
Anniversary Rose, bowl, mixing; white w/decals, vertical pattern, 1½-qt.....................................**$55.00**
Anniversary Rose, cup, snack; white w/decals, 5-oz **$5.00**
Anniversary Rose, plate, dinner; white w/decals, 10".**$12.00**
Anniversary Rose, sugar bowl, white w/decals, w/lid ..**$15.00**
Blue Mosaic, creamer, white w/decals..........................**$8.00**
Blue Mosaic, platter, white w/decals, 9x12" **$17.50**
Blue Mosaic, soup plate, white w/decals, 6⅝"...........**$14.00**
Bubble, bowl, berry; crystal iridescent, 4" **$4.00**
Bubble, candlesticks, Forest Green, pr **$37.50**
Bubble, flat soup, Sapphire Blue, 7¾"........................**$15.00**
Bubble, pitcher, Royal Ruby, ice lip, 64-oz **$60.00**
Bubble, stem, juice; Royal Ruby, 4-oz **$10.00**
Bubble, sugar bowl, crystal iridescent.........................**$6.00**
Bubble, tumbler, lemonade; Royal Ruby, 16-oz **$16.00**
Charm, bowl, dessert; Royal Ruby, 4¾"........................**$8.00**
Charm, cup & saucer, ivory **$17.00**
Charm, plate, salad; Forest Green, 6⅝" **$10.00**
Classic, bowl, crystal, deep, 11" **$25.00**
Classic, chip & dip, white, 5½" & 11" bowls.............**$35.00**
Classic, plate, Royal Ruby, 14½".............................**$35.00**
Early American Prescut, ashtray, 5".............................**$10.00**
Early American Prescut, bowl, console; 9" **$15.00**
Early American Prescut, bowl, salad; 10¾" **$12.00**
Early American Prescut, coaster................................**$2.00**
Early American Prescut, creamer **$3.00**
Early American Prescut, pitcher, 40- to 48-oz, 2 styles, ea.**$55.00**
Early American Prescut, plate, 4-part w/swirl dividers, 11" **$150.00**

Early American Prescut, salt & pepper shakers, plastic tops, pr..**$6.00**
Fishscale, bowl, dessert; ivory, shallow, 5½" **$10.00**
Fishscale, bowl, vegetable; ivory w/red, 8¾".............**$35.00**
Fishscale, platter, ivory w/blue, 11¾" **$60.00**
Fleurette, bowl, chili; white w/decals, 5"....................**$20.00**
Fleurette, mug, white w/decals **$75.00**
Fleurette, plate, bread & butter; white w/decals, 6¼"....**$14.00**
Forest Green, ashtray, 5¾" sq.....................................**$9.00**
Forest Green, bowl, vegetable; oval, 8½"...................**$21.00**
Forest Green, punch cup, round **$2.25**
Forest Green, stem, cocktail; 3½-oz...........................**$10.00**
Forest green, stem, goblet, 9-oz.................................**$10.00**
Forest Green, stem, sherbet; 6-oz...............................**$9.00**
Forest Green, tumbler, fancy, 9-oz **$6.00**
Forest Green, tumbler, iced tea; 13-oz........................**$7.50**
Forest Green, vase, bud; 9".......................................**$10.00**
Forget-Me-Not, bowl, dessert; white w/decals, 4⅝".....**$8.00**
Forget-Me-Not, casserole, white w/decals, oval, w/lid, 1½-qt...**$24.00**
Forget-Me-Not, loaf pan, white w/decals....................**$25.00**
Game Bird, bowl, vegetable; white w/decals, 8¼".....**$60.00**

Game Bird, mug, decal on white, 1959 – 62, eight-ounce, $8.00. (Photo courtesy Gene Florence)

Game Bird, sugar bowl, white w/decals, w/lid **$70.00**
Game Bird, tumbler, juice; white w/decals, 5-oz **$35.00**

Golden Shell, plate, 10", $6.00; dessert bowl, $3.50; cup and saucer, $4.25. Add $5.00 for original box. (Photo courtesy Gene Florence)

Harvest, creamer, white w/decals...................$7.00

Harvest, plate, 10", $10.00; cup and saucer, $5.00; platter, $15.00. (Photo courtesy Gene Florence)

Honeysuckle, cup & saucer, white w/decals.................$5.50
Honeysuckle, plate, dinner; white w/decals, 9⅛".........$6.00
Honeysuckle, soup plate, white w/decals, 6⅝" $9.00
Jane Ray, bowl, oatmeal; Vitrock, 5⅞".......................$18.00
Jane Ray, cup, Vitrock...$20.00
Jane Ray, plate, dinner; ivory, 9⅛"............................$45.00
Lace Edge, bowl, milk white, footed, 11"...................$15.00
Lace Edge, cake plate, milk white, 13" $15.00
Lace Edge, plate, salad; milk white, 8¼".....................$7.00
Laurel, bowl, vegetable; ivory or white, 8¼" $40.00
Laurel, plate, serving; gray, 11" $20.00
Laurel, sugar bowl, peach lustre, footed.....................$4.00
Meadow Green, bowl, mixing; white w/decal, 2½-qt..$10.00
Meadow Green, casserole, white w/decal, crystal lid, 2-qt..$9.00
Meadow Green, mug, white w/decal, 8-oz $3.00
Oatmeal Prescut, cup & saucer..................................$4.00
Oatmeal Prescut, tumbler, water; 9-oz $2.00
Philbe, bowl, cereal; pink or green, 5½"....................$45.00
Philbe, creamer, crystal, footed, 3¼"..........................$70.00
Philbe, plate, sandwich; pink or green, 10" $75.00
Philbe, platter, blue, closed handles, 12"..................$175.00
Philbe, sherbet, crystal, 3¾".....................................$75.00
Philbe, tumbler, iced tea; pink or green, footed, 15-oz..$85.00
Pineapple Prescut, box, cigarette or dresser; 4¾".......$15.00
Pineapple Prescut, butter dish, round.........................$15.00
Primrose, baking pan, white w/decal, w/lid, 5x9"......$18.00
Primrose, cake pan, white w/decal, 8" sq $12.00
Primrose, comport, Lace Edge, white w/decal, footed, 11"...$150.00
Primrose, plate, dinner; white w/decal, 9⅛" $7.00
Rainbow, creamer, pastel, footed $15.00
Rainbow, plate, sherbet; primary color, 6¼" $6.00
Rainbow, stem, pastel, 10-oz....................................$10.00
Rainbow, tumbler, juice; primary color, 5-oz $12.00
Royal Ruby, bowl, fruit; 4¼"......................................$5.50
Royal Ruby, creamer, flat $12.00
Royal Ruby, ice bucket..$35.00
Royal Ruby, plate, salad; 7¾" $6.00
Royal Ruby, sherbet, footed.......................................$8.00
Royal Ruby, tumbler, water; footed, 10-oz, 5"............$6.50
Royal Ruby, vase, 9"..$17.50
Sheaves of Wheat, cup & saucer, crystal $7.00

Sheaves of Wheat, tumbler; water, crystal, 9-oz..........$15.00
Shell, bowl, dessert; milk white, 4¾" $4.00
Shell, cup, demitasse; Aurora (mother-of-pearl), 3¼-oz .$25.00
Shell, platter, milk white, oval, 11½x15½" $40.00
Soreno, ashtray, aquamarine, 4¼" $5.00
Soreno, bowl, chip/salad; Honey Gold, 8½" $6.50
Soreno, pitcher, juice; Avocado or milk white, 28-oz...$6.00
Soreno, water bottle, crystal, spout cap, 48-oz.............$6.00
Swirl, bowl, dessert/fruit; Azur-ite, 4⅞" $12.00
Swirl, bowl, dessert/fruit; pink, 4⅞".............................$9.00
Swirl, plate, salad; ivory or white, 7⅜"........................$8.00
Swirl, plate, salad; Sunrise, 7⅜"..................................$8.00
Swirl, plate, serving; ivory or white, 11".....................$25.00
Swirl, sugar bowl, Azur-ite, flat, tab handles..............$10.00
Swirl, tumbler, juice; pink, 5-oz...................................$6.00
Three Bands, bowl, fruit; ivory, 4⅞".............................$10.00
Three Bands, cup & saucer, ivory, 8-oz......................$17.50
Three Bands, plate, dinner; ivory, 9⅛".........................$25.00
Turquoise Blue, bowl, soup/salad; 6⅝".......................$25.00
Turquoise Blue, cup $5.00
Turquoise Blue, mug, 8-oz..$10.00
Turquoise Blue, sugar bowl.......................................$8.00
Wheat, bowl, chili; white w/decals, 5" $25.00
Wheat, casserole, white w/decals, knob lid, 2-qt $15.00
Wheat, custard, low or dessert; white w/decals, 6-oz ..$3.00
Wheat, mug, white w/decals $50.00
Wheat, tumbler, tea; white w/decals, 11-oz.................$8.00

Angels

Angels, Birthday

Not at all hard to find and still reasonably priced, birthday angels are fun to assemble into twelve-month sets, and since there are many different series to look for, collecting them can be challenging as well as enjoyable. Generally speaking, angels are priced by the following factors: 1) company — look for Lefton, Napco, Norcrest, and Enesco marks or labels (unmarked or unknown sets are of less value); 2) application of flowers, bows, gold trim, etc. (the more detail, the more valuable); 3) use of rhinestones, which will also increase the price; 4) age; and 5) quality of the workmanship involved, detail, and accuracy of painting.

#1194, angel of the month series, white hair, 5", ea, from $18 to...$20.00
#1294, angel of the month, white hair, 5", ea, from $18 to $20.00
#1300, boy angels, wearing suit, white hair, 6", ea, from $22 to..$25.00
#1600 Pal Angel, month series of both boy & girl, 4", ea, from $10 to..$15.00
Arnart, Kewpies, in choir robes, w/rhinestones, 4½", ea, from $12 to..$15.00
Enesco, angels on round base w/flower of the month, gold trim, ea, from $15 to...$18.00

High Mountain Quality, colored hair, 7", ea, from $30 to **$32.00**

Kelvin, C-230, holding flower of the month, 4½", ea, from $15 to...**$20.00**

Kelvin, C-250, holding flower of the month, 4½", ea, from $15 to...**$20.00**

Lefton, #0130, Kewpie, 4½", ea, from $35 to **$40.00**

Lefton, #0489, holding basket of flowers, 4", ea, from $25 to...**$30.00**

Lefton, #0556, boy of the month, 5½", ea, from $25 to..**$30.00**

Lefton, #0574, day of the week series (like #8281 but not as ornate), ea, from $25 to **$28.00**

Lefton, #0627, day of the week series, 3½", ea, from $28 to...**$32.00**

Lefton, #0985, flower of the month, 5", ea, from $28 to..**$32.00**

Lefton, #1323, angel of the month, bisque, ea, from $18 to **$22.00**

Lefton #1411, 4", from $28.00 to $32.00. (Photo courtesy Loretta De Lozier)

Lefton, #1987, angel of the month, ea, from $30 to ...**$35.00**

Lefton, #2600, birthstone on skirt, 3¼", ea, from $25 to..**$30.00**

Lefton, #3332, bisque, w/basket of flowers, 4", ea, from $25 to...**$30.00**

Lefton, #5146, birthstone in skirt, 4½", ea, from $22 to..**$28.00**

Lefton, #6224, applied flower/birthstone on skirt, 4½", ea, from $18 to...**$25.00**

Lefton, #6883, sq frame, day of the week & months, 3¼x4", ea, from $28 to...**$32.00**

Lefton, #6949, day of the week series in oval frame, 5", ea, from $28 to..**$32.00**

Lefton, #6985, musical, sm, ea, from $40 to.............**$45.00**

Lefton, #8281, day of the week series, applied roses, ea, from $30 to..**$35.00**

Lefton, AR-1987, w/ponytail, 4", ea, from $18 to........**$22.00**

Lefton, 1987J, w/rhinestones, 4½", ea, from $25 to....**$30.00**

Napco, A1360-1372, angel of the month, ea, from $20 to ..**$25.00**

Napco, A1917-1929, boy angel of the month, ea, from $20 to...**$25.00**

Napco, A4307, angel of the month, sm, ea, from $22 to ...**$25.00**

Napco, C1361-1373, angel of the month, ea, from $22 to.**$25.00**

Napco, C1921-1933, boy angel of the month, ea, from $20 to...**$25.00**

Napco, S1291, day of the week 'Belle,' ea, from $22 to ..**$25.00**

Napco, S1307, bell of the month, ea, from $22 to......**$25.00**

Napco, S1361-1372, angel of the month, ea, from $20 to..**$25.00**

Napco, S1392, oval frame angel of the month, ea, from $25 to...**$30.00**

Napco, S401-413, angel of the month, ea, from $20 to .**$25.00**

Napco, S429, day of the week angel (also available as planters), ea, from $25 to...............................**$30.00**

Napco, C1917, boy angel of the month, 4½", from $20.00 to $25.00.

Norcrest, F-120, angel of the month, 4½", ea, from $18 to ..**$22.00**

Norcrest, F-15, angel of the month, on round base w/raised pattern on dress, 4", ea, from $18 to **$22.00**

Norcrest, F-167, bell of the month, 2¾", ea, from $8 to..**$12.00**

Norcrest, F-210, day of the week angel, 4½", ea, from $18 to...**$22.00**

Norcrest, F-23, day of the week angel, 4½", ea, from $18 to...**$22.00**

Norcrest, F-340, angel of the month, 5", ea, from $20 to......**$25.00**

Norcrest, F-535, angel of the month, 4½", ea, from $20 to...**$25.00**

Relco, 4¼", ea, from $15 to **$18.00**

Relco, 6", ea, from $18 to **$22.00**

SR, angel of the month, w/birthstone & 'trait' of the month (i.e. April - innocence), ea, from $20 to **$25.00**

TMJ, angel of the month, w/flower, ea, from $20 to ..**$25.00**

Ucagco, white hair, 5¾", from $12 to **$15.00**

Wales, wearing long white gloves, white hair, Made in Japan, 6⅜", ea, from $25 to...**$28.00**

Angels, Zodiac

These china figurines were made and imported by the same companies as the birthday angels. Not as many companies made the Zodiac series, though,, which makes them harder to find. Because they're older and were apparently never as popular as the month pieces, they were not made or distributed as long as the birthday angels. Examples tend to be more individualized due to each sign having a specific characteristic associated with it.

Japan, wearing pastel dress w/applied pink rose on head, standing on cloud base w/stars, 4½", ea, from $15 to........**$20.00**

Japan, wearing pastel dress w/rhinestones on gold stars, applied pink rose on head, 4", ea, from $20 to ...**$25.00**

Josef, holds tablet w/sign in gold, 1960-1962, ea, from $30
to **$40.00**
Josef, no wings, sign written in cursive on dress, 4", ea, from
$30 to...**$40.00**
Lefton, K8650, applied flowers & gold stars, 4" when standing (1946-1953), ea, from $40 to **$45.00**

Napco S980, 4", from $20.00 to $22.00; Napco A2646, 5", from $22.00 to $25.00; Napco S1259, planter series, 4", from $25.00 to $28.00. (Photo courtesy Denise and James Atkinson)

Semco, gold wings, applied roses & pleated ruffle on front
edge of dress, 5", ea, from $20 to **$25.00**

Aprons

America's heartland offers a wide variety of aprons, ranging from those once worn for kitchen duty or general household chores to fancier styles designed for cocktail parties. Today they can be found in an endless array of styles and in fabrics ranging from feed sacks to fine silk with applied rhinestones. Some were embroidered or pieced, some were even constructed of nice handkerchiefs. Aprons were given and received as gifts; often they were cherished and saved. Some of these are now surfacing in today's market. You may find some in unused condition with the original tags still attached.

Condition is important when assessing the value of vintage aprons. Unless very old, pass up on those that are stained and torn. Hand sewn examples are worth more than machine- or commercial-made aprons, and if they retain the tags from their original maker, you can double their price. Some labels themselves are collectible. Children's and young ladies' dress aprons command very high prices, as often they were recycled into quilt patches and dust cloths.

Perhaps no other area of Americana evokes as much nostalgia as vintage aprons. Our advisor's favorite, he says, is a grandmother's that has become stained from cookie baking and worn soft from use. He recommends tying them onto your old caned dining chair or as he does, to the grandfather clock in his kitchen, giving the impression that the wearer is only temporarily absent.

Advisor: Darrell Thomas (See Directory, Aprons)

Adult's cocktail, baby blue w/many hand-sewn white & pink
roses, 1930s...**$25.00**
Adult's cocktail, sheer white fabric w/pink & white rhinestones, flower bouquet in back, beautiful hand detailing,
1940s...**$65.00**
Adult's shoulder style, white cotton & crocheted lace, worn
at wedding reception, classic style, 1940s **$55.00**
Adult's shoulder type, pink w/black trim, kitten sewn into
pocket, heavy cotton, 1940s **$25.00**
Adult's shoulder type, white cotton w/Coon Chicken Inn on
front, 1940s Black Americana **$45.00**
Adult's waist style, beautiful Christmas motif, red, very fancy,
1940s-50s **$13.00**
Adult's waist style, Easter, w/eggs & sm Spring flowers, very
nice, 1950s...**$15.00**
Adult's waist style, Halloween orange gingham w/sewn-on
black cats, 1950s **$14.00**
Adult's waist type, black gingham w/beautiful lace attachments, hand & machine sewn, 1940s....................**$25.00**

Adult's waist type, cotton with chenille hearts and flowers, pink heart in center, ca 1940s – 50s, $20.00.

Adult's waist type, lace, synthetics & cottons, some w/lace
trim, very dressy/frilly, 1920s to 1960s, ea from $12.50
to **$25.00**
Adult's waist type, lg peaches & apples sewn together to
construct full apron, interesting design, machine made,
1950-60 ....**$15.00**
Adult's waist type, many styles, various colors of gingham, ca
1930s to 1960s, ea from $5 to............................**$12.50**
Adult's waist type, rose handkerchiefs w/sheer yellow cottons, dressy & frilly, 1950s **$35.00**
Child's over-the-neck type, green cotton w/allover brightly
colored flower bouquets, handmade/lots of stitches,
1920s..**$85.00**
Child's waist type, green gingham w/purple flowers, 1 pocket, 1940s..**$45.00**
Child's waist type, white muslin w/blue stitches around
pockets, 1930s...**$35.00**

Young adult's full coverage, red polka-dot fabric w/machine-sewn cherries attached at pockets, 1950s **$32.50**

Young adult's over-the-shoulder type, peach & orange cotton muslin w/hand-attached & sewn fruits, 1930s......**$42.50**

Young adult's waist type, gray gingham w/pink roses, 2 pockets, machine sewn, 1950s **$10.00**

Young adult's waist type, pink gingham windmills & tulips stitched onto print, 1940s......................**$12.50**

Young adult's waist type, sheer light blue fabric abounding w/yellow French-knot flowers, sm pleats, 1940s .**$22.50**

Ashtrays

Ashtrays, especially for cigarettes, did not become widely used in the United States much before the turn of the century. The first examples were simply receptacles made to hold ashes for pipes, cigars, and cigarettes. Later, rests were incorporated into the design. Ashtrays were made in a variety of materials. Some were purely functional, while others advertised or entertained, and some stopped just short of being works of art. They were made to accommodate smokers in homes, businesses, or wherever they might be. Today their prices range from a few dollars to hundreds. Since today so many people buy and sell on eBay and other Internet auction auction sites, there is much more exposure to ashtray collecting. Also these auction prices must be considered when determining the value of an item. Many of the very fine ashtrays from the turn of the century do not command the same price as they did in the early 1990s unless the maker's name is widely known. And now, in the twenty-first century, many of the old ashtrays are actually antiques. This may contribute to the continued fluctuation of prices in this still new collectibles field. For further information see *Collector's Guide to Ashtrays, Second Edition, Identification and Values,* by Nancy Wanvig.

See also specific glass companies and potteries; Japan Ceramics; Tire Ashtrays; World's Fairs.

Advisor: Nancy Wanvig (See Directory, Ashtrays)

Advertising, Benedictine, green bottle cut in half & made into tray, label still on bottle, 7½" L **$24.00**

Advertising, Camel, cobalt glass half-circle w/name in yellow & green leaves in center, 8"....................................**$35.00**

Advertising, Chrysler Belvidere Assembly, blue-painted metal w/silver logo embossed in center, 5" dia..............**$27.50**

Advertising, General Electric, dark green motor form w/GE logo embossed on blue base, 5⅜" dia.................**$58.00**

Advertising, Gillette Safety Razor, copper-plated steel, No Stropping..., 4¼" **$42.00**

Advertising, International House of Pancakes, amber glass w/brown letters in center, 3½" sq **$7.00**

Advertising, Mack Truck, gold Mack figural (4") on chrome tray, 1970, 7" dia....................................**$45.00**

Advertising, Old Forester Now at 86 & 100 Proof!, milk glass, 5¼" dia...**$5.00**

Advertising, Quaker State, ceramic, green letters and red logo, 6¾", $30.00. (Photo courtesy Nancy Wanvig)

Advertising, Registered Polled Herefords, clear glass w/white decal on back, 4⅛" sq.......................**$6.00**

Advertising, Rotary International, clear glass w/blue & yellow cogwheel emblem & name, 5" dia **$8.00**

Advertising, Rubbermaid 25th Anniversary 1934-1959, dust-pan shape, 5" W **$20.00**

Advertising, Schlitz, tan ceramic, brown logo & picture, 5½" dia **$25.00**

Advertising, University of Virginia, tan ceramic, brown picture in center, 4½" dia.............................**$9.00**

Advertising, White Horse Scotch, horse & name on rise, Wade England, 6"..**$41.00**

Art glass, black, in stand w/brass legs, rim & rest across top, some moriage, 2½" H.............................**$40.00**

Art glass, Murano, shades of blue, artist signed, heavy, 4¼" dia **$125.00**

Art glass, St Clair, 5 multicolored flowers, marked, 4" dia..**$70.00**

Brass, embossed Zodiac symbols, glass insert w/snufferette, 1950s, 7⅜" dia.....................................**$18.00**

China, Royal Doulton, The Gleaners, Old English scenes, 4¾"..**$60.00**

Cloisonne, frog, brass cells, rest in mouth, 3½".........**$85.00**

Glass, Anchor Hocking, Manhattan, 1938-43, 4" dia ...**$12.00**

Glass, Cambridge, amethyst w/golf-ball stem, 3½" H.**$62.00**

Glass, Daisy & Button, blue cup on 3 legs, 2¼"..........**$9.00**

Glass, Federal, Diana, amber iridescent, 1937-41, 4⅛" sq..**$9.00**

Glass, Fostoria, Mayfair, frosted, 3⅞" sq **$11.00**

Glass, Hazel Atlas, windmill & checkerboard, green w/match holder center, 4" dia **$14.00**

Glass, LE Smith, #503, black amethyst, w/match holder, 6½" dia **$15.00**

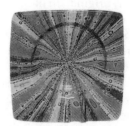

Glass, radiating rays on slumped form, marked Higgins on rim, after 1964, 5¼", $55.00. (Photo courtesy Nancy Wanvig)

Glass, Westmoreland, Panelled Grape, milk glass, 1950-70s, 4" sq..**$18.00**

Jasperware, Wedgwood, pink w/white grape leaf border, 4½"..**$22.00**

Lustreware, Japan, pink flowers on 5" sides of triangle..**$15.00**

Metal, chrome-plated fretwork, machine-cut outside, cobalt glass insert, Hong Kong, 4" dia **$25.00**

Novelty, Betty & Barney, ceramic, Hanna-Barbera Productions, 1961, 8⅛"..............................**$98.00**

Novelty, Black face, ceramic, bee on tip of nose, heavy eyebrows, eyes rolled up, Japan, 4" **$55.00**

Novelty, cat face, ceramic, gold slanted eyes, open mouth, holes in nose, Japan, 3⅝"..................**$31.00**

Novelty, God Bless America, pot metal w/copper finish, flag & eagle in relief, 5⅛".................................**$8.00**

Novelty, hobo in top hat, holes in cup and tie, marked Cerami-Dreams by Vera, Japan, 6¼", $36.00. (Photo courtesy Nancy Wanvig)

Novelty, Lyndon Johnson signature on white ceramic cowboy hat, 6½" L......................................**$15.00**

Novelty, penguin, ceramic, smokes comes out of left eye, Japan, 7" **$40.00**

Novelty, raised skeleton, pottery, Ashes to Ashes, 7" dia..**$30.00**

Novelty, Scottie dog, combination cigarette holder and ashtray, marked Gobel Germany, 7", from $75.00 to $100.00. (Photo courtesy Candace Sten Davis and Patricia J. Baugh)

Novelty, skunk, ceramic w/real fur on tail, For Little Butts & Big Stinkers, 4½" H **$12.00**

Novelty, top hat, cobalt glass, 2 rests, 2½" **$14.00**

Porcelain, Rosenthal, white w/embossed decor on outside, 1950s, 4¼".......................................**$24.00**

Pot metal, cowboy w/copper finish, Japan, 5"...........**$15.00**

Pottery, Red Wing, duck figural, orange, 4" **$32.00**

Pottery, Rookwood, fish figural at side of rim, blue, 1945, 6" dia **$165.00**

Souvenir, Cincinnati Reds, red logo & lettering on clear glass, 4½"...**$15.00**

Souvenir, Knoxville World's Fair, fair scenes on white, 1982, 4" dia...**$7.00**

Souvenir, New York, scenes from Niagara Falls, ceramic, 7⅝" **$7.00**

Autographs

'Philography' is an extremely popular hobby, one that is very diversified. Autographs of sports figures, movie stars, entertainers, and politicians from our lifetime may bring several hundred dollars, depending on rarity and application, while John Adams's simple signature on a document from 1800, for instance, might bring thousands. A signature on a card or cut from a letter or document is the least valuable type of autograph. A handwritten letter is generally the most valuable, since in addition to the signature you get the message as well. Depending upon what it reveals about the personality who penned it, content can be very important and can make a major difference in value.

Many times a polite request accompanied by an SASE to a famous person will result in receipt of a signed photo or a short handwritten note that might in several years be worth a tidy sum!

Obviously as new collectors enter the field, the law of supply and demand will drive the prices for autographs upward, especially when the personality is deceased. There are forgeries around, so before you decide to invest in expensive autographs, get to know your dealers.

Over the years many celebrities in all fields have periodically employed secretaries to sign their letters and photos. They have also sent out photos with preprinted or rubber stamped signatures as time doesn't always permit them to personally respond to fan mail. With today's advanced printing, even many long-time collectors have been fooled with a mechanically produced signature.

Newspaper: *Autograph Times*
2303 N 44th St., #225, Phoenix, AZ 85008
602-947-3112 or fax: 602-947-8363

Adamson, Joy; ink signature on 3x6" card **$69.00**

Arnold, Tom; signed color photo, 8x10"...................**$32.00**

Bacon, Kevin; signed color photo from Hollow Man, 8x10" **$32.00**

Baldwin, Faith; handwritten letter, chatty 3 pages to friend, postmarked 1975......................................**$59.00**

Baldwin, Stephen; signed color photo as Barney Rubble, 8x10"..**$28.00**

Baum, Vicki; ink signature on white card, dated 1958, 3x5" **$39.00**

Begley, Ed Jr; signed black & white photo, 8x10"......**$12.00**

Bergen, Edgar; fountain pen ink signature on pink album page, his own name & 'Charlie' **$65.00**

Black, Karen; signed black & white photo in scene from Invaders From Mars, 8x10" **$16.00**

Buzzi, Ruth; signed color photo, 8x10" **$24.00**

Calhoun, Rory; ink signature on pink album page **$42.00**

Carey, MacDonald; inscribed black & white glossy photo, bold signature, 8x10" **$35.00**

Carney, Art; signed black & white photo as The Archer in TVs Batman, 8x10" **$16.00**

Coburn, Charles; ink signature on inscribed album page ..**$50.00**

Craig, Yvonne; signed color photo as Batgirl, 8x10" ..**$28.00**

Curtice, Harlow; ink signature on sepia photo, as president of General Motors, 8x10" **$39.00**

Damon, Matt; signed color photo from The Talented Mr Ripley, 8x10" **$32.00**

Davis, Geena; signed color photo, 8x10" **$32.00**

Dempsey, Jack; ink signature on album page **$75.00**

DeWitt, Joyce; signed color photo, 8x10" **$24.00**

DeWolfe, Billy; ink signature on lg album page, 1950s, 5x6" **$38.00**

Diller, Phyllis; signed color photo, 8x10" **$20.00**

Doherty, Shannen; signed color photo, 8x10" **$30.00**

Drysdale, Don; signed black & white lithograph, in white uniform, printed by Meadow Gold Milk, postcard size **$59.00**

Dunbar, Dixie; inscribed & signed sepia 8x10" photo ..**$45.00**

Evans, Dale; ink signature on album page, 1940s **$44.00**

Friedman, Herbet; dark ink signature on lg white cachet ..**$35.00**

Fullerton, Gordon; signed NASA color lithograph, in space suit w/flag & globe, 8x10" **$59.00**

Furness, Betty; signed sepia photo, ca 1934, 5x7" **$49.00**

Garr, Teri; signed black & white photo, 8x10" **$20.00**

Gobel, George; ink signature on white card **$35.00**

Gordon, Ruth; signed sepia photo, early, 8x10" **$49.00**

Hopper, Dennis; signed color photo, 8x10" **$32.00**

Hu, Kelly; signed color photo, 8x10" **$32.00**

Javits, Jacob; signed black & white photo, as US Senator, ca 1960s, 8x10" **$49.00**

Kristofferson, Kris; signed color photo of scene from Blade, 8x10" **$36.00**

Landon, Michael; ink signature on album page, 2½x5½" ..**$100.00**

Lawrence, David L; ink signature on sepia photo, 5x8" .**$39.00**

Lawrence, Vicki; signed black & white photo, 8x10" .**$16.00**

Lee, Christopher; signed color photo as Dracula, 8x10" ..**$52.00**

Lewis, Ted; signature on sepia photo, ca 1930s, 8x10" **$69.00**

Liotta, Ray; signed color photo, 8x10" **$36.00**

Lombardo, Guy; inscribed & signed black & white glossy photo, 8x10" **$75.00**

Lowe, Rob; signed color photo, 8x10" **$28.00**

Luce, Clair Booth; signature on calling card as Ambassador of the United States of America, w/1956 postmarked envelope **$45.00**

MacArthur, James; signed color photo as Dano from Hawaii Five-O, 8x10" **$25.00**

MacMurray, Fred; ink signature on white card, 3x5" .**$39.00**

Mantle, Mickey; ink signature on pink album page .**$225.00**

Martin, Tony; inscribed & signed sepia photo, 5½x7" **$34.00**

McMurtry, Tom; inscribed & signed black & white photo as test pilot standing before X-24B, 1970s, 8x10" **$45.00**

Montgomery, Robert; ink signature on white card, 3x5" ...**$39.00**

Myers, Mike; signed photo as Dr Evil in Austin Powers, 8x10" **$30.00**

Grateful Dead (Jerry Garcia and Bob Weir), album cover, minor wear, from $300.00 to $400.00. (Photo courtesy Early American History Auctions)

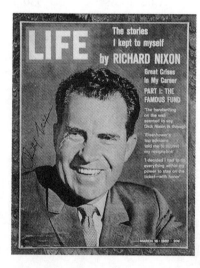

Nixon, Richard; signed on cover of *Life*, **March 16, 1962, EX, from $300.00 to $400.00.** (Photo courtesy Early American History Auctions)

Hackett; Buddy; signed color scene of Scuttle in Disney's Little Mermaid, 8x10" **$24.00**

Hewitt, Jennifer Love; signed color photo, 8x10" **$32.00**

Hirsch, Judd; signed color photo of scene from Taxi, 8x10" **$20.00**

Oberon, Merle; boldly signed sepia photo, 5x7" **$69.00**

Page, Patti; signed black & white photo, 8x10" **$12.00**

Parks, Bert; ink signature on white card, dated 1961, 3x5" ..**$37.00**

Parsons, Estelle; signed black & white movie pose, 8x10" ...**$16.00**

Peerce, Jan; ink signature on white card, dated 1966, 4x6" .**$39.00**

Peppard, George; ink signature on white card, dated 1967, 3x5" **$35.00**

Petty, Lori; signed color movie scene, 8x10" **$30.00**

Previn, Andre; boldly inscribed & signed black & white photo, dated 1968, 8x10" **$55.00**

Randolf, Jennings; inscribed & signed sepia photo, ca 1970, 8x10" **$39.00**

Remick, Lee; ink signature on white card, dated 1963, 3x5" **$45.00**

Reynolds, Debbie; signed color photo scene from Singin' In the Rain, 8x10" **$25.00**

Rutherford, Ann; signed sepia photo, ca 1940s, 8x10" .**$49.00**

Savage, Fred; signed color photo w baseball & bat, 8x10" ..**$24.00**

Schneider, John; signed color photo, 8x10" **$30.00**

Shannon, Molly; signed color photo from movie Superstar, 8x10" **$28.00**

Sizemore, Tom; signed color movie scene from Pearl Harbor, 8x10" **$32.00**

Skelton, Red; ink signature on white card, dated 1964, 3x5" **$35.00**

Slater, Christian; signed color movie scene, 8x10" **$30.00**

Spinks, Leon; signed black & white boxing pose, 8x10" ..**$15.00**

St Johns, Adela Rogers; bold ink signature on album page **$38.00**

Stewart, Patrick; signed color movie scene, 8x10" **$68.00**

Travolta, John; signed black & white glossy photo as Danny from Grease, 8x10" **$75.00**

Vanderbilt, Amy; bold ink signature on black & white photo, 1950s, 8x10" **$39.00**

Warren, Earl; ink signature on lg piece of white paper .**$75.00**

Wayne, John; publicity still, black and white, bold signature, 9½x7", from $600.00 to $800.00. (Photo courtesy Early American Historical Auctions)

Yankoff, Ventsislav; inscribed ink signature on sm piece of paper, dated 22 VII 1955 ....**$45.00**

Automobilia

Automobilia remains a specialized field, attracting antique collectors and old car buffs alike. It is a field that encompasses auto-related advertising and accessories like hood ornaments, gear shift and steering wheel knobs, sales brochures, and catalogs. Memorabilia from the high-performance, sporty automobiles of the sixties is very popular with baby boomers. Unusual items have been setting auction records as the market for automobilia heats up. Note: Badges

vary according to gold content — 10k or sterling silver examples are higher than average. Dealership booklets (Ford, Chevy, etc.) generally run about $2.00 to $3.00 per page, and because many reproductions are available, very few owner's manuals sell for more than $10.00. Also it should be mentioned here that there are many reproduction clocks and signs out there. Any 'Guard' badges with round Ford logos are fake. Buyers beware. See also License Plates; Tire Ashtrays.

Advisor: Leonard Needham (See Directory, Automobilia)

Bank, Thunderbird, metal 1955 replica, Banthrico Inc Chicago USA on bottom, 7" L, EX+ **$30.00**

Banner, OK/A Variety of late Model Values!/4th Quarter Clearance, football player & lg football on yellow, 33x115", EX **$350.00**

Book, My Life and Work, Henry Ford w/Samuel Crowther, Doubleday, NY, 1st edition, 1922, VG **$125.00**

Book, 75 Years of Chevrolet, George H Dammann, Crestling Publishing, 1st edition, 1985, VG **$30.00**

Booklet, General Motors User's Guide, yellow, black & white cover, ca 1946, G **$12.00**

Booklet, Gentle Art of Motoring, Cadillac, 1948, 12-page, EX **$12.00**

Booklet, List of Parts, Ford, 1913, G **$120.00**

Brochure, AMC dealer's, 1973, 40-page, 9¼x9¼", VG ..**$18.00**

Brush, upholstery; Dietrich Motor Car Co, round w/Cadillac & LaSalle emblems on white, celluloid, 3½" dia, NM ..**$140.00**

Catalog, Pep Boys 1957 Catalog/New Low Prices/Auto Accessories & Parts-Tires-Bikes, 88-page, EX **$30.00**

Clock, Cadillac, neon, emblem on black dot, yellow border, metal frame, 18", EX, $950.00.

Dash trim kit, Ford Focus, 15 pcs **$130.00**

Display, Fulton Accelerator & Fulton Pedal Pads for Ford Cars, wood & metal, 10x7x14", VG+ **$65.00**

Display, Jointite Cork Gaskets for Ford Cars, wood board w/curved top displays various gaskets, 37x18", VG+ .**$55.00**

Emblem, Chevelle, 6" **$22.50**

Emergency kit, Ford, tin container holding original bulbs & fuses, 3½x2½x1½", EX **$85.00**

Folder, 1974 Opel Manta, 4-page, 7½" sq.....................**$4.00**

Hood latch, Ford, V8, chrome, 1930s, VG **$40.00**

Hood ornament, Cadillac, all chrome, EX **$30.00**

Hood ornament, devil thumbing nose, chrome, VG+ .**$200.00**

Hub caps, 1965 Ford Galaxie, 15", EX, 4 for **$250.00**

Hubcap emblem, LaSalle, LaS on red circle, 3" dia, VG..**$30.00**

Lamp, Chevrolet, plastic, modernistic style w/blue bow-tie decals on white shade, black base, electric, 14", EX..............**$50.00**

Letter opener, 1942 Packard handle, metal, reverse shows ribbon scroll work, 11", EX....................................**$60.00**

Licence plate attachment, Marathon Best in the Long Run, man running, red, white & black, 5x3¾", NM **$80.00**

License plate attachment, Ford Good Drivers League 1940 Member, blue & white enamel on tin, 6x6¼", EX+ .**$100.00**

License plate attachment, Mobil California World's Fair, pegasus, red & white die-cut embossed tin, 6⅜x5⅜", M **$125.00**

Manual, Automatic Overdrive, Chrysler operating instructions, 1952, 24-page, 5x7", EX **$12.00**

Manual, owner's; AMC Gremlin/Hornet/Javelin/Matador/Ambassador, 1974, EX **$12.00**

Manual, owner's; Chrysler, 1964, VG **$20.00**

Manual, owner's; Delta 88 1982 Oldsmobile, 2nd edition, January 1982, 5x9" **$10.00**

Manual, owner's; Desoto, 1933, VG **$60.00**

Manual, owner's; Kaiser, 1st edition, 1947, G **$20.00**

Manual, owner's; 1973 Ford Maverick, 72-page, 8½x4"..**$7.00**

Manual, repair; Chevrolet, Independence Model, 1931, 276-page, G...**$45.00**

Oiler can, Nash General Use Oil, 4-oz tin w/plastic cap on center needle-like spout, EX+.............................**$110.00**

Padlock, Ford script oval logo engraved on front, plate covers keyhole, w/Ford key, 3", EX, A......................**$55.00**

Paperweight, Model T, brass, open windows, 5", EX+ ..**$25.00**

Pin, lapel; Buick 1903-1953, red, white & blue cloisonne detail on gold-tone w/early car in center, ½" dia, NM..**$40.00**

Pin, lapel; Chevrolet Corvette, cloisonne detail on gold, late 1950s, ½" dia, NM+ **$135.00**

Pin, lapel; Ford logo, cloisonne style, 1½" L.................**$4.00**

Pin-back button, New Chevrolet Six, lady's portrait on blue, 1929, EX...**$65.00**

Postcard, Dodge Brothers auto w/oval rear window, real photo, ca 1922, EX **$10.00**

Promotional car, 1965 Ford Mustang, teal w/M chrome on bumpers & hub caps...**$110.00**

Radiator emblem, Auburn, ca 1920s, G **$50.00**

Radiator emblem, Chevrolet logo, blue & white enamel on metal, ca 1940, 1½x4", EX **$30.00**

Radiator emblem, Ford, V8, triangular shape, red on gray paint, 2-pc, ca 1933, VG.......................................**$120.00**

Radiator emblem, Ford name in oval, 1930s, 1x2", G .**$60.00**

Radiator grille badge, Old Trails/Insured Indianapolis, arrowhead shape w/red & white cloisonne inlay, 3x6", NM........**$60.00**

Shift knob, Ford, red Bakelite, w/working thermometer.**$110.00**

Sign, Buick Is Where Service Is Good/Prices Are Fair/Let Us Prove It!, die-cut embossed shield, red & silver, 18x17", EX **$100.00**

Sign, Factory Engineered Parts, 2-sided porcelain w/Pontiac Indian head logo, red & black on white, 24" dia, EX..........**$1,500.00**

Sign, Mercedes Benz, porcelain, round, name & leaf sprays encircle 3-pointed emblem, blue & white, 8½" dia, NM...**$30.00**

Sign, OK Used Cars & Trucks/Satisfaction/Value/Selection, plastic light-up w/rounded ends, 11x23x4", EX.**$325.00**

Sign, Recommended By Keystone Automobile Club/Largest in the East, 2-sided porcelain oval, orange, blue & white, 20", VG **$550.00**

Steak knife set, Chrysler, Cut Into Their Sales, stainless steel w/wooden handles, w/pamphlet, EX (w/wooden box)..**$40.00**

Steering wheel, Ford F250 XLT, 1959.....................**$110.00**

Stereo viewer, Pontiac, plastic, complete w/handled case & index card w/all colors & models, 1950s, VG+..**$150.00**

Tachometer, Sears Allstate Transistorized..., metal & plastic, 3½" dia, EXIB...**$50.00**

Thermometer, Chevrolet, First in Sales/First in Service, self-framed metal w/curved ends, red, white & blue, 39", VG+...**$85.00**

Thermometer, Ditzler Automotive Finishes, dial type, tin face w/glass front, red, yellow, blue & white, 12" dia, VG+..**$150.00**

Token, General Motors Motorama, gold-tone metal, minor scratches, 1954, G **$18.00**

Valve covers, Ford Mustang, w/running horse, M **$125.00**

Water bag, Minnequa Water Bag, flax canvas w/Indian graphics, rope handle, Pueblo Tent & Awning Co, 10x15", EX+ **$50.00**

Wax can, Ford Polishing Wax/M-220-A, round tin w/pry lid, 8-oz, EX+ **$30.00**

Wrench, hub cap; Chevrolet, minor rust/dings, G **$10.00**

Wrench, open end, Dodge Brothers DB mark w/casting #24, EX..**$10.00**

Wrench, open end; Cadillac, ⅝" & 11¹⁄₁₆", 6" **$80.00**

Wrench set, Ford, 7-pc w/6 open-ended wrenchs & 1 monkey wrench, VG+...**$40.00**

Autumn Leaf Dinnerware

A familiar dinnerware pattern to just about all of us, Autumn Leaf was designed by Hall China for the Jewel Tea Company who offered it to their customers as premiums. In fact, some people erroneously refer to the pattern as 'Jewel Tea.' First made in 1933, it continued in production until 1978. Pieces with this date in the backstamp are from the overstock that was in the company's warehouse when production was suspended. There are matching tumblers and stemware all made by the Libbey Glass Company, and a set of enameled cookware that came out in 1979. You'll find blankets, tablecloths, metal canisters, clocks, playing cards, and many other items designed around the Autumn Leaf pattern. All are collectible.

Since 1984 the Hall company has been making special items for the National Autumn Leaf Collectors Club. These pieces are designated as such by the 'Club' marking that is accompanied by the date of issue. Limited edition items (also by Hall) are being sold by China Specialties, a company in Ohio; but once you become familiar with the old pieces, these are easy to identify, since the molds have been redesigned or were not previously used for Autumn Leaf production.

For further study, we recommend *The Collector's Encyclopedia of Hall China* by Margaret and Kenn Whitmyer. For information on company products, see Jewel Tea.

Advisor: Gwynneth M. Harrison (See Directory, Autumn Leaf)

Club: National Autumn Leaf Collectors' Club
Gwynneth Harrison
P.O. Box 1, Mira Loma, CA 91752-0001; 909-685-5434
e-mail: morgan99@pe.net

Newsletter: *Autumn Leaf*
Bill Swanson, Editor
807 Roaring Springs Dr.
Allen, TX 75002-2112; 972-727-5527
e-mail: bescome@attbi.com

Apron, oil cloth, from $600 to **$700.00**
Baker, cake; Heatflow clear glass, Mary Dunbar, 1½-qt, from $65 to...**$85.00**
Baker, French; 1936-76, 3-pt, from $18 to **$20.00**
Baker, French; 1966-76, 2-pt, from $150 to **$175.00**
Baker, individual; oval, Fort Pitt, 1966-76, 12-oz, from $200 to...**$225.00**
Baker, souffle; 1966-76, 4⅛", from $10 to **$12.00**
Baker, souffle; 1978, 4½", from $75 to.........................**$80.00**
Bean pot, 1 handle, 2¼-qt, from $700 to.............**$1,000.00**
Bean pot, 2 handles, 1960-76, from $225 to **$250.00**
Blanket, Vellux, Autum Leaf color, 1979-??, king size, from $180 to...**$220.00**
Book, Autumn Leaf Story, from $40 to **$80.00**
Bottle, Jim Beam, broken seal, from $80 to **$110.00**
Bowl, cereal; 1938-76, 6", from $8 to...........................**$12.00**
Bowl, cream soup; 1950-76, from $30 to.....................**$40.00**
Bowl, divided vegetable; Royal Glasbake, milk white, from $125 to...**$150.00**
Bowl, mixing; New Metal, 3-pc set, 1980-??, from $250 to..**$275.00**
Bowl, Royal Glasbake, milk white, 4-pc set, from $400 to..**$500.00**
Bowl, salad; 1937-76, 9", from $15 to **$20.00**
Bowl, vegetable; oval, Melmac, from $40 to **$50.00**
Bowl, vegetable; oval, 1939-76, from $15 to **$25.00**
Bowl, vegetable; 1937-39, 9", from $150 to..............**$175.00**
Bread box, metal, 1937-41, from $600 to **$900.00**
Butter dish, ruffled top, regular, 1959-60, 1-lb **$500.00**
Butter dish, wings top, 1961-??, ¼-lb **$2,000.00**
Cake plate, on metal stand, 1958-69, from $150 to ..**$225.00**
Cake safe, decor top, 1935-41, from $25 to................**$50.00**
Calendar, club gift, 1985 ....**$175.00**
Calendar, 1940s & newer, ea, from $100 to..............**$200.00**
Candlesticks, metal, Douglas, pr, from $70 to..........**$100.00**
Candy dish, metal base, from $450 to **$500.00**
Canister, Autumn Leaf color, white plastic lid, Douglas, from $8 to..**$10.00**
Canisters, copper top, 4-pc set, from $500 to **$800.00**
Canisters, sq, 4-pc set, 1935-42, from $295 to..........**$350.00**

Casserole, round, w/lid, 1935-76, 2-qt, from $30 to ...**$45.00**
Casserole, Royal Glasbake, milk white, oval, w/lid, 4-qt, from $135 to..**$150.00**
Casserole, Royal Glasbake, milk white, round, w/lid, 2-qt, from $135 to..**$150.00**

Casserole, with lid, 1935 – 1976, two-quart, 9" diameter, from $30.00 to $45.00.

Cleanser can, from $750 to **$1,200.00**
Clock, electric, #11D831, 1956-69, from $400 to.......**$550.00**
Coaster, metal, 3⅛", from $5 to **$8.00**
Coffee dispenser, 1941, from $200 to **$400.00**
Coffeepot, Rayed, 1937-49, 9-cup, from $30 to...........**$45.00**
Coffeepot, Rayed, 1937-76, 8-cup, from $30 to...........**$45.00**
Cookbook, NALCC (club pc), 1984 ....**$45.00**
Cover, bowl; plastic, 1950-61, 8-pc set, from $75 to.**$100.00**
Cover, toaster; plastic, Mary Dunbar, 1950-61 ....**$50.00**
Creamer & sugar bowl, Melmac, from $30 to **$40.00**
Cup, coffee; Jewel's Best, from $20 to..........................**$30.00**
Cup, custard; Heatflow clear glass, Mary Dunbar.......**$60.00**
Cup, custard; Radiance, 1936-76, from $6 to...............**$10.00**
Cup, tea; regular, Ruffled-D, 1936-76, from $4 to **$6.00**
Drip jar, 1936-76, from $15 to.......................................**$20.00**
Dutch oven, metal & porcelain, w/lid, 1979-??, 5-qt, from $125 to...**$175.00**
Flatware, stainless steel, 1960-68, per pc, from $25 to..**$30.00**
Fork, pickle; Jewel Tea, from $40 to............................**$75.00**
Goblet, gold & frost on clear glass, footed, Libbey, 1960-61, 10-oz, from $60 to **$75.00**
Gravy boat/pickle dish, w/underplate, 1942-76, from $40 to..**$55.00**
Hot pad, round, metal back, 1937-??, from $15 to **$20.00**
Hot pad, round, red or green back, 1946-??, 7¼", from $20 to..**$30.00**
Jug, utility; Rayed, 1937-76, from $20 to.....................**$25.00**
Marmalade, 3-pc set, 1938-39, from $100 to **$125.00**
Mug, conic, 1966-76, from $50 to..................................**$65.00**
Mug, Irish coffee; 1966-76, from $90 to.....................**$150.00**
Mustard, 3-pc set, 1938-39, from $100 to **$125.00**
Napkin, muslin, 16" sq, from $30 to **$50.00**
Pan, loaf; Mary Dunbar, from $100 to **$125.00**
Pan frying; stoneware glass top, Mary Dunbar, from $145 to..**$175.00**

Percolator, Douglas, 1960-62 ....**$350.00**

Pitcher, syrup; club pc, 1994, from $55 to.................**$95.00**

Place mats, set of 8, from $150 to.........................**$325.00**

Plate, pie (baker); 1937-76, from $20 to **$35.00**

Plate, salad; Melmac, 7", from $12 to.......................**$20.00**

Plate, 1938-76, 6", from $5 to..................................**$8.00**

Plate, 1938-76, 8", from $16 to................................**$20.00**

Plate, 1938-76, 9", from $8 to................................**$12.00**

Plate, 1938-76, 10", from $12 to..............................**$18.00**

Platter, oval, Melmac, 14", from $40 to **$50.00**

Platter, oval, 1938-76, 11½", from $18 to **$20.00**

Platter, oval, 1938-76, 13½", from $20 to **$28.00**

Playing cards, Autumn Leaf, double deck, 1943-46, from $150 to...**$200.00**

Pressure cooker, metal, Mary Dunbar, from $90 to ..**$125.00**

Range set, salt & pepper shakers w/grease jar, 1936-76, from $50 to...**$60.00**

Salt & pepper shakers, Casper, regular, ruffled, 1939-76, from $20 to...**$30.00**

Saucepan, w/lid, metal, 1979-??, 2-qt, from $70 to....**$100.00**

Saucer, regular, Ruffled D, 1936-76, from $1 to **$3.00**

Scales, Jewel Family, from $100 to.............................**$200.00**

Scales, Jewel Imperial or American, from $150 to....**$200.00**

Shelf liner, paper, 1945-??, complete roll (108"), from $25 to...**$50.00**

Shelf liner, plastic, 1946-57, complete roll, from $125 to ...**$130.00**

Stack set, 4-pc, 1951-76, from $80 to **$100.00**

Sweeper, Little Jewel, from $175 to...........................**$210.00**

Tablecloth, plastic, 1950-53, 54" sq, from $120 to **$150.00**

Tablecloth, sailcloth, 1955-58, 62" sq, from $95 to ...**$140.00**

Teapot, Aladdin, 1942-76, from $50 to.......................**$70.00**

Teapot, French, club pc, 1992, from $75 to **$95.00**

Teapot, long spout, Rayed, 1935, from $75 to **$95.00**

Teapot, Newport, 1933, from $200 to **$250.00**

Tidbit, 2-tier, 1954-69, from $80 to............................**$100.00**

Towel, tea; 1956-57, 16x33", from $50 to **$60.00**

Toy, circus train, 1950, from $900 to **$1,200.00**

Toy, Jewel truck, green, 1970, from $350 to............**$425.00**

Toy, Jewel truck, semi trailer, brown, 1954-57, from $1,000 to **$1,500.00**

Trash can, red, metal, from $750 to......................**$1,200.00**

Tray, coffee service; oval, 1934-??, 18¾", from $75 to..**$100.00**

Tray, red, metal, from $75 to.....................................**$100.00**

Tray, wood & glass, from $125 to.............................**$140.00**

Tumbler, glass, Brockway, 1975-76, 9-oz, from $30 to..**$45.00**

Tumbler, gold & frost on clear glass, Libbey, 1960-61, 15-oz, from $50 to...**$65.00**

Tumbler, iced-tea; frosted glass, Libbey, 1940-49, 5½", from $15 to...**$20.00**

Vase, bud; regular decal, 1940, from $225 to............**$275.00**

Warmer, round, 1956-60, from $125 to **$160.00**

Avon

You'll find Avon bottles everywhere you go! But it's not just the bottles that are collectible — so are items of jewelry, awards, magazine ads, catalogs, and product samples. Of course, the better items are the older ones (they've been called Avon since 1939 — California Perfume Company before that), and if you can find the mint in the box, all the better.

For more information we recommend *Hastin's Avon Collector's Price Guide* by Bud Hastin. See also Cape Cod.

Bell, Miss Nashville, lady in pink & black dress, 5⅜", M..**$40.00**

Bottle, Lady Avon, 1987 NAAC Chicago Convention, limited edition of 1,200, MIB..**$40.00**

Brush & comb set, Her Prettiness Line, 1970s, NM (VG box)...**$110.00**

Cake plate, Currier & Ives winter scene w/gold trim, footed, 4½x9½", M...**$40.00**

Figurine, Avon Lady, National Association Avon Club, #1906, 1977, M...**$95.00**

Figurine, Clark Gable as Rhett Butler, Images of Hollywood Series, 5¾", M...**$40.00**

Figurine, Elvis Presley, w/guitar & case behind, 1987, 7", NMIB..**$40.00**

Figurine, Mrs Albee, 1978 President Club, porcelain, 9" (not including parasol), M...**$110.00**

Figurine, Poor Man, Nativity Collection, signed & dated 1990, MIB..**$55.00**

Figurine, Standing Angel, Nativity Collectibles Series, 1987, NM (EX box)...**$60.00**

Figurine, 1979 Mini Albee award, 3", NN+ **$70.00**

Foot massager, Scott T Massager, Scotty dog shape, black w/red plaid body, fabric bone in mouth, 14", EX (original box)...**$40.00**

Nativity set, O Holy Night, porcelain, 1989-90, NMIBs..**$90.00**

Necklace, Lil' Orphan Annie, 2-sided heart-shaped pendant w/chain, 1982, M...**$45.00**

Stein, Racing Car, handcrafted in Brazil for Avon, 1989, 9", NM..**$35.00**

Stein, Star Wars, 1988, M (w/certificate of authenticity)..**$55.00**

Tea set, Currier & Ives winter scene w/gold trim, pot w/lid, creamer, sugar w/lid, 4 cups & saucers, 13-pc, 1977, M...**$60.00**

Thimbles, American Fashion Silhouettes, 8 pcs, ea in separate box, w/mahogany display rack, NM (in set box) **$80.00**

Wild Country After Shave, in George Washington cologne decanter, 6½", empty, in original box, $30.00. (Photo courtesy Monsen and Baer)

Barbie Doll and Her Friends

Barbie was first introduced in 1959, and soon Mattel found themselves producing not only dolls but tiny garments, fashion accessories, houses, cars, horses, books, and games as well. Today's Barbie collectors want them all. Though the early Barbie dolls are very hard to find, there are many of her successors still around. The trend today is toward Barbie exclusives — Holiday Barbie dolls and Bob Mackie dolls are all very 'hot' items. So are special-event Barbie dolls.

When buying the older dolls, you'll need to do a lot of studying and comparisons to learn to distinguish one Barbie doll from another, but this is the key to making sound buys and good investments. Remember, though, collectors are sticklers concerning condition; compared to a doll mint in box, they'll often give an additional 20% if that box has never been opened (or as collectors say 'never removed from box,' indicated in our lines by 'NRFB')! As a general rule, a mint-in-the-box doll is worth from 50% to 100% more than one mint, no box. The same doll, played with and in only good condition, is worth half as much (or less than that). If you want a good source for study, refer to one of these fine books: *A Decade of Barbie Dolls and Collectibles, 1981 – 1991,* by Beth Summers; *The Wonder of Barbie* and *The World of Barbie Dolls* by Paris and Susan Manos; *The Collector's Encyclopedia of Barbie Dolls and Collectibles* by Sibyl DeWein and Joan Ashabraner; *Barbie Doll Fashion, Vol I* and *Vol II,* by Sarah Sink Eames; *Barbie Exclusives, Books I and II,* by Margo Rana; *The Barbie Doll Boom, 1986 – 1995,* and *Collector's Encyclopedia of Barbie Doll Exclusives and More* by J. Michael Augustyniak; *The Barbie Doll Years, 5th Edition,* by Patrick C. Olds; *The Story of Barbie* by Kitturah Westenhouser; *Barbie, The First 30 Years, 1959 Through 1989,* by Stefanie Deutsch; and *Schroeder's Collectible Toys, Antique to Modern.* (All are published by Collector Books.)

Dolls

Barbie, #1, 1958-59, blond or brunette hair, MIB, ea from $5,000 to..**$6,500.00**
Barbie, #2, 1959, blond or brunette hair, MIB, ea from $5,000 to..**$6,000.00**
Barbie, #3, 1960, blond hair (extra long), original swimsuit, NM **$1,100.00**
Barbie, #3, 1960, blond or brunette hair, original swimsuit, NM, ea **$950.00**
Barbie, #4, 1960, blond or brunette hair, original swimsuit, M, ea from $450 to **$500.00**
Barbie, #5, 1961, blond hair, MIB, from $550 to.......**$650.00**
Barbie, #5, 1961, red hair, original swimsuit, NM **$375.00**
Barbie, #6, blond hair, original swimsuit, EX...........**$250.00**
Barbie, American Girl, 1964, platinum cheek-length hair, original swimsuit, NM...**$650.00**
Barbie, American Girl, 1964, red hair, replica swimsuit, NM..**$600.00**
Barbie, Amethyst Aura, 1997, Bob Mackie, NRFB **$115.00**
Barbie, Antique Rose, 1996, FAO Schwarz, NRFB **$195.00**
Barbie, Blue Elegance, 1992, Hills, MIB **$40.00**
Barbie, Brazilian, 1989, Dolls of the World, NRFB......**$75.00**
Barbie, Bubble-Cut, 1962, blond or brunette hair, NRFB, ea **$400.00**
Barbie, Calvin Klein, 1996, Bloomingdale's, NRFB **$65.00**
Barbie, Chinese, 1993, Dolls of the World, NRFB.......**$50.00**
Barbie, City Shopper, 1996, Macy's, MIB **$75.00**
Barbie, Country Looks, 1993, Ames, MIB **$25.00**
Barbie, Dream Princess, 1992, Sears Exclusive, NRFB..**$40.00**
Barbie, Elizabethan, 1994, Great Eras, MIB **$50.00**
Barbie, English, 1992, Dolls of the World, NRFB........**$65.00**
Barbie, Flight Time, 1990, NRFB **$35.00**
Barbie, Gold Medal Skater, 1976, MIB **$85.00**
Barbie, Grecian Goddess, 1996, Great Eras, NRFB **$55.00**

Barbie, Growing Pretty Hair, 1971, M (EX box), $220.00. (Photo courtesy McMasters Doll Auctions)

Allan, 1964 – 1967, painted red hair, MIB, $145.00. (Photo courtesy McMasters Doll Auctions)

Barbie, Holiday, 1988, NRFB, minimum value.......**$1,000.00**
Barbie, Holiday, 1989, NRFB **$250.00**

Barbie, Holiday, 1990, NRFB $250.00
Barbie, Holiday, 1991, NRFB $250.00
Barbie, Holiday, 1992, NRFB $150.00
Barbie, Holiday, 1993, NRFB $200.00
Barbie, Holiday, 1994, NRFB $175.00
Barbie, Holiday, 1995, NRFB $75.00
Barbie, Holiday, 1996, NRFB $50.00
Barbie, Holiday, 1997, NRFB $35.00
Barbie, Irish, 1984, Dolls of the World, NRFB..........$125.00
Barbie, Loving You, 1984, MIB............................$40.00
Barbie, Magic Curl (Black), 1982, MIB.....................$35.00
Barbie, Masquerade Ball, 1993, Bob Mackie, NRFB .$400.00
Barbie, My Size, 1993, MIB...............................$175.00
Barbie, Nigerian, 1990, Dolls of the World, NRFB......$60.00
Barbie, Night Dazzle, 1994, JC Penney Exclusive, NRFB ..$55.00
Barbie, Oreo Fun, 1997, NRFB $35.00
Barbie, Oscar de la Renta, 1998, Bloomingdale's, NRFB....$80.00
Barbie, Patriot, 1995, American Stories Collection, NRFB...$35.00
Barbie, Peaches 'N Cream, 1985, MIB.....................$35.00
Barbie, Pink Ice, 1996, Toys R Us, MIB.....................$95.00
Barbie, Quick Curl Miss America, 1976, MIB $125.00
Barbie, Royal Invitation, 1993, Spiegel, NRFB.............$85.00
Barbie, Sapphire Dreams, 1995, Toys R Us, NRFB $80.00
Barbie, Sara Lee, 1993, MIB $65.00
Barbie, Silver Screen, 1994, FAO Schwarz, NRFB $200.00
Barbie, Sparkle Eyes (Black), 1992, NRFB...............$40.00
Barbie, Swan Lake Ballerina, 1991, NRFB $200.00
Barbie, Theatre Elegance, 1994, Spiegel, NRFB $175.00
Barbie, Twirly Curls, 1983, MIB...........................$45.00
Barbie, Winter Royale, Pace Club, 1993, NRFB..........$75.00
Cara, Ballerina, 1976, MIB................................$75.00

Casey, Twist 'N Turn, 1967, NMIB, $450.00. (Photo courtesy McMasters Doll Auctions)

Chris, 1967, blond hair, original outfit, NM $125.00
Christie, All American, 1991, MIB.........................$25.00
Christie, Beauty Secrets, 1980, MIB $60.00
Christie, Kissing, 1979, MIB $65.00
Francie, Busy, 1972, NRFB.................................$425.00
Kelley, Quick Curl, 1972, NRFB $175.00

Ken, Army, 1993, Stars 'N Stripes, NRFB $35.00
Ken, Beach Blast, 1989, NRFB.............................$25.00
Ken, Crystal, 1984, NRFB.................................$40.00
Ken, Fashion Jeans, 1982, MIB............................$35.00
Ken, Ice Capades, 1990, NRFB............................$40.00
Ken, Sport & Shave, 1980, MIB............................$40.00
Ken, Superstar, 1977, MIB.................................$95.00
Midge, Earring Magic, 1993, NRFB........................$30.00
Midge, Winter Sports, 1995, Toys R Us, MIB...............$40.00
PJ, Deluxe Quick Curl, 1976, MIB..........................$65.00
PJ, Free Moving, 1976, MIB................................$85.00
PJ, Sun Lovin' Malibu, 1979, MIB..........................$50.00

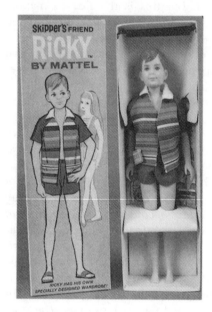

Ricky, painted red hair, 1964, MIB, $110.00. (Photo courtesy McMasters Doll Auctions)

Skipper, Dream Date, 1990, NRFB $25.00
Skipper, Growing Up, 1976, MIB $100.00
Skipper, Hollywood Hair, 1993, NRFB.......................$30.00
Skipper, Pepsi Spirit, 1989, NRFB...........................$70.00
Skooter, 1963, brunette hair, original swimsuit & bows, MIB $175.00

Skooter, 1965, titian hair, straight legs, MIB, $225.00. (Photo courtesy McMasters Doll Auctions)

Stacey, Twist 'N Turn, 1968, blond hair, NRFB **$900.00**

Steffie, Walk Lively, 1965, MIB, from $250.00 to $275.00. (Photo courtesy McMasters Doll Auctions)

Steffie, Walk Lively, 1968, original outfit & scarf, NM ...**$175.00**
Teresa, Country Western Star, 1994, NRFB **$30.00**
Teresa, Rappin' Rockin', 1992, NRFB **$45.00**
Tutti, 1974, blond hair, original outfit, EX **$60.00**
Whitney, Style Magic, 1989, NRFB **$35.00**

Accessories

Case, Barbie, Stacey, Francie & Skipper, pink hard plastic, rare, NM, from $75 to **$100.00**
Case, Barbie & Midge, wearing Rain Coat & Sorority Meeting outfits, pink vinyl, NM, from $45 to **$55.00**
Case, Barbie on Madison Avenue, black w/pink handle, FAO Schwarz, 1992, M **$40.00**
Case, Bubble Cut Barbie wearing Solo in the Spotlight, pink vinyl, 1963, rare, NM, from $75 to **$85.00**
Case, Circus Star Barbie, FAO Schwarz, 1995, M **$95.00**
Case, Miss Barbie, white vinyl, w/original wig, wig stand & mirror, rare, EX **$150.00**

Case, Skipper, blue background, 1964, rare, NM, $150.00. (Photo courtesy Mike's General Store)

Case, Skooter, Skooter wearing Country Picnic & chasing butterflies, blue vinyl, rare, from $125 to **$175.00**
Case, Tuttie, train in background, orange vinyl w/plastic handle & closure, 1974, NM.....................................**$150.00**
Furniture, Barbie & the Beat Dance Cafe, 1990, MIB.**$35.00**
Furniture, Barbie Cookin' Fun Kitchen, MIB **$50.00**
Furniture, Barbie Dream Glow Vanity, 1986, MIB **$20.00**
Furniture, Barbie Dream Store Makeup Department, 1983, MIB **$40.00**
Furniture, Barbie Mountain Ski Cabin, Sears Exclusive, MIB...**$50.00**
Furniture, Barbie's Apartment, 1975, MIB.................**$140.00**
Furniture, Francie & Casey Housemates, 1966, complete, NM **$200.00**
Furniture, Go-Together Chaise Lounge, MIB.............**$75.00**
Furniture, Ice Capades Skating Rink, 1989, MIB.........**$70.00**
Furniture, Movietime Prop Shop, 1989, MIB **$50.00**
Furniture, Pink Sparkles Armoire, 1990, NRFB...........**$25.00**
Furniture, Superstar Barbie Beauty Salon, 1977, MIB.**$55.00**
Furniture, Susy Goose, Ken Wardrobe, M **$50.00**
Furniture, Tuttie Playhouse, 1966, M **$100.00**
Furniture, Work Center, 1985, MIB...........................**$30.00**

Outfit, Ken, King Arthur, MIP, $325.00. (Photo courtesy June Moon)

Outfit, Barbie, All American Girl, #3337, 1972, complete, M..**$75.00**
Outfit, Barbie, Barbie in Switzerland, #822, 1964, NRFB..**$250.00**
Outfit, Barbie, Blue Royalty, Barbie, #1469, 1970, MIB **$250.00**
Outfit, Barbie, Brunch Time, #1628, complete, NM..**$125.00**
Outfit, Barbie, Cinderella, #872, complete, NM........**$150.00**
Outfit, Barbie, City Sophisticate, #2671, 1979, NRFB..**$25.00**
Outfit, Barbie, Cloud 9, #1489, 1969-70, complete, M ..**$200.00**
Outfit, Barbie, Dream Wrap, #1476, 1969-70, complete, M **$150.00**
Outfit, Barbie, Evening In, #3406, 1971, NRFB **$150.00**
Outfit, Barbie, Galaxy A Go-Go, #2742, 1986, NRFB..**$30.00**
Outfit, Barbie, Hurray for Leather, #1477, 1969, NRFB ..**$75.00**
Outfit, Barbie, Knit Hit, #1804, 1968, complete, M **$75.00**
Outfit, Francie, First Things First, #1252, 1966, NRFB..**$115.00**
Outfit, Francie, Get Ups 'N Go Ice Skater, #7845, 1974-75, MIP..**$75.00**
Outfit, Francie, In-Print, #1288, 1967, NRFB.............**$150.00**

Outfit, Francie, Midi Bouquet, #3446, 1971, NRFB ...**$125.00**

Outfit, Francie, Satin Happenin', #1237, 1970, NRFB..**$75.00**

Outfit, Francie & Casey, Cool-It!, 1968, MIP..........**$50.00**

Outfit, Francie & Casey, Pink Lightning, #1231, 1969-70, MIB **$250.00**

Outfit, Ken, Arabian Nights, #0774, 1964, NRFB.......**$200.00**

Outfit, Ken, Fun on Ice, #791, 1963, NRFB...............**$125.00**

Outfit, Ken, Get-Ups 'N Go Doctor, #7705, 1973, MIP..**$75.00**

Outfit, Ken, Ken in Mexico, #0778, 1964, NRFB.......**$175.00**

Outfit, Ken, Morning Workout Fashion Pak, 1964, NRFB..**$50.00**

Outfit, Ken, Special Date, #1401, complete, NM.........**$85.00**

Outfit, Ken, White Is Right Fashion Pak, 1964, NRFB...**$40.00**

Outfit, Ken & Brad, Sun Fun Fashion Pak, 1971, MIP..**$75.00**

Outfit, Ken Ski Champion, #798, 1963, NRFB...........**$100.00**

Outfit, Skipper, Beach Peachy, #1938, 1967, NRFB ..**$150.00**

Outfit, Skipper, Daisy Crazy, #1732, 1970, complete, M...**$150.00**

Outfit, Skipper, Dream-Ins, #3293, 1972, MIB...........**$175.00**

Outfit, Skipper, Dressed in Velvet, #3477, 1971, NRFB..**$125.00**

Outfit, Skipper, Real Sporty, #1961, NRFB................**$200.00**

Outfit, Skipper, School's Cool, #1976, 1969-70, MIB.**$200.00**

Outfit, Skipper, Ship Ahoy, #1918, complete, M, minimum value, $75.00.

Outfit, Skipper, Summer Slacks Fashion Pak, 1970, MIP..**$75.00**

Outfit, Skipper & Fluff, Sporty Shorty Fashion Pak, 1971, MOC..**$65.00**

Outfit, Slipper, Hearts 'N Flowers, #1945, 1967, NRFB .**$300.00**

Outfit, Tutti, Clowning Around, #3606, 1967, NRFB.**$195.00**

Outfit, Tutti & Chris, Sea-Shore Shorties, #3614, 1968-69, complete, M **$125.00**

Vehicle, Allan's Roadster, 1964, aqua, MIB................**$500.00**

Vehicle, Barbie & Ken Dune Buggy, pink, Irwin, 1970, MIB **$250.00**

Vehicle, Barbie Silver 'Vette, MIB **$30.00**

Vehicle, Barbie Travelin' Trailer, MIB........................**$40.00**

Vehicle, Star 'Vette, red, 1977, MIB **$100.00**

Gift Sets

Army Barbie & Ken, Stars & Stripes, 1993, MIB.........**$60.00**

Barbie & Her Horse Dancer, Canada, MIB................**$75.00**

Barbie & Ken Campin' Out, 1983, MIB......................**$75.00**

Barbie Loves Elvis, 1996, NRFB...............................**$75.00**

Barbie's Olympic Ski Village, MIB...........................**$75.00**

Dance Sensation Barbie, 1985, MIB **$35.00**

Halloween Party Barbie & Ken, Target, 1998, NRFB ..**$65.00**

Malibu Barbie Beach Party, M (M case)....................**$75.00**

Night Night Sleep Tight Tutti, NRFB **$300.00**

Pretty Pairs Nan 'N Fran, 1970, NRFB.....................**$250.00**

Walking Jamie Strollin' in Style, NRFB.....................**$450.00**

Barbie and Ken Campin' Out, 1983, NRFB, $100.00. (Photo courtesy Beth Summers)

Miscellaneous

Barbie & Me Dress-up Set, MIB **$100.00**

Barbie Beauty Kit, 1961, complete, M **$125.00**

Barbie Dough Dessert Maker, 1994, MIB...................**$40.00**

Bicycle, Camp Barbie, 1985, 16", NM........................**$85.00**

Book, Happy Go Lucky Skipper, Random House, 1963, hardcover, EX **$35.00**

Coloring book, Barbie & Ken, 1963, unused, NM **$50.00**

Game, Barbie Queen of the Prom, Mattel, 1962, MIB..**$80.00**

Ornament, Holiday Barbie, Hallmark, 1994, 2nd edition, MIB **$35.00**

Paper dolls, Barbie, Whitman #4601, 1963, uncut, M.**$85.00**

Puzzle, jigsaw; Skipper & Skooter, 100 pcs, 1965, MIB..**$30.00**

Tea set, Barbie 25th Anniversary, 1984, complete, M...**$150.00**

Wagon, Camp Barbie, 1995, 34", EX **$50.00**

Wristwatch, 30th Anniversary, 1989, MIB...................**$80.00**

Barware

From the decade of the 1990s, the cocktail shaker has emerged as a hot new collectible. These micro skyscrapers are now being saved for the enjoyment of future generations, much like the 1930s buildings saved from destruction by landmarks preservation committees of today.

Cocktail shakers — the words just conjure up visions of glamour and elegance. Seven hard shakes over your right shoulder and you can travel back in time, back to the glamor of Hollywood movie sets with Fred Astaire and Ginger Rogers and luxurious hotel lounges with gleaming chrome; back to the world of F. Scott Fitzgerald and *The Great Gatsby*; or watch *The Thin Man* movie showing William Powell instruct a bartender on the proper way to shake a martini — the reveries are endless.

An original American art form, cocktail shakers reflect the changing nature of various styles of art, design, and architecture of the era between WWI and WWII. We see the graceful lines of Art Nouveau in the early '20s being replaced by the rage for jagged geometric modern design. The geometric cubism of Picasso that influenced so many designers of the '20s was replaced with the craze for streamline design of '30s. Cocktail shakers of the early '30s were taking the shape of the new deity of American architecture, the skyscraper, thus giving the appearance of movement and speed in a slow economy.

Cocktail shakers served to penetrate the gloom of depression, ready to propel us into the future of prosperity like some Buck Rogers rocket ship — both perfect symbols of generative power, of our perpetration into better times ahead.

Cocktail shakers and architecture took on the aerodynamically sleek industrial design of the automobile and airship. It was as Norman Bel Geddes said: 'a quest for speed.' All sharp edges and corners were rounded off. This trend was the theme of the day, as even the sharp notes of jazz turned into swing.

Cocktail shakers have all the classic qualifications of a premium collectible. They are easily found at auctions, antique and secondhand shops, flea markets, and sales. They can be had in all price ranges. They require little study to identify one manufacturer or period from another, and lastly they are not easily reproduced.

The sleek streamline cocktail shakers of modern design are valued by collectors of today. Those made by Revere, Chase, and Manning Bowman have taken the lead in this race. Also commanding high prices are those shakers of unusual design such as penguins, zeppelins, dumbbells, bowling pins, town crier bells, airplanes, even ladies' legs. They're all out there, waiting to be found, waiting to be recalled to life, to hear the clank of ice cubes, and to again become the symbol of elegance.

For more information we recommend *Vintage Bar Ware, An Identification and Value Guide*, by Stephen Visakay (Collector Books).

Advisor: Steve Visakay (See Directory, Barware)

Cocktail cup, clear glass rooster figural w/red details, 1930s-40s, 3½x3¼" dia, from $20 to............**$25.00**

Cocktail cup, green Catalin w/chrome stem, ca 1930, 5¾x2¾", from $8 to............**$10.00**

Cocktail cup, ruby glass on chrome base, Farberware, 5", from $7 to............**$10.00**

Cocktail cup, ruby glass w/sterling trim, footed, 3⅜", from $7 to............**$12.00**

Cocktail glass, enameled rooster on clear footed cone form, 1930s, 3¼" to 3½", ea from $3 to............**$8.00**

Cocktail picks, bowling pin handles, chrome & plastic set of 10 on holder w/ball finial, 1940s, 4", from $15 to............**$25.00**

Decanter pump, glass w/black & gold enamel, top-hat cap, 1940s, from $65 to............**$75.00**

Ice bucket, clear glass, Cape Cod, Imperial Glass, #160/63, 6½"............**$195.00**

Ice bucket, clear glass, First Love, Duncan & Miller, #30, 6"............**$110.00**

Ice bucket, green, with lid, Fry, from $225.00 to $245.00; yellow, with lid, Fenton, from $145.00 to $155.00. (Photo courtesy Gene Florence)

Ice chopper, cobalt glass w/silk-screened recipes, 1930s, 11½", from $45 to............**$75.00**

Ice tub, clear glass, American, Fostoria, w/liner, 6½"............**$95.00**

Ice tub, clear glass, Janice, footed, New Martinsville, 6"............**$100.00**

Ice tub, green glass (Moongleam), Octagon, Heisey, #500............**$80.00**

Ice tub, pink glass, Spiral Flutes, handles, Duncan & Miller............**$60.00**

Jigger, shot; musical, silver plate w/red bands, Cone, Napier, 6x2⅝", from $35 to............**$45.00**

Mixer, chrome w/jade Catalin mounts, Manning-Bowman, ca 1928, 10¾", from $200 to............**$250.00**

Set, chrome-plated brass, Zephyr shaker, 4 cups w/red Catalin bases & round tray, Revere Copper & Brass Co, from $250 to............**$300.00**

Set, hammered chrome w/black composition handle, Krome Kraft, 1940s-60s, 10¼" shaker+6 footed cups, from $65 to............**$95.00**

Set, nickel plate, Paris pattern, teapot-like 10" shaker, Wm Rogers & Sons, ca 1927, +6 5" cups, from $100 to............**$150.00**

Set, silver plate, simulated cowhide grain, leather straps, golf theme, Derby SP Co No 1921, complete, from $1,900 to............**$2,500.00**

Shaker, aluminum & red Bakelite, Zeeronater NY Beverage Cooler, 14½", from $85 to............**$110.00**

Shaker, amber glass, chrome top, ca 1937, 11½", from $55 to............**$65.00**

Shaker, brass artillery shell form, inscribed presentation, dated 1904, 3-pc, from $150 to............**$250.00**

Shaker, chrome, Farberware, 1930s, 10", from $28 to............**$38.00**

Shaker, chrome skyscraper w/Catalin knob, unmarked, 12½", from $150 to.................................**$175.00**

Shaker, chrome w/orange Catalin trim, Krome Kraft, early 1940s-1960s, 12¾", from $45 to **$55.00**

Shaker, chrome w/plastic top cap, standing dumbbell form, 1930s, 12", from $95 to **$120.00**

Shaker, chromium-plated skyscraper style with walnut trim, Manning-Bowman, 1936, from $65.00 to $75.00. (Photo courtesy Stephen Visakay)

Shaker, clear glass w/enamel sailboats, chrome top, Hazel Atlas, from $35 to **$65.00**

Shaker, clear glass w/red & white enamel decor, chrome top, unmarked, 1930s-40s, from $35 to **$45.00**

Shaker, clear glass w/silver overlay hunt scene, Sterling outlined in design, Heisey, 1940s-50s, 14", from $175 to **$275.00**

Shaker, clear molded glass, 1940s-50s, 3-pc, party size, 14¼", from $65 to...**$75.00**

Shaker, clear or colored glass, from Imperial's No 451 line, 1930s, ea from $45 to...**$65.00**

Shaker, cobalt glass w/football player silver overlay, 1930s, party size, 12½", from $75 to **$125.00**

Shaker, cobalt glass w/polo scene silver overlay, chrome top, 1930s, from $125 to **$175.00**

Shaker, cobalt glass w/white windmill scene, Hazel Atlas, from $25 to..**$35.00**

Shaker, frosted glass w/silkscreen decor, 1930s, party size, 13", from $65 to **$75.00**

Shaker, glass lined w/chrome outer casing, Ritz, Monarch Aluminum, 1937, 12¾", from $75 to **$95.00**

Shaker, green glass pitcher-like form w/chrome top & Catalin finial, Cambridge Glass Co.(?), 13", from $125 to..**$150.00**

Shaker, green glass w/etched rooster, silver-plated top w/cork, unmarked, 1926, 10½", from $65 to........**$75.00**

Shaker, heavy molded glass, chrome top, ca 1950s, 11x3½", from $35 to..**$55.00**

Shaker, heavy pressed glass w/cranberry flashing, silver-plated top, 1930s, 11", from $125 to **$150.00**

Shaker, nickel plated, 12-sided, Jos Henrichs...Pat Feb 22, 1910, 12¾", from $150 to....................................**$175.00**

Shaker, nickel plated w/engraved & enameled rooster, Meriden...Patented Jan 11, 1927, spout cap missing, from $125 to...**$145.00**

Shaker, pressed & cut glass w/chrome top, New Martinsville(?), 1930s, from $75 to **$95.00**

Shaker, ribbed glass w/painted black horizontal bands, Czechoslovakia, 1930s, from $95 to....................**$110.00**

Shaker, ruby glass, lady's leg form w/chrome top & removable chrome high-heel slipper, West Virginia Specialty, 15½"..**$400.00**

Shaker, ruby glass, Shake Well Before Using, sterling trim, 9", from $75 to...**$95.00**

Shaker, ruby glass w/copper top, Thirst Extinguisher, extinguisher form, silkscreened recipes, 1940s, 11½", from $65 to...**$95.00**

Shaker, ruby glass w/tavern scene in silver overlay, chrome top, 1930s, from $65 to **$85.00**

Shaker, silver overlay roosters on ruby glass, chrome top, shouldered cylinder, ca 1930, 12", from $250 to...**$295.00**

Shaker, silver overlay ships on clear glass, silver-plated lid, cobalt glass foot, 1925-29, 9¼", from $75 to......**$110.00**

Shaker, silver plate, stamped Italy, 11½", from $95 to..**$135.00**

Shaker, silver plate, unmarked, jumbo party size, 1930s, 13x5", from $55 to **$75.00**

Shaker, silver plate w/figual rooster finial, cork stopper, Bernard Rice & Sons, 1920s, 14", from $95 to ...**$125.00**

Shaker, silver plate w/red bands, Cone, Napier, 9x3¾", from $75 to...**$95.00**

Shaker, silver-plated pinch-bottle style, engraved roosters, Meriden...Patented Jan 11, 1927, 8½", from $175 to..**$250.00**

Soda siphon, chrome w/enameled top, Soda King Syphon, 10", from $125 to **$195.00**

Traveling bar, nickel plated, cocktail shaker form, Germany, ca 1928, 8", 9-pc, from $75 to.............................**$95.00**

Tumbler, highball; lady w/palette decal (palette becomes clear when filled w/drink), ca 1941, 4¾", from $10 to...**$12.00**

Bauer Pottery

The Bauer Pottery Company is one of the best known of the California pottery companies and is noted for both its artware and its dinnerware. Over the past ten years, Bauer Pottery has become particularly collectible, and prices have risen accordingly. Bauer actually began operations in Kentucky in 1885, but in 1910 they moved to Los Angeles where they continued in business until they closed in 1962. The company produced several popular dinnerware lines, including La Linda, Monterey, and Brusche Al Fresco. Most popular (and most significant) was the Ringware line begun in 1932, which preceded Fiesta as a popular solid-color, everyday dinnerware. The earliest pieces are unmarked, although to collectors they are unmistakable, due in part to their distinctive glazes, which have an almost primitive charm due to their drips, glaze misses, and color variations.

Another dinnerware line popular with collectors is Speckleware, a term that refers to a 1950s-era speckled glaze used on several different kinds of pottery other than dinnerware, including vases, flowerpots, and kitchenware. Though not as popular as Ringware, it holds its value well and is usually available at much lower prices than Ring. Keep an eye out for other flowerpots and mixing bowls as well, as they are common garage-sale items.

Artware by Bauer is not so easy to find any more, but it is worth seeking out because of its high values. So-called oil jars sell for upwards of $1,500.00, and Rebekah vases routinely fetch $400.00 or more. Matt Carlton is one of the most desirable designers of handmade ware.

Colors are particularly important in pricing Bauer pottery, especially Ringware. Burgundy, cobalt blue, delph blue, and ivory are generally at the high end. Black and white glazes on Ringware items are worth as much as twice the prices listed here. Common colors in dinnerware are orange-red, jade green, and Chinese yellow. An in-depth study of colors and values may be found in *The Collector's Encyclopedia of Bauer Pottery* by Jack Chipman (Collector Books).

Advisors: Michele and Frank Miele (See Directory, Bauer)

Art Pottery, #2000 Hi-Fire and Matt Carlton

Hi-Fire, garden vase, California orange-red, Fred Johnson, 18", minimum value, $750.00. (Photo courtesy Jack Chipman)

Hi-Fire vase, #10 Stock, chartreuse **$125.00**
Hi-Fire vase, Ring cylinder, 10", from $125 to...........**$175.00**
Matt Carlton vase, carnation; jade green, 10"............**$350.00**
Matt Carlton vase, fan form, 3¾", from $75 to..........**$150.00**
Matt Carlton vase, Rebekah, 12", from $900 to a minimum of..**$1,500.00**
Matt Carlton vase, signature style, Chinese yellow, 12", minimum value **$1,500.00**

Brusche

Al Fresco, bowl, fruit; speckled or solid, 5", from $10 to...**$12.00**

Al Fresco, creamer & sugar bowl, speckled or solid ..**$25.00**
Al Fresco, mug, w/handle, solid colors, 8-oz.............**$10.00**
Al Fresco, plate, dinner; speckled or solid, 10", from $12 to **$15.00**
Contempo, cup & saucer, Spice Green.......................**$12.00**
Contempo, mug, Kitchenware, Gloss Pumpkin, 8-oz.**$15.00**
Contempo, teapot, beige...**$65.00**

Cal-Art and Garden Pottery

Flowerpot, Cal-Art Swirl #3 (3"), gloss glazes, from $20 to **$25.00**
Jardiniere, Cal-Art Swirl #12 (12"), speckled pink.....**$125.00**
Jardiniere, Cal-Art Swirl #6 (6"), gloss glazes, from $50 to **$60.00**
Spanish Pot, #4 (4"), speckled colors, from $18 to.....**$25.00**
Spanish Pot, Hi-Fire, #5 (5"), gloss white **$35.00**
Swan, Cal-Art, matt white, med, 9" **$65.00**
Vase, Cal-Art 'Robot Midget,' burgundy, 4"................**$35.00**

Gloss Pastel Kitchenware (aka GPK)

Aladdin teapot, all colors, 8-cup, from $160 to.........**$200.00**
Cookie jar (aka Beehive), all colors, from $95 to.....**$150.00**
Mixing bowl, #24, all colors, from $30 to...................**$40.00**
Pitcher, w/ice lip, all colors, 2-qt, from $75 to...........**$90.00**

Other Bauer Dinnerware

La Linda, cereal bowl, from $15 to **$30.00**
La Linda, gravy boat, gloss colors **$25.00**
La Linda, jumbo cup & saucer, gloss green................**$45.00**
Monterey, cup & saucer, from $18 to **$25.00**
Monterey, gravy boat, from $40 to............................**$65.00**
Monterey, plate, dinner; burgundy, 9" **$25.00**
Monterey Moderne, mug, w/handle, 10-oz, from $20 to..**$30.00**
Monterey Moderne, teapot, 6-cup, from $65 to **$95.00**

Plainware

Bean pot, individual; from $135 to **$185.00**
Bowl, mixing; #3, other colors, 2-gal, minimum value ..**$350.00**
Bowl, mixing; #3, yellow, 2-gal.................................**$175.00**
Creamer, individual; handmade by Matt Carlton, yellow ..**$95.00**
Ramekin, from $15 to **$25.00**

Ringware (Ring)

Bowl, Double Ring, Mixing #18, jade green **$130.00**
Bowl, Double Ring, Mixing #24, cobalt blue **$90.00**
Bowl, low salad; light blue, 9" **$60.00**
Bowl, low salad; orange-red, 9" **$75.00**
Carafe, w/copper raffia-wrapped handle, orange-red..**$120.00**
Casserole, individual; jade green, rare, 5½" **$250.00**
Cookie jar, delph blue, w/lid.....................................**$350.00**
Cookie jar base (no lid), delph blue..........................**$110.00**
Cup & saucer set, cobalt blue....................................**$50.00**

Cup & saucer set, delph blue $45.00

Pitcher, ice water; two-quart, from $165.00 to $200.00. (Photo courtesy Jack Chipman)

Plate, dessert; Chinese yellow, 6½" $15.00
Plate, dinner; jade green, 9½" $35.00
Plate, dinner; orange-red, 9½" $30.00
Plate, salad; cobalt blue, 7½" $30.00
Salt & pepper shakers, squat style, jade green, pr......$45.00
Tumbler, no handle, cobalt blue, 12-oz $50.00
Tumblers, w/handles, Chinese yellow, 12-oz, set of 6, minimum value $180.00

Speckled Kitchenware

Buffet server, speckled white, no frame $40.00
Casserole, speckled pink, w/frame, 1½-qt $40.00
Casserole, speckled pink, w/frame, 2-qt....................$60.00
Mug, Kitchenware, speckled green, 8-oz....................$15.00
Pelican pitcher, speckled blue, 20-oz.........................$45.00
Pelican pitcher, speckled yellow, 20-oz $35.00
Teapot, Monterey Moderne style, speckled green $45.00

Other Miscellaneous Bauer

Fish cookie jar, Cemar turned Bauer, speckled green....$75.00
Hi-Fire, mixing bowl set, various colors, 4-pc, from $150 to $200.00
Oil jar, jade green, 16", minimum value $850.00
Tuna baker, w/original stand 'Chicken of the Sea,' burgundy..$45.00
Vase, stock, #677 Tracy Irwin design, speckled white, 12½" $175.00

Beanie Babies

The popularity of Ty Beanie Babies is not as intense and values for them are not as high as during the years 1996 – 2000, when crazed collectors swarmed stores for the newest releases and prices soared for many Beanie Babies. However, collectors will still find value in the rare and exclusive Beanie Babies, as well as some of the retired regular issues. There are many other bean bag animals on the market, many of which are very similar to Ty Beanie Babies, and collectors need to learn the characteristics that distinguish Ty Beanie Babies from counterfeits and/or reproductions.

The most important thing to know is that there are different swing tags (heart-shaped paper tags, usually attached to the animal's ear, but also to arms, legs, or wings) and tush tag styles (sewn into the tush of the animal), and these indicate year of issue. Ty Beanie Babies were introduced in 1994, and the earliest their tags date is 1993.

#1 Swing tag: single heart-shaped tag; comes on Beanie Babies with tush tags dated 1993. (Photos courtesy Amy Sullivan)

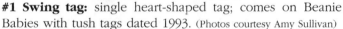

#2 Swing tag: heart-shaped; folded, with information inside; narrow letters; comes on Beanie Babies with tush tags dated 1993. (Photos courtesy Amy Sullivan)

#3 Swing tag: heart-shaped; folded, with information inside; wider letters; comes on Beanie Babies with tush tags dated 1993 and 1995. (Photos courtesy Amy Sullivan)

#4 Swing tag: heart-shaped; folded, with information inside; wider lettering with no gold outline around the 'ty'; yellow star on front; first tag to include a poem and birth date; comes on Beanie Babies with tush tags dated 1993, 1995, and 1996. (Photos courtesy Amy Sullivan)

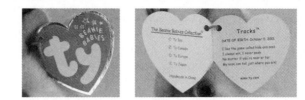

#5 Swing tag: heart-shaped; folded, with information inside; different font on front and inside; birth month spelled out, no style numbers, website listed; comes on Beanie Babies with tush tags dated 1993, 1995, 1996, 1997, 1998, and 1999. (Photos courtesy Amy Sullivan)

#9 Swing tag: shows five smaller holographic stars above the words 'Beanie Babies' in fine yellow print. Inside information identical to #6 and #7 swing tags; comes on Beanie Babies with tush tags dated 2001 and 2002. (Photo courtesy Amy Sullivan)

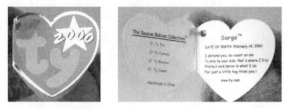

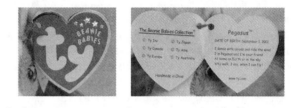

#6 Swing tag: features holographic star with '2000' across star; inside: Ty, Inc., Ty Canada, Ty Europe, and Ty Japan; birthdate, website address and poem in smaller font than #5; new safety precaution on back, smaller font and UPC; comes on Beanie Babies with tush tags dated 2000. (Photos courtesy Amy Sullivan)

#10 Swing tag: same as #9 tag except inside lists two more locations of Ty, Inc., on left-handed side: Ty Asia and Ty Australia. (Photo courtesy Amy Sullivan)

Early tush tags (dated 1993 and 1995) do not have the Beanie's name on them; after 1995 Beanie Baby names were printed on both swing tags and tush tags. The earlier Beanie Babies have white tags with black writing with the year of issue, 'Ty Inc,' and manufacturing information on the tag; later tush tags are white with red writing and list the Beanie Baby's name along with manufacturing information.

Variations on #6 Swing tags: The twelve Zodiac Beanie Babies, released in September 2000, have all the characteristics of the sixth generation swing tag with the exception of the word 'Zodiac' on the front of the swing tag, which replaces the star and 2000. The interiors of the three Holiday Beanie Babies' tags released in October 2000 have a blue background and white snowflakes.

#7 Swing tag: identical to #6 tag except 'Beanies' is written across the holographic star instead of '2000.' This tag appears in UK Beanie Babies (photo not available); comes on Beanie Babies with tush tags dated 2000.

Removing tags from the more current Beanie Babies or having ripped, creased, or damaged tags decreases the value of the animal. However, most of the rarer 1994, 1995, and 1996 issues are still quite valuable with a damaged tag or even without a swing tag, due to their scarcity.

Remember that Ty produces several other plush lines, some of which are even stuffed with pellets. You need to be able to determine what product you have. Beginning collectors often confuse Teenie Beanie Babies and Beanie Buddies with Beanie Babies. Beanie Babies are approximately 6" to 10" in length/height (though Slither the snake is even longer!) Teenie Beanie Babies debuted in April 1997 as Happy Meal Toys in McDonald's restaurants and are smaller versions of Beanie Babies. Beanie Buddies are larger versions of Beanie Babies and are made of a more plush fabric. Sometimes Ty produced a Beanie Baby, Teenie Beanie Baby, *and* a Beanie Buddy, all with the same name and look, with the exception of the size. It is important to know which type of animal you own! Ty produced Teenie Beanie Baby versions of the rare Beanie Babies in 1999, and these certainly do not have the same values as the rare Beanie Babies by the same names!

#8, Swing tag: shows a ¼" holographic star with the word 'Beanie' and 'Baby' below in fine yellow print. Inside information identical to #6 swing tag; comes on Beanie Babies with tush tags dated 2000 and 2001. (Photo courtesy Amy Sullivan)

Our prices are for mint or near-mint condition Beanie Babies with both swing tag and tush tags intact and in perfect condition. Values for Beanie Babies missing a hang tag decrease by up to 50% and up to 75% if missing both swing and tush tags. For Beanie Babies with a #1, #2, or #3 swing tag, add 30% to 40% to the prices suggested below. Style numbers are the last four digits in the UPC code located on the back of the Beanie Baby's swing tag.

Advisor: Amy Sullivan (See Directory, Beanie Babies)

Key: R — retired   # — style number
BBOC — Beanie Babies Official Club

#1 Bear, red w/#1 on chest, issued only to Ty sales reps, 253 made, R, minimum value..................................**$5,000.00**

Addison, #4362, given to fans at Chicago Cubs vs AZ Diamondbacks game at Wrigley Field, May 20, 2001, R, from $10 to..**$15.00**

Ally, #4032, alligator, R..**$45.00**

Almond, #4246, bear, R, from $5 to **$7.00**

Amber, #4243, tabby cat, gold, R, from $5 to.............**$10.00**

America, #4506, bear, blue, R, proceeds sent to American Red Cross for relief to victims of September 11, from $7 to..**$15.00**

America, #4409, bear, white, R, from $7 to **$14.00**

America, #4412, bear, red, R, from $15 to **$25.00**

Ants, #4195, anteater, R, from $5 to **$10.00**

Ariel, #4288, fundraising bear for the Elizabeth Glaser Pediatric AIDS Foundation, R, from $5 to...............**$8.00**

Aruba, #4314, angelfish, R, from $5 to......................**$7.00**

Aurora, #4271, polar bear, R, from $5 to **$7.00**

Baby Boy, #4534, It's a Boy, bear, blue, from $5 to.....**$8.00**

Baby Girl, #4535, It's a Girl, bear, pink, from $5 to.....**$8.00**

Baldy, #4074, eagle, R, from $5 to **$10.00**

Bam, #4544, ram, from $5 to **$7.00**

Bananas, #4316, orangutan, R, from $5 to **$7.00**

Bandito, #4543, raccoon, grey, from $5 to **$7.00**

Batty, #4035, bat, pink or tie-dyed, R, from $5 to........**$8.00**

BB, #4253, birthday bear, R, from $5 to **$10.00**

Beak, #4211, kiwi bird, R, from $5 to **$7.00**

Beani, #4397, cat, gray, R, from $5 to **$7.00**

Beanie baby of the month, Ty Internet store offer, 12 different Beanies offered to members each month of 2003, each from $8 to..**$10.00**

Bernie, #4109, St Bernard, R, from $5 to **$8.00**

Bessie, #4009, cow, brown, R, from $20 to.................**$35.00**

Birthday bears (2001), named by months, #4370 through #4372; #4386 through #4393; #4547, all R, ea from $5 to........**$7.00**

Birthday bears (2002), named by months, w/hats, August R, from $5 to **$10.00**

Blackie, #4011, bear, R, from $8 to **$15.00**

Blizzard, #4163, tiger, white, R, from $9 to **$13.00**

Bones, #4001, dog, brown, R, from $10 to..................**$20.00**

Bongo, #4067, monkey, 1st issue, brown tail, R, from $20 to...**$50.00**

Bongo, #4067, monkey, 2nd issue, tan tail, R, from $10 to **$15.00**

Bonsai, #4567, chimpanzee, from $5 to....................**$7.00**

Booties, #4536, kitten, black, from $5 to **$7.00**

Bride, #4528, bear, from $5 to **$10.00**

Brigitte, #4374, poodle, pink, R, from $5 to **$7.00**

Britannia, #4601, British bear, UK exclusive, R, minimum value **$45.00**

Brownie, #4010, bear, w/swing tag, R, minimum value ..**$1,480.00**

Bruno, #4183, terrier, R, from $5 to..............................**$7.00**

Bubbles, #4078, fish, yellow & black, R, minimum value..**$30.00**

Buckingham, #4603, bear, UK exclusive, R, minimum value **$75.00**

Bucky, #4016, beaver, R, from $10.00 to $20.00. (Photo courtesy Amy Sullivan)

Bumble, #4045, bee, R, minimum value....................**$200.00**

Bunga Raya, #4615, Asia-Pacific flower bear, Malaysia exclusive, yellow, from $20 to..**$35.00**

Bushy, #4285, lion, R, from $5 to **$7.00**

Butch, #4227, bull terrier, R, from $6 to......................**$8.00**

Buzzie, #4354, bee, R, from $5 to **$7.00**

Buzzy, #4308, buzzard, R, from $5 to **$7.00**

Canyon, #4212, cougar, R, from $5 to........................**$7.00**

Carrots, #4512, rabbit, R, from $7 to **$9.00**

Cashew, #4292, bear, brown, R, from $5 to **$8.00**

Cassie, #4340, collie, R, from $5 to **$7.00**

Caw, #4071, crow, R, from $275 to........................**$325.00**

Celebrate, #4385, 15-year anniversary bear, R, from $7 to..**$10.00**

Celebrations, #4620, The Queen's Golden Jubilee bear, R, UK, Australia, New Zealand & Canada exclusive, from $10 to **$50.00**

Champion, #4408, 32 different versions representing teams in 2002 World Cup soccer tournament, all R, from $7 to..........**$20.00**

Charmer, unicorn, from $5 to **$7.00**

Cheddar, #4525, mouse holding cheese, R, from $7 to ..**$10.00**

Cheeks, #4250, baboon, R, from $5 to......................**$7.00**

Cheery, #4359, Sunshine bear, R, from $7 to **$10.00**

Cheezer, #4301, mouse, R, from $6 to **$8.00**

Chickie, #4509, chick, R, from $7 to **$10.00**

Chilly, #4012, polar bear, R, minimum value **$700.00**

China, #4315, panda bear, R, from $5 to **$7.00**

Chinook, #4604, bear, Canada exclusive, R, from $20 to..**$25.00**

Chip, #4121, calico cat, R, from $5 to **$7.00**

Chipper, #4259, chipmunk, R, from $5 to...................**$7.00**

Chocolate, #4015, moose, R, from $8 to....................**$12.00**

Chops, #4019, lamb, R, from $50 to...........................**$80.00**

Cinders, #4295, bear, black, R, from $5 to..................**$7.00**

Classy, #4373, bear, 'The People's Beanie,' R, from $8 to.**$10.00**

Claude, #4083, crab, tie-dyed, R, from $5 to **$8.00**

Clover, #4503, bear, white w/shamrocks, R, from $7 to.**$10.00**

Clubby, bear, blue, BBOC exclusive, R, from $15 to..**$20.00**

Clubby II, bear, purple, BBOC exclusive, R, from $12 to ..**$15.00**

Clubby III, #4993, bear, brown, BBOC exclusive, R, from $10 to..**$20.00**

Clubby IV, #4996, bear, purple, BBOC exclusive, R, from $10 to..**$15.00**

Clubby V, bear, pink, BBOC exclusive, from $7 to **$10.00**

Color Me Beanie, bear that can be decorated by owner, from $7 to..**$15.00**

Congo, #4160, gorilla, R, from $5 to **$7.00**

Coral, #4079, fish, tie-dyed, R, minimum value...........**$50.00**

Coral Casino, bear given to club members only, R, minimum value **$1,000.00**

Cottonball, #4511, rabbit, R, from $6 to.........................**$9.00**

Courage, #4515, German Shepherd, all profits donated to NY Police & Fire widow's/children's benefit fund, R, from $6 to....**$8.00**

Creepers, #4376, skeleton, R, from $5 to.......................**$8.00**

Crunch, #4130, shark, R, from $5 to..............................**$7.00**

Cubbie, #4010, bear, brown, R, from $15 to **$20.00**

Cupid, #4502, dog, white, R, from $7 to.......................**$9.00**

Curly, #4052, bear, brown, R, from $8 to **$10.00**

Dad-e, #4413, e-Beanie offered only through Ty Internet Store, R, minimum value **$10.00**

Daffodil, bear, #4624, Ty Europe exclusive, from $10 to..**$50.00**

Daisy, #4006, cow, black & white, R, from $10 to......**$20.00**

Darling, #4368, dog, R, from $5 to **$8.00**

Dart, #4352, frog, R, from $5 to...................................**$7.00**

Dearest, #4350, bear, peach, R, from $8 to **$10.00**

Derby, #4008, horse, 1st issue, fine yarn mane & tail, R, minimum value **$650.00**

Derby, #4008, horse, 2nd issue, coarse mane & tail, R, from $10 to..**$15.00**

Derby, #4008, horse, 3rd issue, white star on forehead, R, from $6 to..**$8.00**

Derby, #4008, horse, 4th issue, white star on forehead, fur mane & tail, R, from $5 to **$7.00**

Diddley, #4383, dog, green, R, from $5 to **$7.00**

Digger, #4027, crab, 1st issue, orange, R, minimum value ..**$325.00**

Digger, #4027, crab, 2nd issue, red, R, minimum value....**$45.00**

Dinky, #4341, dodo bird, R, from $5 to **$7.00**

Dinosaurs, from left to right: Steg, #4087, stegosaurus, R, minimum value, $320.00; Bronty, #4085, brontosarus, blue, R, minimum value, $320.00; Rex, #4086, tyrannosaurus, R, minimum value, $300.00. (Photo courtesy Amy Sullivan)

Dizzy, #4365, dalmatian, R, 5 versions w/different colored ears & spots, ea from $6 to..............................**$15.00**

Doby, #4110, doberman, R, from $5 to **$8.00**

Doodle, #4171, rooster, tie-dyed, R, from $15 to........**$20.00**

Dotty, #4100, dalmatian, R, from $6 to **$8.00**

Early, #4190, robin, R, from $5 to **$7.00**

Ears, #4018, rabbit, brown, R, from $10 to.................**$20.00**

Echo, #4180, dolphin, R, from $8 to **$12.00**

Eggbert, #4232, baby chick, R, from $5 to....................**$7.00**

Eggs, #4337, Easter bear, pink, R, from $7 to.............**$12.00**

Eggs II, #4516, Easter bear, blue, R, from $8 to.........**$10.00**

England, #4608, bear, UK exclusive, R, from $20 to...**$35.00**

Erin, #4186, green bear, R, from $8.00 to $11.00. (Photo courtesy Amy Sullivan)

Eucalyptus, #4240, koala, R, from $5 to........................**$7.00**

Ewey, #4219, lamb, R, from $5 to **$7.00**

Ferny, #4618, Asia-Pacific flower bear, black, New Zealand exclusive, R, from $20 to....................................**$30.00**

Fetch, #4189, golden retriever, R, from $6 to **$8.00**

Fetcher, #4298, chocolate lab, R, from $6 to **$8.00**

Flash, #4021, dolphin, R, minimum value **$30.00**

Flashy, #4339, peacock, R, from $5 to **$8.00**

Fleece, #4125, lamb, white w/cream face, R, from $5 to..**$8.00**

Fleecie, #4279, lamb, cream w/purple neck ribbon, R, from $5 to..**$8.00**

Flip, #4012, cat, white, R, from $15 to **$30.00**

Flitter, #4255, butterfly, pastel, R, from $6 to **$8.00**

Float, #4343, butterfly, R, from $6 to.............................**$8.00**

Floppity, #4118, bunny, lilac, R, from $8 to **$12.00**

Flutter, #4043, butterfly, tie-dyed, R, minimum value ...**$275.00**

Fortune, #4196, panda bear w/red ribbon around neck, R, from $5 to..**$7.00**

Fraidy, #4379, cat, black & orange, R, from $6 to.........**$8.00**

Frankenteddy, #4562, 2002 Halloween bear, R, from $7 to.**$10.00**

Freckles, #4066, leopard, R, from $5 to **$7.00**

Freiherr von Schwarz, #4611, bear, Germany exclusive, R, from $60 to...**$80.00**

Frigid, #4270, king penguin, R, from $6 to...................**$8.00**

Frills, #4367, hornbill bird, R, from $7 to **$10.00**

Frisbee, #4508, dog, gray, from $6 to **$8.00**

Frolic, #4519, dog, R, from $7 to...............................**$10.00**
Fuzz, #4237, bear, R, from $8 to................................**$11.00**
Garcia, #4051, bear, tie-dyed, R, from $85 to...........**$110.00**
Germania, #4236, German bear, UK exclusive, R, from $15 to..**$20.00**
Giganto, #4384, mammoth, R, from $6 to.....................**$8.00**
Gigi, #4191, poodle, R, from $5 to...............................**$7.00**
Gizmo, #4541, lemur, R, from $6 to **$8.00**
Glory, #4188, American bear w/stars, R, from $15 to..**$20.00**
Glow, #4283, lightning bug, R, from $5 to **$7.00**
Goatee, #4235, mountain goat, R, from $5 to..............**$7.00**
Gobbles, #4034, turkey, R, from $5 to **$7.00**
Goldie, #4023, goldfish, R, from $15 to **$30.00**
Goochy, #4230, jellyfish, R, from $5 to **$7.00**
Grace, #4274, bunny, praying, R, from $6 to **$8.00**
Gracie, #4126, swan, R, from $6 to **$8.00**
Graf von Rot, #4612, bear, Germany exclusive, R, from $70 to..**$90.00**
Groom, #4529, bear, from $7 to **$10.00**
Groovy, #4256, bear, R, from $6 to **$8.00**
Grunt, #4092, razorback pig, red, R, minimum value.**$45.00**
Hairy, #4336, spider, brown w/hair, R, from $6 to **$8.00**
Halo, #4208, angel bear, R, from $7 to **$10.00**
Halo II, #4269, angel bear, R, from $7 to **$12.00**
Happy, #4061, hippo, 1st issue, gray, R, minimum value....**$330.00**
Happy, #4061, hippo, 2nd issue, lavender, R, from $10 to...**$25.00**
Harry, #4546, bear, from $7 to.......................................**$10.00**
Haunt, #4377, 2001 Halloween bear, black, R, from $6 to..**$8.00**
Herder, #4524, sheep dog, from $6 to **$8.00**
Hero, #4351, bear, brown, w/necktie, R, from $6 to **$8.00**
Hippie, #4218, rabbit, tie-dyed, R, from $6 to **$8.00**
Hippity, #4119, bunny, mint green, R, from $7 to **$9.00**
Hissy, #4185, coiled snake, R, from $5 to.....................**$7.00**
Holiday Teddy (1997), #4200, R, from $20 to **$30.00**
Holiday Teddy (1998), #4204, R, from $20 to **$30.00**
Holiday Teddy (1999), #4257, R, from $10 to **$15.00**
Holiday Teddy (2000), #4332, R, from $10 to **$15.00**
Holiday Teddy (2001), #4395, R, from $8 to **$10.00**
Holiday Teddy (2002), #4564, R, from $8 to **$10.00**
Honks, #4258, goose, from $5 to **$7.00**
Hoofer, #4518, Clydesdale horse, from $5 to **$8.00**
Hoot, #4073, owl, R, from $20 to **$30.00**
Hope, #4213, bear, praying, R, from $6 to **$8.00**
Hopper, #4342, rabbit, R, from $5 to **$7.00**
Hoppity, #4117, bunny, pink, R, from $10 to.............**$20.00**
Hornsly, #4345, triceratops, R, from $5 to **$7.00**
Howl, #4310, R, from $5 to..**$7.00**
Huggy, #4306, bear, R, from $6 to **$8.00**
Humphrey, #4060, camel, R, minimum value **$450.00**
Iggy, #4038, iguana, all issues, R, from $6 to **$8.00**
Inch, #4044, worm, felt antenna, R, from $65 to **$75.00**
Inch, #4044, worm, yarn antenna, R, from $10 to **$20.00**
India, #4291, tiger, R, from $5 to.................................**$7.00**
Inky, #4028, octopus, 1st issue, tan, no mouth, R, minimum value **$350.00**

Inky, #4028, octopus, 2nd issue, tan, w/mouth, R, minimum value **$300.00**
Inky, #4028, octopus, 3rd issue, pink, R, from $10 to **$15.00**
Issy, #4404, bear, New York City Four Seasons Hotel exclusive to guests, from $200 to.......................**$250.00**
Issy, #4404, bear, R, retail stores, from $8 to..............**$15.00**
Jabber, #4197, parrot, R, from $5 to **$10.00**
Jake, #4199, mallard duck, R, from $5 to **$7.00**
Jester, #4349, clown fish, R, from $6 to **$8.00**

Jinglepup, #9394, dog with Santa cap, R, from $7.00 to $15.00. (Photo courtesy Amy Sullivan)

Jolly, #4082, walrus, R, from $5 to **$7.00**
Kaleidoscope, #4348, cat, rainbow-colored, R, from $6 to..**$8.00**
Kanata, bear, Ty Canada exclusive, inside swing tag has flag of one of the Canadian provinces or territories, from $20 to..**$30.00**
Kicks, #4229, soccer bear, R, from $8 to **$10.00**
Kirby, #4396, dog, white, R, from $6 to......................**$10.00**
Kissme, #4504, bear w/hearts, R, from $7 to..............**$10.00**
Kiwi, #4070, toucan, R, minimum value **$70.00**
Knuckles, #4247, pig, R, from $5 to **$7.00**
Kooky, #4357, cat, purple, blue & white, R, from $5 to...**$7.00**
Kuku, #4192, cockatoo, R, from $5 to **$8.00**
Lefty, #4057, donkey w/American flag, blue-gray, R, minimum value **$110.00**
Lefty 2000, #4290, donkey, red, white & blue, R, USA exclusive, from $6 to...**$8.00**
Legs, #4020, frog, R, from $10 to **$20.00**
Libearty, #4057, bear w/American flag, white, R, minimum value **$160.00**
Liberty, #4531, American bear, 3 versions, red, white & blue-heads, all R, ea from $10 to...................**$15.00**
Lightning, #4537, horse, from $6 to.............................**$8.00**
Lips, #4254, fish, R, from $5 to **$7.00**
Lizzy, #4033, lizard, 1st issue, tie-dyed, R, minimum value...**$275.00**
Lizzy, #4033, lizard, 2nd issue, blue, R, from $15 to ..**$20.00**
Loosy, #4206, Canada goose, R, from $5 to **$7.00**
Lucky, #4040, ladybug, 1st issue, 7 spots, R, minimum value **$100.00**

Lucky, #4040, ladybug, 2nd issue, 21 spots, R, minimum value **$200.00**

Lucky, #4040, ladybug, 3rd issue, 11 spots, R, from $10 to **$15.00**

Luke, #4214, Labrador puppy, R, from $5 to **$7.00**

Mac, #4225, cardinal, R, from $5 to..........................**$7.00**

Magic, #4088, dragon, R, from $15 to **$30.00**

Manny, #4081, manatee, R, minimum value...............**$45.00**

Maple, #4600, bear, Ty Canada exclusive, R, minimum value **$35.00**

Mattie, #4521, cat, R...**$.09**

MC Beanie, brown bear w/MasterCard logo, R, free w/first use of Ty MasterCard, from $50 to **$80.00**

MC Beanie II, orange bear w/MasterCard logo, free w/first use of Ty MasterCard, from $50 to **$70.00**

Mel, #4162, koala, R, from $5 to...............................**$7.00**

Mellow, #4344, multicolored pastel bear, R, from $5.00 to $8.00. (Photo courtesy Amy Sullivan)

Midnight, #4355, panther, R, from $5 to **$7.00**

Millennium, #4226, bear, R, from $8 to.......................**$10.00**

Mistletoe, #4500, bear, red, R, from $6 to.....................**$8.00**

Mom-e, #4411, e-Beanie offered only through Ty Internet store, R, minimum value **$10.00**

Mooch, #4224, spider monkey, R, from $5 to **$7.00**

Morrie, #4282, eel, R, from $5 to..............................**$7.00**

Mr, #4363, groom bear, R, from $7 to **$10.00**

Mrs, #4364, bride bear, R, from $7 to **$10.00**

Mugungwha, #4617, Asia-Pacific flower bear, white, Korea exclusive, R, from $20 to.................................**$35.00**

Mum, #4517, Mother's Day bear, pink, R, from $10 to ..**$15.00**

Mystic, #4007, unicorn, 1st issue, soft fine mane & tail, R, minimum value...**$100.00**

Mystic, #4007, unicorn, 2nd issue, coarse yarn mane & brown horn, R, from $10 to................................**$15.00**

Mystic, #4007, unicorn, 3rd issue, iridescent horn, R, from $6 to **$8.00**

Mystic, #4007, unicorn, 4th issue, iridescent horn, rainbow fur mane & tail, R, from $5 to **$7.00**

Nana, #4067, 1st issue of Bongo the monkey, R, minimum value **$940.00**

Nanook, #4104, husky dog, R, from $5 to....................**$7.00**

Nectar, #4361, hummingbird, R, from $10 to..............**$20.00**

Neon, #4239, sea horse, tie-dyed, R, from $5 to........**$10.00**

Nibbler, #4216, rabbit, cream, R, from $5 to **$10.00**

Nibbly, #4217, rabbit, brown, R, from $5 to................**$7.00**

Niles, #4284, camel, R, from $5 to............................**$7.00**

Nip, #4003, cat, 1st issue, gold w/white face & tummy, R, minimum value...**$250.00**

Nip, #4003, cat, 2nd issue, all gold, R, minimum value ..**$325.00**

Nip, #4003, cat, 3rd issue, gold w/white paws, R, from $15 to **$25.00**

Nipponia, #4605, bear, Japan exclusive, R, from $35 to ..**$48.00**

Nuts, #4114, squirrel, R, from $5 to............................**$7.00**

Oats, #4305, horse, R, from $5 to...............................**$7.00**

Osito, #4244, Mexican bear, USA exclusive, R, from $8 to .**$10.00**

Panama, #4520, tree frog, R, from $5 to **$7.00**

Patriot, #4360, bear, red, white & blue, 2 versions w/flag on bottom of right or left foot, R, ea from $10 to **$20.00**

Patti, #4025, platypus, 1st issue, maroon, R, minimum value **$285.00**

Patti, #4025, platypus, 2nd issue, purple, R, from $10 to..**$20.00**

Paul, #4248, walrus, R, from $5 to **$7.00**

Peace, #4053, bear, tie-dyed, embroidered peace sign, R, from $8 to **$15.00**

Peanut, #4062, elephant, light blue, R, from $8 to **$12.00**

Peanut, #4062, elephant, royal blue (manufacturing mistake), R, minimum value **$1,375.00**

Pecan, #4251, bear, gold, R, from $5 to......................**$7.00**

Peekaboo, #4303, turtle, R, from $5 to........................**$7.00**

Pegasus, #4542, winged horse, from $7 to **$10.00**

Peking, #4013, panda bear, R, minimum value.........**$630.00**

Pellet, #4313, hamster, R, from $5 to..........................**$7.00**

Periwinkle, #4400, e-Beanie bear, blue, R, from $6 to...**$10.00**

Pierre, #4607, bear, Canada exclusive, R, from $20 to...**$30.00**

Pinchers, #4026, lobster, R, from $8 to **$12.00**

Pinky, #4072, flamingo, R, from $8 to **$10.00**

Pompey, #4625, soccer bear, Ty Europe exclusive, available only through the Portsmouth football club, from $50 to ..**$100.00**

Poofie, #4505, dog, R, from $7 to **$10.00**

Poopsie, #4381, bear, yellow, R, from $8 to...............**$10.00**

Pops, #4522, bear w/American flag tie, R, from $7 to...**$10.00**

Pops, #4522, bear w/British flag tie, UK exclusive, R, from $15 to..**$30.00**

Pops, #4522, bear w/Canadian flag tie, Canada exclusive, R, from $15 to..**$30.00**

Poseidon, #4356, whale shark, from $5 to....................**$7.00**

Pouch, #4161, kangaroo, R, from $5 to **$7.00**

Pounce, #4122, cat, brown, R, from $5 to **$7.00**

Pounds, #4530, elephant, R, from $7 to......................**$10.00**

Prance, #4123, cat, gray stripe, R, $5 to......................**$7.00**

Prickles, #4220, hedgehog, R, from $5 to **$7.00**

Prince, #4312, bullfrog, R, from $5 to **$7.00**

Princess, #4300, bear, purple, commemorating Diana, Princess of Wales, PVC or PE pellets, R, from $8 to.............**$15.00**

Prinz von Gold, #4613, bear, Germany exclusive, R, from $20 to **$30.00**

Propeller, #4366, flying fish, R, from $5 to **$7.00**

Puffer, #4181, puffin, R, from $5 to **$7.00**

Pugsly, #4106, pug dog, R, from $5 to......................**$7.00**

Pumkin', #4205, pumpkin, R, from $6 to....................**$8.00**

Punchers, #4026, 1st issue of Pinchers the lobster, R, minimum value **$1,450.00**

Purr, #4346, kitten, gray, R, from $5 to **$7.00**

Quackers, #4024, duck, 1st issue, no wings, R, minimum value **$750.00**

Quackers, #4024, duck, 2nd issue, w/wings, R, from $10 to **$15.00**

Radar, #4091, bat, black, R, minimum value **$55.00**

Rainbow, #4037, chameleon, 4 versions, R, ea from $5 to .**$10.00**

Regal, #4358, King Charles spaniel, R, from $6 to **$8.00**

Rescue, #4514, dalmatian, all profits donated to NY Police & Fire widow's & children's benefit fund, R, from $5 to..**$10.00**

Righty, #4085, elephant w/American flag, gray, R, minimum value **$120.00**

Righty 2000, #4289, elephant, red, white & blue, R, USA exclusive, from $6 to...**$8.00**

Ringo, #4014, raccoon, tan, R, from $10 to **$15.00**

Roam, #4209, buffalo, R, from $5 to **$7.00**

Roary, #4069, lion, R, from $6 to.............................**$8.00**

Rocket, #4202, blue jay, R, from $5.........................**$7.00**

Romance, #4398, bear, pink, R, from $8 to **$10.00**

Rose, bear, #4622, Ty Europe exclusive, from $10 to..**$30.00**

Rover, #4101, dog, red, R, from $10 to.....................**$15.00**

Roxie, #4334, reindeer, red or black nose, R, from $7 to...**$10.00**

Rufus, #4280, dog, R, from $5 to.............................**$7.00**

Runner, #4304, mustelidae, R, from $6 to **$8.00**

Rusty, #4563, red panda, from $5 to.........................**$7.00**

Sakura, #4602, Japanese bear, Japan exclusive, R, minimum value **$90.00**

Sakura II, #4619, Asia-Pacific flower bear, pink, Japan exclusive, from $15 to.......................................**$30.00**

Sammy, #4215, bear, tie-dyed, R, from $5 to.............**$7.00**

Sampson, #4540, dog, from $7 to............................**$10.00**

Santa, #4203, R, from $10 to **$15.00**

Sarge, #4277, German shepherd, R, from $5 to............**$7.00**

Scaly, #4263, lizard, R, from $5 to...........................**$7.00**

Scared-e, orange Halloween cat, R, Ty Internet store exclusive, from $8 to **$15.00**

Scary, #4378, witch, R, from $6 to **$8.00**

Scat, #4231, cat, R, from $5 to **$7.00**

Schweetheart, #4252, orangutan, R, from $5 to...........**$7.00**

Scoop, #4107, pelican, R, from $6 to **$8.00**

Scorch, #4210, dragon, R, from $5 to.......................**$8.00**

Scotland, #4609, bear, Scotland exclusive, R, from $65 to **$85.00**

Scottie, #4102, Scottish terrier, R, from $7 to..............**$10.00**

Scurry, #4281, beetle, R, from $5 to.........................**$7.00**

Seadog, #4566, Newfoundland dog, from $5 to...........**$7.00**

Seamore, #4029, seal, white, R, minimum value.........**$55.00**

Seaweed, #4080, otter, brown, R, from $15 to **$20.00**

Sequoia, #4516, grizzly bear, R, from $6 to **$8.00**

Serenity, #4533, dove, R, from $7 to.......................**$12.00**

Shamrock, #4338, bear, R, from $8 to......................**$10.00**

Sheets, #4260, ghost, R, from $5 to **$7.00**

Sherbet, bear, 3 versions, pink, yellow or green, R, from $7 to..**$10.00**

Siam, #4369, Siamese cat, R, from $5 to **$8.00**

Side-Kick, #4532, dog, from $7 to...........................**$10.00**

Signature bear (1999), #4228, R, from $8 to...............**$10.00**

Signature bear (2000), #4266, R, from $8 to...............**$12.00**

Signature bear (2001), #4375, R, from $8 to...............**$12.00**

Signature bear (2002), #4565, R, from $5 to...............**$10.00**

Silver, #4242, tabby cat, gray, R, from $5 to...............**$7.00**

Sizzle, #4399, bear, red, R, from $7 to **$10.00**

Slayer, #4307, frilled dragon, R, from $5 to................**$7.00**

Sledge, #4538, hammerhead shark, R, from $5 to.........**$8.00**

Slippery, #4222, seal, gray, R, from $5 to..................**$7.00**

Slither, #4031, snake, R, minimum value **$630.00**

Slowpoke, #4261, sloth, R, from $5 to......................**$7.00**

Sly, #4115, fox, 1st issue, all brown, R, minimum value..**$65.00**

Sly, #4115, fox, 2nd issue, brown w/white belly, R, from $10 to...**$15.00**

Smart, #4353, 2001 graduation owl, R, from $5 to........**$7.00**

Smarter, #4526, 2002 graduation owl, R, from $6 to.....**$8.00**

Smooch, #4335, bear, R, from $15 to **$20.00**

Smoochy, #4039, frog, R, from $5 to.........................**$7.00**

Sneaky, #4278, leopard, R, from $5 to.......................**$7.00**

Sniffer, #4299, beagle, R, from $5 to........................**$7.00**

Snip, #4120, Siamese cat, R, from $5 to....................**$7.00**

Snort, #4002, bull, red w/cream feet, R, from $7 to ...**$10.00**

Snowball, #4201, snowman, R, from $10 to **$12.00**

Snowgirl, #4333, snowgirl, R, from $10 to...................**$12.00**

Soar, #4410, eagle w/American flag wings, available only through Ty Internet store, R, from $10 to...........**$15.00**

Spangle, #4245, American bear, red, white or blue face, R, from $10 to...**$20.00**

Sparky, #4100, dalmatian, R, minimum value............**$50.00**

Speckles, #4402, bear, e-Beanie offered through Ty website, R, from $6 to **$10.00**

Speedy, #4030, turtle, R, from $15 to.......................**$18.00**

Spike, #4060, rhinoceros, R, from $5 to....................**$7.00**

Spinner, #4036, spider, striped, R, from $5 to **$7.00**

Splash, #4022, whale, R, minimum value **$30.00**

Spooky, #4090, ghost, orange neck ribbon, R, minimum value **$20.00**

Spot, #4000, dog, 1st issue, no spot on back, R, minimum value **$650.00**

Spot, #4000, dog, 2nd issue, black spot on back, R, from $15 to...**$30.00**

Spring, #4513, bunny, light blue, R, from $6 to...........**$8.00**

Springy, #4272, bunny, lavender, R, from $5 to...........**$7.00**

Spunky, #4184, cocker spaniel, R, from $6 to..............**$8.00**

Squealer, #4005, pig, R, from $10 to........................**$15.00**

Squirmy, #4302, worm, green, R, from $5 to **$7.00**

Starlett, #4382, cat, white, R, from $5 to...................**$7.00**

Stilts, #4221, stork, R, from $5 to...........................**$7.00**

Sting, #4077, stingray, R, minimum value..................**$50.00**

Stinger, #4193, scorpion, R, from $5 to **$7.00**

Stinky, #4017, skunk, R, from $10 to **$15.00**

Stretch, #4182, ostrich, R, from $5 to **$7.00**

Stripes, #4065, 1st issue, gold tiger w/thin stripes, R, minimum value **$175.00**

Stripes, #4065, 2nd issue, tiger, caramel, wide stripes, R, from $10 to **$15.00**

Strut, #4171, rooster, R, from $7 to................................**$9.00**

Sunny, #4401, e-Beanie bear, yellow-orange, R, from $7 to **$9.00**

Swampy, #4273, alligator, R, from $5 to **$7.00**

Swirly, #4249, snail, R, from $5 to **$7.00**

Swoop, #4268, pterodactyl, R, from $5 to......................**$7.00**

Tabasco, #4002, bull, red feet, R, minimum value......**$50.00**

Tank, #4031, armadillo, 1st issue, no shell, 7 lines, R, minimum value..**$50.00**

Tank, #4031, armadillo, 2nd issue, no shell, 9 lines, R, minimum value **$100.00**

Tank, #4031, armadillo, 3rd issue, w/shell, R, minimum value **$65.00**

Ted-e, brown bear, e-Beanie available only through Ty Internet store, R, from $5 to **$10.00**

Teddy, #4050, bear, brown, new face, R, from $40 to..**$50.00**

Teddy, #4050, bear, brown, old face, R, minimum value..**$625.00**

Teddy, #4051, bear, teal, new face, R, minimum value **$625.00**

Teddy, #4051, bear, teal, old face, R, minimum value **$600.00**

Teddy, #4052, bear, cranberry, new face, R, minimum value **$625.00**

Teddy, #4052, bear, cranberry, old face, R, minimum value **$600.00**

Teddy, #4055, bear, violet, new face, R, minimum value..**$625.00**

Teddy, #4055, bear, violet, old face, R, minimum value....**$600.00**

Teddy, #4056, bear, magenta, new face, R, minimum value **$625.00**

Teddy, #4056, bear, magenta, old face, R, minimum value **$600.00**

Teddy, #4057, bear, jade, new face, R, minimum value..**$625.00**

Teddy, #4057, bear, jade, old face, R, minimum value ...**$600.00**

Teddy, #4347, 100th Year Anniversary bear w/gold medal around neck, from $7 to **$15.00**

Thank You bear, given to Ty authorized retailers to display in their stores, R, from $210 to............................**$275.00**

The Beginning, #4267, bear, white w/silver stars, R, from $10 to **$20.00**

The End, #4265, bear, black, R, from $12 to..............**$18.00**

Thistle, #4623, bear, Ty Europe exclusive, from $10 to..**$30.00**

Tiny, #4234, chihuahua, R, from $6 to **$8.00**

Tiptoe, #4241, mouse, R, from $5 to...............................**$7.00**

Tooter, #4559, dinosaur, from $6 to **$8.00**

Toothy, #4523, tyrannosaurus, R, from $6 to................**$8.00**

Tracker, #4198, basset hound, R, from $6 to **$8.00**

Tracks, #4507, lynx, R, from $6 to **$8.00**

Tradee, #4403, e-Beanie offered only through Ty Internet store, R, from $8 to...**$10.00**

Trap, #4042, mouse, R, minimum value **$300.00**

Tricks, #4311, dog, R, from $5 to **$7.00**

Trumpet, #4276, elephant, R, from $5 to **$7.00**

Tuffy, #4108, terrier, R, from $5 to **$8.00**

Turk-e, turkey, Ty Internet store exclusive, from $8 to ..**$10.00**

Tusk, #4076, walrus, R, from $35 to...........................**$48.00**

Twigs, #4068, giraffe, R, from $10.00 to $15.00. (Photo courtesy Amy Sullivan)

Ty Billionaire bear (1998), brown, new face, dollar sign on chest, issued only to Ty employees, R, minimum value..**$800.00**

Ty Billionaire II bear (1999), purple, BB on chest, issued only to Ty employees, R, minimum value **$950.00**

Ty Billionaire III bear (2000), orange, issued only to Ty employees, R, minimum value **$790.00**

Ty Billionaire IV bear (2001), brown, issued only to Ty employees, R, minimum value **$780.00**

Ty Billionaire IV bear (2002), blue, issued only to Ty employees, R, minimum value..**$750.00**

Ty Employee Christmas bear (1997), violet, new face, R, minimum value..**$1,500.00**

Ty 2K bear, #4262, R, from $8 to **$12.00**

Unity, #4606, Ty Europe exclusive, R, from $20 to **$35.00**

USA, #4287, American bear, USA exclusive, R, from $8 to...**$10.00**

Valentina, #4233, bear, fuchsia w/white heart, R, from $6 to.**$8.00**

Valentino, #4058, bear, white w/red heart, R, from $8 to.....**$12.00**

Vanda, #4614, Asia-Pacific flower bear, blue, Singapore exclusive, R, from $22 to..**$35.00**

Velvet, #4064, panther, R, from $12 to.........................**$15.00**

Waddle, #4075, penguin, R, from $10 to **$12.00**

Wales, #4610, bear, red, Wales exclusive, R, from $65 to..**$90.00**

Wallace, #4264, bear, green, R, from $7 to **$9.00**

Wattlie, #4616, Asia-Pacific flower bear, green, Australia exclusive, from $23 to...**$40.00**

Waves, #4084, whale, R, from $6 to **$8.00**

Web, #4041, spider, black, R, minimum value **$350.00**

Weenie, #4013, dachshund, R, from $10 to **$12.00**

Whiskers, #4317, terrier, R, from $5 to...........................**$7.00**

Whisper, #4187, deer, R, from $5 to...............................**$7.00**

Wiggly, #4275, octopus, R, from $5 to **$7.00**
Wise, #4194, 1998 graduation owl, R, from $6 to **$8.00**
Wiser, #4238, 1999 graduation owl, R, from $5 to **$7.00**
Wisest, #4286, 2000 graduation owl, R, from $5 to......**$7.00**
Woody, #4539, brown bear, from $5 to **$8.00**
Wrinkles, #4103, bulldog, R, from $6 to........................**$8.00**
Zero, #4207, penguin, w/Christmas cap, R, from $5 to ..**$7.00**
Ziggy, #4063, zebra, R, from $10 to **$15.00**
Zip, #4004, cat, 1st issue, black w/white face & tummy, R,
    minimum value **$230.00**
Zip, #4004, cat, 2nd issue, all black, R, minimum value..**$320.00**
Zip, #4004, cat, 3rd issue, black w/white paws, R, from $8
    to...**$12.00**
Zodaic Goat, #4329, R, from $5 to **$7.00**
Zodaic Horse, #4324, R, from $5 to **$7.00**
Zodiac Dog, #4326, R, from $5 to **$7.00**

Zodiac dragon, #4322, R, from $5.00 to $7.00. (Photo courtesy Amy Sullivan)

Zodiac Monkey, #4328, R, from $5 to...........................**$7.00**
Zodiac Ox, #4319, R, from $5 to **$7.00**
Zodiac Pig, #4327, R, from $5 to **$7.00**
Zodiac Rabbit, #4321, R, from $5 to **$7.00**
Zodiac Rat, #4318, R, from $5 to **$7.00**
Zodiac Rooster, #4325, R, from $5 to **$7.00**
Zodiac Snake, #4323, R, from $5 to **$7.00**
Zodiac Tiger, #4320, R, from $5 to **$7.00**
Zoom, turtle, from $6 to...**$8.00**

Beatles Collectibles

Possibly triggered by John Lennon's death in 1980, Beatles fans (recognizing that their dreams of the band ever reuniting were gone along with him) began to collect vintage memorabilia of all types. Recently some of the original Beatles material has sold at auction with high-dollar results. Handwritten song lyrics, Lennon's autographed high school textbook, and even the legal agreement that was drafted at the time the group disbanded are among the one-of-a-kind multi-thousand dollar sales recorded.

Unless you plan on attending sales of this caliber, you'll be more apt to find the commercially produced memorabilia that literally flooded the market during the '60s and beyond when the Fab Four from Liverpool made their unprecedented impact on the entertainment world. A word about their 45 rpm records: They sold in such mass quantities that unless the record is a 'promotional' (made to send to radio stations or for jukebox distribution), they have very little value. Once a record has lost much of its original gloss due to wear and handling, becomes scratched or has writing on the label, its value is minimal. Even in near-mint condition, $4.00 to $6.00 is plenty to pay for a 45 rpm (much less if it's worn), unless the original picture sleeve is present. (An exception is the white-labeled Swan recording of 'She Loves You/I'll Get You'). A Beatles picture sleeve is usually valued at $30.00 to $40.00, except for the rare 'Can't Buy Me Love,' which is worth more than ten times that amount. (Beware of reproductions!) Albums of any top recording star or group from the '50s and '60s are becoming very collectible, and the Beatles are among the most popular. Just be very critical of condition! An album must be in at least excellent condition to bring a decent price.

For more information we recommend *The Beatles, Second Edition,* by Barbara Crawford, Hollis Lamon, and Michael Stern (Collector Books).

See also Celebrity Dolls; Magazines; Movie Posters; Records; Sheet Music.

Advisor: Bojo/Bob Gottuso (See Directory, Character and Personality Collectibles)

Newsletter: *Beatlefan*
P.O. Box 33515, Decatur, GA 30033; Send SASE for information

Ashtray, china, EX/M, $250.00; G, $175.00. (Photo courtesy Barbara Crawford, Hollis Lamon, and Michael Stern)

Balloon, various colors, sealed in package **$75.00**
Banner, Hallmark stamps promo, 3x18", VG+............**$50.00**
Beach towel, by Cannon, NM...................................**$160.00**
Belt buckle, metal w/photo under plastic, EX **$40.00**
Binder, vinyl 3-ring, various colors, NM, minimum value ..**$150.00**
Binder, vinyl 3-ring, white, NM **$110.00**
Book, Fun-Kit, 1964, M **$55.00**
Book, Lennon Remembers, hardback, 1971, NM........**$30.00**

Book, Love Letters to the Beatles, 1964, EX...............$25.00
Book, True Story of the Beatles, Bantam paperback, 1964, M...$10.00
Bracelet, black & white photos on brass mount, EX (beware of repros)...$90.00
Brunch bag, blue vinyl w/zippered top, 8"..............$450.00
Bubble bath container, Soakie, Paul or Ringo, NM, ea...$110.00

Button, EX/NM, $50.00; G, $35.00. (Photo courtesy Barbara Crawford, Hollis Lamon, and Michael Stern)

Calendar, John & Yoko, 1970, black & white images, w/record, NM..$25.00
Calendar, photo of group in doorway, 1964, complete, 19x11", VG+...$125.00
Candy dish, Paul, pottery w/gilt edge, UK...............$150.00
Cap, brown corduroy w/Ringo image, EX................$150.00
Card, Fan Club Member, 1964.....................................$39.00
Cards, Mod Fashion, 8x5½", pr..................................$15.00
Cartoon Colorforms, complete in box w/instructions, NM..$750.00
Clutch purse, cloth w/leather strap & allover pictures.....$240.00
Clutch purse, white vinyl w/leather strap, group photo..$140.00
Collectors' stamps, 1964 Hallmark Edition, 5 for........$10.00
Coloring book, Saalfield, unused, NM.........................$95.00
Concert book, 1964, USA, 12x12".................................$40.00
Concert book, 1965, USA, 12x12".................................$35.00
Cork stopper, figural head, 1 of ea Beatle, Germany, ea..$250.00
Disk-Go case, plastic 45 rpm record holder..............$175.00
Doll, vinyl, John or George w/instrument, Remco, 4", ea..$125.00
Doll, vinyl, Paul or Ringo w/instrument, Remco, 4", ea........$75.00
Dolls, blow-up; set of 4, EX.......................................$140.00
Dress, Holland, 3 styles, NM......................................$600.00
Eyeglasses case, John, facsimile signature, England...$75.00
Greeting cards, Yellow Submarine, MIB....................$190.00
Halloween mask, John Lennon.....................................$125.00
Handkerchief, With Love From Me to You — The Beatles, group in center bordered by song titles & instruments, 11", EX..$50.00
Hummer, cardboard, faces & signatures on tube, 11", EX..$185.00
Magazine, Life, Paul & Linda on cover, 1971, NM......$18.00

Magnet, From Me to You, 1990s, 2x3", EX....................$5.00
Nodders, composition, Carmascots, 1964, 8", set of 4, EX in original box...$750.00
Nodders, composition, Carmascots, 1964, set of 4, VG.....$55.00
Paperweight, Official Beatles Fan, multicolor, 1970s, EX..$35.00
Pendant, black & white group photo w/first names in gold on back, no chain, VG+..$60.00
Pin-back button, I'm an Official Beatles Fan, green duck, 2"..$25.00
Pins, Yellow Submarine, hand-painted brass, 8 for....$50.00
Plate, bamboo, w/color picture of group, 12".........$135.00
Playing cards, group pictures in suits, complete w/2 jokers, G+ (fair box)...$160.00
Pop-up book, Yellow Submarine, NM.........................$45.00
Press book, Let It Be, 6-page, EX................................$75.00
Record box (45s), green w/white top, black handle, Airflite, VG+...$315.00
Record sleeve, Can't Buy Me Love, rare, M..............$525.00
Scarf, red w/black photos, leatherette cord, EX.........$70.00
Sheet music, I Want To Hold Your Hand, 1968.........$20.00
Stamps, set of 100 in booklet, 20 of group & 20 ea individual in color, Hallmark, unused, VG+....................$35.00
Thimble, Fenton, baked-on image, 1990s, EX.............$15.00
Throw blanket, Sgt Pepper, 1990s, 53x65", M.............$35.00
Tie-tac set, NEMS, 1964, MOC (watch for repros)......$75.00
Tumbler, plastic w/inset photo & lips at top, 6¼", VG (watch for repros)...$75.00
Wallet, vinyl w/photos, by SSP, VG+.........................$100.00

Beatrix Potter

Since 1902 when *The Tale of Peter Rabbit* was published by Fredrick Warne & Company, generations have enjoyed the adventures of Beatrix Potter's characters. Beswick issued ten characters in 1947 that included Peter Rabbit, Benjamin Bunny, Squirrel Nutkin, Jemima Puddleduck, Timmy Tiptoes, Tom Kitten, Mrs. Tittlemouse, Mrs. Tiggywinkle, Little Pig Robinson, and Samuel Whiskers. The line grew until it included figures from other stories. Duchess (P1355) was issued in 1955 with two feet that were easily broken. Later issues featured the Duchess on a base and holding a pie. This was the first figure to be discontinued in 1967. Color variations on pieces indicate issue dates as do the different backstamps that were used. Backstamps have changed several times since the first figures were issued. There are three basic styles: Beswick brown, Beswick gold, and Royal Albert — with many variations on each of these. Unless stated otherwise, figures listed here are Beswick brown.

Advisor: Nicki Budin (See Directory, Beatrix Potter)

And This Pig Had None, B6.......................................$60.00
Aunt Petitoes, B3...$55.00
Aunt Petitoes, B6...$75.00
Benjamin Bunny, ears in, 3B......................................$55.00
Benjamin Bunny, ears out, B3..................................$195.00

Benjamin Bunny Sat on a Bank, B6............................$45.00
Benjamin Bunny Sat on a Bank, head turned, 3B....$115.00
Benjamin Wakes Up, B6...$55.00
Cecily Parsley, B6...$65.00
Cecily Parsley, 3A..$95.00
Chippy Hackee, C3...$75.00
Christmas Stocking, B6...$250.00
Cottontail, B6...$45.00
Cousin Ribby, B3..$55.00
Cousin Ribby, B6..$50.00
Diggory Diggory Delvet, B3...................................$50.00
Flopsy, Mopsy, Cottontail; B2..............................$195.00
Foxy Whiskered Gentleman, B3.............................$75.00
Goody & Timmy Tiptoes, B6.................................$150.00
Goody Tiptoes, B3..$60.00
Hunca Munca, B2-gold...$175.00
Hunca Munca, B3..$65.00
Hunca Munca, C3..$65.00
Hunca Munca Spills the Beads, B6 ....$65.00
Hunca Munca Sweeping, B3...................................$65.00
Jemima Puddleduck, B10..$50.00
Jemima Puddleduck, B2...$160.00
Jemima Puddleduck, B3..$55.00
Jemima Puddleduck, B8..$95.00
Jemima Puddleduck, Made a Feather Nest, B3 ....$65.00
Jemima Puddleduck Made a Feather Nest, B6 ....$45.00
John Joiner, B6...$55.00
Johnny Townmouse, B3..$55.00
Johnny Townmouse, C3..$65.00
Little Pig Robinson, B3..$45.00
Little Pig Robinson Spying, B6.............................$125.00
Little Pig Robinson Spying, C3.............................$175.00
Miss Dormouse, B6...$85.00
Miss Moppet, 3B..$55.00
Mother Ladybird, B6...$115.00
Mr Alderman Ptolemy, B6......................................$65.00
Mr Benjamin Bunny, 3B...$40.00
Mr Benjamin Bunny & Peter Rabbit, B3 ....$125.00
Mr Benjamin Bunny & Peter Rabbit, B6 ....$75.00
Mr Drake Puddleduck, B3......................................$50.00
Mr Jackson, B3..$55.00
Mr Jackson, B6..$65.00
Mr Jeremy Fisher, B3...$65.00
Mr Jeremy Fisher, C3...$70.00
Mr Jeremy Fisher Digging, B4..............................$195.00
Mrs Flopsy Bunny, B3..$65.00
Mrs Rabbit, 2B...$450.00
Mrs Rabbit, 3B...$60.00
Mrs Rabbit & Bunnies, 3B......................................$85.00
Mrs Rabbit & Peter, B6..$65.00
Mrs Tiggy Winkle, B3...$55.00
Mrs Tiggy Winkle Washing, B8A...........................$125.00
Mrs Tittlemouse, 3C...$45.00
No More Twists, B6..$55.00
Old Mr Bouncer, B6 ....$55.00
Old Mr Bouncer, C3 ....$85.00
Old Mr Brown, B3..$60.00

Old Woman in Shoe, B3..$45.00
Old Woman in Shoe Knitting, B3............................$95.00
Old Woman in Shoe Knitting, B6............................$45.00
Peter in Gooseberry Net, B6...................................$75.00
Peter Rabbit, B10...$50.00
Peter Rabbit, B3..$95.00
Pickles, 3A...$450.00

Pigling Bland, maroon jacket, first version, B3, $225.00.

Poorly Peter Rabbit, B3...$75.00
Poorly Peter Rabbit, B6...$65.00
Rebeccah Puddle-Duck, B3.....................................$40.00
Ribby, 3A...$75.00
Ribby, 3B...$65.00
Ribby & the Patty Pan, B6.....................................$45.00
Sally Henny Penny, B3...$75.00
Samuel Whiskers, B3..$45.00
Sir Isaac Newton, 3B..$450.00
Tabitha Twitchet, B3..$75.00
Tabitha Twitchet, B6..$40.00
Tabitha Twitchet & Miss Moppet, B3.....................$175.00
Tabitha Twitchet & Miss Moppet, B6.....................$150.00
Thomasina Tittlemouse, 3B...................................$110.00
Timmy Tiptoes, 3B...$65.00
Timmy Willie, B3...$45.00
Timmy Willie, B6...$65.00
Tom Kitten, B10...$50.00
Tom Kitten, B3...$85.00
Tom Kitten, B4...$75.00
Tom Thumb, B3..$65.00
Tom Thumb, B6..$55.00
Tom Thumb, 3C...$115.00

Beer Cans

In January of 1935 the Continental Can Co. approached a New Jersey brewery with the novel idea of selling beer in cans. After years of research, Continental had perfected a plastic coating for the inside of the can which prevented the beer from contacting and adversely reacting to metal.

Consumers liked the idea, and throw-away beer cans soon replaced returnable bottles as the most popular container in which to purchase beer.

The first beer can was a steel flat top which actually bore a picture of the newly invented 'can opener' and instructions on how to use it. Because most breweries were not equipped to fill a flat can, a 'cone top' was invented to facilitate passage through the bottle filler. By the 1950s the cone top was obsolete. Ten years later, can companies introduced a 'tab top' can which made the can opener unnecessary. Aluminum cans and cans ranging in size from six-ounce to one-gallon were popularized during the 1960s.

Beer can collecting reached its heyday during the 1970s. Thousands of collectors bought, drank, and saved cans throughout America. Unfortunately, the number of collectors receded, creating a huge supply of cans with minimal demand. There are many valuable beer cans today — however, they pre-date 1970. A post-1970 can worth more than a few dollars is rare.

Values are based on cans in conditions as stated. A can with flaws — rust, fading, or scratches — may still have value; however, it is generally much less than its excellent condition counterpart. Unless noted otherwise, all of the cans we list here are the 12-ounce size. The letters 'IRTP' in some of our descriptions stand for 'Internal Revenue Tax Paid.'

Newsletter: *Beer Cans and Brewery Collectibles*
Beer Can Collectors of America
747 Merus Ct., Fenton, MO 63026-2092
Fax/phone: 314-343-6486; e-mail: bcca@bcca.com;
http://www.bcca.com Subscription: $30 per year for US residents; includes six issues and right to attend national CANvention®

Cone top, Fort Schuylar Lager, Utica Brewing, Utica NY, EX **$100.00**
Cone top, Goetz Country Club Beer, MK Goetz Brewing, St Joseph MO, 1950s, VG+ **$32.00**
Cone top, Iroquois Beer, Iroquois Brewing, Buffalo NY, VG **$40.00**
Cone top, Martin's Beer, Yakina Valley Brewing, Selah, EX...**$265.00**
Cone top, Old German Brand, Cumberland Brewing, Cumberland MD, 1940s, G **$20.00**
Cone top, Old Virginia Special, Virginia Brewing, Roanoke VA, 1950s, VG **$40.00**
Cone top, Peerless Beer, Lacrosse Brewing, Lacrosse WI, 1950s, EX **$80.00**
Cone top, Stegmaier's Gold Medal Beer, Stegmaier Brewing, Wilkes-Barre PA, 1950s, EX............................**$85.00**
Cone top, Uchtorff Beer, Uchtorff Brewing, Davenport IA, 1950s, EX..**$200.00**
Cone top, Wiemand Extra Pale, Pacific Brew & Malt, San Jose, 1940s, NM **$130.00**
Cone top (low profile), Beverwyck Ale, gold background, Beverwyck Brewing, Albany NY, 1930s, NM......**$120.00**

Cone top (low profile), Blatz Milwaukee Beer, red letters, Blatz Brewing, Milwaukee WI, 1930s, VG **$58.00**
Cone top (low profile), Cran Rootbeer, Minneapolis Brewing, Minneapolis MN, 1930s, EX **$190.00**
Cone top (low profile), Pacific Lager Beer, Ranier Brewing, San Francisco, 1930s, EX....................................**$200.00**
Cone top (low profile), Ranier Special Export, Ranier Brewing, San Francisco CA, 1930s, EX **$65.00**
Crowntainer, Hudepohl Chevy Ale, Hudepohl Brewing, Cincinnati OH, 1940s, EX.................................**$750.00**
Crowntainer, Leinenkugels Chippewa Pride Beer, Leinenkugels Brewing, Chippewa Falls WI, VG...**$50.00**
Crowntainer, Old Ox Head Ale, Standard Brewing, Rochester NY, 1940s, EX+ **$190.00**

Flat tops: Club House Premium Beer, Grace Brothers Brg., Santa Rosa, CA, EX, $80.00; Regal Bock Beer, Regal Amber Brg., San Francisco, CA, EX, $65.00; Lone Star Beer, Lone Star Brg., San Antonio, TX, EX+, $85.00.

Flat top, A-1 Pilsner, Arizona Brewing, Phoenix AZ, 1950s, 10-oz, EX **$43.00**
Flat top, Atlas Prager Beer, Atlas Brewing, Chicago IL, 1950s, VG **$30.00**
Flat top, Burgermeister Beer, San Francisco Brewing, San Francisco CA, VG **$8.00**
Flat top, Dodger Lager Beer, Maier Brewing, Los Angeles CA, 1950s, EX **$55.00**
Flat top, Duquesne Pilsner Beer, Duquesne Brewing, Pittsburgh PA, 1950s, NM **$27.50**
Flat top, Esslinger Parti-Quiz, Esslinger Brewing, Philadelphia PA, 1950s, NM...**$125.00**
Flat top, Frankenmuth Mel-O-Dry Beer, Frankenmuth Brewing, Frankenmuth MI, 1940s, NM...................**$40.00**
Flat top, Gold Prize Beer, Gulf Brewing, Houston TX, 1950s, VG **$45.00**
Flat top, Grace Brother Dark Beer, Grace Bros Brewing, Santa Rosa CA, 1940s, G **$50.00**
Flat top, Jacob Rupert Knickerbocker Beer, Jacob Rupert Brewing, New York NY, 1930s, VG....................**$65.00**
Flat top, Mile Hi Life, Tivoli Brewing, Denver CO, 1950s, EX **$48.00**
Flat top, Old Dutch Lager, Maier Brewing, Los Angeles CA, 1950s, EX..**$45.00**
Flat top, Pilsner's Malt Crest Brew, Metropolis Brewing, Trenton NJ, 1940s, EX **$50.00**

Flat top, Schaefer Light Beer, Schaefer Brewing, New York NY, 1940s, VG **$18.00**

Flat top, Senators Club Premium Beer, Columbus Brewing, Shanandoah PA, 1950s, EX **$60.00**

Flat top, Walter's Pilsner Beer, Walter Brewing, Pueblo CO, 1950s, EX **$30.00**

Flat top, Wiedemann Fine Beer, Wiedemann Brewing, Newport KY, 1950s, NM **$7.00**

Pull tab, Black Pride Beer, West Bend Brewing, West Bend WI, 1970s, NM **$12.00**

Pull tab, El Rancho Beer, General Brewing, Los Angeles CA, 1970s, NM **$22.50**

Pull tab, Golden Lion Beer, Burger Meister Brewing, San Francisco CA, 1970s, NM....................................**$30.00**

Pull tab, Hausbrau Lager Beer, Maier Brewing, Los Angeles CA, 1960s, NM **$55.00**

Pull tab, Hiew Brau, Tivoli Brewing, Denver CO, EX **$12.50**

Pull tab, Old Bohemian, Eastern Brewing, Hammonton NJ, 1960s, EX **$45.00**

Pull tab, Ox Bow Beer, Walter Brewing, Puebelo CO, 1970s, EX..**$30.00**

Pull tab, Suntory Beer, #624 Golfer, Suntory Brewing, Japan, 1970s, M..**$40.00**

Zip top, Kentucky Malt Liquor, Gertel Brewing, Louisville KY, NM **$38.00**

Zip top, Sebewaing Beer, Sebewaing Brewing, Sebewaing MI, 1960s, NM **$45.00**

Bellaire, Marc

Marc Bellaire, originally Donald Edmund Fleischman, was born in Toledo, Ohio, in 1925. He studied at the Toledo Museum of Art under Ernest Spring while employed as a designer for the Libbey Glass Company. During World War II while serving in the Navy, he traveled extensively throughout the Pacific, resulting in his enriched sense of design and color.

Marc settled in California in the 1950s where his work attracted the attention of national buyers and agencies who persuaded him to create ceramic lines of his own, employing hand-decorated techniques throughout. As a result, he founded a studio in Culver City. There he produced high quality ceramics often decorated with ultra-modern figures or geometric patterns and executed with a distinctive flair. His most famous pattern was Mardi Gras, decorated with slim dancers on spattered or striped colors of black, blue, pink, and white. Other major patterns were Jamaica, Balinese, Beachcomber, Friendly Island, Cave Painting, Hawaiian, Bird Isle, Oriental, Jungle Dancer, and Kashmir. (Kashmir usually has the name Ingle on the front and Bellaire on the back.)

It is to be noted that Marc was employed by Sascha Brastoff during the '50s. Many believe that he was hired for his creative imagination and style.

During the period 1951 – 1956, Marc was named one of the top ten artware designers by *Giftwares Magazine*. After 1956 he taught and lectured on art, design, and ceramic decorating techniques from coast to coast. Many of his pieces were one of a kind, and his work was commissioned throughout the United States.

During the 1970s he worked from his studio in Marin County, California. He eventually moved to Palm Springs where he set up his final studio/gallery. There he produced large pieces with a Southwest style. Mr. Bellaire died in 1994.

Advisor: Marty Webster (See Directory, California Pottery)

Ashtray, Bird Isle, black birds on cream, 8" **$85.00**
Ashtray, Clown, multicolor on cream, 7" **$65.00**
Ashtray, Jamaica, musicians on brown, 10x14" **$85.00**
Ashtray, Still Life, matt fruits & leaves, 10x15" **$100.00**
Box, Jamaica, man w/guitar, free-form, B46, 8" **$135.00**
Box, Mardi Gras, 10" dia **$200.00**
Compote, Cave Painting, 4-footed, 6x12" **$125.00**
Cookie jar, Stick People, wooden lid, 10" **$150.00**
Platter, Friendly Island, 10" **$135.00**
Platter, Hawaiian, 3 figures on orange, 7x13" **$125.00**

Platter, reclining lady, 14" long, from $125.00 to $175.00.

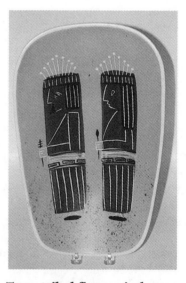

Tray, tribal figures in brown on gold, 15" long, $125.00.

Vase, Balinese Women, hourglass shape, 8" **$125.00**
Vase, Black Cats, hourglass shape, 8" **$125.00**
Vase, Stick People, irregular beak-like opening, 12"...**$250.00**

Bells

Bell collectors claim that bells rank second only to the wheel as being useful to mankind. Down through the ages bells have awakened people in the morning, called them to meals and prayers, and readied them to retire at night. We have heard them called rising bells, Angelus Bells (for deaths), noon bells, Town Crier bells (for important announcements), and curfew bells. Souvenir bells are often the first type collected, with interest spreading to other contemporaries, then on to old, more valuable bells. As far as limited edition bells are concerned, the fewer made per bell, the better. (For example a bell made in an edition of 25,000 will not appreciate as much as one from an edition of 5,000.)

Newsletter: *The Bell Tower*
The American Bell Association
P.O. Box 19443, Indianapolis, IN 46219

**Ormolu, stork and wolf handle (from La Fontaine poem), nodder type, French, 4½",
$425.00. (Photo courtesy Dorothy Malone Anthony)**

Bisque, Mrs Christmas Mouse, marked Jasco Taiwan, 4½" ..**$6.00**
Brass, classic shape, heavy, 6¼"..................................**$25.00**
Brass, lady in ornate robe & headdress figural, thick walls, old, 5" **$65.00**
Brass, Napoleon a Wagram, L'Embereur Bataille de Waterloo, Napoleon finial on handle, 6½x3"........................**$55.00**
Brass, wooden handle, old patina, 10x4½" **$45.00**
Bronze, Cleopatra figural by Gerry Ballantyne, 1990, limited edition, 6", NM..**$130.00**
Bronze, school teacher figural, Gerry Ballantyne, 1981, 6"...**$130.00**
Cast iron, #2, w/yoke & clapper, 14" dia, EX.............**$55.00**
Ceramic, girl figural, holding ruffled skirt, gold trim, unmarked, 4¾"..**$45.00**
Ceramic, girl holding flowers figural, applied roses & trim on skirt, Japan, 3"..**$12.50**
China, Primrose, Shelley England, Fine Bone China .**$315.00**
Crystal, engraved pinwheel pattern, Yugoslovia label, 5" ..**$22.00**
Glass, amberina w/crystal handle, brass clapper, 7½" ..**$55.00**

Glass, blue w/embossed angelfish, palms, swordfish & sailboat, replaced clapper, 6" **$14.00**
Glass, bluejay on pine branch painted on frost, unmarked, 6½"..**$15.00**
Glass, Christmas decor, Waterford, 1984, 4½", MIB..**$120.00**
Glass, ruby-flashed crystal, unmarked, 6"...................**$20.00**
Metal, Kentucky No 7, cow decal, Sargent & Co, New Haven, Conn USA, 3¼x2½" **$55.00**
Metal, lady in bustled dress w/holstered gun & feathered hat, gold finish, Lowell Davis, 2½", MIB....................**$130.00**
Porcelain, Dickens caroler figural, Hallmark **$40.00**
Porcelain, Dutch girl figural, blue & white windmill on skirt, water buckets act as clapper, Albert Price..., 3¾" ..**$15.00**
Porcelain, girl figural, heart-shaped hat, red hearts on white skirt, spaghetti trim, unmarked, 3" **$12.50**
Porcelain, lady in blue dress figural, #3806 Germany, 3¾", EX..**$25.00**
Porcelain, mule in harness, Schmid, Lowell Davis, 1990, 2" **$45.00**
Porcelain, Weihnachts-Glocke '85, Christmas, Hutchenreuther, 1985 limited edition, MIB **$42.50**
Silver, Aunt Jemima figural, souvenir of Charleston SC, Holland Novelty Co, 4" **$40.00**
Silver, Old Colonial, Towle, 6½" **$65.00**
Silver, Spanish Tracery, Gorham, 1970, 7" **$50.00**
Silver w/engraved brass handle, Buccellati limited edition, 3½x2" **$75.00**
Silver-plated, engraved decor, ring-like finial, International Silver Co, 3½" **$12.00**
Silver-plated, sleigh type, Wallace, 1973, MIB (no brochure) **$200.00**

**Wood, intricate marquetry, 9¼",
$30.00. (Photo courtesy Dorothy Malone Anthony)**

Black Americana

There are many avenues one might pursue in the broad field of Black Americana and many reasons that might entice one to become a collector. For the more serious, there are documents such as bills of sale for slaves, broadsides, and other historical artifacts. But by and far, most collectors enjoy attractive advertising pieces, novelties and kitchenware items, toys and dolls, and Black celebrity memorabilia.

It's estimated that there are at least 50,000 collectors around the country today that specialize in this field. There are large auctions devoted entirely to the sale of Black Americana. The items they feature may be as common as a homemade potholder or a magazine or as rare as a Lux Dixie Boy clock or a Mammy cookie jar that might go for several thousand dollars. In fact, many of the cookie jars have become so valuable that they're being reproduced; so are salt and pepper shakers, so beware.

For further study, we recommend *Black Collectibles Sold in America* by P.J. Gibbs.

See also Advertising, Aunt Jemima; Condiment Sets; Cookie Jars; Postcards; Salt and Pepper Shakers; Sheet Music; String Holders.

Advisor: Judy Posner (See Directory, Black Americana)

Advertising page, Chream of Wheat (sic), Peace & Plenty, Edward Brewer, 1923, 13x10⅜"..............................**$16.00**

Advertising page, Cream of Wheat, Chream (sic) of Wheat Is Ready, James Montgomery Flagg, 1917, 14x10¼"..**$16.00**

Album, Authentic Minstrel Show, fine cover art, long playing, EX..**$16.00**

Album, Uncle Remus Stories, EX graphics on back & front of cover, 1940s, 78 rpm, EX **$50.00**

Ashtray, Club Harlem, red printing on clear glass, EX...**$30.00**

Ashtray, Levy's Rye, You Don't Have To Be Jewish..., pottery, boy w/lg pc of bread, 1960s.................................**$95.00**

Bank, Lucky Joe, molded clear glass w/tin lid, Nash's Prepared Mustard giveaway, 1940s-50s, 4½", EX.**$45.00**

Biscuit tin, Southern Biscuit Co, butler serving family on plantation porch, pastels, 1926", 3½x10" dia, EX.**$60.00**

Book, Gigi & Gogo, Edgard Liger-Belair, Luiz Sa illustrations, told in 4 languages, 1943, 15 pages, 8¾x6¼", EX .**$90.00**

Book, Josephine Baker, Hammond, hardback, 1988, 11x8½", EX, w/dust jacket..**$30.00**

Book, Little Alexander, Besse Schiff, Wartburg Press, hardcover, 1955, 30 pages, 10x8", EX...........................**$90.00**

Book, Little Washingtons Holidays, Lillian Elizabeth Roy, Paul S Johst illustrations, 1925, 1st edition, EX.............**$60.00**

Book, Treasury of Stephen Foster, hardbound, 1946, 1st edition, EX w/dust jacket...**$50.00**

Book, Turkey Trott & Black Santa, KG Dyer, Platt & Munk, 1942, 1st edition, EX w/dust jacket.....................**$125.00**

Book, You Funny Little Noddy, Enid Blyton, hardbound, 1950, 7½x5½", EX...**$30.00**

Brooch, lady's face, black on gold-tone metal w/green stones, rhinestones on turban, Art Deco style, 2" **$50.00**

Canister, Luzianne Coffee, Mammy litho on tin, 2-lb size, M **$68.00**

Catalog, Dennison's Minstrel Show, EX graphics, 1940s, 63 pages, 6¾x4¾", EX..**$95.00**

Cookbook, Southern Cookbook, Howard Weeden verse, ethnic images & dialect, 1930s, 6x9" **$65.00**

Cookie jar, Coon Chicken Inn, smiling face figural, copyright '92, USA..**$135.00**

Doll, baby, jointed bisque, tufted hair w/pink bow, original white diaper, 1930s, 6", EX **$125.00**

Doll, black hard plastic w/beads & fur, marked PMIJHB, 4¾"..**$18.00**

Doll, boy, stuffed cloth, corduroy bibs, hat, embroidered face, 1940s-50s, 15", EX.....................................**$135.00**

Doll, Golliwog, stuffed cloth, vintage, 33", EX...........**$95.00**

Dutch oven, Old Vir-gin-a No-Burn Dutch Oven, ethnic image on box, Jeannette Steel Corp, 1930s, box: 11x12x3½"..**$195.00**

Egg cup, sailor w/accordion figural, porcelain, #446, marked Foreign, 2¾", NM...**$125.00**

Figurine, Black Native Jungle Imp, Irene Nye, pottery w/original plastic necklace & earrings, #201, 3½" **$75.00**

Figurine, girl w/banjo beside palm tree, chenille on wooden base, Japan, 1950s, 3¾"......................................**$15.00**

Film, Our Gang, Styme on cover w/other members, 8mm, 1950s, EX in 5" sq box **$30.00**

Game, Sambo, tin over cardboard, 21x13½", G, $140.00. (Photo courtesy Collectors Auction Services)

Game, Tops 'n Tails, 48 cards form 24 pictures, EXIB (caricature graphics)..**$75.00**

Measuring cup, pottery face, red ball nose, Al Jolson-type mouth, 1-cup..**$17.50**

Mug, pottery face, embossed features, side-glance eyes, cold-painted lips, shiny, unmarked, 3½".......................**$40.00**

Picture record, Blue Tail Fly, 78 rpm, original colorful sleeve, 10¼" sq, EX..**$40.00**

Postcard, Mammy, The Tea Cup's Fortune Telling, Harry Roseland, framed size: 6⅞x9¾"..............................**$30.00**

Salt & pepper shakers, Luzianne Mammy, green skirt, 4⅝", pr, from $95 to..**$125.00**

Salt & pepper shakers, Mammy w/broom, gold trim, Norcrest label, #H424, 4¼", pr.......................................**$395.00**

Souvenir, figure resting on cotton ball in basket, ca 1930s – 1940s, $75.00. (Photo courtesy M. Davern)

Spice shaker set, pottery, Black Chef, stamped Japan, corks on bottoms, 4", set of 4 in original wooden rack **$95.00**

Swizzle sticks, Zulu-Lulu, set of 6 on original 8½x11" card **$35.00**

Tablecloth, printed figures eating watermelon, blue border, 51" sq, NM...**$150.00**

Tablecloth, printed multicolor figures on white, lime-green border, 51" sq, NM...**$150.00**

Tile, Low Water on the Mississippi, Currier & Ives scene, delicately Painted 24k Gold by Gungott Art Studios, 6⅛" **$95.00**

Tin container, boy being pecked by goose, litho graphics, 3½x6" dia, NM **$85.00**

Token, Green River Whiskey, man on horse embossed on gold-tone metal, 1¼" dia..**$45.00**

Towel, kitchen; father plays banjo as children dance, print on white w/red border, VG **$55.00**

Towel, kitchen; youth playing banjo printed on white, 26½x15", M...**$55.00**

Wall pocket, chef on cookstove, marked Hollywood, from $60.00 to $75.00.

Whisk broom, wooden bellhop handle, multicolor paint, 1930s, NM...**$90.00**

Black Cats

Kitchenware, bookends, vases, and many other items designed as black cats were made in Japan during the 1950s and exported to the United States where they were sold by various distributors who often specified certain characteristics they wanted in their own line of cats. Common to all these lines were the red clay used in their production and the medium used in their decoration — their features were applied over the glaze with cold (unfired) paint. The most collectible is a line marked (or labeled) Shafford. Shafford cats are plump and pleasant looking. They have green eyes with black pupils; white eyeliner, eyelashes, and whiskers; and red bow ties. The same design with yellow eyes was marketed by Royal, and another fairly easy-to-find 'breed' is a line by Wales with yellow eyes and gold whiskers. You'll find various other labels as well. Some collectors buy only Shafford, while others like them all.

When you evaluate your black cats, be critical of their paint. Even though no chips or cracks are present, if half of the paint is missing, you have a half-price item (if that). Collectors are very critical. These are readily available on Internet auctions, and unless pristine, they realize prices much lower than ours. Remember this when using the following values which are given for cats with near-mint to mint paint.

Ashtray, flat face, Shafford, hard-to-find size, 3¾"......**$50.00**

Ashtray, flat face, Shafford, 4¾" **$18.00**

Ashtray, head shape, not Shafford, several variations, ea from $12 to...**$15.00**

Ashtray, head shape w/open mouth, Shafford, 3", from $25 to...**$30.00**

Bank, seated cat w/coin slot in top of head, Shafford, from $225 to..**$275.00**

Bank, upright cat, Shafford-like features, marked Tommy, 2-part, from $150 to...**$175.00**

Cigarette lighter, Shafford, 5½" **$175.00**

Cigarette lighter, sm cat stands on book by table lamp...**$65.00**

Condiment set, upright cats, yellow eyes, 2 bottles & pr of matching shakers in wireware stand, row arrangment...**$95.00**

Condiment set, 2 joined heads, J&M bows w/spoons (intact), Shafford, 4", from $95 to.....................................**$120.00**

Condiment set, 2 joined heads, yellow eyes, not Shafford **$65.00**

Cookie jar, cat's head, fierce expression, yellow eyes, brown-black glaze, heavy red clay, rare, lg **$250.00**

Cookie jar, cat's head, Shafford, from $80 to **$100.00**

Creamer & sugar bowl, cat-head lids are salt & pepper shakers, yellow eyes variation, 5⅜" **$50.00**

Creamer & sugar bowl, Shafford **$45.00**

Cruet, slender form, gold collar & tie, tail handle **$12.00**

Cruet, upright cat w/yellow eyes, open mouth, paw spout **$30.00**

Cruets, oil & vinegar; cojoined cats, Royal Sealy, 1-pc (or similar examples w/heavier yellow-eyed cats), 7¼"..**$40.00**

Decanter, long cat w/red fish in his mouth as stopper...**$75.00**

Decanter, upright cat holds bottle w/cork stopper, Shafford...**$50.00**

Decanter set, upright cat, yellow eyes, +6 plain wines .**$35.00**

Decanter set, upright cat, yellow eyes, +6 wines w/cat faces **$50.00**

Demitasse pot, tail handle, bow finial, Shafford, 7½"..**$165.00**

Desk caddy, pen forms tail, spring body holds letters, 6½" **$8.00**

Egg cup, cat face on bowl, pedestal foot, Shafford, from $95 to **$125.00**

Grease jar, sm cat head, Shafford, scarce, from $95 to ..**$110.00**

Ice bucket, cylindrical w/embossed yellow-eyed cat face, 2 sizes, ea **$75.00**

Measuring cups, 4 sizes on wooden wall-mount rack w/painted cat face, Shafford, rare, from $350 to................**$400.00**

Mug, Shafford, cat handle w/head above rim, standard, 3½" **$55.00**

Mug, Shafford, scarce, 4", from $70 to **$80.00**

Paperweight, cat's head on stepped chrome base, open mouth, yellow eyes, rare...............................**$75.00**

Pincushion, cushion on cat's back, tongue measure ..**$25.00**

Pitcher, milk; Shafford, 6" and 6½", $150.00 for either size.

Pitcher, squatting cat, pour through mouth, Shafford, rare, 5", 14½" circumference **$90.00**

Pitcher, squatting cat, pour through mouth, Shafford, scarce, 4½", 13" circumference..**$75.00**

Pitcher, squatting cat, pour through mouth, Shafford, very rare, 5½", 17" circumference................................**$250.00**

Planter, cat & kitten in a hat, Shafford-like paint........**$30.00**

Planter, cat sits on knitted boot w/gold drawstring, Shafford-like paint, Elvin, 4¼x4½" **$30.00**

Planter, upright cat, Shafford-like paint, Napco label, 6"...**$20.00**

Pot holder caddy, 'teapot' cat, 3 hooks, Shafford, from $170 to..**$195.00**

Salad set, spoon & fork, funnel, 1-pc oil & vinegar cruet & salt & pepper shakers on wooden wall-mount rack, Royal Sealy..**$200.00**

Salt & pepper shakers, long crouching cat, shaker in ea end, Shafford, 10"...**$165.00**

Salt & pepper shakers, range size; upright cats, Shafford, scarce, 5", pr...**$65.00**

Salt & pepper shakers, round-bodied 'teapot' cat, Shafford, pr, from $125 to...**$140.00**

Salt & pepper shakers, seated, blue eyes, Enesco label, 5¾", pr **$15.00**

Salt & pepper shakers, upright cats, Shafford, 3¾" (watch for slightly smaller set as well), pr **$25.00**

Spice set, triangle, 3 rounded tiers of shakers, 8 in all, in wooden wall-mount triangular rack, very rare...**$450.00**

Spice set, 4 upright cat shakers hook onto bottom of wire-ware cat-face rack, Shafford, rare.......................**$450.00**

Spice set, 6 sq shakers in wooden frame, Shafford..**$175.00**

Spice set, 6 sq shakers in wooden frame, yellow eyes..**$125.00**

Stacking tea set, mama pot w/kitty creamer & sugar bowl, yellow eyes..**$85.00**

Stacking tea set, 3 cats w/red collar, w/gold ball, yellow eyes, 3-pc **$80.00**

Sugar bowl/planter, sitting cat, red bow w/gold bell, Shafford-like paint, Elvin, 4" **$25.00**

Teapot, bulbous body, head lid, green eyes, Shafford, lg, 7" **$75.00**

Teapot, bulbous body, head lid, green eyes, Shafford, med size, from $40 to **$45.00**

Teapot, bulbous body, head lid, green eyes, Shafford, sm, 4"-4½" **$30.00**

Teapot, cat face w/double spout, Shafford, scarce, 5", from $200 to...**$250.00**

Teapot, cat's face, yellow hat, blue & white eyes, pink ears, lg, from $40 to **$50.00**

Teapot, crouching cat, paw up to right ear as spout, green jeweled eyes, 8½" L...**$80.00**

Teapot, panther-like appearance, gold eyes, sm.........**$20.00**

Teapot, upright, slender cat (not ball-shaped), lift-off head, Shafford, rare, 8"...**$250.00**

Teapot, upright cat w/paw spout, yellow eyes & red bow, Wales, 8¼"...**$60.00**

Teapot, yellow eyes, 1-cup...**$30.00**

Teapot, yellow-eyed cat face embossed on front of standard bulbous teapot shape, wire bail **$60.00**

Thermometer, cat w/yellow eyes stands w/paw on round thermometer face..**$30.00**

Toothpick holder, cat on vase atop book, Occupied Japan **$12.00**

Tray, flat face, wicker handle, Shafford, rare, lg.......**$185.00**

Utensil rack, flat-backed cat w/3 slots for utensils, cat only...**$125.00**

Wall pocket, flat-backed 'teapot' cat, Shafford..........**$125.00**

Wine, embossed cat's face, green eyes, Shafford, sm.**$75.00**

Blair Dinnerware

After graduating from the Cleveland School of Art in the 1930s, William H. Blair became an employee of the Purinton Pottery Company in Wellsville, Ohio, and later in Shippenville, Pennsylvania. His sister Dorothy was married to Bernard Purinton (founder of the Purinton Pottery Company). Bill Blair was responsible for designing most of Purinton's early lines, including both of their most recognized patterns, Apple and Intaglio. In 1946 he left the Purinton Pottery Company and opened his own pottery, Blair Ceramics, in Ozark, Missouri. William Blair designed his dinnerware line with a modernistic look utilizing square and rectangular shapes, with many items accented by twisted rope handles. Gay Plaid, Blair's signature pattern, features large bold stripes of dark green, chartreuse, and brown on ivory slip. Other patterns such as Spiced Pear, Leaves, Yellow and Gray Plaid, Bamboo, and Rick Rack, were produced in smaller quantities. The two most elusive patterns, Bird and Brick, were manufactured from red clay, and their shapes were rounded. Both Bird and Brick are intaglio-style designs, meaning that the motif is etched into the pottery. Blair Ceramics was sold by Neiman-Marcus and several other fine department stores in New York and Chicago. The pottery closed in 1955 after a devastating fire.

Almost all items produced by Blair Ceramics (except for the smaller pieces) were marked 'Blair, Decorated by Hand.' Although this appears to be a signature, it is only a facsimile that was applied with an ink stamp. A few experimental plates and tumblers have surfaced which have been artist signed with Mr. Blair's personal signature, 'William H. Blair' or simply 'Blair.' These pieces are rare and command premium prices.

Advisor: Joe McManus (See Directory, Dinnerware)

Club/Newsletter: *Purinton News & Views*
PO Box 153
Connellsville, PA 15425
A quarterly newsletter devoted to enthusiasts of Purinton Pottery and Blair Ceramics

Pitcher, water; Gay Plaid, with ice lip, from $50.00 to $60.00.

Beer mug, Bird, from $90 to...**$100.00**
Beer mug, Fish, signed William H Blair, rare, minimum value **$150.00**
Beer mug, Gay Plaid, from $45 to............................**$55.00**
Bowl, covered onion soup; Leaves, from $20 to **$25.00**
Bowl, Gay Plaid, sq, 8", from $20 to...........................**$25.00**

Casserole, individual; Gay Plaid, w/lid, from $35 to ..**$40.00**
Coffee server, Gay Plaid, from $40 to..........................**$50.00**
Cookie jar, Gay Plaid, wooden lid, from $100 to **$125.00**
Creamer, Bamboo, from $25 to **$30.00**
Creamer, Gay Plaid, from $20 to **$25.00**
Creamer & sugar bowl, Gay Plaid, mini, from $40 to...**$50.00**
Cup & saucer, Bird, from $30 to **$40.00**
Cup & saucer, Brick, from $30 to................................**$35.00**
Cup & saucer, Gay Plaid, from $8 to **$10.00**
Cup & saucer, Leaves, from $10 to **$12.00**
Pitcher, Bird, w/ice lip, from $100 to.......................**$125.00**
Plate, dinner; Bird, from $40 to **$50.00**
Plate, dinner; Fruit, signed William H Blair, rare, minimum value **$350.00**
Plate, dinner; Gay Plaid, from $10 to.........................**$15.00**
Plate, dinner; Leaves, from $10 to **$15.00**
Plate, dinner; Spiced Pear, from $30 to.......................**$40.00**
Plate, dinner; Yellow & Gray Plaid, from $10 to........**$15.00**
Plate, salad; Bamboo, from $6 to **$8.00**
Plate, salad; Bird, from $20 to **$25.00**
Plate, salad; Brick, from $20 to...................................**$25.00**
Plate, salad; Gay Plaid, from $6 to **$8.00**
Platter, Gay Plaid, sq, 10", from $18 to.....................**$20.00**
Relish dish, Bird, oblong, minimum value **$125.00**
Relish dish, Fish (experimental pattern), oblong, minimum value **$125.00**
Relish dish, Gay Plaid, oblong, 12" L, from $18 to.....**$20.00**
Salt & pepper shakers, Bamboo, short, pr, from $12 to .**$14.00**
Salt & pepper shakers, Gay Plaid, conical, tall, pr, from $50 to **$60.00**
Salt & pepper shakers, Gay Plaid, short, pr, from $12 to..**$14.00**
Salt & pepper shakers, Leaves, short, pr, from $12 to ..**$14.00**
Sugar bowl, Gay Plaid, w/lid, from $20 to..................**$25.00**
Sugar bowl, Yellow & Gray Plaid, w/lid, from $20 to..**$25.00**
Tumbler, Bird, from $25 to **$35.00**
Tumbler, Gay Plaid, from $10 to **$12.00**
Tumbler, Leaves, from $12 to **$15.00**
Water cooler, Bamboo, rare, 5-gal, minimum value .**$175.00**
Water cooler, Gay Plaid, rare, 5-gal, minimum value .**$200.00**
Water cooler, Yellow & Gray Plaid, rare, minimum value..**$175.00**

Blue Danube

A modern-day interpretation of the early Meissen Blue Onion pattern, Blue Danube is an extensive line of quality dinnerware that has been produced in Japan since the early 1950s and distributed by Lipper International of Wallingford, Connecticut. It is said that the original design was inspired by a pattern created during the Yuan Dynasty (1260 – 1368) in China. This variation is attributed to the German artist Kandleva. The flowers depicted in this blue-on-white dinnerware represent the ancient Chinese symbols of good fortune and happiness. The original design, with some variations, made its way to Eastern Europe where it has been produced for about two hundred years. It is regarded today as one of the world's most famous patterns.

At least one hundred twenty-five items have at one time or another been made available by the Lipper company, making it the most complete line of dinnerware now available in the United States. Collectors tend to pay higher prices for items with the earlier banner mark (1951 to 1976), and reticulated (openweave) pieces bring a premium. Unusual serving or decorative items generally command high prices as well. The more common items that are still being produced usually sell for less than retail on the secondary market.

The banner logo includes the words 'Reg US Pat Off' along with the pattern name. In 1976 the logo was redesigned and the pattern name within a rectangular box with an 'R' in circle to the right of it was adopted. Very similar lines of dinnerware have been produced by other companies, but these two marks are the indication of genuine Lipper Blue Danube. Among the copycats you may encounter are Mascot and Vienna Woods — there are probably others.

Advisor: Lori Simnioniw (See Directory, Dinnerware)

Ashtray, 3¾" **$4.00**
Ashtray, 7¾", from $30 to **$35.00**
Au gratin, 6½", from $9 to **$12.00**
Baker, oval, 10", from $50 to **$55.00**
Bell, 6" **$25.00**
Biscuit jar, 9", from $50 to..........................**$60.00**
Bone dish/side salad; crescent shape, banner mark, 9", from $18 to..**$24.00**
Bowl, cereal; banner mark, 6", from $9 to **$14.00**
Bowl, Chinese; 11½", from $50 to **$60.00**
Bowl, cream soup; w/lid, from $25 to...........**$30.00**
Bowl, dessert; 5½", from $8 to **$10.00**
Bowl, divided vegetable; 11x7½", from $50 to **$62.00**
Bowl, fruit/berry; 1⅛x5½", from $8 to **$12.00**
Bowl, heart shape, 2¼x8½" **$65.00**
Bowl, lattice edge, 9", from $50 to..............**$60.00**
Bowl, low pedestal skirted base, shaped rim, banner mark, 2x9x12", from $70 to **$80.00**
Bowl, rice; 4½", from $10 to........................**$12.00**
Bowl, salad; 9", from $35 to **$42.00**
Bowl, soup; 8½", from $15 to **$18.00**
Bowl, vegetable; oval, 10" L, from $30 to......**$40.00**
Bowl, vegetable; round, w/lid, from $75 to.....**$100.00**
Bowl, vegetable; 3¼x10", from $50 to..........**$70.00**
Bowl, vegetable; 9", from $40 to **$50.00**
Bowl, wedding; w/lid, footed, sq, 8½x5", from $55 to...**$65.00**
Box, white lacquerware, gold label w/rectangular logo, 2¼x4½"..**$30.00**
Butter dish, round, 8½" **$85.00**
Butter dish, ¼-lb, from $22 to **$28.00**
Cache pot, w/handles, 8x8" **$45.00**
Cake pedestal, lattice edge, rectangular mark, 5x10" .**$75.00**
Cake pedestal, 4x10" **$55.00**
Cake plate, sq, w/handles, from $80 to..........**$95.00**
Cake server & knife, from $25 to..................**$30.00**

Candelabrum, four-light, 12x11", $225.00.

Candlesticks, 2½", from $35.00 to $45.00 for the pair.
(From the collection of Elaine France)

Candlesticks, 6½", pr, from $40 to **$50.00**
Candy dish, open, 8", from $28 to **$32.00**
Candy dish, w/lid, from $50 to......................**$60.00**
Casserole, individual; banner mark, 6" across handles ...**$30.00**
Casserole, round, w/lid, 7¼", from $60 to.....**$70.00**
Casserole, round, w/lid, 8¾", from $65 to.....**$75.00**
Casserole, round, 1-qt, w/lid, 6¼", from $50 to.........**$60.00**
Chamber stick, Old Fashioned, 4x6" dia....................**$25.00**
Cheese board, wooden, w/6" dia tile & glass dome from $25 to **$35.00**
Chop plate, 12" dia, from $50 to **$60.00**
Chop plate, 14" dia, from $60 to **$70.00**
Chop plate, 16", from $75 to **$85.00**
Coasters, set of 4, from $25 to......................**$35.00**
Coffee mug, 3⅛", set of 4, from $60 to **$75.00**
Coffeepot, embossed applied spout, ornate handle, 7½", from $60 to **$70.00**
Coffeepot, 6", from $45 to **$55.00**
Compote, 4", from $65 to............................**$75.00**
Compote, 13", from $75 to..........................**$85.00**
Condiment bowl, 2½" deep, w/saucer, 6¾", from $22 to ..**$28.00**
Cookie jar, from $65 to **$75.00**
Creamer, bulbous, 3½", from $18 to **$22.00**
Creamer, ovoid, 3½", from $18 to **$22.00**
Creamer & sugar bowl, 'y' handles, bulbous, 4¾", 3½", from $38 to..**$42.00**
Cup & saucer, angle handle, scalloped rims, from $7 to..**$9.00**

Cup & saucer, demitasse **$10.00**
Cup & saucer, farmer's; 4x5" (across handle), from $15 to.**$20.00**
Cup & saucer, flat handle, 2½", from $10 to **$12.00**
Cup & saucer, Irish coffee; cylindrical cup, from $12 to .**$16.00**
Cup & saucer, 2¾", from $18 to **$22.00**
Cutting board, 14x9½", +stainless steel knife **$45.00**
Dish, deep, w/lug handles, 8¾", from $18 to **$22.00**
Dish, leaf shape, 5¾x4" **$20.00**
Ginger jar, 5", from $35 to **$40.00**
Goblet, clear glass w/Blue Danube design, 7¼", set of 12,
    from $80 to **$100.00**
Gravy boat, double spout, w/undertray, 3½x6", from $35
    to **$40.00**
Gravy boat, 6⅜x9¾", from $65 to **$75.00**
Hurricane lamp, glass mushroom globe **$75.00**
Ice bucket, from $20 to **$30.00**
Ice cream scoop, cutting blade, no mark **$50.00**
Inkstand, 2 lidded inserts, shaped base, banner mark, 9"
    L **$300.00**
Mug, soup; 4 for **$65.00**
Mustard/mayonnaise, from $70 to **$75.00**
Napkin holders, set of 4, from $30 to **$35.00**
Napkins, Sunnyweave, set of 4, from $25 to..............**$30.00**
Pitcher, bulbous w/flared spout, fancy handle, 5¼", from $25
    to..**$30.00**
Pitcher, bulbous w/flared spout, fancy handle, 6¼" ...**$40.00**
Pitcher, milk; 'y' handle, 5¼", from $25 to **$30.00**
Plate, bread & butter; 6¾" **$6.00**
Plate, collector; from $40 to **$48.00**
Plate, cookie; 10", from $38 to **$42.00**
Plate, deviled eggs; from $80 to **$90.00**
Plate, lattice rim, 8" **$15.00**
Plate, triangular, 9¾" L **$50.00**
Plate, 8½", from $8 to **$11.00**
Plate, 10¼", from $10 to...**$15.00**
Platter, 12x8½", from $40 to **$52.00**
Platter, 14x10", from $60 to **$65.00**
Platter, 15½" sq, from $200 to **$250.00**
Relish, 2-part, 7¼", from $32 to **$38.00**
Relish, 7¾", from $20 to **$25.00**
Salt & pepper shakers, dome top w/bud finial, bulbous bot-
    tom, 5", pr **$40.00**
Salt & pepper shakers, 5 holes in salt, 3 in pepper, 5", pr,
    from $25 to **$30.00**
Salt box, wooden lid, 4¾x4¾" **$55.00**
Snack plate & cup **$25.00**
Soap dish, from $8 to **$12.00**
Souffle, 7½", from $40 to **$50.00**
Soup ladle, from $35 to **$45.00**
Soup tureen, oval, w/lid, from $135 to.....................**$150.00**
Spooner, 4¾x4" **$50.00**
Sugar bowl, ovoid, w/lid, 5", from $26 to **$32.00**
Sugar bowl, w/lid, mini, from $20 to **$25.00**
Sweetmeat dish, 7½", from $35 to **$42.00**
Tablecloth, 50x70", +4 napkins **$95.00**
Tazza, attached pedestal foot, banner mark, 4½x15", from
    $85 to **$95.00**

Tea tile/trivet, 6" **$25.00**
Teakettle, enamel, wooden handle, w/fold-down metal sides,
    9x9½" **$25.00**
Teapot, 'y' handle, 6½", from $60 to.........................**$70.00**
Tidbit tray, 2-tier, from $40 to **$50.00**
Tidbit tray, 3-tier, from $50 to **$75.00**
Toothbrush holder, from $15 to **$18.00**
Tray, oblong, 10¼", from $40 to **$50.00**
Tray, rectangular, pierced handles, 14½" **$105.00**
Tray, 5-sided, 12", from $40 to **$50.00**
Tumbler, china, 3⅜", from $8 to **$10.00**
Undertray, for soup tureen, from $50 to....................**$55.00**
Vase, bud; 6", from $15 to **$18.00**
Vase, scalloped rim w/embossed decor, round foot, wide
    body, no mark, 6" **$20.00**
Vase, 9", from $40 to **$50.00**
Vase, 10", from $65 to **$75.00**

Soup tureen, with underplate and ladle, from $220.00 to $250.00. (From the collection of Elaine France)

Blue Garland

During the 1960s and 1970s, this dinnerware was offered as premiums through grocery stores. Its ornate handles, platinum trim, and the scalloped rims on the flat items and the bases of the hollow ware pieces when combined with the 'Haviland' backstamp suggested to most supermarket shoppers that they were getting high quality dinnerware for very little. And indeed the line was of good quality, but the company that produced it had no connection at all to the famous Haviland company of Limoges, France, who produced fine china there for almost one hundred years. The mark is Johann Haviland, taken from the name of the founding company that later became Philip Rosenthal and Co. This was a German manufacturer who produced chinaware for export to the United States from the mid-1930s until well into the 1980s. Today's dinnerware collectors find the delicate wreath-like blue flowers and the lovely shapes very appealing.

This line may also be found with the Thailand – Johann Haviland backstamp, a later issue. Our values are for the dinnerware with the Bavarian backstamp. The Thailand line will usually sell for at least 30% less.

Bell, 5½x3¼", from $35 to $50.00
Beverage server (teapot/coffeepot), w/lid, 11", from $70 to...$90.00
Bowl, fruit; 5⅛", from $2.50 to $3.00
Bowl, oval, 11¼", from $50 to.........................$60.00

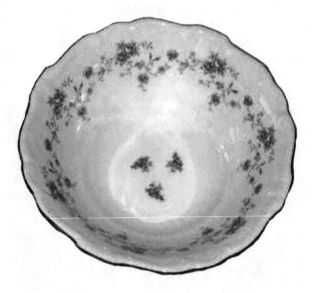

Bowl, serving; 3x8½", from $25.00 to $32.00.

Bowl, soup; 7½", from $9 to $12.00
Bowl, vegetable; round, w/lid, from $70 to $85.00
Bowl, vegetable; round, 2¾x8½", from $28 to $35.00
Butter dish, w/lid, ¼-lb, from $70 to $85.00
Butter pat, 3½", from $10 to $1.50
Candle holders, 4", pr, from $80 to..........................$100.00
Chamber stick, metal candle cup & handle, 6" dia.....$75.00
Coaster, 3½", from $8 to $10.00
Creamer, from $15 to..$18.00
Cup & saucer, flat, from $8 to $12.00
Cup & saucer, footed, from $8 to...........................$12.00
Dish, serving; flat, 10¾x7¾" $60.00
Gravy boat, w/attached underplate, from $35 to........$45.00
Gravy boat, w/separate underplate, from $35 to........$45.00
Mug, coffee; 3½" $5.00
Plate, bread & butter; 6¼", from $2 to.......................$3.00
Plate, dinner; 10", from $9 to.................................$11.00
Plate, salad; 7¾", from $7 to....................................$9.00
Platter, 13", from $30 to..$35.00
Platter, 14½", from $35 to $45.00
Platter, 15¼", from $45 to $55.00
Salt & pepper shakers, 4¼", pr, from $40 to $55.00
Sugar bowl, w/lid, from $18 to $22.00
Teakettle, porcelain w/stainless steel lid.....................$25.00
Teapot, w/lid, 7", from $75 to $90.00

Tidbit, 1-tier, from $35 to $45.00
Tidbit, 2-tier, from $40 to $50.00
Tidbit, 3-tier, 13¾", from $45 to $65.00

Blue Ridge Dinnerware

Blue Ridge has long been popular with collectors, and prices are already well established, but that's not to say there aren't a few good buys left around. There are! It was made by a company called Southern Potteries, who operated in Erwin, Tennessee, from sometime in the latter '30s until the mid-'50s. They made many hundreds of patterns, all hand decorated. Some collectors prefer to match up patterns, while others like to mix them together for a more eclectic table setting.

One of the patterns most popular with collectors (and one of the most costly) is called French Peasant. It's very much like Quimper with simple depictions of a little peasant man with his staff and a lady. But they also made many lovely floral patterns, and it's around these where most of the buying and selling activity is centered. You'll find roosters, plaids, and simple textured designs, and in addition to the dinnerware, some vases and novelty items as well.

Very few pieces of dinnerware are marked except for the 'china' or porcelain pieces which usually are. Watch for a similar type of ware often confused with Blue Ridge that is sometimes (though not always) marked Italy.

The values suggested below are for the better patterns. To evaluate the French Peasant line, double these figures; for the simple plaids and textures, deduct 25% to 50%, depending on their appeal.

If you'd like to learn more, we recommend *The Best of Blue Ridge Dinnerware* by Betty and Bill Newbound.

Advisors: Bill and Betty Newbound (See Directory, Dinnerware

Newsletter: *National Blue Ridge Newsletter*
Norma Lilly
144 Highland Dr., Blountsville, TN 37617

Ashtray, individual, from $18 to $20.00
Baking dish, plain, 8x13", from $22 to $25.00
Basket, aluminum edge, 10", from $30 to $35.00
Batter jug, from $65 to $75.00
Bonbon, divided, center handle, china, from $85 to.......$100.00
Bowl, cereal/soup; premium, 6", from $25 to.............$30.00
Bowl, salad; 10½x11½", from $60 to $75.00
Bowl, vegetable; premium, w/lid, from $125 to.......$175.00
Box, cigarette; w/4 ashtrays, from $125 to...............$150.00
Box, Seaside, china, from $170 to.............................$175.00
Butter dish, Woodcrest, from $45 to $55.00
Butter pat/coaster, from $30 to.................................$35.00
Candy box, china, 6" dia, from $125 to....................$150.00
Casserole, w/lid, from $45 to.....................................$50.00

Child's cereal bowl, from $125 to $150.00
Child's mug, from $150 to $175.00
Child's plate, from $125 to...................................$175.00
Child's play tea set, complete, from $375 to $400.00
Creamer, Colonial, sm, from $12 to......................$15.00
Creamer, demitasse; china, from $80 to.....................$95.00
Cup & saucer, demitasse; earthenware, from $45 to ..$70.00
Demitasse pot, china, from $250 to $300.00
Gravy boat, from $25 to $30.00
Gravy tray, from $50 to $70.00
Pie baker, from $35 to $45.00
Pitcher, Antique, china, 5", from $85 to...................$100.00

Pitcher, Charm House, from $190.00 to $220.00. (Photo courtesy Betty and Bill Newbound)

Pitcher, Sculptured Fruit, china, from $85 to $95.00
Plate, advertising, lg, from $300 to.............................$350.00

Plate, Forked-Tailed Flycatcher, from Colonial Birds salad set, from $75.00 to $80.00. (Photo courtesy Betty and Bill Newbound)

Plate, round or sq, 7", from $15 to............................$18.00
Plate, salad; flower, 8¼", from $30 to $35.00
Ramekin, w/lid, 7½", from $30 to.............................$35.00
Relish, deep shell, china, from $80 to $85.00
Relish, Palisades shape, from $40 to $50.00
Server, wood or metal center handle, from $30 to $40.00
Shakers, Apple, 2¼", pr, from $40 to.........................$50.00
Shakers, Good Housekeeping, pr, from $95 to........$125.00
Shakers, tall, footed, china, pr, from $75 to $100.00
Sherbet, from $35 to...$40.00
Sugar bowl, demitasse; china, from $50 to................$60.00
Sugar bowl, Fifties shape, w/lid, from $15 to $20.00
Sugar bowl, rope handle, w/lid, from $15 to.............$20.00
Tea tile, round or sq, 3", from $35 to $40.00
Teapot, ball shape, from $175 to $200.00
Teapot, Colonial, from $100 to $150.00
Teapot, Fine Panel, china, from $175 to...................$225.00
Teapot, Woodcrest, from $175 to $225.00

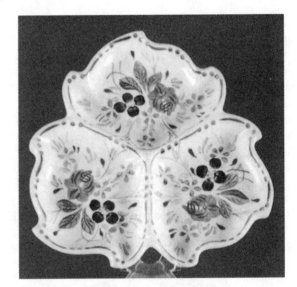

Tray, snack; Irresistible, Martha shape, from $150.00 to $160.00. (Photo courtesy Betty and Bill Newbound)

Tray, waffle set; 9x13", from $100 to $125.00
Vase, Boot, 8", from $95 to......................................$100.00
Vase, Ruffle Top, china, 9½", from $90 to.................$125.00

Blue Willow Dinnerware

Blue Willow dinnerware has been made since the 1700s, first by English potters, then Japanese, and finally American companies as well. Tinware, glassware, even paper 'go-withs' have been produced over the years — some fairly recently, due to on-going demand. It was originally copied from the early blue and white wares made in Nanking and Canton in China. Once in awhile you'll see some pieces in black, pink, red, or even multiple colors.

Obviously the most expensive will be the early English wares, easily identified by their backstamps. You'll be most likely to find pieces made by Royal or Homer Laughlin, and even though comparatively recent, they're still collectible, and their prices are very affordable.

For further study we recommend *Blue Willow Identification and Value Guide* by Mary Frank Gaston.

See also Homer Laughlin; Royal China.

Advisor: Mary Frank Gaston

Newsletter: *American Willow Report*
Lisa Kay Henze, Editor
P.O. Box 900, Oakridge, OR 97463. Bimonthly newsletter, subscription: $15 per year, out of country add $5 per year

Newsletter: *The Willow Word*
Mary Berndt, Publisher
P.O. Box 13382, Arlington, TX 76094; Send SASE for information about subscriptions and the International Willow Collector's Convention

Ashtray, advertisement for Schweppes Table Waters, English, unmarked, 4" dia, from $40 to.............................**$50.00**
Baking dish, oven proof, marked Japan, 2½x5", from $30 to **$35.00**
Banked, stacking pig figures (3), Japan, 7", from $65 to...**$75.00**
Biscuit jar, metal handle, unmarked Japan, 6", from $150 to **$175.00**
Bowl, sauce; 1 handle, 7" L, from $25 to **$30.00**
Bowl, vegetable; rectangular, unmarked English, 8¾x7", from $80 to...**$100.00**
Bowl, vegetable; rectangular, w/lid, unmarked, 10½x6", from $120 to..**$150.00**
Bread bowl, reversed Traditional center, unmarked Japan, 15", from $200 to **$225.00**
Butter pat, marked England, 3½", from $25 to **$30.00**

Candle holder, Gibson & Son (English), 5" diameter, from $150.00 to $175.00. (Photo courtesy Mary Frank Gaston)

Canisters, barrel shapes, graduated sizes, Japan, set of 4, from $350 to..**$450.00**

Canisters, tin, sq sides, graduated sizes, unmarked, set of 4, from $120 to..**$140.00**
Charger, Traditional, Royal China, 12¼", from $30 to...**$40.00**
Clock, tin, marked Smith's, made in Great Britain, from $150 to **$165.00**
Compote, Shenango China, 3x6" dia, from $50 to......**$60.00**
Cosy pot (stacking teapot), 2-cup pot w/creamer & sugar bowl, Japan, from $130 to **$150.00**
Creamer, Made in Japan, 3½", from $10 to **$15.00**
Creamer, scalloped rim, marked England, 2", from $40 to **$50.00**
Cup, known as Texas Cup, marked Japan, 5½x8½", from $90 to **$100.00**
Cup, punch; Two Temples II, butterfly border, pedestal foot, unmarked English, 3", from $55 to.......................**$65.00**
Cup & saucer, demitasse; marked Japan, 2½", 4½", from $14 to **$18.00**
Cup & saucer, Two Temples II, from $25 to **$35.00**
Drainer, meat; Turner Center pattern, unmarked English, 14¼x10¼", from $350 to **$400.00**
Flatware, plastic & stainless steel, Japan, 4-pc place setting, from $45 to...**$55.00**
Juicer/reamer, Moriyama mark, 6x7", from $300 to ..**$350.00**
Ladle, unmarked, 12¼", from $175 to....................**$200.00**
Muffin dish, knob final, illegible English mark, 3½x9" dia, from $150 to **$175.00**
Olive & vinegar cruets, Japan, 6", pr, from $90 to....**$110.00**
Pitcher, Two Temples II w/butterfly border, gold band, English, 4½", from $100 to **$125.00**
Plate, Advertising: Ye Olde Cheshire Cheese..., Traditional pattern, Wedgwood & Co mark, 7¾", from $60 to **$70.00**
Plate, hot water; Traditional center & border, exterior decor, English mark, 11", from $300 to **$350.00**
Plate, soup; Traditional center & border, Shenango China mark, 9", from $20 to **$25.00**
Plate, Traditional pattern, reticulated edge, unmarked English, 7¼", from $150 to **$175.00**
Plate, Variant center pattern, pictorial border, unmarked, 6", from $8 to...**$12.00**
Platter, pictorial border, National China, Co, from $35 to....**$45.00**
Relish, 5 sections, Shenango China mark, 8½", from $40 to..**$50.00**
Salad bowl, unmarked Japan, 3½x10", w/ceramic & wood fork & spoon, from $120 to **$140.00**
Sherbet, Two Temples II pattern w/butterfly border, Made in Japan, 3½x3¾", from $40 to **$50.00**
Teakettle, Blue Willow Pantry Collection, Taiwan **$30.00**
Tumbler, clear glass, unmarked, 4-5", ea, from $15 to ..**$20.00**

Bookends

You'll find bookends in various types of material and designs. The more inventive their modeling, the higher the price. Also consider the material. Cast-iron examples, especially if in original polychrome paint, are bringing very high prices right now. Brass and copper are good as well, though elements of design may override the factor of materials altogether. If they are signed by the designer or marked by the manufacturer, you can boost the price. Those with a decidedly Art Deco appearance are often good sellers. The consistent volume of common to moderately uncommon bookends that are selling online has given the impression that some are more easily available than once thought. Hence, some examples have not accrued in value. See *Collector's Guide to Bookends* by Louis Kuritzky (Collector Books) for more information.

Advisor: Louis Kuritzky (See Directory, Bookends)

Club: Bookend Collector Club
Louis Kuritzky
4510 NW 175h Pl. 7
Gainesville, FL 32605; 352-377-3193
Quarterly full-color newsletter: $25 per year

Atlas, painted chalk on polished stone base, JB Hirsch, ca 1940, 7¾", pr...**$135.00**
Back-to-Back Girls, brass, ca 1940, 7¾", pr **$175.00**

Charioteer, gray metal on polished stone base, attributed to J.B. Hirsch, 5", $275.00. (Photo courtesy Louis Kuritzky)

Flamingo, painted cast iron, unmarked Everstyle, 1948, 5¼", pr **$125.00**
Galleon, painted gray metal, Made in Occupied Japan, ca 1946, 6¾", pr...**$75.00**
Grazing Pony, painted gray metal, ca 1930, 5¼", pr ..**$110.00**
Linden Hall, painted gray metal, ca 1960, 3", pr.........**$25.00**
Maiden, gray metal, Frankart shop mark, ca 1930, 6", pr..**$225.00**
Moon Rabbit (rabbit in crescent), brass, ca 1935, 5", pr....**$110.00**
Oak Leaf, painted gray metal, PM Craftsman, ca 1965, 6½", pr...**$45.00**
Pensive Hound, painted gray metal, Ronson, ca 1930, Company tag #16031, 3¾", pr **$95.00**
Pirate couple, painted gray metal, K&O, ca 1932, 10½", pr...**$175.00**
Rooks, turquoise glaze, Rookwood, marked IXII 2275, William McDonald's initials, 1940, 5¼", pr.........**$400.00**
Sailfish & Wave, painted gray metal, Jennings #1258, ca 1928, 5", pr...**$110.00**
Ski Queen, gray metal w/enameling, K&O, ca 1932, pr..**$175.00**
Soldier w/Sabre, painted gray metal w/celluloid face & knee on polished stone base, JB Hirsch, ca 1931, 8¼", pr..**$275.00**
Up to My Neck (horse head), clear glass, ca 1940, 5", pr....**$75.00**
Wolfhound, clear glass, New Martinsville, ca 1940, 7", pr..**$200.00**

Woman on couch, gray metal w/celluloid face, marked JBH, ca 1930, 4¾", pr..**$300.00**

Books

Books have always fueled the mind's imagination. Before television lured us out of the library into the TV room, everyone enjoyed reading the latest novels. Western, horror, and science fiction themes are still popular to this day — especially those by such authors as Louis L'Amour, Steven King, and Ray Bradbury, to name but a few. Edgar Rice Burrough's Tarzan series and Frank L. Baum's Wizard of Oz books are regarded as classics among today's collectors. A first edition of a popular author's first book (especially if it's signed) is avidly sought after, so is a book that 'ties in' with a movie or television program.

On the whole, ex-library copies and book club issues (unless they are limited editions) have very low resale values.

Besides the references in the subcategory narratives that follow, for further study we also recommend *Huxford's Old Book Value Guide* (Collector Books); *Collector's Guide to Children's Books, 1850 to 1950, Vols I, II,* and *III,* by Diane McClure Jones and Rosemary Jones; and *Whitman Juvenile Books* by David and Virginia Brown. All are published by Collector Books.

Big Little Books

The Whitman Publishing Company started it all in 1933 when they published a book whose format was entirely different than any other's. It was very small, easily held in a child's hand, but over an inch in thickness. There was a cartoon-like drawing on the right-hand page, and the text was printed on the left. The idea was so well accepted that very soon other publishers — Saalfield, Van Wiseman, Lynn, World Syndicate, and Goldsmith — cashed in on the idea as well. The first Big Little Book hero was Dick Tracy, but soon every radio cowboy, cartoon character, lawman, and space explorer was immortalized in his own adventure series.

When it became apparent that the pre-teen of the '50s preferred the comic-book format, Big Little Books were finally phased out; but many were saved in boxes and stored in attics, so there's still a wonderful supply of them around. You need to watch condition carefully when you're buying or selling. For further information we recommend *Big Little Books, A Collector's Reference and Value Guide*, by Larry Jacobs (Collector Books).

Newsletter: *Big Little Times*
Big Little Book Collectors Club of America
Larry Lowery
P.O. Box 1242, Danville, CA 94526; 415-837-2086

Alice in Wonderland, Whitman #759, NM....................**$55.00**
Andy Panda & Tiny Tom, Whitman #1425, NM.........**$40.00**
Blondie, Baby Dumpling & All; Whitman #1487, EX..**$25.00**

Bonanza, Bubble Gum Kid, Whitman #2002, 1967, EX..**$12.00**

Bringing Up Father, Whitman #1133, NM....................**$60.00**

Buck Jones in the Fighting Rangers, Whitman #1188, EX..**$35.00**

Charlie Chan, Whitman #1478, 1939, EX **$35.00**

Chester Gump Finds the Hidden Treasure, Whitman #766, EX **$35.00**

Dick Tracy & the Mad Killer, Whitman #1436, NM.....**$55.00**

Dick Tracy Out West, Whitman #723, NM.................**$100.00**

Eddie Canter in An Hour w/You, Whitman #774, 1934, NM...**$75.00**

Flash Gordon & the Witch Queen of Mongo, Whitman #1190, NM **$45.00**

Flash Gordon in the Ice World of Mongo, Whitman #1443, 1942, EX...**$45.00**

Jungle Jim, Whitman #1138, VG................................**$15.00**

Lone Ranger & the Secret Killer, Whitman #1431, EX...**$45.00**

Mickey Mouse the Mail Pilot, Whitman #731, EX **$65.00**

Og Son of Fire, #1196, Whitman, NM, $35.00.

Popeye & the Quest for the Rainbird, Whitman #1459, EX...**$35.00**

Smilin' Jack & the Escape From Death Rock, Whitman #1445, VG...**$10.00**

Smilin' Jack & the Stratosphere Ascent, Whitman #1152, 1937, EX...**$35.00**

Tarzan & the Ant Men, Whitman #1444, EX...............**$40.00**

Tarzan Lord of the Jungle, Whitman #1407, NM.........**$45.00**

Tarzan the Fearless, Whitman #769, 1934, NM **$100.00**

Uncle Ray's Story of the United States, Whitman #722, VG **$15.00**

Children's Miscellaneous Books

Aaron & the Green Mountain Boys, Patricia Lee Gauch, Coward, McCann & Geoghegan, 1972, 63 pages, hardbound, VG..**$20.00**

Across Five Aprils, Irene Hunt, Follett, 1964, 223 pages, pictorial binding, hardbound, VG...............................**$10.00**

Agib & the Honey Cakes, Kathleen Lines, Henry Z Walck, 1972, 48 pages, Wilkinson illustrations, hardbound, w/dust jacket, EX...**$15.00**

Alicia Has a Bad Day, Lisa Jahn-Clough, Houghton Mifflin, 1994, 1st edition, hardbound, w/dust jacket, EX.**$15.00**

Alphabet for Joanna: A Poem, Horas Gregory, Holt Rinehart, 1963, sm format, hardbound, VG.........................**$10.00**

Amelia's Nine Lives, Lorna Balian, Abingdon Press, 1986, oblong, hardbound, w/dust jacket, VG................**$10.00**

Angel & the Donkey, James Reeves, McGraw-Hill, 1970, later edition, slim, hardbound, w/dust jacket, EX **$15.00**

Angel & the Soldier Boy, Peter Collington, wordless picture book, Knopf, 1987, 1st edition, hardbound, NM..**$30.00**

Angelina's Baby Sister, Katherine Holabird, Potter, 1991, 1st edition, hardcover, w/dust jacket, VG..................**$15.00**

Animals Born Alive & Well, Ruth Heller, Grosset & Dunlap, 1987, hardbound, w/dust jacket, VG...................**$12.00**

Arabian Nights: Three Tales, Degorah Nourse Lattimore, Cotler, 1995, 1st edition, oversized picture book, w/dust jacket, NM..**$10.00**

At the Mouth of the Luckiest River, Arnold A Griese, Crowell, 1969, 65 pages, cloth binding, w/dust jacket, EX .**$15.00**

Ava Maria, Rachel Field, Random House, 1940, cloth binding, hardbound, VG **$15.00**

Bad Case of Animal Nonsense, Jonathan Allen, Godine, 1981, cloth binding, graphics on front cover, 1st edition, w/dust jacket..**$15.00**

Bear That Heard Crying, Natalie Kinsey-Warnock, Cobblehill, 1993, 1st edition, hardbound, w/dust jacket, NM .**$15.00**

Bearskinner, Brimm Brothers, Atheneum, 1977, 1st American edition, pictorial binding, NM................................**$15.00**

Bemba, an African Adventure; Andree Clair, Harcourt Brace, 1962, 158 pages, early printing, hardbound, w/dust jacket **$10.00**

Big Squeak, Little Squeak; Robert Krause, Orchard, 1996, 1st edition, slim picture book, hardbound, w/dust jacket, VG **$20.00**

Bolivar, Hardie Gramatky, Putnam's Sons, 1961, 62 pages, pink cloth binding, w/dust jacket, EX..................**$10.00**

Bossy the Calf Who Lost Her Tinker Bell, GA Cooke, McLoughlin, 1941, color pictorial binding, hardbound, EX **$10.00**

Can I Keep Him, Steven Kellogg, Dial, 1977, 7th printing, slim, hardbound, w/dust jacket, EX **$25.00**

Captain Hook, Bernard Brett, Collins, London, no date, 64 pages, hardcover w/dust jacket, EX **$15.00**

Christmas Crocodile, Bonny Becker, David Small illustrator, Simon & Schuster, 1998, 1st edition, w/dust jacket, NM..**$10.00**

Contented Little Pussy Cat, Frances Ruth Keller, Platt & Munk, 1959, hardbound, VG **$12.00**

Country Bunny & the Little Golden Shoes, Du Bose Heyward, Houghton Mifflin, 1939, hardbound, contemporary reprint, NM...**$10.00**

Country Mail Is Coming, Max Fatchen, Little Brown, 1987, 64 pages, 1st edition, hardbound, w/dust jacket, EX..**$10.00**

Crippled Lamb, Max Lucado, World Printing, Liz Bonham illustrations, hardbound, w/dust jacket, NM........**$15.00**

Daniel Boone, Felix Sutton, Grosset Dunlap, 1956, 69 pages, pictorial binding, hardbound, NM **$10.00**

Dash & Dart, Mary & Conrad Buff, Viking, 1962, 75 pages, 11th printing, hardbound, former library copy, w/dust jacket..**$10.00**

Diamond Champs, Matt Christopher, Little Brown, 1977, 1st edition, w/dust jacket, NM...**$30.00**

Diary of a Horse, Claire Golle, Thomas Yoseloff, 1956, 40 pages, 1st edition, Marc Chagall drawings, VG....**$20.00**

Dinosaur Bob & His Adventure w/the Family Lazardo, William Joyce, Harper Collins, 1995, 1st edition, oblong, VG..**$10.00**

Dinosaurs, Lee Bennett Hopkins, Harcourt Brace, 1987, 47 pages, softcover, signed/inscribed by author, EX.**$12.00**

Discovery at the Rio Camuy, Russell & Jeanne Gurnee, Crown, 1974, 183 pages, indexed, hardbound, w/dust jacket, VG..**$10.00**

Dr Frick & His Fractions, Henry W Ford, Holt Rinehart, 1965, magician & rabbit cover, G **$10.00**

Dr Gravity, Dennis Haseley, Farrar, 1992, 322 pages, 1st edition, hardbound, w/dust jacket, VG.....................**$10.00**

Egon, Larry Bograd, Macmillan, 1980, 1st edition, hardbound, w/dust jacket, EX..**$10.00**

Fairy w/the Long Nose, Claude Boujon, McElderry, 1987, 1st American edition, w/dust jacket, EX **$15.00**

Family Howl, Betty Dinneen, Macmillan, 1981, 89 pages, 1st edition, cloth spine/boards, dust jacket, VG **$10.00**

First Rains, Peter Bonnici, Lisa Kopper illustrator, Carol Rhoda, 1985, unnumbered pages, VG **$12.00**

French Are Coming, Wilma Pitchford Hays, Colonial Williamsburg, 1965, 102 pages, hardbound, w/dust jacket, VG..**$15.00**

Friendly Tales for Children, Ella H Hay, Midwest, 1946, 64 pages, cloth binding, hardbound, VG **$15.00**

Fun in Bed for Children, Virginia Kirkus, Simon & Schuster, 1935, 137 pages, 1st edition, hardbound, w/dust jacket, VG..**$10.00**

Gift-Giver's Cookbook, Jane Green, Simon & Schuster, 1971, 191 pages, VG...**$10.00**

Good-Natured Bear, Richard Henry Horne, Macmillan, 1927, 1st American edition, scissor-cuts by Lisl Hummel, VG...**$20.00**

Goodmorning Good Night, Ivan Gantschev, Neugebauer, 1991, 1st edition, hardbound, w/dust jacket, EX .**$15.00**

Grandma's Joy, Eloise Greenfield, Philomel, 1980, hardbound, 1st edition, w/dust jacket, signed by author, NM..**$20.00**

Grandmother Cat & the Hermit, Elizabeth Coatsworth, Macmillan, 1970, 86 pages, Weekly Reader Edition, EX...**$10.00**

Grandpa's Face, Eloise Greenfield, Philomel, 1988, later printing, hardbound, NM..**$10.00**

Hawk in Silver, Mary Gentle, Lathrop, Lee & Shephard, 1977, 237 pages, 1st American edition, hardbound, dust jacket, EX..**$10.00**

Heidi, Clara M Burd/Johanna Spyri, Winston, 1924, pictorial label on cloth, w/dust jacket, EX **$30.00**

Herbie Jones & the Dark Attic, Suzy Kline, Putnam's Sons, 1992, 101 pages, 1st edition, hardbound, w/dust jacket, VG...**$15.00**

His Great Adventure, Robert Herrick, Macmillan, 1913, 408 pages, 1st edition, hardbound, frontispiece, G.....**$10.00**

Hole Is To Dig, First Book of First Definitions; Ruth Krauss, Harper & Brothers, 1952, later edition, hardbound, EX **$15.00**

Horse of Air, Lindsey Campbell, Routledge & Kegan Paul, London, 1957, green cloth, 1st edition, VG **$10.00**

In Grandpa's House, Philip Sendak, Harper & Row, 1985, stated as 1st edition, hardcover, w/dust jacket, NM **$15.00**

Is Anybody There?, Eve Bunting, Harper Collins, 1988, 170 pages, Book Club reprint, hardbound, w/dust jacket, EX...**$20.00**

It's Nothing to a Mountain, Sid Hite, Holt, 1994, 214 pages, hardcover, w/dust jacket, NM...............................**$12.00**

Jambo Means Hello: Swahili Alphabet Book, Muriel Feelings, Dutton, 1974, 4th printing, hardbound, EX **$20.00**

Jazz Fish Hen, Howie Green, Tuttle, 1992, 48 pages, hardbound, 1st printing, w/dust jacket, EX.................**$10.00**

Jesse & Able, Rachel Isadora, Greenwillow, 1981, 1st edition, hardbound, NM w/VG dust jacket **$10.00**

Jibby the Cat, Felix Salten, Julian Messner, 1948, 177 pages, 1st edition, cloth binding, hardbound, G.............**$20.00**

King's Falcon, Paula Fox, Bradbury Press, 1969, 57 pages, 1st edition, hardbound, w/dust jacket, VG.................**$15.00**

Legend of Jimmy Spoon, Kristiana Gregory, Harcourt Brace, 1990,1 65 pages, 1st edition, hardbound, w/dust jacket, NM...**$15.00**

Leif the Unlucky, Erik Christian Haugaard, Houghton Mifflin, 1982, 206 pages, 1st edition, hardbound, w/dust jacket, VG...**$10.00**

Lester's Overnight, Kay Chorao, Dutton, 1977, 1st edition, hardbound, w/dust jacket, NM **$12.00**

Little Bear & the Papagini Circus, Margaret Greaves, Dial, 1986, 1st edition, 1st printing, hardbound, NM....**$15.00**

Little Red Engine Goes Carolling, Diana Ross, Faber & Faber, 1971, reprint, hardbound, VG...............................**$10.00**

Loretta & the Little Fairy, Gerda M Scheidl, North-South, 1993, 64 pages, 1st edition, pictorial binding, hardbound, NM **$12.00**

Magic at Midnight, Phyllis Arkle, Funk & Wagnalls, 1968, 80 pages, 1st American edition, hardbound, w/dust jacket, EX..**$10.00**

Magic Number, Harold Goodwin, Bradbury Press, 1969, 1st edition, hardbound, w/dust jacket, VG.................**$10.00**

Mariel of Redwall, Brian Jacques, Philomel, 1988, 431 pages, 3rd printing, w/dust jacket, NM...............................**$30.00**

Marvelous Misadventures of Sebastian, Alexander Lloyd, Dutton, 1970, 1st edition, signed/inscribed by author, NM.....**$35.00**

Maxine in the Middle, Holly Keller, Greenwillow, 1989, 1st edition, hardbound, w/dust jacket, NM........................**$10.00**

Mitz & Fritz of Germany, Madeline Brandeis, Grosset & Dunlap, 1933, 160 pages, hardbound, photo illustrations, G...**$10.00**

Mother Goose: A Collection of Classic Nursery Rhymes, M Hague, Holt Rinehart, 1984, 1st edition, hardbound, w/dust jacket, NM...**$20.00**

Mother Goose's Nursery Rhymes, Allen Atkinson, Knopf, 1984, 87 pages, hardbound, 1st edition, EX.........**$15.00**

Mr Budge Builds a House, Gareth Adamson, Chilton, 1968, hardbound, color pictorial binding, EX+ **$10.00**

Munching Peter & Other Stories, Rose Fylman, Ginn, 1934, 300 pages, blue cloth binding, hardbound, VG ...**$10.00**

My Father's Dragon, Ruth Stiles Gannett, Random House, 1948, Weekly Reader Edition, early reprint, NM ..**$10.00**

My Friend Johnny, Vana Earle, Lathrop, 1952, 1st edition, hardbound, w/dust jacket, EX **$15.00**

Mystery of Navajo Moon, Timothy Green, Northland, 1991, 1st edition, hardbound, oversized, w/dust jacket, EX...**$12.00**

Nana Upstairs & Nana Downstairs, Tomie de Paola, Putnam's Sons, 1973, 13th printing, NM...............**$10.00**

Next Place, Warren Hanson, Waldman House, 1997, 4th printing, oblong, w/dust jacket, signed/inscribed by author, NM..**$15.00**

Nicky's Lopsided, Lumpy But Delicious Orange, Phyllis Green, Addison Wesley, 1978, 111 pages, 1st edition, hardcover, NM..**$10.00**

Night Daddy, Charles Grodin, Random House, 1993, 1st edition, picture book, hardbound, w/dust jacket, inscribed, EX **$10.00**

No Dragons on My Quilt, Jean Ray Laury, American Quilter's Society, 1990, 1st edition, hardbound, NM...........**$20.00**

Not So Long Ago, Ruth Langland Holberg, Crowell, 1939, 131 pages, 1st edition, hardbound, G **$20.00**

Ogden Nash's Musical Zoo, Ogden Nash, Little Brown, 1947, 47 pages, 1st edition, hardbound, VG **$15.00**

One Morning, Yohji Izawa, Picture Studio, 1985, 1st edition, hardcover, w/dust jacket, NM...............................**$25.00**

Opening Night, Rachel Isadora, 1984, hardbound, w/dust jacket, EX...**$10.00**

Our Eddie, Sulamith IshKishor, Pantheon, 1969, 183 pages, 1st edition, hardbound, w/dust jacket, VG...........**$10.00**

Out of the Dust, Karen Hesse, Scholastic Press, 1997, 227 pages, 1st edition, 2nd printing, w/dust wrapper, NM **$45.00**

Planet of Junior Brown, Virginia Hamilton, Macmillan, 1971, 210 pages, 3rd printing, w/dust jacket, VG **$10.00**

Plantation Doll, Cora Cheney, Henry Holt, 1955, 136 pages, hardbound pictorial cloth, NM...............................**$15.00**

Pooh's Honey Bee Counting Book, Walt Disney, 1994, hardbound, 1st edition, EX.......................................**$10.00**

Power Boys Adventure, The Mystery of the Million Dollar Penny, **Mel Lyle, 1965, illustrated, Whitman, 212 pages, EX, $6.00.** (Photo courtesy David and Virginia Brown)

Power Twins, Ken Follett, Morrow, 1990 reprint, 90 pages, 1st edition, hardbound, EX.....................................**$10.00**

Princess & the Lion, Elizabeth Coatsworth, Antelope Books/Hamish Hamilton, 1974 printing, hardbound, w/dust jacket, NM..**$15.00**

Puffin Island, Ada & Frank Graham, Cowles, 1971, 140 pages, 1st edition, signed by both authors, hardcover, w/dust jacket, EX...**$20.00**

Puffin Island, Ada & Frank Graham, Cowles, 1971, 140 pages, 1st edition, w/dust jacket, signed by authors, NM...**$20.00**

Random House Book of Fairy Tails, Amy Ehrlich, Random House, 1985, later printing, 208 pages, hardbound, w/dust jacket, EX..**$12.00**

Rex Lee Rough Rider of the Air, Thomson Burtis, Grosset & Dunlap, 1930, 218 pages, green cloth w/airplane graphic front, EX..**$10.00**

Riddle Book, Lily Lee Dootson, Rand McNally, 1925, 160 pages, pictorial tan cloth cover, VG **$15.00**

Ring o' Roses, Leslie L Brook, nursery rhyme picture book, Frederick Warne, ca 1900-10s, G **$35.00**

Rosie the Dancing Elephant, Maureen Daly, LF Bjorklund illustrations, Dodd Mead, 1967, 43 pages, hardbound, w/dust jacket, EX..**$15.00**

Samantha & the Swan, Cecile Curtis, Hodder & Stoughton, London, 1965, 38 pages, 1st English edition, G- dust jacket, VG **$15.00**

Self-Portrait w/Wings, Susan Green, Little Brown, 1989, 206 pages, 1st edition, hardbound, w/dust jacket, EX **$12.00**

Selfish Giant & Other Stories, Kate Seredy & Wilhelmina Harper, McKay, 1935, 1st edition, hardbound, VG .**$35.00**

Sharing Susan, Eve Bunting, Harper Collins, 1991, 122 pages, early printing, hardbound, w/dust jacket, inscribed, NM **$20.00**

Shoo-Fly Pie, Mildred Jordan, Knopf, 1944, 118 pages, cloth spine, decorative boards, 1st edition, G **$10.00**

Sir Alva & the Wicked Wizard, Priscilla & Otto Friedrich, Lothrop, Lee & Shepard, 1960, later printing, hardbound, VG **$10.00**

Small Big Bad Boy, Irina Hale, Viking, 1991, 1st edition, slim picture book, hardbound, VG..............................**$10.00**

Son for a Day, Corinne Gerson, Atheneum, 1980, 140 pages, 1st edition, hardbound, VG....................................**$10.00**

Stellaluna, Janell Cannon, pop-up/mobile, Harcourt Brace, 1997, 1st edition, hardbound, NM **$10.00**

Stranger in the Forest, Carol Brink, Macmillan, 1959, 314 pages, 1st edition, hardbound, w/dust jacket, EX..**$30.00**

Summer of My German Soldier, Bette Green, Dial Press, 1973, later printing, 230 pages, hardbound, w/dust jacket, EX **$15.00**

Talking Earth, Jean Craighead George, Harper & Row, 1983, 151 pages, stated as 1st edition, hardbound, EX..**$10.00**

Tangled Butterfly, Marion Dane Bauer, Houghton Mifflin, 1980, 162 pages, hardbound, NM.........................**$10.00**

Tell It - Make It Book, Shari Lewis, Tarcher, 1972, 113 pages, oblong, hardbound, w/dust jacket, VG................**$10.00**

The Town That Went South, Clive King, Macmillan, 1959, 118 pages, stated as 1st edition, hardbound, w/dust jacket, EX...**$10.00**

Tim Mouse & the Major, Judy Brook, Lothrop, 1973, 1st American edition, Gold Library Edition label to dust jacket, EX **$10.00**

Tin Soldier, Hans Christian Anderson, McLoughlin Bros, 1945, hardbound, w/dust jacket, EX **$12.00**

Trouble in Bugland, William Kotzwinkle, David Godine, 1983, 152 pages, 1st edition, hardbound, w/dust jacket, EX...**$15.00**

The Two Jungle Books, **Rudyard Kipling, 1950, Garden City, color paste-on pictorial on red cover, EX, $20.00.** (Photo courtesy Diane McClure Jones and Rosemary Jones)

Up North in Winter, Deborah Hartley, Dutton, 1986, 1st edition, 1st printing, hardbound, w/dust jacket, NM **$15.00**

Varnell Roberts, Superpigeon; Genevieve Gray, Houghton Mifflin, 1975, 113 pages, 1st edition, hardbound, w/dust jacket, EX..**$15.00**

Very Windy Day, Elizabeth MacDonald, William Morrow, 1992, Tambourine Library Edition, oblong, hardbound, VG...**$10.00**

William the Backwards Skunk, Chuck Jones, Crown, 1986, 1st edition, hardbound, w/dust jacket, NM **$65.00**

Winkle Twinkle Pup & Other Stories, Sari Sari, McLoughlin, 1941, pictorial binding, VG **$12.00**

Witch Watch, Paul Coltman, Gillian McClure illustrations, Farrar Straus Giroux, 1989, 1st American edition, w/dust jacket, NM...**$15.00**

Yellow Butter Purple Jelly Red Jam Black Bread, Mary Ann Hoberman, Viking, 1981, 1st edition, hardbound, w/dust jacket, VG...**$15.00**

Juvenile Series Books

Betty Gordon in the Land of Oil, AB Emerson, Cupples & Leon, 1920, 210 pages, hardbound w/Betty on front board, VG..**$12.00**

Betty Gordon in Washington, AB Emerson, Cupples & Leon, 1920, 210 pages, Betty on front board, frontispiece, VG..**$12.00**

Bobbsey Twins & the Greek Hat Mystery, Laura Lee Hope, Grosset & Dunlap, 1964, 176 pages, hardbound, VG.**$15.00**

Bobbsey Twins & the Talking Fox Mystery, Laura Lee Hope, Grosset & Dunlap, 1970, 175 pages, hardbound, G.....**$15.00**

Bobbsey Twins Big Adventure at Home, Laura Lee Hope, Grosset & Dunlap, 1960, 176 pages, hardbound, VG **$12.00**

Bobbsey Twins on the Sun-moon Cruise, Laura Lee Hope, Grosset & Dunlap, 1975, 181 pages, hardbound, VG **$65.00**

Bobby Benson in the Tunnel of Gold, Peter Dixon, Hecker H-O, 1936, 72 pages, color pictorial wrappers, EX.....**$15.00**

Borrowers Afield, Mary Norton, 1955, early reprint, 215 pages, hardbound, colorful dust jacket, EX..........**$10.00**

Combat Nurses of WWII, Wyatt Blassingame, #116 Landmark Books, Random House, 1967, 184 pages, cloth bound, NM **$45.00**

Donna Parker in Hollywood, Marcia Martin, Whitman, 1961, 282 pages, hardbound, VG **$10.00**

Elsie's Children, Martha Finley, Dodd Mead, 1905, 323 pages, hardbound, G..**$8.00**

Elsie's Motherhood, Martha Finley, Grosset & Dunlap, early reprint, 348 pages, hardbound, VG **$8.00**

Enchanted Valley, Adventures of Sassy & Rowdy; Marvin E Jones, Eakin Press, 1990, hardbound, EX.............**$10.00**

Frank in the Mountains, Harry Castlemon, Rocky Mountain Series, Winston, 1896, 277 pages, G **$10.00**

G-Men Smash the Professor's Gang, William Engle, Grosset & Dunlap, 1936, 205 pages, hardbound, VG............**$15.00**

Gory Gary Strikes Back, Adventures of Sassy & Rowdy; Marvin E Jones, Eakin Press, 1990, 85 pages, hardbound, EX...**$10.00**

Great Airport Mystery, FW Dixon, Hardy Boys Series, Grosset & Dunlap, 1930, 210 pages, hardbound, dust jacket, VG...**$15.00**

Happy Hollisters & the Mystery at Missle Town, Jerry West, Doubleday, 1961, 186 pages, hardbound, w/dust jacket, VG...**$10.00**

Happy Hollisters & the Old Clipper Ship, Jerry West, Doubleday, 1956, hardbound, w/dust jacket, VG ..**$10.00**

Little Men, Life at Plumfield w/Jo's Boys, Louisa May Alcott, Goldsmith, no date, hardbound, 253 pages, w/dust jacket, G..**$10.00**

Mystery of the Golden Horn, Phyllis A Whitney, Philadelphia: Westminster, 1962, 1st edition, Vicki Stewart adventure, EX...**$40.00**

On the Banks of Plum Creek, Helen Sewell/Laura Ingalls Wilder, Harper & Row, 1937, 239 pages, hardbound, NM **$85.00**

Sugar Creek Gang Goes Camping, Paul Hutchens, Eerdmans, 1944, 95 pages, hardbound, w/dust jacket, VG ...**$10.00**

Taffy & Melissa Mollases, Carylyn Haywood, Morrow, 1969, 190 pages, 1st edition, hardbound, signed by author, NM **$35.00**

Little Golden Books

Everyone has had a few of these books in their lifetime; some we've read to our own children so many times that we still know them word for word, and today they're appearing in antique malls and shops everywhere. The first were printed in 1942. These are recognizable by their blue paper spines (later ones had gold foil). Until the early 1970s, they were numbered consecutively; after that they were unnumbered.

First editions of the titles having a 25¢ or 29¢ cover price can be identified by either a notation on the first or second pages or a letter on the bottom right corner of the last page (A for 1, B for 2, etc.). If these are absent, you probably have a first edition.

Condition is extremely important. To qualify as mint, these books must look just as good as they looked the day they were purchased. Naturally, having been used by children, many show signs of wear. If your book is only lightly soiled, the cover has no tears or scrapes, the inside pages have only small creases or folded corners, and the spine is still strong, it will be worth about half as much as one in mint condition. A missing cover makes it worthless. Additional damage would of course lessen the value even more.

A series number containing an 'A' refers to an activity book, while a 'D' number identifies a Disney story.

For more information we recommend *Collecting Little Golden Books* by Steve Santi (who provided us with our narrative material).

Activity book, 1955-63, hardcover, paper doll book w/paper dolls, EX **$35.00**
Activity book, 1955-63, hardcover, stamps, complete, EX..**$15.00**
Activity book, 1955-63, hardcover, wheel book w/wheel, EX **$10.00**
Annie Oakley & the Rustlers, 32215, A edition, NM...**$20.00**
Bambi Friends of the Forest, 3101-59, A edition, EX....**$4.00**
Band-Aid book, 1950-79, Helen Gaspard or Kathryn Jackson, Malvern illustrations, w/out band-aid insert, EX ..**$10.00**
Bozo & the Hide 'N Seek Elephant, #598, D edition, EX.**$6.00**
Brave Cowboy Bill, #93, B edition, no puzzle, EX.....**$15.00**
Bunny's Magic Tricks, #441, A edition, EX................**$25.00**
Cinderella's Friends, #D115, F edition, VG................**$14.00**
Corky, #486, A edition, VG **$12.00**
Eager Reader Series, 1974-75, boxed set of 8, EX......**$35.00**
Exploring Space, #342, A edition, EX **$14.00**
Friendly Book, #199, A edition, EX...........................**$12.00**
General titles, later editions w/nonfiction titles, EX, ea ..**$5.00**
General titles, later editions w/popular comic strip characters, EX, ea **$8.00**
General titles, 1950s 1st editions, antique gold foil spine w/leaves & flower pattern, hardcover, ea............**$15.00**
General titles, 1960s editions, antique gold foil spine w/leaves & flower pattern, hardcover, ea............**$12.00**
General Titles, 1969-75 later printings, gold foil spine w/animal pattern, ea **$4.00**
General titles, 1969-75 1st editions, gold foil spine w/animal pattern, hardcover, ea **$8.00**
Giant Little Golden Book, 1957-59, Disney titles, EX, ea ..**$20.00**
Giant Little Golden Book, 1957-59, individual titles, ea **$10.00**
Giant w/the Three Golden Hairs, #219, 1955, EX.......**$12.00**
Hansel & Gretel, 317, D edition, VG **$14.00**

Jig-Saw Puzzle Book, 1949-50, various authors & illustrations, w/intact puzzle, EX, ea **$45.00**
Jig-Saw Puzzle Book, 1949-50, various authors & illustrations, w/out puzzle, ea...**$10.00**
Little Brown Bear, #304-60, A edition, EX **$6.00**
Mickey Mouse Heads for the Sky, #100-60, A edition, EX..**$4.00**
Mrs Brisby & the Magic Stone, #110-38, B edition, EX.**$2.00**

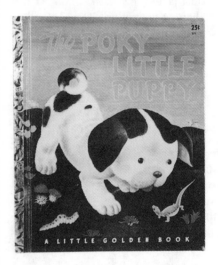

Poky Little Puppy, 1942, first printing, NM, $24.00. (Photo courtesy June Moon)

Popular illustrators Garth Williams & Eloise Wilkin, later editions, ea **$10.00**
Popular illustrators Garth Williams & Eloise Wilkin, 1st editions, ea **$20.00**

Movie and TV Tie-Ins

Air Force One, Max Allan Collins, Ballantine paperback, Harrison Ford cover, 1997, NM................................**$4.00**
Amorous Adventures of Moll Flanders, Daniel Defoe, Signet #D2559, EX..**$5.00**
Another Day in Paradise, Eddie Little, Viking Press, 1st American edition, 1st printing, w/dust jacket, NM..**$13.00**
Banyon, Warner, TV pilot version, NM **$12.00**
Bat Masterson, Bantam, paperback, Gene Barry cover, NM..**$10.00**
Battlestar Galactica, Cylon Death Machine, Berkley, paperback, #2 in series, NM **$8.00**
Battlestar Galactica: The Photostory, Glen A Larsen, Berkley Multi-Media Special, 1st printing, 1979, EX.............**$4.00**
Black Sheep Squadron, Devil in the Slot; Bantam, paperback, 1st in series, NM **$10.00**
Bonanza, One Man w/Courage, Media, paperback, NM..**$15.00**
Boulevard Nights, Dewey Gram, Warner Books #90-106, 1st printing, 1979, EX **$4.00**
Buckaroo Banzai, Earl Mac Rauch, Pocket Books, 1st printing, 1948, NM **$50.00**
Burke's Law - Who Killed the Madcap Milicent, Pocket, paperback, NM..**$12.00**
Charlie's Angels - Killing Kind, Ballantine, paperback, 2nd in series, NM **$8.00**
Dark Shadows - Victoria Winters, Paperback Library, photo cover, 2nd in series, NM **$10.00**

Death in the Doll's House (movie title: Shadow on the Wall), Lees & Lawrence, Dell Mapback #352, Ann Southern cover, EX **$4.00**

Dr Quinn Medicine Woman, Teresa Warfield, Boulevard books, paperback, Jane Seymour cover, NM........**$30.00**

Dr Strangelove or: How I Learned To Stop Worrying & Love the Bomb, Peter George, Bantam #H3079, 5th printing, 1965, EX **$6.00**

Fantastic Voyage, Isaac Asimov, Bantam, 20th printing, EX...**$4.00**

From Russia w/Love, Ian Fleming, Signet D2030, 19th printing, EX **$4.00**

Girl From UNCLE - Birds of a Feather Affair, Signet, paperback, 1st in series, NM **$15.00**

Golden Child, George C Chesbro, Pocket Books, Eddie Murphy cover, EX **$5.00**

Gunsmoke - Cheyenne Vengeance, Award, 4th in series, NM...**$7.00**

Island of Dr Moreau, Joseph Silva, Ace, Burt Lancaster & Michael York on cover, EX.................................**$6.00**

Jurassic Park, Michael Chrichton, Ballantine Books, March 1999 reissue, paperback, 400 pages, NM.................**$8.00**

Knight Rider - Trust Doesn't Rust, Pinnacle, 2nd in series, NM **$10.00**

Land of the Giants, Pyramid, paperback, NM **$12.00**

Lando Calrissian & the Flamewind of Oseon, Neil L Smith, Ballantine Del Rey, 1st printing, 1983, Schimdt cover, EX **$4.00**

Live & Let Die, Ian Fleming, Signet #P2730, 27th printing, EX...**$4.00**

M*A*S*H Trivia: Unofficial Quiz Book, George St John, Warner Books, 1st printing, 1983, EX.....................**$4.00**

Man From UNCLE - Killer Spores, Dell, paperback, 3rd in series, NM **$10.00**

Man in the Iron Mask, Alexandre Dumas, Signet, 1998 reprint, paperback, 495 pages, M **$6.00**

Men in Black: A Novel, Steve Perry, Bantam, 1997, paperback, movie cover, NM..................................**$3.00**

Miami Vice - The Florida Burn, Avon, paperback, 1st in series, NM **$10.00**

Mod Squad - The Hit, Pyramid, paperback, 5th in series, NM **$8.00**

Notorious Landlady, Irving Shulman, Gold Medal, Kim Novak & Jack Lemmon cover, EX **$5.00**

Phantom of the Paradise, Bjarne Rostaing, Dell #7175, EX..**$12.00**

Planet of the Apes - Man the Fugitive, Award, paperback, 1st in series, NM **$10.00**

Rat Patrol - Desert Danger, Paperback Library, 2nd in series, NM **$15.00**

Six Million Dollar Man - Solid Gold Kidnapping, Warner, paperback, 2nd in series, NM **$12.00**

Sooner or Later, Bruce & Carole Hart, Avon, 12th printing, EX **$7.00**

Star Trek - Where No Man Has Gone Before, Bantam, paperback photo novel, NM...................................**$20.00**

Those Magnificent Men in Their Flying Machines, John Burke, Pocket Books #50189, 1st printing, 1965, EX.............**$5.00**

Zarak, AJ Bevan, Avon T-150, paperback, EX..............**$5.00**

Bottle Openers

A figural bottle opener is one where the cap lifter is an actual feature of the subject being portrayed — for instance, the bill of a pelican or the mouth of a four-eyed man. Most are made of painted cast iron or aluminum; others were chrome or brass plated. Some of the major bottle-opener producers were Wilton, John Wright, L&L, and Gadzik. They have been reproduced, so beware of any examples with 'new' paint. Condition of the paint is an important consideration when it comes to evaluating a vintage opener.

For more information, read *Figural Bottle Openers, Identification Guide*, by the Figural Bottle Opener Collectors. Number codes in our descriptions correspond with their book.

Advisor: Charlie Reynolds (See Directory, Bottle Openers)

Club: Figural Bottle Opener Collectors
Linda Fitzsimmons
9697 Gwynn Park Dr., Ellicott City, MD 21043; 301-465-9296

Newsletter: *Just for Openers*
John Stanley
3712 Sunningdale Way, Durham, NC 27707-5684; 919-419-1546. Quarterly newsletter covers all types of bottle openers and corkscrews

Alligator & boy, F-133, painted cast iron, 1947, 2¾x3⅞", EX..**$220.00**

Amish boy, F-31, cast iron, EX **$200.00**

Anchor chain, F-228, steel, 6⅞" L...............................**$70.00**

Bear head, F-426, painted cast iron, 1950, 4x3", EX.**$130.00**

Beer drinker, F-192, cast iron, rare **$1,800.00**

Black Face Crowley, F-404, cast iron, wall mount....**$650.00**

Buffalo, N-523, bronze, wall mount, 1984, 5⅜x2¾" ..**$90.00**

Clown head, F-417, multicolor painted cast iron, laughing, common, 1950, 4¾", EX.......................................**$85.00**

Cocker Spaniel, F-80, multicolor paint on cast iron, 2¾x3¾", EX **$120.00**

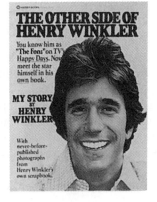

The Other Side of Henry Winkler (**Happy Days**), **Warner Bros. Inc, 1976, from $10.00 to $15.00.** (**Photo courtesy Greg Davis and Bill Morgan**)

Cowboy signpost, F-14, painted cast iron, 1 leg up, 1950, EX **$135.00**

Double-Eye (4-eyed man), F-414, multicolor paint on cast iron, EX..**$50.00**

Dragon, F-145, cast iron w/greenish finish **$300.00**

Drunk on lamp/sign post, F-9, aluminum, EX..........**$250.00**

Elephant, F-46, red paint on cast iron, ca 1940, G **$60.00**

Elephant standing on base, F-58, brass, 2⅛x3"..........**$50.00**

False teeth, F-420, red & white painted cast iron, wall mount, common, 1954, 2⅜x3¾"......................................**$70.00**

Fish, F-165, abalone shell inlay on gold metal, VG **$55.00**

Fish (shark?), F-154, cast metal, Schlitz stamped on side, 7", EX **$80.00**

Geisha, F-186, cast iron w/black paint **$180.00**

Goat, F-72, painted cast iron, sitting on green base, 4x2½" **$35.00**

Grass Skirt Greek, F-43, cast iron, EX......................**$450.00**

Lion head, F-430, cast iron w/gold paint, wall mount, rare..**$2,000.00**

Lobster, F-169, red painted cast iron, 4⅜" L................**$37.50**

Mallard duck on base, painted cast iron, Wilton **$50.00**

Mexican cactus, F-24, multicolor paint on cast iron, man sitting w/head down leaning on cactus, 1954, 2⅞", EX **$460.00**

Monkey, F-89, cast iron w/black & white paint, EX.**$225.00**

Nude atop globe, F-179, chrome, 4½" **$75.00**

Owl, F-127, cast iron w/black paint..........................**$160.00**

Parrot, F-108, multicolor paint on cast iron, marked JW, EX **$60.00**

Pelican, F-129, multicolor paint on cast iron, 3¼", VG ..**$75.00**

Pelican, F-131, orange, white & green paint on cast iron, 3", VG..**$195.00**

Rhino, F-76, chrome on cast iron, marked Japan **$300.00**

Road runner, F-124, pot metal w/copper finish........**$600.00**

Sailor, F-17, multicolor paint on cast iron, holds sign reading Sailor's Ball '56, 1950s, 3¾"......................................**$80.00**

Sailor, F-18, aluminum, painted colors, VG..............**$235.00**

Sea horse, F-142, brass, 3¼x1⅜"..............................**$105.00**

Snake, F-144, steel, 1988, 5¼" L................................**$25.00**

Wagon wheel, N-532, bronze, wall mount, 1987, 3¼x2½" .**$85.00**

Boyd Crystal Art Glass

After the Degenhart glass studio closed (see the Degenhart section for information), it was bought out by the Boyd family, who added many of their own designs to the molds they acquired from the Degenharts and other defunct glasshouses. They are located in Cambridge, Ohio, and the glass they've been pressing in the more than 350 colors they've developed since they opened in 1978 is marked with their 'B in diamond' logo. All the work is done by hand, and each piece is made in a selected color in limited amounts — a production run lasts only about twelve weeks or less. Items in satin glass or an exceptional slag are especially collectible, so are those with hand-painted details, commanding as much as 30% more.

Beware: Boyd has recently re-issued some of the closed issues, confusing the pricing structure as well as collectors!

Airplane, Aqua Diamond, $20.00.

Airplane, Banana Cream Carnival................................**$20.00**

Airplane, Classic Black, 1991 ....**$20.00**

Airplane, Cobalt Blue Carnival, 1992 ....**$20.00**

Angel, Fantasia **$19.00**

Angel, Harvest Gold **$19.00**

Angel, Lemon Custard **$17.00**

Angel, Marshmallow **$17.00**

Angel, Moss Green **$17.00**

Angel, Peacock Blue Carnival................................**$17.00**

Angel, Purple Frost..**$17.00**

Angel #07, Green Bouquet **$17.00**

Baby Shoe, Peacock Blue **$8.00**

Beaded Oval Toothpick, Rubina................................**$15.00**

Bernie Eagle, Cobalt Blue **$10.00**

Bird Salt, Rubina **$12.00**

Bird Salt, Russett Green **$10.00**

Bird Salt, Tomato Creme **$10.00**

Bow Slipper, Alpine Blue **$8.00**

Bow Slipper, Millennium White **$8.00**

Brian Bunny, Peach Lustre................................**$15.00**

Bunny Salt, Alice Blue................................**$25.00**

Bunny Salt, Aqua Diamond **$18.00**

Bunny Salt, Cornsilk **$25.00**

Bunny Salt, Mint Green **$25.00**

Bunny Salt, Pocono Blue **$25.00**

Caprice Box, Heavenly Blue **$22.00**

Cat Slipper, Millennium Surprise **$10.00**

Cat Slipper, Rosie Pink **$9.00**

Daisy & Button Toothpick, Rubina................................**$15.00**

Doberman Head, Dogwood Slag, 1979 ....**$25.00**

Elephant Head Toothpick, Persimmon Slag/Candy Swirl .**$18.00**

Forget-Me-Not Toothpick, Cobalt Blue **$15.00**

Forget-Me-Not Toothpick, Tomato Creme **$15.00**

Hen on Nest Covered Dish, Azure Blue, 3" **$25.00**

Hen on Nest Covered Dish, Budding Pink, 3"...........**$25.00**

Hen on Nest Covered Dish, Caramel Slag, 5" **$45.00**

Hen on Nest Covered Dish, Olde Lyme Green, 3" **$25.00**

JB Scottie, Cornsilk..**$20.00**
JB Scottie, Nutmeg..**$15.00**
Kitten on Pillow, Butterscotch.....................................**$20.00**
Kitten on Pillow, Magic Marble....................................**$15.00**
Kitten on Pillow, Purple Variant...................................**$20.00**
Louise Colonial Lady Doll, Bermuda, hand-painted in White..**$45.00**
Louise Colonial Lady Doll, Holly Green......................**$30.00**
Louise Colonial Lady Doll, Mardi Gras (slag).............**$20.00**
Louise Colonial Lady Doll, Purple Variant...................**$35.00**
Lucky Unicorn, Olde Lyme Green................................**$18.00**
Miss Cotton the Kitten, Cobalt Blue.............................**$15.00**
Miss Cotton the Kitten, Windsor Blue...........................**$15.00**
Nancy, Avocado...**$7.00**
Nancy, Capri Blue..**$8.00**
Nancy, Harvest Gold...**$7.00**
Nancy, Peacock Blue Carnival......................................**$8.00**
Owl, Crown Tuscan..**$15.00**
Owl, Lavender 'n Lace...**$15.00**
Owl, Lemonade...**$15.00**
Pooch, Sandpiper..**$15.00**
Robin Covered Dish, Buckeye Satin, 5".......................**$22.00**
Robin Covered Dish, Vaseline, 5".................................**$18.00**
Robin Covered Dish, Wintergreen Slag, 5"..................**$35.00**
Sammy Squirrel, Cambridge Blue..................................**$10.00**
Sly the Fox, Avocado...**$10.00**
Sly the Fox, Fantasia...**$11.00**
Sports Car, Peacock Blue...**$12.00**
Swan, Aqua Diamond, 3"...**$15.00**
Swan, Thistlebloom, 3"...**$15.00**
Taffy, Avocado...**$16.00**
Taffy, Harvest Gold..**$16.00**
Tractor, Cardinal Red...**$20.00**
Tractor, Cobalt Blue...**$15.00**
Tractor, Vaseline...**$20.00**
Zack the Elephant, Cornsilk...**$20.00**
Zack the Elephant, English Yew....................................**$20.00**
Zack the Elephant, Violet Slate....................................**$20.00**

Boyds Bears and Friends

The cold-cast sculptures designed by Gary M. Lowenthal such as we've listed here have become very dear to the heart of many collectors who enthusiastically pursue his Bearstones, Folkstones, and Dollstones lines, particularly first editions (1Es). Counterfeits do exist. Be sure to watch for the signature bear paw print on Bearstones, the star on Folkstones, and the shoe imprints on the Dollstones. To learn more about the entire line of Boyd's Collectibles, we recommend this Internet price guide: *Rosie's Secondary Market Price Guide to Boyds Bears & Friends*, www.RosieWells.com.

Bearstones, 1993, Bailey w/suitcase, 1E/2000...........**$125.00**
Bearstones, 1993, Clara the Nurse, 2E/2022, MIB.....**$150.00**
Bearstones, 1993, Grenville & Nevil, The Sign, white bottom, #2099..**$35.00**

Bearstones, 1993, Moriarity, in cat suit, original version, 1E/2005...**$215.00**
Bearstones, 1993, Nevil, 4E/2002..............................**$70.00**
Bearstones, 1994, Bailey & Wixie...To Have & To Hold, 4E/2017..**$55.00**
Bearstones, 1994, Maynard the Santa Moose, 11E/1018, MIB...**$45.00**
Bearstones, 1994, Maynard the Santa Moose, 7E/2238..**$50.00**
Bearstones, 1994, Sebastian's Prayer, 1E/39 (R, 1996)...**$90.00**
Bearstones, 1995, Bailey the Baker w/Sweetie Pie, 1E/1763..**$325.00**
Bearstones, 1995, Otis, Tax Time; 14E/2262, MIB......**$35.00**
Bearstones, 1995, Wilson the Wonderful Wizard of Wuz, 11E/2261..**$37.50**
Bearstones, 1996, M Harrison's Birthday, 3E/2275......**$40.00**
Bearstones, 1997, Grace & Jonathan Born To Shop, 5E/228306...**$35.00**
Bearstones, 1998, Elvira & Chauncey Fitzbruin, 1E/95, MIB...**$35.00**
Bearstones, 1998, Margot the Ballerina, regular edition, 2E/227709...**$37.50**
Bearstones, 1998, Serendipity as the Guardian Angel, 1E/2846M (NM box)...**$70.00**
Bearstones, 1999, Gwain Love Is the Master Key, 1E/228317...**$40.00**
Dollstones, Katherine w/Amanda & Edmund, 22E/3505.**$45.00**
Dollstones, 1995, Betsy w/Edmund, 1E/1783, MIB.....**$35.00**
Dollstones, 1996, Candice w/Matthew, 1E/4691, MIB..**$30.00**
Dollstones, 1996, Jennifer w/Priscilla, 1E/4535, MIB..**$30.00**
Dollstones, 1996, Megan w/Elliot & Annie, 1E/3504, MIB..**$30.00**
Dollstones, 1998, Shannon & Wilson, 1E/4230, MIB..**$28.00**
Dollstones, 1999, Melissa w/Katie & Desiree, The Ballet Musical, 1E/272003...**$40.00**
Dollstones, 2000, Afternoon Stroll, 1E/3557...............**$40.00**
Dollstones, 2000, Samantha w/Connor, 1E/3559.........**$24.00**
Folkstones, 1994, Athena the Wedding Angel.............**$22.50**
Folkstones, 1995, Ernest Hemmingmoose, #11E/2835..**$45.00**
Folkstones, 1995, Jan Claude & Jacque the Skiers, 1E/2815..**$20.00**
Folkstones, 1995, Na-Nick of the North.......................**$22.00**
Folkstones, 2000, Sam, Libby & Ellis, 1E/2886...........**$45.00**

Brastoff, Sascha

Who could have predicted when Sascha Brastoff joined the Army's Air Force in 1942 that he was to become a well-known artist! It was during his service with the Air Force that he became interested in costume and scenery design, performing, creating Christmas displays and murals, and drawing war bond posters.

After Sascha's stint in the Armed Forces, he decided to follow his dream of producing ceramics and in 1947 opened a small operation in West Los Angeles, California. Just six years later along with Nelson Rockefeller and several other businessmen with extensive knowledge of mass production techniques he built a pottery on Olympic Boulevard in Los Angeles.

Brastoff designed all the products while supervising approximately 150 people. His talents were so great they enabled him to move with ease from one decade to another and successfully change motifs, mediums, and designs as warranted. Unusual and varying materials were used over the years. He created a Western line that was popular in the 1940s and early 1950s. Just before the poodle craze hit the nation in the 1950s, he had the forsight to introduce his poodle line. The same was true for smoking accessories, and he designed elegant, hand-painted dinnerware as well. He was not modest when it came to his creations. He knew he was talented and was willing to try any new endeavor which was usually a huge success.

Items with the Sascha Brastoff full signature are always popular, and generally they command the highest prices. He modeled obelisks; one with a lid and a full signature would be regarded as a highly desirable example of his work. Though values for his dinnerware are generally lower than for his other productions, it has its own following. The Merbaby design is always high on collectors' lists. An unusual piece was found last year — a figural horse salt shaker, solid white with assorted stars. More than likely it was made as part of a set, possibly the Star Steed pattern. It was marked 'Sascha' under the glaze between the front legs.

The 1940 Clay Club pieces were signed either with a full signature or 'Sascha.' In 1947 Sascha hired a large group of artists to hand decorate his designs, and 'Sascha B' became the standard mark. Following the opening of his studio in 1953, a chanticleer, the name Sascha Brastoff, the copyright symbol, and a hand-written style number (all in gold) were used on the bottom, with 'Sascha B.' on the front or topside of the item. (Be careful not to confuse this mark with a full signature, California, U.S.A.). Costume designs at 20th Century Fox (1946 – 47) were signed 'Sascha'; war bonds and posters also carried the signature 'Sascha' and 'Pvt.' or 'Sgt. Brastoff.'

After Brastoff left his company in 1962, the mark became a 'R' in a circle (registered trademark symbol) with a style number, all handwritten. The chanticleer may also accompany this mark. Brastoff died on February 4, 1993. For additional information consult *The Collector's Encyclopedia of Sascha Brastoff* by Steve Conti, A. DeWayne Bethany, and Bill Seay. Another source of information is *The Collector's Encyclopedia of California Pottery (Second Edition)* by Jack Chipman. Both are published by Collector Books.

Advisor: Lonnie Wells (See Directory, Brastoff)

Ashtray, Abstract, free-form, #F-2, 8" L **$40.00**
Ashtray, orange, gold & green design, free-form, #C-30 ...**$60.00**
Bowl, Aztec (or Mayan), floral, 3-footed, 2¼x7¾x5½"..**$45.00**
Bowl, Aztec (or Mayan), free-form, rooster mark, 3x9x6"..**$95.00**
Bowl, Mosaic, free-form, rooster mark, #M21, 2½x4"..**$35.00**
Bowl, Star Steed, 3-footed sunfish shape, #C-14, 2½x9¾x8½" **$110.00**
Box, fruit & leaves on brown, Sascha B on top of lid, 5" L...**$60.00**
Box, Minos, 9" L, NM **$95.00**

Box, Mosaic, dog finial, 6½" sq, NM **$165.00**
Cache pot, petal-like design w/dark greens, pinks, mauves, black & white..**$65.00**
Cigarette holder, Jewel Bird, pipe form, w/gold trim, 3½x5½"..**$50.00**
Dish, Aztec (or Mayan), #03, rooster mark, 5½" sq....**$38.00**
Dish, Aztec (or Mayan), #03B, rooster mark, 7" sq.....**$50.00**
Dish, Jewel Bird, free-form, #F42, 10" dia **$85.00**
Dish, Rooftops, #C-8, rooster mark, 2¾x13x6"..........**$95.00**
Dish, Star Steed, 7½" sq...**$65.00**
Humidor, Abstract, stainless steel lid, #F-20, rare, 6½"..**$65.00**
Plate, Chi Chi Bird, 8½" **$100.00**
Plate, dinner; Golden Classic **$90.00**
Shell dish, gold & white drip accents, #S-52, NM.......**$65.00**
Vase, Aztec (or Mayan), gold horse, #066, 5½x8½" ..**$125.00**
Vase, elk, #082, 8"..**$75.00**
Vase, gold & white rings w/white drip-like design, cylindrical, #V-3, 12" **$125.00**
Vase, Rooftops, cylindrical, #047, 8½" **$115.00**
Vase, Totem Pole, #082, 8"...**$75.00**
Vase, Vanity Fair, #F24, 10x5" **$155.00**
Vase, walrus, brown & gray, #082, 8" **$75.00**
Vases, gold leaves on white w/yellow speckles, sq sides, 9¼", pr...**$265.00**
Wall pocket, Provincial Rooster, #P-1, 4x5" **$95.00**

Brayton Laguna

This company's products have proven to be highly collectible for those who appreciate their well-made, diversified items, some bordering on the whimsical. Durlin Brayton founded Brayton Laguna Pottery in 1927. The marriage between Durlin and Ellen (Webb) Webster Grieve a few years later created a partnership that brought together two talented people with vision and knowledge so broad that they were able to create many unique lines. At the height of Brayton's business success, the company employed over 125 workers and 20 designers.

Durlin's personally created items command a high price. Such items are hand turned, and those that were made from 1927 to 1930 are often incised 'Laguna Pottery' in Durlin's handwriting. These include cups, saucers, plates of assorted sizes, ashtrays, etc., glazed in eggplant, lettuce green, purple, and deep blue as well as other colors. Brayton Laguna's children's series (created by Lietta J. Dodd) has always been favored among collectors. However, many lines such as Calasia (artware), Blackamoors, sculpture, and the Hillbilly line are picking up large followings of their own. The sculptures, Indian and Peruvian pieces including voodoo figures, matadors, and drummers, among others, were designed by Carol Safholm. Andy Anderson created the Hillbilly series, most notably the highly successful shotgun wedding group. He also created the calf, bull, and cow set, which is virtually always found in the purple glaze, though very rarely other colors have been reported as well. Webton Ware is a good line for those who want inexpensive pottery and a Brayton

Laguna mark. These pieces depict farmland and country-type themes such as farmers planting, women cooking, etc. Some items — wall pockets, for instance — may be found with only a flower motif; wall hangings of women and men are popular, yet hard to find in this or any of Brayton's lines. Predominantly, the background of Webton Ware is white, and it's decorated with various pastel glazes including yellow, green, pink, and blue.

More than ten marks plus a paper label were used during Brayton's history. On items too small for a full mark, designers would simply incise their initials. Webb Brayton died in 1948, and Durlin died just three years later. Struggling with and finally succumbing to the effect of the influx of foreign pottery on the American market, Brayton Laguna finally closed in 1968.

For further study, read *The Collector's Encyclopedia of California Pottery (Second Edition)* by Jack Chipman (Collector Books).

See also Cookie Jars.

Advisor: Lee Garmon (See Directory, Elvis Presley Memorabilia)

Candle holder, Blackamoor, sitting on blue rug, 5", from $75 to **$90.00**
Figurine, donkey & cart, ceramic & wood, donkey: 6x4", cart: 10" L...**$125.00**
Figurine, Figaro (cat), begging, 3½".........................**$110.00**
Figurine, fox, late 1930s, 4x4".................................**$85.00**
Figurine, Gay Nineties Bar, 3 men posing, 8½x7½".**$110.00**
Figurine, Gay Nineties series, Bedtime, couple in night clothes, 8¾"...**$150.00**

Figurine, Gay Nineties series, Seashore Honeymoon, 9", from $100.00 to $125.00.

Figurine, lady w/basket, lavender dress, hat over arm, 8½"..**$80.00**
Figurine, lady w/wolfhounds, ca 1943, 11"...............**$120.00**
Figurine, Matilda, holds 2 planter baskets by strap across shoulder, 1930-37, 7⅝"...**$100.00**
Figurine, Pluto, howling, 6".....................................**$125.00**

Figurine, Pluto, sniffing, 3½".....................................**$100.00**
Figurine, Purple Cow family: cow, calf & bull (6"), from $350 to...**$450.00**
Figurine, Sambo, 7¾"...**$300.00**
Figurines, Zizi & Fifi, pr, NM....................................**$495.00**
Flower holder, Sally, 7½"..**$40.00**
Planter, Blackamoor kneeling, NM............................**$125.00**
Salt & pepper shakers, peasant couple, marked, pr...**$57.50**
Vase, hat form w/pink roses & blue ribbon, 1943, 3x4"..**$30.00**

Breweriana

Breweriana refers to items produced by breweries which are intended for immediate use and discard, such as beer cans and bottles, as well as countless items designed for long-term use while promoting a particular brand. Desirable collectibles include metal, cardboard, and neon signs; serving trays; glassware; tap handles; mirrors; coasters; and other paper goods.

Breweriana is generally divided into two broad categories: pre- and postprohibition. Preprohibition breweries were numerous and distributed advertising trays, calendars, etched glassware and other items. Because American breweries were founded by European brewmasters, preprohibition advertising often depicted themes from that region. Brewery scenes, pretty women, and children were also common.

Competition was intense among the breweries that survived prohibition. The introduction of canned beer in 1935, the postwar technology boom, and the advent of television in the late 1940s produced countless new ways to advertise beer. Moving signs, can openers, enameled glasses, and neon are prolific examples of postprohibition breweriana.

A better understanding of the development of the product as well as advertising practices of companies helps in evaluating the variety of breweriana items that may be found. For example, 'chalks' are figural advertising pieces which were made for display in taverns or wherever beer was sold. Popular in the 1940s and 1950s, they were painted and glazed to resemble carnival prizes. Breweries realized in addition to food shopping, women generally assumed the role of cook — what better way to persuade women to buy a particular beer than a cookbook? Before the advent of the bottle cap in the early 1900s, beer bottles were sealed with a porcelain stopper or cork. Opening a corked bottle required a corkscrew which often had a brewery logo.

Prior to the advent of refrigeration, beer was often served at room temperature. A mug or glass was often half warm beer and half foam. A 1" by 8" flat piece of plastic was used to scrape foam from the glass. These foam scrapers came in various colors and bore the logo of the beer on tap.

Before prohibition, beer logos were applied to glassware by etching the glass with acid. These etched glasses often had ornate designs that included a replica of the actual brewery or a bust of the brewery's founder. After prohibition, enameling became popular and glasses were generally 'painted' with less ornate designs. Mugs featuring beer advertising date back to the 1800s in America; preprohibition versions were generally made of pottery or glass. Ceramic mugs became popular after prohibition and remain widely produced today.

Tap handles are a prominent way to advertise a particular brand wherever tap beer is sold. Unlike today's ornate handles, 'ball knobs' were prominent prior to the 1960s. They were about the size of a billiard ball with a flat face that featured a colorful beer logo.

See also Bar Ware; Beer Cans.

Club: Beer Can Collectors of America
747 Merus Ct., Fenton, MO 63026
Annual dues: $27; although the club's roots are in beer can collecting, this organization offers a bimonthly breweriana magazine featuring many regional events and sponsors an annual convention; www.bcca.com

Baseball cap, Rolling Rock Light, mesh back, cloth patch, Latrobe Brewing Co, Latrobe PA, M **$10.00**
Book, Beer Poster Book, Will Anderson, copyright 1977, 11x16", EX **$95.00**
Buckle, belt; Budweiser, solid brass, Tiffany type, w/belt ring & clip on back, EX **$45.00**
Clock, Bud Light, neon, 19" dia, EX **$175.00**

Clock, Duquensne Beer, reverse-painted glass with metal housing, lights up, 19x25x5½", EX, $425.00. (Photo courtesy Collectors Auction Service)

Coaster, Atlantic Tavern Pale, red & white printed pressed paper, Atlantic Brewing Co, Chicago IL, modern...**$7.00**
Coaster, Blue Bonnet Lady, pressed paper, 2-sided, Pabst Brewing Co, Milwaukee WI, 4¼" dia, EX.............**$5.00**
Coaster, Cream Ale - Pilsner Beer, pressed paper, Louis F Neuweiler's Sons, Allentown PA, 4" sq, NM **$6.00**
Coaster, Hamm's Beer, w/bear, blue & white pressed paper, St Paul MN, 3" sq **$5.00**
Coaster, Hanley's, metal, 3" dia, M **$20.00**
Coaster, Jos Schlitz Old Milwaukee, red & white pressed paper, Milwaukee WI, 3" dia.......................**$2.50**

Coaster, Powder Horn Blended Whiskey, pressed paper, Hartford Conn, 4" dia **$5.00**
Coaster, Schaefer Fine Beer, pressed paper, F&M Schaefer Brewing, New York NY, 4¼" dia, NM.....................**$4.00**
Cooler, Falstaff, red & white painted aluminum, w/original opener & ice pick mounted in lid, G...................**$30.00**
Cooler, Storz, red & white enamel on metal, 16x21x10", VG **$65.00**
Counter, Alley's & Pfaff's Beer, New Bedford & NE League Official baseball schedule, preprohibition, EX...**$175.00**
Crate, Cold Spring Ales, 1930s – 1940s, EX................**$36.00**
Crate, Suffolk Brewing Co, Boston Mass, preprohibition, EX **$47.50**
Crown cap, Bavaria's Beer, red, white & black..........**$10.00**
Crown cap, Dawson's Ale, red & yellow.....................**$15.00**
Crown cap, Frankenmuth Beer, red w/white lettering .**$7.50**
Crown cap, Jacob Ruppert Knickerbocker Beer, red & white **$5.00**
Crown cap, Old Dutch Beer, red & white **$8.00**
Drinking glass, Reuter Pilsner Beer, Boston MA, clear glass w/white lettering, footed, preprohibition, M......**$120.00**
Foam scraper, Rheingold, white, NM **$25.00**
Foam scraper, Schaefer, red, M.................................**$25.00**
Foam scraper, white blank...**$12.00**
Hat, Old Schmidt's, paper, C Schmidt & Sons, Philadelphia PA, 1960s, NM..**$15.00**
Letterhead, El Dorado Brewing Valley Brew, Stockton CA, 1913, 5½x8", NM..**$15.00**
Match cover, Stegmaier, can & bottle, Stegmaier Brewing, Wilkes-Barre PA, NM **$5.00**
Menu, Reingold, chalk board, early, 15x18", EX.........**$75.00**
Menu, Rubsam & Horrmann Beer & Ale, New York NY, ca 1940, 11x7", NM..**$12.00**
Mug, Alley's Ale, Boston MA, embossed metal, preprohibition, EX+ **$175.00**
Mug, Anheuser-Busch, AB logo, no date or marks, M .**$35.00**
Mug, cobalt & gray stoneware w/stylized vine decor, Wick-Werke, ca 1937, 5¾", M..................................**$70.00**
Mug, Hamm's Bear, Octoberfest, Ceramart 1973, M ...**$45.00**
Mug, pewter, gun handle w/barrel stub protruding opposite side, Wilton **$50.00**
Mug, Reingold, plastic, M...**$7.00**
Pete's Wicked Mardi Gras, Lucite, 2-sided, Pete's Brewing, Palo Alto CA, 10", NM..**$20.00**
Pocket calendar, Pabst, advertising the Eddie Canter show on NBC, 1947, NM..**$10.00**
Pocketknife, Stroh's Beer, red on yellow plastic, 3½", EX...**$25.00**
Print, Pearl Brewing, Take a Shot at JR, glossy paper, 1980, 14½x20", NM..**$254.00**
Register lamp, Blatz Milwaukee, plastic & metal, working, 8x9" **$75.00**
Sign, Ballantine Ale, bottle & lovely lady, cardboard standup, 1969, 10¾x14", NM..**$30.00**
Sign, Black Horse Beer, tin over cardboard, easel back, Black Horse Brewery, Lawrence MA, 1960s, 10¼x11¾", EX .**$20.00**
Sign, Drink Wagner's Augustiner Special, red, white & green printed paper, 1920s, 8½x12", EX **$35.00**

Sign, Hampden New England's Favorite Ale, printer's proof for diecut, c 1947, 19x12½" +frame, M **$75.00**

Sign, Iron City Beer, barbershop quartet, plastic w/cardboard back, easel stand, 3-D, 15½x9", VG **$40.00**

Sign, Miller Genuine Draft, neon, bright colors, 32x34", NM **$200.00**

Sign, Miller High Life, light in metal case, 9x27", EX..**$75.00**

Sign, Rolling Rock, Northern Dancer, Kentucky Derby winner, pressed board w/cardboard stand, 1964, 11x14", NM **$37.50**

Sign, Stegmaier Wilkes Barre Plastic, plastic & paper, 11x9", NM **$55.00**

Stein, Anheuser-Busch, Birds of Prey, Germany, 1991, M..**$100.00**

Stein, Anheuser-Busch, Ceramarte, Brew House, Collector's Club Members only, 2000, 10", MIB.................**$75.00**

Stein, Anheuser-Busch, Ceramarte, Faust, American Originals Series, limited edition, MIB..................................**$120.00**

Stein, Anheuser-Busch, Ceramarte, International Association of Chiefs of Police 100th Anniversary, 1993, 5½", M....**$85.00**

Stein, Anheuser-Busch, Ceramarte, Owl, Birds of Prey series, pewter lid w/eagle finial, 10½", M **$85.00**

Stein, Anheuser-Busch, Ceramarte, 1996 collector's club member, Brazil, M **$100.00**

Stein, F Hollender & Co Brewery, NY & Chicago, preprohibition, M **$150.00**

Stein, Falstaff International Museum of Brewing, 1971, w/paper hang tag & descriptions, 10¾", M........**$125.00**

Stein, Mettlach #1526, Princeton, preprohibition, .5 litre, M **$185.00**

Stein, Mettlach #2900, Quilmes Brewery Argentina, preprohibition, M **$375.00**

Stein, Mettlach 31997, George Ehrets Brewery, preprohibition, M **$335.00**

Tap handle, Blitz Weinhard Beer, wood w/metal insert 1 side, Blitz-Weinhard Brewery, Portland OR, 1970s, 14", EX.**$20.00**

Tap handle, Coors Light, ball style, 7", NM **$18.00**

Tap handle, Coors Light, decal on painted wood, Adolph Coors Brewing, Golden CO, 11¼", NM **$20.00**

Tap handle, Killian's Red, horse head in shamrock, Lucite, 2-sided, Coors Brewing Co, Golden CO, 8½", NM .**$20.00**

Tap handle, Miller Lite, golf theme, wood & plastic, 2-sided, Miller Brewing, Milwaukee WI, M.......................**$20.00**

Tap handle, Pig's Eye Pilsner, composition pirate head figural, 3-sided plastic decal inserts, 11½", NM **$50.00**

Tap handle, red decal on painted wood, Anheuser-Busch, St Louis MO, 2-sided, 11¼", M...................................**$20.00**

Tap handle, Sonoma Mountain Amber Lager, black painted wood w/plastic decaled shield, Sonoma Mountain Brewery, 11¼"..**$22.00**

Tap handle, Stroh's Beer, red & yellow Lucite, 2-sided, Stroh Brewing Co, Detroit MI, 4½", NM **$12.50**

Tap knob, Busch Beer, Lucite, 2-sided, Anheuser-Busch, St Louis MO, NM **$6.00**

Tap knob, Molson Golden, Lucite, 2-sided, Molson Brewing, Canada, 5 34/", NM..**$5.00**

Tip tray, Miller Brewing, lady on moon, 1950s, 6½x4½", NM **$20.00**

Tray, Blatz, bottle-man waiter, Blatz Brewing, Milwaukee WI, 1964, 13" dia, NM **$40.00**

Tray, Eagle Monarch Ale, bottle on wood-grain look, Eagle Brewing, Utica NY, light rust, 12" dia, VG..........**$145.00**

Tray, Ebling Extra, Christy Girl, Ebling Brewing Co, New York NY, 1934, 13" dia, VG **$125.00**

Tray, Esslinger's, sm waiter, white background, yellow trim, 1950s, 13" dia, EX..**$30.00**

Tray, Esslinger's Ale, winking Red Cap serving, multicolor on yellow, 1940s, 12" dia, NM **$140.00**

Tray, Fox Head 400, stylized fox head, Waukesha WI, 1950s, 13" dia, EX...**$75.00**

Tray, G Heileman Brewing, 5 factory scenes 1977 commemorative, 13" dia, EX...**$17.50**

Tray, Knickerbocker, standing patriot, Jacob Ruppert, New York NY, 1950s, 12" dia, EX................................**$17.50**

Tray, Muehlebach Pilsner Serve the Finest, Geo Muehlebach Brewing, Kansas City MO, 1940s, 13" dia, NM.....**$70.00**

Tray, Old Stock Ale, red & white, Philadelphia Brewing, 1930s, 12" dia, NM...**$160.00**

Tray, Pabst Blue Ribbon, ribbon w/hops & barley wreath, Pabst Brewing Co, Milwaukee WI, 1970s, 12½x15" oval, NM **$27.50**

Tray, Pabst Blue Ribbon Blended 33 to 1, light & dark blue, 1950s, 13" dia, NM **$35.00**

Tray, Ruppert Knickerbocker Beer, Colonial Man, 13" dia, EX **$18.00**

Tray, Schlitz Beer, circles & sqs encircle logo on white, 1968, 12" dia, NM **$25.00**

Tray, Simon Pure, red & white, William Simon Brewery, Buffalo NY, 13" dia, EX **$17.50**

Tray mat, Genesee Beer, lady holds tray w/glass, lake beyond, 10¾" dia, NM..**$15.00**

Breyer Horses

Breyer horses have been popular children's playthings since they were introduced in 1952, and you'll see several at any large flea market. Garage sales are good sources as well. The earlier horses had a glossy finish, but after 1968 a matt finish came into use. You'll find smaller domestic animals too. They are evaluated by condition, rarity, and desirability; some of the better examples may be worth a minimum of $150.00. Our values are for average condition; examples in mint condition are worth from 10% to 15% more.

For more information and listings, see *Schroeder's Collectible Toys, Antique to Modern*, and *Breyer Animal Collector's Guide* by Felicia Browell. (Both are published by Collector Books.)

Adios (Best Tango Quarter Horse), shaded bay, Traditional scale, 1997 ....**$30.00**

Andalusian Mare (Sears), alabaster, Classic scale, 1984 .**$20.00**

Arabian Foal, chestnut, Classic scale, 1973-82.............**$13.00**

Arabian Mare, bay, Stablemate scale, 1975-88...............**$9.00**

Arabian Stallion, bay, Stablemate scale, 1975-88.........**$10.00**

Belgian, chestnut, Traditional scale, 1965-80 .... **$40.00**

Black Stallion (Black Stallion Returns Set), black, Classic scale, 1983-93 .... **$15.00**

Bucking Bronco, black, Classic scale, 1966-73 & 1975-76.. **$42.00**

Citation, bay, Stablemate scale, 1975-81 .... **$8.00**

Clydesdale Foal, chestnut, Traditional scale, 1969-89 . **$18.00**

Cutting Horse, bay w/black points, Classic scale, 1997-99 (w/out calf) **$22.00**

Duchess (Black Beauty Family), bay w/points, Classic scale, 1980-93 .... **$15.00**

El Pastor Paso Fino, bay w/black points, Traditional scale, 1974-81 .... **$35.00**

Family Arabian Mare, wood-grain, Traditional scale, 1963-67 .... **$65.00**

Five-Gaiter (American Saddlebred), dapple gray, black & red ribbons, Traditional scale, 1987-88 .... **$65.00**

Foundation Stallion (Azteca), dapple gray, Traditional scale, 1980-87 .... **$35.00**

Fury Prancer, wood-grain, Traditional scale, 1958-62 . **$350.00**

Ginger (Toys R Us/Sweet Memories), brown appaloosa, Classic scale, 1997 .... **$20.00**

Grazing Foal, palomino, Traditional scale, 1964-81 .... **$28.00**

Hanoverian, dark bay w/black points, Traditional scale, 1980-84 .... **$35.00**

Indian Pony, dark bay appaloosa w/black points, Traditional scale, 1973-85 .... **$35.00**

Johar (Toys R Us/Drinkers of the Wind), rose gray, Classic scale, 1993 .... **$18.00**

John Henry (JC Penney/Cowboy Pride Three-Piece Horse Set), bay roan, Traditional scale, 1998 .... **$25.00**

Keen (Equestrian Team Gift Set), chestnut, Classic scale, 1980-93 .... **$15.00**

Khemosabi, red bay w/black points, Traditional scale, 1990-95 .... **$28.00**

Lady Phase (Breezing Dixie Appaloosa Mare), dark bay w/white blanket, limited edition, Traditional scale, 1988......... **$65.00**

Legionario III, alabaster, Traditional scale **$30.00**

Man O'War, red chestnut, Classic scale, 1975-90 .... **$20.00**

Merrylegs (Black Beauty Family), dapple gray, Classic scale, 1980-93 .... **$15.00**

Morganglanz, chestnut, Traditional scale, 1980-87 ...... **$28.00**

Old Timer, alabaster (w/hat), Traditional scale, 1966-76.. **$50.00**

Pace, Dan Patch, red bay w/black points, Traditional scale, 1990 .... **$45.00**

Polo Pony, bay w/black points, 1976-82 .... **$40.00**

Proud Arabian Foal, glossy alabaster, Traditional scale, 1956-60 .... **$28.00**

Proud Arabian Stallion (Sundown), sorrel, Traditional scale, 1995-96 .... **$30.00**

Quarter Horse Foal (Quarter Horse Family), light bay w/black points, Classic scale, 1974-93 .... **$12.00**

Quarter Horse Gelding, buckskin w/black points, Traditional scale, 1961-80 .... **$45.00**

Quarter Horse Stallion, palomino, Stablemate scale, 1976-88 .... **$9.00**

Quarter Horse Yearling, sandy bay blanket appaloosa, Traditional scale, 1971-88 .... **$40.00**

Rearing Stallion, bay w/black points, Classic scale, 1965-80 .... **$25.00**

Roemer (Toys R Us/Sandstone), light bay, Traditional scale, 1998 .... **$40.00**

Running Foal, smoke w/white points, Traditional scale, 1963-70 .... **$32.00**

Running Mare, wood-grain, Traditional scale, 1963-65 . **$150.00**

San Domingo, chestnut pinto, Traditional scale, 1978-87 .. **$35.00**

Sham, red bay, Traditional scale, 1984 – 1988, $45.00. (Photo courtesy Carol Karbowiak Gilbert)

Shetland Pony, bay w/black points, Traditional scale, 1973-88 .... **$20.00**

Silky Sullivan, brown w/darker mane & tail, Classic scale, 1975-90 .... **$18.00**

Stock Horse Stallion (Tobiano Pinto), black, Traditional scale, 1981-88 .... **$28.00**

Swamps (Hawk), black, Classic scale, 1991 .... **$18.00**

Thoroughbred Mare, black, Stablemate scale, 1975-88 .. **$8.00**

Thoroughbred Mare, dark chestnut bay, Traditional Scale, #3155, 1973 – 1984, $50.00. (Photo courtesy Carol Karbowiak Gilbert)

Thoroughbred Mare (JC Penney Pride & Joy), light chestnut, Traditional scale, 1998 .... **$32.00**

Touch of Class, bay w/black points, Traditional scale, 1986-88 ....$30.00

Western Pony, palomino, w/saddle, Traditional scale, 1968-73 ....$28.00

Other Animals

Black Angus Bull, standing, black, 1978-current.........$20.00

Cow (Holstein), black & white, 1972-89.....................$25.00

Elephant, battleship gray, w/out boy...........................$65.00

Kitten, gray-point Siamese, 1966-71 ....$50.00

Moose, med brown, 1966-96 ....$25.00

Pronghorn Antelope, 1971-76 ....$65.00

Rin-Tin-Tin, brown, 1958-66 ....$40.00

Texas Longhorn Bull, sorrel, 1961-89.........................$25.00

British Royal Commemoratives

While seasoned collectors may prefer the older pieces using 1840 (Queen Victoria's reign) as their starting point, even present-day souvenirs make a good inexpensive beginning collection. Ceramic items, glassware, metalware, and paper goods have been issued on the occasion of weddings, royal tours, birthdays, christenings, and many other celebrations. Food tins are fairly easy to find, and range in price from about $30.00 to around $75.00 for those made since the 1950s.

We've all seen that items related to Princess Diana have appreciated rapidly since her untimely and tragic demise, and in fact collections are being built exclusively from memorabilia marketed both before and after her death. For more information, we recommend *British Royal Commemoratives* by Audrey Zeder.

Advisor: Audrey Zeder (See Directory, British Royalty Commemoratives)

Plate, Royal Wedding Bouquet, Commemorating the Marriage of His Royal Highness The Prince of Wales to Lady Diana Spencer, 29th July, 1981, Royal Doulton, $45.00.

Album, Royal Family by Panini, completely filled, 1984 ....$50.00

Beaker, Charles/Diana wedding, footed base, black w/24k portrait & decor, Prinknash...................................$55.00

Beer mat, pub; Elizabeth II, 1977, cardboard, 4x4" $5.00

Book, The Queen & Princess Anna, Lisa Sheridan, 1959, hardback..$25.00

Bookmark, Charles/Diana wedding, white leather w/gold portrait & decor $25.00

Bookmark, Prince Edward wedding, white leather w/gold decor, 9x1½" $15.00

Bottle, beer; Charles/Diana 1981 wedding, George Gale & Company, empty...$25.00

Bowl, Charles/Diana wedding, black & white portrait, multi-color heart decor, ⅞"x5½..............................$35.00

Calendar, Elizabeth II coronation, perpetual standup, multi-color portrait, 7x5" $45.00

Coin, Princess Diana, 1999 5-pound, special pack, Royal Mint..$30.00

Cup & saucer, Princess Diana memorial, multicolor portrait & decor...$40.00

Dish, memorial, Princess Diana, iridescent glass, 3½" ...$30.00

Doll, Princess Diana, multicolor cardboard doll w/magnetic dresses, 1997 ....$20.00

Egg cup, Elizabeth II 2002 Jubilee, black silhouette, footed...$15.00

Ephemera, Elizabeth II 1977 Jubilee paper plate, blue w/Jubilee insignia $5.00

Horse brass, Charles/Diana wedding, embossed portrait & decor on brass $35.00

Jewelry, Princess Diana earrings, multicolor portrait, silver-tone bezel...$35.00

Magazine, Observer, Elizabeth II 1983 visit to California, 3-13-83 ....$30.00

Medallion, Charles/Diana wedding, relief portrait, gilded, velvet case, 1¾" $50.00

Medallion, Princess Elizabeth 1947 wedding, pot metal, 1⅝" $50.00

Miniature, photo album of 1982 royal family, 1¼x2" .$35.00

Mug, Charles/Diana wedding, shaded blue portrait/decor, straight sides, Spode...$75.00

Mug, Charles/Diana 1981 wedding, black portrait in red heart frame, stoneware...$25.00

Mug, Elizabeth II 1972 wedding anniversary, multicolor decor, footed, Aynsley...$65.00

Mug, Elizabeth II 2002 Jubilee, multicolor Queen portrait on maroon $20.00

Mug, Prince William 1997 confirmation, multicolor portrait & decor, limited edition 80 ....$125.00

Mug, Princess Diana memorial, multicolor portrait, rose decor, bone china, Nelson $35.00

Mug, Princess Diana 30th birthday, multicolor portrait & decor, limited edition of 5,000, Aynsley..............$150.00

Newspaper, Princess Diana memorial, The Sun, 9-1-97..$20.00

Novelty, Charles/Diana wedding foil sticker, multicolor decor, 5½x5"...$6.00

Novelty, Elizabeth II coronation pocketknife, multicolor decor, 5x2½" $45.00

Novelty, Princess Diana memorial tree ornament, glass sphere, multicolor portrait..............................**$15.00**

Photograph, Princess Elizabeth & Margaret, black & white, 7½x6"..**$50.00**

Pin-back button, Charles/Diana wedding, black & white portrait, red, white & blue trim, 1½" **$15.00**

Pitcher, Elizabeth II coronation, treacle w/embossed tan portrait & decor, 4"..................................**$45.00**

Plate, Charles/Diana wedding, multicolor portrait, embossed design on rim, 9½" **$65.00**

Plate, Charles/Diana 1981 wedding, multicolor portrait & decor, green border, 8½" **$45.00**

Plate, Princess Diana 1987 memorial, black portrait & decor, LE 125, 7½" **$45.00**

Postcard, Elizabeth II 2002 Jubilee, Queen portrait+5 previous monarchs **$5.00**

Postcard, Princess Diana 1977 memorial, multicolor portrait, WPI, boxed set of 12.................**$25.00**

Postcard, Princess Margaret 2002 Memorial, multicolor portrait, doves & rose....................**$5.00**

Postcard, Queen Mother 2000 Millennium Queen, multicolor portrait & family tree **$5.00**

Pressed glass, Charles/Diana wedding plate, portrait & decor on lavender, 3½"....................**$30.00**

Print, Elizabeth II, multicolor portrait w/Corgi dogs, 11¾x8½"...............................**$12.00**

Puzzle, Elizabeth II, multicolor collage coronation tins, 247-pcs, 11x17" **$25.00**

Scrapbook, Charles/Diana wedding, silver w/blue decor, unused, 12x9½" **$45.00**

Spoon, Diana, multicolor portrait w/tiara, silver plate, ca 1982 ....**$25.00**

Spoon, King George VI, relief portrait/decor, 4¼" **$30.00**

Teapot, Elizabeth II 2002 Jubilee, head shape, gold crown, 8" **$95.00**

Teapot, Queen Mother's 90th birthday, multicolor portrait wearing yellow, bone china, 2-cup......**$75.00**

Thimble, Charles/Diana wedding, blue Prince of Wales feather design, Highland, MIB **$35.00**

Thimble, Elizabeth II 2002 Jubilee, young Queen portrait, multicolor decor........................**$6.00**

Tin, Charles/Diana wedding, multicolor portrait & decor on cream, 4¼x3x3".....................**$35.00**

Tin, Charles/Diana wedding, pastel multicolor portrait & decor, Jameson, 9x2½" **$45.00**

Tin, George VI coronation, multicolor portrait & decor, octagonal, 5x4"........................**$40.00**

Tin, Queen Elizabeth Coronation, full-face portrait, 7"..**$25.00**

Towel, Elizabeth II 2002 Jubilee, Queen portrait, multicolor guards **$10.00**

Tray, Charles/Diana wedding, multicolor portrait/royal residences, 14x14".......................**$50.00**

Tray, Charles/Diana wedding, multicolor portrait & decor, light blue border, 19x12" **$55.00**

Trinket box, George VI Canada visit, footed, w/lid, Adams **$75.00**

Brock of California

This was the trade name of the B.J. Brock Company, located in Lawndale, California. They operated from 1947 until 1980, and some of the dinnerware lines they produced have become desirable collectibles. One of the most common themes revolved around country living, farmhouses, barns, chickens, and cows. Patterns were Rooster, California Farmhouse, and California Rustic. Shapes echoed the same concept — there were skillets, milk cans, and flatirons fashioned into sugar bowls, creamers, and salt and pepper shakers. The company marketed a three-piece children's set as well. Also look for their '50s modern line called Manzanita, with pink and charcoal branches on platinum. With interest in this style of dinnerware on the increase, this should be one to watch.

Bowl, California Farmhouse, 6¾" **$5.00**

Bowl, California Farmhouse, 10¾".............................**$20.00**

Bowl, Forever Yours, 8¾" **$24.00**

Bowl, salad; California Farmhouse, 3-footed, 7x10½" ..**$20.00**

Butter dish, California Farmhouse, shaped like flatiron, green handle, 9" L **$42.50**

Canister, tea; California Farmhouse, wooden lid, 5½x4¼x3¼"...**$45.00**

Casserole, French; California Farmhouse, w/rooster, 3x8½" dia w/5" handle **$45.00**

Coffeepot, California Farmhouse, with rooster, 9½", from $60.00 to $70.00.

Condiment set, California Farmhouse, w/rooster, set of 4 w/original lids & spoons.....................**$40.00**

Creamer & sugar bowl, California Farmhouse, w/rooster, w/lid **$22.50**

Cup & saucer, California Farmhouse.........................**$12.00**

Dish, palm tree, water & birds, cream w/misty rose edge, 4½x8½"...**$35.00**

Egg cup, California Farmhouse, chicken on fence, 3½"....**$25.00**

Gravy boat, Forever Yours...**$20.00**

Mug, coffee; Forever Yours, 3¼" $16.00
Plate, California Farmhouse, w/rooster, 6¾" $5.00
Plate, California Farmhouse, 11" $15.00
Plate, Forever Yours, 10¾" $15.00
Platter, California Farmhouse, w/rooster, 11" $17.50
Platter, California Farmhouse, 14¼x9¼" $22.50
Platter, Forever Yours, 13½x17¼" $40.00
Salt & pepper shakers, California Farmhouse, w/rooster, 2¾",
    pr $15.00
Saucepan, California Farmhouse, w/lid, 7¼" dia $25.00
Tray, serving; California Farmhouse, 13" dia $25.00
Tray, tidbit; California Farmhouse, 3-tiered w/metal stem,
    13½" tall...$45.00

Bubble Bath Containers

There's no hotter area of collecting today than items from the '50s through the '70s that are reminiscent of kids' early TV shows and hit movies, and bubble bath containers fill the bill. Most of these were made in the 1960s. The Colgate-Palmolive Company produced the majority of them — they're the ones marked 'Soaky' — and these seem to be the most collectible. Each character's name is right on the bottle. Other companies followed suit; Purex also made a line, so did Avon. Be sure to check for paint loss, and look carefully for cracks in the brittle plastic heads of the Soakies. Our values are for examples in excellent to near mint condition.

For more information, we recommend *Schroeder's Collectible Toys, Antique to Modern* (published by Collector Books).

Advisors: Matt and Lisa Adams (See Directory, Bubble Bath Containers)

Alvin (Chipmunks), Colgate-Palmolive, white A on red sweater, w/puppet, neck tag & contents, M.........$50.00
Alvin (Chipmunks), DuCair Bioscence, holding microphone, w/contents, M $25.00
Atom Ant, Purex, 1965, NM $70.00
Baba Looey, Purex, 1960s, brown w/blue scarf & green hat, NM $35.00
Baba Looey, Roclar (Purex), 1977, NM......................$15.00
Bamm-Bamm, Purex, black or green suspenders, NM, ea...$35.00
Barney, Kid Care, 1994, yellow hat & puppy slippers, NM $8.00
Barney Rubble, Roclar (Purex), brown outfit w/yellow accents, MIB $25.00
Batman, Colgate-Palmolive, 1966, NM $75.00
Batmobile, Avon, 1978, blue & silver w/decals, EX....$20.00
Beauty & the Beast, Cosrich, original tag, M, ea from $5 to $8.00
Betty Bubbles, Lander, 1960s, NM.............................$15.00
Bozo the Clown, Colgate-Palmolive, 1960s, NM $30.00
Broom Hilda, Lander, 1977, EX $30.00
Bullwinkle, Fuller Brush, 1970s, NM..........................$60.00

Care Bear, AGC, 1984, NM...$10.00
Cecil (Beany & Cecil), Purex, 1962, NM $25.00
Charlie Brown, Avon, red baseball outfit, NM $20.00

Deputy Dawg, Colgate-Palmolive, 9¾", EX, from $20.00 to $25.00.

Dino & Pebbles, Cosrich, 1994, NM...........................$15.00
Donald Duck, Colgate-Palmolive, 1960s, M.................$30.00
Dum Dum, Purex, 1964, white w/pink accents, rare, EX ..$100.00
ET, Avon, 1984, NM..$15.00
Fred Flintstone, Milvern (Purex), 1960s, red outfit w/black accents, EX+ $30.00
Garfield, Kid Care, lying in tub, NM $10.00
Goofy, Colgate-Palmolive, 1960s, red, white & black w/cap head, NM $20.00
Gumby, M&L Creative Packaging, 1987, NM...............$30.00
Holly Hobbie, Benjamin Ansehl, 1980s, several variations, M, ea $15.00
Huckleberry Hound, Knickerbocker (Purex), bank, red & black, original neck tag, 15", M..........................$60.00
Jasmine (Aladdin), Cosrich, w/bird or mirror, original tag, M, ea $6.00
King Louie (Jungle Book), Colgate-Palmolive, 1960s, slip over, NM $15.00
Little Mermaid, Kid Care, 1991, tail up, NM $10.00
Little Orphan Annie, Lander, 1977, NM, from $25 to..$30.00
Magilla Gorilla, Purex, 1960s, NM $35.00
Mickey Mouse, Avon, 1969, MIB.................................$30.00
Mickey Mouse as Band Leader, Colgate-Palmolive, 1960s, NM $30.00
Miss Piggy, Muppet Treasure Island, Calgon, 1996.....$10.00
Morocco Mole, Purex, 1966, rare, EX $100.00
Mr Robottle, Avon, 1971, MIB.....................................$20.00
Pebbles & Dino, Cosrich, Pebbles riding Dino, M $6.00
Peter Potamous, Purex, 1960s, purple w/white or yellow shirt, w/contents & original tag, M, ea..................$25.00
Popeye, Colgate-Palmolive, 1977, blue w/white accents, NM $35.00
Power Rangers, Kid Care, 1996, any character, M.........$8.00
Raggedy Ann, Lander, 1960s, NM...............................$65.00
Ricochet Rabbit, Purex, movable arms, VG.................$35.00
Secret Squirrel, Purex, 1966, rare, VG........................$45.00

Smokey Bear, Colgate-Palmolive, 1960s, NM $25.00
Snoopy Flying Ace, Avon, 1969, MIB..........................$20.00
Snow White, Colgate-Palmolive, 1960s, movable arms, NM...$35.00
Speedy Gonzales, Colgate-Palmolive, 1960s, EX........$30.00
Superman, Avon, 1978, w/cape, MIP $40.00
Teenage Mutant Ninja Turtles, Kid Care, 1990, any character, M, ea...$8.00
Thumper, Colgate-Palmolive, 1960s, EX $25.00
Tweety Bird on Cage, Colgate-Palmolive, NM $30.00
Woodsy Owl, Lander, early 1970s, EX $35.00
Yogi Bear, Purex, powder/bank, green hat & yellow tie, NM...$30.00

Buttons

Collectors refer to buttons made before 1918 as 'old,' those from 1918 on they call 'modern.' Age is an important consideration, but some modern buttons are very collectible too. You might find some still in your Grandmother's button jar, and nearly any flea market around will have some interesting examples.

Some things you'll want to look for to determine the age of a button is the material it is made of, the quality of its workmanship, the type of its decoration, and how it was constructed. Early metal buttons were usually made in one piece of steel, copper, or brass. Old glass buttons will have irregularities on the back, while the newer ones will be very smooth. 'Picture' buttons with animals and people as their subjects were popular in the last quarter of the nineteenth century. Many were quite large and very fancy. As a rule, those are the most valuable to collectors.

For more information, refer to *Anitque and Collectible Buttons, Vol. I* and *Vol. II*, by Debra J. Wisniewski and *Painted Porcelain Jewelry and Buttons* by Dorothy Kamm. All are published by Collector Books.

Aurora borealis, late 1950s to early 1960s, med, ea, from $4 to $6.00
Aurora borealis, late 1950s to early 1960s, sm, ea, from $2 to $3.00
Brass face w/cut-steel trim, mounted in steel cup by pins $5.00
Celluloid disk w/pierced brass escutcheon loop shank & plate $10.00
Celluloid overlay w/cut design in 2 or more colors, from $2 to $4.00
Coconut shell, carved fish, palm or pineapple (others), 1930s-60s, ea, from $5 to $8.00
Enameled roses w/champlevè border..........................$40.00
Enameled stork scene on brass $28.00
Glass, black w/white & goldstone overlay, from $3 to $8.00
Glass w/paint trims, gold or silver lustre, or rhinestones, 1930s-1960s, ea, from $2 to....................................$4.00
Japanned brass, engraved decor, from $2 to.................$3.00

Jelly Belly, metal fish, reptile, bird or mammal w/glass center, some w/rhinestone eyes, ea............................$12.00
Metalized plastic, common shape (animal's head, rope, bow tie, etc), ea, from $1 to...$2.00
Pewter w/floral decor, sm, from $2 to $3.00
Plastic, animal (realistic), celluloid shank, 1950s, ea.....$2.00
Plastic, autumn leaves, self shank, set of 5 ....$10.00
Plastic, imitation tortoise shell, from $4 to....................$6.00
Plastic, solid color animal w/rhinestone eyes, ea, from $1 to $1.50
Plastic w/rhinestones, 1930-1950s, from $4 to..............$7.00
Transparent glass, colored or clear, made in Germany, Austria or Czechoslovakia, 1930s-1940s, extra lg ...$3.00
Transparent glass, colored or clear, made in Germany, Austria or Czechoslavakia, 1930s-1940s, smaller sizes, ea, 50¢ to $2.00

Cake Toppers

In many ways, these diminutive couples reflect our culture — they actually capture miniature moments in time, and their style of dress reflects the many changes made in fashion down through the years. The earliest cake toppers (from before the turn of the twentieth century) were made of sugar and disintegrated rapidly. Next came bridal couples of carved wood, usually standing on plaster (gum paste) bases. When molded, this material could be made into lovely platforms and backdrops for the tiny figures. It was sometimes molded into columns with gazebo-style or lattice roofs under which the dainty couples stood hand in hand. Good Luck horseshoes representing all the best wishes for the bridal couple were popular as well.

By the 1920s and 1930s, plaster bases were still in use, but a flower bower replaced the columns and horseshoes. These bowers were constructed of wire and trimmed with cloth flowers, often lilies of the valley. The bridal figures of this period were usually porcelain or chalkware, and the brides' gowns became sleek and elegant, reflecting the Art Deco trend in fashion. Gone was the bustle and the prim pose. The groom looked equally elegant in black tie and tails. The pair now often took on a 'high society' air.

Then in the mid-1930s appeared the exact opposite — kewpies. These child-like figures with their wide-eyed, innocent faces were popular cake toppers well into the 1940s.

During WWII, military toppers became popular. It was now the groom who drew the most attention. He was dashing and patriotic in an Armed Forces uniform, and all branches of the military were represented. To complement the theme, a 48-star American flag or a red, white, and blue ribbon was often suspended from the center of the bower.

After the war, the bridal couple and the base they stood on were made of plastic — the latest rage. As for flowers and trim, there seemed no limit. Cabbage roses, strings of pearls, and huge gatherings of white netting added the final trim to oversized backdrops of hearts, cupids, birds, and bells. In the new millennium, fine china or delicate porcelain have become the materials of choice.

Cake toppers are fragile. Look them over carefully before purchasing. Expect to find them in all stages of completeness and condition. Chips, dents, broken parts, crumbling bases, or soiled clothing all seriously devalue a piece. Those in questionable or poor condition (unless extremely rare) are basically worthless. Prices suggested in the following listings apply to cake toppers that are complete with base, bower (or other finishing top), flowers, trim, and lace or clothing if applicable. A collectible topper should reflect minimal wear and obvious care.

Advisor: Jeannie Greenfield (See Directory, Cake Toppers)

Kewpie couple, bisque & molded plaster base **$100.00**
Kewpie couple, celluloid w/crepe-paper clothes, bride wears headband, 3" **$50.00**
Marine dress uniform on groom, bisque, 4½".............**$40.00**
Military couple arm-in-arm on plaster (gum paste) base, cloth bower of flower & leaves on wire, 48-star flag in center **$75.00**
Sailor uniform on groom, all plaster, 4½"....................**$40.00**
World War II military couple, plaster w/paper base ...**$45.00**
1900s couple on plaster (gum paste) base, bower of cloth flowers w/painted plaster centers **$90.00**
1920s couple, all bisque, bride in dropped-waist gown, 4" **$50.00**
1930s couple on raised & sculpted base, cupola roof & columns w/lilies-of-the-valley trim, heavy, 10".....**$75.00**
1930s porcelain kewpies (crepe-paper attire) embrace under bower of cloth flowers, plaster embossed/sculptured base, 3" **$50.00**
1930s porcelain kewpies on cardboard platform w/wire crepe-paper arch, crepe-paper tux, satin dress, 4" **$50.00**
1940s couple, basalt carved figures, 1-pc **$20.00**
1940s couple, 3 lg bells on sides as backdrop, ea w/cloth flowers w/green velvet leaves & silver paper in centers ..**$40.00**
1940s couple holding hands stands before table w/wedding ring, bower of cloth flowers & bell, plaster & chalkware..**$50.00**

1940s couple, plaster and chalkware with silver metal bell, $40.00. (Photo courtesy Jeannie Greenfield)

1950s couple, heart-theme base, lg heart w/netting, flower center & upturned bell w/white glitter as backdrop, plastic **$20.00**

Calculators

It is difficult to picture the days when a basic four-function calculator cost hundreds of dollars, especially when today you get one free by simply filling out a credit application. Yet when they initially arrived on the market in 1971, the first of these electronic marvels cost from $300.00 to $400.00. All this for a calculator that could do no more than add, subtract, multiply, and divide.

Even at that price there was an uproar by consumers as calculating finally became convenient. No longer did you need to use a large mechanical monster adding machine or a slide rule with all of its complexity. You could even put away your pencil and paper for those tough numbers you couldn't 'do' in your head.

With prices initially so high and the profit potential so promising, several hundred companies jumped onto the calculator bandwagon. Some made their own; many purchased them from other (often overseas) manufacturers, just adding their own nameplate. Since the product was so new to the world, most of the calculators had some very different and interesting body styles.

Due to the competitive nature of all those new entries to the market, prices dropped quickly. A year and a half later, prices started to fall below $100.00 — a magic number that caused a boom in consumer demand. As even more calculators became available and electronics improved, prices continued to drop, eventually forcing many high-cost makers (who could not compete) out of business. By 1978 the number of major calculator companies could be counted on both hands. Fortunately calculators are still available at almost every garage sale or flea market for a mere pittance — usually 25¢ to $3.00.

For more information refer to *A Guide to HP Handheld Calculators and Computers* by Wlodek Mier-Jedrzejowicz, *Collector's Guide to Pocket Calculators* by Guy Ball and Bruce Flamm (both published by Wilson/Barnett), and *Personal Computers and Pocket Calculators* by Dr. Thomas Haddock.

Note: Due to limited line length, we have used these abbreviations: flr — fluorescent; fct — function.

Advisor: Guy D. Ball (See Directory, Calculators)

Website: www.vintagecalculators.com

Alco, #888, 4-fct, flr, 3-AA batteries, c 1973, 3x5½" **$40.00**
Anita, #811 version 1, 4-fct, memory, %, red LED, 3-AAA batteries, round keys, England, 2¾x4¾"...................**$65.00**
APF, #RS-1 (aka Kel-Co), 4-fct, %, horse-race handicapping calculator, red LED, 9V battery, Hong Kong, 2¾x5½" .**$40.00**
Bohn, Omnitrex, 4-fct, %, green-tube display, 5-AA batteries, 1973, 2-tone case, Taiwan, 4x6½" **$37.50**

Bradford, #8DPS, 4-fct, %, square root, green flr, 2-AA batteries, Japan, 3x5½" **$45.00**

Busicom, Handy L3-I20A, 1971, very rare (original price $395.00), from $200.00 to $300.00.
(Photo courtesy Guy Ball)

Calstar, #DT-10, 4-fct, memory, %, 10-digit flr, 2 D batteries, Taiwan, 6½x7" **$30.00**

Canon, Palmtronic 8 mini, 4-fct, %, flr, 2 AA batteries, Japan, 1976, 2½x3⅝" **$45.00**

Casio, #101MR, 4-fct, memory, %, square root, green flr, 4 AA batteries, decimal slide switch, Japan, 1974, 4½x6½" **$25.00**

Century, Centurion, 4-fct, red LED, sealed battery, brown case w/black & red keys, Mexico, 3x5¼" **$65.00**

Commodore, #385R, 4-fct, %, red LED, sealed battery, CMB logo, England, 3x4" **$50.00**

CompuChron, Calculator Watch, 4-fct, %, red LED, 4-button battery, hard-edged case, 1½x1¾" **$150.00**

Craig, #4509, 4-fct, AA battery, purple cover LED, Japan, 1974, 2¾x5½" **$45.00**

Daltone, Opti-Cal 1, 4-fct, memory, %, 4 AA batteries, black w/silver top, 1973-74, 3½x5¾" **$80.00**

Eldorado, #8KB, 4-fct, flr, sealed battery, mustard color, lg portable desk-top, 1972, 5¾x9" **$55.00**

Elite, #4000M, 4-fct, memory, %, green flr, 4 AA batteries, 3½x6" **$45.00**

Enterprex, #605, 4-fct, %, red LED, 2 AA batteries, 3x5" .**$40.00**

Falcon, #F600, 4-fct, memory, %, square root, green flr, 2 AA batteries, black case, 3x5" **$45.00**

Hanimex, #2170, 4-fct, memory, %, square fct, reciprical, green flr, 2 AA batteries, Hong Kong, 3½x5½" **$45.00**

Hewlett-Packard, #25C, science fct, 49-step programmable, red LED, continuous data, 1976, 2¾x5" **$70.00**

Ibico, #076, 4 fct, memory, %, sq fct, reciprical, flr, 4 AAA batteries, Japan, 3x5" **$35.00**

Keystone, #98, 4-fct, memory, %, flr, sealed battery, ca 1974-75, 3¼x5¼" **$55.00**

Kings Point, #9202, 4-fct, memory, %, blue flr, 4 C batteries, case similar to Soundesign 8300, Japan, 4½x7½"...**$45.00**

Litronix, #1000 (aka Triton 1000), 4-fct, red LED, 3 AA batteries, decimal slide switch, black case, 3x6" **$40.00**

Lloyd's #304, 4-fct, %, square root, flr, 4 AA batteries, Taiwan, 3½x5½" **$22.50**

Microlith, #205 (aka Scientific), science fct, green flr, 9V battery, early F fct key, Hong Kong, 1974, 3x5¼" **$70.00**

Mini Master, 4-fct, red LED, sealed battery, 4 slide switches, sturdy, 1971, 3¾x6¾" **$175.00**

Monroe-Litton, #10, 4-fct, paper tape display, sealed battery, stylized case, 1972, 4x8½" **$90.00**

National Semiconductor, #500, 4-fct, memory, green flr & paper printer, sealed battery, Japan, 3x5½" **$45.00**

Novus, #4515 (aka Mathematician PR), science fct, memory, programmable, red LED, sealed battery, ca 1975, 3x6" **$30.00**

Plustron, #308, 4-fct, red LED, 9V battery, gray w/round blue & white keys, 3x4" **$45.00**

Qualitron, #1443, 4-fct, memory, square root, green flr, 4 AA batteries, Taiwan, 3x5½" **$40.00**

Radio Shack, #EC-312 (aka Astro), 4-fct & biorhythm calculations, flr, 2 AA batteries, Taiwan, 3x4½" **$60.00**

Radofin, #8P, 4-fct, %, red LED, 9V battery, same case as 1610, Hong Kong, 2½x5" **$40.00**

Rockwell, #9TR, 4-fct, %, red LED, 9V battery, green case & keys, Mexico, 3x6" **$45.00**

Royal, Digital IV, 4-fct, red LED, sealed battery, ca 1972, 3¼x6¾" **$120.00**

Santron, #400, 4-fct educational w/clown face, red & green LEDs for eyes, 9V battery, Taiwan **$40.00**

Sears, #82 (aka 711.58151), 4-fct, %, red LED, 9V battery, case similar to APF mark 82, Hong Kong, 2½x5" **$30.00**

Sharp, #EL-501, science fct, green flr, 2 AA batteries, Japan, similar to EL-500, 3x5½" **$25.00**

Silver Reed, #8, 4-fct, %, square root, green flr, 2-AA batteries, Japan, 3¼x5" **$45.00**

Spectrum, #SP-70, science fct, 14-digit display, sealed battery, case similar to Kings Point, 1974, 3½x6¾" **$50.00**

Summit, SL-8MR, 4-fct, memory, %, red LED, sealed battery, slanted display case, 1975, 2¾x4¾" **$35.00**

Texas Instruments, #TI-5050, 4-fct, %, paper tape printer, sealed battery, mini desk-top, 1975, 4x8½" **$35.00**

Texas Instruments, SR-51-II, science & financial fcts, red LED, sealed battery pack, looks like SR-16-II, 1976, 3x6"..**$25.00**

Triumph, #88T (aka EC25), science fct, green flr, 4 AA batteries, looks like various Adler models, 3x4¾" **$55.00**

Unisonic, #830A, 4-fct, %, square root, green flr, 4 AAA batteries, looks like #711E, Japan, 3x5" **$15.00**

Unitrex, #901MR, 4-fct, memory, %, square root, flr, 2 AA batteries, Korea, 3¼x5½" **$35.00**

Voesa, #3000, 4-fct, memory, %, red LED, 9V battery, same case as Bohsei #3000, Hong Kong, 2¾x5¼" **$12.50**

California Raisins

Since they starred in their first TV commercial in 1986, the California Raisins have attained stardom through movies, tapes, videos, and magazine ads. Today we see them everywhere on the secondary market — PVC figures, radios, banks, posters — and they're very collectible. The PVC figures were introduced in 1987. Originally there were four, all issued for retail sales — a singer, two conga dancers, and a saxophone player. Before the year was out, Hardee's, the fast-food chain, came out with the same characters, though on a slightly smaller scale. A fifth character, Blue Surfboard (horizontal), was created, and three 5½" Bendees with flat pancake-style bodies appeared.

In 1988 the ranks had grown to twenty-one: Blue Surfboard (vertical), Red Guitar, Lady Dancer, Blue/Green Sunglasses, Guy Winking, Candy Cane, Santa Raisin, Bass Player, Drummer, Tambourine Lady (there were two styles), Lady Valentine, Boy Singer, Girl Singer, Hip Guitar Player, Sax Player with Beret, and four Graduates (styled like the original four, but on yellow pedestals and wearing graduation caps). And Hardee's issued an additional six: Blue Guitar, Trumpet Player, Roller Skater, Skateboard, Boom Box, and Yellow Surfboard.

Still eight more characters came out in 1989: Male in Beach Chair, Green Trunks with Surfboard, Hula Skirt, Girl Sitting on Sand, Piano Player, AC, Mom, and Michael Raisin. They made two movies and thereafter were joined by their fruit and vegetable friends, Rudy Bagaman, Lick Broccoli, Banana White, Leonard Limabean, and Cecil Thyme. Hardee's added four more characters in 1991: Anita Break, Alotta Style, Buster, and Benny.

All Raisins are dated with these exceptions: those issued in 1989 (only the Beach Scene characters are dated, and they're actually dated 1988) and those issued by Hardee's in 1991.

For more information we recommend *Schroeder's Collectible Toys, Antique to Modern* (Collector Books).

Applause, Captain Toonz, w/blue boom box, yellow glasses & sneakers, Hardee's 2nd Promotion, 1988, sm, M, from $1 to..**$3.00**

Applause, FF Strings, w/blue guitar & orange sneakers, Hardee's 2nd Promotion, 1988, sm, M, from $1 to..**$3.00**

Applause, Michael Raisin, Special Edition, 1989, M, $15.00.

Applause, SB Stuntz, w/yellow skateboard & sneakers, Hardee's 2nd Promotion, 1988, sm, M, from $1.....**$3.00**

Applause, Trumpy Trunote, w/trumpet & blue sneakers, Hardee's 2nd Promotion, 1988, sm, M, from $1 to ..**$3.00**

Applause, Waves Weaver I, w/yellow surfboard connected to foot, Hardee's 2nd Promotion, 1988, sm.................**$3.00**

Applause, Waves Weaver II, w/yellow surfboard not connected to foot, Hardee's 2nd Promotion, 1988, sm, M ...**$2.00**

Applause-Claymation, Banana White, yellow dress, Meet the Raisins 1st Promotion, 1989, M..............................**$20.00**

Applause-Claymation, Lick Broccoli, green & black w/red & orange guitar, Meet the Raisins 1st Promotion, 1989, M **$20.00**

Applause-Claymation, Rudy Bagaman, w/cigar, purple shirt & flipflops, Meet the Raisins 1st Promotion, 1989, M **$20.00**

CALRAB, Blue Surfboard, board connected to foot, Unknown Promotion, 1988, M...**$35.00**

CALRAB, Blue Surfboard, board in right hand, not connected to foot, Unknown Promotion, 1987, M...........**$50.00**

CALRAB, Christmas Issue, 1988, w/candy cane, M.....**$12.00**

CALRAB, Christmas Issue, 1988, w/red hat, M...........**$12.00**

CALRAB, Guitar, red guitar, 1st Commercial Issue, 1988, M...**$8.00**

CALRAB, Hands, left hand points up, right hand points down, Post Raisin Bran Issue, 1987, M...................**$2.00**

CALRAB, Hands, pointing up w/thumbs head, Hardee's First Promotion, 1987, sm, M...**$3.00**

CALRAB, Hands, pointing up w/thumbs touching head, 1st Key Chains, 1987, M...**$5.00**

CALRAB, Microphone, right hand in fist w/microphone in left, Post Raisin Bran Issue, 1987, M **$2.00**

CALRAB, Microphone, right hand points up w/microphone in left, Hardee's First Promotion, 1987, M **$3.00**

CALRAB, Microphone, right hand points up w/microphone in left, First Key Chains, 1987, M...........................**$5.00**

CALRAB, Saxophone, gold sax, no hat, First Key Chains, 1987, M **$5.00**

CALRAB, Saxophone, gold sax, no hat, Hardee's First Promotion, sm, M...**$3.00**

CALRAB, Saxophone, inside of sax painted red, Post Raisin Bran Issue, 1987, M **$2.00**

CALRAB, Singer, microphone in left hand not connected to face, First Commercial Issue, 1988, M.....................**$6.00**

CALRAB, Sunglasses, index finger touching face, First Key Chains, 1987, M...**$5.00**

CALRAB, Sunglasses, index finger touching face, orange glasses, Hardee's First Promotion, 1987, M.............**$3.00**

CALRAB, Sunglasses, right hand points up, left hand points down, orange glasses, Post Raisin Bran Issue, 1987, M...**$2.00**

CALRAB, Sunglasses II, eyes not visible, aqua glasses & sneakers, First Commercial Issue, 1988, M **$4.00**

CALRAB, Sunglasses II, eyes visible, aqua glasses & sneakers, First Commercial Issue, 1988, M..........................**$35.00**

CALRAB, Winky; hitchhiking pose & winking, First Commercial Issue, 1988, M **$6.00**

CALRAB-Applause, AC, 'Gimme-5' pose, Meet the Raisins Edition, 1989, M....................$225.00

CALRAB-Applause, Alotta Style, purple boom box, Hardee's Fourth Promotion, 1991, sm, MIP (w/collector's card)....................$15.00

CALRAB-Applause, Anita Break, shopping w/Hardee's bags, Hardee's Fourth Promotion, 1991, sm, MIP (w/collector's card)....................$15.00

CALRAB-Appaluse, Bass Player, gray slippers, Second Commercial Issue, 1988, M $8.00

CALRAB-Applause, Benny, bowling ball & bag, Hardee's Fouth Promotion, 1991, sm, MIP (w/collector's card).........$15.00

CALRAB-Applause, Boy in Beach Chair, orange glasses, brown base, Beach Theme Edition, 1988, M........$20.00

CALRAB-Applause, Boy w/Surfboard, purple board, brown base, Beach Theme Edition, 1988, M....................$20.00

CALRAB-Applause, Boy w/Surfboard, not connected to foot, brown base, Beach Theme Edition, 1988, M..........$20.00

CALRAB-Applause, Cecil Thyme (Carrot), Meet the Raisins Second Edition, 1989, M $250.00

CALRAB-Applause, Drummer, Second Commercial Issue, 1988, M $10.00

CALRAB-Applause, Girl w/Boom Box, purple glasses, green shoes, Beach Theme Edition, 1988, M....................$20.00

CALRAB-Applause, Girl w/Tambourine, green shoes & bracelet, Beach Theme Edition, 1988, M $15.00

CALRAB-Applause, Girl w/Tambourine (Ms Delicious), yellow shoes, Second Commercial Issue, 1988, M....$15.00

CALRAB-Applause, Hip Band Guitarist (Hendrix), w/headband & yellow guitar, Third Commercial Issue, 1988, M....................$30.00

CALRAB-Applause, Hip Band Guitarist (Hendrix), w/headband & yellow guitar, Second Key Chains, 1988, sm, M....................$65.00

CALRAB-Applause, Hula Girl, yellow shows & bracelet, green skirt, Beach Theme Edition, 1988, M..........$20.00

CALRAB-Applause, Lenny Lima Bean, purple suit, Meet the Raisins Second Edition, 1989, M....................$175.00

CALRAB-Applause, Microphone (female), yellow shoes & bracelet, Third Commercial Issue, 1988, M...........$12.00

CALRAB-Applause, Microphone (female), yellow shoes & bracelet, Second Key Chains, 1988, sm, M $45.00

CALRAB-Applause, Microphone (male), left hand extended w/open palm, Second Key Chains, 1988, sm, M..$45.00

CALRAB-Applause, Mom, yellow hair, pink apron, Meet the Raisins Second Edition, 1989, M, from $150 to..$200.00

CALRAB-Applause, Piano, blue piano, red hair, green sneakers, Meet the Raisins First Edition, 1989, M $35.00

CALRAB-Applause, Saxophone, black beret, blue eyelids, Third Commercial Issue, 1988, M....................$15.00

CALRAB-Applause, Singer (female), reddish purple shoes & bracelet, Second Commercial Issue, 1988, M........$12.00

CALRAB-Applause, Sunglasses, Graduate w/index fingers touching face or Sax Player, Graduate Key Chains, 1988, M, ea $85.00

CALRAB-Applause, Valentine, boy holding heart, Special Lover's Edition, 1988, M $8.00

CALRAB-Applause, Valentine, girl holding heart, Special Lover's Edtion, 1988, M $8.00

CALRAB-Claymation, Sunglasses, Singer, Hands, Saxophone, Graduate on yellow base, Post Raisin Bran, 1988, ea from $45 to....................$65.00

Miscellaneous

Bank, no mark, 6½", from $25.00 to $30.00. (Photo courtesy Beverly and Jim Mangus)

Activity book, M....................$20.00

Bank, cereal box w/lid, plastic, EX, from $10 to........$15.00

Baseball cap, 1988, EX $5.00

Beach towel, CALRAB, M....................$35.00

Book, Raisin the Roof, 1988, EX....................$12.00

Bulletin board, Singer & Conga Line or Beach Scene, Rose Art, 1988, MIP, ea $25.00

Clay Factory, Rose Art, 1988, complete, MIB $40.00

Colorforms, MIB....................$25.00

Coloring book, California Raisins on Tour, Marvel, 1988, unused, EX $12.00

Crayon-By-Number Set, Rose Art, 1988, complete, MIB..$40.00

Doll, vinyl w/suction cups, 1987, lg version, EX $5.00

Doll, vinyl w/suction cups, 1987, sm version, EX......$10.00

Doorknob hanger, various images, 9x4", M, ea.............$7.00

Official Fan Club Watch Set, MIP $30.00

Puppet, female figure w/yellow or green shoes, Bendy/Sutton Happenings, 1988, MIB, ea $30.00

Puppet, male figure w/yellow shoes & glasses, Bendy/Sutton Happenings, 1988, MIB....................$35.00

Record, Signed Sealed Delivered, 45 rpm, 1989, EX (EX picture sleeve)....................$20.00

Sandwich Stage, Del Monte Fruit Snacks, MIB, from $50 to $75.00

Sleeping bag, purple, 1988, EX $40.00

Tote bag, yellow w/Conga Line, 1987, EX $20.00

Umbrella, lady raisins on the beach, 1988, EX...........$45.00

Camark Pottery

Camark Pottery was manufactured in CAMden, ARKansas, from 1927 to the early 1960s. The pottery was founded by Samuel J. 'Jack' Carnes, a native of east-central Ohio familiar with Ohio's fame for pottery production. Camark's first wares were made from Arkansas clays shipped by Carnes to John B. Lessell in Ohio in early to mid-1926. Lessell was one of the associates responsible for early art pottery making. These wares consisted of Lessell's lustre and iridescent finishes based on similar ideas he pioneered at Weller and other potteries. The variations made for Camark included versions of Weller's Marengo, LaSa, and Lamar. These 1926 pieces were signed only with the 'Lessell' signature. When Camark began operations in the spring of 1927, the company had many talented, experienced workers including Lessell's wife and step-daughter (Lessell himself died unexpectedly in December 1926), the Sebaugh family, Frank Long, Alfred Tetzschner, and Boris Trifonoff. This group produced a wide range of art pottery finished in glazes of many types, including lustre and iridescent (signed LeCamark), Modernistic/Futuristic, crackles, and combination glaze effects such as drips. Art pottery manufacture continued until the early 1930s when emphasis changed to industrial castware (molded wares) with single-color, primarily matt glazes.

In the 1940s Camark introduced its Hand Painted line by Ernst Lechner. This line included the popular Iris, Rose, and Tulip patterns. Concurrent with the Hand Painted Series (which was made until the early 1950s), Camark continued mass production of industrial castware — simple, sometimes nondescript pottery and novelty items with primarily glossy pastel glazes — until the early 1960s.

Some of Camark's designs and glazes are easily confused with those of other companies. For instance, Lessell decorated and signed a line in his lustre and iridescent finishes using porcelain (not pottery) blanks purchased from the Fraunfelter China Company. Camark produced a variety of combination glazes including the popular drip glazes (green over pink and green over mustard/brown) closely resembling Muncie's — but Muncie's clay is generally white while Camark used a cream-colored clay for its drip-glaze pieces. Muncie's are marked with a letter/number combination, and the bottoms are usually smeared with the base color. Camark's bottoms have a more uniform color application.

For more information, we recommend the *Collector's Guide to Camark Pottery* by David Edwin Gifford, Arkansas pottery historian, and also author of *Collector's Encyclopedia of Niloak Pottery*. (Both books are published by Collector Books.)

Advisor: Tony Freyaldenhoven (See Directory, Camark)

Artware

Candle holder, blue & white stipple, Arkansas die stamp, 1 14", from $30 to **$50.00**
Compote, Delphinium Blue, footed, unmarked, 3¼x7", from $15 to...**$25.00**

Pitcher, green to blue matt, slim, early circular mold mark, 9", from $150 to..**$200.00**
Pitcher, Royal Blue, unmarked, 3", from $10 to..........**$15.00**
Pitcher, solid green w/embossed floral decor, angular handle, upright rim, unmarked, 10¾", from $80 to.........**$100.00**
Planter, Orange Green Overflow, unmarked, 5", from $80 to **$100.00**
Vase, Autumn (rich brown), fan form, 1st block letter, 6", from $30 to...**$40.00**
Vase, Black & White Overflow, flared rim, footed, 1st block letter, 6", from $30 to...**$40.00**
Vase, blue & gray mottle, stepped Deco design, unmarked, 9¼", from $225 to...**$275.00**

Vase, Brown Stipple, 11", from $250.00 to $300.00; Vase, Green and Blue, no mark, 10¼", from $250.00 to $300.00. (Photo courtesy David Gifford)

Vase, bud; Delphinium Blue, brown Arkansas sticker, 8½", from $20 to..**$25.00**
Vase, Frosted Green, flared rim, footed, 1st block letter, 7¾", from $30 to...**$40.00**
Vase, Frosted Green, flared/ruffled rim, footed, 1st block letter, 5½", from $40 to **$60.00**
Vase, Ivory, shouldered, slim, 1st block letter, 10¼", from $60 to..**$80.00**
Vase, Rose Green Overflow, ring handles, 1st block letter, 4½", from $60 to...**$80.00**
Vase, Sea Green (bright, solid), rim-to-hip handles, unmarked, 4½", from $30 to.................................**$40.00**

Hand-Painted Ware

Basket, Lechner's Bas Relief Iris, yellow, mold mark: 805R USA, 9½", from $100 to **$120.00**
Basket, Lechner's Bas Relief Morning Glory II, blue, unmarked, 9¾", from $100 to............................**$120.00**
Bowl, Festoon of Roses, pink, 2nd Arkansas inventory sticker, mold mark: 553 USA, 4¾x11¾", from $150 to...**$200.00**

Bowl, Lechner's Bas Relief Iris, blue, unmarked, 5½x14",
from $80 to...**$100.00**

Vase, Festoon of Roses, blue, sm handles, unmarked, 8¼",
from $80 to...**$100.00**

Vase, Festoon of Roses, low handles, footed, mold mark: 544
USA, 7½", from $80 to **$100.00**

Vase, Festoon of Roses, yellow, mold mark: 808R USA, 6¾",
from $80 to...**$100.00**

Industrial Castware

Cup & saucer, Seafoam Green, flower form, Camark ink
stamp/unmarked, 2¼", 4¼", from $15 to.............**$20.00**

Figurine, camel, Royal Blue, 1st block letter, 3½", from $80
to...**$100.00**

Figurine, cat, Emerald Green, head turned to side, tail straight
out, mold mark: Camark, 16" L, from $60 to.........**$80.00**

Figurine, deer, burgundy, 2nd Arkansas inventory sticker,
4½x8½", from $60 to......................................**$80.00**

Figurine, horse on base, Delphinium Blue, 2nd Arkansas
inventory sticker, 8x10", from $80 to **$100.00**

Figurine, lion, burgundy, Lions Club Camden Ark, unmarked,
3½x2¼", from $15 to......................................**$20.00**

Figurine, razorback hog, burgundy, mold mark: 117 USA,
4¼", from $15 to...**$20.00**

Figurine, swan, Royal Blue, open back, unmarked, 4¾", from
$10 to...**$15.00**

Fishbowl holder, Tropical Fish, Mirror Black, unmarked, 8¼",
from $150 to...**$200.00**

Fishbowl holder, Wistful Cat, mirror black, unmarked, 9",
from $60 to...**$80.00**

Plaque, horse's head, Lechner decorated, blue/silver
Arkansas sticker, 7", from $100 to **$120.00**

Salt & pepper shakers, S&P shapes, Mirror Black w/gold trim,
unmarked, 2¾", pr, from $30 to **$40.00**

Shoe, Emerald Green, mold mark: 785 USA, 2", from $10
to **$15.00**

Vase, flower form, gold & yellow, circle Nor-So I, 9¼", from
$40 to...**$50.00**

Cambridge Glassware

If you're looking for a 'safe' place to put your investment
dollars, Cambridge glass is one of your better options. But as
with any commodity, in order to make a good investment,
knowledge of the product and its market is required. There
are two books we would recommend for your study, *Colors
in Cambridge Glass,* put out by the National Cambridge
Collectors Club, and *The Collector's Encyclopedia of Elegant
Glass* by Gene Florence.

The Cambridge Glass Company (located in Cambridge,
Ohio) made fine quality glassware from just after the turn of
the century until 1958. They made thousands of different
items in hundreds of various patterns and colors. Values
hinge on rarity of shape and color. Of the various marks they
used, the 'C in triangle' is the most common. In addition to
their tableware, they also produced flower frogs representing
ladies and children and models of animals and birds that are
very valuable today.

Club: National Cambridge Collectors, Inc.
P.O. Box 416
Cambridge, OH 43725-0416
www.cambridgeglass.org
Master membership $20.00; associate members $3.00.

#520, Peach Blo or green, bowl, cereal/grapefruit; #466,
6½" **$32.50**

#520, Peach Blo or green, gravy/sauce baot...............**$75.00**

#520, Peach Blo or green, plate, luncheon; 8"..........**$18.00**

#520, Peach Blo or green, stem, sherbet; #3060, 7"....**$22.50**

#520, Peach Blo or green, tumbler, low foot, #3095, 12-
oz **$30.00**

#704, any color, bowl, soup; 8½"..........................**$30.00**

#704, any color, celery dish, #908, 11"...................**$35.00**

#704, any color, cup, demitasse; #925....................**$35.00**

#704, any color, mayonnaise set, #169, 3-pc **$75.00**

#704, any color, plate, service; 10½"......................**$75.00**

#704, any color, stem, #3075, 9-oz........................**$28.00**

#704, any color, tumbler, whiskey; #3075, 2-oz **$35.00**

Apple Blossom, crystal, creamer, footed....................**$20.00**

Apple Blossom, crystal, plate, tea; 7½"....................**$12.00**

Apple Blossom, crystal, relish, 4-part, 12" **$45.00**

Apple Blossom, crystal, stem, tall sherbet, #3130, 6-oz .**$18.00**

Apple Blossom, crystal, sugar bowl, footed **$20.00**

Apple Blossom, pink or green, bonbon, handles, 5½"...**$40.00**

Apple Blossom, pink or green, pitcher, #3130, 64-oz...**$350.00**

Apple Blossom, pink or green, platter, rectangular, tab handles, 13½"...**$150.00**

Apple Blossom, pink or green, tumbler, footed, #3400, 12-
oz **$50.00**

Apple Blossom, yellow or amber, ashtray, heavy, 6"..**$125.00**

Apple Blossom, yellow or amber, cup, AD................**$65.00**

Apple Blossom, yellow or amber, plate, bread & but-
ter; sq...**$10.00**

Apple Blossom, yellow or amber, tumbler, #3025, 10-
oz **$30.00**

Candlelight, crystal, bowl, 4-toed, flared, #3900/62,
12" **$90.00**

Candlelight, crystal, bowl, 4-toed, flared rim,
#3900/54, 10" **$75.00**

Candlelight, crystal, candlestick, 3-light, #1338, 6"......**$95.00**

Candlelight, crystal, candy jar, w/lid, round, #3900/165 .**$150.00**

Candlelight, crystal, creamer, #3900/41......................**$25.00**

Candlelight, crystal, icer, cocktail; #968, 2-pc...........**$120.00**

Candlelight, crystal, plate, handles, #3900/131, 8" **$30.00**

Candlelight, crystal, plate, rolled rim, #3900/166, 14".**$85.00**

Candlelight, crystal, stem, cocktail; #78701, 4-oz **$35.00**

Candlelight, crystal, stem, tall sherbet, #3776, 7-oz **$28.00**

Caprice, blue or pink, bowl, fruit; #18, 5" **$75.00**

Caprice, blue or pink, bowl, salad; cupped, #80, 13" .**$195.00**

Caprice, blue or pink, candlestick, keyhole, 3-light, #638..**$75.00**

Caprice, blue or pink, cup, #17.................................**$35.00**

Caprice, blue or pink, stem, low oyster cocktail; blown, #300, 4½" **$50.00**

Caprice, crystal, ashtray, 3-footed, shell form, 2¾" **$8.00**

Caprice, crystal, bowl, jelly; handles, #151, 5" **$15.00**

Caprice, crystal, butter dish, #52, ¼-lb **$235.00**

Caprice, crystal, candlestick, 2-light, #72, 6" **$40.00**

Caprice, crystal, creamer, individual, #40....................**$12.00**

Caprice, crystal, mustard, w/lid, #87, 2-oz.................**$60.00**

Caprice, crystal, plate, cabaret; 4-footed, #32, 11" **$30.00**

Caprice, crystal, stem, claret, blown, #301, 4½-oz......**$50.00**

Caprice, crystal, tumbler, tea; footed, #300, 12-oz **$20.00**

Caprice, tumbler, blue or pink, tumbler, table; flat, #310, 10-oz **$65.00**

Chantilly, crystal, bowl, celery/relish; 3-part, 9" **$35.00**

Chantilly, crystal, cocktail icer, 2-pc **$65.00**

Chantilly, crystal, creamer, scalloped edge, individual, #3900..**$15.00**

Chantilly, crystal, hat, lg **$295.00**

Chantilly, crystal, mustard, w/lid **$65.00**

Chantilly, crystal, pitcher, upright..............................**$225.00**

Chantilly, crystal, salt & pepper shakers, flat, pr.........**$30.00**

Chantilly, crystal, stem, water; #3779, 9-oz.................**$28.00**

Chantilly, crystal, vase, flower; footed, 13"................**$150.00**

Chantilly stems, #3625: low sherbet, seven ounce, $18.00; goblet, ten ounce, $28.00; low oyster cocktail, 4½ ounce, $20.00.

Cleo, blue, creamer, Decagon....................................**$35.00**

Cleo, blue, mayonnaise, footed **$75.00**

Cleo, blue, plate, Decagon, handles, 7"......................**$30.00**

Cleo, blue, server, center handle, 12" **$65.00**

Cleo, blue, tumbler, footed, #3022, 12-oz...................**$95.00**

Cleo, pink, green, yellow or amber, candlestick, 2-light..**$65.00**

Cleo, pink, green, yellow or amber, ice tub **$125.00**

Cleo, pink, green, yellow or amber, pitcher, #38, 3½-pt...**$225.00**

Cleo, pink, green, yellow or amber, plate, Decagon, handles, 11" **$40.00**

Cleo, pink, green, yellow or amber, stem, cocktail; #3115, 3½" **$25.00**

Cleo, pink, green, yellow or amber, tumbler, footed, #3115, 8-oz..**$25.00**

Daffodil, crystal, basket, handles, low foot, #55, 6"....**$35.00**

Daffodil, crystal, comport, pulled stem #532, 6" **$65.00**

Daffodil, crystal, relish, 3-part, #214, 10" **$65.00**

Daffodil, crystal, stem, oyster cocktail; #1937, 5-oz **$20.00**

Daffodil, crystal, vase, footed, 36004, 8".....................**$95.00**

Decagon, blue, bowl, relish; 2-part, 11" **$40.00**

Decagon, blue, mayonnaise, handles, w/liner & ladle .**$45.00**

Decagon, blue, plate, 7½"..**$12.00**

Decagon, blue, stem, cocktail; 3½-oz **$24.00**

Decagon, blue, sugar bowl, scalloped rim **$20.00**

Decagon, pastel color, basket, handles, upturned sides, 7" **$15.00**

Decagon, pastel color, bowl, vegetable; oval, 9½" **$35.00**

Decagon, pastel color, cup....................................**$6.00**

Decagon, pastel color, plate, salad; 8½" **$15.00**

Decagon, pastel color, tray, center handle, 12"..........**$30.00**

Diane, crystal, bowl, bonbon; handles, footed, 7".....**$38.00**

Diane, crystal, bowl, cream soup; w/liner, #3400 ......**$35.00**

Diane, crystal, butter dish, round.............................**$165.00**

Diane, crystal, cocktail shaker, metal top **$135.00**

Diane, crystal, decanter, ball form............................**$235.00**

Diane, crystal, plate, handles, 13½" **$45.00**

Diane, crystal, plate, salad; 8" **$14.00**

Diane, crystal, stem, wine; #3122, 2½-oz **$35.00**

Diane, crystal, tumbler, footed, #3135, 10-oz **$22.00**

Diane, crystal, tumbler, juice; footed, 5-oz **$40.00**

Elaine, crystal, bowl, bonbon; handles, footed, 6"......**$25.00**

Elaine, crystal, bowl, celery/relish; 5-part, 12" **$65.00**

Elaine, crystal, creamer, several styles, ea...................**$20.00**

Elaine, crystal, pitcher, ball form, 80-oz....................**$295.00**

Elaine, crystal, plate, torte; 14" **$65.00**

Elaine, crystal, salt & pepper shakers, footed, pr........**$40.00**

Elaine, crystal, stem, claret; #3121, 4½-oz **$50.00**

Elaine, crystal, stem, sherry; #3104, 2-oz **$195.00**

Elaine, crystal, tumbler, water; footed, #1402, 9-oz **$20.00**

Elaine, crystal, vase, keyhole, footed, 9" **$145.00**

Flower frog, Rose Lady, light emerald, 8½", $200.00. (Photo courtesy Lee Garmon and Dick Spencer)

Gloria, crystal, basket, handles, sides up, 6" **$30.00**

Gloria, crystal, bowl, celery/relish; 5-part, 12" **$60.00**

Gloria, crystal, bowl, cereal; 6" sq................................**$35.00**

Gloria, crystal, comport, tall, 7" **$45.00**

Gloria, crystal, pitcher, middle indent, 67-oz **$225.00**

Gloria, crystal, plate, salad; tab handles, 10".............**$45.00**

Gloria, crystal, salt & pepper shakers, short, pr..........**$45.00**

Gloria, crystal, stem, cordial; #3135, 1-oz **$75.00**

Gloria, crystal, tumbler, footed, #3115, 12-oz..............**$30.00**

Gloria, crystal, vase, keyhole base, flared rim, 14"....**$175.00**

Gloria, green, pink or yellow, bowl, cranberry; 3½"..**$65.00**

Gloria, green, pink or yellow, bowl, cream soup; w/round liner...**$65.00**

Gloria, green, pink or yellow, bowl, relish; handles, 2-part, 8"...**$45.00**

Gloria, green, pink or yellow, plate, dinner; sq........**$110.00**

Gloria, green, pink or yellow, stem, cordial; #3120, 1-oz .**$155.00**

Gloria, green, pink or yellow, tumbler, footed, #3115, 12-oz **$50.00**

Imperial Hunt scene, colors, bowl, 3-part, 8½" **$95.00**

Imperial Hunt Scene, colors, creamer, flat...................**$50.00**

Imperial Hunt Scene, colors, ice tub...........................**$95.00**

Imperial Hunt Scene, colors, salt & pepper shakers, pr .**$175.00**

Imperial Hunt Scene, crystal, bowl, cereal; 6"............**$20.00**

Imperial Hunt scene, crystal, candlestick, keyhole, 3-light **$45.00**

Imperial Hunt Scene, crystal, creamer, footed.............**$20.00**

Imperial Hunt Scene, crystal, ice bucket **$65.00**

Imperial Hunt Scene, crystal pitcher, w/lid, #711, 76-oz.**$165.00**

Imperial Hunt Scene, crystal, stem, wine; #1402, 2½-oz..**$65.00**

Imperial Hunt Scene, crystal, sugar bowl, footed **$20.00**

Imperial Hunt Scene, crystal, tumbler, flat, #1402, 15-oz ..**$35.00**

Marjorie, crystal, bowl, nappy; #4111, 4"....................**$20.00**

Marjorie, crystal, comport, #4004, 5" **$35.00**

Marjorie, crystal, creamer, straight sides, flat, #1917/18 ...**$50.00**

Marjorie, crystal, stem, claret; #7606, 4½-oz...............**$55.00**

Marjorie, crystal, tumbler, #8858, 8-oz **$20.00**

Mt Vernon, amber or crystal, ashtray, oval, #71, 6x4½"...**$12.00**

Mt Vernon, amber or crystal, bottle, toilet water; sq, #18, 7-oz **$75.00**

Mt Vernon, amber or crystal, bowl, preserve; #76, 6".**$12.00**

Mt Vernon, amber or crystal, bowl, salad; #120, 10½"..**$25.00**

Mt Vernon, amber or crystal, box, w/lid, #17, 4" sq..**$32.50**

Mt Vernon, amber or crystal, celery dish, #79, 10½" ..**$15.00**

Mt Vernon, amber or crystal, comport, #11, 7½" **$25.00**

Mt Vernon, amber or crystal, pickle dish, 1-handle, #78, 6"...**$12.00**

Mt Vernon, amber or crystal, plate, salad; #5, 8½" **$7.00**

Mt Vernon, amber or crystal, salt & pepper shakers, tall, #89, pr...**$25.00**

Mt Vernon, amber or crystal, tumbler, barrel shape, #13, 12-oz **$15.00**

Portia, crystal, bowl, individual nut; 4-footed, 3"........**$60.00**

Portia, crystal, candlestick, 5" **$30.00**

Portia, crystal, celery/relish, tab handles, 3-part, 9"..**$50.00**

Portia, crystal, cigarette holder, urn shape..................**$60.00**

Portia, crystal, comport, 5½"..**$50.00**

Portia, crystal, ivy ball, 5¼" **$75.00**

Portia, crystal, plate, 8½" sq **$15.00**

Portia, crystal, stem, claret; #3121, 4½-oz **$50.00**

Portia, crystal, stem, wine; #3130, 2½-oz....................**$40.00**

Portia, crystal, tumbler, juice; #3126, 5-oz **$20.00**

Portia, crystal, vase, globular, 5"..................................**$65.00**

Rosalie, amber, bowl, bonbon; handles, 5½" **$15.00**

Rosalie, amber, bowl, handles, 10"...............................**$40.00**

Rosalie, amber, candy dish, w/lid, 6".............................**$75.00**

Rosalie, amber, plate, bread & butter; 6¾" **$7.00**

Rosalie, amber, plate, 8⅜"...**$10.00**

Rosalie, amber, sugar bowl, footed..............................**$13.00**

Rosalie, amber, tumbler, footed, #3077, 12-oz............**$25.00**

Rosalie, blue, pink or green, bowl, fruit; 5½" **$20.00**

Rosalie, blue, pink or green, bottle, French dressing ..**$150.00**

Rosalie, blue, pink or green, candlestick, 2 styles, 4", ea **$35.00**

Rosalie, blue, pink or green, comport, almond; footed, 6"...**$45.00**

Rosalie, blue, pink or green, ice tub..............................**$85.00**

Rosalie, blue, pink or green, platter, 12" **$85.00**

Rosalie, blue, pink or green, salt cellar, footed, 1½"..**$65.00**

Rosalie, blue, pink or green, sugar shaker................**$325.00**

Rose Point, crystal, ashtray, #721, 2½" sq...................**$35.00**

Rose Point, crystal, ashtray, oval, #3500/131, 4½" **$65.00**

Rose Point, crystal, bowl, bonbon; handles, #3400/1179, 5½"...**$40.00**

Rose Point, crystal, bowl, cream soup; w/liner, #3400 .**$175.00**

Rose Point, crystal, bowl, crimped rim, #1351, 10½" .**$85.00**

Rose Point, crystal, bowl, handles, #1402/89, 6".........**$45.00**

Rose Point, crystal, bowl, nut; 4-footed, #3400/71, 3" ..**$75.00**

Rose Point, crystal, bowl, oblong, footed, #3500/118, 12"...**$175.00**

Rose Point, crystal, cake plate, tab handles, 13½"......**$75.00**

Rose Point, crystal, candlestick, keyhole, 2-light, #3400/647, 6"..**$45.00**

Rose Point, crystal, candy box, tall stem, w/lid, #3121/3, 5⅜"..**$175.00**

Rose Point, crystal, cigarette box, #615 ....**$150.00**

Rose Point, crystal, creamer, flat, ...**$150.00**

Rose Point, crystal, cup, punch; 5-oz...........................**$37.50**

Rose Point, crystal, ice bucket, #1402/52 ....**$225.00**

Rose Point, crystal, mayonnaise set, #3500/59, w/liner & ladle **$75.00**

Rose Point, crystal, pitcher, ice lip, #3400/100, 76-oz..**$215.00**

Rose Point, crystal, salt & pepper shakers, round, glass base, individual, #1470, pr................................**$95.00**

Rose Point, crystal, stem, cocktail; plain stem, #7801.**$45.00**

Rose Point, crystal, stem, low sherbet; #3121, 6-oz **$22.00**

Rose Point, crystal, tumbler, cordial; #3400/1341, 1-oz..**$110.00**

Rose Point, crystal, vase, globular, #3400/103, 6½" **$95.00**

Valencia, crystal, basket, handles, footed, #3500/55, 6".**$30.00**

Valencia, crystal, candy dish, w/lid, #3500/103 ....**$135.00**

Valencia, crystal, honey dish, w/lid, #3500/139 ....**$150.00**

Valencia, crystal, plate, #3500/67, 12" **$40.00**

Valencia, crystal, relish, 3-compartment, #3500/68, 5½" ..**$25.00**

Valencia, crystal, salt & pepper shakers, #3400/18, pr **$65.00**

Valencia, crystal, stem, claret; #1402 ....**$50.00**

Wildflower, crystal, bowl, bonbon; handles, footed, 6" ...**$17.50**
Wildflower, crystal, bowl, celery/relish; 3-part, #3900/126, 12" **$40.00**
Wildflower, crystal, creamer, individual, #3900/40 ......**$20.00**
Wildflower, crystal, pitcher, ball form, #3400/38, 80-oz ..**$165.00**
Wildflower, crystal, plate, bonbon; handles, #3900/130, 7" **$17.50**
Wildflower, crystal, plate, torte; #3900/167, 14" **$45.00**
Wildflower, crystal, stem, cordial; #3121, 1-oz **$57.50**
Wildflower, crystal, sugar bowl, #3900/41 ....**$14.00**
Wildflower, crystal, tumbler, water; #3121, 10-oz........**$22.00**
Wildflower, crystal, vase, flower; footed, #278, 11" **$95.00**

Cameras

Camera collecting as an investment or hobby continues to grow in popularity. The large number of older cameras that have recently been offered for sale in Internet auctions has created a good buyer's market, and excellent cameras can often be purchased that offer great potential for future increases in value.

Buying at garage sales, flea markets, auctions, or estate sales are ways to add to collections, although it is rare to find an expensive classic camera offered through these outlets. However, buying at such sales to resell to dealers or collectors can be profitable if one is careful to buy quality items, not common cameras that sell for very little at best, especially when they show wear. A very old camera is not necessarily valuable, as value depends on availability and quality. Knowing how to check out a camera or to judge quality will pay off when building a collection or when buying for resale.

Some very general guidelines follow, but for the serious buyer who intends to concentrate on cameras, there are several reference books that can be obtained. Most are rather expensive, but some provide good descriptions and/or price guidelines.

There are many distinct types of cameras to consider: large format (such as Graflex and large view cameras), medium format, early folding and box styles, 35mm single-lens-reflex (SLR), 35mm range finders, twin-lens-reflex (TLR), miniature or sub-miniature, novelty, and other types — including the more recent 'point-and-shoot' styles, Polaroids, and movie cameras. Though there is a growing interest in certain types, we would caution you against buying common Polaroids and movie cameras for resale, as there is very little market for them at this time. However, from a collector's standpoint, you can get some great buys on these types of cameras, so now is a great time to build an extensive collection.

Most pre-1930s, folding and box-type cameras were produced, which today make good collector items. Most have fairly low values because they were made in vast numbers. Many of the more expensive classics were manufactured in the 1930 – 1955 period and include primarily the Rangefinder type of camera and those with the first built-in meters. The most prized of these are of German or Japanese manufacture, valued because of their innovative designs and great optics. The key to collecting these types of cameras is to find a mint-condition item or one still in the original box. In camera collecting, quality is the most important aspect.

This updated listing includes only a few of the various categories and models of cameras from the many thousands available and gives current average retail prices for working models with average wear. Note that cameras in mint condition or like new with their original boxes may be valued much higher, while very worn examples with defects (scratches, dents, torn covers, poor optics, nonworking meters or range finders, torn bellows, corroded battery compartments, etc.) would be valued far less. A dealer, when buying for resale, will pay only a percentage of these values, as he must consider his expenses for refurbishing, cleaning, etc., as well as sales expenses. Again, remember that quality is the key to value, and prices on some cameras vary widely according to condition.

Typical collector favorites are old Alpa, Canon, Contax, Nikon, Leica, Rolleiflex, some Zeiss-Ikon models, Exakta, and certain Voigtlander models. For information about these makes as well as models by other manufacturers, please consult the advisor.

Advisor: C.E. Cataldo (See Directory, Cameras)

Agfa, Billy, early 1930s..**$15.00**
Agfa, box type, 1930-50, from $10 to **$30.00**
Agfa, Isolette **$20.00**
Agfa, Karat-35, 1940..**$35.00**
Agfa, Optima, 1960s, from $20 to................................**$50.00**
Aires, 35III, 1958...**$35.00**
Alpa, Standard, 1946-52, Swiss.............................**$1,500.00**
Ansco, Cadet **$5.00**
Ansco, Folding, Nr 1 to Nr 10, ea, from $10 to **$40.00**
Ansco, Memar, 1954-58 ....**$20.00**
Ansco, Memo, 1927 type..**$100.00**
Ansco, Speedex, Standard, 1950....................................**$15.00**
Ansco, Super Speedex, 3.5 lens, 1953-58 ....**$175.00**
Argoflex, Seventy-five, TLR, 1949-58 ....**$7.00**
Argus A2F, 1940 ....**$20.00**
Argus C3, Black brick type, 1940-50 ....**$10.00**
Argus C4, 2.8 lens w/flash **$30.00**
Asahi Pentax, Original, 1957..**$200.00**
Asahiflex 1, 1st Japanese SLR **$500.00**
Baldi, by Balda-Werk, 1930s..**$30.00**
Bell & Howell Dial-35 ....**$50.00**
Bell & Howell Foton, 1948...**$1,200.00**
Bolsey, B2 ....**$20.00**
Braun Paxette I, 1952 ....**$30.00**
Burke & James, Cub, 1914..**$20.00**
Canon A-1 ....**$165.00**
Canon AE-1, from $70 to **$110.00**
Canon AE-1P, from $90 to..**$130.00**
Canon F-1 ....**$225.00**
Canon IIB, 1949-53 ....**$250.00**
Canon III...**$250.00**
Canon IV, 1950-52 ....**$300.00**

Canon J, 1939-44, from $4,000 to...........................**$6,000.00**
Canon L-1, 1956-57..**$400.00**
Canon P, 1958-61..**$300.00**
Canon Rangefinder IIF, ca 1954...............................**$350.00**
Canon S-II, Seiki-Kogaku, 1946-47, from $600 to **$800.00**
Canon S-II, 1947-49..**$375.00**
Canon T-50, from $50 to...**$85.00**
Canon TL, from $60...**$80.00**
Canon TX...**$60.00**
Canon VT, 1956-57..**$300.00**
Canon 7, 1961-64..**$450.00**
Canonet QL1, from $25 to **$40.00**
Ciroflex, TLR, 1940s..**$30.00**
Compass Camera, 1938, from $1,000 to **$1,300.00**
Conley, 4x5 Folding Plate, 1905...............................**$150.00**
Contessa 35, 1950-55, from $100 to **$150.00**
Contex II or III, 1936, from $300 to...........................**$450.00**
Detrola Model D, Detroit Corp, 1938-40....................**$20.00**
Eastman Folding Brownie Six-20................................**$12.00**
Eastman Kodak Baby Brownie, Bakelite **$10.00**
Eastman Kodak Bantam, Art Deco, 1935-38...............**$35.00**
Eastman Kodak Box Brownie 2A..................................**$7.00**
Eastman Kodak Box Hawkeye No 2A...........................**$8.00**
Eastman Kodak Hawkeye, plastic.................................**$8.00**
Eastman Kodak Medalist, 1941-48, from $140 to **$200.00**
Eastman Kodak No 1 Folding Pocket camera **$20.00**
Eastman Kodak No 3A Folding Pocket camera...........**$30.00**
Eastman Kodak Pony 135 ....**$10.00**
Eastman Kodak Retina II...**$65.00**
Eastman Kodak Retina IIa...**$90.00**
Eastman Kodak Retina IIIc, from $125 to.................**$180.00**
Eastman Kodak Retina IIIC, from $250 to **$450.00**
Eastman Kodak Retinette, various models, ea, from $20
   to **$50.00**
Eastman Kodak Signet 35..**$20.00**
Eastman Kodak Signet 80..**$60.00**
Eastman Kodak 35, 1940-51..**$25.00**
Eastman Premo, many models exist, ea, from $30 to...**$200.00**
Eastman View Cameras, early 1900s, from $100 to ..**$200.00**
Edinex, by Wirgen **$30.00**
Exakta II, 1949-50...**$130.00**
Exakta VX, 1951...**$85.00**
FED 1, USSR, postwar, from $45 to............................**$60.00**
FED 1, USSR, prewar, from $80 to.............................**$135.00**
Fujica AX-3 ....**$80.00**
Fujica AX-5 ....**$125.00**
Fujica ST-701...**$70.00**
Graflex Pacemaker Crown Graphic, various sizes, ea, from
   $80 to..**$150.00**
Graflex Speed Graphic, various sizes, ea, from $100 to .**$200.00**
Hasselblad 1000F, 1952-57, from $500 to **$700.00**
Herbert-George, Donald Duck, 1946 ....**$35.00**
Kodak No 2 Folding Pocket Brownie, 1904-07 ....**$40.00**
Konica Autoreflex TC, various models, ea, from $60 to ..**$90.00**
Konica FS-1 ....**$75.00**
Konica III Rangefinder, 1956-59 ....**$125.00**
Kowa H, 1963-67 ....**$35.00**

Leica II, 1963-67...**$450.00**
Leica IID, 1932-38, from $250 to...............................**$400.00**
Leica IIIf, 1950-56, from $300 to **$500.00**
Leica M3, 1954-66, from $600 to...........................**$1,100.00**
Mamiya-Sekor 500TL, 1966..**$25.00**
Mamiyaflex, TLR, 1951, from $125 to.......................**$150.00**
Mercury Model II, CX, 1945.......................................**$35.00**

Mercury II, CX, half-frame, 1945, 35mm, $50.00. (Photo courtesy C.E. Cataldo)

Minolta Autocord, TLR **$100.00**
Minolta HiMatic Series, various models, ea, from $25 to ..**$30.00**
Minolta SR-7 ....**$50.00**
Minolta SRT-101, from $50 to.....................................**$70.00**
Minolta SRT-202, from $50 to.....................................**$90.00**
Minolta X-700...**$155.00**
Minolta XD-11, 1977..**$140.00**
Minolta XG-1, XG-7, XG-9, XG-A, ea, from $50 to.....**$80.00**
Minolta 35, early Rangefinder models, 1947-50, ea, from $250
   to..**$500.00**
Minolta-16, miniature, various models, ea, from $15 to..**$30.00**
Minox B, spy camera **$125.00**
Miranda Automex II, 1963...**$70.00**
Nikkormat (Nikon), various models, ea, from $80 to ..**$150.00**
Nikon EM, from $60 to...**$80.00**
Nikon F, various finders & meters, ea, from $150 to.**$275.00**
Nikon FG..**$125.00**
Nikon FM..**$160.00**
Nikon S Rangefinder, 1951-54, from $350 to............**$700.00**
Nikon S2 Rangefinder, 1954-58, from $300 to..........**$500.00**
Nikon S3 Rangefinder, 1958-60, from $500 to........**$1,200.00**
Olympus OM-1 ....**$120.00**
Olympus OM-10..**$65.00**
Olympus Pen EE, compact half-frame **$35.00**
Olympus Pen F, compact half-frame SLR, from $150 to .**$200.00**
Pax M3, 1957...**$40.00**
Pentax K-1000, from $70 to **$100.00**
Pentax ME..**$75.00**
Pentax Spotmatic, many models, ea, from $40 to.....**$150.00**
Petri FT, FT-1000, FT-EE & similar models, ea **$70.00**
Petri-7, 1961..**$20.00**
Plaubel-Makina II, 1933-39..**$200.00**
Polaroid, most models, ea, from $5 to.......................**$10.00**

Polaroid SX-70...**$35.00**
Polaroid 110, 110A, 110B, ea from $30 to.................**$50.00**
Polaroid 180, 185, 190, 195, ea, from $100 to...........**$250.00**
Praktica FX, 1952-57..**$40.00**
Praktica Super TL...**$50.00**
Realist Stereo, 3.5 lens...**$100.00**
Regula, King, various models, fixed lens, ea..............**$25.00**
Regula, King, various models, interchangeable lens, ea..**$75.00**
Ricoh Diacord 1, TLR, built-in meter, 1958.................**$75.00**
Ricoh KR-30..**$90.00**
Ricoh Singlex, 1965 ....**$80.00**
Rollei 35, miniature, Germany, 1966-70, from $175 to .**$275.00**
Rollei 35, miniature, Singapore, from $100 to...........**$175.00**
Rolleicord II, 1936-50, from $70 to..........................**$90.00**
Rolleiflex Automat, 1937 model **$125.00**
Rolleiflex SL35M, 1978, from $75 to........................**$100.00**
Rolleiflex 3.5E..**$300.00**
Samoca 35, 1950s...**$25.00**
Sereco 4x5, Folding Plate, Sears, 1901, from $90 to.**$135.00**
Spartus Press Flash, 1939-50 ....**$10.00**

Subminiature 'Hit' Novelty, $20.00.
(Photo courtesy C.E. Cataldo)

Taron 35, 1955 ....**$25.00**
Tessina, miniature, from $300 to **$500.00**
Tessina, miniature in colors, from $400 to **$700.00**
Topcon Super D, 1963-74 ....**$125.00**
Topcon Uni **$40.00**
Tower 45, Sears, w/Nikkor lens **$200.00**
Tower 50, Sears, w/Cassar lens **$20.00**
Univex-A, Univ Camera Co, 1933............................**$25.00**
Voigtlander Bessa, various folding models, 1931-49, ea, from
    $15 to..**$35.00**
Voigtlander Bessa, w/rangefinder, 1936...................**$140.00**
Voigtlander Brilliant, TLR, metal body version, 1933..**$30.00**
Voigtlander Vitessa L, 1954, from $150 to.................**$250.00**
Voigtlander Vitessa T, 1957 ....**$200.00**
Voigtlander Vito II, 1950..**$50.00**
Yashica A, TLR **$45.00**
Yashica Electro-35, 1966......................................**$25.00**
Yashica FX-70...**$70.00**
Yashicamat 124G, TLR, from $150 to **$250.00**

Zeiss Baldur Box Tengor, Frontar lens, 1935, from $35 to.**$150.00**
Zeiss Ikon Juwell, 1927-39.....................................**$500.00**
Zeiss Ikon Nettar, folding Roll Film, various sizes, ea, from
    $20 to..**$35.00**
Zeiss Ikon Super Ikonta B, 1937-56.........................**$150.00**
Zenit A, USSR, from $20 to.....................................**$35.00**
Zorki, USSR, 1950-56, from $30 to **$50.00**
Zorki-4, USSR Rangefinder, 1956-73........................**$65.00**

Candlewick Glassware

This is a beautifully simple, very diverse line of glassware made by the Imperial Glass Company of Bellaire, Ohio, from 1936 to 1982. (The factory closed in 1984.) From all explored written material found so far, it is known that Mr. Earl W. Newton brought back a piece of the French Cannonball pattern upon returning from a trip. The first Candlewick mold was derived using that piece of glass as a reference. As for the name Candlewick, it was introduced at a Wheeling, West Virginia, centennial celebration in August of 1936, appearing on a brochure showing the crafting of 'Candlewick Quilts' and promoting the new Candlewick line.

Imperial did cuttings on Candewick; several major patterns are Floral, Valley Lily, Starlight, Princess, DuBarry, and Dots. Remember, these are *cuts* and should not be confused with etchings. (Cuts that were left unpolished were called Gray Cut — an example of this is the Dot cut.) The most popular Candlewick etching was Rose of Sharon (Wild Rose). All cutting was done on a wheel, while etching utilized etching paper and acid. Many collectors confuse these two processes. Imperial also used gold, silver, platinum, and hand painting to decorate Candlewick, and they made several items in colors.

With over 740 pieces in all, Imperial's Candlewick line was one of the leading tableware patterns in the country. Due to its popularity with collectors today, it is still number one and has the distinction of being the only single line of glassware ever to have had two books written about it, a national newsletter, and over fifteen collector clubs across the USA devoted to it exclusively.

There are reproductions on the market today — some are coming in from foreign countries. Look-alikes are often mistakenly labeled Candlewick, so if you're going to collect this pattern, you need to be well informed. Most collectors use the company mold numbers to help identify all the variations and sizes. The *Imperial Glass Encyclopedia, Vol. 1*, has a very good chapter on Candlewick. Other references are *Candlewick, The Jewel of Imperial*, by Mary Wetzel-Tomalka; and *Elegant Glassware of the Depression Era* by Gene Florence (Collector Books).

Advisor: Kathy Doub (See Directory, Imperial Glass)

Newsletter: *The Candlewick Collector* (Quarterly)
Virginia R. Scott, Editor
Subscriptions, $7.00 direct to
Connie Doll
17609 Falling Water Rd., Strongsville, OH 44136; 440-846-9610
e-mail: CWCollector@AOL.com

Ashtray, heart, #400/173, 5½" **$12.00**
Ashtray, round, #400/19, 2¾" **$9.00**
Ashtray, set, sq, nesting, #400/650, 3-pc...................**$130.00**
Ashtray, sq, #400/652, 4½".......................................**$40.00**

Birthday cake plate, 13", 400/160, $550.00.

Bowl, bouillon; handles, #400/126...........................**$50.00**
Bowl, centerpiece; flared, #400/13B, 11" **$65.00**
Bowl, cottage cheese; 6"..**$25.00**
Bowl, float, #400/92F, 12"...**$40.00**
Bowl, heart, #400/49H, 9"..**$135.00**
Bowl, ivy; high, bead foot, #3400/188, 7" **$225.00**
Bowl, jelly; w/lid, #400/59, 5½" **$75.00**
Bowl, nappy, 4-footed, #400/74B, 8½" **$75.00**
Bowl, relish; 2-part, #400/84, 6½"..............................**$25.00**
Bowl, relish; 5-part, #400/56, 13½"............................**$55.00**
Bowl, salad; #400/75B, 10½".....................................**$40.00**
Bowl, sq, #400/231, 5" **$100.00**
Bowl, 3-part, w/lid, #400/216, 10" **$495.00**
Bowl, 3-toed, #400/205, 10"..**$165.00**
Cake stand, high foot, #400/103D, 11" **$95.00**
Candle holder, flower, 2-bead stem, #400/66F, 4".....**$110.00**
Candle holder, heart shape, #400/40HC, 5"...............**$110.00**
Candle holder, mushroom, #400/86 ....**$35.00**
Candle holder, 3-way, beaded base, #400/115...........**$125.00**
Candy box, #400/59, 5½" dia **$45.00**
Candy box, beaded foot, w/lid, #400/140 ....**$595.00**
Clock, 4" dia..**$395.00**
Coaster, w/spoon rest, #400/226 ....**$16.00**
Compote, 2-bead stem, #400/66B, 5½"......................**$22.00**
Compote, 3-bead stems, #400/220, 5".......................**$85.00**
Creamer & sugar bowl, #400/31...............................**$25.00**
Creamer & sugar bowl, domed foot, #400/18...........**$295.00**
Cup, coffee; #400/37..**$7.50**
Cup, tea; #400/35 ....**$8.00**
Fork & spoon set, #400/75...**$35.00**
Ice tub, #400/63, 5½x8"..**$110.00**
Icer, seafood/fruit cocktail; #3800 line, 1-bead stem, 2-pc..**$90.00**
Ladle, marmalade; 3-bead stem, #400/130.................**$12.00**

Mayonnaise set, plate, heart bowl & spoon, #400/49, 3-pc .**$35.00**
Oil cruet, bead base, #400/164, 4-oz **$55.00**
Oil cruet, bulbous bottom, #400/275, 6-oz................**$60.00**
Pitcher, #400/24, 80-oz..**$125.00**
Pitcher, plain, #400/416, 20-oz..................................**$40.00**
Pitcher, short, round, #400/330, 14-oz **$275.00**
Plate, canape; w/off-center indent, #400/36, 6" **$15.00**
Plate, crimped, handles, #400/145C, 12"..................**$40.00**
Plate, crimped, handles, #400/62C, 8½".....................**$22.00**
Plate, crimped, handles, #400/72C, 10"......................**$35.00**
Plate, salad; #400/3D, 7"..**$8.00**
Plate, salad; oval, #400/38, 9" **$40.00**
Plate, serving; cupped edge, #400/75V, 12½".............**$30.00**
Plate, torte; handles, #400/113D, 14" **$40.00**
Plate, triangular, #400/266, 7½"................................**$250.00**
Platter, #400/131D, 16"...**$225.00**
Rose bowl, #400/142K, 7"...**$395.00**
Salad set, round plate, flared bowl, fork & spoon, #400/75B, 4-pc..**$95.00**
Salt & pepper shakers, beaded feet, bulbous, chrome lids, #400/96, pr **$10.00**
Salt & pepper shakers, individual, #400/109, pr **$11.00**
Salt cellar, 18 beads, #400/61, 2"...............................**$10.00**
Sauce boat, #400/169..**$125.00**
Snack jar, bead foot, w/lid, #400/139/1......................**$550.00**
Stem, champagne/sherbet; #3800, 4-oz.......................**$18.00**
Stem, cocktail; #4000...**$22.00**
Stem, cordial; #3800, 1-oz..**$45.00**
Stem, iced-tea goblet; #4000, 11-oz **$40.00**
Stem, parfait; #3400, 6-oz...**$58.00**
Stem, tall sherbet; #400/190, 5-oz **$15.00**
Stem, water goblet, #3400, 9-oz..................................**$20.00**
Stem, water; #400/190, 10-oz **$18.00**
Stem, wine; #3400, 4-oz..**$20.00**
Tray, fruit; center handle, #400/68F, 10½"..................**$175.00**
Tray, upturned handles, #400/42E, 5½".......................**$20.00**
Tumbler, #400/15, 10-oz...**$195.00**
Tumbler, #400/19, 10-oz...**$12.00**
Tumbler, iced tea; #400/18, 12-oz..............................**$80.00**
Tumbler, juice; #400/19, 5-oz.....................................**$10.00**
Tumbler, low sherbet; #400/19, 5-oz...........................**$18.00**
Vase, #400/198, 6" dia **$300.00**
Vase, bead foot, sm neck, ball, #400/25, 4"................**$50.00**
Vase, bead foot, straight sides, #400/22, 10" **$195.00**
Vase, fan; bead handles, #400/87F, 8".......................**$35.00**

Candy Containers

Most of us can recall buying these glass toys as a child, since they were made well into the 1960s. We were fascinated by the variety of their shapes then, just as collectors are today. Looking back, it couldn't have been we were buying them for the candy, though perhaps as a child those tiny sugary balls flavored more with the coloring agent than anything else were enough to satisfy our 'sweet tooth.'

Glass candy containers have been around since our country's centennial celebration in 1876 when the first two, the Liberty Bell and the Independence Hall, were introduced. Since then they have been made in hundreds of styles, and some of them have become very expensive. The leading manufacturers were in the East — Westmoreland, Victory Glass, J.H. Millstein, Crosetti, L.E. Smith, Jack Stough, T.H. Stough, and West Bros. made perhaps 90% of them — and collectors report finding many in the Pennsylvania area. Most are clear, but you'll find them in various other colors as well.

Plastic parts were incorporated into candy containers as early as the 1940s, and by 1960 virtually all were made entirely of this inexpensive, colorful, and versatile material. Children were soon clamoring for these new all-plastic containers, many of which seemed as much a toy as a mere candy container. Today most of these are imported from China and Mexico. Shapes vary from vehicles of all sorts to cartoon, movie, and TV characters, TV sets, and telephones, to holiday decorations and household items. Collector interest is apparent in shops and malls as well as on the Internet.

If you're going to deal in candy containers of either the vintage glass variety or modern plastics, you'll need a book that will show you all the variations available. Vintage candy container buffs will find *Collector's Guide to Candy Containers* by Douglas M. Dezso, J. Leon Poirier, and Rose D. Poirier to be a wonderful source of pictures and information. D&P numbers in our listings refer to that book. Published by Collector Books, it is a must for beginners as well as seasoned collectors. Other references are *The Compleat American Glass Candy Containers Handbook* by Eilkelberner and Agadjaninian (revised by Adele Bowden) and Jenny Long's *Album of Candy Containers, Vol. 1* and *Vol. 2,* published in 1978 – 83, now out of print. Plastic containers are well represented in *Modern Candy Containers & Novelties* by Jack Brush and William Miller, also by Collector Books.

Because of their popularity and considerable worth, many of the original glass containers have been reproduced. Beware of any questionable glassware that has a slick or oily touch. Among those that have been produced are Amber Pistol, Auto, Carpet Sweeper, Chicken on Nest, Display Case, Dog, Drum Mug, Fire Engine, Independence Hall, Jackie Coogan, Kewpie, Mail Box, Mantel Clock, Mule and Waterwagon, Peter Rabbit, Piano, Rabbit Pushing Wheelbarrow, Rocking Horse, Safe, Santa, Santa's Boot, Station Wagon, and Uncle Sam's Hat. Others are possible.

Our values are given for candy containers that are undamaged, in good original paint, and complete (with all original parts and closure). Repaired or repainted containers are worth much less.

See also Christmas; Easter; Halloween.

Club/Newsletter: *The Candy Gram*
Candy Container Collectors of America
Betty MacDuff, Membership Chairperson
2711 De La Rosa Street
The Villages, FL 32159
www.candycontainer.org

Modern

Airplane (double tail), blue plastic, paper closure, West Germany, 7/16x3x2⅞", from $4 to **$5.00**

Barrel of Monkeys, plastic w/paper label, Hasbro, made in Mexico, 3½x2¼", from $4.50 to **$6.00**

Bugs Bunny Pocket Pack, gumball dispenser, Processed Plastic Co, made in China, 3½", from $4.50 to.......**$5.50**

Cannon, yellow & red plastic, West Germany embossed on barrel, 1x¾x2⅜", from $5.50 to **$7.00**

Duck, plastic, Wizard Candy Pet, Wizard Toys, made in China, 2⅞", from $3 to **$4.00**

Flying Saucer, plastic, 4-color, push alien's head to dispence candy, battery operated, Bee International, 3⅜x4" dia...**$4.00**

Hulk gumball dispenser, plastic, Imaginings 3, made in China, 5⅝", from $3.50 to **$5.50**

Jelly Belly Truck, plastic, w/clear trailer & cardboard label, back doors open, Goelitz, 5¾" L, from $9 to.......**$10.50**

Jump Shot gumball dispenser, Bee International, made in China, 3¾x2¾x2⅜", from $5 to.............................**$6.50**

Mr Freeze, plastic, Creative Confection Concepts, made in China, 4", from $5 to **$6.50**

Parrot, colorful plastic, eyes move when shaken, whistle in tail, Allen Mitchel, Hong Kong, 4⅝", from $5 to....**$7.00**

Power Ranger, red & white, marked 1993 Saban, made in China, 3⅞", from $5 to **$7.00**

Rabbit, clear plastic figure w/hands together in front, Pieces of Heaven, West Germany, 8", from $10 to.........**$15.00**

Roller Skates, plastic w/plastic string attached to back of shoe, push closure, Topps, 1991, 2¼", from $5 to.**$8.00**

Soldier, black top & bottom, clear middle, paper litho face & chest, HILCO Corporation c 1992 Made in China, 6"..**$4.00**

Sweet Tarts Candy Camera, yellow plastic, Tapper, made in China, 3x4⅝x1⅛", from $3 to **$4.50**

Taffy Apple, red apple w/worm (closure), Creative Confection Concepts, made in Mexico, 2⅜x3⅛x2¼", from $4 to...**$6.50**

Vintage

Army Bomber, star-in-circle insignia, wax push-in closure, HJ Millstein/Jeannette, D&P 76, ca 1944, 4⅛", from $35 to...**$50.00**

Bell, Stough's; vertical ribs at lower third, in cardboard rest, D&P 96, ca 1944, 2¼", complete, from $300 to ...**$350.00**

Car, Boyd; various colors, D&P 159 ....**$30.00**

Car, Little Sedan; marked 3 DR JS Co & numbered, D&P 171..**$35.00**

Chicago Bus, 8 windows ea side, red tin snap-on closure, D&P 149, 1940s, 1⅞x5x1½", from $400 to **$450.00**

Chick in Shell Auto, 12 raised vents ea side, 8 spokes on wheels, D&P 8, ca 1922, 2⅜x4¼", from $200 to....**$250.00**

Chicken on Oblong Basket, Victory Glass Co, D&P 11, ca 1930, 3x2⅞x1⅝", from $60 to **$75.00**

Clarinet, red & white striped tube at top, D&P 448....**$35.00**

Clock, Candy Bank; all plastic, D&P 479....................**$40.00**

Dog, Hound w/Lg Glass Hat; seated, D&P 27 ....$20.00

Dog, Scottie, looking straight ahead, D&P 35 ....$25.00

Dog w/Umbrella, wearing coat & bow tie, black Bakelite screw-on hat-form lid, D&P 37, ca 1940, 2⅞", from $60 to..**$80.00**

Fire Engine, Fire Department in Circle, D&P 253 ....$50.00

Fire Engine, Mini; w/driver, no steering wheel, D&P 258..**$25.00**

Gun, Medium w/Hook Grip; screw head in grip, D&P 396 ....**$35.00**

Gun, Stough's Whistling Jim - Straight Grip, D&P 402 .**$25.00**

Gun, Waffle Grip; Stough, D&P 406..........................**$25.00**

Hearse #2, heavy glass w/open top, lines on hood, tin slide-on closure, D&P 165A, 2¾x4¼x2⅛", from $100 to..**$150.00**

Hound w/Large Glass Hat, push-in closure reads TH Stough Co..., D&P 27, ca 1957, 3½x2¾x1¾", from $35 to..**$50.00**

Jeep, D&P 410, 4¼" long, from $25.00 to $35.00.

Kettle on Three Feet, horizontal ribs, original closure, D&P 307 ....**$45.00**

Koala, stippled figural w/black plastic screw-on cap (at base), marked San Diego Zoo, D&P 49, 6¾", from $15 to..**$20.00**

Lamp, clear plastic w/cork closure in base, D&P 340, ca 1950, 4x2½", from $60 to **$75.00**

Lamp, Mini Kerosene; boot base, D&P 337................**$15.00**

Lantern, Aluminum Top & Bottom; beaded ribs, D&P 343 ....**$35.00**

Lantern, Dec 20'04 - Medium; shaker top, D&P 351 ..**$30.00**

Lantern, embossed ribs, metal top & base, marked W Glass Co Grapeville PA, D&P 375, 3¾x2¾x1⅞", from $40 to..**$45.00**

Lantern, Pat Apld for; Made in USA, D&P 359............**$20.00**

Locomotive, Curved Line 888; D&P 490 ....**$30.00**

Locomotive, Stough's E3S Wide Cab; D&P 505...........**$30.00**

Military Cap, D&P 388...**$25.00**

Nurser, Plain Oval; Crosetti, D&P 124......................**$20.00**

Nurser w/Glass Nipple, rolled cardboard plug, Jeannette, D&P 120, 2¾", from $40 to................................**$60.00**

Peter Rabbit, Jeannette, D&P 60 ....**$30.00**

Porch Swing, metal swing on stand (bag was tied to seat w/ribbon), D&P 315, ca 1933-36, 4⅛x4x2¼", from $200 to..**$250.00**

Racer #12, straps over hood, 2 vents ea side, no dividers, tin snap-on closure, D&P 476, ca 1942, 5⅜", from $175 to..**$220.00**

Santa's Boot - Glass; embossed strap, D&P 273..........**$20.00**

Snowman w/Pipe, plastic, E Rosen Co, D&P 290, ca 1945, 5", from $10 to..**$15.00**

Tank, Two Cannons; D&P 413 ....**$35.00**

Village Engine Co No 23, tin litho firehouse form, red or gray roof, D&P 138, 2⅞x2⅝x1¾", from $125 to **$150.00**

Cape Cod by Avon

You can't walk through any flea market or mall now without seeing a good supply of this lovely ruby red glassware. It was made by Wheaton Glass Co. and sold by Avon from 1975 until it was discontinued in 1993. A gradual phasing-out process lasted for approximately two years. The small cruet and tall candlesticks, for instance, were filled originally with one or the other of their fragrances, the wine and water goblets were filled with scented candle wax, and the dessert bowl with guest soap. Many 'campaigns' featured accessory tableware items such as plates, cake stands, and a water pitcher. Though still plentiful, dealers tell us that interest in this glassware is on the increase, and we expect values to climb as supplies diminish.

For more information we recommend *Avon's Cape Cod*, by Debbie and Randy Coe.

Advisor: Debbie Coe (See Directory, Cape Cod)

Bell, Hostess; marked Christmas 1979, 6½".................**$22.50**

Bell, Hostess; unmarked, 1979-80, 6½".....................**$18.50**

Bowl, dessert; 1978-90, 6½"....................................**$14.50**

Bowl, rimmed soup; 1991, 7½" **$24.50**

Bowl, vegetable; marked Centennial Edition 1886-1986, 8¾"..**$35.00**

Bowl, vegetable; unmarked, 1986-90, 8¾" **$30.00**

Box, trinket; heart form, w/lid, 1989-90, 4"................**$19.50**

Butter dish, w/lid, 1983-84, ¼-lb, 7" L.......................**$24.50**

Cake knife, red plastic handle, wedge-shaped blade, Regent Sheffield, 1981-84, 8" **$15.00**

Candle holder, hurricane type w/clear chimney, 1985...**$45.00**

Candlestick, 1975-80, 8¾", ea **$12.50**

Candlestick, 1983-84, 2½", ea **$9.75**

Candy dish, 1987-90, 3½x6" dia **$19.50**

Christmas ornament, 6-sided, marked Christmas 1990, 3¼"..**$14.50**

Creamer, footed, 1981-84, 4"...................................**$12.50**

Cruet, oil; w/stopper, 1975-80, 5-oz.........................**$12.50**

Cup & saucer, 15th Anniversary, marked 1975-1990 on cup, 7-oz..**$24.50**

Cup & saucer, 1990-93, 7-oz...................................**$19.50**

Decanter, w/stopper, 1977-80, 16-oz, 10½" **$18.00**

Goblet, claret; 1992, 5-oz, 5¼" **$14.00**

Goblet, saucer champagne; 1991, 8-oz, 5¼" **$15.00**

Goblet, water; 1976-90, 9-oz...................................**$9.50**

Goblet, wine; 1977-80, 3-oz, 4½" **$3.00**
Mug, pedestal foot, 1982-84, 5-oz, 5"................**$12.50**
Napkin ring, 1989-90, 1¾".................................**$9.50**
Pie plate/server, 1992-93, 10¾" dia **$38.50**
Pitcher, water; footed, 1984-85, 60-oz...............**$49.50**
Plate, bread & butter; 1992-93, 5½" **$10.00**
Plate, cake; pedestal foot, 1991, 3½x10¾" dia **$50.00**
Plate, dessert; 1980-90, 7½".................................**$8.00**
Plate, dinner; 1982-90, 11" **$30.00**
Platter, oval, 1986, 13" **$59.50**
Relish, rectangular, 2-part, 1985-96, 9½" **$19.50**
Salt & pepper shakers, marked May 1978, ea **$9.50**
Salt & pepper shakers, unmarked, 1978-80, ea **$7.50**
Sauce boat, footed, 1988, 8" L **$29.50**
Sugar bowl, footed, 1980-83, 3½" **$12.50**
Tidbit tray, 2-tiered (7" & 10" dia), 1987, 9¾".............**$56.50**
Tumbler, straight-sided, footed, 1988, 8-oz, 3½"........**$12.00**
Tumbler, straight-sided, 1990, 12-oz, 5½" **$14.50**
Vase, footed, 1985, 8" **$24.00**

Cardinal China Company

This was the name of a distributing company who had their merchandise made to order and sold it through a chain of showrooms and outlet stores in several states from the late 1940s through the 1950s. (Although they made some of their own pottery early on, we have yet to find out just what they themselves produced.) They used their company name to mark cookie jars (some of which were made by the American Bisque Company), novelty wares, and kitchen items, many of which you'll see as you make your flea market rounds. *The Collector's Encyclopedia of Cookie Jars* by Joyce and Fred Roerig (Collector Books) shows a page of their jars, and more can be seen in *American Bisque* by Mary Jane Giacomini (Schiffer).

Cake plate, gold-plated, marked Cardinal China Co Warranted 22K Made in USA, 10¼".................**$10.00**
Cheese dish, cheese wedges (various types) on white, rectangular, 5x3¾".................................**$8.00**
Cheese plate, mouse atop slab of cheese, 13x10" **$15.00**
Corn holder, corn husks, marked Corn Husks by Cardinal China, 9", 4 for.................................**$10.00**
Crumber set, airbrushed leaves, wood-handled brush w/plastic bristles, 2-pc.................................**$12.50**
Doorstop, Keystone Cop, American Bisque, 8"..........**$95.00**
Dresser dish, Doxie-dog, from $15 to.................**$18.00**
Egg dish, rooster in bright pastels, green painted scallops at rim, 2 sm & 1 lg well, 6" dia **$15.00**
Egg timer, windmill, 4½".................................**$45.00**
Flower holder, turquoise on white, doughnut shape, 7" .**$8.00**
Gravy boat, roses, 2⅝x7¾".................................**$10.00**
Measuring spoon holder, cottage w/peaked roof, applied thermometer.................................**$15.00**
Measuring spoon holder, flowerpot, plain (not basketweave) base.................................**$10.00**

Measuring spoon holder, flowerpot w/basketweave base, w/spoons.................................**$12.00**
Measuring spoon holder, Measure Boy.................**$25.00**
Measuring spoon holder, windowsill-planter shape w/plastic spoons as flowers **$15.00**
Ring holder, elephant figural, shamrock, flat back w/hole for hanging.................................**$12.00**
Salt & pepper shakers, Chinese man & lady, green & yellow, pr.................................**$20.00**
Scissors holder, nest w/chicken figural.................**$22.00**
Shrimp boats, 4¾" L w/cardboard sail on wooden pole, various colors, set of 4, from $65 to **$75.00**
Spoon rest, double sunflower form, 6x5½", from $7 to .**$10.00**
Spoon rest, rooster on white, triangular, 1950s **$15.00**
String holder, nest w/chicken figural **$25.00**
Switch plate, bluebirds, Good Morning/Good Night, 5¼x4".................................**$22.00**
Teabag holder, single 5-petal flower face.................**$6.00**

Carnival Chalkware

From about 1910 until sometime in the 1950s, winners of carnival games everywhere in the United States were awarded chalkware figures of Kewpie dolls, the Lone Ranger, Hula girls, comic characters, etc. The assortment was vast and varied. The earliest were made of plaster with a pink cast. They ranged in size from about 5" up to 16".

They were easily chipped, so when it came time for the carnival to pick up and move on, they had to be carefully wrapped and packed away, a time consuming, tedious chore. When stuffed animals became available, concessionists found that they could simply throw them into a box without fear of damage, and so ended an era.

Today the most valuable of these statues are those modeled after Disney characters, movie stars, and comic book heroes.

Chalkware figures are featured in *The Carnival Chalk Prize, Vols I* and *II*, and *A Price Guide to Chalkware/Plaster Carnival Prizes*, all written by Thomas G. Morris. Along with photos, descriptions, and values, Mr. Morris has also included a fascinating history of carnival life in America.

Our values are for examples in excellent to near-mint condition.

Advisor: Tom Morris (See Directory, Carnival Chalkware)

Air raid warden, standing, holding American flag, ca 1940, 14".................................**$120.00**
Army soldier, standing beside pillar saluting, marked Luchini, ca 1941, 14".................................**$90.00**
Bell hop, copyright JY Jenkins Studio, Venice CA, ca 11/1946, 13".................................**$85.00**
Bulldog, sitting, ca 1930-45, 16" **$95.00**
Cannon, sailor at base saluting, marked Remember Pearl Harbor, ca 1940, 11x11x5" **$95.00**
Cat bank, sitting figure, marked Bank, ca 1940-50, 8½".................................**$35.00**
Cowboy holding hat, ca 1935-45, 8½" **$35.00**

Dog, sitting, known as Bonzo, Bimbo or Bozo, some marked Jenkins, ca 1925-45, 8½" **$45.00**

Dog ashtray, sitting figure, marked Rin Tin Tin, ca 1935-45, 10¼" **$45.00**

Donald Duck as Uncle Scrooge holding money bag, ca 1940-50, 8" **$55.00**

Dopey, standing w/hands on tummy, ca 1937-50, 13" ...**$95.00**

Fan dancer w/hands behind head, w/feathers, marked Art, ca 1935-45, 12½" **$125.00**

Girl, I Love Me type, pink chalk, hand painted, ca 1915-30, 11½" **$60.00**

Girl, standing w/hands between knees, w/wig & lg eyes, hand painted, marked 1919, 10"..........................**$175.00**

Gorilla, King Kong, not marked, fists on chest, flat back, ca 1930-40, 6¼"...**$45.00**

Horse, standing circus type w/feather plume on head, ca 1935-45, 11"...**$45.00**

Hula girl w/hands under breasts, added skirt, ca 1940-50, 17"...**$200.00**

Jeff, cartoon character created by Bud Fisher, variations found, ca 1925-40, 5½-6", ea **$115.00**

Kewpie w/both hands on tummy, fat, ca 1935-45, 7½" ..**$25.00**

Kewpie-type girl, standing, jointed arms, original dress & wig, ca 1920-30, 12" **$165.00**

Lady, standing, jointed arms, crepe-paper dress & wig, ca 1920-30, 12"...**$185.00**

Lighthouse lamp, w/light inside, ca 1935-45, 15½" ...**$95.00**

Lovebirds, kissing, marked Eagle Love, ca 1940-50, 6¼" ..**$35.00**

Mae West, marked AL Venice Dolls, ca 1935-45, 14" ...**$165.00**

Mexican w/lg sombrero, marked Pancho or Happy Days, flat back, ca 1935-45, 11½".............................**$45.00**

Oriental lady, marked Ming Toy, Jenkins Studio, Venice CA, 8/1924, 13" **$195.00**

Pig bank, standing, happy countenance, ca 1940-50, 7"..**$25.00**

Pluto, sitting, Disney cartoon dog, unmarked, ca 1930-40, 6" **$50.00**

Popeye, standing w/left arm across chest, ca 1935-50, 15½" **$195.00**

Sailor girl w/hands in pockets, wearing jumpsuit & billed cap, Jenkins, 11/1924, 13½" **$95.00**

Scottie dog, sitting, pointed ears, lady bug on nose, ca 1935-45, 5" **$35.00**

Ship lamp, 3-D schooner, light on the inside, ca 1930-40, 14¾" **$145.00**

Shriner, standing w/cane, arm in sling, marked Just Joined, ca 1930-40, 10½"...**$45.00**

Three Little Pigs ashtray, Disney cartoon characters, ca 1935-45, 6½x5¼" **$45.00**

Cash Family, Clinchfield Artware

Some smaller East Tennessee potteries are beginning to attract collector attention. Clinchfild Artware produced by the Cash family of Erwin is one of them. The pottery was started in 1945 when the family first utilized a small building behind their home where they made three pottery pieces: a rolling-pin planter, a small elephant-shaped pitcher, and a buttermilk jug. Eventually they hired local artists to hand paint their wares. Cash products are sometimes confused with those made by the better-known Blue Ridge Pottery, due to the fact that many of the area's artisans worked first at one local company then another, and as a result, a style emerged that was typical of them all. Molds were passed around as local companies liquidated, adding to the confusion. But Cash's production was limited to specialty and souvenir pieces; the company never made any dinnerware.

For more information see *The Collector's Encyclopedia of Blue Ridge Dinnerware* by Bill and Betty Newbound (Collector Books).

Character jug, American Indian chief's head, tomahawk handle, bright multicolors **$225.00**

Character jug, lady w/dark hair forms handle, 1945, 6" .**$55.00**

Creamer & sugar bowl, yellow-brown & brown flowers, 5¼x6", 5½" **$32.50**

Ginger jar, cobalt blue w/continuous brush strokes, 4½" ..**$22.50**

Jug, Iris, lavender on white, sweeping handle loops above, body, 5¾" **$47.50**

Mug, kitten face embossed/glazed on side, 4"...........**$35.00**

Mug, Pine Cone, 4¼"...**$16.00**

Pitcher, Antique Violets, scalloped incurvate rim, 5" ..**$25.00**

Pitcher, blue flower clusters on white, ball shape, 6½x5" **$45.00**

Pitcher, elephant figural with hand-painted flowers, 4", $50.00.

Pitcher, pink dogwood, Karen shape, bulbous w/flat area where handle joins body, 5½"..........................**$32.50**

Pitcher, Sculptured Fruit, flat rim, 7" **$65.00**

Pitcher, white ear of corn figural w/green leaves at spout, green stem-like handle, 5" **$35.00**

Pitcher, white ear of corn figural w/leaves at base, green handle, miniature, 2"...................................**$22.00**

Pitcher & bowl, blue daisy-like flowers, 1945, 12", 17" ..**$75.00**

Planter, Baby's Book, book form w/lamb on front, pink & blue on white w/sm greenery, 4¼x4½x2⅜" **$24.50**

Planter, Scottie dog, white w/black details, 7" **$65.00**

Planter, swan figural, 10x11"..**$30.00**

Sugar bowl, orange-yellow flowers w/green leaves, light
  green trim at rim & handle, 5¼x6".......**$32.50**

Vase, Falling Leaves variation, waisted, 6"............**$24.50**

Vase, trumpet flowers & hummingbird, angular rim,
  9x4½" **$55.00**

Cat Collectibles

Cat collectibles continue to grow in popularity as cats continue to dominate the world of household pets. Cat memorabilia can be found in almost all categories, and this allows for collections to grow rapidly! Most cat lovers/collectors are attracted to all items and to all breeds, though some do specialize. Popular categories include Siamese, black cats, Kitty Cucumber, Kliban, cookie jars, teapots, books, plates, postcards, and Louis Wain.

Because cats are found throughout the field of collectibles and antiques, there is some 'crossover' competition among collectors. For example: Chessie, the C&O Railroad cat, is collected by railroad and advertising buffs; Felix the Cat, board games, puppets, and Steiff cats are sought by toy collectors. A Weller cat complements a Weller pottery collection just as a Royal Doulton Flambe cat fits into a Flambe porcelain collection.

Since about 1970 the array and quality of cat items have made the hobby explode. And, looking back, the first half of the twentieth century offered a somewhat limited selection of cats — there were those from the later Victorian era, Louis Wain cats, Felix the Cat, the postcard rage, and the kitchen-item black cats of the 1950s. But prior to 1890, cat items were few and far between, so a true antique cat (100-years old or more) is scarce, much sought after, and when found in mint condition, pricey. Examples of such early items would be original fine art, porcelains, and bronzes.

There are several 'cat' books available on today's market; if you want to see great photos representing various aspects of 'cat' collecting, you'll enjoy *Cat Collectibles* by Pauline Flick, *Antique Cats for Collectors* by Katharine Morrison McClinton, *American Cat-alogue* by Bruce Johnson, *Collectible Cats, Book II,* by Marbena "Jean" Fyke, and *The Cat Made Me Buy It* and *The Black Cat Made Me Buy It*, both by Muncaster and Yanow.

See also Black Cats; Character Collectibles; Cookie Jars; Holt Howard; Lefton.

Advisor: Karen Shanks (See Directory, Cat Collectibles)

Club: Cat Collectors

Newsletter: *Cat Talk*
Karen Shanks, President
PO Box 150784, Nashville, TN 37215
615-297-7403; www.catcollectors.com;
email: musiccitykitty@yahoo.com
Subscription $20 per year US or $27 Canada.

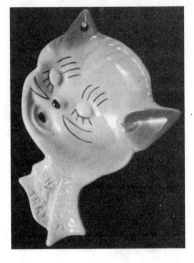

Ashtray/spoon rest, ceramic, ca 1940s, 7½", from $12.00 to $15.00. (Photo courtesy Marbena Fyke)

Bank, ceramic, orange cat figural, Laurel Burch,
  8x5½"...**$25.00**

Bedspread, cat in center, pink & white, baby's crib size,
  60x40", M..**$25.00**

Box, kitten atop trash can, multicolor w/decorative trim,
  Limoges, 2½"".......................................**$40.00**

Candle holder, 3 cats & 8 mice singing around base, cold cast
  resin, multicolor, 4x6", MIB.................**$27.50**

Cross-stitch chart, Siamese, w/black & white instructions for
  making wall hanging or pillow................**$16.50**

Figurine, clear crystal, Princess House, 1970s, original label
  on base **$15.00**

Figurines, Siamese, white w/green eyes, ceramic, ArtMark
  label, 11", pr.......................................**$30.00**

Knife rest, flat figural, white porcelain, Germany, 5¼"..**$60.00**

Lamp, figural cat base, tail raised, holds shade, green eyes
  light up, 15x7"....................................**$50.00**

Pincushion, silver figural, marked Sterling 925, 2"......**$20.00**

Squeeze toy, white w/pink & blue details, Arrow Rubber &
  Plastic Co, 1960, EX.............................**$20.00**

Tile, kitten w/yarn, Lowell Herrero, 1992, 4¼x4½"....**$18.00**

Character Cats

Cat in the Hat, bank, Cat in red car w/friend passenger, rubber & plastic, Stellar Gifts, 1997, M.......................**$15.00**

Cat in the Hat, book, The Cat in the Hat, 1957, 61 pages,
  EX..**$25.00**

Cat in the Hat, book, The Cat in the Hat Comes Back, 61
  pages, 1957, EX...................................**$20.00**

Cat in the Hat, box, hinged lid, w/Whozits, Midwest of
  Cannon Falls, MIB **$15.00**

Cat in the Hat, Christmas ornament, stamp, 1999, M.**$15.00**

Cat in the Hat, cigarette case, clear gloss enamel over picture
  of Cat & Whozits, 3x4", NM..................**$18.00**

Cat in the Hat, dictionary, I Can Read It All By Myself
  Beginner's Book, PD Eastman, 1964, VG+..........**$20.00**

Cat in the Hat, doll, talker, working, Mattel, 1970s, NM....**$250.00**

Cat in the Hat, doorstop, cast iron, w/Whozits, 1998,
  MIB **$25.00**

Cat in the Hat, Dr. Suess, plush figure, 1983, Coleco, $75.00. (Photo courtesy June Moon)

Cat in the Hat, Grow Chart, M $15.00

Cat in the Hat, guitar, plastic, turn crank for music, Mattel, 1970, 14", VG $40.00

Cat in the Hat, musical jack-in-the-box, plays For He's a Jolly Good Fellow, Mattel, 1970, from $75 to $100.00

Chessie, crib toy, figural, plush, musical, 1958, EXIB.$95.00

Chessie, embroidery kit, Columbia-Minerva, 1976, 14x11", EX $30.00

Chessie, mirror, Peake, Chessie's Old Man, 2x3" $12.00

Chessie, playing cards, 2 decks, 1 says Sleep Like a Kitten, other says, Peake-Chessie's Old Man, 1946, EXIB...$40.00

Chessie, pocketknife, Chessie on 1 side of blade, 1985 on other, Barlow, NMIB...$30.00

Chessie, printer's block, EX $30.00

Chessie, scarf, silk, red w/Chessie, black border, 22" sq, EX...$35.00

Felix the Cat, book, Felix the Cat, McLoughlin Bros, 24 pages, 1931, VG+...$120.00

Felix the Cat, clock, Kit Cat Clock, red cat w/swinging tail, Felix pictured in instructions, original, 15¼x4", NMIB $45.00

Felix the Cat, cookie jar, figure stands beside stack of cookies, Treasure Craft, retired, MIB.............................$50.00

Felix the Cat, doll, felt w/straw filling, wire frame, jointed head, 1920s, 13", VG+ $230.00

Felix the Cat, figural paperweight, lead painted black & white, Felix on base, 2¼", VG+............................$80.00

Felix the Cat, figurine, black & white on white base, Wade Ceramics, numbered certificate, 1997, NM...........$25.00

Felix the Cat, figurine, celluloid, black w/white features, Made in Japan, 1930s, 2", EX...............................$50.00

Felix the Cat, figurine, wood w/original strings, leather ears, jointed body, Sullivan, 1925, EX....................$165.00

Felix the Cat, mug, Felix Kept On Walking in black on white, EX..$80.00

Felix the Cat, music box, Felix playing piano on base w/city scene, Enesco, 1987, EX......................................$120.00

Felix the Cat, puzzle, dexterity; Felix in black on white, marked Industrial Sunday, Germany, 1926, VG+ .$80.00

Felix the Cat, squeaker, rubber body w/metal squeaker, Irwin, 1950s, EX..$90.00

Figaro, figurine, black & white on brown base w/Figaro, wooden, 1¼", EX..$55.00

Figaro, figurine, Goebel, w/sticker, 2½", VG+ $60.00

Figaro, pitcher, milk; shaped as ball of yarn w/3-D cat at bottom, yellow, American Bisque, 8¼", EX............$145.00

Garfield, bank, ceramic, piggy bank shape, Paws, MIB .$45.00

Garfield, bank, head w/Miami football helmet on, NFL licensed product, solid vinyl, MIB.......................$40.00

Garfield, box, pewter w/Garfield on lid & I Love You inside, Selangor Pewter, 1978, EX $70.00

Garfield, cookie jar, figural seated w/cookie jar, #E-5932, Made in Japan, 1978, 8½", MIB..........................$55.00

Garfield, cookie jar, Garfield coming out of chimney, Enesco, 1981, 5", NM...$80.00

Garfield, doll, in Canadian Mountie clothes, holding Canadian flag, plush, Dakin, 9", NM (original tags)................$42.50

Garfield, doll, Jack 'n the Beanstalk, plush, NM $55.00

Garfield, doll, plush, w/rubber duck on chest & swimming mask on face, Fun Farm, Dakin, 8½", M (original tags).....$60.00

Garfield, doll, The Big Bad Wolf, plush, Furry Tales tag, MIB $55.00

Garfield, figurine, I'm the Boss, That's Why, seated in green chair, Enesco, 1981, NM.......................................$50.00

Garfield, figurine, Let's Get Fiscal, w/Odie, Enesco, 1978, M (original tag)...$50.00

Garfield, figurine, smiling into mirror, wearing dentist's coat, Enesco, 1978, 2½", NM.......................................$70.00

Garfield, figurine, Town Hall, Garfield & friends sing in front of courthouse w/Noel on roof, Danbury Mint, MIB......$80.00

Garfield, fish tank, figural w/clear stomach as tank, red rocks inside, electric, EX...$55.00

Garfield, toothbrush holder, figurine w/hole in back, Enesco, 1981, M...$45.00

Garfield, Wacky Wobbler, orange plastic, MIB...........$60.00

Garfield, wall light, head & front feet, porcelain w/metal base, EX...$110.00

Kitty Cucumber, bell, 3 kittens in winter scene w/1989, street light as handle, Schmid, 7", EX...........................$50.00

Kitty Cucumber, figurine, fisherman in green overalls, pole in 1 hand, big fish in other, Schmid, 1985, 3¼", EX....$35.00

Kitty Cucumber, figurine, Kitty w/cat doll, birthday cake & present, marked Priscilla, 3½", EX $80.00

Kitty Cucumber, music box, Kitty & Ginger skating, plays winter Wonderland, Schmid, 1987, from $80 to...$90.00

Kitty Cucumber, music box, 2 kittens making snowman, plays Winter Wonderland, 6", from $80 to $90.00

Kitty Cucumber, ornament, ice skater w/blue hat & coat & red scarf, Schmid, 1986, 3", EX............................$45.00

Kliban, bank, wearing red sneakers, 6½", from $40 to..$55.00

Kliban, book, Kliban's Calendar Cats, 1981, 11¼x9½", EX (EX plastic slipcover)..$25.00

Kliban, book, Never Eat Anything Bigger Than Your Head, 1976, 1st edition, EX..$15.00

Kliban, bookends, 1 cat on top & 1 by bookcase, 1 in wastebasket & 1 playing w/mouse, Sigma, 5¾x8½", EX, pr...$135.00

Kliban, bowl, cats in red sneakers walk around white bowl, Kiln Craft Tableware Ironstone, 6" **$15.00**

Kliban, box, cat on back rests on lg red heart, Sigma, from $150 to..**$175.00**

Kliban, box, soaking in tub of blue water, Sigma, from $100 to..**$150.00**

Kliban, candle holder, cat climbing tree, Sigma, 8¼", EX, from $30 to...**$50.00**

Kliban, candy dish, oval, tummy is bowl, Sigma, 9¼", from $75 to...**$100.00**

Kliban, candy dish, 3-D cat curved around side of bowl, 11" L, from $100 to **$125.00**

Kliban, clock, cat in red sneakers, round, battery-operated, 8½" dia, M...**$30.00**

Kliban, cloth print, 4 cats indulge in Chinese food, 16x19", M...**$25.00**

Kliban, cookie jar, cat in top of red stool playing guitar, Sigma, 1970s, 10¼x4¼" dia, from $75 to.............**$90.00**

Kliban, creamer, figural, Sigma, from $50 to **$60.00**

Kliban, doll, plush, on surfboard, wearing Hawaiian-style pants, 7x14¾x4½", EX..**$35.00**

Kliban, doll, plush black & gray cat w/green, orange & yellow fish in lap, 12", M..**$45.00**

Kliban, jar, cat in pr of pants, banana sticking out of pocket, 6x8", EX...**$95.00**

Kliban, mug, as lifeguard, California below, Gift Creations, 1989, MIB **$35.00**

Kliban, mug, cat in Christmas tree, Season's Greetings.**$20.00**

Kliban, mug, cat on shore listening to seashell, California below, Gift Creations Inc, 1989, EXIB..................**$45.00**

Kliban, mug, cat putting golf ball, mouse waiting in hole, Gift Creations, 1989, MIB...**$25.00**

Kliban, mug, cat wearing Santa hat as handle on white cylinder, Sigma **$75.00**

Kliban, mug, cat's face, Sigma, from $15 to **$20.00**

Kliban, ornament, cat in Santa hat driving train w/presents in back, 1981, 3x3", NM...............................**$40.00**

Kliban, picture frame, Love a Cat, 3-D cat by 7½x5" white frame, Sigma...**$65.00**

Kliban, pin, cat in red sneakers, enameled, Workman Publishing of NYC, 1¼" **$25.00**

Kliban, place mat, many cats in various sizes, EX......**$25.00**

Kliban, pot holder, cat hiding behind bouquet of roses on white, 7x10", EX...**$15.00**

Kliban, puzzle, jigsaw; Snowcat, 100+ pcs, Great American Puzzle Factory, 1997, 7x9", MIB **$20.00**

Kliban, salt & pepper shakers, posed as Nipper listening to gramaphone, Sigma, 3", pr................................**$175.00**

Kliban, sleeping bag, cat in red sneakers, 78", M.......**$20.00**

Kliban, sugar bowl, figural, head as lid, black & white w/red base, Sigma, 1970s, from $80 to........................**$120.00**

Kliban, teapot, cat in airplane, head is lid, Sigma **$375.00**

Kliban, teapot, dressed in tuxedo, unmarked, 8½", EX ..**$135.00**

Kliban, teapot/demitasse pot, upright cat in Santa hat, 7¾", from $175 to...**$225.00**

Kliban, toaster cover, variety of cats in red sneakers on ivory, 10¼x12x4", M..**$20.00**

Kliban, towel, cat on stool playing guitar w/Love To Eat Them Mouses lyrics, cloth, Barth & Dreyfuss, 16x25" **$15.00**

Kliban, towel set, cat in red sneakers, bath, hand & wash size, EX...**$35.00**

Kliban, wall plaque, rectangular w/embossed cat, from $70 to **$90.00**

Cat-Tail Dinnerware

Cat-Tail was a dinnerware pattern popular during the late '20s until sometime in the '40s. So popular, in fact, that ovenware, glassware, tinware, even a kitchen table was made to coordinate with it. The dinnerware was made primarily by Universal Potteries of Cambridge, Ohio, though a catalog from Hall China circa 1927 shows a three-piece coffee service, and others may have produced it as well. It was sold for years by Sears, Roebuck and Company, and some items bear a mark that includes their name.

The pattern is unmistakable: a cluster of red cattails (usually six, sometimes one or two) with black stems on creamy white. Shapes certainly vary; Universal used at least three of their standard mold designs, Camwood, Old Holland, Laurella, and possibly others. Some Cat-Tail pieces are marked Wheelock on the bottom. (Wheelock was a department store in Peoria, Illinois.)

If you're trying to decorate a '40s vintage kitchen, no other design could afford you more to work with. To see many of the pieces that are available and to learn more about the line, read *The Collector's Encyclopedia of American Dinnerware* by Jo Cunningham (Collector Books).

Advisors: Barbara and Ken Brooks (See Directory, Dinnerware)

Batter pitcher, from $150.00 to $175.00; Mixing bowl, 8", $23.00. (Photo courtesy Barbara and Ken Brooks)

Bowl, footed, 9½"..**$20.00**
Bowl, mixing; 8" **$23.00**
Bowl, Old Holland shape, marked Wheelock, 6" **$7.00**
Bowl, salad **$25.00**

Bowl, soup; flat rim, 7¾"......................................**$15.00**
Bowl, soup; tab handles, 8"..................................**$17.50**
Bowl, straight sides, 6¼".......................................**$12.00**
Bowl, vegetable; oval, 9".......................................**$27.50**
Bowl, w/lid, part of ice box set, 4"....................**$12.00**
Bowl, w/lid, part of ice box set, 5"....................**$15.00**
Bowl, w/lid, part of ice box set, 6"....................**$18.50**
Butter dish, 1-lb..**$30.00**
Cake cover & tray, tinware.................................**$35.00**
Cake plate, Mt Vernon...**$25.00**
Canister set, tin, 4-pc...**$60.00**
Casserole, w/lid...**$30.00**
Coffeepot, electric..**$150.00**
Coffeepot, 3-pc..**$70.00**
Cookie jar, from $75 to.......................................**$100.00**
Cracker jar, barrel shape, from $75 to...............**$85.00**
Creamer..**$20.00**
Cup & saucer, from $6 to.....................................**$10.00**
Custard cup...**$9.00**
Gravy boat, from $18 to..**$25.00**
Jug, ball; ceramic-topped cork stopper..............**$37.50**
Jug, canteen..**$38.00**
Jug, side handle, cork stopper.............................**$38.00**
Jug, 1-qt, 6"..**$25.00**
Match holder, tinware...**$35.00**
Pickle dish/gravy boat liner.................................**$20.00**
Pie plate..**$30.00**
Pie server, hole in handle for hanging, marked Universal
    Potteries...**$25.00**
Pitcher, glass w/ice lip, from $75 to **$125.00**
Pitcher, milk/utility..**$22.50**
Plate, chop...**$35.00**
Plate, dinner; Laurella shape, from $15 to........**$20.00**
Plate, luncheon; 9"..**$35.00**
Plate, salad or dessert; round................................**$6.50**
Plate, sq, 7¼"...**$7.00**
Platter, oval, tab handles, 13⅜"..........................**$30.00**
Platter, oval, 11½", from $15 to..........................**$20.00**
Platter, oval, 14¾"..**$55.00**
Platter, round, tab handles, 11"...........................**$30.00**
Salad set (fork, spoon & bowl), from $50 to.......**$60.00**
Salt shaker, Salt or Pepper, glass, made by Tipp, lg, ea, from
    $25 to...**$35.00**
Saucer, Old Holland shape, marked Wheelock.....**$6.00**
Scales, metal..**$37.00**
Shaker set (salt, pepper, flour & sugar shakers), glass, on red
    metal tray, made by Tipp, from $60 to........**$65.00**
Stack set, 3-pc w/lids, from $35 to......................**$40.00**
Sugar bowl, w/lid, from $20 to **$25.00**
Syrup, red top..**$70.00**
Tablecloth..**$90.00**
Teapot, 4-cup...**$35.00**
Tray, for batter set..**$75.00**
Tumbler, juice; glass...**$30.00**
Tumbler, marked Universal Potteries, scarce, from $65 to..**$70.00**
Tumbler, water; glass..**$35.00**
Waste can, step-on, tinware..................................**$35.00**

Catalin Napkin Rings

Bakelite (developed in 1910) and Catalin (1930s) are very similar materials — identical, in fact, in chemical composition. Both are phenol resin, and both were made in the same wonderful colors that found favor in American kitchens from the 1930s until the 1950s. In particular, figural napkin rings made of this material have become very collectible. Those most desirable will have an inlaid eye or some other feature of a second color.

Band, lathe turned, amber, red or green, 1¾"..............**$8.00**
Band, plain, amber, red or green, 2", ea..................**$6.00**
Band, plain, colors, 2", set of 6, MIB **$40.00**
Camel, inlaid eye rod...**$120.00**
Camel, no inlaid eyes..**$95.00**
Chicken, no inlaid eyes...**$40.00**
Chicken, no inlaid eyes, amber w/green beak..........**$60.00**
Donald Duck, w/decal, from $135 to....................**$160.00**
Duck, inlaid eye rod...**$75.00**
Duck, no inlaid eyes **$60.00**
Elephant, ball on head...**$135.00**
Elephant, inlaid eye rod...**$100.00**
Fish, inlaid eye rod...**$80.00**
Fish, no inlaid eyes...**$55.00**
Mickey Mouse, w/decal, from $135 to...................**$170.00**
Rabbit, inlaid eye rod...**$75.00**
Rabbit, no inlaid eyes...**$60.00**
Rocking horse, inlaid eye rod..................................**$75.00**
Rocking horse, no inlaid eyes **$65.00**
Rooster, inlaid eye rods..**$110.00**
Rooster, no inlaid eyes...**$80.00**
Schnauzer, sitting, inlaid eye rods..........................**$75.00**
Schnauzer dog, sitting, no inlaid eyes **$55.00**
Scottie dog, no eye rod..**$55.00**
Scottie dog, standing, inlaid eye rod.......................**$75.00**

Ceramic Arts Studio

American-made figurines are very popular now, and these are certainly among the best. They have a distinctive look you'll soon learn to identify with confidence, even if you happen to pick up an unmarked piece. They were first designed in the 1940s and sold well until the company closed in 1955. (After that, the new owner took some molds to Japan and produced them over there for a short time.) The company's principal designer was Betty Harrington, who modeled the figures and knicknacks that so many have grown to love. In addition to the company's marks (there were at least seven, possibly more), many of the later pieces she designed carry their assigned names inscribed on the bottom as well.

The company also produced a line of metal items to accessorize the figurines. These were designed by Liberace's stepmother, Zona, who was also Betty's personal friend and art director of the figurine line.

Though prices continue to climb, once in a while one of many unmarked bargains can be found, but first you must familiarize yourself with your subject!

Advisor: BA Wellman (See Directory, Ceramic Arts Studio)
e-mail: bawellman@dishinitout.com

Club/Newsletter: CAS Collectors
P.O. Box 46
Madison, WI 53701-0046
www.CAScollectors.com
Membership: $18.00 per year, quarterly newsletter included
Convention to be held in Madison, August 21 – 24, 2003

Bank, Mr & Mrs Blankety Blank, 4½", pr	**$215.00**
Bank, Paisley Pig, 3"	**$150.00**

Bells: Summer Belle, 5¼", $90.00; Lilibelle, 6½", $145.00; Winter Belle, 5¼", $90.00.

Bowl, Space, aqua, round/stylized, 5¼"	**$80.00**
Candle holder, Bedtime Boy, 4¾"	**$95.00**
Candle holder, Triad Girl, left or right; from $90 to	**$125.00**
Figurine, Alice, sitting on knees, 4½", from $250 to	**$295.00**
Figurine, Bali-Hai, standing, 8"	**$135.00**
Figurine, Benny, baby elephant, 3¼"	**$75.00**
Figurine, Blessing Angel, hand down, 5¾"	**$100.00**
Figurine, Bright Eyes, cat, 3"	**$40.00**
Figurine, bunny, 1¾"	**$50.00**
Figurine, Calico Cat, 3"	**$40.00**
Figurine, Chinese Boy & Girl, 3", pr	**$65.00**
Figurine, Chubby St Francis, 8½"	**$165.00**
Figurine, Colonial Man, 6½"	**$65.00**
Figurine, Cupid on flower	**$75.00**
Figurine, Daisy, donkey, 5½"	**$150.00**
Figurine, Dutch Boy & Girl, 4½", pr, from $50 to	**$65.00**
Figurine, Egyptian Woman, 9½"	**$325.00**
Figurine, Elsie, elephant, 5"	**$95.00**
Figurine, frog, singing, 2"	**$45.00**
Figurine, Guitar Boy, 5"	**$75.00**

Figurine, Hans, Dance Boy, 5½"	**$70.00**
Figurine, Hansel & Gretel, 1-pc, 3", from $65 to	**$100.00**
Figurine, Isaac, 10"	**$165.00**
Figurine, lamb, plain	**$50.00**
Figurine, lamb w/bow, 4"	**$65.00**
Figurine, Little Bo Peep, 5½"	**$35.00**
Figurine, Little Jack Horner #2, 4"	**$80.00**
Figurine, longhorn ox, 3" L	**$90.00**
Figurine, lovebirds, 1-pc, 2¾"	**$45.00**
Figurine, Lucindy, 7"	**$65.00**
Figurine, Mary, 6¼"	**$49.00**
Figurine, mermaid mother on rock, 4"	**$185.00**
Figurine, Minnehaha	**$125.00**
Figurine, Mrs Skunky, 3"	**$55.00**
Figurine, Our Lady of Fatima	**$165.00**
Figurine, panda w/hat	**$60.00**
Figurine, pekingese, 3"	**$95.00**
Figurine, Peter Pan & Wendy, 5¼", pr	**$250.00**
Figurine, Pioneer Sam & Suzie, 5½", 5", pr	**$95.00**
Figurine, Pixie Girl, kneeling, 2½"	**$65.00**
Figurine, Polish Boy & Girl, 6½", pr	**$120.00**
Figurine, Praying Boy Angel, on knees, 3¼"	**$100.00**
Figurine, Rose, ballerina tying shoe	**$95.00**
Figurine, spaniel pup, sitting, 2"	**$45.00**
Figurine, spring colt, 3½"	**$125.00**
Figurine, squirrel w/jacket, 2¼"	**$45.00**
Figurine, Swan Lake Man, 7"	**$250.00**
Figurine, Toby Horse, 2¾"	**$110.00**
Figurine, tortoise w/hat, crawling, 2½" L	**$125.00**
Figurine, Wing Sang, woman, 6", from $40 to	**$60.00**
Head vase, Barbie, blond, 7"	**$175.00**
Head vase, Becky, 5¼"	**$165.00**
Head vase, Mei-Ling, 5"	**$150.00**
Honeypot, w/bee, 4"	**$150.00**
Metal accessory, arched window for religious figure, 6½"	**$75.00**
Metal accessory, artist palette w/shelves, left & right, 13" L	**$95.00**
Metal accessory, beanstalk for Jack, rare	**$165.00**
Metal accessory, birdcage w/perch, 14"	**$85.00**
Metal accessory, box, diamond shape, 15½x14"	**$55.00**
Metal accessory, corner spider web for Miss Muffet, flat back, 4"	**$95.00**
Metal accessory, frame w/shelf, 22" sq	**$55.00**
Metal accessory, garden shelf, from Mary Contrary, 4x12"	**$95.00**
Metal accessory, pocket step shelf, w/planter, round, 8"	**$75.00**
Metal accessory, pyramid shelf	**$75.00**
Metal accessory, rainbow arch w/shelf, black, 13½x19x5½"	**$120.00**
Metal accessory, sofa, for Maurice & Michelle, from $60 to	**$80.00**
Metal accessory, star for angel, flat black	**$80.00**
Metal accessory, triple ring for birds (shelf sitting), 15"	**$75.00**
Miniature, Aladdin's lamp, 2" L	**$75.00**
Miniature, pitcher, Adam & Eve, 3"	**$60.00**
Miniature pitcher, Pine Cone, 3¾"	**$65.00**
Plaque, Dancing Dutch Boy & Girl, pr	**$165.00**
Plaque, Greg & Grace, 9½", 9", pr	**$145.00**

Plaque, Hamlet, 8" **$225.00**
Plaque, Manchu & Lotus, 8", pr.................**$190.00**
Plaque, Shadow Dancers A & B, 7", pr **$185.00**
Plaque, Zor, 9" **$65.00**
Razor blade bank, Tony, #319, 4¾" **$95.00**
Salt & pepper shakers, baby chick in nest, snuggle, pr..**$75.00**
Salt & pepper shakers, Blackamoor, 4¾", pr..............**$95.00**
Salt & pepper shakers, covered wagon & oxen, ea 3" L,
   pr **$80.00**
Salt & pepper shakers, fish on tail, pr **$125.00**
Salt & pepper shakers, fox & goose, snuggle, 3¼", 2¼",
   pr **$225.00**
Salt & pepper shakers, monkey mother & baby, snuggle,
   pr **$125.00**
Salt & pepper shakers, Sabu & elephant, 2¾", 5", pr ..**$285.00**
Salt & pepper shakers, Santa Claus & Christmas tree, 2¼",
   pr **$150.00**
Salt & pepper shakers, sea horse & seaweed, snuggle, pr..**$185.00**
Salt & pepper shakers, Sooty & Taffy, Scottie dogs, pr....**$65.00**
Salt & pepper shakers, Wee Chinese Boy & Girl, 3", pr ..**$35.00**
Shelf sitter, boy w/dog, 5¼" **$65.00**
Shelf sitter, Budgie, bird................................**$40.00**
Shelf sitter, canary, singing, 5"................................**$90.00**
Shelf sitter, cowboy, 4¾"................................**$85.00**
Shelf Sitter, Dutch Boy, 4½"................................**$35.00**
Shelf sitter, Harmonica Boy, 4"................................**$75.00**
Shelf sitter, Maurice & Michelle, 7", pr................**$165.00**
Shelf sitter, Nip & Tuck, 4¼", 4", pr................**$60.00**
Shelf sitter, tom cat, blue eyes, 4¾"................**$100.00**
Shelf sitter, Tuffy, cat family #2, 5¼"................**$90.00**
Vase, bud; bamboo, 6" **$25.00**

Character and Promotional Drinking Glasses

In any household, especially those with children, I would venture to say, you should find a few of these glasses. Put out by fast-food restaurant chains or by a company promoting a product, they have for years been commonplace. But now, instead of glass, the giveaways are nearly always plastic. If a glass is offered at all, you'll usually have to pay 99¢ for it.

Some are worth more than others. Among the common ones are Camp Snoopy, B.C. Ice Age, Garfield, McDonald's, Smurfs, and Coca-Cola. The better glasses are those with super heroes, characters from Star Trek and '30s movies such as 'Wizard of Oz,' sports personalities, and cartoon characters by Walter Lantz and Walt Disney. Some of these carry a copyright date, and that's all it is. It's not the date of manufacture.

Many collectors are having a good time looking for these glasses. If you want to learn more about them, we recommend *Tomart's Price Guide to Character and Promotional Drinking Glasses* by Carol Markowski, and *Collectible Drinking Glasses, Identification and Values*, by our advisors Mark Chase and Michael Kelly (Collector Books).

There are some terms used in the descriptions that may be confusing. 'Brockway' style refers to a thick, heavy glass that tapers in from top to bottom. 'Federal' style, on the other hand, is thinner, and the top and bottom diameters are the same.

Advisors: Mark Chase and Michael Kelly (See Directory, Character and Promotional Drinking Glasses)

Newsletter: *Collector Glass News*
P.O. Box 308
Slippery Rock, PA 16057; 724-946-2838; Fax: 724-946-9012 or e-mail: cgn@glassnews.com; www.glassnews.com

Al Capp, Dogpatch USA, ruby glass, oval portraits of Daisy or Li'l Abner, ea from $25 to................................**$30.00**
Al Capp, Shmoos, USF, 1949, Federal, 3 different sizes (3½", 4¾", 5¼"), from $10 to................................**$20.00**
Al Capp, 1975, footed, Daisy Mae, Li'l Abner, Mammy, Pappy, Sadie, ea from $40 to..............................**$80.00**
Al Capp, 1975, footed, Joe Btsfplk, from $60 to.........**$90.00**
Animal Crackers, Chicago Tribune/NY News Syndicate, 1978, Eugene, Gnu, Lana, Dodo, ea from $7 to.............**$10.00**
Animal Crackers, Chicago Tribune/NY News Syndicate, 1978, Louis, scarce, from $25 to **$35.00**
Apollo Series, Marathon Oil, Apollo 11, 12, 13, 14, ea from $2 to...**$4.00**
Apollo Series, Marathon Oil, carafe, from $6 to..........**$10.00**
Arby's, Bicentennial Cartoon Series, 1976, 10 different, 6", ea from $20 to..**$20.00**
Avon, Christmas Issue, 1969-72, 4 different, ea from $2 to..**$5.00**
Battlestar Galactica, Universal Studios, 1979, 4 different, ea from $7 to..**$10.00**
BC Ice Age, Arby's, 1981, 6 different, ea from $3 to....**$5.00**
Burger Chef, Burger Chef & Jeff, Now We're Glassified!, from $15 to...**$25.00**
Burger Chef, Friendly Monster Series, 1977, 6 different, ea from $20 to...**$35.00**
Burger Chef, Presidents & Patriots, 1975, 6 different, ea from $7 to..**$10.00**
Burger King, Dallas Cowboys, Dr Pepper, 6 different, ea from $7 to...**$15.00**
Burger King, Mardi Gras, 1988, white glass mug w/red & yellow logo, from $8 to **$10.00**
Burger King, Mardis Gras, 1989, black glass mug w/white logo, from $8 to....................................**$10.00**
Burger King, Put a Smile in Your Tummy, features Burger King mascot, from $8 to................................**$10.00**
Burger King, Where Kids Are King Series, pitcher, clear glass w/white label featuring Burger King & phrase, from $35 to **$40.00**
Burger King, Where Kids Are King Series, set of 4 glasses matching pitcher listed above, ea from $3 to.........**$5.00**
Charles Dickens' A Christmas Carol, Subway, 1980s, 4 different, ea from $4 to **$6.00**
Children's Classics, Libbey Glass Co, Alice in Wonderland, Gulliver's Travels, Tom Sawyer, ea from $10 to...**$15.00**
Children's Classics, Libbey Glass Co, Moby Dick, Robin Hood, Three Musketeers, Treasure Island, ea from $10 to **$15.00**

Children's Classics, Libbey Glass Co, The Wizard of Oz, from $25 to..**$30.00**

Dick Tracy, Domino's Pizza, M **$185.00**

Dick Tracy, 1940s, frosted, 8 different characters, 3" or 5", ea from $50 to..**$75.00**

Disney Characters, 1989, frosted juice, face images of Daisy, Donald, Goofy, Mickey, Minnie, Scrooge, ea from $5 to..**$9.00**

Disney Characters, 1990, frosted tumbler, faces images of Daisy, Donald, Goofy, Mickey, Minnie, Scrooge, ea from $5 to..**$8.00**

Disney Film Classics, McDonald's/Coca-Cola/Canada, Cinderella, Fantasia, Peter Pan, Snow White & the Seven Dwarfs, ea **$15.00**

Domino's Pizza, Avoid the Noid, 1988, 4 different, ea .**$7.00**

Donald Duck, Donald Duck Cola, 1960s-70s, from $15 to..**$20.00**

Elsie the Cow, Borden, Elsie & Family in 1976 Bicentennial Parade, patriotic colors, from $5 to..............**$7.00**

Elsie the Cow, Borden, 1950s, white head image on waisted style, from $15 to..**$20.00**

Elsie the Cow, Borden, 1960, yellow daisy image, from $10 to..**$12.00**

ET, Pizza Hut, 1982, footed, 4 different, from $2 to **$4.00**

Flintstone Kids, Pizza Hut, 1986, 4 different, ea from $2 to..**$4.00**

Flintstones, Welch's, 1962 (6 different), 1963 (2 different), 1964 (6 different), ea from $8 to..........................**$12.00**

Ghostbusters II, Sunoco/Canada, 1989, 6 different, ea from $5 to..**$8.00**

Goonies, Godfather's Pizza/Warner Bros, 1985, 4 different, ea from $4 to..**$8.00**

Great Muppet Caper, McDonald's, 1981, 4 different, 6", ea **$2.00**

Hanna-Barbera, Pepsi, 1977, Dynomutt, Flintstones, Josie & The Pussycats, Mumbly, Scooby, Yogi & Huck, ea from $20 to..**$35.00**

Happy Days, Dr Pepper, 1977, Fonzie, Joanie, Potsie, Ralph, Richie, ea from $8 to..**$12.00**

Happy Days, Dr Pepper/Pizza Hut, 1977, Fonzie or Richie, ea from $10 to..**$15.00**

Happy Days, Dr Pepper/Pizza Hut, 1977, Joanie, Potsie, Ralph, ea from $8 to..**$12.00**

Harvey Cartoon Characters, Pepsi, 1970s, action pose, Baby Huey, Hot Stuff, Wendy, ea from $8 to **$15.00**

Harvey Cartoon Characters, Pepsi, 1970s, static pose, Baby Huey, Casper, Hot Stuff, Wendy, ea from $12 to ..**$20.00**

Harvey Cartoon Characters, Pepsi, 1970s, static pose, Richie Rich, from $15 to..**$25.00**

Harvey Cartoon Characters, Pepsi, 1970s, static pose, Sad Sack, scarce, from $25 to..**$35.00**

Holly Hobbie, American Greetings/Coca-Cola, Christmas, 1980, 4 different: Christmas Is..., Wrap Each..., etc, ea from $3 to..**$5.00**

Holly Hobbie, American Greetings/Coca-Cola, Christmas, 1981, 3 different: Tis the Season..., A Gift..., etc, ea from $2 to **$4.00**

Holly Hobbie, American Greetings/Coca-Cola, Christmas, 1982, 3 different: Wishing You..., Share..., etc, ea from $2 to..**$4.00**

Honey, I Shrunk the Kids, McDonald's, 1989, plastic, 3 different, ea from $1 to..**$2.00**

Hopalong Cassidy's Western Series, ea from $25 to ...**$30.00**

Howdy Doody, Welch's/Kagran, 1950s, 6 different, embossed bottom, ea from $15 to..**$20.00**

Indiana Jones & the Temple of Doom, 7-Up (w/4 different sponsors), 1984, set of 4 from $8 to **$15.00**

Indiana Jones: The Last Crusade, white plastic, 4 different, ea from $2 to..**$4.00**

Jungle Book, Disney/Canada, 1966, 6 different, numbered, 5", ea from $40 to..**$75.00**

Jungle Book, Disney/Canada, 1966, 6 different, numbered, 6½", ea from $30 to..**$60.00**

Jungle Book, Disney/Pepsi, 1970s, Bagheera or Shere Kahn, unmarked, ea from $60 to **$90.00**

Jungle Book, Disney/Pepsi, 1970s, Mowgli, unmarked, from $40 to..**$50.00**

Jungle Book, Disney/Pepsi, 1970s, Rama, unmarked, from $50 to..**$60.00**

Keebler Soft Batch Cookies, 1984, 4 different, ea from $7 to..**$10.00**

Leonardo TTV Collector Series, Pepsi, Underdog, Go-Go Gopher, Simon Bar Sinister, Sweet Polly, 6", ea from $15 to..**$25.00**

Leonardo TTV Collector Series, Pepsi, Underdog, Simon Bar Sinister, Sweet Polly, 5", ea from $8 to **$15.00**

Mark Twain Country Series, Burger King, 1985, 4 different, ea from $8 to..**$10.00**

Masters of the Universe, Mattel, 1983, He-Man, Man-at-Arms, Skeletor, Teels, ea from $5 to **$10.00**

Masters of the Universe, Mattel, 1986, Battle Cat/He-Man, Man-at-Arms, Orko, Panthor/Skeletor, ea from $3 to........**$5.00**

McDonald's, Hawaiians & Their Sea Series, 1980s, smoke-tinted glass w/white graphics, 4 different, ea from $6 to..**$8.00**

McDonald's, McDonaldland Action Series, 1977, 6 different, ea..**$5.00**

McDonald's, Olympics, 1984, clear glass mugs w/painted-on graphics, 4 different featuring various events, ea from $5 to..**$7.00**

Mickey Mouse, Happy Birthday, Pepsi, 1978, Clarabelle & Horace, from $15 to **$20.00**

Mickey Mouse, Happy Birthday, Pepsi, 1978, Daisy & Donald, from $12 to..**$15.00**

Mickey Mouse, Happy Birthday, Pepsi, 1978, Donald, Goofy, Mickey, Minnie, Pluto, Uncle Scrooge, ea from $6 to..**$10.00**

Mickey Mouse, Through the Years, K-Mart, glass mugs w/4 different images (1928, 1937, 1940, 1955), ea from $3 to..**$5.00**

Mickey Mouse, Through the Years, Sunoco/Canada, 1988, 6 different (1928, 1938, 1940, 1955, 1983, 1988), ea from $6 to..**$10.00**

Mister Magoo, Polanar Jelly, many different variations & styles, ea from $25 to..**$35.00**

Norman Rockwell, Saturday Evening Post Series, Country Time Lemonade, 4 different, w/authorized logo, ea from $3 to...**$5.00**

Norman Rockwell, Saturday Evening Post Series, Country Time Lemonade, 4 different, no logo, ea from $3 to...**$5.00**

Pac-Man, Bally Midway MFG/AAFES/Libbey, 1980, Shadow (Blinky), Bashfuk (Inky), Pokey (Clyde), Speedy (Pinky), ea $4 to...**$6.00**

Pac-man, Bally Midway MFG/Libbey, 1982, 5⅜" flare top or mug, 6" flare top, ea from $2 to.............................**$4.00**

PAT Ward, Collector Series, Holly Farms Restaurants, 1975, Boris, Bullwinkle, Natasha, Rocky, ea from $30 to...**$50.00**

PAT Ward, Pepsi, 1970s, Boris, Mr Peabody, Natasha, 5", ea from $10 to...**$15.00**

PAT Ward, Pepsi, late 1970s, static pose, Boris and Natasha, from $20.00 to $25.00; Snidley Whiplash, from $15.00 to $20.00.

PAT Ward, Pepsi, 1970s, Bullwinkle, brown lettering, no Pepsi logo, 6", from $20 to **$25.00**

PAT Ward, Pepsi, 1970s, Bullwinkle, 5", from $25 to..**$30.00**

PAT Ward, Pepsi, 1970s, Bullwinkle w/balloon, Dudley Do-Right in Canoe, Rocky in circus, 5", ea from $10 to...**$15.00**

PAT Ward, Pepsi, 1970s, Dudley-Do-Right, black lettering, 6", from $15 to...**$20.00**

PAT Ward, Pepsi, 1970s, Dudley-Do-Right, red lettering, no Pepsi logo, 6", from $15 to **$20.00**

PAT Ward, Pepsi, 1970s, Dudley-Do-Right, 5", from $15 to..**$20.00**

PAT Ward, Pepsi, 1970s, Rocky, black or white lettering, 6", from $15 to...**$20.00**

PAT Ward, Pepsi, 1970s, Rocky, brown lettering, no Pepsi logo, 6", from $20 to **$25.00**

PAT Ward, Pepsi, 1970s, Rocky, 5", from $20 to **$25.00**

PAT Ward, Pepsi, 1970s, Snidley Whiplash, 5", from $10 to...**$15.00**

Peanuts Characters, McDonald's, 1983, Camp Snoopy, 5 different, ea from $1 to...**$2.00**

Peanuts Characters, McDonalds, 1983, Camp Snoopy, white plastic w/Lucy or Snoopy, ea from $5 to................**$8.00**

Peanuts Characters, milk glass mug, At Times Life Is Pure Joy (Snoopy & Woodstock dancing), from $3 to..........**$5.00**

Peanuts Characters, milk glass mug, Snoopy for President, 4 different, numbered & dated, ea from $5 to..........**$8.00**

Peanuts Characters, plastic, I Got It! I Got It!, I Have a Strange Team, Let's Break for Lunch, ea from $5 to **$8.00**

Pepsi, Historical Advertising Posters, 1979, 4 different, black & white, ea from $8 to...**$10.00**

Pepsi, Twelve Days of Christmas, 1976, ea from $1 to....**$3.00**

Pillsbury, Doughboy w/various musical instruments, 1991, mail-in premium, from $6 to................................**$12.00**

Pocahontas, Burger King, 1995, 4 different, MIB, ea **$3.00**

Popeye, Kollect-A-Set, Coca-Cola, 1975, Popeye, from $7 to...**$10.00**

Popeye, Kollect-A-Set, Coca-Cola, 1975, 6 different, any except Popeye, ea from $5 to...**$7.00**

Rescuers, Pepsi, 1977, Bernard, Bianca, Brutus & Nero, Evinrude, Orville, Penny, ea from $8 to **$15.00**

Rescuers, Pepsi, 1977, Madame Medus or Rufus, ea from $25 to...**$30.00**

Ringling Bros Circus Clown Series, Pepsi, 1980s, 8 different, ea **$12.00**

Ringling Bros Circus Poster Series, Pepsi, 1980s, 6 different, ea **$20.00**

Roger Rabbit, McDonald's, 1988, plastic, ea from $1 to...**$3.00**

Smurf's, Hardee's, 1982 (8 different), 1983 (6 different), ea from $1 to...**$3.00**

Star Trek, Dr Pepper, 1976, 4 different, ea from $20 to..**$25.00**

Star Trek, Dr Pepper, 1978, 4 different, ea from $30 to..**$40.00**

Star Trek II: The Search for Spock, Taco Bell, 1984, 4 different, ea from $3 to...**$5.00**

Star Trek: The Motion Picture, Coca-Cola, 1980, 3 different, ea from $10 to...**$15.00**

Star Wars Trilogy: Empire Strikes Back, Burger King/Coca-Cola, 1980, 4 different, ea from $7 to **$10.00**

Star Wars Trilogy: Return of the Jedi, Burger King/Coca-Cola, 1983, 4 different, ea from $6 to **$8.00**

Star Wars Triology: Star Wars, Burger King/Coca-Cola, 1977, 4 different, ea from $12 to...................................**$15.00**

Super Heroes, Marvel, 1978, flat bottom, Captain America, Hulk, Spider-Man, Thor, ea from $100 to...........**$150.00**

Super Heroes, Marvel, 1978, flat bottom, Spider-Woman, from $175 to...**$250.00**

Super Heroes, Marvel/7 Eleven, 1977, footed, Captain America, Fantastic Four, Howard the Duck, Thor, ea from $20 to...**$35.00**

Super Heroes, Pepsi Super (Moon) Series, DC Comics, 1976, Green Arrow, from $20 to...**$30.00**

Super Heroes, Pepsi Super (Moon) Series, DC Comics or NPP, 1976, Batgirl, Batman, Shazam!, ea from $10 to......**$15.00**

Superman, NPP/M Polanar & Sonn, 1964, 6 different, various colors, 4¼" or 5¾", ea from $20 to......................**$35.00**

Universal Monsters, Universal Studio, 1980, footed, Creature, Dracula, Frankenstein, Mummy, Mutant, etc, ea from $100 to...**$160.00**

Urchins, Coca-Cola/American Greeting, 1976-78, baseball, bicycling, golf, skating, swimming, tennis, ea from $3 to **$5.00**

Walter Lantz, Pepsi, 1970s, Chilly Willy or Wally Walrus, ea from $35 to..**$55.00**

Walter Lantz, Pepsi, 1970s-80s, Anty/Miranda, Chilly/Smelley, Cuddles/Oswald, Wally/Homer, ea from $30 to...**$40.00**

Walter Lantz, Pepsi, 1970s-80s, Woody Woodpecker/Knothead & Splinter, from $15 to..............................**$20.00**

Warner Bros, Arby's Adventure Series, 1988, footed, Bugs, Daffy, Porky, Sylvester & Tweety, ea from $35 to.**$45.00**

Warner Bros, Pepsi, 1973, white plastic, Bugs, Daffy, Porky, Road Runner, Sylvester or Tweety, ea from $3 to..**$5.00**

Warner Bros, Pepsi, 1973, 12-oz, Bugs, Porky, Road Runner, Sylvester, Tweety, ea from $10 to **$15.00**

Warner Bros, Pepsi, 1973, 16-oz, Cool Cat, black lettering, from $10 to..**$15.00**

Warner Bros, Pepsi, 1976, Beaky Buzzard & Cool Cat w/kite or Taz & Porky w/fishing pole, ea from $8 to.....**$10.00**

Warner Bros, Pepsi, 1976, Foghorn Leghorn & Henry Hawk, from $10 to...**$15.00**

Warner Bros, Pepsi, 1979, Collector's Series, Bugs Bunny, Daffy Duck, Porky, Road Runner, Sylvester, Tweety, ea $7 to **$10.00**

Warner Bros, Welch's, 1974, action poses, 8 different, phrases around top, ea from $2 to.................................**$4.00**

Warner Bros, Welch's, 1976-77, 8 different, names around bottom, ea from $5 to...**$7.00**

Welch's, Dinosaur Series, 1989, 4 different, ea..............**$2.00**

Wendy's, Clara Pella (Where's the Beef?) or Clara Pella (no phrase), ea from $4 to...**$6.00**

Western Heroes, Annie Oakley, Buffalo Bill, Wild Bill Hickok, Wyatt Earp, ea from $8 to.........................**$12.00**

Western Heroes, Lone Ranger, from $10 to.................**$15.00**

Wild West Series, Coca-Cola, Buffalo Bill, Calamity Jane, ea from $10 to..**$15.00**

Wizard of Id, Arby's, 1983, 6 different, ea from $7 to ..**$10.00**

Ziggy, 7-Up Collector Series, 4 different, ea from $4 to .**$70.00**

Character Banks

Since the invention of money there have been banks, and saving it has always been considered a virtue. What better way to entice children to save than to give them a bank styled after the likeness of one of their favorite characters! Always a popular collectible, mechanical and still banks have been made of nearly any conceivable material. Cast-iron and tin banks are often worth thousands of dollars. The ones listed here were made in the past fifty years or so, when ceramics and plastics were the materials of choice. Still, some of the higher-end examples can be quite pricey!

For more information see *Collector's Guide to Banks* by Jim and Beverly Mangus; several are shown in *The Collector's Encyclopedia of Cookie Jars* (there are three in the series) by Fred and Joyce Roerig. All of these books are published by Collector Books.

See also Advertising Character Collectibles; Cowboy Collectibles; Star Wars.

Advisor: Robin Stine (See Directory, Cleminson)

Little Lulu, plastic, Play Pal Plastics, 7½", $30.00. (Photo courtesy June Moon)

Abu (monkey from Aladdin), ceramic, Schmid, Disney, 5¾", MIB **$48.00**

Annie, ceramic, w/dog, Applause, 1982, 6½x6¾" **$60.00**

Beetle Bailey, ceramic, Enesco, King Features Syndicate, 1999, 7½", MIB..**$28.00**

Big Al, ceramic, playing guitar, Walt Disney Productions, 7¼"..**$65.00**

Browser, ceramic, upright dragon, Nintendo, 1993, 11", MIB **$85.00**

Bubbles Marineland Whale, ceramic, 1960s, 4x7½"....**$48.00**

Charlie Brown, ceramic/composition, w/baseball glove, United Features Syndicate Inc, 1971, 7¾".............**$85.00**

Cool Cash (of Shirt Tails), ceramic, penguin in yellow shirt, Hallmark, 1981 ....**$40.00**

Daffy Duck in Money Safe, ceramic, The Good Company, Warner Brothers, 1989, 7x4".................................**$68.00**

Darth Vader, ceramic, black head only, Lucasfilm LTD, 1996, 6¼"...**$48.00**

Dolly Dingle, ceramic head figural, 1980s...................**$45.00**

Donald Duck as Santa, ceramic, Enesco, Disney, 6x5½", MIB **$28.00**

Donald Duck in Boat, ceramic, Enesco, Disney, 5¾", MIB..**$28.00**

Dr Mario, ceramic, musical, Nintendo, 1993, 11", MIB ..**$85.00**

Droopy Dog, ceramic, Japan, 7"...............................**$18.00**

Eager Beaver, ceramic, Hallmark go-with to the Ricky Raccoon cookie jar **$45.00**

ET Heartlight, ceramic, full figure, money slot in his back, rubber stopper, 6" **$32.00**

Frosty the Snowman, ceramic, American Bisque, 1950s, 6½", EX..**$65.00**

Goofy Around the World, ceramic, Disney, 1993, 7", MIB..**$85.00**

Hubert the Lion, ceramic, Lefton, Made in Japan, 8"..**$65.00**

Humpty Dumpty, ceramic, cold paint, 7", EX.............**$35.00**

Humpty Dumpty & Little Bo Peep, ceramic, painted figures on white pig shape, unmarked, 3x5".................**$35.00**

Hunchback of Notre Dame, ceramic, Enesco, Disney, 9¼", MIB **$45.00**

Jerry (from Tom & Jerry), ceramic, in cheese wedge, Metro Goldwyn Mayer, 1981, 4x4x5½" **$68.00**

Jetsons, ceramic, Elroy, Orbitty & Astro asleep in bed, Hanna-Barbera, 1986, 3½x4x6½", MIB **$175.00**

Little Mermaid, ceramic, limited edition, Disney, 8½", MIB...**$68.00**

Little Red Riding, ceramic, Italy N43, 8¼" **$95.00**

Lucy, ceramic/composition, w/baseball bat, United Features Syndicate Inc, 1971, 7¾" **$85.00**

Luigi, ceramic, musical, Nintendo, 1993, 11", MIB......**$85.00**

Mario, rubber figural, 6½" **$5.00**

Mary & Her Lamb, ceramic, Russ Berrie & Co, 6", MIB..**$35.00**

Mickey Mouse Cracking Safe, ceramic, Disney, 6"......**$48.00**

Mickey Mouse Holding Pig, ceramic, Disney, 8½" **$42.00**

Mickey Mouse in Pick-Up Truck, ceramic, Walt Disney Productions, 5x5" **$48.00**

Mickey Mouse in Race Car, ceramic, Walt Disney Productions, 5x5" **$48.00**

Minnie Mouse Holding Pig, ceramic, Disney, 8½"......**$45.00**

Miss Piggy, ceramic, long blue gown, Henson & Assoc, Sigma, 8" **$55.00**

Mrs Potts, ceramic, Schmid, Disney, 6", MIB............**$95.00**

Muppets Cookie Monster, ceramic, Applause.............**$55.00**

Paddington Bear, ceramic, Eden Toys, 1980, NM **$52.50**

Paddington Bear, ceramic, Schmid, 1980s, 5½x3½" ..**$85.00**

Rolly, ceramic, dalmatian puppy, Disney, 7"..............**$65.00**

Ronald McDonald, ceramic, McDonald's Corp, 1993, 8x7", MIB **$55.00**

Smurf, ceramic, 9½"..**$60.00**

Snoopy & Woodstock, ceramic, bird finial, marked Snoopy c 1958 1966 1972 United Features Syndicate Inc, 8½"..**$62.00**

Snoopy 'Lollipop,' composition, Aviva, 1973, 6" **$42.00**

Snoopy on Doghouse, ceramic, marked Snoopy c 1958 1966 United Features Syndicate Inc, 7x3¾x3¾"............**$35.00**

Sylvester & Tweety Birdcage, ceramic, MIB **$78.00**

Tazmanian Devil, ceramic, The Good Company, scarce .**$135.00**

Tom (from Tom & Jerry), old composition style, tall, standing, EX **$95.00**

Tom & Jerry w/Barrel, composition, older pc, EX......**$85.00**

Tweety Bird, ceramic, Warner Brothers Studio Store, 1997, 12x5", MIB..**$48.00**

Uncle Sam, ceramic, bust w/hands on lapels, unmarked, 6¾"..**$65.00**

Wizard of Oz Cowardly Lion, ceramic, Enesco, 1988, 5¾" **$35.00**

Wizard of Oz Scarecrow, ceramic, Enesco, 1988, 7"...**$35.00**

Wizard of Oz Tin Man, ceramic, Enesco, 1988, 6¾"...**$35.00**

Woodsey Owl, Give a Hoot Don't Polute, ceramic, McCoy **$145.00**

Woodstock, ceramic, United Features Syndicate, 1972, 6" from $30 to **$35.00**

Woody Woodpecker, ceramic, Applause.....................**$22.00**

Woody Woodpecker, ceramic, Walter Lantz, Applause, 1957, 7", from $25 to **$40.00**

Yoshi, ceramic, musical, Nintendo, 1993, 11", MIB.....**$85.00**

Ziggy Don't Break My Heart, ceramic, figure atop lg red heart, 6½" **$42.00**

Ziggy Holding Pig, ceramic, Tom Wilson, Universal Press Syndicate, MCMLXXXI, 7"......................................**$48.00**

Character Clocks and Watches

There is growing interest in the comic character clocks and watches produced from about 1930 into the 1950s and beyond. They're in rather short supply simply because they were made for children to wear (and play with). They were cheaply made with pin-lever movements, not worth an expensive repair job, and many were simply thrown away. The original packaging that today may be worth more than the watch itself was usually ripped apart by an excited child and promptly relegated to the wastebasket.

Condition is very important in assessing value. Unless a watch is in like-new condition, it is not mint. Rust, fading, scratching, or wear of any kind will sharply lessen its value, and the same is true of the box itself. Good, excellent, and mint watches can be evaluated on a scale of one to five, with excellent being a three, good a one, and mint a five. In other words, a watch worth $25.00 in good condition would be worth five times that amount if it were mint ($125.00). Beware of dealers who substitute a generic watch box for the original. Remember that these too were designed to appeal to children and (99% of the time) were printed with colorful graphics.

Some of these watches have been reproduced, so be on guard. For more information, we recommend *Comic Character Clocks and Watches* by Howard S. Brenner, and *Schroeder's Collectible Toys, Antique to Modern* (Collector Books).

See also Advertising and Promotional Wristwatches.

Advisor: Howard Brenner (See Directory, Character Clocks and Watches)

Clocks

Batman, 1993, alarm 'voice' says 'Gotham City in trouble, Call for Batman,' Batlight shines on ceiling, battery-op, NM ..**$40.00**

Dig 'Em Alarm Clock, 1979, NM...................................**$35.00**

Foghorn Leghorn & Henry Hawk, Foghorn w/brass drum, Henry w/trumpet, battery-op, 5x6½", M...............**$38.00**

Mickey's Clockshop, Walt Disney, 1993, animated, musical, lights up, electric, MIB **$60.00**

Partridge Family Wall Clock, Time Setters, 1972, full-color photo image, 10" dia, NM, from $200 to **$250.00**

Road Runner, Seth Thomas, 1970, folding travel alarm, 3" dia when closed, MIB..**$185.00**

Simpson Wall Clock, JPI, Simpson family on black background, white frame, 11x9", M **$40.00**

Snoopy Alarm Clock, Citizen, 1980s, Snoopy & Woodstock w/umbrellas, light blue plastic base, double bell, 5" dia, NM...**$20.00**

Snoopy Alarm Clock, Equity, 1980s, Snoopy w/baseball & bat, white metal case w/silver trim, 4" dia, MIB, from $75 to **$100.00**

Snoopy Cuckoo Clock, Japan, 1983, Woodstock is cuckoo bird, NM, from $175.00 to $200.00. (Photo courtesy Andrea Podley and Derrick Bang)

Snoopy Pendulum Clock, Citizen, 1980s, Snoopy & Woodstock on face, plastic casing, 13", from $95 to **$135.00**

Tweety & Sylvester, animated, talking, wireless remote for demo, battery-op, 9x22½", NM...........................**$170.00**

Woody Woodpecker Alarm Clock, Walter Lantz, 1st issue, Woody in chef's hat in front of Woody's Cafe tree, EX (EX box) **$300.00**

Pocket Watches

Bart Simpson, 1997, manufactured for Marks & Spencer (English store), brushed steel, sports diver style, MIP **$70.00**

Big Bad Wolf, EX...**$950.00**

Buster Brown, 1928, EX...**$175.00**

Buster Brown, 1960s, VG...**$75.00**

Popeye, Fossil, silver-tone w/matching chain, w/hand-painted ceramic figure of Wimpy, M (in litho tin 'can' package) **$75.00**

Snoopy, Fossil, gold-tone, limited edition of 500, w/hand-decorated red ceramic dog dish & original paperwork, MIB **$135.00**

Wristwatches

Bambi, Birthday Series, US Time, 1949, NM **$265.00**

Batman, LCD digital, battery, Quintel, DC Comics, 1989, M on blister card **$25.00**

Betty Boop, red & white woven cloth band, 1980s, NM ..**$35.00**

Bill Clinton, color image w/stars & stripes behind him, gold-filled case, leather band, M....................................**$24.00**

Cinderella, animated hands/arms, yellow band, Bradley, Walt Disney Productions, 1972, M **$80.00**

Cinderella, Swiss movement, wind-up, gold-tone polished case, bright blue band, Bradley, W Disney Productions, 1975, M...**$65.00**

Daisy Duck, Birthday Series, US Time, 1948, EX+....**$245.00**

Dale Evans Queen of the West, 1st version, sq face, original leather band, Ingraham, late 1940s, non-working but EX..**$135.00**

Dopey, Birthday Series, US Time, 1948, NM.............**$275.00**

Jabba the Hut, Bradley, Lucas Films, ca 1983, M........**$60.00**

Knight Rider, quartz, Armotron, NM **$95.00**

Little Orphan Annie, leather band, New Haven Watch Co, 1948, NM **$95.00**

Mickey Mouse, case in clear Lucite bubble, Swiss movement, wind-up, Bradley/Walt Disney Productions, oversize, 1976, EX **$110.00**

Mickey Mouse, rare bangle style, gold-tone metal, stem wind, Bradley, Walt Disney Productions, 1977, EX **$110.00**

Mickey Mouse Auto Racer, inner ring resembles full tachometer, Swiss movement, rubber band, Bradley, Disney, 1970, M...**$175.00**

Mickey Mouse Bobbin' Head, head moves w/ea tick, Bradley, Disney, 1978, rare, M **$295.00**

Mickey Mouse Football Player, Swiss movement, wind-up, polished chrome case, red leather band, Bradley, Disney, 1978, M...**$110.00**

Minnie Mouse, lavender dress & gloves, Walt Disney Productions, stem wind, blue leather band, 1960s, NM...**$145.00**

Miss Piggy, Swiss J-jewel movement, lavender band, Picco Inc, Hanson Associates Inc, 1979, M...................**$115.00**

Peter Rabbit, Swiss 17-jewel movement, Bradley Time Division, 1980, EX...**$60.00**

Roy Rogers, brown leather band, MIB......................**$265.00**

R2D2 & C3PO, Swiss movement, stem wind, Bradley, 20th Century Fox Film Corporation, regular size, 1977, MIB **$78.00**

R2D2 & C3PO, Swiss movement, stem wind, oversized version, Bradley, 20th Century Fox, 1977, MIB.......**$148.00**

Sam the Olympic Eagle, quartz digital, Ballanda, 1984, NM..**$40.00**

Snoopy Red Baron, stem wind, black base metal case, Timex, c 1965 United Feature Syndicate Inc, NM...........**$175.00**

Spider-Man Super-Hero Man, Dabs, 1981, MIB, from $50.00 to $75.00. (Photo courtesy Bill Bruegman)

Spiro Agnew, eyes do not move, Dirty Time, 2nd issue, late 1960s, NM...**$145.00**

Spiro Agnew, Peace Time Co, Swiss made, red, white & blue band, yellow-plated bezel, stainless steel back, M in package **$115.00**

Superman, gold-tone top w/stainless steel back, yellow hands, blue strap, Dabs & Co/DC Comics, 1977, EX..........**$70.00**

Superman, 1993 limited edition, MOC.....................**$375.00**

Surf Time, Bradley Time, stem wind, gray leather band, 1970s, M...**$75.00**

Tarzan, Swiss 15-jewel movement, black suede & cream strap, Bradley, Licensed by Edgar Rice Burroughs, 1983, EX **$110.00**

Uncle Sam, stem wind, gold-tone case top, stainless steel back, red, white & blue cloth band, 1972, NM **$88.00**

Character Collectibles

Any popular personality, whether factual or fictional, has been promoted through the retail market to some degree. Depending on the extent of their fame, we may be deluged with this merchandise for weeks, months, even years. It's no wonder, then, that the secondary market abounds with these items or that there is such wide-spread collector demand for them today. There are rarities in any field, but for the beginning collector, many nice items are readily available at prices most can afford. Disney characters, Western heroes, TV and movie personalities, super heroes, comic book characters, and sports greats are the most sought after.

For more information, we recommend *Character Toys and Collectibles* by David Longest; *Toys of the Sixties* and *Superhero Collectibles: A Pictorial Price Guide,* both by Bill Bruegman; *Collector's Guide to TV Memorabilia, 1960s and 1970s,* by Greg Davis and Bill Morgan; and *Howdy Doody* by Jack Koch. *Schroeder's Collectible Toys, Antique to Modern,* published by Collector Books, contains an extensive listing of character collectibles with current market values.

See also Advertising Characters; Beatles Collectibles; Bubble Bath Containers; California Raisins; Cat Collectibles; Character and Promotional Drinking Glasses; Character Watches; Coloring Books; Cookie Jars; Cowboy Character Collectibles; Disney Collectibles; Dolls, Celebrity; Elvis Presley Memorabilia; Movie Posters; Paper Dolls; Pez Candy Containers; Pin-Back Buttons; Puzzles; Rock 'n Roll Memorabilia; Shirley Temple; Star Wars; Toys; Vandor.

Note: Our listings are often organized by the leading character with which they're associated (for example, Pokey is in the listings that begin Gumby) or the title of the production in which they appear (Mr. T. is with A-Team listings).

A-Team, Grenade Toss, Placo, 1983, MIB (sealed) **$75.00**

Abbott & Costello, dolls, Who's on First, Ideal, 1984, 12", MIB **$100.00**

Addams Family, doll, Lurch, vinyl w/cloth outfit, Remco, 1964, NM **$65.00**

Addams Family, hand puppet, Morticia, cloth body w/vinyl head, Ideal, 1965, NM **$65.00**

Alf, finger puppet, plush, Coleco, 1987, M (EX box) .**$15.00**

Atom Ant, push-button puppet, Kohner, 1960s, EX....**$25.00**

Banana Splits, harmonica, Larami, 1973, MOC...........**$50.00**

Banana Splits, slide-tile puzzle, Roalex, MIP............**$100.00**

Batman, Batarang, black plastic, came w/utility belt, Ideal, 1966, 8", NM...**$100.00**

Batman, Batcuffs, came w/utility belt, Ideal, 1966, 4", NM..**$100.00**

Batman, coins, set of 20, Transogram, 1966, MOC **$50.00**

Batman, flashlight, plastic figure, Nasta, 1981, 4", MIC..**$15.00**

Batman, hand puppet, blue vinyl, Ideal, 1965, MOC .**$50.00**

Batman, hat/mask, felt hat w/drop-down mask, Pow! patch on front, 1966, NM **$25.00**

Batman, Hot-Line Batphone, red plastic w/decals, Marx, 1966, 8", NMIB **$500.00**

Batman, Official Batman Chute, NPPI, 1966, MOC.....**$40.00**

Batman, pocket puppet, Durham, 1970s, 10", MOC ...**$35.00**

Batman, Print Putty, 1966, MOC...................................**$25.00**

Batman, Stardust Touch of Velvet Art, Hasbro, 1966, complete, NMIB **$100.00**

Batman, Super Top, 1977, MOC.....................................**$30.00**

Batman, Thingmaker, for rings & rubber stamps, Mattel, 1965, EX..**$35.00**

Battlestar Galactica, yo-yo, plastic tournament shape w/paper sticker seal, 1970s, MIP **$16.00**

Beany & Cecil, Beany-Copter, Mattel, 1960s, MOC...**$140.00**

Beany & Cecil, bowling game, w/10 Cecil figures as pins & 2 balls, unused, EX+ (VG+ box) **$225.00**

Beany & Cecil, Cecil & His Disguise Kit, Mattel, 1962, MIB (sealed)..**$125.00**

Betty Boop, standee, cardboard, life-size, EX **$30.00**

Beverly Hillbillies, slide-tile puzzle, 1960s, MOC........**$60.00**

Beverly Hills 90210, license plate, any character, Fantasy Plates, 1991, M, ea **$5.00**

Bionic Woman, Bionic Beauty Salon, MIB, $50.00. (Photo courtesy Martin and Carolyn Berens)

Bionic Woman, tattoos & stickers, complete w/8 stickers & 28 tattoos, Kenner, 1976, MIP **$20.00**

Blondie & Dagwood, dexterity puzzle, paper litho under glass w/red metal case, 1940s, 5x3", EX **$25.00**

Bonzo, pull toy, Chein, litho tin, 7", NM...................**$400.00**

Bozo the Clown, Decal Decorator Kit, Meyercord, 1950s, unused, EXIB **$40.00**

Bozo the Clown, doll, talker, Mattel, 1963, 18", VG+ .**$50.00**

Bozo the Clown, yo-yo, plastic tournament shape w/paper sticker seal, Roalex, 1960s, NM+ **$30.00**

Brady Bunch, Brain Twisters, Larami, 1973, MOC......**$25.00**

Brady Bunch, Hex-A-Game, Larami, 1973, MOC, from $30 to **$40.00**

Brady Bunch, Outdoor Fun Set, several different, Larami, 1973, MIB, ea from $40 to **$50.00**

Brady Bunch, Pick 'N Play, Larami, 1973, MOC, from $50 to **$60.00**

Brady Bunch, tambourine, Larami, 1973, MOC..........**$25.00**

Bugs Bunny, doll, stuffed cloth w/plastic face, Warner Bros, 1950s, NM, from $75 to..**$125.00**

Bugs Bunny, doll, stuffed cloth w/plastic face, wearing bib overalls & plaid shirt, M&H Novelty, 1950, 19", EX **$60.00**

Bugs Bunny, figure, litho tin, standing w/arm full of carrots, Warner Bros, 1950s, EX..**$75.00**

Bugs Bunny, Magic Rub-Off Pictures, Whitman, EXIB ..**$75.00**

Bugs Bunny, Magic Slate, Golden, 1987, MIP (sealed).**$5.00**

Bugs Bunny, mug, molded plastic w/sm round handle, ears wrap around rim, painted features, 4", 1960s, NM..**$15.00**

Bugs Bunny, paper cups, Bugs Bunny & Pals Cold Cups, set of 25 8-oz, Warner Bros, 1950s, unused, M (EX box).**$150.00**

Bugs Bunny, Toot-A-Tune, plastic flute, Warner Bros, MIB..**$150.00**

Captain America, bath puppet, MIP **$40.00**

Captain America, Official Utility Belt, Remco, 1979, MIB..**$20.00**

Captain America, playset, complete w/shield, mask, handcuffs, keys, dart gun, MIP (sealed)........................**$65.00**

Captain Kangaroo, TV Eras-O-Board Set, Hasbro, 1956, complete, M (VG box) **$30.00**

Care Bears, figures, 10 different characters, Kenner, 1984, 3", MOC, ea..**$15.00**

Care Bears, phonograph, 1983, MIB, $125.00.
(Photo courtesy Martin and Carolyn Berens)

Casper the Friendly Ghost, jack-in-the-box, litho tin, plays theme song, Mattel, 1960, EX **$75.00**

Casper the Friendly Ghost, Stitch-A-Story, Hasbro, 1967, MOC (sealed) **$50.00**

Charlie's Angels, backpack, vinyl w/group photo on top flap, Travel Toys, 1977, M, from $65 to..........................**$75.00**

Charlie's Angels, Beauty Hair Care Set, HG Toys, 1977, MIB, from $125 to..**$150.00**

Charlie's Angels, playset, Toy Factory, MIB (sealed), from $100 to..**$125.00**

Charlie's Angels, Rainy Day Set, Travel Toys, Inc, 1977, MIB **$175.00**

Charlie's Angels, record player, 1970s, NM..................**$75.00**

Charlie's Angels, walkie-talkies, LJN, 1976, rare, NRFB, from $300 to..**$350.00**

Child's Play, doll, Chucky, Play by Play, 1992, 15", EX ..**$25.00**

Chipmunks, kite, Roalex, 1960s, MIP..........................**$65.00**

CHiPs, bullhorn, plastic, Placo Toys, 1977, M, from $25 to...**$35.00**

CHiPs, Colorforms, 1981, MIB **$25.00**

CHiPs, Motorcycle Helmet Set, HG Toys, 1979, rare, MIB.**$100.00**

CHiPs, sunglasses, Fleetwood, 1977, MOC..................**$15.00**

Daffy Duck, doll, stuffed plush, Mighty Star, 1971, 19", NM..**$25.00**

Daffy Duck, Silly Putty, Ja-Ru, 1980, MOC **$5.00**

Dennis the Menace, hand puppet, cloth body w/vinyl head, EX..**$40.00**

Dennis the Menace, phonograph, Hank Ketcham, 1960s, NM, from $100 to..**$150.00**

Dennis the Menace, Stuff 'N Lace Doll, Standard Toycraft, MIP **$40.00**

Dennis the Menace & Ruff, ornament set, 1977, MIB...**$20.00**

Dick Tracy, barrette, Bonnie Braids, 1951, 1", NMOC ..**$35.00**

Dick Tracy, Candid Camera, complete w/instructions, Seymour/New York News, 1950s, EXIB **$100.00**

Dick Tracy, Colorforms Cartoon Kit, 1962, complete, EXIB **$75.00**

Dick Tracy, figure, Bonnie Braids, plastic, Charmore, 1951, 1¼", NMOC **$50.00**

Dick Tracy, greeting cards, several styles w/neon backgrounds, Norcross, 1960s, NM, ea **$20.00**

Dick Tracy, hand puppet, cloth & vinyl, complete w/red cord, Ideal, 1961, NMIB **$125.00**

Dick Tracy, magnifying glass, Larami, 1979, MOC......**$20.00**

Dr Dolittle, Animal Fist Faces, EXIB **$40.00**

Dr Dolittle, Numbered Pencil Coloring Set, Hasbro #3633, M (sealed)...**$30.00**

Dr Dolittle, periscope, Bar-Zim, NMIP **$30.00**

Dracula, doll, Hamilton Presents, 14", MIB **$25.00**

Dukes of Hazzard, backpack, denim-type material w/image of the General Lee, Remco, 1981, NM..................**$40.00**

Dukes of Hazzard, Colorforms, 1981, NMIB **$30.00**

Dukes of Hazzard, guitar, plastic w/original decals, VG..**$35.00**

Dukes of Hazzard, yo-yo, plastic butterfly shape w/chrome finish, imprint seal, Duncan, 1980s, MIP..............**$25.00**

ET, doll, plush, Showtime, 1982, 8", NM.......................**$6.00**

ET, night light, figural w/glowing chest, MIB.............**$15.00**

ET, photo album, M (sealed) **$12.00**

Family Affair, Buffy Fashion Wig, Amsco, 1971, MIB ..**$100.00**

Fat Albert & the Cosby Kids, figures, Bill, Bucky or Rudy, Tedro Enterprises, 1982, MOC, ea **$30.00**

Flash Gordon, slide-tile puzzle, Defenders of the Earth, Ja-Ru, 1985, MOC...**$18.00**

Flintstones, bubble pipe, Bamm-Bamm, 1960s, 8", EX ..**$20.00**

Flintstones, Color-By-Numbers, Pebbles & Bamm-Bamm, Transogram, 1963, MIB (sealed) **$70.00**

Flintstones, doll, Baby Pebbles & Cave House, 1964, 8", MIB **$275.00**

Flintstones, doll, Bamm-Bamm, plastic & vinyl w/cloth clothes, Ideal, 1960s, 16", MIB, from $150 to.....**$200.00**

Flintstones, doll, Fred, vinyl, 12", NM.........................**$70.00**

Flintstones, doll, Pebbles, plastic & vinyl w/cloth outfit, Ideal, 1967, 12", MIB, from $150 to.........................**$200.00**

Flintstones, figure, any character, bendable, Just Toys, MOC, ea **$10.00**

Flintstones, Play Fun Set, Whitman, 1965, complete, EXIB **$65.00**

Flintstones, push-button puppet, Pebbles, Kohner, 1960s, EX **$25.00**

Flintstones, Quick Score Target, 1977, MOC **$25.00**

Flintstones, xylophone, 1978, MOC. **$25.00**

Flipper, color-by-number set, Hasbro, 1966, complete, NMIB, from $50 to **$60.00**

Flipper, doll, stuffed plush w/sailor hat, Knickerbocker, 1976, 17", EX **$30.00**

Flipper, riding toy, plastic figure w/red wheels & handles, Irwin, 1965, NM, from $125 to **$150.00**

Foghorn Leghorn, hand puppet, plush, Warner Bros, 1970s, NM **$30.00**

Foghorn Leghorn, tray, cartoon image of carriage ride in Central Park NY, Warner Bros, rectangular, M **$30.00**

Foodini, dexterity puzzle, American Metal, 1950s, rare, NM **$125.00**

Frankenstein/Phantom, flicker ring, M **$35.00**

Full House, doll, Jesse, Tiger, 1993, 11½", MIB **$40.00**

Full House, doll, Michelle, talker, cloth & vinyl, 15", MIB...**$40.00**

Gilligan's Island, ball cap, stitched logo, American Needle, EX **$10.00**

Gilligan's Island, note pad, Gilligan & Skipper on cover, glossy, 1960s, unused, M..**$75.00**

Goldilocks, Storykins, Hasbro, 1967, MIB, from $75 to ..**$100.00**

Green Hornet, Electric Drawing Set, Lakeside, 1966, complete, NMIB **$250.00**

Green Hornet, Follow the Colors Magic Rub-Off, Whitman, complete, EXIB **$200.00**

Green Hornet, kite, Roalex, 1967, MIP **$200.00**

Green Hornet, movie viewer, 1966, MOC **$75.00**

Gumby & Pokey, figures, bendable, Lewco/Perma Toys, 12" & 8½", M, ea from $15 to **$20.00**

Happy Days, beanbag, red & white panels w/image of Fonz giving thumbs-up sign, 1970s, NM......................**$125.00**

Happy Days, Colorforms, Fonz, unused, EXIB **$30.00**

Happy Days, doll, Fonz, stuffed cloth, Samet & Wells, 1976, 16", NM **$30.00**

Happy Days, Flip-A-Knot, 1977, MIP **$15.00**

Hardy Boys, phonograph, Shaun Cassidy, electric or battery-op versions, Vanity Fair, 1978, NM, ea.................**$75.00**

Hogan's Heroes, writing tablet, 1965, unused, NM.....**$30.00**

Howdy Doody, Bee-Knee-Kit, 1950s, NMIB...............**$65.00**

Howdy Doody, Color TV Set, complete w/5 rolls of film, NMIB..**$100.00**

Howdy Doody, costume playset, Princess Summerfall-Winterspring, Wonderland, 1950s, unused, NMIB..**$100.00**

Howdy Doody, film, A Trip to Fun Land, 8mm, Castle Films, 1950s, NMIB **$65.00**

Howdy Doody, hand puppet, Zany Toys, 1952, NMIB.**$50.00**

Howdy Doody, paint set, Milton Bradley, complete, NMIB **$200.00**

Howdy Doody, pinball game, Ja-Ru, 1987, MOC **$15.00**

HR Pufnstuf, bop bag, Coleco, 1970, MIP **$50.00**

HR Pufnstuf, pillow doll, 1970s, M, from $65 to........**$75.00**

Huckleberry Hound, figure, squeeze vinyl, Dell, 1962, 7", MIP..**$50.00**

Huckleberry Hound, Flip Show, 1961, EXIB **$40.00**

Huckleberry Hound, push-button puppet, Kohner, NM..**$45.00**

Huckleberry Hound, wastebasket, litho metal w/images of Huck, Yogi, Quick Draw & TV Friends, Hanna-Barbera, 1960s, VG..**$175.00**

Hugga Bunch, tray, litho metal, 1984, VG.................**$10.00**

Incredible Hulk, Hide-A-Way Play Case, Sears Exclusive, 1978, MIB **$75.00**

Incredible Hulk, Official Utility Belt, Remco, 1979, MIB..**$20.00**

Incredible Hulk, slide-tile puzzle, APC, 1977, MOC ...**$10.00**

Incredible Hulk, train set, 1979, NMIB......................**$50.00**

Incredible Hulk, wallet, vinyl, 1976, unused, NM.......**$20.00**

Inspector Gadget, Colorforms Shrinky Dinks, 1983, MIB .**$30.00**

James Bond, Electric Drawing Set, Lakeside, 1966, few pcs missing o/w EXIB **$125.00**

James Bond, wallet, vinyl, Glidrose Productions, 1966, NM...**$80.00**

Jetsons, doll, George, stuffed cloth, Nanco, 1989, 13", EX **$10.00**

Jetsons, figure, any character, bendable, Just Toys, MOC, ea **$10.00**

Jetsons, Slate & Chalk Set, 1960s, unused, MIB........**$100.00**

Josie & the Pussycats, Comic-Stiks, Deco Mfg, 1972, MOC...**$40.00**

Josie & the Pussycats, guitar, plastic, Larami, 1973, MOC, from $50 to **$75.00**

Josie & the Pussycats, Pendant Jewelry Set, Larami, 1972, MOC...**$30.00**

Julia, Dress-Up Kit, Colorforms, 1969, MIB **$50.00**

Julia, Hospital Set, Transogram, 1970, complete, NMIB, from $75 to..**$100.00**

Justice League of America, paint-by-number set, Hasbro, 1967, complete, EXIB.....................................**$150.00**

Kaptain Kool & the Kongs, magic slate, Whitman, 1978, MOC, from $35 to **$45.00**

Kaptain Kool & the Kongs, pencil-by-number set, Hasbro, 1977, unused, NMIB, from $40 to **$50.00**

Kermit the Frog, push-button puppet, Sony/Japan, 4", MOC...**$25.00**

King Kong, Colorforms Panoramic Play Set, 1976, complete, EXIB **$25.00**

Knight Rider, kite, 1982, MIP (sealed)........................**$25.00**

Knight Rider, Self-Inking Stamp Set, Larami, 1982, complete, MOC...**$30.00**

Kojak, Harbor Patrol Set, Continental Plastics, 1978, MOC...**$30.00**

Kung Fu, target set, Multiple, 1975, MOC, from $40 to..**$50.00**

Land of the Giants, Spaceship Spindrift, Remco, 1968, MIB..**$60.00**

Land of the Lost, Moonbase Rocket, Larami, 1975, MOC, from $30 to **$40.00**

Land of the Lost, Secret Look-Out, Larami, 1975, MIP, from $30 to **$40.00**

Land of the Lost, Stink, pull string talker, MIB, $85.00. (Photo courtesy June Moon)

Lassie, A Day in the Life of Lassie Play Kit, Plas-Trix, 1956, unused, NMIB **$200.00**

Lassie, doll, stuffed cloth, Knickerbocker, 14" L, EX.**$150.00**

Laugh-In, flicker rings, set of 5, EX.....................**$20.00**

Laurel & Hardy, wind-up figures, plastic, 1970, 5" & 6", NM, pr **$125.00**

Laverne & Shirley, Bowling Game, Harmony, 1977, MOC, from $30 to...**$40.00**

Laverne & Shirley, Secretary Set, Harmony, 1977, MOC, from $25 to...**$35.00**

Leave It to Beaver, ball cap, Beaver, stitched graphics, American Needle, 1994, EX...................................**$10.00**

Li'l Abner, flying saucer, blue vinyl w/multicolored Li'l Abner decal insert, 1954, 9" dia, NM **$50.00**

Linus the Lion-Hearted, doll, talker, Mattel, 1965, 21", VG...**$85.00**

Little House on the Prairie, Colorforms, 1978, MIB, from $40 to...**$50.00**

Little House on the Prairie, doll, Carrie, Knickerbocker, 1978, MIB **$35.00**

Little House on the Prairie, tea set, 26 pcs, Ohio Art, 1980, MIB **$100.00**

Little Lulu, crossword puzzle book, Whitman, 1974, unused, M **$50.00**

Little Lulu, perfume set, NMOC **$60.00**

Little Lulu & Tubby, figures, bisque, 1971, NM, pr.....**$12.00**

Little Orphan Annie & Sandy, figure, plaster, copyright 1973, scarce, M, from $300 to.......................................**$400.00**

Little Red Riding Hood, doll, rubber w/washable synthetic hair, Deluxe Reading, 1955, 23", MIB **$125.00**

Love Boat, puffy stickers, several variations, Imperial, 1982, MIP, ea **$10.00**

Love Boat, Travel Stamp Set, Imperial, 1983, MOC **$20.00**

M*A*S*H, canteen, Tristar, 1981, EX **$10.00**

M*A*S*H, dog tags, Tristar, 1981, MOC **$10.00**

Magilla Gorilla, doll, stuffed plush, Nanco, 1990, 7", NM...**$15.00**

Magilla Gorilla, figure, squeeze vinyl w/painted features, Screen Gems/Spain, 1967, 8", VG **$125.00**

Magilla Gorilla, pull toy, rubber, Ideal, 1964, 9", NM .**$55.00**

Magnum PI, handcuffs, 1981, MOC.............................**$20.00**

Man From UNCLE, Secret Print Putty, Colorforms, NMOC .**$35.00**

Man From Atlantis, Dip Dot Painting Kit, Kenner, 1977, NRFB...**$130.00**

Marvel Super Heroes, checkers set, Hasbro, 1976, MIP (sealed) **$50.00**

Marvel Super Heroes, light-up drawing desk, plastic, Lakeside, 1976, EXIB **$40.00**

Marvel Super Heroes, notebook, Mead, 1970s, unused, M ..**$25.00**

Marvel Super Heroes, record case, 1977, 18x15", EX .**$25.00**

Mighty Mouse, Launcher Pistol, Ja-Ru, 1981, MOC **$15.00**

Mighty Mouse, magic slate, Lowe, 1950s, NM.............**$50.00**

Mod Squad, Instant Intercom, white plastic walkie-talkies, Larami, 1973, MOC **$50.00**

Mork & Mindy, Colorforms Dress-Up Set, 1979, MIB.**$25.00**

Mork & Mindy, gumball machine, Mork From Ork, Hasbro, 1980, MIB, from $40 to..**$50.00**

Mork & Mindy, paint-by-number set, Craft Master, 1979, complete, NMIB **$25.00**

Mortimer Snerd, hand puppet, brown & white checked body w/composition head, 1950s, EX+ **$100.00**

Mother Goose, dishes, plastic, 26 pcs, Ideal, 1940s, MIB..**$150.00**

Mr Ed, hand puppet, plush, talker, Mattel, 1962, MIP..**$150.00**

Mr Magoo, doll, stuffed cloth w/vinyl head, felt jacket & knitted scarf, Ideal, 1964, 15", EX, minimum value....**$75.00**

Munsters, hand puppet, Grandpa, cloth body w/vinyl head, Ideal, 1964, EX+...**$100.00**

Munsters, hand puppet, Herman, cloth body w/vinyl head, talker, EX **$75.00**

Muppet Babies, doll, Kermit or Miss Piggy, Hasbro, 1985, 12", MIB, ea **$35.00**

Muppets, Miss Piggy Latch Hook Kit, MIB (sealed)....**$55.00**

Muppets, stick puppet, Kermit the Frog, plastic, Fisher-Price, 1979, 3½", MOC **$5.00**

My Favorite Martian, Magic Trick Set, Gilbert, 1964, EXIB...**$200.00**

Nancy Drew, fan club kit, FCCA, 1978, complete, NM (NM folder) **$65.00**

Nancy Drew, Mystery Pictures To Color, 1977, M.......**$15.00**

New Zoo Revue, doll, any character, stuffed plush w/vinyl head, Rushton, 1970s, NM, from $30 to...............**$40.00**

New Zoo Revue, figure, any character, bendable, Imperial, 1973, MIB, ea from $15 to **$20.00**

New Zoo Revue, musical mobile, Young Designs, 1971, MIB, from $50 to...**$75.00**

Olive Oyle, hand puppet, cloth body w/vinyl head, 1950s, 10", M, from $50 to..**$60.00**

Oswald Rabbit, magic slate, Saalfield, 1962, EX..........**$20.00**

Partridge Family, bulletin board, red cork w/white music staff logo, 1970s, 18x24", EX, from $75 to.........**$100.00**

Partridge Family, doll, Laurie, Remco, 1973, rare, 16", MIB...**$250.00**

Patty Duke, Charm Jewelry Set, Standard Toykraft, 1963, complete, NMIB **$75.00**

Peanuts, Colorforms, Star Snoopy, MIB......................**$25.00**

Peanuts, Deluxe Peanuts Playset, Determined/Helm Toy, 1975, MIB, from $225 to **$300.00**

Peanuts, diary, Happiness Is Having Secrets, image of Snoopy, Hallmark, 1990s, M $10.00

Peanuts, doll, Snoopy, stuffed cloth, Ideal, 1970s, 13½", MIB, from $50 to...$60.00

Peanuts, doll, Snoopy as chef, rag-type, 6", VG..........$10.00

Peanuts, dolls, Linus, Lucy or Peppermint Patty, stuffed cloth, Ideal, 1970s, 13½", MIB, ea from $40 to..............$50.00

Peanuts, figure, Snoopy as baseball player, PVC, 1984, 8½", NM, from $35 to...$45.00

Peanuts, hand puppet, Woodstock, velveteen w/yarn feathers, Determined, 1970s, 6", NM, from $15 to $20.00

Peanuts, jump rope, Snoopy, white plastic, MIP.........$15.00

Peanuts, marionette, Charlie Brown, Pelham, 1970s, 8", MIB, from $75 to...$100.00

Peanuts, Snoopy Felt Pen Picture Set, Craftmaster, 1979, complete, NMIB $15.00

Peanuts, tea set, 12 pcs, Chein, 1969, MIB, from $200 to..$250.00

Peanuts, whistle, Woodstock, Hallmark, 1976, MIP $50.00

Pee Wee's Playhouse, Colorforms Playhouse Transfer Rub-Ons, MIP (sealed) $12.00

Phantom of the Opera, Rub-Ons Magic Picture Transfers, Hasbro, 1966, complete, NMIB..............................$75.00

Pink Panther, Silly Putty, Ja-Ru, 1980, MOC............$10.00

Pinky Lee, paint set, Gabriel, 1950s, complete, NMIB..$75.00

Pinky Lee, party packet, 1950s, complete, M (NM mailer) $10.00

Planet of the Apes, doll, Cornelius, rubber, 1973, 6", EX+ $40.00

Planet of the Apes, squirt gun, Cornelius, plastic, AHI, 1970s, M $150.00

Pogo, figures, Pogo & friends, vinyl, 6 different characters, Procter & Gamble premiums, 1969, up to 5½", NM, ea...........$15.00

Pogo, mugs, plastic, set of 6 ea w/different character, 4", 1960s, NM, ea...$18.00

Popeye, ashtray, figure of Popeye holding pipe in mouth & other hand on hip, lustreware w/gold trim, 1930s, 7", EX, A...$275.00

Popeye, doll, Popeye, stuffed cloth w/vinyl head & arms, Uneeda, 1979, 8", MIB, from $35 to.....................$45.00

Popeye, figure, celluloid, 1940s, 5", EX.....................$125.00

Popeye, Pencil-By-Number Set, 1959, unused, MIB ...$35.00

Popeye, puffy magnet, EX $15.00

Popeye, slide-tile puzzle, 1960s, MOC.......................$35.00

Porky Pig, bubble gum machine, plastic figure, Banko Matic, 1970s, 9½", EXIB..$25.00

Porky Pig, figure, Sun Rubber, 1950s, 6", EXIB $100.00

Punky Brewster, doll, Galoob, 1984, 18", NRFB $40.00

Quick Draw McGraw, wall plaque, figure of Quick Draw playing bass fiddle, multicolored, Hanna-Barbera, NM $100.00

Raggedy Ann, coin purse, vinyl figure w/zipper closure, Hallmark, NM, from $15 to $20.00

Raggedy Ann, cologne doll, styrofoam w/cloth clothes & yarn hair over plastic bottle, Giftique, 1977, NM .$20.00

Raggedy Ann, Colorforms Dollhouse, 1974, complete, MIB, from $25 to...$30.00

Raggedy Ann, Colorforms Pop-Up Tea Party, complete, MIB, from $30 to...$40.00

Raggedy Ann, finger puppet, Bobbs-Merrill, 1977, MOC...$20.00

Raggedy Ann, pajama bag doll, stuffed cloth w/yarn hair, Knickerbocker, 1960s, 27", NM............................$80.00

Raggedy Ann, yo-yo, plastic tournament shape w/imprint seal, 1970s, MIP...$18.00

Raggedy Ann & Andy, dolls, 75th Anniversary edition, Applause, 1992, 19", M (M box), pr, from $160 to..$175.00

Raggedy Ann & Andy, Fun-Filled Playtime Box, Whitman, 1976, complete, NMIB.....................................$30.00

Raggedy Ann & Andy, Paste & Stick Set, Whitman, 1968, MIB $30.00

Raggedy Ann & Andy, phonograph, Vanity Fair, 1974, NMIB, from $45 to...$55.00

Raggedy Ann & Andy, pinball game, plastic, Arco, 1978, 11", NM (VG box), from $25 to $30.00

Raggedy Ann & Andy, tea set, litho metal, 9 pcs, Chein, 1972, MIB $30.00

Raggesy Ann & Andy, hand puppets, cloth w/yarn hair, Knickerbocker, 1973, 10", MIP, ea $25.00

Rainbow Brite, Color Cottage, MIB (sealed)...............$30.00

Rainbow Brite, dolls, Lurky, Spark Sprite or Twink Sprite, 10", NMIB, ea $20.00

Richochet Rabbit, pull toy, rubber, Ideal, 1960s, 9", EX+..$50.00

Road Runner, Magic Cartoon Board, 1971, unused, M.....$25.00

Rocky & Bullwinkle, blackboard, die-cut figure at top, Frolic Toys, 1970s, 12x16", VG..............................$50.00

Rocky & Bullwinkle, Castanets, Larami, 1972, MOC...$20.00

Rocky & Bullwinkle, Colorforms #146, unused, NMIB..$85.00

Rocky & Bullwinkle, figures, any character, Wham-O, MOC, ea $25.00

Rocky & Bullwinkle, telescope, Larami, 1970s, MOC .$25.00

Rookies, Action Accessory Set, 1976, MIB..................$25.00

Rookies, helmet, plastic w/sticker on top, 1970s, VG...$15.00

Rootie Kazootie, hand puppet, cloth body w/vinyl head, 1953, 10", EX..$30.00

Ruff & Ready, Spelling Game, unused, 1958, M $35.00

Scooby Doo, necklace, King's Island, MOC $30.00

Scrappy, xylophone pull toy, paper litho on wood, EX ..$375.00

Sesame Street, doll, Big Bird, talker, Playskool, 1970s, 22", VG...$25.00

Sesame Street, doll, Cookie Monster, stuffed plush, Hasbro, 1970s, 12", VG...$15.00

Sesame Street, doll, Ernie, stuffed cloth, 18", EX $20.00

Sesame Street, snack set, Chilton Globe, 1988, complete, MIB $20.00

Shari Lewis, Electric Drawing Set, 1962, complete, NMIB..$75.00

Simpsons, bookmarker, paper, 'Read Man,' pictures the family reading, 6", NM..$3.00

Simpsons, doll, Bart, stuffed cloth w/vinyl head, Vivid Imaginations, 10", M...$35.00

Simpsons, doll, Bart, talker, stuffed cloth & vinyl, Dandee, 18", MIB..$75.00

Simpsons, doll, Bubble Blowin' Lisa, Mattel, complete, 10½", MIB $85.00

Simpsons, doll, rag-type, any character, Dandee, 11", NM, ea $18.00

Simpsons, key chain, PVC figure of Bart on silver-tone ring, Street Kids, M $3.00

Simpsons, Lisa Simpson Double Stamp Set, Jaru, MOC..$15.00

Simpsons, pajama bag, stuffed cloth Bart figure holding toothbrush & pillow, 24", M..................$40.00

Simpsons, punch ball set, National Latex Products, MIP ..$5.00

Simpsons, Trace 'N Color Drawing Set, Toymax, complete, NMIB..................$85.00

Simpsons, Write 'N Wipe, several variations, Rose Art, MIB (sealed), ea $15.00

Simpsons, 3-D Chess Set, MIB (sealed) $35.00

Six Million Dollar Man, Bionic Action Club Kit, Kenner, 1973, complete, M, from $50 to..................$75.00

Six Million Dollar Man, paint-by-number set, Craft Master, 1975, MIB, from $30 to..................$40.00

Six Million Dollar Man, Poster Put-Ons, Bi-Rite, 1978, MIP..................$15.00

Six Million Dollar Man, wrist radio, Illco, 1976, MIB, from $200 to..................$250.00

Smurfs, banner, Happy Smurfday, MIP..................$20.00

Smurfs, Colorforms, complete, EXIB..................$35.00

Smurfs, sewing cards, MIB (sealed)..................$25.00

Snuffy Smith, figures, pink plastic, set of 4, Marx, 1950s, NM..................$65.00

Spider-Man, binder, paper w/colorful image of several characters, Mead, 1970s, NM..................$40.00

Spider-Man, doll, stuffed cloth w/vinyl head, Amsco, 1976, 8", EX..................$40.00

Spider-Man, roller skates, plastic, 1970s, MIP (sealed)...$40.00

Spider-Man, Sharp Shooter, Larami, 1978, MOC..................$40.00

Spider-Man, TV chair, inflatable vinyl, Carlin Playthings, 1978, MIB, from $50 to..................$75.00

Starsky & Hutch, iron-on transfers, various styles, 1970s, MIP, ea from $20 to..................$25.00

Starsky & Hutch, Mini Target Set, Fleetwood, 1976, MOC, from $40 to..................$50.00

Starsky & Hutch, 3-D viewer, Fleetwood, 1977, MIP, from $25 to..................$35.00

Super Friends, Magnetic Target, 1980, MOC..................$20.00

Superman, doll, Applause, 18", NM..................$25.00

Superman, Fun Poncho, Ben Cooper, 1976, MIP (sealed)..$30.00

Superman, kite, Hi-Flier, 1984, MIP..................$30.00

Superman, push-button puppet, Kohner, 1966, NM..$125.00

Superman, scrapbook, Saalfield, 1940, unused, NM..$200.00

Superman, slide-tile puzzle, APC, 1977, MOC..................$10.00

Superman, Sparkle Paints, w/5 pictures to paint, 1966, NMIB..................$65.00

Superman, wallet, colorful graphics on yellow vinyl, w/magic pad & pencil, etc, 1966, NM..................$85.00

Superman, yo-yo, plastic slimline w/view lens, flasher seal, Duncan, 1980s, NM..................$20.00

Sylvester the Cat, roly poly, EX..................$25.00

Tarzan, Magic Rub-Off Picture Set, Whitman, 1966, complete, VG (VG box)..................$25.00

Tasmanian Devil, doll, stuffed plush, 1980, 13", EX ...$15.00

Teenage Mutant Ninja Turtles, cereal bowl, painted ceramic, Mirage Studios, 1990, M..................$8.00

Teenage Mutant Ninja Turtles, tote bag, repeated design, Mirage Studio, 1989, 14x8", NM..................$20.00

Teenage Mutant Ninja Turtles, water bopper, inflatable vinyl, 1990, 36", MIP..................$25.00

Three Stooges, flasher ring, Curly, Larry or Moe, EX, ea ..$20.00

Tom & Jerry, checkers game, Ja-Ru, 1990, MOC..................$10.00

Tom & Jerry, crayon-by-number set, Transogram, 1965, MIB (sealed)..................$65.00

Tom & Jerry, figure, painted plaster, 5", EX..................$85.00

Tom Corbett Space Cadet, belt buckle, black leather w/encircled name & metal rocket ship, 1950s, EX..................$45.00

Tom Corbett Space Cadet, Field Glasses, black metal w/colorful images, 1952, NMIB..................$125.00

Tom Corbett Space Cadet, Model-Craft Molding & Coloring Set, complete, MIB..................$165.00

Topo Gigio, hand puppet, American Character, 1960s, 12", NRFB..................$125.00

Tweety Bird, lantern, tin & glass, battery-op, Amico, 1950s, 5½", EX..................$85.00

Uncle Wiggily, doll, stuffed cloth w/original clothes, Georgene, 20", NM..................$550.00

Underdog, harmonica, yellow plastic w/figure at both ends, 1975, 8", EX..................$20.00

Underdog, yo-yo, plastic tournament shape w/paper sticker seal, 1992, MIP..................$18.00

Universal Monsters, charm, any character, M, ea..................$10.00

Universal Monsters, Flicker Stickers, set of 6, 1991, MOC..$15.00

Welcome Back Kotter, chalkboard, Board King, 1976, 18½x24½", NM..................$50.00

Welcome Back Kotter, Colorforms, 1976, MIB..................$30.00

Welcome Back Kotter, Poster Art Kit, Board King, 1976, MIP (sealed), from $35 to..................$45.00

Wizard of Oz, Magic Kit, Fun Inc, 1960s, complete, NMIB..................$50.00

Wizard of Oz, trinket box, ruby slippers, Presents, 1999, MIB..................$15.00

Wolfman, doll, vinyl w/cloth outfit, Hamilton Presents, 1992, 14", EX..................$30.00

Wolfman, flashlight key chain, Basic Fun, 1995, MOC..$12.00

Wonder Woman, figure, painted plastic, Ideal, 1966, 4", EX..................$45.00

Wonder Woman, hand puppet, plastic body w/vinyl head, Ideal, 1966, 11", NM..................$25.00

Wonder Woman, music box, figure on round base, painted composition, 1978, 7x4½" dia, M..................$40.00

Woody Woodpecker, kazoo, plastic figure, Linden, 1960s, 7", EX..................$25.00

Woody Woodpecker, ring, cloisonne, 1970s, M..................$15.00

Yogi Bear, doll, Boo Boo, stuffed cloth, Knickerbocker, 1973, MIB (sealed)..................$35.00

Yogi Bear, doll, plush w/felt hat, collar & tie, 17", EX..$50.00

Yogi Bear, lamp, figural base w/images of Yogi's friends in circus motif on shade, EX..................$200.00

Yogi Bear, mug, painted plastic, 1962, NM..................$20.00

Yogi Bear, pillow doll, w/bells inside, 15", EX..................$20.00

Yogi Bear, slippers, corduroy, 1962, unused, NMIB ...**$70.00**

Yogi Bear, yo-yo, litho tin tournament shape w/image of Yogi & Boo-Boo, 1970s, NM **$10.00**

Cherished Teddies

First appearing on dealers' shelves in the spring of 1992, Cherished Teddies found instant collector appeal. They were designed by artist Priscilla Hillman and produced in the Orient for the Enesco company. Besides the figurines, such as those we've listed below, the line includes waterballs, frames, plaques, and bells.

Seth and Sarabeth, retired, from $25.00 to $30.00.

Allison & Alexandra, Two Friends Mean Twice the Love, 1998, retired **$25.00**

Arthur (August), Smooth Sailing, holding sailboat, 1995, retired **$15.00**

Beth, Happy Holidays Deer Friend, riding deer rocker, Christmas 1992 (suspended 1995) **$45.00**

Chantel & Fawn, We're Kindred Spirits, 1999 limited edition (closed) **$40.00**

Clarence, Santa Spells Christmas Joy, seated on blocks, 1998, Parade of Gifts Exclusive **$35.00**

Gina, Where Friends Gather Magic Blossoms, 2000, retired **$15.00**

John, Bear in Mind You're Special, seated in chair, 1996, retired **$25.00**

Kelsie, Be the Apple of My Eye, holding apple, 1997, retired **$18.00**

Lee, You're a Bear's Best Friend, w/puppy, 1997 limited edition **$15.00**

Margy, I'm Wrapping Up a Little Holiday Joy To Send Your Way, 1998 Avon Exclusive **$25.00**

Mayor Wilson T Beary, w/key to city, 1995 Membears only **$50.00**

Nathaniel & Nellie, It's Twice as Nice w/You, 1992, retired..**$50.00**

Paula, Helping Others Is the Best Part of My Job, stethoscope around neck, 2001 Avon Exclusive **$20.00**

Pinocchio, You've Got My Heart on a String, hanging from strings as a puppet, 2000, retired **$25.00**

Rebecca, Let Heaven & Nature Sing, w/2 bunnies, 2001 limited edition (closed)..**$25.00**

Christmas Collectibles

Christmas is nearly everybody's favorite holiday, and it's a season when we all seem to want to get back to time-honored traditions. The stuffing and fruit cakes are made like Grandma always made them, we go caroling and sing the old songs that were written two hundred years ago, and the same Santa that brought gifts to the children in a time long forgotten still comes to our house and yours every Christmas Eve.

So for reasons of nostalgia, there are thousands of collectors interested in Christmas memorabilia. Some early Santa figures are rare and may be very expensive, especially when dressed in a color other than red. Blown glass ornaments and Christmas tree bulbs were made in shapes of fruits and vegetables, houses, Disney characters, animals, and birds. There are Dresden ornaments and candy containers from Germany, some of which were made prior to the 1870s, that have been lovingly preserved and handed down from generation to generation. They were made of cardboard that sparkled with gold and silver trim.

Artificial trees made of feathers were produced as early as 1850 and as late as 1950. Some were white, others blue, though most were green, and some had red berries or clips to hold candles. There were little bottle-brush trees, trees with cellophane needles, and trees from the '60s made of aluminum.

Collectible Christmas items are not necessarily old, expensive, or hard to find. Things produced in your lifetime have value as well. To learn more about this field, we recommend *Christmas Ornaments, Lights and Decorations, Vols I, II,* and *III,* by George Johnson (Collector Books).

Bar set, painted wood Santas, ca 1950s, from $20.00 to $30.00.

Bulb, apple, painted milk glass, embossed leaves at top of oval, Japan, 2½", from $10 to **$15.00**

Bulb, bear sitting on haunches, painted milk glass, Japan, ca 1950, 2¾", from $75 to **$85.00**

Bulb, berry, painted clear glass, exhaust tip, bumpy round shape, 1¾", from $15 to **$20.00**

Bulb, bird in birdcage, painted milk glass, Japan, ca 1935-55, 2", from $10 to..**$15.00**

Bulb, bird in birdhouse, painted milk glass, Japan, ca 1935-50, 1½", from $15 to..**$20.00**

Bulb, bulldog in vest, painted milk glass, grumpy look, Japan, 2¾", from $90 to..**$110.00**

Bulb, candle, clear glass, round shaft w/'dripping wax,' smooth 'flame' w/exhaust tip, 3", from $25 to.....**$30.00**

Bulb, candle, milk glass shaft w/clear glass 'flame,' China, 3¾", from $20 to..**$25.00**

Bulb, candle, milk glass w/clear 'flame,' Czechoslovakia, 4", from $5 to..**$10.00**

Bulb, candle, milk glass w/embossed lines, Japan, 2½", from $10 to..**$15.00**

Bulb, cats (2) in basket, painted milk glass, Japan, 2¼", from $55 to..**$65.00**

Bulb, chick, painted clear glass, fluffy body & sm head, 1½", from $25 to..**$35.00**

Bulb, chick, painted clear glass, wings folded, 1½", from $25 to..**$35.00**

Bulb, clover blossom, painted milk glass, marked SK (Japan), 1¾", from $30 to..**$35.00**

Bulb, cross, molded clear glass w/wide flat arms, Japan, 3", from $20 to..**$25.00**

Bulb, cross on egg shape, milk glass, embossed radiating lines, Japan, 2¼", from $35 to..**$40.00**

Bulb, dog clown, painted milk glass, Japan, 3¼", from $175 to..**$200.00**

Bulb, dog in polo outfit, painted milk glass, Japan, ca 1950, 2¾", from $25 to..**$35.00**

Bulb, dragon on lantern, painted milk glass, Japan, 2¼", from $10 to..**$15.00**

Bulb, elephant w/trunk down, painted milk glass, Japan, ca 1935, 2½", from $20 to..**$30.00**

Bulb, fish, painted clear glass, football shape, tail at base, Japan, 2¾", from $10 to..**$12.00**

Bulb, fish w/tail, painted clear or milk glass, base in nose, Japan, 2⅜", from $25 to..**$35.00**

Bulb, flower in a seashell, painted milk glass, Japan, 2¼", from $75 to..**$85.00**

Bulb, gourd man, painted milk glass, double-sided, V-shaped mouth & bow tie, Japan, 2½", from $25 to.........**$30.00**

Bulb, hippo girl, painted milk glass, wearing dress, Japan, 4½", from $175 to..**$200.00**

Bulb, horse head in horseshoe, painted milk glass, Japan, 2¼", from $55 to..**$65.00**

Bulb, lion in suit w/pipe, painted milk glass, Japan or Canada, ca 1935 & 1955, 2½", from $25 to.........**$35.00**

Bulb, lion w/tennis racket, painted milk glass, w/shirt & pants, Japan, ca 1935 & 1955, 2¾", from $20 to..**$30.00**

Bulb, monkey w/stick, painted milk glass, Perma-Lite, Japan, 2¼", from $70 to..**$80.00**

Bulb, mushroom, painted milk glass, 2", from $20 to.......**$25.00**

Bulb, Oriental cat man, painted milk glass, wearing jacket, pants & sm cap, flowers in hands, Japan, 2¾", from $70 to.**$80.00**

Bulb, owl in vest & top hat, painted clear or milk glass, wings folded, Japan, 2¼", from $90 to..**$110.00**

Bulb, parakeet, painted milk glass, wings folded, marked SK (Japan), 3¾", from $8 to..**$10.00**

Bulb, peacock, painted milk glass, full feathers form disc behind embossed bird, double-sided, 1950s, Japan, 1¼"..**$50.00**

Bulb, pig in hooded basket, painted clear glass, Japan, 2", from $100 to..**$125.00**

Bulb, pine cone, painted clear glass, embossed detail, crushed glass trim, Czech, recent, 2¼", from $5 to..............**$10.00**

Bulb, rabbit begging, painted clear glass, American, 1950s, miniature, 1½", from $50 to..**$75.00**

Bulb, rooster in tub, painted milk glass, Japan, 2¼", from $40 to..**$50.00**

Bulb, rosebud, painted milk glass, Japan, miniature, 1½", from $5 to..**$8.00**

Bulb, Scottie, painted milk glass, sitting w/front legs straight, Japan, 2½", from $35 to..**$45.00**

Bulb, songbird, painted milk glass, sitting, base in bottom, Japan, 3", from $8 to..**$10.00**

Bulb, squirrel eating nut, painted clear glass, American, ca 1950, 1½", from $50 to..**$75.00**

Candy box, reindeer lithograph on cardboard, USA, 4½", from $5 to..**$10.00**

Candy box, Santa lithograph on cardboard, USA, 5¾", from $5 to..**$10.00**

Candy container, ball, printed paper on cardboard, Germany, 1960s, 3-3½", from $10 to..**$15.00**

Candy container, bell, paper w/scrap decoration, 1930s, 5½" wide, from $25 to..**$30.00**

Candy container, book, light blue paper w/gold trim, opens along page's edge, 3", from $30 to..**$40.00**

Candy container, cornucopia, plain colored paper, 1940-50s, 3-10", ea from $12 to..**$25.00**

Candy container, egg, printed or lithographed paper on pressed cardboard, 1½", from $10 to..**$25.00**

Candy container, lady's hat box, printed paper, 2½-3", from $100 to..**$125.00**

Candy container, peanut, embossed paper w/realistic appearance, Japan, 2½", from $45 to..**$55.00**

Candy container, potato, brown paper w/embossed eyes, opens along seam, 2½", from $45 to..**$55.00**

Candy container, Santa w/pack in right hand, plastic, Irwin, ca 1950, 4", from $18 to..**$20.00**

Candy container, Santa waving, white opaque & translucent red & clear plastic, ca 1960, 3½", from $12 to.....**$15.00**

Candy container, Santa's boot, pressed paper, US Zone, late 1940s-early 1950s, 6", from $20 to..**$30.00**

Candy container, snow ball, crushed glass on cardboard sphere, ca 1980-90s, 2½-3¼", from $3 to................**$4.00**

Candy container, trunk w/curved top, printed paper on light cardboard stock, 3", from $25 to..**$35.00**

Chain of angels, plastic 3-D angels w/musical instruments, Japan, ca 1970, 9', from $4 to..**$5.00**

Chain of beads, plastic, faceted beads, Japan or China, 1960s-70s, 9', from $3 to..**$4.00**

Chain of beads, plastic, round beads, Japan or China, 1960s-70s, 9', from $2 to..**$3.00**

Decoration, acrylic oval w/etched Christmas scene, 1970s-80, 3", from $1 to **$2.00**

Decoration, angel child, plastic, Japan, late 1940s-50s, 1¾-2¼", ea from $3 to..**$4.00**

Decoration, angel on cloud w/star, celluloid, Made in West Germany, 2", from $5 to..**$6.00**

Decoration, ball, plastic, faceted, Bradford Plastics, 1950-60, 2½", from $1 to...**$2.00**

Decoration, ball, plastic, indented w/different colored ring at middle where halves join, 1940-50, 2¼", from $5 to .**$6.00**

Decoration, ball, plastic, molded in 2 parts, hanging loop at top, ca 1930, 2¾", from $5 to **$6.00**

Decoration, Santa in sleigh, plastic, molded in 1 pc, Germany or Japan, 3½", from $45 to **$55.00**

Decoration, Santa w/pack, plastic, Irwin, 5¼", from $50 to..**$60.00**

Decoration, Santa waving w/lantern, plastic, Made in Japan, 4¾", from $35 to..**$45.00**

**Lanterns, Japan, ca 1950s: snowman, 5",
MIB, $50.00; Santa face, 5", MIB, $65.00.**

Light cover, Santa w/hands on stomach, plastic, ca 1950, 4¾", from $15 to..**$18.00**

**Night light, Rudolph, E.M.C. Art, 12" long, from
$45.00 to $50.00.** (Photo courtesy George Johnson)

Ornament, ball, plastic, wedge-shaped indents & scallops, Bradford, 1955-60, 2¾", from $2 to.........................**$3.00**

Ornament, ball, plastic w/holly leaves in side, American or Japanese, ca 1960s-70s, 2¼", from $1 to.................**$1.50**

Ornament, ball, styrofoam covered w/satin or velvet, 1980s, 2½-3", from 25¢ to..**$.50**

Ornament, ball frame, plastic w/embossed holly leaves & spun glass, American, 1955-60, 3½", from $2 to **$3.00**

Ornament, barrel, silvered plastic w/embossed ribs, American, 1950s, 2½", from $5 to **$6.00**

Ornament, bell, honeycomb paper on cardboard, 3", from $2 to...**$3.00**

Ornament, bell, honeycomb paper on cardboard, 11", from $5 to...**$6.00**

Ornament, bell, silvered plastic w/embossed holly leaves & spun glass, American, ca 1960, 3¾", from $2 to **$3.00**

Ornament, bell, solid-colored plastic, Bradford Plastics ca 1950, 2-3¼", from 25¢ to..**$.75**

Ornament, bird, glitter on cardboard, removable head, Japan, ca 1960, 2¾-3½", from $3 to...................................**$5.00**

Ornament, boot, printed Santa & Merry Christmas on vinyl, 1950s, 5½", from $20 to **$25.00**

Ornament, cat, fluorescent plastic, USA, 1940s-50s, 3¼", from $15 to..**$17.00**

Ornament, church, crushed glass on cardboard, Czechoslovakia, 3¾", from $15 to **$20.00**

Ornament, church, silvered plastic, sq w/steeple & cross, Shiny Brite, ca 1950, 4¼", from $8 to **$10.00**

Ornament, elf, plastic, pointed ears, sinister look, 3¼", from $15 to..**$18.00**

Ornament, geometric prism, plastic kite shape w/8 reflective sides, ca 1965, 5½", from $1 to **$1.50**

Ornament, house, 6-sided, foil over paper, Wilmsen of Philadelphia, ca 1935, 2¼", from $10 to **$15.00**

Ornament, icicle, translucent plastic, molded hook at top, American, ca 1960, 5½", from 25¢ to ....**$.50**

Ornament, icicle, twisted clear plastic, American, 1960s, 5", from 50¢ to..**$1.00**

Ornament, lion, fluorescent plastic, USA, 1940s-50s, from $6 to **$8.00**

Ornament, musical instrument, silvered plastic, American, 1950s, 4¼-4¾", ea from $4 to...............................**$5.00**

Ornament, pine cone, foil-covered papier-mache, 3-D, B Wilmsen of Philadelphia, ca 1935, 2", from $10 to...**$15.00**

Ornament, Santa, plastic w/rabbit fur trim, pebbles in back make it rattle, spring at hanger, 4¾", from $15 to .**$18.00**

Ornament, Santa in sled w/running deer, plastic, EX detail, hole in back for candy, 1950s, 4" L, from $20 to.**$25.00**

Ornament, snowflake, white or blue fluorescent plastic, American, 2", ea from $1 to....................................**$1.50**

Ornament, star in a ring, colored translucent plastic, ca 1950, 3¾", from $3 to..**$5.00**

Ornament, surprise ball, paper, when unwound toy/trinket found inside, Japan, 1950s, 3½", from $5 to **$8.00**

Ornament, teapot, silvered plastic w/embossed details, ca 1960, 3", from $8 to..**$9.00**

Christmas Tree Pins

Once thought of as mere holiday novelties, Christmas tree pins are now considered tiny prizes among costume jewelry and Christmas collectors. Hollycraft, Weiss, Lisner, and other famous costume jewelry designers created beautiful trees. Rhinestones, colored 'jewels', and lovely enameling make Christmas tree pins tiny works of art, and what used to be purchased for a few dollars now may command as much as one hundred, especially if signed. Pins are plentiful and prices vary. Buyers should be aware that many fakes and repros are out there. Many 'vintage looking' pins are actually brand new and retail for less than $10.00. Know your dealer, and if you are unsure, let it pass.

If you'd like to learn more about them, we recommend *Christmas Pins, Past & Present,* by Jill Gallina (Collector Books).

Brooks, body resembles harp strings, multicolor stones, from $45 to..**$65.00**
Carnegie, conical shape w/inset multicolor stones, lg red stone at base, 1960s, from $75 to.........................**$85.00**
De Nicola, silver soft-flowing tree w/gold rope garland & balls, 1960s-60s, from $75 to..............................**$95.00**
Eisenberg, gold Victorian style w/multicolor stones & star top, 1st issued in 1992, from $50 to.....................**$65.00**
Hobè, white rhinestones w/numerous multicolor stones, 1980s reissue, from $35 to.................................**$45.00**
Hollycraft, bright multicolored rhinestones w/white rhinestone garland, from $45 to..............................**$65.00**
Hollycraft, filigree body w/multicolor rhinestones, matching earrings, from $125 to..........................**$175.00**
Hollycraft, gold-tone ribbon-like design, early 1960s, from $75 to..**$95.00**

Kenneth Lane, pastel-colored hand-set rhinestones, 1960s, from $100.00 to $125.00. (Photo courtesy Jill Gallina)

Jolle, gold porcupine-like shape w/pearls & rhinestones, from $45 to..**$65.00**
Mylu, gold w/red stones, dangling green balls along bottom, from $45 to..**$60.00**
Unsigned, gold-tone metal w/white rhinestones, 1990s, from $18 to..**$25.00**

Unsigned, partridge in pear tree, fine enameling, 1950s, from $35 to..**$50.00**
Weiss, geometric shape, multicolor rhinestones, 1950s, lg, from $125 to..**$225.00**
Weiss, green enameling & angular garland w/rhinestones, star atop w/red stone, ca 1950s-60s, from $45 to.........**$65.00**
Weiss, multicolor stones, mother-of-pearl-like candles, ca 1950s, from $95 to..**$125.00**

Trifari, set with jelly-like Swarovski crystals designed exclusively for that company, ca 1961, from $85.00 to $110.00. (Photo courtesy Jill Gallina)

Cigarette Lighters

Collectors of tobacciana tell us that cigarette lighters are definitely hot! Look for novel designs (figurals, Deco styling, and so forth), unusual mechanisms (flint and fuel, flint and gas, battery, etc.), those made by companies now defunct, advertising lighters, and quality lighters made by Ronson, Dunhill, Evans, Colibri, Zippo, and Ronson. For more information we recommend *Collector's Guide to Cigarette Lighters* by James Flanagan (Collector Books).

Newsletter: *On the Lighter Side*
Judith Sanders
Route 3, 136 Circle Dr., P.O. Box 1733
Quitman, TX 75783; 903-763-2795; SASE for information

Advertising, chromium w/decals on front & back, Japan, 1960s, 2¼x1½", from $5 to..................................**$10.00**
Advertising, Coors, painted metal, table size w/disposable butane pocket lighter, 1970s, 3½x1¾", from $10 to..**$20.00**
Advertising, GE Supply Co, brass & enamel, Park Industries, late 1950s, pocket size, 2¼x1½", from $10 to......**$20.00**
Advertising, Mindy's Rigging Specialists, chrome & enamel, Barlow, 1960s, pocket size, 2¼x1½", from $15 to..**$20.00**
Advertising, tube-style, chromium & enamel, pocket size, Redlite, 1940s, 3x⅜" dia, from $20 to...................**$30.00**
Animal, brass wolf dressed as cowboy, w/match striker, mid-1930s, table size, 5½x2", from $250 to..............**$300.00**
Animal, camel, metal, Japan, late 1940s, table size, 2x3", from $25 to..**$40.00**
Animal, donkey, brass, lighter on back, Japan, mid-1950s, 2x2½", from $15 to..................................**$20.00**

Animal, elephant, painted metal, Strikalite, late 1940s, 3x3½", from $25 to...**$35.00**

Art Deco, chrome & enamel ashtray stand, late 1940s, 22x8½" dia at base, from $25 to...........................**$40.00**

Camera/lighter combination, uses split roll of 35mm film, Camera-Lite, 1940s, 2¼x1¾", from $300 to........**$500.00**

Case/lighter combination, brass w/marble-like lid, Marhill of NY, 1950s, 5¼x2⅛", from $45 to...........................**$60.00**

Case/lighter combination, chromium w/US Army Air Corp emblem in blue enamel w/gold, Evans, 1940s, 4¼x2½", $75 to...**$100.00**

Case/lighter combination, Lektrocase, chromium & wooden slats, Glolite Corp, mid-1930s, 3x3⅞", from $80 to...........**$100.00**

Case/lighter combination, Pal, chromium & tortoise enamel, Ronson, ca 1941, 4⅛x2", from $50 to..................**$80.00**

Decorative, bronze-finished golf caddy, bag comes off the base (lighter), 1930s, 7x4¼", from $300 to.........**$350.00**

Decorative, chromium with gold trim, Prince, ca 1955, 2⅝", from $15.00 to $25.00. (Photo courtesy James Flanagan)

Decorative, Cupid, gold cherubs on black enamel, Ronson, ca 1956, 2¼x1¾", from $35 to...............................**$50.00**

Decorative, marble base w/gold-plated lighter top, Alfred Dunhill, ca 1955, 2½x3¾", from $275 to............**$325.00**

Figural, dog w/front paws on fence looking at book, brass, Occupied Japan, ca 1948, 2⅝x2⅜", from $80 to..**$120.00**

Figural, elephant, painted metal w/brass lift-arm, mid-1930s, table size, 3⅜x4⅞", from $30 to...........................**$40.00**

Figural, horse w/bridle & reins, painted ceramic, Japan, ca 1955, table size, 5½x5½", from $15 to..................**$25.00**

Figural, poodle handle, gold-tone metal, mid-1960s, table model, 2¾x2" dia, from $10 to...............................**$25.00**

Flashlight/lighter combination, chromium, battery operated, Magna, 1950s, pocket size, 2¼x2", from $35 to...**$50.00**

Flashlight/lighter combination, chromium, battery operated, Made in Japan, pocket model, 2⅞x1½", from $15 to............**$25.00**

Flashlight/lighter combination, chromium & leather, pocket model, ca 1960, 2x1½", from $20 to.....................**$30.00**

Novelty, bomb, brass, 1940s, 4x1¼" dia, from $40 to...**$60.00**

Novelty, canteen, plastic, butane, cap removes to reveal lighter, Germany, 1980s, pocket size, 2¼x1⅜", from $15 to..**$25.00**

Novelty, Gremlin, ceramic figure, Aircraft Novelty Co, 1930s, 4¼x4", from $75 to...**$100.00**

Novelty, metal boot, lever on back opens lighter, ca 1920s, 1¾", from $60.00 to $100.00. (Photo courtesy James Flanagan)

Novelty, plastic & metal striker type, late 1980s, pocket size, 2x1¼", from $5 to...**$10.00**

Occupied Japan, chromium & ceramic elephant, ca 1948, table size, 3½x4", from $75 to...........................**$110.00**

Occupied Japan, chromium typewriter, lights by pressing space bar, ca 1948, 1¾x3½", from $150 to.........**$175.00**

Occupied Japan, silver-plated cowboy, head is hinged to reveal lighter, ca 1948, 4x1¾", from $90 to........**$115.00**

Occupied Japan, silver-plated cowboy boot w/sunburst & floral decor, ca 1950, 2⅛x2⅞", from $50 to.........**$70.00**

Pocket, brass, butane, Scripto, late 1950s, 2½x1¼", +gift box, from $20 to...**$35.00**

Pocket, brass & enamel, butane, Battat, late 1970s, 2⅞x1⅛", from $15 to...**$25.00**

Pocket, brass w/ostrich hide band, Elgin American, 1950s, 1¾x1⅜", from $40 to...**$60.00**

Pocket, chromium, butane, pipe lighter, Savinelli, 1970s, 2¾x1⅛", from $20 to...**$40.00**

Pocket, chromium, butane, pipe lighter w/tamper bottom, Colibri, late 1960s, 3¼x½" dia, from $20 to.........**$40.00**

Pocket, chromium, Goldwyn, late 1950s, 1⅜x1⅝", from $10 to...**$20.00**

Pocket, chromium, lift-arm, Tee-Vee, mid-1930s, 2¼x1", from $15 to...**$25.00**

Pocket, chromium, lift-arm type, Golden Wheel, late 1940s, 1x⅞", from $20 to...**$30.00**

Pocket, chromium, striker type, Match King, 1950s, 1¾x1⅜", from $40 to...**$60.00**

Pocket, chromium & enamel, Imaco, late 1950s, 2¼x1½", from $20 to...**$30.00**

Pocket, chromium pistol w/mother-of-pearl grips, Japan, 1950s, 1½x2", from $25 to...................................**$40.00**

Pocket, D-Day Commemorative, black finish, Zippo, ca 1994, 2½x1½", M in tin, from $20 to............................**$40.00**

Pocket, gold-tone metal, musical, Crown, late 1940s, 2⅝x1⅜", from $20 to...**$40.00**

Pocket, pinup girl enameled on side, Supreme, 1950s, 2x1⅝",
from $20 to...**$35.00**

Pocket, silver-plated metal w/gold-tone etched wheat, Zippo,
ca 1994, 2¼x1½", from $20 to.............................**$30.00**

Pocket, Sport, chromium & blue leather, Ronson, ca 1956,
2x1¾", M in gift box, from $25 to........................**$40.00**

Pocket, Trickette, brass & rhinestones, Wisner, 1950s, pocket
size, 1½x1¾", from $25 to **$40.00**

Table, brass with floral and gold trim, Evans, 1940s, 5", from $25.00 to $40.00. (Photo courtesy James Flanagan)

Table, chromium nude w/Bakelite ashtray, Harry Davis
Molding Co, ca 1935, 5x6¾", from $40 to **$60.00**

Table, chromium w/embossed nude, ca 1988, 3x1¾", from
$15 to..**$30.00**

Table, Gloria, plastic & brass, batteries & butane, mid-1960s,
7¼x4¼" at base, from $30 to..............................**$50.00**

Table, Miss Cutie, gold-tone plastic, Negbaur, mid-1950s,
4¾x1½" dia at base, from $25 to **$50.00**

Cleminson Pottery

One of the several small potteries that operated in California during the middle of the century, Cleminson was a family-operated enterprise that made kitchenware, decorative items, and novelties that are beginning to attract a considerable amount of interest. At the height of their productivity, they employed 150 workers, so as you make your rounds, you'll be very likely to see a piece or two offered for sale just about anywhere you go. Prices are not high; this may be a 'sleeper.'

They marked their ware fairly consistently with a circular ink stamp that contains the name 'Cleminson.' But even if you find an unmarked piece, with just a little experience you'll easily be able to recognize their very distinctive glaze colors. They're all strong, yet grayed-down, dusty tones. They made a line of bird-shaped tableware items that they marketed as 'Distlefink' and several plaques and wall pockets that are decorated with mottoes and Pennsylvania Dutch-type hearts and flowers.

In Jack Chipman's *The Collector's Encyclopedia of California Pottery, Second Edition,* you'll find a chapter devoted to Cleminson Pottery. Roerig's *The Collector's Encyclopedia of Cookie Jars* has additional information. (Both of these books are published by Collector Books.)

See also Clothes Sprinkler Bottles; Cookie Jars.

Ashtray, You're the Big Wheel, 8" **$15.00**

Bowl, Gram's bowl, w/lid, bowl alone: 2½" high **$27.00**

Creamer, rooster figural, 5½", from $40 to **$48.00**

Cup, clown head w/conical hat lid, bright colors, from $60
to..**$80.00**

Cup, Morning After/Never Again, comic face w/ice-bag
lid **$20.00**

Hors d'ouvres set, Galagray, seven inserts: three bells, three heart shapes, and one round, on wooden lazy Susan base, $80.00.

Plaques, multicolor flowers, white ribbons for hanging,
6½x6½", pr..**$30.00**

Plate, hand-painted fruit, 7½", from $15.00 to $25.00.

Range set, Cherry, 5" grease jar & 6" salt & pepper shakers,
3-pc set...**$30.00**

Razor blade bank, barber's face, from $25 to **$35.00**

Ring holder, bulldog, 3x3", from $35 to......................**$45.00**

Salt & pepper shakers, apples & Salt & Pepper in lg letters,
6", pr..**$20.00**

Sock darner, girl, Darn It, w/original ribbon..............**$55.00**

**String holder, heart shape with verse,
$45.00. (Photo courtesy Ellen Bercovici)**

String holder, winking man's head, wearing hat, 1930s, 5½x5½"..**$80.00**
Toothbrush holder, baby's face, 4", from $55 to.........**$70.00**
Wall pocket, black kettle w/heart & verse..................**$30.00**
Wall pocket, coffeepot, w/verse, 8½" **$30.00**
Wall pocket, pitcher & bowl, w/verse, 8x7"..............**$28.00**
Wall pocket, pitcher form, 8¼"..................................**$27.50**

Clothes Sprinkler Bottles

With the invention of the iron, clothes were sprinkled with water, rolled up to distribute the dampness, and pressed. This created steam when ironing, which helped to remove wrinkles. The earliest bottles were made of hand-blown clear glass. Ceramic figurals were introduced in the 1920s; these had a metal sprinkler cap with a rubber cork. Later versions had a true cork with an aluminum cap. More recent examples contain a plastic cap. A 'wetter-downer' bottle had no cap but contained a hole in the top to distribute water to larger items such as sheets and tablecloths. These were filled through a large opening in the bottom and plugged with a cork. Some 'wetter-downers' are mistaken for shakers and vice versa. In the end, with the invention of more sophisticated irons that produced their own steam (and later had their own sprayers), the sprinkler bottle was relegated to the attic or, worse yet, the trash can.

The variety of subjects depicted by figural sprinkler bottles runs from cute animals to laundry helpers and people who did the ironing. Because of their whimsical nature, scarcity, and desirability as collectibles, we have seen a rapid rise in the cost of these bottles over the last couple of years.

See also Kitchen Prayer Ladies.

Advisor: Ellen Bercovici (See Directory, Clothes Sprinkler Bottles)

Cat, marble eyes, American Bisque, from $300.00 to $400.00. (Photo courtesy Ellen Bercovici)

Cat, variety of designs & colors, handmade ceramic, from $75 to..**$150.00**
Chinese man, Sprinkle Plenty, white, green & brown, holding iron, ceramic, from $95 to.............................**$150.00**
Chinese man, Sprinkle Plenty, yellow & green, ceramic, Cardinal China Co, from $25 to.............................**$50.00**
Chinese man, towel over arm, ceramic, from $300 to..**$400.00**
Chinese man, variety of designs & color, handmade ceramic, from $50 to...**$150.00**
Chinese man, white & aqua, ceramic, California, Cleminsons, from $40 to...**$50.00**
Chinese man, white & aqua w/paper shirt tag, ceramic, California, Cleminsons, from $75 to....................**$100.00**
Chinese man w/removable head, ceramic, from $250 to...**$400.00**
Clothespin, face w/stenciled eyes & airbrushed cheeks, ceramic, marked Cardinal **$400.00**
Clothespin, face w/stenciled eyes & airbrushed cheeks & lips, from $200 to **$250.00**
Clothespin, hand decorated, ceramic, from $150 to.**$400.00**
Clothespin, red, yellow & green plastic, from $20 to.**$40.00**
Dearie Is Weary, ceramic, Enesco, from $350 to **$500.00**
Dutch girl, ceramic, Cardinal China, variety of color combinations...**$300.00**
Elephant, pink & gray, ceramic, from $60 to **$85.00**
Elephant, trunk forms handle, ceramic, American Bisque, from $400 to...**$600.00**
Elephant, white & pink w/shamrock on tummy, ceramic, from $100 to...**$150.00**
Emperor, variety of designs & colors, handmade ceramic, from $150 to...**$200.00**
Fireman **$3,000.00**
Iron, blue flowers, ceramic, from $100 to **$150.00**
Iron, green ivy, ceramic, from $50 to **$75.00**
Iron, green plastic, from $35 to...................................**$55.00**
Iron, lady ironing, ceramic, from $45 to.....................**$75.00**
Iron, man & woman farmer, ceramic, from $200 to.**$275.00**
Iron, souvenir of Aquarena Springs, San Marcos TX, ceramic, from $200 to...**$300.00**

Iron, souvenir of Florida, pink flamingo, ceramic, from $250 to...**$325.00**
Iron, souvenir of Wonder Cave, ceramic, from $250 to ..**$300.00**
Mammy, ceramic, from $250 to.............................**$350.00**
Mary Maid, all colors, plastic, Reliance, from $15 to ..**$35.00**
Mary Poppins, ceramic, California, Cleminsons, from $250 to...**$450.00**
Myrtle, ceramic, Pfaltzgraff, from $250 to.................**$350.00**
Peasant woman, w/laundry poem on label, ceramic, from $200 to...**$300.00**
Poodle, gray, pink or white, ceramic, from $200 to .**$300.00**
Rooster, green, tan & red detailing over white, Sierra Vista, ceramic, from $85 to **$125.00**

Dutch Boy and Girl, from $175.00 to $250.00 each. (Photo courtesy Ellen Bercovici)

Clothing and Accessories

Watch a 'golden oldie' movie, and you can't help admiring the clothes — what style, what glamour, what fun! Due in part to the popularity of old movie classics and great new movies with retro themes, there's a growing fascination with the fabulous styes of the past — and there's no better way to step into the romance and glamour of those eras than with an exciting piece of vintage clothing!

'OOOhhh, it don't mean a thing, if it ain't got that S-W-I-N-G!' In 1935, Benny Goodman, 'King of Swing,' ushered in the swing era from Los Angeles's Polmar Ballroom. After playing two standard sets, he switched to swing, and the crowd went crazy! Swing era gals' clothing featured short full or pleated skirts, wide padded shoulders and natural waistlines. Guys, check out those wild, wide ties that were worn with 'gangster-look' zoot suits!

Clothes of the 1940s though the 1970s are not as delicate as their Victorian and Edwardian counterparts; they're easier to find and much more affordable! Remember, the more indicative of its period, the more desirable the item. Look for

pieces with glitz and glamour — also young, trendy pieces that were expensive to begin with. Look for designer pieces and designer look-alikes. Although famous designer labels are hard to find, you may be lucky enough to run across one! American designers like Adrian, Claire McMardell, Charles James, Mainboucher, Hattie Carnegie, Norell, Pauline Trigere, and Mollie Parnis came to the fore during World War II. The '50s were the decade of Christian Dior; others included Balenciaga, Balmain, Chanel, Jacques Heim, Nona Ricci, Ann Fogarty, Oleg Cassini, and Adele Simpson. In the '60s and '70s, Mary Quant, Betsey Johnson, Givenchy, Yves St. Laurent, Oscar de la Renta, Galanos, Pierre Cardin, Rudi Gernreich, Paco Rabanne, Courreges, Arnold Scassi, Geoffrey Beene, Emilio Pucci, Zandra Rhodes, and Jessica McClintock (Gunne Sax) were some of the names that made fashion headlines.

Pucci, Lilli Ann of California, Eisenberg, and Adele Simpson designs continue to be especially sought after. Look for lingerie — '30s and '40s lace/hook corsets and '50s pointy 'bullet' bras (like the ones in the old Maidenform Dream ads). For both men and women, '70s disco platform shoes (the wilder, the better), cowboy shirts and jackets, also fringed 'hippie' items. For men, look for bowling shirts, '50s 'Kramer' shirts, and '40s and '50s wild ties, especially those by Salvadore Dali.

Levi jeans and jackets made before 1971 have a cult following, especially in Japan. Among the most sought-after denim Levi items are jeans with a capitol 'E' on a *red* tab or back pocket. The small 'e' jeans are also collectible; these were made during the late 1960s and until 1970 (with two rows of single stitching inside the back pocket). Worth watching for as well are the 'red line' styles of the '80s (these have double-stitched back pockets). Other characteristics to look for in vintage Levis are visible rivets inside the jeans and single pockets and silver-colored buttons on jackets with vertical pleats. From the same era, Lee, Wrangler, Bluebell, J.C. Penney, Oxhide, Big Yanks, James Dean, Doublewear, and Big Smith denims are collectible as well.

As with any collectible, condition is of the utmost importance. 'Deadstock' is a term that refers to a top-grade item that has never been worn or washed and still has its original tags. Number 1 grade must have no holes larger than a pinhole. A torn belt loop is permissible if no hole is created. There may be a few light stains and light fading. The crotch area must have no visible wear, and the crotch seam must have no holes. And lastly, the item must not have been altered. Unless another condition is noted within the lines, values in the listing here are for items in number 1 grade. There are also other grades for items that have more defects.

While some collectors buy with the intent of preserving their clothing and simply enjoy having it, many buy it to wear. If you do wear it, be very careful how you clean it. Fabrics may become fragile with age.

For more information, refer to *Vintage Hats and Bonnets, 1770 – 1970, Identifications and Values,* by Sue Langley; *Ladies' Vintage Accessories* by LaRee Johnson Bruton; *Antique and Vintage Clothing, 1850 – 1940,* by

Diane Snyder Haug; *Collector's Guide to Vintage Fashions* (all by Collector Books) and *Vintage Fashions for Women, the 1950s & '60s,* by Kristina Harris (Shiffer); *Clothing and Accessories From the '40s, '50s, and '60s,* by Jan Lindenberger (Schiffer); *Vintage Denim* by David Little; *Fashion Footwear, 1800 – 1970* by Desire Smith; *Plastic Handbags* by Kate E. Dooner; *Fit to Be Tied, Vintage Ties of the '40s and Early '50s,* by Rod Dyer and Ron Spark; and *The Hawaiian Shirt* by H. Thomas Steele. For more information about denim clothing and vintage footwear see *How to Identify Vintage Apparel for Fun and Profit*, which is available from Flying Deuce Auction & Antiques (see Auction Houses).

Prices are a compilation of shows, shops, and Internet auctions. They are retail values and apply to items in excellent condition. Note: Extraordinary items bring extraordinary prices!

Advisors: Ken Weber, Clothing (www.vintagemartini.com); Flying Duce Auctions, Vintage Denim (See Directory, Clothing and Accessories)

Newsletter: *Costume Society of America*
55 Edgewater Dr., P.O. Box 73
Earleville, MD 21919
Phone: 1-800-CSA-9447 or fax: 410-275-8936
www.costumesocietyamerica.com

Newsletter: *The Vintage Connection*
904 North 65 Street
Springfield, OR 97478-7021

1940s Women's Day Wear

Playsuit, green cotton with fish print, EX, $145.00. (Photo courtesy Vintage Martini)

Blouse, chartreuse chiffon, short sleeves, pleated front, back snaps, no label, EX..$48.00
Blouse, white organza, embroidered flowers, button front, short puff sleeves, EX...$60.00

Dress, beige & white rayon, dot print, short gathered sleeves, matching belt, no label, EX....................................$58.00
Dress, burgundy wool crepe, scoop neckline, padded shoulders, hip drape, 'Miss Plaza,' EX............................$68.00
Dress, cream rayon, Disney Pinocchio print, short sleeves, button front, belt, VG...$225.00
Dress, floral print cotton, black peplum & collar, short sleeves, EX...$65.00
Dress, navy wool gabardine, long sleeves, sailor collar, Navy patches, full skirt, VG..................................$85.00
Dress, printed cotton, black halter top w/spread collar, multicolor striped skirt, no label, EX...........................$58.00
Pants, blue chambray, white piping, sailor styling, wide leg, VG...$60.00
Playsuit, green & white leaf print, white pique cotton trim, matching overskirt no label, EX.......................$85.00
Suit, black & red wool tweed, Persian lamb collar, button front, matching belt, Morness of London, EX.......$75.00
Suit, red gabardine, tab & button decorations, patch pockets, turn-back cuffs, slender skirt, EX $125.00
Swimsuit, black lycra w/gold ribbon trim, gold neck strap, no label, EX...$55.00

1940s Women's Coats and Jackets

Coat, brown tweed, tailored, spread collar, patch pockets, button front, EX..$64.00
Fur coat, silver mouton, satin lining, long sleeves, button front, EX..$125.00
Fur collar, stone martins, 6 bodies w/legs, mouth clasps, snap legs, EX..$48.00
Jacket, black wool, contrast faille collar & peplum, tab pockets, Lilli Ann of Paris, EX $125.00
Jacket, green gabardine, long sleeves, turn-back cuffs, back belt, inset pockets, shawl lapels, VG $65.00

1940s Women's Evening Wear

Dress, black rayon crepe, full length, floral sequin applique on hip, no label, EX..$165.00
Dress, black taffeta, boustier bodice, slender skirt, overskirt in multistripe satin, EX............................$150.00
Dress, burgundy velvet bodice, short sleeves, V-waistline, full striped taffeta skirt, EX.........................$95.00
Dress, dinner; black & silver stripes, button front, short puff sleeves, black crepe overskirt, EX.....................$75.00
Dress, dinner; fuchsia crepe, short sleeves, peplum, sequin flowers on front of bodice, VG $85.00
Dress, ivory crepe, entirely beaded, sleeveless, matching bolero & belt, VG...$85.00
Dress, ivory jersey w/yellow & brown floral print, sleeveless, peplum, VG...$145.00

1940s Women's Lingerie

Bra, black satin, strapless, quilted cup, velvet lining, EX..$45.00

Nightgown, lavender rayon, ruffled shoulder straps, attached belt, inset lace, EX **$38.00**

Nightgown, peach satin, bias cut, lace yoke, cap sleeves, ribbon belt, EX **$65.00**

Pajamas, white rayon w/navy fan print, short sleeves, button front, EX **$48.00**

Slip, white silk satin, lace yoke, bias cut, Yolanda, EX .. **$45.00**

Tap pants, peach silk, lace gussets, elastic waist, EX . **$35.00**

1940s Women's Accessories

Hat, black straw topper, daisies cover brim & crown, El Rita Hats, VG **$45.00**

Hat, brown felt, sculpted front, bird-of-paradise curves around face, Elsie Raine Miller, EX **$52.00**

Hat, turban style, natural woven straw & purple crepe, Sally Victor, VG **$85.00**

Shoes, burgundy suede pumps, decorative top-stitching, EX **$58.00**

Shoes, gold & silver leather, top-stitched vamp, open toe, ankle strap, VG **$85.00**

Shoes, navy suede platforms, open toe, ankle straps, EX .. **$225.00**

Shoes, purple satin and gold platform sandals, rhinestone clasps, VG, $235.00. (Photo courtesy Vintage Martini)

Shoes, 2-tone lavender linen wedgies, open toe, sling back, Sbicca California, EX **$65.00**

Stockings, tan silk, seamed, in package, Schiaparelli, EX **$125.00**

1950s Women's Day Wear

Blouse, white cotton, spread collar, button front, dart fitted, short lace sleeves, EX **$38.00**

Dress, beach wear, white terry cloth w/butterfly print, boustier bodice, full skirt, EX **$85.00**

Dress, black silk, spread collar, rose silk inset & side drape, full skirt, Jacques Fath, EX **$325.00**

Dress, green floral cotton, strapless, boned bodice, full flounced skirt, EX **$75.00**

Dress, rainbow striped voile, shawl collar, sleeveless, full skirt, EX **$58.00**

Dress, rose print cotton, gathered bodice, full skirt, sleeveless, EX **$75.00**

Dress, white linen w/multicolor embroidered butterflies, no label, VG **$62.00**

Dress, 2-pc, purple brocade jacket, scoop neckline w/collar, ¾-sleeves, accordion pleated skirt, EX **$98.00**

Dress, 2-pc black velvet, hand-painted irises, matching sequins, no label, VG **$145.00**

Dress, 2-pc blue wool knit, ¾-sleeves, matching belt, ribbed skirt, VG **$65.00**

Pants, green gabardine, Western-cut pockets & belt loops, tapered legs, EX **$75.00**

Skirt, circle; black felt w/pink velvet applique leaves & cording, no label, VG **$125.00**

Skirt, circle; hand painted and signed by Emilio Pucci, VG, $875.00. (Photo courtesy Vintage Martini)

Suit, black faille, double breasted, ¾-sleeves, dart fitted skirt, EX **$85.00**

Suit, black wool felt, removable velvet inset collar & cuffs, Lilli Ann, Paris, EX **$265.00**

1950s Women's Coats and Sweaters

Coat, swing style, black crepe w/satin lining, Peter Pan collar, satin necktie, EX **$85.00**

Coat, swing style, black wool w/black velvet stripes, button front, satin lining, Lilli Ann of Paris, EX **$245.00**

Jacket, navy gabardine w/white beaded leaves, notched lapels, button front, VG **$75.00**

Raincoat, silk floral print in green & pink, ¾-sleeves, attached hood, Bergdorff Goodman, EX **$85.00**

Sweater, gray cashmere w/pearl buttons, silver beading across neckline & bust, EX **$65.00**

Sweater, ivory cashmere w/white beaded bows, white mink collar, EX $145.00

Sweater set, 2-pc (w/shell), orlon w/pearl buttons, VG .$35.00

1950s Women's Evening Wear

Blouse, multicolored silk, short sleeves, Emilio Pucci, EX $235.00

Dinner gown, printed purple & turquoise floral silk, raised waist, short sleeves, EX $68.00

Dress, beige satin w/rows of sequins, bronze cummerbund & back overskirt, Emma Domb, EX $425.00

Dress, black silk faille, halter bodice w/lace insets, full skirt, gathered cummerbund, no label, VG $125.00

Dress, cocktail; beige lace halter, full skirt, matching belt, VG $65.00

Dress, cocktail; black taffeta, boustier bodice, sarong-style skirt w/lg side bow, no label, EX $75.00

Dress, cocktail; green floral bubble skirt w/green cummerbund, sleeveless, EX $125.00

Dress, dinner; blue & purple floral print silk, short sleeves, high waist, Edward Abbot, EX $62.00

Dress, dinner; brown satin w/brown lace bodice & overskirt, scoop neckline, sleeveless, EX $108.00

Dress, formal; white net w/ruffled flowers, boustier bodice, floor length, no label, EX $145.00

Dress, pink brocade, tea length, sweetheart neckline, sleeveless, tiered net down back, scalloped edging, EX..........$125.00

Hostess set, checked taffeta jacket, satin pants, EX, $135.00. (Photo courtesy Vintage Martini)

1950s Women's Lingerie

Crinoline, black net w/ivory satin stripes, VG $28.00

Crinoline, purple net w/satin edges, very full, 6 layers, EX $75.00

Girdle, peach satin brocade w/black lace, EX $35.00

Girdle, white satin long line, bullet bra, lace back, EX .$85.00

Pajamas, blue & white rayon, embroidered 'counting sheep' on pocket, TV Jama by Saucy Sandy, EX $45.00

Slip, navy rayon w/lace border, EX.............................$16.00

1950s Women's Accessories

Belt, red velvet, lg rhinestone decorations, velvet-covered buckle, VG $18.00

Gloves, elbow-length pink suede, blue beaded flowers on top edge, VG..$35.00

Gloves, pink & black taffeta plaid, black palms, VG..$28.00

Hat, black headband w/gray organza bow, EX $18.00

Hat, braided ivory raffia w/pie-wedge shapes, wide brim, VG $45.00

Hat, saucer, beige fur felt, gold embroidered applique on front, Merri-Soie, VG.......................................$32.00

Shoes, black velvet mules, wood wedge, beaded & sequin toes, Woo King Shoes, VG $48.00

Shoes, navy suede & patent vinyl spring-o-lators, Ferncraft Exclusives, EX $45.00

Shoes, olive green crocodile stilettos, wing tops with large buttons, Hebert Levine, VG, $65.00. (Photo courtesy Vintage Martini)

Shoes, white leather sandals, floral bow & heel, open toe, sling back, Kornhauser of Palm Beach, EX..........$58.00

Stockings, seamed, tan, velvet swords & rhinestones on ankles, EX..$45.00

1960s – 70s Women's Day Wear

Dress, black & white knit, color blocked, button front, Pauline Trigere, VG $85.00

Dress, red & green wool, button front, long sleeves, Givenchy, 1960s, VG $225.00

Dress, white cotton halter, full length, embroidered roses, lace waist yoke, 1970s, EX...................................$55.00

Dress, 2-pc, olive knit w/white sailor collar, sleeveless, A-line skirt, 1960s, EX..$45.00

Dress, 3-pc, A-line skirt, shell & box jacket w/¾-sleeves, pink mohair, dart fitted, 1960s, EX..............................$58.00

Dress, 3-pc blue floral chiffon halter & maxi skirt, white twill jacket w/chiffon accents, 1970s, EX $75.00

Pants, green twill cigarette style, dart fitted, side zipper, VG $32.00

Short set, gray, blue, and purple abstract print, blouse, shorts, and skirt, Pucci, 1960s, $495.00. (Photo courtesy Lisa Albertson)

1960s – 70s Women's Coats

Coat, green wool, button front, sm mink collar, turn-back cuffs, EX $45.00

Coat, ice blue leather, double breasted, patch pockets, white faux fur collar & trim, 1970s, EX.....................$158.00

Coat, sleeveless vest style, wing collar, white rabbit w/ermine-style black tips, button front, 1970s, VG $100.00

Coat, trapeze style, black wool, long sleeves, rolled collar lined in red satin, Pauline Trigere, 1960s, EX $225.00

Coat, trench; brown faille w/faux raccoon lining & collar, patch pockets, 1970s, EX $45.00

Coat, yellow leather w/brown satin Peter Pan collar, brass buttons, ¾-sleeves, EX $60.00

Jacket, black heat-press velvet, button front, fox collar, 1960s, EX...$48.00

1960s – 70s Women's Evening Wear

Dress, black crepe w/bodice covered in black payettes, dropped waist, sleeveless, 1960s, EX $65.00

Dress, black French lace, long sleeves, full skirt, attached crinoline, Oscar de la Renta, 1960s, EX.............$975.00

Dress, cocktail; black crepe w/sequin skirt & ostrich-trimmed hem, Lilli Diamond of California, EX $85.00

Dress, cocktail; trapeze style, black crepe shift w/lace overlay, back satin bow, sleeveless, VG $65.00

Dress, cocktail; white rayon w/ostrich feather trim, accordion pleated skirt, ribbon belt, 1960s, EX $125.00

Dress, evening; beige crepe w/silver loop beaded bodice, sarong skirt, 1960s, EX $150.00

Dress, multicolor diagonal stripes, pique cotton, full skirt, halter bodice, Lanvin, 1970s, VG.....................$235.00

Pantsuit, black crochet, long sleeves, zipper front, winged collar, 1960s, EX...$85.00

1960s – 70s Women's Accessories

Boot tights (all-in-one boots & tights), purple, chunk heels, EX $45.00

Boots, go-go; white vinyl w/back zipper, 1960s, EX.$65.00

Boots, green vinyl w/yellow stripes, Braniff Airlines Uniform, zip back, Herbert Levine, VG $158.00

Gloves, black satin w/embroidered roses, elbow length, VG..$45.00

Hat, blue tone-on-tone satin, turban shape, original hatbox, Hattie Carnegie, 1960s, EX................................$75.00

Hat, navy pleated chiffon & straw, wide brim folds back, white organza flower on front, Henri, 1970, VG..$148.00

Purse, brown snakeskin, Judith Leiber, EX...............$495.00

Purse, brown suede, lg sq, suede arm strap, long fringe, 1970s, EX..$35.00

Purse, evening; silver lame leather, chain handle, rhinestone clasp, 1960s, EX $38.00

Purse, French magazine, 1960s, EX..........................$145.00

Purse, wood box w/hand-painted owl & rhinestones, Enid Collins, 1960s, EX $45.00

Shoes, 'disco' platforms, silver w/rhinestone decorations, EX..$85.00

Shoes, clear plastic spring-o-lators, Lucite heel w/gold rhinestones, open toes, VG $48.00

Shoes, pale green stilettos, sling back, back bows, Jacque Heim, VG $125.00

Shoes, red flocked velvet stilettos, 3" heel, Holiday by Wise, VG..$45.00

Shoes, turquoise & silver brocade stilettos, pearl decoration on toe, EX $35.00

1940s – 70s Men's Wear

Jacket, black & gray wool tweed, single breasted, Kingsridge, 1950s, EX..$65.00

Jacket, bomber; leather & suede w/embroidery, reversible, 1950s, EX..$595.00

Jacket, Ricky style, ivory & black-flecked wool w/black insets & vents in back, long sleeves, 1950s, EX $325.00

Overcoat, tan cashmere w/black velvet collar, tan lapels, button front, D'Milano, 1950s, EX............................$125.00

Pants, aqua w/pin stripes, pleated front, high waisted, cuffs, 1940s, EX..$85.00

Robe, burgundy satin w/star print, spread collar, notched lapels, rope belt, 1940s, EX..................................$75.00

Robe, wool, Western motif, rope belt, 1950s, EX $95.00

Shirt, beige wool gabardine w/black diamonds, spread collar, short sleeves, Eaton's of Cal, 1950s, EX..........$32.00

Shirt, bowling; green cotton/rayon, short sleeve, back vents, league patch on arm, 1950s, EX............................$55.00

Shirt, pink wool gabardine w/brown stitching, spread collar, 1940s, EX..$85.00

Shoes, brown crocodile, lace-ups, cap toe, 1950s, EX..$215.00

Shoes, brown leather & white suede spectators, 1950s, EX..$135.00

Suit, brown sharkskin, single breasted, shawl collar, flat-front pants, 1960s, EX.................**$195.00**

Suit, navy gabardine, double-breasted, wide collar, notched lapels, pleated front, dead stock, 1940s, EX.......**$158.00**

Suit, orange wool w/velvet lapels & pocket flaps, spread collar, wide legs, 1970s, EX **$85.00**

Swimsuit, tan & red Hawaiian print w/palm trees, elastic waist, 1950s, VG **$22.00**

Tie, peek-a-boo, brown & yellow satin w/pinup girl lining, 1950s, EX.......................................**$165.00**

Tie, red & green satin, Christmas print, 1940s, EX **$65.00**

Vintage Denim

Jacket, Hercules, indigo, red tag, medium, EX............**$85.00**

Jacket, Lee 101-LJ, dark w/hege, rare, sm, EX..........**$400.00**

Jacket, Lee 91-B, indigo, M.....................................**$260.00**

Jacket, Levi 1st edition, blanket lined, leather patch (poor but complete), medium/lg, EX.....................**$700.00**

Jacket, Levi 506 1st edition, medium color w/silver buckle, slight wear, medium, VG **$600.00**

Jacket, Levi 507 XX 2nd edition, complete paper patch, EX color/contrast, medium, EX **$325.00**

Jacket, Levi 507 XX 2nd edition, paper patch, XL, NM..**$650.00**

Jeans, Big Smith Buckaroo, ½ red lines, Talon 42 zipper, G color & hege, medium, EX....................**$55.00**

Jeans, Lee Riders, center tag, red/black, crotch rivet, button fly, EX contrast/color, professional repair, sm....**$600.00**

Jeans, Lee 101 Z, medium color, medium lg, EX+......**$45.00**

Jeans, Levi, shorthorn tag, western style, side sipper, 1940s, sm, deadstock **$20.00**

Jeans, Levi 501, big E, medium color, slight hege, minor stains/wear, medium.................................**$475.00**

Jeans, Levi 501, big E, medium color w/G contrast & slight hege, some damage, medium............................**$400.00**

Jeans, Levi 501, big E, medium dark w/slight contrast & hege, medium, EX...**$175.00**

Jeans, Levi 501, red lines, #6 underlined, sm, NM....**$120.00**

Jeans, Levi 501, red lines, dark color w/hege, medium, NM **$150.00**

Jeans, Levi 501, red lines, medium color w/hege, medium, NM **$110.00**

Jeans, Levi 501, red lines, medium-light color, medium, EX+...**$30.00**

Jeans, Levi 501, single-stitched, G color & hege, sm, EX..**$130.00**

Jeans, Levi 501, single-stitched, leather patch, EX color, slight contrast & hege, lg, M.........................**$850.00**

Jeans, Levi 501, sm e, double-stitched red lines, medium-light color, sm, NM.................................**$35.00**

Jeans, Levi 501, sm e, single-stitched, G color & contrast, slight hege, medium, EX.............................**$200.00**

Jeans, Levi 501 RL, #6 button, EX contrast & hege, slight damage, medium **$120.00**

Jeans, Levi 501 XX, leather patch (attached), G color, hege & contrast, slight stain, lg..........................**$850.00**

Jeans, Levi 501 XX, leather patch (not attached), very dark, medium, EX **$1,200.00**

Jeans, Levi 501 XX, paper patch, medium dark, EX contrast, slight hege, medium, EX **$725.00**

Jeans, Levi 505, sm e, single-stitched, paper tags, sm, M..**$220.00**

Jeans, Levi 505, sm e, single-stitched, very dark, medium, NM **$250.00**

Jeans, Levi 505, sm e, single-stitched, w/flashers, sm, M..**$225.00**

Jeans, Levi 717, big E, indigo, boot cut, EX hege & contrast, some damage, sm **$125.00**

Jeans, Wrangler Bluebell, dark blue, medium, NM...**$125.00**

Shirt, Levi, western style, short horn tag, medium, NM..**$150.00**

Shirt, Sears Roebuck, indigo, western style, 1960s, medium, EX **$125.00**

Work jacket, Dubbleware, 3-pocket, 1930s, medium, EX..**$275.00**

Work jacket, Headlight, 3-pocket, 'change button,' top pocket cropped, 1930s, medium, NM **$900.00**

Coca-Cola Collectibles

Coca-Cola was introduced to the public in 1886. Immediately an advertising campaign began that over the years and continuing to the present day has literally saturated our lives with a never-ending variety of items. Some of the earlier calendars and trays have been known to bring prices well into the four figures. Because of these heady prices and the extremely widespread collector demand for good Coke items, reproductions are everywhere, so beware! Some of the items that have been reproduced are pocket mirrors (from 1905, 1906, 1908 – 11, 1916, and 1920), trays (from 1899, 1910, 1913 – 14, 1917, 1920, 1923, 1926, 1934, and 1937), tip trays (from 1907, 1909, 1910, 1913 – 14, 1917, and 1920), knives, cartons, bottles, clocks, and trade cards. In recent years, these items have been produced and marketed: an 8" brass 'button,' a 27" brass bottle-shaped thermometer, cast-iron toys and bottle-shaped door pulls, Yes Girl posters, a 12" 'button' sign (with one round hole), a rectangular paperweight, a 1949-style cooler radio, and there are others. Look for a date line.

In addition to reproductions, 'fantasy' items have also been made, the difference being that a 'fantasy' never existed as an original. Don't be deceived. Belt buckles are 'fantasies.' So are glass doorknobs with an etched trademark, bottle-shaped knives, pocketknives (supposedly from the 1933 World's Fair), a metal letter opener stamped 'Coca-Cola 5¢,' a cardboard sign with the 1911 lady with fur (9" x 11"), and celluloid vanity pieces (a mirror, brush, etc.).

When the company celebrated its 100th anniversary in 1986, many 'centennial' items were issued. They all carry the '100th Anniversary' logo. Many of them are collectible in their own right, and some are already expensive.

If you'd really like to study this subject, we recommend these books: *Goldstein's Coca-Cola Collectibles* by Sheldon Goldstein; *Collector's Guide to Coca-Cola Items, Vols I* and *II*, by Al Wilson; *Petretti's Coca-Cola Collectibles Price Guide* by Allan Petretti; *B.J. Summers' Pocket Guide to Coca-Cola; B.J. Summers' Guide to Coca-Cola;* and *Comemorative Bottles* by Bob and Debra Henrich.

Advisor: Craig Stifter (See Directory, Soda Pop Collectibles)

Club: Coca-Cola Collectors Club
PMB 609, 4780 Ashform Dunwoody Rd, Suite A9166
Atlanta, GA 30338. Annual dues: $30

Ashtray, metal sq w/molded cigarette holder, EX.......**$30.00**
Banner, canvas, Coca-Cola Brings You Edgar Bergen With Charley McCarthy Sunday Evenings.., graphics, 1950s, 42x60", EX+.......................**$1,100.00**
Blotter, Friendliest Drink on Earth, hand-held bottle over image of Earth, 1956, NM+ **$15.00**
Bookends, brass half-bottle shape on flat base, 1963, 8", NM, pr **$325.00**
Boomerang, 1950s, EX.......................**$35.00**
Bottle, display; clear glass w/white lettering, plastic cap, 1960s, 20", EX **$100.00**
Bottle carrier, aluminum banded construction w/red Drink Coca-Cola on sides, wire handle w/red wood grip, 1950s, EX......................**$100.00**
Bottle carrier, 6-pack, bent wood w/rounded corners, red stamped logo, curved wood handle, 1940s, VG ..**$125.00**
Bottle opener, flat metal bottle shape, 1950s, M........**$25.00**
Calendar, 1969, Things Go Better w/Coke, man whispering in girl's ear at table on front sheet, incomplete, EX **$35.00**
Calendar, 1970, Coke bottles on party table in foreground w/couples dancing in background, complete, EX+ .**$60.00**
Calendar, 1974, Santa on Dec 1973 page w/Coca-Cola girls on inside pages, complete, NM+ **$20.00**
Calendar, 1982, 4 young ladies in leotards taking a break w/Coke on January page, complete, NM+..............**$8.00**

Clock, light-up, ca 1930s – 1940s, working, EX, $7,500.00. (Photo courtesy Gary Metz)

Clock, round light-up w/black numbers on white around red center dot w/Drink...In Bottles, metal frame, Swihart, 15", NM.......................**$925.00**
Clock, sq w/green numbers & dots around fishtail logo (Drink Coca-Cola), glass front, metal frame, 1960s, 15", NM **$325.00**

Clock, vertical w/red numbers on reverse glass sq face, Drink Coca-Cola light-up panel below, 1960s, VG.......**$200.00**
Decal, Drink Coca-Cola in Bottles in red & yellow on red rectangle w/curved corners, 1950s, 9x15", NM **$45.00**
Desk set, mini cooler on plastic base flanked by 2 pen holders, EX+ **$100.00**

Display, cardboard die-cut Santa, 1945, 14x9", EX, $225.00.

Doll, Frozen Coca-Cola mascot, stuffed cloth, 1960s, NM..**$150.00**
Doll, Santa, cloth body w/rubber face & hands, vinyl boots & belt, Rushton Star Creations, 1950s, 15", no bottle o/w EX **$140.00**
Door push bar, tin, Coke Adds Life..., wave logo at left, black background, 1970s, 3x32", EX+ **$35.00**
Fan, cardboard w/wooden handle, Have a Coke, Sprite boy peering around lg Coke bottle on white, 1950s, EX..........**$85.00**
Festoon, square dance, 5-pc, 1957, VG+ (original envelope) **$1,400.00**
Fountain glass, clear bell shape w/white Drink Coca-Cola, 1940-60s, EX.......................**$15.00**
Frisbee, white plastic w/red Coke Adds Life to...Having Fun, red & white wave logo, 1960s, M **$15.00**
Game, Dominoes, Coke bottle embossed on backs, 1940s, complete, NMIB **$65.00**
Game, Double Six Dominos, complete in original brown vinyl case w/Sprite Boy logo, 1970s, EX **$35.00**
Game, Dragon Checkers, 1940s, NMIB.......................**$50.00**
Lighter, flip-top w/fishtail logo, 1960, NM.................**$125.00**
Matchbook, World's Fair New York/Visit the Coca-Cola Tower, w/graphics, 1964, EX **$10.00**
Matchbook holder w/matches, metal sq upright 3-sided holder w/red button logo & Be Really Refreshed!, 1959, EX **$150.00**
Mechanical pencil, mother-of-pearl finish w/advertising, NM **$100.00**
Menu board, cardboard w/wood-tone border, Sign of Good Taste logo, bottles in lower corners, 1959, 28x19", EX+ **$200.00**
Menu board, tin oblong w/curved ends & menu slots on either side of red button attached in center, 1950s, 14x62", VG **$450.00**

Model kit, Vending Machine (hot rod), 1970, MIB (sealed) **$75.00**

Napkin holder, metal, Have a Coke 5¢ w/image of Sprite Boy & fountain glass, 1950, VG **$800.00**

Patch, fishtail logo w/Drink Coca-Cola in Bottles in yellow & white on red cloth, 1960s, EX+ **$10.00**

Pen holder & bottle lighter, Bakelite, round base w/center pen holder & lighter on side, 1950s, EX............**$200.00**

Pencil holder, replica of 1896 ceramic syrup dispenser, 1960s, 7", EX...**$175.00**

Pillow, race-car shape, stuffed print cloth w/other advertising & #16, 'Goodyear' tires, 1970s, 15", NM **$100.00**

Playing cards, Be Really Refreshed, masquerade party, 1960, NMIB...**$165.00**

Playing cards, Coca-Cola Adds Life to...Everything Nice, 1976, MIB (sealed)...**$30.00**

Postcard, shows image of the Coca-Cola Pavilion at the New York World's Fair w/fair goers & inset of globe, 1964, EX..**$10.00**

Radio, can shape w/wave logo, 1970s, EX+.............**$50.00**

Radio, red plastic, 1950s, EX/NM, $800.00.

Radio, vending machine, wood-grain front w/wave logo upper right, 1970s, EX...**$175.00**

Record, Trini Lopez Sings His Greatest Hits/Presented for Fresca by Your Local Bottler of Coca-Cola, 45 rpm, 1967, EX...**$20.00**

Sign, cardboard, Enjoy That Refreshing New Feeling, bongo couple w/bottles, aluminum frame, 1960s, 39x22", VG **$85.00**

Sign, cardboard, Hospitality, 2 young ladies offering young man on sofa a Coke, 1947, 20x36", NM+ **$800.00**

Sign, cardboard, It's Twice Time/Twice the Convenience, couple on scooter, 1960s, 32x67", NM+.............**$200.00**

Sign, cardboard, Now! For Coke, trapeze artist reaching for bottle of Coke, gold frame, 1959, 20x36", VG....**$300.00**

Sign, cardboard, Recapture the '20s on Trays for Coca-Cola, image of 1923 girl & 3 trays on brown, 1970s, 31x20", EX+ **$20.00**

Sign, cardboard, We're Bringing Back the Good Ole Trays..., 4 tray images on red oval on white, 1970s, 23x18½", NM..**$20.00**

Sign, cardboard stringer, Have a Float With... lettered around white life preserver w/center graphics, 1960s, 10", EX **$85.00**

Sign, cardboard stringer, Santa w/3 bottles in ea hand framed by wreath, 1950s, EX+.............................**$50.00**

Sign, cardboard trolley, Yes, sunbather in white 2-pc suit eyeing hand-held bottle, disk logo on white, 1946, 11x28", VG..**$325.00**

Sign, celluloid disk, Coca-Cola lettered in white over bottle on red, gold border, 1950s, 9" dia, NM **$200.00**

Sign, motion, plastic & metal resembling the end of a barrel w/disk logo, green motion lights, deep frame, 1950s, NM **$925.00**

Sign, neon, Drink Coca-Cola, round w/neon border, plastic & metal, red & white, 1950s, NM.....................**$450.00**

Sign, paper cutout, No Trick! Just Treat!, image of girl w/2 glasses of Coke looking at jack-'o-lantern, 1960s, 15", NM+ **$80.00**

Sign, porcelain, curved corners, Coca-Cola Sold Here Ice Cold, white & yellow on red, yellow border, 1955, 12x29", EX...**$250.00**

Sign, porcelain, Fountain Service/Drink Coca-Cola, button on red-striped center band, white ground, 1950s, 12x30", EX..**$175.00**

Sign, porcelain truck cab, Drink Coca-Cola in Bottles, red on white, 1940s-50s, 10x51", EX+ **$375.00**

Sign, tin, 1964, 12x32", NM, $225.00. (Photo courtesy Gary Metz)

Sign, tin, curved corners, Drink Coca-Cola Trade Mark Reg, white on red w/white border, 1970s, 12x24", NM+ .**$25.00**

Sign, tin, rolled edge, Coke Adds Life to...Everthing Nice on white next to red & white wave logo, 1960s, oblong, EX **$200.00**

Sign, tin button, Coca-Cola in white on red, 1950s, 48", VG **$400.00**

Sign, tin button w/arrow, red button w/Drink Coca-Cola, horizontal silver arrow, 1950-60s, 18" dia, EX....**$750.00**

Sign, tin curb w/metal footed frame, 2-sided, Drink...Enjoy That...New Feeling on fishtail logo above bottle, 33", VG **$350.00**

Sign, tin flange, red fishtail on white w/thin green stripes, curved outer corners, 2-sided, 1960s, 15x18", VG .**$325.00**

Syrup can, 1-gal, red paper label w/red Coca-Cola on white circle w/3 bands on either side, sm spout opening, 1940s, EX..**$300.00**

Syrup dispenser, red streamline w/Drink Coca-Cola Ice Cold, Have a Coke lettered on tap, EX **$375.00**

Thermometer, masonite, Thirst Knows No Season, bottle & slanted bulb, 1944, 17", EX.................................**$500.00**

Thermometer, plastic, gauge atop cube base w/wave logo, 1980s, EX.................................**$25.00**

Thermometer, tin, button (red) at top of white vertical panel w/gray lines ea side, Quality Refreshment, 1950s, 9", EX.................................**$285.00**

Thermometer, tin, double bottles flank bulb, gold version, 16", EX.................................**$475.00**

Thermometer, tin bottle shape, gold, 1956, 8", EX **$40.00**

Toy car, tin, red w/white logo, friction, Taiyo, 1960s, 10½", EX **$250.00**

Toy truck, Big Wheel, tin & plastic, battery-op, Taiyo, 10", MIB **$125.00**

Toy truck, Cragstan Tiny Truck, tin w/plastic cab, red w/yellow litho bed, friction, 1950s-60s, 4", EX.................................**$150.00**

Toy truck, delivery, red & white w/wave logo, chrome hubs, Buddy L #5117, 1970s, 9", VG+ **$40.00**

Toy truck, Matchbox Series #37, diecast, yellow w/red trim, Lesney, 1950s-60s, 2¼", NMIB.................................**$115.00**

Toy truck, VW, diecast, red w/white bed cover, Budgie, 1980s, NMIB **$70.00**

Toy van, VW, red & white litho tin w/bottle cases showing on sides, friction, Taiyo, 1950s, 7½", VG.................................**$225.00**

Tray, 1950 – 1952, Red-Head Girl, fairly scarce, $200.00.

Tray, 1958, wicker picnic basket & wicker tray w/Coke bottles on 2-wheeled pull cart, 11x13", EX.................................**$25.00**

Tray, 1961, Coke Refreshes You Best/Here's a Coke for You, Coke poured into glass surrounded by flowers, 11x13", EX.................................**$30.00**

Tray, 1972, early Duster Girl at steering wheel on white, red rim, 15x11", EX **$15.00**

Vendor, red-painted wood stadium type w/strap, white Drink Coca-Cola logo, 1950s, NM **$325.00**

Whistle, plastic, Merry Christmas...Memphis Tenn, 1950, EX.................................**$25.00**

Yo-yo, plastic slim-line shape w/molded seal, Russell, 1977, MIP.................................**$28.00**

Yo-yo, plastic tournament shape w/imprinted seal, Duncan Imperial, 1980s, NM.................................**$15.00**

Yo-yo, wood tournament shape w/painted seal, Russell, 1960s, NM.................................**$120.00**

Coloring and Activity Books

Coloring and activity books representing familiar movie and TV stars of the 1950s and 1960s are fun to collect, though naturally unused examples are hard to find. Condition is very important, of course, so learn to judge their values accordingly. Unused books are worth as much as 50% to 75% more than one only partially colored. Several examples are shown in *Cartoon Toys & Collectibles, Identification and Value Guide,* by David Longest, and for those featuring the stars of TV shows, you'll enjoy *Collector's Guide to TV Memorabilia, 1960s & 1970s,* by Greg Davis and Bill Morgan. Both publications are available from Collector Books.

A-Team Coloring Book, 1983, some pages colored, VG+...**$10.00**

Alice in Wonderland Coloring Book, 1970s, unused, NM...**$15.00**

Andy Griffith Show Coloring Book, Saalfield, unused, EX..**$50.00**

Atom Ant Coloring Book, Watkins-Strathmore, 1967, some pages colored, EX.................................**$10.00**

Batman Sticker Book, Whitman, 1966, unused, EX **$45.00**

Batman w/Robin the Boy Wonder Dot-to-Dot & Coloring Book, Vasquez Bros, 1967, unused, NM, from $50 to..........**$75.00**

Beatles Coloring Book, Saalfield, unused, EX..........**$125.00**

Betty Grable Paint Book, Whitman, 1947, unused, EX..**$55.00**

Bewitched Fun & Activity Book, Treasure Books #8908, 1965, unused, NM.................................**$25.00**

Bionic Woman Fun Coloring Book, Treasure Books, 1976, unused, NM, from $15 to **$20.00**

Brady Bunch Coloring Book, Whitman, 1973, unused, EX, from $25 to.................................**$35.00**

Brave Little Taylor Paint & Coloring Book, Whitman, 1938, some pages colored, VG **$75.00**

Bullwinkle Coloring Book, 1969, unused, NM...........**$25.00**

Buzz Corry Coloring Book, Ralston Purina, 1953, some pages colored, scarce, EX **$75.00**

Chilly Willy Coloring Book, Saalfield, 1962, unused, NM ..**$35.00**

Daffy Duck Coloring Book, Watkins-Strathmore, 1963, unused, M.................................**$35.00**

Daniel Boone Coloring Book, Whitman, 1961, unused, EX...**$25.00**

Dick Van Dyke Coloring Book, Saalfield, 1963, unused, EX..**$40.00**

Donny & Marie Sticker Book, Whitman, 1977, unused, NM.**$20.00**

Doris Day Coloring & Cut-Out Book, Whitman, 1953, some pages used, 15x11", EX.................................**$215.00**

Dudley Do-Right Comes to the Rescue Coloring Book, Saalfield, 1969, unused, M **$35.00**

Elizabeth Taylor Coloring Book, Whitman, 1954, some pages colored, EX.................................**$40.00**

Ellsworth Elephant Coloring Book, Saalfield, 1962, unused, NM **$30.00**

Fantastic Four vs Frightful Four Coloring Book, Marvel, 1983, unused, NM **$8.00**

Figaro & Cleo Story Paint Book, Whitman, 1940, unused, NM **$75.00**

Flipper Paintless Paint Book, Whitman, 1964, unused, NM **$25.00**

Flying Nun Coloring Book, Saalfield, 1968, unused, NM **$35.00**

Gene Autry Cowboy Adventures Coloring Book, Merrill, 1941, unused, EX **$85.00**

George of the Jungle Coloring Book, Whitman, 1968, unused, EX **$30.00**

Gilligan's Island Coloring Book, Whitman, 1965, unused, NM **$50.00**

Gloria Jean Coloring Book, Saalfield, 1941, some pages colored, VG **$30.00**

Green Hornet Coloring Book, Whitman, 1966, unused, NM **$60.00**

Gulliver's Travels Coloring Book, Saalfield, 1939, some pages colored, VG+ **$45.00**

Gumps Paint Book, Art Co, 1931, unused, EX+ **$90.00**

Happy Days Coloring Book, Waldman, 1983, unused, NM **$12.00**

Hayley Mills in Search of the Castaways Coloring Book, Whitman, 1962, EX **$25.00**

Heart Family Coloring Book, Golden, 1985, unused, NM..**$10.00**

Heckle & Jeckle Coloring Book, Treasure Books, 1957, unused, EX **$15.00**

Howdy Doody Coloring Book, Whitman, 1952, VG...**$15.00**

Huckleberry Hound Coloring Book, Whitman, 1959, some pages colored, EX **$15.00**

Humpty Dumpty Coloring Book, Lowe, 1950s, unused, NM......................................**$10.00**

I Love Lucy Coloring Book (Lucy, Ricky & Little Ricky), Dell, 1955, unused, NM......................................**$75.00**

Incredible Hulk at the Circus Coloring Book, 1977, unused, M **$25.00**

Jackie Gleason's TV Show Coloring Book, Abbott, 1956, unused, VG **$40.00**

Jeanette MacDonald Costume Parade Paint Book, Merrill, 1941, unused, EX **$30.00**

Jiminy Cricket, A Story Paint Book, Walt Disney, 1939, from $65.00 to $95.00. (Photo courtesy David Longest)

John Wayne Coloring Book, Saalfield, 1951, some pages colored, rare, EX **$85.00**

Julia, A Coloring Book, Saalfield, #9523, 1968, blue or red cover, NM, from $20.00 to $25.00. (Photo courtesy Greg Davis and Bill Morgan)

King Arthur Sticker Book, Golden, 1966, unused, VG..**$15.00**

Land of the Lost Coloring Book, Whitman, #1045, 1975, $25.00. (Photo courtesy Greg Davis and Bill Morgan)

Land of the Lost Sticker Book, Whitman, 1975, unused, NM......................................**$50.00**

Leave It to Beaver Coloring Book, Saalfield, 1958, unused, EX......................................**$60.00**

Little Lulu & Tubby Tom Paint Book, 1946, unused, VG..**$40.00**

Little Orphan Annie Coloring Book, Artcraft, 1974, unused, NM **$20.00**

Lucille Ball & Desi Arnez Coloring Book, Whitman, 1953, unused, EX......................................**$100.00**

Man From UNCLE Coloring Book, Whitman, 1967, unused, NM **$40.00**

Marty Mouse Coloring & Activity Book, Waldman, 1964, some pages used, EX **$20.00**

Mickey & Donald Paint Book, Whitman, 1949, unused, EX......................................**$45.00**

Mighty Hercules Sticker Book, Lowe, 1963, unused, EX ..**$25.00**

Million Dollar Duck Coloring Book, Whitman, 1971, unused, EX......................................**$15.00**

Moon Mullins Crayon & Paint Book, McLoughlin Bros, 1932, unused, EX...$65.00

Munsters Sticker Book, Whitman, 1965, unused, M....$75.00

Nanny & the Professor Coloring Book, Saalfield, 1971, unused, NM...$20.00

New Zoo Revue Press-Out & Play Album, Artcraft, 1974, unused, NM...$25.00

Osmonds Coloring Book, Artcraft, 1973, unused, EX.$35.00

Our Gang Coloring Book, Saalfield/Hall Roach Studios, 1933, unused, EX...$20.00

Ozzie's Girls Coloring Book, Saalfield, 1973, unused, EX...$20.00

Patty Duke Coloring Book, Whitman, 1966, unused, NM..$25.00

Pixie & Dixie Stencil Book, Golden, 1960, unused, NM..$20.00

Pluto & the Lost Bone Coloring Book, 1981, some pages colored, EX..$10.00

Popeye Great Big Paint & Crayon Book, Mc Loughlin Bros, 1935, unused, NM...............................$165.00

Porky Pig Coloring Book, Leon Schlesinger, 1930s, unused, EX, from $150 to...............................$175.00

Raggedy Ann & Andy Activity Book, Whitman, unused, NM..$15.00

Rambo Coloring Book, 1979, unused, M.....................$15.00

Rocky Jones Coloring Book, Whitman, 1951, some pages colored, EX...$40.00

Roger Ramjet Coloring Book, Whitman, 1966, unused, NM..$40.00

Roy Rogers Paint Book, Whitman, 1944, unused, NM..$50.00

Scooby Doo's All Star Laugh-A-Lympics Coloring book, Rand McNally, 1978, EX...............................$15.00

Shirley Temple's Bust Book, Saalfield, 1959, unused, VG..$50.00

Six Million Dollar Man Press-Out Book, Stafford Pemberton, 1977, M, from $50 to $75.00

Skippy Coloring Book, Whitman, 1970, unused, EX ..$12.00

Sleeping Beauty Magic Forest Coloring Book, Watkins-Strathmore, 1959, some pages colored, NM.........$25.00

Snoopy & Woodstock Coloring Book, Allan Publishing Inc, 1982, unused, NM......................................$8.00

Sonic Hedge Hedgehog Paint & Marker Book, Golden Book, 1993, unused, EX...............................$15.00

Tammy & Her Friends Cut-Out Coloring Book, Whitman, 1965, unused, EX...$30.00

Tiny Chatty Twins Coloring Book w/Cut-Out Dolls, Whitman Authorized Edition, 1960s, unused, NM...............$40.00

Tom Terrific Coloring Book, Treasure Books, 1957, unused, EX...$25.00

Tom Terrific w/Mighty Manfred the Wonder Dog, Treasure Books, 1957, unused, EX $25.00

Top Cat Activity Book, Charlton, 1971, unused, NM..$25.00

Underdog Coloring Book, Whitman, 1965, unused, VG..$20.00

Voyage to the Bottom of the Sea Coloring Book, Whitman, 1965, some pages colored, EX....................$35.00

Wagon Train Coloring Book, Whitman, 1959, some pages colored, EX...$25.00

Walt Disney's Magic Forest Coloring Book, Watkins-Strathmore, 1959, some pages colored, EX..........$15.00

Welcome Back Kotter Coloring Book, Whitman, 1977, unused, NM...$8.00

Welcome Back Kotter Sticker Fun, Whitman, 1977, unused, M...$15.00

Winky Dink's Coloring Dot Book, Whitman, 1955, some pages colored, EX.................................$30.00

Yogi Bear Coloring Book, Charlton, 1971, unused, NM.$25.00

Zorro Coloring Book, Whitman, 1958, unused, VG....$30.00

Comic Books

Though just about everyone can remember having stacks and stacks of comic books as a child, few of us ever saved them for more than a few months. At 10¢ a copy, new ones quickly replaced the old, well-read ones. We'd trade them with our friends, but very soon, out they went. If we didn't throw them away, Mother did. So even though they were printed in huge amounts, few survive, and today they're very desirable collectibles.

Factors that make a comic book valuable are condition (as with all paper collectibles, extremely important), content, and rarity, but not necessarily age. In fact, comics printed between 1950 and the late 1970s are most in demand by collectors who prefer those they had as children to the earlier comics. They look for issues where the hero is first introduced, and they insist on quality. Condition is first and foremost when it comes to assessing worth. Compared to a book in excellent condition, a mint issue might bring six to eight times more, while one in only good condition would be worth less than half the price. We've listed some of the more collectible (and expensive) comics, but many are worth very little. You'll really need to check your bookstore for a good reference book before you get actively involved in the comic book market.

Amazing Spider-Man and Dr. Doom, Marvel Comics #5, EX, $150.00.

Alice Cooper, Tales From the Inside, Marvel Premier #50, 1979, VG+..$25.00

Annie Oakley & Tagg, Dell #575, EX.........................$25.00

Archie Comics, Archie Publications #4, 1943, VG.....$325.00

Atomic Mouse, #1, VG+ $75.00

Banana Splits, #3, VG+..$10.00

Batman & Robin Battle Mutiny in the Big House, DC Comics #46, 1948, scarce, EX................................$150.00

Beatles Summer Love, #47, EX $50.00

Beatles Yellow Submarine, Gold Key, 1968, w/poster, NM, from $150 to..$200.00

Ben Casey, #5, VG..$10.00

Best of Donald Duck & Scrooge, Dell #2, 1967, EX...$30.00

Beverly Hillbillies, Dell #5, NM, from $75 to $100.00

Bewitched, Dell, 1965 – 1969, from $40.00 to $50.00 each. (Photo courtesy Greg Davis and Bill Morgan)

Bill Boyd Western, #9, VG $25.00

Black Rider, Marvel #8, photo cover, EX.................$100.00

Blaze Carson, #2, VG $30.00

Bonanza, Dell #210, 1962, EX $125.00

Brady Bunch, Dell #2, 1970, NM...............................$50.00

Brave & the Bold, Dell #43, EX+ $225.00

Bugs Bunny Halloween Parade, Dell Giant #1, EX ..$100.00

Captain Marvel Jr, Master Comics #73, 1946, G...........$30.00

Captain Midnight, Dell #37, EX $85.00

Chip 'n Dale, Dell Four-Color #581, VG $10.00

Cisco Kid, Dell #17, VG+ $20.00

Crazy, Marvel #1, 1972, NM $25.00

Daktari, #1, VG+ $12.00

Dale Evans Queen of the West, Dell #479, EX $100.00

Dark Shadows, Gold Key #15, 1972, EX.....................$15.00

Davy Crockett Frontier Fighter, Dell #3, 1955, EX $15.00

Dennis the Menace, Dell #20, EX...............................$15.00

Dick Tracy Monthly, Dell #18, EX..............................$35.00

Donald Duck in Mathmagicland, Dell #1198, EX........$45.00

Donald Duck Lost in the Andes, Dell #223, 1949, EX ..$175.00

Earth Man on Venus, Avon, 1951, EX $325.00

Elmer Fudd, Dell #689, NM $25.00

F-Troop, Dell #4, 1967, VG $20.00

Family Affair, Gold Key #1, 1970, NM $40.00

Flash Gordon, Dell #5, 1967, EX $100.00

Flintstones Bedrock Bedlam, Dell Giant #48, 1961, NM ..$450.00

Gene Autry, Dell #51, VG $20.00

Gentle Ben, Dell #4, 1968, photo cover, EX................$10.00

Grandma Duck's Farm Friends, Dell #873, NM..........$40.00

Happy Days, Gold Key #1, 1979, M............................$15.00

Hawkman, DC Comics #1, 1964, NM..........................$500.00

Hercules Unchained, Dell Four-Color #1121, VG+ $25.00

Hogan's Heroes, Dell #8, 1967, EX $40.00

Horse Soldiers, Dell, 1959, G+....................................$20.00

Howdy Doody, Dell #4, 1950, EX $40.00

HR Pufnstuf, Gold Key #2, 1971, EX...........................$40.00

Huckleberry Hound, Dell #10, 1961, VG $10.00

Human Torch Battling the Submarines, #8, 1942, NM ..$2,500.00

Hunchback of Notre Dame, Dell #854, 1957, EX........$40.00

I Dream of Jeanie, Dell #1, 1966, NM, from $50 to....$75.00

I Love Lucy, Dell #25, 1959, NM $35.00

Iron Man, Dell #10, NM $25.00

Jesse James, Dell Four-Color #757, G+ $15.00

Jetsons, Gold Key #35, EX $15.00

John Carter of Mars, Gold Key #1, 1964, VG $20.00

Jungle Jim, Dell #112, 1949, G $10.00

Justice League of America, Dell #6, VG $50.00

Katzenjammer Kids, Dell #32, 1946, VG $35.00

KISS, Marvel #1, 1977, EX $40.00

Lad the Dog, Dell Movie Classic #1303, 1961, VG+....$55.00

Lady & the Tramp, Dell #1, 1955, VG.........................$30.00

Lassie, Dell #27, NM...$15.00

Leave It to Beaver, Dell Silver Age Classic #999, 1959, VG+ $55.00

Li'l Abner, Dell #61, 1947, NM...................................$195.00

Littlest Outlaw, Dell Four-Color #609, VG+ $15.00

Lone Ranger, Dell #161, 1960, NM $75.00

Lone Ranger Movie, Dell Giant, 1956, EX+ $50.00

Man From UNCLE, Dell #8, VG $15.00

Man in Space, Dell Four-Color #716, VG....................$20.00

Mandrake the Magician, Dell #5, NM..........................$12.00

Marge's Little Lulu & Tubby at Summer Camp, Dell Giant #2, 1958, VG+..$35.00

Marvel Family Battles the Hissing Horror, Marvel #74, 1952, VG $25.00

Mary Poppins, Gold Key, 1964, EX $20.00

MGM's Mouse Musketeers, Dell #728, NM $15.00

Mickey Mouse & the Mystery Sea Monster, Wheaties premium, 1950, NM..$15.00

Minnie Mouse Girl Explorer, Wheaties premium, 1951, NM $15.00

Moby Dick, Dell #717, 1956, EX.................................$25.00

Monkees, Dell #1, 1967, NM......................................$40.00

Munsters, Dell #4, EX $15.00

Mutt & Jeff, Dell #24, VG+...$30.00

My Favorite Martian, Dell #3, EX...............................$30.00

Nanny & the Professor, Dell #1, 1970, NM.................$25.00

Old Ironsides w/Johnny Tremain, Dell #874, 1957, EX ...$15.00

Oswald the Rabbit, Dell #102, EX...............................$30.00

Outlaws of the West, Dell #15, VG $15.00

Peter Pan, Dell #926, 1958, VG $20.00

Peter Panda, Dell #31, 1958, EX................................$20.00

Pixie & Dixie & Mr Jinks, Dell Four-Color #1196, 1961, EX $15.00

Pogo Possum, Dell #1, 1949, G $75.00

Raggedy Ann & Andy, Gold Key #2, 1972, NM $25.00

Rawhide, Dell #1160, 1960, VG+ $30.00

Rawhide Kid, Dell #12, EX..$35.00

Red Ryder, Dell #69, 1949, NM.......................$35.00
Restless Gun, Dell Four-Color #1146, VG................$25.00
Rifleman, Dell #5, 1960, photo cover, EX..............$35.00
Rin-Tin-Tin & Rusty, Dell Four-Color #523, 1953, VG ..$15.00
Robin Hood, Dell #413, 1952, EX......................$30.00
Shadow, DC Comics #1, 1973, EX.......................$15.00
Sheena Queen of the Jungle, Jumbo Comics #140, 1950,
 VG...$30.00
Silver Surfer, Marvel #4, 1969, VG...................$65.00
Simpsons, Bongo Comic Group #8, NM+...................$5.00
Six Million Dollar Man, Charlton #1, 1976, NM.........$15.00
Snagglepuss, Gold Key #2, 1964, VG...................$10.00
Space Busters, Dell #2, 1952, EX....................$150.00
Spider-Man, Marvel #1, Golden Edition, NM...........$375.00

Star Trek, Gold Key 10210-806, 1968, M, $150.00.

Steve Canyon, Dell Four-Color #641, 1955, NM..........$35.00
Superboy, Dell #89, VG $60.00
Superman, DC Comics #25, 1941, VG $225.00
Tales of Suspense, Marvel Silver Age #46, 1964, VG+ $25.00
Tales of the Crypt, Dell #40, NM.....................$90.00
Tales To Astonish, Marvel #22, 1961, VG $35.00
Tarzan, Dell #27, 1951, EX...........................$35.00
That Darn Cat, Gold Key, 1965, photo cover, EX.......$20.00
This Is Your Life Donald Duck, Dell #1109, NM $125.00
Tom & Jerry Back to School, Dell Giant #1, 1956, NM...$100.00
Tom Mix, Fawcett #2, VG $110.00
Top Cat, Dell #3, 1962, VG $12.00
Top Cat, Gold Key #5, 1963, NM $30.00
Tweety & Sylvester, Dell #11, NM.....................$20.00
Uncle Remus & His Tales of Brer Rabbit, Dell Four-Color
 #129, 1946, EX $55.00
Underworld Crime, Dell #3, 1952, EX+.................$60.00
Wacky Witch, Gold Key #7, 1972, NM $5.00
Weird Fantasy, Dell #11, VG+.........................$45.00
Wild Bill Elliot, Dell #9, EX+ $45.00
Wild Wild West, Dell #2, 1966, EX....................$15.00
Wyatt Earp, Dell #860, NM............................$75.00
Yogi Bear Jellystone Jollies, Gold Key #11, 1963, EX.$15.00

Zane Grey's Outlaw Trail, Dell Four-Color #511, 1954,
 EX $25.00
101 Dalmatians, Dell Four-Color #1183, 1961, EX $25.00

Compacts and Purse Accessories

When 'liberated' women entered the work force after WWI, cosmetics, previously frowned upon, became more acceptable, and as a result the market was engulfed with compacts of all types and designs. Some went so far as to incorporate timepieces, cigarette compartments, coin holders, and money clips. All types of materials were used — mother-of-pearl, petit-point, cloisonne, celluloid, and leather among them. There were figural compacts, those with wonderful Art Deco designs, souvenir compacts, and some with advertising messages.

Carryalls were popular from the 1930s to the 1950s. They were made by compact manufacturers and were usually carried with evening wear. They contained compartments for powder, rouge, and lipstick, often held a comb and mirror, and some were designed with a space for cigarettes and a lighter. Other features might have included a timepiece, a tissue holder, a place for coins or stamps, and some even had music boxes. In addition to compacts and carryalls, solid perfumes and lipsticks are becoming popular collectibles as well.

For further study, we recommend *Vintage and Vogue Ladies' Compacts*, *The Estée Lauder Solid Perfume Compact Collection*, and *Vintage and Contemporary Purse Accessories*, all by Roselyn Gerson; and *Collector's Encyclopedia of Compacts, Carryalls and Face Powder Boxes, Volumes I* and *II*, by Laura Mueller.

Advisor: Roselyn Gerson (See Directory, Compacts)

Newsletter: The Compacts Collector Chronicle
Powder Puff
P.O. Box 40
Lynbrook, NY 11563
Subscription: $25 (4 issues, USA or Canada) per year

Carryalls

Elgin, gold-tone leaping gazelles, braided/tasseled handle,
 hinged mirror, 4½x2½", from $125 to.................$150.00
Evans, gold-tone w/linear bark-like design & faux gems
 on lid, single access, snake wrist chain, 5½x3⅛",
 from $125 to $150.00
Evans, gold-tone w/rose & gold-tone lid ribbing, double
 access, glued-in mirror, oversize, 6¾x3¼", from $150
 to $175.00
Evans, mother-of-pearl w/gold-tone ribs, double access,
 glued-in mirror, 5½x3¼", from $150 to $175.00
Evans, Sunburst, gold-tone, double access, mesh wrist strap,
 glued-in mirror, no lighter, 3¼" sq, $100 to $125.00
Evans, Waves, gold-tone, double access, snake wrist chain,
 glued-in mirror, 5½x3⅛", from $150 to $175.00

Kigu (UK), gold-tone w/faux engraving, double access, snake wrist chain, framed mirror, 3¾x3", from $75 to **$100.00**

Mondaine, black enamel on white metal w/hinged lid inset for rouge, framed mirror, wrist cord, 4x3", from $125 to..**$150.00**

Terri, gold-tone oval luggage case form w/faux black Moroccan leather finish, silk wrist cord w/band slide, 3¾"..**$150.00**

Unmarked, brushed gold-tone w/rhinestown crown bijou lid, double access, hinged pop-up lipstick tube, 5¼", from $65 to **$75.00**

Volupté, gold-tone w/incised lines & faux gems, lip-lock closure, music box, glued-in mirror, 6", from $250 to............**$300.00**

Volupté, silver- & gold-tone w/chevron & faux gems, single access, Art Moderne style, detachable carrier, 6", from $125 to..**$150.00**

Volupté, silver- & gold-tone w/strewn daisies & rhinestones, rope handle, hinged mirror, 5¼", complete, from $150 to **$175.00**

Volupté, silver-tone w/black enameling & rhinestone swag, single access, detachable carrier w/wristband, 6", from $150 to..**$170.00**

Compacts

Italy, 800 silver vermeil with enamel swirls, 3", $275.00.

American Beauty, silver-tone w/post-Deco gazelles on lid, double access, glued-in mirror, 2⅞x2½", from $75 to..**$100.00**

Belle Ayre, clear faceted plastic flapjack w/blue glued-in mirror inset, 5" dia, from $125 to **$150.00**

Dorette, snakeskin, red case, clip closure, glued-in mirror, 3¾x3¼", from $75 to..**$100.00**

Dorothy Gray, gold-tone picture-hat flapjack w/embossed garden hat on lid, glued-in mirror, 3⅞" dia, from $150 to **$175.00**

Elgin American, gold-tone w/incised musical instruments, music box, glued-in mirror, ca 1953, 2¾x1¾", from $125 to..**$150.00**

Evans, Patrician, gold-tone plaid w/watch inset in lid, double hinged mirrors, ca 1948, 2½" sq, from $125 to..**$150.00**

Germany, gold-tone, tambour opener w/black & gold plastic slats, framed tray mirror, 3¼x2⅜", from $125 to......**$150.00**

Henriette, brushed gold-tone w/attached blue plastic disk w/Seabees logo by Disney artist, glued-in mirror, 2½" sq **$175.00**

Henriette, gold-tone jack-in-the box case w/black kid bellows sides, framed mirror, 3" sq, from $150 to..**$175.00**

Henriette, painted wood w/white lambs at play on lid, pin hinges, glued-in mirror, 4x3", from $75 to..........**$100.00**

Henriette, Questioning Game Ball, daisy petals under domed plastic lid w/Yes/No/Maybe, framed mirror, 2x2", from $150 to **$175.00**

Lady Vanity, gold-tone horseshoe, cartoon lid by A Honeywell, talon zipper closure, snakeskin hinge, 3¾", from $75 to..**$100.00**

Lady Vanity, yellow Lucite w/black Moroccan leather lid (stamped USN), glued-in mirror, puff w/logo, 4x2¾", from $100 to..**$125.00**

Lucien Lelong, Circassian walnut w/coin purse closure, inlay lid logo, brushed aluminum interior, 4" sq, from $225 to..**$250.00**

Miahati, clear plastic w/reverse lid inset of shell flowers, glued-in mirror, 3" sq, from $75 to......................**$100.00**

Pilcher, gold-tone w/celluloid lid plaque of Empire State Building decal, framed mirror, 3½x2⅜", from $100 to............**$125.00**

Pilcher, red Lucite w/etched florals, metallic push-pc closure, glued-in mirror, 4½" sq, from $125 to **$150.00**

Polly Bergen, purple marbled plastic w/gold-tone turtle on lid, gold foil back label, framed mirror, 3¼x2½", up to..**$40.00**

Quinlan, 24k gold-plate w/embossed fleur-de-lis, framed mirror, 3" dia, w/white-beaded carrier pouch, from $125 to..**$150.00**

Revlon, gold-tone presentation gift set w/gold-thread brocade bag & gold foil box, box: 10x6x1¼", from $125 to..**$150.00**

Revlon, Love Pat, blue plastic with blonde girl and white daisies, 4¼" diameter, from $35.00 to $45.00. (Photo courtesy Roselyn Gerson/Photographer Alvin Gerson)

Rex Fifth Avenue, leather w/faux alligator pattern & mock tortoise-shell backing, plastic lip closure, 4" sq, from $150 to..**$175.00**

Rho-Jan, purple marbled plastic flapjack, high dome, glued-in mirror, 5" dia, from $150 to............................**$175.00**

Richard Hudnut, gold-tone w/faux gemstones & sun ray motif, framed mirror, 2¼" dia lipstick, 2½x2¼", from $75 to...**$100.00**

Unknown, alligator, black case w/slide-out tray mirror, clip closure, Made in Argentina in powder well, 3" sq, from $75 to.................................**$100.00**

Unknown, leather horseshoe w/embossed ostrich skin look, zipper closure, Ivorene interior, 4x3⅞", from $125 to...**$150.00**

Unknown, silver-tone w/champlevè enameling of Chicago Skyline & World's Fair Chicago 1933-1934, 2½x1⅝", from $125 to...**$150.00**

Unmarked, solid ivory w/cherry blossom carvings on lid, gold-tone interior, framed mirror, 2¾x2", from $125 to...**$150.00**

Unmarked, walnut w/diagonal lid marquetry, mystery opener, glued-in mirror, 3⅜" sq, from $75 to..............**$90.00**

Varsity, tan leather over white metal w/stamped gilt US Airforce insignia, glued-in mirror, 4½x3½", from $125 to...**$150.00**

Zell, blond wooden flapjack w/maroon plastic lid inset w/affixed horse ornament, glued-in mirror, 4¼" dia, from $75 to...**$100.00**

Zell, silver-tone w/enameled US Army eagle, planes, landing field, hangers, boat, framed mirror, 3¼x1¾", from $175 to...**$200.00**

Lipsticks

Atomette, polished gold-tone with rhinestone owl, mirror on top, 2¼", from $50.00 to $70.00. (Photo courtesy Roselyn Gerson/Photographer Alvin Gerson)

Black baked enamel w/glittery 'can-can' girls, 2¼", from $35 to...**$50.00**

Black Bakelite w/rhinestones & gold beading, 2¼", from $40 to...**$60.00**

Black fabric-covered tube w/petit-point roses, 2¼", from $15 to...**$25.00**

Christy, black enamel & silver-tone tube, 1¾", from $15 to...**$20.00**

Coty, gold-tone w/green enamel bands, 2½", from $45 to.**$55.00**

Delta, white enamel tube, 1⅞", from $15 to..............**$20.00**

Elizabeth Arden, gold-tone w/pearls & rhinestones on lid, letter 'E' repeats at base, 2½", from $20 to..........**$30.00**

Elizabeth Post, red, white & blue cardboard tube, 2½", from $15 to...**$25.00**

Florenza, brushed gold-tone tube w/green cabochon stones, 2", from $35 to...**$50.00**

Gold-tone filigree w/green stones, cabochon green stone on lid, 2¼", from $45 to.................................**$65.00**

Hampden, gold-tone w/applied filigree set w/red, blue & green stones, 2", from $35 to...........................**$50.00**

Hampden, purple or blue translucent tube w/rhinestones decor at base, 2¼", from $30 to.........................**$40.00**

Helena Rubinstein, Cracker Jack, black & gold-tone stripes w/center gold-tone band w/red rhinestones, 2¾", from $45 to...**$65.00**

Jannifer Cosmetics Inc, black plastic sq tube w/encircling gold band, mirror on front lid, 3", from $15 to....**$25.00**

Lillie Dache, brushed gold-tone w/applied plastic figures on swing, 2½", from $45 to.................................**$55.00**

Lucien Lelong, rabbit-fur covered tube, 2¼", from $45 to...**$65.00**

Polly Bergen, brushed-gold-tone, 3", in presentation box, from $10 to...**$20.00**

Richard Hudnut, silver-tone octagon shape, 1⅞", from $10 to...**$15.00**

Robert, gold-tone w/mobe pearl set on lid, framed w/golden leaves & rhinestones, 2¾", from $40 to..............**$60.00**

Sand-finished gold-tone w/applied sparkle flowers, 2¼", from $15 to...**$25.00**

Schiaparelli, Schiap Atomic, shocking pink, white & silver plastic tube, 2¼", MIB, from $35 to....................**$50.00**

Silver w/hand-engraved & decorated rope design, 2", from $45 to...**$75.00**

Sterling w/faceted amethyst stone centered on lid, 2¼", from $100 to...**$125.00**

Unmarked, gold-tone w/filigree, rhinestones & pearls at top, 2¼", from $45 to.................................**$60.00**

Weisner of Miami, pearls & aurora borealis rhinestones, 2¼", from $45 to...**$65.00**

Yardley, Bond Street refill, wooden tube w/red, white & blue transfer, 2", MIB, from $10 to.........................**$15.00**

Yves Saint Laurent, heart shape w/colored heart-shaped stone centered on lid, from $90 to....................**$125.00**

Mirrors

Accessocraft, gold-tone, forward/backward tilting mirror/ light combination, 5¼x2" dia, from $15 to...........**$25.00**

Blue enameling w/pink rose, faux jade handle, decorative retainer, 5¾", from $15 to.................................**$25.00**

Debbie J Palmer, polished gold-tone, Contented Cat, sleeping cat shape, 1¾x2½", 1995.................................**$30.00**

Florenza, antique white & gold w/portrait of lady on yellow enamel disk at back of mirror, 2½" L, from $45 to...**$65.00**

Florenza, antique white & gold-tone w/raised floral decor, 4", from $20 to...**$25.00**

Florenza, white- & gold-tone w/faux pearls forming flower centers along w/smaller red & stones, 4½", from $35 to **$55.00**

Gold-tone, hand-crafted ea side w/red & clear rhinestones, 5" L, from $25 to **$35.00**

Gold-tone & black enamel w/gold swirls in center, 4½", from $15 to..**$25.00**

Gold-tone filigree w/black marbleized cabochon stone, pearls & rhinestones, 4" L, from $30 to **$40.00**

Gold-tone filigree w/twisted wire ring holder, green velvet center, beveled mirror w/wire retainer, 4", from $50 to **$60.00**

Gold-tone plastic w/Colonial transfer on plastic disk, 4½", from $15 to...**$20.00**

Gold-tone w/astrological sign on black disk, 5", from $15 to **$25.00**

Gold-tone w/embossed decor, lg green stone cabachon amid sm multicolor stones, 4½" L, w/fabric case, from $20 to **$35.00**

Gold-tone w/enameled menorah & symbols of 12 tribes of Israel, framed retainer, 5½", from $40 to **$50.00**

Gold-tone w/pink enameling & red & clear rhinestones ea side, 4½" L, from $25 to..**$35.00**

Gold-tone w/raised metal filigree & turquoise stones, scalloped retainer, 4¼" L, from $20 to **$30.00**

Italy, flowers painted on mini mosaics & framed w/gold-tone wire filigree, loop & hook for hanging, 5¼", from $35 to..**$45.00**

Limoges, courting scene on white enamel, signed Fragonard, colored stones set in handle, beveled mirror, 4", from $25 to..**$30.00**

Petit-point gold-tone oval, framed mirror, 5", from $20 to.**$30.00**

Silver-tone, round, engine-turned, framed mirror, 3¼", from $20 to..**$35.00**

Silver-tone w/leaves in relief set w/cabochon coral stones, framed mirror retainer, 5x2½", from $25 to.........**$35.00**

Silver-tone w/raised leaves & colored stones, beveled mirror, mini, 4x1⅝", from $15 to **$20.00**

Sterling silver shield shape, engine turned, monogram on cartouch, beveled mirror, 4", from $75 to............**$90.00**

Solid Perfumes

Avon, gold-tone, designed to resemble mandolin, 2¼x1", from $30 to..**$40.00**

Avon, gold-tone flower basket compact/pin combination set w/rhinestones, 1½x1⅛", from $15 to...................**$25.00**

Avon, polished gold-tone, resembles book w/engraved designs, 1⅜x1¼", from $25 to **$35.00**

Avon, Wee Willy Winter plastic pin-pal, 1974, 2½" **$20.00**

Blanchard, black plastic perfume locket, golden cut-out disk on lid, gold-plated chain, contains Evening Star, 1¾" **$15.00**

Brushed silver-tone, designed to resemble cherries, leaves set w/red stones, 1⅝x1¼", from $35 to......................**$45.00**

Corday, Golden Intaglio, gold-tone compact, contains Toujours Moi creme perfume, 1½" dia, from $35 to................**$45.00**

Coty, gold-tone flower w/centered blue cabochon stone, contains Imprevu, 1½", in fitted presentation box, from $30 to..**$40.00**

Estee Lauder, beige kitten compact, contains Beautiful, 2x1½"...**$55.00**

Estee Lauder, Cat's Meow, frosted pink translucent cat w/silver ribbon & rhinestones on pillow, contains Pleasures, 2"..**$60.00**

Estee Lauder, clear Lucite, resembles pear, contains Aliage, 3x1¾", from $85 to..**$135.00**

Estee Lauder, clear Lucite w/facets to give illusion of diamond solitaire ring inside box, 1¾x1¾", from $40 to **$60.00**

Estee Lauder, enameled butterfly w/purple & yellow stones, contains White Linen, 1994, 2x2" **$55.00**

Estee Lauder, glass slipper (red, white or black), contains White Linen, Knowing or Beautiful, 1995, 2x2¼" ..**$90.00**

Estee Lauder, oblong gold-tone perfume compact w/scroll-design lid, contains Estee, 3⅞x1", from $25 to **$30.00**

Estee Lauder, red & cobalt enamel Collector's Egg, gold pedestal, red tassel, contains Beautiful, 1995, 2x1¼" dia..........**$75.00**

Estee Lauder, silver-tone heart shape centered on gold-tone heart, contains White Linen, 1½x1¾", from $35 to..**$45.00**

Estee Lauder, Starry Nights, blue enamel w/gold stars & rhinestones, contains Beautiful, 1994, 1¾" dia.....**$70.00**

Florenza, gold-tone set w/cabochon turquoise stones, twist closure, 1½" dia, from $15 to **$25.00**

Florenza, silver-tone bullfrog pendant, 2x1¼", from $35 to..**$45.00**

Fuller Brush, gold-tone fish pin, set w/blue eyes, 1¾x1¾", from $25 to..**$35.00**

Givenchy, brushed gold-tone shell w/twist closure, 1⅞x1⅞", from $20 to..**$25.00**

Gold-tone duck w/lg red stone eyes, rhinestones & black enamel stripes, from $40 to **$50.00**

Gold-tone egg w/alternating rows of pink crystals & pearls, 2x1", from $75 to **$90.00**

Gold-tone w/disk of woman in relief on lid, 1½" sq, from $35 to..**$45.00**

Gold-tone 4-leaf clover pin/pendant w/faceted green stones suspended from a bow, 1¼", from $40 to............**$50.00**

Grandiflorum, round nickel-plated compact w/engraved florals, mirror in lid, contains Angelica, 1996, 1½" dia..........**$40.00**

Guy Laroche, gold-tone shell, contains Fidji, 2½x2½", from $30 to..**$40.00**

Helena Rubinstein, gold-tone compact w/centered faceted green stone, 1x1½", from $15 to **$20.00**

Houbigant, white plastic heart w/pink plastic bow centered on lid, contains Chantilly, 2⅜x2½", from $25 to..**$35.00**

Kenneth Jay Lane, gold-tone lid w/carved faux jade disk centered on lid, 1997, 2x1¾"......................................**$30.00**

Max Factor, Golden Matchbox, scrolled-design lid, pull-out drawer, contains Hypnotique, 1½x2x1⅛", from $65 to **$80.00**

Polished textured gold-tone, resembles pig, green stones for eyes, 1x2", from $50 to..**$75.00**

Revlon, Frivolous Fragrant Frog, gold-tone w/green enamel eyes, 1½x½", from $40 to **$50.00**

Revlon, gold-tone filigree octagon w/lady's portrait in center, contains Ciara, 1¾", from $30 to **$40.00**

Revlon, green enamel & gold-tone pendant, contains Moon Drops, 2⅛x2", from $35 to....................................**$45.00**

Revlon, silver-tone compact/pendant, contains Intimate, 2" dia, from $30 to **$40.00**

Sarah Coventry, gold-tone, resembles turtle, lid set completely w/faceted amethyst stone, 1¾x1½", from $30 to...**$40.00**

Stephen B, silver-tone mini compact, 1x1¼", from $25 to **$35.00**

Striated gold-tone w/leaves on stems, leaves form legs, ¼x1¼", from $35 to...**$45.00**

Textured gold-tone, resembles peanut, 2x1", from $40 to ..**$50.00**

Textured gold-tone pin, resembles swan, eye set w/green stone, 1½x1¾", from $40 to.......................................**$50.00**

Viviane Woodward, iridescent blue enamel, resembles purse w/twist closure, 2x1½", from $45 to **$65.00**

Yves Saint Laurent, gold-tone box w/faux brown leather & YSL logo, 1½x1¼", from $30 to.............................**$40.00**

Cookbooks and Recipe Leaflets

Cookbook collecting is not new! Perhaps one of the finest books ever written on the subject goes back to just after the turn of the century when Elizabeth Robins Pennell published *My Cookery Books*, an edition limited to 330 copies; it had tipped-in photographs and was printed on luxurious, uncut paper. Mrs. Pennell, who spent much of her adult life travelling in Europe, wrote a weekly column on food and cooking for the *Pall Mall Gazette* and as a result reviewed many books on cookery. Her book was a compilation of titles from her extensive collection which was later donated to the Library of Congress. That this book was reprinted in 1983 is an indication that interest in cookbook collecting is strong and ongoing.

Books on food and beverages, if not bestsellers, are at the least generally popular. Cookbooks published by societies, lodges, churches, and similar organizations offer insight into regional food preferences and contain many recipes not found in other sources. Very early examples are unusually practical, often stressing religious observances and sometimes offering medical advice. Recipes were simple combinations of basic elements. Cookbooks and cooking guides of World Wars I and II stressed conservation of food. In sharp contrast are the more modern cookbooks often authored by doctors, dietitians, cooks, and domestic scientists, calling for more diversified materials and innovative combinations with exotic seasonings. Food manufacturers' cookbooks abound. By comparing early cookbooks to more recent publications, the fascinating evolution in cookery and food preparation is readily apparent.

Because this field is so large and varied, we recommend that you choose the field you find most interesting and specialize. Will you collect hardbound or softcover? Some collectors zero in on one particular food company's literature — for instance, Gold Medal Flour and Betty Crocker, the Pillsbury Flour Company's Pillsbury Bake-Offs, and Jell-O. Others look for more general publications on chocolate, spices and extracts, baking powers, or favored appliances. Fund-raising, regional, and political cookbooks are other types to consider.

Our advisor, Col. Bob Allen, has written *A Guide to Collecting Cookbooks*, a compilation of four large collections resulting in a much broader overview than is generally possible in a book of this type. It contains more than 300 color illustrations and in excess of 5,000 titles with current values. We also recommend *Price Guide to Cookbooks and Recipe Leaflets* by Linda Dickinson. Both are published by Collector Books.

Our suggested values are based on cookbooks in very good condition; remember to adjust prices up or down to evaluate examples in other conditions.

Advisor: Bob Allen (See Directory, Cookbooks)

Club/Newsletter: *Cookbook Gossip*
Cookbook Collectors Club of America, Inc.
Bob and Jo Ellen Allen
P.O. Box 56
St. James, MO 65559-0056

Newsletter: *The Cookbook Collector's Exchange*
Sue Erwin
P.O. Box 89
Magalia, CA 95954

Around the World Cook Book, 1951, $10.00. (Photo courtesy Col. Bob Allen)

Alice B Toklas Cookbook, 1954, Alice B Toklas, Sir Francis Rose, illustrated, hardbound, 296 pages **$45.00**

America Regional Cookbook, 1932, Sheilla Hibben, hardback **$35.00**

America's Cookbook, 1938, 1941, Home Institute, New York Herald Tribune, hardback **$25.00**

American Cooker Recipe Book, 1926, softback **$20.00**

American Everyday Cookbook, 1st edition, 1955, Agnes Murphy, Food Editor of the New York Post, approximately 500 pages **$20.00**

American Heritage Cookbook 1st edition, 1964, history of American eating & drinking, illustrated, hardback, 640 pages...**$25.00**

Arm & Hammer - Good Things To Eat, 1940s, 6x3¼" give-away, 15 pages...**$8.00**

Around the World Cookbook for Young People, 1966, Mildred O Knopfs, hardback **$15.00**

Art & Secrets of Chinese Cookery, 1932, LaChoy Food Products, booklet, 15 pages.........................**$14.00**

Bakers Review - National Monthly of the Baking Industry, 1958, August, softback, 70 pages.........................**$10.00**

Best Chocolate & Cocoa Recipes, 1931, Walter Baker & Co, General Foods, 60 pages............................**$15.00**

Best in Cookery in the Middle West, 1956, Grace Grosvenor Clark, Doubleday, hardback **$20.00**

Better Homes & Gardens - Table Settings & Accessories, 1944, softback, 50 pages **$12.50**

Better Homes & Gardens Bread Cookbook, 1963, hardback, 160 pages...**$12.50**

Better Homes & Gardens Cookbook, 1930, 1937, Home Service Bureau, 3-ring binder, hardback..............**$30.00**

Betty Crocker, Festive Fixings With a Foreign Flair, 1963, softback, 23 pages **$6.00**

Betty Crocker, Gold Medal Flour Cookbook, 1917, soft cover, 74 pages **$30.00**

Betty Crocker, Party Book, 1st edition, 1st printing, 1960, hardback, spiral, 176 pages.........................**$10.00**

Betty Crocker, Pie Parade, 1957, softback, 38 pages **$8.00**

Betty Crocker's Cookbook, 1969, hardback, 5-ring binder..**$10.00**

Bible Cookbook, 1958, Marian Maeve O'Brien, Bethony Press, St Louis, hardback............................**$20.00**

Blueberry Hill Menu Cookbook, 1963, Elsie Masterton, hardback, 374 pages **$20.00**

Bond Bread - Name Your Favorite Recipe Book, 1925, softback **$14.00**

Boston School Kitchen Text Book, 1887, Mrs DA (Mary J) Lincoln, hardback 237 pages **$90.00**

Brunches & Coffees 1969, Marion Courtney, hardback ...**$15.00**

C&H Cane Sugar Presents 'Drivert' Fondant Icings, 1957, 28 pages **$8.00**

Calorie Saving Recipes With Sucary, 1955, booklet **$80.00**

Calumet Cookbook, 1923, 27th edition, 80 pages **$14.00**

Campbell's Great Restaurant Cookbook, 1969, Doris Townsend, Rutledge Books, hardback, 160 pages.**$15.00**

Carnation - Baking Secrets, 1953, Mary Blake, 8 pages ..**$8.00**

Casserole Treasury, 1964, Lousene R Brunner, hardback, 310 pages...**$15.00**

CBS Radio Booklet - Kate Smith's Favorite Recipes, 1939 .**$14.00**

Choice Candy Recipes, 1929, Lucy G Allen, Little Brown & Co, hardback..**$35.00**

Clean Plates, 1964, Cooking for Young Children, Mitzi F Perry-Miller, hardback............................**$15.00**

Complete American Cookbook, 1957, Stella Stanard, revised, hardback, 512 pages **$20.00**

Connecticut Home Record, 1917, County Farm Bureau, sm booklet...**$20.00**

Cookbook by Reddie Wilcolater, 1946, Wilcolater Co, softback **$12.50**

Cooking Is Fun, 1955, Gas Range, booklet **$10.00**

Cooking on a Ration, 1943, Mills, hardback...............**$30.00**

Cooking With Cold, 1933, Kelvinator, booklet...........**$15.00**

Copper Kettle Cookbook, 1963, Martha Dixon, hardback ..**$15.00**

Daily Food for Christians, 1898, DeWolfe Fiske Co, hardback **$55.00**

Daniel Webster Flour Cookbook, 1907, softback, 120 pages...**$25.00**

Different Salads Featuring Rose Apple Recipes, 1930, Kehoe Preserving Co, booklet **$20.00**

Dormeyer Electric Mix Treasures, 1947, Ethel Allison, prepared especially for Your Dormeyer Mixer, booklet, 34 pages...**$12.50**

Easter Idea Book, 1954, Charlotte Adams, Lenten dishes, ham, eggs, centerpieces, softback **$10.00**

Eat Italian Once a Week, 1967, Vernon Jarratt, hardback .**$15.00**

Eggs at Any Meal, 1931, US Dept of Agriculture, Leaflet No 39, 8 pages **$15.00**

Electric Cookbook, 1910, Portland Railway, Light & Power Co, 82 pages...**$20.00**

Everyday Cookbook, 1889, 1892, Miss E Neil, Chicago, hardback **$45.00**

Exciting World of Rice Dishes, 1959, General Foods Kitchens, General Foods Corp, booklet, 20 pages **$10.00**

Family Circle's New Home Canning Guide, 1940s, 32 pages...**$6.00**

Family's Food, 1931, Lauman, McKay & Zuill, hardback ..**$35.00**

Famous Dishes From Every State, 1936, Frigidare Corp, Dayton OH, booklet, 40 pages............................**$15.00**

Farm & Home Cookbook & Housekeeper's Assistant, 1909, by Farm & Home Magazine, hardback **$55.00**

Fine Art of Chinese Cooking, 1962, Dr Lee Su Jan, Gramercy Publishing, hardback, 234 pages **$10.00**

Fish & Seafood Cookery, 1930s, Mid-Central Fish Co, Kansas City MO, softback **$15.00**

Fleischmann's Compressed Yeast & Good Health, 1917...**$20.00**

Fleishmann's Yeast - Delicious Recipes, 1920s, people in evening clothes on cover **$14.00**

Fondue, Chafing Dish & Casserole Cookery, 1969, Margaret Deeds Murphy, New York, hardback...................**$15.00**

Food & Nutrition, 1967, Life Science Library, hardback, 200 pages...**$10.00**

Food Fit for a King Recipes, 1939, Majestic Waterless Low Heat Cookware, softback **$15.00**

French Chef Cookbook, 1968, Julia Child, hardback..**$30.00**

Frigidaire Recipe Book, 1931, hardback **$15.00**

General Foods Cookbook, 1st edition, 1932, hardback, 370 pages...**$35.00**

Gentleman's Companion or Around the World With Knife, Fork & Spoon, 1946, Chas H Baker Jr, simulated leather covers...**$12.50**

Going Wild in the Kitchen, 1965, Gertrude Parke, David McKay Co, Inc, hardback, 329 pages...................**$15.00**

Golden Anniversary Cookbook, 1949, First Presbyterian Church, Napponsee IN, spiral bound......................**$8.00**

Good Food & How To Prepare It, 1920, 1930, George E Conforth, hardback, 228 pages.............................**$25.00**

Good Housekeeping, Party Pie Book, Plain & Fancy, #7, 1958, 64 pages, softback **$8.00**

Good Housekeeping Institute Meals Tested & Approved, 1930, 5th edition, hardback, 254 pages **$15.00**

Good Housekeeping's Quick & Easy Cookbook, 1958, Consolidated Book Publishers, hardback **$20.00**

Graham Kerr Cookbook, 1966, 1969, Galloping Gourmet, hardback **$15.00**

Hamilton Ross Modern Cookbook, 1940, K Camille & Den Dooven, hardback, 238 pages **$25.00**

Health in the Household or Hygenic Cookery, 1886, Susanna W Doods, AM, DD, hardback................................**$60.00**

Heinz Book of Salads, 1925, HJ Heniz Co, softback, 90 pages...**$20.00**

Hints to Housewives, 1917, Mayor Mitchell's Food Committee, hardback..**$35.00**

Home Canning by the One-Period Cold Pack Method, June, 1917, May 1918, 40 pages **$20.00**

Honey for Breakfast, 1950s, qualities of honey, American Honey Institute, 6-page fold-out..............................**$6.00**

Horsford Almanac & Cookbook, 1879, 46 pages........**$50.00**

Hospitality Cookbook, 1960, hardback **$15.00**

Housekeepers Cookbook, 1894, Housekeeping Publishing Co, hardback, 687 pages......................................**$70.00**

How To Bake by the Ration Book - Swan's Down Wartime Recipes, 1943, cakes, quick breads, desserts, 23 pages................**$12.50**

How To Can Meat, Game & Poultry, 1930s, Ball Corporation, 5x8½"..**$10.00**

How To Get the Most Out of the Food You Buy, 1941, National Nutrition Program, General Electric, booklet, 22 pages...**$12.50**

Howdy Doody Cookbook, 1952, Welch Grape Juice Co, softback **$25.00**

Hows & Whys of Cooking, 1938, Evelyn Halliday & Isabel Nobel, University of Chicago Principal, hardback, 252 pages...**$45.00**

The I Hate To Cook Book, 1960, $15.00. (Photo courtesy Col. Bob Allen)

Ida Bailey Allen's Money-Saving Cookbook, 1st edition, 1940, hardback, 481 pages..**$35.00**

International Harvester Refrigerator Recipes, 1949, Irma Harding, International Harvester Co, softback **$10.00**

It's a Picnic, 1st edition, 1969, Nancy Fair McIntyre, hardback, 150 pages...**$15.00**

Jell-O, Through the Menu With Jell-O, 1927, 20 pages ..**$15.00**

Jell-O - It's So Simple, America's Most Famous Dessert, 1922, Rockwell cover...**$20.00**

Jell-O - Joy's of Jello-O, Story of Jell-O & Why It Grew, 1st edition, 1961, 95 pages...**$6.00**

Jewel Tea, Jewel Cookbook, 1950s **$10.00**

Joy of Cooking, 1931, 1936, 1941, 1942, 1943, 1946, 1952, Irma S Rombauer, illustrated by Becker, Bobbs Merril, 1,011 pgs...**$15.00**

Junior League of Charleston, South Carolina; 1953, 7th printing, hardback, 330 pages.....................................**$17.50**

Kitchen Tested Recipes, 1933, Sunbeam Mixmaster, softback **$15.00**

La Cuisine Creole, 1st edition, 1885, Lafcadio Hearn, devoted to New Orleans dishes, hardback, rare..............**$400.00**

Little Cookbook, 1950s, Jean Allen tested recipe, 10 pages **$8.00**

Low Fat, Low Cholesterol Diet, 1951, Gofman Dobin, hardback, 371 pages **$15.00**

Lowney's Chocolate Recipes, 1912, revised hardback, 426 pages...**$40.00**

Making the Most of Your Electrolux With Practical Recipes, 1935, Servel Inc, softback, 48 pages **$12.50**

Margaret Rudkin Pepperidge Farm Cookbook, 1st edition, 1963, hardback, 440 pages.....................................**$25.00**

Men in Aprons, 1944, Lawrence A Keating, hardback, 186 pages...**$25.00**

Mrs Apple Yard's Kitchen, 1942, Louise Andrews Kent, hardback **$35.00**

My Best Recipes, 1934, Mary Hale Martin, Libby McNeill & Libby, softback, 87 pages.....................................**$15.00**

Mystery Chef's Own Cookbook, 1934, 1943, Longman Green, hardback, 366 pages.....................................**$25.00**

New Dishes From Left Overs, 1935, Coral Smith, hardback...**$30.00**

New New Can-Opener Cookbook, 1951, 1952, 1959, 1968, Poppy Cannon, hardback, 314 pages...................**$15.00**

Old World Foods for New World's Families, 1946, spiral bound **$20.00**

Our Favorite Recipes Cookbook, 1930, St Paul's Episcopal Church Parrish, Steubenville OH...........................**$12.00**

Peter Hunt's Cape Cod Cookbook, 1957, 1962, Peter Hunt, hardback, 181 pages...**$15.00**

Peter Pan Peanut Butter Cook Book, 1963, Derby Foods Inc, softback, 26 pages **$6.00**

Pillsbury, 12th Grand National Bake Off - 100 Recipes, 1961, 96 pages **$25.00**

Pillsbury - Best One-Dish Cookbook From Pillsbury's Bake-off Collection, 1960, 53 pages.............................**$8.00**

Pillsbury's 5th Baking Contest - 100 Grand National Recipes, 1954, 96 pages **$15.00**

Pillsbury's 100 Prize-Winning Recipes, 1950, $60.00. (Photo courtesy Col. Bob Allen)

Potluck Party Recipes, 1960, Thora H Campbell, hardback .**$15.00**

Principles of Food Preparation, 1930, Mary D Chambers, hardback **$35.00**

Rawleigh's Good Health Guide & Cookbook, 1929, 32 pages .**$18.00**

Reasons for Using & Recipes for Preparing Woodcock Macaroni, ca 1910, softback **$20.00**

Recipes at Moderate Cost, 2nd edition, 1943, Constance C Hart, spiral bound...**$25.00**

Recipes for Today, 1943, Consumer Service Dept, General Foods, softback, 40 pages.......................................**$12.50**

Royal Baker & Pastry Cook, 1902, Chefs of the New York Cooking School, 44 pages.....................................**$25.00**

Rumford Fruit Cookbook, 1927, Lily Haxworth Wallace, 48 pages...**$18.00**

Salad Bowl, 1929, Martha Adams, Best Foods Co, Home Economics Service, softback **$20.00**

Salads, Sandwiches & Chaffing Dish Dainties, 1st Edition, 1899, Janet McKenzie Hill, hardback, 250+ pages.............**$75.00**

Sara & Aggies Household Handy Book, 1938, softback, 31 pages..**$14.00**

Science of Food & Cookery, 1921 HS Anderson, hardback, 297 pages...**$45.00**

Sixty (60) Minute Chef, 1947, Lillian Beuno McCue & Carol Truax, hardback **$25.00**

Soups, Salads & Desserts - The Story of Dick's Surprise, 1918, Burt Onley's Products, softback, 32 pages............**$20.00**

Specialties of the House, 1960, Elizabeth H Grossman, Simon Schuster, hardback, 96 pages.................................**$15.00**

Spry - Aunt Jenny's Favorite Recipes, 1943, 49 pages ..**$8.00**

Stillmeadow Sampler, 1959, Gladys Tabor, hardback .**$25.00**

Sunbeam Mixmaster, 1957, instructions & recipe book, softback, 42 pages **$6.00**

Teenager's Menu Cookbook, 1969, Charlotte Adams, hardback **$15.00**

Treasure of Great Recipes, 1st edition, 1965, Vincent & Mary Price, Doubleday, hardback, 455 pages................**$75.00**

Treasury of Meat Recipes, 1940, National Live Stock & Meat Board, Dept of Home Economics, softback, 40 pages **$10.00**

Universal CookBook, 1899, Universal Food Chopper, softback **$30.00**

Waterless Cookware Instruction & Recipe Book, 1927, softback **$15.00**

Watkins Cookbook, 1945, Elaine Allen, hardback, spiral, 288 pages..**$17.50**

West Coast Cookbook, Helen Evans Brown, 1952 reprint, hardback, 437 pages...**$12.50**

White House Cookbook, 1887, 1890, Mrs FL Gillette & Hugo Ziemann, c RS Peale for Werner Co, hardback, 570 pages **$75.00**

Williamsburg Art of Cookery, 3rd edition, 1942, Mrs Helen Bullock, hardback, signed...................................**$20.00**

Woman's Day Cook Book of Favorite Recipes, 1963, $5.00. (Photo courtesy Col. Bob Allen)

Woman's Day Cookbook of Sandwiches, Appetizers, 1963, softback..**$5.00**

Woman's Exchange Recipes, 1946, Stella V Hough in collaboration w/Kay Kopera, hardback **$25.00**

Cookie Cutters

In recent years, cookie cutters have come into their own as worthy kitchen collectibles. Prices on many have risen astronomically, but a practiced eye can still sort out a good bargain. Advertising cutters and product premiums, especially in plastic, can still be found without too much effort. Aluminum cutters with painted wood handles are usually worth several dollars each, if in good condition. Red and green are the usual handle colors, but other colors are more highly prized by many. Hallmark plastic cookie cutters, especially those with painted backs, are always worth considering, if in good condition.

Be wary of modern tin cutters being sold for antique. Many present-day tinsmiths chemically antique their cutters, especially those done in a primitive style. These are often sold by others as 'very old.' Look closely because most tinsmiths today sign and date these cutters.

Angel, aluminum w/cut-out handle, 5" **$5.00**

Bird, metal w/red riveted handle (possibly repainted), Holey Tole **$10.00**

Chicken, heavy metal, flat back, 2¾x3½"......................$12.50

Christmas stocking, Aunt Chick's, red plastic.............$30.00

Christmas tree, Santa, star & stocking, red plastic, Aunt Chick's, set of 4, MIB, from $60 to........................$70.00

Cinderella, Prince, Jaq & Gus, red plastic, HRM, set of 4 ..$30.00

Diamond, scalloped edge, tin w/green wood handle, 2⅜x2¼"..$12.50

Dove, heavy metal, flat back w/1 hole, 2½x4¾"........$14.00

Gingerbread boy, red plastic, marked Design Pat 127026, 4¾x3½"...$12.00

Gingerbread house set: roof wall, rectangle, chimney & scallop, copper, Boston Mountain Copper Co, M in VG box...$25.00

Gingerbread man, stainless steel, flat back, lg $20.00

Heart, aluminum, flat back w/riveted handle, Swans Down, 2½"..$15.00

Hebrew alphabet set, tin, 1-pc construction, complete .$32.50

Heinz pickle, tin w/attached loop handle, 5½"............$8.50

Horse, tin, open back, Davis Baking Powder, 3¾x3"..$34.50

Lion, aluminum, flat back, Holey Tole, 2½x4½"........$12.00

Lion, heavy metal, flat back w/1 hole, 3x4"................$14.00

Man stands, wearing hat, tin, open back, marked Germany beneath hands, 5¾"..$55.00

MGM Cartoon Characters, Tom & Jerry, Lucky Ducky, Barney Bear, Droopy & Tuffy, red plastic, Loew's, 1956, MIB..$85.00

Mickey Mouse, boy, girl, star, moon & heart shapes w/in circle, Germany, 6" dia..$100.00

Mighty Morphin Power Ranger, yellow plastic, 3½" $3.00

Miss Piggy & Kermit the Frog, plastic, Henson Associates Inc, 3x3", 4x3", pr..$30.00

Nativity set, red plastic, from 3½" to 4", HRM Made in USA, NM in partial box..$25.00

Old lady, heavy metal, flat back, 10" $10.00

Peanuts Gang, Hallmark, set of 4, MIB.......................$30.00

Rabbit, tin, 4"x5½", $38.00.

Raggedy Ann, red plastic, 4"..$21.50

Reindeer, aluminum w/cut-out handle, 3¼"..................$5.00

Republican elephant, tin w/straight strap handle, 2x3", MIB...$25.00

Santa, aluminum w/cut-out handle, 4x2"......................$7.00

Santa, aluminum w/green wooden knob $10.00

Scalloped flower-like shape, aluminum w/green wood handle, 2⅝" dia..$12.50

Scooby Doo, yellow plastic, Hallmark, 1970s, 4x3"....$15.00

Scottie, heavy copper-colored metal, no back, 1x4½x6¼".$10.00

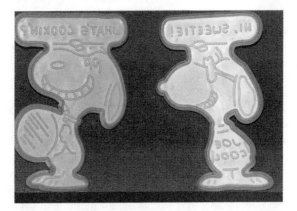

Snoopy, Peanuts Characters Corp c 1958 United Features Syndicate Inc, 1974, set of two, $10.00. (Photo courtesy Rosemary Henry)

Snowflakes, Williams Sonoma, from 1½" to 3", set of 5..$25.00

Snowman, heavy metal, flat back w/3 holes, #55, 6x4"...$28.00

Snowman or Gingerbread Boy, 8", MIB, $10.00.

Turkey, aluminum w/cut-out handle, 3x4" $5.00

Turkey, heavy metal, flat back w/2 holes, 3x4".........$24.00

Watering can, heavy metal, flat back, 4¾x5½" $25.00

Witch on broomstick, copper-colored aluminum, 5¼x5"..$17.00

Cookie Jars

This is an area that for years saw an explosion of interest that resulted in some very high prices. Though the market has leveled off to a large extent, rare cookie jars sell for literally thousands of dollars. Even a common jar from a good manufacturer will fall into the $40.00 to $100.00 price range. At the top of the list are the Black-theme jars, then come the cartoon characters such as Popeye, Howdy Doody, or the Flintstones — in fact, any kind of a figural jar from an American pottery is collectible.

The American Bisque company was one of the largest producers of these jars from 1930 until the 1970s. Many of their jars have no marks at all; those that do are simply marked 'USA,' sometimes with a mold number. But their airbrushed colors are easy to spot, and collectors look for the molded-in wedge-shaped pads on their bases — these say 'American Bisque' to cookie jar buffs about as clearly as if they were marked.

The Brush Pottery (Ohio, 1946 – 71) made cookie jars that were decorated with the airbrush in many of the same colors used by American Bisque. These jars are strongly holding their values, and the rare ones continue to climb in price. McCoy was probably the leader in cookie-jar production. Even some of their very late jars bring high prices. Abingdon, Shawnee, and Red Wing all manufactured cookie jars, and there are a lot of wonderful jars by many other companies. Joyce and Fred Roerig's books *The Collector's Encyclopedia of Cookie Jars, Vols. I, II,* and *III,* cover them all beautifully, and you won't want to miss Ermagene Westfall's *An Illustrated Value Guide to Cookie Jars II,* another wonderful reference. All are published by Collector Books.

Warning! The marketplace abounds with reproductions these days. Roger Jensen of Rockwood, Tennessee, is making a line of cookie jars as well as planters, salt and pepper shakers, and many other items which for years he marked McCoy. Because the 'real' McCoys never registered their trademark, he was able to receive federal approval to begin using this mark in 1992. Though he added '#93' to some of his pieces, the vast majority of his wares are undated. He used old molds, and novice collectors are being fooled into buying the new for 'old' prices. Here are some of his reproductions that you should be aware of: McCoy Mammy, Mammy With Cauliflower, Clown Bust, Dalmatians, Indian Head, Touring Car, and Rocking Horse; Hull Little Red Riding Hood; Pearl China Mammy; and the Mosaic Tile Mammy. Within the past couple of years, though, one of the last owners of the McCoy Pottery Company was able to make a successful appeal to end what they regarded as the fradulent use of their mark (it seems that they at last had it registered), so some of the later Jensen reproductions have been marked 'Brush-McCoy' (though this mark was never used on an authentic cookie jar) and 'B.J. Hull.' Besides these forgeries, several Brush jars have been reproduced as well (see Roerig's books for more information), and there are others. Some reproductions are being made in Taiwan and China, however there are also jars being reproduced here in the states.

Cookie jars from California are getting their fair share of attention right now, and then some! We've included several from companies such as Brayton Laguna, Treasure Craft, Vallona Starr, and Twin Winton. Westfield's and Roerig's books have information on all of these. Advisor Mike Ellis is the author of *Collector's Guide to Don Winton Designs* (Collector Books); and another of our advisors, Bernice Stamper, has written *Vallona Starr Ceramics,* which we're sure you will enjoy.

Advisors: Jim and Beverly Mangus, Shawnee (See Directory, Shawnee); Mike Ellis, Twin Winton (See Directory, Twin Winton); Bernice Stamper, Vallona Star (See Directory, Vallona Star); Lois Wildman, Vandor (See Directory, Vandor).

Newsletter: *Cookie Jarrin' With Joyce*
R.R. 2, Box 504
Walterboro, SC 29488

A Little Company, Bella (Dancer), 1955, 12" **$150.00**
A Little Company, Carmella, limited edition of 750, 1997, 13½" **$180.00**
A Little Company, Duet, limited edition of 750, 1997, 14" .**$190.00**
A Little Company, Ruby, limited edition of 500, 1995, 13".**$180.00**
Abingdon, Bo Peep, #694, from $250 to **$275.00**
Abingdon, Choo Choo (Locomotive), #651 .... **$150.00**
Abingdon, Clock, #653, 1949 .... **$100.00**
Abingdon, Daisy, #677, 1949 .... **$50.00**
Abingdon, Fat Boy, #495 .... **$250.00**
Abingdon, Hippo, decor, #549, 1942 .... **$325.00**
Abingdon, Hobby Horse, 3602 .... **$185.00**
Abingdon, Humpty Dumpty, decor, #663 .... **$250.00**
Abingdon, Jack-in-Box, #611 .... **$275.00**
Abingdon, Little Girl, #693, from $60 to **$75.00**
Abingdon, Miss Muffet, 3622 .... **$205.00**
Abingdon, Money Bag, #588 .... **$75.00**
Abingdon, Mother Goose, #695 .... **$295.00**
Abingdon, Old Lady, decor, #471, minimum value ..**$300.00**
Abingdon, Pineapple, #664 .... **$95.00**
Abingdon, Pumpkin, #674, 1949, minimum value **$325.00**
Abingdon, Three Bears, #696, from $90 to **$100.00**
Abingdon, Wigwam, #665 .... **$250.00**
Abingdon, Windmill, #678, from $200 to **$225.00**
Advertising, Archway Van, Made in China on foil label, 5¾x10" **$16.00**
Advertising, Betty Crocker, cylinder, made in Taiwan, Welcome Industrial Corp **$90.00**
Advertising, Big Boy, paper label: Big Boy Elias Bros Inc made by Wolfe Studio Michigan c 1997 .... **$200.00**
Advertising, Chips Ahoy, cylinder **$45.00**
Advertising, Doughboy, cylinder, glass w/glass lid, Anchor Hocking (unmarked) **$18.00**
Advertising, Dryer's Grand Ice Cream, cylinder, Treasure Craft **$95.00**
Advertising, Entenmann's Chef, Made in Brazil, marked JCK, 1992 .... **$250.00**
Advertising, Hard Rock Hotel Bear, Lotus 1997 China, paper label: Handcrafted...For Lotus Made in China **$36.00**
Advertising, Keebler Hollow Tree, Keebler Co 1981, manufactured by Friendship Pottery ca 1993 ....**$40.00**
Advertising, Montezuma, Olmeca Tequila on front of headband otherwise unmarked **$175.00**
Advertising, MooTown Snackers, comic cow w/sign & apron **$175.00**
Advertising, Mother's Oats, Blackbird Pottery Armana IA, 1992 limited edition **$225.00**
Advertising, Mrs Field's Chocolate Chip, Niccum **$175.00**

Advertising, Nick at Nite Television, Treasure Craft, w/certificate of authenticity **$600.00**

Advertising, Pillsbury Best Flour Sack, Benjamin & Medwin, 1988 ....**$75.00**

Advertising, Quaker Graindrops, marked Weiss Hand Painted Made in Brazil c 1981 The Quaker Oats Co......**$225.00**

Advertising, Stack of Oreo Cookies, The Nabisco Classics Collection, Made in China.................................**$30.00**

American Bisque, Bear, #CJ-701 ....**$60.00**

American Bisque, Chest, #CJ562 ....**$175.00**

American Bisque, Chick, #CJ-702 ....**$125.00**

American Bisque, French Poodle, #CJ-751 ....**$125.00**

American Bisque, Hen with Chick, marked USA, 9", $150.00. (Photo courtesy Fred and Joyce Roerig)

American Bisque, Puppy, #CJ-754 ....**$70.00**

American Bisque, Teakettle (Martha & George), embossed couple on side, green w/gold trim.................................**$50.00**

Artistic Potteries, Chef, #30, 10½" **$475.00**

Artistic Potteries, Mammy, #31, 9½".................................**$675.00**

Benjamin & Medwin, Betty Boop, King Features/Fleischer Studios, 1995 ....**$35.00**

Benjamin & Medwin, Charlie Brown, Made in Taiwan .**$45.00**

Benjamin & Medwin, Felix the Cat, Felix the Cat Productions, Taiwan, 1991 ....**$50.00**

Benjamin & Medwin, Lucy, Made in Taiwan.................................**$45.00**

Benjamin & Medwin, Snoopy Doghouse, Made in Taiwan **$40.00**

Benjamin & Medwin, Snoopy Pilot, Snoopy pilot, seated w/goggles, Made in China **$45.00**

Brayton Laguna, chicken shape, 10".................................**$400.00**

Brayton Laguna, Wedding Ring Granny (+) **$500.00**

Brush, Antique Touring Car.................................**$700.00**

Brush, Boy w/Balloons **$800.00**

Brush, Chick in Nest (+) **$400.00**

Brush, Cinderella Pumpkin, #W32 ....**$250.00**

Brush, Circus Horse, green (+).................................**$950.00**

Brush, Clown, yellow pants.................................**$200.00**

Brush, Clown Bust, #W49 ....**$300.00**

Brush, Cookie House, #W31.................................**$125.00**

Brush, Covered Wagon, dog finial, #W30 (+), minimum value **$550.00**

Brush, Cow w/Cat on Back, brown, #W10 (+).........**$125.00**

Brush, Cow w/Cat on Back, purple (+), minimum value **$1,000.00**

Brush, Davy Crockett, no gold, marked USA (+)......**$300.00**

Brush, Dog & Basket.................................**$250.00**

Brush, Donkey Cart, ears down, gray, #W33 ....**$400.00**

Brush, Donkey Cart, ears up, #W33, minimum value .**$800.00**

Brush, Elephant With Ice Cream Cone, has been reproduced, $500.00. (Photo courtesy Ermagene Westfall)

Brush, Elephant w/Monkey on Back, minimum value .**$5,000.00**

Brush, Fish, #W52 (+) **$500.00**

Brush, Formal Pig, gold trim, #W7 Brush USA (+) ...**$475.00**

Brush, Formal Pig, no gold, green hat & coat (+)....**$300.00**

Brush, Gas Lamp, #K1.................................**$75.00**

Brush, Granny, pink apron, blue dots on skirt.........**$325.00**

Brush, Granny, plain skirt (+), minimum value **$400.00**

Brush, Happy Bunny, white, #W25.................................**$225.00**

Brush, Hen on Basket, unmarked.................................**$125.00**

Brush, Hillbilly Frog (+), minimum value **$4,500.00**

Brush, Humpty Dumpty, w/beany & bow tie (+).....**$275.00**

Brush, Humpty Dumpty, w/peaked hat & shoes......**$225.00**

Brush, Laughing Hippo, #227 (+).................................**$750.00**

Brush, Little Angel (+).................................**$800.00**

Brush, Little Boy Blue, gold trim, #K25, sm.............**$700.00**

Brush, Little Boy Blue, no gold, #K24 USA, sm........**$550.00**

Brush, Night Owl.................................**$125.00**

Brush, Old Clock, #W10.................................**$150.00**

Brush, Old Shoe, #W23 (+) **$125.00**

Brush, Panda, #W21 (+).................................**$250.00**

Brush, Peter, Peter Pumpkin Eater, #W24.................................**$300.00**

Brush, Peter Pan, gold trim, lg (+).................................**$800.00**

Brush, Peter Pan, no gold, sm.................................**$550.00**

Brush, Puppy Police (+).................................**$585.00**

Brush, Raggedy Ann, #W16 ....**$475.00**

Brush, Sitting Pig (+).................................**$400.00**

Brush, Smiling Bear, #W46 (+) **$350.00**

Brush, Squirrel on Log, #W26.................................**$100.00**

Brush, Squirrel w/Top Hat, black coat & hat...........**$275.00**

Brush, Stylized Owl...**$350.00**
Brush, Stylized Siamese, #W41 ....**$450.00**
Brush, Teddy Bear, feet apart.................................**$250.00**
Brush, Teddy Bear, feet together.............................**$200.00**
Brush, Treasure Chest, #W28.................................**$170.00**

California Originals, Little Red Riding Hood, #320 USA, from $325.00 to $375.00. (Photo courtesy Fred and Joyce Roerig)

Clay Art, Amazing Grace, lady singing & clapping hands, 1995 ....**$35.00**
Clay Art, Barnyard Santa, Made in Taiwan, 1993........**$45.00**
Clay Art, Catfish, Made in Philippines, 1990................**$45.00**
Clay Art, Humpty Dumpty, 1991 ....**$125.00**
Clay Art, Jazz Player, man playing sax, 1995...............**$35.00**
Clay Art, Mama Cat, Clay Art San Francisco, Made in Taiwan, 1992 ....**$45.00**
Clay Art, Marilyn Monroe, Made in China, 1996 ....**$60.00**
Clay Art, Ragtime Piano Player, 1995 ....**$50.00**
Clay Art, Road Hog, Made in China, 1995...................**$50.00**
Clay Art, Teddy Bear, Made in Taiwan, 1991 ....**$45.00**
Clay Art, Wizard of Oz, Turner Entertainment Co, MGM 1966 c 1990 ....**$80.00**
Cleminson, Christmas Cookie House, 7".....................**$35.00**

Cleminson, King of Hearts, from $300.00 to $325.00. (Photo courtesy Fred and Joyce Roerig)

Cleminson, Mother's Best...**$375.00**
Cleminson, Potbellied Stove **$225.00**

DeForest of California, Barrel, Cookies on front, #553..**$30.00**
DeForest of California, Clown, marked on sides of shoes in back **$175.00**
DeForest of California, Cookie King, 1957, minimum value..**$800.00**
DeForest of California, Elephant, heart on chest **$45.00**
DeForest of California, Henny (Dandee Hen)...........**$225.00**
DeForest of California, Lil Angel, 1947 ....**$775.00**
DeForest of California, Owl..**$55.00**
DeForest of California, Padre, Thou Shalt Not Steal along bottom of robe **$95.00**
DeForest of California, Pig, Goodies on tummy, 1956 .**$125.00**
DeForest of California, Pig Head, unmarked..............**$55.00**
DeForest of California, Poodle, 1960 ....**$50.00**
DeForest of California, Puppy **$55.00**
DeForest of California, Ranger Bear...........................**$45.00**
Doranne of California, Bear Essentials, #BE-19..........**$60.00**
Doranne of California, Cow on Moon, #J 2, USA.....**$375.00**
Doranne of California, Doctor, #CJ-130 ....**$275.00**
Doranne of California, Donkey, red tie, #CJ-108 ....**$60.00**
Doranne of California, Elephant, #CJ-144 ....**$60.00**
Doranne of California, School Bus, #CJ-120..............**$175.00**
Enesco, Bear, holds lavender heart lettered Cookies, 1993 ....**$95.00**
Enesco, Clown Head, Japan, #E-5835 ....**$150.00**
Enesco, Frosty Snowman, Made in Taiwan ROC, 1994 .**$60.00**
Enesco, Lucy 'n Me Bear, Lucy King.........................**$150.00**
Enesco, Mary's Moo Moo, Mary Rhyner, Made in Taiwan, 1993 ....**$50.00**
Enesco, Mickey Mouse in face of clock, M **$95.00**
Enesco, Superman, Warner Bros, 1997, Made in China...**$40.00**
Enesco, Sweet Pickles Alligator, 1981 ....**$175.00**

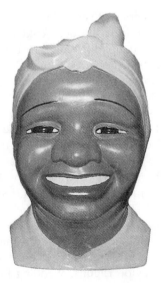

Gilner, Mammy Head, unmarked, from $1,200.00 to $1,400.00. (Photo courtesy Fred and Joyce Roerig)

Goebel, Cat, head only, 1983 ....**$125.00**
Goebel, Hilda Hippo, Richard Scarry, 1988..............**$125.00**
Goebel, Lion, head only, 1983....................................**$80.00**
Goebel, Owl, head only, 1983....................................**$80.00**
Goebel, Pig, head only, 1983 ....**$125.00**
Hallmark, Friendship Garden, Mary Engelbreit, 1993.**$80.00**

Hallmark, Maxine, J Wagner $25.00
Hallmark, Trevor Bear, Made in China, 1994 ....$35.00
Hanna-Barbera, Barney Rubble $55.00
Hanna-Barbera, Dino & Pebbles $55.00
Hanna-Barbera, Flintstone House................................$55.00
Hanna-Barbera, Fred Flintstone $55.00
Happy Memories, Elvis Presley, black leather jacket & guitar $300.00
Happy Memories, Hopalong Cassidy & Topper, w/gun, 15½", minimum value $400.00
Happy Memories, James Dean, w/cigarette, 1994 ....$315.00
Happy Memories, Marilyn Monroe, 1995, 15" $315.00
Happy Memories, Scarlet O'Hara, green dress, 1996, 13¼" $300.00
Hirsch, Basketball, WH Hirsch Mfg Co Made in USA $125.00
Hirsch, Chef, WH Hirsch Mfg Co USA Los Angeles Calif ...$275.00
Hirsch, Cow, marked WH Hirsch Co Calif USA $150.00
Hirsch, Gingerbread House, unmarked $60.00
Hirsch, Nun, on knees w/rosary $325.00
Hirsch, Peck o' Cookies, hen figural w/tail feather finial, marked..$225.00
Hirsch, Planet, rocket finial, marked WH '55 c $85.00
Hirsch, Rabbit, marked WH c '58................................$40.00
Hirsch, Treasure Chest, all brown, marked WH c '58...$70.00
JC Miller, Andrew McClellan, Black military figure...$125.00
JC Miller, Sarah, Black lady w/hair covered w/red scarf tied in lg bow, hand to face, head & shoulders only .$95.00
JC Miller, Sister Ruth, singing praises in blue choir robe, gold trim...$50.00
JC Penney Home Collection, Goldilocks & Three Bears .$38.00
JC Penney Home Collection, Mary Had a Little Lamb ..$38.00
JC Penney Home Collection, Old Woman in Shoe $38.00
JC Penney Home Collection, Santa & Rudolph, Made in China $35.00
Lefton, Bluebird Love Nest, #7525, 11" $250.00
Lefton, Bossie Cow, #6594.......................................$150.00
Lefton, Boy, chef's hat, head only, #396, 8⅜" $225.00
Lefton, French Girl, 31174, paper label, 9" $300.00
Lefton, Girl, hair covered w/scarf, bow finial, #397, 8⅜"..$225.00
Lefton, Scotch Girl, plaid band along skirt, paper label, #1173, 9" $300.00
MacMillan, Raggedy Ann, 1993, Taiwan, 1993 ....$95.00
Maddux of California, Baby Birds on Bough, from $45 to $55.00
Maddux of California, Chipmunk on Stump, C Romanelli, from $130 to...$145.00
Maddux of California, Queen, #2104, from $150 to .$175.00
Maddux of California, Strawberry................................$25.00
Maurice Ceramics, Mammy (Nanna reproduction), marked WD 40 USA, 11"...$35.00
May Department Store Company, Bear, 1996.............$30.00
May Department Store Company, Stocking, Made in China, 1996 ....$38.00
McCoy, Animal Crackers..$100.00
McCoy, Apollo, #260, 1970-71, minimum value.....$1,000.00
McCoy, Apple, 1967...$60.00
McCoy, Asparagus...$50.00

McCoy, Barrel, Cookies sign on lid............................$75.00
McCoy, Basket of Eggs..$40.00
McCoy, Basket of Potatoes..$40.00

McCoy, Bear With Cookie in Vest, no cookies, 1945, from $75.00 to $85.00. (Photo courtesy Fred and Joyce Roerig)

McCoy, Betsy Baker (+), from $250 to $300.00
McCoy, Black Kettle, w/immovable bail, hand-painted flowers $40.00
McCoy, Blue Willow Pitcher $75.00
McCoy, Bobby Baker..$65.00
McCoy, Burlap Bag, red bird on lid............................$50.00
McCoy, Caboose $150.00
McCoy, Cat on Coal Scuttle $175.00
McCoy, Chef, donut (+) $250.00
McCoy, Chilly Willy $85.00
McCoy, Chipmunk...$125.00
McCoy, Christmas Tree, minimum value $800.00
McCoy, Churn, 2 bands..$35.00
McCoy, Clown Bust (+)...$75.00
McCoy, Clyde Dog..$250.00
McCoy, Coalby Cat...$375.00
McCoy, Coca-Cola Can...$100.00
McCoy, Coca-Cola Jug...$85.00
McCoy, Coffee Mug...$45.00
McCoy, Colonial Fireplace $85.00
McCoy, Cookie Bank, 1961..$165.00
McCoy, Cookie Boy...$225.00
McCoy, Cookie Jug, cork stopper, brown & white.....$40.00
McCoy, Cookie Jug, double loop $35.00
McCoy, Cookie Jug, single loop, 2-tone green rope...$35.00
McCoy, Cookie Log, squirrel finial, from $35 to $45.00
McCoy, Cookie Mug...$45.00
McCoy, Cookie Safe...$65.00
McCoy, Cookstove, black or white..............................$35.00
McCoy, Corn, single ear...$175.00
McCoy, Corn, standing ears in row, yellow or white, 1977 ....$85.00
McCoy, Covered Wagon...$95.00
McCoy, Cylinder, red flowers.....................................$45.00
McCoy, Dalmatians in Rocking Chair (+) $275.00
McCoy, Davy Crockett (+) $50.00
McCoy, Dog on Basketweave, from $75 to $90.00

McCoy, Drum, red $90.00
McCoy, Dutch Boy..$65.00
McCoy, Dutch Girl, boy on reverse, rare..................$250.00
McCoy, Dutch Treat Barn..$50.00
McCoy, Eagle on Basket, from $35 to.......................$50.00
McCoy, Early American Chest (Chiffoniere) $85.00
McCoy, Elephant...$200.00
McCoy, Engine, black..$175.00
McCoy, Flowerpot, plastic flower on top $500.00
McCoy, Forbidden Fruit, from $65 to.......................$90.00
McCoy, Freddy Gleep (+), minimum value..............$500.00
McCoy, Friendship 7..$200.00
McCoy, Frog on Stump $75.00
McCoy, Fruit in Bushel Basket, from $65 to..............$80.00
McCoy, Gingerbread Boy...$75.00
McCoy, Grandfather Clock $90.00
McCoy, Granny..$120.00
McCoy, Hamm's Bear (+)..$225.00
McCoy, Happy Face $80.00
McCoy, Hen on Nest, from $85 to $95.00
McCoy, Hillbilly Bear, rare (+), minimum value $900.00
McCoy, Hobby Horse (+), from $125 to...................$150.00
McCoy, Hot Air Balloon...$40.00
McCoy, Indian, brown (+) $350.00
McCoy, Indian, majolica..$400.00
McCoy, Kangaroo, blue..$300.00
McCoy, Keebler Tree House $70.00
McCoy, Kettle, bronze, 1961 ....$40.00
McCoy, Kissing Penguins, from $100 to $125.00
McCoy, Kitten on Basketweave $90.00
McCoy, Kittens on Ball of Yarn $85.00
McCoy, Koala Bear $85.00
McCoy, Kookie Kettle, black $35.00
McCoy, Lamb on Basketweave....................................$90.00
McCoy, Liberty Bell $75.00
McCoy, Little Clown $75.00
McCoy, Lollipops..$80.00
McCoy, Mammy, Cookies on base, white (+) $150.00
McCoy, Milk Can, Spirit of '76.................................$45.00
McCoy, Modern...$65.00
McCoy, Monk $50.00
McCoy, Mother Goose..$150.00

McCoy, Mouse on Clock, $40.00.

McCoy, Mrs & Mrs Owl, from $75 to.........................$90.00
McCoy, Mushroom on Stump $55.00
McCoy, Nursery, decal of Humpty Dumpty, from $70
    to $80.00
McCoy, Oaken Bucket, from $25 to............................$45.00
McCoy, Orange $55.00
McCoy, Owl..$50.00
McCoy, Pear, 1952 ....$85.00
McCoy, Pears on Basketweave $70.00
McCoy, Pepper, yellow..$40.00
McCoy, Picnic Basket, from $65 to $75.00
McCoy, Pig, winking...$300.00
McCoy, Pineapple $80.00
McCoy, Pineapple, Modern..$90.00
McCoy, Pirate's Chest, from $125 to $145.00
McCoy, Popeye, cylinder $200.00
McCoy, Potbelly Stove, black.....................................$30.00
McCoy, Puppy, w/sign $85.00
McCoy, Raggedy Ann $110.00
McCoy, Red Barn, cow in door, rare, minimum value ..$350.00
McCoy, Rooster, white, 1970-1974............................$60.00
McCoy, Rooster, 1955-1957 ....$95.00
McCoy, Round w/Hand-Painted Leaves......................$45.00
McCoy, Sad Clown..$85.00
McCoy, Snoopy on Doghouse (+), marked United Features
    Syndicate...$200.00
McCoy, Snow Bear, from $65 to.................................$75.00
McCoy, Spaniel in Doghouse, bird finial...................$250.00
McCoy, Strawberry, 1955-1957..................................$65.00
McCoy, Strawberry, 1971-1975..................................$45.00
McCoy, Teapot, 1972...$60.00
McCoy, Tepee, slant top $350.00
McCoy, Tepee, straight top (+)..................................$300.00
McCoy, Tilt Pitcher, black w/roses.............................$50.00
McCoy, Timmy Tortoise $45.00
McCoy, Tomato $60.00
McCoy, Touring Car...$100.00
McCoy, Traffic Light..$50.00
McCoy, Tudor Cookie House $125.00
McCoy, Tulip on Flowerpot......................................$150.00
McCoy, Turkey, natural colors..................................$250.00
McCoy, Upside Down Bear, panda $50.00
McCoy, WC Fields $200.00
McCoy, Wedding Jar $90.00
McCoy, Windmill...$100.00
McCoy, Wishing Well..$40.00
McCoy, Woodsy Owl, from $250 to $300.00
McCoy, Wren House, side lid $175.00
McCoy, Yosemite Sam, cylinder $150.00
McMe, Cathy, 1994 ....$150.00
McMe, Dale Evans, 1994 ....$160.00
McMe, Florence Mildred, prayerful girl beside baby
    buggy $125.00
McMe, Gene Autry, 1995..$195.00
McMe, Larry, Curley or Moe, 1996, ea $130.00
McMe, Oliver Hardy, 1996 ....$125.00
McMe, Roy Rogers, 1994..$160.00

McMe, Stan Laurel, 1996 ....**$125.00**

McMe, Trigger, w/Roy on back, rearing, 1995 ....**$225.00**

McMe Productions, Uncle Justin, Black face w/yellow hat, 1993 ....**$90.00**

Metlox, Apple, Golden Delicious, 9½", from $150 to ...**$175.00**

Metlox, Barn, Mac's, from $250 to **$275.00**

Metlox, Barrel, w/green apple lid, from $100 to **$125.00**

Metlox, Barrel, w/red apple lid (aka Apple Barrel), 3¾-qt, 11" **$75.00**

Metlox, Basket, Natural; w/cookie lid (aka Cookie Basket), 10½", from $40 to **$50.00**

Metlox, Basket, white w/basket lid, from $35 to **$45.00**

Metlox, Bear, Ballerina, from $100 to **$125.00**

Metlox, Bear, Beau, from $60 to **$75.00**

Metlox, Bear, Panda, w/lollipop, from $400 to **$450.00**

Metlox, Bear, Teddy, white, 3-qt, from $40 to **$45.00**

Metlox, Beaver, Bucky, from $125 to.........................**$150.00**

Metlox, Bluebird on Stump, stain finish, from $65 to.**$75.00**

Metlox, Cat, Calico, green w/pink ribbon, from $175 to .**$200.00**

Metlox, Children of the World, Cookie Creations Series, 2-qt, from $125 to...**$150.00**

Metlox, Cookie Boy, 9", from $275 to **$300.00**

Metlox, Debutante, minimum value...........................**$400.00**

Metlox, Dina-Stegosaurus, Year of Dinosaur Series, from $150 to **$175.00**

Metlox, Dog, Bassett, from $325 to...........................**$350.00**

Metlox, Duck, Francine, from $225 to **$250.00**

Metlox, Duck Blues, from $100 to **$125.00**

Metlox, Dutch Girl, minimum value...........................**$350.00**

Metlox, Egg Basket, from $175 to **$200.00**

Metlox, Flamingo, minimum value.............................**$350.00**

Metlox, Frog, The Prince, from $175 to.....................**$200.00**

Metlox, Goose, Lucy, from $125 to **$150.00**

Metlox, Granada Green, 3-qt, from $35 to **$45.00**

Metlox, Grape, from $200 to **$250.00**

Metlox, Hen, blue, from $250 to **$300.00**

Metlox, Hen & Chick, minimum value **$350.00**

Metlox, Humpty Dumpty, no feet, 11", minimum value..**$500.00**

Metlox, Humpty Dumpty, seated, w/feet, from $250 to ..**$275.00**

Metlox, Kitten, says Meow (aks Tattle-Tale), 2¾-qt, 10", from $125 to **$150.00**

Metlox, Lighthouse, from $275 to **$300.00**

Metlox, Little Red Riding Hood, minimum value...**$1,250.00**

Metlox, Loveland, from $65 to...................................**$75.00**

Metlox, Mammy, Cook, blue, from $475 to..............**$500.00**

Metlox, Mammy, Cook, red, from $725 to.................**$750.00**

Metlox, Mediteree, 2½-qt, from $35 to **$45.00**

Metlox, Merry Go Round, from $250 to **$275.00**

Metlox, Mona-Monoclonius, Year of the Dinosaur, aqua or rose, ea from $150 to **$175.00**

Metlox, Mouse, Chef Pierre, from $75 to...................**$100.00**

Metlox, Mushroom Cottage, from $225 to **$250.00**

Metlox, Owl, brown, 2½-qt, from $90 to....................**$95.00**

Metlox, Pear, from $125 to..**$150.00**

Metlox, Penguin, Frosty, short or long coat, from $150 to **$175.00**

Metlox, Pig, Slenderella, from $125 to **$150.00**

Metlox, Pineapple, 3¾-qt, from $75 to **$100.00**

Metlox, Pretty Anne, 2½-qt, from $175 to **$200.00**

Metlox, Rabbit, Easter Bunny, solid chocolate, minimum.**$350.00**

Metlox, Rabbit on Cabbage, 3-qt, 10", from $125 to.**$150.00**

Metlox, Raccoon, Cookie Bandit, bisque, 2¾-qt, from $125 to **$150.00**

Metlox, Rag Doll, girl, 2½-qt, from $175 to..............**$200.00**

Metlox, Rex-Tyrannosaurus, Year of the Dinosaur Series, from $150 to **$175.00**

Metlox, Rocking Horse, 11", minimum value...........**$450.00**

Metlox, Santa Head, from $350 to............................**$375.00**

Metlox, Squirrel on Pine Cone, stain finish, 3-qt, 11", minimum value **$400.00**

Metlox, Strawberry, 3½-qt, 9½", from $85 to **$95.00**

Metlox, Sunflowers, Cookie Creations Series, 2-qt, from $65 to..**$85.00**

Metlox, Topsy, solid blue apron, from $425 to.........**$450.00**

Metlox, Walrus, brown & white, from $350 to.........**$375.00**

Metlox, Whale, white, from $300 to.........................**$350.00**

Metlox, Woodpecker on Acorn, 3-qt, from $375 to..**$400.00**

New Rose Collection, Cotton Ginny, girl in basket of cotton **$125.00**

New Rose Collection, John Henry............................**$135.00**

New Rose Collection, Mammy, signed Rose Saxby **$55.00**

New Rose Collection, Sambo & Tiger.......................**$150.00**

New Rose Collection, Watermelon Girl **$135.00**

North American Ceramics, Airplane, movable propellers, unmarked **$625.00**

North American Ceramics, Corvette, marked ACC J9 c 1986, NAC USA in circular design.......................**$150.00**

North American Ceramics, Double-Decker Bus, Piccadilly Circus & State Street on side panels **$375.00**

North American Ceramics, Engine, NAC USA, #DCJ32, c 1987...**$70.00**

North American Ceramics, Motorcycle w/Rider, Dave Deal, c 1988, minimum value...**$750.00**

Pfaltzgraff, Benjamin Franklin, limited edition **$275.00**

Pfaltzgraff, character face, Muggsy Line, minimum value .**$250.00**

Pfaltzgraff, Star Trek, cylinder, 1993.........................**$45.00**

Purinton, Fruit, red trim, oval, 9"..............................**$60.00**

Purinton, Heather Plaid, oval, 9½"............................**$60.00**

Purinton, Normandy Plaid, oval, 9½".........................**$60.00**

Red Wing, Bob White, unmarked **$200.00**

Red Wing, Carousel, unmarked.................................**$350.00**

Red Wing, Crock, white **$80.00**

Red Wing, Dutch Girl (Katrina), yellow w/brown trim.**$175.00**

Red Wing, Friar Tuck, cream w/brown, marked **$175.00**

Red Wing, Friar Tuck, green, marked.......................**$175.00**

Red Wing, Friar Tuck, yellow, unmarked.................**$150.00**

Red Wing, Grapes, cobalt or dark purple, ea **$275.00**

Red Wing, Grapes, green...**$135.00**

Red Wing, Jack Frost, short, unmarked **$250.00**

Red Wing, Jack Frost, tall, unmarked.......................**$300.00**

Red Wing, King of Tarts, multicolored, marked (+) .**$325.00**

Red Wing, King of Tarts, white, unmarked..............**$200.00**

Red Wing, Peasant design, embossed/painted figures on aqua **$110.00**

Red Wing, Peasant design, embossed/painted figures on brown $120.00

Red Wing, Pierre (chef), blue, brown or pink, unmarked, ea $150.00

Red Wing, Pineapple, yellow $135.00

Regal, Cat, from $345 to......$385.00

Regal, Churn Boy $250.00

Regal, Clown, green collar, from $650 to $675.00

Regal, Cookie Barn, Old McDonald's Farm, from $295 to......$325.00

Regal, Davy Crockett, from $450 to $495.00

Regal, Diaper Pin Pig, from $450 to $540.00

Regal, Dutch Girl, from $600 to $655.00

Regal, Dutch Girl, peach trim......$720.00

Regal, Fi-Fi Poodle, from $600 to......$655.00

Regal, Fisherman, from $650 to......$720.00

Regal, French Chef, from $350 to......$400.00

Regal, Goldilocks (+)......$340.00

Regal, Harpo Marx $1,080.00

Regal, Hobby Horse, from $250 to $270.00

Regal, Hubert Lion, from $720 to $850.00

Regal, Humpty Dumpty, red......$250.00

Regal, Little Miss Muffet, from $315 to $350.00

Regal, Majorette, from $425 to......$500.00

Regal, Oriental Lady w/Baskets, from $585 to......$625.00

Regal, Quaker Oats $115.00

Regal, Three Bears......$175.00

Regal, Toby Cookies, unmarked, from $675 to......$700.00

Regal, Tulip......$270.00

Regal, Uncle Mistletoe......$765.00

Robinson-Ransbottom, apple decor on orange, marked RRPCo Roseville Ohio 312, 1970s, 8", from $100 to......$125.00

Robinson-Ransbottom, blue spongeware, marked RRPCo Roseville O, 1960, 10", from $30 to......$40.00

Robinson-Ransbottom, Bud, Army man, brown, flat unglazed bottom 1942-43, 12", from $150 to......$175.00

Robinson-Ransbottom, Chicken, brown w/red comb, 1958, 11", from $100 to......$125.00

Robinson-Ransbottom, Chicken, white w/red comb, marked RRPCo Roseville O USA, 1958, 11", from $125 to......$135.00

Robinson-Ransbottom, circus tigers on lid, vertical striped bottom, marked RRPCo Roseville Ohio, 1955, 10", from $75 to......$100.00

Robinson-Ransbottom, Cow Jumped Over the Moon, no mark, 1949, 1957-59, 11", from $125 to......$150.00

Robinson-Ransbottom, Dutch Boy, marked RRPCo Roseville Ohio #423, 1956, 13", from $175 to......$200.00

Robinson-Ransbottom, Dutch Girl, marked RRPCo Roseville Ohio, 1956, 12", from $175 to......$200.00

Robinson-Ransbottom, Dutch Girl, w/gold trim, marked RRPCo Roseville Ohio, 1956, 12", from $250 to.$300.00

Robinson-Ransbottom, Hootie, marked RRPCo Roseville Ohio, #354, 1954-59, 12", from $100 to......$125.00

Robinson-Ransbottom, Jack, Navy man, in blue w/white hat, flat unglazed bottom, 1942-43, 12", from $175 to......$200.00

Robinson-Ransbottom, Joco the Monkey, from $325.00 to $375.00. (Photo courtesy Fred and Joyce Roerig)

Robinson-Ransbottom, Log w/Squirrel, marked RRPCo Roseville O, from $250 to $300.00

Robinson-Ransbottom, Ol' King Cole, red coat, 10½", from $350 to......$400.00

Robinson-Ransbottom, Ol' King Cole, yellow coat, 10½", from $200 to......$225.00

Robinson-Ransbottom, Oscar, green hat, Oscar on bottom, 10", from $65 to $75.00

Robinson-Ransbottom, Peter, Peter, Pumpkin Eater, w/gold trim, 1957-59, 8½", from $225 to......$250.00

Robinson-Ransbottom, Plymouth Colony, white w/blue decor, plain bottom, 1970, 8", from $50 to......$60.00

Robinson-Ransbottom, Santa Claus, Merry Christmas to All in red, marked USA, 1960s, 8½", from $150 to $200.00

Robinson-Ransbottom, Sheriff Pig, no mark, glazed bottom, 1954-59, 12", from $100 to......$125.00

Robinson-Ransbottom, Whale, white, pink & blue w/yellow eyelids, blue hat, RRPCo Roseville O, 1959, 8", from $600 to......$700.00

Shawnee, Bean Pot, snowflake, marked USA $70.00

Shawnee, Drum Major, gold trim, USA 10, $700.00. (Photo courtesy Joyce and Fred Roerig)

Shawnee, Dutch Boy, cold paint, marked USA......$70.00

Shawnee, Dutch Boy (Happy), blue crisscross stripes w/decals & gold, marked USA $385.00

Shawnee, Dutch Boy (Happy), patches w/gold, marked USA......$525.00

Shawnee, Dutch Girl, cold paint, marked USA **$140.00**

Shawnee, Dutch Girl, quilted skirt, airbrushed green, marked Great Northern #1026 ....**$420.00**

Shawnee, Fruit Basket, marked Shawnee #84 ....**$225.00**

Shawnee, Muggsy the Dog, blue scarf, hand-painted black detail w/gold, marked Pat Muggsy USA **$910.00**

Shawnee, Puss 'n Boots, long tail, decals w/gold, marked Pat Puss 'n Boots **$630.00**

Shawnee, Sailor Boy, black scarf, marked USA **$140.00**

Shawnee, Sailor Boy, gold scarf w/decals, marked USA .**$770.00**

Shawnee, Smiley the Pig, clover buds, marked Pat Smiley USA **$500.00**

Shawnee, Smiley the Pig, shamrocks, green bib, marked USA **$280.00**

Shawnee, Smiley the Pig, strawberries w/gold, marked USA **$700.00**

Shawnee, Winnie the Pig, apples w/gold, marked USA ..**$910.00**

Shawnee, Winnie the Pig, peach collar, marked Pat Winnie USA **$350.00**

Shawnee, Winnie the Pig, peach collar w/gold, marked Pat Winnie USA **$700.00**

Sierra Vista, Elephant, marked **$150.00**

Sigma, Agatha, Tastesetter, David Straus **$200.00**

Sigma, Beaver Fireman, Cara Marks...the Tastesetter ..**$275.00**

Sigma, Chef w/Dog, Tastesetter C MCMLXXXIV **$95.00**

Sigma, Chick, Cara marks for Sigma the Tastesetter **$95.00**

Sigma, Cubs Bear, Krazy Kids & Kritters...MCMLXXXIV .**$150.00**

Sigma, Fat Cat, Tastesetter MCMLXXXV **$325.00**

Sigma, Goose, paper label, 353 ....**$95.00**

Sigma, Hortense, Tastesetter c By Sigma, David Strauss **$175.00**

Sigma, Kabuki, from $125.00 to $175.00. (Photo courtesy Ermagene Westfall)

Sigma, Kermit in TV, Henson Assoc **$425.00**

Sigma, Panda Chef, Cara Marks for Sigma the Tastesetter ..**$95.00**

Sigma, Popcorn Vendor, Tastesetter on paper label, minimum value **$450.00**

Sigma, Rabbit, cylinder, Tastesetter C MCMLXXXII Towle Company **$45.00**

Sigma, Rag Doll, Tastesetter c MCMLXXXIV **$225.00**

Sigma, Santa, Tastesetter, c MCMLXXXIV **$95.00**

Sigma, Senorita, Siesta Tastesetter, David Straus **$350.00**

Sigma, Snowman, Dennis Kyte for Sigma Tastesetter ...**$125.00**

Sigma, Victoria, Tastesetter, David Straus **$255.00**

Sigma, Wind in the Willows, 1981 ....**$150.00**

Star Jar, Cowardly Lion, 1994.....................................**$300.00**

Star Jar, Dorothy & Toto, 1994 ....**$375.00**

Star Jar, Glinda, 1994..**$300.00**

Star Jar, Herman Munster, 1996 ....**$275.00**

Star Jar, King Kong, Turner Entertainment, 1996 ......**$275.00**

Star Jar, Munchkin Mayor, 1994, 13½" **$375.00**

Star Jar, Professor Marvel, 1994, 14½" **$375.00**

Star Jar, Scarecrow, 1994 ....**$300.00**

Star Jar, Wicked Witch, 1994......................................**$375.00**

Star Jar, Winged Monkey, 1994, 13⅝" **$375.00**

Treasure Craft, Bear, Made in USA inside lid **$40.00**

Treasure Craft, Bunny, white w/multicolor bouquet ..**$60.00**

Treasure Craft, Droopy Dog **$375.00**

Treasure Craft, Eightball, Made in USA......................**$80.00**

Treasure Craft, Golf Ball, Made in USA **$50.00**

Treasure Craft, Hobby Horse, mark in side lid **$50.00**

Treasure Craft, Kermit Serenading Miss Piggy, Henson Mexico **$75.00**

Treasure Craft, Miss Piggy, Henson............................**$50.00**

Treasure Craft, Seymour J Snailsworth **$425.00**

Treasure Craft, Soccer Ball, Made in USA...................**$45.00**

Twin Winton, Apple, wood finish, unmarked..........**$125.00**

Twin Winton, Bear Sheriff (TW-55), 11" **$60.00**

Twin Winton, Boxing Kangaroo (unlisted in catalogs but verified by designer), fully painted, no mark, minimum value **$500.00**

Twin Winton, Butler (TW-60), **$300.00.** (Photo courtesy Mike Ellis)

Twin Winton, Chipmunk (TW-45), bag of acorns over shoulder, 10" **$60.00**

Twin Winton, Cookie Car (Cable Car, TW-98), 7x12".**$60.00**

Twin Winton, Cookie Catcher (TW-52), 8x13" **$85.00**

Twin Winton, Cookie Elf (TW-57), signed MAC **$200.00**

Twin Winton, Cookie Guard (TW-96), 12" **$350.00**

Twin Winton, Cookie Nut (TW-83), squirrel atop, 9x10" ..**$55.00**

Twin Winton, Cookie Time (TW-81), mouse atop clock, 14"...**$40.00**

Twin Winton, Cop (Keystone, TW-249), Collector Series, 12½"...**$225.00**

Twin Winton, Dog (Circus, TW-93) on Drum, 12" ...**$175.00**

Twin Winton, Dog in Basket (TW-71), 10"...............**$85.00**

Twin Winton, Donkey (TW-288), straw hat, multicolor..**$290.00**

Twin Winton, Dutch Girl (TW-247), Collector Series, 12"..**$200.00**

Twin Winton, Elephant (Sailor, TW-28), Collector Series, 12" **$250.00**

Twin Winton, Elf Bakery (TW-50), seated on stump, 12"..**$50.00**

Twin Winton, Gorilla (TW-39), in hat, tie & suspenders, 12" **$350.00**

Twin Winton, Hen on Basket (TW-61), 8½" **$100.00**

Twin Winton, Hotei (TW-78), 12½" **$85.00**

Twin Winton, Jack-in-the-Box (TW-48), 13½"...........**$400.00**

Twin Winton, Kitten in Basket (TW-70), 10".............**$65.00**

Twin Winton, Lighthouse (TW-42), 13" **$400.00**

Twin Winton, Little Lamb (TW-266), Collector's Series, blue apron **$125.00**

Twin Winton, Mopsy (Raggedy Ann, TW-242), Collector's Series **$150.00**

Twin Winton, Noah's Ark (TW-94), 10" **$75.00**

Twin Winton, Owl (Scholar, TW-91), 12" **$40.00**

Twin Winton, Pirate Fox (TW-246), multicolor.........**$175.00**

Twin Winton, Poodle Cookie Counter (TW-64), 13x7½"..**$85.00**

Twin Winton, Pot O' Cookies (TW-58), 8x13" **$25.00**

Twin Winton, Rabbit (TW-87), 13" **$75.00**

Twin Winton, Rooster (TW-68), crowing, 12" **$75.00**

Twin Winton, Shaggy Pup TW-40), red bow, unmarked, rare...**$400.00**

Twin Winton, Stove (TW-65), 8x13"...........................**$75.00**

Twin Winton, Walrus (TW-63), clown hat & collar, 11"...**$350.00**

Twin Winton, Ye Olde Cookie Bucket (TW-59), 9" **$25.00**

Vandor, Betty Boop Holiday, yellow bracelet, 1994 ...**$50.00**

Vandor, I Love Lucy, 4 figures in blue & white convertible, 1996 ....**$150.00**

Viacom, Real Monsters, 1996 ....**$36.00**

Viacom, Tommy Pickles (Rugrat), 1996 ....**$40.00**

Wade, Brew Gaffer, An Original Design for Lyons Tetley By Wade England **$150.00**

Wade, Peasant, 1991, 10½"...**$110.00**

Warner Bros, Animaniacs, Made in China, 1994 ....**$110.00**

Warner Bros, Baseball Bugs, Taiwan, 1993 ....**$45.00**

Warner Bros, Bugs Bunny Head, China, 1996.............**$75.00**

Warner Bros, Bugs Miranda, Made in China, 1994 ...**$110.00**

Warner Bros, Daffy Duck, Hey Who Ate All the Cookies?, 1997 ....**$40.00**

Warner Bros, Foghorn-Leghorn w/Dog & Henry Hawk, 1996..**$75.00**

Warner Bros, Kansas City Chief Taz, 1994...................**$55.00**

Warner Bros, London Tour Bus, 1995 ....**$75.00**

Warner Bros, Marc Anthony & Pussyfoot, 1995, 9x10" ..**$75.00**

Warner Bros, Marvin the Martian Head, 1995 ....**$35.00**

Warner Bros, Michael Jordan/Bugs Bunny Space Jam, 1996...**$100.00**

Warner Bros, New York Giants Taz, 1994 ....**$55.00**

Warner Bros, Pinky & the Brain, 1996, 12½" **$75.00**

Warner Bros, Porky Pig in TV, 1995, 10½x8½"...........**$65.00**

Warner Bros, Summer Olympics, 1996 ....**$125.00**

Warner Bros, Sylvester Head, Applause, 1994.............**$80.00**

Warner Bros., Taz, Applause, 1994, from $65.00 to $75.00. (Photo courtesy Fred and Joyce Roerig)

Warner Bros, Tazmanian Devil Head, 1996.................**$65.00**

Warner Bros, Wile E Coyote, Taiwan, 1993.................**$45.00**

World Bazaars, Snowman, w/broom & red bird, Made in China...**$35.00**

World Bazaars, Snowman Decorating Tree, Made in China **$35.00**

Coors Rosebud Dinnerware

Golden, Colorado, was the site for both the Coors Brewing Company and the Coors Porcelain Company, each founded by the same man, Adolph Coors. The pottery's inception was in 1910, and in the early years they manufactured various ceramic products such as industrial needs, dinnerware, vases, and figurines; but their most famous line and the one we want to tell you about is 'Rosebud.'

The Rosebud 'Cook 'n Serve' line was introduced in 1934. It's very easy to spot, and after you've once seen a piece, you'll be able to recognize it instantly. It was made in solid colors — rose, blue, green, yellow, ivory, and orange. The rose bud and leaves are embossed and hand painted in contrasting colors. There are nearly fifty different pieces to collect, and bargains can still be found; but prices are accelerating, due to increased collector interest. For more information we recommend *Coors Rosebud Pottery* by Robert Schneider and *Collector's Encyclopedia of Colorado Pottery, Identification and Values,* by Carol and Jim Carlton.

Note: Yellow and white tends to craze and stain. Our prices are for pieces with minimal crazing and no staining. To evaluate pieces in blue, add 10% to the prices that follow;

add 15% for items in ivory. Rosebud is prone to have factory flaws, and the color on the Rosebuds may be of poor quality. When either of these factors are present, deduct 10%.

Advisor: Rick Spencer (See Directory, Silverplated Flatware)

Newsletter: *Coors Pottery Newsletter*
Robert Schneider
3808 Carr Pl. N
Seattle, WA 98103-8126

Apple baker, w/lid	**$55.00**
Ashtray	**$175.00**
Baking pan, 12¼x8¼"	**$75.00**
Basket, 9¼"	**$60.00**
Bowl, mixing; no rosebuds, 3-pt	**$45.00**
Bowl, oatmeal	**$35.00**
Bowl, pudding; 2 sm ear handles, 2-pt, from $35 to	**$40.00**
Bowl, vegetable; deep	**$35.00**
Cake knife	**$85.00**
Cake plate, from $40 to	**$45.00**
Casserole, Dutch; lg	**$95.00**
Casserole, Dutch; sm	**$72.00**
Casserole, straight sides, 5"	**$50.00**
Casserole, straight sides, 8"	**$65.00**
Creamer	**$30.00**
Cup & saucer	**$45.00**
Egg cup	**$50.00**
Honey pot, w/spoon	**$300.00**
Jar, utility; w/lid	**$85.00**
Loaf pan, from $40 to	**$50.00**
Pie plate	**$35.00**

Pitcher, water; with lid, $150.00.

Plate, dinner; 10¼"	**$95.00**
Plate, 5"	**$8.00**
Plate, 8"	**$25.00**
Ramekin, handled	**$35.00**
Refrigerator set	**$130.00**

Salt & pepper shakers, individual; sm, pr	**$70.00**
Salt & pepper shakers, kitchen; slanted or pillar style, lg, pr	**$65.00**
Sugar bowl, w/lid	**$40.00**
Sugar shaker	**$75.00**
Teapot, 6-cup, from $160 to	**$185.00**
Tumbler, footed or w/handle, from $105 to	**$130.00**
Water server, w/stopper	**$120.00**

Coppercraft Guild

During the 1960s and 1970s, the Coppercraft Guild Company of Taunton, Massachusetts, produced a variety of copper and copper-tone items which were sold through the home party plan. Though copper items such as picture frames, flowerpots, teapots, candle holders, and trays were their mainstay, they also made molded wall decorations such as mirror-image pairs of birds on branches and large floral-relief plaques that they finished in metallic copper-tone paint. Some of their pictures were a combination of the copper-tone composition molds mounted on a sheet copper background. When uncompromised by chemical damage or abuse, the finish they used on their copper items has proven remarkably enduring, and many of these pieces still look new today. Collectors are beginning to take notice!

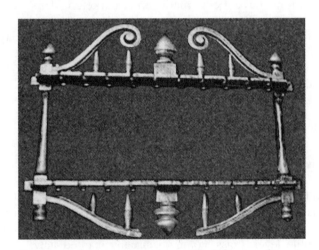

Spoon rack, copper-tone finish on heavy molded plastic, 12x14", from $18.00 to $22.00.

Bank, bell form, wooden handle screws into top, 8½x3⅜"	**$18.00**
Bowl, embossed florals, 2x11"	**$25.00**
Bowl, fruit; flared rim, footed, 4½x9"	**$16.50**
Bowl, punch; smooth footed form w/flared rim, 6x15"	**$30.00**
Candle holder, hurricane style, 10", MIB	**$20.00**
Candle holder/wall sconce, embossed leaf-shaped back w/metal ring, 13x7"	**$22.00**
Casserole, glass bowl insert, copper base & lid, black finial, scrolling handles, 4x9"	**$25.00**
Chafing dish, w/lid & stand, MIB w/original papers	**$75.00**
Coffeepot, black wooden stick handle, black finial, 8x5" w/4¾" handle	**$25.00**

Ice bucket, lion heads w/rings form handles, w/lid, 7½x7" $35.00

Plaque, embossed woman & girls at well, acorn border, 13" dia $20.00

Plaque, embossed/tooled bamboo, orange & gold enameling on black background, rectangular walnut frame, 23½x9½" $55.00

Plaque, The Last Supper, 10x20" $25.00

Plaque, Traveler's Rest, 10x14" $35.00

Pot, bail handle, 4x3" $12.00

Tray, flared rim w/rope trim, marked, 16¼" $45.00

Tray, shallow ruffled rim, handles, 1x14" dia $25.00

Water set, 8¼" water pot w/8 2¾" cups & 18" dia tray, all marked w/foil stickers...$70.00

Wine bucket, wide trumpet neck, footed, 10x7".........$30.00

Corkscrews

When the corkscrew was actually developed remains uncertain (the first patent was issued in 1795), but it most likely evolved from the worm on a ramrod or cleaning rod used to draw wadding from a gun barrel and found to be equally effective in the sometimes difficult task of removing corks from wine bottles. Inventors scurried to develop a better product, and as a result, thousands of variations have been made and marketed. This abundance and diversification invariably began to attract collectors, whose ranks are burgeoning. Many of today's collectors concentrate their attention on one particular type — those with advertising, a specific patent, or figural pullers, for instance.

Our advisor has written a very informative book, *Bull's Pocket Guide to Corkscrews* (Schiffer), with hundreds and full-color illustrations and current values.

Advisor: Donald A. Bull (See Directory, Corkscrews)

Bull's head, brass plated, from $30 to $40.00

Champagne tap combination, New Century, Williamson Co, from $50 to $70.00

Double lever, brass, common, usually marked Italy, sometimes w/advertising, from $15 to...........................$30.00

Finger pull, 2- or 3-finger, w/cap lifter added, depending on mark, ea from $5 to......................................$50.00

Finger pull, 4-finger w/foil cutter/wire breaker at handle, may have cap lifter, ea from $50 to $75.00

Five-in-one tool, Napier, cap lifter, corkscrew, funnel, drink measure & bottle resealer, from $60 to.................$75.00

Folding bow, common, produced since the 18th century, unmarked, ea from $10 to $50.00

Folding bow, w/foil cutter added, from $100 to.......$200.00

Lazy tong (aka concertina, compound lever or zigzag), cast handle, unmarked, from $80 to.........................$100.00

Ornate frame, brass, Italian, modern, from $50 to......$60.00

Parrot figural, solid brass, web helix tail, 6¼", from $75 to...$100.00

Picnic type, brass hex head w/machined-in cap lifter, sheath forms handle, unmarked, from $25 to $35.00

Pocket folding, So-Ezy Made in USA Pat Pend, from $40 to..$50.00

Pocket folding, Tip Top, Williamson of Newark NJ, no advertising, from $40 to....................................$60.00

Prong puller, Converse, common wood handle w/nickel-plated brass sheath, from $25 to $35.00

Prong puller, San Bri, black metal w/plastic sheath, from $30 to..$40.00

Schlitz Beer advertising, cast wire breaker above bell, Williamson, from $30.00 to $50.00. (Photo courtesy Donald A. Bull)

Spring type (addition to handle design), all steel, unmarked, from $60 to..$100.00

Syroco, man in top hat figural, known as Old Codger, Codger & Topper, painted pressed wood composition, from $90 to $150.00

T-handle, celluloid ivory, from $50 to $60.00

T-handle, iron, marked Picon, from $50 to $60.00

T-handle, metal, various simple designs, unmarked, ea from $10 to...$15.00

T-handle, wood, simple style, direct pull, unmarked, ea from $10 to...$75.00

Waiter's friend, single knife blade & foil cutter, unmarked, from $50 to..$60.00

Waiter's friend, single knife blade only, various advertising, ea from $15 to...$25.00

Williamson's Don't Swear, opener combination w/Catalin sheath, worm turned in & out, not pulled or pushed, from $25 to..$50.00

Cottage Ware

Made by several companies, cottage ware is a line of ceramic table and kitchen accessories, each piece styled as a cozy cottage with a thatched roof. At least four English potteries made the ware, and you'll find pieces marked 'Japan' as well as 'Occupied Japan.' You'll also find pieces styled as windmills and water wheels. The pieces preferred by collectors are marked 'Price Brothers' and 'Occupied Japan.' They're compatible in coloring as well as in styling, and values run about the same. Items marked simply 'Japan' are worth considerably less.

Bell, Price Brothers, minimum value $150.00
Biscuit jar, wicker handle, Maruhon Ware, Occupied Japan, 6½", from $80 to $90.00
Butter dish, Price Bros, from $45 to $60.00
Butter dish, round, Beswick England, w/lid, 3½x6", from $75 to..$100.00
Chocolate cup & saucer, straight sides, Price Bros, 3¾", 5⅜", from $35 to..$45.00
Chocolate pot, Price Bros, from $125 to....................$145.00
Condiment set, mustard pot, salt & peppers in row arrangement, Price Bros, 6", from $40 to $50.00
Condiment set, 3-part cottage on shaped tray w/applied bush, Price Bros, 4½", from $60 to $80.00
Cookie jar/canister, cylindrical, Price Bros, 8½x5", from $100 to..$135.00
Cookie jar/canister, cylindrical, Price Bros, 8x3¾" (rare size) $275.00
Cookie/biscuit jar, Occupied Japan, from $75 to $95.00
Creamer & sugar bowl, Price Bros, 2½x4½", from $40 to..$50.00
Cup & saucer, Price Bros, 3⅜", 5½", from $45 to.......$55.00
Demitasse pot, Price Bros, from $85 to $110.00
Egg cup set, Price Bros, 4 on 6" sq tray, from $50 to.....$65.00
Grease jar, Occupied Japan, from $25 to....................$38.00
Hot water pot, Westminster England, 8½x4" $50.00
Marmalade & jelly, 2 houses cojoined, Price Bros, from $75 to..$85.00
Mug, Price Bros, 3⅞", from $35 to $50.00
Pitcher, embossed cottage, lg flower on handle, Price Bros, from $125 to..$150.00
Pitcher, tankard; round, Price Bros, 7⅞", from $110 to..$135.00

Platter, Price Bros., 12x7½", $65.00.

Sugar box, for cubes, Price Bros, 5¾" L, from, $35 to..$50.00
Teapot, Keele Street, w/creamer & sugar bowl, from $75 to..$95.00
Teapot, Occupied Japan, 6½", from $40 to $55.00
Toast rack, 4-slot, Price Bros, 5½"............................$75.00

Cow Creamers

Cow creamers (and milk pitchers) have been around since before the nineteenth century, but, of course, those are rare. But by the early 1900s, they were becoming quite commonplace. In many of these older ones, the cow was standing on a platform (base) and very often had a lid. Not all cows on platforms are old, however, but it is a good indication of age. Examples from before WWII often were produced in England, Germany, and Japan.

Over the last fifty years there has been a slow revival of interest in these little cream dispensers, including the plastic Moo cows, made by Whirley Industries, U.S.A, that were used in cafes during the '50s. With the current popularity of anything cow-shaped, manufacturers have expanded the concept, and some creamers now are made with matching sugar bowls. If you want to collect only vintage examples, you'll have to check closely to make sure they're not new.

Advisor: Shirley Green (See Directory, Cow Creamers)

Advertising, iridescent white, Worthing Parade, foreign, 4½x6"..$28.00
Advertising, Jell-O, multicolored, 5x6½"....................$175.00
Arthur Wood, ironstone, w/sailboat on side, England, marked, 5½x7"..$85.00
Burleigh, calico, Staffordshire England, ca 1975, 7" L, from $65 to..$75.00
Burleigh, lazy cow, blue & white, on base, 5x6½".....$60.00
C Cooke, w/suckling calf on platform, w/lid, 5x6½".$225.00
China, Blue Onion design, blue & white, sitting, 4x3½"...$20.00
Crown Devon, recumbent Jersey (impressed on side), #1074, 4x7"..$15.00
Czech, dark brown & white (head only) w/blue eyes & horns, handle on back of neck, head bent down, #1337, 6½"..$43.00
Czech, marigold iridescent, reclining cow on base, 5½x7" ..$55.00
Delft style, blue sailing ship (left side) on white, unmarked, ca 1950s..$45.00
English, GT Yarmouth printed on side of reclining brown & grey cow w/horns, no mark, 7" L $42.00
English, Newquay printed on side of reclining brown cow w/detailed face, 3½x6"..$28.00
Germany, white upright cow w/pink around snout (spout), red collar supports gold bell, thin porcelain, marked, 4½".$85.00
Goebel, brown & white, full bee mark, 4x6" $35.00
Guernsey printed on side, brass bell at neck, slash-type mouth, brown & white w/black hooves, from $20 to..........$35.00
Holstein, black & white, K403 on bottom, 4½x8" $48.00
Jackfield type, red clay, on platform, w/lid, 19th century, 5½x7"..$175.00
Japan, brown & white, sitting, 3¼", from $15 to $25.00
Japan, brown & white, tail handle, black mark, 5¼", from $22 to..$35.00
Japan, brown to cream, shiny, 5¼" L, from $22 to.....$35.00
Japan, ironstone, black ring around eyes (known as Bull's Eye), crudely molded, reddish spots, green bell, 6" $30.00

Japan lusterware, creamer and sugar bowl on platforms, ca 1950s, 4¼x6", from $75.00 to $90.00 for the set. (Photo courtesy Shirley Green)

Unmarked (very common), ca 1950s, with matching salt and pepper shakers, $40.00. (Photo courtesy Shirley Green)

Japan, recumbent cow w/muted orange, yellow & brown flowers, black hooves, marked, 7½" L...................**$35.00**

Japan, Texas longhorn, lustre, creamer & sugar bowl, w/lid, 5x6½"...**$125.00**

Japan, yellow & white, 2½", from $15 to **$20.00**

Leersum castle image on side, brown & white, unmarked, ca 1960, 6", from $32 to **$38.00**

Lefton, creamer & sugar bowl, tan w/white markings, 4x5½"...**$42.00**

McMaster, pottery, creamer & sugar bowl, 4x6".........**$37.00**

Occupied Japan, green & tan, lg body, 6x5"..............**$65.00**

Souvenir, Arms of University & City of Oxford shield, cream & orange lustre, marked Foreign, 1950s, 6" L, from $35 to **$40.00**

Souvenir, historical building on side of standing brown & white cow, metal bell on cord, porcelain, Bavaria, 1930s, 6"...**$38.00**

Staffordshire, multicolored chintz, on platform, w/lid, 5½x7"...**$135.00**

Stafforshire Ware, Kent, Made in England, on platform, w/lid, 1940s-50s, scarce, 4¾x7", from $100 to..............**$150.00**

TG Green, reclining, tan, England, 4x6"......................**$37.00**

Unmarked, for child's tea set, white porcelain, 1½x2"...**$15.00**

Unmarked, recumbent w/legs tucked under, glossy white, 1920s, 6"..**$50.00**

Unmarked, sitting, tail forms handle, floral decor on white, 1960s, 5½x8", from $55 to **$65.00**

Unmarked, stands w/tail curled, glossy brown, old, 2¼x3"...**$25.00**

Unmarked, white standing cow w/design similar to Desert Rose around back opening, black hooves, gold trim, 1960s, 7" L...**$35.00**

Unmarked, white w/brown splashes, black hooves, brown horns, head up, pink mouth open wide, ca 1950, 7" L...**$15.00**

Unmarked Germany, brown & white, wide open naturalistic mouth, 6" L...**$15.00**

Unmarked Germany, standing shaded gray cow w/horns & wrinkled skin at neck, lg naturalistic open mouth, 1960s, 7" L..**$40.00**

Cowboy Character Collectibles

When we come across what is now termed cowboy character toys and memorabilia, it rekindles warm memories of childhood days for those of us who once 'rode the range' (often our backyards) with these gallant heroes. Today we can really appreciate them for the positive role models they were. They sat tall in the saddle; reminded us never to tell an un-truth; to respect 'women-folk' as well as our elders, animal life, our flag, our country, and our teachers; to eat all the cereal placed before us in order to build strong bodies; to worship God; and have (above all else) strong values that couldn't be compromised. They were Gene, Roy, and Tex, along with a couple of dozen other names, who rode beautiful steeds such as Champion, Trigger, and White Flash.

They rode into a final sunset on the silver screen only to return and ride into our homes via television in the 1950s. The next decade found us caught up in more western adventures such as Bonanza, Wagon Train, The Rifleman, and many others. These set the stage for a second wave of toys, games, and western outfits.

Annie Oakley was one of only a couple of cowgirls in the corral; Wild Bill Elliott used to drawl, 'I'm a peaceable man'; Ben Cartwright, Adam, Hoss, and Little Joe provided us with thrills and laughter. Some of the earliest collectibles are represented by Roy's and Gene's 1920s predecessors — Buck Jones, Hoot Gibson, Tom Mix, and Ken Maynard. There were so many others, all of whom were very real to us in the 1930s – 1960s, just as their memories and values remain very real to us today.

Remember that few items of cowboy memorabilia have survived to the present in mint condition. When found, mint or near-mint items bring hefty prices, and they continue to escalate every year. Our values are for examples in good to very good condition.

For more information we recommend these books: *Roy Rogers, Singing Cowboy Stars, Silver Screen Cowboys, Hollywood Cowboy Heroes,* and *Western Comics: A Comprehensive Reference,* all by Robert W. Phillips. Other books include *Collector's Guide to Hopalong Cassidy*

Memorabilia by Joseph J. Caro, *Collector's Reference & Value Guide to The Lone Ranger* by Lee Felbinger, *W.F. Cody Buffalo Bill* by James W. Wojtowicz, and *Roy Rogers and Dale Evans Toys & Memorabilia* by P. Allan Coyle.

See also Toys, Guns; Toys, Rings.

Club/Newsletter: The Old Cowboy Picture Show
George F. Coan
PO Box 66
Camden, SC 29020; 803-432-9643

Club/Newsletter: Cowboy Collector
Joseph J. Caro, Publisher
P.O. Box 7486
Long Beach, CA 90807

Club/Newsletter: Hopalong Cassidy Fan Club International and *Hopalong Cassidy Newsletter*
Laura Bates, Editor
6310 Friendship Dr.
New Concord, OH 43762-9708; 614-826-4850

Newsletter: *The Lone Ranger Silver Bullet*
P.O. Box 553
Forks, WA 98331; 206-327-3726

Bat Masterson, Indian Fighter playset, multiple, complete, NM (NM box)..**$200.00**
Bonanza, Foto Fantastiks Coloring Set, Eberhard Faber, 1965, complete, M (EX box)....................................**$100.00**
Buffalo Bill Jr, belt & buckle, aluminum & plastic, Flying A Productions, 1950s, EX..**$45.00**
Cheyenne, cowboy gloves, fringed w/name & image of horse head, unused, M....................................**$50.00**
Corporal Rusty (Rin-Tin-Tin), outfit, Iskin/Screen Gems, 1955, w/gun & holster, EX (EX box) **$225.00**
Dale Evans, outfit: skirt, vest, blouse & holster, Yankeeboy, EX (EX box) **$265.00**
Daniel Boone, Woodland Whistle, Autolite, 1964, NMIB..**$65.00**
Davy Crockett, bank, bust figure w/rifle, copper-tinted metal, 1950s, 5", NM (EX box)..............................**$125.00**
Davy Crockett, bank, plaster figure, VG...................**$125.00**
Davy Crockett, Dart Gun Target Set, Knickerbocker, 1950s, complete, NRFB **$75.00**
Davy Crockett, tool kit, litho tin chest, complete w/tools & manual, Liberty Steel, 1955, M............................**$450.00**
Gabby Hayes, Target Set, complete, EX (EX box)....**$300.00**
Gunsmoke, outfit, Mat Dillon, Seneca, 1958, complete, EX (EX box) **$125.00**
Hopalong Cassidy, dominoes, Milton Bradley, 1950, complete, EX (EX box), from $75 to........................**$100.00**
Hopalong Cassidy, sparkler, plastic bust figure w/metal plunger, 3½", EX..**$275.00**
Lone Ranger, horseshoe, rubber, Gardner Games, 1950, complete, NMIB, from $175 to **$195.00**
Lone Ranger, Legend of, playset, HG Toys, 1978, MIB (sealed)..**$50.00**

Lone Ranger, movie viewer, Lone Ranger Rides Again, 1940, lg, NMIB, from $200 to **$250.00**
Lone Ranger, Mysterious Prospector Playset, Gabriel, 1976, complete, scarce, NM (NM box)........................**$100.00**
Lone Ranger, telescope, 1946, NMIB, from $150 to..**$200.00**
Rifleman, hat, Tex-Felt Co, 1958, EX......................**$70.00**
Rin Tin Tin & Rusty, belt buckle, EX......................**$65.00**
Roy Rogers, Burn-Rite Wood Burning Set, Rapaport Bros, complete, NM (EX box) **$175.00**
Roy Rogers, Crayon Set, Standard Toykraft, 1950s, complete, VG (VG box)..**$75.00**
Roy Rogers, horseshoe set, NMIB **$145.00**
Roy Rogers, movie, Silver Fox Hunt, Hollywood Film Ent, 1950s, 8mm, VG+..**$60.00**
Roy Rogers, outfit, Merit Playsuits, 1950s, complete, NMIB **$350.00**
Roy Rogers, riding horse, plush trigger w/molded plastic face, Reliable Toy, Canada, 26" L, EX+ **$400.00**
Roy Rogers Riders, harmonica, 1955, 4", NMOC.........**$95.00**

Texas Ranger, spurs, MIB, $50.00; gloves, M, $40.00. (Photo courtesy Dunbar Gallery)

Tonto, Castile Soap figure, Kirk Guild, 1939, 4", EXIB ..**$55.00**

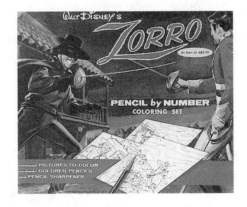

Zorro, Pencil by Number, includes seven uncolored pictures, pencils, EXIB, $65.00. (Photo courtesy June Moon)

Cracker Jack Toys

In 1869 Frederick Rueckheim left Hamburg, Germany, bound for Chicago, where he planned to work on a farm for his uncle. But farm life did not appeal to Mr. Rueckheim, and after the Chicago fire, he moved there and helped clear the debris. With another man whose popcorn and confectionary business had been destroyed in the fire, Mr. Rueckheim started a business with one molasses kettle and one hand popper. The following year, Mr. Rueckheim bought out his original partner and sent for his brother, Louis. The two brothers formed Rueckheim & Bro. and quickly prospered as they continued expanding their confectionary line to include new products. It was not until 1896 that the first lot of Cracker Jack was produced — and then only as an adjunct to their growing line. Cracker Jack was sold in bulk form until 1899 when H.G. Eckstein, an old friend, invented the wax-sealed package, which allowed them to ship it further and thus sell it more easily. Demand for Cracker Jack soared, and it quickly became the main product of the factory. Today millions of boxes are produced — everyone with a prize inside.

The idea of prizes came along during the time of bulk packaging; it was devised as a method to stimulate sales. Later, as the wax-sealed package was introduced, a prize was given (more or less) with each package. Next, the prize was added into the package, but still not every package received a prize. It was not until the 1920s that 'a prize in every package' became a reality. Initially, the prizes were put in with the confection, but the company feared this might pose a problem, should it inadvertently be mistaken for the popcorn. To avoid this, the prize was put in a separate compartment and, finally, into its own protective wrapper. Hundreds of prizes have been used over the years, and it is still true today that there is 'a prize in every package.' Prizes have ranged from the practical girl's bracelet and pencils to tricks, games, disguises, and stick-anywhere patches. To learn more about the subject, you'll want to read *Cracker Jack Toys, The Complete Unofficial Guide for Collectors*, and *Cracker Jack, The Unauthorized Guide to Advertising Collectibles*, both by our advisor, Larry White.

Note: Words printed in upper case lettering actually appear on the toy.

Advisor: Larry White (See Directory, Cracker Jack)

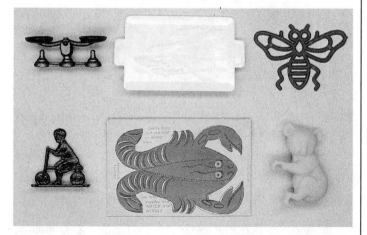

Scales, metal, $75.00; Tray, plastic, $11.00; outline figure, plastic, $8.00; Stand-up boy on scooter, metal, $27.00; Lobster game, paper, $35.00; Koala bear, plastic, $8.00. (Photo courtesy Larry White)

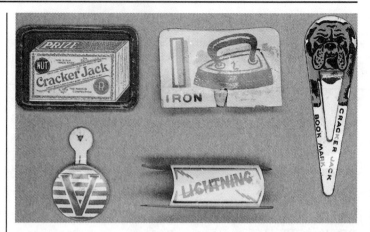

Tray, $135.00; Alphabet stand-up, $140.00; Bulldog bookmark, $19.50; Victory label button, $45.00; Lightning sled, $65.00. (Photo courtesy Larry White)

Kangaroo punch-out, $9.50; Fish plate, $7.50; Comic character stand-up HERBY, $87.50; Tankard charm, $55.00. (Photo courtesy Larry White)

A-MAZE PUZZLE, plastic/paper, dexterity game, about 1" sq...**$5.00**
ANIMANIACS STICKER MADNESS, paper, any of 24....**$2.50**
ANIMATED JUNGLE BOOK, paper, pop-up book....**$125.00**
Astronaut, plastic, CJ CO, 1 of 10................................**$19.50**
Aviation wings, metal, CRACKER JACK AIR CORPS ...**$65.00**
BADGE FUN, paper, B SERIES 75, any of 21 ....**$2.00**
Baseball card, Joe Jackson, 1914, EX...................**$11,500.00**
Baseball card, paper, 1914, 1 of 144, typical...............**$55.00**
Baseball player, plastic, CJ CO, any of 11 ....**$8.75**
BIKE STICKER, paper, series ID 1380, any...................**$2.50**
BIRDS TO COLOR, paper, paint book.........................**$75.00**
Booklet, paper, HUB A DUB-DUB, JACK & JILL, etc.**$40.00**
Bookmark, plastic, set #40, any of 14 ....**$3.50**
Box prize, paper, insert separator w/game, etc, any of 40 ....**$27.50**
Boy eating Cracker Jack, paper, mechanical prize, about 3" **$395.00**
BREAKFAST SET, agateware in matchbox **$37.50**

Button, metal, US ARMY QUARTERMASTER, gold or silver wash..$11.50

Button, Victorian lady pin-back, celluloid over metal, 1 of 37...$100.00

BUTTON CLIP-ON, plastic, series 1375, any $8.50

Ceramic figure, FAS JAPAN, various comic characters, painted..$27.50

Ceramic figure, JAPAN, various, about 2" to 3" tall, some paint...$9.50

Charm, pot metal, horse, cat, dog, rabbit, etc.............$9.50

CHILDRENS NOTES, book, paper, about 2" high, early ..$45.00

Clam shell w/water flowers inside, about 1½"...........$50.00

Comb, plastic, marked, thick, Canadian $12.50

Compass, paper & metal, about 1½" dia, balance on needlepoint..$97.50

Coupon, paper, The Cracker Jack Embroidery Outfit.$75.00

CRACKER JACK BANK, metal, book shape................$275.00

CRACKER JACK NURSERY GAMES, paper, book, about 2¼x3"..$127.50

CRACKER JACK PUZZLE BOOK, paper, series 3......$115.00

CRACKER JACK RIDDLES, paper, book w/jester on cover ..$12.50

Decal, plastic/paper, Z-1138, bunny, bear, etc...........$17.50

Dirigible, metal w/celluloid blimp, charm..................$78.50

DRAWING STENCILS, paper, rabbit, flower etc $35.00

Eraser boy, paper, Jack at blackboard writes/erases slogan..$295.00

FELT PATCH, felt on paper, series ID 1383, any color or design...$4.50

Fish plaque, vacuform plastic, grouper, salmon, etc ..$20.00

FLICK-A-WINK, paper, marked, game $35.00

Fortune Teller, celluloid Sailor Jack in paper envelope, various colors..$125.00

Fortune Teller, metal, disk w/letters & attributes $45.00

Frog, paper w/metal jumping mechanism, about 3"...$125.00

FROG CHIRPER, metal, copright 1946 Cloudcrest $20.00

GLOW IN THE DARK STICKERS, paper, 1972 copyright ..$5.50

GOOFY ZOO, paper, wheeled zoo animal poses $35.00

Hat, paper, ME FOR CRACKER JACK........................$295.00

Hoe, metal w/wood handle, about 6" L.......................$9.50

HOLD UP TO LIGHT, plastic, astronaut, egg, etc.......$15.00

JIG-SAW PUZZLE, paper, dirigible, knights, etc, 1931 copyright $145.00

JIG-SAW PUZZLE, paper, 6 sections, boy fishing, etc...$9.50

MAGICARD, paper, D SERIES #44, any of 15.............$17.50

Match shooter, metal, hand gun, rifle, machine gun, japanned..$27.50

MINUTE MOVIES, paper, flip book of moving animal, any of 12 ....$15.00

Nit, plastic, R & L Australia, Laugh, Fun, Flap, etc........$9.50

NURSERY RHYMES & RIDDLES, paper, booklet.........$87.50

Palm puzzle, paper & celluloid, cow over moon, etc ..$95.00

Paper dolls, paper, JANE & JIMMY CUT-OUT TWINS..$145.00

PENCIL HOLDER, paper, marked, about 2x4".............$78.00

PHONEY PENNY 1C, metal w/gold wash....................$30.00

Post card, paper, CJR-1, miniature of 1908 designs, any of 12 ....$7.50

Post card, paper, Cracker Jack Bears, 1908, any of 16...$27.50

PUT...TAKE, metal spinner, about 1½".......................$20.00

RIDDLE BOOK, paper, series 1335, any of 18 ....$3.50

Riddle card, paper, Cracker Jack Riddles, any of 20.....$9.50

RING TOSS, game, paper, Makatoy $24.00

Sailboat, plastic put-together....................................$6.50

Scale, metal, gold bottom, red pans..........................$35.00

SCORE COUNTER, paper, baseball game counter....$125.00

SEND A MESSAGE BY DOT & DASH, paper, game...$29.50

Serving tray, plastic, 5 fishes, thick, Canadian $11.00

Slide cars, paper, CRACKER JACK MOVIES, Jack/Bingo, etc $135.00

SMITTY, vacuform plastic, 1 of various comic characters ..$13.50

Stand-up, plastic, marked NOSCO, various figures.......$2.50

Stand-up, plastic 3-dimensional, Sailor Jack, 2000 copyright $2.50

Stand-up, tin litho metal, OFFICER, about 3" $17.50

SUPER SLATE, paper & plastic, B SERIES 49, any of 30...$4.50

SWINGING FROG, paper, 1 of 4, monkey, parrot, skeleton..$40.00

TAG ALONGS, plastic, SERIES #72, any of 15 ....$5.00

TATTOOS, paper, series Z-1366, any of 9.......................$.75

TELE-VIZ, paper, wheel prize about 2" sq $85.00

Telescope, plastic, POKEMON, series CJ #20, any of 24 .$4.50

Top, TWO TOPPERS, metal w/wood dowel, Jack & Angelus..$50.00

Traffic sign, plastic, CJ CO, STOP, NARROW BRIDGE, etc..$9.50

TRANSFER FUN, paper, B SERIES 35, any of 20...........$7.50

TWIG & SPRIG, paper, booklet, any title $97.50

Visor, paper, marked, about 6½' across.....................$95.00

Whistle, metal, airplane shape w/eagle design $65.00

Whistle, metal, SIMPLEX FLUTE $6.75

Whistle, paper, BLOW FOR MORE w/PRIZE box pictured..$67.50

Whistle, plastic, 2-tube, about 3" L, any 2-color...........$2.75

WORDS OF WISDOM, paper, book, about 3x5" $275.00

WRITE MOVIE STAR'S NAME HERE, paper, movie star card $27.50

YOU'RE IT, metal, finger pointing spinner.................$17.50

ZEPHYR, metal, TOOTSIETOY, about 2½" $17.50

Zodiac coin, plastic, 1 of 12......................................$8.75

Crackle Glass

At the height of productivity from the 1930s through the 1970s, nearly five hundred companies created crackle glass. As pieces stayed in production for several years, dating an item may be difficult. Some colors, such as ruby red, amberina, cobalt, and cranberry, were more expensive to produce. Smoke gray was made for a short time, and because quantities are scarce, prices tend to be higher than on some of the other colors, amethyst, green, and amber included. Crackle glass is still being produced today by the Blenko Glass Company, and it is being imported from Taiwan and China as well. For further information on other glass companies and values we recommend *Crackle Glass, Identification and Value Guide, Book I* and *Book II*, by Stan and Arlene Weitman (Collector Books).

Advisors: Stan and Arlene Weitman (See Directory, Crackle Glass)

Decanter, green with royal blue pulled-back handle, Rainbow, 1940s – 1960s, 14½", from $100.00 to $125.00. (Photo courtesy Stan and Arlene Weitman)

Cruet, amber w/matching pulled-back handle, amber 3-ball stopper, Rainbow, 1940s-60s, 4¼", pr, from $80 to **$100.00**

Cruet, amberina w/amber pulled-back handle, amber 3-ball stopper, Rainbow, 1940s-60s, 6½", from $75 to .**$100.00**

Cruet, ruby w/amber handle, amber teardrop stopper, Pilgrim, 1949-69, 6½", from $75 to **$85.00**

Cruet, sea green, no handle, 1-ball sea green stopper, Pilgrim, 1949-69, 6", from $75 to **$85.00**

Decanter, amberina, tall slim neck, flared rim, red teardrop stopper, Blenko, 1960s, 13", from $100 to **$125.00**

Decanter, crystal w/olive geen stopper, pinched sides, Blenko, 1940s-50s, 10½", from $100 to **$125.00**

Decanter, sea green, clear teardrop stopper, strawberry-like pressed mark (Pilgrim), 1949-69, 12", from $100 to.**$125.00**

Decanter, topaz, shouldered, fine crackle, ball stopper, Rainbow, late 1940s-60s, 8½", from $80 to **$100.00**

Decanter, topaz w/clear ribbed drop-over handle, bulbous, 2-ball topaz stopper, Pilgrim, 1949-69, 6¼", pr, $110 to...**$135.00**

Fish vase, topaz, Hamon, 1940s – early 1970s, 9", from $75.00 to $85.00. (Photo courtesy Stan and Arlene Weitman)

Fruit, apple, cobalt w/green leaf & stem, Blenko, 1950s-60s, 4½", from $70 to...**$110.00**

Fruit, apple, ruby w/green leaf & stem, Blenko, 1950s-60s, 3½", from $60 to...**$100.00**

Fruit, pear, pale Sea Green, Blenko, 1950s-60s, 5", from $60 to...**$100.00**

Jug, dark amber w/clear drop-over handle, Pilgrim, 1949-69, 6¾", from $75 to...**$80.00**

Jug, lemon-lime w/clear drop-over handle, Pilgrim, 1949-69, 4", from $35 to..**$40.00**

Liqueur glass, topaz w/low clear drop-over handle, slim cylinder, Pilgrim, 1949-69, 4", from $40 to...........**$45.00**

Mug, amber w/dark amber drop-over handle, unknown maker, late 1950s-early 1960s, 6¼", from $25 to..**$30.00**

Perfume bottle, light blue w/matching flower stopper, probably European, 4½", from $50 to **$75.00**

Pitcher, amberina w/amber drop-over handle, wide flared rim, waisted, Kanawha, 1957-87, 3¼", from $40 to...**$45.00**

Pitcher, amberina w/amber pulled-back handle, waisted, Rainbow, late 1940s-60s, 5", from $55 to.............**$60.00**

Pitcher, amberina w/orange drop-over handle, applied serpentine at neck, unknown maker & date, 5½", from $55 to..**$60.00**

Pitcher, amethyst w/matching pulled-back handle, inverted cone shape w/sm foot, Pilgrim, 1949-69, 4¼", from $50 to...**$55.00**

Pitcher, blue w/clear angular drop-over handle, frilly rim, Pilgrim, 1949-69, 3½", from $45 to.......................**$50.00**

Pitcher, blue w/clear pulled-back handle, cylindrical, Pilgrim, 1949-69, 4", from $25 to...**$30.00**

Pitcher, blue w/matching pulled-back handle, curving/flaring rim, unknown maker, 4¾", from $55 to **$60.00**

Pitcher, blue w/matching pulled-back handle, cylindrical w/sm foot, Kanawha, 1957-87, 4", from $35 to....**$40.00**

Pitcher, charcoal w/matching drop-over handle (rare color), unknown maker & date, bulbous, 4½", from $55 to...**$60.00**

Pitcher, crystal w/matching drop-over handle, slim waisted form w/angular rim, Pilgrim, 12½", from $100 to **$125.00**

Pitcher, dark amber w/clear drop-over handle, can neck, Pilgrim, 1949-69, 5", from $35 to **$40.00**

Pitcher, dark amber w/matching drop-over handle, pear shape, Pilgrim, 1949-69, 4", from $35 to **$40.00**

Pitcher, dark blue w/matching drop-over handle, waisted, mold blown, unknown maker & date, 5¼", from $25 to...**$30.00**

Pitcher, emerald green w/clear low drop-over handle, Pilgrim, 1949-69, 4", from $35 to.....................................**$40.00**

Pitcher, emerald green w/matching pulled-back handle, long slim neck, unknown maker & date, 5½", from $55 to...**$60.00**

Pitcher, gold w/matching handle, cylindrical w/flared rim, Rainbow, 1940s-60s, 3½", from $35 to.................**$40.00**

Pitcher, gold w/matching pulled-back handle, mold blown, Kanawha, 1957-87, 5¼", from $45 to **$50.00**

Pitcher, green w/matching pulled-back handle, Williamsburg Glass Co label, 1950-60, 4¾", from $55 to **$60.00**

Pitcher, lemon-lime w/matching drop-over handle, teardrop shape, Pilgrim, 1949-69, 3¾", from $35 to **$40.00**

Pitcher, olive green w/clear drop-over handle, can neck, Pilgrim label on body, 1949-69, 4¾", from $45 to..**$50.00**

Pitcher, olive green w/matching drop-over handle, wide mouth, Blenko, 1960s, 5¾", from $50 to **$55.00**

Pitcher, olive green w/matching pulled-back handle, lg air bubbles/crooked handle, Jamestown, 1950s, 5", from $20 to..**$30.00**

Pitcher, olive-green w/matching pulled-back handle, frilly top (5½" wide), Blenko, 1960s, 8¼", from $95 to **$110.00**

Pitcher, ruby, amber drop-over handle, waisted but fat, folded-down rim, unknown maker & date, 4½", from $55 to..**$60.00**

Pitcher, ruby w/amber pulled-back handle, long cylindrical neck, no pouring spout, Pilgrim, 1949-69, 4½", from $40 to..**$45.00**

Pitcher, ruby w/clear drop-over handle, teardrop shape, narrow rim, Pilgrim, 1949-69, 3¾", from $40 to **$45.00**

Pitcher, ruby w/clear drop-over handle, trumpet neck, Pilgrim, 1949-69, 3½", from $40 to......................**$45.00**

Pitcher, ruby w/clear drop-over handle, trumpet neck, Pilgrim, 1949-69, 3¾", from $40 to......................**$45.00**

Pitcher, ruby w/clear drop-over handle, waisted, flat rim w/sm spout, Pilgrim, 1949-69, 3¼", from $40 to..**$45.00**

Pitcher, tangerine, waisted, drop-over handle, Pilgrim, 1940-69, 3½", from $40 to..**$45.00**

Pitcher, tangerine w/amber drop-over handle, cylindrical neck, Pilgrim, 1949-69, 4¾", from $40 to..............**$45.00**

Pitcher, tangerine w/amber drop-over handle, high waist, pinched rim, Rainbow, 1940s-60s, 6", from $70 to..**$75.00**

Pitcher, tangerine w/clear drop-over handle, left-handed (spout at 45 degree angle from handle), 1949-69, 3¾"..........**$50.00**

Pitcher, tangerine w/matching pulled-back handle, Pilgrim, 1949-69, 4", from $40 to......................................**$45.00**

Pitcher, topaz w/amber pulled-back handle, slim neck, Rainbow, late 1940s-60s, 8", from $80 to..............**$90.00**

Pitcher, topaz w/matching drop-over handle, hourglass shape, unknown maker & date, 3½", from $20 to............**$25.00**

Pitcher, topaz w/matching pulled-back handle, trumpet neck, Hamon, 1966-70s, 3¼", from $35 to......................**$40.00**

Pitcher, Wheat w/matching drop-over handle, ovoid, Blenko, 1960s, 9¾", from $75 to......................................**$100.00**

Tumbler, lemonade; clear w/dark amber drop-over handle, unknown maker, 5¼", from $35 to **$50.00**

Vase, amberina, slim teardrop w/flared rim, Kanawha, 1959-87, 5½", from $55 to..**$60.00**

Vase, amberina (Blenko's tangerine), hourglass shape, Blenko, 1961, 7", from $80 to..................................**$85.00**

Vase, amethyst, double-neck (folded to meet in center forming 2 necks), Blenko, 1940s-50s, 4", from $60 to.**$85.00**

Vase, amethyst, pinched rim, fine crackling, Pilgrim, 1949-69, 4", from $65 to..**$80.00**

Vase, amethyst, 4-ruffle rim, can neck, bulbous body, unknown maker & date, 4", from $60 to.............**$85.00**

Vase, black amethyst w/applied serpentine at neck, unknown maker & date, 8¼", from $135 to......**$150.00**

Vase, blue, applied blue decoration at waist, Pilgrim, 1949-69, 5", from $50 to..**$65.00**

Vase, blue, flared cylinder w/slightly shaped rim, Pilgrim, 1949-69, 4½", from $45 to......................................**$50.00**

Vase, emerald green, bottle neck w/flared rim, Hamon, late 1940s-70s, 9¾", from $65 to..................................**$80.00**

Vase, lemon-lime, applied decor at neck, folded rim, Pilgrim, 1949-69, 5", from $50 to..................................**$65.00**

Vase, sea green, pinched rim, lg crackling, Blenko, late 1940s-50s, 3¾", from $55 to..................................**$75.00**

Vase, sea green w/clear drop-over angle handles, Blenko, 1940s-50s, 7½", from $85 to..............................**$100.00**

Vase, tangerine, stick neck, 4-ruffle rim, Rainbow, 1940s-60s, 5¼", from $65 to..**$70.00**

Vase, tangerine (amberina), footed, crimped rim, Blenko, 1950s, 8", from $120 to..**$145.00**

Vase, topaz, ruffled rim, flat disc foot, Bischoff, 1942-63, 10¼", from $110 to..**$135.00**

Vase, yellow (Jonquil), flared/slightly shaped rim, Blenko, 1940s-50s, 11", from $110 to..............................**$135.00**

Wine goblet, olive green, long stem, unknown maker, 5¾", from $50 to..**$75.00**

Cuff Links

Cuff link collecting continues to be one of the fastest growing hobbies. Few collectibles are as affordable, available, and easy to store. Cuff links can often be found at garage sales, thrift shops, and flea markets for reasonable prices.

People collect cuff links for many reasons. Besides being a functional and interesting wearable, cuff links are educational. The design, shape, size, and materials used often relate to events, places, and products, and they typically reflect the period of their manufacture: examples are Art Deco, Victorian, Art Nouveau, Modern, etc. They offer the chance for the 'big find' which appeals to all collectors. Sometimes pairs purchased for small amounts turn out to be worth substantial sums.

Unless otherwise noted, the following listings apply to cuff links in excellent to mint condition.

Advisor: Gene Klompus (See Directory, Cuff Links)

Club: The National Cuff Link Society

Newsletter: *The Link*
Gene Klompus, President
P.O. Box 5700
Vernon Hills, IL 60010
Phone or fax: 847-816-0035; Dues $30 per year; write for free booklet, *The Fun of Cuff Link Collecting*
e-mail: Genek@cufflink.com

Website: www.cufflink.com

Amethyst rectangles (⅝x⅜") set in 14k gold frames, initialed................**$75.00**

Art Deco sterling circlet w/blue enamel, black rim border, seed pearl in center, 2-sided................**$190.00**

Art Deco 14k gold circlets w/intricate pattern & segmented black enamel borders, 2-sided, marked, ⅝" dia.**$200.00**

Cuff links, tie bar and money clip, base metal, ca 1950, EX, $55.00. (Photo courtesy Gene Klompus)

Devil's head, sterling silver, 1950s, ¾", 95.00.
(Photo courtesy Gene Klompus)

Dirksen campaign, elephant heads, rhinestones & enamel, +lapel pin................**$45.00**

Esso Oil Drop, Happy Motoring, figural man on gold-tone mount, 1"................**$35.00**

Mico Mosaic w/multicolor flowers in blue, ca 1930s, ½x½", +tie pin................**$110.00**

Mother-of-pearl circlets w/engraved pattern & white gold trim, 14k yellow gold backs, ½" dia................**$75.00**

Old Pawn Navajo petrified wood & sterling, ca 1950s, 1⅜x1⅛"................**$150.00**

Oliver Tractor 50 series, metal tractor shapes, original..**$85.00**

Oval plaque w/mythological King Tridon on horse, molded plastic, Swank, 1"................**$40.00**

Platinum plated w/round onyx cabachon, Mont Blanc, ⅝"..**$135.00**

Roulette wheels, red & black numbers, button spins wheel & causes metal ball to revolve, Monte Carlo, MIB................**$75.00**

Royal Rangers, enamel emblem on wood-tone sq w/rounded corners................**$35.00**

Silver .925, ball on ea end of rod, Tiffany................**$50.00**

Silver circlet w/lg pearl set in center, marked Mikimoto, +tie bar, MIB................**$125.00**

Sterling circlet w/relief Viking ship, GI in dotted circle (Georg Jensen), sm................**$185.00**

Sterling sq set w/enameled view of jockey on horse, #925S HH (Hans Hansen), stud backs, 1960s, 1x⅞"....**$190.00**

14k gold oval w/relief griffin, marked, 4.10 dwt, ⅞x⅝"................**$50.00**

1972 Olympics logo, silver-tone base metal, toggle back, ¾" diameter, $125.00. (Photo courtesy Gene Klompus)

Cup and Saucer Sets

Lovely cups and saucers are often available at garage sales and flea markets, and prices are generally quite reasonable. If limited space is a consideration, you might enjoy starting a collection, since they're easy to display en masse on a shelf or one at a time as a romantic accent on a coffee table. English manufacturers have produced endless bone china cups and saucers that are more decorative than functional and just as many that are part of their dinnerware lines. American manufacturers were just about as prolific as were the Japanese. Collecting examples from many companies and countries is a wonderful way to study the various ceramic manufacturers. Our advisors have written *Collectible Cups and Saucers, Identification and Values, Books I and II* (Collector Books), with hundreds of color photos organized by six collectible categories: early years (1700 – 1875), cabinet cups, nineteenth and twentieth century dinnerware, English tablewares, miniatures, and mustache cups and saucers.

Advisors: Jim and Susan Harran (See Directory, Cups and Saucers)

Breakfast, Rolls Royce car on footed cup w/loop handle, Elizabethan Fine Bone China, 1964-present, from $30 to................**$40.00**

Coffee, stylized red transfer, tapered coffee can w/loop handle, Gafle Porcelain...Sweden, 1950s, from $30 to..........**$35.00**

Demitasse, Colonial, footed cup w/French Loop handle, Lenox, 1950s, from $40 to................**$50.00**

Demitasse, Dresden flower band, straight cup w/loop handle & low thumb rest, Schumann...US Zone, 1945-49, from $40 to................**$50.00**

Demitasse, gold swirled lines separate cherubs & flowers, straight cup w/winged-maiden handle, Capodimonte, 1930-present..**$60.00**

Demitasse, Golden Orchid, artist signed, bucket-shaped cup w/foot rim, ornate handle, Stouffer Co, 1938-46, from $50 to..**$60.00**

Demitasse, Husk pattern made for Williamsburg, footed creamware cup w/feathered loop handle, Wedgwood, 1950s, from $25 to.......................................**$35.00**

Demitasse, mixed floral on white w/gold, 3-footed cup w/high gooseneck handle, Pirkenhammer, 1918-45, from $40 to..**$50.00**

Demitasse, strawberry cup with leaf-shaped saucer, Cemar, California, 1946 – 1957, from $40.00 to $50.00. (Photo courtesy Jim and Susan Harran)

Demitasse, turquoise, straight cup w/question mark handle, Van Briggle, 1950s, from $60 to.............................**$90.00**

Miniature coffee, gray w/gold trim, straight-sided cup w/loop handle, Bing & Grondahl, ca 1948, from $40 to ..**$50.00**

Miniature tea, Indian Tree, round cup w/loop handle, Coalport, 1960 to present, from $50 to.................**$70.00**

Miniature tea, Lily of the Valley, straight-sided cup w/loop handle, Shelley, 1945-66, from $175 to..............**$200.00**

Miniature tea, paisley chintz, cup w/broken loop handle, Grosvenor China, 1961-69, from $100 to............**$150.00**

Tea, Blossom Time, pastoral scene, 8-lobed footed cup w/loop handle & thumb rest, Royal Albert, 1945, from $40 to..**$50.00**

Tea, blue bachelor buttons, footed & slightly waisted cup w/broken loop handle, Royal Vale, 1962+, from $30 to..**$40.00**

Tea, blue band w/gilt scrolls & jewels on white, footed cup w/ornate handle, Mitterteich Porcelain...US Zone, from $45 to **$60.00**

Tea, blue forget-me-nots form band on white, cup, saucer & desert plate, Paragon, 1957+, from $60 to............**$75.00**

Tea, Cairo, blue & white bird on branch decoration, pedestal foot, scalloped, Coalport, 1949-59, from $40 to ...**$50.00**

Tea, daffodils on white, waisted & footed cup w/broken loop handle, Hammersley, ca 1939-50s, from $35 to ...**$45.00**

Tea, Dainty Pink, Dainty shape, Shelley, 1945-66, from $75 to...**$100.00**

Tea, deep turquoise w/gold trim, footed cup w/8 puffly flutes & curled handle, Royal Albert, 1945+, from $35 to...**$45.00**

Tea, Dresden-style flowers on white w/gold, round cup w/loop handle, Noritake, 1940s, from $25 to.......**$30.00**

Tea, floral transfer border, cup w/French loop handle, Taylor & Kent Ltd, ca 1939-49, from $35 to **$45.00**

Tea, gold flowers on coral, cup w/scalloped foot & ornate handle, Hutschenreuther, ca 1928-43, from $75 to..**$80.00**

Tea, gold leafy designs on bands of turquoise & white, low Doris shape, Aynsley, 1950s, from $30 to............**$40.00**

Tea, gold work on pink & white, gilt inside cup, Royal Doulton, ca 1902-1956, from $125 to.................**$175.00**

Tea, grapes & autumn leaves w/gold on white, footed cup w/ornate handle, Tirschenreuth Bavaria, 1903-81, from $40 to..**$55.00**

Tea, green roses on pale green, footed & scalloped cup w/feather handle, Paragon, 1939-49, from $35 to ..**$45.00**

Tea, green w/heavy gold floral paste, footed/ribbed cup w/broken loop handle, Hammersley & Co, ca 1912-39, from $125 to...**$150.00**

Tea, hand-painted flowers on maroon, scalloped foot & rim, coiled loop handle, Princess China, Occupied Japan, from $30 to...**$40.00**

Tea, Katherine, pink & white w/gold, tapered cup w/scalloped foot, fancy handle, Weimar, 1975-present, from $60 to...**$70.00**

Tea, Maclean, flowers/plaid ribbon & crest, footed cup w/kicked loop handle, Royal Stafford, 1952-present, from $40 to..**$50.00**

Tea, mixed flowers on black w/white band, footed & scalloped cup w/high loop handle, Paragon, 1939-49, from $40 to..**$50.00**

Tea, molded heart-shaped reserves with purple flowers, gold trim, Lefton, ca 1949 – 1955, from $30.00 to $40.00. (Photo courtesy Jim and Susan Harran)

Tea, Nouveau poppies, 4-panel waisted cup w/loop handle & thumb rest, Limoges, ca 1900-1941, from $50 to....**$60.00**

Tea, Old Avesbury, gold & white, Chelsea shape, Royal Crown Derby, ca 1969, from $50 to....................**$60.00**

Tea, orange enameled flowers w/gold on white, footed cup w/coiled handle, New Chelsea China Co, 1951-61, from $35 to..**$40.00**

Tea, peaches & blossoms on white, pear-shaped cup w/broken loop handle, Regency China, 1953-present, from $30 to..**$35.00**

Tea, pink & white floral transfer on pale peach in cup & on saucer, low Doris shape, Aynsley, 1950-present, from $35 to **$40.00**

Tea, Pompador, green & white w/gold florals, scalloped & footed cup w/ear handle, Rosenthal US Zone, 1945-49, from $50 to...**$60.00**

Tea, red w/gold decoration & highlights, round cup w/ring handle, Alka-Kunst Alboth & Kaiser Bavaria, 1927-53, from $50 to...**$75.00**

Tea, rose transfer inside pedestaled cup w/broken loop handle & inside saucer, Lefton China, 1949-55, from $40 to..**$50.00**

Tea, rose transfer on white w/gold, fluted cup w/angular handle & flat thumb rest, Salsbury Crown China, 1951, from $30 to...**$40.00**

Tea, Shamrock, Belleek Pottery, ca 1955-65, w/dessert plate, from $100 to..**$125.00**

Tea, yellow w/gold flowers on rim, York shape, Aynsley, 1950s, from $30 to...**$40.00**

Tea, yellow w/violets inside cup, gold trim, 12-fluted, Adderleys Ltd, ca 1962, from $35 to **$40.00**

Czechoslovakian Glass and Ceramics

Established as a country in 1918, Czechoslovakia is rich in the natural resources needed for production of glassware as well as pottery. Over the years it has produced vast amounts of both. Anywhere you go, from flea markets to fine antique shops, you'll find several examples of their lovely pressed and cut glass scent bottles, Deco vases, lamps, kitchenware, tableware, and figurines.

More than thirty-five marks have been recorded; some are ink stamped, some etched, and some molded in. Paper labels have also been used. *Czechoslovakian Glass and Collectibles* by Diane and Dale Barta and Helen M. Rose, and *Made in Czechoslovakia* by Ruth Forsythe are two books we highly recommend for further study.

Club: Czechoslovakian Collectors Guild International
P.O. Box 901395
Kansas City, MO 64190

Ceramics

Canister, Sugar, Delft-style windmill scene, rectangular..**$45.00**
Creamer, cow figural, yellow & white lustre, 6¼" **$110.00**
Creamer, duck figural, open bill forms spout, 3¾".....**$60.00**
Creamer, hen w/bonnet figural, 4"............................**$45.00**
Creamer, lady figural, 6¼"......................................**$85.00**
Creamer, parrot figural, 4½".....................................**$55.00**

Creamer, swan's head & neck forms handle, 5⅛" **$75.00**
Creamer, white lustre w/cat figural handle, 4⅜"........**$75.00**
Creamer & sugar bowl, pink lustre, w/lid, 3¼", 4"....**$50.00**
Dresser box, courting couple on lid, cobalt body, mirror inside lid, 3¼" **$65.00**
Figurine, Deco-style lady, shiny white, 9¾".............**$250.00**
Figurine, elephant, w/blanket on back, 4½"............**$150.00**

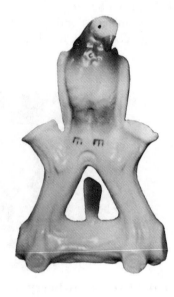

Flower holder, bird on double-branch base, 5½", $50.00. (Photo courtesy Dale and Diane Barta and Helen M. Rose)

Flower holder, bird on stump w/3 openings, 5⅜"......**$40.00**
Flower holder, bird perched along side of open log, 3½"..**$40.00**
Salt & pepper shakers, Mexican couple w/yellow hats, 2¾", pr..**$30.00**
Vase, painted florals on white, cylindrical, 4⅜" **$100.00**

Vase, striated golden lustre glaze with black Art Deco motifs, 10", from $100.00 to $110.00. (Photo courtesy Dale and Diane Barta and Helen M. Rose)

Wall pocket, bird among apples, 4¾" **$65.00**
Wall pocket, bird perched at birdhouse, 5½".............**$60.00**
Wall pocket, multicolor peacock painted on dark blue, 7¼" **$125.00**
Wall pocket, woodpecker along trunk form, 7¾".......**$70.00**

Glassware

Bowl, crystal bubbly glass w/applied blue ornamentation, 4"...**$375.00**

Bowl, painted flowers & stripes on clear footed cylinder, 4¼"..**$90.00**

Candlestick, cameo, black vines on orange, disk foot, slim, 12½"...**$650.00**

Candlestick, cased, yellow w/black edge on ruffled rim, slim, 8½"...**$75.00**

Candlestick, pink w/applied green serpentine decor, 8".**$65.00**

Candy basket, light green, varicolored w/matching handle, 8"...**$200.00**

Candy basket, mottled colors, crystal twisted thorn handle, 7"...**$220.00**

Decanter, green w/painted decor, 7⅝".........................**$75.00**

Figurine, religious figure praying, clear frost, 3⅞"....**$145.00**

Perfume bottle, amber cut to clear, atomizer, 8½"....**$200.00**

Perfume bottle, crystal w/long slim stopper, 5¼".....**$125.00**

Perfume bottle, green w/stepped sides, green frosted stopper, 5⅛"...**$130.00**

Perfume bottle, intaglio-cut lady with flower basket in stopper, 6½", from $350.00 to $450.00. (Photo courtesy Monsen and Baer)

Perfume bottle, topaz w/cut crystal spear-shaped stopper, 5½"...**$170.00**

Pitcher, cobalt w/enameled exotic bird, lid, 11¼"....**$350.00**

Puff box, blue frost, mold-blown flowers, 3¼"...........**$95.00**

Puff box, pink casket shape, 2⅝"..................................**$75.00**

Puff box, pink w/diamond quilt, 6-sided, 4⅜".........**$300.00**

Vase, bud; red w/silver & black decor, inverted cone shape w/black disk foot, 11¼".......................................**$110.00**

Vase, cased, mottled colors, black rim, sm foot, 8½".**$85.00**

Vase, cased, red w/black painted decor, 8½"...........**$120.00**

Vase, cased, varicolored w/green aventurine, trumpet neck, flared foot w/embossed ribs, 7".........................**$150.00**

Vase, cased, white opaque w/red opaque overlay, 5½".**$95.00**

Vase, cased, white w/crystal handle, waisted, sm tiered foot, 7½"...**$65.00**

Vase, cobalt, trumpet neck, 7"...................................**$100.00**

Vase, cobalt cut to clear, 10¼"...................................**$350.00**

Vase, fan; cased, mottled colors w/white interior, flared foot, 8¼"...**$200.00**

Vase, fan; orange w/yellow overlay, 8".....................**$200.00**

Vase, jack-in-the-pulpit; yellow cased w/mottled multicolors at base, 7½"...**$95.00**

Vase, mottled colors, stick neck, 8⅛"..........................**$85.00**

Vase, pink mottled, 9¼"...**$150.00**

Dakin

Dakin has been in the toy-making business since the 1950s and has made several lines of stuffed and vinyl dolls and animals. But the Dakins that collectors are most interested in today are the licensed characters and advertising figures made from 1968 through the 1970s. Originally there were seven Warner Brothers characters, each with a hard plastic body and a soft vinyl head, all under 10" tall. The line was very successful and eventually expanded to include more than fifty cartoon characters and several more that were advertising related. In addition to the figures, there are banks that were made in two sizes. Some Dakins are quite scarce and may sell for over $100.00 (a few even higher), though most will be in the $30.00 to $60.00 range. Dakin is now owned by Applause, Inc.

Condition is very important, and if you find one still in the original box, add about 50% to its value. Figures in the colorful 'Cartoon Theatre' boxes command higher prices than those that came in a clear plastic bag or package (MIP). More Dakins are listed in *Schroeder's Collectible Toys, Antique to Modern*, published by Collector Books.

Alice in Wonderland, w/Alice, Mad Hatter & White Rabbit, artist Faith Wick, 18", MIB.................................**$150.00**

Bamm-Bamm, Hanna-Barbera, 1970, w/club, EX.......**$30.00**

Banana Splits, Second Banana, Hanna-Barbera, 1970, EX, $35.00.

Barney Rubble, Hanna-Barbera, 1970, EX...................**$40.00**

Bugs Bunny, Warner Bros, 1971, MIP $30.00
Bugs Bunny, Warner Bros, 1976, MIB (TV Cartoon Theater box) $40.00
Daffy Duck, Warner Bros, 1976, MIB (TV Cartoon Theater box) $40.00
Dream Pets, Midnight Mouse, cloth, original tag, EX.$15.00
Elmer Fudd, Warner Bros, 1968, hunting outfit w/rifle, EX $125.00
Elmer Fudd, Warner Bros, 1978, MIP (Fun Farm bag)..$60.00
Garfield, 1981, 6½", EX $10.00
Goofy, Disney, cloth clothes, EX....................................$20.00
Goofy Gram, Bull, I'm Mad About You, EX $25.00
Goofy Gram, Frog, Happy Birthday, EX.......................$25.00
Goofy Gram, Tiger, To a Great Guy, EX $25.00
Hoppy Hopperroo, Hanna-Barbera, 1971, EX+..........$75.00
Huey Duck, Disney, straight or bent legs, EX.............$30.00
Louie Duck, Disney, straight or bent legs, EX $30.00

Merlin the Mouse, Warner Bros., 1970, EX+, $25.00.

Olive Oyle, King Features, 1974, cloth clothes, MIP...$50.00
Oliver Hardy, Larry Harmon, 1974, EX+......................$30.00
Pink Panther, Mirisch-Freleng, 1971, EX+ $50.00
Pinocchio, Disney, 1960s, EX $20.00
Popeye, King Features, 1976, MIB (TV Cartoon Theater box)..$50.00
Porky Pig, Warner Bros, 1976, MIB (TV Cartoon Theater box)..$40.00
Ren & Stimpy, water squirters, Nickelodeon, 1993, EX..$10.00
Speedy Gonzales, Warner Bros, MIB (TV Cartoon Theater box) $50.00
Stan Laurel, Larry Harmon, 1974, EX+ $30.00
Sylvester, Warner Bros, 1978, MIP (Fun Farm bag) $20.00
Tasmanian Devil, Warner Bros, 1978, rare, NM $300.00
Tiger in Cage, bank, 1971, EX.......................................$25.00
Top Banana, Warner Bros, NM.......................................$25.00
Underdog, Jay Ward, 1976, MIB (TV Cartoon Theater box) $150.00
Wile E Coyote, Warner Bros, 1976, MIB (TV Cartoon Theater box)...$40.00
Yogi Bear, Hanna-Barbera, 1970, EX...........................$60.00
Yosemite Sam, Warner Bros, 1968, MIB.......................$40.00

Advertising

Bay View Bank, 1976, EX+ $30.00
Bob's Big Boy, 1974, w/hamburger, EX+ $150.00
Buddig Bull, Buddig Meats, 1970s, cloth, EX..............$20.00
Cocker Spaniel, Crocker National Bank, 1979, cloth, 12", VG..$20.00
Diaperene Baby, Sterling Drug Co, 1980, EX..............$40.00
Freddie Fast Gas Attendant, 1976, M $75.00
Glamour Kitty, 1977, w/crown, EX $200.00
Hobo Joe, bank, Hobo Joe's Restaurant, EX $60.00
Kernal Renk, American Seeds, 1970, rare, EX+........$300.00
Li'l Miss Just Rite, 1965, EX+ $60.00

Little Liberty Bell, 1975, MIP, $60.00. (Photo courtesy Jim Rash)

Quasar Robot Bank, 1975, NM $125.00

Sambo's Restaurant, 1974, 8¾", EX/NM, $80.00.

Sambo's Tiger, 1974, vinyl, EX+ $125.00
Smokey the Bear, 1976, M $25.00

St Bernard, Christian Bros Candy, 1982, cloth, VG **$20.00**
Woodsy Owl, 1974, MIP **$60.00**

Decanters

The first company to make figural ceramic decanters was the James Beam Distilling Company. Until mid-1992 they produced hundreds of varieties in their own US-based china factory. They first issued their bottles in the mid-'50s, and over the course of the next twenty-five years, more than twenty other companies followed their example. Among the more prominent of these were Brooks, Hoffman, Lionstone, McCormick, Old Commonwealth, Ski Country, and Wild Turkey. In 1975, Beam introduced the 'Wheel Series,' cars, trains, and fire engines with wheels that actually revolved. The popularity of this series resulted in a heightened interest in decanter collecting.

There are various sizes. The smallest (called miniatures) hold two ounces, and there are some that hold a gallon! A full decanter is worth no more than an empty one, and the absence of the tax stamp doesn't lower its value either. Just be sure that all the labels are intact and that there are no cracks or chips. You might want to empty your decanters as a safety precaution (many collectors do) rather than risk the possibility of the inner glaze breaking down and allowing the contents to leak into the porous ceramic body.

All of the decanters we've listed are fifths unless we've specified 'miniature' within the description.

See also Elvis Presley Collectibles.

Newsletter: *Beam Around the World*
International Association of Jim Beam Bottle and Specialties Clubs
Shirley Sumbles, Executive Administrator
2015 Burlington Ave., Kewanee, IL 61443; 309-853-3370

Newsletter: *The Ski Country Collector*
1224 Washington Ave., Golden, CO 80401

Aesthetic Specialties (ASI), Automotive, Cadillac, 1903, white, 1979 ....**$72.00**
Aesthetic Specialties (ASI), Automotive, Model T Ice Cream Truck, 1980...**$79.00**
Aesthetic Specialties (ASI), Automotive, Oldsmobile, 1920, gold, 1980..**$160.00**
Aesthetic Specialties (ASI), Sports, Bing Crosby 41st, otter, 1981 ....**$65.00**
Aesthetic Specialties (ASI), Sports, Kentucky Derby, 1979 ..**$40.00**
Aesthetic Specialties (ASI), Transportation, Stanley Steamer, 1911, black, 1981 ....**$78.00**
Anniversary, Atlanta, 1972...**$19.00**
Anniversary, Cotton Carnival, 1973 ....**$24.00**
Anniversary, Happy Birthday, white, 1974 ....**$15.00**
Anniversary, John Lennon, 1980...................................**$24.00**
Anniversary, Ohio Presidents, 1972............................**$13.00**
Anniversary, Washington Monument, 1973.................**$23.00**

Armagnac, Lantern, 1955..**$8.00**
Armagnac, Windmill, 1950 ....**$36.00**
Beam, Animal, Ape - King Kong, 1976.......................**$22.00**
Beam, Animal, Bear, Travelodge, 1972 ....**$15.00**
Beam, Animal, Burmese Cat, 1967 ....**$12.00**
Beam, Animal, Fox, Berkley Club, blue, 1967.............**$49.00**
Beam, Animal, Great Dane, 1976 ....**$18.00**
Beam, Animal, Horse w/Foal, Oh! Kentucky, 1982 ....**$80.00**
Beam, Animal, Koala Bear, Australia, gray, 1973 ....**$15.00**
Beam, Animal, Ram, w/thermometer, 1958 ....**$42.00**
Beam, Automotive, Cadillac, '59 Blue Salesman's Special, 1992 ....**$195.00**
Beam, Automotive, Cadillac, '59 Pink Convertible, 1991 ....**$60.00**
Beam, Automotive, Chevrolet, '53 Corvette, white, 1989 .**$175.00**
Beam, Automotive, Chevrolet, '55 Corvette, Apollo White, Angelo's Liquors, 1991 ....**$190.00**
Beam, Automotive, Chevrolet, '57 Bel Air Convertible, red, 1990 ....**$96.00**
Beam, Automotive, Chevrolet, '57 Bel Air Hardtop, black, 1987 ....**$90.00**
Beam, Automotive, Chevrolet, '57 Bel Air Hardtop, turquoise w/white top, 1988..**$70.00**
Beam, Automotive, Chevrolet, '63 Corvette, silver-blue Stingray, New York......................................**$115.00**
Beam, Automotive, Chevrolet, '69 Camaro, yellow w/black top, Pennsylvania, 1988...**$90.00**
Beam, Automotive, Chevrolet, '69 Camaro Convertible, Fathom Green, 1988..**$172.00**

Beam, Automotive, Chevrolet, 1978 Corvette Pace Car, black and silver, 1987, $250.00.

Beam, Automotive, Chevrolet, '78 Corvette, red, 1984 .**$80.00**
Beam, Automotive, Dodge, '70 Challenger, blue, 1992..**$179.00**
Beam, Automotive, Dodge, '70 Hot Rod, yellow, 1992 ...**$55.00**
Beam, Automotive, Duesenberg, light blue, 1981.....**$110.00**
Beam, Automotive, Ford, '56 Thunderbird, gray, 1986 ...**$100.00**
Beam, Automotive, Ford, '56 Thunderbird, yellow, 1986 ...**$110.00**
Beam, Automotive, Ford, '64 Mustang, white, 1985 ...**$75.00**
Beam, Automotive, Ford, 1903 Model A, red w/black trim, 1978 ....**$49.00**
Beam, Automotive, Ford, 1913 Model T, black, 1974 .**$55.00**
Beam, Automotive, Ford, 1928-35 Model A, olive green coupe, 1980...**$55.00**
Beam, Automotive, Ford, 1928-35 Model A V-8 Pick-U-, black, Angelo's Liquors, 1990 ....**$90.00**

Beam, Automotive, Mercedes Benz, '74 SL, Champagne Gold, Angelo's Liquors, 1988 .... **$60.00**

Beam, Bird, Bald Eagle (reissued 1967-68), 1966 .... **$12.00**

Beam, Bird, Blue Goose, 1979 .... **$15.00**

Beam, Bird, Blue Jay, 1969 .... **$9.00**

Beam, Bird, Mallard Duck, 1957 .... **$20.00**

Beam, Bird, Woodpecker, 1969 .... **$9.00**

Beam, Casino, Barney's Slot Machine, 1978 .... **$40.00**

Beam, Casino, Golden Gate, 1969 .... **$65.00**

Beam, Casino, Harold's Club, Silver Opal, 1957 .... **$25.00**

Beam, Casino, Harold's Club, VIP, 1977 .... **$25.00**

Beam, Centennial, Alaska Purchase, 1966 .... **$9.00**

Beam, Centennial, Indianapolis, 1971 .... **$7.00**

Beam, Centennial, Washington State Bicentennial, 1976 .. **$18.00**

Beam, Convention, Buffalo, Lockhart Buffalo, 1998 .... **$59.00**

Beam, Convention, Race Car #2, yellow, 2001 .... **$55.00**

Beam, Convention, Waterman, yellow, 1980 .... **$29.00**

Beam, Ducks Unlimited, #1, Mallard, 1974 .... **$40.00**

Beam, Ducks Unlimited, #12, Redhead, 1986 .... **$62.00**

Beam, Ducks Unlimited, #16, Canada Goose, 1990 .... **$60.00**

Beam, Ducks Unlimited, #2, Wood Duck, 1975 .... **$38.00**

Beam, Ducks Unlimited, #3, Mallard Hen, 1977 .... **$45.00**

Beam, Ducks Unlimited, #5, Canvasback Drake, 1979 .. **$47.00**

Beam, Ducks Unlimited, #7, Green-Winged Teal Pair, 1981 .... **$43.00**

Beam, Ducks Unlimited, #9, American Widgeon Pair, 1983 .... **$65.00**

Beam, Executive, Prestige, 1967 .... **$11.00**

Beam, Executive, Sovereign, 1969 .... **$9.00**

Beam, Fish, Crappie, 1979 .... **$29.00**

Beam, Fish, Largemouth Bass, 1973 .... **$22.00**

Beam, Fish, Perch, 1980 .... **$27.00**

Beam, Fish, Trout Unlimited, 1977 .... **$19.00**

Beam, Fish, Walleye, 1987, $28.00.

Beam, Horse Racing, Churchill Downs, 95th Derby, pink roses, 1969 .... **$24.00**

Beam, Horse Racing, Duidoso Downs, pointed ears, 1968 .... **$35.00**

Beam, People, American Cowboy (not pewter version), 1981 .... **$20.00**

Beam, People, Buffalo Bill, 197 .... **$16.00**

Beam, People, Indian Chief, 1980 .... **$20.00**

Beam, People, Viking, 1973 .... **$16.00**

Beam, Sports, Baseball '100 Years,' 1969 .... **$35.00**

Beam, Sports, Bing Crosby 29th, 1970 .... **$16.00**

Beam, Sports, Clint Eastwood, Tennis, 1973 .... **$26.00**

Beam, Sports, Sports Car Club of America, smooth, 1976 . **$14.00**

Beam, States, Delaware, 1972 .... **$10.00**

Beam, States, Kentucky, brown head, 1967 .... **$15.00**

Beam, States, Oregon, 1967 .... **$23.00**

Beam, Train, Casey Jones, Engine w/Tender (tender is not a bottle), 1989 .... **$45.00**

Beam, Train, Casey Jones Box Car, green, 1990 .... **$30.00**

Beam, Train, General Combination Car, 1988 .... **$49.00**

Beam, Train, General Wood Tender #3, 1988 .... **$125.00**

Beam, Train, Grant Baggage Car, 1982 .... **$60.00**

Beam, Train, JB Turner Caboose #285, yellow, 1985 . **$95.00**

Beam, Train, JB Turner Tank Car, 1983 .... **$65.00**

Beam, Train, JB Turner Wood Tender #249 (tender is not a bottle), 1982 .... **$75.00**

Beam, Transportation, '29 Model A Police Car, blue, 1982 .... **$120.00**

Beam, Transportation, '34 Police Patrol Car, black & white, 1989 .... **$150.00**

Beam, Transportation, Fire Truck Pumper 1934, 1987 .. **$120.00**

Beam, Transportation, Mississippi 1867 Steam Pumper Engine, 1977 .... **$125.00**

Beam, Transportation, Semi Truck/Tractor Trailer, beige, Angelo's Liquors, 1991 .... **$75.00**

Bell's, Christmas, Cellerman's Art, 1995 .... **$50.00**

Bell's, Christmas, We Wish You, 1988 .... **$325.00**

Bell's, Royal, Prince Charles 50th, 1998 .... **$55.00**

Bells, Royal, Andrew & Sarah, 1986 .... **$90.00**

Cyrus Noble, Bartender, 1971 .... **$112.00**

Cyrus Noble, Bartender, 1974, mini **$19.00**

Cyrus Noble, Blacksmith, 1974 .... **$45.00**

Cyrus Noble, Blacksmith, 1976, mini **$17.00**

Cyrus Noble, Carousel, White Charger, 1979 .... **$55.00**

Cyrus Noble, Dolphin, 1979 .... **$48.00**

Cyrus Noble, Mine Shaft, 1978 .... **$38.00**

Cyrus Noble, Mine Shaft, 1979, mini **$19.00**

Cyrus Noble, Whiskey Drummer, 1975 .... **$35.00**

Cyrus Noble, Whiskey Drummer, 1977 .... **$19.00**

Double Springs, Animal, Bull, 1969 .... **$14.00**

Double Springs, Automotive, Bentley 1927 Touring Car, 1972 .... **$45.00**

Double Springs, Automotive, Duesenberg 1921 Phaeton, 1978 .... **$30.00**

Double Springs, Bicentennial, Iowa, 1976 .... **$52.00**

Eam, Sports, WGA Western Open, 1971 .... **$17.00**

Ezra Brooks, Animal, Beaver, 1972 .... **$12.00**

Ezra Brooks, Animal, Clydesdale Horse, 1974 .... **$25.00**

Ezra Brooks, Animal, Ram, 1972 .... **$18.00**

Ezra Brooks, Animal, Setter w/Bird, 1970 .... **$17.00**

Ezra Brooks, Automotive, Indy Car, Gould #1, 1982 .. **$80.00**

Ezra Brooks, Automotive, Sprint Race Car #21, 1971 .**$85.00**
Ezra Brooks, Automotive, 1957 Corvette, blue, 1976..**$120.00**
Ezra Brooks, Bird, Canadian Loon, 1979 ....**$30.00**
Ezra Brooks, Bird, quail, 1970 ....**$11.00**
Ezra Brooks, Casino, Bucket of Blood.........................**$15.00**
Ezra Brooks, Casino, Gold Nugget Rooster, 1969 ....**$28.00**
Ezra Brooks, Casino, Slot Machine, 1971 ....**$25.00**
Ezra Brooks, Clown, Bust #1, Smiley, 1979.................**$32.00**
Ezra Brooks, Clown, w/Accordion, 1971 ....**$27.00**
Ezra Brooks, Fish, Dolphin, Amvet, 1974 ....**$10.00**
Ezra Brooks, Fish, Trout & Fly, 1970 ....**$19.00**
Ezra Brooks, Organization, American Legion, Chicago, 1972 ....**$5.00**
Ezra Brooks, Organization, American Legion, Seattle, 1983 ....**$30.00**
Ezra Brooks, Organization, Bare Knuckle Fighter, 1971 .**$32.00**
Ezra Brooks, Organization, VFW, Illinois #2, 1983......**$25.00**
Ezra Brooks, People, Farmer, Iowa, 1977.....................**$27.00**
Ezra Brooks, People, Minuteman, 1975 ....**$15.00**
Ezra Brooks, People, Tennis Player, 1973.....................**$15.00**
Ezra Brooks, Sports, Greensboro Open, 1972.............**$24.00**
Ezra Brooks, Sports Mascot, Bucky Badger, Boxer, 1973..**$30.00**
Ezra Brooks, Sports Mascot, Trojan Horse, 1974........**$22.00**
Ezra Brooks, Train, Iron Horse, 1969...........................**$12.00**
Famous Firsts, Animal, Bear w/Baby, 1981, mini........**$35.00**
Famous Firsts, Animal, Squirrel, 1981, mini.................**$32.00**
Famous Firsts, Automotive, '53 Corvette, 1975, 500ML..**$95.00**
Famous Firsts, Automotive, Ferrari, Blue, 1975 ....**$50.00**
Famous Firsts, Automotive, Renault Racer #3, 1969....**$65.00**
Famous Firsts, Transportation, China Clipper, 1979..**$125.00**
Famous Firsts, Transportation, Winnie May Plane, 1972, pt...**$75.00**
Garnier, Automotive, Citroen, 1970 ....**$25.00**
Garnier, Automotive, Indy 500 #1, 1970 ....**$42.00**
Garnier, Automotive, 1913 Alfa Romeo, 1969.............**$25.00**
Garnier, Bird, Cardinal, 1969 ....**$15.00**
Garnier, Bird, Meadowlark, 1969.................................**$15.00**
Garnier, Dog, Cocker Spaniel, 1970 ....**$19.00**
Garnier, Dog, Springer Spaniel, 1970 ....**$19.00**
Grenadier, Club Bottle, Robert E Lee, 1974................**$29.00**
Grenadier, Club Bottle, Robert E Lee, 1974, mini **$20.00**
Grenadier, Horse, American Saddle Bred, 1978..........**$49.00**
Grenadier, Horse, Arabian, 1978.................................**$49.00**
Grenadier, Soldier, Napoleonic, Murat, 1970 ....**$21.00**
Grenadier, Soldier - Bicentennial, Brunswick, Dragoons, 1976...**$20.00**
Grenadier, Soldier - British Army, African Rifle Corps, 1970 ....**$35.00**
Grenadier, Soldier - Civil War, Confederate Captain, 1970 ....**$33.00**
Hoffman, Animal, Bear & Cub, 1978.............................**$65.00**
Hoffman, Animal, Boston Terrier, 1978, mini...............**$26.00**
Hoffman, Animal, Kangaroo & Koala Bear, 1978........**$40.00**
Hoffman, Animal, Quarter Horse, mini, 1979..............**$16.00**
Hoffman, Animal, Sammy Siamese, 1981, 50ML..........**$14.00**
Hoffman, Animal, Springer Spaniel, 1979 ....**$58.00**
Hoffman, Animal, Wolf & Raccoon, 1978 ....**$51.00**

Hoffman, Automotive, AJ Foyte #2, 1972 ....**$125.00**
Hoffman, Automotive, Rutherford #3, 1974................**$95.00**
Hoffman, Birds, Canada Geese, 1980, ½-pt.................**$18.00**
Hoffman, Birds, Loon Decoy, 1978.............................**$31.00**
Hoffman, Mr Lucky #1, Cobbler, 1973 ....**$26.00**
Hoffman, Mr Lucky #1, Sandman, 1974, mini **$12.00**
Hoffman, Mr Lucky #2, Charmer, 1974 ....**$25.00**
Hoffman, Mr Lucky #2, Guitarist, 1975, mini...............**$14.00**
Hoffman, Mr Lucky #3, Blacksmith, 1976 ....**$34.00**
Hoffman, Mr Lucky #3, Stockbroker, 1976, mini.........**$16.00**
Hoffman, Mr Lucky #4, Carpenter, 1979 ....**$32.00**
Hoffman, Mr Lucky #4, Tailor, 1979, mini **$13.00**
Hoffman, Mr Lucky #5, Farmer, 1980...........................**$29.00**
Hoffman, Pistol, 45 Automatic, 1978, pt **$26.00**
Hoffman, Rodeo, Bareback Rider, 1978 ....**$45.00**
Hoffman, Rodeo, Rodeo Championship Saddle, 1978..**$59.00**
Hoffman, Sport Helmet, Auburn Tigers, 1981 ....**$30.00**
Hoffman, Sport Mascot, LSU Tiger #1, 1978...............**$35.00**
Jack Daniels, Silver Coronet, 1986...............................**$45.00**
Jack Daniels, Tribute to Tennessee, 1982, 1.75L **$29.00**
Jack Daniels, 125th Anniversary, 1990 ....**$50.00**
Lionstone, Automotive, Corvette, 1984, 1.75L **$100.00**
Lionstone, Automotive, Turbo Car STP, red, 1972 ......**$57.00**
Lionstone, Bicentennial, Betsy Ross, 1975 ....**$26.00**
Lionstone, Bicentennial, Valley Forge, 1975 ....**$29.00**
Lionstone, Bird, Doves of Peace, 1977 ....**$36.00**
Lionstone, Bird, Pintail Duck w/Base, 1981 ....**$49.00**
Lionstone, Circus, Burmese Girl, 1973 ....**$25.00**

Lionstone, Fireman, #1, $125.00. (Photo courtesy Roy Willis)

Lionstone, Firefighter, #1 Fireman, yellow hat, 1972...**$132.00**
Lionstone, Firefighter, #2 Fireman w/Child, 1974 ....**$95.00**
Lionstone, Firefighter, #3 Fireman, Down Pole, 1975 ..**$100.00**
Lionstone, Firefighter, #4 Fireman, Emblem, 1978 ......**$31.00**
Lionstone, Firefighter, #5 Fireman, Emblem, 1979 ......**$32.00**
Lionstone, Old West, Bath, 1976.................................**$70.00**
Lionstone, Old West, Country Doctor, 1969 ....**$22.00**
Lionstone, Old West, Indian, Proud, 1969 ....**$22.00**
Lionstone, Old West, Lonely Luke, 1974.....................**$32.00**

Lionstone, Safari, Gazelles, 1977 ....$20.00
McCormick, Automotive, Dune Buggy, Shrine, 1976..$38.00
McCormick, Automotive, 1937 Packard, black, 1980..$55.00
McCormick, Bicentennial, Ben Franklin, 1975............$25.00
McCormick, Bicentennial, Betsy Ross, 1975 ....$25.00
McCormick, Bird, Canada Goose, 1984 ....$39.00
McCormick, Bird, Wood Duck, 1984, mini $19.00
McCormick, Bull, Black Angus, 1975, mini $25.00
McCormick, Bull, Charlois, 1974................................$25.00
McCormick, Bull, Longhorn, 1975, mini $29.00
McCormick, Confederate, Jeb Stewart, 1976...............$62.00
McCormick, Confederate, Jefferson Davis, 1976 ....$62.00
McCormick, Entertainer, Hank Williams Sr, 1980 .....$140.00
McCormick, Entertainer, Jimmie Durante, 1981..........$65.00
McCormick, Frontiersman, Davy Crockett, 1975 ....$25.00
McCormick, Gunfighter, Bat Masterson, 1972............$32.00
McCormick, Gunfighter, Black Bart, 1974...................$35.00
McCormick, Sport, Air Race Propeller, 1971...............$21.00
McCormick, Sport, Muhammad Ali, 1980 ....$165.00
McCormick, Sport, Texas Tech Raiders, 1972.............$42.00
Mike Wayne, Christmas Tree, green, 1979..................$69.00
Mike Wayne, John Wayne Bust, 1980 ....$55.00
Mike Wayne, Pheasant, 1981 ....$22.00
Old Bardstown, Bulldog, 1980 ....$155.00
Old Bardstown, Iron Worker, 1978............................$27.00
Old Bardstown, Wildcat, #1, 1978.............................$69.00
Old Commonwealth, Coal Miner, #2 Miner w/Pick, 1976..$39.00
Old Commonwealth, Coal Miners, #1 Coal Miner, 1975.....$89.00
Old Commonwealth, Fireman (Modern), #2 Nozzleman,
    1983 ....$72.00
Old Commonwealth, Fireman (Old), #1 Cumberland Valley,
    1976 ....$112.00
Old Commonwealth, Football Mascot, Clemson Tiger,
    1979 ....$43.00
Old Crow, Chess, Bishop...$15.00
Old Crow, Chess, Knight...$15.00
Pacesetter, Camaro Z28, black, 1982 ....$48.00
Pacesetter, Case Tractor, mini $35.00
Pacesetter, Corvette, gold, 1978, mini $50.00
Pacesetter, Corvette Stingray, dark blue, moving wheels,
    1975 ....$68.00
Pacesetter, John Deer Tractor #1, 1982.....................$149.00
Ski Country, Animal, American Elk, 1980..................$205.00
Ski Country, Animal, Badger, 1981............................$51.00
Ski Country, Animal, Fox on Log, 1974 ....$96.00
Ski Country, Animal, Skunk Family, 1978, mini..........$31.00
Ski Country, Bird, Barn Swallow, 1977 ....$50.00
Ski Country, Bird, Blue Wing Teal, 1976 ....$256.00
Ski Country, Bird, Cardinal, 1979 ....$75.00
Ski Country, Bird, King Elder Duck, 1977 ....$61.00
Ski Country, Bird, Pelican, 1976, mini $55.00
Ski Country, Bird, Spectacled Owl, 1976, mini $88.00
Ski Country, Bird, Turkey, 1976 ....$120.00
Ski Country, Bird, White Falcon, 1977, mini $49.00
Ski Country, Bird, Wood Duck, banded, 182, mini.....$50.00
Ski Country, Brown Bear, 1974 ....$38.00
Ski Country, Ceremonial Dancer, Antelope Dancer, 1982..$77.00

Ski Country, Ceremonial Dancer, Butterfly Dancer, 1987,
    mini $35.00
Ski Country, Ceremonial Dancer, Wolf Dancer, 1981,
    mini..$48.00
Ski Country, Christmas, Bob Cratchit, 1977 ....$54.00
Ski Country, Christmas, Scrooge, 1979......................$58.00
Ski Country, Christmas, Woodland Trio, 1990 ....$69.00
Ski Country, Circus, Circus Elephant, 1974.................$44.00
Ski Country, Circus, Clown, 1974, mini $39.00
Ski Country, Circus, Tomb Thumb, 1974....................$33.00
Ski Country, Fire Engine, Ahrens-Fox, red & gold, 1981..$225.00
Ski Country, Fish, Brown Trout, 1976, mini $50.00
Ski Country, Fish, Salmon, 1977 ....$40.00
Ski Country, Grand Slam Animal, Dall Sheep, 1980 .$175.00

Ski Country, Animal, Raccoon, 1975, $55.00.

Wild Turkey, Series #1, #1 Male, Standing, 1971 ......$155.00
Wild Turkey, Series #1, #3 On the Wing, 1982, mini .$19.00
Wild Turkey, Series #2, #1 Lore, 1979.......................$32.00
Wild Turkey, Series #2, #2 Lore, 1980.......................$32.00
Wild Turkey, Series #2, #3 Lore, 1981.......................$44.00
Wild Turkey, Series #3, #1 In Flight, 1983.................$100.00
Wild Turkey, Series #3, #3 Turkey & Bobcat, 1984, mini....$39.00
Wild Turkey, Series #3, #3 Fighting, 1983 ....$145.00
Wild Turkey, Series #4, #2, Turkey & Raccoon, 1984.$90.00
Wild Turkey, Series #4, #4 Turkey & Fox, 1985.........$90.00
Wild Turkey, Series #4, #9 Turkey & Skunk, 1986 .....$99.00

DeForest of California

This family-run company (operated by Jack and Margaret DeForest and sons) was located in California; from the early 1950s until 1970 they produced the type of novelty ceramic kitchenware and giftware items that state has become known for. A favored theme was their onion-head jars, bowls, ashtray, etc., all designed with various comical expressions. Some of their cookie jars were finished in a brown wood-tone glaze and were very similar to many produced by Twin Winton.

See also Cookie Jars.

Bank, Goody, pig figural, brown or pink, 1956, from $225 to...**$275.00**

Bean pot, pig figural, pink w/blue bow finial, Beans on lid, 1956, from $125 to.................................**$150.00**

Candy dish, pig figural, bow on lid, marked Candy on side, 1959, from $65 to.................................**$75.00**

Condiment, Cheezy or Big Cheese, cheese wedge shape w/smiling face, ea from $25 to............................**$35.00**

Condiment, crying face, Onion on Derby-hat lid, from $25 to...**$35.00**

Condiment, hamburger form w/smiling face, Relish on top of bun, 1956, from $25 to.............................**$30.00**

Condiment, smiling face, Horse Radish on hat lid, from $25 to...**$35.00**

Covered dish, peanut w/squirrel finial, from $15 to...**$20.00**

Creamer, pig figural, pink or brown, 1956, ea from $20 to...**$25.00**

Dip set, Peter Porker line, Dippy Pig, pig's head in center of tray, brown or pink, 1956, from $75 to **$95.00**

Garlic jar, smiling male face, Garlic on green hat lid, c 1956, from $25 to...**$30.00**

Hors d'oeuvres, pig figural w/holes in back, from $25 to...**$30.00**

Jam jar, smiling face w/brown hair, Jam on yellow hat lid, ca 1957, from $25 to.................................**$30.00**

Lazy Susan, Perky Pig, from $175.00 to $200.00.
(Photo courtesy Fred and Joyce Roerig)

Mayonnaise jar, happy girl face w/blond pigtails, May o'Naise on green hat lid, c 1957.......................**$30.00**

Pitcher, pig's head figural, brown or pink, 2-25, from $65 to **$75.00**

Plate, chop; Bar-B-Cutie, onion face, 15", from $65 to **$75.00**

Plate, dinner; Bar-B-Cutie, onion face, 11", from $35 to...**$45.00**

Platter, Hammy, pig's face, 1956, from $60 to............**$70.00**

Range set, Perky (pig's face), drippings jar w/salt & pepper shakers, unmarked, 3-pc set, from $75 to **$95.00**

Relish jar, Hammy Jr pig's face w/bow tie, pink or brown, 1947, 9x10", from $55 to **$65.00**

Rolling pin, Caution, Don't Dalley in This Galley, face on white, multicolor handles, from $55 to..................**$65.00**

Salt & pepper shakers, Bar-B-Cutie, onions, pr, from $20 to...**$30.00**

Salt & pepper shakers, cheese wedges, unmarked, pr, from $25 to...**$30.00**

Spoon rest, boy & girl faces form 2 rests, from $40 to...**$50.00**

Tea set, floral decor on shaded brown, stacking, 3-pc, from $40 to...**$50.00**

Tureen, Bar-B-Cutie, onion face, w/ladle, 8x12", from $175 to...**$195.00**

Degenhart

John and Elizabeth Degenhart owned and operated the Crystal Art Glass Factory in Cambridge, Ohio. From 1947 until John died in 1964, they produced some fine glassware. John was well known for his superior paperweights, but the glassware that collectors love today was made after '64, when Elizabeth restructured the company, creating many lovely moulds and scores of colors. She hired Zack Boyd, who had previously worked for Cambridge Glass, and between the two of them, they developed almost 150 unique and original color formulas.

Complying with provisions she had made before her death, close personal friends at Island Mould and Machine Company in Wheeling, West Virginia, took Elizabeth's moulds and removed the familiar 'D in a heart' trademark from them. She had requested that ten of her moulds be donated to the Degenhart Museum, where they remain today. Zack Boyd eventually bought the Degenhart factory and acquired the remaining moulds. He has added his own logo to them and is continuing to press glass very similar to Mrs. Degenhart's.

For more information, we recommend *Degenhart Glass and Paperweights* by Gene Florence, published by the Degenhart Paperweight and Glass Museum, Inc., Cambridge, Ohio.

Club: Friends of Degenhart
Degenhart Paperweight and Glass Museum
P.O. Box 186, Cambridge, OH 43725
614-432-2626. Individual membership: $5 per year; membership includes newsletter, *Heartbeat*, a quarterly publication and free admission to the museum

Beaded Oval Toothpick, Lavender Slag.......................**$30.00**

Bernard & Eldena, Amethyst Carnival, pr...................**$15.00**

Bernard & Eldena, Ice Blue Carnival, pr **$15.00**

Bird on Nest, Milk Glass **$50.00**

Bird Salt, Bittersweet **$20.00**

Bird Salt, Lavender Green Slag **$35.00**

Bird Toothpick, Milk White...**$15.00**

Bird w/Cherry Salt, Dark Custard Slag........................**$25.00**

Daisy & Button Toothpick, Vaseline............................**$30.00**

Elizabeth Degenhart Portrait Plate, Amberina **$35.00**

Elizabeth Degenhart Portrait Plate, Amethyst..............**$50.00**

Elizabeth Degenhart Portrait Plate, Caramel Slag........**$15.00**

Elizabeth Degenhart Portrait Plate, Clear....................**$30.00**

Forget Me Not Toothpick, Crown Tuscan....................$27.50
Forget-Me-Not Toothpick, Brownie..........................$21.00
Forget-Me-Not Toothpick, Ivory $21.00
Forget-Me-Not Toothpick, Misty Green....................$22.50
Forget-Me-Not Toothpick, Sparrow Slag....................$22.50

Gypsy Pot Toothpick Holder, Bittersweet, $35.00.

Heart Jewel Box, Cobalt....................................$25.00
Heart Toothpick, Milk White $15.00
Hen Covered Dish, Amber, 3½" $30.00

Hen Covered Dish, Tomato, $80.00.

Little Brave, Milk Glass....................................$10.00
Little Brave, Purple $10.00
Little Buckaroo, Purple Slag..............................$10.00
Ohio Plate, Old Custard $15.00
Owl, Blue Milk Glass......................................$16.50
Owl, Chad's Blue, from $45 to $50.00
Owl, Cobalt Carnival $125.00
Owl, Custard $45.00
Owl, Custard #2 ....$50.00
Owl, Dark Rose $45.00
Owl, Delft Blue..$55.00
Owl, Fog Opaque..$60.00

Owl, Light Bluefire $45.00
Owl, Louise Lavender......................................$16.50
Owl, Milk Blue..$45.00
Owl, Periwinkle $50.00
Owl, Pink $50.00
Owl, Pink Milk Glass......................................$15.00
Owl, Red Carnival $110.00
Owl, Smoky..$50.00
Owl, Violet $55.00
Owl, Yellow Vaseline......................................$20.00
Paperweight, multicolor floral w/5 teardrop controlled bubbles, 1950s, John Degenhart, 3¼x3½" $250.00
Paperweight, single flower on green bed, John Degenhart, 1950s, 3x3" $250.00
Paperweight, 5 multicolor flowers w/controlled bubble center, John Degenhart, 1950s, 2½x2½"..................$175.00
Pooch, Blue Bell..$22.00
Pooch, Buttercup $15.00
Pooch, Elizabeth Blue $15.00
Pooch, Ivory Slag..$15.00
Pooch, Rose Marie $25.00
Pooch, Royal Violet $17.50
Pooch, Ruby Red $25.00
Pooch, Sahara Sand $15.00

Pooch, Tomato Slag, $40.00.

Priscilla, Amber..$125.00
Priscilla, Amber Satin....................................$150.00
Priscilla, Amethyst Heather Bloom......................$100.00
Priscilla, April Green $100.00
Priscilla, Bittersweet Slag................................$150.00
Priscilla, Blue Carnival..................................$170.00
Priscilla, Cobalt $100.00
Priscilla, Dark Amethyst $150.00
Priscilla, Jade..$150.00
Shoe Skate, Sapphire Blue $35.00
Sweetheart Toothpick, Amber............................$20.00
Sweetheart Toothpick, April Green $25.00
Tomahawk, Amethyst $25.00
Tomahawk, Amethyst Carnival $30.00

Tomahawk, Cobalt Blue Carnival **$50.00**
Turkey Covered Dish, Amberina **$30.00**
Turkey Covered Dish, Amethyst................................**$35.00**
Turkey Covered Dish, Caramel Slag...........................**$75.00**

deLee Art Pottery

Jimmie Lee Adair Kohl founded her company in 1937, and it continued to operate until 1958. She was the inspiration, artist, and owner of the company for the twenty-one years it was in business. The name deLee means 'of or by Lee' and is taken from the French language. She trained as an artist at the San Diego Art Institute and UCLA where she also earned an art education degree. She taught art and ceramics at Belmont High School in Los Angeles while getting her ceramic business started. Jimmie Lee died on September 9, 1999, at the age of 93, after having lived a long and wonderfully creative life.

The deLee line included children, adults, animals, birds, and specialty items such as cookie jars, banks, wall pockets, and several licensed Walter Lantz characters. Skunks were a favorite subject, and more of her pieces were modeled as skunks than any other single animal. Her figurines are distinctive in their design, charm, and excellent hand painting; when carefully studied, they can be easily recognized. Jimmie Lee modeled almost all the pieces — more than 350 in all.

The beautiful deLee colors were mixed by her and remained essentially the same for twenty years. The same figurine may be found painted in different colors and patterns. Figurines were sold wholesale only. Buyers could select from a catalog or visit the deLee booth in New York and Los Angeles Gift Marts. All figurines left the factory with name and logo stickers. The round Art Deco logo sticker is silver with the words 'deLee Art, California, Hand Decorated.' Many of the figures are incised 'deLee Art' on the bottom.

The factory was located in Los Angeles during its twenty-one years of production and in Cuernavaca, Mexico, for four years during WWII. Production continued until 1958, when Japanese copies of her figures caused sales to decline. For further study we recommend *deLee Art* by Joanne and Ralph Schaefer and John Humphries.

Advisors: Joanne and Ralph Schaefer (See Directory, deLee)

Bank, Money Bunny, pink & white w/blue purse, 9", from $90 to..**$95.00**
Candle holder, Star, singing angel, 4½", from $25 to...**$35.00**
Cookie jar, Cookie, girl wearing chef's hat, words painted on apron, 12", from $250 to.......................................**$400.00**
Figurine, Amigo, donkey, freckles on nose, 5", from $50 to **$60.00**
Figurine, boy w/sailboat, round silver sticker on his back, 4", from $65 to...**$85.00**

Figurine, Bunny Hug, rabbit w/arms extended, flowers on white body, 5½", from $30 to...............................**$35.00**
Figurine, Butch, sailor boy, 1942, 6", from $40 to **$60.00**
Figurine, Can-Can Dancer, swinging skirt, 14", from $150 to **$175.00**
Figurine, Corny, boy w/fish, 5¼", from $65 to **$85.00**
Figurine, Daisy, red roses on bodice, white skirt w/red trim, sticker w/name, ca 1950, 8"..................................**$20.00**
Figurine, Ferdinand, seated bull, 1938, 5", from $50 to..**$65.00**
Figurine, girl in sunsuit holding starfish, #40, 7", from $85 to **$125.00**
Figurine, girl kneeling & saying prayers, flesh-toned paint, #39, 3", from $65 to...**$125.00**
Figurine, Happy, elephant, pink & white w/pink & blue flowers, from $40 to **$50.00**

**Figurine, horse with flower wreath, 5",
from $60.00 to $75.00.** (Photo courtesy
Joanne and Ralph Schaefer and John Humphries)

Figurine, June, seated w/open book, 4", from $65 to...**$85.00**
Figurine, Kitty, coy look, w/sticker, 4", from $35 to...**$45.00**
Figurine, Leilani, Island girl in 2-pc bathing suit, seated, 9", from $200 to..**$300.00**
Figurine, Nina, laced vest, lavender flowers on skirt, 6"...**$25.00**
Figurine, Olga, ballerina on tummy, rare, 3½", from $150 to **$175.00**
Figurine, Pancake, panda bear, black & white, seated, 6", from $50 to..**$65.00**
Figurine, poodle, silver 'spaghetti' fur, 6½", from $70 to...**$90.00**
Figurine, Sadie, pig, hand painted **$25.00**
Figurine, skunk, from 2¼-3½" L, ea, from $20 to.......**$35.00**
Figurine, Smoothie, cocker spaniel, sitting, 4", from $25 to...**$35.00**
Figurine, Stinkie, skunk, 4".......................................**$24.00**
Figurine, Waddles, realistic paint w/airbrushing & hand finishing, 1950s, ½" sticker, from $25 to **$35.00**

Figurines, Buddy and Sis, from $45.00 to $60.00 each. (Photo courtesy Joanne and Ralph Schaefer and John Humphries)

Figurines, Sadie and Cy, 3" and 2½", $60.00 for the pair.
(Photo courtesy Joanne and Ralph Schaefer and John Humphries)

Head vase, girl w/short ponytails, 2 holes at top of head, 5½", from $65 to **$85.00**
Planter, Annabelle, flower trim, 8", from $35 to..........**$45.00**
Planter, Annie, blond w/blue bow & flowers on dress, holds basket w/opening, 1940, 10", from $65 to............**$85.00**
Planter, Audrey, opening in basket hanging from left arm, 1940, 7", from $40 to **$65.00**
Planter, Buddy, blue shirt, basket on shoulder forms planter, 7", from $45 to **$60.00**
Planter, Hank, purple outfit, pillar planter behind, 7½", from $35 to..**$50.00**
Planter, Hattie, blue bodice & flowered skirt, w/sticker, 7½" **$25.00**
Planter, Hattie, pink roses on bodice & along hem, #40, 7½", from $30 to...**$45.00**
Planter, Johnny, holding flowers, pillar planter at his back, 8½", from $50 to **$60.00**
Planter, Katrina, brown hair & shoes, 6½", from $35 to .**$45.00**
Planter, lamb, white w/blue bell, unmarked, 8", from $45 to **$60.00**

Planter, Linda, crown of hat has opening, 7½", from $35 to **$50.00**
Planter, Lizzie, tipping hat, planter behind & to the right, 9", from $35 to...**$50.00**
Planter, Lou, 2 openings, green bow & waist, dainty flower decor, 7", from $35 to...**$50.00**
Planter, Maria, green & purple flowers, 1940s, 6¾"....**$20.00**
Planter, Mary, lamb at side, holds vase (planter), 1938, 6½", from $50 to...**$65.00**
Planter, Mr Chips, chipmunk, opening in acorn he holds, 1940, 4½", from $25 to..**$35.00**
Planter, Pat, opening in uplifted skirt, decoration on pantaloons, 1940, 6¼-7", from $25 to **$40.00**
Planter, Peanuts, elephant holding drum w/opening, 1948, 7", from $75 to..**$95.00**
Planter, Pedro, Mexican boy w/guitar, 8", from $30 to **$45.00**
Planter, Sahara Sue, opening in saddle, 5", from $60 to ..**$85.00**
Planter, Sally, holding chick, opening in bonnet, 1938, 6½", from $35 to...**$45.00**
Planter, Sonny, green jacket, lg planter behind, 8", from $50 to **$65.00**
Planter, Sue, holds bouquet, opening at back, 8", from $50 to **$60.00**
Vase, girl leaning over edge of flower-petal vase (2½x3½"), unmarked, 5", from $75 to...............................**$125.00**

Delft

Collectors have been in love with the quaint blue and white Delftware for many years. It was originally made in the Dutch city of Delft (hence its name), but eventually it was also produced in England and Germany. Antique Delft can be very expensive, but even items made in the twentieth century are very collectible and much less pricey. Thousands of Delft pieces are being imported every year from the Netherlands, ranging from souvenir grade to excellent quality ware made under the Royal Delft label. All of our examples are from more recent production, such as you might find at garage sales and flea markets.

Bank, Canal House Bank of Amsterdam, 7¼x3".........**$25.00**
Cake plate, windmill scene, pedestal foot, Holland, 3¾x10¾"..**$45.00**
Canisters, windmills, scalloped, Ter Steege, set of 4 ..**$55.00**
Charger, horse & coach scene, 15¼"............................**$46.00**
Cheeseboard, ceramic, 10¾x6¾", w/ceramic-handled knife **$40.00**
Clock, mantel; windmill, Holland, battery operated, 5x8¼" **$50.00**
Coaster set, windmill & swans, 3½", 8 for..................**$35.00**
Coffee filter holder, Dewitt, 6½x7".............................**$30.00**
Coffee grinder, windmill scene, mounted on wooden board, 1930s..**$125.00**
Creamer, cow figural, 10¾x8½"....................................**$30.00**
Cup & saucer, windmill scene, scalloped-rim saucer, Steege, 4 for **$32.00**

Decanter, pitcher-like shape, Levert & Co, Amsterdam Holland, 5" dia **$47.00**

Earrings, windmill cabochon on sterling mount, clip style, 1", pr...**$20.00**

Lamp, boudoir; windmill scene, paper shade w/rick-rack trim, 8" **$25.00**

Lamp; windmill scene, electric, matching shade, Holland, 9" **$40.00**

Mug, windmill scene, horses & wagon, made for Heinekin, 5½" **$30.00**

Pitcher & bowl, windmill scene, Holland, 9", 8".........**$45.00**

Plaques, Porceleyne, 6", set of five, from $225.00 to $250.00. (Photo courtesy Michael Sessman)

Plate, Ann Frank House, 7¼" **$30.00**
Plate, floral, 10¼"...**$30.00**
Plate, shoemaker making wooden shoes, 9½"............**$25.00**
Plate, sleigh scene, 12¾"...**$40.00**
Plate, windmill & people, Holland, 10¼" **$40.00**
Spoon rack, windmill scene, holds 6 spoons, Dewitt, 8x4" .**$24.00**
Stein, windmill scene & floral spray, 6½"...................**$25.00**
Teapot, windmill scene, 10¼".....................................**$25.00**
Wafer jar, 7 styles of windmills, 4½x3¾" **$25.00**

Depression Glass

Since the early '60s, this has been a very active area of collecting. Interest is still very strong, and although values have long been established, except for some of the rarer items, Depression glass is still relatively inexpensive. Some of the patterns and colors that were entirely avoided by the early wave of collectors are now becoming popular, and it's very easy to reassemble a nice table setting of one of these lines today.

Most of this glass was manufactured during the Depression years. It was inexpensive, mass produced, and available in a wide assortment of colors. The same type of glassware was still being made to some extent during the '50s and '60s, and today the term 'Depression glass' has been expanded to include the later patterns as well.

Some things have been reproduced, and the slight variation in patterns and colors can be very difficult to detect. For instance, the Sharon butter dish has been reissued in original colors of pink and green (as well as others that were not original); and several pieces of Cherry Blossom, Madrid, Avocado, Mayfair, and Miss America have also been reproduced. Some pieces you'll see in 'antique' malls and flea markets today have been recently made in dark uncharacteristic 'carnival' colors, which, of course, are easy to spot.

For further study, Gene Florence has written several informative books on the subject, and we recommend them all: *The Pocket Guide to Depression Glass, The Collector's Encyclopedia of Depression Glass,* and *Very Rare Glassware of the Depression Years* (Collector Books).

See also Anchor Hocking and other specific companies.

Adam, green, tumbler, 4½" **$30.00**
Adam, pink, ashtray, 4½" **$30.00**
Adam, pink, cake plate, footed, 10" **$30.00**
Adam, pink, lamp **$495.00**
Adam, pink, pitcher, round base, 32-oz......................**$75.00**
Adam, pink or green, bowl, cereal; 5¾"......................**$55.00**
Adam, pink or green, creamer....................................**$28.00**
Adam, pink or green, saucer, sq, 6" **$6.00**

Adam, pink or green, water pitcher, 8", $45.00.

Adams Rib, any iridescent color, creamer...................**$45.00**
Adams Rib, any non-iridescent color, bowl, salad; 3-footed, 8" **$45.00**
Adams Rib, any non-iridescent color, plate, lunch **$18.00**
Addie, any color other than black, cobalt, jade or red, tumbler, water; footed, 9-oz **$15.00**
Addie, black, cobalt, jade or red, mayonnaise, 5".......**$25.00**
Amelia, Rubigold, bowl, sq, 5½" **$30.00**
Amelia, smoke, tumbler, 4" **$50.00**
American Pioneer, crystal, pink or amber, goblet, cocktail; 3-oz, 3¾" **$40.00**
American Pioneer, crystal, pink or green, cup...........**$12.00**
American Pioneer, crystal, pink or green, pilsner, 11-oz, 5¾"..**$150.00**

American Pioneer, crystal or pink, bowl, w/lid, 8¾" ..**$125.00**
American Pioneer, crystal or pink, goblet, water; 8-oz, 6" .**$45.00**
American Pioneer, crystal or pink, sugar bowl, 3½" ...**$20.00**
American Pioneer, crystal or pink, tumbler, 12-oz, 5" **$50.00**
American Pioneer, green, candy jar, w/lid, 1-lb **$110.00**
American Pioneer, green, plate, w/handles, 6" **$15.00**
American Pioneer, green, tumbler, 8-oz, 4" **$55.00**
American Sweetheart, Monax, bowl, soup; flat, 9½" ..**$90.00**
American Sweetheart, Monax, plate, chop; 11" **$25.00**
American Sweetheart, Monax, salt & pepper shakers, footed,
    pr **$475.00**
American Sweetheart, pink, bowl, berry; flat, 3¾" **$85.00**
American Sweetheart, pink, plate, salad; 8" **$14.00**
American Sweetheart, pink, platter, oval, 13" **$55.00**
American Sweetheart, pink, sugar bowl, open, footed **$15.00**
American Sweetheart, pink or Monax, plate, salver; 12" .**$24.00**
American Sweetheart, red, bowl, console; 18" **$1,100.00**
American Sweetheart, smoke & other trims, plate, luncheon;
    9" **$45.00**
Aunt Polly, blue, bowl, berry; lg, 7⅞" **$50.00**
Aunt Polly, blue, pitcher, 48-oz, 8" **$225.00**
Aunt Polly, blue, plate, luncheon; 8" **$20.00**
Aunt Polly, green or iridescent, bowl, 2x4¾" **$18.00**
Aunt Polly, green or iridescent, candy, footed, w/handles ..**$30.00**
Aunt Polly, green or iridescent, creamer **$35.00**
Aunt Polly, green or iridescent, sugar bowl **$25.00**
Aurora, cobalt or pink, creamer, 4½" **$25.00**
Aurora, cobalt or pink, tumbler, 10-oz, 4¾" **$27.50**
Avocado, crystal, bowl, oval, w/handles, 8" **$11.00**
Avocado, crystal, pitcher, 64-oz **$350.00**
Avocado, green, bowl, preserve; w/handle, 7" **$35.00**
Avocado, green, sherbet **$70.00**
Avocado, pink, bowl, w/handles, 5¼" **$30.00**
Avocado, pink, cake plate, w/handles, 10¼" **$55.00**
Avocado, pink, creamer, footed **$35.00**
Avocado, pink, tumbler **$195.00**
Beaded Block, crystal, pink, green or amber, bowl, jelly;
    w/handles, 4⅞" to 5" **$20.00**
Beaded Block, crystal, pink, green or amber, bowl, pickle;
    w/handles, 6½" **$30.00**
Beaded Block, crystal, pink, green or amber, plate, round,
    8¾" **$30.00**
Beaded Block, ice blue, bowl, sq, 5½" **$35.00**
Beaded Block, milk white, bowl, celery; 8¼" **$60.00**
Berlin, crystal, basket **$27.50**
Berlin, crystal, bowl, round, 7" **$20.00**
Berlin, crystal, creamer **$20.00**
Berlin, crystal, plate, lunch; 9" **$15.00**
Block Optic, green, butter dish, w/lid, 3x5" **$50.00**
Block Optic, green, mug **$40.00**
Block Optic, green, plate, grill; 9" **$95.00**
Block Optic, green, salt & pepper shakers, footed, pr ...**$45.00**
Block Optic, green, tumbler, footed, 10-oz, 6" **$35.00**
Block Optic, green, vase, blown, 5¾" **$350.00**
Block Optic, green or pink, bowl, salad; 7¼" **$175.00**
Block Optic, green or pink, goblet, wine; 4½" **$40.00**
Block Optic, green or pink, plate, sandwich; 10¼" **$25.00**

Block Optic, green or pink, tumbler, flat, 9½-oz, 3¹³⁄₁₆" ..**$15.00**
Block Optic, green or pink, whiskey, 2-oz, 2¼" **$32.00**
Block Optic, pink, pitcher, 54-oz, 8½" **$50.00**
Block Optic, yellow, plate, dinner; 9" **$45.00**
Block Optic, yellow, sherbet, 5½-oz, 3¼" **$10.00**
Bowknot, green, bowl, cereal; 5½" **$35.00**
Bowknot, green, plate, salad; 7" **$15.00**
Bowknot, green, sherbet, low footed **$25.00**
Cameo, crystal or platinum, bowl, sauce; 4¼" **$6.00**
Cameo, crystal or platinum, cup, 2 styles **$5.50**
Cameo, crystal or platinum, tumbler, water; 9-oz, 4" **$9.00**
Cameo, green, bowl, cereal; 5½" **$40.00**
Cameo, green, butter dish, w/lid **$250.00**
Cameo, green, cookie jar, w/lid **$65.00**
Cameo, green, goblet, water; 6" **$65.00**

**Cameo, green, luncheon plate, 8", $15.00; yellow,
$11.00; pink, $35.00. (Photo courtesy Gene Florence)**

Cameo, green, pitcher, syrup or milk; 20-oz, 5¾" **$295.00**
Cameo, green, plate, grill; closed handles, 10½" **$75.00**
Cameo, green, platter, closed handles, 12" **$30.00**
Cameo, green, tumbler, flat, 10-oz, 4¾" **$30.00**
Cameo, green, vase, 5¾" **$250.00**
Cameo, pink, cake plate, flat, 10½" **$175.00**
Cameo, pink, plate, sandwich; 10" **$55.00**
Cameo, yellow, bowl, console; 3-legged, 11" **$125.00**
Cameo, yellow, plate, grill; 10½" **$10.00**
Cameo, yellow, sherbet, molded, 3⅛" **$40.00**
Cameo, yellow, tumbler, footed, 9-oz, 5" **$17.50**
Cherry Blossom, delphite, creamer **$22.00**
Cherry Blossom, delphite, platter, oval, 11" **$45.00**
Cherry Blossom, green, bowl, cereal; 5¾" **$47.50**
Cherry Blossom, green, plate, dinner; 9" **$28.00**
Cherry Blossom, green, tray, sandwich; 10½" **$33.00**
Cherry Blossom, green or delphite, plate, sherbet; 6" ..**$10.00**
Cherry Blossom, pink, butter dish, w/lid **$90.00**
Cherry Blossom, pink, sugar bowl **$14.50**
Cherry Blossom, pink, tumbler, flat, PAT, 12-oz, 5" **$75.00**

Cherryberry, crystal or iridescent, bowl, 2x6¼" $50.00
Cherryberry, crystal or iridescent, butter dish, w/lid.....$150.00
Cherryberry, crystal or iridescent, sugar bowl, lg $15.00
Cherryberry, pink or green, creamer, lg, 4⅝"..............$42.50
Cherryberry, pink or green, plate, sherbet; 6"............$12.00
Cherryberry, pink or green, sherbet..........................$10.00
Chinex Classic, browntone or plain ivory, bowl, soup; 7¾" $12.50
Chinex Classic, browntone or plain ivory, plate, sandwich or cake; 11½" $7.50
Chinex Classic, castle decorated, plate, sherbet; 6¼" ...$7.50
Chinex Classic, castle decorated, saucer $6.00
Chinex Classic, decal decorated, bowl, cereal; 5¾"......$9.00
Chinex Classic, decal decorated, butter dish $75.00
Circle, green, bowl, 5¼"..$20.00
Circle, green, bowl, 9⅜"..$35.00
Circle, green, pitcher, 80-oz $35.00
Circle, green, sherbet, 4¾" $7.00
Circle, green, tumbler, tea; 10-oz, 5" $18.00
Circle, pink, plate, luncheon; 8¼" $10.00
Circle, pink, plate, sherbet/saucer; 6" $5.00
Circle, pink, sherbet, 3⅛" $10.00
Cloverleaf, black, creamer, footed, 3⅝" $18.00
Cloverleaf, green, sugar bowl, footed, 3⅝" $10.00
Cloverleaf, green or yellow, plate, sherbet; 6" $10.00
Cloverleaf, pink, green or yellow, bowl, dessert; 4"...$40.00
Cloverleaf, pink, tumbler, flat, flared, 10-oz, 3¾" $30.00
Cloverleaf, yellow, plate, luncheon; 8" $14.00
Colonial, crystal, bowl, berry; lg, 9".........................$25.00
Colonial, crystal, plate, grill; 10" $15.00
Colonial, crystal, plate, saucer/sherbet......................$3.00
Colonial, crystal, tumbler, 11-oz, 5⅛" $22.00
Colonial, green, bowl, cream soup; 4½" $80.00
Colonial, green, plate, luncheon; 8½"........................$11.00
Colonial, green, stem, cocktail; 3-oz, 4"....................$25.00
Colonial, pink, bowl, berry; 3¾" $60.00
Colonial, pink, cup..$10.00
Colonial, pink, sugar bowl, 4½".................................$25.00
Colonial, pink, tumbler, footed, 3-oz, 3¼" $17.00
Colonial, pink or green, whiskey, 1½-oz, 2½".........$16.00
Colonial Block, crystal, bowl, 7"................................$10.00
Colonial Block, crystal, creamer $6.00
Colonial Block, pink or green, butter dish................$45.00
Colonial Block, pink or green, sherbet........................$8.00
Colonial Block, white, sugar bowl $8.00
Colonial Fluted, green, bowl, berry; 4"......................$12.00
Colonial Fluted, green, cup..$8.00
Colonial Fluted, green, plate, sherbet; 6" $4.00
Colonial Fluted, green, sugar bowl $10.00
Columbia, crystal, bowl, salad; 8½" $22.00
Columbia, crystal, butter dish, w/lid..........................$20.00
Columbia, crystal, plate, snack $30.00
Columbia, crystal, tumbler, water; 9-oz......................$30.00
Columbia, pink, cup $25.00
Columbia, pink, plate, luncheon; 9½" $35.00
Coronation, green, sherbet..$85.00
Coronation, pink, bowl, no handles, 4¼"..................$80.00

Coronation, pink, plate, luncheon; 8½" $4.50
Coronation, pink, tumbler, footed, 10-oz, 5" $30.00
Coronation, royal ruby, bowl, berry; lg, w/handles, 8" ..$20.00
Crackle, crystal, bowl, console $20.00
Crackle, crystal, cup $10.00
Crackle, crystal, pitcher, cone, footed, 9" $45.00
Crackle, crystal, plate, snack; cloverleaf $13.00
Crackle, crystal, tumbler, juice; straight sides $8.00
Cremax, blue or decorated, bowl, cereal; 5¾" $10.00
Cremax, blue or decorated, plate, bread & butter; 6¼" ..$4.00
Cremax, creamer..$4.50
Cremax, sugar bowl, open..$4.50
Crow's Foot, amber, plate, round, 8" $4.50
Crow's Foot, black or blue, bowl, sq, 4⅞".................$30.00
Crow's Foot, black or blue, vase, 4½x4"....................$80.00
Crow's Foot, red, creamer, footed..............................$12.50
Crow's Foot, red, platter, 12" $55.00
Cube, green, butter dish, w/lid...................................$65.00
Cube, pink, plate, luncheon; 8" $9.00
Cube, pink, sugar bowl, 3" $7.00
Cube, pink or green, candy jar, w/lid, 6½" $30.00
Cube, pink or green, coaster, 3¼" $10.00
Cupid, green or pink, bowl, fruit; 10¼" $215.00
Cupid, green or pink, creamer, flat............................$175.00
Cupid, green or pink, cup $75.00
Cupid, green or pink, saucer......................................$25.00
Della Robbia, any color, bowl, finger; 5"..................$35.00
Della Robbia, any color, cup, punch $15.00
Della Robbia, any color, plate, salad; 7¼"................$25.00
Della Robbia, stem, champagne; 6-oz........................$28.00
Diamond Quilted, blue or black, bowl, cereal; 5" $15.00
Diamond Quilted, pink or green, plate, sandwich; 14" ...$15.00
Diana, crystal, bowl, cream soup; 5½" $12.00
Diana, crystal, sugar bowl, open, oval........................$9.00
Diana, crystal or amber, plate, bread & butter; 6".........$2.00
Diana, pink, coaster, 3½"...$8.00
Dogwood, green, cake plate, heavy, solid foot, 13".$150.00
Dogwood, monax or cremax, cup, thick....................$45.00
Dogwood, pink, bowl, berry; 8½" $65.00
Dogwood, pink, plate, luncheon; 8" $7.00
Dogwood, pink, tumbler, decorated, 12-oz, 5" $75.00
Doric, delphite, sherbet, footed..................................$10.00
Doric, green, bowl, cereal; 5½" $90.00
Doric, green, plate, sherbet; 6" $7.00
Doric, pink, butter dish, w/lid....................................$80.00
Doric, pink, tumbler, footed, 12-oz, 5" $90.00
Doric, pink or green, bowl, berry; 4½" $12.00
Doric, pink or green, candy dish, w/lid, 8"................$42.00
Doric, pink or green, coaster, 3" $20.00
Doric, pink or green, plate, grill; 9" $25.00
Doric, pink or green, sugar bowl................................$15.00
Doric & Pansy, green or teal, creamer......................$115.00
Doric & Pansy, green or teal, plate, dinner; 9" $40.00
Doric & Pansy, pink or crystal, bowl, berry; lg, 8" $33.00
Doric & Pansy, pink or crystal, sugar bowl, open......$85.00
English Hobnail, pink or green, bowl, celery; 9".......$32.00
English Hobnail, pink or green, bowl, finger; 4½".....$15.00

English Hobnail, pink or green, bowl, nappy; cupped, 8" .$30.00
English Hobnail, pink or green, tumbler, water; 8-oz...$22.00
English Hobnail, turquoise or ice blue, bottle, toilet; 5-oz..$50.00
English Hobnail, turquoise or ice blue, candlestick, round base, 9" $50.00
English Hobnail, turquoise or ice blue, plate, round, 8½" .$25.00
Fancy Colonial, any color, bowl, nappy or olive; 5" ..$15.00
Fancy Colonial, any color, stem, goblet; deep, 8-oz...$25.00
Fire-King, blue, plate, luncheon; 8" $47.50
Fire-King, crystal, bowl, cereal; 5½" $20.00
Fire-King, pink or green, tumbler, footed, 10-oz, 5¼" $80.00
Floral, delphite, creamer, flat $77.50
Floral, delphite, tumbler, water; footed, 7-oz, 4¾" ...$195.00
Floral, green, butter dish, w/lid..............................$95.00
Floral, green, relish dish, 2-part, oval $24.00
Floral, jadite, refrigerator dish, sq, w/lid, 5" $50.00
Floral, pink, bowl, vegetable; w/lid, 8" $50.00
Floral, pink, plate, dinner; 9" $20.00
Floral, pink, tumbler, juice; footed, 5-oz, 4" $20.00
Floral & Diamond Band, green, butter dish, w/lid...$130.00
Floral & Diamond Band, pink, bowl, berry; 4½" $10.00
Floral & Diamond Band, pink, creamer, sm...............$10.00

Floral and Diamond Band, pink, pitcher, 8", $115.00; green $135.00. (Photo courtesy Gene Florence)

Floral & Diamond Band, pink or green, plate, luncheon; 8"..$45.00
Floral & Diamond Band, pink or green, tumbler, water; 4" $25.00
Florentine No 1, cobalt, saucer...............................$17.00
Florentine No 1, crystal or green, bowl, berry; lg, 8½" ..$30.00
Florentine No 1, crystal or green, tumbler, iced tea; footed, 12-oz, 5¼" $28.00
Florentine No 1, yellow, coaster/ashtray, 3¾"...........$20.00
Florentine No 1, yellow, cup $13.00
Florentine No 1, yellow, tumbler, juice; footed, 5-oz, 3¾"..$25.00
Florentine No 1, yellow or pink, bowl, vegetable; oval, w/lid, 9½" $75.00
Florentine No 2, cobalt, comport, ruffled, 3½" $65.00
Florentine No 2, crystal, green or pink, platter, oval, 11" $16.00
Florentine No 2, crystal or green, bowl, cream soup; 4¾"..$18.00
Florentine No 2, crystal or green, plate, sherbet; 6" $4.00

Florentine No 2, crystal or green, tumbler, footed, 9-oz, 5" $30.00
Florentine No 2, crystal or green, tumbler, tea; 12-oz, 5" $35.00
Florentine No 2, pink, bowl, berry; lg, 8"................$32.00
Florentine No 2, yellow, bowl, shallow, 7½" $95.00
Florentine No 2, yellow, plate, grill; 10¼"..................$18.00
Florentine No 2, yellow, salt & pepper shakers, pr....$50.00
Flower Garden w/Butterflies, amber or crystal, candy dish, flat, w/lid, 6" $130.00
Flower Garden w/Butterflies, amber or crystal, tray, oval, 5½x10"..$55.00
Flower Garden w/Butterflies, black, bowl, rolled edge, w/base, 9" $200.00
Flower Garden w/Butterflies, black, candlesticks, 8", pr..$325.00
Flower Garden w/Butterflies, black, plate, indented, 10" .$100.00
Flower Garden w/Butterflies, blue or canary yellow, plate, 7" $30.00
Flower Garden w/Butterflies, pink, green or blue-green, comport, 2⅞" H $23.00
Flower Garden w/Butterflies, pink, green or blue-green, creamer..$75.00
Flower Garden w/Butterflies, pink, green or blue-green, powder jar, flat, 3½" $80.00
Flower Garden w/Butterflies, pink, green or blue-green, saucer..$25.00
Flute & Cane, crystal, bowl, fruit; 4½" $10.00
Flute & Cane, crystal, creamer...............................$15.00
Flute & Cane, crystal, oil bottle, w/stopper, 6-oz........$45.00
Flute & Cane, crystal, sugar bowl, w/lid...................$25.00
Fortune, pink or crystal, bowl, salad or lg berry; 7¾" ...$25.00
Fortune, pink or crystal, saucer $5.00
Fruits, green, saucer..$5.50
Fruits, green, tumbler, 12-oz, 5" $165.00
Fruits, green or pink, sherbet $12.00
Fruits, pink, bowl, berry; 4½" $28.00
Georgian, green, bowl, berry, 4½" $9.00
Georgian, green, bowl, deep, 6½" $68.00
Georgian, green, butter dish, w/lid..........................$85.00
Georgian, green, creamer, footed, 4" $17.00
Georgian, green, plate, sherbet; 6" $7.00
Georgian, green, saucer..$3.00
Georgian, green, sugar bowl, footed, 4"....................$17.00
Gothic Garden, any color, bowl, tab handle, 9" $65.00
Gothic Garden, any color, candy dish, flat...............$125.00
Gothic Garden, any color, plate, tab handle, 11".......$65.00
Hex Optic, pink or green, bowl, mixing; 7¼" $15.00
Hex Optic, pink or green, bowl, mixing; 10".............$28.00
Hex Optic, pink or green, pitcher, footed, 48-oz, 9" ..$50.00
Hex Optic, pink or green, saucer............................$3.00
Hex Optic, pink or green, tumbler, footed, 5¾".........$10.00
Hex Optic, pink or green, tumbler, 12-oz, 5" $7.00
Hobnail, crystal, bowl, cereal; 5½"............................$4.00
Hobnail, crystal, bowl, salad; 7" $4.50
Hobnail, crystal, pitcher, milk; 18-oz.........................$22.00
Hobnail, crystal, whiskey, 1½-oz.............................$6.00
Hobnail, pink, plate, luncheon; 8½" $7.50

Hobnail, pink, sherbet................................$5.00
Homespun, pink or crystal, bowl, closed handles, 4½" .$18.00
Homespun, pink or crystal, plate, sherbet; 6" $8.00
Homespun, pink or crystal, sugar bowl, footed.........$12.50
Indiana Custard, bowl, flat soup; 7½"....................$35.00
Indiana Custard, plate, bread & butter; 5¾" $7.00
Indiana Custard, platter, oval, 11½"......................$40.00
Indiana Custard, sugar bowl $12.00
Iris, crystal, bowl, cereal; 5"..............................$115.00
Iris, crystal, goblet, 8-oz, 5½".............................$26.00
Iris, crystal or iridescent, tumbler, footed, 6".............$20.00
Iris, iridescent, bowl, fruit; ruffled, 11½" $14.00
Iris, iridescent, saucer.....................................$9.00
Iris, transparent green or pink, creamer, footed $150.00
Jubilee, pink, cup...$40.00
Jubilee, pink, tray, cake; w/handles, 11"..................$65.00
Jubilee, yellow, creamer $20.00
Jubilee, yellow, stem, cordial; 1-oz, 4"...................$250.00
Kaleidoscope, blue, bowl, berry; 5"........................$15.00
Kaleidoscope, blue, sugar bowl $25.00
Kaleidoscope, green or pink, plate, grill; 9½"............$17.50
Laced Edge, opalescent, bowl, vegetable; 9" $110.00
Laced Edge, opalescent, bowl, 5⅞"........................$37.50
Laced Edge, opalescent, creamer $40.00
Laced Edge, opalescent, plate, luncheon; 12" $80.00
Laced Edge, opalescent, saucer $15.00
Lake Como, white w/blue scene, bowl, flat soup $105.00
Lake Como, white w/blue scene, cup, regular $30.00
Lake Como, white w/blue scene, plate, salad; 7¼"....$22.50
Lake Como, white w/blue scene, salt & pepper shakers,
   pr $45.00
Largo, amber or crystal, bowl, 7½" $20.00
Largo, amber or crystal, plate, 8"..........................$10.00
Largo, blue or red, cake plate, pedestal $95.00
Laurel, blue, bowl, cereal; 6".................................$28.00
Laurel, blue, cup..$22.00
Laurel, green or decorated rim, bowl, soup; 7⅞".......$40.00
Laurel, green or decorated rim, sugar bowl, tall........$25.00
Laurel, white opal, ivory or blue, plate, sherbet; 6" ...$10.00
Laurel, white opal or ivory, sherbet......................$12.00
Lincoln Inn, any color, cup................................$12.00
Lincoln Inn, blue or red, bonbon, oval, handled........$16.00
Lincoln Inn, blue or red, comport............................$30.00
Lincoln Inn, blue or red, plate, 8"...........................$15.00
Lincoln Inn, blue or red, tumbler, footed, 12-oz........$50.00
Lincoln Inn, colors other than blue or red, bowl, cereal;
   6" $9.00
Lincoln Inn, colors other than blue or red, nut dish, foot-
   ed $12.00
Lincoln Inn, colors other than blue or red, sugar bowl..$14.00
Line #555, crystal, bowl, w/handles, 9" $20.00
Line #555, crystal, cup......................................$8.00
Line #555, crystal, plate, 6" $5.00
Line #555, crystal, tray, center handle, 11" $30.00
Little Jewel, colors, creamer................................$15.00
Little Jewel, crystal, bowl, 6½"..............................$10.00
Little Jewel, crystal, sugar bowl $8.00

Lois, crystal, green or pink, bowl, salad; flat rim, 10"...$40.00
Lois, crystal, green or pink, plate, dinner....................$35.00
Lorain, crystal or green, bowl, salad; 7¼" $50.00
Lorain, crystal or green, plate, dinner; 10¼" $60.00
Lorain, yellow, plate, sherbet; 5½"........................$12.50
Lorain, yellow, sugar bowl, footed.........................$27.50
Lotus, amber, crystal or white, creamer $22.00
Lotus, amber, crystal or white, sherbet, tulip bell.......$22.00
Lotus, amethyst, plate, flared, 13".........................$65.00
Lotus, blue, green or pink, bowl, cupped, 9" $85.00
Madrid, amber, bowl, cream soup; 4¾"....................$18.00
Madrid, amber, cookie jar, w/lid $45.00
Madrid, amber, plate, sherbet; 6"..........................$5.00
Madrid, amber, tumbler, footed, 10-oz, 5½"...............$33.00
Madrid, blue, cup $16.00
Madrid, blue, platter, oval, 11½"...........................$24.00
Madrid, green, bowl, salad; 8"..............................$17.50
Madrid, green, butter dish, w/lid...........................$90.00
Madrid, green, sugar bowl...................................$14.00
Madrid, pink, cake plate, round, 11¼" $10.00
Manhattan, crystal, ashtray, round, 4" $12.00
Manhattan, crystal, coaster, 3½".............................$16.00
Manhattan, crystal, plate, salad; 8½".......................$17.00
Manhattan, crystal, relish tray, 5-part, 14"................$30.00
Manhattan, crystal, vase, 8"................................$25.00
Manhattan, pink, bowl, closed handles, 8".................$28.00
Manhattan, pink, cup, rare................................$275.00
Manhattan, pink, plate, saucer/sherbet.....................$75.00
Maya, colors, bowl, flared rim, 7" $35.00
Maya, colors, plate, mayonnaise; 7".........................$20.00
Maya, crystal, cake plate, pedestal $35.00
Maya, crystal, tray, tab handles............................$25.00
Mayfair (Federal), amber, creamer, footed...................$13.00
Mayfair (Federal), amber or green, saucer..................$4.00
Mayfair (Federal), crystal, plate, grill; 9½" $8.50
Mayfair (Federal), green, bowl, sauce; 5" $15.00
Mayfair (Open Rose), blue, bowl, vegetable; w/lid, 10" ..$150.00
Mayfair (Open Rose), blue, pitcher, 60-oz, 8"..........$195.00
Mayfair (Open Rose), blue, sandwich server, center han-
   dle $85.00
Mayfair (Open Rose), blue, tumbler, water; 9-oz, 4¼" .$110.00
Mayfair (Open Rose), blue, vase, sweet pea.............$135.00
Mayfair (Open Rose), green or yellow, plate, luncheon,
   8½"..$85.00
Mayfair (Open Rose), green or yellow, sugar bowl, foot-
   ed $210.00
Mayfair (Open Rose), pink, bowl, cream soup; 5" $65.00
Mayfair (Open Rose), pink, cup $20.00
Mayfair (Open Rose), pink, goblet, cocktail; 3-oz, 4"...$110.00
Mayfair (Open Rose), pink, salt & pepper shakers, flat,
   pr $65.00
Mayfair (Open Rose), yellow, bowl, vegetable; 10" .$135.00
Mayfair (Open Rose), yellow, plate, grill; w/handles,
   11½" $125.00
Miss America, crystal, butter dish, w/ lid.................$210.00
Miss America, crystal, tumbler, iced tea; 14-oz, 5¾"...$30.00
Miss America, green, plate, 6¾"..............................$14.00

Miss America, pink, celery dish, 10½" long, $42.00.

Miss America, pink, comport, 5"....................$30.00
Miss America, pink, sugar bowl $25.00
Miss America, royal ruby, creamer, footed $225.00
Miss America, royal ruby, plate, salad; 8½".............$165.00
Moderntone, amethyst, bowl, berry; lg, 8¾" $40.00
Moderntone, amethyst, plate, sandwich; 10½".............$40.00
Moderntone, amethyst, plate, sherbet; 5⅞" $5.00
Moderntone, cobalt, bowl, cream soup; ruffled, 5" $65.00
Moderntone, cobalt, creamer.......................$12.00
Moderntone, cobalt, sugar bowl.................$13.00
Monticello, crystal, bowl, deep, 12"................$30.00
Monticello, crystal, bowl, finger; 4½"...............$10.00
Monticello, crystal, bowl, round, 6" $10.00
Monticello, crystal, plate, flat, 17"...............$55.00
Monticello, crystal, stem, cocktail................$12.50
Moondrops, blue or red, bowl, 3-legged, ruffled, 9½" ...$70.00
Moondrops, blue or red, candlesticks, ruffled, 5", pr.$40.00
Moondrops, blue or red, goblet, wine; 4-oz, 4"..........$20.00
Moondrops, blue or red, plate, luncheon; 8½"..........$17.00
Moondrops, blue or red, saucer $4.00
Moondrops, blue or red, tumbler, 12-oz, 5⅛"...........$30.00
Moondrops, colors other than blue or red, bowl, cream soup;
    4¼" $40.00
Moondrops, colors other than blue or red, bowl, pickle;
    7½" $20.00
Moondrops, colors other than blue or red, butter dish,
    w/lid...$275.00
Moondrops, colors other than blue or red, mug, 12-oz,
    5⅛" $23.00
Moondrops, colors other than blue or red, plate, sandwich;
    w/handles, 14" $25.00
Moondrops, colors other than blue or red, sugar bowl,
    3½" $11.00
Mt Pleasant, amethyst, black or cobalt, bowl, fruit; scalloped,
    10" $45.00
Mt Pleasant, amethyst, black or cobalt, bowl, sq, w/handles,
    6" $18.00
Mt Pleasant, amethyst, black or cobalt, cake plate,
    1¼"x10½" $40.00

Mt Pleasant, amethyst, black or cobalt, cup $14.00
Mt Pleasant, amethyst, black or cobalt, tumbler, footed ..$28.00
Mt Pleasant, pink or green, bowl, scalloped, w/handles,
    8"...$19.00
Mt Pleasant, pink or green, creamer $18.00
Mt Pleasant, pink or green, plate, w/handles, 8" $11.00
Mt Vernon, crystal, bowl, lily; 6" $15.00
Mt Vernon, crystal, bowl, 3-footed, 10"....................$25.00
Mt Vernon, crystal, cake plate, 11" $20.00
Mt Vernon, crystal, decanter $35.00
Mt Vernon, crystal, sugar bowl, lg.......................$12.00
New Century, green or crystal, bowl, berry; lg, 8" $28.00
New Century, green or crystal, creamer $15.00
New Century, green or crystal, plate, salad; 8½"........$14.00
New Century, green or crystal, sugar bowl $10.00
New Century, pink, cobalt or amethyst, cup..............$20.00
New Century, pink, cobalt or amethyst, tumbler, 12-oz,
    5¼"..$30.00
Newport, amethyst, plate, sherbet; 5⅞" $8.00
Newport, amethyst, tumbler, 9-oz, 4¼"...................$40.00
Newport, cobalt, bowl, berry; 4¾".......................$25.00
Newport, cobalt, platter, oval, 11¾"......................$50.00
No 610 Pyramid, crystal, bowl, oval, 9½"..................$30.00
No 610 Pyramid, crystal, pink or green, tumbler, footed, 2
    styles, 8-oz....................................$55.00
No 610 Pyramid, pink, bowl, berry; 4¾" $35.00
No 610 Pyramid, yellow, creamer $40.00
No 612 Horseshoe, green, bowl, cereal; 6½" $30.00
No 612 Horseshoe, green, relish, 3-part, footed $30.00
No 612 Horseshoe, yellow, bowl, vegetable; 8½" $35.00
No 612 Horseshoe, yellow, plate, luncheon; 9⅜".......$16.00
No 616 Vernon, crystal, cup...............................$10.00
No 616 Vernon, green or yellow, saucer $4.00
No 618 Pineapple & Floral, amber or red, platter, closed han-
    dle, 11".......................................$18.00
No 618 Pineapple & Floral, crystal, amber or red, bowl,
    cream soup.....................................$22.00
No 618 Pineapple & Floral, crystal, bowl, berry; 4¾"..$25.00
No 618 Pineapple & Floral, crystal, tumbler, 8-oz, 4¼" ..$32.00
Normandie, amber, bowl, cereal; 6½".....................$25.00
Normandie, amber, tumbler, iced tea; 12-oz, 5"..........$45.00
Normandie, iridescent, plate, grill; 11" $9.00
Normandie, pink, creamer, footed $14.00
Old Cafe, crystal, pink or royal ruby, cup..................$12.00
Old Cafe, crystal or pink, bowl, open handles, 6½" ..$15.00
Old Cafe, crystal or pink, pitcher, 36-oz, 6" $125.00
Old Cafe, royal ruby, vase, 7¼".........................$50.00
Old Colony, pink, bowl, plain, 9½"..........................$32.00
Old Colony, pink, comport, 7" $30.00
Old Colony, pink, creamer $30.00
Old Colony, pink, sugar bowl $30.00
Old English, pink, green or amber, bowl, flat, 9½"....$35.00
Old English, pink, green or amber, creamer..............$17.50
Old English, pink, green or amber, vase, footed, 8x4½"...$55.00
Olive, blue or red, candy jar, w/lid.......................$40.00
Olive, emerald or pink, bowl, shallow, 7"..................$15.00
Olive, emerald or pink, plate, 8" $8.00

Orchid, crystal, ice bucket, 6".............................**$95.00**
Orchid, red, black or blue, comport, 3¼x6¼" **$55.00**
Orchid, red, black or blue, vase, 8".....................**$275.00**
Orchid, yellow, bowl, sq, 8¾".............................**$75.00**
Ovide, Art Deco, saucer..................................**$20.00**
Ovide, black, creamer **$6.50**
Ovide, black or green, salt & pepper shakers, pr......**$27.50**
Ovide, decorated white, bowl, cereal; 5½" **$13.00**
Oyster & Pearl, crystal or pink, bowl, deep fruit; 10½"..**$25.00**
Oyster & Pearl, royal ruby, bowl, w/handles, 6½" **$27.50**
Parrot, amber, bowl, berry; lg, 8".......................**$90.00**
Parrot, amber, tumbler, 12-oz, 5½" **$165.00**
Parrot, green, plate, sherbet; 5¾"........................**$35.00**
Parrot, green, salt & pepper shakers, pr.................**$295.00**
Party Line, any color, bowl, mixing; 7".................**$20.00**
Party Line, any color, bowl, vegetable; flared, 11".....**$35.00**
Party Line, any color, creamer, 7-oz....................**$10.00**
Party Line, any color, plate, 8"..........................**$10.00**
Party Line, any color, syrup, 8-oz.......................**$45.00**
Party Line, any color, tumbler, wine; 3-oz.............**$12.00**
Patrician, amber or crystal, bowl, berry; 5" **$14.00**
Patrician, amber or crystal, plate, dinner; 10½"...........**$8.00**
Patrician, amber or crystal, sherbet.....................**$13.00**
Patrician, green, plate, salad; 7½".......................**$20.00**
Patrician, green, sugar bowl **$15.00**
Patrician, pink, bowl, cereal; 6"..........................**$25.00**
Patrick, pink, creamer **$65.00**
Patrick, pink, sugar bowl **$65.00**
Patrick, pink or yellow, goblet, cocktail; 4".............**$80.00**
Patrick, yellow, plate, sherbet; 7".......................**$12.00**
Peacock & Wild Rose, all colors, bowl, console; 11"...**$185.00**
Peacock & Wild Rose, all colors, candy dish, w/lid, 7" ..**$250.00**
Peacock & Wild Rose, all colors, creamer, round handle,
    4½" **$55.00**
Peacock & Wild Rose, all colors, relish tray, 3-part..**$110.00**
Peacock & Wild Rose, all colors, saucer................**$20.00**
Peacock & Wild Rose, all colors, tumbler, 3" **$60.00**
Peacock Reverse, all colors, bowl, sq, 4⅞" **$45.00**
Peacock Reverse, all colors, creamer, flat, 2¾".......**$100.00**
Peacock Reverse, all colors, plate, sherbet; 5¾".......**$25.00**
Peacock Reverse, all colors, sugar bowl, flat, 2¾"....**$100.00**
Pebbled Rim, amber, green or pink, bowl, berry.........**$8.00**
Pebbled Rim, amber, green or pink, plate, dinner; 9" **$10.00**
Penny Line, any color, candle holder **$20.00**
Penny Line, any color, pitcher...........................**$55.00**
Penny Line, any color, sugar bowl......................**$12.50**
Penny Line, any color, tumbler, tea; 12-oz **$14.00**
Petalware, cremax, monax florette or fired-on decorations,
    creamer, footed **$12.50**
Petalware, cremax or monax, plate, salad; 8"...........**$6.00**
Petalware, crystal, plate, salver; 11"......................**$4.50**
Petalware, pink, plate, salver; 12" **$15.00**
Petalware, red trim floral, saucer.......................**$10.00**
Pillar Optic, amber, green or pink, plate, luncheon; 8" ..**$12.00**
Pillar Optic, crystal, cup................................**$10.00**
Pillar Optic, crystal, tumbler, water; 9-oz.............**$2.50**
Pillar Optic, royal ruby, sugar bowl, footed..............**$65.00**

Primo, yellow or green, cup.............................**$13.00**
Primo, yellow or green, plate, grill; 10"...............**$18.00**
Princess, green, ashtray, 4½"............................**$75.00**
Princess, green, sugar bowl..............................**$10.00**
Princess, green or pink, plate, grill; 9½"................**$20.00**
Princess, pink, bowl, salad; octagonal, 9"..............**$55.00**
Princess, topaz or apricot, coaster......................**$115.00**
Princess, topaz or apricot, plate, salad; 8"............**$15.00**
Queen Mary, crystal, ashtray, round, 3¼"...............**$3.00**
Queen Mary, crystal, creamer, footed..................**$25.00**
Queen Mary, crystal, tumbler, footed, 10-oz, 5".........**$35.00**
Queen Mary, pink, bowl, cereal; 6".....................**$28.00**
Queen Mary, pink, cigarette jar, oval, 2x3".............**$7.50**
Queen Mary, pink, relish tray, 3-part, 12" **$18.00**
Radiance, amber, bowl, relish; 3-part, 8" **$35.00**
Radiance, amber, butter dish **$210.00**
Radiance, amber, cup, footed...........................**$12.00**
Radiance, ice blue or red, bowl, bonbon; footed, 6" .**$35.00**
Radiance, ice blue or red, comport, 6".................**$35.00**
Radiance, ice blue or red, sugar bowl **$25.00**
Raindrops, green, bowl, fruit; 4½".......................**$6.00**
Raindrops, green, sugar bowl............................**$7.50**
Reeded, amber, bottle, bitters; 3-oz....................**$35.00**
Reeded, amber, plate, server; flat, 14".................**$32.50**
Reeded, dark green, bowl, nappy; 8"....................**$30.00**
Reeded, pink, pitcher, ice lip, 80-oz...................**$60.00**
Reeded, pink, vase, ball shape, rose, 6"................**$45.00**
Ribbon, black, plate, luncheon; 8".....................**$14.00**
Ribbon, green, candy dish w/lid **$45.00**
Ring, crystal, bowl, soup; 7"............................**$10.00**
Ring, crystal, goblet, 9-oz, 7¼".........................**$12.00**
Ring, green or decorated, bowl, berry; lg, 8"..........**$12.00**
Ring, green or decorated, tumbler, water; footed, 5½"...**$12.00**
Rock Crystal, colors other than crystal or red, bowl, salad;
    scalloped edge, 10½" **$50.00**
Rock Crystal, colors other than crystal or red, creamer, foot-
    ed, 9-oz..**$32.00**
Rock Crystal, colors other than crystal or red, sugar bowl,
    open, 10-oz..**$22.00**
Rock Crystal, crystal, bowl, scalloped edge, 5"..........**$22.00**
Rock Crystal, crystal, candlesticks, tall, 8", pr **$100.00**
Rock Crystal, crystal, spooner..........................**$45.00**
Rock Crystal, red, bowl, roll tray; 13".................**$125.00**
Rock Crystal, red, goblet, iced tea; low foot, 11-oz....**$67.50**
Rock Crystal, red, tumbler, whiskey; 2½-oz.............**$50.00**
Romanesque, amber, bowl, 10½".......................**$45.00**
Romanesque, crystal, tray, snack.......................**$15.00**
Rose Cameo, green, bowl, cereal; 5" **$22.00**
Rose Cameo, green, plate, salad; 7" **$15.00**
Rosemary, amber, bowl, berry; 5" **$6.00**
Rosemary, amber or green, saucer......................**$5.00**
Rosemary, green, platter, oval, 12".....................**$25.00**
Rosemary, pink, bowl, cream soup; 5"..................**$45.00**
Roulette, crystal, pitcher, 65-oz, 8"....................**$30.00**
Roulette, pink or green, tumbler, iced tea; 12-oz, 5⅛" ...**$35.00**
Round Robin, green, creamer, footed **$12.50**
Round Robin, iridescent, sherbet.......................**$10.00**

Roxana, white, bowl, 4½x2⅜".....................................**$20.00**
Roxana, yellow, bowl, cereal; 6"............................**$20.00**
Royal Lace, blue, bowl, vegetable; oval, 11"............**$70.00**
Royal Lace, crystal, bowl, straight edge, 3-legged, 10"....**$35.00**
Royal Lace, crystal, salt & pepper shakers, pr............**$42.00**

Royal Lace, green, cracker jar, $100.00; pink, $60.00.

Royal Lace, green, cup...**$20.00**
Royal Lace, pink, cookie jar, w/lid.............................**$60.00**
Royal Lace, pink, sugar bowl.......................................**$20.00**
Royal Ruby, red, bowl, berry; Old Cafe, 3¾"...............**$9.00**
Royal Ruby, red, creamer, footed **$9.00**
Royal Ruby, red, cup, round **$6.00**
Royal Ruby, red, tray, 6x4½".......................................**$12.50**
S Pattern, crystal, bowl, cereal; 5½" **$5.00**
S Pattern, crystal, plate, luncheon; 8¼".....................**$7.00**
S Pattern, yellow, amber or crystal w/trims, plate, grill ..**$8.00**
S Pattern, yellow, amber or crystal w/trims, tumbler, 5-oz, 3½" **$8.00**
Sandwich, amber or crystal, bowl, berry; 4½"..............**$3.50**
Sandwich, amber or crystal, plate, dinner; 10½".........**$8.00**
Sandwich, pink or green, decanter, w/stopper **$150.00**
Sandwich, red, creamer...**$45.00**
Sandwich, teal blue, butter dish, domed, w/lid **$155.00**
Sharon, amber, butter dish w/lid................................**$50.00**
Sharon, amber, plate, salad; 7½"................................**$15.00**
Sharon, green, creamer, footed...................................**$22.50**
Sharon, pink, bowl, berry; 5".......................................**$14.00**
Sharon, pink, tumbler, footed, 15-oz, 6½"..................**$60.00**
Ships, blue/white, cup, plain, Moderntone **$11.00**
Ships, blue/white, plate, sherbet; 5⅞" **$30.00**
Ships, blue/white, tumbler, juice; 5-oz, 3¾"................**$14.00**
Sierra, green, cup..**$16.00**
Sierra, pink, bowl, berry; lg, 8½" **$35.00**
Sierra, pink, sugar bowl **$22.00**
Sierra, pink or green, salt & pepper shakers, pr.........**$45.00**
Spiral, green, bowl, mixing; 7" **$15.00**
Spiral, green, ice or butter tub....................................**$30.00**

Spiral, green, saucer **$2.00**
Spiral, green, vase, footed, 5¾".....................................**$55.00**
Square Hazen, crystal, pink or green, plate, salad; 8" ..**$12.50**
Square Hazen, ruby, bowl, soup/salad; sq, 7"............**$22.50**
Starlight, crystal or white, bowl, salad; 11½"...............**$28.00**
Starlight, crystal or white, cup **$5.00**
Starlight, crystal or white, plate, luncheon; 8½"..........**$5.00**
Starlight, pink, plate, sandwich; 13" **$18.00**
Strawberry, crystal or iridescent, comport, 5¾"..........**$18.00**
Strawberry, crystal or iridescent, sugar bowl, lg **$22.00**
Strawberry, pink or green, bowl, berry; 4"...................**$12.00**
Strawberry, pink or green, tumbler, 8-oz, 3⅝" **$40.00**
Sunburst, crystal, plate, dinner; 9¼"...........................**$22.00**
Sunburst, crystal, sugar bowl......................................**$10.00**
Sunflower, pink, plate, luncheon; 8"............................**$35.00**
Sunflower, pink or green, tumbler, footed, 8-oz, 4¾"....**$35.00**
Sunshine, pink or green, bowl, w/handles, hex edge, 8" .**$55.00**
Sunshine, pink or green, sugar bowl, round, footed..**$22.50**
Swirl, delphite, cup..**$10.00**
Swirl, delphite, plate, 10½"...**$25.00**
Swirl, pink, butter dish...**$200.00**
Swirl, pink, sherbet, low footed **$18.00**
Swirl, ultramarine, bowl, footed closed handles, 10"..**$35.00**
Swirl, ultramarine, salt & pepper shakers, pr..............**$45.00**
Tea Room, green, candlesticks, low, pr.......................**$80.00**
Tea Room, green, sherbet, low, footed.......................**$25.00**
Tea Room, green or pink, bowl, finger **$70.00**
Tea Room, green or pink, tumbler, footed, 6-oz.........**$35.00**
Tea Room, pink, plate, luncheon, 8¼" **$30.00**
Tea Room, pink, relish, divided **$20.00**
Thistle, green, bowl, cereal; 5½"..................................**$35.00**
Thistle, pink, plate, luncheon; 8"..................................**$22.00**
Top Notch, all colors, creamer **$25.00**
Top Notch, all colors, plate, serving tray....................**$35.00**
Tulip, amethyst or blue, saucer **$7.00**
Tulip, crystal or green, bowl, oval, oblong, 13¼".......**$90.00**
Twisted Optic, blue or canary yellow, bowl, salad; 7" ..**$25.00**
Twisted Optic, blue or canary yellow, creamer **$15.00**
Twisted Optic, blue or canary yellow, plate, 12".......**$20.00**
Twisted Optic, pink, green or amber, candlesticks, 2 styles, 3", pr **$50.00**
Twisted Optic, pink, green or amber, plate, cracker; 9½" .**$18.00**
Twisted Optic, pink, green or amber, vase, flat rim, 7¼" ..**$40.00**
US Swirl, green, bowl, berry; 4⅜".................................**$5.50**
US Swirl, green, plate, salad; 7⅞".................................**$5.50**
US Swirl, green or pink, butter dish, w/lid **$120.00**
US Swirl, green or pink, pitcher, 48-oz, 8" **$85.00**
US Swirl, pink, comport..**$30.00**
US Swirl, pink, vase, 6½"...**$25.00**
Victory, black, amber, pink or green, bowl, cereal; 6½"..**$14.00**
Victory, black, amber, pink or green, creamer............**$15.00**
Victory, black, amber, pink or green, sugar bowl.......**$15.00**
Victory, blue, bowl, console; 12"..................................**$65.00**
Victory, blue, plate, salad; 7".......................................**$20.00**
Vitrock, white, bowl, cereal; 7½"..................................**$8.00**
Vitrock, white, plate, luncheon; 8¾".............................**$5.00**
Vitrock, white, platter, 11½" **$35.00**

Waterford, crystal, bowl, berry; 4¾"	$7.00
Waterford, crystal, goblet, Miss America shape, 5½"	$40.00
Waterford, crystal, plate, sandwich; 13¾"	$13.00
Waterford, pink, creamer, oval	$12.00
Waterford, pink, sugar bowl	$12.50
Windsor, crystal, bowl, berry; 4¾"	$4.00
Windsor, crystal, candy jar, w/lid	$20.00
Windsor, crystal, plate, chop; 13⅝"	$15.00
Windsor, crystal, tumbler, footed, 4"	$8.00
Windsor, green, bowl, cream soup; 5"	$29.00
Windsor, green, cup	$12.50
Windsor, green, salt & pepper shakers, pr	$55.00
Windsor, pink, ashtray, 5¾"	$38.00
Windsor, pink, cake plate, footed, 10¾"	$25.00
Windsor, pink, powder jar	$60.00

Disney

The largest and most popular area in character collectibles is without doubt Disneyana. There are clubs, newsletters, and special shows that are centered around this hobby. Every aspect of the retail market has been thoroughly saturated with Disney-related merchandise over the years, and today collectors are able to find many good examples at garage sales and flea markets.

Disney memorabilia from the late '20s and '30s was marked either 'Walt E. Disney' or 'Walt Disney Enterprises.' After about 1940 the name was changed to 'Walt Disney Productions.' This mark was in use until 1984 when the 'Walt Disney Company' mark was introduced, and this last mark has remained in use up to the present time. Some of the earlier items have become very expensive, though many are still within the reach of the average collector.

During the '30s, Mickey Mouse, Donald Duck, Snow White and the Seven Dwarfs, and the Three Little Pigs (along with all their friends and cohorts) dominated the Disney scene. The last of the '30s' characters was Pinocchio, and some 'purists' prefer to stop their collections with him.

The '40s and '50s brought many new characters with them — Alice in Wonderland, Bambi, Dumbo, Lady and the Tramp, and Peter Pan were some of the major personalities featured in Disney's films of this era.

Even today, thanks to the re-releases of many of the old movies and the popularity of Disney's vacation 'kingdoms,' toy stores and department stores alike are full of quality items with the potential of soon becoming collectibles.

If you'd like to learn more about this fascinating field, we recommend *Schroeder's Collectible Toys, Antique to Modern*, published by Collector Books.

See also Character and Promotional Drinking Glasses; Character Banks; Character Watches; Cowboy Character Memorabilia; Dolls, Mattel; Enesco; Games; Hagen-Renaker; Pin-Back Buttons; Puzzles; Salt and Pepper Shakers; Toys; Valentines; Wade.

Note: In the following listings, many of the characters have been sorted by the name of the feature film in which they appeared.

Advisor: Judy Posner (See Directory, Character and Personality Collectibles)

Aladdin, doll, Genie, stuffed cloth w/vinyl head, Mattel, 1992, 11", MIB	$25.00
Aladdin, doll, Jasmine, stuffed cloth w/vinyl head, Mattel, 1993, 14", MIB	$20.00
Aladdin, figure, any character, Mattel, 5", MOC, ea	$10.00
Aladdin, salt & pepper shakers, Genie & Magic Lamp, Treasure Craft, M, stacking pr	$35.00
Aladdin, Water Jewel Magic Gift Set, Mattel, 1994, MIB	$65.00
Alice in Wonderland, bank, ceramic, Leeds, NM	$175.00
Alice in Wonderland, figure, Alice, ceramic, Japan (originally sold in the theme parks), 1970s, 6", M	$30.00
Alice in Wonderland, figure, Alice, Disneykin, 1st series, Marx, 1960s, M	$8.00
Aristocats, doll, Duchess, stuffed plush, 1970, 15", NM	$50.00
Bambi, ashtray, Thumper figure, ceramic, Goebel, #DIS 8, 1950s, 4", M	$225.00
Bambi, bookmark, Prevent Forest Fires, State Forest Service/WDP, 1940s, 6¼", NM	$30.00
Bambi, Colorforms, 1966, complete, NMIB	$20.00
Bambi, planter, ceramic, Bambi standing on lg green base, Leeds, 1940s, 5", NM+	$45.00
Bambi, salt & pepper shakers, Flower the skunk figures, ceramic, Goebel, 1950s, 2¾", M, pr	$175.00
Chip & Dale Rescue Rangers, hand puppet, Helm Products, NM, pr	$60.00
Cinderella, planter, Cinderella figure holding up apron as planter pot, ceramic, Evan K Shaw, 1950s, 7¼", NM	$400.00
Cinderella, planter, Prince figure leaning on 'brick wall' planter, ceramic, Evan K Shaw, 1950s, 7¼", M	$325.00
Cinderella, purse, green slipper w/zipper closure, 1970s, 5", MIP	$20.00
Daisy Duck, figure, bisque, croquet player, WDP, 1960s, 4", EX	$40.00
Daisy Duck, figure, Disneykin, 1st series, Marx, 1960s, M	$8.00
Disney, embroidery set, features Disney characters, complete, EXIB	$50.00

Disney, globe, ca 1945, $225.00. (Photo courtesy Joel Cohen)

Disney, Magic Erasable Picture, Transogram, 1950s, unused, MIB **$50.00**

Disney, seed packets, ea w/8" plastic plant identifier featuring various characters, Colorforms, 1977, unused, NM, ea **$12.00**

Disney, Weebles figures, 1973, $12.00 each. (Photo courtesy June Moon)

Disney World, bumper sticker, Walt Disney World 15 Years, 1986, M **$15.00**

Disney World, vehicle, cast metal replica of EPCOT tourist vehicle (GM Test Track), 1/64th scale, 1998, MIB...**$25.00**

Disneyland, certificate for piloting the USS Mark Twain steamboat on Rivers of America Frontierland, 1970s, unused, M...**$65.00**

Disneyland, scrapbook, softcover, Whitman, 1955, unused, scarce, EX..**$50.00**

Disneyland, tea set, American, 1950s, MIB, $250.00. (Photo courtesy Dunbar Gallery)

Donald Duck, booklet, Automotive Quiz, 12 pages, Sunoco Oil premium, 1941, EX...**$50.00**

Donald Duck, bread wrapper, waxed paper, Debus, 1952, NM **$25.00**

Donald Duck, cereal bowl, yellow plastic w/alphabet & numbers on rim, Post Bran Flakes, 1930s, 5½", NM **$60.00**

Donald Duck, doctor kit, WDP, 1940s, EXIB **$125.00**

Donald Duck, doll, Dancing Donald, stuffed cloth w/vinyl head, Hasbro, 1977, 18", EX **$35.00**

Donald Duck, Dress Buttons, plastic, encircled figures of Donald, set of 3, EX (VG+ Mickey Mouse Dress Buttons card).**$75.00**

Donald Duck, figure, ceramic, head cocked looking up, arms down in front, tail up, American Pottery, 1940s, 6½", M **$225.00**

Donald Duck, figure, ceramic, hockey player on skates, Goebel, #DIS 123, 1950s, 4½", M......................**$250.00**

Donald Duck, figure, plastic, Jumpkins, Kohner, 1960s, 5", MOC **$40.00**

Donald Duck, figure, squeeze rubber, facing forward w/1 arm down & 1 arm bent, Sun Rubber, 1949, 10", EX+..**$45.00**

Donald Duck, figure, Weebles, 1973, EX.....................**$15.00**

Donald Duck, hat, mesh w/vinyl beak, rolls eyes & quacks when squeezed, rare, 10", EX.............................**$125.00**

Donald Duck, magic slate, Whitman, 1970s, NM........**$25.00**

Donald Duck, marionette, Pelham, EXIB **$100.00**

Donald Duck, paint box, litho tin, shows Donald painting, Transogram, 1948, EX...**$50.00**

Donald Duck, slippers, stuffed head of Donald on top, Trimfoot/WDP, 1940s-50s, EX **$65.00**

Donald Duck, tea set, lithographed tin, MIB, from $250.00 to $350.00. (Photo courtesy Dunbar Gallery)

Donald Duck's Nephew, figure, ceramic, hockey player on skates w/stick, Goebel, #DIS 124, 1950s, 3½", M .**$225.00**

Dumbo, figure, ceramic, on round base, Goebel, #DIS 722, 1950s, 4", M...**$325.00**

Dumbo, hand puppet, cloth body w/vinyl head, Gund, 1955, 9", NM (EX box) **$65.00**

Dumbo, wall plaques, Dumbo & Timothy, diecut cardboard, WDP, Copyright 1951, 9x14" & 8¼", pr **$40.00**

Ferdinand the Bull, figure, bisque, Japan, 1930s, 3", VG ..**$45.00**

Ferdinand the Bull, figure, composition, Knickerbocker, 10", NM **$400.00**

Ferdinand the Bull, soap figure, Kerk Guild Bath Product, 1938, unused, VG+ (VG+ box) **$45.00**

Goofy, figure, Jumpkins, plastic, Kohner, 1960s, 5", MOC ..**$40.00**

Goofy, yo-yo, wood w/paper seal, tournament shape, hallmark, 1970s, MOC **$30.00**

Hunchback of Notre Dame, Colorforms, MIB (sealed)...**$10.00**

Hunchback of Notre Dame, dolls, Esmerelda, Frollo, Phoebus or Quasimodo, vinyl, Applause, 1996, 9", MIB, ea **$12.00**

Jose Carioca, figure, ceramic, American Pottery, 1940s, 6", NM **$150.00**

Jose Carioca, figure, ceramic, Mexico, 1940s, 4¼", NM ..**$125.00**

Jungle Book, doll, Baloo, stuffed velvet & felt, Japan, 6", NM..**$50.00**

Jungle Book, figure, Bagheera, Disneykin, 2nd series, Marx, 1960s, M................................**$15.00**

Jungle Book, figure, Shere Khan, Disneykin, 2nd series, Marx, 1960s, M................................**$15.00**

Jungle Book, figure, Sonny (baby elephant), Disneykin, 2nd series, Marx, 1960s, M................................**$15.00**

Lady & the Tramp, Colorforms Cartoon Kit, 1962, complete, NMIB................................**$35.00**

Lady & the Tramp, figures, Lady & Tramp, stuffed suede w/felt ears, leather accents, WDP, 1970s, pr........**$45.00**

Lion King, spoon rest, Timon, Treasure Craft, M........**$20.00**

Lion King, yo-yo, Simba, plastic, Spectra Star, 1994, MOC...**$6.00**

Ludwig Von Drake, Do-It-Yourself Needlepoint, Hassenfeld, unused, MIB................................**$35.00**

Mary Poppins, tea set, plastic, 1964, MIB................**$100.00i**

Mickey Mouse, ashtray, Mickey seated on triangular dish playing concertina, ceramic lustreware, 2¾", NM, A....**$170.00**

Mickey Mouse, belt buckle, brass w/colorful pie-eyed Mickey, 1970s, 2¼" sq, EX+................................**$25.00**

Mickey Mouse, brush, wood handle w/black metal trim featuring pie-eyed Mickey, WDE/Henry L Hughes Co, 1930s, EX................................**$75.00**

Mickey Mouse, Build-Up Blocks, Eldon, 1950s, complete, M (NM tower-like box)................................**$50.00**

Mickey Mouse, Candy Factory, Remco, 1973, NMIB..**$75.00**

Mickey Mouse, Colorforms Rub 'N Play Magic Transfer Set, 1978, unused, MIB................................**$30.00**

Mickey Mouse, doll, talker, stuffed cloth, 50 Year Anniversary, Horsman, 1980s, MIB................**$65.00**

Mickey Mouse, doll, walker, Hasbro, 1975, 20", VG...**$25.00**

Mickey Mouse, figure, bisque, on sled, 1970s, 4", M..**$30.00**

Mickey Mouse, figure, bisque, w/kite, 1970s, 4", M...**$30.00**

Mickey Mouse, figure, pewter, Sorcerer, Hudson, 1986, 2½", M................................**$75.00**

Mickey Mouse, gumball machine, plastic head form on red base, Hasbro, 1968, NM................................**$50.00**

Mickey Mouse, lamp base figure, ceramic, standing on base w/name, no lamp works, Dan Brechner Co, 1960s, 8", M................................**$100.00**

Mickey Mouse, limited edition plate, Schmidt, 1972 – 78, from $50.00 to $60.00.

Mickey Mouse, marionette, Pelham, 11", EX............**$150.00**

Mickey Mouse, mirror, patriotic theme, Sentinel Creations, 1972, 16½", EX................................**$125.00**

Mickey Mouse, music box, cowboy, Schmid, M........**$75.00**

Mickey Mouse, pin cushion, ceramic Mickey holding cushion, Japan, 4¼", NM................................**$85.00**

Mickey Mouse, push-button puppet, playing drums, Kohner, 1948, EX................................**$95.00**

Mickey Mouse, riding toy, Mickey Mouse Bus Lines, litho tin & wood, Gong Bell, 1955, rare, 20", EXIB......**$1,400.00**

Mickey Mouse, ventriloquist doll, Horsman, 1973, NM.**$70.00**

Mickey Mouse, wastebasket, litho tin, Chein, 1974, 13", EX................................**$25.00**

Mickey Mouse & Minnie, bookends, composition figures, multicolored, Determined Productions, 1970s, 6½", EX, pr................................**$75.00**

Mickey Mouse & Minnie, candy dish, lustreware w/wicker-type handle, Mickey serving Minnie on white, blue rim, Japan, 6" dia, EX................................**$110.00**

Mickey Mouse & Minnie, dolls, Nostalgia Mickey & Nostalgia Minnie, plush, w/Disneyland & WDP tags, 1980s, 14", NMIB, pr................................**$75.00**

Mickey Mouse & Minnie, figures, ceramic, Mickey offering Minnie a bouquet of flowers, Goebel, 1988, M, pr..**$300.00**

Mickey Mouse Club, CB Radio, Durham Industries, 1977, MIB................................**$25.00**

Mickey Mouse Club, magazine, Vol II, #5, August 1957, NM................................**$18.00**

Mickey Mouse Club, magic slate, w/16-page activity/story book inside, Strathmore, 1954, NM+................**$20.00**

Mickey Mouse Club, Mousegetar Jr, plastic, Mattel, 1950s, EX................................**$125.00**

Mickey Mouse Club, Mousekartooners, Mattel, 1950s, EXIB................................**$65.00**

Mickey Mouse Club, projector, Newsreel, plastic w/metal tripod, battery-op, Mattel, 1950s, 9¼", EX+............**$75.00**

Mickey Mouse Club, projector, plastic, Stephens, 1950s, complete, MIB................................**$125.00**

Mickey Mouse Club, stamp book, by Kathleen N Daly, Golden Press, 1956, EX................................**$40.00**

Minnie Mouse, doll, stuffed cloth w/leather-type shoes, Gund, 1940s, scarce, 18", VG................................**$275.00**

Minnie Mouse, doll, Sun Rubber, 1950s, 10", VG........**$65.00**

Minnie Mouse, Minnie Picture Toast, Hoan Products, 1988, M (EX card)................................**$25.00**

Minnie Mouse, slide-tile puzzle, plastic, Marx, 1950s, 3½" sq, VG+ (VG+ box featuring Mickey & MM Club house)................................**$40.00**

Minnie Mouse, wall pocket, head form, Disneyland, 1970s, M................................**$100.00**

Monty (Mickey's Nephew), figure, Disneykin, 1st series, Marx, 1960s, M................................**$8.00**

Mouseketeers, doll, blond girl, vinyl, all original, Horsman, M................................**$45.00**

Mouseketeers, mouse ears, black plastic headband type w/white embossed lettering, Kohner/WDP, 1956, NM+................................**$40.00**

Mouseketeers, Mouseketeers Television, litho tin w/paper scroll, 1950s, VG................$150.00

Nightmare Before Christmas, figure, Evil Scientist, Hasbro, 1993, MOC................$130.00

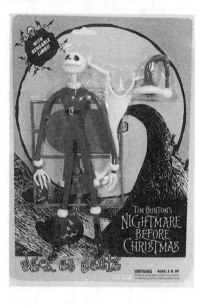

Nightmare Before Christmas, Jack Skellington as Santa, Hasbro, 1993, MOC, from $75.00 to $100.00.

Nightmare Before Christmas, figures, Mayor or Sally, Hasbro, 1993, MOC, ea................$100.00

Pagemaster, doll, Richard, plush, Applause, 1994, 11", M................$15.00

Pagemaster, key chains, PVC, set of 5, Applause, 1994, MOC................$10.00

Peter Pan, figure, Peter Pan, ceramic, sitting on rock, Japan, 1960s-70s, 5", EX+................$40.00

Peter Pan, finger puppet, 1960s, VG................$25.00

Peter Pan, place mat, vinyl, shows Tinkerbell & the magic castle, 1960s, 12x18", EX................$25.00

Peter Pan, towel set, Styled by Gildex, 1950s, MIP (sealed) $65.00

Pinocchio, brooch, painted plastic Pinocchio figure, NEMO, 1940, 2", EX (VG card) $40.00

Pinocchio, clicker, Jiminy Cricket, yellow plastic head figure, 1950s, NM................$20.00

Pinocchio, figure, Figaro, porcelain, gray & white, National, 1940s, 2¼", M................$55.00

Pinocchio, figure, Gepetto, wood fiber, Multi-Products, 1940s, 2½", EX+................$65.00

Pinocchio, figure, Gepetto, wood fiber, Multi-Products, 1940s, 5½", EX+................$90.00

Pinocchio, figure, Gideon, bisque, 1940s, 3", EX+......$45.00

Pinocchio, figure, Gideon, wood fiber, Multi Products, 1940s, 2", EX+................$65.00

Pinocchio, figure, Jiminey Cricket, wood fiber, United Fund Campaign Award on base, Multi Products, 1940, 5½", NM $250.00

Pinocchio, figure, Pinocchio, bisque, 1940s, 3", EX+..$75.00

Pinocchio, figure, Pinocchio, bisque, 1940s, 4", EX+..$100.00

Pinocchio, figure, Pinocchio, ceramic, walking w/school books & apple, Japan, 1950s, 4½", VG................$50.00

Pinocchio, figure, Pinocchio, porcelain (glazed), Japan, 1940s, 2¾", EX................$30.00

Pinocchio, hand puppet, Pinocchio, velvety cloth body w/plastic head, rubber boots, Gund, 1960s, 11", EX+........$50.00

Pinocchio, tumbler, Jiminy Cricket head figure, light blue plastic w/flicker eyes, WDP, 1950s, 4", NM+........$30.00

Pluto, nodder, plastic, Hong Kong, 1960s, 2½", M.....$18.00

Pluto, push-button puppet, wood w/plastic head, Kohner, 5", NMIB................$95.00

Pluto, rocking chair, stuffed vinyl w/wooden rockers, Pluto & pups on chair back, 1950s, 32", EX................$150.00

Pluto, salt & pepper shakers, white ceramic w/red & black cold paint, EX, pr................$40.00

Pocahontas, salt & pepper shakers, Percy & Meeko, Tiawan, M, pr................$30.00

Rocketeer, beach towel, AMC Theatres promo, NM...$20.00

Rocketeer, roll-along figures, PVC, set of 3, Applause, 1990, M................$15.00

Rocketeer, sleeping bag, NM................$20.00

Rocketeer, wallet, Pyramid Handbag Co, M................$20.00

Sleeping Beauty, crib mobile, plastic, Kenner, 1958, complete, EXIB................$30.00

Sleeping Beauty, plaques, 5-pc set, WDP, 1959, MIB..$125.00

Snow White & the Seven Dwarfs, birthday cake candle holders, pewter, figural, Reed & Barton, 1980s, complete set, NMIB................$125.00

Snow White and the Seven Dwarfs, charm bracelet, Disney mark, from $125.00 to $140.00.

Snow White & the Seven Dwarfs, doll set, 7 Dwarfs, plush, Snow White's 50th Anniversary promo from Sears, 1978, 7", M................$75.00

Snow White & the Seven Dwarfs, glo-in-the-dark print, w/forest friends, multicolor, 1940s, original frame, 11x9", EX................$50.00

Snow White & the Seven Dwarfs, plate, any in First Edition Series, 1 of 15,000, 1980s, 8½", M, ea................$50.00

Snow White & the Seven Dwarfs, trinket box, Dopey, ceramic w/gold trim, 2½x2x2", EX................................**$60.00**
Three Little Pigs, switch plate, plastic, 1950s, MIP......**$35.00**
Toy Story, Mr Potato Head, Hasbro, MIP....................**$20.00**
Toy Story, pull toy, Slinky Dog, MIB..........................**$20.00**

Toy Story, Talking Woody, cloth with vinyl head and hands, Thinkway, MIB, $45.00. (Photo courtesy Mark Mazzetti)

Winnie the Pooh, figure, Pooh, plush, Disney's Classic Pooh Collection, Gund, 1990s, 5½", M (NM box)..........**$30.00**
101 Dalmatians, Colorforms, complete w/booklet, 1962, NMIB...**$40.00**
101 Dalmatians, teapot, Roly, Treasure Craft, M.........**$35.00**

Dog Collectibles

Dog lovers appreciate the many items, old and new, that are modeled after or decorated with their favorite breeds. They pursue, some avidly, all with dedication, specific items for a particular accumulation or a range of objects, from matchbook covers to bronzes.

Perhaps the Scottish terrier is one of the most highly sought-out breeds of dogs among collectors; at any rate, Scottie devotees are more organized than most. Both the Aberdeen and West Highland Terriers were used commercially; often the two are found together in things such as magnets, Black & White Scotch Whiskey advertisements, jewelry, and playing cards, for instance. They became a favorite of the advertising world in the 1930s and 1940s, partly as a result of the public popularity of President Roosevelt's dog, Fala. For information on Scottish terriers see *A Treasury of Scottie Dog Collectibles, Identification and Values,* Vol I – III, by Candace Sten Davis and Patricia Baugh (Collector Books).

Poodles were the breed of the 1950s, and today items from those years are cherished collectibles. Trendsetter teeny-boppers wore poodle skirts, and the 5-&-10¢ stores were full of pink poodle figurines with 'coleslaw' fur. For a look back at these years, we recommend *Poodle Collectibles of the '50s and '60s* by Elaine Butler (L-W Books).

Many of the earlier collectibles are especially prized, making them expensive and difficult to find. Prices listed here may vary as they are dependent on supply and demand, location, and dealer assessment.

Advisor: Elaine Butler, Poodles (See Directory, Poodle Collectibles)

Club: Heart of America Scottish Terrier Club
Julia Dahn
P.O. Box 204
Old Monroe, MO 63369

Basset Hound, cache pot, 2 sad-faced dogs w/pot in back, marked Japan, 4½", EX..**$5.00**
Basset Hound, cookie jar, black w/red tongue, tail as lid finial, unmarked, 5½x10", NM.............................**$40.00**
Bassett Hound, figurine, seated, ivory w/brown highlights, comic face, 1940s-1950s, 2⅝".................................**$6.00**
Border Collie, door knocker, brass, name plate below, 2½x2"..**$30.00**
Border Collie, figurine, painted metal, marked ENG, 1¼x1⅛", EX..**$30.00**
Boston Terrier, figurine, marked Styson Porcelain USA, 7¾x7", M..**$90.00**
Bulldog, bank, painted cast iron, marked Kaiser on red collar, coin slot in back of head, 7", EX.................**$450.00**
Bulldog, box, figurine on lid, French Limoges, EX...**$120.00**
Bulldog, figurine, Mack on collar, marked C Mack Trucks Inc, Limited Edition Keith Smykal Assoc NYC, 5¾x7½", EX..**$105.00**
Bulldog, figurine, porcelain, marked #7420, 9½x11¼", EX...**$1,280.00**
Bulldog, postcard, bulldog & flag, silk, WWI era, NM .**$75.00**
Cocker Spaniel, ashtray, copper-tone metal w/figural dog on side, 4x5" w/2x3¾" dog, EX...............................**$25.00**
Cocker Spaniel, ashtray, white w/sleeping dog on side, Frankoma #402, Sapulpa clay, 1980-81, 7⅜x5¾", EX.**$90.00**
Cocker Spaniel, bookends, metal dog w/marble disk behind, 3½x4½x3½", pr..**$50.00**
Cocker Spaniel, bookends, wooden, Barwood, 5¾x3¾x3½", pr..**$30.00**
Cocker Spaniel, coaster, Sunshine Beer, advertising war bonds, 3½x3½", EX..**$30.00**
Cocker Spaniel, doorstop, cast iron, Hubley, 4¼x7"...**$145.00**
Cocker Spaniel, figural fence finial, 6¾x9", EX...........**$20.00**
Cocker Spaniel, figurine, black, Coopercraft, 7", EX...**$40.00**
Cocker Spaniel, figurine, black & white, Beswick, NM ..**$45.00**
Cocker Spaniel, figurine, black & white, marked Melba, EX..**$25.00**
Cocker Spaniel, figurine, blonde color, Unique Design, 6½x8½", EX...**$25.00**
Cocker Spaniel, figurine, brown & white, lying down, Home Interiors, 1986, 8x15x7", EX................................**$30.00**
Cocker Spaniel, figurine, dog lying down w/paper in mouth, Chase Japan foil label, 6½x4½x5½".....................**$35.00**

Cocker Spaniel, figurine, Living Stone, 1985, 9", EX...**$25.00**

Cocker Spaniel, figurine, puppy, brown, Licthen Ware, EX..**$18.00**

Cocker Spaniel, figurine, sitting on green cushion, Capodimonte, 5", EX **$40.00**

Cocker Spaniel, hankerchief, dog w/2 shoes, Dessin Dep, 12x12", NM **$40.00**

Cocker Spaniel, music box, dog sitting surrounded by flowers, Gorham, EX...............................**$10.00**

Cocker Spaniel, planter, 3 puppies side-by-side, marked C720, 4½x4", EX **$20.00**

Cocker Spaniel, plate, 2 puppies chewing on baseball glove, chewed ball on ground, 23k gold rim, Jim Lamb, 8½" dia **$40.00**

Collie, child's cup, dog jumps through hoop that monkey in red coat holds, Made in Bavaria, 2½", EX............**$50.00**

Newfoundland, bank, glossy black w/green collar, standing w/rock-like structure between legs, ESD Japan #21509, 5½x8"...**$35.00**

Pekingese, doorstop, brown on green base, marked #353, 5x5", EX...**$130.00**

Pekingese, doorstop, Hubley, 9x14½", NM...........**$1,600.00**

Pekingese, figurine, ivory w/blue hat & shawl, Szeiler, 3⅞", EX...**$45.00**

Pekingese, figurine, Sandicast, 1984, 5x8", EX **$25.00**

Pekingese, pin tray, head only, brown w/blue accents, Wade, 3x3¾", EX...**$18.00**

Pekingese, postcard, Top Hat & Tails, England, 1950s, EX **$25.00**

Poodle, magnifying glass, enclosed in round metal case w/black dog (2") w/gold collar on top, EX.........**$30.00**

Poodle, radio, black, lying down, radio in zippered tummy, 1950s, 9x9", EX **$50.00**

Dalmatian, figurine, Lefton, #1641, from $50.00 to $60.00. (Photo courtesy Loretta DeLozier)

Poodle, serving tray, marked Made in Calif. U.S.A., from $10.00 to $15.00. (Photo courtesy Elaine Butler)

English Setter, tie rack 2 dogs on top lying down, 18 holders, Syrocco, 6¼x13½", EX **$40.00**

German Shepherd, figurine, lying down w/open mouth, marked #5108, 9½x17½", EX...............................**$110.00**

German Shepherd, Jell-O mold, tin, German, 2¾x4½", EX **$25.00**

German Shepherd, wall plaque, head, marked Germany, bronzed cast iron, 6½" dia, EX......................**$175.00**

Great Dane, figurine, lying down, black & white, yellow eyes & red collar, ca pre-WWII, 5" L, M.......................**$25.00**

Husky, button, face reverse painting, brass flat loop shank, 1930s, ½" dia, VG...**$25.00**

Husky, figurine, dog w/butterfly on nose, hand-blown glass, marked Deanne Norris, mounted on slate, 2½x7x4", M...**$50.00**

Husky, figurine, snowbabies w/husky, Dept 56, 7½x4", NM...**$35.00**

Husky, pen holder, husky team w/sled full of cargo & person w/heavy coat, carved ivory, 5⅛x2¼", EX **$105.00**

Labrador Retreiver, mug, clear glass w/embossed image, 1880s, 3½", EX **$80.00**

Scottie, bowl, white w/5 red dogs, Hazel Atlas, 2¼x5" dia **$55.00**

Scottie, ice tub, clear w/8 black Scotties & red checked bottom border, 1940s, 4¼x5¾" dia, EX.....................**$55.00**

Scottie, tumbler, Hazel Atlas Glass Co., ca 1940s, from $12.00 to $18.00. (Photo courtesy Candace Sten Davis and Patricia Baugh)

Setter, puzzle, Tense Moment, 2 dogs hunting, Perfect Picture
   Puzzle #25, 1940s, EXIB **$20.00**
Spaniel, covered box, white w/white dog w/black highlights,
   egg shape, Enesco, 1980, ...**$25.00**
Terrier, button, 2 dogs, 1 above the other, Syrocco, 1940s,
   1½" **$5.00**
Terrier, creamer, black & white, Made in Japan, 3¼", EX ..**$30.00**

Dollhouse Furniture

Some of the mass-produced dollhouse furniture you're
apt to see on the market today was made by Renwal and
Acme during the 1940s and Ideal in the 1960s. All three of
these companies used hard plastic for their furniture lines
and imprinted most pieces with their names. Strombecker
furniture was made of wood, and although it was not
marked, it has a certain recognizable style to it. Remember
that if you're lucky enough to find it complete in the original
box, you'll want to preserve the carton as well.

Advisor: Judith Mosholder (See Directory Dollhouse Furniture)

Acme/Thomas, carriage, blue w/blue top & white wheels or
   black w/pink top & white wheels, ea **$6.00**
Acme/Thomas, cradle, pink & blue w/molded storks &
   babies **$8.00**
Acme/Thomas, doll, baby in diaper, 2" **$4.00**

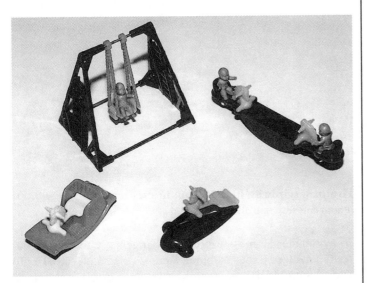

Acme, single swing, $20.00; seesaw, $10.00; Tommy horse, $18.00; Shoofly, $10.00. (Photo courtesy Jundy Mosholder)

Allied/Pyro, cupboard, corner; aqua **$8.00**
Allied/Pyro, piano, black w/white keyboard **$12.00**
Ardee, chair, dining; red w/ivory **$5.00**
Babyland Nursery, any pc, blue or pink, ea **$5.00**
Best, doll, baby; sitting, 2" **$3.00**
Blue Box, bed, light brown w/blue spread **$5.00**
Blue Box, piano, w/stool **$15.00**
Blue Box, vanity w/heart-shaped mirror **$4.00**

Cheerio, any hard plastic pc, ea **$4.00**
Cheerio, any soft plastic pc, sm, ea **$2.00**
Commonwealth, lamppost, w/street sign & mailbox, red..**$15.00**
Commonwealth, spade, pink **$4.00**
Fisher-Price, clock, grandfather; brown **$10.00**
Fisher-Price, dest set #262 ....**$6.00**

Fisher-Price, dinette set, pedestal table and four chairs, 1978 – 1983, MIB, $4.00. (Photo courtesy Brad Cassity)

Fisher-Price, doll (boy) #277, MOC **$2.50**
Ideal, chair, bedroom; blue w/pink skirt **$30.00**
Ideal, chair, kitchen; white w/red seat **$15.00**
Ideal, china closet, dark brown swirl or dark marbleized
   maroon, ea **$15.00**
Ideal, doll, baby; painted diaper **$10.00**
Ideal, highboy, dark marbleized maroon **$15.00**

Ideal, living room chairs, $15.00 each; tilt-top table, $45.00; floor lamp, $25.00; fireplace, $35.00; floor radio, $10.00; sofa, $20.00; coffee table, $10.00; end table/night stand, $6.00. (Photo courtesy Judith Mosholder)

Ideal, stove, ivory w/black **$15.00**

Ideal, tub, corner; blue w/yellow.................................$18.00
Ideal, vanity, ivory w/blue.......................................$18.00
Ideal Petite Princess, cabinet #4418-0, in original box...$12.00
Ideal Petite Princess, chair, guest dining #4414-9.........$8.00
Ideal Petite Princess, chair, hostess dining #4415-6......$8.00
Ideal Petite Princess, clock, grandfather #4423-0.........$15.00
Ideal Petite Princess, dish rack #4508-8.....................$10.00
Ideal Petite Princess, hamper #4499-0.......................$30.00
Irwin Interior Decorator, sink, yellow w/orange...........$5.00
Irwin Interior Decorator, toilet, light green.................$5.00
Jaydon, chest of drawers, reddish brown swirl............$6.00
Jaydon, piano w/bench, reddish brown swirl.............$12.00
Kage, clock, table; walnut w/ivory shade...................$10.00
Kage, refrigerator, white w/black detail......................$8.00
Marx, buffet, hard plastic, w/molded fruit, tan, ½" scale..$3.00
Marx, chair, kitchen; soft plastic, ivory, ¾" scale.........$3.00
Marx, china cupboard, hard plastic, dark brown or dark
    maroon swirl, ½" scale, ea...............................$3.00
Marx, playpen, soft plastic, pink, ¾" scale..................$3.00
Marx, toilet, hard plastic, peach, ¾" scale..................$5.00
Marx, vanity, soft plastic, yellow, ¾" scale..................$3.00
Marx Little Hostess, chair, rocker; reddish brown.......$12.00
Marx Little Hostess, clock, grandfather; red...............$18.00
Marx Little Hostess, fireplace, ivory........................$20.00
Marx Little Hostess, table, tilt-top; black..................$12.00
Marx Newlywed, vanity, deep pink & blue................$15.00
Mattel Littles, chair, living room; w/footstool & plant, in orig-
    inal box...$15.00
Mattel Littles, doll, Belinda w/4 chairs & pop-up room set-
    ting, in original box....................................$25.00
Mattel Littles, doll, Littles Family (Mr & Mrs Little & baby), in
    original box...$22.00
Nancy Forbes, bed, walnut...................................$4.00
Nancy Forbes, cabinet, floor; walnut.......................$4.00
Nancy Forbes, chair, kitchen; white........................$2.00
Nancy Forbes, night stand, walnut.........................$2.00
Plasco, bench, vanity; brown, dark brown, ivory or pink,
    ea...$3.00
Plasco, buffet, brown, marbleized reddish brown, tan or tan
    w/yellow detail, ea.......................................$4.00
Plasco, buffet, med maroon swirl or very dark maroon swirl,
    ea...$5.00
Plasco, doll, baby; pink......................................$25.00
Plasco, highboy, tan..$8.00
Plasco, sink, bathroom; pink................................$4.00
Reliable, bench, piano; brown...............................$8.00
Reliable, radio, floor; rust..................................$15.00
Reliable, table, kitchen; ivory..............................$12.00
Renwal, bench, piano/vanity; brown or light brown swirl,
    ea...$2.00
Renwal, bench, piano/vanity; light green.................$4.00
Renwal, chair, club; dark green w/brown base.........$10.00
Renwal, clock, kitchen; ivory...............................$20.00
Renwal, doll, father; metal rivets, blue suit..............$30.00
Renwal, doll, father; plastic rivets, all tan................$25.00
Renwal, highchair, ivory.....................................$30.00
Renwal, ironing board, blue or pink, ea...................$7.00

Renwal, piano, marbelized brown..........................$35.00
Renwal, sink, opening door, ivory w/red..................$18.00

Renwal, seesaw #21, $25.00; slide #20, $20.00; kiddie car #27, $55.00; doll, $25.00; tricycle #7, $20.00. (Photo courtesy Judith Mosholder)

Strombecker, bowl, silver or yellow, ¾" scale, ea......$10.00
Strombecker, chair w/ottoman, light brown flocked, 1"
    scale...$25.00
Strombecker, night stand, light green or pink, ¾" scale, ea..$6.00
Strombecker, scale, blue or green, ¾" scale, ea.........$15.00
Strombecker, toilet, ivory, ¾" scale........................$10.00
Strombecker, urn, green or yellow, ¾" scale, ea........$10.00
Superior, potty chair, white or bright blue, ¾" scale, ea..$8.00
Superior, sofa, brown, pale green, red or turquoise, ¾" scale,
    ea...$5.00
Superior, vanity w/mirror, red, ¾" scale..................$5.00

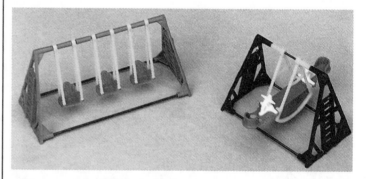

Thomas, triple swing, $60.00; horse-head swing, $80.00.
(Photo courtesy Bob and Marcie Tubbs)

Tomy Smaller Homes, armoire, w/hangers................$15.00
Tomy Smaller Homes, cabinet, stereo......................$15.00
Tomy Smaller Homes, sink, kitchen; double bowl, 1
    rack..$3.00
Tomy Smaller Homes, vanity................................$15.00
Tomy Smaller Homes, vanity stool..........................$6.00
Tootsietoy, chair, bedroom rocker; pink...................$18.00
Tootsietoy, lamp, floor; gold................................$40.00
Tootsietoy, table, living room; gold........................$20.00
Wolverine, sofa, pink..$3.00
Wolverine, television, brown.................................$3.00
Young Decorator, lamp, floor; green shade...............$60.00
Young Decorator, playpen, pink.............................$45.00
Young Decorator, sofa, 4 sections, rose....................$60.00

Dolls

Doll collecting is one of the most popular hobbies in the United States. Since many of the antique dolls are so expensive, modern dolls have come into their own and can be had at prices within the range of most budgets. Today's thrift-shop owners know the extent of 'doll mania,' though, so you'll seldom find a bargain there. But if you're willing to spend the time, garage sales can be a good source for your doll buying. Granted most will be in a 'well loved' condition, but as long as they're priced right, many can be re-dressed, rewigged, and cleaned up. Swap meets and flea markets may sometimes yield a good example or two, often at lower-than-book prices.

Modern dolls, those from 1935 to the present, are made of rubber, composition, magic skin, synthetic rubber, and many types of plastic. Most of these materials do not stand up well to age, so be objective when you buy, especially if you're buying with an eye to the future. Doll repair is an art best left to professionals, but if yours is only dirty, you can probably do it yourself. If you need to clean a composition doll, do it very carefully. Use only baby oil and follow up with a soft dry cloth to remove any residue. Most types of wigs can be shampooed with wig shampoo and lukewarm water. Be careful not to matt the hair as you shampoo, and follow up with hair conditioner or fabric softener. Comb gently and set while wet, using small soft rubber or metal curlers. Never use a curling iron or heated rollers.

In our listings, unless a condition is noted in the descriptions, values are for dolls in excellent condition.

For further study, we recommend these books: *Collector's Guide to Dolls of the 1960s and 1970s* by Cindy Sabulis; *Collector's Guide to Horsman Dolls* by Don Jenson; *Doll Values, Antique to Modern* and *Modern Collectible Dolls* by Patsy Moyer; *Effenbee Dolls* by Patricia Smith; *Small Dolls of the 40s and 50s* by Carol Stover; *Talking Toys of the 20th Century* by Kathy and Don Lewis; All these references are published by Collector Books.

See also Barbie and Friends; Shirley Temple; Toys (Action Figures and GI Joe).

Magazine: *Doll Castle News*
37 Belvidere Ave., P.O. Box 247
Washington, NJ 07882
908-689-7042 or Fax: 908-689-6320
www.dollcastlenews.com

Newsletter: *Doll News*
United Federation of Doll Clubs
10900 North Pomona Ave.
Kansas City, MO 64153
816-891-7040; www.ufdc.org

Newsletter: *Modern Doll Club Journal*
Jeanne Niswonger
305 W Beacon Rd., Lakeland, FL 33803

Annalee

Barbara 'Annalee' Davis was born in Concord, New Hampshire, on February, 11, 1915. She started dabbling at doll making at an early age, often giving her creations to friends. She married Charles 'Chip' Thorndike in 1941 and moved to Meredith, New Hampshire, where they started a chicken farm and sold used auto parts. By the early 1950s, with the chicken farm failing, Annalee started crafting her dolls on the kitchen table to help make ends meet. She designed her dolls by looking into the mirror, drawing faces as she saw them, and making the clothes from scraps of material. Annalee died in April 2002.

The dolls she developed are made of wool felt with hand-painted features and flexible wire frameworks. The earlier dolls from the 1950s had a long white red-embroidered tag with no date. From 1959 to 1964, the tags stayed the same except there was a date in the upper right-hand corner. From 1965 to 1970, this same tag was folded in half and sewn into the seam of the doll. In 1970 a transition period began. The company changed its tag to a satiny white tag with a date preceded by a copyright symbol in the upper right-hand corner. In 1975 they made another change to a long white cotton strip with a copyright date. In 1982 the white tag was folded over, making it shorter. Many people mistake the copyright date as the date the doll was made — not so! It wasn't until 1986 that they finally began to date the tags with the year of manufacture, making it much easier for collectors to identify their dolls. Besides the red-lettered white Annalee tags, numerous others were used in the 1990s, but all reflect the year the doll was actually made.

For many years the company held a June auction on the premises; this practice has been discontinued. Annalee's signature can increase a doll's value by as much as $300.00, sometimes more. She had personally signed no dolls for several years. Chuck (her son) and Karen Thorndike are now signing them.

Remember, these dolls are made of wool felt. To protect them, store them with moth balls, and avoid exposing them to too much sunlight, since they will fade. Our advisor has been a collector for almost twenty years and a secondary market dealer since 1988. Most of these dolls have been in her collection at one time or another. She recommends 'if you like it, buy it, love it, treat it with care, and you'll have it to enjoy for many years to come.'

Our values are suggested for dolls in very good to excellent condition, not personally autographed by Annalee herself.

Advisor: Jane Holt (See Directory, Dolls)

Newsletter: *The Collector*
Annalee Doll Society
P.O. Box 1137, 50 Reservoir Rd., Meredith, NH 03253-1137
1-800-433-6557

1976, Bicentennial Boy and Girl Mice, 7", $150.00 for the pair. (Photo courtesy Jane Holt)

1976, Bunnies (2) w/Basket, 7" $50.00
1976, Colonial Drummer Boy, tricorn hat, 1 year in production, 18" $250.00
1976, Colonial Drummer Boy, tricorn hat, 1 year in production, 10" $125.00
1977, Leprechaun, dark green w/shamrock vest, 10" .$60.00
1978, Pilgrim Boy & Girl, 1 year in production, 18", pr..$225.00
1982, Ballooning Santa, 7" $95.00

1982, I'm #10 Girl (one year in production), 7", $95.00. (Photo courtesy Jane Holt)

1983, Duck w/Kerchief, 12" $50.00
1984, Mrs Claus, 5" $30.00
1984, Sweetheart Duck, 5" $30.00
1985, Pilot Duckling, 5" $40.00
1985, Valentine Bear, heart on T-shirt, 18" $95.00
1986, Christmas Morning Kid, 7" $25.00
1986, Cupid Kid, in hot air balloon, 7" $95.00
1987, Kitten w/Yarn & Basket, 10" $50.00
1988, Cat w/Mouse, 18" $75.00
1989, Mrs Claus, 7" $35.00
1990, Girl (or Boy) on Sled, 18" $95.00
1990, Snowy Owl, 10" $50.00
1991, Aviator Frog, aviator hat w/goggles, holds flag, 10" ..$45.00
1991, Christmas Swan, 18" $75.00

1991, Country Boy Bunny w/Wheelbarrow, 10" $45.00
1991, Pilgrim Boy & Girl Mouse, green, no basket, 12", pr..$50.00
1991, Thorny the Ghost, 18" $95.00
1992, Jacob Marley, w/plaque, 10" $115.00
1992, Uncle Sam w/5" child, 12" $250.00
1993, Baseball Pitcher, 10" $45.00
1993, Spring Boy Rooster, 7" $40.00
1994, Devil Kid, 12" $65.00
1995, Ghost Mouse, 7" $30.00
1995, Indian Boy, holds spear, brown shirt & pants, 7"...$40.00
1996, Skeleton Kid, 30" $125.00
1996, St Patrick's Day Boy, 7"......................................$35.00
1996, Witch Mouse, 7" $30.00
1997, Haunted Tree, 15" $75.00
1997, Hearth & Home Santa, 7".....................................$45.00
1998, Bride & Groom, 3", pr...$50.00
1998, Sweetheart Boy Elf, 10" $35.00
1999, Mr & Mrs Santa Stringing Lights, 7", pr.............$60.00
2000, Irish Lamb, w/shamrock in mouth, 10" $45.00

1984, 1986, 1987, Cardholder Santa, 18", $50.00 each. (Photo courtesy Jane Holt)

Betsy McCall

The tiny 8" Betsy McCall doll was manufactured by the American Character Doll Company from 1957 through 1963. She was made from high-quality hard plastic with a bisque-like finish and hand-painted features. Betsy came in four hair colors — tosca, red, blond, and brunette. She had blue sleep eyes, molded lashes, a winsome smile, and a fully jointed body with bendable knees. On her back there is an identification circle which reads McCall Corp. The basic doll wore a sheer chemise, white taffeta panties, nylon socks, and Mary Jane-style shoes, and could be purchased for $2.25.

There were two different materials used for tiny Betsy's hair. The first was a soft mohair sewn into fine mesh. Later the rubber skullcap was rooted with saran which was more suitable for washing and combing.

Betsy McCall had an extensive wardrobe with nearly one hundred outfits, each of which could be purchased separately. They were made from wonderful fabrics such as velvet, taffeta, felt, and even real mink. Each ensemble came with the appropriate footwear and was priced under $3.00. Since none of Betsy's clothing was tagged, it is often difficult to identify other than by its square snap closures (although these were used by other companies as well).

Betsy McCall is a highly collectible doll today but is still fairly easy to find at doll shows. The prices remain reasonable for this beautiful clothes horse and her many accessories. For further information we recommend *Betsy McCall, A Collector's Guide*, by Marci Van Ausdall.

Advisor: Marci Van Ausdall (See Directory, Dolls)

Newsletter: *Betsy's Fan Club*
Marci Van Ausdall
P.O. Box 946, Quincy, CA 95971-0946
e-mail: dreams707@aol.com; Subscription $16.00 per year or send $4 for sample copy

Doll, American Character, 14", M, $265.00. (Photo courtesy Patsy Moyer)

Doll, American Character, Linda McCall (Betsy's cousin), vinyl, Betsy face, rooted hair, 1959, all original, 36" **$350.00**
Doll, American Character, Sandy McCall, nude/played with, 1959, 39" **$50.00**
Doll, American Character, Sandy McCall, vinyl, molded hair, sleep eyes, red blazer/navy shorts, all original, 1959, 39" **$350.00**
Doll, American Character, vinyl, rooted hair, jointed, brown sleep eyes, all original, 1961, 22" **$250.00**
Doll, American Character, vinyl, rooted hair, jointed, sleep eyes, 1961, nude/played with, 22" **$30.00**

Doll, American Character, vinyl, rooted hair, Patti Playpal-style body, 1959, all original, 36" **$325.00**
Doll, Horsman, vinyl w/rigid plastic teen body, jointed wrists, sleep eyes, rooted hair, all original, 1974, 29" **$275.00**
Doll, Horsman, vinyl w/rigid teen body, jointed wrists, sleep eyes, rooted hair, nude, 1974, 29" **$75.00**
Doll, Horsman, vinyl/rigid plastic, sleep eyes, all original, 1967, 12½" **$50.00**
Doll, Ideal, vinyl head, strung hard plastic Toni body, rooted saran wig, all original, 14", NM **$250.00**
Doll, Rothchile, hard plastic, sleep eyes, tied ribbon emblem 35th on back, all original, 1986, 8" **$35.00**

Celebrity Dolls

Celebrity and character dolls have been widely collected for many years, but they've lately shown a significant increase in demand. Except for rarer examples, most of these dolls are still fairly easy to find at doll shows, toy auctions, and flea markets, and the majority are priced under $100.00. These are the dolls that bring back memories of childhood TV shows, popular songs, favorite movies and familiar characters. Mego, Mattel, Remco, and Hasbro are among the largest manufacturers.

Condition is a very important worth-assessing factor, and if the doll is still in the original box, so much the better! Should the box be unopened (NRFB), the value is further enhanced. Using mint in box as a standard, deduct 30% to 35% for one that is mint (no box). Increase the price for 'never removed from box' examples by about 40%. Values for dolls in only good or poorer condition drop at a rapid pace.

For further information, we recommend *Collector's Guide to Celebrity Dolls* by David Spurgeon.

See also Elvis Presley Memorabilia.

Beverly Hills 90210, Dylan, Brandon, Kelly, Brenda, or Donna, Mattel, 1991, any 12" figure with accessories, $65.00. (Photo courtesy June Moon)

Bionic Woman/Lindsay Wagner, Kenner, 1980, MIB.**$175.00**

Blues Brothers, Jake & Elwood in black trench coats, 27", 1977, MIB **$150.00**

Bobby Orr, Regal, 1975, rare, 12", MOC...................**$800.00**

Brooke Shields, blue sweater & white pants, LJN, 1982, NRFB...**$45.00**

Brooke Shields, pink sweater & gray pants, LJN, 1982, NRFB...**$40.00**

Brooke Shields, Prom Party, LJN, 1982, rare, MIB, from $150.00 to $200.00. (Photo courtesy Henri Yunes)

Buffy/Annissa Jones, Mattel, 1967, 5", w/3" Mrs Beasley doll, MIB **$250.00**

Cher, original pink gown, Mego, 1976, EX.................**$45.00**

Christy Brinkley, Real Models Collection, Matchbox, 1989, 11½", NRFB **$55.00**

CJ/Pamela Anderson Lee, Toy Island, 1997, 11½", NRFB .**$35.00**

Dennis Rodman, Wedding Day clothes, Street Players, 1995, 11½", MIB...**$65.00**

Diana Ross, vinyl, gold lamè dress, black Crissy shoes, Ideal, 1970s, 17", NM **$275.00**

Dolly Parton, black jumper or cowgirl outfit, Eegee 2nd edition, 1987, 11½", NRFB, ea **$50.00**

Dolly/Carol Channing, Naco Dolls, 1962, rare, 11½", MIB **$350.00**

Dorothy Hamill, red olympic outfit w/medal, 1977, 11½", NRFB **$75.00**

Dorothy/Judy Garland, 50th Anniversary of Wizard of Oz, Multitoys, 1984, rare, MIB **$100.00**

Drew Carey, Creation, 1998, 11½", NRFB...................**$30.00**

Drew Carey & Mimi Bobeck, he w/briefcase & mug, she w/purse & mirror, Creation Entertainment, 9", MIB, pr...**$100.00**

Elvis, Burning Love, World Doll, 1984, 21", MIB **$110.00**

Elvis Presley, Jailhouse Rock, w/guitar, Hasbro, 1993, NRFB **$55.00**

Elvis Presley, Teen Idol, w/guitar, Hasbro, 1993, NRFB .**$55.00**

Farrah Fawcett, pink halter dress, Mego, 12", NM **$25.00**

Flo-Jo, pink & blue athletic outfit w/bag, LJN, 1989, 11½", MIB **$85.00**

George Burns, Effanbee, in tux, w/stand, 1996, MIB .**$125.00**

Grandpa Munster/Al Lewis, Remco, 1964, 6", MIB...**$200.00**

Herman Munster/Fred Gwynne, Remco, 1964, MIB.**$150.00**

Honeymooners, Ralph, Alice & Ed, vinyl, Exclusive Toy Products, 9", M (sealed) set of 3 ....**$120.00**

Jaclyn Smith, Charlie's Angels, Hasbro, 1970s, MOC, $40.00. (Photo courtesy June Moon)

Jaclyn Smith, Mego, 1977, NRFB (damage to box)...**$295.00**

James Dean, City Streets Dean, DSI, 1994, MIB..........**$55.00**

James Dean, vinyl, Exclusive Premiere Limited Edition Collector's Series, original jeans & red jacket, 9", M .**$60.00**

Jeannie/Barbara Eden, Remco, 1972, 6½", NRFB **$100.00**

Jerry Springer, 1990s, 12", MIB...**$30.00**

John Wayne, Spirit of the West outfit, Effanbee Great Legends Series, 1981, 17", MIB...**$125.00**

Julia/Diahann Caroll, 2-pc nurse uniform, Mattel, 1969, 11½", NRFB...**$200.00**

Kevin/Macully Caulkin, screams, THQ Inc, 1989, MIB..**$25.00**

Kris/Cheryl Ladd, jumpsuit & scarf, Hasbro, 1977, 8½", MOC...**$40.00**

Lucille Ball as Carmen Miranda, CBS Inc/Desilu, Hamilton Collection, 18", w/certificate, MIB **$100.00**

Mama Cass, Hasbro, all original, 1967, 4", M **$95.00**

Marie Osmond, Mattel, 1976, 30", MIB **$115.00**

Marilyn Monroe, Silver Sizzle, 1993, MIB **$55.00**

Marilyn Monroe, There's No Business Like Show Business, Tristar, 1982, 17", NRFB...**$85.00**

Marilyn Monroe, Tristar, 1982, 17", NRFB.................**$85.00**

MC Hammer, purple outfit, Mattel, 1991, 11½", MIB..**$70.00**

Michael Jackson, Grammy Awards outfit, LJN, 1984, NRFB...**$65.00**

Mr T, talker, vest & jeans, Galloob 2nd edition, 1982, 12", MIB **$75.00**

Nanny/Fran Drescher, gold skirt outfit, Street Player, 1995, MIB **$65.00**

Nanny/Fran Drescher, turquoise outfit, Street Player, 1995, MIB **$65.00**

Patty Duke, vinyl, w/phone, all original, Horsman, 1965, M...**$185.00**

Pinky Lee, plastic & compo, all original, Juro, 1950s, 24", EX+ **$395.00**

Redd Fox, cloth, talker, Shindana, 1977, MIB.............**$45.00**

Sabrina/Kate Jackson, red & white dress, Mattel, 1978, 11½",
NRFB...**$60.00**

Shirley Temple, Glad Rags to Riches outfit, Ideal, 1984, 16",
MIB **$125.00**

Shirley Temple, printed flower dress w/blue hair ribbons,
Ideal, 1930s, 18", EX, from $700 to **$800.00**

Simpson family, Homer, Marge, Bart, Lisa & Maggie, plastic,
Burker King, 1990, w/tags, complete set of 55 ....**$95.00**

Sonny Bono, Mego, 1975, NRFB **$110.00**

Sonny Bono, Mego, 1976, NRFB **$95.00**

Sylvester Stallone, Over the Top outfit, Lewco Toys, 1986,
20", NRFB **$35.00**

Sally Ann Howes as Truly Scrumptious, Chitty Chitty Bang Bang, talking, pink dress, Mattel, 1968, rare, MIB, $450.00. (Photo courtesy Henri Yunes)

Truly Scrumptious/Sally Ann Howes, white dress, Mattel,
1969, 11½", MIB **$400.00**

Twiggy, Mattel, 1967, rare, 11½", MIB.....................**$400.00**

Wayne Gretzky, The Great Gretzky/Le Magnifique, Mattel,
1982, 11½", MIB **$150.00**

Wonder Woman/Linda Carter, Mego, 1970s, M in G box .**$225.00**

Chatty Cathy and Other Mattel Talkers

One of the largest manufacturers of modern dolls is the Mattel company, the famous maker of the Barbie doll. But besides Barbie, there are many other types of Mattel dolls that have their own devotees, and we've tried to list a sampling of several of their more collectible lines.

Next to Barbie, the all-time favorite doll was Mattel's Chatty Cathy. She was first made in the 1960s, in blond and brunette variations, and much of her success can be attributed to that fact that she could talk! By pulling the string on her back, she could respond with eleven different phrases. The line was expanded and soon included Chatty Baby, Tiny Chatty Baby and Tiny Chatty Brother (the twins), Charmin' Chatty, and finally Singing Chatty. They all sold successfully for five years, and although Mattel reintroduced the line in 1969 (smaller

and with a restyled face), it was not well received. For more information we recommend *Chatty Cathy Dolls, An Identification & Value Guide,* by our advisors, Kathy and Don Lewis.

In 1960 Mattel introduced their first line of talking dolls. They decided to take the talking doll's success even further by introducing a new line — cartoon characters that the young TV viewers were already familiar with.

Below you will find a list of the more popular dolls and animals available. Most MIB (mint-in-box) toys found today are mute, but this should not detract from the listed price. If the doll still talks, you may consider adding a few more dollars to the price.

Advisors: Kathy and Don Lewis (See Directory, Dolls)

Baby Colleen, Sears Exclusive, 1965, 15½", MIB **$100.00**

Baby Flip-Flop, JC Penney Exclusive, 1970, MIB........**$85.00**

Baby Sing-A-Song, 1969, 16½", MIB **$150.00**

Baby Small Talk, 1968, MIB.....................................**$125.00**

Charmin' Chatty, 1963, 25", MIB..............................**$275.00**

Chatty Baby, Black, w/pigtails, M.........................**$1,500.00**

Chatty Baby, brunette hair, red pinafore over white romper,
original tag, MIB **$250.00**

Chatty Baby, early, ring around speaker, blond hair, blue
eyes, M **$250.00**

Chatty Baby, open speaker, brunette hair, brown eyes,
M **$375.00**

Chatty Cathy, brunette hair, brown eyes, M.............**$375.00**

Chatty Cathy, early, brunette hair, blue eyes, M **$85.00**

Chatty Cathy, later issue, open speaker, brunette hair, brown
eyes, M **$850.00**

Chatty Cathy, mid-year or transitional, brunette hair, blue
eyes, M **$650.00**

Chatty Cathy, patent pending, brunette hair, blue eyes,
M...**$750.00**

Chatty Cathy, soft vinyl head and rooted ponytails (very unusual), 20", MIB, from $550.00 to $600.00. (Photo courtesy Cris Johnson/Patsy Moyer)

Cynthia, M $45.00
Hi Dottie, Black, 1972, complete w/telephone, NM ...$75.00
Singin' Chatty, blond hair, M $250.00
Sister Belle, 1961, MIB $200.00
Teachy Keen, Sears Exclusive, 1966, 16", MIB.......$2,125.00
Timey Tell, MIB $110.00
Tiny Chatty baby, Black, M $650.00
Tiny Chatty Baby, blond hair, blue eyes, M.............$250.00
Tiny Chatty Baby, brunette hair, brown eyes, M $300.00

Dawn Dolls by Topper

Made by Deluxe Topper in the 1970s, this 6" fashion doll was part of a series sold as the Dawn Model Agency. They're becoming highly collectible, especially when mint in the box. They were issued already dressed in clothes of the highest style, or you could buy additional outfits, many complete with matching shoes and accessories.

Advisor: Dawn Diaz (See Directory, Dolls)

Dawn's Apartment, complete w/furniture $50.00
Doll, Dancing, Glori, NRFB............................$30.00
Doll, Dancing Angie, NRFB $30.00
Doll, Dancing Dale, NRFB $50.00
Doll, Dancing Dawn, NRFB $30.00
Doll, Dancing Gary, NRFB............................$40.00
Doll, Dancing Jessica, NRFB $30.00
Doll, Dancing Ron, NRFB $40.00
Doll, Dancing Van, NRFB..............................$50.00

Doll, Dawn Model Agency, Daphne, jointed waist, snapping knees, painted green eyes, NRFB, $75.00; loose, played with, from $10.00 to $15.00.

Doll, Dawn Head to Toe, NRFB, from $75 to...........$100.00
Doll, Dawn Majorette, NRFB.......................................$75.00
Doll, Denise, NRFB...$75.00
Doll, Dinah, NRFB..$75.00
Doll, Gary, NRFB..$30.00
Doll, Jessica, NRFB $30.00
Doll, Kip Majorette, NRFB...$45.00

Doll, Longlocks, NRFB $30.00
Doll, Maureen, Dawn Model Agency, red & gold dress, NRFB $75.00
Doll, Ron, NRFB $30.00
Outfit, Bell Bottom Flounce, #0717, NRFB $25.00

Outfit, Peach Keen, #0822, 1969, MOC, $15.00.
(Photo courtesy Gloria Anderson/Patsy Moyer)

Holly Hobbie

In the late 1960s a young homemaker and mother, Holly Hobbie, approached the American Greeting Company with some charming country-styled drawings of children as proposed designs for greeting cards. Her concepts were well received by the company, and since that time thousands of Holly Hobbie items have been produced. Nearly all are marked HH, H. Hobbie, or Holly Hobbie.

Advisor: Donna Stultz (See Directory, Dolls)

Newsletter: *Holly Hobbie Collectors Gazette*
c/o Donna Stultz
1455 Otterdale Mill Rd.
Taneytown, MD 21787-3032; 410-775-2570
hhgazette@hotmail.com
Subscription: $25 per year for 6 bimonthly issues; includes free 50-word ad per issue, 'Free' sample issue available!

Doll, Country Fun Holly Hobbie, 1989, 16", NRFB.....$20.00
Doll, Grandma Holly, Knickerbocker, cloth, 14", MIB $20.00
Doll, Grandma Holly, Knickerbocker, cloth, 24", MIB $25.00
Doll, Holly Hobbie, Heather, Amy or Carrie, Knickerbocker,
     cloth, 6", MIB, ea $10.00
Doll, Holly Hobbie, Heather, Amy or Carrie, Knickerbocker,
     cloth, 9", MIB, ea $10.00
Doll, Holly Hobbie, Heather, Amy or Carrie, Knickerbocker,
     cloth, 16", MIB, ea $20.00
Doll, Holly Hobbie, Heather, Amy or Carrie, Knickerbocker,
     cloth, 27", MIB, ea $25.00

Doll, Holly Hobbie, Heather, Amy or Carrie, Knickerbocker, cloth, 33", MIB, ea **$35.00**

Doll, Holly Hobbie, 1988, scented, clear ornament around neck, 18", NRFB **$30.00**

Doll, Holly Hobbie, 25th Anniversary collector's edition, Meritus, 1994, 26", MIB **$25.00**

Doll, Holly Hobbie Day 'N Night, Knickerbocker, cloth, 14", MIB **$15.00**

Doll, Holly Hobbie Dream Along, Holly, Carrie or Amy, Knickerbocker, cloth, 9", MIB, ea **$10.00**

Doll, Holly Hobbie Talker, cloth, 4 sayings, 16", MIB ..**$25.00**

Doll, Little Girl Holly, Knickerbocker, cloth, 1980, 15", MIB...**$20.00**

Doll, Robby, Knickerbocker, cloth, 16", MIB...............**$20.00**

Doll, Robby, Knickerbocker, cloth, 9", MIB.................**$15.00**

Dollhouse, M...**$200.00**

Sewing Machine, Durham, 1975, plastic & metal, battery-op, 5x9", EX...**$25.00**

Sing-A-Long Electric Parlor Player, Vanity Fair, 1970s, complete w/booklet, scarce, NMIB **$45.00**

Doll, Holly Hobbie, all vinyl with painted eyes, marked KTC 1975/Made in Taiwan on head and back, Knickerbocker, 11", from $12.00 to $15.00. (Photo courtesy Patsy Moyer)

Ideal Dolls

The Ideal Toy Company made many popular dolls such as Shirley Temple, Betsy Wetsy, Miss Revlon, Toni, and Patti Playpal. Ideal's doll production was so enormous that since 1907 over 700 different dolls have been 'brought to life,' made from materials such as composition, latex rubber, hard plastic, and vinyl.

Since Ideal dolls were mass produced, most are still accessible and affordable. Collectors often find these dolls at garage sales and flea markets. However, some Ideal dolls are highly desirable and command high prices — into the thousands of dollars. These sought-after dolls include the Samantha doll, variations of the Shirley Temple doll, certain dolls in the Patti Playpal family, and some Captain Action dolls.

The listing given here is only a sampling of Ideal dolls made from 1907 to 1989. This listing reports current, realistic selling prices at doll shows and through mail order. Please remember these values are for dolls in excellent condition with original clothing.

For more information please refer to *Collector's Guide to Ideal Dolls, Second Edition,* by Judith Izen, published by Collector Books.

See also Advertising Characters; Shirley Temple; and Dolls' subcategories: Betsy McCall, Celebrity Dolls, and Tammy.

Club: Ideal Collectors Club
Judith Izen
P.O. Box 623, Lexington, MA 02173
Subscription: $20 per year for 4 issues; includes free wanted/for sale ads in each issue

Baby Coos, hard plastic head, magic skin body, sleep eyes, 1948-53, 14", EX..**$15.00**

Baby Crissy, vinyl, foam-filled limbs, auburn grow hair, all original, 1973-76, 24", M **$150.00**

Bizzie Lizzie, vinyl, jointed body, blond hair, w/power pack & accessories, 1971-72, 18", M..............................**$60.00**

Bonnie Braids, vinyl head, magic skin 1-pc body, painted hair & eyes, coos when squeezed, 1951-53, 11½", EX..**$35.00**

Chelsea (Jet Set), vinyl, posable, rooted straight hair, mod clothes & shoes, 1967, 24", M..................................**$50.00**

Deanna Durbin, jointed composition, brown human hair wig, sleep eyes, felt tongue, all original, 1938-41, 15", EX...**$125.00**

Kissy Baby, all vinyl, bent legs, all original, 1963-64, 22", EX..**$55.00**

Patti Playpal, marked Ideal Doll/G-35 on head, hard-to-find orange-red rooted saran hair, walker, original clothes, ca 1960 – 1961, 35", M, $500.00. (Photo courtesy Cornelia Ford/Patsy Moyer)

Patti Playpal, vinyl, jointed wrists, sleep eyes, curly or straight hair, original clothes, 1959-62, 35", M.................**$350.00**

Saucy Walker, hard plastic, walker, flirty eyes, teeth, crier, saran wig, plastic curlers, all original, 1951-55, 16", M......**$225.00**

Snoozie, vinyl & cloth reissue of 1933 doll, Swiss music box, all original, 1949, 11", M...**$75.00**

Sparkle Plenty, plastic head, magic skin body, yarn hair, 1947-50, 14", VG **$50.00**

Suzy Play Pal, vinyl, jointed body, rooted curly blond saran hair, sleep eyes, original dotted dress, 1959, 28", M........**$325.00**

Tara, Black, vinyl, long black hair that grows, sleep eyes, all original, 1976, 15½", M **$170.00**

Tickletoes, compo, rubber & cloth, squeaker, flirty sleep eyes, organdy dress, 1928-39, 17", EX..................$75.00

Tiffany Taylor, vinyl w/rooted hair, teenage body, all original, 1974-76, 19", M.................................$75.00

Jem

The glamorous life of Jem mesmerized little girls who watched her Saturday morning cartoons, and she was a natural as a fashion doll. Hasbro saw the potential in 1985 when they introduced the Jem line of 12" dolls representing her, the rock stars from Jem's musical group, the Holograms, and other members of the cast, including the only boy, Rio, Jem's road manager and Jerrica's boyfriend. Each doll was poseable, jointed at the waist, head, and wrists, so that they could be positioned at will with their musical instruments and other accessory items. Their clothing, their makeup, and their hairdos were wonderfully exotic, and their faces were beautifully modeled. The Jem line was discontinued in 1987 after being on the market for only two years.

Doll, Roxy, complete, M, $50.00; NRFB, $65.00.
(Photo courtesy Lee Garmon)

Accessory, Glitter 'n Gold Roadster, M.....................$150.00

Accessory, Jem/Jerrica, star earrings, MIB..................$35.00

Accessory, KJEM guitar, M...$25.00

Accessory, New Wave waterbed, M............................$35.00

Clothes, Award Night, On Stage Fashions, MIP (sealed)..$30.00

Clothes, City Lights, Flip Side Fashions, MOC............$20.00

Clothes, Let the Music Play, Smashin' Fashions, MOC..$35.00

Clothes, Music Is Magic, MIP (sealed).........................$30.00

Clothes, Rappin' Rio Fashion, photo card, MOC........$45.00

Clothes, Set Your Sails, 2nd year, photo on card, MOC..$35.00

Clothes, Twilight in Paris, On Stage Fashions, MIP (sealed)...$25.00

Doll, Aja, Hologram, 2nd issue, M.............................$90.00

Doll, Ashley, Starlight Girl, no wrist or elbow joints, 11", M..$40.00

Doll, Danse, Hologram, M...$45.00

Doll, Flash 'n Sizzle Jem, M...$30.00

Doll, Glitter 'n Gold Rio, NRFB..................................$35.00

Doll, Jem/Jerrica, 1st issue, M....................................$30.00

Doll, Kimber, Hologram, 1st issue, M.........................$40.00

Doll, Krissie, Starlight Girl, no wrist or elbow joints, 11"...$65.00

Doll, Pizzazz, Misfits, 1st issue, NRFB........................$65.00

Doll, Pizzazz, Misfits, 2nd issue, M............................$55.00

Doll, Rock 'n Curl Jem, NRFB.....................................$30.00

Doll, Shana, Hologram, 1st issue, NRFB...................$175.00

Doll, Stormer, Misfits, 2nd issue, M...........................$60.00

Doll, Synergy, Hologram, M..$45.00

Liddle Kiddles

These tiny little dolls ranging from ¾" to 4" tall were made by Mattel from 1966 until 1979. They all had poseable bodies and rooted hair that could be restyled, and they came with accessories of many types. Some represented storybook characters, some were flowers in perfume bottles, some were made to be worn as jewelry, and there were even spacemen Kiddles.

Serious collectors prefer examples that are still in their original packaging and will often pay a minimum of 30% (to as much as 100%) over the price of a doll in excellent condition with all her original accessories. A doll whose accessories are missing is worth from 65% to 70% less.

Advisor: Dawn Diaz (See Directory, Dolls)

Club: Liddle Kiddle Klub
Laura Miller
3639 Fourth Ave., La Crescenta, CA 91214

Animiddles, NM, $40.00 each. (Photo courtesy Cindy Sabulis)

Aqua Funny Bunny, #3532, complete, EX..................$35.00

Baby Din-Din, #3820, complete, M............................$75.00

Beat-A-Diddle, #3510, MIP.......................................$500.00

Cinderiddle's Palace, 35068, plastic window version, M..$50.00

Florence Niddle, #3707, complete, M.........................$75.00

Flower Ring Kiddle, #3744, MIP..................................$50.00

Heart Charm Bracelet Kiddle, #3747, MIP..................$50.00

Howard Biff Biddle, #3502, NRFB.............................$300.00

Kiddle & Kars Antique Fair Set, 3#806, NRFB..........$300.00

Lady Crimson, #A3840, 1970 – 1971, MIB, $100.00.
(Photo courtesy Tamela Storm and Debra Van Dyke)

Lenore Limousine, #3743, complete, M........................$60.00
Liddle Kiddle Kottage, #3534, EX................................$25.00
Liddle Kiddles Talking Townhouse, #5154, MIB.........$50.00
Liddle Red Riding Hiddle, #3546, complete, M.........$150.00
Lola Rocket, #3536, MIP..$75.00
Lorelei Locket, #3717, MIP..$75.00
Lou Locket, #3757, MIP..$75.00
Lucky Lion, #3635, complete, M....................................$50.00
Luvvy Duvvy Kiddle, #3596, MIP $75.00
Nurse 'N Totsy Outfit, #LK7, MIP $25.00
Pink Funny Bunny, #3532, MIP.....................................$100.00
Rapunzel & the Prince, #3783, MIP..............................$200.00
Rosemary Roadster, 33642, complete, M.....................$60.00
Sleep 'N Totsy Outfit, #LK5, MIP $25.00

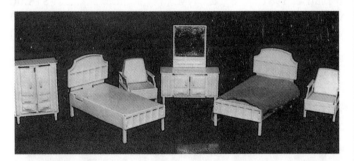

Snap-Happy Bedroom set, #5172, 1969, M, $15.00. (Photo courtesy Tamela Storm and Debra Van Dyke)

Snap-Happy Furniture, #5171, MIP $30.00
Surfy Skediddle, #3517, complete, M $75.00
Tessie Tractor, ##671, complete, NM...........................$150.00
Vanilla Lilly, #2819, MIP $25.00
Windy Fliddle, #3514, complete, M..............................$85.00

Littlechap Family

In 1964 Remco Industries created a family of four fashion dolls that represented an upper-middle class American family. The Littlechaps family consisted of the father, Dr. John Littlechap, his wife, Lisa, and their two children, teenage daughter Judy and pre-teen Libby. Interest in these dolls is on the rise as more and more collectors discover the exceptional quality of these fashion dolls and their clothing.

Advisor: Cindy Sabulis (See Directory, Dolls)

Carrying case, EX..$40.00
Doll, Dr John, MIB $60.00
Doll, Judy, EX, from $15 to $20.00
Doll, Judy, MIB $65.00
Doll, Libby, EX from $15 to...$20.00
Doll, Libby, MIB...$45.00
Doll, Lisa, MIB $60.00
Dolls, Dr John or Lisa, all original, EX, ea $30.00
Family room, bedroom or Dr John's office, EX, ea ..$125.00
Outfit, Dr John, NRFB, from $30 to............................$50.00
Outfit, Judy, complete, EX, from $25 to $40.00
Outfit, Judy, NRFB, from $35 to $75.00

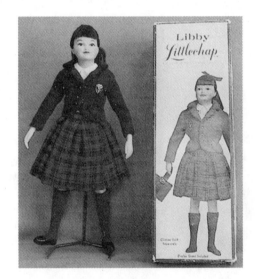

Libby doll, in original terry cloth cover-up, EX, $35.00; Three-Piece Blazer outfit, $35.00. (Photo courtesy Cindy Sabulis)

Outfit, Libby, NRFB, from $35 to................................$50.00
Outfit, Lisa, NRFB, from $35 to $75.00

Nancy Ann Storybook Dolls

This company was in business as early as 1936, producing painted bisque dolls with mohair wigs and painted eyes. Later they made hard plastic 8" Muffie and Miss Nancy Ann Style Show dolls. Debby (11") and Lori Ann (7½") had vinyl heads and hard plastic bodies. In the 1950s and 1960s, they produced a 10½" Miss Nancy Ann and Little Miss Nancy Ann, both vinyl high-heeled fashion-type dolls.

Around the World Series, English Flower Girl, all bisque, EX...$150.00

Audrey Ann, toddler, marked Nancy Ann Storybook 12, 6",
EX...**$250.00**
Baby, bisque body, plastic arms & legs, painted eyes, 1947-
49, 3½-4½", EX **$45.00**
Baby, hard plastic, black sleep eyes, ca 1949, 3½-4½",
EX...**$40.00**
Baby, hard plastic, black sleep eyes, christening dress only,
ca 1953, 3½-4½", EX, ea **$40.00**
Baby, molded socks, bisque star-shaped hands, 1940, 3½-
4½", EX, ea..**$60.00**
Baby, 1-pc head, body & legs, fist hands, 1943-47, 3½-4½",
ea **$60.00**
Baby Sue Sue, vinyl, nude, 1960s **$35.00**
Big & Little Sister Series, hard plastic, EX, ea.............**$30.00**
Child, hard plastic, black sleep eyes, 1949, 5", EX **$15.00**
Child, molded socks, molded bangs, 1939, 3½-4½", EX,
ea...**$75.00**
Child, molded socks & bangs, 1939, 5", EX **$125.00**
Child, molded socks only, 1940, 5", EX......................**$50.00**
Child, pudgy or slim tummy, 1941-42, 5", EX............**$20.00**
Child, 1-pc head, body & legs, 1943-47, 5", EX.........**$25.00**
Debbie, hard plastic, school dress, name on wrist tag, 10",
MIB **$400.00**

Debby, in cowgirl outfit with Miss America banner, 1955, $225.00. (Photo courtesy Maureen Fukushima/Patsy Moyer)

Little Miss Nancy Ann, day dress, 1959, 8½", MIB......**$50.00**
Little Miss Nancy Ann, nude, 1959, 8½" **$25.00**
Lori Ann, vinyl, 7½", EX...**$45.00**
Mammy & baby, marked Japan 1146 or America mold, 5",
EX **$150.00**
Masquerade Series, Ballet Dancer, all bisque, MIB...**$800.00**
Miss Nancy Ann, vinyl head, rooted hair, rigid vinyl body,
high-heeled feet, nude, 1959, 10½".................**$25.00**
Muffie, hard plastic, reissued in 1968+, MIB............**$105.00**
Muffie, vinyl head, molded or painted upper lashes, rooted wig,
walker or bend-knee walker, 1955-56, 8", EX **$60.00**
Nancy Ann Style Show, vinyl head, plastic body, all original,
complete, 18", M...**$500.00**
Operetta or Hit Parade Series, bisque or plastic, MIB, ea ..**$175.00**

Powder & Crinoline series, all bisque, EX, ea.............**$60.00**
Sports Series, EX...**$300.00**
Topsy, Black, jointed bisque w/plastic eyes, EX........**$50.00**

Raggedy Ann and Andy

Raggedy Ann dolls have been made since the early part of the twentieth century, and over the years many companies have produced their own versions. They were created originally by Johnny Gruelle, and though these early dolls are practically nonexistent, they're easily identified by the mark, 'Patented Sept. 7, 1915.' P.F. Volland made them from 1920 to 1934; theirs were very similar in appearance to the originals. The Mollye Doll Outfitters were the first to print the now-familiar red heart on her chest, and they added a black outline around her nose. These dolls carry the handwritten inscription 'Raggedy Ann and Andy Doll/Manufactured by Mollye Doll Outfitters.' Georgene Averill made them ca 1938 to 1950, sewing their label into the seam of the dolls. Knickerbocker dolls (1963 to 1982) also carry a company label. The Applause Toy Company made these dolls for two years in the early 1980s, and they were finally taken over by Hasbro, the current producer, in 1983.

Please note that our values are for dolls in excellent/near-mint condition. If your doll has been played with but is still in good condition with a few minor flaws (as most are), you'll need deduct about 75% from these prices. Refer to *The World of Raggedy Ann Collectibles* by Kim Avery (Collector Books).

Advisor: Kim Avery

Applause, 1981-83, 8", EX/NM.....................................**$15.00**
Applause, 1981-83, 17", EX/NM....................................**$50.00**
Applause, 1981-83, 48", EX/NM...................................**$175.00**

Applause, Raggedy Ann and Andy pair, 1986, 12", EX/NM, $28.00 to $32.00 each. (Photo courtesy Kim Avery)

Bobbs-Merrill, ventriolquist dummy, hard plastic head & hands, foam body, printed face, 1974, 30", EX/NM **$175.00**

Georgene Novelties, Ann or Andy, orange yarn hair, I Love You on chest, 1930s, 15", EX/NM, ea **$350.00**

Georgene Novelties, Ann or Andy, orange yarn hair, I Love You on chest, 1940s, 18", EX/NM, ea **$325.00**

Georgene Novelties, Ann or Andy, orange yarn hair, I Love You on chest, 1940s, 21", EX/NM, ea **$400.00**

Georgene Novelties, Ann or Andy, orange yarn hair, I Love You on chest, 1950s, 18", EX/NM, ea **$300.00**

Georgene Novelties, Ann or Andy, orange yarn hair, I Love You on chest, 1960-63, 18", EX/NM, ea **$150.00**

Georgene Novelties, Awake/Asleep Ann & Andy, 1940s, 12", EX/NM, pr **$650.00**

Georgene Novelties, Beloved Belindy, 1950s, 15", EX/NM.**$750.00**

Knickerbocker, Ann, printed features, yarn hair, sewn-in tag, 1970s, 15", EX/NM **$80.00**

Knickerbocker, Ann, printed features, yarn hair, sewn-in tag, 1970s, 24", EX/NM **$135.00**

Knickerbocker, Ann, printed features, yarn hair, sewn-in tag, 1970s, 30-36", EX/NM, ea.....................**$300.00**

Knickerbocker, Ann, printed features, yarn hair, sewn-in tag, 1980s, 16", EX/NM **$25.00**

Knickerbocker, Ann, printed features, yarn hair, sewn-in tag, 1980s, 24", EX/NM **$55.00**

Knickerbocker, Ann, printed features, yarn hair, sewn-in tag, 1980s, 30-36", EX/NM, ea....................**$110.00**

Knickerbocker, Ann, Talking, printed features, yarn hair, sewn-in tag, 1960s, EX/NM **$265.00**

Knickerbocker, Ann or Andy, printed features, yarn hair, sewn-in tag, 1960s, 15", EX/NM, ea **$300.00**

Knickerbocker, Ann or Andy, printed features, yarn hair, sewn-in tag, 1960s, 30-36", EX/NM, ea **$500.00**

Knickerbocker, Beloved Belindy, ca 1965, 15", MIB..**$1,600.00**

Nasco/Bobbs-Merrill, cloth head w/hard plastic body, printed features, apron marked Raggedy Ann, 1972, 24", EX/NM **$150.00**

Strawberry Shortcake and Friends

Strawberry Shortcake came on the market with a bang around 1980. The line included everything to attract small girls — swimsuits, bed linens, blankets, anklets, underclothing, coats, shoes, sleeping bags, dolls and accessories, games, and many other delightful items. Strawberry Shortcake and her friends were short lived, lasting only until the mid-1980s.

Online Clubs:
The Strawberryland Town Square
The Strawberry Swap Shop

Big Berry Trolley, 1982, EX...**$40.00**
Doll, Angel Cake, 6", MIB..**$25.00**
Doll, Apple Dumpling, 6", MIB **$25.00**
Doll, Apricot, 15", NM...**$35.00**
Doll, Baby Needs a Name, 15", NM............................**$35.00**
Doll, Berry Baby Orange Blossom, 6", MIB **$35.00**

Doll, Butter Cookie, 6", MIB.............................**$25.00**
Doll, Cafe Ole, 6", MIB **$35.00**
Doll, Cherry Cuddler, 6", MIB..........................**$35.00**
Doll, Lime Chiffon, 6", MIB.............................**$25.00**
Doll, Mint Tulip, 6", MIB.................................**$25.00**
Doll, Raspberry Tart, 6", MIB...........................**$25.00**
Doll, Strawberry Shortcake, 12", NRFB **$45.00**
Doll, Strawberry Shortcake, 15", NM.................**$35.00**
Dollhouse Furniture, attic, 6-pc, rare, M.............**$150.00**
Dollhouse Furniture, bathroom, 5-pc, rare, M.............**$65.00**
Dollhouse Furniture, bedroom, 7-pc, rare, M.............**$90.00**
Dollhouse Furniture, kitchen, 11-pc, rare, M **$100.00**
Dollhouse Furniture, living room, 6-pc, rare, M .:........**$85.00**
Figure, Almond Tea w/Marza Panda, PVC, 1", MOC..**$15.00**
Figure, Cherry Cuddler w/Gooseberry, Strawberryland Miniatures, MIP, from $15 to **$20.00**
Figure, Lemon Meringue w/Frappo, PVC, 1", MOC....**$15.00**
Figure, Lime Chiffon w/balloons, PVC, 1", MOC **$15.00**
Figure, Merry Berry Worm, MIB **$35.00**

Figure, Purple Pieman and Berry Bird, poseable, 1982, 8½", MIB, $35.00. (Photo courtesy Patsy Moyer)

Figure, Raspberry Tart w/bowl of cherries, MOC **$15.00**
Figure, Sour Grapes w/Dregs, Strawberryland Miniatures, MIP, from $15 to **$20.00**
Ice Skates, EX..**$35.00**
Motorized Bicycle, EX **$95.00**
Roller Skates, EX..**$35.00**
Sleeping Bag, EX **$25.00**
Storybook Play Case, M **$35.00**
Stroller Coleco, 1981, M **$85.00**
Telephone, Strawberry Shortcake figure, battery-operated, EX...**$85.00**

Tammy and Friends

In 1962 the Ideal Novelty and Toy Company introduced their teenage Tammy doll. Slightly pudgy and not quite as sophisticated-looking as some of the teen fashion dolls on the market at the time, Tammy's innocent charm captivated consumers. Her extensive wardrobe and numerous accessories added to her popularity with children. Tammy had a car, a house, and her own catamaran. In addition, a large number of companies obtained licenses to issue products using the 'Tammy' name. Everything from paper dolls to nurses' kits were made with Tammy's image on them. Her success was not confined to the United States; she was also successful in Canada and several European countries.

Advisor: Cindy Sabulis (See Directory, Dolls)

Doll, rare carrot top, MIB, $75.00. (Photo courtesy Cindy Sabulis)

Accessory Pak, #9179-3, w/plate of crackers, juice, glasses, sandals & newspaper, NRFP $20.00
Accessory Pak, #9183-80, w/camera, luggage case & airline ticket, NRFP...$15.00
Accessory Pak, #9188-80, w/tennis racket, score book, ball & sneakers, NRFP...$15.00
Accessory Pak, unknown #, w/frying pan, electric skillet & lids, NRFP, from $45 to...$50.00
Case, Dodi, green background, EX $30.00
Case, Misty, pink & white background, EX.................$25.00
Case, Misty & Tammy, hatbox style, EX $30.00
Case, Pepper, green or coral background, front snap closure, EX, ea...$15.00
Case, Pepper, yellow or green background, EX, ea ...$20.00
Case, Pepper & Dodi, blue background, front opening, EX..$30.00
Case, Pepper & Patti, Montgomery Ward's Exclusive, red background, EX $50.00
Case, Tammy Beau & Arrow, hatbox style, blue or red, EX, ea $40.00
Case, Tammy Evening in Paris, blue, black or red background, EX, ea $20.00

Case, Tammy Model Miss, double trunk, red or black, EX, ea $25.00
Case, Tammy Model Miss, hatbox style, blue or black, EX, ea $30.00
Case, Tammy Model Miss, red or black background, EX, ea...$25.00
Case, Tammy Traveler, red or green background, EX, ea..$45.00
Doll, Bud, MIB, minimum value $600.00
Doll, Dodi, MIB $75.00
Doll, Glamour Misty the Miss Clairol Doll, MIB........$150.00
Doll, Grown Up Tammy, MIB $85.00
Doll, Grown Up Tammy (Black), MIB, minimum value.$300.00
Doll, Misty, MIB...$100.00
Doll, Patti, MIB..$200.00
Doll, Pepper, carrot-colored hair, MIB $75.00
Doll, Pepper, MIB..$65.00
Doll, Pepper, trimmer body & smaller face, MIB........$75.00
Doll, Pepper (Canadian version), MIB $75.00
Doll, Pos'n Dodi, M in decorated box $150.00
Doll, Pos'n Dodi, M in plain box $75.00
Doll, Pos'n Misty & Her Telephone Booth, MIB.......$125.00
Doll, Pos'n Pepper, MIB..$75.00
Doll, Pos'n Pete, MIB...$125.00
Doll, Pos'n Salty, MIB...$125.00
Doll, Pos'n Tammy & Her Telephone Booth, MIB ...$100.00
Doll, Pos'n Ted, MIB...$100.00
Doll, Tammy, MIB $85.00
Doll, Tammy's Dad, MIB...$65.00
Doll, Tammy's Mom, MIB..$75.00
Doll, Ted, MIB...$50.00
Outfit, Dad & Ted, pajamas & slippers, #9456-5, MIB..$20.00
Outfit, Pepper & Dodi, Light & Lacy, #9305-4, MIP....$45.00
Outfit, Tammy, Career Girl, #9945-7, complete, M $75.00
Outfit, Tammy, Jet Set, #9155-3 or #9943-2, MIP, ea...$55.00
Outfit, Tammy, Pizza Party, #9115-7 or #9924-2, complete, M...$30.00
Outfit, Tammy's Mom, Evening in Paris, #9421-9, complete, M...$35.00
Pak clothing, #9221-3, w/skirt, shoes & hanger, NRFP.$20.00
Pak clothing, #9243-7, w/sheath dress, black belt, shoes & hanger, NRFP.......................................$30.00
Pepper's Jukebox, M $65.00
Pepper's Treehouse, MIB...$150.00
Tammy Dress-Up Kit, Colorforms, 1964, complete, MIB ..$30.00
Tammy Hair Dryer, sq or round case, NM $50.00
Tammy's Bed, Dress & Chair, MIB $85.00
Tammy's Car, MIB...$75.00
Tammy's Ideal House, EX..$100.00
Tammy's Jukebox, M...$50.00
Tammy's Magic Mirror Fashion Show, Winthrop-Atkins, NRFB...$50.00

Tressy

Tressy was American Character's answer to Barbie. This 11½" fashion doll was made from 1963 to 1967. Tressy had a unique feature — her hair 'grew' by pushing a button on her stomach. She and her little sister, Cricket, had numerous fashions and accessories.

Advisor: Cindy Sabulis (See Directory, Dolls)

Apartment, M	**$150.00**
Beauty Salon, M	**$125.00**
Case, Cricket, M	**$30.00**
Case, Pre-Teen Tressy, M	**$30.00**
Case, Tressy, M	**$30.00**

Cricket doll and accessory set, NRFB, $200.00.
(Photo courtesy Cindy Sabulis)

Doll, Tressy, loose in original dress	**$35.00**
Doll, Tressy in Miss America Character outfit, NM	**$65.00**
Doll, Tressy w/Magic Make-up Face, M	**$25.00**
Doll Clothes Pattern, M	**$10.00**
Gift Pack, w/doll & clothing, NRFB, minimum value	**$100.00**
Hair Accessory Pak, NRFB, ea	**$20.00**
Hair Dryer, M	**$40.00**
Hair or Cosmetic Accessory Kits, minimum value, ea	**$50.00**
Millinery, M	**$150.00**
Outfits, MOC, ea from $30 to	**$40.00**
Outfits, NRFB, minimum value, ea	**$65.00**

Uneeda Doll Co., Inc.

The Uneeda Doll Company was located in New York City and began making composition dolls about 1917. Later a transition was made to plastics and vinyl. Unless another condition is noted within the description, our values are for dolls that are mint in their original boxes.

Baby Dollikins, vinyl head, hard plastic jointed body, drinks & wets, 1960, 21", EX **$45.00**

Baby Dollikins, vinyl head, hard plastic jointed body, drinks & wets, 1960, 21", MIB **$200.00**
Baby Trix, vinyl head, hard plastic body, 1965, 19", EX..**$8.00**
Baby Trix, vinyl head, hard plastic body, 1965, 19", M.**$30.00**
Bareskin Baby, hard plastic & vinyl, 1968, 12½", EX ...**$5.00**
Bareskin Baby, hard plastic & vinyl, 1968, 12½", M.**$20.00**
Blabby, hard plastic & vinyl, 1962+, 14", EX **$7.00**
Coquette, Black, hard plastic & vinyl, 1963+, 16", M.**$36.00**
Coquette, hard plastic & vinyl, 1963+, 16", EX.............**$7.00**
Dollikin, hard plastic & vinyl, multi-jointed, marked Uneeda/2S, 1957+, 19", EX **$135.00**
Fairy Princess, hard plastic & vinyl, 1961, 32", MIB .**$110.00**
Freckles, vinyl head, hard plastic body, marked 22 on head, 1960, 32", EX **$25.00**
Jennifer, vinyl & plastic, rooted side-part hair, painted features, teen body, mod clothing, 18", EX **$7.00**
Magic Meg w/Hair that Grows, vinyl & plastic, rooted hair, sleep eyes, 16", M **$25.00**
Pir-thilla, vinyl, rooted hair, sleep eyes, blows balloons, 1958, 12½", M **$12.00**
Pollyanna, for Disney, 1960, 17", MIB **$200.00**
Pollyanna, for Disney, 1960, 31", EX...........................**$40.00**
Purty, vinyl & plastic, painted features, long rooted hair, 1973, 11", EX **$7.00**

Saranade rooted blond ponytail, blue sleep eyes, fully jointed vinyl and hard plastic, speaker in tummy, complete, MIB, $350.00.
(Photo courtesy Michael Stitt/Patsy Moyer)

Saranade, vinyl & hard plastic, rooted blond hair, blue sleep eyes, speaker in tummy, phonograph & record, 1962, 21", EX **$15.00**
Tiny Teen, vinyl, 6-pc hard plastic body, rooted hair, pierced ears, 1957-59, 10½", MIB **$135.00**

Vogue Dolls, Inc.

Vogue Dolls Incorporated is one of America's most popular manufacturers of dolls. In the early 1920s through the mid-1940s, Vogue imported lovely dolls of bisque and composition, dressing them in the fashionable designs hand sewn by Vogue's founder, Jennie Graves. In the late '40s through the early '50s, they became famous for their wonderful hard plastic dolls, most notably the 8" Ginny doll. This adorable toddler doll skyrocketed into nationwide attention in the early '50s as lines of fans stretched around the block during store promotions, and Ginny dolls sold out regularly. A Far-Away-Lands Ginny was added in the late '50s, sold well through the '70s, and is still popular with collectors today. In fact, a modern-day version of Ginny is currently being sold by the Vogue Doll Company, Inc.

Many wonderful dolls followed through the years, including unique hard-plastic, vinyl, and soft-body dolls. These dolls include teenage dolls Jill, Jan, and Jeff; Ginnette the 8" baby doll; Miss Ginny; and the famous vinyl and soft-bodied dolls by noted artist and designer E. Wilkin. It is not uncommon for these highly collectible dolls to turn up at garage sales and flea markets.

Over the years, Vogue developed the well-deserved reputation as 'The Fashion Leaders in Doll Society' based on their fine quality sewing and on the wide variety of outfits designed for their dolls to wear. These outfits included frilly dress-up doll clothes as well as action-oriented sports outfits. The company was among the first in the doll industry to develop the concept of marketing and selling separate outfits for their dolls, many of which were 'matching' for their special doll lines. The very early Vogue outfits are most sought after, and later outfits are highly collectible as well. It is wise for collectors to become aware of Vogue's unique styles, designs, and construction methods in order to spot these authentic Vogue prizes on collecting outings.

Values here are only a general guide. For further information we recommend *Collector's Guide to Vogue Dolls* by Judith Izen and Carol J. Stover (Collector Books).

Baby Dear, redesigned vinyl head & limbs, cloth body, crier, 1965, 12", MIB.........................**$75.00**
Baby Dear, vinyl head & limbs, cloth body, 1960-64, 18", M...**$225.00**
Baby Dear-One, redesigned vinyl head & limbs, cloth body, closed mouth, 1965, 1967-80, 25", M **$65.00**
Baby Dear-One/Bobby Dear-One, vinyl head & limbs, cloth body, painted lower teeth, sleep eyes, 1962-63, 25", M **$250.00**
Baby Hug, soft plastic & vinyl, sleep eyes, 1964-65, M..**$30.00**
Baby Wide Eyes, vinyl, sleep eyes, 1976-82, M **$65.00**
Brikette, vinyl, ball-jointed wrist, turn swivel waist, elongated neck swivels at base, 1959-61, 22", M...........**$200.00**
Crib Crowd, hard plastic, painted eyes & lashes, green dotted Swiss romper, w/plastic toy, 1951, 8", M, from $475 to over **$500.00**
Crib Crowd, Ruthie, hard plastic, painted eyes, yellow organdy gown, 1949, 8", M, from $475 to over .**$500.00**
Dream Baby, vinyl, sculpted hair, sleep eyes, 1961, 16", M **$60.00**
Ginnette, vinyl, jointed, open mouth, painted eyes, 1955-56, 8", M **$150.00**
Ginny, bent-knee walker, formal gown, 1957-59, 8", M, minimum value **$225.00**
Ginny, bent-knee walker, Sugar 'N Spice, 1960, 8", M..**$275.00**

Ginny, hard plastic, painted eyes, Cinderella, 1948-50, 8", M, minimum value...**$400.00**
Ginny, hard plastic, painted eyes, Holiday outfit, 1948-50, 8", M, minimum value.....................................**$400.00**
Ginny, straight-leg walker, molded lashes, Bon-Bons, 1955, 8", M, minimum value...**$400.00**
Ginny, straight-leg walker, Coronation Queen, 1954, 8", M, minimum value...**$750.00**
Ginny, straight-leg walker, molded lashes, formal dress, 1956, 8", M, from $350 to..**$400.00**
Ginny, straight-leg walker, painted lashes, My First Corsage, 1954, 8", M, from $350 to.....................................**$400.00**
Ginny, strung, sleep eyes, all original, 1950-53, 8", from $375 to..**$450.00**
Ginny, strung, sleep eyes, school or play outfit, 50-53, 8", M...**$110.00**
Ginny, strung, sleep eyes, Square Dance outfit, 1950-53, 8", M, minimum value..**$425.00**
Ginny, vinyl, non-walker, rooted hair, sleep eyes, Far-Away Lands outfit, 1965-72, 8", M.............................**$80.00**
Ginny, vinyl, non-walker, rooted hair, sleep eyes, molded lashes, USA, 1965-72, 8", M, minimum value **$100.00**
Ginny, vinyl, walker, rooted hair, blue sleep eyes, jointed neck, arms & legs, 1960, 36", M......................**$250.00**
Ginny, vinyl head, bent-knee walker, 1963-65, 8", M, minimum value **$150.00**
Ginny Baby, all vinyl, jointed arms & legs, sleep eyes, Saran or molded hair, drinks & wets, 1959-60, 18", M, from $30 to..**$45.00**
Ginny Baby, vinyl, platinum pixie hair, sleep eyes, 1964-65, 12", M, from $20 to...**$40.00**
Jan, vinyl, straight legs, sleep eyes, swivel waist, 1959-60, 10½", MIB...**$120.00**
Jeff, vinyl, blue sleep eyes, painted-on black hair, 1958-60, 11", MIB...**$150.00**

Jill, blond ponytail, all original, M, $200.00. (Photo courtesy Bonnie Groves)

Jill, hard plastic, bent-knee walker, sleep eyes, metal loops in ears for earrings, basic dress, 1957-60, 10½", M **$150.00**

Jill, hard plastic, bent-knee walker, sleep eyes, metal loops in ears for earrings, gown, 1957-58, 10½", M, from $150 to **$225.00**

Jill, hard plastic, bent-knee walker, sleep eyes, metal loops in ears for earrings, Theater Time, 1959, 10½", MIB..**$300.00**

Jill (All New), vinyl, rooted hair, sleep eyes, high-heel feet, 1962, M, from $150 to **$175.00**

Jimmy, vinyl, jointed, open mouth, painted eyes, loose, 8", M **$60.00**

Jimmy, vinyl, jointed, open mouth, painted eyes, 1958, 8", MIB, from $125 to **$150.00**

Li'l Imp, vinyl & hard plastic, bent-knee walker, sleep eyes, orange hair & freckles, 1959-60, 11", M............**$150.00**

Li'l Loveable Imp, vinyl, straight legs, sleep eyes, rooted hair, 1964-65, 11", M **$65.00**

Little Miss Ginny, all vinyl, 1-pc body & legs, 1965, 12", M, from $20 to..**$40.00**

Littlest Angel, all vinyl, 1969-80, 11", M **$25.00**

Littlest Angel, all vinyl, 1969-80, 15", MIB **$55.00**

Littlest Angel, vinyl & hard plastic, bent-knee walker, sleep eyes, 1961-63, 10½", M...**$65.00**

Miss Ginny, hard plastic, 1962-64, 16", M..................**$80.00**

Sunshine Baby, composition molded hair, blue dimity dress w/embroidery, 1943-47, 8", M **$400.00**

Sweetheart Jill, vinyl, rooted hair, sleep eyes, high-heeled feet, 1963, 10½", M, from $150 to **$175.00**

Toddles, Clown, composition, red & navy blue polka dot outfit, 1942, 8", M, from $250 to...........................**$300.00**

Toddles, composition, pink shorts set & shoes, 1943, 8", M, from $250 to...**$300.00**

Toddles, Uncle Sam, composition, right arm bent, wig, 1943, 7½", M, from $250 to **$300.00**

Too Dear, vinyl head & limbs, closed mouth, rooted hair, 1963-65, 17", M **$250.00**

Wee Imp, hard plastic, bent-knee walker, sleep eyes, orange Saran wig, 1960, 8", M, from $300 to.................**$400.00**

Door Knockers

Though many of the door knockers you'll see on the market today are of the painted cast-iron variety (similar in design to doorstop figures), they're also found in brass and other metals. Most are modeled as people, animals, and birds; and baskets of flowers are common. All items listed are cast iron unless noted otherwise. Prices shown are suggested for examples without damage and in excellent original paint.

Advisor: Craig Dinner (See Directory, Door Knockers)

Alsation Wolf Dog (German Shepherd), brass, 5x4", EX...**$60.00**

Bathing beauty w/finger at mouth, green 1920s swimsuit, unmarked 'Fish' pc, 5¼", beware of very good reproductions **$795.00**

Birdhouse, cream w/red roof, green & cream trees, cream backplate, signed Hubley #629, 3⅜x2⅝"............**$425.00**

Birds at birdhouse, cast iron, back plate embossed w/leaves & flowers, 3¾", EX, from $400 to **$425.00**

Buster Brown and Tige, cream shirt and pants, cream dog with black spots, #200, 4⅜x2", $635.00. (Photo courtesy Craig Dinner)

Bloodhound's head, brass, ca 1940, English, 3¼x2¼", EX...**$95.00**

Butterfly, black, green, yellow & pink, under pink rose, cream & purple backplate, 3½x2½"....................**$275.00**

Butterfly on sunflower, multicolor paint, 4x2½" **$525.00**

Cardinal on twigs, multicolor paint, rare, 5x3"..........**$285.00**

Castle, cream w/3 flags, blue sky, green trees, gold band, white oval backplate, 4x3"....................................**$285.00**

Cottage in woods, white cottage w/red roof, green trees in background, Judd #629, 3¼", EX, from $300 to.**$350.00**

Dog, brown, at entrance to cream doghouse, pink dish in front of dog, dark brown backplate, 4x3" **$785.00**

Dragon, tooled wrought iron, w/strike, 6½" **$115.00**

Flower basket, yellow ribbon, white basket, pink & blue flowers w/green leaves, yellow & white backplate, 4x2½"...**$95.00**

George Washington, multicolor paint, Waverly..., 4½x2¾" **$85.00**

Highlander w/bagpipes, brass, marked Made in Great Britain, 6"...**$85.00**

Ivy basket, light & dark green ivy in yellow basket, white backplate, 4½x2½" **$175.00**

Liberty bell, cast iron, ca 1920, 3¼", EX....................**$225.00**

Little girl knocking on door, blue dress, brown hat w/black ribbon, holds black doll in left hand, rare, 3¾x2¾".....**$725.00**

Mammy w/laundry basket over head, red & white dotted bandana, multicolored clothes, breast are knocker, rare, 7¼" **$1,750.00**

Morning Glory, green leaves back plate, Judd #608, 3¼", EX..**$285.00**

Nickolas House, famous Salem Mass home, painted green white, signed Sarah Symonds, 4x6", EX.............**$635.00**

Parrot, multicolored paint on cast iron, ca 1890, 4½x3", EX ..**$125.00**

Parrot faces right, on brown branch, multicolored feathers, green leaves, cream & green backplate, 4¾x2¾"..............**$125.00**

Parrot on branch, multicolor paint, Hubley, 4¾x2¾" ..**$125.00**

Poinsettia, red and green on white backing, Hubley, #627, 3½x2½", M, $525.00; Pear on floral and leaf backing, yellow-orange, green, and red details, 3¼x3", M, $310.00. (Photo courtesy Bertoia Auctions)

Red-headed Woodpecker, on tree trunk base, cast iron, EX..**$75.00**

Rooster, white variation, 4½x3"...............................**$275.00**

Roses, pink & cream w/green leaves, brown stems, cream oval backplate, signed Hubley #626, 3x4"..........**$445.00**

Spider, orange, black & yellow, on gray & black web, w/yellow, black & brown fly, 3½x1⅞"......................**$750.00**

The Fat Boy, English character in oval plaque, bronze, marked #11258, 3½x1¾", EX................................**$65.00**

Woman wearing bonnet, detailed profile, Judd #619, 4", EX **$425.00**

Woman's head wearing bonnet, Hubley #619, 4¼x3", EX **$385.00**

Zinnias, multicolor paint, marked Pat Pend LVL, rare, 3¾x2½" **$550.00**

Doorstops

There are three important factors to consider when buying doorstops — rarity, desirability, and condition. Desirability is often a more important issue than rarity, especially if the doorstop is well designed and detailed. Subject matter often overlaps into other areas, and if they appeal to collectors of Black Americana and advertising, for instance, this tends to drive prices upward. Most doorstops are made of painted cast iron, and value is directly related to the condition of the paint. If there is little paint left or if the figure has been repainted or is rusty, unless the price has been significantly reduced, pass it by.

Be aware that Hubley, one of the largest doorstop manufacturers, sold many of their molds to the John Wright Company who makes them today. Watch for seams that do not fit properly, grainy texture, and too-bright paint; and watch for reproductions!

The doorstops we've listed here are all of the painted cast-iron variety unless another type of material is mentioned

in the description. Values are suggested for original examples in near-mint condition and paint and should be sharply reduced if heavy wear is apparent. Recent auctions report even higher prices realized for examples in pristine condition. For further information, we recommend *Doorstops, Identification and Values,* by Jeanne Bertoia.

Club: Doorstop Collectors of America
Jeanie Bertoia
1881 Spring Rd.
Vineland, NJ 08361; 856-692-1881; Membership $20.00 per year, includes two *Doorstoppers* newsletters and convention. Send two-stamp SASE for sample.

Blowfish, full figure, no base, Hubley, 8x7¼", from $450 to **$575.00**

Buddha, 7x5¾", from $200 to....................................**$275.00**

Castle, atop mountain w/winding road, 8", from $350 to..**$425.00**

Cat, arched back, head down & tail up, rectangular base, Sculptured Metal Studios, 1928, from $275 to....**$350.00**

Cat Sleeping, full figure, National Foundry, 3½x9½", from $275 to..**$350.00**

Clown, seated on sq base, multicolored diamond suit w/white ruffled collar, cJo, 8", from $550 to......**$650.00**

Cockatoo on Branch, full figure, 14", from $200 to..**$275.00**

Cocker Spaniel, standing, Hubley, 6¾x11", from $275 to..**$350.00**

Colonial Lady, in hat & shawl holding flowers, #37, Hubley, 8", from $200 to...**$275.00**

Conestoga Wagon, #100, 8x11", from $100 to..........**$175.00**

Cottage with flowers and cut-out windows, painted cast iron, paint worn but good, 12" long, $200.00. (Photo courtesy Bertoia Auctions)

Deco Woman, standing w/hands clasped behind head, rectangular base, 17", from $475 to.........................**$550.00**

Dutch Boy, standing w/hands in pockets, sq base, 11", from $450 to..**$650.00**

Dutch Girl, hands clasped looking down, 6", from $150 to **$225.00**

Dutch Girl, standing w/hands on hips, lg shoes, 9¾", from $325 to..**$400.00**

El Capitan, 7¾", from $175 to **$250.00**

Elephant, trunk down, B&H, 10x11¾", from $250 to **$350.00**

Fantail Fish, #464, Hubley, 9¾x6", from $175 to **$250.00**

Fawn, stylized, standing on rock-shaped base, #6, Taylor Cook, 1930, 10x6", from $250 to.........................**$375.00**

French Girl, standing holding out skirt, #23, Hubley, 9¼", from #250 to...........................**$325.00**

Frog, stylized, 6½x4½", from $100 to.......................**$150.00**

Geisha, standing, no base, full figure, Hubley, 10¼", from $500 to.................................**$750.00**

Giraffe, side view, standing on base, wedge, #S-110, 13½x5¼", from $250 to............................**$300.00**

Girls Reading, seated back-to-back, 5x8½", from $750 to...**$1,000.00**

Graf Zeppelin, w/2 towers & hangar on beveled base, 8¼x13", from $550 to.............................**$650.00**

Horse & Rider Jumping Fence, #79, Eastern Specialty Co, 8x11¾", from $400 to.............................**$475.00**

Horse Performing, beveled base w/scrolled element, 10½x12¼", from $125 to....................................**$200.00**

House, single story, #1288, cJo, 8x4½", from $150 to .**$225.00**

Huckleberry Finn, walking w/stick & bucket in hand, grassy base, Littco Products, 12½", from $550 to.........**$650.00**

Hummingbird, wings at side, full figure, 4x7", from $250 to **$325.00**

Kittens (3) in a Basket, M Rosenstein Copyright 1932 Lancaster PA USA, 7x10", from $400 to..............**$475.00**

Lighthouse, full figure, hexagonal stepped base, 13½", from $150 to..**$225.00**

Maid of Honor, in lg hat w/floral bouquet holding up hem of skirt, flared base, 8¼", from $300 to..................**$375.00**

Man in Chair, English, 10x6", from $250 to..............**$325.00**

Old Woman, profile view, holding flower basket & closed parasol, oblong base, #7796, B&H, 11x7", from $600 to......**$1,000.00**

Organ Grinder, standing sideways, monkey at feet, 10", from $375 to...**$450.00**

Owl on Books, Eastern Specialty Mfg Co, 9¼", from $550 to...**$750.00**

Pansy Bowl, #265, Hubley, 7x6½", from $125 to **$175.00**

Peacock, frontal view w/fanned tail, 6¼x6¼", from $150 to...**$225.00**

Penguin, standing in top hat & tails, full figure, Hubley, 10½", from $350 to...**$475.00**

Petunias & Asters in Basket, #470, Hubley, 9½x6½", from $125 to...**$175.00**

Pirate w/Sword, standing w/legs apart, beveled base, 12", from $475 to..**$550.00**

Poppy Basket, stylized, #E110, CH Co, 10½x9½", from $325 to...**$450.00**

Puppies (3) in a Basket, Copyright 1932 M Rosenstein Lancaster PA USA, 7x7½", from $350 to.............**$475.00**

Rabbit, side view, sitting upright, B&H, 15½x8½", from $750 to...**$1,000.00**

Rhumba Dancer, Black tropical girl standing in layered ruffled skirt & head scarf tied on top of head, 11", from $600 to...**$850.00**

Rose Basket, looped handle, 12½x7", from $250 to.**$300.00**

Senorita, standing in long dress & shawl looking sideways w/hand on hip & holding flower basket, 11¼", from $350 to...**$500.00**

Squirrel w/Nut, side view, EMIG 1382, 8x5½", from $175 to **$250.00**

Swan, standing on oval base, full figure, National Foundry, 5¾x4½", from $200 to...**$275.00**

Tulips in Pot, lg ribbon bow, Hubley, 12¾x7", from $275 to...**$350.00**

Turkey, side view, walking, 13x11", from $750 to...**$1,000.00**

Turtle, full figure, 17x4¼", from $375 to **$450.00**

Violet Bowl, Hubley, 6¼x4¼", from $125 to **$175.00**

Wirehaired Terrier, sitting on base, #476, Hubley, 12¾", from $500 to..**$600.00**

Wolfhound, side view, seated, head up, Spencer/Guilford Conn, 6½", from $200 to...................................**$275.00**

Woman Skier, standing w/legs crossed & skis in crook of arm, hand in pocket, 12½", from $500 to **$750.00**

Woman w/Flower Baskets, standing in long dress, 8"..**$275.00**

Parrot, rare, cast iron with excellent paint, 11½", from $450.00 to $550.00; white cockatoo, rare, cast iron with excellent paint, 11", from $500.00 to $600.00; rooster, cast iron with strong vibrant paint in pristine conditon, from $425.00 to $500.00. (Photo courtesy Bertoia Auctions)

Parrot on Branch, #1010, Blodgett Studio, from $250 to..**$325.00**

Duncan and Miller Glassware

Although the roots of the company can be traced back as far as 1865 when George Duncan went into business in Pittsburgh, Pennsylvania, the majority of the glassware that collectors are interested in was produced during the twentieth century. The firm became known as Duncan and Miller in 1900. They were bought out by the United States Glass Company who continued to produce many of the same designs through a separate operation which they called the Duncan and Miller Division.

In addition to crystal, they made some of their wares in a wide assortment of colors including ruby, milk glass, some opalescent glass, and a black opaque glass they called Ebony. Some of their pieces were decorated by cutting or etching. They also made a line of animals and bird figures.

Advisor: Roselle Schleifman (See Directory, Elegant Glass)

Canterbury, ashtray, crystal, club shape, 3" $8.00

Canterbury, basket, crystal, oval, handled, 3½" $25.00

Canterbury, basket, crystal, oval, handled, 11½" $75.00

Canterbury, bowl, crystal, flared, 8x2½" $17.50

Canterbury, bowl, crystal, flared, 12x3½" $30.00

Canterbury, bowl, crystal, star shape, handle, 5½x1¾" ..$10.00

Canterbury, bowl, fruit nappy; crystal, 5" $8.00

Canterbury, candlestick, crystal, 3-light, 6" $30.00

Canterbury, candy dish, crystal, 3-part, 3-handled, w/lid, 8x3½" $35.00

Canterbury, cheese stand, crystal, 5½x3½" $10.00

Canterbury, decanter, crystal, w/stopper, 32-oz, 12" ...$65.00

Canterbury, ice bucket or vase, crystal, 6" or 7" $40.00

Canterbury, mayonnaise, crystal, 6x3¼" $17.50

Caribbean, bowl, blue, folded side, handled, 5x7" $37.50

Caribbean, bowl, flower; blue, oval, handled, 10¾" ..$80.00

Caribbean, bowl, vegetable; crystal, flared edge, 9¼" ..$30.00

Caribbean, creamer, blue $25.00

Caribbean, ice bucket, crystal, handled, 6½" $75.00

Lily of the Valley, plate, 9", $45.00. (Photo courtesy Gene Florence)

Caribbean, pitcher, ice lip; clear, 9", $225.00; blue, $650.00.

Caribbean, plate, cheese/cracker; crystal, handled, 3½"x11" dia $40.00

Caribbean, plate, dinner; crystal, 10½" $65.00

Caribbean, salt dip, blue, 2½" $25.00

Caribbean, stem, cordial; crystal, 1-oz, 3" $75.00

Caribbean, tray, blue, round, 12¾" $50.00

First Love, ashtray, crystal, #30, 5x3¼" $24.00

First Love, bowl, crystal, #30, 11x1¾" $55.00

First Love, bowl, rose; crystal, #115, 3x5" $40.00

First Love, cake plate, crystal, #115, 14" $50.00

First Love, cheese stand, crystal, #111, 3x5¼" $25.00

First Love, honey dish, crystal, #91, 5x3" $30.00

First Love, plate, crystal, #115, 6" $12.00

First Love, tray, celery; crystal, #91, 11" $40.00

First Love, urn, crystal, #529, 7" $37.50

First Love, vase, crystal, #507, 10" $95.00

Lily of the Valley, candy dish, crystal, w/lid $85.00

Lily of the Valley, sugar bowl, crystal $25.00

Nautical, ashtray, crystal, 6" $12.50

Nautical, cigarette holder, blue $35.00

Nautical, comport, opalescent, 7" $595.00

Nautical, salt & pepper shakers, crystal, pr $35.00

Sandwich, bowl, grapefruit; crystal, footed, w/fruit cup liner, 5½" $17.50

Sandwich, bowl, salad; crystal, shallow, 12" $40.00

Sandwich, cup, tea; crystal, 6-oz $10.00

Sandwich, plate, torte; crystal, 12" $45.00

Sandwich, stem, ice cream; crystal, 5-oz, 4¼" $12.50

Sandwich, vase, crystal, flat base, crimped, 4½" $25.00

Spiral Flutes, bowl, almond; amber, green or pink, 2" ..$13.00

Spiral Flutes, bowl, nappy; amber, green or pink, 7" .$15.00

Spiral Flutes, candle, amber, green or pink, 11½" $125.00

Spiral Flutes, ice tub, amber, green or pink, handled ...$60.00

Spiral Flutes, oil, amber, green or pink, w/stopper, 6-oz ..$195.00

Spiral Flutes, plate, pie; amber, green or pink, 6" $3.00

Spiral Flutes, platter, amber, green or pink, 13" $50.00

Spiral Flutes, stem, wine; amber, green or pink, 3½-oz, 3¾" $17.50

Spiral Flutes, vase, amber, green or pink, 6½" $20.00

Tear Drop, bowl, dessert nappy; crystal, 6" $6.00

Tear Drop, candlestick, crystal, 4" $9.00

Tear Drop, celery, crystal, 3-part, 12" $20.00

Tear Drop, creamer, crystal, 3-oz $5.00

Tear Drop, nut dish, crystal, 2-part, 6" $11.00

Tear Drop, plate, canape; crystal, 6" $10.00

Tear Drop, stem, champagne; crystal, 5-oz, 5" $10.00

Tear Drop, tumbler, crystal, flat, 9-oz, 4¼" $8.00

Terrace, ashtray, cobalt or red, sq, 4¾" $95.00

Terrace, bowl, crystal or amber, footed, flared rim, 10x3¾" $55.00

Terrace, candy urn, crystal or amber, w/lid $135.00

Terrace, plate, crystal or amber, 6" $12.00

Terrace, plate, sandwich; crystal or amber, handled, 11" ..$40.00

Terrace, stem, wine; crystal or amber, #5111½, 3-oz, 5¼" ..$32.50

Terrace, tumbler, cobalt or red $40.00
Terrace, vase, crystal or amber, footed, 10"..............$115.00

Early American Prescut

This was a line of inexpensive but good quality glassware made during the 1960s and 1970s by Anchor Hocking. It was marketed through dime-stores and houseware stores, and as is obvious judging from the plentiful supplies available at today's garage sale and flea markets, it sold very well. If you like it, now's the time to buy! For more information, refer to Gene Florence's book called *Collectible Glassware of the 40s, 50s, and 60s* (Collector Books).

Ashtray, #700/690, 4" $5.00
Bowl, round, #767, 7¼".........................$6.00
Bowl, salad; #788, 10¾"......................$12.00
Butter dish, w/lid, #705, ¼-lb $6.00
Cake plate, footed, #706, 13½"...................$30.00
Candy dish, w/lid, #744, 5¼".....................$10.00
Coaster, 700/702.................................$2.50
Creamer, #754....................................$3.00
Cruet, w/stopper, #711, 7¾" $6.00
Pitcher, #791, 60-oz.............................$17.00
Plate, deviled egg/relish; #750, 11¾" $35.00
Plate, snack; #780, 10"..........................$10.00
Punch set, 15-pc $35.00
Relish, divided, tab handle, #770, 10" $20.00
Relish, oval, 2-part, #778, 8½" $5.00
Shakers, metal tops, 700/699, pr.................$6.00
Sugar bowl, w/lid #753 ....$4.00

Tray, 12", $12.50; plate, 11", $12.00; syrup/server, 12-ounce, $20.00. (Photo courtesy Gene Florence)

Tumbler, #731, 10-oz, 4½" $4.00
Vase, #741, 8½"..................................$7.00

Easter Collectibles

The egg (a symbol of new life) and the bunny rabbit have long been part of Easter festivities; and since early in the twentieth century, Easter has been a full-blown commercial event. Postcards, candy containers, toys, and decorations have been made in infinite varieties. In the early 1900s many holiday items were made of papier-mache and composition and imported to this country from Germany. Rabbits were made of mohair, felt, and velveteen, often filled with straw, cotton, and cellulose.

Candy container, plastic, clown on wheels, hollow, Rosbro/Tico, 1950s, 6"...........................$50.00
Candy container, plastic, rabbit driving 3-wheeled cart w/basket on back, Rosbro, 7"...............$70.00
Candy container, yellow rabbit in red hat & shorts holding yellow basket w/red & blue crisscrosses, Rosbro, 1950s $40.00
Chick, dressed, cardboard w/spring neck, West Germany/US Zone, 1940-50........................$65.00

Decoration, fold-out tissue paper and cardboard, 9", $18.00.

Egg, molded cardboard, Germany, ca 1930s, from 3-7", from $65 to..................................$85.00
Egg, molded cardboard, West Germany/US Zone, 1940-60, from 3-8", from $25 to.......................$40.00

Plastic rabbits, 6", from $12.00 to $18.00 each.

Rabbit, celluloid, dressed, from 3-5", M......................**$65.00**

Rabbit, celluloid, pulling wagon, M **$125.00**

Rabbit, cotton batten w/paper ears, Japan, 1930-50, from 2-5"...**$30.00**

Rabbit, cotton batten w/paper ears, Japan, 1930-50, 6"..**$45.00**

Rabbit, dressed, cardboard w/spring neck, West Germany/US Zone, 1940-50...**$80.00**

Rabbit, pulp, begging, US, 1940-50, w/base...............**$55.00**

Rabbit, pulp, next to lg basket, US, 1930-50 ....**$75.00**

Rabbit, pulp, sitting w/basket on back, US, 1940-50 ..**$75.00**

Tin, Peter Rabbit Easter scenes, marked Tin Deco on bottom, 4½x2½x2", from $135 to......................................**$150.00**

Toy, Egg Wagon, rabbit pulling egg-shaped cart, Chein, 1930s, 4¼x8¼x4¼", EX..**$55.00**

Toy, Walking Duck Cart, Fisher-Price, #305, 1957-64, EX ..**$40.00**

Egg Cups

Egg cups were once commonplace kitchen articles that were often put to daily use. These small egg holders were commonly made in a variety of shapes from ceramics, glass, metals, minerals, treen, and plastic. They were used as early as ancient Rome and were very common on Victorian tables. Many were styled like whimsical animals or made in other shapes that would specifically appeal to children. Some were commemorative or sold as souvenirs. Still others were part of extensive china or silver services.

Recent trends in US dietary patterns have caused egg cups to follow butter pats and salt dishes into relative obscurity. Yet today in other parts of the world, especially Europe, many people still eat soft-boiled eggs as part of their daily ritual, so the larger china companies in those locations continue to produce egg cups.

Though many are inexpensive, some are very pricey. Sought-after categories (or cross-collectibles) include Art Deco, Art Pottery, Black Memorabilia, Chintz, Golliwogs, Majolica, Personalities, Pre-Victorian, Railroad, and Steamship. Single egg cups with pedestal bases are the most common, but shapes vary to include buckets, doubles, figurals, hoops, and sets of many types.

Pocillovists, as egg cup collectors are known, are increasing in numbers every day. For more extensive listings we recommend *Egg Cups: An Illustrated History and Price Guide*, by Brenda C. Blake (Antique Publications); and *Schroeder's Antiques Price Guide* (Collector Books).

Advisor: Brenda C. Blake (See Directory, Egg Cups)

Newsletter: *Egg Cup Collector's Corner*
Dr. Joan George, Editor
67 Stevens Ave., Old Bridge, NJ 08857; Subscription $20 per year for 4 issues; sample copies available at $5 each

Bunnies (3) encircle cup, ea dressed w/suit, bow tie & umbrella, applied flowers, 2¾"............................**$20.00**

Chef, red nose, black mustache, white hat forms top of cup, ceramic, unmarked **$22.00**

Ducks (3 along rim), white ceramic w/applied flowers & painted details, unmarked, 2¼"............................**$22.00**

Egg cup couples, heads/hats are salt and pepper shakers, from $30.00 to $35.00 each. (Photo courtesy Helene Guarnaccia)

Floral, blue on white porcelain, attributed to Japan, 2⅜" ..**$15.00**

Floral, multicolored spray on white swirl mold, Marlow, Minton, double, 3½"...**$45.00**

Floral, Old Country Rose, Royal Albert, bone china...**$18.00**

Floral, peonies & sm yellow flowers w/green leaves on white, Wm Guerin & Co, Limoges, 4 for............**$125.00**

Floral, Petite Fleur, floral sprig on white, Villeroy & Boch, pr..**$30.00**

Geisha Girl pattern, crudely made, Made in Japan ink stamp, 2⅜" **$12.00**

Man & shoulder head & shoulders, tops are shakers, wooden w/hand-painted features, stamped Japan, 1950s, 2⅝", pr..**$35.00**

Mr Jinx (cat) & bluebird on white w/red trim, Ridgway Potteries, Trade Mark in GB Screen Gems Inc, 1¾"................**$55.00**

Peter Rabbit depicted on green watering can shape, 2¾"...**$18.00**

Pig mother nursing sm pigs, scene w/fence & bird on white, Staffordshire England...**$32.00**

Polka dots, contrasting dots on pastel, 1960s, 2½", set of 4 ea in a different color...**$35.00**

Popeye & Olive Oyl on gold lustre, Japan mark, 1930s, 3⅜"..**$125.00**

Popeye figural, multicolor porcelain, Japan mark, 1930s.**$175.00**

Rabbit, pink bisque w/white embossed flowers, applied rabbit & multicolor flowers at foot, unmarked, 2¾"....**$18.00**

Running legs in brown shoes, Carlton England, 1980 ..**$50.00**

Tonto embossed & painted on white, Keele St Pottery Co...Lone Ranger Inc 1961, 2½" **$95.00**

Union Pacific Winged Streamliner, brown on white w/gold band at top, Scammell's Trenton China **$5.00**

Walking feet in blue shoes, Carlton, 1973, 2¼" **$38.00**

1920s man painted on white, attached saucer **$20.00**

Egg Timers

Egg timers are comprised of a little glass tube (pinched in the center and filled with sand) attached to a figural base, usually between 3" and 5" in height. They're all the rage today among collectors. Most figural egg timers reached their heyday in the 1940s. However, Germany produced many beautiful and detailed timers much earlier. Japan followed suit by copying many German designs. Today, one may find timers from the United Kingdom as well as many foreign ports. The variety of subjects represented by these timers is endless. Included are scores of objects, animals, characters from fiction, and people in occupational or recreational activities. Timers have been made in many materials including bisque, china, ceramic, chalkware, cast iron, tin, brass, wood, and plastic.

Although they were originated to time a three-minute egg, some were also used to limit the duration spent on telephone calls as a cost-saving measure. Frequently a timer is designed to look like a telephone, or a phone is depicted on it.

Since the glass tubes were made of thin, fine glass, they were easily broken. You may recognize a timer masquerading as a figurine by the empty hole that once held the tube. Do not pass up a good timer just because the glass is missing. These can be easily replaced by purchasing a cheap egg timer with a glass tube at your local grocery story.

Listings are for ceramic timers in excellent to mint condition with their glass tubes attached.

Advisor: Ellen Bercovici (See Directory, Egg Timers)

Bear, timer inserted to look like milk bottle, American Bisque...**$95.00**
Bear dressed as chef w/towel over arm, Japan, 4".....**$50.00**
Bellhop, green, Japan, 4½"...**$40.00**
Bellhop on phone, Japan, 3".......................................**$40.00**
Black chef sitting w/right hand raised holding timer, many sizes & shadings, German.....................................**$95.00**
Black chef standing w/frying pan, chalkware, Japan .**$95.00**
Black chef standing w/lg fish, timer in fish's mouth, Japan, 4¾"...**$125.00**
Bobby policeman, black outfit, German......................**$95.00**
Bobby policeman, blue outfit, Japan, from $95 to ...**$125.00**
Boy skiing, German, 3" **$50.00**
Boy stands on head (plastic) which fills w/sand, Cooley Lilly sticker, 3¾"...**$40.00**
Boy w/black cap stands & holds black bird, unmarked, 3½"...**$50.00**
Boy w/black cloak & cane, German, 3¾" **$50.00**
Boy w/red cap stands & holds different glass tubes in both hands, wooden, unmarked, 4½"..........................**$35.00**
Bunny rabbit, floppy ears, timer in mouth, Japan, from $75 to...**$95.00**
Cat, timer sits in his back, wooden.............................**$30.00**
Cat holding plate w/hole to hold timer which removes to change, Japan, 3¾"...**$50.00**
Cat standing by base of grandfather clock, German, 4¾"..**$65.00**
Cat w/ribbon at neck, German.....................................**$65.00**
Chef, combination music box, wooden, lg **$175.00**
Chef, winking, white clothes, timer in back, turn upside down to tip sand, 4", from $30 to **$50.00**

Chef holding large orange egg, 3¼", from $50.00 to $65.00.

Chef & lady baker, incised crown mark, ca 1935-49, from $85 to...**$100.00**
Chef in white on blue base holding spoon, German, 4" ..**$50.00**
Chef in yellow pants, white jacket, blue trim, holds platter of food, Japan, 3½" **$50.00**
Chef standing in blue w/white apron, towel over right arm, timer in jug under left, Japan, 4½".......................**$40.00**
Chicken, wings hold tube, German, 2¾", from $50 to ..**$65.00**
Chicken on nest, green plastic, England, 2½"............**$25.00**
Clown on phone, standing, yellow suit, Japan, 3¾"...**$65.00**
Clown sitting w/legs to side, timer in right hand, German, 3¼", from $85 to...**$95.00**
Colonial lady w/bonnet, variety of dresses & colors, German, 3¾"...**$50.00**
Colonial man in knickers, ruffled shirt, waistcoat hides hat, Japan, 4¾"...**$65.00**
Dutch boy kneeling, Japan, 2½" from $30 to.............**$40.00**
Dutch boy standing, German, 3½"..............................**$50.00**
Dutch girl on phone, standing, blue & white, Japan, 3¾" ...**$50.00**
Dutch girl w/flowers, walking, chalkware, unmarked, 4½".**$65.00**
Fisherman, fish wrapped around neck, timer in fish's mouth, German...**$95.00**
Geisha, German, 4½" **$85.00**
Goebel, double, chefs, man & woman, German, 4"...**$85.00**
Goebel, double, Mrs Pickwick, green, German, 4"...**$195.00**
Goebel, double, rabbits, various color combinations, German, 4½", from $50 to **$100.00**
Goebel, double, roosters, various color combinations, German, 4" **$100.00**
Goebel, lg owl w/holder on side, from $65 to **$95.00**
Goebel, little girl w/chick on tip of her shoe, from $95 to...**$125.00**
Goebel, single, chimney sweep, German, 4¼", from $50 to.**$70.00**
Goebel, single, Friar Tuck, German, 4".....................**$50.00**
Golliwog, bisque, English, 4½" **$200.00**
Kitchen maid w/measuring spoons, DAVAR, from $100 to.**$125.00**
Kitten w/ball of yarn, chalkware...............................**$50.00**

Leprechaun, shamrock on base, brass, Ireland, 3¼", from $25 to **$35.00**

Lighthouse, blue, cream & orange lustre, German, 4½" ..**$85.00**

Mammy, tin, lithographed picture of her cooking, pot holder hooks, unmarked, 7¾", from $150 to **$195.00**

Mexican boy playing guitar, German, 3½" **$50.00**

Mouse, brown 'Chef' on white apron, Josef Originals **$35.00**

Mouse, yellow & green, chalkware, Josef Originals, Japan, 1970s, 3¼" **$25.00**

Mrs Santa Claus, timer sits in bag next to her.............**$75.00**

Newspaper boy, Japan, 3¾" **$50.00**

Parlor maid w/cat, Japan, 4" **$50.00**

Penguin, chalkware, England, 3¾", from $25 to.........**$40.00**

Pixie, Enesco, Japan, 5½"...**$25.00**

Rabbit holding carrot, timer in basket, Japan..............**$50.00**

Sailboat, lustreware, German **$75.00**

Sailor, blue, German, 4" **$50.00**

Sailor w/sailboat, German, 4" **$50.00**

Santa Claus & present, Sonsco/Japan, 5½"..................**$75.00**

Scotsman w/bagpipes, plastic, England, 4½" **$35.00**

Sea gull, ceramic with lustre finish, German, $75.00. (Photo courtesy Ellen Bercovici)

Sultan, Japan, 3½"...**$50.00**

Telephone, black glaze on clay, Japan, 2"...................**$35.00**

Telephone, candlestick type on base w/cup for timer, wooden, Cornwall Wood Prod, So Paris ME.................**$25.00**

Veggie man or woman, bisque, Japan, 4½", ea **$95.00**

Welsh woman, German, 4½" **$50.00**

Windmill w/dog on base, Japan, 3¾" **$85.00**

Elvis Presley Memorabilia

Since he burst upon the '50s scene wailing 'Heartbreak Hotel,' Elvis has been the undisputed 'king of rock 'n roll.' The fans that stood outside his dressing room for hours on end, screamed themselves hoarse as he sang, or simply danced until they dropped to his music are grown-up collectors today. Many of their children remember his comeback performances, and I'd venture to say that even their grandchildren know Elvis on a first-name basis.

There has never been a promotion in the realm of entertainment to equal the manufacture and sale of Elvis merchandise. By the latter part of 1956, there were already hundreds of items that appeared in every department store, drugstore, specialty shop, and music store in the country. There were bubble gum cards, pin-back buttons, handkerchiefs, dolls, guitars, billfolds, photograph albums, and scores of other items. You could even buy sideburns from a coin-operated machine. Look for the mark 'Elvis Presley Enterprises' (along with a 1956 or 1957 copyright date); you'll know you've found a gold mine. Items that carry the 'Boxcar' mark are from 1974 to 1977, when Elvis's legendary manager, Colonel Tom Parker, promoted another line of merchandise to augment their incomes during the declining years. Upon his death in 1977 and until 1981, the trademark became 'Boxcar Enterprises, Inc., Lic. by Factors ETC. Bear, DE.' The 'Elvis Presley Enterprises, Inc.' trademark reverted back to Graceland in 1982, which re-opened to the public in 1983.

Due to the very nature of his career, paper items are usually a large part of any 'Elvis' collection. He appeared on the cover of countless magazines. These along with ticket stubs, movie posters, lobby cards, and photographs of all types are sought after today, especially those from before the mid-'60s.

Though you sometimes see Elvis 45s with $10.00 to $15.00 price tags, unless the record is in near mint to mint condition, this is just not realistic, since they sold in such volume. In fact, the picture sleeve itself (if it's in good condition) will be worth more than the record. The exceptions are, of course, the early Sun label records (he cut five in all) that collectors often pay in excess of $500.00 for. In fact, a near-mint copy of 'That's All Right' (his very first Sun recording) realized $2,800.00 at an auction held a couple of years ago! And some of the colored vinyls, promotional records, and EPs and LPs with covers and jackets in excellent condition are certainly worth researching further. For instance, though his *Moody Blue* album with the blue vinyl record can often be had for under $25.00 (depending on condition), if you find one of the rare ones with the black record you can figure on about ten times that amount! For a thorough listing of his records as well as the sleeves, refer to *Official Price Guide to Elvis Presley Records and Memorabilia* by Jerry Osborne.

For more general information and an emphasis on the early items, refer to *Elvis Collectibles* and *Best of Elvis Collectibles* by Rosalind Cranor, P.O. Box 859, Blacksburg, VA 24063 ($19.95+$1.75 postage each volume). Also available: *Elvis Presley Memorabilia* by Sean O'Neal (Schiffer).

Special thanks to Art and Judy Turner, Homestead Collectibles (see Directory, Decanters) for providing information on decanters. See also Magazines; Movie Posters; Pin-back Buttons; Records.

Advisor: Lee Garmon (See Directory, Elvis Presley Memorabilia)

Ashtray, black & white photo of Elvis w/hands clasped, white border w/gold rim, EPE, 1956, NM $350.00

Belt, white w/image in pink circle & 1 playing guitar, song titles in green, Elvis Presley in pink, EPE, 1956, NM **$315.00**

Book, autograph; The Partnership Behind the Legend, by & signed by Colonel Tom Parker, 32 pages, photos & info, EX...**$80.00**

Calendar, RCA, heavy stock, 1963, NM **$55.00**

Cigarette lighters, 25th Anniversary of Elvis' Death, Zippo, set of 4, MIB **$75.00**

Cookie jar, 1968 Comeback, Vandor, MIB **$75.00**

Decanter, McCormick, 1978, Elvis '77, plays Love Me Tender, 750 ml **$125.00**

Decanter, McCormick, 1978, Elvis Bust, no music box, 750 ml **$75.00**

Decanter, McCormick, 1979, Elvis '55, plays Loving You, 750 ml **$125.00**

Decanter, McCormick, 1979, Elvis '77 Mini, plays Love Me Tender, 50 ml **$55.00**

Decanter, McCormick, 1979, Elvis Gold, plays My Way, 750 ml, $175.00. (Photo courtesy Lee Garmon)

Decanter, McCormick, 1980, Elvis '55 Mini, plays Loving You, 50 ml **$65.00**

Decanter, McCormick, 1980, Elvis '68, plays Can't Help Falling in Love, 750 ml **$125.00**

Decanter, McCormick, 1980, Elvis Silver, plays How Great Thou Art, 750 ml **$175.00**

Decanter, McCormick, 1981, Aloha Elvis, plays Blue Hawaii, 750 ml **$150.00**

Decanter, McCormick, 1981, Elvis Designer I White (Joy), plays Are You Lonesome Tonight, 750 ml **$150.00**

Decanter, McCormick, 1981, Elvis '68 Mini, plays Can't Help Falling in Love, 50 ml **$55.00**

Decanter, McCormick, 1982, Aloha Elvis Mini, plays Blue Hawaii, 50 ml **$175.00**

Decanter, McCormick, 1982, Elvis Designer II White (Love), plays It's Now or Never, 750 ml **$125.00**

Decaner, McCormick, 1982, Elvis Karate, plays Don't Be Cruel, 750 ml...**$350.00**

Decanter, McCormick, 1983, Elvis Designer III White (Reverence), 750 ml...............................**$250.00**

Decanter, McCormick, 1983, Elvis Gold Mini, plays My Way, 50 ml...**$125.00**

Decanter, McCormick, 1983, Elvis Silver Mini, plays How Great Thou Art, 50 ml **$95.00**

Decanter, McCormick, 1983, Sgt Elvis, plays GI Blues, 750 ml...**$295.00**

Decanter, McCormick, 1984, Elvis & Rising Sun, plays Green Green Grass of Home, 750 ml...............**$495.00**

Decanter, McCormick, 1984, Elvis Designer I Gold, plays Are You Lonesome Tonight, 750 ml................**$175.00**

Decanter, McCormick, 1984, Elvis Designer Gold II, plays It's Now or Never, 750 ml...............................**$195.00**

Decanter, McCormick, 1984, Elvis Karate Mini, plays Don't Be Cruel, 50 ml...**$125.00**

Decanter, McCormick, 1984, Elvis on Stage, plays Can't Help Falling in Love, 50 ml (decanter only)...............**$195.00**

Decanter, McCormick, 1984, Elvis w/Stage, 50 ml (complete w/separate stage designed to hold decanter).....**$450.00**

Decanter, McCormick, 1984, Elvis 50th Anniversary, plays I Want You, I Need You, I Love You, 750 ml.......**$495.00**

Decanter, McCormick, 1984, Sgt Elvis Mini, plays GI Blues, 50 ml **$95.00**

Decanter, McCormick, 1985, Elvis Designer I White, plays Are You Lonesome Tonight, 50 ml......................**$125.00**

Decanter, McCormick, 1985, Elvis Designer III Gold, plays Crying in the Chapel, 750 ml..............................**$250.00**

Decanter, McCormick, 1985, Elvis Teddy Bear, plays Let Me Be Your Teddy Bear, 750 ml **$695.00**

Decanter, McCormick, 1986, Elvis & Gates of Graceland, plays Welcome to My World, 750 ml **$150.00**

Decanter, McCormick, 1986, Elvis & Rising Sun Mini, plays Green Green Grass of Home, 50 ml **$250.00**

Decanter, McCormick, 1986, Elvis Designer I Gold Mini, plays Are You Lonesome Tonight, 50 ml............**$150.00**

Decanter, McCormick, 1986, Elvis Designer I Silver Mini, plays Are You Lonesome Tonight, 50 ml............**$135.00**

Decanter, McCormick, 1986, Elvis Hound Dog, plays Hound Dog, 750 ml **$695.00**

Decanter, McCormick, 1986, Elvis Season's Greetings, plays White Christmas, 375 ml **$195.00**

Decanter, McCormick, 1986, Elvis Teddy Bear Mini, plays Let Me Be Your Teddy Bear, 50 ml **$295.00**

Decanter, McCormick, 1986, Elvis 50th Anniversary Mini, plays I Want You, I Need You, I Love You, 50 ml **$250.00**

Decanter, McCormick, 1987, Elvis Memories, casstte player base, lighted top, extremely rare, 750 ml, from $1,000 to.**$1,200.00**

Doll, '68 Comeback, Hasbro, 1993, MIB.....................**$30.00**

Doll, Aloha From Hawaii, white outfit w/300+ genuine rhinestones, Danbury Mint, 18", EX.............................**$75.00**

Doll, Celebrity Collection, Supergold Elvis, #1 in series of 4, vinyl, 21", MIB...**$75.00**

Doll, gold suit, made by Gemmy, EPE, plays Blue Christmas, 19", MIB...**$65.00**

Doll, Phoenix Elvis, vinyl, World Doll Co, 21", MIB...**$90.00**

Flight log page, Los Angeles to Las Vegas, w/Certificate of Authenticity, EX **$85.00**

Guitar, toy; Rock 'n Roll & Elvis's image, Selcol, 1960s, 20", NMIB...**$650.00**

Lobby card, Jailhouse Rock, 1956, 11x14", VG+ **$75.00**

Lobby card, King Creole, 1958, 11x14", EX................**$80.00**

Lobby card, Wild in the Country, 1961, 14x17", EX....**$55.00**

Menu, Las Vegas Hilton, Summer Festival Menu '75, EX **$465.00**

Overnight bag, pink w/images overall, EPE, 1956, EX.....**$135.00**

Plate, Heartbreak Hotel, Delphi, 1992, MIB **$35.00**

Plate, Viva Las Vegas, Bruce Emmett's Elvis on the Big Screen series, Delphi, 1992, 8½", MIB **$60.00**

Postage stamps, full sheet of 29¢ stamps (40 total), M..**$55.00**

Poster, Ed Parker's Elvis Presely Memorial Karate Championship, 1978, EX **$80.00**

Profile plaque, Clay Art, 10", from $150.00 to $175.00. (Photo courtesy Lee Garmon)

Record, For LP Fans Only, Victor 1990, 1959, EX.....**$130.00**

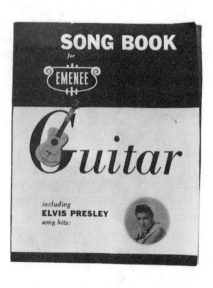

Song book, included with the 'Love Me Tender' guitar by Emenee, NM, $80.00. (Photo courtesy Rosalind Cranor/ Ramona Griffin)

Suitcase, black & white photos overall, brown leather trim, 17x21", NM..**$70.00**

Teapot, white suit, on 1 knee, guitar strap is handle, guitar end is spout, South West Ceramics, England, 8½" **$235.00**

Telephone, in gold outfit w/microphone & stand, sings & dances, plays Hound Dog, 12" Elvis on stage, 1998, NMIB..**$45.00**

Ticket, Alabama & Mississippi Fair & Dairy Show, 1956, EX...**$80.00**

Ticket, Indiana State University, September 16, 1977, NM..**$30.00**

Ticket, June 18, 1977, Kemper Arena, Kansas City MO, unused, M...**$135.00**

Tour book, Jail House Rock tour, 1956, 12 pages, 8x10", NM **$160.00**

Enesco

Enesco is a company that imports and distributes ceramic novelty items made in Japan. Some of their more popular lines are the Human Beans, Partners in Crime Christmas ornaments, Eggbert, Dutch Kids, and Mother in the Kitchen (also referred to as Kitchen Prayer Ladies, see also that category). Prices are climbing steadily. Several Enesco items are pictured in *The Collector's Encyclopedia of Cookie Jars, Volumes 1, 2,* and *3,* by Joyce and Fred Roerig (Collector Books).

Figurines, Human Beans, large, from $15.00 to $18.00, small, from $7.00 to $10.00; bank, Human Beans, from $35.00 to $45.00. (Photo courtesy Joyce and Fred Roerig)

Bank, Sad Hound, 6½"...**$18.00**

Condiment jar, Missy Mouse, #E-1167, 4" **$20.00**

Creamer & sugar bowl, Hopper the Frog, 3½", pr **$35.00**

Figurine, Brambly Hedge, canopy bed w/rabbit, bedside table w/candle & snack, top of canopy has miscellaneous items, 4x4x6"...**$60.00**

Figurine, Country Cousins Tree House, girl hanging on ladder w/boy & squirrel on top, 1985, 7".................**$55.00**

Figurine, Country Cousins Tree Tire Swing, girl in tire swing, boy in top of tree & puppy & kitten below, 7x8", 1981 ....**$50.00**

Figurine, Disney Thanksgiving, Minnie w/cornucopia of fruit, #22-655, 3¼" **$8.00**

Figurine, fireman w/wings, Heavenly Host series, #271977, 4½"...**$3.00**

Figurine, Golf Is a Blast, dog w/dynamite strapped to golf bag, Dog Gone Golf series, #299251, 4½".............**$7.00**

Figurine, Hanging In There, koala in eucalyptus tree, bear & tree are ceramic, branch is bronze, 1983, 3¾" **$65.00**

Figurine, I'm a...Human Bean, big blue shoes, 4¼" ...**$15.00**

Figurine, I'm So Attached to You, girl puppet w/toy bear, No Strings Attached series, #109002, 3½" **$3.00**

Figurine, Jennie, Country Fair, #E-4151, 4½" **$15.00**

Figurine, Kinka girl, blue dress w/embossed white shawl, lg hat w/white feather, tan purse, #121215 on sticker, 7" **$60.00**

Figurine, Kinka girl in pink dress w/ruffle bottom, pink flower wreath in hair, holding lavender butterfly, #119075...**$90.00**

Figurine, Little Deere, Big Smile, pig on John Deere riding mower, Mary's Moo Moo, #674559, 2½" **$8.00**

Figurine, Loxley Castle, Sherwood Forest Collection, MIB..**$90.00**

Figurine, Marvin, in diaper, on back, #E-2779C, 2½" .**$10.00**

Figurine, Miss Biddy, w/purse & umbrella, unmarked, 5½" **$18.00**

Head vase, Abraham Lincoln, dated 1809-1865 ....**$145.00**

Head vase, Barbie, in nurses uniform, 1990s, 8".........**$55.00**

Head vase, Evening Splendor, 1996, MIB **$50.00**

Head vase, lady w/pink turtleneck & blue vest, light pink bow in hair, 7¼" **$350.00**

Music box, Carousel Royale, illuminated & action, plays cassettes, MIB..**$265.00**

Music box, Eggbert Golf Birdie, plays 'Tee' for Two, 1989..**$60.00**

Music box, Enchanted Clocktower, storybook nursery rhyme characters, multi-action, electric, NMIB..............**$425.00**

Music box, Ferris Wheel, illuminated & action, 13", MIB..**$210.00**

Music box, Home on the Range, old-time kitchen stove w/mice working, plays Whistle While You Work, MIB **$180.00**

Music box, Kriss Krinkle in jack-in-the-box, plays O Tannenbaum, #1586/7500, EX **$80.00**

Music box, On Cue, pool table w/mice playing, plays The Entertainer, 9½x5½", MIB **$175.00**

Music box, Sleeping Beauty in jack-in-the-box, 1986, MIB .**$100.00**

Music box, Typing Letter to Santa, mice on old-style typewriter, plays Jolly Old St Nicholas, #E-207, M **$75.00**

Music box, We're in the Money, cats play in cash register, illuminated & action, MIB.......................................**$110.00**

Napkin/recipe card holder, Dearie Is Weary on lady's apron, foil label, 6½" **$60.00**

Ornament, Garfield dressed in fuzzy reindeer outfit, 1988, MIB **$50.00**

Planter, Angel in the Clouds, #E-7012, 4" **$22.00**

Replica, 1911 Die-Cast Antique Replica Race Car, Vintage Collection, 1995, on base, 12"............................**$55.00**

Salt & pepper shakers, Dutch Treat, boy & girl ea sit on wooden shoe, #E-5816, 2½", pr **$12.00**

Salt & pepper shakers, The Bar Hounds, black & gold, 3¾", pr...**$55.00**

Spoon rest, Beaver Dam, red & gold label, 5¾".........**$20.00**

Spoon rest, Humpty Dumpty, Mr or Mrs, C-8355, 6¾"..**$50.00**

Teapot, Mickey Mouse riding horse, from film Two Gun Mickey, lid on 1 cactus & spout on other **$70.00**

Teapot, Winkin' Kitten, unmarked, 5" **$45.00**

Tea set, Lucy & Me, teapot, creamer & sugar bowl, 1980s, NM **$45.00**

Wall pocket/head vases, smiling elves w/big puffy cheeks, labels intact, 5½", pr..**$60.00**

Wedding set, bride, groom, best man, bridesmaid, junior bridesmaid, flower girl & ring bearer, 1983.........**$70.00**

Spoon holder, Mary Poppins, musical, $175.00.

Eye Winker

Designed along the lines of an early pressed glass pattern by Dalzell, Gilmore, and Leighton, Eye Winker was one of several attractive glassware assortments featured in the catalogs of L. G. Wright during the '60s and '70s. The line was extensive and made in several colors: amber, blue, green, crystal, and red. It was probably pressed by Fostoria, Fenton, and Westmoreland, since we know these are the companies that made Moon and Star for Wright, who was not a glass manufacturer but simply a distributing company. Red and green are the most desirable colors and are priced higher than the others we mentioned. The values given here are for red and green, deduct about 20% for examples in clear, amber, or light blue.

Though prices may have softened slightly due to Internet influence, this line is still very collectible; and as the increased supply made available through online auctions gradually diminishes, we expect values to return to the level they were several months ago.

Advisor: Sophia Talbert (See Directory, Eye Winker)

Ashtray, allover pattern, 4½" dia, from $20 to **$25.00**

Bowl, 4 toes, 2½x5", from $22 to...............................**$28.00**

Butter dish, allover pattern, 4½" dia lid, 6" base, from $50 to **$65.00**

Candy dish, allover pattern, disk foot, w/lid, 5¼x5½"....**$45.00**

Candy dish, oval, 4-toed, 5x3½".................................**$25.00**

Celery or relish, ruffled rim, oblong, 9½x5"...............$40.00
Compote, allover pattern except for plain flared rim & foot, patterned lid, 7x5".................................**$50.00**
Compote, allover pattern except for plain flared rim & foot, 7x7"..**$30.00**
Compote, allover pattern w/plain flared rim, patterned lid, 10½x6"+finial..**$70.00**

Compote, ruffled rim, four-sided, 6x10", from $50.00 to $60.00. (From the collection of Sophia Talbert)

Creamer & sugar bowl, allover pattern, disk foot, sm, 3¼"..**$350.00**
Fairy lamp, allover pattern, disk foot, 2-pc, from $40 to ..**$60.00**
Goblet, plain rim & foot, 6¼"...............................**$25.00**
Marmalade, w/lid, 5¼x4"...................................**$45.00**
Pitcher, ruffled rim, plain foot, 1-qt, from $70 to........**$75.00**
Pitcher, 28-oz, 7¾", minimum value **$50.00**
Salt & pepper shakers, 4", pr................................**$30.00**
Salt cellar, allover pattern, ruffled rim, 1¾"...............**$10.00**
Sherbet, plain rim & foot, 4½"..............................**$20.00**
Toothpick holder, allover pattern, ruffled rim, 2¼" **$15.00**
Tumbler, 8-oz, from $20 to...**$28.00**

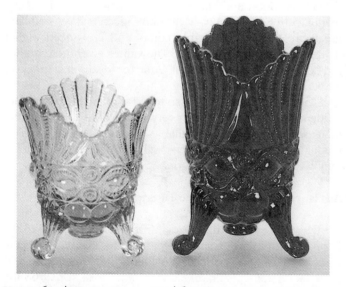

Vase, 6", $50.00; Vase, 8", $60.00. (From the collection of Sophia Talbert)

Fans, Electric

Vintage fans can be fascinating collectibles with various complex working parts and styling varying from the very basic to the most wonderful Art Deco designs. Values hinge on age, style, condition, and manufacturer. To qualify as excellent, a fan must retain its original paint (with only a few blemishes). It must be clean and polished, the original cord must be present, and it must be in good working order with no replacement parts. If you're interested in this field of collecting, we recommend *Collector's Guide to Electric Fans* by John M. Witt (Collector Books).

Dominion #2017, 12" blades (4), stamped steel base, 2-speed rotary switch, light blue finish, 1952, EX **$20.00**
Emerson, 16" Parker blades (4) on stamped steel hub, blue & silver badge, 1941, EX..**$40.00**
Emerson #16646, oscillating, smooth step base, cast-iron motor, 12" Parker blades (4), brass guard & badge, 1912, EX.....**$300.00**
Emerson #24466, 12" brass blades (6) on brass hub, brass guard, 1917-18, EX **$350.00**
Emerson #2450-G, 10" Parker flat black blades (4), glossy black body, toggle switch, 1951, EX.....................**$15.00**
Emerson #73638, 16" Parker Improved blades (4), pyramid badge, 1932, EX..**$75.00**
Emerson Northwind #444A, pot metal base, 8" windmill blades, 2-speed w/AC/DC motor, 1926, EX..........**$45.00**
General Electric, 6" stamped brass blades (4) w/steel guard, AC/DC motor, hunter green paint, 1924, EX........**$35.00**
General Electric #FM10V41, 10" Vortalex blades (3), sea-green metallic finish, ca 1950, EX **$25.00**
General Electric #19X263, 10" steel blades (4), 2-speed slide switch w/continuous oscillator, 1928, EX **$25.00**

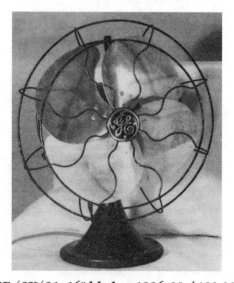

GE 49X491, 16" blades, 1936, M, $130.00; EX, $65.00. (Photo courtesy John M. Witt)

General Electric #75X423, 12" blades (4), hunter green w/brass & green badge, 3-speed slide switch, 1938, EX...**$45.00**

Gilbert #A-54, 12" overlapping blades (4), Art-Deco look, 2-speeds, oscillator, 1940, EX.................................**$175.00**

Hunter/Century, 12" blades (4), stamped steel motor housing, 3-speed, oscillator, 1939, EX.........................**$20.00**

Knapp-Monarch Model #3-503, 12" overlapping blades (4), streamlined look, brown wrinkle finish, 1940, EX..**$45.00**

Montgomery Ward #86K5324, 12" chrome-plated blades (4), cast-iron base, steel motor housing, 2-speed, 1945, EX...**$35.00**

Polar Cub G, 5" gold blades (4), ribbed cast-iron base, 1-speed plug-in type, 1921, EX................................**$65.00**

R&M #D10-A6-01, 10" overlapping blades (4), lg center button covers hub, oscillator, 1940, EX.....................**$65.00**

Signal Junior, 10" blades (4), universal motor, oscillator, light green, 1939, EX.......................................**$25.00**

StarRight, 10" polished brass blades (4), lime green glossy, 8-sided base, 3-speed slide switch, oscillator, 1933, EX..**$55.00**

Victor, 16" aluminum blades (6), S-type guard held by steel struts, w/breeze spreader, 1936, EX.....................**$85.00**

Wagner Electric #5260, 10" blades (4), stamped steel w/cast-iron motor housing, 3 speeds, oscillator, 1931, EX.**$25.00**

Westinghouse, 310-A-3 Power-Aire, 10" blades (4), 1941-49, EX...**$30.00**

Westinghouse #803008-A, 10" blades (4), 3-speed, oscillator, 1933, EX..**$25.00**

Fast-Food Collectibles

Since the late 1970s, fast-food chains have been catering to their very young customers through their kiddie meals. The toys tucked in each box or bag have made a much longer-lasting impression on the kids than any meal could. Today it's not just the toys that are collectible, but also boxes, promotional signs used by the restaurant, the promotional items themselves (such as Christmas ornaments you can buy for 99¢, collector plates, glass tumblers, or stuffed animals), and the 'under 3' (safe for children under 3) toys their toddler customers are given on request.

There have been three kinds of promotions: 1) national — every restaurant in the country offering the same item, 2) regional, and 3) test market. While, for instance, a test market box might be worth $20.00, a regional box might be $10.00, and a national, $1.00. Supply dictates price.

To be most valuable, a toy must be in the original package, just as it was issued by the restaurant. Beware of dealers trying to 'repackage' toys in plain plastic bags. Most original bags were printed or contained an insert card. Vacuform containers were quickly discarded, dictating a premium price. Toys without the original packaging are worth only about one-half to two-thirds as much as those mint in package, which are the values we give in our listings.

Toys representing popular Disney characters draw cross-collectors, so do Star Trek, My Little Pony, and Barbie toys. It's not always the early items that are the most collectible, because some of them may have been issued in such vast amounts that there is an oversupply of them today. At the same time, a toy only a year or so old that might have been quickly withdrawn due to a problem with its design will already be one the collector will pay a good price to get.

Prices have dropped due to the influence of the Internet, and the values in our listings reflect the softer market. If you'd like to learn more about fast-food collectibles, we recommend *Tomart's Price Guide to Kid's Meal Collectibles* by Ken Clee; *The Illustrated Collector's Guide to McDonald's® Happy Meal® Boxes, Premiums and Promotions©, McDonald's® Happy Meal Toys in the USA, McDonald's® Happy Meal Toys Around the World,* and *Illustrated Collector's Guide to McDonald's® McCAPS,* all by Joyce and Terry Losonsky; *McDonald's® Collectibles* by Gary Henriques and Audre DuVall; and *Schroeder's Collectible Toys, Antique to Modern* (Collector Books).

See also California Raisins.

Note: Unless noted otherwise, values are given for MIP items (when applicable).

Club: McDonald's© Collector Club
1153 S Lee St., PMB 200
Des Plaines, IL 60016-6503
Membership: $15 per year for individual or out of state, $7 for juniors, or $20 per family or International members; includes annual dated lapel pin, quarterly newsletter, and annual members directory; send LSASE for club information, chapter list, and publication list; www.mcdclub.com

Newsletter: *Sunshine Express* (monthly)
and club's Sunshine Chapter
Bill and Pat Poe founders and current officers
220 Dominica Circle E.
Niceville, FL 32578-4085
Club membership: as per above
850-897-4163; fax: 850-897-2606
e-mail: BPOE@cox.net

Newsletter: *Collecting Tips*
Meredith Williams
Box 633, Joplin, MO 64802. Send SASE for information.

Arby's, Barbar's World Tour, finger puppets, 1990, ea..**$3.00**

Arby's, Looney Tunes Car Tunes, 1989, ea....................**$3.00**

Arby's, Looney Tunes Characters, 1988, standing, ea ...**$5.00**

Arby's, Mr Men, ea...**$5.00**

Barbar's World Tour, storybooks, 1991, ea **$3.00**

Barbar's World Tour, vehicles, 1990, ea **$3.00**

Bone Age, 1989, 4 different, ea **$5.00**

Burger King, Capitol Critters, 1992, 4 different, ea **$2.00**

Burger King, Lion King, 1994, 7 different, ea...............**$3.00**

Burger King, Minnie Mouse, 1992 ....**$2.00**

Burger King, Pocahontas, 1995, 8 different, ea **$3.00**

Burger King, Pocahontas, 1996, finger puppets, 6 different, ea...**$3.00**

Burger King, Rodney Reindeer & Friends, 1986, 4 different, ea...**$3.00**

Burger King, Simpsons, 1990, M (no package), $2.00 each.

Burger King, Teenage Mutant Ninja Turtles Bike Gear, 1993, ea...$3.00
Burger King, Toy Story, 1995, Woody............................$3.00
Burger King, Z-Bots w/Pogs, 1994, 5 different, ea........$2.00
Burger King, 1991, ea...$3.00
Burger King, 1994, 7 different, ea $3.00
Burger King, 1995, finger puppets, 6 different, ea........$3.00
Dairy Queen, Baby's Day Out Books, 1994, 4 different, ea..$5.00
Dairy Queen, Bobby's World, 1994, 4 different, ea $2.00
Dairy Queen, Radio Flyer, 1991, miniature wagon $3.00
Dairy Queen, Tom & Jerry, 1993, 4 different, ea $3.00
Denny's, Adventure Seekers Activity Packet, 1993, ea..$2.00
Denny's, Flintstones Plush Figures, 1989, Fred & Wilma or Barney & Betty, ea...$3.00
Denny's, Flintstones Plush Figures, 1989, Pebbles & Bamm-Bamm, pr..$5.00
Denny's, Jetson's Space Cards, 1992, 6 different, ea.....$2.00
Dominos Pizza, Avoid the Noid, 1988, 3 different, ea..$2.00
Dominos Pizza, Noid, 1989, bookmark..........................$5.00
Good Gobblin', 1989, 3 different, ea............................$3.00
Hardee's, Apollo Spaceship, 1995, 3-pc set.................$12.00
Hardee's, Balto, 1995, 6 different, ea $2.00
Hardee's, Bobby's World (At the Circus), 1996, 5 different, ea $2.00
Hardee's, Dinosaur in My Pocket, 1993, 4 different, ea..$2.00
Hardee's, Flintstones First 30 Years, 4 different, ea.......$2.00
Hardee's, Halloween Hideway, 1989, 4 different, ea....$2.00
Hardee's, Micro Super Soakers, 1994, 4 different, ea....$2.00
Hardee's, Shirt Tales, 1990, plush figures, 5 different, ea .$2.00
Hardee's, Swan Princess, 1994, 5 different, ea $2.00
Hardee's, X-Men, 1995, 6 different, ea..........................$2.00
Hunchback of Notre Dame, 1995, hand puppet, 4 different, ea $10.00
Jack-in-the Box, Bendable Buddies, 1991, 5 different, ea..$2.00
Jack-in-the-Box, Garden Fun Seed Packages, 1994, 3 different, ea $3.00
Jack-in-the-Box, Jack Pack Make-A-Scene, 1990, 3 different, ea...$3.00
Long John Silver's, Fish Car, 1989, 3 different, ea.........$2.00
Long John Silver's, I Love Dinosaurs, 1993, 4 different, ea ..$2.00

Long John Silver's, Treasure Trolls, 1992, pencil toppers, 4 different, ea $2.00
McDonald's, Airport, 1986, Ronald McDonald seaplane ..$5.00
McDonald's, Babe, 1996, plush animals, 6 different, MIP, ea $2.00
McDonald's, Barbie/Hot Wheels, 1993, Hot Wheels, any including under age 3, ea $2.00
McDonald's, Barbie/Hot Wheels, 1994, Camp Teresa...$3.00
McDonald's, Bedtime, 1989, drinking cup, M...............$2.00
McDonald's, Bedtime, 1989, Ronald, set of 4 ....$3.00
McDonald's, Changables, 1987, 6 different, ea.............$2.00
McDonald's, Circus Parade, 1991, ea............................$2.00
McDonald's, Feeling Good, any including under age 3, ea...$2.00
McDonald's, Friendly Skies, 1991, Ronald or Grimace, ea...$3.00
McDonald's, Hook, 1997, 4 different, ea......................$2.00
McDonald's, Lego Building Set, 1986, helicopter or airplane, ea..$2.00
McDonald's, Lego Building Set, 1996, race car or tanker boat, ea..$3.00
McDonald's, Looney Tunes Quack-Up Cars, 1993, 4 different, ea..$2.00
McDonald's, New Archies, 1988, 6 different, ea...........$6.00
McDonald's, Power Rangers, 1995, any including under age 3, ea $2.00

McDonald's, Ronald McDonald Slippers, $25.00. (Photo courtesy Gary Henriques and Audre DuVall)

McDonald's, Tale Spin, 1990, any including under age 3, ea...$2.00
McDonald's, Turbo Macs, 1988, any including under age 3, ea...$2.00
McDonald's, Water Games, 1992, ea $2.00
McDonald's, Zoo Face, 4 different, ea $2.00
McDonald's, 101 Dalmatians, 1991, 4 different, ea $2.00
McDonald's, 101 Dalmatians, 1996, snow dome ornaments, 4 different, ea $2.00
McDonald's Rescue Rangers, 1995, any including under age 3, ea $2.00
Pizza Hut, Beauty & the Beast, 1992, hand puppets, 4 different, ea $2.00
Pizza Hut, Brain Thaws, 1995, 4 different, ea $2.00
Pizza Hut, Eureeka's Castle, 1990, hand puppets, 3 different, ea..$2.00

Pizza Hut, Marvel Comics, 1994, 4 different, ea............**$2.00**
Pizza Hut, Squirt Toons, 1995, 5 different, ea **$2.00**
Sonic, Airtoads, 6 different, ea..**$2.00**
Sonic, Animal Straws, 1995, 4 different, ea....................**$2.00**
Sonic, Bone-A-Fide Friends, 1994, 4 different, ea **$2.00**
Sonic, Creepy Strawlers, 1995, 4 different, ea **$2.00**
Sonic, Go Wild Bills, 1995, 4 different, ea.....................**$2.00**
Sonic, Totem Pal Squirters, 1995, 4 different, ea...........**$2.00**
Subway, Battle Balls, 1995-96, 4 different, ea................**$2.00**
Subway, Bump in the Night, 1995, 4 different, ea........**$2.00**
Subway, Explore Space, 1994, 4 different, ea...............**$2.00**
Subway, Hurricanes, 1994, 4 different, ea **$2.00**
Subway, Santa Claus, 1994, under age 3, Comet the Reindeer..**$2.00**
Subway, Tom & Jerry, 1995, 4 different, ea...................**$2.00**
Taco Bell, Congo, 1995, watches, 3 different, ea **$3.00**
Taco Bell, Happy Talk Sprites, 1983, Spark, Twinkle, or Romeo, plush, ea **$3.00**
Taco Bell, Pebble & the Penguin, 1995, 3 different, ea ..**$2.00**
Target Markets, Muppet Twisters, 1994, 3 different, ea ..**$2.00**
Target Markets, Targetters, 1992 (5 different), 1994 (5 different w/rooted hair), ea **$2.00**

Wendys, Alien Mix-up Characters, 1990, $3.00 each.

Wendy's, All Dogs Go to Heaven, 1989, 6 different, ea .**$2.00**
Wendy's, Animalinks, 1995, 6 different, ea **$2.00**
Wendy's, Dino Games, 1993, 3 different, ea.................**$2.00**
Wendy's, Felix the Cat, 1990, under age 3, rub-on set .**$2.00**
Wendy's, Glo-Ahead, 1993, any including under age 3, ea **$2.00**
Wendy's, Mighty Mouse, 1989, 6 different, ea **$2.00**
Wendy's, Wacky Windups, 1991, 5 different, ea............**$2.00**
Wendy's, Yogi Bear & Friends, 1990, 6 different, ea.....**$2.00**
White Castle, Bow Biters, 1989, Blue Meany.................**$1.00**
White Castle, Castle Dude Squirters, 1994, 3 different, ea .**$3.00**
White Castle, Fat Albert & the Cosby Kids, 1990, 4 different, ea...**$5.00**
White Castle, Super Balls, 1994, 3 different, ea............**$2.00**

Fenton Glass

Located in Williamstown, West Virginia, the Fenton company is still producing glassware just as they have since the early part of the century. Nearly all fine department stores and gift shops carry an extensive line of their beautiful products, many of which rival examples of finest antique glassware. The fact that even some of their fairly recent glassware has collectible value attests to its fine quality.

Over the years they have made many lovely colors in scores of lines, several of which are very extensive. Paper labels were used exclusively until 1970. Since then some pieces have been made with a stamped-in logo.

Numbers in the descriptions correspond with catalog numbers used by the company. Collectors use them as a means of identification as to shape and size. If you'd like to learn more about the subject, we recommend *Fenton Glass, The Second Twenty-Five Years,* and *Fenton Glass, The Third Twenty-Five Years,* by William Heacock; *Fenton Glass, The 1980s,* by James Measell; and *Fenton Art Glass, 1907 to 1939,* and *Fenton Art Glass Patterns, 1939 to 1980,* both by Margaret and Kenn Whitmyer.

Club: Fenton Art Glass Collectors of America, Inc.
Newsletter: Butterfly Net
P.O. Box 384
Williamstown, WV 26187; Full membership $20 per year; $5 for each associate membership; children under 12 free

Club: Pacific Northwest Fenton Association
P.O. Box 881
Tillamook, OR 97141, 503-842-4815
e-mail: shirley@oregoncoast.com
website: www.glasscastle.com/pnwfa.htm; Subscription: $23 per year; includes quarterly informational newsletter and exclusive piece of Fenton glass

Baskets

Apple Blossom, #7336-AB, 6½", from $150 to **$185.00**
Aqua Crest, #192, 7", from $95 to **$125.00**
Block & Star, #5637-MI, from $30 to **$35.00**
Blue Ridge, #1922, 10", from $250 to **$290.00**
Cactus, #3439-MI, 9", from $45 to **$55.00**
Coin Dot, blue opalescent, #1522, 10", from $145 to ..**$165.00**
Coin Dot, blue opalescent, #1925, 6", from $200 to.**$250.00**
Coin Dot, cranberry, #203, 7", from $85 to **$115.00**

Coin Dot, lime opal, #1437, 1952 – 1954, 7", from $150.00 to $185.00.
(Photo courtesy Margaret and Kenn Whitmyer)

Crest, Black Rose, #7237-BR, 7", from $145 to.........**$185.00**
Crystal Crest, #36, cone, 8", from $110 to **$145.00**
Gold Crest, #1923, 7", from $100 to..........................**$125.00**
Gold Crest, #37, miniature fan, sq, 2½", from $90 to ..**$110.00**
Hobnail, amber, #3837-AR, 7", from $20 to.................**$25.00**
Hobnail, blue opalescent, 13½", from $300 to..........**$400.00**
Hobnail, blue pastel, #3837-BP, 7", from $45 to.........**$55.00**
Hobnail, cranberry, #3637-CR, deep, 7", from $200 to ..**$225.00**
Hobnail, green pastel, #3834-GP, 4½", from $35 to....**$40.00**
Hobnail, milk glass, #3638-MI, 8½", from $30 to.......**$38.00**
Hobnail, orange, #3638-OR, 8½", from $25 to **$30.00**
Hobnail, Peach Blow, #3830-PB, 10", from $100 to..**$150.00**
Silver Crest, #7339-SC, divided, from $75 to..............**$90.00**
Spiral Optic, blue opalescent, #3137-BO, from $50 to..**$60.00**

Bells

American Legacy, Heritage Green, #G1665HG, 1982-83..**$24.00**
Beauty, Periwinkle Blue, #9665PQ, 1986....................**$22.00**
Berries & Blossoms on Opal Satin, #1773RK...............**$32.00**
Blue Dogwood on Cameo Satin, #9462BD, basketweave..**$36.00**
Bow & Drape, Tulips, #9266TL, 4½"..........................**$22.00**
Burmese w/blue butterfly & multicolor flowers, ruffled
    edge **$80.00**
Cardinal in the Churchyard on Opal Satin, Birds of Winter
    Series, #7668BC, 1987.....................................**$36.00**
Christmas Faith, #7667XS, 1986 ....**$65.00**
Christmas Message, #7669VZ, musical, 1988 ....**$55.00**
Cross, Crystal Velvet, #9761VE, 1989........................**$24.00**
Garden of Eden, Cobalt Marigold Carnival, #9663NK,
    1985 ....**$35.00**
Hobby Horse on Custard Satin, Childhood Treasures,
    #1760HQ, petite **$22.00**
Majestic Flight on White Satin, #7618EE **$85.00**
Pastel Violets, #7668VC, 1987 ....**$32.00**
Smoke & Cinders on White Satin, #7667TL................**$90.00**
Strawberry pattern on Misty Blue, 6½".......................**$32.00**
Wisteria, Connoisseur, #7666ZW, hand-painted, 1988...**$85.00**

Carnival Glass

Note: Carnival glass items listed here were made after 1970.

Basket, Sunburst, amethyst, #8636CN, 1983 ....**$36.00**
Bowl, Butterfly & Berry, #C8428XB, QVC, black, footed,
    1989 ....**$65.00**
Comport, Pinwheel, Teal Marigold, #8227OI...............**$26.00**
Pitcher, Hobnail, black, #3008XB, 1990 ....**$75.00**
Pitcher, Plytec, Cobalt Marigold, #9461INK, 1987, 32-oz..**$45.00**
Pitcher, Sunburst, Cobalt Marigold, #8667NK, 1985 ...**$35.00**
Plate, Garden of Eden, Cobalt Marigold, #9614NK, 1985, 8"..**$35.00**
Toothpick holder, Cactus, Red Sunset, #3495RN.................**$28.00**

Crests

Apple Blossom, bowl, relish; #7333-AB, heart shape, from
    $85 to...**$90.00**

Aqua, salver, #600, 12", from $45 to **$65.00**
Black, basket, #7237-BC, 7", from $145 to **$165.00**
Black Rose, vase, tulip; #7250-BR, 8", from $110 to.**$125.00**
Blue, bonbon, #7428-BC, 8", from $45 to...................**$55.00**
Blue Ridge, vase, flared, #188-7, from $60 to.............**$70.00**
Crystal, basket, #1924, 5", from $75 to......................**$95.00**
Crystal, bottle, #192, 7", from $100 to.......................**$125.00**
Crystal, bowl, oval, #1522, 10", from $65 to..............**$75.00**
Emerald, comport, low footed, #7329-EC, from $50 to..**$55.00**
Flame, candle holder, #7474-FC, from $45 to.............**$60.00**
Flame, comport, footed, #7249-FC, from $65 to.........**$85.00**
Gold, bowl, regular, #682, 9½", from $25 to...............**$35.00**
Gold, jar, candy or bath powder; #192, w/lid, from $55
    to...**$65.00**
Gold, top hat, #1924, 5", from $25 to **$32.00**
Ivory, vase, cornucopia; #1523, from $60 to **$80.00**
Jug, handled, #192, 8", from $90 to **$125.00**
Peach, basket, #192, 7", from $60 to.........................**$80.00**
Peach, bottle, vanity; #192-A, from $45 to..................**$48.00**
Peach, bowl, double crimped, #203, 7", from $20 to .**$25.00**
Rose, cup, #680, from $35 to....................................**$40.00**
Rose, plate, #680, 6", from $16 to.............................**$18.00**
Rose, vase, sq or triangular, #201, 5", from $40 to **$45.00**
Silver, ashtray, #7377-SC, from $35 to **$45.00**
Silver, basket, #1924, 5", from $65 to........................**$85.00**
Silver, basket, cone, #36, 6¼", from $35 to **$40.00**
Silver, bonbon, #7428-SC, 8", from $18 to **$22.00**
Silver, bottle, vanity; #711, from $55 to **$65.00**
Silver, bowl, #5823-SC, 11", from $50 to **$60.00**
Silver, bowl, banana; #7324-SC, from $38 to **$42.00**
Silver, bowl, dessert; deep, #680, from $15 to **$18.00**
Silver, cake plate, footed, #680, 13", from $35 to........**$45.00**
Silver, chip & dip, #7303-SC, from $65 to..................**$85.00**
Silver, creamer, #1924, 5", from $25 to......................**$32.00**
Silver, epergne set, #7202-SC, from $65 to **$90.00**
Silver, ivy ball, footed, #7232-SC, from $40 to **$45.00**
Silver, Jamestown, vase, tulip; #7250-SJ, 8", from $100 to..**$115.00**

Silver, jug, #7467, 70-ounce, from $200.00 to $250.00. (Photo courtesy Margaret and Kenn Whitmyer)

Silver, nut dish, footed, #680, from $22 to **$27.00**

Silver, planter, 3-tier, #680, from $60 to **$80.00**
Silver, plate, #681, 9", from $25 to **$30.00**
Silver, puff box, #711, w/lid, from $40 to....................**$55.00**
Silver, salt & pepper shakers, #7206-SC, pr, from $85 to...**$90.00**
Silver, sherbet, footed, #680, from $20 to **$25.00**
Silver, Spanish Lace, salt & pepper shakers, footed, #3508-SC, ea, from $40 to...**$45.00**
Silver, tidbit, 3-tier, #7295-SC, from $55 to.................**$65.00**
Silver, torte plate, #7216-SC, 16", from $50 to **$65.00**
Silver, vanity set, #711, from $150 to **$175.00**
Silver, vase, #4517, 10", from $75 to **$90.00**
Silver, vase, #5859-SC, 8", from $35 to........................**$45.00**
Silver, vase, #7262-SC, 12", from $100 to.....................**$145.00**
Silver, vase, double crimped, #203, 4½", from $15 to...**$18.00**
Silver, vase, tulip; triangle, #192-A, 9", from $28 to **$35.00**
Silver, Violets in the Snow, ashtray, #7377-DV, from $45 to **$55.00**
Silver, Yellow Rose, candle holder, #7271-YR, from $25 to **$30.00**

Figurals and Novelties

Apple, Dusty Rose Overlay, #5019OD, 1984...............**$35.00**
Bear cub, Hearts & Flowers, #5151FH **$28.00**
Bear cub, Holly Berry, #5233HL, reclining **$28.00**
Bear Cub, Provincial Bouquet, #5151FS, hand-painted...**$28.00**
Bird, Happiness; Colonial Amber, #5197CA **$18.00**
Bird, Happiness; Lilac, #5197LX.................................**$28.00**
Bird, Holly Berry, #5115HL...**$28.00**
Boot, Daisy & Button, #1990OI **$24.00**

Bridesmaid Doll, Almost Heaven Blue Slag, #5228, $45.00.

Butterfly, Ruby Carnival, FAGCA, 1989 ....**$50.00**
Butterfly candy box, Colonial Amber, #9280CA **$26.00**
Butterfly on stand, Periwinkle Blue, #5171PW...........**$24.00**
Cat, black w/hand-painted Copper Rose, #C5165KP, QVC, 1991 ....**$28.00**
Cat, Holly Berry, #5165HL..**$28.00**
Cat, Strawberries on French Opalescent, #5165SF **$32.00**
Dog, scottie; crystal, #5214CY, 1986............................**$17.00**
Dog, spaniel; Vintage decor on Cameo Satin, #5159SP, 1982...**$26.00**
Doll, Shell Pink, Gracious Touch, #5228PE **$28.00**

Duckling, Tulips, #5169TL..**$28.00**
Egg, Tulips, #5140TL **$28.00**
Elephant, Berries & Blossoms on Opal Satin, #5158RK..**$28.00**
Elephant, Frosted Asters on Blue Satin, #5158FA........**$29.00**
Elephant, multicolored, #5012, 1984 ....**$35.00**
Fawn, Thistles & Bows, #5160EQ, 1986.......................**$28.00**
Fawn, Vintage decor on Cameo Satin, #5160NF, reclining, 1982 ....**$24.00**
Fawn, Winterberry, #5160BQ, 1987.............................**$28.00**
Fox, Cobalt Marigold Carnival, #5226NK....................**$28.00**
Hobby Horse, Winterberry, #5135BQ, 1988 ....**$24.00**
Iceberg, Inspirations, blue, #8740II, 5x6", 1988..........**$32.00**
Kissing Kids, Crystal Velvet, boy or girl, #5101VE, 1981, ea..**$26.00**
Kitten, Pastel Violets, #5119VC **$28.00**
Light, electric; Pink Velvet, girl, #9605VP....................**$48.00**
Lion, Blue Royale, #5241KK, 1990...............................**$25.00**
Mouse, Hearts & Flowers, #5148FH **$28.00**
Mouse, Vintage decor on Cameo Satin, brown, #5148NJ, 1982..**$20.00**
Ornament, ruby, #1714RU, AL Randall Co, 1982 ....**$15.00**
Owl, Jade Green, #5168JA **$32.00**
Panda, Vintage decor on Cameo Satin, #5151PJ, 1982..**$24.00**
Penguin, multicolored, #5014, 1984 ....**$36.00**
Pig, Natural Animals, #5220QP, 1985-86 ....**$26.00**
Praying Angel, Opal Satin w/blue highlights, #5114AB, AL Randall Co, 1985 ....**$24.00**
Puppy, Pastel Violets, #5225VC **$28.00**
Red Clown on Opal Satin, #5111NL, 1985 ....**$36.00**
Ring holder, Fine Cut & Block, Dusty Rose, #9144DK .**$7.00**
Santa fairy light, Holly Berry, #5106HL.......................**$40.00**
Santa in Chimney, Opal Carnival, #5235DS, hand-painted, AL Randall Co, 1988.............................**$360.00**
Slipper, Burmese, Love Bouquet, #9591WQ, 1986......**$24.00**
Snail, Cobalt Marigold Carnival, #5134NK, 1985 ....**$28.00**
Squirrel, Meadow Blooms on Opal Satin, #5215JU, 1986..**$28.00**
Swan, Shell Pink w/hand-painted floral, #C5161EQ, QVC, 1988 988 ....**$32.00**
Swan, Teal Royale, #5127OC, open **$18.00**
Toothpick holder, Purple Stretch, #7590VY, Levay, 1981 .**$29.00**
Top hat, Hobnail, milk glass, #3991MI........................**$12.00**
Whale, Berries & Blossoms on Opal Satin, #5152RK..**$28.00**

Hobnail

Ashtray, blue opalescent, #3873-BO, oval, from $15 to..**$18.00**
Ashtray, Colonial Blue, #3776-CB, round, from $12 to...**$14.00**
Bell, Cameo opalescent, #3667-CO, 6", from $25 to..**$28.00**
Berry dish, milk glass, #3928-MI, from $11 to.............**$13.00**
Bonbon, blue opalescent, #3921-BO, star, 5", from $18 to **$22.00**
Bonbon, French opalescent, #3935-FO, 2-handled, oval, 5", from $12 to...**$15.00**
Bowl, cranberry, special, 7", from $35 to **$40.00**
Bowl, dessert; blue opalescent, #3828-BO, sq, from $30 to...**$35.00**

Bowl, dessert; French opalescent, #3838-FO, sq, from $25 to.......................................**$28.00**

Bowl, milk glass, #3625-MI, oval, 8", from $20 to **$25.00**

Bowl, topaz opalescent, footed, shallow, 11", from $100 to.......................................**$145.00**

Butter, amber, #3977-AR, ¼-lb, from $20 to...............**$25.00**

Cake plate, French opalescent, footed, 12", from $75 to ..**$85.00**

Cake plate, milk glass, #3913-MI, footed, from $35 to..**$40.00**

Candle holder, milk glass, #3673-MI, footed, ea, from $18 to.......................................**$22.00**

Creamer & sugar bowl, cranberry, #3901-CR, from $75 to...**$85.00**

Creamer & sugar bowl, milk glass, #3901-MI, from $18 to.**$22.00**

Cruet, #3863, 7¾", $50.00. (Photo courtesy Gene Florence)

Goblet, water; topaz opalescent, from $35 to.............**$40.00**

Jam & jelly set, crystal, #3915-CY, from $18 to **$20.00**

Jug, syrup; milk glass, #3762-MI, 12-oz, from $20 to..**$22.00**

Oil & vinegar set, French opalescent, #3916-FO, on tray, from $85 to.......................................**$93.00**

Plate, salad; blue opalescent, #3918-BO, 8", from $14 to..**$18.00**

Plate, topaz opalescent, 8", from $25 to **$30.00**

Shaker, kitchen; black, #3602-BK, from $12 to **$15.00**

Toothpick holder, Colonial Blue, #3795-CB, from $12 to .**$14.00**

Tray, fan; French opalescent, 10½", from $30 to **$35.00**

Vase, hand; blue opalescent, 6", from $65 to.............**$85.00**

Vase, handkerchief; milk glass, #3651-MI, 6½", from $20 to **$22.00**

Lamps

Boudoir, Hobnail, opal, from $60 to............................**$80.00**

Courting, electric; Diamond Optic, Colonial Blue, from $100 to.......................................**$125.00**

Courting, oil; Diamond Optic, Colonial Amber, from $75 to **$80.00**

Double Ball, Rose, milk glass, #9204-MI, 24", from $120 to **$150.00**

Fairy, candle; Swirled Feather, French Satin, #2090-FA, from $150 to.......................................**$175.00**

Fairy, electric; Swirled Feather, Green Satin, #2092-GA, from $275 to.......................................**$325.00**

Fairy, Hobnail, blue opalescent, from $35 to.............**$40.00**

Fairy, Hobnail, Colonial Blue, footed, 3-pc, from $50 to ..**$60.00**

Fairy, Hobnail, custard, from $25 to **$35.00**

Fairy, Hobnail, green transparent, footed, 3-pc, from $35 to.......................................**$45.00**

Fairy, Lily of the Valley, Cameo opalescent, from $30 to..**$35.00**

Fairy, Spiral Optic, blue opalescent, from $45 to.......**$50.00**

Gone-With-The-Wind, Poppy, Silver Crest, from $250 to..**$275.00**

Hurricane, Diamond Optic, ruby overlay, #170, from $100 to.......................................**$140.00**

Hurricane, Hobnail, blue pastel, 11", from $100 to ..**$130.00**

Hurricane, Hobnail, milk glass, w/handled base, from $40 to.......................................**$45.00**

Hurricane, Spiral Optic, Steigel Blue, #170, w/base, from $175 to.......................................**$185.00**

Hurricane, Swirled Feather, Cranberry Satin, #2098-RA, from $300 to.......................................**$350.00**

Mariner's, Hanging Heart, turquoise iridescent, 20¼", from $400 to.......................................**$600.00**

Mariner's, Violets in the Snow, 19", from $200 to.....**$250.00**

Oil, Hobnail, Colonial Amber, from $45 to.................**$55.00**

Student, Decorated Hobnail, 1974 – 1976, 21", from $200.00 to $250.00. (Photo courtesy Margaret and Kenn Whitmyer)

Student, Hobnail, cranberry, 19", from $200 to.........**$250.00**

Student, Rose, Colonial Amber, 19", from $85 to......**$100.00**

Table, Violets in the Snow, Silver Crest, 33", from $175 to **$200.00**

Miscellaneous

Apothecary jar, Hobnail, Colonial Amber, from $45 to..**$50.00**

Ashtray, Hobnail, milk glass, #3878, octagonal, 6½" .**$12.00**

Boot, Hobnail, milk glass, #3992, 4" **$14.00**

Bowl, banana; Cactus, from $35 to **$40.00**

Bowl, cereal; Hobnail, milk glass, from $40 to **$45.00**

Bowl, finger or deep dessert; Silver Crest, #680, 5"....**$22.50**

Bowl, Hobnail, French opalescent, flared, 9", from $30 to **$35.00**

Bowl, Hobnail, rose pastel, sq, 9", from $45 to **$55.00**

Bowl, Hobnail, topaz opalescent, cupped, 9", from $90 to **$125.00**

Bowl, peanut; Hobnail, milk glass, #3627, octagonal, 6x6"..**$18.50**

Bowl, salad; Emerald Glo, 10"..................................**$30.00**

Bowl, salad; Silver Crest, #680, 10" **$50.00**

Boxtle, vanity; Hobnail, French opalescent, from $225 to...**$250.00**

Butter & cheese, Hobnail, milk glass, #3677, w/lid, 4¼"..**$160.00**

Butter dish, Hobnail, amber, ¼-lb, from $20 to.........**$25.00**

Cake plate, Thumbprint, Colonial Amber, footed, from $10 to...**$14.00**

Candle holder, Valencia, Colonial Green, from $8 to .**$10.00**

Candlestick, Diamond Lace, #1948, cornucopia, from $40 to...**$45.00**

Candlestick, Ivory Crest, #951, cornucopia, from $35 to .**$40.00**

Candy box, Hobnail, Blue Marble, slipper, w/lid, from $40 to...**$50.00**

Candy box, Hobnail, milk glass, #3600, w/lid, 6" **$35.00**

Candy box, Silver Crest, from $45 to **$55.00**

Candy box, Waffle, milk glass, from $30 to.................**$35.00**

Cologne bottle, Hobnail, cranberry opalescent, w/wooden stopper, from $75 to..**$85.00**

Comport, Gold Crest, footed, from $25 to...................**$28.00**

Cream pitcher, Vasa Murrhina, Blue Mist, from $40 to ...**$45.00**

Creamer, Emerald Crest, clear reeded handles, #7231 ..**$35.00**

Creamer, Silver Crest, ruffled top **$55.00**

Creamer & sugar bowl, Daisy & Button, milk glass, from $20 to...**$25.00**

Cruet, Emerald Glo...**$30.00**

Cruet, Hanging Heart, turquoise iridescent, from $165 to..**$185.00**

Cruet, Hobnail, green opalescent, from $250 to **$300.00**

Cup, child's; Hobnail, milk glass, #489 ....**$60.00**

Decanter, Coin Dot, French opalescent, #894, handled, from $200 to...**$250.00**

Decanter, Spiral Optic, cranberry, from $400 to **$500.00**

Epergne set, Cactus, from $225 to...........................**$250.00**

Epergne set, Hobnail, milk glass, 2-pc, from $60 to...**$75.00**

Ginger jar, Block Optic, #893, from $250 to **$300.00**

Ginger jar, Spiral Optic, cranberry, #893, w/base & lid, from $350 to...**$395.00**

Goblet, wine; Historic America, Fort Dearborn, from $25 to **$30.00**

Goblet, wine; Hobnail, ruby, from $18 to **$22.00**

Ivy ball, Diamond Optic, w/base, #705, from $160 to....**$180.00**

Jar, apothecary; Hobnail, milk glass, #3689, w/lid, 11" ...**$135.00**

Jardiniere, Hobnail, milk glass, #3898, scalloped, 6" ..**$35.00**

Jardiniere, Hobnail, milk glass, 3½", from $14 to **$18.00**

Jug, Coin Dot, cranberry, #1353, crimped, 70-oz, from $275 to...**$295.00**

Jug, Silver Crest, #711, squat, from $75 to.................**$85.00**

Jug, syrup; Hobnail, coral, 12-oz, from $35 to **$45.00**

Lavabo, Hobnail, milk glass, from $100 to **$125.00**

Mayonnaise set, Block & Star, from $20 to.................**$28.00**

Mustard, Emerald Crest, w/lid & spoon......................**$85.00**

Napkin rings, Hobnail, milk glass, set of 4, from $100 to..**$140.00**

Oil bottle, Aqua Crest, #680, from $150 to...............**$185.00**

Oil bottle, Silver Crest, #680 ....**$85.00**

Plate, Silver Crest, #680, 10".....................................**$40.00**

Plate, Silver Crest, #680, 6½", from $8 to **$10.00**

Puff box, Hobnail, French opalescent, w/wooden lid, from $20 to...**$25.00**

Puff box, Hobnail, turquoise, from $50 to...................**$60.00**

Punch bowl, Silver Crest, from $300 to **$400.00**

Relish dish, Silver Turquoise Crest, heart shape, handled, from $40 to...**$45.00**

Rose jar, Coin Dot, cranberry, #893, from $250 to....**$350.00**

Salt & pepper shakers, Hobnail, milk glass, #3806, flat, 3", pr...**$20.00**

Salt & pepper shakers, Teardrop, turquoise, pr, from $35 to...**$40.00**

Sherbet, Hobnail, blue opalescent, from $20 to..........**$25.00**

Syrup pitcher, Hobnail, milk glass, #3660, 12-oz, 5¼"..**$35.00**

Tidbit, Silver Crest, #680, 3-tier plates......................**$50.00**

Toothpick holder, Hobnail, Blue Bell, from $22 to.....**$27.00**

Tumbler, Coin Dot, Honeysuckle, #1353, barrel, 10-oz, from $40 to...**$45.00**

Tumbler, Diamond Optic, ruby overlay, #1353, 10-oz, from $25 to...**$27.00**

Urn, Hobnail, Colonial Amber, w/lid, 11", from $75 to ..**$85.00**

Urn, Hobnail, milk glass, w/lid, 11", from $185 to...**$225.00**

Vanity set, Crystal Crest, #192, 3-pc, from $220 to....**$275.00**

Vase, Apple Blossom, double crimped, 8", from $55 to..**$75.00**

Vase, Block & Star, 9", from $30 to **$45.00**

Vase, bud; Hobnail, crystal, 8", from $6 to **$8.00**

Vase, Daisy & Button, green pastel, footed, cupped, 8", from $45 to...**$50.00**

Vase, handkerchief; Hobnail, blue opalescent, 6", from $40 to...**$45.00**

Vase, Hobnail, milk glass, #3654, 3-toed, 5"...............**$12.50**

Vase, Honeycomb, blue, #1721, pinched, 8½", from $60 to **$70.00**

Vase, Silver Crest, #186, bulbous base, 8"...................**$40.00**

Vase, Spiral Optic, Cameo opalescent, 6½", from $20 to .**$25.00**

Vase, Spiral Optic, French opalescent, #1523, cornucopia, from $75 to...**$95.00**

Wedding jar, Hobnail, milk glass, from $25 to **$28.00**

Fiesta

You still can find Fiesta, but it's hard to get a bargain. Since it was discontinued in 1973, it has literally exploded onto the collectibles scene, and even at today's prices, new collectors continue to join the ranks of the veterans.

Fiesta is a line of solid-color dinnerware made by the Homer Laughlin China Company of Newell, West Virginia. It was introduced in 1936 and was immediately accepted by the American public. The line was varied. There were more than fifty items offered, and the color assortment included red (orange-red), cobalt, light green, and yellow. Within a short time, ivory and turquoise were added. (All these are referred to as 'original colors.')

As tastes changed during the production years, old colors were retired and new ones added. The colors collectors refer to as '50s colors are dark green, rose, chartreuse, and gray, and today these are very desirable. Medium green was introduced in 1959 at a time when some of the old standard shapes were being discontinued. Today, medium green pieces are the most expensive. Most pieces are marked. Plates were ink stamped, and molded pieces usually had an indented mark.

In 1986 Homer Laughlin reintroduced Fiesta, but in colors different than the old line: white, black, cobalt, rose (bright pink), and apricot. Many of the pieces had been restyled, and the only problem collectors have had with these new colors is with the cobalt. But if you'll compare it with the old, you'll see that it is darker. Turquoise, periwinkle blue, yellow, and Seamist green were added next, and though the turquoise is close, it is a little greener than these original. Lilac and persimmon were later made for sale exclusively through Bloomingdale's department stores. Production was limited on lilac (not every item was made in it), and once it was discontinued, collectors were clamoring for it, often paying several times the original price. Sapphire blue, a color approximating the old cobalt, was introduced in 1996 — also a Bloomingdale's exclusive, and the selection was limited. Then came Chartreuse (a little more vivid than the chartreuse of the '50s); Gray was next, then Juniper (a rich teal); Cinnabar (maroon); a strong yellow called Sunflower, a dark bluish-purple they've aptly named Plum; and the last new color to be added is like the much coveted medium green – a shade they call Shamrock.

Items that have not been restyled are being made from the original molds. This means that you may find pieces with the old mark in the new colors (since the mark is an integral part of the mold). When an item has been restyled, new molds had to be created, and these will have the new mark. So will any piece marked with the ink stamp. The new ink mark is a script 'FIESTA' (all letters upper case), while the old is 'Fiesta.' Compare a few, the difference is obvious. Just don't be fooled into thinking you've found a rare cobalt juice pitcher or individual sugar and creamer set, they just weren't made in the old line. And if you find a piece with a letter H below the mark, you'll know that piece is new.

For further information, we recommend *The Collector's Encyclopedia of Fiesta, Ninth Edition,* by Sharon and Bob Huxford, and *Post86 Fiesta* by Richard Racheter.

Note: Our values are for vintage items only.

Newsletter: *Fiesta Collector's Quarterly*
China Specialties, Inc.
Box 471, Valley City, OH 44280; $12 (4 issues) per year

Club: Homer Laughlin Collectors Club (HLCC)
Homer Laughlin China Collector's Association (HLCCA)
P.O. Box 26021
Crystal City, VA 22215-6021
Dues $25.00 single, $40.00 couple; includes magazine

Ashtray, '50s colors	**$88.00**
Ashtray, red, cobalt or ivory	**$65.00**
Ashtray, yellow, turquoise or light green	**$48.00**
Bowl, covered onion soup; cobalt or ivory	**$725.00**
Bowl, covered onion soup; red	**$750.00**
Bowl, covered onion soup; turquoise, minimum value	**$8,000.00**
Bowl, covered onion soup; yellow or light green	**$650.00**
Bowl, cream soup; '50s colors	**$75.00**
Bowl, cream soup; med green, minimum value	**$4,200.00**
Bowl, cream soup; red, cobalt or ivory	**$62.00**

Bowl, cream soup; yellow, turquoise, or light green, $38.00.

Bowl, dessert; 6", '50s colors	**$52.00**
Bowl, dessert; 6", med green	**$600.00**
Bowl, dessert; 6", red, cobalt or ivory	**$52.00**
Bowl, dessert; 6", yellow, turquoise or light green	**$40.00**
Bowl, footed salad; red, cobalt, ivory or turquoise	**$400.00**
Bowl, footed salad; yellow or light green	**$340.00**
Bowl, fruit; 4¾", '50s colors	**$40.00**
Bowl, fruit; 4¾", med green	**$525.00**
Bowl, fruit; 4¾", red, cobalt or ivory	**$35.00**
Bowl, fruit; 4¾", yellow, turquoise or light green	**$28.00**
Bowl, fruit; 5½", '50s colors	**$40.00**
Bowl, fruit; 5½", med green	**$80.00**
Bowl, fruit; 5½", red, cobalt or ivory	**$35.00**
Bowl, fruit; 5½", yellow, turquoise or light green	**$28.00**
Bowl, fruit; 11¾", red, cobalt, ivory or turquoise	**$340.00**
Bowl, fruit; 11¾", yellow or light green	**$275.00**
Bowl, individual salad; med green, 7½"	**$120.00**
Bowl, individual salad; red, turquoise or yellow, 7½"	**$90.00**
Bowl, nappy; 8½", '50s colors	**$65.00**
Bowl, nappy; 8½", med green	**$145.00**
Bowl, nappy; 8½", red, cobalt, ivory or turquoise	**$58.00**
Bowl, nappy; 8½", yellow or light green	**$42.00**
Bowl, nappy; 9½", red, cobalt, ivory or turquoise	**$65.00**
Bowl, nappy; 9½", yellow or light green	**$52.00**
Bowl, Tom & Jerry; ivory w/gold letters	**$260.00**
Bowl, unlisted salad; red, cobalt or ivory, minimum value	**$1,200.00**
Bowl, unlisted salad; yellow	**$110.00**
Candle holders, bulb; red, cobalt, ivory or turquoise, pr	**$140.00**
Candle holders, bulb; yellow or light green, pr	**$110.00**
Candle holders, tripod; red, cobalt, ivory or turquoise, pr	**$650.00**
Candle holders, tripod; yellow or light green, pr	**$485.00**
Carafe, red, cobalt, ivory or turquoise	**$340.00**
Carafe, yellow or light green	**$255.00**

Casserole, French; standard colors other than yellow, from $690 to..**$725.00**
Casserole, French; yellow **$300.00**
Casserole, '50s colors **$300.00**
Casserole, med green, minimum value.....................**$900.00**
Casserole, red, cobalt or ivory.................................**$225.00**
Casserole, yellow, turquoise or light green **$165.00**
Coffeepot, demitasse; red, cobalt, ivory or turquoise ...**$550.00**
Coffeepot, demitasse; yellow or light green.............**$425.00**
Coffeepot, '50s colors..**$350.00**
Coffeepot, red, cobalt or ivory **$255.00**
Coffeepot, yellow, turquoise or light green **$195.00**
Compote, sweets; red, cobalt, ivory or turquoise **$100.00**
Compote, sweets; yellow or light green **$80.00**
Compote, 12", red, cobalt, ivory or turquoise **$200.00**
Compote, 12", yellow or light green **$150.00**
Creamer, individual; red..**$365.00**
Creamer, individual; turquoise or cobalt...................**$345.00**
Creamer, individual; yellow **$80.00**
Creamer, regular; '50s colors....................................**$40.00**
Creamer, regular; med green **$90.00**
Creamer, regular; red, cobalt or ivory **$35.00**
Creamer, regular; yellow, turquoise or light green **$22.00**
Creamer, stick-handled; red, cobalt, ivory or turquoise.....**$72.00**
Creamer, stick-handled; yellow or light green............**$48.00**
Cup, demitasse; '50s colors.......................................**$375.00**
Cup, demitasse; red, cobalt or ivory **$80.00**
Cup, demitasse; yellow, turquoise or light green........**$68.00**
Cup, see teacup
Egg cup, '50s colors **$160.00**
Egg cup, red, cobalt or ivory.....................................**$72.00**
Egg cup, yellow, turquoise or light green **$60.00**
Lid, for mixing bowl #1–#3, any color, minimum value..**$770.00**
Lid, for mixing bowl #4, any color, minimum value....**$1,000.00**
Marmalade, red, cobalt, ivory or turquoise **$325.00**
Marmalade, yellow or light green **$245.00**
Mixing bowl #1, red, cobalt, ivory or turquoise **$245.00**
Mixing bowl #1, yellow or light green **$180.00**
Mixing bowl #2, red, cobalt, ivory or turquoise **$130.00**
Mixing bowl #2, yellow or light green **$115.00**
Mixing bowl #3, red, cobalt, ivory or turquoise **$135.00**
Mixing bowl #3, yellow or light green **$125.00**
Mixing bowl #4, red, cobalt, ivory or turquoise **$160.00**
Mixing bowl #4, yellow or light green **$130.00**
Mixing bowl #5, red, cobalt, ivory or turquoise **$185.00**
Mixing bowl #5, yellow or light green **$160.00**
Mixing bowl #6, red, cobalt, ivory or turquoise **$275.00**
Mixing bowl #6, yellow or light green **$215.00**
Mixing bowl #7, red, cobalt, ivory or turquoise **$410.00**
Mixing bowl #7, yellow or light green **$350.00**
Mug, Tom & Jerry; '50s colors..................................**$100.00**
Mug, Tom & Jerry; ivory w/gold letters.....................**$65.00**
Mug, Tom & Jerry; red, cobalt or ivory **$82.00**
Mug, Tom & Jerry; yellow, turquoise or light green...**$60.00**
Mustard, red, cobalt, ivory or turquoise **$265.00**
Mustard, yellow or light green **$210.00**
Pitcher, disk juice; gray, minimum value................**$3,000.00**

Pitcher, disk juice; Harlequin yellow.........................**$60.00**
Pitcher, disk juice; red..**$600.00**
Pitcher, disk juice; yellow **$48.00**
Pitcher, disk water; '50s colors **$280.00**
Pitcher, disk water; med green, minimum value ...**$1,200.00**
Pitcher, disk water; red, cobalt or ivory....................**$170.00**
Pitcher, disk water; yellow, turquoise or light green ..**$125.00**
Pitcher, ice; red, cobalt, ivory or turquoise **$160.00**
Pitcher, ice; yellow or light green **$140.00**

Pitcher, jug, two-pint; '50s colors, $150.00.

Pitcher, jug, 2-pt; red, cobalt or ivory **$120.00**
Pitcher, jug, 2-pt; yellow, turquoise or light green **$88.00**
Plate, cake; red, cobalt, ivory or turquoise, minimum value.**$1,000.00**
Plate, cake; yellow or light green, minimum value ..**$900.00**
Plate, calendar; 1954 or 1955, 10" **$45.00**
Plate, calendar; 1955, 9" **$50.00**
Plate, chop; 13", '50s colors.....................................**$100.00**
Plate, chop; 13", med green......................................**$375.00**
Plate, chop; 13", red, cobalt or ivory **$60.00**
Plate, chop; 13", yellow, turquoise or light green......**$42.00**
Plate, chop; 15", '50s colors.....................................**$145.00**
Plate, chop; 15", red, cobalt or ivory **$80.00**
Plate, chop; 15", yellow, turquoise or light green......**$50.00**
Plate, compartment; 10½", '50s colors **$75.00**
Plate, compartment; 10½", red, cobalt or ivory...........**$45.00**
Plate, compartment; 10½", yellow, turquoise or light green ..**$40.00**
Plate, compartment; 12", red, cobalt or ivory.............**$60.00**
Plate, compartment; 12", yellow or light green..........**$55.00**
Plate, deep; '50s colors...**$58.00**
Plate, deep; med green **$140.00**
Plate, deep; red, cobalt or ivory **$60.00**
Plate, deep; yellow, turquoise or light green **$38.00**
Plate, 6", med green **$20.00**
Plate, 6", red, cobalt or ivory **$7.00**
Plate, 6", yellow, turquoise or light green **$5.00**
Plate, 6", '50s colors...**$9.00**
Plate, 7", '50s colors...**$13.00**
Plate, 7", med green **$32.00**
Plate, 7", red, cobalt or ivory **$10.00**
Plate, 7", yellow, turquoise or light green **$9.00**
Plate, 9", '50s colors...**$22.00**

Plate, 9", med green $45.00
Plate, 9", red, cobalt or ivory $18.00
Plate, 9", yellow, turquoise or light green $12.00
Plate, 10", '50s colors $52.00
Plate, 10", med green $135.00
Plate, 10", red, cobalt or ivory $40.00
Plate, 10", yellow, turquoise or light green $32.00
Platter, '50s colors $58.00
Platter, med green $175.00
Platter, red, cobalt or ivory $45.00
Platter, yellow, turquoise or light green $35.00
Relish tray, gold decor, complete, minimum value ... $250.00
Relish tray base, red, cobalt, ivory or turquoise $100.00
Relish tray base, yellow or light green $75.00
Relish tray center insert, red, cobalt, ivory or turquoise ... $60.00
Relish tray center insert, yellow or light green $50.00
Relish tray side insert, red, cobalt, ivory or turquoise ... $60.00
Relish tray side insert, yellow or light green $50.00
Salt & pepper shakers, '50s colors, pr $45.00
Salt & pepper shakers, med green, pr $185.00
Salt & pepper shakers, red, cobalt or ivory, pr $30.00
Salt & pepper shakers, yellow, turquoise or light green,
    pr $22.00
Sauce boat, '50s colors $78.00
Sauce boat, med green $180.00
Sauce boat, red, cobalt or ivory $85.00
Sauce boat, yellow, turquoise or light green $48.00
Saucer, demitasse; '50s colors $110.00
Saucer, demitasse; red, cobalt or ivory $22.00
Saucer, demitasse; yellow, turquoise or light green ... $18.00
Saucer, '50s colors $6.00
Saucer, med green $12.00
Saucer, original colors $4.00
Sugar bowl, individual; turquoise $365.00
Sugar bowl, individual; yellow $125.00
Sugar bowl, w/lid, '50s colors, 3¼x3½" $75.00
Sugar bowl, w/lid, med green, 3¼x3½" $225.00
Sugar bowl, w/lid, red, cobalt or ivory, 3¼x3½" $58.00
Sugar bowl, w/lid, yellow, turquoise or light green,
    3¼x3½" $48.00
Syrup, red, cobalt, ivory or turquoise $425.00
Syrup, yellow or light green $375.00
Teacup, '50s colors $38.00
Teacup, med green $60.00
Teacup, red, cobalt or ivory $35.00
Teacup, yellow, turquoise or light green $25.00
Teapot, lg; red, cobalt, ivory or turquoise $260.00
Teapot, lg; yellow or light green $210.00
Teapot, med; '50s colors $325.00
Teapot, med; med green, minimum value $1,200.00
Teapot, med; red, cobalt or ivory $225.00
Teapot, med; yellow, turquoise or light green $165.00
Tray, figure-8; cobalt $100.00
Tray, figure-8; turquoise or yellow $400.00
Tray, utility; red, cobalt, ivory or turquoise $42.00
Tray, utility; yellow or light green $38.00
Tumbler, juice; chartreuse or dark green $600.00

Tumbler, juice; red $60.00
Tumbler, juice; rose $65.00
Tumbler, juice; yellow, turquoise or light green $40.00
Tumbler, water; red, cobalt, ivory or turquoise $85.00
Tumbler, water; yellow or light green $65.00
Vase, bud; red, cobalt, ivory or turquoise $125.00
Vase, bud; yellow or light green $85.00
Vase, 8", red, cobalt, turquoise or ivory, minimum value ... $700.00
Vase, 8", yellow or light green, minimum value $600.00
Vase, 10", red, cobalt, ivory or turquoise, minimum value ... $950.00
Vase, 10", yellow or light green, minimum value $850.00
Vase, 12", red, cobalt, ivory or turquoise, minimum value ... $1,300.00
Vase, 12", yellow or light green, mininum value ... $1,100.00

Kitchen Kraft

Bowl, mixing; 6", light green or yellow $72.00
Bowl, mixing; 6", red or cobalt $78.00
Bowl, mixing; 8", light green or yellow $85.00
Bowl, mixing; 8", red or cobalt $95.00
Bowl, mixing; 10", light green or yellow $115.00
Bowl, mixing; 10", red or cobalt $125.00
Cake plate, light green or yellow $55.00
Cake plate, red or cobalt $65.00
Cake server, light green or yellow $145.00
Cake server, red or cobalt $155.00
Casserole, individual; light green or yellow $150.00
Casserole, individual; red or cobalt $160.00
Casserole, 7½", light green or yellow $85.00
Casserole, 7½", red or cobalt $90.00
Casserole, 8½", light green or yellow $105.00
Casserole, 8½", red or cobalt $115.00
Covered jar, lg; light green or yellow $320.00
Covered jar, lg; red or cobalt $225.00
Covered jar, med; light green or yellow $280.00
Covered jar, med; red or cobalt $295.00
Covered jar, sm; light green or yellow $285.00
Covered jar, sm; red or cobalt $300.00
Covered jug, light green or yellow $280.00
Covered jug, red or cobalt $290.00
Fork, light green or yellow $125.00
Fork, red or cobalt $135.00
Metal frame for platter $26.00
Pie plate, Spruce green $305.00
Pie plate, 9", light green or yellow $45.00
Pie plate, 9", red or cobalt $48.00
Pie plate, 10", light green or yellow $45.00
Pie plate, 10", red or cobalt $48.00
Platter, light green or yellow $70.00
Platter, red or cobalt $75.00
Platter, spruce green $350.00
Salt & pepper shakers, light green or yellow, pr $100.00
Salt & pepper shakers, red or cobalt, pr $110.00
Spoon, ivory, 12", minimum value $500.00
Spoon, light green or yellow $135.00
Spoon, red or cobalt $145.00
Stacking refrigerator lid, ivory $225.00

Stacking refrigerator lid, red or cobalt, $85.00; unit, light green or yellow, $48.00; unit, red or cobalt, $58.00.

Stacking refrigerator lid, light green or yellow...........**$75.00**
Stacking refrigerator unit, ivory **$210.00**

Finch, Kay

Wonderful ceramic figurines signed by sculptor-artist-decorator Kay Finch are among the many that were produced in California during the middle of the last century. She modeled her line of animals and birds with much expression and favored soft color combinations often with vibrant pastel accents. Some of her models were quite large, but generally they range in size from 12" down to a tiny 2". She made several animal 'family groups' and some human subjects as well. After her death a few years ago, prices for her work began to climb.

She used a variety of marks and labels, and though most pieces are marked, some of the smaller animals are not; but you should be able to recognize her work with ease, once you've seen a few marked pieces.

For more information, we recommend *Kay Finch Ceramics, Her Enchanted World,* by Mike Nickel and Cindy Horvath (Schiffer); and *The Collector's Encyclopedia of California Pottery, Second Edition,* by Jack Chipman (Collector Books). Please note: Prices below are for items decorated in multiple colors, not solid glazes, unless noted.

Advisors: Mike Nickel and Cindy Horvath (See Directory, Kay Finch)

Figurine, Baby Ambrosia, kitten, natural colors, #5166, 5½" **$200.00**
Figurine, Baby Bunny, #5303, 3½"..........................**$125.00**
Figurine, bull, #6211, 6¼".....................................**$300.00**
Figurine, Casey Jones, Jr, #5013, 5½"....................**$200.00**
Figurine, Chanticleer, rooster, #129, 11"................**$300.00**
Figurine, Circus Baby Elephant, #5365, 2¼" **$350.00**
Figurine, Dog Show Westie, #4833...........................**$400.00**
Figurine, Dog Show Yorkie, #4851............................**$500.00**
Figurine, Dog Show Yorkshire Terrier, 2½x3"..........**$650.00**
Figurine, Grumpy, pig, #165, 7½"...........................**$275.00**

Figurine, guppy, #174, 2½" L **$125.00**
Figurine, Hear No Evil, kitten, #4863, 3" **$125.00**
Figurine, Jezebel, contented cat, #179, 6x9"............**$275.00**
Figurine, Kneeling Madonna, #4900, 6" **$100.00**
Figurine, long-eared dog, #5926, 6".........................**$175.00**
Figurine, peasant boy & girl, #113, #117, 6¾", pr **$100.00**
Figurine, seababy, #162, 2½x3½".............................**$175.00**
Figurine, singing angel, #34802, 4½" **$175.00**
Figurine, sleeping bear, #5004, 4½" **$200.00**
Figurine, standing donkey, Florentine White, #839, 9½"..**$300.00**
Figurine, swallow on perch, 5"................................**$175.00**
FIgurine, turkey, #5843, 4½".................................**$175.00**
FIgurine, Winkie Pig, #185, 3¾x4" **$95.00**
Figurines, penguin family, Pete, Polly & Pee Wee, #466, #467, #468, 7¼", 4¾", 3¼" **$410.00**
Plaque, butterfly, #5720, 14".................................**$225.00**
Stein, attached poodle, #5488.................................**$450.00**
String holder, dog w/bow over left ear, wall mount, 4½x4" **$400.00**
Tea tile, Yorkshire Terrier embossed, 5½" sq.............**$95.00**
Toby jug, Santa w/hat lid, 5½"................................**$150.00**
Tumbler, embossed afghan design, signed Kay & Brayden, 6"..**$250.00**
Wall pocket, girl, gold gloss **$250.00**

Figurine, draft horse, #130B, 4½", $100.00.

Fishbowl Ornaments

Prior to World War II, every dime store had its bowl of small goldfish. Nearby were stacks of goldfish bowls — small, medium, and large. Accompanying them were displays of ceramic ornaments for these bowls, many in the shape of Oriental pagodas or European-style castles. The fish died, the owners lost interest, and the glass containers along with their charming ornaments were either thrown out or relegated to the attic. In addition to pagodas and castles, other ornaments included bridges, lighthouses, colonnades, mermaids, and fish. Note that figurals such as mermaids are difficult to find.

Many fishbowl ornaments were produced in Japan between 1921 and 1941, and again after 1947. The older Japanese items often show clean, crisp mold designs with visible detail of the item's features. Others were made in Germany and some by potteries in the United States. Aquarium pieces made in America are not common. Those produced in recent years are usually of Chinese origin and are more crude, less colorful, and less detailed in appearance. In general, the more detail and more colorful, the older the piece. A few more examples are shown in *Collector's Guide to Made in Japan Ceramics* by Carole Bess White (Collector Books).

Advisor: Carole Bess White (See Directory, Japan Ceramics)

Bathing beauty in green suit on yellow lustre shell, red Japan mark, 2¼", from $50 to **$85.00**

Bathing beauty in green suit on orange coral, black Japan mark, 4", from $20.00 to $30.00. (Photo courtesy Carole Bess White)

Bathing beauty on shell, cinnamon & white lustre, red Japan mark, 3", from $40 to **$60.00**
Boy on dolphin, multicolored, black Japan mark, 3¾", from $25 to...**$40.00**
Castle, multicolored, black Japan mark, 2¼", from $18 to **$25.00**
Castle, multicolored, black Japan mark, 3¾", from $22 to **$30.00**
Castle, multicolored (worn paint), black Japan mark, 3", from $3 to...**$5.00**
Castle, multicolored shiny, no mark, 4½", from $20 to ..**$32.00**
Castle, tan lustre w/green & white rocks, red Japan mark, 5¼", from $20 to..**$28.00**
Coral, shiny orange w/shadow of black sea diver, red Japan mark, 3½", from $18 to **$28.00**
Diver, orange, black mark, 3¼", from $15 to.............**$25.00**
Diver, white, black Japan mark, 4¾", from $15 to......**$25.00**
Fish, multicolored, black Japan mark, 2½", from $15 to...**$25.00**
Fish (2) on base, multicolored, black Japan mark, 3¼", from $15 to...**$25.00**
Mermaid, painted bisque, black Japan mark, 4¾", from $45 to...**$65.00**
Mermaid on conch shell, multicolored, black Japan mark, 3½", from $35 to...**$50.00**

Mermaid on snail, multicolored, red Japan mark, 4", from $45 to **$65.00**
Nude lady on starfish, painted bisque, black Japan mark, 4½", from $75 to...**$125.00**
Pagoda, multicolored, black Japan mark, 3½", from $18 to **$28.00**
Torii gate, multicolored, black Japan mark, 3¾", from $18 to **$30.00**

Fisher-Price

Probably no other toy manufacturer is as well known among kids of today as Fisher-Price. Since the 1930s they've produced wonderful toys made of wood covered with vividly lithographed paper. Plastic parts weren't used until 1949, and this can sometimes help you date your finds. These toys were made for play, so very few older examples have survived in condition good enough to attract collectors. Watch for missing parts and avoid those that are dirty. Edge wear and some paint dulling is normal and to be expected. Our values are for toys with minimum signs of such wear. Mint condition examples will bring considerably higher prices, of course, and if the original box is present, add from 20% to 40% more.

For more information we recommend *Modern Toys, American Toys, 1930 – 1980,* by Linda Baker; *Fisher-Price, A Historical, Rarity Value Guide,* by John J. Murray and Bruce R. Fox (Books Americana); and *Schroeder's Collectible Toys, Antique to Modern,* published by Collector Books.

Advisor: Brad Cassity (See Directory, Toys)

Club: Fisher-Price Collector's Club
Jeanne Kennedy
1442 N Ogden, Mesa, AZ 85205; Monthly newsletter with information and ads; send SASE for more information

Museum: Toy Town Museum
636 Girard Ave., PO Box 238, East Aurora, NY 14052
Monday through Saturday, 10-4.

Adventure People Alpha Star, #326, 1983-84...............**$30.00**
Adventure People Daredevil Sport Plane, #306............**$8.00**
Adventure People Mountain Climbers, #351, 1976-79...**$20.00**
Adventure People Sea Explorer, #310, 1975-80...........**$25.00**
Adventure People Wild Safari Set, #304, 1975-78........**$55.00**
Amusement Park, #932, 1963-65 ....**$300.00**
Bulldozer, #311, 1976-77 ....**$25.00**
Bunny Cart, #5, 1948-49 ....**$75.00**
Bunny Cart, #406, 1950-53 ....**$50.00**
Bunny Drummer, #512, 1942 ....**$225.00**
Bunny Engine, #703, 1954-56 ....**$100.00**
Chatter Telephone, #747, 1962-67 ....**$30.00**
Copter Rig, #344, 1981-84 ....**$15.00**
Dandy Dobbin, #765, 1941-44 ....**$200.00**
Donald Duck Drum Major, #400, 1946-48 ....**$275.00**
Ducky Flip Flap, #715, 1964-65 ....**$65.00**

Egg Truck, #749, 1947......................................**$225.00**
Elsie's Dairy Truck, 1948-49.....................**$700.00**
Fuzzy Fido, #444, 1941-44 ....**$225.00**
Gold Star Stagecoach, #175, 1954-55 & Easter 1956 .**$250.00**
Happy Hauler, #732, 1968-70......................**$35.00**
Happy Hippo, #151, 1962-63 ....**$85.00**
Husky Construction Crew, #317, 1978-80 ....**$30.00**
Husky Dump Truck, #302, 1978-84 ....**$20.00**

McDonald's Restaurant, #2552, 1990, 1st version........**$70.00**
Molly Moo Cow, #132, 1972-78 ....**$25.00**
Molly Moo-Moo, #190, 1956 & Easter 1957 ....**$225.00**
Mother Goose, #164, 1964-66 ....**$35.00**
Music Box Iron, #125, 1966 ....**$45.00**

Husky Farm Set, #331, 1981 – 1983, EX+, $25.00. (Add from 20% to 40% for box.) (Photo courtesy Brad Cassity)

Oscar the Grouch, #177, 1977 – 1984, EX+, $20.00. (Add 20% to 40% for box.) (Photo courtesy Brad Cassity)

Husky Race Car Rig, #320, 1979-82.............................**$30.00**
Ice Cream Wagon, #778, 1940 & Easter 1941 ....**$350.00**
Jack & Jill TV Radio, #155, 1968-70, wood & plastic..**$40.00**
Jingle Giraffe, #472, 1956.............................**$225.00**
Jolly Jalopy, #724, 1965 ....**$15.00**
Juggling Jumbo, #735, 1958-59 ....**$225.00**
Jumbo Rolo, #755, 1951-52 ....**$225.00**
Junior Circus, #902, 1963-70 ....**$225.00**
Katie Kangaroo, #158, 1976-77 ....**$25.00**
Katy Kackler, #140, 1954-56 & Easter 1957.................**$85.00**
Kitty Bell, #499, 1950-51 ....**$125.00**
Lift & Load Railroad, #943, 1978-79.............................**$50.00**
Little People Garage Squad, #679, 1984-90, MIP........**$15.00**
Little People Jetliner, #2360, 1986-88.............................**$10.00**
Little People Main Street, #2500, 1986-90 ....**$50.00**

Pick-Up & Peek Puzzle, #500, 1972-86 ....**$10.00**
Picnic Basket, #677, 1975-79...........................**$30.00**
Play Family Car & Camper, #686, 1968-70, MIB **$130.00**
Play Family Castle, #993, 1974-77, 1st version **$100.00**
Play Family Dog, #663, 1966-70, black, MIP **$120.00**
Play Family Dog, #663, 1966-70, tan, MIP **$170.00**
Play Family Fun Jet, #183, 1st version **$25.00**
Play Family Lift & Load Depot, #942, 1977-79 ....**$50.00**
Play Family Patio Set, #726, 1970-73, MIP **$75.00**
Pound & Saw Bench, #728, 1966-67 ....**$25.00**
Power Tow, #4580, 1985-86...........................**$20.00**

Little People Playground, #2525, 1986 – 1990, EX+, $15.00. (Add from 20% to 40% for box.) (Photo courtesy Brad Cassity)

Prancy Pony, #617, 1965 – 1970, EX+, $30.00. (Add 20% to 40% for box.) (Photo courtesy Brad Cassity)

Puffy Engine, #444, 1951-54..**$85.00**
Push Bunny Cart, #401, 1942.....................................**$225.00**
Queen Buzzy Bee, #444, 1959, red litho **$40.00**
Scoop Loader, #300, 1975-77 ....**$25.00**

Teddy Zilo, #734, 1964, EX+, $65.00. (Add 20% to 40% for box.) (Photo courtesy Brad Cassity)

Three Men in a Tub, #142, 1970-73, w/bell **$20.00**
Tuggy Turtle, #139, 1959-60 & Easter 1961 ....**$100.00**
Tumble Tower Game, #118, 1972-75 ....**$10.00**
Winnie the Pooh TV-Radio, #175, 1971-73, Sears only ...**$65.00**

Wood Sailboat Kit, #706, 1982 – 1985, EX+, $25.00. (Add 20% to 40% for box.) (Photo courtesy Brad Cassity)

Woodsey's Log House, #960, 1979-81, complete.........**$25.00**
Ziggy Zilo, #737, 1958-59..**$75.00**

Fishing Lures

There have been literally thousands of lures made since the turn of the century. Some have bordered on the ridiculous, and some have turned out to be just as good as the manufacturers claimed. In lieu of buying outright from a dealer, try some of the older stores in your area — you just might turn up a good old lure. Go through any old tackle boxes that might be around, and when the water level is low, check out the river banks.

If you have to limit your collection, you might want to concentrate just on wooden lures, or you might decide to try to locate one of every lure made by a particular company. Whatever you decide, try to find examples with good original paint and hardware. Though many lures are still very reasonable, we have included some of the more expensive examples as well to give you an indication of the type you'll want to fully research if you think you've found a similar model. For such information, we recommend *Fishing Lure Collectibles, Volume 1,* by Dudley Murphy and Rick Edmisten and *Volume 2* by Dudley and Deanie Murphy; *The Heddon Legacy* by Bill Roberts and Rob Pavey; *Modern Fishing Lure Collectibles, Volumes 1* and *2,* by Russell E. Lewis; *The Fishing Lure Collector's Bible*, by R.L. Streater with Rick Edmisten and Dudley Murphy; *19th Century Fishing Lures* by Arlan Carter; *Collector's Guide to Creek Chub Lures & Collectibles* by Harold E. Smith, M.D.; and *Commercial Fish Decoys* by Frank R. Baron. All are published by Collector Books.

Advisor: Dave Hoover (See Directory, Fishing Lures)

Club: NFLCC Tackle Collectors
Drew Reese, contact
197 Scottsdale Circle
Reeds Spring, MO 65737; Send SASE for more information about membership and their publications: *The National Fishing Lure Collector's Club Magazine* and *The NFLCC Gazette*

All Star, Musky Gee-Wiz Frog, wooden core, single hook, 1930, 5½", from $200 to...**$250.00**
Arbogast, Tin Liz Hickory Shad, lead bodied, painted eyes, no fins or tail, single hook, 1938, 2⅛", from $40 to....**$60.00**
Bite-Em-Bait, Lipped Wiggler, adjustable lip, painted tack eyes, 2 trebles, 1930, 3½", from $40 to..................**$60.00**
CA Clark, Little Eddie #1000, red & yellow w/red dot on tail, 2 treble hooks, 1946, 1¾", from $15 to **$30.00**
Danielson, Danielson Minnow, cast aluminum, 2 single hooks pop out when line is pulled, 1927, 4¼", from $150 to..**$200.00**
Drake, Sea Bat, red & yellow, no eye detail, adjustable diving fins, 2 trebles, 1932, 3⅛", from $45 to............**$75.00**
Haas, Haas' Liv-Minno, 3 wooden sections & hinged metal tail, 2 trebles, 1935, 4¾", from $150 to...............**$200.00**
Han-Craft, Plunk-O Lure, glass eyes, metal top fin, fish-shaped tail, 2 trebles, 1939, 3¼", from $50 to....**$100.00**
Heddon, Laguna Runt L-10, black & red dots on cream, 2 trebles, 1939, 2½", from $75 to..............................**$100.00**
Heddon, Munk-Mouse #F4200, reverse lip, spotted flock paint, 2 trebles, 1942, 2¾", from $150 to............**$200.00**
Heddon, Musky Surfusser #350, fat body, heavy duty toilet seat hook rigs, 2 trebles, 1937, 4", from $200 to..**$250.00**

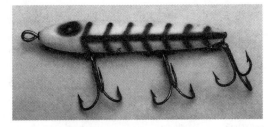

Heddon, Saltwater Torpedo #30, 1947, glass eyes, no spinner, 4", from $30.00 to $50.00.
(Photo courtesy Dudley Murphy and Rick Edmisten)

Heddon, Tad Polly #5100 (aka Tad Polly Runt), 2 trebles, 1938, 3", from $75 to..............................**$150.00**

Jamison, Smacker, red head & white body, 1 single dressed hook, 1934, 6", from $10 to.......................**$15.00**

Keeling, Spinnered Surface Lure, brown stripes on yellow, slim, 2 trebles, ca 1930, 3¾", from $75 to..........**$125.00**

Keeling, Tip Top, front or rear mounted propeller, green to yellow, 2 trebles, 1925, 3¾", from $40 to.............**$50.00**

Kellman, Cicada Plug, cvd wood w/feathers under wings, rubber legs, 1 single hook, 1930, 2⅜", from $100 to ..**$150.00**

Kellman, Mouse, clipped bucktail body w/mouse tail & nose, single hook, 1930, 2½", from $100 to.................**$125.00**

Moonlight/Paw Paw, Moonlight Pikaroon Musky, red to yellow w/black stripe, 3 trebles, 1926, 5¼", from $150 to **$200.00**

Moonlight/Paw Paw, Moonlight Weighted Bucktail Bait, stainless spinner, hair tail, double hook, 1930, 1¼", $75 to..**$100.00**

Moonlight/Paw Paw, Paw Paw Sucker Minow, lg head, painted to imitate sucker, 3 trebles, 1937, 4¼", from $50 to...**$75.00**

Pflueger, Baby Scoop #9300, glass-eyed Scoop w/3 bladed propellers, 2 trebles w/short wire leader, 1935, 3", from $40 to...**$65.00**

Pflueger, Catalina Minnow, slim w/2 belly weights, single hook, 1930, 4⅛", from $75 to............................**$100.00**

Pflueger, Flocked Mouse, 1950, 2¾", from $150.00 to $200.00. (Photo courtesy Dudley Murphy and Rick Edmisten)

Shakespeare, Frog Skin Bait, frog skin stretched over wooden body, 2 trebles, 1930, 3¾", from $50 to..........**$75.00**

Shakespeare, Jim Dandy Floating Minnow, yellow w/glass eyes, floppy marked propellers, 3 trebles, 1930, 3⅞", from $50 to...**$75.00**

Shakespeare, Striped Bass Wobbler #6636, 2 lg trebles, 1938, 6", from $100 to......................................**$125.00**

Shakespeare, Swimming Mouse Jr #6580, black dots on yellow, 2 trebles, 1930, 2¾", from $30 to.................**$45.00**

South Bend, Bass-Oreno #973, yellow w/red stripe, glass eyes, fat, 3 trebles, 1927, 3½", from $10 to..........**$40.00**

South Bend, Feathered Weedless Spinner Hook #565, painted eyes, single dressed hook, 1929, 4½", from $10 to...**$25.00**

South Bend, Plug-Oreno #959, glass eyes, green & yellow, 2 single hooks, 1929, 2½", from $100 to...............**$150.00**

South Bend, Plunk-Oreno #929, concave mouth, painted tack eyes, red & yellow w/single dressed hook, 1939, 2", from $20 to...**$40.00**

South Bend, Tarp-Oreno #979, painted tack eyes, 2 single hooks, 1938, 8", from $50 to................................**$75.00**

Strike Master, Surface Killer, glass eyes, thin propellers, cup hook rigging, 3 trebles, 1928, 3¾", from $75 to....**$100.00**

Winchester, Fantail Chub, red, vaguely resembles Heddon Tad Polly, 2 trebles, 1930, 4", from $150 to **$200.00**

Wright & McGill, Flapper Crab, molded composition, hair antenna, rubber legs, 1 treble, 1930, 2½", from $50 to...**$75.00**

Fitz & Floyd

If you've ever visited a Fitz & Floyd outlet store, you know why collectors find this company's products so exciting. Steven Speilberg has nothing on their designers when it comes to imagination. Much of their production is related to holidays, and they've especially outdone themselves with their Christmas lines. But there are wonderful themes taken from nature featuring foxes, deer, birds, or rabbits, and others that are outrageously and deliberately humorous. Not only is the concept outstanding, so is the quality.

See also Cookie Jars.

Bowl, white, cat taking nap in lid, marked Cat Nap on bottom, 1977, 5x3"......................................**$100.00**

Butter dish, turkey stretched out across lid on white box, 1990, MIB..**$80.00**

Cake stand, Old World Rabbits, wicker-weave design w/flowers & vines, pedestal foot, 4¼x13¼" dia ..**$85.00**

Candy basket, stump decor, rabbit on handle, blue bow around stump, 1991, 9x8" dia, MIB...................**$115.00**

Coffeepot, St Nicholas, 9x11½" **$200.00**

Covered box, cat shape, yellow w/blue & white spots, blue shoes, 1985, 6½x4"...**$90.00**

Creamer & sugar bowl, rabbit figurals, standing creamer, sugar bowl lying down, 1991, MIB.....................**$80.00**

Figurine, reindeer, w/harness & straps, 18".............**$100.00**

Figurine, rooster, black & white w/red comb, Garden Gourmet Collection, MIB **$120.00**

Mug, jack-'o-lantern with vulture handle, from $45.00 to $55.00. (Photo courtesy Pamela Apkarian-Russell)

Mug, St Nicholas, 4" $160.00
Pitcher, cat figural, French King motif, 10x10" $220.00
Plate, dinner; Cloisonne Peony, white center, black border w/pink & rose flowers & green leaves, 10¼" $85.00
Plate, dinner; St Nicholas, white w/green garland border w/Santa, 10¼", from $85 to $125.00
Plate, Les Bands pattern, white w/blue ringed border, 10¼" $50.00
Salt & pepper shakers, Cats a Courting, 4½"..............$85.00

Salt and pepper shakers, comical Santas, from $25.00 to $35.00 for the pair.

Salt & pepper shakers, wedge of cheese w/2 mice sticking head out of top, 1980...$85.00
Serving dish, white basketweave w/pansy border & 3 rabbit figural feet, 1991, 11½"......................................$80.00
Serving dish, white w/grapes & leaves border & twig-like handles, 3-section, 2x9x21"...............................$100.00
Sugar bowl, St Nicholas, w/lid $160.00
Teapot, bear figural, tree branch at rear serves as handle, 1994, 6½x10"..$135.00
Teapot, Hat Party, 2 frogs hugging on lid, wood-grain effect w/berries, blossoms & vines, MIB......................$95.00
Teapot, kangaroo shape, head finial, gray, w/2 matching cups, 6¼x6½" $170.00

Teapot, Kittens a Courting, kittens in & around cottage, 1992, 10x6x7½" $90.00
Teapot, moose figural, 20-oz, 6½x9½" $210.00
Teapot, Moscow Russian Cathedral, marked #798/5000, 1994, 8½x9¾x 5¾" $340.00
Vase, Kittens a Courting, kittens in & around cottage, 1992, 9" $100.00
Vase, Nautilus shell shape w/3 shell-shaped feet, white & rose, 8½x11" $130.00
Vase, rabbit family in stump, Mr Rabbit in top hat w/little rabbits around stump, 14x11" $175.00

Florence Ceramics

During the '40s, Florence Ward began modeling tiny ceramic children as a hobby at her home in Pasadena, California. She was so happy with the results that she expanded, hired decorators, and moved into a larger building where for two decades she produced the lovely line of figurines, wall plaques, busts, etc., that have become so popular today. The 'Florence Collection' featured authentically detailed models of such couples as Louis XV and Madame Pompadour, Pinkie and Blue Boy, and Rhett and Scarlett. Nearly all of the Florence figures have names which are written on their bases.

Many figures are decorated with 22k gold and lace. Real lace was cut to fit, dipped in a liquid material called slip, and fired. During the firing it burned away, leaving only hardened ceramic lace trim. The amount of lace work that was used is one of the factors that needs to be considered when evaluating a 'Florence.' Size is another. Though most of the figures you'll find today are singles, a few were made as groups, and once in awhile you'll find a lady seated on a divan. The more complex, the more expensive.

There are Florence figurines that are very rare and unusual, i.e., Mark Anthony, Cleopatra, Story Hour, Grandmother and I, Carmen, Dear Ruth, Spring and Fall Reverie, Clocks, and many others. These may be found with high prices; however, there are bargains still to be had.

Our wide range of values reflects the amounts of detailing and lace work present. If you'd like to learn more about the subject, we recommend *The Complete Book of Florence, A Labor of Love,* by Barbara and Jerry Kline, our advisors for this category, and Margaret Wehrspaun. (Ordering information may be found in the Directory.) Other references include *The Collector's Encyclopedia of California Pottery, Second Edition,* by Jack Chipman; and *The Florence Collectibles, An Era of Elegance,* by Doug Foland.

Advisors: Jerry and Barbara Kline (See Directory, Florence Ceramics)

Club: Florence Ceramics Collectors Club (FCCS)
Jerry Kline
PO Box 468
Bennington, VT 05201
802-442-3336 or fax: 802-442-7354
Website: www.sweetpea.net; e-mail: sweetpea@sweetpea.net

Amelia, 8¼", from $275 to................................**$300.00**
Angel, 7¾", from $140 to................................**$150.00**
Ava, flower holder, 10½", from $300 to................**$350.00**
Bea, 7¼", from $150 to................................**$175.00**
Belle, 8", from $140 to................................**$150.00**
Butch, 5½", from $200 to................................**$225.00**
Charmaine, hands away, 8½", from $275 to............**$375.00**
Cindy, fancy, 8", from $425 to................................**$475.00**
Colleen, 8", from $350 to................................**$400.00**

Cynthia, lace and fur trim, blue and white with 22k gold, 9¼", $750.00. (Photo courtesy Jack Chipman)

Delia, hand showing, from $200 to............**$250.00**
Diana, powder box, 6¼", from $550 to..............**$600.00**
Don, prom boy, 9½", from $425 to................**$475.00**
Elaine, Godey girl, matt, 6", from $60 to..............**$70.00**
Ellen, from $225 to................................**$250.00**
Emily, flower holder, 8", from $100 to................**$125.00**
Ethel, plain, 7¼", from $160 to................**$180.00**
Fern, flower holder, no gold, 7", from $150 to........**$160.00**
Gary, 8½", from $160 to................................**$175.00**
Girl (bust), traditional, 12", from $200 to................**$225.00**
Halloween Child, 4", from $600 to............**$700.00**
Irene, 6", from $60 to................................**$70.00**
Josephine, from $350 to................................**$375.00**
Joy, child, 6", from $175 to................................**$200.00**
Judy, 9", from $450 to................................**$500.00**
Kay, flower holder, 7", from $60 to............**$70.00**
Kiu, 11", from $250 to................................**$275.00**
Lea, flower holder, 6", from $80 to................**$100.00**
Lillian, 7¼", from $135 to................................**$150.00**
Linda Lou, red or teal, 7¾", from $375 to................**$425.00**
Madonna, 10", from $150 to................................**$175.00**
Margot, rare, 8½", from $650 to................**$700.00**
Mary, seated, 7½", from $650 to................**$700.00**
Merry Maids, Betty, Jane or Rosie, shell bowl, ea, from $200 to................................**$250.00**
Mimi, flower holder, 6", from $70 to................**$80.00**
Nita, 8", from $500 to................................**$575.00**

Pamela, 7¼", from $350 to................................**$400.00**
Pinkie, 12", from $400 to................................**$450.00**
Priscilla & John Alden, pr, from $550 to................**$600.00**
Reggie, 7½", from $400 to................................**$450.00**
Sarah, 7½", from $130 to................................**$140.00**
Sherri, 8", from $450 to................................**$500.00**

Shirley, applied compact, rose and fur trim, 22k gold accents, 8", $375.00. (Photo courtesy Jack Chipman)

Sue, 6", from $60 to................................**$70.00**
Tess, teenager, 7¼", from $500 to................**$550.00**
Toy, 9", from $325 to................................**$350.00**

Victor, 10", from $275.00 to $325.00.

Vivian, 10", from $350 to................................**$400.00**
Wood Nymph, from $400 to................................**$450.00**
Yvonne, plain, 8¾", from $425 to................**$500.00**

Flower Frogs

Flower frogs reached their peak of popularity in the United States in the 1920s and 1930s. During that time nearly every pottery and glasshouse in the Unted States produced some type of flower frog. At the same time ceramic flower frogs were being imported from Germany and Japan. Dining tables and sideboards were adorned with flowers sparingly placed around dancing ladies, birds, and aquatic animals in shallow bowls.

In the 1930s garden clubs began holding competitions in cut flower arranging. The pottery and glass flower frogs proved inadequate for the task and a new wave of metal flower frogs entered the market. Some were simple mesh, hairpin, and needle holders; but many were fanciful creations of loops, spirals, and crimped wires.

German and Japanese imports ceased during World War II, and only a very few American pottery and glass companies continued to produce flower frogs into the 1940s and 1950s. Metal flower frog production followed a similar decline; particularly after the water soluble florist foam, Oasis, was invented in 1954. For further information we recommend *Flower Frogs for Collectors* (Schiffer) by our advisor, Bonnie Bull.

Advisor: Bonnie Bull (See Directory, Flower Frogs)

Bird on stump, yellow & black on lustre base, Made in Japan, 2¼" **$45.00**

Birds (3) on branch, white ceramic w/gold trim, unmarked **$35.00**

Black amethyst glass, 2½x4" **$35.00**

Clear glass oval, 4¾x6" **$10.00**

Clear glass w/3 tiny feet, ¾x2½" dia **$12.50**

Dome shape, mulberry-glazed pottery, Van Briggle, artist's marks **$85.00**

Grecian classical figure, yellow roses in brown hair, Dresden, 9½x4", NM **$370.00**

Green Depression glass, 5" dia, NM **$25.00**

Heron, clear glass, Cambridge, 9" **$115.00**

Jug form, green-glazed pottery, AR Cole (unmarked), 1940s, 4½x4½" **$55.00**

Junque Boat, metal, 2½x6½", EX **$42.00**

Lily form, silver-plate, Leonard, 3x7", EX **$22.00**

Lotus, lead, US Pat No 1916588, 3¼x6", EX **$55.00**

Lovebirds, multicolor lustre, Noritake, 7¼" **$250.00**

Madonna figural, green-glazed pottery, Nicodemus, 10x3½", w/1½x10" bowl **$525.00**

Mottled earth tones, marked Fulper, 1x2x½" **$65.00**

Mushroom form, mottled greens, browns & beige, ceramic, 2-pc, Made in Japan sticker, 3¾" **$8.00**

Needle frog w/cage dome, green metal, Dazey Mfg No 173 Needlesharp **$48.00**

Nude Deco lady w/curving drape, white ceramic, unmarked Germany, 1930s, 6¼" **$95.00**

Nude lady, pastels on white ceramic, Germany, 1930s, 7½" **$245.00**

Nude lady, white ceramic, Made in Western Germany, 1940s-50s, 6" **$175.00**

Nude lady dancing w/draped scarf, pastels on white ceramic, Registered Germany, 1930s, 8" **$255.00**

Nude lady holds scarf wide, shiny white, Registered Germany 314138/2, 1930s, 8" **$240.00**

Nude lady w/arms folded, white ceramic, marked 10077 IV, 6" **$145.00**

Nude lady w/bowl, shiny white, 6¼", w/5" bowl & 2 candlesticks, ca 1940s, 4-pc set **$165.00**

Nude lady w/flowing drape, green, unmarked (attributed to Camark), 1940s, 9" **$95.00**

Nude lady w/3 openings behind her, white ceramic, Metlox, 1940s-50s **$75.00**

Nude with floral garland seated on large lotus flower base, Germany, 7½", $95.00.

Parrot, multicolor on pierced pearl lustre base, Made in Japan, 2¼" **$45.00**

Parrots in tree, multicolor ceramic, unmarked, 5" **$49.00**

Pitcher shape, beige w/cobalt tulips & leaves, 9 holes on stoneware body, unmarked, 4¾" **$15.00**

Robin perched on open trunk, multicolor on white ceramic, Made in Czecho-slovakia, 4" **$25.00**

Turtle form, turquoise, Van Briggle, 5" dia, NM **$125.00**

Wire ware, original green paint, marked Blue Ribbon Flower Holder Co, Cuyahoga Falls, 2½x3" **$15.00**

Yellow ware, plain, no marks or decor, molded raised feet, Weller, 3¼" **$28.00**

Fostoria

This was one of the major glassware producers of the twentieth century. They were located first in Fostoria, Ohio, but by the 1890s had moved to Moundsville, West Virginia. By the late '30s, they were recognized as the largest producers of handmade glass in the world. Their glassware is plentiful today and, considering its quality, not terribly expensive.

Though the company went out of business in the mid-'80s, the Lancaster Colony Company continues to use some of the old molds — herein is the problem. The ever-popular American and Coin Glass patterns are currently in production, and even experts have trouble distinguishing the old from the new. Before you invest in either line, talk to dealers. Ask them to show you some of their old pieces. Most will be happy to help out a novice collector. Read *Elegant Glassware of the Depression Era* by Gene Florence; *Fostoria Glassware, 1887 – 1982,* by Frances Bones; *Fostoria, An Identification and Value Guide, Volume II,* by Ann Kerr; and *Fostoria Stemware, The Crystal for America Series,* by Milbra Long and Emily Seate.

You'll be seeing a lot of inferior 'American' at flea markets and (sadly) antique malls. It's often priced as though it is American, but in fact it is not. It's been produced since the 1950s by Indiana Glass who calls it 'Whitehall.' Watch for pitchers with only two mold lines, they're everywhere. (Fostoria's had three.) Remember that Fostoria was handmade, so their pieces were fire polished. This means that if the piece you're examining has sharp, noticeable mold lines, be leery. There are other differences to watch for as well. Fostoria's footed pieces were designed with a 'toe,' while Whitehall feet have a squared peg-like appearance. The rays are sharper and narrower on the genuine Fostoria pieces, and the glass itself has more sparkle and life. And if it weren't complicated enough, the Home Interior Company sells 'American'-like vases, covered bowls, and a footed candy dish that were produced in a foreign country, but at least they've marked theirs.

Coin Glass was originally produced in crystal, red, blue, emerald green, olive green, and amber. It's being reproduced today in crystal, green (darker than the original), blue (a lighter hue), and red. Though the green and blue are 'off' enough to be pretty obvious, the red is very close. Beware. Here are some (probably not all) of the items currently in production: bowl, 8" diameter; bowl, 9" oval; candlesticks, 4½"; candy jar with lid, 6¼"; creamer and sugar bowl; footed comport; wedding bowl, 8¼". Know your dealer!

Numbers included in our descriptions were company-assigned stock numbers that collectors use as a means to distinguish variations in stems and shapes.

Newsletter/Club: *Facets of Fostoria*
Fostoria Glass Society of America
P.O. Box 826, Moundsville, WV 26041
Membership: $12.50 per year

American, crystal, ashtray, sq, 5"	**$45.00**
American, crystal, bottle, condiment/ketchup; w/stopper	**$145.00**
American, crystal, bowl, centerpiece; 9½"	**$50.00**
American, crystal, bowl, cream soup; handled, 5"	**$45.00**
American, crystal, bowl, jelly; 4¼"	**$15.00**
American, crystal, bowl, pickle; oblong, 8"	**$15.00**
American, crystal, bowl, relish boat; 2-part, 12"	**$20.00**
American, crystal, bowl, vegetable; oval, 2-part, 10"	**$35.00**

American, crystal, bowl, wedding; sq, pedestal foot, w/lid, 8"	**$110.00**
American, crystal, box, hairpin; w/lid, 3½x1¾"	**$325.00**

American, crystal, candle holder, two-light, on bell base, 6", $125.00.

American, crystal, cigarette box, w/lid, 4¾"	**$40.00**
American, crystal, comport, w/lid, 5"	**$25.00**
American, crystal, cup, flat	**$7.50**
American, crystal, goblet, iced tea; #2056, low foot, 12-oz, 5¾"	**$15.00**
American, crystal, ice bucket, w/tongs	**$60.00**
American, crystal, jam pot, w/lid	**$65.00**
American, crystal, picture frame	**$15.00**
American, crystal, plate, torte; 14"	**$75.00**
American, crystal, syrup, w/drip-proof top	**$35.00**
Baroque, blue, ashtray	**$16.00**
Baroque, blue, candlestick, 5½", ea	**$60.00**
Baroque, crystal, bowl, celery; 11"	**$18.00**
Baroque, crystal, bowl, w/handles, 4"	**$11.00**
Baroque, crystal, plate, sandwich; center handle, 11"	**$25.00**
Baroque, crystal, plate, 6"	**$3.00**
Baroque, yellow, bowl, 3-footed, 7"	**$25.00**
Baroque, yellow, mustard, w/lid	**$50.00**
Brocade #287 Grape, blue, candy box, #2331, 3-part, w/lid	**$185.00**
Brocade #287 Grape, green, bowl, #2297, A, 3-footed	**$70.00**
Brocade #287 Grape, orchid, vase, #4103, bulbous, 3" or 4"	**$80.00**
Brocade #289 Paradise, green or orchid, bowl, centerpiece; #2329, round, 13"	**$140.00**
Brocade #290 Oakleaf, crystal, bowl, dessert; #2375, w/handles, 10"	**$80.00**
Brocade #290 Oakleaf, crystal, ice bucket, #2378	**$100.00**
Brocade #290 Oakleaf, crystal, plate, lettuce; #2315, 13"	**$60.00**
Brocade #290 Oakleaf, crystal, stem, claret; #877, 4-oz	**$35.00**
Brocade #290 Oakleaf, ebony, candlestick, #2395, scroll, 3", ea	**$75.00**
Brocade #290 Oakleaf, green or rose, finger bowl, #869	**$70.00**
Brocade #72 Oakwood, orchid or blue, bowl, #2394, flared rim, 3-toed, 12"	**$115.00**

Brocade #73 Palm Leaf, rose or green, candlestick, trindle, #2383, ea $145.00

**Coin, crystal, pitcher, #1372/453, 6¼",
$55.00. (Photo courtesy Gene Florence)**

Colony, crystal, bowl, salad; 7¾.........................$22.50
Colony, crystal, candlestick, 9", ea $30.00
Colony, crystal, plate, luncheon; 8".....................$12.00
Colony, crystal, sugar bowl, 3½"...........................$8.00

**Deer, standing, blue, $55.00. (Photo
courtesy Lee Garmon and Dick Spencer)**

Fairfax, amber, bowl, lemon; w/handles, 9"...........$10.00
Fairfax, amber, plate, bread; oval, 12" $25.00
Fairfax, green or topaz, bowl, soup; 7" $40.00
Fairfax, green or topaz, tumbler, footed, 12-oz, 6" $18.00
Fairfax, rose, blue or orchid, ashtray, 2½" $15.00
Fairfax, rose, blue or orchid, plate, canape.............$20.00
Fuchsia, crystal, bowl, #2395, 10".........................$95.00
Fuchsia, crystal, cake plate, 10"...........................$65.00
Fuchsia, crystal, candlestick, #2375, 3", ea $35.00
Fuchsia, crystal, plate, luncheon; #2440, 8"............$22.00
Fuchsia, wisteria, stem, cordial; #6004, ¾-oz $150.00

Fuchsia, wisteria, tumbler, juice; #6004, footed, 5-oz .$40.00
Hermitage, amber, green or topaz, ashtray, #2449........$5.00
Hermitage, azure, bowl, fruit; #2449 ½, 5".................$15.00
Hermitage, crystal, bottle, oil; #2449, 3-oz $20.00
Hermitage, wisteria, bowl, #2449, footed, 10"...........$115.00
June, crystal, bowl, cereal; 6½" $25.00
June, crystal, bowl, 10"...$35.00
June, rose or blue, bowl, baker; oval, 9".................$150.00
June, rose or blue, plate, dinner; sm, 9½"................$50.00
June, topaz, creamer, footed....................................$20.00
June, topaz, tumbler, footed, 12-oz, 6".....................$40.00
Kashmir, blue, finger bowl..$40.00
Kashmir, blue, plate, salad; round, 7" $7.00
Kashmir, yellow or green, bowl, soup; 7" $35.00
Kashmir, yellow or green, plate, grill; 10" $35.00
Kashmir, yellow or green, stem, juice; footed, 5-oz ...$15.00
Lafayette, blue, burgundy or Empire Green, creamer, footed,
4½"..$40.00
Lafayette, burgundy, bowl, relish; 2-part, 6½" $45.00
Lafayette, crystal or amber, bowl, cereal; 6"...............$20.00
Lafayette, crystal or amber, plate, 8" $10.00
Lafayette, crystal or amber, platter, 12" $40.00
Lafayette, Empire Green, bowl, sweetmeat; 4½".........$33.00
Lafayette, rose, green or topaz, bowl, olive; 6½" $25.00
Lafayette, rose, green or topaz, cup..........................$18.00
Lafayette, rose, green or topaz, sugar bowl, footed, 3⅝"..$25.00
Lafayette, wisteria, bowl, fruit; 5" $32.50
Lafayette, wisteria, saucer..$5.00

**Meadow Rose, crystal, pitcher, #2666, 32-
ounce, $225.00. (Photo courtesy Gene Florence)**

Navarre, crystal, bowl, #2496, handled, footed, 10½"...$85.00
Navarre, crystal, bowl, nut; #2496, 3-footed, 6¼".......$20.00
Navarre, crystal, ice bucket, #2375, 6" $150.00
Navarre, crystal, relish, #2496, 4-part, 10"..................$55.00
New Garland, amber or topaz, bowl, footed, 11".......$50.00
New Garland, amber or topaz, lemon dish, w/handles..$15.00
New Garland, amber or topaz, sugar bowl $12.50
New Garland, rose, celery, 11"...................................$30.00
New Garland, rose, plate, 9"......................................$35.00

New Garland, rose, stem, claret; #6002 ....**$32.50**
Pioneer, azure or orchid, ashtray, 3¾" **$24.00**
Pioneer, azure or orchid, comport, 8" **$35.00**
Pioneer, blue, bouillon, flat **$14.00**
Pioneer, crystal, amber or green, bowl, cereal; 6" **$10.00**
Pioneer, crystal, amber or green, plate, chop; 12" **$18.00**
Pioneer, crystal, amber or green, platter, 15" **$27.50**
Pioneer, ebony, cup, footed **$12.50**
Pioneer, ebony, plate, 9" **$14.00**
Pioneer, rose or topaz, sugar bowl, footed **$12.00**
Rogene, crystal, comport, #5078, 6" **$30.00**
Rogene, crystal, jug 7, #2270 ....**$150.00**
Rogene, crystal, mayonnaise bowl, #766 ....**$25.00**
Rogene, crystal, oil bottle, #1495, w/cut stopper, 5-oz ..**$55.00**
Rogene, crystal, plate, 6" **$7.50**
Rogene, crystal, plate, 8" **$15.00**
Rogene, crystal, stem, grapefruit; #945½ **$27.50**
Rogene, crystal, sugar bowl, #1851, flat **$22.50**
Rogene, crystal, tumbler, table; #4076, flat **$14.00**
Rogene, stem, cordial; #5082, ¾-oz **$40.00**
Royal, amber or green, bowl, soup; #2350, 7¾" **$30.00**
Royal, amber or green, candlestick, #2324, 9", ea **$75.00**
Royal, amber or green, grapefruit, w/insert **$90.00**
Royal, amber or green, tumbler, #859, flat, 12-oz **$30.00**
Seville, amber, bowl, soup; #2350, 7¾" **$20.00**
Seville, amber, plate, luncheon; #2350, 8½" **$6.00**
Seville, green, candlestick, #2324, 4", ea **$22.00**
Seville, green, stem, wine; #870 ....**$28.00**
Sun Ray, crystal, bowl, fruit; 5" **$8.00**
Sun Ray, crystal, candy jar, w/lid **$45.00**
Sun Ray, crystal, onion soup, w/lid **$40.00**
Sun Ray, crystal, sugar bowl, footed **$12.00**
Trojan, rose, ashtray, #2350, sm **$30.00**
Trojan, rose, bowl, #2395, 10" **$115.00**
Trojan, rose, goblet, wine; #5099, 3-oz, 5½" **$60.00**
Trojan, topaz, bowl, bouillon; #2375, footed **$18.00**
Trojan, topaz, candlestick, #2395½, scroll, 5", ea **$65.00**
Trojan, topaz, sugar bowl, #2375½, footed **$20.00**
Versailles, blue, bowl, #2394, footed, 12" **$85.00**
Versailles, pink or green, bowl, soup; #2375, 7" **$80.00**
Versailles, pink or green, ice dish, #2451 ....**$35.00**
Versailles, yellow, cup, after dinner; #2375 ....**$40.00**
Versailles, yellow, plate, chop; #2375, 13" **$50.00**
Vesper, amber, candy jar, #2331, 3-part, w/lid **$125.00**
Vesper, amber, plate, dinner; 10½" **$82.00**
Vesper, blue, comport, 8" **$85.00**
Vesper, blue, plate, bread & butter; #2350, 6" **$12.00**
Vesper, green, bowl, fruit; #2350, 5½" **$12.00**
Vesper, green, ice bucket, #2378 ....**$65.00**
Vesper, green, stem, water goblet; #5093 ....**$28.00**

Franciscan Dinnerware

Franciscan is a trade name of Gladding McBean, used on their dinnerware lines from the mid-'30s until it closed its Los Angeles-based plant in 1984. They were the first to market 'starter sets' (four place settings), a practice that today is commonplace.

Two of their earliest lines were El Patio (simply styled, made in bright solid colors) and Coronado (with swirled borders and pastel glazes). In the late '30s, they made the first of many hand-painted dinnerware lines. Some of the best known are Apple, Desert Rose, and Ivy. From 1941 to 1977, 'Masterpiece' (true porcelain) china was produced in more than 170 patterns.

Many marks were used, most included the Franciscan name. An 'F' in a square with 'Made in U.S.A.' below it dates from 1938, and a double-line script 'F' was used in more recent years.

For further information, we recommend *The Collector's Encyclopedia of California Pottery, Second Edition,* by Jack Chipman.

Note: To evaluate maroon items in El Patio and Coronado, add 10% to 20% to suggested prices.

Advisors: Mick and Lorna Chase, Fiesta Plus (See Directory, Dinnerware)

Desert Rose, creamer, regular, $22.00; sugar bowl, regular, $32.00.

Apple, bowl, cereal; 6" **$16.50**
Apple, ashtray, individual **$22.00**
Apple, bowl, mixing; sm **$182.50**
Apple, butter dish **$50.00**
Apple, cup & saucer, tea **$17.50**
Apple, pitcher, milk **$82.50**
Apple, platter, 14" **$72.50**
Apple, shakers, tall, pr **$82.50**
Apple, teapot **$138.00**
Apple, tumbler, 10-oz **$35.00**
Coronado, bowl, casserole; w/lid, from $85 to **$125.00**
Coronado, bowl, cream soup; w/underplate, from $40 to ..**$50.00**
Coronado, bowl, nut cup; from $16 to **$18.00**
Coronado, bowl, salad; lg, from $35 to **$50.00**
Coronado, creamer, from $12 to **$15.00**
Coronado, plate, chop; 12½" dia, from $25 to **$35.00**
Coronado, plate, 6½", from $6 to **$10.00**
Coronado, plate, 8½", from $12 to **$15.00**
Coronado, salt & pepper shakers, pr, from $20 to **$35.00**
Coronado, teapot, from $65 to **$95.00**

Desert Rose, ashtray, oval..$125.00
Desert Rose, bell, Danbury Mint $125.00
Desert Rose, bowl, cereal; 6"......................................$15.00
Desert Rose, bowl, mixing; med $165.00
Desert Rose, bowl, soup; footed $32.00
Desert Rose, butter dish..$45.00
Desert Rose, coffeepot $125.00
Desert Rose, cookie jar $295.00
Desert Rose, cup & saucer, demitasse.........................$35.00
Desert Rose, goblet, footed $195.00
Desert Rose, mug, barrel, 12-oz $35.00
Desert Rose, napkin ring..$65.00
Desert Rose, pitcher, water; 2½-qt $125.00
Desert Rose, plate, grill $95.00
Desert Rose, plate, 9½"...$20.00
Desert Rose, platter, 14"...$55.00
Desert Rose, tumbler, 10-oz $32.00
El Patio, bowl, fruit..$7.00
El Patio, gravy boat $32.00
El Patio, relish, 3-section..$75.00
El Patio, sherbet $25.00
Forget-Me-Not, bowl, soup $18.00
Forget-Me-Not, plate, 8½"..$12.00

Fresh Fruit, baking dish, one-quart, $255.00. (Photo courtesy Mick and Lorna Chase)

Ivy, bowl, divided vegetable...$55.00
Ivy, bowl, rimmed soup..$52.50
Ivy, plate, chop; 12" $90.00
Ivy, relish, oval, 10"...$35.00
Ivy, sherbet..$30.00
Ivy, tile..$65.00
Meadow Rose, bowl, cereal; 6" $15.00
Meadow Rose, bowl, salad; 10".....................................$115.00
Meadow Rose, box, cigarette..$125.00
Meadow Rose, candle holders, pr.................................$145.00
Meadow Rose, creamer, regular $18.00
Meadow Rose, cup & saucer, jumbo..............................$65.00
Meadow Rose, egg cup $35.00
Meadow Rose, piggy bank $295.00

Meadow Rose, plate, coupe dessert..............................$40.00
Meadow Rose, plate, 8½"...$12.00
Meadow Rose, platter, turkey; 19"................................$295.00
Meadow Rose, shaker & pepper mill, pr...................$295.00
Meadow Rose, teapot..$125.00
Meadow Rose, thimble...$75.00
Poppy, creamer...$45.00
Poppy, pickle tray, 9"...$42.50
Poppy, plate, 8½"...$18.00
Starburst, ashtray, individual $20.00
Starburst, bowl, soup/cereal $13.00
Starburst, butter dish..$45.00
Starburst, casserole, lg...$100.00

Starburst, coffeepot, $150.00.

Starburst, gravy ladle $30.00
Starburst, mug, sm $60.00
Starburst, oil cruet..$75.00
Starburst, plate, dinner $12.00
Starburst, relish, 3-part, 9"..$35.00
Starburst, salt & pepper shakers, bullet shape, lg, pr.$50.00
Starburst, sugar bowl..$25.00
Starburst, tumbler, 6-oz, from $40 to..........................$50.00

Frankoma

John Frank opened a studio pottery in Norman, Oklahoma, in 1933. The bowls, vases, coffee mugs, shakers, etc., he created bore the ink-stamped marks 'Frank Pottery' or 'Frank Potteries.' At this time, only a few hundred pieces were produced. Within a year, Mr. Frank had incorporated. Though not everything was marked, he continued to use these marks for two years. Items thus marked are not easy to find and command high prices. In 1935 the pot and leopard mark was introduced.

The Frank family moved to Sapulpa, Oklahoma, in 1938. In November of that year, a fire destroyed everything. The pot and leopard mark was never re-created, and today collectors avidly search for items with this mark. The rarest of all Frankoma marks is 'First Kiln a Sapulpa 6-7-38,' which was applied to only about one hundred pieces fired on that date.

Grace Lee Frank worked beside her husband, creating many limited edition Madonna plates, Christmas cards, advertising items, birds, etc. She died in 1996.

Clay is important in determining when a piece was made. Ada clay, used until 1953, is creamy beige in color. In 1953 they changed over to a red brick shale from Sapulpa. Today most clay has a pinkish-red cast, though the pinkish cast is sometimes so muted that a novice might mistake it for Ada clay.

Rutile glazes were created early in the pottery's history; these give the ware a two-tone color treatment. However the US government closed the rutile mines in 1970, and Frank found it necessary to buy this material from Australia. The newer rutile produced different results, especially noticeable with their Woodland Moss glaze.

Upon John Frank's death in 1973, their daughter Joniece became president. Though the pottery burned again in 1983, the buildings were quickly rebuilt. Due to so many setbacks, however, the company found it necessary to file Chapter 11 in order to remain in control and stay in business. Mr. Richard Bernstein purchased Frankoma in 1991; it continues to operate.

Frank purchased Synar Ceramics of Muskogee, Oklahoma, in 1958; in late 1950, the name was changed to Gracetone Pottery in honor of Grace Lee Frank. Until supplies were exhausted, they continued to produce Synar's white clay line in glazes such as Alligator, Woodpine, White Satin, Ebony, Wintergreen, and a black-and-white straw combination. At the Frankoma pottery, an 'F' was added to the stock number on items made at both locations. New glazes were Aqua, Pink Champagne, and black, known as Gunmetal. Gracetone was sold in 1962 to Mr. Taylor, who had been a long-time family friend and manager of the pottery. Taylor continued operations until 1967. The only dinnerware pattern produced there was Orbit, which is today hard to find. Other Gracetone pieces are becoming scarce as well.

If you'd like to learn more, we recommend *Frankoma Pottery, Value Guide and More,* by Susan Cox; and *Frankoma and Other Oklahoma Potteries* by Phyllis and Tom Bess.

Club/Newsletter: Frankoma Family Collectors Association
c/o Nancy Littrell
P.O. Box 32571, Oklahoma City, OK 73123-0771
Membership dues: $25; includes newsletter and annual convention

Bookend, Dreamer Girl (Weeping Lady), #427, 5⅜", from $225 to..**$275.00**
Bookends, Charger Horse, Desert Gold, Ada clay, 1934-60, pr...**$250.00**
Christmas card, 1950-51, ea from $125 to **$150.00**
Christmas card, 1954 ....**$110.00**
Christmas card, 1972...:..**$35.00**
Christmas card, 1980-82, ea **$25.00**
Flower bowl, ridged shoulder, Frank Potteries, from $300 to **$350.00**
Jug, Bar-B-Que, Prairie Green, 4"................................**$65.00**

Lazy susan, Wagon Wheel, tan, Ada clay, complete...**$60.00**
Leaf dish, Prairie Green, #227, lg **$40.00**
Mug, Elephant, 1969, from $65 to **$85.00**
Mug, Elephant or Donkey, 1977-90, ea from $20 to...**$30.00**
Pitcher, Guernsey, Peacock Blue, Ada clay, 5" **$75.00**
Pitcher, Plainsman, White Sand, w/ice lip, 2-qt, NM..**$35.00**
Plate, salad; Mayan Aztec, 7" **$12.00**
Plate, salad; Westwind, White Sand, 7" **$7.50**

Plate, Teenagers of the Bible, Jesus the Carpenter, $35.00.

Salt & pepper shakers, Mayan-Aztec, White Sand, pr, NM **$20.00**
Sculpture, Cat, Prairie Green, mini, 3" **$110.00**
Sculpture, Gardener Girl, blue dress, #710, 5¾".......**$125.00**
Sculpture, Greyhound, Flame Orange, red clay, 14½" L....**$275.00**
Sculpture, Indian Chief, Ada clay, #142, 8", from $200 to..**$225.00**
Sculpture, Puma, seated, black gloss, Ada clay, #114, 6½" ..**$95.00**
Sculpture, Two Girls, early 1940s, 5", from $700 to .**$800.00**

Sugar bowl, Mayan-Aztec, with lid, 4", from $12.00 to $15.00; matching teapot, 4¼", from $18.00 to $22.00.

Tumbler, Prairie Green, #5L...**$8.00**
Vase, bud; Snail, Flame, Sapulpa clay, #39.................**$29.00**
Vase, collector; #V-1, from $125 to **$150.00**
Vase, collector; #V-5, 1973, 13"...................................**$85.00**
Vase, collector; #V-14, from $75 to..............................**$85.00**
Vase, Fawn, Deco form, #51, 6¾x3¾"........................**$215.00**

Vase, Prairie Green, w/handles, #71, 10½"..................$67.50
Vase, Tall Ram's Head, #74, 9¼", from $100 to **$150.00**
Vase, Thunderbird, Osage Brown, Ada clay, mini, 3½"..**$135.00**
Wall pocket, Phoebe, Prairie Green, Ada clay, #730, 7½"..**$150.00**
Wall pocket, Wagon Wheel, 7" **$50.00**

Freeman-McFarlin

This California-based company was the result of a union between Gerald McFarlin and Maynard Anthony Freeman, formed in the early 1950s and resulting in the production of a successful line of molded ceramic sculptures (predominately birds and animals, though human figures were also made) as well decorative items such as vases, flowerpots, bowls, etc. Anthony was the chief designer, and some of the items you find today bear his name. Glazes ranged from woodtones and solid colors to gold leaf, sometimes in combination. The most collectible of the Freeman-McFarlin figures were designed by Kay Finch, who sold some of her molds to the company in the early 1960s. The company produced these popular sculptures in their own glazes without Kay's trademark curlicues, making them easy for today's collectors to distinguish from her original work. This line was so successful that in the mid-'60s the company hired Kay herself, and until the late '70s, she designed numerous new and original animal models. Most were larger and more realistically detailed than the work she did in her own studio. She worked for the company until 1980. Her pieces are signed.

In addition to the signatures already mentioned, you may find pieces incised 'Jack White' or 'Hetrick,' both freelance designers affiliated with the company. Other marks include paper labels and an impressed mark 'F.McF, Calif USA,' often with a date.

Ashtray, teal green w/black rim & exterior, #219, 12¾x9¼" **$17.50**
Figurine, bear, seated, light brown w/black-tipped ears, 1¾" **$18.00**
Figurine, deer on leaf, souvenir of Mt Ranieir Wn (sic), 1½x3" **$22.00**
Figurine, doe, recumbent, 1950s, 1½"..................**$14.00**
Figurine, horse, brown w/dark mane & tail, rearing, 2⅞"...**$35.00**
Figurine, kitten, black matt w/glossy eyes, 1¾x4½"...**$18.00**
Figurine, mouse, standing, light gray, marked Anthony USA, 5½"..**$18.00**
Figurine, owl, gold, 5x5".......................................**$15.00**
Figurine, Persian cat, gold, #175, 8¾"..........................**$75.00**
Figurine, puppy, lying down, gold, #446, 2¼x6"........**$50.00**
Figurine, Siamese cat, seated, chocolate point, 5½" ...**$65.00**
Figurine, skunk, bobbing head, 2½"............................**$32.00**
Figurine, turtle, gold w/olive green inserts on back, #162, 8x8" **$35.00**
Figurine, unicorn, lying down, white, #139, 1970s, 7"..**$60.00**
Figurines, Butch & Biddy (same molds as Kay Finch pr), paper labels, pr..**$35.00**
Figurines, coyotes, gold leaf, #144, #145, 10", 9", pr ...**$130.00**

Figurines, ducks, white with amber beaks, black eyes, marked Anthony, 7½" and 5", $50.00 for the pair.

Mushrooms, gold, #370 (7"), #371 (5"), #372 (unmarked, 2½"), set **$35.00**
Pillow for sleeping kitten or puppy, 1950s, 1½"..........**$9.00**
Planter, blue w/green drip, footed, 10½" **$30.00**
Planter, hippo, lg open mouth, dark gray w/pink mouth & white teeth...**$15.00**
Urn, green, horizontal ribbing, 2 scrolled handles, 10¼x5¼" **$25.00**
Wall plaque, tropical fish, pink & gray w/black stripes, 7x4½" **$17.50**
Wall plaques, mermaids, turquoise tails, blonde hair, 1 lg, 3 sm **$195.00**

Furniture

A piece of furniture can often be difficult to date, since many seventeenth- and eighteenth-century styles have been reproduced. Even a piece made early in the twentieth century now has enough age on it that it may be impossible for a novice to distinguish it from the antique. Sometimes cabinetmakers may have trouble identifying specific types of wood, since so much variation can occur within the same species; so although it is usually helpful to try to determine what kind of wood a piece has been made of, results are sometimes inconclusive. Construction methods are usually the best clues. Watch for evidence of twentieth-century tools — automatic routers, lathes, carvers, and spray guns.

For further information we recommend *Antique Oak Furniture* by Conover Hill; *Collector's Guide to Oak Furniture* by Jennifer George; *Heywood-Wakefield Modern Furniture* by Steven Rouland and Roger Rouland; *Collector's Encyclopedia of American Furniture, Volumes I* and *II,* and *Furniture of the Depression Era,* both by Robert and Harriett Swedberg;

and *American Oak Furniture* by Katherine McNerney. All are published by Collector Books.

Armchair, laminated hardwood w/original leather seat & back, attributed to Breuer, ca 1935, EX **$400.00**

Armchair, molded birch w/web seat, 1950s, 31x23x21", EX, pr **$200.00**

Armchair, oak w/spindle back, saddle seat, Boston type, 42" **$175.00**

Bed, dark wood, headboard w/attached night stand, sm footboard, 1950s, full size, EX **$100.00**

Bed, day; oak Country, pencil-post legs, pine apron, 13x68x26" **$70.00**

Bed, iron w/brass trim, old white repaint, single side rails, 60" **$150.00**

Bed, painted beechwood w/carved crest & upholstered head & footboard, ca 1940, twin size, pr **$1,200.00**

Bed, sleigh; weathered red unknown wood (dark stain), 1950s, full size **$425.00**

Bookcase, golden oak, 2 1-pane doors, adjustable shelves, sm gallery & apron, 58x36x12½" **$795.00**

Bookcase, quartersawn oak, stacked, 4-shelf, drawer in base, 53" **$440.00**

Bookcase, walnut, step-back w/double doors, single drawer in base, 76x42x19" **$1,200.00**

Cabinet, china; blond finish, sliding glass doors, 4 drawers, 2 doors, 1950s, EX **$110.00**

Cabinet, china; burled walnut, double doors over bombe base, ca 1935-40, 83x68x18", EX **$2,500.00**

Cabinet, kitchen, double doors over 2 drawers over 2 panel doors, ca 1915, refinished, 69x38x18" **$900.00**

Cabinet, solid pine, 4-pane glass door, modern reproduction w/sq nails, 29x19x12" **$165.00**

Chair, dark patterned fabric, chrome base, Knoll style, 1960s, 30x33x33", VG, pr.. **$400.00**

Chair, side; golden oak, 4-slat back w/simple turnings, saddle seat, side braces, 38" **$125.00**

Chair, side; oak, step-cown crest, vase splat, plank saddle seat, 32", 4 for **$900.00**

Chair, side; oak thumb-back w/5 spindles, refinished, 31½" **$100.00**

Chair, side; oak 3-slat ladder-back, replaced rush seat, VG **$170.00**

Chair, side; white oak, bentwood balloon back, side braces, 34" **$125.00**

Chair, side; white paint w/fabric seat ('shabby chic look'), Berkey & Gay, 1940s, pr **$250.00**

Chair, swivel seat, black leather sling on tubular metal frame, 1950s, 36x20x24", EX................................... **$200.00**

Chair, swivel; black vinyl & fabric upholstery, brushed aluminum base w/chrome frame, 1970s **$100.00**

Chair, wire w/chromed steel rod construction w/open back, 1970s, 31x20½x21", VG **$70.00**

Chair & ottoman, orange fabric upholstery, sculptural form, 1960s, VG **$400.00**

Chifferobe, bow-front drawers, hat box, beveled mirror, ca 1920s, refinished **$1,200.00**

Coat tree, 6 turned pegs, 4 turned legs, brass accents, 1930s, 55½" **$245.00**

Couch, rattan, curved back w/horizontal poles at sides, red & green highlights, repairs, 34x67", G **$200.00**

Desk, mahogany, embossed leather top, kneehole, Vanleigh NY, 1930s, 30x46x24", EX **$400.00**

Desk, mahogany, kidney shape, 5 drawers ea side, refinished, 1930s, 30x46" **$500.00**

Desk, wicker w/oak top, ornate openwork sides, white paint, 34x28x17", +32" matching chair **$395.00**

Footstool, quartersawn oak, carved paw feet, reupholstered, 22x14" **$150.00**

Highchair, spindle back, original dark finish, 1940s, EX ..**$195.00**

Hutch, china; oak, 2 single pane doors over shelf over 2 drawers over 2 doors, 2-pc, ca 1960s, 74x59x18".......... **$400.00**

Lamp, floor; chromed metal base w/frosted glass shade, 1960s, 58x12" dia, EX **$200.00**

Lamp, table; brass tripod base w/perforated metal & linen shade, 1950s, 20x15" dia, pr **$300.00**

Lamp, table; brushed aluminum base w/frosted glass shade, 1960s, 16x9" dia, EX **$100.00**

Lamp, table; dumbbell form, white lacquered metal w/tilt mercury on/off switch on Lucite ring, 1960s, 21x5" dia, VG...**$100.00**

Plant stand, oak, splayed legs, narrow apron, sm shelf, 18x18" sq **$145.00**

Plant stand, oak w/black marble top, 24½x11½" dia, EX ..**$150.00**

Rocker, golden oak, applied carvings, 7-spindle back, curved apron, caned seat, 37½" **$275.00**

Rocker, oak, pressed back, hand-tooled leather seat, 12 spindles, restored, 38" **$695.00**

Rocker, teak frame w/caned back, 1950s, 27x29x31", VG **$250.00**

Secretary, ash/poplar Country, double doors, 3 drawers, fall-front lid, paneled door, 89x42" **$525.00**

Secretary, oak, drop front, glass-fronted curio on side, refnished, 53x40x12½" **$675.00**

Sewing stand, wicker, white paint, complete w/carrying handles, ca 1930, 27½x15x11", EX **$225.00**

Shelf, knotty pine, dark stain, 10x30x7" **$30.00**

Sideboard, birch, 4 drawers & 2 doors, Heywood-Wakefield, 48", EX **$375.00**

Sideboard, maple, dovetail drawers, folding doors, 1950s, EX **$175.00**

Sideboard, quartersawn golden oak, 4 drawers, double doors, mirror back, 64x56x25" **$450.00**

Sideboard, rosewood, convex curved front, 4 sliding doors, Danish Modern, 32x79x20½" **$240.00**

Spoon rack, old dark pine, 3 shelves designed to hold 18 spoons, 14½x9¾", EX **$30.00**

Stool, shoeshine box; dark oak, ca 1930s, 15x15x11½"...**$65.00**

Table, coffee; green laminate top in limed-oak frame, 1940s, 16x36" sq, EX **$200.00**

Table, coffee; lacquered sqs form top, ebonized base, 1980s, 12½x43¼" sq, EX.. **$650.00**

Table, coffee; reverse-painted mirrored top w/5-leg wooden base w/scrolled feet, refinished, 1940s, 15x34" dia, EX.. **$500.00**

Table, coffee; triform Lucite base, clear glass top, 1970s, 16¼x35½" dia **$110.00**

Table, console; walnut top & lower shelf, tubular black enamel metal frame, 1950s, 29x60x16", EX **$150.00**

Table, console; walnut w/brass ormolu, ca 1940, 30x51x17", EX **$600.00**

Table, dining; oak, quartersawn column legs, 47x48", +3 12" leaves...**$1,495.00**

Table, dining; quarter-cut legs w/bell cups, ball feet, serpentine stretchers, 29x47½" dia **$925.00**

Table, drop-leaf; walnut, old varnish, 69", +3 10" leaves .**$1,200.00**

Table, occcasional; oak, Queen Anne-style legs w/tiger oak grain, original finish, 19½x13¾", EX..................**$125.00**

Table, side; chrome octagonal frame w/glass top, 19½x24", pr **$250.00**

Table, side; Deco-style walnut top, lacquered base, Meuller, 1930s, 26x26" dia, VG **$280.00**

Table, side; oak, scalloped top, cabriole legs, narrow apron, 17x14" sq **$195.00**

Table, side; rustic white cedar log construction, 4-leg w/stretcher, 20x18" dia **$125.00**

Table, wrought iron w/curled incised legs supporting ceramic tile top, 1950s, 19x23" sq, VG **$240.00**

Tables, nesting; white paint w/floral decal, 1950s, largest: 21x25½x19½", set of 3 ....**$45.00**

Vanity, oak, serpentine front, beveled mirror, restored/refinished, 66x34x20" **$695.00**

Washstand, yellow poplar & pine, old dark finish, 1 drawer, backsplash, shelf, 32x22x16½" **$345.00**

Games

Games from the 1870s to the 1970s and beyond are fun to collect. Many of the earlier games are beautifully lithographed. Some of their boxes were designed by well-known artists and illustrators, and many times these old games are appreciated more for their artwork than for their entertainment value. Some represent a historical event or a specific era in the social development of our country. Characters from the early days of radio, television, and movies have been featured in hundreds of games designed for children and adults alike.

If you're going to collect games, be sure that they're reasonably clean, free of water damage, and complete. Most have playing instructions printed inside the lid or on a separate piece of paper that include an inventory list. Check the contents, and remember that the condition of the box is very important too.

If you'd like to learn more about games, we recommend *Board Games of the '50s, '60s & '70s* by Stephanie Lane and *Schroeder's Collectible Toys, Antique to Modern*, published by Collector Books.

Club: Association of Game and Puzzle Collectors
PMB 321, 197 M Boston Post Road West
Marlborough, MA 01752

$10,000 Pyramid, Milton Bradley, 1972, EXIB **$15.00**

All American Skittle Score-Ball, Aurora, 1974, EXIB ...**$35.00**

Alvin & the Chipmunks Acorn Hunt, Hasbro, 1960, EXIB.**$35.00**

Annie Oakley, Game Gems/T Cohn, 1965, EXIB.......**$50.00**

Astro Launch, Ohio Art, 1963, EXIB.....................**$75.00**

Batman & Robin Target, Hasbro, 1966, MIB **$200.00**

Beverly Hillbillies, Standard Toykraft, 1963, NMIB **$50.00**

Brady Bunch, Whitman, 1973, MIB........................**$100.00**

Bullwinkle Target & Ring Toss, Parks Plastics, 1961, EXIB ..**$75.00**

Cabby, Selchow & Righter, 1950s, EXIB **$75.00**

Camp Granada, Milton Bradley, 1965, MIB **$45.00**

Charlie 'N Me Robot, Topper, 1967, EXIB **$45.00**

Chutes Away, Gabriel, 1978, EXIB **$65.00**

Clue, Parker Bros, 1949, original issue, VG (VG box)..**$50.00**

Dark Shadows, Milton Bradley, 1969, NMIB **$40.00**

Dating Game, Hasbro, 1967, EXIB **$30.00**

Dick Van Dyke, Standard Toykraft, 1964, EXIB **$75.00**

Doctor Dolittle Marble Maze, Hasbro, 1967, EXIB......**$40.00**

Don't Spill the Beans, Schaper, 1967, MIB (sealed)....**$25.00**

Dragnet, Transogram, 1955, NMIB **$65.00**

Elliot Ness & the Untouchables, Transogram, 1961, EXIB .**$65.00**

Ellsworth Elephant, Selchow & Righter, 1960, EXIB...**$50.00**

Feely Meely, Milton Bradley, 1967, EXIB....................**$30.00**

Fess Parker Target, Transogram, 1965, EXIB **$55.00**

Flintstones Target Set, Lido, 1962, EXIB **$75.00**

Flip-It 7-11, Aurora, 1973, EXIB................................**$45.00**

Frantic Frogs, Milton Bradley, 1965, EXIB **$30.00**

Game of Politics, Parker Bros, 1952, VG (VG box)....**$40.00**

Get Smart Skittle Pool, Aurora, 1972, NMIB **$55.00**

Gidget, Standard Toykraft, 1965, MIB, from $75 to ..**$100.00**

Gilligan's Island, Game Gems/T Cohn, 1965, EXIB..**$225.00**

Goofy Finds His Marbles, Whitman, 1970s, EXIB **$25.00**

Green Acres, Standart Toykraft, 1965, NMIB.............**$125.00**

Groucho's TV Quiz, Pressman, 1954, EXIB **$75.00**

Gunsmoke Target, Park Plastics, 1958, EXIB.............**$100.00**

Happy Days, Parker Bros, 1976, EXIB **$20.00**

Have Gun Will Travel, Parker Bros, 1959, EXIB **$75.00**

High Dice, Bettye-B, 1956, EXIB **$40.00**

Hollywood Squares, Ideal, 1974, EXIB **$25.00**

Hoppity Hopper, Milton Bradley, 1964, EXIB **$45.00**

Howdy Doody 3-Ring Circus, Harett-Gilmar, 1950, EXIB .**$60.00**

Huckleberry Hound Tumble Race, Transogram, 1961, EXIB...**$30.00**

Hulla Baloo Electric Teen Game, Remco, 1965, NMIB ..**$75.00**

Ironside, Ideal, 1967, EXIB **$100.00**

James Bond Secret Agent 007, Milton Bradley, 1960s, EXIB..**$30.00**

KISS on Tour, EXIB **$50.00**

Knight Rider, Parker Bros, 1983, NMIB....................**$20.00**

Kreskin's ESP, Milton Bradley, EXIB........................**$10.00**

Lavern & Shirley, MIB (sealed) **$25.00**

Let's Face It, Hasbro, 1955, EXIB **$30.00**

Limbo Legs, Milton Bradley, 1969, EXIB....................**$35.00**

Little Orphan Annie Pursuit, Selchow & Righter, 1970s, MIB **$20.00**

Little Rascals Clubhouse Bingo, Gabriel, 1958, NMIB..**$100.00**

Love Boat, Ungame, 1980, VG (VG box) **$20.00**

M*A*S*H Trivia, Golden, 1984, EXIB **$15.00**

Major Matt Mason Space Exploration, Mattel, 1967, EXIB **$75.00**

Marvel Super Heroes Strategy, Milton Bradley, 1980, EXIB . **$35.00**

Mary Hartman, Mary Hartman, Reiss, 1977, NMIB **$40.00**

Melvin the Moon Man, Remco, 1959, EXIB **$65.00**

Miami Vice, Pepper Lane, 1984, EXIB **$25.00**

Mickey Mouse Canasta Jr, Russell, 1950, EXIB **$50.00**

Milton the Monster, Milton Bradley, 1966, NMIB **$30.00**

Monday Night Baseball, Aurora, 1973, EXIB **$35.00**

Monopoly Deluxe, Parker Bros, 1964, EXIB **$45.00**

Moon Tag, Parker Bros, 1957, EXIB **$85.00**

Mr Magoo Visits the Zoo, Lowell, 1961, EXIB **$50.00**

My Favorite Martian, Transogram, 1963, VG (VG box) . **$65.00**

Nancy Drew Mystery, Parker Bros, 1957, EXIB **$90.00**

Nodding Nancy, Parker Bros, VG (VG box) **$85.00**

Official Baseball, Milton Bradley, 1966, EXIB **$100.00**

Overland Trail, Transogram, 1960, EXIB **$65.00**

Peter Pan, Transogram, 1953, EXIB **$40.00**

Peter Rabbit, Gabriel, 1946, EXIB **$75.00**

Pirates of the Caribbean, Parker Bros, 1967, EXIB **$25.00**

Poison Ivy, Ideal, 1969, VG (VG box) **$40.00**

Popeye Ball Toss, Transogram, 1966, EXIB **$65.00**

Prince Valiant, Transogram, 1955, EXIB **$45.00**

Raggedy Ann, Milton Bradley, 1974, EXIB **$20.00**

Rat Patrol Desert Combat, Transogram, 1966, NMIB .. **$125.00**

Rex Mars Space Target, Marx, 1950s, EXIB **$125.00**

Rosey the Robot, Transogram, 1962, EXIB **$85.00**

Sam Snead Tee Off, 1973, VG (VG box) **$35.00**

Scooby Doo Where Are You?, Milton Bradley, 1973, EXIB.. **$30.00**

Sea Hunt, Lowell, 1961, EXIB **$65.00**

Sharpshooter, Cadaco, 1965, EXIB **$65.00**

Shenanigans, Milton Bradley, 1964, EXIB **$50.00**

Silly Safari, Topper, 1966, EXIB **$50.00**

Snoopy & the Red Baron, Milton Bradley, 1970, MIB .. **$40.00**

Snoopy Snack Attack, Gabriel, 1980, MIB **$25.00**

Space Age, Parker Bros, 1953, EXIB **$75.00**

Space: 1999, Milton Bradley, 1976, VG (VG box) **$30.00**

Spider-Man, Milton Bradley, 1967, EXIB **$50.00**

Square Mile, Milton Bradley, 1962, EXIB **$45.00**

Starsky & Hutch Detective, Milton Bradley, 1976, MIB . **$30.00**

Sub Attack, Milton Bradley, 1965, EXIB **$35.00**

Superman Marble Maze, Hasbro, 1966, EXIB **$75.00**

Sword in the Stone, Parker Bros, 1963, EXIB **$30.00**

Tennesee Tuxedo, Transogram, 1963, EXIB **$135.00**

Thunderbirds, Waddington, 1965, EXIB **$65.00**

Tic-Tac Dough, Transogram, 1956, EXIB **$40.00**

Tin Can Alley, Ideal, 1976, EXIB **$50.00**

To Tell the Truth, Lowell, 1957, EXIB **$40.00**

Tom & Jerry, Parker Bros, 1948, EXIB **$50.00**

Top Secret, National Games, 1956, EXIB **$65.00**

Toy Town, Milton Bradley, 1962, EXIB **$50.00**

Travels of Jamie McPheeters, Ideal, 1963, EXIB **$45.00**

Truth or Consequences, Gabriel, 1955, EXIB **$35.00**

Untouchables, target game, Marx, 1960, EXIB **$200.00**

Virginian Transogram, 1962, EXIB **$85.00**

Voice of the Mummy, Milton Bradley, 1971, EXIB ... **$150.00**

Walt Disney's Adventureland, Parker Bros, 1956, EXIB .. **$40.00**

Walt Disney's Tiddly Winks, Whitman, 1963, NMIB ... **$10.00**

Wide World of Travel Game, Parker Bros, 1957, NMIB . **$35.00**

Wolfman Mystery, Hasbro, 1963, EXIB **$150.00**

Woody Woodpecker Ring Toss Game, 1958, MIB **$100.00**

World's Fair, Milton Bradley, 1964, EXIB **$40.00**

Yogi Bear & Huckleberry Hound Bowling Set, Transogram,
    1960, EXIB **$50.00**

You Don't Say, Milton Bradley, 1963, EXIB **$20.00**

Zorro, Whitman, 1965, NMIB **$50.00**

Wally Gator, board game, Transogram, EX (EX box), from $50.00 to $65.00. (Photo courtesy Bill Bruegman)

Gas Station Collectibles

Items used and/or sold by gas stations are included in this very specialized area of advertising collectibles. Those with an interest in this field tend to specialize in memorabilia from a specific gas station like Texaco or Signal. This is a very regional market, with items from small companies that are no longer in business bringing the best prices. For instance, memorabilia decorated with Gulf's distinctive 'orange ball' logo may sell more readily in Pittsburgh than in Los Angeles. Gas station giveaways like plastic gas pump salt and pepper sets and license plate attachments are gaining in popularity with collectors. If you're interested in learning more about these types of collectibles, we recommend *Gas Station Memorabilia* by B.J. Summers and Wayne Priddy, published by Collector Books.

See also Ashtrays; Automobilia.

Advisor: Scott Benjamin (See Directory Gas Station Collectibles)

Newsletter: *Petroleum Collectors Monthly*
Scott Benjamin and Wayne Henderson, Publishers
PO Box 556, LaGrange, OH 44050-0556; 440-355-6608
Subscription: $35.95 per year in US, Canada: $44.50; International: $71.95 (Samples: $5)
Website: www.pcmpublishing.com or www.oilcollectibles.com

Ashtray, Champion Spark Plugs, Sillimanite makes
    Champion..., white dish w/spark plug in center, 1920s-
    30s, 4" dia., EX **$110.00**

Bank, Shell lettered on yellow plastic shell form, 4x4x2",
    NM **$85.00**

Bank, Sinclair Power X gas pump, plastic, red & white, 4½", EX..**$50.00**

Blotter, Texaco Motor Oil, ...Saves Power & Leaves No Deposit, shows garage man w/side hood up on car & star logo, 6", M...**$110.00**

Brush, upholstery; Brush Past 'Em With Indian Gas... on wooden top, 8", EX+...**$160.00**

Calendar, En-Ar-Co & En-Ar-Co Penn Motor Oil, diecut cb boy holding up chalk board w/rope border, 1939, 8x5", NM **$30.00**

Calendar, Socony Gasoline & Motor Oil Co, 1929, pictures service man at pump w/car behind, incomplete, 22", VG+ **$325.00**

Chart, Gargoyle/Mobiloil, cloth w/metal strips, 2 sheets, recommends oil for various vehicles from 1923-26, 32x20", EX **$190.00**

Chart, gasoline prices from 1 to 20 gallons, 2-sided wooden box w/hinged lid, paper price inserts, 12x7", EX .**$200.00**

Clipboard, Shell, metal w/heavy cast clam shell logo at top, 1920s-30s, 8½x4", EX+ **$225.00**

Clock, Champion Dependable Spark Plugs, molded plastic Champion panel above round clock w/spark plug, 24x25", VG...**$50.00**

Clock, Pennzoil, lighted, numbers 12-2-4-6-8-10 & red dots around yellow oval logo, Pam, 15" dia, NM **$450.00**

Clock, Texaco, round lighted wall style w/numbers around star logo on plastic face, dome cover, 15" dia, EX+.......**$650.00**

Cookie tin, Gilmore Oil, station giveaway, lion's head encircled by Christmas holly wreath on yellow, 10" dia, EX+ **$50.00**

Credit card application display box, DX Credit Card Applications/But Modern!..., black & red on white, 9x6x2", NM **$50.00**

Customer record box, Mobil Lubrication, red metal recipe type w/white label on top, flying horse logo, 10x9x7", EX..**$30.00**

Display, Bowes 'Seal-Fast' Auto Lamps, metal w/reverse-painted glass front, lights up, 12x8x5", VG+ **$375.00**

Display rack, Shell, metal fold-out type w/9 product display holes, top handle, yellow name on red enamel, 28x16x17", EX...**$135.00**

Display rack, Sinclair Auto Specialties, wire rack w/white-on-red tin sign, 3-tiered, coiled top handle, 34x18x15", VG+ **$50.00**

Display rack, Texaco/Products for Car & Home, sign atop 4-footed pole w/3 metal wire baskets, 47", EX+ ...**$130.00**

Fan, Shell Products/Shell Petroleum Corp, diecut shell shape w/tropical beach scene on wooden stick, 14x8", VG+ **$40.00**

First aid kit, Flying Red Horse/Mobilgas-Mobiloil, red, white & blue tin litho, late 1940s, EX+...........................**$85.00**

Glassware set, Fisk Tires Starter Set/Styled by Libbey, set of 4 in original carton, ea w/different saying, 5", EX......**$40.00**

Globe, Flying A Gasoline, red logo w/black trim on round white lenses, white gill body, NM+....................**$600.00**

Globe, Pioneer, round w/red script lettering on white lens w/high profile black body, 15", G+ **$120.00**

Globe, Sinclair Dino, plastic body with two lenses, 13½" diameter, EX, $190.00. (Photo courtesy Collectors Auction Service)

Globe, Standard Oil white crown form, 1-pc w/screw neck, 16½", NM+ **$600.00**

Globe, TP Ethyl Gasoline, round w/yellow, black & white Ethyl logo in center of red TP logo on white, 1930s-40s, 15", EX+..**$2,300.00**

Grease bucket, Diamond Grease/Half Bushel/30 Lbs Net Weight painted label on side of galvanized bucket w/bail handle, EX **$40.00**

Grease can, Monogram Oils & Lubricants/Stand Up!/No 2 Cup Grease, 5-lb, pry lid, bail handle, black, white & red, VG+ **$150.00**

Grease can, Sinclair Axle Grease, 1-lb, green & white w/vertically striped background, slip lid, 2½x4½" dia, VG..**$50.00**

Hat, attendant's; Hancock, stitched cloth logo on tan canvas w/black visor, VG+..**$100.00**

Hat, attendant's; Sunset Ethyl Gasoline/Sunset Oil Company advertising on yellow cloth 'garrison' style, NM+ ..**$225.00**

Map holder, Marathon, Ask About Our Free Travel Bureau Service, metal wall-mount, 4 rows, 1950s-60s, 20x11x2", VG...**$275.00**

Map holder, Texaco Touring Service, green metal wall-mount box w/You're Welcome below red emblem, 9x4x2", VG+ **$70.00**

Mileage chart, Texaco, Tour w/Texaco in all 48 States, board w/wood scroll posts & paper roll chart, 6x13x½", EX.**$100.00**

Oil bottle, Gargoyle Mobiloil BB, 1-qt, 4-sided embossed clear glass w/metal screw-on funnel pour spout, 14", EX...**$300.00**

Oil bottle, Standard Oil, 1-qt, clear glass w/embossed logo, 15", EX **$50.00**

Oil bottle, Standard/Polarine, 1-qt, 2 painted labels on clear glass, w/metal funnel scew-on pour spout, 16", EX.**$75.00**

Oil bottle, 1-qt clear glass w/The Master lid, fitted wire pouring holder, 14", EX..**$120.00**

Oil bottles w/rack, 8 various 1-qt clear glass bottles in wire rack w/center open-diamond handle, 13x18x9", EX.......**$620.00**

Oil can, Air Speed Reconditioned Motor Oil, 1-qt, orange on yellow, image of plane in flight, rare, NM **$775.00**

Oil can, Conoco Motor Oil (Heavy), 1-gal, 2 top corner spouts & handle, yellow, w/logo, 11", VG.........**$800.00**

Oil can, Gargoyle Mobiloil BB (Heavy), 1-qt, top spout w/original foil seal w/Gargoyle, paper label, 7½", EX.........**$200.00**

Oil can, Gargoyle Mobiloil Arctic/Light Medium Body, 1-qt, sq w/pour spout, paper label, 1891 copyright, 7½", EX **$210.00**

Oil can, Hi-Val-Ue Motor Oil, 1-qt, orange & black on silver w/oil derrick, plane & truck, EX $165.00

Oil can, Mohawk Chiefton Motor Oil, 1-qt, white w/blue & orange, EX...$110.00

Oil can, Mohawk Petroleum Co/Mohawk Motor Oil, 1-qt, white & black on red, VG..................................$300.00

Oil can, Old Dutch Lubricant, 5-qt, round w/spout & bail handle on dome top, white & 2-tone blue, VG .$210.00

Oil can, Oneida Motor Oil, 1-gal, round w/top spout & fold-down handle, blue & white on yellow, 9½", EX.$175.00

Oil can, Penn Seal 100% Pennsylvania Motor Oil (30¢), 1-qt, orange & blue w/white trim, 1930s, NM $75.00

Oil can, Red Indian Motor Oil, 1-gal, round, white, red & black, VG+ $160.00

Oil can, Shell Motor Oil, 1-gal, top spout & handle, yellow front w/yellow & red checked sides, Shell logo, 11", VG $500.00

Oil can, Texaco Home Lubricant, oval w/top center needle-like pour spout, white label & star logo on green, 5", NM $650.00

Oil can, Tiopet Motor Oil, 5-qt, red, white & blue, 11x4x6½", EX $625.00

Oil rack, Socony Upperlube Oil, 4-legged rack w/embossed tin sign, red, white & black, 40x18x3", VG $210.00

Oil rack, Sunoco Motor Oil/Mercury Made, porcelain & wood footed 2-step stand w/wire bottle holder atop, 23x22x19", EX...$1,000.00

Pencil case, Texaco Fire Chief, red plastic gas pump form w/labels, hinged lid, rubber pump hose on side, Hasbro, EX+ $180.00

Pump, Atlantic White Flash, restored, 80", EX, $850.00. (Photo courtesy Collectors Auction Service)

Salt & pepper shakers, Shell TCP gas pumps, plastic, red & yellow, 3", NM, pr $100.00

Sign, Amoco, diecut metal oval torch emblem, red, white & blue, 36x44", VG+...$90.00

Sign, Conoco, diecut porcelain inverted triangle emblem pump sign, blue & white, 9x10", EX+ $165.00

Sign, Gargoyle Mobiloil 35¢ a Quart From Bulk/Vacuum Oil Co, embossed tin, orange & black on white, w/logo, 18x14", EX..$235.00

Sign, Grizzly Gasoline/Dubbs Cracked/Perfect Performance/ Watch Your Miles, lg bear, 2-sided tin, arched top, 36", G+...$2,050.00

Sign, Ladies/Gentlemen restroom signs, Shell, porcelain w/cut-out corners, red on orange w/red border, 2x10", VG/NM, pr...$250.00

Sign, Red Crown Gasoline, diecut porcelain pump sign w/crown atop rectangular panel, red on yellow, 14x12", NM+ $1,600.00

Sign, Sohio High Test Anti-Knock Ethel Gasoline, metal side-walk sign on pedestal stand, white & black on red, 54", EX $1,950.00

Sign, Standard Oil Products, white-on-blue porcelain 2-sided sidewalk sign w/red pedestal frame & stand, 67", VG+..$425.00

Sign, Standard Red Crown Gasoline/Starts Your Car 'Just Like That!,' cardboard, red & black on white, 12x42", G+..$30.00

Sign, Sunoco Winter Oil & Transep/For Quicker Start!, paper, shows Mickey Mouse as pilgrim shooting at turkey, 29", EX $750.00

Sign, Texaco porcelain star, red, for 1950s-60s station, 16x15x2", NM..$200.00

Sign, Veedol Motor Oil 100% Pennsylvania Supreme Quality 30¢ a Qt, embossed tin, orange & white on black, 9x9", VG+..$350.00

Soap dispenser, Atlantic Refining Co, metal w/impressed logo, wall mount, 6", G+.............................$50.00

Soap dispenser, chrome-plated metal cylinder w/plastic window, 9", VG+...$70.00

Thermometer, Atlas Wiper Blades, half-dial type in rectangular metal box w/wire hanger, 8x14", VG $100.00

Thermometer, Champion/World's No 1 Seller, plastic spark plug shape, 21x8", VG+ $20.00

Thermometer, Fleet-Wing Petroleum Products, embossed tin, yellow, curved top, 6½x2", NMIB $75.00

Thermometer, Shellzone Anti-Freeze/Permanent Type, tin, yellow on red, yellow Shell logo below, curved ends, 17", EX...$375.00

Tie clip, Sunoco diamond emblem, blue enameled lettering & line trim on gold-tone metal, W&H Co on back, 1x2", VG+..$25.00

Uniform, Texaco, green cloth w/short sleeves, hexagonal pocket patch, VG..$40.00

Wind sock, Texaco, red vinyl w/white lettering & star logo, 142x36" dia, EX...$360.00

Gay Fad Glassware

What started out as a home-based 'one-woman' operation in the late 1930s within only a few years had grown into a substantial company requiring much larger facilities and a staff of decorators. The company, dubbed Gay Fad by her husband, was founded by Fran Taylor. Originally they decorated kitchenware items but later found instant success with the glassware they created, most of which utilized frosted backgrounds and multicolored designs such as tulips, state themes, and Christmas motifs. Some pieces were decorated with 22-karat gold and sterling silver. In addition to the frosted glass which collectors quickly learn to associate with this company, they also became famous for their 'bentware' — quirky cocktail glasses whose stems were actually bent.

Some of their more collectible lines are Beau Brummel — martini glasses with straight or bent stems featuring a funny-faced drinker wearing a plaid bow tie; Gay Nineties — various designs such as can-can girls and singing bartenders; 48 States — maps with highlighted places of interest; Rich Man, Poor Man (or Beggar Man, Thief, etc.); Bartender (self-explanatory); Currier & Ives — made to coordinate with the line by Royal China; Zombies — extra tall and slim with various designs including roses, giraffes, and flamingos; and the sterling silver- and 22-karat gold-trimmed glassware.

Until you learn to spot it a mile away (which you soon will), look for an interlocking 'G' and 'F' or 'Gay Fad,' the latter mark indicating pieces from the late 1950s to the early 1960s. The glassware itself has the feel of satin and is of very good quality. It can be distinguished from other manufacturers' wares simply by checking the bottom — Gay Fad's are frosted; generally other manufacturers' are not. Hand-painted details are another good clue. (You may find similar glassware signed 'Briard'; this is not Gay Fad.) Listings below include Fire-King and Federal Glass pieces that were decorated by Gay Fad.

This Ohio-based company was sold in 1963 and closed altogether in 1965. Be careful of condition. If the frosting has darkened or the paint is worn or faded, it's best to wait for a better example.

Advisor: Donna S. McGrady (See the Directory, Gay Fad)

Ashtray, Trout Flies, clear...**$8.00**
Batter bowl, Fruits, milk white, signed w/F (Federal Glass), handled..**$55.00**
Bent tray, Phoenix Bird, clear, signed Gay Fad, 13¾" dia .**$17.00**
Bent tray, Stylized Cats, clear, signed Gay Fad, 11½" dia...**$24.00**
Bent trays, classic design, paper label, 2 sq trays in metal frame..**$22.00**
Beverage set, Apple, frosted, 86-oz ball pitcher & 6 13-oz round bottom tumblers **$145.00**
Beverage set, Colonial Homestead, frosted, 85-oz pitcher & 6 12-oz tumblers...**$72.00**
Beverage set, Magnolia, clear, 86-oz pitcher & 6 13-oz tumblers **$75.00**
Bowl, chili; Fruits, 2¼x5"...**$14.00**
Bowl, mixing; Poinsettia, red w/green leaves on Fire-King Ivory Swirl, 8"...**$45.00**
Bowl, splash-proof; Fruits, Fire-King, 4¼x6½"............**$55.00**
Bowls, nesting; Fruits, Fire-King, 6", 7½", 8¾", set of 3 .**$45.00**
Canister set, Red Rose, red lids, white interior, 3-pc ..**$60.00**
Casserole, Apple, open, oval, Fire-King Ivory, 1-qt **$45.00**

Casserole, Apple, w/lid, Fire-King Ivory, 1-qt **$65.00**
Casserole, Fruits, divided, oval, Fire King, 11¾".........**$40.00**
Casserole, Fruits, w/lid, Fire-King, 1-qt.......................**$35.00**
Casserole, Peach Blossom, w/au gratin lid, Fire-King, 2-qt...**$35.00**
Casserole, Rosemaling (tulips) on lid, clear, 2-qt, w/black wire rack...**$30.00**
Chip n' Dip, Horace the Horse w/cart, knife tail, 3 bowls, double old-fashion glass as head, signed Gay Fad..**$60.00**
Cocktail set, Poodle, metal frame 'body' w/martini mixer, double old-fashion glass as head & 4 5-oz glasses, signed Gay Fad...**$58.00**
Cocktail shaker, Ballerina Shoes, red metal screw-top lid, frosted, 32-oz, 7"...**$20.00**
Cocktail shaker, full-figure ballerina, frosted, 28-oz, 9"..**$35.00**
Cruet set, Oil & Vinegar, Cherry, clear.....................**$17.00**
Decanter set, Gay '90s, Scotch, Rye, Gin & Bourbon, frosted or white inside **$85.00**
Goblet, Bow Pete, Hoffman Beer, 16-oz.....................**$15.00**
Ice tub, Gay '90s, frosted **$21.00**
Juice set, Tommy Tomato, frosted, 36-oz pitcher & 6 4-oz tumblers..**$47.50**
Loaf pan, Apple, Fire-King Ivory.................................**$35.00**
Luncheon set, Fantasia Hawaiian Flower, 1 place setting (sq plate, cup & saucer)...**$15.00**
Luncheon set, Ivy, sq plate, cup & saucer, tumbler, clear, 1 complete place setting, 4-pc....................................**$24.00**
Martini mixer, 'A Jug of Wine...,' w/glass stirring rod, clear, signed Gay Fad, 10⅝" **$18.00**
Mix-A-Salad set, Ivy, 22-oz shaker w/plastic top, garlic press, measuring spoon, recipe book, MIB....................**$70.00**
Mug, Fruits, stackable, Fire-King, 3"............................**$12.00**
Mug, Notre Dame, frosted, 16-oz **$15.00**
Mug set, Here's How in a different language on ea mug, frosted, 12-pc...**$68.00**
Pilsner set, Gay 90s, portraits: Mama, Papa, Victoria, Rupert, Aunt Aggie, Uncle Bertie, Gramps & Horace, frosted, 8-pc..**$80.00**

Pitcher, Currier & Ives, $60.00. (Photo courtesy Donna McGrady)

Pitcher, juice; Ada Orange, frosted, 36-oz **$22.00**

Pitcher, martini; cardinal & pine sprig, frosted, w/glass stirrer, 42-oz **$35.00**

Pitcher, Rosemaling (tulips), white inside, 32-oz **$28.00**

Plate, Fruits, lace edge, Hazel Atlas, 8½" **$17.50**

Punch set, pink veiling, bowl & 8 cups in white metal frame...**$65.00**

Range set, Rooster, salt, pepper, sugar & flour shakers, frosted w/red metal lids, 8-oz, 4-pc **$120.00**

Refrigerator container, Distlefink on white, Fire-King, w/lid, 4x8" **$50.00**

Salad set, Fruits, frosted, lg bowl, 2 cruets, salt & pepper shakers, 5-pc **$50.00**

Salad set, Outlined Fruits, lg bowl, 2 cruets, salt & pepper shakers, frosted, 5-pc..**$65.00**

Salt & pepper shakers, Morning Glory, frosted w/red plastic tops, pr **$16.00**

Stem, bent cocktail, Beau Brummel, clear, signed Gay Fad, 3½-oz **$12.00**

Stem, bent cocktail, Souvenir of My Bender, frosted, 3-oz ..**$11.00**

Tea & toast, Magnolia, sq plate w/cup indent & cup, clear **$14.00**

Tom & Jerry set, Christmas bells, milk white, marked GF, bowl & 6 cups...**$70.00**

Tumbler, Bob White, brown, turquoise & gold on clear, signed Gay Fad, 10-oz...**$12.00**

Tumbler, Christmas Greetings From Gay Fad, frosted, 4-oz ..**$17.00**

Tumbler, Hors D'oeuvres, clear, 14-oz **$10.00**

Tumbler, Kentucky state map (1 of 48), pink, yellow or lime, frosted, marked GF, 10-oz **$6.00**

Tumbler, Oregon state map on pink picket fence, clear, marked GF..**$6.00**

Tumbler, Pegasus, gold & pink on black, 12-oz **$10.00**

Tumbler, Say When, frosted, 4-oz **$8.00**

Tumbler, Zombie, flamingo, frosted, marked GF, 14-oz .**$18.00**

Tumbler, Zombie, giraffe, frosted, marked GF, 14-oz .**$16.00**

Tumbler, 1948 Derby Winner Citation, frosted, 14-oz **$50.00**

Tumblers, angels preparing for Christmas, frosted, 12-oz, set of 8...**$72.00**

Tumblers, Dickens Christmas Carol characters, frosted, 12-oz, set of 8..**$50.00**

Tumblers, Famous Fighters (John L Sullivan & the others), frosted, 16-oz, 8-pc set **$85.00**

Tumblers, French Poodle, clear, 17-oz, set of 8 in original box **$96.00**

Tumblers, Game Birds & Animals, clear, 12-oz, 8-pc set, MIB **$65.00**

Tumblers, Ohio Presidents, frosted, 12-oz, set of 8 ....**$55.00**

Tumblers, Rich Man, Poor Man (nursery rhyme), frosted, marked GF, 16-oz, set of 8......................................**$80.00**

Tumblers, Sports Cars, white interior, 12-oz, 8-pc set...**$45.00**

Vanity set, butterflies in meadow, pink inside, 5-pc...**$60.00**

Vase, Red Poppy, clear, footed, 10" **$24.00**

Waffle set, Blue Willow, 48-oz waffle batter jug & 11½-oz syrup jug, frosted, pr **$95.00**

Waffle set, Little Black Sambo, frosted, 48-oz waffle batter jug, 11½-oz syrup jug..**$275.00**

Waffle set, Peach Blossoms, 48-oz waffle batter jug & 11½-oz syrup jug, frosted, pr **$40.00**

Waffle set, Red Poppy, frosted, 48-oz waffle batter jug, 11½-oz syrup jug **$24.00**

Wine set, Grapes, decanter & 4 2½-oz stemmed wines, clear, 5-pc **$40.00**

Geisha Girl China

The late nineteenth century saw a rise in the popularity of Oriental wares in the US and Europe. Japan rose to meet the demands of this flourishing ceramics marketplace with a flurry of growth in potteries and decorating centers. These created items for export which would appeal to Western tastes and integrate into Western dining and decorating cultures, which were distinct from those of Japan. One example of the wares introduced into this marketplace was Geisha Girl porcelain.

Hundreds of different patterns and manufacturers' marks have been uncovered on Geisha Girl porcelain tea and dinnerware sets, dresser accessories, decorative items, etc., which were produced well into the twentieth century. They all share in common colorful decorations featuring kimono-clad ladies and children involved in everyday activities. These scenes are set against a backdrop of lush flora, distinctive Japanese architecture, and majestic landscapes. Most Geisha Girl porcelain designs were laid on by means of a stencil, generally red or black. This appears as an outline on the ceramic body. Details are then completed by hand-painted washes in a myriad of colors. A minority of the wares were wholly hand painted.

Most Geisha Girl porcelain has a colorful border or edging with handles, finials, spouts, and feet similarly adorned. The most common border color is red which can range from orange to red-orange to a deep brick red. Among the earliest border colors were red, maroon, cobalt blue, light (apple) green, and Nile green. Pine green, blue-green, and turquoise made their appearance circa 1917, and a light cobalt or Delft blue appeared around 1920. Other colors (e.g. tan, yellow, brown, and gold) can also be found. Borders were often enhanced with gilded lace or floral decoration. The use of gold for this purpose diminished somewhat around 1910 to 1915 when some decorators used economic initiative (fewer firings required) to move the gold to just inside the border or replace the gold with white or yellow enamels. Wares with both border styles continued to be produced into the twentieth century. Exquisite examples with multicolor borders as well as ornate rims decorated with florals and geometrics can also be found.

Due to the number of different producers, the quality of Geisha ware ranges from crude to finely detailed. Geisha Girl porcelain was sold in sets and open stock in outlets ranging from the five-and-ten to fancy department stores. It was creatively used for store premiums, containers for store products, fair souvenirs, and resort memorabilia. The fineness of detailing, amount of gold highlights, border color, scarcity of form and, of course, condition all play a role in establishing the market value of a given item. Some patterns are scarcer than others, but most Geisha ware collectors seem not to focus on particular patterns.

The heyday of Geisha Girl porcelain was from 1910 through the 1930s. Production continued until the World War II era. During the 'Occupied' period, a small amount of wholly hand-painted examples were made, often with a black and gold border. The Oriental import stores and catalogs from the 1960s and 1970s featured some examples of Geisha Girl porcelain, many of which were produced in Hong Kong. These are recognized by the very white porcelain, sparse detail coloring, and lack of gold decoration. The 1990s has seen a resurgence of reproductions with a faux Nippon mark. These items are supposed to represent high quality Geisha ware, but in reality they are a blur of Geisha and Satsuma-style characteristics. They are too busy in design, too heavily enameled, and bear a variety of faux Nippon marks. Once you've been introduced to a few of these reproductions, you'll be able to recognize them easily.

Note: Colors mentioned in the following listings refer to borders.

Advisor: Elyce Litts (See Directory, Geisha Girl China)

Master nut bowl, Basket A, apple green, footed, 6", $25.00. (Photo courtesy Elyce Litts)

Ashtray, Temple A, spade-shape, multicolor $25.00
Biscuit jar, leaving the Teahouse, fluted, bulbous, red w/gold $45.00
Bonbon dish, Battledore, mum shaped, olive green ..$22.00
Bowl, berry; Oni Dance A, 9-lobed, scalloped, red-orange w/gold, individual..$12.00
Bowl, salad; Garden Bench A, 9-lobed, red, 7¼" $25.00
Butter pat, Basket of Mums B, red-orange w/gold, 3¼"..$10.00
Cocoa pot, Temple A, multicolor border, Nippon $125.00
Cracker jar, Checkerboard, cobalt, 3-footed $85.00
Cracker jar, Spider Puppet, footed, lobed, cobalt w/gold ..$65.00
Creamer, Porch, red-orange, modern $10.00

Cup & saucer, after dinner; Basket B, dark apple green w/gold, straight sides $16.00
Cup & saucer, tea; Bamboo Trellis, dark green $15.00
Gravy boat & underplate, Rice Harvesters, leaf shape w/gold...$32.00
Hatpin holder, Long-Stemmed Peony, ribbed hourglass form, cobalt w/gold...$45.00
Nappy, Mother & Daughter, lobed, gold lacing, fan-shaped reserves...$30.00
Relish dish, Picnic A, multicolor border, wholly hand-painted...$30.00
Ring tree, Garden Bench Q, gold hand on decorated base..$55.00
Salt & pepper shaker, Dressing, red, pr......................$20.00
Toothbrush holder, Flute, red-orange, 4"....................$28.00

GI Joe

The first GI Joe was introduced by Hasbro in 1964. He was 12" tall, and you could buy him with blond, auburn, black, or brown hair in four basic variations: Action Sailor, Action Marine, Action Soldier, and Action Pilot. There was also a Black doll as well as representatives of many other nations. By 1967 GI Joe could talk, all the better to converse with the female nurse who was first issued that year. The Adventure Team series (1970 – 1976) included Black Adventurer, Talking Astronaut, Sea Adventurer, Talking Team Commander, Land Adventurer, and several variations. At this point, their hands were made of rubber, making it easier for them to grasp the many guns, tools, and other accessories that Hasbro had devised. Playsets, vehicles, and clothing completed the package, and there were kid-size items designed specifically for the kids themselves. The 12" dolls were discontinued by 1976.

Brought out by popular demand, Hasbro's 3¾" GI Joes hit the market in 1982. Needless to say, they were very well accepted. In fact, these smaller GI Joes are thought to be the most successful line of action figures ever made. Loose figures (those removed from the original packaging) are very common, and even if you can locate the accessories that they came out with, most are worth only about $3.00 to $10.00. It's the mint-in-package items that most interest collectors, and they pay a huge premium for the package. There's an extensive line of accessories that goes with the smaller line as well. Many more are listed in *Schroeder's Collectible Toys, Antique to Modern* published by Collector Books.

Note: A/M was used in the description lines as an abbreviation for Action Man.

12" Figures and Accessories

Accessory, Action Marine Communications Post Poncho Set, #7701, MIP...$175.00
Accessory, Adventure Team Aerial Recon, MIP..........$50.00
Accessory, Adventure Team Diving Helmet, EX $14.00

Accessory, Adventure Team Face Mask, red, EX $20.00
Accessory, Adventure Team Flight Suit, orange, EX ...$25.00
Accessory, Adventure Team Training Tower, complete, EX.$125.00
Accessory, Air Force Dress Tunic, VG $25.00
Accessory, Astronaut Booties, EX...........................$15.00
Accessory, Binoculars, red w/string, EX $14.00
Accessory, British Helmet, EX.................................$18.00
Accessory, Crash Crew Jacket, silver, EX $28.00
Accessory, Deck Commander Set, #7621, MIP $125.00
Accessory, Japanese Helmet, EX..............................$28.00
Accessory, Marine Medic Set, MIP...........................$150.00
Accessory, Rocket Firing Bazooka, MIP.....................$70.00
Accessory, Russian Medal, A/M, EX $10.00
Accessory, Scramble Crash Helmet, #7810, MIP.........$50.00
Accessory, Scramble Parachute Pack, #7811, MIP.......$45.00
Accessory, Scramble Pilot Jumper, EX $80.00
Figure, Action Marine, 30th Anniversary, 1994, NRFB ...$80.00
Figure, Action Pilot, complete, NM (EX+ box).........$400.00
Figure, Action Pilot, 30th Anniversary, 1994, NRFB..$100.00
Figure, Adventure Team Air Adventurer, complete, NM (EX
   box) $325.00
Figure, Adventure Team Eagle Eye Land Commander, mov-
   ing eyes, MIP $100.00
Figure, Adventure Team Mike Power Atomic Man, MIP..$150.00
Figure, Adventure Team Smoke Jumper, complete, EX ...$175.00
Figure, Australian Jungle Fighter, complete, EX........$265.00
Figure, Bullet Man, complete, NM $300.00
Figure, Crash Crew Fire Fighter, complete, NM $475.00
Figure, Danger of the Depths, complete, M.............$500.00
Figure, Fight for Survival w/Polar Explorer, complete,
   NMIB..$325.00
Figure, Fighter Pilot, complete, EX $425.00
Figure, German Stormtrooper, complete, VG...........$350.00
Figure, Green Beret, complete, M.............................$500.00
Figure, Hidden Missile Discover w/Spaceman, complete,
   NMIB..$200.00
Figure, Man of Action, Kung Fu hands, complete, MIB .$325.00
Figure, Marine Beachhead Assault, complete, EX.....$250.00
Figure, Marine Demolition, complete, NM $300.00
Figure, Mountain Troops, complete, VG $165.00
Figure, Mouth of Doom w/Jungle Explorer, complete,
   NMIB..$275.00
Figure, Russian Soldier, complete, NM $550.00
Figure, Smoke Jumper, complete, M.........................$375.00
Figure, West Point Cadet, complete, EX $265.00
Figure, World War I Aviator, mail-in, MIB..................$60.00
Vehicle, Adventure Team Big Trapper, EX $60.00
Vehicle, Adventure Team Sandstorm Jeep, green, EXIB ..$275.00
Vehicle, British Armored Car, Irwin, EX...................$275.00
Vehicle, Fire Engine, A/M, MIP................................$75.00
Vehicle, Iron Knight Tank, EX $135.00

3¾" Figures and Accessories

Accessory, Ammo Dump Unit, 1985, EX (EX pkg) $20.00
Accessory, Cobra Emperor w/Air Chariot, 1986, NRFB .$60.00
Accessory, Crusader Space Shuttle, 1988, NRFB $175.00

Accessory, Free Fall, 1990, NMOC $18.00
Accessory, GI Joe Combat Infantry, Hasbro, NMIB $75.00
Accessory, Jet Pack Jump & Platform, 1982, MIP (Canadian).$50.00
Accessory, Mauler MBT Tank, 1985, NRFB................$80.00
Accessory, Missile Defense Unit, 1984, MIP $20.00
Accessory, Mobile Missile System, complete, EX $45.00
Accessory, Mountain Howitzer, 1984, w/accessories, EX $8.00
Accessory, Q-Force Battle Gear, Action Force, MIP $5.00
Accessory, Skyhawk, complete, EX (G box) $18.00
Accessory, Tiger Cat w/Frostbite, 1988, complete, EX..$20.00
Figure, Annihilator, 1989, NMOC............................$20.00
Figure, Armadillo, 1988, w/accessories, NM $14.00
Figure, Backblast, 1988, NMOC................................$20.00
Figure, Barbecue, 1985, EX (EX card)........................$50.00
Figure, Barricade, w/accessories, NM $14.00
Figure, Blizzard, 1988, NMOC..................................$18.00
Figure, Budo, 1988, EX (EX card) $20.00
Figure, Charbroil, 1988, red eyes, MOC....................$15.00
Figure, Chuckles, 1987, MOC $26.00
Figure, Cobra Commander, 1983, MIP $125.00
Figure, Cobra Soldier, 1983, MIP $60.00
Figure, Croc Master, 1987, EX (EX card)....................$30.00
Figure, D-Day, 1995, MOC...$8.00
Figure, Dial-Tone, 1986, EX (EX card) $22.00
Figure, Dr Mindbender, 1986, EX (EX card)...............$20.00
Figure, Eco War Cesspool, w/accessories, EX $10.00
Figure, Eels, 1985, MOC...$55.00
Figure, Ferret, 1988, w/accessories, EX......................$8.00
Figure, Frostbite, 1985, w/accessories, NM................$12.00
Figure, Ghostrider, 1988, w/accessories, NM.............$12.00
Figure, Gung-Ho, w/accessories, NM.........................$12.00
Figure, Hydro-Viper, 1988, NMOC $25.00
Figure, Iceberg, 1986, NMOC...................................$20.00
Figure, Joe Colton, 1994 mail-in, w/accessories, M $15.00
Figure, Low-Light, 1986, NMOC $25.00
Figure, Maverick, 1988, MOC....................................$30.00
Figure, Mega Marine Blast-Off, 1993, MOC $18.00
Figure, Metal-Head, 1990, MOC................................$15.00
Figure, Night Creeper, w/accessories, VG $12.00
Figure, Recoil, 1989, MOC.......................................$15.00
Figure, Road Pig, 1988, MOC...................................$20.00
Figure, Sneak Peek, 1987, EX (EX card).....................$18.00
Figure, Tele-Viper, 1985, MOC..................................$42.00
Figure, Wild Bill, 1992, MOC....................................$14.00
Figure, Zap, 1982, straight arm, NMOC $100.00

Gilner

Gilner was a California company that operated in Culver City from the mid-1930s until 1957. They produced florist ware, figurines, and other types of decorative pottery. Their pixie line is very popular with today's collectors.

Cookie jar, brown bear sitting, 13"............................$35.00
Dish, leaf shape, brown w/brown native sitting, 3¾x8"..$30.00
Dish, leaf shape w/pixie in chartreuse sitting on edge, 6½"...$30.00

Figurine, pixie in blue doing splits touching toes.......**$35.00**

Figurine, pixie in green, seated w/knees up, left arm on knee w/hand to face, right arm resting on knee, 2x2x2".**$23.00**

Figurine, pixie in green, seated w/legs apart, knees up & hands on knees, 2½"......................................**$27.50**

Figurine, pixie in green holding sign behind him that reads I Love You, 2½".................................**$30.00**

Figurine, pixie in maroon, seated by stump, 2¾".......**$20.00**

Figurine, pixie in maroon, seated holding knees to chest, 2½"..**$23.00**

Figurine, pixie in red, on knees w/arms out, 2⅝"......**$30.00**

Figurine, pixie in red, reclining w/elbow on ground w/head in hand, 2x4½"...**$25.00**

Figurine, pixie standing on leaf, 4", $50.00.

Planter, Native Village hut, 6½x5¾".............................**$55.00**

Planter, red pixies kneel & kiss on chartreuse stump, 3½x5"...**$35.00**

Salt & pepper shakers, chartreuse Merry Maid & red Happy People pixies, pr...**$35.00**

Shelf sitter, pixie in green **$30.00**

Vase, bud; female pixie in chartreuse kneeling against stump, 6x6"...**$40.00**

Vase, bud; male pixie on stump, 7½x5" **$45.00**

Wall pocket, clock w/2 pixies kissing, 7x5½x4¼"......**$45.00**

Wall pocket, pixie in banana bunch, 7½" W..............**$35.00**

Wall pocket, pixie on grapes, 5¾x5" **$60.00**

Wall pocket, pixie on strawberry, 5¾x5"....................**$45.00**

Wall pocket, red strawberry w/green leaves, 5½x3½"..**$20.00**

Glass Knives

Popular during the Depression years, glass knives were made in many of the same colors as the glass dinnerware of the era — pink, green, light blue, crystal, and more rarely, amber or white (originally called opal). Some were hand painted with flowers or fruit. The earliest boxes had poems printed on their tops explaining the knife's qualities in the pre-stainless steel days: 'No metal to tarnish when cutting your fruit, and so it is certain this glass knife will suit.' Eventually, a tissue flyer was packed with each knife, which elaborated even more on the knife's usefulness. 'It is keen as a razor, ideal for slicing tomatoes, oranges, lemons, grapefruit, and especially constructed for separating the meaty parts of grapefruit from its rind...' Boxes add interest by helping identify distributors as well as commercial names of the knives.

When originally sold, the blades were ground to a sharp cutting edge, but due to everyday usage, the blades eventually became nicked. Collectors will accept reground, resharpened blades as long as the original shape has been maintained.

Documented US glass companies that made glass knives are the Akro Agate Co., Cameron Glass Corp., Houze Glass Corp., Imperial Glass Corp., Jeannette Glass Co., and Westmoreland Glass Co.

Internet final-bid auction prices indicate what a person is willing to pay to add a new or different piece to a personal collection and may not necessarily reflect any price guide values.

Aer-Flo, amber, 7½"...**$300.00**

Aer-Flo, crystal, 7½"...**$40.00**

Aer-Flo, green, 7½"...**$85.00**

Aer-Flo, pink, 7½"...**$90.00**

Block, crystal, 8¼"...**$25.00**

Buffalo Knife Co, green, 9¼"..**$60.00**

Candlewick, crystal, 8½" **$400.00**

Dagger, crystal, 9¼"..**$150.00**

Dur-X (3-leaf), blue, 8½-9", ea **$45.00**

Dur-X (3-leaf), pink, 8½-9"..**$40.00**

Dur-X (5-leaf), green, 8½"...**$45.00**

Pinwheel, crystal...**$12.00**

Plain handle, crystal, 8½"..**$15.00**

Plain handle, green, 8½"..**$35.00**

Steelite, crystal, 8½"...**$35.00**

Steelite, pink, 8½"...**$75.00**

Stonex, amber, 8½", $250.00. (Photo courtesy Michele A. Rosewitz)

Stonex, green, 8½" **$80.00**

Stonex, opal, 8½" **$350.00**

Vitex (Star & Diamond), blue, 8½-9", ea **$30.00**

Vitex (Star & Diamond), pink, 8½-9", ea....................**$30.00**

3 Star, blue, 8½"...**$35.00**

Golden Foliage

In 1935 Libbey Glass was purchased by Owens-Illinois but continued to operate under the Libbey Glass name. After

World War II, the company turned to making tableware and still does today. Golden Foliage is just one of the many patterns made during the 1950s. It is a line of crystal glassware with a satin band that features a golden maple leaf as well as other varieties. The satin band is trimmed in gold, above and below. Since this gold seems to have easily worn off, be careful to find mint pieces for your collection. This pattern was made in silver as well.

Advisor: Debbie Coe (See Directory, Cape Cod)

Creamer & sugar bowl **$15.00**
Drink set, includes 6 jiggers & brass-finished caddy ..**$49.00**
Drink set, includes 8 tumblers (9-oz), ice tub & brass-finished
    caddy **$75.00**
Drink set, includes 8 tumblers (9-oz) & brass-finished
    caddy **$48.00**
Goblet, cocktail; 4-oz..**$6.50**
Goblet, cordial; 1-oz **$9.50**
Goblet, pilsner; 11-oz **$10.00**
Goblet, sherbet; 6½-oz..**$5.00**
Goblet, water; 9-oz **$7.50**
Ice tub, in metal 3-footed frame................................**$22.50**

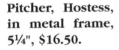

Pitcher, Hostess, in metal frame, 5¼", $16.50.

Salad dressing set, includes 3 bowls (4") & brass-finished
    caddy **$19.50**
Tumbler, beverage; 12½-oz..**$9.50**
Tumbler, cooler; 14-oz..**$9.50**
Tumbler, jigger; 2-oz..**$7.00**
Tumbler, juice; 6-oz **$5.00**
Tumbler, old fashioned; 9-oz **$6.00**
Tumbler, water; 10-oz..**$8.50**

Granite Ware

Though it really wasn't as durable as its name suggests, there's still a lot of granite ware around today, though much of it is now in collections. You may even be able to find a bargain. The popularity of the 'country' look in home decorating and the exposure it's had in some of the leading decorating magazines has caused granite ware prices, especially on rare items, to soar in recent years.

It's made from a variety of metals coated with enameling of various colors, some solid, others swirled. It's color, form, and, of course, condition that dictates value. (To evaluate items with wear and chipping, be sure to drastically reduce our values in proportion to the amount of damage.) Swirls of cobalt and white, purple and white, green and white, and brown and white are unusual, but even solid gray items such as a hanging salt box or a chamberstick can be expensive, because pieces like those are rare. Decorated examples are uncommon — so are children's pieces and salesman's samples.

For further information, we recommend *The Collector's Encyclopedia of Granite Ware, Colors, Shapes, and Values,* by Helen Greguire (Collector Books).

Asparagus boiler, gray lg mottle, marked Extra Agate
    Nickel-Steel-Ware L&G Mfg Co, insert missing,
    7¾x11x7¾", EX **$195.00**
Baking pan, blue & white fine mottle, white interior, cobalt
    trim, molded handles, 2¼x12¼x19¼", EX..........**$145.00**
Baking pan, lavender-blue & white lg swirl, white interior,
    molded handles, eyelet, 2x9½x8¼", EX................**$95.00**
Bowl, mixing; apple green w/tangerine inside, Harmonizing
    Colors Vollrath Ware, 4½x8¾", NM....................**$25.00**
Bowl, mixing; yellow & white lg swirl inside & out, black
    trim, ca 1950, 4⅞x9¾", M **$50.00**
Bowl, soup/cereal; solid yellow w/white interior, black trim,
    2⅝x6", NM..**$25.00**
Bread pan, cobalt & white lg mottled, white interior, seamed
    ends, oblong, NM **$345.00**
Bucket, berry; cream w/green, wire bail, seamless, 5x3½",
    EX **$145.00**
Bucket, black & white lg swirl inside & out, black trim,
    wooden bail, seamed body, 7½x7½", EX..........**$575.00**
Bucket, blue & white med mottle, white interior, dark blue
    trim & ears, w/lid, seamed, 5½x6", NM..............**$275.00**
Butter dish, blue & white med mottle, white interior,
    3½x7⅛", NM **$650.00**
Coaster, blue & white lg swirl, white interior, cobalt trim,
    triple coated, Blue Diamond Ware, 4" dia, NM..**$295.00**
Coffeepot, cream w/green trim, weld handle, seamed body,
    7¾x5½", NM **$95.00**
Coffeepot, red & white lg swirl, black trim, white interior,
    seamed body, ca 1950, 9½x5½", EX..................**$245.00**
Coffeepot, red inside & out, black trim & handles, bulbous,
    9x5¼", NM..**$105.00**
Coffeepot, redipped dark blue w/white flecks over original green &
    white Chrysolite, white interior, black trim, 11", EX.....**$165.00**
Coffeepot, solid aqua, white interior, black trim & handle,
    glass Pyrex insert, ca 1930, 9x5½", NM **$85.00**
Colander, blue shading to light blue back to blue, white interior,
    fancy perforations, Bluebelle Ware, 5⅛x8¾", M........**$185.00**
Colander, solid yellow w/dark blue trim, black handles, pierced
    bottom & sides, Japan, ca 1970, 5x10⅛", EX..............**$30.00**
Corn pot, solid yellow inside & out, brown trim, handles & lid,
    ceramic on Steel 11½-Qt...1988, 9½x11¼", M............**$20.00**

Creamer, solid white, cobalt trim, squatty, 3¾x4", M....**$145.00**

Cup, custard; blue & white lg swirl, white interior, cobalt trim, Blue Diamond Ware, 2⅛x4¼", EX.............**$195.00**

Cup, custard; blue shading to light blue & back to blue, Bluebelle Ware, 2½x3⅞", EX....................................**$75.00**

Cup, custard; cream w/green trim, 2¼x3⅜", NM........**$55.00**

Cup, dark blue & white med mottled relish, white interior, dark blue trim, riveted handle, 2⅜x4", EX...........**$55.00**

Cup, muffin; gray lg mottle, 1¼x3¼", NM...................**$85.00**

Dishpan, blue & white lg splash-type mottling, white interior, black riveted handles & trim, 5x14½", EX **$185.00**

Double boiler, gray med mottle, seamless, wooden bail handles, marked L&G Mfg Co, 11¾x9¼", EX...........**$115.00**

Foot tub, dark gray med mottle, seamed, oval, 8¾x18¾x12⅞", EX..**$195.00**

Fry pan, brown & white med mottle inside & out, black handle & trim, Onyx Ware, 1⅛x7¼", EX....................**$195.00**

Fudge pan, lavender-cobalt & white lg swirl, white interior, cobalt trim, 6½x9½", EX......................................**$195.00**

Funnel, blue & white med mottle, gray interior w/fine blue flecks, seamless body, 4¾x3¼" dia, EX.............**$165.00**

Grater, cream & green, handled, flat, 1x4½x6½", NM..**$165.00**

Griddle, gray med mottle, riveted handles, marked Granite Iron Ware....July 21 96, ¾x10x21", EX...............**$195.00**

Kettle, gray large mottle, flared sides, bail handle, 7x15¾", G+, $145.00. (Photo courtesy Helen Greguire)

Kettle, lavender-blue & white med swirl, white interior, Berlin style w/black trim, seamless, 7¼x9½", EX............**$210.00**

Measure, solid blue, white lettering & interior, marked GM in circle, 1-cup, 2¼x2" dia, G **$30.00**

Milk can, brown & white med mottle inside & out, black trim, seamed body, wooden bail, Onyx Enamel Ware, 9x5¼", EX **$135.00**

Mug, blue & white lg swirl w/black trim, white interior, 3½x3⅞", NM **$95.00**

Mug, brown & white lg swirl, white interior, cobalt trim, riveted handles, seamless, 3⅛x4", EX **$155.00**

Mug, brown shading to beige w/western scenes, ca 1970, 3⅛x3½", M **$45.00**

Mug, dark green & white lg mottle, white interior, cobalt trim, Chrysolite, 2¾x2¾", EX.............................**$135.00**

Mug, farmer's; blue & white lg swirl, white interior, black trim & handle, seamless, 4½x4¼", EX...............**$295.00**

Pail, water; blue & white lg mottle, white interior, black trim, ears & wooden handle, 8⅞x11¼", NM...............**$275.00**

Pail, water; gray lg mottle, seamless body, wooden bail, 9⅜x11⅞", EX..**$95.00**

Pie plate, green & white lg swirl, white interior, cobalt trim, Emerald Ware, 1¼x8⅞", EX....................................**$115.00**

Pitcher, water; gray lg mottle, weld handle, seamless, 10⅝x7", NM...**$295.00**

Plate, light blue & white med swirl inside & out, ¾x10", EX **$95.00**

Pudding pan, solid white w/cobalt trim, Tru-Blu Quality Enamelware... label, eyelet, 1½x7", M **$35.00**

Roaster, black & white fine mottle inside & out, metal damper on lid (embossed Lisk), 8½x18½x12", EX.............**$60.00**

Roaster, light blue & white lg swirl, white interior, black trim & handles, w/lid, 5¾x11¾" dia (+handles), M ..**$250.00**

Roaster, solid red lid w/ridges, black bottom, seamless, 6½x9½", EX..**$65.00**

Sauce pan, blue & white lg swirl, white interior, dark blue trim & handle, Berlin-style, w/lid, 8x10¼" dia, EX......**$175.00**

Sauce pan, red & white lg mottle inside & out, seamless, wooden handle, ca 1960, 3x4⅝" dia, NM.............**$75.00**

Sauce pan, solid reddish-orange, white interior, black trim & handle, ca 1960, 2¾x6" dia, EX.........................**$20.00**

Scoop, solid med blue, white interior, 2⅜x5¼", NM........**$155.00**

Spoon, blue & white lg mottle, white interior, black handle, 13", EX..**$110.00**

Spoon, dark green & white lg mottle, white bowl interior, 2⅜x15", EX..**$195.00**

Stew pan, blue & white med swirl w/white interior, black riveted handles & trim, 3⅛x10⅛", NM....................**$210.00**

Strainer, solid white w/cobalt trim, riveted handles, perforated sides & bottom, 1⅜x5½", EX............................**$65.00**

Tea steeper, brown & white med relish, white interior, cobalt trim, riveted handle, seamless, 4⅞x4", EX.........**$195.00**

Tea strainer, gray med mottle, pierced bottom, ⅞x4" dia, NM **$95.00**

Teakettle, blue & white lg swirl, white interior, black trim & ears, wooden bail, 8x7¼", EX **$295.00**

Teakettle, green veins of lg mottling w/white overall lumpy effect, white interior, green trim, Elite Austria, 7½", G..**$130.00**

Teakettle, light gray lg mottle, seamed body & spout, wooden bail, 6½x8½", EX...**$225.00**

Teakettle, red & white lg swirl, white interior, black trim & ears, wooden handle, Bakelite knob, 1950s, 5x5½", NM **$295.00**

Teakettle, red & white lg swirl, white interior, black trim, ears & handle, seamless, ca 1930, 7¼x7", EX **$295.00**

Teakettle, solid white w/black trim & knob, wooden bail, 8x8", NM..**$95.00**

Teakettle, solid yellow w/white interior, black trim & handle, seamless body, seamed spout, marked Pland-18, 6¼", EX ...**$50.00**

Teapot, dark red & white lg swirl, white interior, black trim, seamed body, ca 1950, 7¾x4¾", NM.................**$195.00**

Teapot, green veins of lg mottling w/overall white lumpy effect, white interior, green trim, Elite Austria, 6x6¼", EX **$245.00**

Teapot, white & light blue lg swirl inside & out, black handle & trim, seamless, 9x5½", EX **$275.00**

Teapot, yellow & white lg swirl, white interior, black trim, seamed, ca 1960, lightweight, 8x5", EX **$120.00**

Tray, gray lg mottle, marked L&G Mfg Co, ⅝x13⅜x9½", NM **$155.00**

Tube mold, solid cobalt w/white interior, ribbed style, 2⅞x8¼", EX..**$95.00**

Tube mold, solid cobalt w/white interior, Turk's head turban style, 3¾x9", EX....................................**$95.00**

Tumbler, reddish-brown & white lg swirl, white interior, cobalt trim, 4¾x3½", M..........................**$350.00**

Wash basin, blue & white lg spatter w/white interior & black trim, eyelet, 2⅝x10¼", EX............................**$145.00**

Wash basin, dark green & white swirl, white interior, cobalt trim, eyelet, Emerald Ware, 3x10⅞", EX............**$195.00**

Griswold Cast-Iron Cooking Ware

Late in the 1800s, the Griswold company introduced a line of cast-iron cooking ware that was eventually distributed on a large scale nationwide. Today's collectors appreciate the variety of skillets, cornstick pans, Dutch ovens, and griddles available to them, and many still enjoy using them to cook with.

Several marks have been used; most contain the Griswold name, though some were marked simply 'Erie.'

If you intend to use your cast iron, you can clean it safely by using any commercial oven cleaner. (Be sure to re-season it before you cook in it.) A badly pitted, rusty piece may leave you with no other recourse than to remove what rust you can with a wire brush, paint the surface black, and find an alternate use for it around the house. For instance, you might use a kettle to hold a large floor plant or some magazines. A small griddle or skillet would be attractive as part of a wall display in a country kitchen. It should be noted that prices are given for pieces in excellent condition. Items that are cracked, chipped, pitted, or warped are worth substantially less or nothing at all, depending on rarity.

Note: The letters PIN in the following listings indicate product identification numbers.

Advisor: Grant Windsor (See Directory, Griswold)

Ashtray, ##00, PIN 570, round, w/matchbook holder, from $10 to..**$15.00**

Bundt cake pan, PIN #935, from $800 to..................**$900.00**

Cake mold, Lamb, #866, from $75 to........................**$100.00**

Cake mold, Large Lamb, PINs 947 & 948, from $325 to..**$375.00**

Cake mold, Rabbit, nickel-plated, from $125 to........**$175.00**

Cake mold, Santa, from $400 to................................**$500.00**

Double broiler, PINs 875 & 876, from $175 to..........**$225.00**

Dutch oven cover, #8, hinged, from $25 to................**$35.00**

Dutch oven display rack, 3-tier, from $900 to **$1,200.00**

Gem pan, #1, slant EPU TM, PIN 940, from $200 to ...**$250.00**

Gem pan, #3, marked slant TM & PIN 942, from $250 to **$300.00**

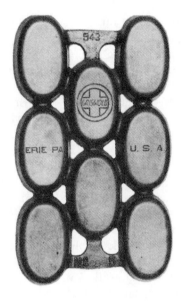

Gem pan, #5, marked Griswold TM Erie PA USA, from $500.00 to $600.00.

Gem pan, #9, Brownie Cake Pan, PIN 947, from $125...**$150.00**

Gem pan, #11, French roll, marked NES No 11, from $30 to **$50.00**

Gem pan, #11, French roll, marked NES oN (error) 11, from $40 to..**$60.00**

Gem pan, #12, marked NO 12, sq corners, from $175 to..**$225.00**

Gem pan, #12, slant/EPU TM, from $300 to **$350.00**

Gem pan, #1270, wheatstick, Best Made (Made for Sears, Roebuck & Co), from $75 to **$125.00**

Gem pan, #1270, wheatstick, Puritan (Made for Sears, Roebuck & Co), from $75 to **$125.00**

Gem pan, #14, Turk Head, PIN 641, from $600 to...**$700.00**

Gem pan, #140, Turk Head, from $125 to **$175.00**

Gem pan, #15, French roll, fully marked, from $125 to..**$150.00**

Gem pan, #16, wide band, aluminum, from $500 to..**$600.00**

Gem pan, #18, popover, wide handle, 6 cups, from $50 to **$75.00**

Gem pan, #19, fully marked, 6-cup golf ball, from $250 to..**$350.00**

Gem pan, #24, breadstick, PIN 957, from $400 to....**$450.00**

Gem pan, #240, Turk Head, from $230 to **$260.00**

Gem pan, #262, cornstick, tea size (watch for reproductions), from $50 to...**$75.00**

Gem pan, #2700, wheatstick, from $275 to..............**$325.00**

Gem pan, #273, cornstick, from $15 to **$25.00**

Gem pan, #50, heart & star, from $1,000 to..........**$1,500.00**

Griddle, #12, gas or vapor, marked Erie Gas Griddle, from $275 to..**$325.00**

Heat regulator, #300, raised markings on 1 side, from $125 to..**$175.00**

Iron, The Erie Fluter, detachable handle, PINs 297 & 298, from $200 to...**$250.00**

Oval roaster, #3, block TMs marked Oval Roaster on lid, from $475 to...**$525.00**

Oval roaster, #4, Block TMs, fully marked cover, w/trivet, from $350 to...**$400.00**

Paperweight, pup, marked #30 Griswold Pup, from $200 to **$300.00**

Pitcher, aluminum, fixed handle, round TM, from $125 to **$175.00**

Skillet, #2, block TM, heat ring, from $1,800 to.....**$2,200.00**

Skillet, #2, block TM, no heat ring, chrome, from $200 to **$250.00**

Skillet, #2, slant/EPU TM, heat ring, from $375 to....**$425.00**

Skillet, #2, slant/EPU TM, Rau Brothers, from $500 to .**$600.00**

Skillet, #2, slant/EPU trademark, no heat ring, from $500 to...**$600.00**

Skillet, #2, slant/Erie TM, from $350 to **$400.00**

Skillet, #3, slant/Erie TM, from $30 to.........................**$40.00**

Skillet, #3, sm TM, hinged, from $25 to....................**$45.00**

Skillet, #3, Square Fry Skillet, PIN 2103 (beware of reproductions), from $75 to...**$125.00**

Skillet, #4, block TM, heat ring, from $375 to..........**$425.00**

Skillet, #4, slant/EPU TM, from $55 to.......................**$75.00**

Skillet, #4, slant/Erie TM, nickel plated, from $40 to..**$60.00**

Skillet, #4, sm TM, late handle, from $15 to...............**$30.00**

Skillet, #5, block TM, heat ring, from $375 to..........**$425.00**

Skillet, #6, block TM, no heat ring, from $10 to.........**$20.00**

Skillet, #8, All-In-One dinner skillet, 3 sections, PIN 1008, from $350 to...**$400.00**

Skillet, #8, sm TM, extra deep, w/hinge, from $35 to...**$45.00**

Skillet, #8, spider TM, from $1,100 to.....................**$1,400.00**

Skillet, #11, block TM, from $125 to..........................**$175.00**

Skillet, #12, block TM, from $75 to...........................**$100.00**

Skillet, #13, block TM, from $1,400 to....................**$1,600.00**

Skillet, #13, slant/EPU TM, from $800 to...............**$1,000.00**

Skillet, #15, oval, w/lid, from $750 to.......................**$900.00**

Skillet, sq utility, PIN 768, w/iron lid PIN 769, from $275 to **$300.00**

Skillet lid, #3, high smooth, from $150 to **$200.00**

Skillet lid, #11, low top writing, from $375 to **$425.00**

Skillet lid, #14, low top writing, from $475 to **$525.00**

Sundial, from $450 to...**$500.00**

Teakettle, #8, spider TM top, from $400 to **$500.00**

Trivet, Classic sad iron, from $50 to...........................**$75.00**

Trivet, Old Lace (coffeepot), sm, PIN 1738, from $200 to...**$250.00**

Trivet, Old Lace (coffeepot), lg, PIN 1739, from $75 to **$125.00**

Trivet, sm decorative, eagle & wreath, PIN 1736, from $20 to...**$25.00**

Wafer iron, w/side-handle base, from $300 to..........**$400.00**

Waffle iron, #11, sq, low bailed base, ball hinge, from $175 to...**$225.00**

Waffle iron, #14, hotel/restaurant size (4 set of paddles), ball hinge, from $700 to...**$900.00**

Waffle iron, #19, heart & star, low bailed base, from $250 to...**$300.00**

Waffle iron, #8, French (3 sets of paddles), finger hinge, from $600 to...**$800.00**

Waffle iron, #9, aluminum, side-handle base, ball hinge, from $30 to...**$50.00**

Guardian Ware

The Guardian Service Company was in business from 1935 until 1955. They produced a very successful line of hammered aluminum that's just as popular today as it ever was. (Before 1935 Century Metalcraft made similar ware under the name SilverSeal, you'll occasionally see examples of it as well.) Guardian Service was sold though the home party plan, and special hostess gifts were offered as incentives. Until 1940 metal lids were used, but during the war when the government restricted the supply of available aluminum, glass lids were introduced. The cookware was very versatile, and one of their selling points was top-of-the-stove baking and roasting — 'no need to light the oven.' Many items had more than one use. For instance, their large turkey roaster came with racks and could be used for canning as well. The kettle oven used for stove-top baking also came with canning racks. Their Economy Trio set featured three triangular roasters that fit together on a round tray, making it possible to cook three foods at once on only one burner; for even further fuel economy, the casserole tureen could be stacked on top of that. Projections on the sides of the pans accommodated two styles of handles, a standard detachable utility handle as well as black 'mouse ear' handles for serving.

The company's logo is a knight with crossed weapons, and if you find a piece with a trademark that includes the words 'Patent Pending,' you'll know you have one of the earlier pieces.

In 1955 National Presto purchased the company and tried to convince housewives that the new stainless steel pans were superior to their tried-and-true Guardian aluminum, but the ladies would have none of it. In 1980 Tad and Suzie Kohara bought the rights to the Guardian Service name as well as the original molds. The new company is based in California, and is presently producing eight of the original pieces, canning racks, pressure cooker parts, serving handles, and replacement glass lids. Quoting their literature: 'Due to the age of the GS glass molds, we are unable to provide perfect glass covers. The covers may appear to have cracks or breaks on the surface. They are not breaks but mold marks and should be as durable as the originals.' They go on to say: 'These glass covers are not oven proof.' These mold marks may be a good way to distinguish the old glass lids from the new, and collectors tell us that the original lids have a green hue to the glass. The new company has also reproduced three cookbooks, one that shows the line with the original metal covers. If you want to obtain replacements, see the Directory for Guardian Service Cookware.

Be sure to judge condition when evaluating Guardian Service. Wear, baked-on grease, scratches, and obvious signs of use devalue its worth. Our prices range from pieces in average to exceptional condition. To be graded exceptional, the interior of the pan must have no pitting and the surface must be bright and clean. An item with a metal lid is worth approximately 25% more than the same piece with a glass lid. To most successfully clean your grungy garage-sale finds, put them in a self-cleaning oven, then wash them in soap and water. Never touch them with anything but a perfectly clean hotpad while they're hot, and make sure they're completely cooled before you put them in water. Abrasive cleansers only scratch the surface.

Advisor: Dennis S. McAdams (See the Directory, Guardian Service Cookware)

Ashtray, glass, w/knight & white stars logo, hostess gift, from $25 to **$30.00**
Beverage urn, w/lid (no screen or dripper), common .**$20.00**

Beverage urn (coffeepot), glass lid, complete with screen and dripper, 15", $50.00. (Photo courtesy Dennis McAdams)

Can of cleaner, unopened..**$15.00**

Cookbooks, Silver Seal, 1936, 48 pages, EX, $45.00; others, from $25.00 to $45.00. (Photo courtesy Dennis McAdams)

Dome cooker, Tom Thumb, glass lid, w/handles, 3½x4⅞" dia, from $25 to **$35.00**

Dome cooker, 1-qt, glass lid, w/handles, 6¾" dia, from $25 to **$45.00**
Dome cooker, 2-qt, glass lid, w/handles, 4½x10½" dia, from $35 to **$50.00**
Dome cooker, 4-qt, glass lid, w/handles, 6½x10½" dia, from $35 to **$55.00**
Fryer, breakfast; glass lid, 10", from $45 to **$60.00**
Fryer, chicken; glass lid, 12", from $75 to **$100.00**
Gravy boat, w/undertray, from $30 to **$50.00**
Griddle broiler, octagonal, w/handles, polished center, 16½" dia, from $20 to **$40.00**
Handle, clamp-on style, from $10 to..........................**$15.00**
Handles, slip-on style, Bakelite, pr, from $20 to........**$35.00**
Ice bucket, glass lid, liner & tongs, 9", from $50 to ...**$90.00**
Kettle oven, glass lid, bail handle, w/rack, 8x12" dia, from $135 to..**$165.00**
Omelet pan, hinged in center, black handle on ea half, from $75 to..**$100.00**
Pot, triangular, w/glass lid, 7" to top of finial, 11" L, from $25 to **$45.00**
Pressure cooker, minimum value **$125.00**
Roaster, glass lid, 4x15" L, from $85 to.....................**$100.00**
Roaster, turkey; glass lid, no rack, 16½" L, from $100 to ..**$125.00**
Roaster, turkey; metal lid, w/rack, 16½" L, from $125 to ..**$165.00**
Service kit, w/3 cleaners, 1 brush, 1 cookbook, 1 clamp-on handle, pr of slip-on handles, steel wool, from $125 to..**$150.00**
Tray, serving; hammered center, w/handles, 13" dia, from $20 to..**$30.00**
Tray/platter, w/handles, hammered surface, also used as roaster cover for stacking, 10x15" L, from $25 to............**$35.00**
Tumblers, glassware, stylized knight & shield in silver, & coasters w/embossed head of knight, 4 of ea in metal rack **$80.00**
Tumblers & ashtray/coasters, glassware w/Guardian logo, white stars & gold trim, hostess gift, 6 of ea, from $275 to .**$325.00**
Tureen, bottom; glass lid, from $40 to........................**$65.00**
Tureen, casserole; glass lid, from $65 to **$90.00**
Tureen, top; glass lid, from $30 to..............................**$45.00**

Gurley Candle Company

Gurley candles were cute little wax figures designed to celebrate holidays and special occasions. They are all marked Gurley on the bottom. They were made so well and had so much great detail that people decided to keep them year after year to decorate with instead of burning them. Woolworth's and other five-and-dime stores sold them from about 1940 until the 1970s. They're still plentiful today and inexpensive.

Tavern Novelty Candles were actually owned by Gurley. They were similar to the Gurley candles but not quite as detailed. All are marked Tavern on the bottom. Prices listed here are for unburned candles with no fading.

Advisor: Debbie Coe (See Directory, Cape Cod)

Christmas, angel, marked Gurley, 3" **$3.50**
Christmas, angel, marked Gurley, 5" **$8.50**
Christmas, baby angel on half moon, marked Gurley, 2½"...**$10.00**
Christmas, Black caroler man w/red clothes, 3".........**$9.50**
Christmas, blue grotto w/star, angel & baby, 4½" **$10.00**
Christmas, caroler man w/red clothes, 7" **$8.50**
Christmas, caroler set: lamppost, girl & boy carolers w/song books, cello player, in package **$35.00**
Christmas, choir boy or girl, 2¾", ea **$6.00**
Christmas, green candelabra w/red candle, 5" **$7.50**
Christmas, grotto w/shepherd & sheep......................**$14.50**
Christmas, lamppost, yellow cap & garland, 5½".........**$6.50**
Christmas, reindeer, marked Tavern, 3½" **$3.50**
Christmas, Rudolph w/red nose, 3" **$3.50**
Christmas, Santa, 6¼" **$12.00**
Christmas, Santa sitting on present on sled, 3" **$13.50**
Christmas, snowman running w/red hat, 3" **$8.50**
Christmas, snowman w/red pipe & green hat, 5".........**$6.00**
Christmas, white church w/choir boy inside, 6" **$14.50**
Christmas, yellow candle in gold chamberstick, 4¾"....**$3.50**
Christmas, 3" deer standing in front of candle, 5".........**$7.50**
Easter, chick, pink or yellow, 3" **$6.00**
Easter, duck, yellow w/purple bow, 5".......................**$9.50**
Easter, pink birdhouse w/yellow bird, 3" **$7.50**
Easter, pink egg w/bunny inside, 3" **$10.00**
Easter, pink egg w/squirrel inside, 3" **$12.00**
Easter, pink winking rabbit w/carrot, 3¼" **$6.00**
Easter, rabbit, pink or yellow, 3" **$5.00**
Easter, white lily w/blue lip & green candle, 3"...........**$5.00**
Halloween, black cat (4") w/orange candlestick beside it ..**$22.50**
Halloween, black owl on orange stump, 3½"..............**$10.00**
Halloween, Frankenstein, later issue but harder to find, 6"..**$24.00**
Halloween, ghost, white, 5" **$20.00**

Halloween, jack-o'-lantern, 4", $8.00.

Halloween, pumpkin w/black cat, 2½" **$9.00**
Halloween, pumpkin-face scarecrow, 5" **$12.00**
Halloween, skeleton, 8½" **$38.00**
Halloween, witch, black, 8" **$22.50**
Halloween, witch w/black cape, 3½" **$9.50**
Halloween, 4" cut-out orange owl w/7½" black candle behind it **$24.00**

Other Holidays, birthday boy, marked Tavern, 3" **$6.00**
Other Holidays, bride & groom, 4½", ea....................**$14.50**
Other Holidays, Eskimo & igloo, marked Tavern, 2-pc **$14.50**
Other Holidays, Western girl or boy, 3", ea................**$9.50**
Thanksgiving, acorns & leaves, 3½"...........................**$6.50**
Thanksgiving, gold sailing ship, 7½" **$12.50**
Thanksgiving, Indian boy & girl, brown & green clothes, 5", pr..**$30.00**
Thanksgiving, Pilgrim girl or boy, 2½", ea **$4.50**
Thanksgiving, turkey, 2½"..**$3.00**
Thanksgiving, turkey, 5¾" **$15.00**

Hadley, M. A.

Since 1940, the M.A. Hadley Pottery (Louisville, Tennessee) has been producing handmade dinnerware and decorative items painted freehand in a folksy style with barnyard animals, baskets, whales, and sailing ships in a soft pastel palette of predominately blues and greens. Each piece is signed by hand with the first two initials and last name of artist-turned-potter Mary Alice Hadley, who has personally created each design. Some items may carry an amusing message in the bottom — for instance, 'Please Fill Me' in a canister or 'The End' in a coffee cup! Examples of this ware are beginning to turn up on the secondary market, and it's being snapped up not only by collectors who have to 'have it all' but by those who enjoy adding a decorative touch to a country-style room with only a few pieces of this unique pottery.

Horses and pigs seem to be popular subject matter; unusual pieces and the older, heavier examples command the higher prices.

Ashtray, Tobacco the Fine Herb on outside rim, tobacco plant in center, 1½x7" **$40.00**
Bank, bunny, 5½" **$28.00**
Bank, dog, white w/blue flowers & chains, 9½" **$65.00**
Bank, pig shape, 5x9" **$45.00**
Bowl, chicken, 5½"..**$13.50**
Bowl, farmer's wife, 4½" **$10.00**
Bowl, grapes, 5⅜"...**$18.50**
Bowl, lamb, 5" **$20.00**
Bust, horse head, white w/blue decor, 9¼" **$65.00**
Canister, Sugar & scrolls, w/lid, 7½x6¾" dia..............**$35.00**
Chowder pot, clouds on pot w/cow & horse on lid, 8½x11" **$85.00**
Coaster, Happy Mother's Day on rim w/flowers in center, 4" **$25.00**
Coaster, Happy New Home, 4"..................................**$15.00**
Coaster, Happy 4th of July, flag & fireworks, 4" **$20.00**
Coaster, To My Valentine w/pink heart trimmed in blue pierced by arrow, 4" **$13.50**
Cup & saucer, Good Morning inside cup, 3½", To You outside; clock face on saucer, 8" dia **$50.00**
Cup & saucer, puppy **$20.00**
Dipper, Little Dipper, 5⅜x2¾x3½" dia **$15.00**

Measuring cup, whale & Hood Canal outside w/1, 2 & 3 inside, sm spout, 3" $18.00
Mug, pig, flared, The End inside, 4¾" $25.00
Mug, rearing horse, Whoa inside $25.00
Mug, ship, Low Tide inside $18.00
Napkin rings, white w/blue decor, horse, cow, bunny & pig, 1 on ea, set of 4............$60.00
Pasta dish, turkey, 2x8" dia............$50.00
Pie plate, lamb, 9½"............$35.00
Pitcher, milk; cow, 6½" $40.00
Plate, chicken, 9" $16.50
Plate, cow, 9¼" $19.50
Plate, cow, 11" $25.00
Plate, duck, 7½"............$15.00

Plate, farmer, 9", $18.00. (Photo courtesy Jack Chipman)

Plate, Happy Birthday & cake on pedestal, 4½".........$13.50
Plate, horse & rider in center w/fence & house on rim, 9"............$25.00
Plate, horse by picket fence, 9" $30.00
Plate, lighthouse, 8"............$25.00
Plate, pig, 9¼"............$20.00
Plate, ship, 11"............$25.00
Pot, lamb, 6x8"............$32.00
Refrigerator magnet, fish shape, 3x3¾" $13.50
Salt & pepper shakers, bird shape, S on 1, P on other, pr.$36.00
Salt & pepper shakers, farmer & farmer's wife, 4¼", pr......$25.00
Salt cellar, bird shape $17.50
Salt crock, Salt & scrolls, Please Fill Me inside, flower on tab handle, 5x5¼" dia............$30.00
Soap dish, pig shape, 3x5"............$30.00
Trivet, snowman, 6"............$20.00
Wall plaque, kitten, 6" $23.50
Wall plaque, rooster, 12¼x3¼"............$28.00

Hagen-Renaker

This California-based company has been in business since 1946, first in Monrovia, later in San Dimas. They're most famous for their models of animals and birds, some of which were miniatures, and some that were made on a larger scale. Many bear paper labels (if they're large enough to accommodate them); others were attached to squares of heavy paper printed with the name of the company. They also used an incised 'HR' and a stamped 'Hagen-Renaker.' In addition to the animals, they made replicas of characters from several popular Disney films under license from the Disney Studio.

Advisor: Gayle Roller (See Directory, Hagen-Renaker)

Newsletter: The Hagen-Renaker Collector's Club Newsletter
c/o Debra Kerr
618 6th Terrace
Palm Beach Gardens, FL 33418

Figurine, Amir, Arabian stallion, #B-707, white w/gray shading, 6" $125.00
Figurine, baby goat, #A-849, white w/gray hooves, black eyes, pink nose & inner ears $1.00
Figurine, baby ostrich, black & grey, 1¼" $10.00
Figurine, baby quail, metal feather, wing detail, ½x¾"..$20.00
Figurine, Bay Mustang (horse), #A-360, matt finish, 2¾"...$100.00
Figurine, bluejay, matt finish, ½x⅝" $20.00
Figurine, Calypso cat, Tom, Siamese, seated, 4⅛" $50.00
Figurine, cat, #B-699, brown tabby w/pink nose, Monrovia, 5" $50.00
Figurine, circus pony, white w/blue harness, head down..$50.00
Figurine, cobra in basket, #A-3082, 3" $25.00
Figurine, draft horse, #A-341, brown & white, black harness w/gold trim, 2¾"............$30.00
Figurine, elephant, #2053, gray w/white tusks, raised trunk, 3¼x4⅜"............$20.00
Figurine, Flower, skunk, Disney, no hole in paw for flowers $40.00
Figurine, frog playing dulcimer, #3183, current, 2".....$25.00
Figurine, Golden Finch, #A-287, wings out at side, ⅝x⅝".$10.00
Figurine, gray whale, #3191............$10.00
Figurine, hedgehog, #A-2074, black & white w/pink nose, black eyes, ⅞x1⅜"............$20.00
Figurine, Indian pony, #3110, brown & white $15.00
Figurine, Jack, white duck, 6½" $30.00
Figurine, Kamiah, Appaloosa mare, 2¾" $25.00
Figurine, Kwei-Li, Siamese cat, #B-667, Designer Workshop, 8"............$35.00
Figurine, Lipizzaner, white w/gray highlights, #A-3169, 3¼"............$30.00
Figurine, Morgan Stallion, A-389, 3"............$125.00
Figurine, Pancho Villa, Chihuahua pup, standing on hind legs, 2"............$25.00
Figurine, Pap, fox, #A-179, walking on hind legs, Monrovia, 2½"............$20.00
Figurine, Patsy, cocker spaniel puppy, Monrovia, 2¾x4"..$25.00
Figurine, Pegasus, standing, #831, white w/gray wings, flowers at neck, current, 2"............$18.00
Figurine, pitbull, #3292, current, 2" $20.00
Figurine, Puss in Boots, 6½"............$400.00

Figurine, Quan-Tiki, Siamese kitten, seated, 4⅛".........**$30.00**

Figurine, raccoon, #A-163, brown, lg, San Dimas, 1¼".**$18.00**

Figurine, Ralph, poodle puppy, white, 2x2"...............**$85.00**

Figurine, San-Su, Siamese cat, lying.....................**$175.00**

Figurine, sandpipper, #3280, 3¼" **$30.00**

Figurine, Sassy, tabby cat, #B-719, 3"...................**$50.00**

Figurine, Siamese kitten, standing on hind legs balanced on tail, Designer Workshop, 3¾" **$30.00**

Figurine, skunk, black & white, lying on back w/tail underneath, 3" **$300.00**

Figurine, Snowflake, fawn (deer), Designer Workshop, 1953.................................**$50.00**

Figurine, swan, #A-380, wings flat against body, 1⅛x2"..**$12.00**

Figurine, Tia Juana Rose, Little Horrible, #D-400, 1¾", MIB **$60.00**

Figurine, toucan on branch, black & white w/orange beak w/black tip, gray branch, 2⅛" **$40.00**

Figurine, Tramp, terrier, Disney's lady & the Tramp, 2¼"..**$50.00**

Figurines, North Pole setting, 3 Eskimos, ice cave & polar bear **$85.00**

Shelf sitter, Alice, Disney's Alice in Wonderland, 1⅞"...**$185.00**

Hall China Company

Hall China is still in production in East Liverpool, Ohio, where they have been located since around the turn of the century. They have produced literally hundreds of lines of kitchen and dinnerware items for both home and commercial use. Many of these have become very collectible.

They're especially famous for their teapots, some of which were shaped like automobiles, basketballs, doughnuts, etc. Each teapot was made in an assortment of colors, often trimmed in gold. Many were decaled to match their dinnerware lines. Some are quite rare, and collecting them all would be a real challenge.

During the 1950s, Eva Zeisel designed dinnerware shapes with a streamlined, ultra-modern look. Her lines, Classic and Century, were used with various decals as the basis for several of Hall's dinnerware patterns. She also designed kitchenware lines with the same modern styling. They were called Casual Living and Tri-Tone. All her designs are very popular with today's collectors, especially those with an interest in the movement referred to as ''50s modern.'

Although some of the old kitchenware shapes and teapots are being produced today, you'll be able to tell them from the old pieces by the backstamp. To identify these new issues, Hall marks them with the shaped rectangular 'Hall' trademark they've used since the early 1970s.

For more information, we recommend *The Collector's Encyclopedia of Hall China*, Third Edition, by Margaret and Kenn Whitmyer (Collector Books).

Club/Newsletter: *Hall China Collector's Club Newsletter*
P.O. Box 360488, Cleveland, OH 44136
Subscription: $13 per year

Arizona, bowl, coupe soup; Tomorrow's Classic, 9"...**$10.00**

Arizona, candlestick, Tomorrow's Classic, 8"...............**$40.00**

Arizona, ladle, Tomorrow's Classic.........................**$22.00**

Arizona, saucer, AD; Tomorrow's Classic.....................**$3.50**

Blue Blossom, ball jug, #1 ....**$165.00**

Blue Blossom, coffeepot, drip; #691 ....**$550.00**

Blue Blossom, custard, Thick Rim.........................**$28.00**

Blue Blossom, shirred egg dish............................**$65.00**

Blue Blossom, water bottle, Zephyr......................**$800.00**

Blue Bouquet, bowl, cereal; D-style, 6".................**$22.00**

Blue Bouquet, bowl, flared, 7¾" **$45.00**

Blue Bouquet, bowl, Radiance, 9".......................**$32.00**

Blue Bouquet, coaster, metal............................**$15.00**

Blue Bouquet, creamer, Boston..........................**$28.00**

Blue Bouquet, jug, Medallion, #3........................**$35.00**

Blue Bouquet, pie baker................................**$70.00**

Blue Crocus, bowl, straight-sided, 6" **$28.00**

Blue Crocus, casserole, Thick Rim.......................**$70.00**

Blue Floral, bowl, 7¾" **$24.00**

Blue Garden, ball jug, #1.............................**$145.00**

Blue Willow, ashtray..................................**$35.00**

Bouquet, bowl, salad; Tomorrow's Classic, lg, 14½"..**$45.00**

Bouquet, candlestick, Tomorrow's Classic, 4½" **$45.00**

Bouquet, creamer, Tomorrow's Classic...................**$14.00**

Bouquet, jug, Tomorrow's Classic, 3-qt **$45.00**

Bouquet, vase, Tomorrow's Classic......................**$95.00**

Buckingham, ashtray, Tomorrow's Classic................**$10.00**

Buckingham, bottle, vinegar; Tomorrow's Classic.......**$95.00**

Buckingham, casserole, Tomorrow's Classic, 1¼-qt....**$40.00**

Buckingham, plate, Tomorrow's Classic, 6".................**$6.00**

Cactus, ball jug, #3 ....**$255.00**

Cactus, custard, Radiance.............................**$24.00**

Cactus, onion soup, individual **$60.00**

Cameo Rose, bowl, cream soup; E-style, 5" **$90.00**

Cameo Rose, bowl, E-style, oval, 10½"...................**$25.00**

Cameo Rose, gravy boat, E-style, w/underplate.........**$32.00**

Cameo Rose, plate, E-style, 7¼" **$9.50**

Cameo Rose, platter, E-style, oval, 13¼" **$22.00**

Cameo Rose, tidbit tray, E-style, 3-tier **$75.00**

Caprice, bowl, open baker; Tomorrow's Classic, 11-oz..**$22.00**

Caprice, egg cup, Tomorrow's Classic **$47.00**

Caprice, vase, Tomorrow's Classic.......................**$75.00**

Carrot & Golden Carrot, bowl, Five Band, 6"............**$25.00**

Carrot & Golden Carrot, casserole, #70, round, 10"....**$75.00**

Carrot & Golden Carrot, teapot, Windshield **$225.00**

Christmas Tree & Holly, bowl, plum pudding; E-style, 4½" **$30.00**

Christmas Tree & Holly, cup, E-style **$22.00**

Christmas Tree & Holly, sugar bowl, E-style, coffee set..**$45.00**

Chrstmas Tree & Holly, saucer, E-style **$4.00**

Clover & Golden Clover, bowl, Thick rim, 8½".........**$35.00**

Clover & Golden Clover, stack set **$135.00**

Crocus, bowl, Radiance, 9" **$40.00**

Crocus, bowl, salad; 9".................................**$22.00**

Crocus, coffeepot, Meltdown...........................**$110.00**

Crocus, mug, flagon style.............................**$90.00**

Crocus, plate, D-style, 7¼"............................**$12.00**

Crocus, pretzel jar..$200.00
Crocus, soap dispenser, metal $125.00

Crocus, square leftover, from $100.00 to $120.00. (Photo courtesy Kenn and Margaret Whitmyer)

Crocus, sugar bowl, Medallion, w/lid $40.00
Crocus, teapot, Streamline $1,800.00
Daisy, cookie jar, Five Band $125.00
Dawn, bottle, vinegar; Tomorrow's Classic $95.00
Dawn, bowl, celery; Tomorrow's Classic, oval............$24.00
Dawn, gravy boat, Tomorrow's Classic......................$45.00
Eggshell, baker, Dot, fish-shape, 13½".......................$65.00
Eggshell, bowl, Dot, ribbed, 8½" $45.00
Eggshell, bowl, salad; Plaid or Swag, 9¾"..................$45.00
Eggshell, custard, Plaid or Swag................................$22.00
Eggshell, onion soup, Dot...$50.00
Eggshell, pretzel jar, Dot w/ivory body $190.00
Fantasy, bean pot, New England, #4 ....$230.00
Fantasy, bowl, fruit; Tomorrow's Classic, footed, lg ...$40.00
Fantasy, drip jar, #1188, open.....................................$65.00
Fantasy, ladle, Tomorrow's Classic $22.00
Fantasy, teapot, Tomorrow's Classic, 6-cup...............$210.00
Fern, bowl, fruit; Century, 5¾" $6.50
Fern, butter dish, Century, w/lid $125.00
Fern, jug, Century..$32.00
Five Band, batter bowl, colors other than red or cobalt..$50.00
Five Band, bowl, red or cobalt, 6" $14.00
Five Band, jug, colors other than red or cobalt, 5".....$25.00
Five Band, syrup, red or cobalt $75.00
Flair, butter dish, Tomorrow's Classic, w/lid $190.00
Flair, marmite, Tomorrow's Classic, w/lid...................$35.00
Flare-Ware, bowl, Gold Lace, 6¾"..................................$8.00
Flare-Ware, casserole, Autumn Leaf, 3-pt....................$22.00
Flare-Ware, cookie jar, Heather Rose $85.00
Flare-Ware, teapot, Radial, 6-cup................................$40.00
Floral Lattice, salt & pepper shakers, canister style, pr..$250.00
French Flower, creamer, Bellevue $25.00
French Flower, jug, Donut...$145.00
Frost Flowers, bowl, baker; Tomorrow's Classic, open, 11-oz $22.00
Frost Flowers, casserole, Tomorrow's Classic, 1¼-qt..$37.00
Frost Flowers, onion soup, Tomorrow's Classic, w/lid..$37.00
Frost Flowers, vase, Tomorrow's Classic.....................$75.00
Gaillardia, bowl, fruit; D-style, 5¼"...............................$8.00
Gaillardia, coffepot, Terrance....................................$55.00

Gaillardia, drip jar, Radiance.....................................$32.00
Game Bird, bowl, fruit; E-style, 5½" $14.00
Game Bird, casserole, E-style, MJ................................$85.00
Game Bird, plate, E-style, 10"......................................$75.00
Game Bird, teapot, Windshield, E-style $315.00
Garden of Eden, ladle, Century...................................$20.00
Garden of Eden, relish, Century, 4-part......................$35.00
Garden of Eden, teapot, Century, 6-cup $160.00
Gold Label, baker, French..$18.00
Gold Label, bowl, salad; 9"...$18.00
Golden Glo, bean pot, New England, 6-pt..................$85.00
Golden Glo, casserole, #102, 7-pt $45.00
Golden Glo, mug, #343...$12.00
Golden Glo, souffle, round, fluted, 16-oz...................$12.00
Golden Glo, sugar bowl, Sani-Grid.............................$20.00
Golden Oak, bowl, cereal; D-style, 6" $8.00
Golden Oak, bowl, straight-sided, 9"...........................$20.00
Golden Oak, custard, straight-sided............................$20.00
Harlequin, bowl, celery; Tomorrow's Classic, oval.....$24.00
Harlequin, casserole, Tomorrow's Classic, 2-qt $65.00
Harlequin, plate, Tomorrow's Classic, 6" $6.00
Harlequin, teapot, Tomorrow's Classic, Thorley $300.00
Heather Rose, bowl, fruit; E-style, 5¼".........................$5.00
Heather Rose, creamer, E-style $10.00
Heather Rose, cup, E-style $7.00
Heather Rose, plate, E-style, 10".................................$12.50
Heather Rose, saucer, E-style $2.00
Holiday, ashtray, Tomorrow's Classic.........................$11.50
Holiday, egg cup, Tomorrow's Classic........................$60.00
Holiday, platter, Tomorrow's Classic, 15"...................$35.00
Homewood, bowl, Radiance, 7½".................................$20.00
Homewood, creamer, Art Deco....................................$25.00
Homewood, cup, D-style $8.00
Lyric, ashtray, Tomorrow's Classic..............................$10.00
Lyric, candlestick, Tomorrow's Classic, 4½" $32.00
Lyric, plate, Tomorrow's Classic, 6"..............................$5.00
Meadow Flower, casserole, Radiance...........................$70.00
Meadow Flower, jug, Five band $70.00
Medallion, bowl, Chinese Red, #3, 6"..........................$16.00
Medallion, casserole, Lettuce $35.00
Medallion, drip jar, Chinese Red $55.00
Medallion, reamer, Lettuce..$400.00
Medallion, teapot, Chinese Red, 64-oz......................$350.00
Morning Glory, bowl, Thick Rim, 7½"..........................$30.00
Mulberry, bowl, celery; Tomorrow's Classic, oval......$24.00
Mulberry, cup, Tomorrow's Classic $11.00
Mulberry, platter, Tomorrow's Classic, 11".................$13.00
Mums, baker, French..$40.00
Mums, bowl, cereal; D-style, 6" $14.00
Mums, canister, Radiance..$600.00
Mums, coffeepot, Terrace..$120.00
Mums, custard, Radiance...$25.00
Mums, gravy boat, D-style $35.00
Mums, salt & pepper shakers, handled, pr.................$50.00
Mums, teapot, Medallion...$200.00
No 488, bowl, Radiance, 9"...$32.00
No 488, bowl, salad; 9"..$40.00

No 488, casserole, Five Band......................$75.00
No 488, cocotte, handled $55.00
No 488, custard, Radiance.........................$25.00
No 488, drip jar, Radiance, w/lid................$45.00
No 488, jug, Rayed $75.00
No 488, plate, D-style, 7".........................$12.00
No 488, punch bowl, Tom & Jerry...............$950.00
No 488, shirred egg dish............................$40.00
No 488, water bottle, Zephyr.....................$900.00
Orange Poppy, bowl, flat soup; C-style, 8½"............$35.00
Orange Poppy, bowl, Radiance, 9" $35.00
Orange Poppy, casserole, oval, 11¾" $75.00
Orange Poppy, leftover, loop handle...........$125.00
Orange Poppy, platter, C-style, oval, 11¼".................$35.00

Orange Poppy, pretzel jar, 7", from $100.00 to $150.00.

Orange Poppy, spoon $120.00
Orange Poppy, wastebasket, metal..............$100.00
Ornage Poppy, teapot, Streamline $350.00
Pastel Morning Glory, cake plate $45.00
Pastel Morning Glory, creamer, New York $25.00
Pastel Morning Glory, gravy boat, D-style..............$35.00
Pastel Morning Glory, saucer, St Denis........$7.50
Pastel Morning Glory, teapot, Aladdin.................$700.00
Peach Blossom, bowl, fruit; E-style, 5¼" $6.50
Peach Blossom, coffeepot, Tomorrow's Classic, 6-cup ..$105.00
Peach Blossom, creamer, Tomorrow's Classic............$13.00
Peach Blossom, jug, Tomorrow's Classic, 3-qt $35.00
Pinecone, bowl, baker; Tomorrow's Classic, open, 11-oz..$22.00
Pinecone, egg cup, Tomorrow's Classic.................$45.00
Pinecone, gravy boat, Tomorrow's Classic $35.00
Pinecone, plate, E-style, 9¼"....................$9.50
Pinecone, plate, Tomorrow's Classic, 6".................$5.50
Prairie Grass, bowl, fruit; E-style, 5¼"...........$5.50
Prairie Grass, creamer, E-style..................$10.00
Prairie Grass, plate, E-style, 10"...............$14.00
Primrose, ashtray, E-style $10.00
Primrose, bowl, flat soup; E-style, 8"...........$12.00
Primrose, bowl, salad; E-style, 9" $16.00

Primrose, jug, E-style, Rayed.....................$22.00
Primrose, plate, E-style, 6½"....................$3.50
Primrose, plate, 10", from $10 to................$12.00
Primrose, sugar bowl, E-style, w/lid............$16.00
Radiance, bowl, ivory, #2, 5¼"..................$6.50
Radiance, canister, red or cobalt, 2-qt..........$230.00
Radiance, stack set, ivory.........................$42.00
Radiance, teapot, red or cobalt, 6-cup..........$350.00
Red Poppy, ball jug, #3............................$120.00
Red Poppy, bowl, D-style, oval, 11¼"..........$55.00
Red Poppy, cake plate $55.00
Red Poppy, custard.................................$20.00
Red Poppy, jug, milk or syrup; Daniel, 4".............$47.00
Red Poppy, mixer cover, plastic..................$45.00
Red Poppy, napkin, linen.........................$25.00
Red Poppy, pretzel jar..............................$600.00
Red Poppy, saucer, D-style $3.00
Red Poppy, teapot, New York.....................$130.00
Red Poppy, tray, metal, round....................$55.00
Red Poppy, tumbler, frosted, glass, 2 styles, ea $25.00
Ribbed, bean pot, Chinese Red $150.00
Ribbed, bowl, Russet, 9½".......................$20.00
Ribbed, casserole, Russet, 9".....................$32.00
Ribbed, ramekin, Chinese Red, 6-oz............$8.50
Rose Parade, bowl, straight-sided, 9" $40.00
Rose Parade, creamer, Sani-Grid.................$22.00
Rose White, sugar bowl, Sani-Grid..............$16.00
Royal Rose, bowl, Thick Rim, 7½"..............$27.00
Satin Black/Hi-White, bowl, celery; Tomorrow's Classic, oval $30.00
Satin Black/Hi-White, creamer, Tomorrow's Classic ...$14.00
Satin Black/Hi-White, plate, Tomorrow's Classic, 8".....$9.50
Satin Black/Hi-White, sugar bowl, Tomorrow's Classic, w/lid $22.00
Sear's Arlington, bowl, fruit; E-style, 5¼"....................$4.50
Sear's Arlington, bowl, vegetable; E-style, w/lid........$35.00
Sear's Arlington, platter, E-style, oval, 13¼"..............$22.00
Sear's Arlington, saucer, E-style $1.50
Sear's Fairfax, bowl, cereal; 5¼".................$4.50
Sear's Fairfax, cup.................................$5.00
Sear's Fairfax, plate, 7¼".........................$5.50
Sear's Fairfax, plate, 10" $9.00
Sear's Monticello, bowl, cream soup; E-style, 5"........$90.00
Sear's Monticello, creamer, E-style.............$9.00
Sear's Monticello, plate, E-style, 8".............$7.50
Sear's Monticello, saucer, E-style $1.50
Sear's Mount Vernon, bowl, cereal; 6¼" $10.00
Sear's Mount Vernon, casserole, w/lid.........$42.00
Sear's Mount vernon, plate, 8"..................$6.00
Sear's Mount Vernon, platter, oval, 15½"...................$30.00
Sear's Richmond/Brown-Eyed Susan, baker, French, flute (BES era only)......................$18.00
Sear's Richmond/Brown-Eyed Susan, creamer $9.00
Sear's Richmond/Brown-Eyed Susan, plate, 6½"..........$3.50
Serenade, bowl, cereal; D-style, 6"..............$8.50
Serenade, bowl, Radiance, 7½".................$16.00
Serenade, casserole, Radiance $40.00

Serenade, dripolator, Kadota, all china, from $135.00 to $150.00. (Photo courtesy Margaret and Kenn Whitmyer)

Serenade, fork...$125.00
Serenade, platter, D-style, 11¼".................$20.00
Serenade, teapot, Aladdin.........................$300.00
Shaggy Tulip, coffeepot, Perk.....................$75.00
Shaggy Tulip, pretzel jar $195.00
Silhouette, bowl, D-style, flared, 3⅝"..........$12.00
Silhouette, bowl, vegetable; D-style, round, 9¼" $32.00
Silhouette, canister, glass w/green decal, 1-gal $27.00
Silhouette, casserole, Medallion..................$40.00
Silhouette, custard, Medallion.....................$27.00
Silhouette, jug, Medallion, #2.....................$22.00
Silhouette, saucer, St Denis.........................$10.00
Silhouette, sifter $55.00
Silhouette, teapot, Streamline $285.00
Spring/Studio 10, bowl, fruit; Tomorrow's Classic, 5¾" ...$6.50
Spring/Studio 10, casserole, Tomorrow's Classic, 2-qt ...$50.00
Spring/Studio 10, marmite, Tomorrow's Classic, w/lid ..$27.00
Springtime, bowl, salad; D-style, 9"............$14.00
Springtime, coffeepot, Washington.............$40.00
Springtime, gravy boat, D-style...................$25.00
Springtime, pie baker $20.00
Stonewall, custard, Radiance........................$27.00
Sudial, casserole, Art Glaze colors, casserole, #3, 5½" ...$32.00
Sundial, batter jug, red or cobalt................$210.00
Sundial, cookie jar, red or cobalt $230.00
Sundial, teapot, Art Glaze colors, 6-cup $275.00
Sunglow, bowl, soup/cereal; Century, 8".....$10.00
Sunglow, plate, Century, 8"...........................$9.50
Sunglow, sugar bowl, Century, w/lid...........$18.00
Tulip, bowl, D-style, oval............................$37.00
Tulip, bowl, Radiance, 6"............................$16.00
Tulip, bowl, Thick Rim, 6"...........................$18.00

Tulip, casserole, tab handles, from $100.00 to $125.00. (Photo courtesy Margaret and Kenn Whitmyer)

Tulip, stack set, Radiance...........................$110.00
Tulip, waffle iron, metal.............................$125.00
Wild Poppy, cocette, handled.......................$95.00
Wild Poppy, mustard, spoon lid.................$295.00
Wild Poppy, tea tile, 6"..............................$120.00
Wildfire, baker, French, fluted $22.00
Wildfire, bowl, fruit; D-style, 5½"..................$6.00
Wildfire, casserole, Thick Rim, Blue Parts $40.00
Wildfire, custard, straight-sided..................$25.00
Wildfire, pie baker $55.00
Wildfire, plate, D-style, 7" $9.50
Wildfire, teapot, Streamline........................$600.00
Yellow Rose, bowl, vegetable; D-style, round, 9¼"....$35.00
Yellow Rose, coffeepot, Kadota bottom........$60.00
Yellow Rose, salt & pepper shakers, handled, pr $44.00
Yellow Rose, saucer, D-style $2.00

Teapots

Airflow, maroon...$100.00
Aladdin, wam yellow, standard gold...........$85.00
Albany, black, standard gold, 6-cup............$60.00
Baltimore, Chinese Red, solid color, 6-cup...$300.00
Boston, cobalt, old gold label $125.00
Cleveland, turquoise, solid color, 6-cup.......$85.00
French, rose, solid color, 4-8 cup................$40.00
Globe, Cadet, solid color, 6-cup................$100.00
Hollywood, canary, standard gold, 6-cup.....$60.00
Illinois, canary, Gold Nebula, 6-cup $200.00
Indiana, ivory, standard gold.....................$275.00
Los Angeles, Dresden, solid colors, 6-cup...$50.00
Melody, ivory, standard gold, 6-cup $175.00
Nautilus, emerald, solid color, 6-cup $255.00
New York, chartreuse, standard gold, 12-cup $50.00

Hallmark

Since the early 1970s when Hallmark first introduced their glass ball and yarn doll ornaments, many lines and themes have been developed to the delight of collectors. Many early ornaments are now valued at several times their original price. This is especially true of the first one issued in a particular series. For instance, Betsy Clark's first edition issued in 1973 has a value today of $125.00 (MIB).

Our values are for ornaments that are mint and in their original boxes.

Advisor: The Baggage Car (See Directory, Hallmark)

Newsletter: The Baggage Car
3100 Justin Dr., Ste. B
Des Moines, IA 50322; 515-270-9080 or Fax 515-223-1398
Includes show and company information along with current listing

Art Masterpiece, 675QX377-2, 2nd edition, 1985, MIB...$14.50
Baby Unicorn, 975QX5486, 1990, MIB.......................$24.50

Baby's First Christmas, 400QX200-1, satin ball, dated 1980, MIB **$30.00**
Betsy Clark, 250QX163-1, satin ball, dated 1975, MIB ..**$42.50**
Betsy Clark, 250XHD110-2, glass ball, dated 1973, 1st edition, MIB **$125.00**
Betsy Clark, 300QX195-1, glass ball, 4th edition, 1976, MIB **$125.00**
Bicentennial '76 Commemorative, 250QX203-1, satin ball, dated 1976, MIB...**$60.00**
Birds of Winter, Cardinals, 225QX205-1, glass ball, dated 1976, MIB **$65.00**
Candy Apple Mouse, 650QX374-2, dated 1985, MIB ..**$14.50**
Carousel, 600QX146-3, handcrafted, 1st edition, dated 1978, MIB **$395.00**
Charmers, 250QX-109-1, glass ball, dated 1974, MIB .**$45.00**
Charmers, 350QX153-5, satin ball, dated 1977, MIB...**$65.00**
Christmas Treat, 500QX134-7, handcrafted, 1979 (reissued in 1980), MIB **$85.00**
Coyote Carols 875QX4993, 1990, MIB **$19.50**
Disney, 350QX133-5, Disney, satin ball, dated 1977, MIB...**$75.00**
Dove, 450QX190-3, twirl-about, handcrafted wind-up, dated 1978, MIB **$85.00**
Drummer Boy, 550QX147-4, handcrafted, dated 1980, MIB...**$95.00**
First Christmas Together, 350QX132-2, satin ball, dated 1977, MIB **$65.00**
Granddaughter, 350QX216-3, satin ball, 1978, MIB **$55.00**
Love, 350QX268-3, glass ball, dated 1978, M in poor box..**$55.00**
Mary Hamilton, 350QX254-7, satin ball, dated 1979, MIB...**$25.00**
Mrs Santa, 125XHd75-2, yarn, 1973, MIB....................**$24.50**
Norman Rockwell, 250QX166-1, satin ball, MIB **$55.00**

Puppy Love, QX-448-4, 1992, second in Keepsake series, 2⅝", MIB, $35.00.

Rabbit, 250QX139-5, rabbit, satin box, 1977, M, no box .**$95.00**
Rockwell, 475QX2296, glass ball, dated 1990, MIB **$24.50**
Rudolph & Santa, 250QX213-1, satin ball, dated 1976, MIB **$95.00**

Santa, 175QX124-1, 1974 (reissued in 1976, 1978), MIB..**$24.50**
Snowflake, 350QX308-3, acrylic, Holiday Highlights, dated 1978, MIB **$65.00**
Snowgoose, 250QX107-1, glass ball, 1974, MIB.........**$75.00**
Special Friends, 575QX372-5, acrylic, dated 1985, MIB ..**$10.00**
Tree Treats - Reindeer, 300QX178-1, handcrafted, dated 1976, MIB **$115.00**
Yesterday's Toys, glass ball, 350QX250-3, glass ball, dated 1978, M (EX box) **$100.00**
Yesteryear - Train, t00QX181-1, handcrafted, dated 1976, MIB **$165.00**
Yesteryears - Jack-in-the-Box, 600QX171-5, handcrafted, dated 1977, MIB...**$125.00**
25th Christmas Together, 350QX269-6, glass ball, dated 1978, MIB **$35.00**

Halloween

Halloween is now the second biggest money-making holiday of the year, and more candy is sold at this time than for any other holiday. Folk artists are making new items to satisfy the demands of collectors and celebrators that can't get enough of the old items. Over one hundred years of celebrating this magical holiday has built a social history strata by strata, and wonderful and exciting finds can be made in all periods! From one dollar to thousands, there is something to excite collectors in every price range, with new collectibles being born every year. For further information we recommend *Collectible Halloween; More Halloween Collectibles; Halloween: Collectible Decorations & Games; Salem Witchcraft and Souvenirs; Postmarked Yesterday, Art of the Holiday Postcard;* and *The Tastes & Smells of Halloween*; also see *Around Swanzey* and *The Armenians of Worcester* (Arcadia). The author of these books is Pamela E. Apkarian-Russell (Halloween Queen), a free-lancer who also writes an ephemera column for *Unravel the Gavel*.

Advisor: Pamela E. Apkarian-Russell (See Directory, Halloween)

Publisher of Newsletter: *Trick or Treat Trader*
P.O. Box 499, Winchester, NH 03470; 603-239-8875;
e-mail: halloweenqueen@cheshire.net;
Internet: http://adam.net/~halloweenqueen/home.html;
Subscription: $15 per year in USA ($20 foreign) for 4 quarterly issues

Candlestick, skeleton head on book, ceramic, Made in Japan, 4x2x2¼" **$16.00**
Candy container, jack-o'-lantern, plastic, Empire Plastic Corp, 1968, 7½x8", NM...**$15.00**
Candy container, jack-o'-lantern w/scowling face, papier-mache, early, 6x7", EX **$155.00**
Costume, Lucy (Peanuts), Collegeville, 1980s, MIB **$15.00**
Decoration, cat w/bow tie, honeycomb tissue w/head diecut, EX...**$24.00**

Decoration, pumpkin, honeycomb paper, black & orange, Made in USA, 8" dia, EX..............$8.00

Decoration, pumpkin, honeycomb paper, Made in USA, 10x12", EX..............$10.00

Decoration, skeleton, black & white compo w/springs as arms & legs, hands & feet on strings, 3⅞" $25.00

Decoration, skeleton, diecut paper, Beistle Co Made in USA, 21½", NM..............$18.00

Decoration, spider, black & white compositon w/spring legs, Japan, EX..............$20.00

Decoration, witch, cardboard diecut w/tissue wings, Made in USA, 9", NM..............$20.00

Diecut, black cat, front & back sections movable, 12x14½" (when in walking position), EX..............$10.00

Diecut, black cat, paper litho on honeycomb tissue base, Made in USA, 12", EX..............$27.50

Diecut, owl, paper litho w/pleated tissue wings, Made in USA, ca 1950s, 8½", EX..............$20.00

Diecut, pumpkin, paper litho, 1940s, 9½"..............$15.00

Diecut, skull & crossbones, tissue eyes & nose, Luhrs USA..............$50.00

Doll, Scarey Witch, M (VG box), $125.00.
(Photo courtesy Pamela Apkarian-Russell)

Earrings, skull, plastic, Russ, pr, MOC..............$4.00

Figure, Nightmare Before Christmas, Sally, MIB.......$450.00

Halloween costume, Big Bird, Ben Cooper, MIB........$20.00

Halloween costume, Buffy & Mrs Beasley, Ben Cooper, 1970, MIB, ea..............$75.00

Halloween costume, Charlie Brown, Determined, 1970s, MIB..............$25.00

Halloween costume, Dick Tracy, Ben Cooper, 1967, complete, EX..............$50.00

Halloween costume, Ed Grimley, Collegeville, 1980s, MIB..$15.00

Halloween costume, Julia, Ben Cooper, 1960s, complete, NMIB, from $40 to..............$60.00

Halloween costume, Oscar the Grouch, Ben Cooper, MIB..$30.00

Halloween costume, Snoopy, Determined, 1970s, MIB..$25.00

Halloween costume, Steve Austin, Ben Cooper, 1974, MIB..$25.00

Halloween costume, Welcome Back Kotter, any character, Collegeville, 1976, MIB..............$35.00

Hat, crepe paper, black cats on orange, M..............$7.50

Horn, black & orange plastic, whistle works well, 5", EX..............$10.00

Horn, litho tin, witches, moon, bats, etc on orange, yellow inside, 10¼", EX..............$47.50

Jack-o'-lantern, cardboard, slot & tab constructions, tissue intact, Made in USA, NM..............$25.00

Jack-o'-lantern, papier-mache, mouth liner, paper eyes, battery-operated, American, 4½x5", EX..............$145.00

Key chain, Nightmare Before Christmas, Jack on tombstone, black enamel..............$12.00

Lantern, jack-o'-lantern on black base, glass, battery-operated, uses 2 C batteries, 5x3" dia, NM..............$125.00

Lapel pin, jack-o'-lantern & cat pops up, Halloween, MOC..............$10.00

Lapel pin, wind-up skeleton head w/moving mouth, Hallmark, MOC..............$10.00

Light bulb, skull & crossbones on milk glass, round..$35.00

Mask, black cat, burlap-like material, some fraying, VG..............$7.00

Mask, paper face w/cut-out released nose, Japan, w/elastic band to go around head, 7½" L, M..............$22.00

Necklace, Night Before Christmas, Jack as Santa, enamel on pewter..............$45.00

Noisemaker, tin litho, good witch & bad witch, wooden handle, 5x4", EX..............$25.00

Noisemaker, tin litho, witch on broomstick & owl in tree, drum shape w/wood handle, EX..............$19.00

Party blower, cardboard paper face w/plastic disk holding moving eyes, Japan, 4½" dia, NM..............$42.50

Pillow, Nightmare Before Christmas, M..............$95.00

Postcard, boy & girl carving jack-o'-lantern & petting black cat, Brundage, Germany, 1912 postmark, EX.......$25.00

Postcard, girl rolling pumpkin, HB Griggs, series #314, Germany, VG..............$20.00

Tablecloth, paper, cats & jack-o'-lanterns, EX............$45.00

Postcard, Whitney (publisher), pre-1920, $25.00. (Photo courtesy Pamela Apkarian-Russell)

Harker Pottery

Harker was one of the oldest potteries in the country. Their history can be traced back to the 1840s. In the '30s, a new plant was built in Chester, West Virginia, and the company began manufacturing kitchen and dinnerware lines, eventually employing as many as three hundred workers.

Several of these lines are popular with collectors today. One of the most easily recognized is Cameoware. It is usually found in pink or blue decorated with white silhouettes of flowers, though other designs were made as well. Colonial Lady, Red Apple, Amy, Mallow, and Pansy are some of their better-known lines that are fairly easy to find and reassemble into sets.

If you'd like to learn more about Harker, we recommend *The Collector's Encyclopedia of American Dinnerware* by Jo Cunningham.

Amy, bean pot, 2¼"	**$16.00**
Amy, bowl, custard; 2x3¼"	**$18.00**
Amy, bowl, utility	**$30.00**
Amy, creamer	**$10.00**
Amy, jug, w/lid, High-Rise	**$75.00**
Amy, pie server	**$27.00**
Amy, platter, 12x11"	**$25.00**
Amy, rolling pin, w/stopper, 15"	**$150.00**
Amy, spoon, 8⅞"	**$30.00**
Amy, stack dish, w/lid, 3x6⅜"	**$35.00**
Amy, sugar bowl, open	**$10.00**
Amy, teapot	**$40.00**
Basket, creamer, 3"	**$12.00**
Basket, plate	**$3.00**
Blue Blossoms, pitcher, Regal	**$25.00**
Boyce, pitcher, Regal, gold trim handle	**$45.00**
Brim, plate, snack	**$8.00**
Calico Tulip, baking dish, individual	**$10.00**
Cameo Rose, bowl, mixing; pink, 9"	**$36.00**
Cameo Rose, bowl, vegetable; pink, 9"	**$16.00**
Cameo Rose, casserole, w/lid	**$40.00**
Cameo Rose, cup	**$12.00**
Cameo Rose, pie baker, 10"	**$30.00**
Cameo Rose, plate, utilty; 11¾"	**$22.00**
Cameo Rose, platter, 12x10⅞"	**$38.00**
Cameo Rose, rolling pin, pink w/white handles	**$130.00**
Cameo Rose, teapot, pink, 4-cup	**$65.00**
Cameo Rose, water jug, 2-qt, 8"	**$75.00**
Cameo Shellware, cup & saucer	**$14.00**
Cherry, salt & pepper shakers, utility; pr	**$20.00**
Chesterton, creamer	**$12.00**
Chesterton, cup	**$3.50**
Chesterton, saucer	**$1.00**
Colonial Lady, bowl, vegetable; 8⅞"	**$18.00**
Colonial Lady, cookie jar, w/lid	**$42.00**
Colonial Lady, rolling pin	**$130.00**
Colonial Lady, salt & pepper shakers, table style, pr	**$28.00**
Colonial Lady, sugar bowl, w/lid	**$18.00**
Compass Rose, creamer, 4⅝"	**$18.00**

Cottage, fork	**$30.00**
Deco Dahlia, pie/cake lifter, 9¼"	**$25.00**
Deco Dahlia, plate, utilty; 12"	**$25.00**

Deco Dahlia, platter, oval, 9½", $18.00.

Emmy, rolling pin, w/stopper, 15"	**$160.00**
Enchantment, creamer	**$10.00**
English Countryside, bowl, utility; lg	**$40.00**
Floral Decal, rolling pin, w/stopper, 15"	**$160.00**
Fruits, pitcher, Regal	**$45.00**
Ivy, batter jug, w/lid, 7"	**$58.00**
Ivy, platter, 12"	**$18.00**
Ivy, salt shaker, Skyscraper, 4⅝"	**$18.00**
Leaf Swirl, casserole, w/lid, w/warmer base, no decor	**$35.00**
Leaf Swirl, coffee server	**$17.00**
Mallow, plate, serving; 12"	**$27.00**
Mallow, plate, 8"	**$12.00**
Mallow, rolling pin, w/stopper, 15"	**$160.00**
Melrose, bowl, advertising, 1¼x5⅞x4½"	**$35.00**
Melrose, bowl, custard; 2x3⅜"	**$18.00**
Modern Tulip, cake plate, w/metal holder, NM	**$20.00**
Modern Tulip, fork, spoon & pie/cake lifter, 3-pc set	**$45.00**
Modern Tulip, rolling pin, w/stopper	**$150.00**
Modern Tulip, sugar bowl, w/lid	**$12.00**
Old Vintage, creamer	**$10.00**
Old Vintage, cup & saucer	**$12.00**
Pansy, bowl, 6"	**$8.00**
Pastel Tulip, cake plate, 11"	**$27.00**
Pastel Tulip, pie baker, 10"	**$25.00**
Pastel Tulip, plate, Gadroon shape, 9"	**$8.00**
Petit Point, bowl, fruit, 5½"	**$5.50**
Petit Point, bowl, mixing; 4⅞x10"	**$26.00**
Petit Point, cup & saucer	**$10.00**
Petit Point, drip jar, w/lid, 4⅞"	**$45.00**
Petit Point, pie baker, 9"	**$30.00**
Petit Point, pie/cake lifter	**$25.00**
Petit Point, plate, bread & butter, 6½"	**$6.00**
Petit Point, platter, oval, 11⅝x9"	**$18.00**
Red Apple I, plate, serving; 12"	**$27.00**
Red Apple II, creamer	**$20.00**

Red Apple II, serving spoon......................................**$35.00**
Rose I, pie baker, 9"...**$27.00**
Rose I, rolling pin...**$130.00**
Rose II, caker server...**$27.00**
Rose II, casserole, w/lid, 8".....................................**$35.00**
Rose II, custard, individual.......................................**$6.00**
Rose Spray, bowl, tab handled.................................**$10.00**
Rose Spray, creamer...**$16.00**
Rose Spray, plate, breakfast; 9"...............................**$12.00**
Rosebud, salt & pepper shakers, pr.........................**$20.00**
Shadow Rose, plate, dinner; 9¼"..............................**$13.00**
Shellridge, creamer..**$10.00**
Slender Leaf, plate, serving.....................................**$17.00**
Slender Leaf, plate, 8"..**$6.00**
Spring Meadow, casserole, w/lid, 5x6½".................**$36.00**
Springtime, plate, 10"...**$8.00**
Springtime, saucer...**$3.00**
Tulip, rolling pin, w/stopper, 15"............................**$160.00**
White Rose, pie baker, Carv-Kraft...........................**$25.00**

Hartland Plastics, Inc.

The Hartland company was located in Hartland, Wisconsin, where during the '50s and '60s they made several lines of plastic figures: Western and Historic Horsemen, Miniature Western Series, and the Hartland Sport Series of Famous Baseball Stars. Football and bowling figures and religious statues were made as well. The plastic, virgin acetate, was very durable and the figures were hand painted with careful attention to detail. They're often marked.

Though prices have come down from their high of a few years ago, rare figures and horses are still in high demand. Dealers using this guide should take these factors into consideration when pricing their items: values listed here are for the figure, horse (unless noted gunfighter), hat, guns, and all other accessories for that particular figure in near-mint condition with no rubs and all original parts. All parts were made exclusively for a special figure, so a hat is not just a hat — each one belongs to a specific figure! Many people do not realize this, and it is important for the collector to be knowledgeable. An excellent source of information is *Hartland Horses and Riders* by Gail Fitch.

In our listings for sports figures, mint to near-mint condition values are for figures that are white or near-white in color; excellent values are for those that are off-white or cream-colored. These values are representative of traditional retail prices asked by dealers; Internet values for Hartlands, as is so often the case nowadays, seem to be in a constant state of flux.

See also *Schroeder's Collectible Toys, Antique to Modern* (Collector Books).

Advisors: James Watson, Sports Figures; Judy and Kerry Irvin, Western Figures (See Directory, Hartland)

Horsemen and Gunfighters

Bat Masterson, gunfighter, NMIB.............................**$500.00**
Bill Longley, NM...**$600.00**

Brave Eagle, NMIB..**$300.00**
Buffalo Bill, NM...**$300.00**
Champ Cowgirl, NM...**$150.00**
Chief Thunderbird, rare shield, NM.........................**$150.00**
Chris Colt, gunfighter, NM......................................**$150.00**
Clay Holister, gunfighter, NM..................................**$225.00**
Dale Evans, purple, NM..**$250.00**
Dan Troop, gunfighter, NM.....................................**$500.00**
Davy Crockett, NM...**$500.00**
General Custer, NMIB...**$250.00**
General George Washington, NMIB..........................**$175.00**
Gil Favor, prancing, NM..**$650.00**
Hoby Gillman, NM..**$250.00**
Jim Bowie, w/tag, NM...**$250.00**
Johnny McKay, gunfighter, NM................................**$800.00**
Lone Ranger, Champ version w/chaps, black breast collar, NM...**$125.00**
Paladin, gunfighter, NM..**$400.00**

Rifleman, Chuck Conners as Lucas McCaine, NMIB, $350.00.

Ronald MacKenzie, NM..**$1,200.00**
Roy Rogers, semi-rearing, NMIB.............................**$600.00**
Seth Adams, NM..**$275.00**
Sgt Preston, repro flag, NM....................................**$650.00**
Tom Jeffords, NM...**$175.00**
Tonto, NM..**$150.00**
Warpaint Thunderbird, w/shield, NMIB....................**$350.00**
Wyatt Earp, w/tag, NMIB..**$250.00**

Sports Figures

Babe Ruth, NM/M, from $175 to..............................**$200.00**
Dick Groat, EX, from $800 to................................**$1,000.00**
Dick Groat, w/bat, NM, minimum value...................**$800.00**
Don Drysdale, EX...**$400.00**
Duke Snider, EX, from $300 to................................**$325.00**
Duke Snider, M, from $500 to..................................**$600.00**
Eddie Mathews, NM/M, from $125 to.......................**$150.00**
Ernie Banks, EX, from $245 to................................**$265.00**
Ernie Banks, 25th Anniversary, MIB..........................**$40.00**

Harmon Killebrew, NM/M, from $400 to...................**$500.00**
Henry Aaron, EX, from $175 to..................................**$190.00**
Henry Aaron, 25th Anniversary, MIB **$50.00**
Little Leaguer, 6", EX, from $100 to...........................**$125.00**
Little Leaguer, 6", NM/M, from $200 to.....................**$250.00**
Louie Aparacio, EX, from $200 to **$225.00**
Louie Aparacio, NM/M, from $250 to **$350.00**
Major Leaguer, 4", EX, from $50 to **$75.00**
Major Leaguer, 4", NM/M, from $100 to **$125.00**
Mickey Mantle, NM...**$350.00**
Nellie Fox, NM/M, from $200 to **$250.00**
Rocky Colavito, NM/M, from $600 to **$700.00**
Roger Maris, EX, from $300 to **$350.00**
Roger Maris, NM/M, from $350 to...............................**$400.00**
Stan Musial, EX, from $150 to **$175.00**
Stan Musial, NM/M, from $200 to...............................**$250.00**

Ted Williams, NM, $235.00.

Warren Spahn, NM/M, from $150 to **$175.00**
Willie Mays, EX, from $150 to **$200.00**
Willie Mays, NM/M, from $225 to **$250.00**
Yogi Berra, w/mask, EX, from $150 to **$175.00**
Yogi Berra, w/mask, NM, from $175 to **$250.00**
Yogi Berra, w/out mask, NM/M, from $150 to.........**$175.00**

Head Vases

These are fun to collect, and prices are still reasonable. You've seen them at flea markets — heads of ladies, children, clowns, even some men, and a religious figure now and then. A few look very much like famous people — there's a Jackie Onassis vase by Inarco that leaves no doubt as to who it's supposed to represent!

They were mainly imported from Japan, although a few were made by American companies and sold to florist shops to be filled with flower arrangements. So if there's an old flower shop in your neighborhood, you might start your search with their storerooms.

If you'd like to learn more about them, we recommend *Head Vases, Identification and Values*, by Kathleen Cole.

Newsletter: *Head Hunters Newsletter*
Maddy Gordon
P.O. Box 83H, Scarsdale, NY 10583; 914-472-0200
Subscription: $24 per year for 4 issues; also holds convention

Child, #S1725A, brunette girl holds umbrella, scarf covers all but bangs, black jumper, 5" **$75.00**
Child, Enesco (paper label), blond girl w/kitten, pink polka-dot bow in hair, pink bodice, 5½" **$45.00**
Child, Enesco (paper label), Delsey Tissue Girl, blond or frosted hair, holds flowers, 5", ea........................**$75.00**
Child, Graduate #609, blond w/black cap & tassel, 5¼" **$45.00**
Child, Inarco #E-1061, blond girl w/ponytail & pink bow, hand to face, white bow at neck, 4½".................**$40.00**
Child, Inarco #E1579, Cleve Ohio, blond girl praying, red pajamas, 1964, 6" **$45.00**
Child, Inarco #E2965, girl w/blond braids, yellow scarf w/lg bow, yellow bodice, 7" **$58.00**
Child, Lefton's (paper Label), blond girl w/flower in hair, green bodice, 6".......................................**$40.00**
Child, Soldier Inarco #E3250, black uniform, sm closed eyes, 6" **$50.00**
Child, unmarked, blond girl in flat-brimmed hat w/applied flower, flower at bodice, 5"..................................**$40.00**
Clown, Inarco #E-2320, blond w/black hat, red nose, red & white mouth, polka-dot tie, 5".............................**$50.00**
Clown, Inarco #E-5071, white face, bald head w/tiny black cap, red nose & mouth, up-turned collar, 4½".....**$40.00**
Clown, National Potteries (paper label), red conical hat w/white ball tip, red ruffled collar, 7"................**$35.00**
Clown, unmarked, orange hair, red mouth & nose, wide ruffle forms base, 4"...**$40.00**

Girl in bow-tied hat, hand to face, Royal Crown, #3411, 7", $300.00. (Photo courtesy Kathleen Cole)

Lady, Rubens #297/M, blond w/flower in hair, leaves on bodice, pearl necklace & earrings, 6½" **$60.00**

Lady, #C6018, blond dressed in pink, white hat w/pink flowers & bow, pearl dangling earrings, 5½" $45.00

Lady, #5854, brown side-swept updo, pearl necklace & earrings, blue bodice w/ruffled collar, 6½" **$150.00**

Lady, Glamour Girl, shiny white w/gold details, 6½" **$20.00**

Lady, Inarco #E1755, Lady Aileen, blond w/jeweled tiara & necklace, 1964, 3½" **$60.00**

Lady, Inarco #E190E/L, blond w/brimmed black hat, hand raised, pearl necklace & earrings, 1961, 8½" **$350.00**

Lady, Inarco #E2782, blond w/flip, white collar on red bodice, 6" **$50.00**

Lady, Japan, blond w/wide-brimmed pink hat, 6 holes in rim to hold flowers, downcast eyes, molded necklace, 5" ...**$45.00**

Lady, Lark (paper label), blond w/sm curls, pearl earrings & necklace, pink bodice w/white collar, 7" **$225.00**

Lady, Lefton's (paper label) #2900, blond w/both hands to bace, flat-brimmed hat, strapless blue bodice, 6"..**$85.00**

Lady, Margo, white hair, ruffled flat-brimmed hat w/applied flower, applied flower at bodice, 6"......................**$50.00**

Lady, Napco #C2636C, blond w/hand to face, strong chin, pearl earrings, necklace & bracelet, 1956, 6½" **$60.00**

Lady, Napcoware #C7314, blond w/loose curls, pearl earrings & necklace, black bodice, 9"......................**$100.00**

Lady, Parma #A219, blond w/side-swept hair, 1 pearl earring, pearl necklace, green bodice, 8½"......................**$300.00**

Lady, Relpo #K1052B, blond w/pearl earrings, wide collar turned up, green flat hat w/pink flower, 5½" **$50.00**

Lady, Relpo #K1679, wide curving brim on blue hat w/bow, pearl earrings & necklace, simple bodice, 7"....**$350.00**

Lady, Rubens #483, blond w/side-swept hair, hand up to face, pink ruffled bodice, pearl necklace & earrings, 6½"..**$65.00**

Lady, Rubens #495, blond w/white-gloved hands crossed at chin, flat-brimmed hat, pearl earrings & necklace, 5¾"..**$65.00**

Lady, unmarked, blond w/brown Derby hat, hand up to face, pearl necklace, brown bodice, 6½"......................**$60.00**

Lady, unmarked, blond w/gold eyelashes, blue hat w/long ribbon at left side, white collar & blue bodice, 4".......**$25.00**

Lady, unmarked, brunette dressed in yellow w/pink applied rose on shoulder, thick black lashes, 6½" **$50.00**

Lady, USA, Deco style, glossy white w/face up, wide-brimmed hat, 8½"................................**$65.00**

Man, unmarked, green Derby hat, black mustache, green suit, 4½"..**$30.00**

Mother & Child, unmarked, blond lady w/baby wrapped in shawl, 1 hand, 5½"................................**$22.50**

Nun, Relpo (paper label), hands up & crossed, white cowl, pale blue-gray bodice & sleeves, 6½"....................**$35.00**

Oriental lady, #3237, Japanese lady w/traditional hairdo, blue bodice w/gold trim, 7½" **$50.00**

Oriental lady, ornate headdress w/gold trim, collar forms sm wing at shoulder, 5"................................**$40.00**

Oriental lady, unmarked, hand to face, ornate hairdo, pink bodice, 4¾" **$40.00**

Oriental lady, unmarked, ornate headdress, Mandarin-style collar on white bodice w/green trim, 8½" **$125.00**

Teen girl, Caffco (paper label), blond frosted bouffant hair-do, green bodice w/bow, 7"................................**$275.00**

Teen girl, Caffco (paper label) #E-3293, blond frosted hair w/yellow bow, yellow bodice w/white collar, 6" ..**$40.00**

Teen girl, Enesco (paper label), blond w/2 ponytails, pink sleeveless bodice, 4"................................**$40.00**

Teen girl, Inarco #E2967, blond w/long flip, blue headband & bodice, 5½"..**$80.00**

Teen girl, Inarco #E3548, blond w/telephone in hand, yellow headband & bodice, white ruffled collar, 5½" **$65.00**

Teen girl, Japan, blond w/2 long curls, blue flowers at ea ear, pearl earrings, ruffled collar, 4½" **$60.00**

Teen girl, Japan, light brown hair, wide-brimmed hat, flower at left ear, blue bodice w/white collar & bow, 6".......**$70.00**

Teen girl, Lark (paper label) #JN-4112, blond w/blue bows in hair, pearl necklace, blue bodice, 5½"..................**$55.00**

Teen girl, Nancy Pew (paper label) #2262, blond w/yellow hat, pearl earrings, yellow bodice, 5½" **$150.00**

Teen girl, Napco #C4072G, blond graduate in white w/gold trim, 6"..**$100.00**

Teen girl, Napcoware (paper label), #C3499, blond w/loose curls, red bow in hair, pearl necklace & earrings, 5½"..**$85.00**

Teen girl, Relpo #K1947, blond w/black hat w/pink bow, pearl necklace, black bodice w/white collar, 5½" **$150.00**

Teen girl, Rubens #4135, blond w/pink-lined hood over head, 5½" **$125.00**

Teen girl, unmarked, blond flip, yellow hat w/irregular dots (mod look), pink bodice w/white insert, 5".........**$85.00**

Heisey Glass

From the late 1800s until 1957, the Heisey Glass Company of Newark, Ohio, was one of the largest, most successful manufacturers of quality tableware in the world. Though the market is well established, many pieces are still reasonably priced; and if you're drawn to the lovely patterns and colors that Heisey made, you're investment should be sound.

After 1901 much of their glassware was marked with their familiar trademark, the 'Diamond H' (an H in a diamond) or a paper label. Blown pieces are often marked on the stem instead of the bowl or foot.

Numbers in the listings are catalog reference numbers assigned by the company to indicate variations in shape or stem style. Collectors use them, especially when they buy and sell by mail, for the same purpose. Many catalog pages (showing these numbers) are contained in *The Collector's Encyclopedia of Heisey Glass, 1896 – 1957,* by Neila Bredehoft. This book and *Elegant Glassware of the Depression Era* by Gene Florence are excellent references for further study. Both are published by Collector Books.

Newsletter: *The Heisey News*
Heisey Collectors of America
169 W Church St., Newark, OH 43055; 612-345-2932

Charter Oak, crystal, bowl, floral; #116, Oak Leaf, 11".......**$30.00**

Charter Oak, Flamingo, candlestick, #116, Oak Leaf, 3"...**$35.00**

Charter Oak, Hawthorne, comport, #3362, low foot, 6"...**$80.00**

Charter Oak, Marigold, stem, luncheon goblet; #3362, low foot, 8-oz...**$60.00**

Charter Oak, Moongleam, plate, dinner; #1246, Acorn & Leaves, 10½"................................**$55.00**

Chintz, crystal, bowl, preserve; footed, handle, 5½" ..**$15.00**

Chintz, crystal, plate, hors d'oeuvre; 2-handled, 12"...**$30.00**

Chintz, Sahara, cup...**$25.00**

Chintz, Sahara, sugar bowl, individual.....................**$30.00**

Colt, standing, 5", $95.00.

Crystolite, crystal, bowl, dessert/sauce; 8" **$30.00**

Crystolite, crystal, cheese, footed, 5½".........................**$27.00**

Crystolite, crystal, jam jar, w/lid **$70.00**

Crystolite, crystal, plate, salad; 7" **$15.00**

Crystolite, crystal, sugar bowl, round.........................**$40.00**

Empress, Alexandrite, saucer, sq **$25.00**

Empress, cobalt, plate, sq, 8".......................................**$70.00**

Empress, Flamingo, bowl, preserve; 2-handled, 5" **$20.00**

Empress, Flamingo, bowl, vegetable; oval, 10"...........**$50.00**

Empress, Moongleam, vase, flared, 8" **$190.00**

Empress, Sahara, plate, muffin; upturned sides, 12"...**$80.00**

Greek Key, crystal, bowl, jelly; shallow, low foot, 4½"..**$40.00**

Greek Key, crystal, bowl, nappy; 8" **$70.00**

Greek Key, crystal, oil bottle, w/#6 stopper, 4-oz **$100.00**

Greek Key, crystal, plate, 7" **$50.00**

Greek Key, crystal, stem, wine; 2-oz **$110.00**

Greek Key, crystal, tumbler, straight sides, 5-oz **$50.00**

Ipswich, crystal, candy jar, w/lid, ¼-lb.....................**$175.00**

Ipswich, crystal, tumbler, cupped rim, flat bottom, 10-oz..**$70.00**

Ipswich, green, sherbet, footed (knob in stem), 4-oz....**$45.00**

Ipswich, pink, creamer...**$70.00**

Ipswich, Sahara, stem, oyster cocktail; footed, 4-oz ...**$50.00**

Lariat, crystal, bowl, celery; handled, 10" **$35.00**

Lariat, crystal, candy, w/lid, 7".....................................**$90.00**

Lariat, crystal, jar, urn; w/lid, 12" **$175.00**

Lariat, crystal, oil bottle, oval, 6-oz **$75.00**

Lariat, crystal, plate, buffet; 21" **$70.00**

Lariat, crystal, stem, claret; blown, 4-oz......................**$28.00**

Lodestar, Dawn, bowl, mayonnaise; 5" **$85.00**

Lodestar, Dawn, sugar bowl **$50.00**

Minuet, crystal, bowl, salad dressings; 6½" **$35.00**

Minuet, crystal, bowl, salad; shallow, 13½"..................**$75.00**

Minuet, crystal, creamer, #1511, Toujours...................**$60.00**

Minuet, crystal, plate, service; 10½".............................**$190.00**

Minuet, crystal, salt & pepper shakers, #10, pr **$75.00**

Minuet, crystal, vase, #4192, 10"................................**$110.00**

New Era, crystal, creamer **$35.00**

**New Era, crystal, goblet, ten-ounce,
$18.00.** (Photo courtesy Gene Florence)

New Era, crystal, tumbler, low, footed, 10-oz **$15.00**

Octagon, crystal, creamer, #500...................................**$10.00**

Octagon, Flamingo, bowl, cream soup; 2-handled **$20.00**

Octagon, Hawthorne, plate, bread; 7" **$20.00**

Octagon, Marigold, dish, frozen dessert; #500 ....**$50.00**

Octagon, Moongleam, tray, celery; 9".........................**$25.00**

Octagon, Sahara, bowl, grapefruit; 6½".......................**$22.00**

Old Colony, Sahara, bowl, salad; sq, 2-handled, 10"..**$55.00**

Old Colony, Sahara, decanter, 1-pt **$325.00**

Old Colony, Sahara, plate, round, 6" **$15.00**

Old Colony, Sahara, stem, cordial; #3390, 1-oz **$125.00**

Old Colony, Sahara, tray, sandwich; center-handled, 12"...**$75.00**

Old Colony, Sahara, tumbler, soda; #3390, footed, 8-oz....**$25.00**

Old Sandwich, cobalt, beer mug, 18-oz **$380.00**

Old Sandwich, crystal, bowl, popcorn; footed, cupped ..**$80.00**

Old Sandwich, Flamingo, creamer, oval **$75.00**

Old Sandwich, Moongleam, tumbler, juice; 5-oz **$25.00**

Old Sandwich, Sahara, plate, sq, 8" **$27.00**

Orchid, crystal, ashtray, 3" **$30.00**

Orchid, crystal, bowl, gardenia; 10" **$75.00**

Orchid, crystal, bowl, lemon; Queen Ann, oval, w/lid, 6" ..**$295.00**

Orchid, crystal, candlestick, Cascade, 3-light...............**$85.00**

Orchid, crystal, candlestick, Flame, 2-light **$160.00**

Orchid, crystal, marmalade, w/lid **$235.00**

Orchid, crystal, plate, mayonnaise; 7".........................**$20.00**

Orchid, crystal, tray, celery; 13"...................................**$60.00**

Plantation, crystal, bowl, celery; 2-part, 13" **$60.00**

Plantation, crystal, bowl, nappy; 5½"..........................$38.00
Plantation, crystal, candlestick, 2-light $90.00
Plantation, crystal, mayonnaise, w/liner, 5¼"............$55.00
Plantation, crystal, salt & pepper shakers, pr.............$70.00
Pleat & Panel, crystal, bowl, nappy; 8"......................$10.00

Pleat and Panel, Flamingo, pitcher, three-pint, $140.00. (Photo courtesy Gene Florence)

Pleat & Panel, Flamingo, sherbet, footed, 5-oz...........$10.00
Pleat & Panel, Moongleam, pitcher, ice lip, 3-pt.......$165.00
Provincial, crystal, bowl, nappy; 5½".........................$20.00
Provincial, crystal, plate, luncheon; 8".......................$15.00
Provincial, Limelight Green, bowl, relish; 4-part, 10"...$195.00
Queen Ann, crystal, bowl, cream soup........................$18.00
Queen Ann, crystal, candlestick, 3-footed, 3".............$50.00
Queen Ann, crystal, ice tub, w/metal handles...........$60.00
Queen Ann, crystal, plate, 9".....................................$12.00
Ridgeleigh, crystal, basket, bonbon; metal handle......$25.00
Ridgeleigh, crystal, bowl, centerpiece; 8"...................$55.00
Ridgeleigh, crystal, cheese, 2-handled, 6"..................$22.00
Ridgeleigh, crystal, creamer.......................................$30.00
Ridgeleigh, crystal, plate, salver; 14"..........................$50.00
Ridgeleigh, crystal, sugar bowl...................................$30.00
Ridgeleigh, crystal, tray, celery; 12"...........................$40.00
Ridgeleigh, crystal, vase, triangular, 8".....................$110.00
Rose, crystal, ashtray, 3"..$37.50
Rose, crystal, bowl, lily; Queen Ann, 7"....................$125.00
Rose, crystal, butter, Waverly, w/lid, 6"....................$210.00
Rose, crystal, creamer, Waverly, individual.................$40.00
Rose, crystal, plate, sandwich; Waverly, 11"...............$60.00
Rose, crystal, stem, sherbet; #5072, 6-oz....................$30.00
Saturn, crystal, bowl, relish; 3-part, 9".......................$20.00
Saturn, crystal, bowl, rose; lg.....................................$40.00
Saturn, crystal, cup...$10.00
Saturn, crystal, sugar shaker......................................$80.00
Saturn, crystal, vase, violet..$35.00
Saturn, Zircon or Limelight, ashtray........................$150.00
Saturn, Zircon or Limelight, mayonnaise...................$80.00
Saturn, Zircon or Limelight, plate, bread; 7"..............$45.00
Stanhope, crystal, bowl, salad; 11".............................$90.00

Stanhope, crystal, cup, w/ or w/out round knob.......$25.00
Stanhope, crystal, stem, claret; #4083, 4-oz...............$25.00
Stanhope, crystal, tumbler, soda; #4083, 5-oz............$20.00
Twist, Alexandrite, stem, saucer champagne; 2-block stem, 5-oz..$30.00
Twist, crystal, bonbon, individual..............................$15.00
Twist, Flamingo, bowl, cream soup/bouillon..............$25.00
Twist, Marigold, cup, zigzag handles.........................$35.00
Twist, Moongleam, bowl, nasturtium; round, 8"........$90.00
Twist, Sahara, oil bottle, w/#78 stopper, 4-oz............$90.00
Victorian, crystal, butter dish, ¼-lb...........................$70.00
Victorian, crystal, plate, 7".......................................$20.00
Victorian, crystal, sugar bowl....................................$30.00
Victorian, crystal, vase, 5½".......................................$60.00
Waverly, crystal, bowl, ice; 2-handled, 6½"................$60.00
Waverly, crystal, bowl, relish; 4-part, round, 9".........$25.00
Waverly, crystal, box, footed, sea horse handle, w/lid, 5".$90.00
Waverly, crystal, cigarette holder...............................$60.00
Waverly, crystal, plate, salad; 7".................................$9.00
Waverly, crystal, tray, celery; 12"...............................$20.00
Yeoman, crystal, plate, cheese; 2-handled...................$5.00
Yeoman, Flamingo, egg cup..$35.00
Yeoman, Hawthorne, bowl, jelly; low, footed, 5".......$30.00
Yeoman, Marigold, ashtray, bow tie, handled, 4".......$35.00
Yeoman, Moongleam, bowl, berry; 2-handled, 8½"...$30.00
Yeoman, Sahara, comport, shallow, high footed, 5"...$37.00

Holt Howard

Now's the time to pick up the kitchenware (cruets, salt and peppers, condiments, etc.), novelty banks, ashtrays, and planters marked Holt Howard. They're not only marked but dated as well; you'll find production dates from the 1950s through the 1970s. (Beware of unmarked copy-cat lines!) There's a wide variety of items and decorative themes; those you're most likely to find will be from the rooster (done in golden brown, yellow, and orange), white cat (called Kozy Kitten), and Christmas lines. Not as easily found, the Pixies are by far the most collectible of all, and in general, Pixie prices continue to climb, particularly for the harder-to-find items.

Internet auctions have affected this market with the 'more supply, less demand' principal (more exposure, therefore in some cases lower prices), but all in all, the market has remained sound. Only the very common pieces have suffered.

Our values are for mint condition, factory-first examples. If any flaws are present, you must reduce the price accordingly.

Christmas

Ashtray, starry-eyed Santa..$35.00
Ashtray, winking Santa, open head holds cigarettes, stomach serves as ashtray, 1959, 5x3", from $40 to............$50.00
Bell, winking Santa, 1958, 4", from $12 to.................$15.00
Beverage set, winking Santa, pitcher & 6 matching cups, from $60 to...$70.00
Bracelet, 4 charms w/Santa faces, 1959, 8"................$70.00

Butter pat, white w/ruffled edge, red holly berry w/2 green leaves, 1959, 2½" **$6.00**

Candelabra, Winter Green, Santa nestled between branching tree **$15.00**

Candle climbers, seated snowman w/tree-style hat, red scarf around neck, pr, from $35 to................................**$45.00**

Candle holder, NOEL in green w/Santa inside O, 8¼x1¼x3" **$25.00**

Candle holder, Santa in convertible, 1959, 3½"..........**$35.00**

Candle holder/planter, 2 Santas play on see-saw, planter in center, Christmas/Greetings on sides **$25.00**

Candle holders, angels, 1 w/red bells in hand & other w/muff, attached holders in back, 1958, 4", M, pr **$85.00**

Candle holders, angels holding stars, 1 reads Happy New Year, other reads Merry Christmas, 1960, pr........**$75.00**

Candle holders, elf girls form letters NOEL w/candles in head, 3½" **$60.00**

Candle holders, reindeer heads, holders on antler tips, #6128L, 5½", pr, from $30 to **$35.00**

Candle holders, Santa on SS Noel boat, 1959, 2¾", pr, from $25 to **$30.00**

Candle holders, Santa w/gift bag, candles go in bags, 3½", pr **$30.00**

Candle holders, seated Santas, 4", pr, from $20 to **$25.00**

Candle holders/bells, 3 Wise Men, 3½", set from $65 to..**$85.00**

Chip & cheese dish, starry-eyed Santa, gold decor, 1960, 12" **$40.00**

Cookie/candy jar, Santa's hat comes off for candy, head comes off for cookies, 8½", from $125 to **$150.00**

Creamer & sugar bowl, winking Santa, stackable, hat is sugar lid, arm is creamer handle, 1959, 4½" **$35.00**

Face dish, starry-eyed Santa, 6¼x6½"..........................**$20.00**

Mug, starry-eyed Santa, straight handle, stackable, from $10 to **$15.00**

Planter, reindeer, $25.00; Salt and pepper shakers, $30.00. (Photo courtesy Pat and Ann Duncan)

Planter, Santa Express, Santa riding train, 6x7½" **$45.00**

Planter/candle holder, starry-eyed Santa, daisy wreath in hands is holder, #6268, 6" **$32.00**

Punch bowl, winking Santa, w/12 matching cups & ladle w/red & white handle...**$175.00**

Salt & pepper shakers, Holly Girls, 4", pr....................**$30.00**

Salt & pepper shakers, Santa holding presents, 2¼", 2¾", pr..**$15.00**

Salt & pepper shakers, Santa inside Christmas tree, 4¼", pr **$18.00**

Salt & pepper shakers, starry-eyed Santa, pr..............**$28.00**

Kozy Kitten

Ashtray, cat on sq plaid base, 4 corner rests, from $60 to.**$75.00**

Butter dish, 2 kittens peek out from under lid, 7", from $100 to..**$125.00**

Coffee jar, Instant Coffee, attached spoon, from $300 to...**$400.00**

Condiment jars, Ketchup, Mustard or Jam 'n Jelly, head finials, 1962, from $150 to....................................**$175.00**

Cookie jar, head form, from $40 to............................**$50.00**

Cookie jar, take lid off & kitten pops up w/sign that reads Just Take 1, 6¼x4¼", NMIB................................**$215.00**

Cottage cheese jar, 2 cats on lid, 4¼x4¼", from $45 to...**$55.00**

Creamer & sugar bowl, stackable, hat is lid, arm is handle, 1959, from $85 to **$100.00**

Letter holder, figural cat w/spring across back, hole in head for pencils..**$50.00**

Memo minder, full-bodied cat, legs cradle note pad, 7", from $75 to...**$100.00**

Powdered cleanser shaker, from $85.00 to $110.00. (Photo courtesy Pat and Ann Duncan)

Salt & pepper shakers, cats in wicker baskets, 3", pr, from $30 to...**$35.00**

Salt & pepper shakers, full-body w/noisemakers in base, 4½" pr, from $35 to...**$45.00**

Salt & pepper shakers, 1 w/red collar, 1 w/blue collar, 1950s, 4¼", pr..**$35.00**

Spice rack, cat heads w/Garlic, Paprika, Nutmeg & Cinnamon, vertical wire wall rack, 10", from $125 to.............**$150.00**

String holder, cat head w/hole in scarf, 4½x4½" , from $40 to **$50.00**

Sugar shaker, cat in apron carries sack w/word Pour, shaker holes in hat, side spout formed by sack, rare....**$125.00**

Tape measure, cat on cushion....................................**$85.00**

Wall pocket, cat w/hole in head, 1959, 7½", from $30 to..**$40.00**

Pixie Ware

Candlesticks, pr, from $50 to **$65.00**

Cherries jar, flat head finial on lid, w/cherry pick or spoon, from $165 to...**$190.00**

Chili sauce, rare, minimum value...........................**$400.00**

Cocktail cherries, flat-head finial w/attached spoon, 1958, from $175 to...**$200.00**

Cocktail olives, winking green head finial on lid, from $135 to...**$165.00**

Cocktail onions, onion-head finial, from $160 to......**$175.00**

Cruets, oil & vinegar; marked Holt Howard 1958, 9½", pr, from $325 to...**$375.00**

Decanter, Devil Brew, striped base, rare, 10½", minimum value **$225.00**

Decanter, Whiskey, w/winking head stopper, minimum value **$225.00**

Decanter, 300 Proof, flat-head stopper w/red nose, minimum value **$225.00**

Dish, flat-head handle w/crossed eyes, & pickle nose, green stripes, minimum value **$100.00**

French dressing bottle, winking flat-head pixie finial, 1959, from $175 to...**$200.00**

Honey, very rare, from $400 to **$500.00**

Hors d'oeuvre, head on body pierced for toothpicks, exaggerated tall hairdo, saucer base, from $225 to **$260.00**

Instant coffee jar, brown-skinned blond head finial, hard to find, from $220 to...**$250.00**

Italian Dressing bottle, round head, from $160.00 to $190.00. (Photo courtesy Pat and Ann Duncan)

Jam 'n Jelly jar, flat-head finial on lid w/attached spoon, 1958, from $65 to...**$85.00**

Ketchup jar, orange tomato-like head finial on lid, from $80 to...**$110.00**

Mayonnaise jar, winking head finial on lid, 5x4¼" dia, from $150 to...**$200.00**

Mustard jar, yellow head finial on lid, from $80 to...**$110.00**

Olive jar, flat-headed finial w/attached pick, from $100 to...**$125.00**

Onions jar, flat onion-head finial on lid, 1958, from $180 to...**$200.00**

Relish jar, male pixie on lid, marked 1959 ....**$250.00**

Russian dressing bottle, from $175 to.......................**$200.00**

Salt & pepper shakers, Salty & Peppy, attached flat head w/painted wood handle, pr, minimum value.....**$250.00**

Sugar bowl, Lil' Sugar w/spoon & pixie lid, +Cream Crock, pr, from $175 to...**$200.00**

Ponytail Princess

Candle holder, girl shares figure-8 platform w/flower-head candle cup, from $50 to **$60.00**

Double tray, from $50.00 to $65.00. (Photo courtesy Pat and Ann Duncan)

Lipstick holder, from $50 to..**$65.00**

Salt & pepper shakers, pr **$45.00**

Rooster

Ashtray, figural rooster w/open-body rectangular receptacle, w/cigarette rest **$15.00**

Bowl, cereal; 6" **$9.00**

Bud vase, figural rooster, from $25 to **$30.00**

Butter dish, embossed rooster, ¼-lb, from $40 to.......**$50.00**

Candle holders, figural roosters, 1960, 5x4", pr, from $35 to **$45.00**

Chocolate pot, tall & narrow w/flaring sides, embossed rooster on front, from $50 to **$60.00**

Cigarette holder, wooden w/painted-on rooster, wall mount, holds several packs **$150.00**

Coffeepot, electric, from $50 to **$70.00**

Coffeepot, embossed rooster, from $40 to...................**$50.00**

Cookie jar, embossed rooster, from $100 to.............**$135.00**

Creamer & sugar bowl, embossed rooster, pr, from $30 to **$45.00**

Cup & saucer **$15.00**

Dish, figural rooster w/open-body receptacle.............**$15.00**

Jam & jelly jar, embossed rooster, from $40 to **$50.00**

Ketchup jar, embossed rooster **$35.00**

Mug, embossed rooster (3 sizes), ea from $5 to.........**$10.00**

Mustard jar, embossed rooster on front, w/lid **$35.00**

Napkin holder..**$40.00**

Pincushion, 3¼x4", from $50 to **$60.00**

Pitcher, embossed rooster on front, cylindrical w/indents on side for gripping, no handle, tall, from $35 to **$45.00**
Pitcher, syrup; embossed rooster on front, tail handle ..**$30.00**
Pitcher, water; flaring sides, tail handle, tall **$50.00**
Plate, embossed rooster, 8½", from $15 to **$22.00**
Platter, embossed rooster, oval, from $28 to **$35.00**
Recipe box, wood w/painted-on rooster, from $75 to .**$100.00**
Salt & pepper shakers, figural, 4½", pr, from $35 to ..**$45.00**
Spoon rest, figural rooster, from $12 to **$15.00**
Tray, facing left, from $15 to **$20.00**
Trivet, tile w/rooster in iron framework, from $30 to...**$40.00**

Miscellaneous

Bank, Coin Clown Bobbing Head, 1958, 6½", from $150 to **$175.00**
Bank, Coin Kitty Bobbing Head, 5½", from $100 to...**$150.00**

Bank, Dandy-Lion, nodder, 6", from $100.00 to $150.00. (Photo courtesy Jim and Beverly Mangus)

Candle holder, Lil' Old Lace or Granny, old lady in blue dress w/bottle & party horn w/holders in back, 1959.........**$40.00**
Candle holders, bride & groom, 4¼", pr **$45.00**
Candle ring, bluebird, 1958, 1¾".................................**$35.00**
Candy dish, Ferris wheel style, 3 red cups/3 pink cups w/white interiors, metal frame w/pink & red base................**$140.00**
Cherry jar, Cherries If You Please lettered on sign held by butler (Jeeves), minimum value **$250.00**
Chip dish, white bowl w/butler head (Jeeves) & painted-on tux, 1960, 5x5½", from $60 to **$85.00**
Cup, coffee/tea; tomato, green leafy handle, 1962, 2½x3½"..**$10.00**
Figurines, pheasants, wings spread, 10x8", 7x5½" & 5½x4", 1958, set..**$80.00**
Marmalade jar, lemon-head finial, #1483, NM **$40.00**
Martini shaker, butler (Jeeves), 9", from $175 to......**$200.00**
Memo clips, Mañana & Urgent! on faces, metal clip/frame, 1⅝x2¼"..**$110.00**
Olives jar, Olives If You Please lettered on sign held by butler (Jeeves), minimum value...............................**$150.00**

Pickles jar, Pickles on lid w/cutout for spoon, sq sides, brown stripes on white w/tan sqs, w/spoon........**$50.00**
Salt & pepper shakers, cowboys, 6½" **$70.00**
Salt & pepper shakers, ear of corn, 4½", pr...............**$30.00**
Salt & pepper shakers, Jolly Girls, flat-head finials, EX **$55.00**
Salt & pepper shakers, Kissing Kids, 2 seated kids, 3¼", pr..**$55.00**

Salt and pepper shakers, Rock 'n Roll kids, heads on springs, $125.00 for the pair. (Photo courtesy Hilma R. Irtz)

Salt & pepper shakers, starry-eyed birds, 4", pr..........**$45.00**
Salt & pepper shakers, yellow birds just out of cracked egg, 4", pr...**$40.00**
Tape dispenser/paper clip holder, duck figural, tape in tail & clips under lid at beak, 1958 ....**$50.00**
Wall pocket, mermaid riding a sea horse, missing chain, 1959, 6¾"..**$70.00**

Homer Laughlin China Co.

The first pottery made by The Laughlin Brothers of East Liverpool, Ohio, rolled off the production linein 1874. Mr. Homer Laughlin bought out his brother Shakespeare's interest in 1877, and the pottery became known as The Homer Laughlin China Company. Over the years, the company has been recognized as the largest producer of American dinnerware and has won numerous awards for quality and design. In keeping with the styles of the time, the early shapes were rather ornate, while the shapes from 1930 through 1970 were of a simpler design. Not only did the Homer Laughlin China Company apply a date to each piece of ware, but many times the name of the shape was also included n the backstamp.

For further information see *The Collector's Encyclopedia of Homer Laughlin Pottery* and *American Dinnerware, 1880s to 1920s*, both by Joanne Jasper (Collector Books). Also recommended is *Homer Laughlin China 1940's and 1950's, Homer*

Laughlin, A Giant Among Dishes, both by Jo Cunningham (Schiffer), and *Homer Laughlin China Identification Guide to Shapes and Patterns,* by Jo Cunningham and Darlene Nossaman (Schiffer). *The Collector's Encyclopedia of Fiesta, Ninth Edition,* by Sharon and Bob Huxford (Collector Books) has photographs and prices of several of the more collectible lines such as listed here.

See also Fiesta.

Advisor: Darlene Nossaman (See Directory, Dinnerware)

Club/Newsletter: Homer Laughlin China Collector's Association (HLCCA)
P.O. Box 26021
Crystal City, VA 22215-6021
Dues $25.00 single; $40.00 couple or family, includes *The Dish* magazine (a 16-page quarterly), free classifieds

Wells plate, from $10.00 to $12.00; Brittany covered sugar bowl, from $12.00 to $15.00; Republic cup and saucer, from $5.00 to $10.00; Seneca plate, from $10.00 to $14.00; Empress creamer, from $12.00 to $14.00. (Photo courtesy Darlene Nossaman)

Brittany Shape

Introduced in 1936; available in Hemlock, Majestic, Sugar Pine, Ivy Chain patterns.

Bowl, fruit; from $4 to	$5.00
Bowl, serving; 9", from $14 to	$16.00
Creamer, from $12 to	$14.00
Plate, 6", from $5 to	$6.00
Plate, 9", from $8 to	$12.00
Plate, 10", from $12 to	$14.00
Platter, 13", from $12 to	$18.00
Sauce boat, from $14 to	$18.00
Saucer, from $2 to	$4.00
Teacup, from $4 to	$6.00
Teapot, from $40 to	$50.00

Empress Shape

Introduced in 1914; available in Cottage Blue, Floral Basket, LaSalle, Springtime patterns. Add 25% for solid colors or Blue Bird decoration.

Bowl, fruit; from $5 to	$8.00
Bowl, serving; round, 8", from $15 to	$18.00
Butter dish, w/lid, from $45 to	$50.00
Casserole, w/lid, from $25 to	$30.00
Plate, 6", from $6 to	$9.00
Plate, 9", from $10 to	$12.00
Plate, 10", from $12 to	$15.00
Platter, 13", from $20 to	$25.00
Sauce boat, from $15 to	$18.00
Saucer, from $4 to	$5.00
Teacup, from $6 to	$8.00
Teapot, from $40 to	$50.00

Seneca Shape

Introduced in 1901; available in American Beauty, Crab Apple, Holly and Berry, Primrose patterns.

Bowl, fruit; from $5 to	$8.00
Bowl, serving; round, 8", from $16 to	$20.00
Casserole, w/lid, 10", from $35 to	$45.00
Creamer, from $12 to	$15.00
Plate, 7", from $8 to	$10.00
Plate, 9", from $10 to	$14.00
Plate, 10", from $12 to	$15.00
Platter, 13", from $25 to	$30.00
Sauce boat, from $15 to	$18.00
Teacup, from $8 to	$12.00
Teapot, from $45 to	$55.00

Wells Shape

Introduced in 1930; available in Buttercup, Modern Laurel, Palm Tree, Pink Clover patterns. Add 25% for Blue Willow teapot or solid-color glazes Sienna Brown, French Rose, and Leaf Green.

Bowl, serving; round, 8", from $8 to	$10.00
Bowl, soup; from $8 to	$10.00
Bowl, 5", from $4 to	$6.00
Butter dish, w/lid, from $35 to	$40.00
Casserole, w/lid, from $35 to	$45.00
Creamer, from $10 to	$14.00
Plate, 6", from $5 to	$7.00
Plate, 10", from $12 to	$14.00
Platter, 13", from $18 to	$22.00
Sauce boat, from $15 to	$18.00
Saucer, from $3 to	$5.00
Teacup, from $6 to	$8.00
Teapot, from $50 to	$60.00

Horton Ceramics

Following the end of WWII, Mr. Horace Horton and his wife, Geri, returned to Mr. Horton's hometown, Eastland, Texas. With good clays nearby, Mr. Horton's keen business ability, and Mrs. Horton's skills in artistic design, they set about establishing a pottery in Eastland. Their wares were marketed mainly to floral shops, variety stores, and department stores. Mrs. Horton designed a logo of a rearing wild horse. Each piece has the mold number on the bottom as well as 'horton ceramics' in lower-case flowing script lettering. The pottery was sold in the early 1960s.

Advisor: Darlene Nossaman (See Directory, Horton Ceramics)

Butter melter, from $15.00 to $20.00.
(Photo courtesy Darlene Nossaman)

Figurine, cat, assorted colors & breeds, 12x6", from $25 to...**$30.00**
Figurine, moccasin, tan w/real buckskin ties, 5½", from $12 to..**$14.00**
Figurine, powder horn, 2-tone brown w/real leather strap, 9", from $12 to..**$14.00**
Jardiniere, green, lime or yellow, #208 pot, 8", from $8 to **$10.00**
Jardiniere, white, pink, black or green, #R12 pot, 12x8", from $10 to...**$12.00**
Jardiniere, white, pink, black or green, #308 Lone Cedar pot, 8x8", from $12 to **$14.00**
Jardiniere, white, pink, black or green, #406 Azalea pot, 5x6", from $8 to..**$10.00**

Planter, #809, from $12.00 to $15.00; planter, W88, from $15.00 to $18.00; planter/vase, #37, from $9.00 to $12.00. (Photo courtesy Darlene Nossaman)

Planter, African Violet, purple, #705, 5", from $8 to ...**$10.00**
Planter, Bamboo, yellow & brown, 12", from $15 to..**$18.00**
Planter, basinette, pink or blue w/gold flowers, 5", from $10 to **$12.00**

Planter, bassinet, pink or blue, #B3, 4x6", from $10 to .**$12.00**
Planter, giraffe, yellow & brown, #G1, 9½", from $15 to..**$18.00**
Vase, black, pink, coral, blue or green, #BV19, 9x1½", from $18 to...**$20.00**
Vase, textured pink, black or turquoise, #C6, 5½x4", from $12 to...**$14.00**
Vase, turquoise, white or black, Lone Cedar, #V14, 10x6", from, $15 to...**$18.00**
Vase, white, black, blue, pink or green, #V955, 9x5½", from $14 to...**$16.00**
Vase, white, pink, black or green, #E6, 6x6", from $10 to.**$14.00**
Wind bell, yellow, brown or coral striped, 6x9", from $20 to..**$25.00**

Hull

Hull has a look of its own. Many lines were made in soft, pastel matt glazes and modeled with flowers and ribbons, and as a result, they have a very feminine appeal.

The company operated in Crooksville (near Zanesville), Ohio, from just after the turn of the century until they closed in 1985. From the 1930s until the plant was destroyed by fire in 1950, they preferred the soft matt glazes so popular with today's collectors, though a few high gloss lines were made as well. When the plant was rebuilt, modern equipment was installed which they soon found did not lend itself to the duplication of the matt glazes, so they began to concentrate on the production of glossy wares, novelties, and figurines.

During the '40s and '50s, they produced a line of kitchenware items modeled after Little Red Riding Hood. Original pieces are expensive today and most are reproduced by persons other than Hull. (See also Little Red Riding Hood.)

Hull's Mirror Brown dinnerware line made from 1960 until they closed in 1985 was very successful for them and was made in large quantities. Its glossy brown glaze was enhanced with a band of ivory foam, and today's collectors are finding its rich colors and basic, strong shapes just as attractive now as they were back then. In addition to table service, there are novelty trays shaped like gingerbread men and fish, canisters and cookie jars, covered casseroles with ducks and hens as lids, vases, ashtrays, and mixing bowls. It's easy to find, and though you may have to pay 'near book' prices at co-ops and antique malls, bargains are out there. It may be marked Hull, Crooksville, O; HPCo; or Crestone.

If you'd like to learn more about this subject, we recommend *The Collector's Encyclopedia of Hull Pottery* and *Ultimate Encyclopedia of Hull Pottery*, both by Brenda Roberts; and *Collector's Guide to Hull Pottery, The Dinnerware Lines*, by Barbara Loveless Gick-Burke.

Advisor: Brenda Roberts (See Directory, Hull)

Bow-Knot, candle holder, cornucopia form, flowers & bow on blue to green, B-17, 4", from $140 to...........**$175.00**
Bow-Knot, vase, flowers & pink bow on blue to green, petal rim, B-2, 5", from $175 to **$220.00**

Butterfly, tea/coffee set, pot, $180.00, creamer and sugar bowl, $95.00 each.

Calla Lily, vase, green to brown, handles, 8", from $185 to **$240.00**

Calla Lily, vase, green to pink, handles, 6", from $140 to **$165.00**

Cinderella Kitchenware, Blossom pitcher, yellow daisy-like flower on white, #29, 16-oz, from $45 to **$70.00**

Cinderella Kitchenware, Bouquet, bowl, 3-color flowers on ivory to yellow, sq, brown ink stamp, 9¾", from $100 to **$125.00**

Dogwood, candle holder, pink to blue, #512, 3¾", from $340 to **$400.00**

Dogwood, vase, cornucopia; yellow to green, #522, 3¾", from $110 to **$135.00**

Ebb Tide, candle holder, shell form, #E-15, 2¾", from $35 to **$50.00**

Ebb Tide, creamer, shell shape, #E-15, 4", from $95 to **$125.00**

Figurine, bear, ivory w/gold trim, 1940s, 1½", from $90 to **$110.00**

Figurine, rabbit, ivory w/gold trim, 1940s, 2¾", from $80 to **$100.00**

Iris, rose bowl, yellow, sm handles, #412, 7", from $170 to **$210.00**

Iris, vase, yellow, handles, waisted, #403, 5", from $40 to **$60.00**

Iris, vase, yellow to pink, trumpet neck, low handles, #402, 7", from $170 to **$220.00**

Magnolia, gloss; candle holder, pink on white, H-24, 4", from $50 to **$65.00**

Magnolia, gloss; sugar bowl, blue on transparent pink, lg open handles, w/lid, H-22, 3¾", from $50 to.......**$70.00**

Magnolia, gloss; vase, pink on pink, waisted, ring handles, footed, H-7, 6½", from $45 to................................**$65.00**

Magnolia, matt; vase, pink, flared rim, angle handles, #13, 4¾", from $50 to **$75.00**

Magnolia, matt; vase, pink, low handles, petal-like top, #9, 10½", from $235 to..**$275.00**

Novelty, Basket Girl, glossy, multicolor, #954, 8", from $35 to..**$45.00**

Novelty, Corky Pig bank, Mirror Brown, 5", from $75 to..**$115.00**

Novelty, flowerpot, embossed ribs, flared sides, #95, 4½", from $15 to..**$20.00**

Novelty, kitten planter, pink bow at neck, #61, 7½", from $40 to..**$55.00**

Novelty, lamb planter, blue bow at neck, #965, 8", from $40 to..**$55.00**

Novelty, parrot planter, pink, green & yellow, #60, 9½x6", from $45 to..**$65.00**

Novelty, pig planter, #60, 5", from $30 to....................**$45.00**

Novelty, piggy bank, white w/pink & blue airbrushing, 3½", from $250 to..**$325.00**

Novelty, poodle planter, pink & green, #114, 8", from $50 to..**$75.00**

Open Rose, jardiniere, pink & yellow rose on pale pink, handles, scalloped rim, #114, 8¼", from $325 to **$415.00**

Open Rose, teapot, pink, ornate handle, #110, 8½", from $350 to..**$450.00**

Open Rose, vase, pink, ornate handles, scalloped rim, footed, #121, 6¼", from $130 to **$160.00**

Open Rose, vase, swan form, pink, #118, 6½", from $175 to..**$215.00**

Orchid, ewer, pink to blue, #311, 13", from $675 to ...**$800.00**

Orchid, vase, pink to blue, handles, #304, 6", from $150 to **$180.00**

Pinecone, vase, pink, handles, 355, 6½", from $175 to...**$225.00**

Poppy, planter, blue to pink, #502, 6½", from $245 to ...**$300.00**

Poppy, vase, green to pink, upturned handles, footed, #606, 10½", from $450 to..**$550.00**

Rosella, sugar bowl, lg open white flowers on ivory, open handles, R-4, 3½", from $45 to **$65.00**

Rosella, vase, cornucopia; lg open white flowers on ivory, R-13, 8½" L, from $125 to **$165.00**

Sueno Tulip, ewer, pink to blue, ornate handle, #109-33, 13", from $465 to..**$540.00**

Sueno Tulip, vase, yellow to blue, handles, #100-33, 10", from $275 to..**$325.00**

Sunglow, flowerpot, pink flowers on bright yellow, #97, 5½", from $30 to..**$40.00**

Sunglow, vase, yellow flowers on pink, rim-to-hip handles, #89, 5½", from $35 to..**$50.00**

Thistle, vase, pink, angle handles, #52, 6½", from $130 to..**$150.00**

Tokay, vase, cornucopia; pink grapes on pink to green, #10, 11", from $55 to **$85.00**

Water Lily, basket, yellow flower on pink to blue, L-14, 10½", from $400 to..**$510.00**

Water Lily, vase, lg flower on pink to brown, handles, footed, L-2, 5½", from $50 to **$70.00**

Wildflower, vase, pink to yellow, low handles, footed, W-3, 5½", from $55 to..**$85.00**

Wildflower, vase, yellow to pink, low handles, #W-12, 9½", from $225 to..**$275.00**

Wildflower (#d series), vase, pink & yellow on pink, handles, footed, #78, 8½", from $350 to.........................**$450.00**

Woodland, basket, flowers on yellow to pink, green branch handle, W9, 8¾", from $250 to **$310.00**

Woodland, candle holder, flower on yellow to green, branch handle, W30, 3½", from $140 to **$170.00**

Dinnerware

Crestone, butter dish, ¼-lb, from $25 to......................**$35.00**
Crestone, carafe, 2-cup, 6½", from $50 to **$65.00**
Crestone, cup & saucer, 7-oz, 5⅞" dia, from $6 to.......**$9.00**
Crestone, French casserole, 9-oz, from $25 to **$35.00**
Crestone, mug, 9-oz, from $4 to...................................**$6.00**

Crestone, pitcher, 6¾", $45.00.

Crestone, plate, 7½", from $4 to...................................**$6.00**
Crestone, plate, 9⅜", from $8 to **$10.00**
Crestone, plate, 10¼", from $10 to..............................**$12.00**
Mirror Almond, ashtray, 8", from $20 to **$25.00**
Mirror Almond, baker, 3-pt, from $15 to **$20.00**
Mirror Almond, bean pot, 2-qt, from $30 to...............**$40.00**
Mirror Almond, creamer, 8-oz, from $12 to.................**$15.00**
Mirror Almond, plate, steak; 11¾", from $20 to..........**$25.00**
Mirror Almond, plate, 9⅜", from $8 to **$10.00**
Mirror Almond, plate, 10¼", from $8 to **$10.00**
Mirror Almond, salt & pepper shakers, 3¾", pr, from $14 to..**$18.00**
Mirror Almond, sauce boat, 5½", from $20 to.............**$30.00**
Mirror Almond, server, w/chicken cover, 13⅜", from $215 to...**$285.00**
Mirror Almond, soup 'n sandwich, from $20 to..........**$25.00**
Mirror Brown, baker, 3-pt, from $15 to **$20.00**
Mirror Brown, bowl, divided vegetable; 10¾", from $25 to **$35.00**
Mirror Brown, bowl, 6½", from $4 to **$5.00**
Mirror Brown, butter dish, ¼-lb, from $20 to **$25.00**
Mirror Brown, coffeepot, 8-cup, from $40 to..............**$55.00**
Mirror Brown, creamer, 8-oz, from $12 to...................**$15.00**
Mirror Brown, custard, from $6 to **$10.00**
Mirror Brown, Dutch oven, 3-pt, from $30 to.............**$40.00**
Mirror Brown, gravy boat, w/saucer, 16-oz, from $35 to..**$50.00**
Mirror Brown, leaf chip 'n dip, 15", from $25 to **$35.00**

Mirror Brown, pie plate, 9¼", from $18 to..................**$24.00**
Mirror Brown, plate, steak; 11¾", from $20 to...........**$35.00**
Mirror Brown, plate, 6½", from $3 to............................**$4.00**
Mirror Brown, plate, 10¼", from $8 to **$10.00**
Mirror Brown, salt & pepper shakers, sm, pr, from $14 to ..**$18.00**
Rainbow, bowl, 6½", from $4 to **$5.00**
Rainbow, bowl, 8", from $20 to **$30.00**
Rainbow, cup & saucer, 6-oz, 5½" dia, from $6 to.......**$9.00**
Rainbow, leaf chip 'n dip, 12¼", from $55 to.............**$85.00**
Rainbow, leaf dish, 7¼", from $12 to **$16.00**
Rainbow, mug, 9-oz, from $4 to......................................**$6.00**
Rainbow, plate, dinner; 10½", from $8 to **$10.00**
Rainbow, plate, luncheon; 8½", from $6 to..................**$8.00**
Rainbow, tidbit tray, 10", from $40 to.........................**$65.00**

Mirror Brown, casserole, hen on nest, 8½x8½", from $75.00 to $100.00.

Imperial Glass

Organized in 1901 in Bellaire, Ohio, the Imperial Glass Company made carnival glass, stretch glass, a line called NuCut (made in imitation of cut glass), and a limited amount of art glass within the first decade of the century. In the mid-'30s, they designed one of their most famous patterns (and one of their most popular with today's collectors), Candlewick. Within a few years, milk glass had become their leading product.

During the '50s they reintroduced their NuCut line in crystal as well as colors, marketing it as 'Collector's Crystal.' In the late '50s they bought molds from both Heisey and Cambridge. Most of the glassware they reissued from these old molds was marked 'IG,' one letter superimposed over the other. When Imperial was bought by Lenox in 1973, an 'L' was added to the mark. The ALIG logo was added in 1981 when the company was purchased by Arthur Lorch. In 1982 the factory was sold to Robert Stahl of Minneapolis. Chapter 11 bankruptcy was filled in October that year. A plant resurgence continued production. Many Heisey by Imperial animals done in color were made at this time. A new mark, the NI for New Imperial, was used on a few items. In November of 1984 the plant closed forever and the assets were sold at liquidation. This was the end of the 'Big I.'

Numbers in the listings were assigned by the company and appeared on their catalog pages. They were used to indicate differences in shapes and stems, for instance. Collectors still use them.

For more information on Imperial we recommend *Imperial Glass* by Margaret and Douglas Archer; *Elegant Glassware of the Depression Era* by Gene Florence; *Imperial Carnival Glass* by Carl O. Burns; and *Imperial Glass Encyclopedia, Vol I, A to Cane, Vol II, Cane to M,* and *Volume III, M to Z,* edited by James Measell.

See also Candlewick.

Note: To determine values for Cape Cod in colors, add 100% to prices suggested for crystal for Ritz Blue and Ruby; Amber, Antique Blue, Azalea, Evergreen, Verde, black, and milk glass are 50% higher than crystal.

Advisor: Kathy Daub (See Directory, Imperial)

Club: National Imperial Glass Collectors' Society, Inc. P.O. Box 534, Bellaire, OH 43906. Dues: $18 per year (+$3 for each additional member of household), quarterly newsletter: *Glasszette,* convention every June; www.imperialglass.org

Ashtray, Cape Cod, 3160/134/1, 4" **$14.00**
Ashtray, Zodiac, milk glass, 9½" **$30.00**
Basket, Crocheted Crystal, basket, 12" **$75.00**

Big Shots, #711, ruby: Magnum mixer, 40-ounce, $100.00; ½-Shot, five-ounce, $25.00.

Bonbon, Fancy Colonial, any color, handles, 5½" **$25.00**
Bottle, condiment; Cape Cod, 6-oz **$65.00**
Bowl, Cape Cod, crimped rim, 9½" **$75.00**
Bowl, Cape Cod, divided, oval, 11" **$80.00**
Bowl, Cape Cod, 12" **$40.00**
Bowl, cream soup; Diamond Quilted, pink or green, 4¾" ..**$15.00**
Bowl, dessert; Cape Cod, tab handles, 4½" **$23.00**
Bowl, Fancy Colonial, any color, handles, 8" **$65.00**

Bowl, finger; Mt Vernon, crystal, 5" **$12.00**
Bowl, heart; Cape Cod, w/handle, 6" **$20.00**
Bowl, mint; Cape Cod, handles, 3" **$20.00**
Bowl, nappy, Cape Cod, 7" **$22.00**
Bowl, punch; Mt Vernon, crystal **$30.00**
Bowl, salad; Reeded, any color, deep, 10" **$45.00**
Bowl, soup; Cape Cod, tab handles, 5½" **$18.00**
Bowl, Star Medallion, green, #671, 8" **$35.00**
Butter dish, Vintage Ruby Grape **$40.00**
Cake plate, Cape Cod, 4-toed, 10" **$100.00**
Cake plate, Collectors Crystal **$30.00**
Candle holder, Cape Cod, flower form, 5" **$60.00**
Candle holder, Crocheted Crystal, single, 6" L **$20.00**
Candy jar, Diamond Quilted, pink or green, footed, w/lid ..**$65.00**
Celery, Cape Cod, 8" **$30.00**
Coaster, Cape Cod, w/spoon rest **$10.00**
Cocktail shaker, reeded, any color, chrome-plated top, 36-oz **$75.00**
Comport, Cape Cod, footed, w/lid **$75.00**
Creamer, Crocheted Crystal, flat **$30.00**
Creamer & sugar bowl, caramel slag, #43530CS **$50.00**
Creamer & sugar bowl, Diamond Quilted, green **$40.00**
Cruet, Cape Cod, w/stopper, 4-oz **$20.00**
Cup, Diamond Quilted, blue or black **$17.50**
Decanter, Mt Vernon, crystal **$35.00**
Figuine, Rooster, amber **$475.00**
Figurine, Airedale, Ultra Blue **$75.00**
Figurine, Champ Terrier, caramel slag, 5¾" **$95.00**
Figurine, Colt, amber, balking **$140.00**
Figurine, Colt, Horizon Blue, kicking **$35.00**
Figurine, Cygnet, caramel, 2½" **$75.00**
Figurine, Donkey, caramel slag **$55.00**
Figurine, Donkey, Ultra Blue **$65.00**
Figurine, Elephant, caramel slag, med **$65.00**
Figurine, Elephant, Nut Brown, sm **$120.00**
Figurine, Hootless Owl, milk glass, glossy **$60.00**
Figurine, Mallard, caramel slag, wings half **$35.00**
Figurine, Marmote Sentinel (woodchuck), caramel slag, 4½" **$40.00**
Figurine, Parlour Pup, terrier, amethyst carnival, 3½" ...**$45.00**
Figurine, Plug Horse, pink, HCA, 1978 ....**$40.00**
Figurine, Scolding Bird, Cathay Crystal **$175.00**
Figurine, Wood Duck, Ultra Blue satin **$55.00**
Figurine/bookend, Fish, ruby, ea **$340.00**
Fork, Cape Cod, #701, early style **$20.00**
Jar, Cape Cod, milk glass, glossy, reed handle, w/spoon ..**$75.00**
Marmalade, Cape Cod, 3-pc set **$32.50**
Mayonnaise bowl, Crocheted Crystal, 5¼" **$12.50**
Mustard, Cape Cod, w/lid & spoon **$22.50**
Pickle, Fancy Colonial, any color, oval, 8" **$30.00**
Pickle dish, milk glass, Doeskin **$20.00**
Pitcher, Cape Cod, blown, 5-pt **$195.00**
Pitcher, Diamond Quilted, pink or green, 64-oz **$50.00**
Pitcher, milk; Grape, 1-pt **$25.00**
Pitcher, Mount Vernon, crystal, 54-oz **$35.00**
Pitcher, Reeded, any color, ice lip, 80-oz **$60.00**
Plate, Cape Cod, 12½" **$70.00**

Plate, crescent salad; Cape Cod, 8" $50.00
Plate, Crocheted Crystal, 9½".................................$7.50
Plate, Crocheted Crystal, 17" $40.00
Plate, luncheon; Diamond Quilted, blue or black, 8".$15.00
Plate, Mt Vernon, crystal, 8" sq.............................$10.00
Plate, salad; Leaf, milk glass, glossy, 8½" $18.00
Plate, serving; Reeded, any color, flat, 14" $32.50
Plate, wall; Windmill, milk glass, 9" $27.00
Relish, Crocheted Crystal, 3-part, 11½" $25.00
Salt & pepper shakers, Fancy Colonial, any color, pr.$75.00
Sherbet, Fancy Colonial, any color, footed jelly, 4¾".$25.00
Stem, champagne, Fancy Colonial, any color, 6-oz $21.00
Stem, cordial; Cape Cod, 1½-oz $10.00
Stem, goblet; Cape Cod, 14-oz $40.00
Stem, parfait; Cape Cod, 5-oz $11.00
Stem, port; Fancy Colonial, any color, deep, 3-oz $30.00
Sugar bowl, Crocheted Crystal, footed.......................$20.00
Sugar bowl, milk glass, dolphin handles, Doeskin $30.00
Sugar bowl, Mt Vernon, crystal, individual $8.00
Syrup, Reeded, any color, ball w/chrome spout & handle ..$90.00
Tray, Cape Cod, for creamer & sugar, 7" $15.00
Tumbler, Crocheted Crystal, footed, 6-oz, 6"...............$20.00
Tumbler, Diamond Quilted, pink or green, footed, 6-oz ..$18.00
Tumbler, iced tea; Cape Cod, footed, 12-oz...............$15.00
Tumbler, juice; Hobnail, milk glass, 6-oz....................$12.00
Tumbler, old-fashioned; Mt Vernon, crystal, 7-oz $10.00
Tumbler, Scroll, milk glass, 12-oz...............................$12.50
Vase, Cape Cod, footed, 6¼" $35.00
Vase, fan; Diamond Quilted, pink or green, dolphin handles...$55.00
Vase, Reeded, any color, ivy ball, footed, 6½"............$55.00

Indiana Glass

In 1971 the Indiana Glass Co. introduced a line of new carnival glass, much of which was embossed with grape clusters and detailed leaves using their Harvest molds. It was first made in blue, and later gold and lime green were added. Prior to 1971 the Harvest molds had been used to produce a snowy white milk glass; blue and green satin or frosted glass; ruby red flashed glass; and plain glass in various shades of blue, amber, and green. Because this line was mass produced (machine-made) carnival, there are still large quantities available to collectors.

They also produced a line of handmade carnival called Heritage, which they made in amethyst and Sunset (amberina). Because it was handmade as opposed to being machine made, production was limited, and it is not as readily available to today's collectors as is the Harvest pattern carnival. There is a significant amount of interest in both lines today. Now that these lines are thirty years old, Grandmother, Mother, and Aunt are leaving a piece or two to the next generation. The younger generation is off and running to complete Granny's collection via the Internet. This has caused a revival of interest in Indiana carnival glass as a collectible.

The company also produced a series of four Bicentennial commemorative plates made in blue and gold carnival: American Eagle, Independence Hall, Liberty Bell, and Spirit of '76. These are valued at $10.00 each unboxed, or $15.00 if in their original box. A large Liberty Bell cookie jar and a small Liberty Bell bank were also made in gold carnival; today the cookie jars are valued at $15.00 to $25.00 while the banks generally sell in the $5.00 to $10.00 range.

This glass is a little difficult to evaluate, since you see it in malls and flea markets with such a wide range of 'asking' prices. On one hand, you have sellers who themselves are not exactly sure what it is they have but since it's 'carnival' assume it should be fairly pricey. On the other hand, you have those who just 'cleaned house' and want to get rid of it. They may have bought it new themselves and know it's not very old and wasn't expensive to start with. (The Harvest Princess Punch Set sold for $5.98 in 1971.) So take heart, there are still bargains to be found, though they're becoming rarer with each passing year. The best buys on Indiana carnival glass are found at garage and estate sales.

In addition to the iridescent lines, Indiana Glass produced a line called Ruby Band Diamond Point, a clear, diamond-faceted pattern with a wide ruby-flashed rim band; some items from this line are listed below. Our values are for examples with the ruby flashing in excellent condition.

See also King's Crown; Tiara.

Advisor: Donna Adler (See Directory, Indiana Glass)

Iridescent Amethyst Carnival Glass (Heritage)

This color is very difficult to find.

Basket, footed, 9x5x7"..$40.00
Butter dish, 5x7½" dia, from $40 to $60.00
Candle holders, 5½", pr, from $30 to..........................$40.00
Center bowl, 4¾x8½", from $30 to.............................$40.00
Goblet, 8-oz, from $15 to...$20.00
Pitcher, 8¼", from $40 to $60.00
Punch set, 10" bowl & pedestal, 8 cups, ladle, 11-pc, from $175 to..$275.00
Swung vase, slender & footed w/irregular rim, 11x3", from $30 to..$40.00

Iridescent Blue Carnival Glass

Basket, Canterbury, waffled pattern, flared sides drawn in at handle, 11x8x12", from $50 to..............................$75.00
Basket, Monticello, allover faceted embossed diamonds, 7x6" sq, from $25 to...$35.00
Butter dish, Harvest, embossed grapes, ¼-lb, 8" L, from $25 to...$40.00
Candle holders, Harvest, compote shape, 4", pr, from $25 to...$35.00
Candy box, Harvest, embossed grapes w/lace edge, w/lid, 6½", from $20 to...$35.00
Candy box, Princess, diamond-point bands, pointed faceted finial, 6x6" dia, from $10 to $15.00

Canister/Candy jar, Harvest, embossed grapes, 7", from $15 to **$35.00**

Canister/Cookie jar, Harvest, embossed grapes, 9", from $80 to **$150.00**

Canister/Snack jar, Harvest, embossed grapes, 8", from $60 to **$125.00**

Center bowl, Harvest, embossed grapes w/paneled sides, 4-footed, common, 4½x8½x12", from $15 to **$20.00**

Cooler (iced tea tumbler), Harvest, embossed grapes, 14-oz, set of 4, from $10 to **$15.00**

Creamer & sugar bowl on tray, Harvest, embossed grapes, 3-pc, from $25 to **$35.00**

Egg/Hors d'oeuvre tray, sectioned w/off-side holder for 8 eggs, 12¾" dia, from $40 to **$50.00**

Garland bowl (comport), paneled, 7½x8½" dia, from $15 to **$20.00**

Goblet, Harvest, embossed grapes, 9-oz, from $10 to ..**$12.00**

Hen on nest, from $15.00 to $25.00.

Pitcher, Harvest, embossed grapes, common, 10½", from $25 to **$40.00**

Plate, Bicentennial; American Eagle, from $10 to **$15.00**

Plate, hostess; Canterbury, allover diamond facets, flared crimped rim, 10", from $20 to **$25.00**

Punch set, Princess, complete w/ladle & hooks, 26-pc ..**$125.00**

Punch set, Princess, incomplete, no ladle or hooks ...**$60.00**

Tidbit, allover embossed diamond points, shallow w/flared sides, 6½" **$15.00**

Wedding bowl (sm compote), Thumbprint, footed, 5x5", from $10 to **$15.00**

Iridescent Gold Carnival Glass

Basket, Canterbury, waffle pattern, flaring sides drawn in at handle terminals, 9½x11x8½", from $40 to **$65.00**

Basket, Monticello, lg faceted allover diamonds, sq, 7x6", from $30 to **$35.00**

Candy box, Harvest, embossed grapes, lace edge, footed, 6½x5¾", from $20 to **$35.00**

Canister/Candy jar, Harvest, embossed grapes, 7", from $25 to **$30.00**

Canister/Cookie jar, Harvest, embossed grapes, 9", from $50 to **$75.00**

Canister/Snack jar, Harvest, embossed grapes, 8", from $40 to **$60.00**

Center bowl, Harvest, oval w/embossed grapes & paneled sides, 4½x8½x12", from $15 to **$20.00**

Console set, Wild Rose, wide naturalistic petals form sides, 9" bowl w/pr 4½" bowl-type candle holders, 3-pc..**$30.00**

Cooler (iced tea tumbler), Harvest, 14-oz, from $8 to ..**$12.00**

Egg plate, 11", from $15 to **$35.00**

Goblet, Harvest, embossed grapes, 9-oz, from $8 to ..**$12.00**

Hen on nest, 5½", from $10 to **$20.00**

Pitcher, Harvest, embossed grapes, 10½", from $24 to ..**$30.00**

Plate, hostess; diamond embossing, shallow w/crimped & flared sides, 10", from $12 to **$20.00**

Punch set, Princess, complete w/ladle & hooks, 26-pc ..**$100.00**

Punch Set, Princess, incomplete, no ladle or hooks ...**$50.00**

Relish tray, Vintage, 6 sections, 9x12¾", from $15 to.**$18.00**

Salad set, Vintage, embossed fruit, apple-shaped rim w/applied stem, 13", w/fork & spoon, 3-pc, from $15 to **$20.00**

Tumbler, Harvest, 4", from $10 to **$15.00**

Wedding bowl, Harvest, embossed grapes, pedestal foot, 8½x8", from $22 to **$28.00**

Wedding bowl (sm compote), 5x5", from $9 to **$12.00**

Iridescent Lime Carnival Glass

Lime green examples are harder to find than either the gold or the blue.

Candy box, Harvest, 6½", from $20.00 to $40.00.

Canister/Candy jar, Harvest, embossed grapes, 7", from $20 to **$30.00**

Canister/Cookie jar, Harvest, embossed grapes, 9", from $50 to **$80.00**

Canister/Snack jar, Harvest, embossed grapes, 8", from $40 to **$60.00**

Center bowl, Harvest, embossed grapes, paneled sides, 4-footed, 4½x8½x12", from $15 to **$20.00**

Compote, Harvest, embossed grapes, 7x6", from $15 to...**$20.00**

Console set, Harvest, embossed grapes, 10" bowl w/compote-shaped candle holders, 3-pc, from $50 to....**$80.00**

Cooler (iced tea tumbler), Harvest, embossed grapes, 14-oz, rare, from $12 to...**$18.00**

Creamer & sugar bowl on tray, Harvest, embossed grapes, 3-pc, from $25 to **$35.00**

Egg plate, 11", from $15 to..................................**$25.00**

Goblet, Harvest, embossed grapes, 9-oz, from $10 to ..**$15.00**

Hen on nest, from $20 to......................................**$25.00**

Pitcher, Harvest, embossed grapes, 10½", from $30 to..**$40.00**

Plate, hostess; allover diamond points, flared crimped sides, 10", from $15 to..**$25.00**

Punch set, Princess, complete w/ladle & hooks, 26-pc ..**$125.00**

Punch set, Princess, incomplete, no ladle or hooks ...**$60.00**

Salad set, Vintage, embossed fruit, apple-shaped rim w/applied stem, 13", w/fork & spoon, 3-pc, from $20 to...**$30.00**

Snack set, Harvest, embossed grapes, 4 cups & 4 plates, 8-pc, from $50 to **$75.00**

Iridescent Sunset (Amberina) Carnival Glass (Heritage)

Basket, footed, 9x5x7", from $30 to...........................**$50.00**

Basket, 9½x7½" sq, from $50 to **$60.00**

Bowl, crimped, 3¾x10", from $40 to **$50.00**

Butter dish, 5x7½" dia, from $35 to...........................**$40.00**

Center bowl, 4¾x8½", from $40 to...........................**$45.00**

Creamer & sugar bowl **$40.00**

Dessert set, 8½" bowl, 12" plate, 2-pc, from $40 to ...**$50.00**

Goblet, 8-oz, from $12 to..**$18.00**

Pitcher, 7¼", from $40 to **$55.00**

Pitcher, 8¼", from $40 to **$50.00**

Plate, 14", from $30 to..**$35.00**

Punch set, 10" bowl, pedestal, 8 cups, & ladle, 11-pc, from $150 to..**$225.00**

Rose bowl, 6½x6½", from $25 to..............................**$35.00**

Swung vase, slender, footed, w/irregular rim, 11x3" ..**$65.00**

Tumbler, 3½", from $10 to.......................................**$15.00**

Patterns

Canterbury, basket, waffle pattern, Lime, Sunset or Horizon Blue, 5½x12", from $35 to **$50.00**

Monticello, basket, lg faceted diamonds overall, Lemon, Lime, Sunset or Horizon Blue, sq, 7x6", from $25 to........**$40.00**

Monticello, basket, lg faceted diamonds overall, Lemon, Lime, Sunset or Horizon Blue, 8¾x10½", from $35 to..**$40.00**

Monticello, candy box, lg faceted overall diamonds, w/lid, Lemon, Lime, Sunset or Horizon Blue, 5¼x6", from $15 to..**$20.00**

Ruby Band Diamond Point, bowl, salad; w/4 servers ..**$45.00**

Ruby Band Diamond Point, butter dish, from $20 to.**$25.00**

Ruby Band Diamond Point, chip 'n dip set, 13" dia, from $18 to..**$25.00**

Ruby Band Diamond Point, comport, 14½" dia, from $15 to..**$25.00**

Ruby Band Diamond Point, cooler (iced tea tumbler), 15-oz, from $8 to..**$10.00**

Ruby Band Diamond Point, creamer & sugar bowl, 4½", from $15 to..**$20.00**

Ruby Band Diamond Point, creamer & sugar bowl, 4¾", on 6x9" tray, from $15 to...**$25.00**

Ruby Band Diamond Point, decanter, 12", $30.00.

Ruby Band Diamond Point, goblet, 12-oz, from $9 to .**$10.00**

Ruby Band Diamond Point, On-the-Rocks, 9-oz, from $8 to..**$10.00**

Ruby Band Diamond Point, pitcher, 8", from $15 to ..**$25.00**

Ruby Band Diamond Point, plate, hostess; 12", from $12 to..**$18.00**

Indianapolis 500 Racing Collectibles

You don't have to be a Hoosier to know that unless the weather interfers, this famous 500-mile race is held in Indianapolis every Memorial day and has been since 1911. Collectors of Indy memorabilia have a plethora of race-related items to draw from and can zero in on one area or many, enabling them to build extensive and interesting collections. Some of the special areas of interest they pursue are autographs, photographs, or other memorabilia related to the drivers; pit badges; race programs and yearbooks; books and magazines; decanters and souvenir tumblers; model race cars; and tickets.

Advisor: Eric Jungnickel (See Directory, Indy 500 Memorabilia)

Belt buckle, 1991, resembles pit pass, bronzed pewter, M..**$15.00**

Book, recap of 1974 Indianapolis 500, Hungness, hardcover, 200+ pages, NM **$20.00**

Book, The Race, Angelo Aneglopolous, 70 pages, EX ...**$50.00**

Coaster set, glass inserts in tin, Indianapolis 500 & race car, set of 6, EX............**$15.00**

Decal, 1954 Indianapolis 500 Mile Classic in white on blue w/red race car, EX............**$20.00**

Flag, Indianapolis Motor Speedway & race car on black & white checks, 1972, cloth w/wooden handle, 18x16", NM...**$8.00**

Folder, Souvenir Postcard; 1914, VG+............**$25.00**

Lapel pin, Indianapolis 500 & race car, enameled, 1993, M............**$15.00**

Matchcover, 1931, Lou Schneider (winner) image, EX .**$28.00**

Model kit, 1950s Indy Racer, Monogram #P12, 1/24 scale, M (NM box)............**$22.50**

Pedal car, 1955 Chevrolet Bel Air convertible, fiberglass body, given as a promotion by a car dealer, EX, $4,500.00.

Pennant, felt w/2 race cars & Souvenir of Indianapolis Speedway on red, 1950s, 26", EX............**$100.00**

Photo, Preston Stroupe behind wheel of race car, 1927, Kirkpatrick Studios, 8x10", EX............**$18.00**

Photo, 1954 Pace Lap, M............**$23.00**

Photo, 1957, Freddie Agabashain, 6x9", EX............**$25.00**

Photo, 1961, AJ Foyt, 8x10", EX............**$30.00**

Photo, 1963, Jim Clark in race car, 11½x9", framed under glass, NM............**$23.00**

Pit badge, 1956, old main gate, bronze, EX............**$70.00**

Pit badge, 1960, image of track & giant Champion Spark Plug, EX............**$75.00**

Pit badge, 1968, EX............**$45.00**

Pit badge, 1981, bronze, on original backing card, EX+..**$45.00**

Pit badge, 1982, Camaro, Chevrolet emblem, checkered flag, bronze, EX............**$30.00**

Pit badge, 1985, Oldsmobile Calais, w/original backing card, NM............**$33.00**

Pit badge, 1987, w/original backing card, EX............**$40.00**

Pit badge, 1988, Oldsmobile Cutlass Supreme, Herff Jones Inc, bronze, EX............**$45.00**

Pit badge, 1993, bronze, M............**$35.00**

Postcard, 1950, Jimmy Bryant in race car, 6x9", EX....**$33.00**

Postcard, 1950s, Paul Russo, 6x9", EX............**$30.00**

Poster, Indianapolis 500 in w/Race Sunday May 27 in red on white w/drivers scene & Time Trials dates, 1970s, 18x22", EX............**$25.00**

Print, The Start, depicts start of 1955 race, 13x19", NM..**$25.00**

Program, 1938, w/insert, VG............**$85.00**

Program, 1948, EX............**$30.00**

Program, 1951, NM............**$45.00**

Program, 1952, VG+............**$30.00**

Program, 1956, w/line-up insert, M............**$30.00**

Program, 1961, VG+............**$20.00**

Program, 1970, EX............**$30.00**

Record, 500 Miles to Glory, actual sounds of 1957 race, EX (EX cover)............**$45.00**

Screwdriver, Proto logo, metal, promotional, 1970s, EX............**$15.00**

Shot glass, clear w/white winged logo w/black letters, gold rim, 1960s, M............**$20.00**

Telephone, commemorating 1986 500, GTE, EX............**$20.00**

Ticket, Press; 1995, Al Unser Jr, NM............**$25.00**

Ticket, 1949, no raincheck, EX............**$22.50**

Ticket, 1957, no raincheck, EX............**$30.00**

Ticket, 1962, AJ Foyt on front, w/raincheck, EX............**$28.00**

Tumbler, AJ Foyt, 1964, 3¼", $20.00.

Tumbler, clear w/black print, crossed flags & car #82 on front w/1911-1965 winners list on back, 4½", EX............**$25.00**

Tumbler, purple carnival glass w/white letters, winners list from 1911-1967, EX............**$15.00**

Tumbler, 1958, clear w/white logo & Tony Hulman in black letters, EX............**$18.50**

Tumblers, clear w/black print, stemmed, w/Hulman family Christmas card, winners list from 1911-1992, set of 4, MIB............**$25.00**

Yearbook, 1946, Floyd Cramer's, M............**$30.00**

Yearbook, 1962, Floyd Cramer's, EX............**$28.00**

Yearbook, 1965, Floyd Cramer's, NM............**$50.00**

Italian Glass

Throughout the century, the island of Murano has been recognized a one of the major glassmaking centers of the world. Companies including Venini, Barovier, Aureliano Toso, Barvini, Vistosi, AVEM, Cenedese, Cappellin, Seguso, and Archimede Seguso have produced very fine art glass, examples of which today often bring several thousand dollars on the secondary market — superior examples much more. Such items are rarely seen at the garage sale and flea market level, but what you will be seeing are the more generic glass clowns, birds, ashtrays, and animals, generally referred to simply as Murano glass. Their values are determined by the techniques used in their making more than size alone. For instance, an item with gold inclusions, controlled bubbles, fused glass patches or layers of colors is more desirable than one that has none of these elements, even though it may be larger. For more information concerning the specific companies mentioned above, see *Schroeder's Antiques Price Guide* (Collector Books).

Ashtray, clown, from $90.00 to $100.00.

Ball, blue murrines, Venini, 3" $950.00

Basket, aqua to green, handles curl up & resemble horns, 8¾" $75.00

Basket, yellow & white latticinio ribbons encased in clear, clear simple handle, 9¾x6½x5½" $325.00

Bookends, 3 multicolor flowers encased in clear dome, lg clear bubble center, Murano, 4", pr $130.00

Bottle, green cased w/latticinio pink & white canes w/black amethyst zanfirico canes, matching ball stopper, Venini, 18" $550.00

Bowl, amber sommerso w/iridescent corroso surface, conical, Murano, 4⅛x10" $315.00

Bowl, amber to red, sq w/pulled rounded points at rim, 9" $50.00

Bowl, amber to red, swirls to 3 pointed edges, heavy, 9" ..$50.00

Bowl, aqua w/applied crystal foot, trifold, paper label, 3½x4½" $50.00

Bowl, biomorphic blob, white glass w/silver foil & colored murrines, folded in on 3 sides, Murano, 7" $100.00

Bowl, bird form, white to mint green, 1940s-50s, 8½" H $70.00

Bowl, black w/white matt finish, folded on 2 sides, blown, 6¾" $50.00

Bowl, center; amber to red, graceful curved rim, Murano, 16" $85.00

Bowl, finger; white opal, ruffled rim w/overall gold inclusions, Venini, 3x4", w/matching underplate $175.00

Bowl, green overshot, green leaf shape, 3x5" $100.00

Bowl, Plume, clear w/internal red filigrana feathers, Archimede Seguso, 2½x8" $350.00

Bowl, white encased in clear, 3 pinched sides, copper fleck internal decor, controlled bubbles, 7" $50.00

Bowl, white filigree netting alternates w/yellow twisted stripes, folded free-form, Murano label, 5" dia...$100.00

Bowl, white w/green trapped rim, internal copper spots & flecks, 2 sides folded inward, Barbini, 7¼" $50.00

Charger, Air Pipes, clear w/spiral bubbled canes, blue rim attached w/incalmo technique, Toso label, 1966, 2x14¾" $750.00

Compote, ruby red, clear grape-cluster handles w/gold inclusions, ruffled ovoid rim, AVEM Murano label $150.00

Flask, violet cased in clear, w/stopper, Venini, 1950s, 9½"..$315.00

Lamp, table; 4 clear segments w/gold leaf, brass base, no shade, 1930s..$650.00

Paperweight, apple, ruby red w/hint of gold on leaf, lg ..$60.00

Paperweight, Inciso, clear cube w/dimples, orange & yellow sommerso layers, Venini, 3" $275.00

Pitcher, cranberry w/diamond optics, crystal handle w/gold inclusions, Murano, 1950s, 11" $195.00

Sculpture, bear, crystal, heavy, Salviati, 6½x8½" $550.00

Sculpture, bird, blue cased, clear bill & plume, white/amethyst cane eyes, Hand Made sticker, 14½"....................$115.00

Sculpture, birds (2) on limb, blue, green, yellow & crystal, Murano, 6½x14" $285.00

Sculpture, Christmas tree, red spiral ribbon in center, Murano, 1950s, 9" $65.00

Sculpture, clown, red bow tie & hat, fat, EX details, Murano, 9x6½" $125.00

Sculpture, clown, red shirt & hat, blue pants, white shirt, amber face, Murano, 6½" $95.00

Sculpture, clown on ball, multicolor on clear ball w/bubbles, Mario Badioli, Murano, 15" $500.00

Sculpture, duck, cobalt & red cased, clear bill, Murano, 6½" $75.00

Sculpture, duck, green, blown, Murano, 10x10½"....$225.00

Sculpture, figure kneeling & offering fruit, amethyst & gold leaf, Murano, 11", pr..$750.00

Sculpture, fish, blue & green w/amber, chevron eye, Murano, 11¾" $195.00

Sculpture, lady, full-skirted gown, cranberry, crystal & gold, Murano, 1950s, 10¾" $325.00

Sculpture, lady dancer, clear frosted style, hands over head/flying skirt, Italy, 10"...................................$140.00

Sculpture, male & female, ea holding gold urn, Camer Glass, Seguso, 12", pr..$1,250.00

Sculpture, native dancer caricature, Made in Italy Murano paper label on base, 13½" $35.00

Sculpture, parrot, blue, green w/clear paperweight base, 10" $85.00

Shade, opaque yellow w/white stripes, Massimo Vignelli, 1950s, 14¼x5" $250.00

Shade, orange w/red, blue & green bands in clear base, Massimo Vignelli, 1950s, 14x5", pr.................$1,600.00

Snifter bowl, amethyst, diamond point design, hollow stem, Murano sticker, 10½x6" $35.00

Stem, champagne; red bowl & foot, clear hollow double-ball stem w/gold foil inclusions, Murano, 6⅛".........**$195.00**

Syrup, green millifiori, Murano, 8"............................**$375.00**

Vase, amber to clear to green, waisted, flared rim, Murano, 1950s, 10"...**$160.00**

Vase, amethyst to amber to clear, folded, 7½"............**$68.00**

Vase, blue millifiori w/crystal overlay, paperweight base, 1950s, 8" **$85.00**

Vase, bud; cobalt swirls in white, Murano, 6¾x3¾"...**$45.00**

Vase, clear to blue to blue-gray pitcher form, blown, rope handle, Murano, 15" **$450.00**

Vase, clear w/green lined basin over solid body w/yellow vertical shaft at base, Antonio Da Ros, Cenedese, 1960, 11x6" **$850.00**

Vase, cobalt encased in clear, slim w/ruffled rim, Murano, 1950s, 15" **$75.00**

Vase, dark aqua w/amber handles & foot, Venini, 1930s, 10" **$200.00**

Vase, emerald to amber, cylindrical w/flared ruffled rim, Murano, 1940s, 11¾"...**$145.00**

Vase, handkerchief; clear w/white threads & gold flecks, 4 pulled points, unknown maker, 4½x4"...............**$25.00**

Vase, handkerchief; red cased in white, Venini Italia engraved signature, 8x12" **$750.00**

Vase, handkerchief; ruby red, Murano, 6½" **$100.00**

Vase, Inciso, purple sommerso, Venini, 13" **$3,250.00**

Vase, jack-in-the-pulpit; amethyst to amber, Venini, 12½"..**$90.00**

Vase, jack-in-the-pulpit; orange to clear, Murano, 1940-50s, 13" **$195.00**

Vase, light smoke crystal, curved dipped center, Made in Italy, 10"...**$65.00**

Vase, multicolor powders cased in clear, applied rigaree collar w/gold leaf, jug form, AVEM, 11x6" **$1,450.00**

Vase, multicolor spatter w/aventurine on amethyst, ruffled rim, rim-to-hip handles, Murano, 5¼"...............**$55.00**

Vase, ruby cased in heavy lead crystal, geometric deisgn w/4 pointed side 'fins,' Murano, 12" **$85.00**

Vase, translucent blue murrina, gourd shape w/slim neck & flared rim, Fratelli Toso, 8" **$1,350.00**

Vase, white to amber base, ruffled rim, classic form, 13½"...**$38.50**

Sculptures, snail, amber in opal shell with spirals and bubbles, paper label (Salviati & Co), 1960s, 7½" long, $300.00; Bird, zigzag canes, white and black with one gold cane and clear applications, Dino Martens, 1954, 10" long, $325.00.

Jade-ite Glassware

For the past few years, Jade-ite has been one of the fastest-moving types of collectible glassware on the market. It was produced by several companies from the 1940s through 1965. Many of Anchor Hocking's Fire-King lines were available in the soft opaque green Jade-ite, and Jeannette Glass as well as McKee produced their own versions.

It was always very inexpensive glass, and it was made in abundance. Dinnerware for the home as well as restaurants and a vast array of kitchenware items literally flooded the country for many years. Though a few rare pieces have become fairly expensive, most are still reasonably priced, and there are still bargains to be had.

For more information we recommend *Anchor Hocking's Fire-King & More*, *Kitchen Glassware of the Depression Years*, and *Collectible Glassware of the 40s, 50s, and 60s*, all by Gene Florence.

Ashtray, Fire-King, sq, 4¼", from $28 to.....................**$30.00**

Ashtray, Jeannette, #530, from $12 to **$15.00**

Baker, Ovenware, Fire-King, 5x1½", from $100 to...**$125.00**

Bottle, water; Jeannette, from $225 to **$250.00**

Bowl, beater; Jeannette, w/beater, from $45 to **$50.00**

Bowl, bon bon; Fire-King, ruffled rim, diamond bottom, 6½", from $40 to...**$55.00**

Bowl, breakfast/cereal; Fire-King, w/red ivy, 16-oz, from $90 to...**$100.00**

Bowl, bulb; Fire-King, in wicker holder, from $25 to.**$30.00**

Bowl, cereal; Shell, Fire-King, 6⅜".............................**$25.00**

Bowl, cereal; 1700 Line, Fire-King, 5⅞".....................**$35.00**

Bowl, chili; Three Bands, Fire-King, 2 bands, 5" **$250.00**

Bowl, dessert; Sheaves of Wheat, Fire-King, 4½" **$85.00**

Bowl, Jeannette, vertical rib, 8", from $35 to **$40.00**

Bowl, mixing; Colonial Kitchen, Fire-King, 6", from $70 to...**$75.00**

Bowl, mixing; Fire-King, splash proof, w/decal flowers, 6¾", from $400 to...**$450.00**

Bowl, mixing; Hocking, 9", from $28 to **$30.00**

Bowl, mixing; Ribbed, Fire-King, 7½", from $25 to....**$30.00**

Bowl, mixing; Swedish Modern, Fire-King, 7¼", from $90 to...**$100.00**

Bowl, oatmeal; Jane Ray, Fire-King, 5⅞".....................**$20.00**

Bowl, soup; Charm, Fire-King, 6"................................**$35.00**

Bowl, vegetable; Three Bands, Fire-King, 8¼"............**$95.00**

Butter dish, Fire-King, w/crystal top, from $110 to ..**$125.00**

Butter dish, Hocking, ¼-lb, from $110 to..................**$125.00**

Butter dish, Jeannette, from $65 to **$75.00**

Canister, flour or sugar; Jeannette, from $50 to **$55.00**

Canister, Jeannette, sq, 48-oz, 5½", ea, from $150 to...**$165.00**

Canister, spice; Jeannette, #5162, 3", ea, from $125 to .**$135.00**

Child's mug, Fire-King, from $200 to......................**$250.00**

Cracker bowl, Jeannette, swirl design, from $30 to....**$35.00**

Crock, Jeannette, #5031, round, 40-oz, from $60 to..**$65.00**

Cup, Hocking, straight, 6-oz, from $9 to **$12.00**

Cup, Ransom, 1700 Line, Fire-King, 9-oz....................**$22.00**

Cup, Restaurant Ware, Fire-King, demitasse **$35.00**

Cup, Sheaves of Wheat, Fire-King..........................$60.00
Cup, Swirl, Fire-King, 8-oz.....................................$40.00
Custard, Ovenware, Fire-King, deep, ruffled top, from $250
    to...$300.00
Custard, Ovenware, Fire-King, individual, 6-oz, from $65
    to...$70.00
Custard, Ovenware, Fire-King, set of 6 in wire holder, from
    $400 to..$450.00
Dessert set, Peach Leaf & Blossom, Fire-King, 2-pc, from $30
    to...$35.00
Dish, candy/dessert; Maple Leaf, Fire-King, from $25 to ..$28.00

**Egg cup, double, Anchor Hocking,
4", from $28.00 to $32.00.**

Flower pot, Fire-King, scalloped top, 3¼", from $25 to $30.00
French casserole, ovenware, Fire-King, 5", w/handle & lid,
    from $450 to..$500.00
Gravy or sauce boat, Restaurant Ware, Fire-King $500.00
Jar, drippings, McKee, 4x5", from $150 to.................$115.00
Jar, grease, Fire-King, screw-on lid, from $75 to.........$85.00
Jar, refrigerator leftover; Hocking, from $55 to $65.00
Jewel box, Fire-King, w/lid, from $75 to.....................$85.00
Jug, ice box; Jeannette, #370, from $325 to $375.00
Loaf pan, Ovenware, Fire-King, 5x9", from $45 to $50.00
Measuring cup, Jeannette, ½-cup, spout, from $150 to...$175.00
Measuring pitcher, Jeannette, 4-cup, from $75 to $85.00
Mug, advertising, Fire-King, North Carolina, from $20 to...$25.00
Mug, chocolate; Restaurant Ware, Fire-King, slim, 6-oz.....$24.00
Mug, Hocking, embossed Fire-King, from $100 to ...$125.00
Mug, Philbe, Fire-King, 8-oz, from $100 to $125.00
Mug, souvenir; Fire-King, 1988 Fire-King Expo, Tulsa, from
    $15 to..$20.00
Mugs, Fire-King, set of 4, in box, from $50 to............$55.00
Pie plate, Ovenware, Fire-King, 9", from $175 to $200.00
Pitcher, ball; plain, Fire-King, 80-oz, from $500 to ...$600.00
Pitcher, Hocking, 16-oz, from $200 to $250.00
Pitcher, milk; Fire-King, 20-oz, from $80 to................$90.00
Plate, Alice, Fire-King, 9½" $28.00
Plate, children's, Fire-King, divided, 7½", from $400 to ..$500.00
Plate, dinner; Shell, Fire-King, 10".............................$25.00

Plate, pie or salad; Restaurant Ware, Fire-King, G297,
    6¾" $12.00
Plate, serving; Restaurant Ware, Fire-King, 10".........$150.00
Platter, Charm, Fire-King, 11x8".................................$55.00
Platter, Jane Ray, Fire-King, 9x12" $25.00
Reamer, orange; Jeannette, light color, #379, lg, from $45
    to...$50.00
Refrigerator container, Fire-King, 4x8", from $45 to ...$50.00
Refrigerator container, Philbe, Fire-King, w/lid, 4½x5", from
    $35 to..$40.00
Salt & pepper shakers, Fire-King, pr, from $80 to $90.00
Salt & pepper shakers, Jeannette, decorated, from $35 to $45.00
Salt box, Jeannette, #5114, from $325 to $350.00
Saucer, Restaurant Ware, Fire-King, demitasse $40.00
Saucer, Swirl, Fire-King, 5¾"....................................$20.00
Saucer, Three Bands, Fire-King, 1 band.....................$75.00
Shakers, flour or sugar, Jeannette, ea, from $50 to.....$60.00
Skillet, Ovenware, Fire-King, 1 spout, 7", from $70 to ..$80.00
Skillet, Ovenware, Fire-King, 2-spout, 7", from $140 to ..$165.00
Sugar bowl, Jane Ray, Fire-King................................$10.00
Sugar bowl, Shell, Fire-King, footed..........................$25.00
Tumbler, water; Jeannette, from $15 to $18.00
Vase, Fire-King, tab handled, 7¾", from $85 to $90.00
Vase, table; Fire-King, 2 shades, from $20 to.............$22.50

Japan Ceramics

This category is narrowed down to the inexpensive novelty items produced in Japan from 1921 to 1941 and again from 1947 until the present. Though Japanese ceramics marked Nippon, Noritake, and Occupied Japan have long been collected, some of the newest fun-type collectibles on today's market are the figural ashtrays, pincushions, wall pockets, toothbrush holders, etc., that are marked 'Made in Japan' or simply 'Japan.' In her books called *Collector's Guide to Made in Japan Ceramics* (there are four in series), Carole Bess White explains the pitfalls you will encounter when you try to determine production dates. Collectors refer to anything produced before WWII as 'old' and anything made after 1952 as 'new.' Backstamps are inconsistent as to wording and color, and styles are eclectic. Generally, items with applied devices are old, and they are heavier and thicker. Often they were more colorful than the newer items, since fewer colors mean less expense to the manufacturer. Lustre glazes are usually indicative of older pieces, especially the deep solid colors. When lustre was used after the war, it was often mottled with contrasting hues and was usually thinner.

Imaginative styling and strong colors are what give these Japanese ceramics their charm, and they also are factors to consider when you make your purchases. You'll find all you need to know to be a wise shopper in the books we've recommended.

See also Blue Willow; Cat Collectibles; Condiment Sets; Flower Frogs; Geisha Girl; Holt Howard; Kreiss; Lamps;

Lefton; Napkin Dolls; Occupied Japan Collectibles; Powder Jars; Toothbrush Holders; Wall Pockets.

Advisor: Carole Bess White (See Directory, Japan Ceramics)

Newsletter: *Made in Japan Info Letter*
Carole Bess White
P.O. Box 819
Portland, OR 97207; Fax: 503-281-2817; Send SASE for information; no appraisals given. e-mail: CBESSW@aol.com

Bowl, candle holders in rim, rosebud flower frog, 6" diameter, from $35.00 to $45.00.

Ashtray, Indian w/pipe, wrapped in blanket, seated on edge of sq dish, multicolored lustre, 4½", from $45 to...**$75.00**

Ashtray, Mexican taking siesta, w/guitar ashtray, multicolored w/tan lustre finish, 1½", from $15 to **$25.00**

Ashtray, toddler w/turtle seated next to rectangular dish w/1 corner rest, multicolored shiny finish, 3", from $20 to **$30.00**

Ashtray set, figural hunt scene on base w/3 stacked horseshoe ashtrays, 5½", from $35 to **$75.00**

Ashtray set, 4 card-suit shapes w/ace from ea suit in center of dish, multicolored lustre finishes, 3½", from $14 to.**$18.00**

Ashtrays, figural hunt scenes w/card suits in horseshoe dishes, multicolored & lustre finishes, 1½", ea from $18 to...**$28.00**

Bank, Hummel-type girl under umbrella, Save for a Rainy Day on grassy base, multicolored matt, 5", from $18 to **$28.00**

Bank, money bag w/$ sign, tied at neck, ruffled rim, incised grid design, opalescent lustre, 4½", from $18 to..**$28.00**

Basket vase, floral motif w/tan lustre interior, blue lustre exterior, pedestal base, side handles, 4", from $35 to ...**$55.00**

Biscuit barrel, Dutch windmill, multicolors on cream, 6½", from $48 to...**$68.00**

Biscuit barrel, round cottage w/thatched roof, floral vine around door, green & brown, 8", from $48 to **$68.00**

Biscuit barrel, white basket-weave w/embossed & green-painted clover, shiny finish, 5¼", from $48 to **$68.00**

Biscuit barrel, yellow w/embossed playing cards in central band, green animal finial, 5½", from $50 to...........**$80.00**

Bookends, colonial couple seated back to back, black & white shiny finish, 6", pr, from $30 to **$45.00**

Bookends, pheasants taking flight from grassy bases, multicolored shiny finish, 5", pr, from $20 to **$30.00**

Bowl, inverted ruffled rim w/rose & leaf handle, scenic interior, multicolored lustre, 7" dia, from $25 to **$40.00**

Cache pot, Big Bad Wolf standing next to house on base, multicolored shiny finish, 5", from $15 to **$25.00**

Cache pot, dog w/lolling tongue upright against ribbed cup, shiny cream finish, 3½", from $15 to **$25.00**

Cache pot, little devil w/arm around nose of gun turret on tank, multicolored shiny finish, 3", from $20 to...**$35.00**

Cache pot, pixie figure seated on edge of vertical leaf pot, multicolored shiny finish, 5¼", from $20 to **$35.00**

Cache pot, Scottie dog w/neck bow, multicolored shiny glazes, 7½", from $20 to **$30.00**

Cache pot, swan on water waves, shiny multicolors on white w/blue water, 4", from $15 to..............................**$25.00**

Cache pot, wishing well w/barrel & bucket on grassy base, multicolored shiny finish, 5", from $15 to **$25.00**

Candlesticks, columns in amber & cream mottled lustre w/black trim around flared bases, 6¼", pr, from $28 to..**$48.00**

Candy dish, figural cartoon-like cat w/legs spread on side of comma-shaped dish, multicolored lustre, 4", from $50 to..**$75.00**

Candy dish, round w/embossed lotus design on sides & lid, matt tan & deep orange w/black trim, 3¼", from $35 to...**$55.00**

Candy dish, 3 geisha girls carrying round bowl, white, orange & black w/gold trim, 4½", from $75 to..**$100.00**

Casserole dish, basket-weave w/embossed floral lid, multicolored shiny finish, 10", from $20 to...................**$35.00**

Cigarette box, Art Deco w/amimal finial, crackle finish over painted design, sq, 5", from $55 to **$80.00**

Cigarette box & ashtray set, doghouse w/dog's head & tail at front & back, 4 ashtrays form roof, matt, 3", from $35 to...**$55.00**

Figurine, dog seated w/head cocked sideways & ears up, bow around neck, green & maroon shiny finish, 5¼", from $25 to..**$35.00**

Figurine, mama bird perched above baby bird (w/mouth open) on branches w/blossoms, multicolored, 4", from $17 to..**$20.00**

Figurine, monkey bent forward scratching head, oval base, incised features, green wash on shiny white, 5", from $25 to..**$35.00**

Flask, flat sided w/embossed drunk against lamppost, Here's to Both of You, multi matt & tan lustre, 5", from $75 to...**$135.00**

Incense burner, elephant w/pagoda on back, multicolored shiny finish, some gold trim, 5¾", from $25 to....**$40.00**

Incense burner, man in suit & vest seated in chair smoking pipe, multicolored shiny finish, 4¼", from $30 to..**$45.00**

Incense burner, sailing ship w/sail marked Incense Burner Bank, multicolored, 4½", from $18 to...................**$28.00**

Lamp, blue lustre tree trunk base w/2 multicolored birds perched on branches, 5½", from $65 to **$95.00**

Lamp, Buddha figure on round base, multicolored Satsuma style, w/domed cage, from $50 to..........................**$80.00**

Leaf dish, curled-up tip, 2 painted flowers by stem, multicolored semi-matt w/gold trim, 6", from $5 to.........**$10.00**

Lemon server, multicolored lustre, 5¾" dia, from $25 to..**$40.00**

Mayonnaise set, tulip-shaped bowl w/petal-shaped plate & spoon, aqua leaves on amber & white lustre, 6½", from $40 to..**$75.00**

Muffineer set, various Art Deco styles & finishes, from $65 to..**$95.00**

Nut cup, Dutch boy leaning against basket, blue, white & orange shiny finish, 2¾", from $18 to...................**$28.00**

Pincushion, dog seated, blue lustre, 3½", from $20 to ..**$30.00**

Pincushion, Santa driving horse-drawn coach, multicolored matt & lustre finish, 3", from $18 to......................**$28.00**

Pitcher, dog shape w/sad eyes & long ears, white & brown shiny finish, 2¾", from $25 to **$35.00**

Pitcher, geometric circle shape w/quarter of circle as cut-out handle, oblong base, semi-matt white, 5½", from $20 to..**$30.00**

Planter, embossed windmill design on sq tapered pot w/under dish, various shiny finishes, Maruyama, 3¼", from $15 to..**$25.00**

Plate, souvenir; hand-painted motifs, various sizes, from $8 to..**$15.00**

Powder box, clown, multicolored lustre finish, 4¼", from $75 to..**$140.00**

Powder box, round basket-weave box in tan lustre w/2 white & black dogs & fruit decal on lid, 4", from $25 to..**$45.00**

Refrigerator set, 3 green stackable boxes w/blue embossed clover design, tab handles, shiny finish, 6½", from $50 to..**$75.00**

Relish dish, floral & weave motif, 3 compartments, scalloped rim, wrapped handle, crackle glaze, 8", from $18 to..**$28.00**

Ring tray, amorous couple on edge of dish, multicolored lustre & shiny finish, 4", from $25 to........................**$40.00**

Sewing kit, candlestick telephone complete w/pincushion, scissors, tape measure, etc, multicolored, 6½", from $35 to..**$45.00**

Shoe, squatty heel, embossed knobby button trim, multicolored lustre, 5¾", from $18 to................................**$28.00**

Snack set, cup & plate (shaped like painter's palette), lustre finish, 7¼", from $15 to..**$25.00**

Sugar shaker, sq w/multicolored Art Deco design & tan lustre, 6½", from $21 to...**$36.00**

Teapot, octagonal 4-footed tulip shape w/ear-shaped handle, orange & yellow lustre w/black trim, 5", from $35 to .**$50.00**

Teapot, round w/inverted lid, angled handle, flat bottom, multicolored floral motif w/blue & tan lustre, 5", from $35 to..**$50.00**

Teapot, round w/2 flat sides, multicolored crackle finish, wrapped handle, 6¾", from $35 to.......................**$55.00**

Teapot, various styles w/multicolored lustre finishes, from $30 to..**$45.00**

Toast rack, rectangular base w/5 curved racks, center has loop finial, blue & tan lustre, 5½" L, from $25 to **$50.00**

Vase, calico hippo w/head tilted upward & mouth wide open, 3¼", from $20 to...**$30.00**

Vase, fan shape w/flared ribbed base, flower & leaf motif on blue, white & orange lustre, black trim, 5", from $35 to..**$55.00**

Vase, multicolor bird on tan lustre floral vase, marked, 10¼", from $50.00 to $75.00. (Photo courtesy Carole Bess White)

Vase, peanut shell form w/ruffled rim & footed base, shiny cream finish, 8¼", from $27 to **$37.00**

Vase, tapered urn w/flared base, lg blue & orange flowers w/black leaf trim on tan lustre, 5½", from $35 to..**$55.00**

Vase, tapered urn w/multicolored stemmed floral motif on white w/yellow, blue & orange stripes & bands, 8", from $28 to **$40.00**

Vase, tree trunk w/2 birds perched on branches, shiny multicolored & lustre finishes, 6¼", from $45 to........**$70.00**

Wall pocket, conical form w/stylized flowers on rust & white stripes, tan lustre top, black trim, 6½", from $65 to..**$95.00**

Jewel Tea Company

At the turn of the century, there was stiff competition among door-to-door tea-and-coffee companies, and most of them tried to snag the customer by doling out coupons that could eventually be traded in for premiums. But the thing that set the Jewel Tea people apart from the others was that their premiums were awarded to the customer first, then 'earned' through the purchases that followed. This set the tone of their business dealings which obviously contributed to their success, and very soon in addition to the basic products they started out with, the company entered the food-manufacturing field. They eventually became one of the country's largest retailers. Today their products, containers, premiums, and advertising ephemera are all very collectible.

Advisors: Bill and Judy Vroman (See Directory, Jewel Tea)

Baking Powder, Jewel, cylindrical tin w/script logo & white lettering, 1950s-60s, 1-lb, from $20 to **$30.00**

Bar Soap, Pine Soap, four green bars in box with embossed pine decoration, MIB, $55.00. (Photo courtesy Bill and Judy Vroman)

Cake decorator set, late 1940s, from $50 to **$65.00**
Candy, Jewel Mints, round green tin, 1920s, 1-lb, $30 to...**$40.00**
Candy, Jewel Tea Spice Jelly Drops, orange box, w/orange & white lettering, from $20 to **$30.00**
Cereal, Jewel Quick Oats, cylindrical box w/white & orange lettering, from $40 to...**$40.00**
Cocoa, Jewel or Jewel Tea, various boxes, ea from $25 to...**$45.00**
Coffee, Jewel Blend, orange & gold w/white lettering & logo, paper label **$40.00**
Coffee, Jewel Private Blend, brown & white lettering, 1-lb, from $15 to...**$25.00**
Coffee, Jewel Special Blend, brown stripes on white, white & orange lettering on brown circle, 2-lb, from $15 to..**$25.00**
Coffee, Royal Jewel, yellow, brown & white, 1-lb, from $20 to..**$35.00**
Coffee, West Coast, orange & brown w/white lettering, bell at top center, 1960s, 2-lb, from $25 to **$35.00**
Dishes, Melmac, 8 place settings, from $150 to **$170.00**
Extract, Jewel Imitation Vanilla, brown box w/orange & white lettering, 1960s, 4-oz, from $20 to **$20.00**
Extract, Jewel Lemon, orange, blue & white, 1916-19, from $40 to..**$50.00**
Flour sifter, litho metal, EX **$485.00**
Garment bag, 1950s, MIP, from $25 to.......................**$30.00**
Laundry, Daintiflakes, pink & blue box marked Soft Feathery Flakes of Pure Mild Soap, from $25 to **$30.00**
Laundry, Daybreak Laundry Set, from $15 to.............**$20.00**

Laundry, Grano Granulated Soap, blue & white box marked Made For General Cleaning, 2-lb, from $25 to.....**$30.00**
Laundry, Pure Gloss Starch, teal & white box, from $25 to **$30.00**
Malted milk mixer, Jewel-T, from $40 to **$50.00**
Mix, Jewel Subrite Mix, Mason jar w/paper label & metal screw lid, 1960s, 26-oz, from $15 to **$25.00**
Mix, Jewel Tea Coconut Dessert, round tan tin w/brown & white logo & lettering, 1930s, 14-oz, from $30 to....**$40.00**
Mix, Jewel Tea Devil's Food Cake Flour, 1920s, 10-oz, from $30 to...**$40.00**
Mix, Jewel Tea Prepares Tapioca, tall sq orange & brown striped tin w/logo & brown lettering, 1930s, from $25 to **$35.00**
Mixer, Mary Dunbar, electric stand w/bowl & original hang tag, white...**$100.00**
Mixer, Mary Dunbar, hand-held w/stand, 1940, from $40 to...**$50.00**
Napkins, paper w/printed pattern, box of 200 ....**$25.00**
Nuts, Jewel Mixed Nuts, round brown-striped tin w/orange & brown lettering, 1960s, 1-lb, from $15 to **$20.00**
Peanut Butter, Jewel Tea, glass jar w/paper label & screw lid, 1930s, 1-lb, from $30 to **$40.00**
Pickle fork, Jewel-T, from $20 to...............................**$25.00**
Razor blades, Jewel-T **$5.00**
Saleman's award, Ephraim Coffee cup & saucer (given to top 400 salesman), 1939, 1-qt, from $175 to.............**$350.00**
Scales, Jewel-T, from $45 to..**$55.00**
Sweeper, Jewel, gold lettering on black, 1930s-40s, from $80 to...**$100.00**
Sweeper, Jewel Little Bissell, from $40 to...................**$50.00**
Sweeper, Jewel Suction Sweeper, early 1900s, lg **$150.00**
sweeper, Jewel Suction Sweeper, 1930s-40s, from $60 to ..**$100.00**
Tea bags, Jewel Tea, dragon logo, gold & brown, 1948...**$65.00**

Jewelry

Today's costume jewelry collectors may range from nine to ninety and have tastes as varied as their ages, but one thing they all have in common is their love of these distinctive items of jewelry, some originally purchased at the corner five-&-dimes, others from department stores and boutiques.

Costume jewelry became popular, simply because it was easily affordable for all women. Today jewelry made before 1954 is considered to be 'antique,' while the term 'collectible' jewelry generally refers to those pieces made after that time. Costume jewelry was federally recognized as an American art form in 1954, and the copyright law was passed to protect the artists' designs. The copyright mark (c in a circle) found on the back of a piece identifies a post-1954 'collectible.'

Quality should always be the primary consideration when shopping for these treasures. Remember that pieces with colored rhinestones bring the higher prices. (Note: A 'rhinestone' is a clear, foil-backed, leaded glass crystal — unless it is a 'colored rhinestone' — while a 'stone' is not foiled.) A complete set (called a parure) increases in value by 20% over the total of its components. Check for a manufacturer's mark, since a signed piece is worth 20% more than one of comparable quality, but not signed. Some of the best designers are Miriam Haskell, Eisenberg, Trifari, Hollycraft, and Joseff.

Early plastic pieces (Lucite, Bakelite, and celluloid, for example) are very collectible. Some Lucite is used in combination with wood, and the figural designs are especially desirable.

There are several excellent reference books available if you'd like more information. Look for *Unsigned Beauties of Costume Jewelry* and *Signed Beauties of Costume Jewelry* by our advisor Marcia Brown. Lillian Baker has written several, including *50 Years of Collectible Fashion Jewelry* and *100 Years of Collectible Jewelry*. Books by other authors include *Collectible Silver Jewelry* and *Costume Jewelry* by Fred Rezazadeh; *Collectible Costume Jewelry* by Cherri Simonds; *Painted Porcelain Jewelry and Buttons* by Dorothy Kamm; *Vintage Jewelry for Investment and Casual Wear* by Karen L. Edeen; *Brilliant Rhinestones* by Ronna Lee Aikins; and video books *Hidden Treasures Series* by Christie Romero and Marcia Brown. All books are available through Collector Books; the videos may be purchased by contacting Marcia Brown.

See also Christmas Tree Pins

Advisor: Marcia Brown (See Directory, Jewelry)

Club/Newsletter: *Vintage Fashion and Costume Jewelry Newsletter Club*
P.O. Box 265, Glen Oaks, NY 11004
Membership: $20 in US; www.lizjewel.com/vf/

Bracelet, Alice Caviness, wide cuff style w/pearls, rhinestones & blue glass stones in various sizes & shapes **$285.00**
Bracelet, bangle; unsigned, black plastic w/diagonal lines of inlaid white rhinestones, hinged, wide **$50.00**
Bracelet, bangle; unsigned, celluloid studded w/2 rows of sm rhinestones, narrow **$85.00**
Bracelet, Castlecliff, golden cuff w/jungle cat, 'fur' texturing & green rhinestone eyes, ¾" band......................**$200.00**
Bracelet, charm; chain w/6 love amulets: cupid's bow, cage w/lovebirds, heart, etc............................**$30.00**
Bracelet, Hollycraft, floral design w/rose-colored rhinestones..**$60.00**
Bracelet, Marcel Boucher, gold-plated arcs w/red cabochons in each, gold cutwork **$80.00**
Bracelet, Regency, 3-row arrangement of light & dark blue rhinestones **$85.00**
Bracelet, Schiaparelli, 3 floweret clusters of pink rhinestones **$140.00**
Bracelet, tiger eye cabochon framed in mesh on 2-bar wrist band, gold-plated........................**$35.00**
Bracelet, tourist's souvenir, chain w/rhinestone-topped letters **$22.00**
Bracelet, unsigned, gold-plated wraparound style widens at ends tipped in sq red channeled rhinestones **$105.00**

Bracelet, unsigned, hinged gold-tone walled style w/florals in relief **$30.00**
Bracelet, unsigned, intense blue faux marquise rhinestones on gold-wire framework, wider on top **$48.00**
Bracelet, unsigned, pink rhinestones, larger stones form 5 spaced bars, 2" wide **$110.00**
Bracelet, unsigned, row of 6 yellow plastic flowers....**$12.00**
Bracelet, unsigned, silver plated w/lg deep purple cabochons **$150.00**
Bracelet, unsigned, single row of hand-set clear rhinestones......................................**$18.00**
Bracelet, unsigned, single row of mixed colored rhinestones on narrow cuff style band................................**$15.00**
Bracelet, unsigned, spring steel wrap stype in summer white w/rhinestone rondels........................**$25.00**
Bracelet, unsigned, wide hinged cuff style w/multi-shaped lavender rhinestones................................**$75.00**
Bracelet, unsigned, wraparound snake w/overlapping scales, silver w/blue marquise rhinestone eyes................**$45.00**
Bracelet, unsigned, 2 strands of pearls, pearl & rhinestone clasp..**$25.00**
Bracelet, unsigned, 3 rows of lg baguette white 'diamonds' enclosed by outside rows of sm chaton rhinestones ..**$65.00**
Bracelet, unsigned, 3 strands of clear round rhinestones..**$55.00**
Bracelet, unsigned, 5 lg clusters of red & iridescent rhinestones of various sizes........................**$80.00**
Bracelet, unsigned, 5 pinwheel arrangements of red navette & fuchsia rhinestones **$52.00**
Bracelet, unsigned, 6 lg topaz stones in various heavy settings dangle from chain, gold-plated **$55.00**
Bracelet, unsigned, 6 rectangular sections, ea w/silver framework & lg faux onyx................................**$48.00**
Bracelet, unsigned, 6 rows of clear round rhinestones .**$78.00**
Bracelet, unsigned, 6 sq of intricate metalwork w/flat-backed gold-flecked red glass stones................................**$45.00**
Bracelet & earrings, Joseff of Hollywood, 4 golden flowers in bracelet, single-flower earrings..........................**$235.00**
Bracelet & earrings, Schiaparelli, gold-tone w/fall-colored rhinestones in lg & sm sizes w/slender leaves...**$145.00**
Bracelet & earrings, unsigned, clusters of rhinestone-centered blue plastic flowers, 7 in single row as bracelet ..**$30.00**
Bracelet & earrings, Weiss, pink rhinestones, single row set w/round & emerald cuts, earrings: 4 lg emerald cuts.................**$110.00**
Brooch, Adele Simpson, sterling turtle w/various shapes of dark & light green rhinestones, 2½" **$155.00**
Brooch, Alice Caviness, lg faceted amber-colored center stone framed w/marquise aurora borealis rhinestones, 2".**$350.00**
Brooch, Barclay, gold-plated anchor set w/gold rhinestones **$65.00**
Brooch, Cadoro, sea creature set w/blue, green & ruby cabochons **$450.00**
Brooch, Castlecliff, sterling crown, openwork w/3 pearls atop, red rhinesones w/diamente accents, 1¾x2" **$170.00**
Brooch, Ciner, pony, red w/rhinestone mane, tail & saddle **$65.00**
Brooch, Coco Chanel, cluster of 3 white flowers w/blue veins & rhinestone centers, hand enameled **$450.00**

Brooch, De Mario, four-strand bow, four pearl drops, $225.00. (Photo courtesy Marcia Brown/photographer Ken Brown)

Brooch, Eisenberg, bow form w/lg pink & lavender rhinestones, edge w/sm white rhinestones **$550.00**

Brooch, Eisenberg, silver-plated Art Nouveau flower form w/lg & sm clear pavé rhinestones......................**$250.00**

Brooch, Eisenberg, 7 huge rhinestones form flower head, sm rhinestones in ribbon, sterling, lg.......................**$450.00**

Brooch, Florenza, gold-plated bird's nest on branch w/3 pear eggs, bl enamel bird.................................**$75.00**

Brooch, Hattie Carnegie, fish, navy blue & rose w/blue cabochons & clear rhinestones....................................**$130.00**

Brooch, Hobé, circle style set w/lg blue aurora borealis stones...**$60.00**

Brooch, Hobé, gold-plated alligator w/red rhinestones...**$50.00**

Brooch, Hollycraft, faux turquoise oval framed w/blue rhinestones...**$70.00**

Brooch, Hollycraft, Nouveau-style mount w/sm enameled flowerheads, 2 lg & many sm green rhinestones.**$110.00**

Brooch, Kenneth Jay Lane, dragonfly w/enamel wings, pink & clear rhinestones in body.........................**$85.00**

Brooch, Kenneth Jay Lane, elephant w/emerald & clear rhinestones, gold-plated w/faux ivory tusks.......**$135.00**

Brooch, Kramer, enameled bee w/green rhinestone eyes..**$95.00**

Brooch, Kramer, lg diamente rhinestones w/sm rhinestone accents in the form of a grape cluster.................**$125.00**

Brooch, Marcel Boucher, exotic bird, gold-plated w/green & blue rhinestones in wings & eye, pavé breast & head feathers **$350.00**

Brooch, Mazer Brothers, enamel peacock w/blue, green & clear rhinestones..**$200.00**

Brooch, Mimi di N, flower form w/lg crystal petals & rhinestone center..**$195.00**

Brooch, Miriam Haskell, open oval set w/pearls & diamente rhinestones, chain bow w/pearl tassels **$325.00**

Brooch, Regency, butterfly set w/lime green rhinestones..**$105.00**

Brooch, Regency, 4-row circlet set w/marquise aurora borealis rhinestones **$135.00**

Brooch, Robert De Mario, gold-tone flower cluster w/frosted pink tube beads & lg pink rhinestones **$230.00**

Brooch, Robert Originals, butterfly, yellow & brown enamel **$50.00**

Brooch, Star Novelty, Remember Pearl Harbor, enamel on gilt w/eagle & lg pearl, clear & colored rhinestone accents **$350.00**

Brooch, Tortolani, swan w/lg faux jade cabochon as body, sm rhinestone accents **$140.00**

Brooches, Trifari: enamel sea horse on pavè coral with faux pearl accents, $295.00; fish, silver plated with faux amethyst belly, $95.00; green enamel coy fish, pavè body, $110.00; red enamel lobster, $78.00. (Photo courtesy Marcia Brown/photographer Ken Brown)

Brooch, Trifari, enameled blue aster w/pink bud & green leaves, clear rhinestone centers...........................**$195.00**

Brooch, Trifari, gold-plated basket filled w/pearl flowers..**$40.00**

Brooch, Trifari, gold-plated lion w/mane of diamente rhinestones...**$180.00**

Brooch, Trifari, gold-plated Zodiac sign: Taurus w/in open ring...**$35.00**

Brooch, Trifari, gold-tone bird w/Lucite belly & blue rhinestones, made for QVC...**$70.00**

Brooch, Trifari, jelly belly spider w/sm rhinestone accents, Lucite belly, sterling silver **$575.00**

Brooch, Trifari, red enamel flower w/gold outlines & white chalk beads in center **$55.00**

Brooch, Trifari, white enamel owl w/green cabochon eyes & rhinestone accents **$130.00**

Brooch, unsigned, airplane w/movable prop, clear rhinestones w/red cockpit & tail flaps, blue enamel wing flaps, sm **$56.00**

Brooch, unsigned, American flag, red, white & blue rhinestones, med **$78.00**

Brooch, unsigned, bunny, gold-tone w/pink rhinestone eyes & pearl tail, sm...**$22.00**

Brooch, unsigned, butterfly, gold-plated outline frame filled w/pink monochromatic rhinestones, lg **$75.00**

Brooch, unsigned, butterfly, lg multicolored teardrop stones, 3 in ea wing, dog-toothed prong setting...........**$130.00**

Brooch, unsigned, calla lilies, hammered texture w/rhinestone stamen, golden stems.....................**$78.00**

Brooch, unsigned, cat, white enamel w/silver X as whiskers, sm.....................**$14.00**

Brooch, unsigned, cat face, allover blue rhinestones .**$36.00**

Brooch, unsigned, daffodil on stem w/2 leaves, 'white diamond' look from late 1930s.....................**$48.00**

Brooch, unsigned, eagle, silver w/red, white & blue rhinestones, 1940s, lg.....................**$68.00**

Brooch, unsigned, enamel carnation w/dimensional petals, pavé diamente stem & leaves.....................**$52.00**

Brooch, unsigned, enameled beetle w/rhinestone eyes ..**$22.00**

Brooch, unsigned, feather style w/white diamond & black chaton rhinestones.....................**$78.00**

Brooch, unsigned, French ivory elephant w/4 rhinestones along spine, 1930s, lg.....................**$250.00**

Brooch, unsigned, frog, Lucite body studded w/clear chatons, enamel feet, cabochon eyes **$42.00**

Brooch, unsigned, giant snowflake of various-size chaton rhinestones **$55.00**

Brooch, unsigned, gold-plated retro style, 6 lg wide baguettes, inner sides of petal-like framework w/pavé diamonds, lg.....................**$105.00**

Brooch, unsigned, golden cornucopia w/6 topaz flowers, lg.....................**$195.00**

Brooch, unsigned, goldfish w/pavé face & black eye, lg ..**$48.00**

Brooch, unsigned, green plastic frog w/silver-tone arms & legs accented by imitation diamonds.....................**$320.00**

Brooch, unsigned, hummingbird, gold-tone w/pink glass cabochon body, pavé rhinestones trim wings......**$32.00**

Brooch, unsigned, Lucite free-form w/4 curving sections, clear rhinestones in opposing 2 ....**$65.00**

Brooch, unsigned, pot-metal grasshopper, enameled, rhinestone accents, 1930s, lg.....................**$135.00**

Brooch, unsigned, prowling gold-tone jungle cat w/green rhinestone eyes & articulated tail **$75.00**

Brooch, unsigned, question mark done in smoky & fuchsia stones, clear teardrop end.....................**$30.00**

Brooch, unsigned, turtle, hand faceted, dentelle, topaz glass 'shell' w/many imitation diamond accents in body.....................**$110.00**

Brooch, unsigned, yellow hydrangea blossom w/clear rhinestone chatons, enameled leaf is swedged to flower .**$52.00**

Brooch, unsigned, 5-petal flower, gold-plated framework w/emerald green chatons.....................**$48.00**

Brooch, unsigned (Austrian), cluster of 3 flocked blossoms, pink w/dark pink enamel pearl-set centers, enameled leaves.....................**$55.00**

Brooch, unsigned (Austrian), lg pink marble cabochon w/rhinestone accents having 3 similar pendant teardrops below.....................**$78.00**

Brooch, Weiss, gold-tone Democratic elephant set w/clear rhinestones, red eye **$75.00**

Brooch, Weiss, pink enamel rose filled w/pink rhinestones.....................**$80.00**

Brooch, Weiss, round w/many lg & sm aurora borealis rhinestones.....................**$110.00**

Brooch & bracelet, unsigned, emerald-cut black rhinestones w/clear accents & mobile frosted glass beads......**$78.00**

Brooch & earrings, Hattie Carnegie, blue plastic filament domes circled w/gold-plated frames...................**$150.00**

Brooch & earrings, Hollycraft, round w/pastel rhinestones in various colors & shapes.....................**$145.00**

Brooch & earrings, Kramer, comma shapes w/opalene cabochons & aurora borealis rhinestones...................**$150.00**

Brooch & earrings, Regency, japanned flower forms w/teal & dark blue rhinestones.....................**$190.00**

Brooch & earrings, Schiaparelli, leaf shapes w/opalene navettes, black & aurora borealis rhinestones....**$125.00**

Brooch & earrings, Schreiner, pink & white cabochons & pink rhinestones, round domed style **$195.00**

Brooch & earrings, Trifari, floral mounts w/4-color pastel rhinestones **$95.00**

Brooch & earrings, unsigned, aurora borealis chatons in 3 layers swedged to gold-plated flower petals........**$45.00**

Brooch & earrings, unsigned, blue & light green navettes form flower & leaf in brooch, 3-stone earrings....**$75.00**

Brooch & earrings, unsigned, crystal beads in circle arrangements, ea topped w/clear rhinestone...................**$65.00**

Brooch & earrings, unsigned, dark blue navettes encircle domed center w/lg & sm blue & green navettes, lg...........**$135.00**

Brooch & earrings, unsigned, iridescent sm blue rhinestones form lover's knot, 3-row earrings, lg chaton accents **$62.00**

Brooch & earrings, unsigned, lg faux baroque pearl cabochons (2 in brooch) w/white diamond rosettes & navettes.....................**$55.00**

Brooch & earrings, unsigned, lilac clusters in white enamel w/green enamel leaves accented w/rhinestones..**$55.00**

Brooch & earrings, unsigned, rows of brown & aurora borealis rhinestones on open-center sq brooch, disk earrings.....................**$72.00**

Brooch & earrings, unsigned, spray arrangement of faux pearls w/rhinestone accents.....................**$55.00**

Brooch & earrings, unsigned, sterling silver flower & leaf mounts set w/lg pastel crystals.....................**$395.00**

Brooch & earrings, unsigned, various shapes & sizes of rhinestones, layered center stones, lg **$95.00**

Brooch & earrings, unsigned, white enamel flower (bud earrings) set w/pastel rhinestones **$62.00**

Brooch & earrings, Weiss, gold-tone 4-leaf clovers set w/gold rhinestones **$70.00**

Brooch & earrings, Weiss, round w/red glass marquise navettes bridged w/arcs of sm clear rhinestones .**$300.00**

Brooch & earrings, Weiss, strawberries w/red & green rhinestones, 2 in brooch, single-berry earrings...........**$145.00**

Brooches, unsigned, ballet dancers, gold-tone w/turquoise enamel costumes, pr.....................**$85.00**

Brooches, unsigned, cutlass & turban joined by 2 chains, rhinestone accents, turban w/2 lg blue rhinestones........**$85.00**

Brooches, unsigned, Maltese crosses set w/clear, blue & citrine rhinestones, set of 2.....................**$85.00**

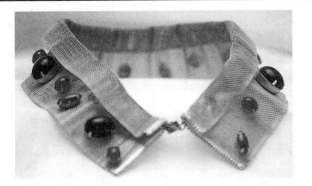

Collar, Hobè, mesh with gold zipper closure, studded with multicolored cabochons, $190.00.
(Photo courtesy Marcia Brown/photographer Ken Brown)

Earrings, Eisenberg, amber & topaz rhinestones w/diamente leaves $140.00

Earrings, Hollycraft, fan shapes w/lg, sm & baguette pink rhinestones $35.00

Earrings, Hollycraft, pink rhinestone studs w/arched drop supporting 3 componets: pink rhinestone egg & 2 faux pearls $75.00

Earrings, Kenneth Jay Lane, faux jade/opal shoulder dusters w/pink & diamente rhinestones ea side, diamente/opal studs $275.00

Earrings, Kramer, Tic-tac-toe style mounts w/diamente rhinestones $55.00

Earrings, Marcel Boucher, X form, 1 side w/diamente pavé chatons, 2nd w/baguettes $75.00

Earrings, Robert Originals, faux pearls w/pink & blue rhinestones, 2 drops hang from lg cluster...................$90.00

Earrings, unsigned, black beads around black imitation jet rhinestones $28.00

Earrings, unsigned, plastic flowers & feathers w/rhinestone accents $20.00

Earrings, unsigned, red plastic fringed leaves & many petaled flowers w/rhinestone centers, 1940s, lg...............$45.00

Earrings, unsigned (Austrian), yellow plastic rigid flower shapes w/7-rhinestone centers $35.00

Fur clip, Netti Rosenstein, red enamel apple w/green leaves having ribs of pink vermeil $165.00

Fur clip, Star Novelty, silver-plated w/emerald-, round- & marquise-cut rhinestones $180.00

Fur clip & earrings, Mazer Brothers, gold-plated feather-like clip mount w/lg aquamarine crystals & sm rhinestones $280.00

Necklace, Alice Caviness, molded imitation Oriental jade pendant w/3 suspended Chinese symbols, gold-plated chain $110.00

Necklace, Alice Caviness, 6-strand gold-plated rope w/center ball of rhinestones, pearls & colored beads, tassel drop $125.00

Necklace, bracelet & earrings, Hobé, multicolored plastic fruit on rope of lg yellow, pink & white round beads $225.00

Necklace, bracelet & earrings, Kramer, gold-tone flattened coil style w/lg diamente rhinestones set in curves.......$210.00

Necklace, bracelet & earrings, Kramer, single rows of clear & pink rhinestones $225.00

Necklace, bracelet & earrings, Trifari, pink plastic row of 'V' shapes $160.00

Necklace, bracelet & earrings, Trifari, silver-plated leaf style $190.00

Necklace, Castlecliff, silver-plated chain & drop w/2 bows, Chinese character & triangle, 14"...........................$90.00

Necklace, Christian Dior, gold-plated flat chain w/diamente rhinestones in frame around dark blue crystal...$295.00

Necklace, Eisenberg, Picasso enameled owl drop on gold-tone chain, white w/gold trim............................$125.00

Necklace, Eisenberg, pink rhinestones form chain, 8 perpendicular pink chatons w/center drop...................$225.00

Necklace, Florenza, silver-plated chain w/Maltese cross drop, amethyst crystals $175.00

Necklace, Hattie Carnegie, 10 strands of tiny to med size crystal beads...$110.00

Necklace, Hobé, Egyptian style, chain w/open & closed links supports bib of interlocking golden rings, lg $275.00

Necklace, Hobé, 2 strands of blue crystals................$125.00

Necklace, Kenneth J Lane, 3 graduated strands of pearls, KJL on clasp $110.00

Necklace, Kramer, double rhinestone chain (baguettes & round cuts) w/lg round drop having 5 vertical rhinestone chains $310.00

Necklace, Marcel Boucher, 5-strand necklace, light green pearls & clear beads, gold-tone feathers at clasp.$80.00

Necklace, Miriam Haskell, 6 strands of sm turquoise triangle beads, turquoise dome clasp w/rhinestone circumference $195.00

Necklace, Robert Originals, 5 strands of lg & sm pink, lavender & purple beads, lg amethyst crystal in clasp.........$325.00

Necklace, Trifari, white beads w/3 bead-set white glass-petaled flowers...$40.00

Necklace, unsigned, bib style w/malachite teardrops surrounded w/clear chatons & navette rhinestones, green earrings.$195.00

Necklace, unsigned, central fan formed of 5 lg citrine baguettes on chain w/2 lg brown chatons & 2 citrine baguettes $25.00

Necklace, unsigned, collar style w/6 scallops ea set w/lg sq-cut frosted & clear green stones framed w/2 chaton rows.$85.00

Necklace, unmarked, double-strand pearls with pavè rhinestone clasp, $48.00. (Photo courtesy Marcia Brown)

Necklace, unsigned, faceted red heart cuts linked w/prong-set pearls in row arrangement **$52.00**

Necklace, unsigned, frosted plastic navettes form flowers on gold-tone w/rhinestone accents............................**$32.00**

Necklace, unsigned, gold-tone chain w/Peking glass urn drop filled w/light green rosettes **$68.00**

Necklace, unsigned, lg lacy butterfly w/3 blue rhinestones, articulated lower wings & applied lower body, on chain **$30.00**

Necklace, unsigned, moonstones alternate w/pavé-set leaves in row arrangement, 1960s....................................**$38.00**

Necklace, unsigned, row of iridescent gold chatons w/5 lg shaded green 'headlights' centering front.............**$45.00**

Necklace, unsigned, silver pot-metal chain of lg links pavé set w/sm rhinestones, lg bell shape at end of dangle..**$105.00**

Necklace, unsigned, single row of chaton rhinestones w/3 spaced lg pear-shaped stones (largest in center).**$90.00**

Necklace, unsigned, single row of rhinestones w/V-shaped sections in center & on ea side **$28.00**

Necklace, unsigned, swan, lg & sm navettes & round rhinestones w/black enamel eyes, beak & feet, lg.......**$80.00**

Necklace, unsigned, 1 row of sq & round green faceted stones..**$45.00**

Necklace, unsigned, 1 strand of faceted pink & fuchsia glass beads w/cranberry rhinestones...............................**$38.00**

Necklace, Weiss, bib style, crisscrossing lines of rhinestones form sqs centered w/lg teardrop diamentes.........**$275.00**

Necklace & bracelet, unsigned, rolled mesh w/spirals of rhinestones, gold-ball terminals **$69.00**

Necklace & bracelet, unsigned, silver blue beads (5 V shapes in necklace) w/dangling blue chatons, wide bracelet....**$98.00**

Necklace & bracelet, unsigned, white lacy fan shapes w/sm rhinestone florettes & scattered pearls in row arrangement **$35.00**

Necklace & earrings, Kramer, lg baguette & round diamente rhinestones, sides w/marquise cut at ea end cross in front **$155.00**

Necklace & earrings, Kramer, silver-plated vine style w/13 stations of 3 white chalk beads ea, 6 beads per earring........**$165.00**

Necklace & earrings, Miriam Haskell, shaded white & blue glass beads in various sizes & shapes.................**$175.00**

Necklace & earrings, Tortalani, gold-tone chain w/drop featuring leaves & 3 faux pearl berries....................**$110.00**

Necklace & earrings, Trifari, 3 strands of faux pearls, leaf-style earrings **$140.00**

Necklace & earrings, unsigned, blue flowers of chaton rhinestones w/navette leaves, 1 ea side of lg central design...**$85.00**

Necklace & earrings, unsigned, peridot rhinestones arch over faux citrines, flowerette in center **$95.00**

Necklace & earrings, unsigned, pink sherbet cabochons in 4 sizes w/pink rhinestones, 3-row rhinestone V in center..**$75.00**

Necklace & earrings, unsigned, pointed collar style set w/lg emerald-cut & chaton rhinestones, bell-shaped drop earrings **$68.00**

Necklace & earrings, unsigned, row of blue & green chatons support 2nd draped row, lg navettes in & between drapes **$105.00**

Necklace & earrings, unsigned, silver mesh 'dog collar' style set w/row of blue chatons **$40.00**

Necklace & earrings, unsigned, white marquise cabochons alternate w/pr of clear chaton rhinestones..........**$40.00**

Necklace & earrings, unsigned, 2 rows of rhinestones w/5 stations centered w/lg round 'emeralds,' lg pear 'emerald' drop **$125.00**

Necklace & earrings, unsigned, 2 strands of beads (inner 1 is shorter) w/cluster of enamel flower & beads on gold rings **$80.00**

Necklace & earrings, unsigned, 2 strands of cranberry glass cabochons w/sm gray chatons as spacers **$78.00**

Necklace & earrings, unsigned, 2 strands of green & blue chatons w/lg center oval support 3 drops each w/lg oval stone **$80.00**

Necklace & earrings, unsigned, 3 strands of yellow beads w/rhinestone accents support cluster of enameled/beaded roses **$86.00**

Necklace & earrings, unsigned, 3-strand, 2 are topaz & clear chatons, inner row: lg green chatons linked w/sm clear stones **$175.00**

Necklace & earrings, wide collar style of round & tubular pink beads forming interlacing loops, simple drop earrings **$425.00**

Necklace & 2 pr earrings, gold-plated w/faceted watermelon glass stones accented by aurora borealis rhinestones **$150.00**

Ring, cocktail; Eisenberg, lg pear form w/pavé diamente rhinestones **$140.00**

Scatter pins, unsigned, rhinestones, 3 loops aside sm flower form, sm, set of 2 ....**$48.00**

Set, Eisenberg, aquamarine plastic w/inset rhinestone ribbons, oval drop on gold chain, brooch, earrings, 1960s **$250.00**

Set, Weiss, silver filigree leaves w/blue & green crystals & aurora borealis, bracelet, brooch & earrings **$195.00**

Johnson Bros.

There is a definite renewal of interest in dinnerware collecting right now, and just about any antique shop or mall you visit will offer a few nice examples of the wares made by this Staffordshire company. They've been in business since well before the turn of the century and have targeted the American market to such an extent that during the 1960s and 1970s, as much as 70% of their dinnerware was sold to distributors in this country. They made many scenic patterns as well as florals, and with the interest today's collectors have been demonstrating in Chintz, dealers tell me that Johnson Brothers' Rose Chintz and Chintz (Victorian) sell very well for them, especially the latter. In addition to their polychrome designs, they made several patterns in both blue and pink transferware.

Though some of their lines, Old Britain Castles, Friendly Village, and Rose Chintz, for instance, are still being produced, most are no longer as extensive as they once were, so the secondary market is being tapped to replace broken items that are not available anywhere else.

Our prices pertain to older pieces only, usually recognizable by the crown in the backstamp. Newer pieces from the 1990s to the present do not carry this crown and are available in any number of retail and outlet stores today. The prices are quite different. While a complete place setting of Old Britain Castles is normally priced at about $50.00, in some outlets you may be able to purchase it for half of that.

In her book *Johnson Brothers Dinnerware Pattern Directory and Price Guide* author Mary Finegan breaks pricing down into three groups: Base Price, One Star, and Two Star. About 90% of Johnson Brothers patterns have proven to be popular sellers and have been made in an extensive range of pieces (with the possible exception of buffet plates and 20" turkey platters, which were produced in holiday patterns only). Some of the patterns you are most likely to encounter and are thus included in the Base Price group are Bird of Paradise, Mount Vernon, Castle on the Lake, Old Bradbury, Day in June, Nordic, Devon Sprays, Old Mill (The), Empire Grape, Pastorale, Haddon Hall, Pomona, Harvest Time, Road Home (The), Indian Tree, Vintage (older version), Melody, and Windsor Fruit. (Also included in this value range are any other patterns not listed below.)

One Star patterns include Autumn's Delight, Coaching Scenes, Devonshire, Fish, Friendly Village, Gamebirds, Garden Bouquet, Hearts and Flowers, Heritage Hall, Indies, Millstream, Olde English Countryside, Rose Bouquet, Sheraton, Tulip Time, and Winchester. Two Star patterns include Barnyard King, Century of Progress, Chintz – Victorian, Dorchester, English Chippendale, Harvest Fruit, His Majesty, Historic America, Merry Christmas, Old Britain Castles, Persian Tulip, Rose Chintz, Strawberry Fair, Tally Ho, Twelve Days of Christmas, and Wild Turkeys.

Prices that follow are base values and apply only to the patterns in the base price group. One and Two Star patterns are in high demand and hard to find, and so fall in the higher ranges of values. They will command a premium of 20% to as much as 50% over the base values. Not all pieces are available in all patterns. In addition to their company logo, much of the dinnerware is also stamped with the pattern name. Today Johnson Brothers is part of the Wedgwood group.

Advisor: Mary J. Finegan (See Directory, Dinnerware)

Bowl, fruit/berry	$8.00
Bowl, soup/cereal	$10.00
Bowl, vegetable; oval	$30.00
Bowl, vegetable; w/lid, minimum value	$90.00
Butter dish, w/lid	$50.00
Coaster	$8.00
Coffee mug	$20.00
Creamer	$30.00
Egg cup	$15.00
Plate, dinner; minimum value	$14.00
Plate, salad; sq or round, minimum value	$12.00

Platter, lg, over 14"	$45.00
Platter, sm, up to 12"	$35.00
Salt & pepper shakers, pr	$40.00
Sauce boat/gravy boat	$40.00
Sugar bowl, open	$30.00
Sugar bowl, w/lid	$40.00
Teacup & saucer	$15.00
Teapot or coffeepot, minimum value	$90.00
Tureen, minimum value	$200.00

Blue Willow (One Star pattern), pitcher/ jug, 6", $45.00. (Photo courtesy Mary Frank Gaston)

Coaching Scenes (One Star pattern), plate, dinner; 10", $18.00.

Millstream (One Star pattern), coffeepot, minimum value, $100.00 (If pink or blue: $125.00).

Josef Originals

Figurines of lovely ladies, charming girls, and whimsical animals marked Josef Originals were designed by Muriel Joseph George of Arcadia, California, from 1945 to 1985. Until 1960 they were produced in California, but production costs were high, and copies of her work were being made in Japan. To remain competitive, she and her partner, George Good, found a company in Japan to build a factory and produce her designs to her satisfaction. Muriel retired in 1982; however, Mr. Good continued production of her work and made some design changes on some of the figurines. The company was sold in late 1985. The name is currently owned by Dakin/Applause, and a limited number of figurines with the Josef Originals name are being made. Those made during the ownership of Muriel are the most collectible. They can be recognized by these characteristics: the girls have a high-gloss finish, black eyes, and most are signed on the bottom. As of the 1970s a bisque finish was making its way into the lineup, and by 1980 glossy girls were fairly scarce in the product line. Brown-eyed figures date from 1982 through 1985; Applause uses a red-brown eye, although they are starting to release copies of early pieces that are signed Josef Originals by Applause or by Dakin. The animals were nearly always made with a matt finish and bore paper labels only. In the mid-1970s they introduced a line of animals with fuzzy flocked coats and glass eyes. Our advisors, Jim and Kaye Whitaker, have three books which we recommend for further study: *Josef Originals, Charming Figurines (Revised Edition); Josef Originals, A Second Look;* and *Josef Originals, Figurines of Muriel Joseph George.* These are all currently available, and each has no repeats of items shown in the other books.

Please note: All figurines have black eyes unless specified otherwise. As with so many collectibles, values have been impacted to a measurable extent since the advent of the Internet.

See also Birthday Angels.

Advisors: Jim and Kaye Whitaker (See Directory, Josef Originals; no appraisal requests please)

A Warm Hello, Thinking of You series, girl on phone, Japan, 5" $50.00
Birthstone Dolls, January to December, Japan, 3½", ea..$25.00
Buggy Bugs series, various poses, wire antenna, Japan, 3¼", ea $15.00
Bunny Hutch series, Japan, 4", ea.................$15.00
Christmas music box, angel, Japan, 7".................$65.00
Doll of the Month (tilt head), California, 3¼" $45.00
Elephant, sitting, Japan, 3¾"..................$20.00
Elephant w/tusks, Japan, 6¾"......................$50.00
First Love series, Tony, Tina, Japan, 5", ea.................$45.00
Gray cat wall plaque, California $45.00
Happy Anniversary music box, Japan, 7¼" $70.00
Happy Home w/dove greeting angel, Japan, 3¾"......$45.00
Hawaii, Small World series, brown eyes, Japan, 4½" .$35.00
Hunter, beautiful standing horse, Japan, 6" $25.00
It's a Wonderful World series, Japan, 3½", ea $35.00

Italian Aristrocrats, lady & escort, Japan, 7", ea $75.00
Jeanne, Colonial Days series (6 in all), Japan, 9"......$110.00
Joseph's Children Johnny, w/marbles, California, 4¾" .$110.00
Kennel Klub series, Yorkshire, etc, Japan, 3", ea........$18.00
Little International series, China, Poland, etc, Japan, 4", ea..$45.00
Love Letter from Love Story - Romance series, Japan, 8"..$115.00
Make Believe series, Japan, 4½", ea $35.00
Mama Ballerina, California, 7" $75.00
Mary Ann & Mamma (various styles), California, 4" & 7", pr $125.00
Mermaid lipstick holder, white w/beige trim, Japan, 4"..$75.00
Mice, various styles & Christmas, 2¾", ea $10.00
Monkeys, Mama & Papa, Japan, 3" $15.00
Music box, Three Coins in Fountain, girl by fountain, Japan, 6" $65.00
Nanette, several colors, half doll w/jewels, California, 5½" $65.00
New Hat from First Time, Japan, 4½"..........................$40.00
Nursery Rhymes series, Miss Mary, Japan, 4" $35.00
Pixie, Christmas Helper, painting toy, Japan, 4¾" $35.00
Pixies, various poses, green trimmed in red & gold, Japan, from 2" to 3¼", ea $30.00
Poodle, from Poodle & Siamese, Japan, 4¼" $30.00
Rose, Flower Girl series, girl w/flower hat, Japan, 4¼" ..$40.00
Rose Garden series (6 different), brown eyes, Japan, 5¼", ea $65.00
Ruby, Little Jewels series, girl w/ruby in crown, Japan, 3½" $35.00
Secret Pal, various colors, girl w/fan, California, 3½".$40.00
Skunk, w/white hair tuft on head, Japan, 2½"............$18.00
Sports Angels series, angels playing various sports, Japan, 2¾", ea....................$35.00
Tabby cat, orange, on base: I Love My Cat, Japan, 3½"..$15.00
Three Kings, Japan, from 8½" - 11", set of 3 ....$70.00
Watusi Lauau series, hunter in pot, natives, etc, Japan, 5", ea $55.00
Wee Ching, Wee Ling, Chinese chldren, boy w/dog, girl w/cat (widely copied), California, ea..................$65.00
Wee Folk, various poses, Japan, 4½", ea....................$20.00
World's Greatest series, bowler, boxer, hunter, Japan, 4½", ea $25.00

Christmas girl with cake, red and green, Japan, $23.00. (Photo courtesy Jim and Kaye Whitaker)

Kanawha

The Kanawha Glass Company of Dunbar, West Virginia, produced a wide variety of fine glassware items from the 1930s until its closure in 1986. Known for fine crackle glass; red, pastel green, and blue slags; and lovely cased-glass pieces, this company's glassware is finding its way into the showcases of today's collectors.

See also Crackle Glass.

Basket, amberina, dark red rim, amber handle, mold blown, 5¼" $55.00
Basket, amberina w/milk glass overlay, amber handle, 5½" $35.00

Bowl, Hobnail, blue slag, ca 1973, 6", from $35.00 to $40.00. (Photo courtesy Ruth and Frank Grizel)

Bowl, milk glass w/blue overlay, Hobnail, crimped ruffled rim, 3¾x7" $25.00
Bowl, yellow crackle, ruffled rim, mold blown, 3x5½" ..$30.00
Candy dish, green crackle, flared crimped rim, flat bottom, mold blown, 3x5½" $30.00
Creamer, amberina w/milk glass interior, amber handle, 4" $35.00
Pitcher, amberina, applied amber handle, slim, paper label, 5½" $12.00
Pitcher, amberina crackle, tall spout, 1950s-50s, lg.....$55.00
Pitcher, aqua crackle, flared spout, blue applied handle, 5" ...$32.00
Pitcher, green crackle, trumpet neck, green handle, mold blown, 5¼" $30.00
Pitcher, milk glass w/light green interior, embossed grapes & leaves, paper label, 3½" $25.00
Pitcher, royal blue crackle, flared rim, footed, 3"........$25.00
Salt & pepper shakers, pink opaque, Hobnail, 5x2¼", pr..$55.00
Sugar bowl, amber crackle, flared rim, mold blown, 3½x3½" $25.00
Vase, amberina crackle, ruffled rim, slim, blown mold, 8"..$70.00
Vase, aqua-blue crackle, paper sticker, 3½" $26.50
Vase, Diamond Quilted, peachblow, crimped ruffled rim, waisted, 7¼" $45.00
Vase, light green over milk glass, pleated ruffled rim, hand-painted flowers, paper label, 4¾" $25.00
Vase, milk glass w/blue satin overlay, hand-painted flowers, pleated ruffled rim, 5" $45.00

Vase, milk glass w/red overlay, Diamonds & Dots, pleated ruffled rim, w/paper label, 5½x6" $50.00
Vase, milk glass w/ruby satin overlay, hand-painted flowers & leaves, pleated ruffled rim, paper label, 5½" ...$45.00
Vase, ruby crackle, slim, flared rim, mold blown, paper label, 8" $45.00
Vase, swung, milk glass, pre-1988, 10½" $10.00

Kaye of Hollywood

This was one of the smaller pottery studios that operated in California during the 1940s — interesting in that people tend to confuse the name with Kay Finch. Kay (Schueftan) worked for Hedi Schoop before striking out on her own; because her work was so similar to that of her former employer's, a successful lawsuit was brought against her, and it was at this point that the mark was changed from Kaye of Hollywood to Kim Ward.

Figurine/planter, blond girl w/2 baskets, #103............$40.00
Figurine/planter, Dutch girl holding 2 pots, #320, 9" .$25.00
Figurine/planter, lady in dark green blouse, white dress w/green flowers, white shawl, 9" $35.00
Figurine/planter, lady w/blue hat, rose blouse & cream dress w/rose & blue flowers, 2 blue baskets under arms, 9" $50.00
Figurine/planter, man in lavender jacket, white shirt & cream pants w/blue & rose flowers, pot behind, #3247, 9½" $40.00
Figurine/planter, Mary Mary Quite Contrary, #3139, 9" .$50.00
Figurine/planter, Victorian lady w/basket, signed Kaye 213 on base, 11½" $35.00
Figurine/planter, pilgrim couple, #3118/#3119, 10½", 11¼", pr..$32.50
Figurine/planter/candle holder, brunette lady in blue, 3 candle holders at back above 2 flower-form pockets, 12", pr $135.00

Soap dish figure, 8", $50.00.
(Photo courtesy Jack Chipman)

Keeler, Brad

California pottery is becoming quite popular among collectors, and Brad Keeler is one of the better known designers. After studying art for a time, he opened his own studio in 1939 where he created naturalistic studies of birds and animals. Sold through giftware stores, the figures were decorated by airbrushing with hand-painted details. Brad Keeler is remembered for his popular flamingo figures and his Chinese Modern Housewares. Keeler died of a heart attack in 1952, and the pottery closed soon thereafter. For more information, we recommend *The Collector's Encyclopedia of California Pottery, 2nd Edition,* by Jack Chipman.

Bowl, green leaves form bowl w/lobster on ea side & claws over edge, #858, 4½x12" dia $250.00
Bowl, 3 shells w/red crab between, #290, 5½x8" dia..$130.00
Figurine, bird, blue w/peach under neck & chest, #17, 6x5" $45.00
Figurine, bird, browns, tans & white, #40, 7"..............$40.00
Figurine, bird, red, on perch, #720, 4⅜"......................$65.00
Figurine, cockatoo, on perch, 11x6½" W $55.00
Figurine, cockatoo, white w/red & orange features, #34 & #35, 8¼", pr..$95.00
Figurine, cocker spaniel puppy, #748, 4½" $60.00
Figurine, crested heron, wings up, #45, 12½"..........$185.00
Figurine, crested heron, wings up, 15" $250.00
Figurine, Little Miss Muffet, 4¼" $60.00
Figurine, Little Red Riding Hood, paper label & stamp, 5" $75.00
Figurine, Mary Mary Quite Contrary, foil label, #977, 5¼" $60.00
Figurine, pheasant hen, #21, 4x8" $40.00
Figurine, quail, 6" $50.00

Figurine, rooster, #74, $85.00.

Figurine, Siamese cat, seated, foil sticker, 5½"............$60.00
Figurine, Wee Willie Winkie, #980 ....$50.00
Figurines, kittens, black w/gray, #772 & #773, 7", 8", pr.$140.00
Plate, serving; green leaves w/red lobster in center, #868, 9x9½" $30.00

Salt & pepper shakers, fish on tail, #149, 4", pr........$125.00
Sauce dish, leaves w/lobster on lid, #870, w/spoon, 5½x4x4½", EX..$85.00
Serving dish, green leaves w/red lobster in center, 9x12½" $60.00
Utensil set, fork & spoon, wood w/lobster claw handles, 11". pr, from $75 to $125.00

Kentucky Derby Glasses

Since the the late 1930s, every running of the Kentucky Derby has been commemorated with a special glass tumbler. Each year at Churchill Downs on Derby day you can buy them filled with mint juleps. In the early days this was the only place where these glasses could be purchased. Many collections were started when folks carried the glasses home from the track and then continued to add one for each successive year as they attended the Derby.

The first glass appeared in 1938, but examples from then until 1945 are extremely scarce and are worth thousands — when they can be found. Because of this, many collectors begin with the 1945 glasses. There are three: the tall version, the short regular-size glass, and a jigger. Some years, for instance 1948, 1956, 1958, 1974, and 1986, have slightly different variations, so often there are more than one to collect. To date a glass, simply add one year to the last date on the winner's list found on the back.

Each year many companies put out commemorative Derby glasses. Collectors call them 'bar' glasses (as many bars sold their own versions filled with mint juleps). Because of this, collectors need to be educated as to what the official Kentucky Derby glass looks like.

These prices are for pristine, mint-condition glasses with no chips or flaws. All colors must be bright and show no signs of fading. Lettering must be perfect and intact, even the list of past winners on the back. If gold trim has been used, it must show no wear. If any of these problems exist, reduce our values by 50% to 75%, depending on the glass and the problem. Many more Kentucky Derby shot glasses, jiggers, cordials, boreals, and shooters in various colors and sizes were produced — too many to list here. But be aware that these may present themselves along the collecting trail.

Advisor: Betty L. Hornback (See Directory, Kentucky Derby and Horse Racing)

1940, aluminum $800.00
1940, French Lick, aluminum.....................................$800.00
1941-1944, plastic Beetleware, ea, from $2,500 to.$4,000.00
1945, jigger...$1,000.00
1945, regular $1,600.00
1945, tall $450.00
1946-47, clear frosted w/frosted bottom, L in circle, ea..$100.00
1948, clear bottom...$225.00
1948, frosted bottom $250.00
1949, He Has Seen Them all, green on frosted $225.00

1950	$450.00
1951	$650.00
1952	$225.00
1953	$175.00
1954	$200.00
1955	$150.00
1956, 1 star, 2 tails	$275.00
1956, 1 star, 3 tails	$400.00
1956, 2 stars, 2 tails	$200.00
1956, 2 stars, 3 tails	$250.00
1957, gold & black on frost	$125.00
1958, Gold Bar	$175.00
1958, Iron Liege	$225.00
1959-60, ea	$100.00
1961	$110.00
1962, Churchill Downs, red, gold & black	$80.00
1963	$70.00
1964	$55.00
1965	$75.00
1966-68, ea	$60.00
1969	$65.00
1970	$70.00
1971	$50.00
1972	$45.00
1973	$55.00
1974, Federal, regular or mistake, ea	$200.00
1974, mistake (Canonero in 1971 listing on back), Libbey	$18.00
1974, regular (Canonero II in 1971 listing on back)	$16.00
1975-76, ea	$16.00
1976, plastic	$16.00
1977	$14.00
1978-79, ea	$16.00
1980	$22.00
1981-82, ea	$14.00
1983-85, ea	$12.00
1986	$14.00
1986 ('85 copy)	$20.00
1987-89, ea	$12.00
1990-92, ea	$10.00
1993-95, ea	$9.00
1996-98, ea	$8.00
1999-2000, ea	$6.00
2001-2002, ea	$5.00
2003	$3.00

Bluegrass Stakes Glasses, Keeneland, Lexington KY

1996	$15.00
1997	$13.00
1998	$12.00
1999-2001, ea	$10.00
2002-2003	$8.00

Breeders Cup Glasses

1985, Aqueduct, not many produced	$300.00
1988, Churchill Downs	$40.00
1989, Gulfstream Park	$70.00
1990, Belmont Park	$45.00
1991, Churchill Downs	$15.00
1992, Gulfstream Park	$30.00
1993, Santa Anita	$35.00
1993, Santa Anita, 10th Running, gold	$40.00
1994, Churchill Downs	$10.00
1995, Belmont Park	$20.00
1996, Woodbine, Canada	$30.00
1997, Hollywood Park	$20.00
1998, Churchill Downs	$10.00
1999, Gulfstream Park	$10.00
2000, Churchill Downs	$9.00
2001, Belmont Park, or 2002, Santa Anita	$8.00
2003, Arlington Park	$7.00

Festival Glasses

1968	$95.00
1984	$20.00
1985-86, no glass made	$.09
1987-88, ea	$16.00
1989-90, ea	$14.00
1991-92, ea	$12.00
1993, very few produced	$75.00
1994-95, ea	$10.00
1996-98, ea	$8.00
1999-2003, ea	$7.00

Jim Beam Stakes Glasses

1980, 6"	$350.00
1981, 7"	$300.00
1982	$275.00
1983	$65.00

1984, $40.00. (Photo courtesy Betty Hornback/Photographer Dean Langdon)

1985-86, ea	**$25.00**
1987-88, ea	**$20.00**
1988-90, ea	**$16.00**
1991-95, ea	**$14.00**
1996-98, ea	**$12.00**
1999, sponsored by 'Gallery Furniture.com'	**$10.00**
2000-2003, Spiral Stakes	**$8.00**

Shot Glasses

1987, 1½-oz, red or black, ea	**$350.00**
1987, 3-oz, black	**$700.00**
1987, 3-oz, red	**$1,500.00**
1988, 1½-oz	**$40.00**
1988, 3-oz	**$60.00**
1989, 3-oz	**$45.00**
1989-91, 1½-oz, ea	**$35.00**
1991, 3-oz	**$40.00**
1992, 1½-oz	**$20.00**
1992, 3-oz	**$25.00**
1993, 1½-oz or 3-oz, ea	**$15.00**
1994, 1½-oz or 3-oz, ea	**$14.00**
1995, 1½-oz or 3-oz, ea	**$14.00**
1996, 1½-oz or 3-oz, ea	**$13.00**
1997, 1½-oz or 3-oz, ea	**$12.00**
1998, 1½-oz or 3-oz, ea	**$10.00**
1999, fluted whiskey, 1½-oz	**$10.00**
2000-2001, fluted whiskey, 1½-oz	**$8.00**
2002-2003, fluted whiskey, 1½-oz	**$6.00**

WAMZ Radio KY Derby Bar Glass, Sponsored by Jim Beam

1991	**$45.00**
1992	**$40.00**
1993	**$25.00**
1994	**$20.00**
1995-96	**$15.00**
1997-99, ea	**$12.00**
2000	**$10.00**
2001, discontinued	**$.09**

Kindell, Dorothy

Yet another California artist that worked during the prolific years of the '40s and '50s, Dorothy Kindell produced a variety of household items and giftware, but today she's best known for her sensual nudes. One of her most popular lines consisted of mugs, a pitcher, salt and pepper shakers, a wall pocket, bowls, a creamer and sugar set, and champagne glasses, featuring a lady in various stages of undress, modeled as handles or stems (on the champagnes). In the set of six mugs, she progresses from wearing her glamorous strapless evening gown to ultimately climbing nude, head-first into the last mug. These are relatively common but always marketable. Except for these and the salt and

pepper shakers, the other items from the nude line are scarce and rather pricey.

Collectors also vie for her island girls, generally semi-nude and very sensuous.

Ashtray, Beachcombers, 11", $60.00. (Photo courtesy Jack Chipman)

Champagne glass, nude stem	**$150.00**
Cigarette box, blue-green w/woman's face in relief, 2x4"	**$380.00**
Head vase, native girl, w/original necklace, 6"	**$105.00**
Mug, nude handles, 1 of the series of 6, common, 5¼"-6", ea, from $30 to	**$40.00**
Shelf sitter, nude w/red drape across lap, red wrap on head, left leg hanging down & right leg underneath, 11½"	**$375.00**
Tumblers, Reconnaisance, The Chase, Mechanized, Delaying Action, Reinforcements, Mission Completed, NM, set of 6	**$920.00**

King's Crown, Thumbprint

Back in the late 1800s, this pattern was called Thumbprint. It was first made by the U.S. Glass Company and Tiffin, one of several companies who were a part of the US conglomerate, through the 1940s. U.S. Glass closed in the late 1950s, but Tiffin reopened in 1963 and reissued it. Indiana Glass bought the molds, made some minor changes, and during the 1970s, they made this line as well. Confusing, to say the least! Gene Florence's *Collectible Glassware of the 40s, 50s, and 60s,* explains that originally the thumbprints were oval, but at some point Indiana changed theirs to circles. And Tiffin's tumblers were flared at the top, while Indiana's were straight. Our values are for the later issues of both companies, with the ruby flashing in excellent condition.

Ashtray, sq, 5¼"	**$35.00**
Bowl, center edge, 3x12½"	**$115.00**
Bowl, crimped, footed	**$110.00**
Bowl, crimped, 4½x11½"	**$125.00**

312

Bowl, mayonnaise; divided, 5" $70.00
Bowl, mayonnaise; 5" $50.00
Bowl, salad; 7⅜" $14.00
Bowl, salad; 9¼" $85.00
Bowl, straight edge.....................................$80.00
Bowl, wedding/candy; footed, 6" $75.00
Candle holder, sherbet type.............................$30.00
Candy box, flat, w/lid, 6" $65.00

**Compote, crimped, footed, 7½x12",
$95.00.** (Photo courtesy Gene Florence)

Compote, flat, sm.......................................$25.00
Compote, 7¼x9¾" $65.00
Cup $8.00
Mayonnaise, 3-pc set....................................$85.00
Plate, bread & butter; 5" $8.00
Plate, party server; 24" $325.00
Plate, snack; w/indent, 9¾" $15.00
Plate, torte; 14½" $100.00
Punch bowl, 2 styles, ea $750.00
Punch set, w/foot, 15-pc................................$1,125.00
Relish, 5-part, 14" $125.00
Stem, claret; 4-oz $14.00
Stem, sundae/sherbet; 5½-oz $9.00
Stem, wine; 2-oz $9.00
Sugar bowl $22.50
Tumbler, iced tea; 11-oz................................$18.00
Tumbler, juice; 4½-oz...................................$14.00
Vase, bud; 9" $125.00

Kitchen Collectibles

If you've never paid much attention to old kitchen appliances, now is the time to do just that. Check in Grandma's basement — or your mother's kitchen cabinets, for that matter. As styles in home decorating changed, so did the styles of appliances. Some have wonderful Art Deco lines, while others border on the primitive. Most of those you'll find still work, and with a thorough cleaning you'll be able to restore them to their original 'like-new' appearance. Missing parts may be impossible to replace, but if it's just a cord that's gone, you can usually find what you need at any hardware store.

Even larger appliances are collectible and are often used to add the finishing touch to a period kitchen. Please note that prices listed here are for appliances that are free of rust, pitting, or dents, and in excellent working condition.

During the nineteenth century, cast-iron apple peelers, cherry pitters, and food choppers were patented by the hundreds, and because they're practically indestructible, they're still around today. Unless parts are missing, they're still usable and most are very efficient at the task they were designed to perform.

A lot of good vintage kitchen glassware is still around and can generally be bought at reasonable prices. Pieces vary widely from custard cups and refrigerator dishes to canister sets and cookie jars. There are also several books available for further information and study. If this area of collecting interests you, you'll enjoy *300 Years of Kitchen Collectibles* by Linda Campbell, and *Kitchen Antiques, 1790 – 1940,* by Kathryn McNerney. Other books include: *Kitchen Glassware of the Depression Years* and *Anchor Hocking's Fire-King & More* by Gene Florence, and *Collector's Encyclopedia of Fry Glassware* by H.C. Fry Glass Society.

See also Aluminum; Anchor Hocking, Clothes Sprinkler Bottles; Glass Knives; Griswold; Kitchen Prayer Ladies; Porcelier; Reamers.

Advisor: Jim Barker, Appliances (See Directory, Appliances)

Appliances

Bean/crock pot, West Bend, brown high-bloss ceramic, chrome-plated steel base, glass lid, ca 1964, NMIB .**$15.00**
Beater/mixer, Weining Made-Rite Co, green Depression-glass bowl, 1930s, 4-cup capacity, NM..........................**$42.50**
Blender, Montgomery Ward, turquoise, 6-cup, 1966, 15½", EX...**$40.00**
Blender, Oster Automatic Pulp Ejector Juicer/Slicer/ Shredder Model 403, 2-speed beehive chrome base, 1960s, MIB..**$100.00**
Blender, Osterizer #448 Beehive, 2-speed, M w/1961 manual **$46.00**
Blender, Osterizer #462H, 2-speed, 5-cup glass jar, EX .**$40.00**
Blender, Vita-Mix Model 517, stainless steel mixing container, chrome dome base w/rubber feet, w/recipe book, NM..**$42.50**
Blender, Waring Model 11-183, chrome w/avocado base trim, glass container, 14-speed, 1000 watt motor, NM ..**$58.00**
Bottle warmer, Vanta, porcelain, pink exterior, EXIB .**$10.00**
Broiler/griddle/toaster, Coleman #5410, cast aluminum, 1960, MIB **$30.00**
Can opener, Can-o-Mat Deluxe AK-345 Rival, wall mount, 1950s, MIB...**$80.00**
Can opener, Sunbeam, pink, 1950s, EX.....................**$35.00**
Can opener/ice crusher, Sunbeam, olive green, 1971, 7", M **$22.00**
Coffee maker, Sunbeam C50 Coffee Master, chrome, lg, EX...**$35.00**

Coffee maker, Sunbeam Model C-50, stainless ball-shape top, 1950s, M w/original filters..................$65.00

Coffee urn, Farberware, chrome w/black handles, pedestal foot, 36-cup, M..................$45.00

Coffee urn, Keystone Chrome Trademark C6502, clear glass lid, w/matching creamer & sugar bowl, NM........$55.00

Crock pot, Montgomery Wards, enameled metal pan, 5 temperature settings, 1970s, NM..................$15.00

Egg cooker, Hankscraft, Fiesta Orange & aluminum, 5½" dia..................$25.00

Egg cooker, Made in Japan, white ceramic dome w/embossed chickens, 120-volt, 5½x5"..................$22.00

Egg cooker, Oster, Bakelite base, 1950s, EX..................$20.00

Egg cooker, Sunbeam, stainless steel & Bakelite, 6½x7" dia, EX..................$42.50

Expresso machine, FAEMA President, green neon tube, 1950s, NM..................$1,900.00

Food warmer, Chase Brass & Copper Co, holds 3 Pyrex canisters..................$35.00

Food warmer, Fire-King on blue-tinted glass lid, 3-pc set: hot plate, pan w/handle & glass lid, 10" H, NM........$15.00

Food warmer, The Quincy, silver-plated, Meriden, 7", EX..$35.00

Grill, Super Star #15 Combination Master Grill, chrome w/red Bakelite handles & feet, 3½x12x7½", NM..................$85.00

Grinder, coffee; Marelli, blue & white swirl (resembles graniteware), heavy, 10½x11", EX..................$45.00

Grinder, Oster Model 516, white enamel, wooden plunger, 1950s, 12", NMIB w/instructions..................$42.50

Heater, Westinghouse, 18", w/14" heater ring..................$35.00

Hot plate, Universal Multi-Therm, 1950s-60s, EX........$75.00

Iron, General Electric, travel, ca 1950, MIB, from $30 to..$50.00

Iron, Westinghouse, ca 1950, 7¾"..................$20.00

Juicer, Atlas Model 240, stainless top, 4.2 amps, EX...$45.00

Juicer, Sunkist Juicit, chrome & white enamel, 4 rubber feet, 1950s, EX..................$60.00

Juicer/extractor, Sunkist Commercial, stainless upper bowl & stainless extractor, enameled label on juicer, 16x8", EX......$85.00

Mixer, Dormeyer #3200, complete w/bowls & juicer, NM..................$60.00

Mixer, General Electric M37, pink, portable, ca 1950s, MIB..................$60.00

Mixer, General Electric 149M Ser. 8 150 watt, three beaters, speed adjustment, two light custard bowls, $125.00

Mixer, Hobart Kitchen Aid K5SS, white enamel, 6-speed, 16½x10¼", EX..................$115.00

Mixer, Kenwood Chef, 2 milk glass bowls, chrome top, 13¼", EX..................$95.00

Mixer, Manning-Bowman, 2 custard glass bowls, juicer, 2 beaters & milk shake stirrer, ca 1940, EX..................$165.00

Mixer, Mixer, Sunbeam Mixmaster Power Plus, Sunbeam Vista on side, 9" bowl, 14¾", NM..................$87.50

Mixer, Sunbeam, 2 jade-ite bowls/jade-ite juicer, w/silver polisher & knife sharpener attachments, EX..................$130.00

Mixer/juicer, Hobart Kitchen Aid Model 30, 10-speed, 1 paddle, 9" bowl, 17x14", EX..................$70.00

Percolator, Corning E-112, avocado w/clear glass, 12-cup, NM..................$45.00

Percolator, General Electric, chrome, fat, black Bakelite handle, 9", EX..................$35.00

Percolator, Samson Adjustable Automatic, c 1937, 12x5", NM..................$47.50

Percolator, Sunbeam Coffeemaster Model C30A, double style, stainless & black Bakelite, 2 settings, EX..................$65.00

Percolator, Universal Automatic w/Flavor Selector, 1950s, 8-cup, MIB..................$50.00

Percolator, Vacuum Coffee; Nicro Model 500, stainless steel, 10"..................$12.00

Popcorn popper, Hamilton Beach Butter-Up Corn Popper, Joe Namath signature & photo on box, MIB........$25.00

Popcorn popper, Kenmore Made-Right, aluminum w/glass lid, ca 1955, NMIB..................$25.00

Popcorn popper, Mirro, aluminum w/black handles, 1950s, EX..................$37.50

Popcorn popper, Popmaster Automatic, Pyrex lid, 10", EX..................$35.00

Popcorn popper, unmarked, aluminum w/glass lid, ca 1950-60s, EX..................$32.50

Popcorn popper, Westbend The Poppery, hot-air popper, 1970s, MIB..................$22.50

Rotisserie broiler, Broil King...No 976, International Appliance Corp, 17", MIB..................$40.00

Rotisserie broiler, Sunbeam Carousel CR, Bakelite base & handles, 16"..................$35.00

Skillet, Farberware, high dome lid, 1978, NM w/booklet.$45.00

Skillet, Revere Ware #8850, temperature control on cord, NM..................$50.00

Skillet, West Bend Miracle Maid, Gem coating, 1970s, NM..................$140.00

Toaster, Dormeyer Automatic Pop-Up, chrome, 2-slice, 1950s, EX..................$70.00

Toaster, General Electric Hotpoint 129T41, side opens, Bakelite handles, side dial, light on top, EX........$75.00

Toaster, Murphy-Richards, Art Deco chrome w/yellow enameling, NM..................$75.00

Toaster, Sunbeam T-35, Bakelite handles, 1950s, EX..$50.00

Toaster, Sunbeam T-9, Art Deco, chrome w/arched top, 2-slice, 8x10", EX..................$60.00

Toaster, Sunbeam T-9, Deco design w/arched top, chrome, 2-slice, NM..................$125.00

Toaster, Sunbeam T20B, Art Deco, chrome, 2-slice, EX...$80.00

Toaster, Toastwell Toaster Co, chrome w/black Bakelite handles, 2-slice, 1940s, NM......................**$115.00**

Toaster, Toastwells, Art Deco, chrome, 1940s, NM.....**$55.00**

Toaster, Torrid, Beardsley Mfg, double-sided, chrome, EX...**$50.00**

Waffle iron, FS Carbon Co, aluminum w/cast-iron base, 110-120 volts, 21x11", EX....................................**$60.00**

Waffle iron, Kenmore Model, chrome w/Bakelite, double unit, 3½x16"..**$55.00**

Waffle iron, Manning-Bowman, 2 rectangle griddles, white handles & feet, 1970s, EX.........................**$35.00**

Waffle iron, Nelson #511, chrome, 1950s, NM...........**$40.00**

Waffle iron, Seneca Co Brighton NY, chrome w/floral pottery insert in lid, MIB......................................**$60.00**

Waffle iron, Sunbeam W-2, chrome, 1950s, EX..........**$52.50**

Waffle/sandwich iron, Electrahot, chrome w/Bakelite handles, EX...**$45.00**

Glassware

Baker, Sapphire Blue, 1-pt, 4½x5", from $7 to.............**$8.00**

Bowl, green transparent, with lid, Jeannette, 9", $50.00. (Photo courtesy Gene Florence)

Bowl, mixing; Beaded Edge, fired-on color, 6", from $18 to..**$20.00**

Bowl, mixing; Beaded Edge, pink, 6", from $30 to....**$35.00**

Bowl, mixing; Crisscross, pink, 10⅛", from $55 to.....**$60.00**

Bowl, mixing; Currier & Ives, Anchorwhite w/decal, 1-qt, from $12.50 to...**$15.00**

Bowl, mixing; fired-on color, Splash Proof, 2-qt, 7⅝", from $14 to...**$16.00**

Bowl, mixing; Modern Tulip, decal on white, 3-qt, from $18 to..**$20.00**

Bowl, mixing; Ribbed, crystal, 5⅜", from $6 to............**$8.00**

Bowl, mixing; Ribbed, Vitrock or red stripe, 7½", from $20 to..**$25.00**

Bowl, mixing; Swirl, Anchorwhite, 7", from $6 to........**$7.50**

Bowl, mixing; Swirl, peach lustre, 8", from $10 to.....**$12.50**

Cake plate, cobalt, Fry, 3-footed, from $125 to........**$140.00**

Candle warmer, Double Red Dots, w/glass votive candle holders signed Fire-King, from $40 to.................**$45.00**

Canister, Dutch scenic decal on clear glass, sq w/tin screw-on lid, from $20 to...**$22.00**

Canister, pink opaque w/embossed ribs, 6½"+lid....**$265.00**

Canisters, Harvest Grape, milk glass, Indiana Glass, 1950s, set of 3 in stepped sizes, largest: 9¾"......................**$125.00**

Casserole, Blue Heaven Ovenware, Anchorwhite w/decal, 1-pt, from $10 to...**$12.00**

Casserole, Candleglow, Anchorwhite w/decal, white lid, 1-qt, from $8 to..**$9.00**

Casserole, fired-on color, w/lid, stick handle, McKee, individual, from $12 to..**$14.00**

Casserole, Sapphire Blue, knob finial, 1-qt, 7¼", from $16 to..**$18.00**

Coffeepot, clear w/silver rings, McKee, from $15 to..**$18.00**

Coffeepot, Pyrex Made in USA, stainless metal band, 4-cup, M...**$55.00**

Cruet, canary yellow, pyramidal, clear stopper, Imperial, from $50 to..**$55.00**

Cruet, Twist, Moongleam (green), Heisey, 4-oz, from $85 to..**$95.00**

Custard cup/baker, Sapphire Blue, 6-oz, from $5 to....**$6.00**

Egg cup, Chalaine Blue, from $25 to.........................**$28.00**

Egg plate, white w/pink trim, 9¾", from $100 to.....**$125.00**

Funnel, clear, 10-oz, 7"......................................**$12.00**

Funnel, clear, 11", from $20 to..............................**$25.00**

Funnel, pink, plain, 4½", from $35 to.......................**$40.00**

Grease jar, Kitchen Aids (red rolling pin, etc on white), from $150 to..**$175.00**

Grease jar, Modern Tulips (black), from $30 to..........**$35.00**

Ladle, amber, flat bottom, from $12 to.......................**$15.00**

Ladle, green, rounded bottom, from $18 to.................**$20.00**

Ladle, Midnight Blue, Cambridge, from $35 to...........**$40.00**

Loaf pan, Chanticleer or Country Kitchen, Anchorwhite w/decal, deep, 5x9", from $8 to.........................**$10.00**

Measuring cup, Cream Dove, crystal, 1-cup, from $30 to..**$38.00**

Measuring cup, Stickney & Poor, crystal, 1-cup, from $30 to..**$38.00**

Measuring cup set, Jennyware, crystal, from $150 to.**$170.00**

Measuring pitcher, green, Hocking, 2-cup, from $40 to..**$45.00**

Measuring pitcher, green w/white dots, Hazel-Atlas, 2-cup, from $45 to..**$50.00**

Measuring pitcher, yellow opaque, 2-cup, from $35 to..**$40.00**

Measuring pitcher/batter jug, custard, McKee, 4-cup, from $50 to..**$55.00**

Meat loaf pan, Fry Ovenglass, rectangular, w/lid, 9", from $85 to..**$95.00**

Mug, Blue Heaven Ovenware, Anchorwhite w/decal, 8-oz, from $8 to..**$10.00**

Refrigerator dish, Blue & Gold Leaf on white, white lid, 4x4", from $5 to..**$6.00**

Refrigerator dish, milk white, oval, 4¼x9", from $22 to..**$25.00**

Refrigerator stack set, Skating Dutch, red on white, 3-pc, from $65 to..**$75.00**

Relish tray, Honeysuckle on white opaque, 3-part, 9¾" dia, from $90 to..**$100.00**

Rolling pin, crystal, w/cork end, from $20 to............**$22.00**

Rolling pin, crystal, wooden screw-on handles (black), from $40 to..**$50.00**

Rolling pin, dark amber, blown, from $100 to.........**$120.00**

Rolling pin, peacock blue, handles are attached to metal rod inside pin, from $275 to......................................**$295.00**

Rolling pin, white clambroth w/wooden screw-on handles, from $125 to..**$135.00**

Salad fork & spoon, amber, from $40 to **$45.00**

Salad fork & spoon, clear w/blue pointed handles, from $75 to...**$80.00**

Salad fork & spoon, clear w/ribbed cobalt handles, from $65 to...**$75.00**

Salt & pepper shakers, black lettering on custard, sq sides, metal lids, pr, from $36 to...............................**$40.00**

Salt & pepper shakers, black lettering on milk glass, metal lids, sq sides, McKee, from $36 to **$40.00**

Salt & pepper shakers, green or blue dots on custard, McKee, pr, from $30 to...**$35.00**

Salt & pepper shakers, Modern Tulips (navy), pr, from $50 to...**$55.00**

Salt & pepper shakers, Red Tulips on white, range size, pr, from $30 to...**$35.00**

Salt & pepper shakers, Roman Arch, black lettering on white, pr, from $40 to...**$50.00**

Sugar shaker, crystal, West Sanitary Automatic Sugar, from $25 to...**$30.00**

Syrup, pink, metal top, Hazel-Atlas, from $65 to........**$75.00**

Syrup, Tally Ho, amber, from $50 to...........................**$55.00**

Teakettle, Corning Ware Cookmates TK-2, white, 1¾-qt, 8x9", M...**$30.00**

Utility dish, Currier & Ives, Anchorwhite w/decal, 6½x10½", from $12 to.................................**$15.00**

Utility pan, Sapphire Blue, 2x10½", from $22.50 to....**$25.00**

Water bottle, cobalt, sloped shoulders, metal lid, 64-oz, 10", from $60 to...**$75.00**

Water bottle, Crisscross, crystal, 32-oz, from $35 to....**$40.00**

Water bottle, Water embossed on clear, sloped shoulders, from $18 to...**$20.00**

Miscellaneous Gadgets

Apple peeler, Goodell, cast iron, 3-prong, crank handle, table-mount, EX **$35.00**

Apple peeler/corer, Little Star, 8" w/handle extended, EX **$15.00**

Apple/potato peeler, Goodell Turntable '98, cast iron w/original green paint, 11", NM.............................**$30.00**

Can opener, Dazey Model 90, red & chrome, vacumatic, rubber seal on bottom, cap remover built in, EX......**$15.00**

Can opener, hook-style opener w/red Bakelite handle, 7" ..**$15.00**

Can opener, Pet Milk, metal circle w/2 prongs to pierce can, 2½" dia, NM **$16.50**

Canister/spice set, flowers on blue lustreware, Japan, 5 canisters, 6 spices & vinegar & oil decanters, NM...**$135.00**

Canisters, apple blossoms on white ceramic, wooden lids, Japan, set of 8 ranging from 4" to 6½", NM.........**$55.00**

Canisters, floral on basketweave, ceramic, Japan, nesting set of 3, NM **$55.00**

Chopper, glass w/snap-on chrome top, red Bakelite handle/plunger, ca 1950s, 12x5" dia, EX.................**$20.00**

Chopper, nut; tin top w/green paint & roses decal fits on lid to clear glass bottom, EX **$30.00**

Chopper, single wedge-like iron blade, wooden handle, EX **$25.00**

Chopper/grinder, Universal No 00, New Britain CT, complete w/2 additional gears to adjust fineness, MIB........**$15.00**

Coffeepot, Rusticana, red transfer, Villeroy & Boch, 1947, 9"...**$40.00**

Coffepot, enamelware, fruits decal on white, black trim, glass knob, black graniteware grounds holder, 9" **$25.00**

Egg beater, Androck, crystal 31-oz bowl, 6¾", EX.....**$55.00**

Egg beater, Dazey Mixerator, syllabub style, plastic lid & glass body w/yellow letters, black wood handles, EX **$35.00**

Egg beater, Ekco on gear, cup is marked No 7218/A&J/Made in USA, 10¼", EX..**$42.50**

Egg beater, Master Pat Aug 24, 09, 10½", $250.00.
(Photo courtesy Don Thornton)

Egg beater, T&S #40, cast iron, EX..............................**$20.00**

Funnel, white porcelain, unmarked, med....................**$17.50**

Grater/grinder, Harras Germany #51, cast iron w/red paint, clamps on table, 10", EX.................................**$20.00**

Ice pick, Hamilton Beach #50, metal, 6 prongs, EX ...**$10.00**

Ice pick, Torrington Ice Breaker, 5¾".........................**$15.00**

Ice shaver/chopper, Swing A Way, chrome plated w/ivory enamel, steel base, ivory handle, EX **$20.00**

Pancake turner, Suzie Flipper Automatic, stainless steel, ca 1950, MIB...**$15.00**

Pastry blender, Androck, bent wires form arc that is attached at ea end of red wooden handle, EX......................**$3.50**

Pea sheller/huller, Mr Pea Huller, hand crank, may be adapted to hand mixer or drill, MIB **$35.00**

Potato masher, Speedy Double-Action, Chadwick Miller, Made in Japan, ca 1969, M in original bag...........**$20.00**

Potato masher/ricer, Handy Things USA, metal basket w/red enameled pliers-like handles, 11" L, NM..............**$10.00**

Potato masher/ricer, metal, resembles pliers w/3½" basket, NM **$15.00**

Rolling pin, metal w/wooden handles, EX age & patina..**$65.00**

Rolling pin, tiger maple (turned), knob-like handles, EX patina, 16"...**$45.00**

Rolling pin, wooden w/blue wooden handles, 18", EX...**$35.00**

Sifter, Androck Handi-Sift, tin, lady baking pie w/little boy, 3-screen, 5½", NM.....................................**$60.00**

Sifter, Androck Handi-Sift, tin w/red morning glories & polka dots, red wooden knob on crank handle, EX......**$25.00**

Sifter, Bromwell, tin w/red apples, EX........................**$22.50**

Sifter, McLaughlin embossed on tin body, crank w/black wooden handle, 6x5", EX..............................$22.50

Spatula, Cutco, #1208 stamped on blade, rosewood handle, 12¼", EX..$20.00

Spatula, green wood handle $15.00

Teakettle, pink anodized aluminum, 1950s, NM.........$38.00

Teakettle, white enamel ware, bulbous teapot shape, beehive shaped hinged lid, NM..............................$30.00

Timer, Lux, Minute Minder, white w/red lettering, M.$20.00

Timer, Lux, Mirro, aluminum w/plastic dial, EX $25.00

Timer, Lux, Presto, white w/black lettering, M $22.50

Timer, Merry Mushroom, Sears Roebuck & Co, Japan, 1976, 5"..$75.00

Whip, Durometal Products, crank style, green wooden handle at top & on crank, EX..............................$20.00

Whisk, Cutco #1060, wireware, 12½".........................$30.00

Kitchen Prayer Ladies

The Enesco importing company of Elk Grove, Illinois, distributed a line of kitchen novelties during the 1960s that they originally called 'Mother in the Kitchen.' Today's collectors refer to them as 'Kitchen Prayer Ladies.' The line was fairly extensive — some pieces are common, others are very scarce. All are designed around the figure of 'Mother' who is wearing a long white apron inscribed with a prayer. She is more commonly found in a pink dress. Blue is harder to find and more valuable. (Our values are for pink; add 30% to 50% more for blue. For examples in white with blue trim, add another 10% to 20%.) This line is pictured in *The Collector's Encyclopedia of Cookie Jars, Book II* and *Book III*, by Joyce and Fred Roerig (Collector Books).

Air freshener $125.00

Bank, Mother's Pin Money, 5½"................................$160.00

Bell $75.00

Candle holders, 4", pr, from $250 to.........................$325.00

Canister, pink, ea $300.00

Cookie jar..$250.00

Creamer, 4"...$60.00

Crumb tray & brush, from $125 to.............................$235.00

Egg timer $75.00

Instant coffee jar, spoon-holder loop on side $120.00

Mug..$80.00

Napkin holder $25.00

Picture frame, minimum value $275.00

Planter $120.00

Plaque, full figure $60.00

Salt & pepper shakers, pr $15.00

Soap dish..$35.00

Spoon holder, upright $50.00

Spoon rest $50.00

Sprinkler bottle, blue, minimum value $600.00

Sprinkler bottle, pink, minimum value $500.00

String holder..$175.00

Sugar bowl, w/spoon $70.00

Teapot..$120.00

Toothpick holder, 4½"..$20.00

Vase, bud...$145.00

Ring holder, 5", $85.00. (Photo courtesy Pat and Ann Duncan)

Kreiss & Co.

Collectors are hot on the trail of figural ceramics, and one area of interest are those unique figurines, napkin dolls, planters, mugs, etc., imported from Japan during the 1950s by the Kreiss company, located in California. Though much of their early production was run of the mill, in the late 1950s, the company introduced unique new lines — all bizarre, off the wall, politically incorrect, and very irreverent — and today it's these items that are attracting the interest of collectors. There are several lines. One is a totally zany group of caricatures called Psycho-Ceramics. There's a Beatnick series, Nudies, and Elegant Heirs (all of which are strange little creatures), as well as some that are very well done and tasteful. Several will be inset with with colored 'jewels.' Many are marked either with an ink stamp or an in-mold trademark (some are dated), so you'll need to start turning likely-looking items over to check for the Kreiss name.

There are two very helpful books on the market: *Kreiss Novelty Ceramics*, written by Mike King (see the Directory, Kreiss); and *The World of Kreiss Ceramics* by Pat and Larry Aikins (L-W Book Sales).

Prices are drastically lower than those we saw for Kreiss figures a few years ago, affected no doubt by Internet trading which has made them so much more accessible. Our values are based on actual online sales.

See also Napkin Ladies.

Ashtray, green guy w/brown pistol in hand & 2 holes in head, w/tag, 4½" $30.00

Ashtray, orange creature w/lg white teeth, 4¼".........$40.00

Bank, blue creature w/black hair, Put Your Money Where My Mouth Is, 5½"..$40.00

Bank/dresser caddy, skunk w/glasses & hat, arms at side .$50.00

Egg cup, orange creature w/lg white teeth, 2½" $60.00

Figure, Beatnik, Man, My Philosophy Is Easy... To Heck With Everything, 5¾", $50.00 to $60.00.

Figurine, bird w/long neck, brown w/black highlights, upturned beak, white hair, Moon Being...............**$40.00**

Figurine, blue creature w/black footprints all over body, lg eyes, tan hair, 5½" **$30.00**

Figurine, blue guy w/yellow ear plugs, Psycho Ceramics, 4¾"...**$22.00**

Figurine, brown guy holding bloody axe, 5¼" **$30.00**

Figurine, coyote family, brown w/blue collars, mother (3¾") chained to 2 pups.................................**$45.00**

Figurine, Dr Seuss bird, white bird walking, red beak, pink hair, Moon Being tag, 5" **$150.00**

Figurine, girl in Christmas dress w/1 hand in muff & other on gift..**$30.00**

Figurine, girl in green dress w/matching purse, bow in hair, white poodle w/spaghetti hair chained to wrist, 6"...**$40.00**

Figurine, green man w/rhinestone eyes holding blue gun to head, 2 holes in head, 5" **$35.00**

Figurine, man in blue & white tux w/pipe cleaners in head, Psycho Ceramics **$35.00**

Figurine, man in blue jacket & hat w/green pants, tag reads Man, You're Sick, Sick, Sick...................................**$30.00**

Figurine, man w/crossed arms, yellow w/brown hair, lg nose, Psycho Ceramics, 9" **$155.00**

Figurine, Old Gray Mare, seated, white w/red striped hat, 5¼"..**$35.00**

Figurine, pink guy w/target on belly, lg pink nose & ears **$35.00**

Figurine, schoolboy in black jacket, brown & white hat, blue shorts, green socks, brown shoes, dirty face, 6"..**$25.00**

Figurine, Spaghetti Poodle, white body w/ears, blue spaghetti legs & tail, sitting in crown, 7¼".......................**$60.00**

Figurine, Split Personality, creature ½ blue & ½ yellow w/tan fur hair, w/tag, 8½" **$160.00**

Figurines, King of Clubs & Queen of Spades, 7", 6½", pr **$50.00**

Figurines, Santa & Holly, Santa chained to green Psycho w/holly decor in hair, Honey, I Discovered...Draft in Chimney **$55.00**

Figurines, Scotty dogs, mother & 2 pups chained together, all in vest, mother having 2 rhinestones, 5½" (mother).......**$40.00**

Lamps

Aladdin lamps have been made continually since 1908 by the Mantle Lamp Company of America, now Aladdin Mantle Lamp Company in Clarksville, Tennessee. Their famous kerosene lamps are highly collectible, and some are quite valuable. Many were relegated to the storage shelf or thrown away after electric lines came through the country. Today many people keep them on hand for emergency light.

Few know that Aladdin Industries, Inc. was one of the largest manufacturers of electric lamps from 1930 to 1956. They created new designs, colorful glass, and unique paper shades. These are not only collectible but are still used in many homes today. Many Aladdin lamps, kerosene as well as electric, can be found at garage sales, antique shops, and flea markets. You can learn more about them in the books *Aladdin Electric Lamps* and *Aladdin — The Magic Name in Lamps, Revised Edition,* written by J.W. Courter, who also periodically issues updated price guides for both kerosene and electric Aladdins.

Advisor: J.W. Courter (See Directory, Lamps)

Newsletter: *Mystic Lights of the Aladdin Knights*
J.W. Courter
3935 Kelley Rd., Kevil, KY 42053. Subscription: $25 (6 issues, postpaid 1st class) per year with current buy-sell-trade information. Send SASE for information about other publications

Aladdin Electric Lamps

Bed, #2302SS, whip-o-lite fluted shade, from $200 to ..**$250.00**
Bedroom, M-70, metal & ceramic, from $20 to...........**$30.00**
Boudoir, G-15, floral base, crystal, 1938-52, from $150 to..**$200.00**
Boudoir, New Series; G-44, Alacite, from $40 to **$50.00**
Bridge, #2058, from $200 to **$275.00**
Bridge, B-135, from $125 to......................................**$175.00**
Floor, #3579, walnut, from $250 to **$275.00**
Floor, #3602, candle arms, reflector, from $175 to....**$250.00**
Floor, Junior; #1062, candle arms, from $175 to.......**$225.00**
Floor, torchere; #4598, from $250 to.........................**$300.00**
Magic Touch, MT-507, ceramic base, from $300 to ..**$350.00**
Pin-Up, G-351, wall medallion, Alacite, from $125 to .**$150.00**
Shade, pleated, for table lamp, minimum value **$300.00**
Smoking stand, #7532, from $200 to.........................**$300.00**
Table, E-305, Vogue base, black, from $550 to.........**$650.00**
Table, G-309, Alacite, illuminated base, tall harp, from $80 to **$90.00**
Table, G-311, Alacite, illuminated base, from $50 to ..**$60.00**
Table, G-34, from $100 to...**$125.00**
Table, 785, Large Vase, green, from $200 to **$250.00**
TV, M-367, black iron base w/shade, from $30 to......**$40.00**
TV, M-469, metal, w/shade, from $25 to.....................**$30.00**

Aladdin Kerosene Mantle Lamps

Caboose Model 21C, B-400, aluminum font, from $75 to ...**$150.00**

Floor Model #12, style #1250, blue & gold, from $200 to ...**$300.00**
Floor Model 12, style #1253, Verde Antique, from $150 to .**$200.00**
Hanging Model #23, aluminum hanger & font, rarer shade from $50 to..**$75.00**
Hanging Model B, flat steel frame, parchment shade, from $200 to..**$275.00**
Shelf Model 23, Lincoln Drape, clear, no oil fill, from $70 to..**$80.00**
Shelf Model 23, Lincoln Drape, clear, oil fill, from $100 to..**$125.00**
Table Model #9, nickel, 2 knob variations, ea from $75 to..**$100.00**
Table Model A, Venetian #103, rose, NM, from $150 to .**$200.00**
Table Model B, Orientale, B-132, rose gold, EX, from $225 to..**$300.00**
Table Model B, Simplicity B-29, green, from $125 to ..**$175.00**
Table Model B, Washington Drape B-52, amber crystal, from $125 to..**$175.00**
Table Model C, clear glass, footed, from $700 to **$800.00**
Table Model 21C, B-139, aluminum font, from $40 to .**$60.00**
Table Model 23, Short Lincoln Drape, amber, from $75 to .**$100.00**

Motion Lamps

Though some were made as early as 1920 and as late as the 1970s, motion lamps were most popular during the 1950s. Most are cylindrical with scenes such as waterfalls and forest fires and attain a sense of motion through the action of an inner cylinder that rotates with the heat of the bulb. Prices below are for lamps with original parts in good condition with no cracks, splits, dents, or holes. Any damage greatly decreases the value. As a rule of thumb, the oval lamps are worth a little more than their round counterparts. **Caution** — some lamps are being reproduced (indicated in our listings by '+'). Currently in production are Antique Autos, Trains, Old Mill, Ships in a Storm, Fish, and three Psychedelic lamps. The color on the scenic lamps is much bluer, and they are in a plastic stand with a plastic top. There are quite a few small motion lamps in production that are not copies of the 1950s lamps.

Advisors: Jim and Kaye Whitaker (See Directory, Lamps)

7-Up, $75.00. (Photo courtesy Jim and Kaye Whitaker)

Antique Autos, Econolite, 1947, 11" (+).....................**$110.00**
Butterflies, Econolite, 1957, 11" (+)..........................**$110.00**
Chicago/London Fire, Econolite, 11"..........................**$165.00**
Disneyland Express, red or yellow plastic, Econolite, 1955, 11"..**$175.00**
Elvgrin Pin-Up Girls...**$375.00**
Firefighters, LA Goodman, 1957, 11"..........................**$200.00**
Fireplace, Econolite, 1958, 11".................................**$125.00**
Forest Fire, Econolite, 1955, 11" **$95.00**
Forest Fire, Rotovue Jr, 1949, 10" **$75.00**
Forest Fire, Scene in Action, 1931, glass/metal, 10" .**$150.00**
Fountain of Youth, Rotovue Jr, 1950, 10" **$110.00**
Fresh Water Fish, Econolite, 1950s, 11" **$110.00**
Hopalong Cassidy, Econolite (Roto-Vue Jr), 1949, 10"..**$300.00**
Indian Chief, Gritt Inc, 1920s, chalk/glass, 11" **$110.00**
Indian Maiden, Gritt Inc, 1920s, chalk/glass, 11"......**$110.00**
Japanese Twilight, Scene in Action, 1931, glass/metal, 13"..**$150.00**
Jet Planes, Econolite, 1950s, 11".................................**$250.00**
Merry Go Round, Rotovue Jr, 1949, 10"....................**$110.00**
Mill Stream, Econolite, 1956, 11" (+).........................**$110.00**
Miss Liberty, Econolite, 1957, 11" **$225.00**
Niagara Falls, Econolite, 1955, 11"..............................**$95.00**
Niagara Falls, Econolite Rainbow, oval, 1960, 11" **$110.00**
Niagara Falls, Rotovue Jr, 1949, 10".............................**$95.00**
Niagara Falls, Scene in Action, 1931, glass/metal, 10" ..**$150.00**
Op Art Lamp, Visual Effects, 1970s, 13" (+) **$50.00**
Oriental Fantasy, LA Goodman, 1957, 11" **$95.00**
Oriental Scene, Econolite, 1959, 11" **$125.00**
Sailboats, LA Goodman, 1954, 14" (+) **$110.00**
Seattle World's Fair, Econolite...................................**$175.00**
Ship/Lighthouse, Scene in Action, 1931, 10" **$165.00**
Snow scene (church or cabin), Econolite, 1957, 11"....**$150.00**
Steamboats, Econolite, 1957, 11" **$110.00**
Totville Train, Econolite, 1948, 11"............................**$150.00**
Trains, Econolite, 1956, 11" (+)...................................**$95.00**
Tropical Fish, Econolite, 1954, 11" **$95.00**
Truck & Bus, Econolite, 1962, 11"..............................**$200.00**
Venice Grand Canal, Econolite, 1963, 11" **$125.00**
White Christmas, Econolite, flat front, 11" **$125.00**

TV Lamps

By the 1950s, TV was commonplace in just about every home in the country but still fresh enough to have our undivided attention. Families gathered around the set and for the rest of the evening delighted in being entertained by Ed Sullivan or stumped by the $64,000 Question. Pottery producers catered to this scenario by producing TV lamps by the score, and with the popularity of anything from the '50s being what it is today, suddenly these lamps are making an appearance at flea markets and co-ops everywhere. For more information, we recommend *TV Lamps* by Tom Santiso.

See also Maddux of California; Morton Potteries, Royal Haeger.

Birds on branches, white w/gold trim, 10".................**$35.00**

Blue jay pr on stonework base w/green leaves, natural colors on bisque **$75.00**
Boy on dolphin, gold paint, Lane & Co, from $95 to..**$105.00**
Clam shell, 14" **$20.00**
Cornucopia, woven, green gloss, bulb inside, from $45 to...**$55.00**
Deer & fawn, both recumbent on wooden base, w/Fiberglas shade, from $75 to...**$90.00**
Duck, flying, black gloss, 12½" L...........................**$50.00**

Exotic bird, coral with gold spray and trim, L-701, 13x12", from $75.00 to $85.00.
(From the collection of John and Peggy Scott)

Exotic bird w/planter, multicolor, porcelain-like, from $85 to...**$100.00**
Fish, stylized, dorsal-fin planter, gold waves, Miller, 1956, 21" **$28.00**
Horse head, black w/white mane, Deco style, light inside, from $75 to...**$95.00**
Horse prancing, holes above stone wall emit light, multicolor porcelain, from $95 to **$110.00**
Horses, gold lustre, on black glass base, sm..............**$35.00**
Mermaid seated before Fiberglas shade, from $85 to..**$110.00**
Panther crouching, black or brown, no base, from $75 to **$100.00**
Panther pr prowling atop naturalistic base, 13" L.......**$30.00**
Stag standing among curling grasses, green, from $75 to...**$95.00**
Stagecoach, green w/much gold detailing, 10" **$22.00**
Swordfish w/planter, lime w/gold, from $95 to........**$110.00**

L.E. Smith

Originating just after the turn of the century, the L.E. Smith company continues to operate in Mt. Pleasant, Pennsylvania, at the present time. In the 1920s they introduced a line of black glass that they are famous for today. Some pieces were decorated with silver overlay or enameling. Using their own original molds, they made a line of bird and animal figures in crystal as well as in colors. The company is currently producing these figures, many in two sizes. They were one of the main producers of the popular Moon and Star pattern which has been featured in their catalogs since the 1960s in a variety of shapes and colors.

See also Eye Winker; Moon and Star.

Aquarium, King Fish, green, 7¼x15" **$275.00**
Bonbon, Mt Pleasant, pink or green, rolled rim, handle, 7" **$16.00**
Bookend, horse, rearing, amber, ea **$38.00**
Bookend, horse, rearing, crystal, ea...........................**$35.00**
Bookend, horse, rearing, ruby, ea...............................**$55.00**
Bowl, Mt Pleasant, black amethyst, 8" **$18.00**
Bowl, Pebbled Rim, any color, oval, 9½" **$28.00**
Bowl, Romanesque, any color, footed, 4¼x10" **$75.00**
Bowl, vegetable; Pebbled Rim, any color, ruffled rim, shallow **$28.00**
Cake plate, Plume, blue **$45.00**
Cake plate, Plume, pink, ruffled rim, footed, 12" **$52.00**
Candle holder, Vintage Grape, milk glass, 2¾x4¾"....**$20.00**
Candle holders, Double Shield, black, 4½x5¾", pr **$55.00**
Covered dish, Conestoga wagon, crystal **$35.00**
Covered dish, Conestoga wagon, milk glass **$80.00**

Covered dish, Turkey, ca 1982, 7", $25.00.

Creamer, Mt Pleasant, black w/silver trim **$12.50**
Creamer & sugar bowl, Mt Pleasant, cobalt, 2¾"........**$42.50**
Cup, Mt Pleasant, pink or green...................................**$9.50**
Cup & saucer, Pebbled Rim, any color **$15.00**
Figurine, camel, crystal..**$50.00**
Figurine, elephant, crystal, 1¾" **$20.00**
Figurine, Fighting Cock, dark blue, 9" **$75.00**
Figurine, Goose Girl, crystal, original, 6" **$25.00**
Figurine, rooster, butterscotch slag, limited edition, #208 ..**$85.00**
Figurine, Scottie, frosted, 2½x6x5" **$35.00**
Figurine, swan, milk glass w/decor, 8½" **$45.00**
Figurine, thrush, blue frost...**$20.00**
Goblet, Bicentennial Soaring Eagle, green, ca 1976, 4 for ..**$20.00**
Goblet, Cherry, ruby, footed, 6½x3⅜".......................**$22.50**
Goblet, water; Pineapple, amberina, 6" **$18.50**
Mayonnaise, Mt Pleasant, amethyst, black or cobalt, 3-footed, 5½" **$30.00**

Nappy, Buttons & Bows, amber, heart shape, 1¾x8x6" ..**$20.00**
Pipe rest, Scottie, fired-on black, 5½" L......................**$20.00**
Pitcher, water; Dogwood, blue or pink **$45.00**
Pitcher, water; Dogwood, green opaque **$45.00**
Planter, Mt Pleasant, blue, 5" **$35.00**
Plate, Cherry, amber crackle, 8".....................................**$7.00**
Plate, Mt Pleasant, pink or green, handles, 8".............**$11.00**
Plate, Octagonal, By Cracky, amber crackle, 8" **$8.50**
Plate, Octagonal, green, 8"...**$5.00**
Plate, party; Cloverleaf, light green, 8½x10½" **$16.00**
Plate, Romanesque, any color, octagonal, 7"................**$7.00**
Plate, Romanesque, any color, octagonal, 10".............**$22.00**
Plate, salad; Pebbled Rim, any color, 7".......................**$6.00**
Platter, Mt Pleasant, cobalt, scroll details on handles, 10" ..**$30.00**
Sherbet, Mt Pleasant, amethyst, black or cobalt..........**$16.00**
Sherbet, Octagonal, crystal crackle, 3x4"......................**$7.00**
Sherbet, Octagonal, med green, 3¼x3½" **$15.00**
Soap dish, swan, crystal **$25.00**
Sugar bowl, Pebbled Rim, any color..............................**$13.00**
Tumbler, Dogwood, blue, 4" **$11.00**
Tumbler, Dogwood, green opaque, 4"...........................**$11.00**
Tumbler, light pink crackle, 4¼" **$12.00**
Vase, fan; Romanesque, any color, 7½" **$55.00**
Vase, Octagonal, vaseline crackle, 7" **$12.00**
Vase, 2 ladies dancing inside heart, black, crimped rim, handles, 7" **$45.00**

Lefton China

China, porcelain, and ceramic items with that now familiar mark, Lefton, have been around since the early 1940s and are highly sought after by collectors in the secondary marketplace today. The company was founded by Mr. George Zoltan Lefton, an immigrant from Hungary. In the 1930s he was a designer and manufacturer of sportswear, but eventually his hobby of collecting fine china and porcelain led him to initiate his own ceramic business. When the bombing of Pearl Harbor occurred on December 7, 1941, Mr. Lefton came to the aid of a Japanese-American friend and helped him protect his property from anti-Japanese groups. Later, Mr. Lefton was introduced to a Japanese factory owned by Kowa Koki KK. He contracted with them to produce ceramic items to his specifications, and until 1980 they made thousands of pieces that were marketed by the Lefton company, marked with the initials KW preceding the item number. Figurines and animals plus many of the whimsical pieces such as Bluebirds, Dainty Miss, Miss Priss, Cabbage Cutie, Elf Head, Mr. Toodles, and Dutch Girl are eagerly collected today. As with any antique or collectible, prices vary depending on location, condition, and availability. For the history of Lefton China, information about Lefton factories, marks, and other identification methods, we highly recommend the *Collector's Encyclopedia of Lefton China, Volumes I, II, III,* and *Lefton Price Guide* by our advisor Loretta DeLozier (Collector Books).

See also Birthday Angels; Cookie Jars.

Advisor: Loretta DeLozier (See Directory, Lefton)

Club: National Society of Lefton Collectors

Newsletter: *The Lefton Collector*
c/o Loretta DeLozier
PO Box 50201
Knoxville, TN 37950-0201
Dues: $25 per year (includes quarterly newsletter)

Ashtray, leaf dish w/applied butterfly or bird, #1237, from $28 to..**$32.00**
Ashtray, swan, Floral Bisque Bouquet, #4744, from $15 to **$20.00**
Ashtray w/attached cigarette holder, Lilac Chintz, leaf form, #1005, 5¼", from $18 to......................................**$22.00**

Bank, lady in mink coat, Money Is Everything, 7½", from $35.00 to $45.00. (Photo courtesy Loretta DeLozier)

Bone dish, Green Heritage, #3708, from $15 to..........**$20.00**
Bookends, tigers seated on right-angled books, #6663, pr, from $30 to...**$40.00**
Candle holder, Green Holly, chamberstick style, #717, from $20 to...**$30.00**
Candy box, Mist Rose, #5538, 3-footed, from $40 to..**$45.00**
Candy box, White Holly, gift box form, #6073, from $32 to..**$38.00**
Candy dish, Floral Mood, 5-pointed leaf shape w/rose design in center, gold edge, #4669, 5¾", from $15 to **$25.00**
Canister set, Sack O'Flour/Sugar/Coffee/Tea, #4084, from $110 to..**$135.00**
Canister set, Sweet Violets, #2875, 4-pc, from $95 to ..**$110.00**
Coffeepot, Festival, #2935, from $135 to **$155.00**
Coffeepot, Rose Chintz, #660, from $165 to.............**$185.00**
Compote, Floral Chintz, #8043, 7", from $18 to.........**$22.00**
Creamer & sugar bowl, Miss Priss, #1508, pr, from $55 to **$65.00**
Creamer & sugar bowl on tray, Rose Chintz, #2044, from $50 to..**$55.00**
Cup & saucer, rose & leaf design on white w/gold trim, #970, from $25 to..**$35.00**
Cup & saucer, rose design on green & white stripes, heavy gold trim, #546, from $35 to **$40.00**

Dish, violet design on white, gold-trimmed scalloped rim, glossy, #2998, 8", from $22 to..................**$28.00**

Dish, White Holly, Christmas tree form, #6071, 8", from $18 to.......................**$22.00**

Egg box, pink airbrushing on white w/ribbon bow & applied flowers on lid, matt finish, #4741, 3¼", from $12 to..................**$18.00**

Figurine, baby girl w/cup, matt finish, #3499, 5½", from $75 to..................**$85.00**

Figurine, calypso dancers, white & pink w/gold sponging & trim, #021, pr, from $125 to..................**$150.00**

Figurine, Christmas dog w/Santa hat & candy cane in mouth, matt finish, #2036, 3", from $8 to.......................**$12.00**

Figurine, cobbler working on shoe, matt finish, #7776, 7¼", from $80 to..................**$85.00**

Figurine, cockatoo, head down & tail up on blossom & leafy round base, matt finish, #1542, 7½", from $85 to..................**$90.00**

Figurine, country doctor examining child seated on lap, matt finish, #5687, 6¾", from $65 to.......................**$75.00**

Figurine, Easter rabbit, white w/brown eyes, nose & feet, #880, from $25 to..................**$35.00**

Figurine, goldfinch on tree stump base, matt finish, #6609, 4½", from $20 to..................**$25.00**

Figurine, Madonna bust, matt pink, #1720, 8", from $30 to..................**$40.00**

Figurine, Mr & Mrs Santa Claus dancing, #02139, 3½", from $20 to..................**$30.00**

Figurine, owl perched on branch, #7556, flowers embossed around branch base, brown tones on white, 12", from $65 to..................**$75.00**

Figurine, peacock w/tail spread on round base, #2336, matt finish, 6", from $55 to..................**$65.00**

Figurine, peacock w/tail trailing back on oblong base, soft colors, #2335, 7¼", from $55 to.......................**$65.00**

Figurine, peasant couple w/jugs, matt finish, #5641, 8", pr, from $110 to..................**$135.00**

Figurine, ruffed grouse, matt brown tones, #2668, pr, from $65 to..................**$75.00**

Figurine, Russian lady, white w/gold trim, #752, 11", from $175 to..................**$225.00**

Figurine, Valentine girl w/bow in hair waving & holding up heart, red & white w/gold sponging, glossy, #376, 4", from $15 to..................**$20.00**

Figurine, Victorian lady w/parasol, glossy finish, gold trim, #1570, 6¼", from $125 to..................**$145.00**

Jam jar, apple teapot form or orange teapot form, glossy finish, #6973, ea from $25 to..................**$35.00**

Jam jar, sq basket w/orange slice & leaves on lid, glossy finish, #5108, 5½", from $12 to..................**$18.00**

Jam jar w/tray & spoon, Festival, #2617, from $35 to...**$45.00**

Mug, Fruits of Italy, #1209, from $5 to.......................**$10.00**

Music box, Heavenly Hobos boy & girl on train engine, plays On the Road Again, #04587, from $65 to.............**$75.00**

Nappy, Green Heritage, leaf form, #1860, from $20 to .**$25.00**

Nappy, roses & leaves in center on white, gold edge, #486, 6¾", from $25 to..................**$30.00**

Night light, girl figure in long pink dress & hat, matt finish, #486, 6", from $40 to..................**$50.00**

Pitcher, Misty Rose, #5692, 7", from $95 to.............**$135.00**

Pitcher & bowl, Green Vintage, #6279, 6¼", from $55 to..................**$65.00**

Planter, ABC block, glossy pastels, #2128, 4", from $8 to..................**$12.00**

Planter, blue jay on log base w/blossom branch, matt finish, #573, 7", from $18 to..................**$28.00**

Planter, clown's head, Freddy the Freeloader look, glossy finish, #4498, 4", from $45 to..................**$55.00**

Planter, cocker spaniel w/glass eyes, brown airbrushing on white, #4672, 7", from $22 to..................**$28.00**

Planter, egg urn, Floral Bisque Bouquet, #5442, 3½", from $12 to..................**$15.00**

Planter, girl w/basket, pink airbrushing, glossy finish, #056, 5½", from $65 to..................**$75.00**

Planter, Home Tweet Home birdhouse, glossy finish, #50261, 5", from $40 to..................**$45.00**

Planter, leprechaun w/pipe & mandolin, glossy finish, #826, 6½", from $20 to..................**$25.00**

Planter, Santa on Reindeer, red & white w/gold trim, #1496, 6", from $20 to..................**$30.00**

Plate, Green Heritage, #3069, 9", from $30 to.............**$35.00**

Platter, Sweet Violets, #2867, from $50 to..................**$60.00**

Punch Bowl, Green Holly, #1367, from $60 to...........**$75.00**

Salt & pepper shakers, Fruits of Italy, #1207, pr.........**$15.00**

Salt & pepper shakers, puppies, brown airbrushing on white, matt finish, #6087, 3¼", from $12 to..................**$18.00**

Salt box, Pink Clover, wooden lid, #2497, from $40 to...**$50.00**

Sleigh, Green Holly, #2637, 10½", from $50 to...........**$55.00**

Teabag holder, Miss Priss, #1516, from $145 to........**$150.00**

Teapot, Bluebird, #438, from $275 to.......................**$325.00**

Teapot, elf head, glossy finish, #3873, from $175 to...**$225.00**

Teapot, Green Vintage, #6711, miniature, from $35 to....**$45.00**

Tidbit tray, Lilac & Chintz, 2-tiered, #1279, from $50 to..**$60.00**

Vase, Green Heritage, ewer, #4072, from $55 to........**$65.00**

Wall plaque, Christy, #448, 7½", from $15 to.............**$20.00**

Vase, Green Holly, lamp shape, #2693, 8½", from $65.00 to $75.00.

Letter Openers

If you're cramped for space but a true-blue collector at heart, here's a chance to get into a hobby where there's more than enough diversification to be both interesting and challenging, yet one that requires very little room for display. Whether you prefer the advertising letter openers or the more imaginative models with handles sculpted as a dimensional figure or incorporating a penknife or a cigarette lighter, for instance, you should be able to locate enough for a nice assortment. Materials are varied as well, ranging from silver plate to wood.

Advisor: Everett Grist (See Directory, Letter Openers)

Brass, Brown & Bigelow, Remembrance Advertising .**$30.00**
Brass, Diversified Industries, stamped B&B.................**$22.00**
Brass, eagle w/cornucopia handle **$15.00**
Brass, enameled bird-headed dragon.........................**$12.00**

Brass, gargoyle handle, embossed blade, $15.00.

Brass, Lincoln head penny handle (2-sided) **$8.00**
Brass, lizard figural, marked China **$10.00**
Brass, lyre handle, stamped Penco, New Bedford MA, made in Taiwan...**$10.00**
Brass, pineapple on handle, engraved decor on blade, marked India **$8.00**
Brass, rose forms handle, embossed decor on blade ...**$8.00**
Brass, smiling Chinese elder forms handle.................**$15.00**
Brass, 12 signs of the Zodiac in blue enamel, Rafi......**$8.00**
Brass, 3-D grasshoper, paperweight handle **$20.00**
Brass, 3-D nude woman handle, Great Smoky Mountains **$18.00**
Brass & pewter, griffin over lion's head **$12.00**
Brass & silver plate, stamped The Viking Sword, Norway **$25.00**
Brass w/enameled flower decor, red tassel.................**$30.00**
Brass w/inlaid bits of colored Bakelite & aluminum wire, stainless blade, Made In Lebanon S&A Haddad...**$45.00**
Bronze, Bennett & Goding Shoe Goods, Metal Arts Co ..**$25.00**
Bronze, dragon decor, Shirokiya, Japan.....................**$12.00**
Bronze & enamel, George Peabody College for Teachers..**$12.00**
Bronze openwork handle, mother-of-pearl blade, Arc de Triomphe **$35.00**
Bronze-colored metal, woman w/vase forms handle .**$18.00**
Cast aluminum, curving abstract shape.........................**$3.00**
Celluloid & steel, pen-knife handle, Vadstena, made in Germany...**$40.00**
Copper, spear shape w/hammered edges **$10.00**
Copper-colored metal, gun form, Washington DC........**$8.00**

Copper-colored metal, stag & tree forms handle, Cherokee Indian Reservation, Japan..........................**$10.00**
Horn, carved scenes, Philippines **$25.00**
Ivory, carved crocodile..**$85.00**
Leather handle w/gold stamping, marked Italy............**$6.00**
Lucite handle encases shell seaweed & sea horse, Florida Gulf Arium, Ft Walton Beach...............................**$18.00**
Lucite handle encases 3 US pennies, paper label: Unique, Canada **$15.00**
Magnifier, red plastic w/brass shield, Annapolis, marked SP, made in USA **$6.00**
Magnifier, clear plastic w/red plastic sheath, ruler on blade, Bausch & Lomb..**$3.00**
Mosaic handle & silver-plated pierced blade..............**$25.00**
Mother-of-pearl, plain..**$15.00**
Pen knife, plastic & steel, knife blade, Great Smoky Mts, Imperial USA **$10.00**
Pewter, eagle figural handle, early **$10.00**
Plastic, beige, Braille alphabet...................................**$10.00**
Plastic, clear w/magnifying blade, in sheath **$3.00**
Plastic, Lincoln Center, New York on handle **$3.00**
Plastic, openwork Oriental design, dagger form...........**$3.00**
Plastic, ruler in blade, Iowa City Iowa **$4.00**
Plastic, white, twisted handle.......................................**$3.00**
Plastic, white w/green Aztec god on handle.................**$4.00**
Plastic, Yellow Pages advertising, black on yellow.......**$3.00**
Plastic & brass, pen & magnifier, souvenir of Laguna Beach **$12.00**
Plastic & steel, cigarette lighter w/fishing fly in body, ruler blade, Mardi Gras '67, Japan................................**$40.00**
Plastic & steel, fish handle, nail clipper & file, Missouri shield w/mule **$10.00**
Plastic & steel, Great Smoky Mountains, knife blade, Imperial USA **$10.00**
Pot metal & steel, Little Rock Arkansas, marked Gish ..**$5.00**
Silver & celluloid, raised owl handle, Tore mark on blade, stamped 830 Silver.......................................**$45.00**
Silver plate, Napoleon over French eagle....................**$10.00**
Stag horn handle, steel blade **$10.00**
Steel, engraved floral, slim/narrow blade **$4.00**
Steel, Siam enameling technique of cross & shield **$20.00**
Walrus bone, carved polar bear..................................**$45.00**
White metal, Catawba College, dagger form **$5.00**
White metal, golf clubs & bag form handle, Metzke 1985..**$15.00**
White metal & steel, sword form, serrated edge on blade..**$10.00**
Wooden, carved grape decor on handle, plain blade...**$6.00**
Wooden, Cherokee NC, dagger form **$5.00**
Wooden, inset turquoise, carnelian & opal **$20.00**

L.G. Wright

Until closing in mid-1990, the L.G. Wright Glass Company was located in New Martinsville, West Virginia. Mr. Wright started his business as a glass jobber and then began buying molds from defunct glass companies. He never made his own glass, instead many companies pressed his wares, among them Fenton, Imperial, Viking, and Westmoreland. Much of L.G. Wright's glass was reproductions of Colonial and Victorian glass and lamps. Many items were made from the original molds, but the designs of some were slightly changed. His company flourished in the 1960s and 1970s. For more information we recommend *The L.G. Wright Glass Company* by James Measell and W.C. 'Red' Roetteis (Glass Press).

Covered dish, turtle, 'Knobby Back,' dark green, 10½", from $135.00 to $145.00.

Barber bottle, Daisy & Fern, cranberry opal satin, from $125 to...**$145.00**
Barber bottle, Hobnail, amber, 4 rows of Hobnails in straight neck, from $120 to **$140.00**
Bowl, banana; Cherry, amber, 2 turned up sides, pedestal foot...**$50.00**
Bowl, berry; Daisy & Button, vaseline opal, 11".......**$115.00**
Bowl, Daisy & Button, blue, 6-crimp rim, sm.............**$20.00**
Bowl, Daisy & Button, clear, 3 peg feet, w/lid...........**$35.00**
Bowl, lily; Panel Grape, blue opal, shallow w/upturned rim, ca 1950s..**$100.00**
Candle holder, Daisy & Button, ruby, sleigh form, sm, from $100 to..**$125.00**
Compote, Beaded Rib, light blue, pedestal foot, lg, from $50 to...**$75.00**
Compote, Cabbage Leaf, blue satin, w/lid **$100.00**
Compote, Daisy & Button, blue, w/lid, sm **$38.00**
Compote, Daisy & Button, vaseline opal, w/lid, sm..**$50.00**
Compote, Dolphin, purple slag, sm **$40.00**
Covered animal dish, any 5" style, caramel slag, from $45 to...**$55.00**
Covered animal dish, any 5" style, purple or blue slag, ea, from $55 to...**$60.00**
Covered animal dish, any 5" style, red slag, from $65 to...**$75.00**
Covered animal dish, Atterbury duck, any color, unmarked, 11", from $70 to **$85.00**
Covered dish, duck on flange base, amethyst w/white head **$65.00**
Covered dish, duck on flange base, milk glass or opaque blue w/milk glass head **$50.00**
Covered dish, flat-iron, amber, 5x8½".........................**$50.00**
Covered dish, hen on nest, #70-8, amethyst w/white head or white w/amethyst head, 8" **$65.00**

Covered dish, hen on nest, #70-8, blue or purple slag, 8", from $100 to..**$125.00**
Covered dish, hen on nest, #70-8, caramel slag, from $75 to..**$100.00**
Covered dish, hen on nest, #70-8, ruby slag, from $165 to..**$195.00**
Covered dish, turtle, 'Knobby Back,' amber, lg...........**$95.00**
Creamer, Honeycomb, cranberry opal, lg...................**$85.00**
Creamer & sugar bowl, Beaded Curtain, Peach Blow ..**$16.50**
Creamer & sugar bowl, Daisy & Button, amberina, from $50 to...**$60.00**
Creamer & sugar bowl, Panel Grape, green, footed, from $40 to..**$50.00**
Creamer & sugar bowl, Quilted, cranberry, from $125 to..**$145.00**
Creamer & sugar bowl, Sweetheart, light blue, footed..**$50.00**
Creamer & sugar bowl, Wildflower, amber, pedestal foot, w/lid, from $70 to...**$85.00**
Cruet, Eye Dot, cranberry opal, fluted, from $145 to .**$165.00**
Cruet, S Pattern, green w/faceted clear stopper, from $70 to..**$90.00**
Cruet, Stars & Stripes, cranberry opal, from $325 to...**$385.00**
Cruet, Thumbprint, cranberry, ovoid shape **$115.00**
Decanter, Grape, dk amethyst, lg................................**$45.00**
Finger bowl, Hobnail, amberina, crimped rim...........**$35.00**
Finger bowl, Honeycomb, cranberry opal, from $50 to ..**$65.00**
Goblet, Horn of Plenty, clear....................................**$20.00**
Goblet, Sawtooth, ruby **$25.00**
Goblet, Stippled Star, amber **$22.50**
Goblet, Sweetheart, ruby...**$25.00**
Hat, Daisy & Button, blue, sm....................................**$17.50**
Hat, Daisy & Button, dark amythest............................**$22.50**
Lamp, Christmas Snowflake, cranberry opal, gold base, round font, ruffled vasiform shade **$345.00**
Lamp, Thumbprint, cranberry w/milk glass base, pear-shaped font & umbrella shade, lg......................**$325.00**
Mustard jar, bull's head as lid, green **$50.00**
Pickle jar, Daisy & Button, amberina, straight sides, silver-metal lid, from $95 to...**$110.00**
Pitcher, milk; Dot, cranberry opal, from $125 to **$140.00**
Pitcher, milk; Swirl, cranberry opal, from $200 to **$250.00**
Pitcher, water; Mary Gregory decoration on med blue, from $165 to...**$195.00**
Pitcher, water; Panel Grape, blue opal, from $95 to...**$110.00**
Pitcher, water; Swirl, cranberry opal, from $235 to ..**$260.00**
Planter, wall mount; Daisy & Button, light blue, canoe shape **$42.00**
Plate, Daisy & Button, blue, 10" **$35.00**
Plate, grape cluster & leaves hand-painted on milk glass, latticework rim..**$110.00**
Plate, Moss Rose on milk glass, latticework rim **$125.00**
Rose bowl, Daisy & Fern, cranberry opal, from $70 to..**$90.00**
Rose bowl, Grape, purple carnival, incruvate rim **$50.00**
Rose bowl, Rib, cranberry opal, from $90 to **$100.00**
Salt & pepper shakers, Three Face, amber satin, pr, from $35 to..**$45.00**
Salt dip, Daisy & Button, green, round w/straight sides..**$10.00**
Shoe, Daisy & Button, amber, pointed top.................**$40.00**

Skillet, Daisy & Button, amberina, sm $35.00

Slipper, Daisy & Button, amber....................................$15.00

Syrup pitcher, Fern, vaseline opal, ca 1965, from $100 to...$125.00

Syrup pitcher, Moss Rose on milk glass, straight sides, silver metal top, from $145 to $165.00

Toothpick holder, Frog, milk glass........................$28.00

Toothpick holder, Sweetheart, ruby $25.00

Tumbler, Dahlia, white carnival................................$95.00

Tumbler, Dot, blue opal...$40.00

Tumbler, Fern, cranberry opal, from $50 to $60.00

Tumbler, Peach Blow w/hand-painted rose lattice $65.00

Tumbler, Rambler Rose, purple carnival, ca 1970s $35.00

Vase, Beaded Curtain, blue overlay, jack-in-the-pulpit rim, lg, from $195 to..$235.00

Vase, Corn, blue opal, modeled as an ear of corn w/husks...$75.00

Vase, Fern, cranberry opal, spherical body w/short cylinder neck & 4-lobe rim, lg, from $195 to $235.00

Vase, Grape, light green, teardrop-shaped body w/crimped 3-lobe rim, med $25.00

Vase, Peach Blow w/embossed cherries, crimped 3-lobe ruffled rim..$235.00

Liberty Blue

'Take home a piece of American history!,' stated an ad from the 1970s for this dinnerware made in Staffordshire, England. Blue and white depictions of George Washington at Valley Forge, Paul Revere, Independence Hall — fourteen historic scenes in all — were offered on different place-setting pieces. The ad goes on to describe this 'unique...truly unusual..museum-quality... future family heirloom.'

For every five dollars spent on groceries you could purchase a basic piece (dinner plate, bread and butter plate, cup, saucer, or dessert dish) for fifty-nine cents on alternate weeks of the promotion. During the promotion, completer pieces could also be purchased. The soup tureen was the most expensive item, originally selling for $24.99. Nineteen completer pieces in all were offered along with a five-year open stock guarantee.

Beware of 18" and 20" platters. These are recent imports and not authentic Liberty Blue. For more information we recommend Jo Cunningham's book, *The Best of Collectible Dinnerware* (Schiffer).

Advisor: Gary Beegle (See Directory, Dinnerware)

Bowl, cereal; 6½", from $12 to.....................................$15.00

Bowl, flat soup; 8¾", from $20 to.................................$22.00

Bowl, fruit; 5", from $6 to...$6.50

Bowl, vegetable; oval, from $40 to $45.00

Bowl, vegetable; round, from $40 to $45.00

Butter dish, w/lid, ¼-lb..$55.00

Casserole, w/lid $125.00

Coaster...$12.50

Creamer, from $18 to..$22.00

Creamer & sugar bowl, w/lid, original box...............$80.00

Cup & saucer, from $7 to...$9.00

Gravy boat, from $32 to...$38.00

Gravy boat liner, from $22 to $30.00

Mug, from $10 to...$12.00

Pitcher, 7½"...$125.00

Plate, bread & butter; 6", from $4 to...........................$4.50

Plate, dinner; 10", from $6 to.......................................$8.00

Plate, luncheon; scarce, 8¾".......................................$24.00

Plate, scarce, 7", from $9 to...$12.00

Platter, 12", from $35 to...$45.00

Platter, 14", $95.00.

Salt & pepper shakers, pr, from $38 to........................$42.00

Soup ladle, plain white, no decal, from $30 to...........$35.00

Soup tureen, w/lid...$425.00

Sugar bowl, no lid $10.00

Sugar bowl, w/lid...$28.00

Teapot, w/lid, from $95 to...$145.00

License Plates

Some of the early porcelain license plates are valued at more than $500.00. First-year plates are especially desirable. Steel plates with the aluminum 'state seal' attached range in value from $150.00 (for those from 1915 to 1920) down to $20.00 (for those from the early 1940s to 1950). Even some modern plates are desirable to collectors who like those with special graphics and messages.

Our values are given for examples in good or better condition, unless noted otherwise. For further information see *License Plate Values* distributed by L-W Book Sales.

Advisor: Richard Diehl (See Directory, License Plates)

Newsletter: *Automobile License Plate Collectors Association*
Richard Dragon
P.O. Box 8400, Warwick, RI 02888-0400.
www.alpca.org

Magazine: *License Plate Collectors Hobby Magazine*
Drew Steitz, Editor
P.O. Box 222
East Texas, PA 18046; phone or fax: 610-791-7979; e-mail: PL8Seditor@aol.com or RVGZ60A@prodigy.com; www.PL8S.com
Issued bimonthly; $18 per year (1st class, USA). Send $2 for sample copy.

1911, Iowa, fair	$100.00
1912, Connecticut, porcelain, truck	$40.00
1915, Indiana	$60.00
1916, Maine, poor	$10.50
1918, Wyoming, repainted	$80.00
1919, Connecticut	$10.50
1923, Idaho	$35.00
1924, Nevada, repainted	$25.00
1924, New Mexico, repainted	$35.00
1925, Florida, repainted	$60.00
1927, New Jersey	$18.50
1927, Oregon, fair	$20.00
1930, Nevada, fair to good	$15.50
1932, Tennessee, poor	$12.50
1936, California, fair	$8.50
1938, California	$20.00
1938, Massachusetts, pr	$27.00
1938, Pennsylvania	$11.50
1939, Minnesota	$11.50
1940, Idaho	$50.00
1940, Illinois	$9.50
1940, Michigan	$15.50
1943, Kansas	$10.50
1943, Kansas, tab	$8.50
1943, Pennsylvania, tab	$10.00
1944, Arkansas, fiberboard	$60.00
1947, Utah, some rust	$14.50
1948, Indiana	$9.50
1950, Pennsylvania	$7.00
1950, Rhode Island	$10.50
1951, Utah	$20.00
1952, Alaska	$100.00
1953, Ohio	$12.50
1954, Kansas	$6.50
1955, Washington	$12.50
1955, Wisconsin	$12.50
1958, Ohio	$7.50
1959, Rhode Island	$9.50
1961, Wyoming	$6.50
1962, New York, pr	$15.00
1963, Montana	$7.50
1963, Washington DC	$12.50
1964, Alaska	$22.00
1965, New York	$12.50
1966, Alaska, totem pole	$12.50
1966, Wisconsin	$4.50
1968, Mississippi	$6.50
1968, South Carolina	$5.50
1970, Virginia, pr	$10.50

1971, Delaware	$5.50
1971, Hawaii	$8.50
1972, Maine	$4.50
1972, Montana	$5.00
1973, Utah, beehive, undated	$10.50
1975, Hawaii	$10.50
1976, Oklahoma, Bicentennial	$10.50
1976, Rhode Island, Ocean State	$10.50
1980, New Mexico	$4.50
1980, West Virginia, blue border map	$12.50
1981, North Carolina, First in Freedom	$10.50
1984, Alabama	$3.50
1986, Louisiana, World's Fair	$15.50
1987, Texas, Sequicentennial	$6.50
1988, California	$8.50
1989, Kentucky, horses	$12.50
1991, Florida, manatee	$20.00
1991, Oklahoma, shield	$5.50
1992, Iowa, Sesquicentennial	$10.50
1994, Georgia, Olympics	$20.00
1994, Montana, Veteran	$9.50
1995, Arizona, cactus	$3.50
1996, Oregon, Trail	$15.00
1997, Vermont	$10.50
1998, Arizona, desert scene	$6.50
1998, South Carolina, bird	$7.50
2000, North Dakota	$5.50

Little Red Riding Hood

This line of novelty cookie jars, canisters, mugs, teapots, and other kitchenware items was made by both Regal China and Hull. Today any piece is expensive. There are several variations of the cookie jars. The Regal jar with the open basket marked 'Little Red Riding Hood Pat. Design 135889' is worth about $375.00 to $450.00. The same with the closed basket goes for at least $75.00 more. An unmarked Regal variation with a closed basket, full skirt, and no apron books at $600.00. The Hull jars are valued at about $350.00 unless they're heavily decorated with decals and gold trim, which can add as much as $250.00 to the basic value.

The complete line is covered in *The Collector's Encyclopedia of Cookie Jars* by Joyce and Fred Roerig (Collector Books), and again in *Little Red Riding Hood* by Mark E. Supnick.

Bank, standing, from $800 to	$900.00
Bank, wall hanging	$1,200.00
Butter dish, from $350 to	$400.00
Canister, cereal	$1,375.00
Canister, salt	$1,100.00
Canister, tea	$700.00
Canisters, coffee, sugar or flour, ea from $600 to	$700.00
Cookie jar, closed basket, from $450 to	$550.00
Cookie jar, open basket, from $375 to	$450.00
Cookie jar, poinsettias, from $700 to	$750.00

Cracker jar, from $600 to $700.00
Creamer, top pour, no tab handle, from $400 to $425.00
Creamer, top pour, tab handle, from $350 to............$375.00
Creamer & sugar bowl, open, 5", from $350 to $400.00
Dresser jar, 8¾", from $350 to $425.00
Lamp, from $1,300 to $1,500.00
Match holder, wall hanging, from $800 to................$850.00
Mustard jar, w/spoon, from $350 to...........................$425.00
Pitcher, milk; 8", from $350 to $425.00
Pitcher, 7", from $400 to $450.00
Planter, hanging, from $375 to $450.00
Salt & pepper shakers, lg, 5", pr, from $125 to.........$150.00
Salt & pepper shakers, Pat Design 135889, med, 4½", pr,
    from $800 to...$900.00
Salt & pepper shakers, 3¼", pr, from $60 to $90.00
Spice jar, sq base, ea from $650 to $750.00

Sugar bowl, with lid, from $300.00 to $425.00.

Sugar bowl lid only, minimum value..........................$175.00
Teapot, from $375 to $450.00
Wolf jar, red base, from $925 to $975.00
Wolf jar, yellow base, from $750 to $800.00

Little Tikes

For more than twenty-five years, this company (a division of Rubbermaid) has produced an extensive line of toys and playtime equipment, all made of heavy-gauge plastic, sturdily built and able to stand up to the rowdiest children and the most inclement weather. As children usually outgrow these items well before they're worn out, you'll often see them at garage sales, priced at a fraction of their original cost. We've listed a few below, along with what we feel would be a high average for an example in excellent condition. Since there is no established secondary market pricing system, though, you can expect to see a wide range of asking prices.

Activity Garden, complete, EX..$85.00

Beauty Salon, complete, EX..$115.00
Bookshelf toy box, blue, EX..$60.00
Canopy bed, w/quilted bedspread & dust ruffle, 14½x12",
    EX $25.00

Castle, with slide, 52x52x13", EX, from $375.00 to $400.00.

Construction Truck Sandbox/Pool, M $75.00
Country Cottage Playhouse, yellow w/blue roof, pink door,
    EX $175.00
Country Kitchen, refrigerator, microwave, dishwasher, stove
    top, sink, fold-out island, 58x21x43"...................$125.00
Cozy Cruiser Trailer/Jogger, MIB................................$135.00
Desk & chair, w/working light, EX $60.00
Dirt Digger Construction Truck, swivels 360 degrees,
    22x11½x23", EX..$65.00
Fire Team, Fire Chief's Car, Ladder Truck & 6 firemen,
    EXIB $70.00
Football Toybox, EX...$65.00
Grand Mansion Dollhouse, no furniture, EX.............$115.00
Hotwheels Adventure Mountain, VG $100.00
Hotwheels Racing Roller Coaster, 40x35x29", EX........$60.00
Laundry Center, washing machine, dryer & ironing board,
    23x12½x31", VG+ $80.00
Little Girl Toybox, EX..$60.00
Mailbox Toy Chest, 27x16x14½", M $85.00
My Size Barbie House, pink w/blue roof, green door, EX..$140.00
Noah's Ark Bed, MIB $115.00
Octopus Merry Go-Round, spinner in middle w/octopus
    face, EX..$95.00
Race Car Bed, red, twin size, NM $310.00
Racing Tire Toybox, MIB $65.00
Ride-on Motorcycle, orange w/black seat, yellow handlebars,
    windshield, EX $90.00
Ride-on Train & Track set, battery-operated, VG+....$110.00
Rocking chair, purple & teal, VG+ $30.00
Sleepytime Express Train Bed, red, yellow & blue, EX ..$140.00
Spaceship Slide Climber, EX $90.00
Tigger Teeter Totter, Tigger spins & sways, EX $55.00
Victorian Toddler Bed, pink & white, EX.................$130.00
Wave Climber, 48" wavy slide, ladder, steering wheel, hiding
    place, 51x42x52" $125.00

Work Bench, complete, EX..............................$90.00
Zebra Rocking Horse/Ride-on, EX.................$55.00

Lladro Porcelains

Lovely studies of children and animals in subtle colors are characteristic of the Lladro porcelains produced in Labernes Blanques, Spain. Their retired and limited editions are popular with today's collectors.

Act II, #5035...$360.00
Angel Tree Topper, #5719, 19990............$260.00
Boy w/Dog, #4522, 7½"...............................$100.00
Boy w/Goat, #4506, from $250 to............$275.00
By My Side, #7645.......................................$190.00
Cellist, #4651...$280.00

Charlie the Tramp, 1984, 11", MIB, $400.00.

Christmas in Here Tree, #6670, 13", MIB..................$380.00
Cinderella, #4828M, 9½" $215.00
Clown Bust, #5130.......................................$275.00
Dancing Class, #5741...................................$115.00
Eve, #1382...$340.00
Fairy Garland, #5860 ....$450.00
Family Roots, #05371, MIB, from $500 to.................$750.00
Flower Song, #7607G, MIB..........................$355.00
Girl on Carousel Horse, #1469, MIB $650.00
Girl to the Fountain, #2023.........................$250.00
Girl w/Cat & Grandfather Clock, #5347.....$330.00
Girl w/Cats, #01309, 9½"............................$180.00
Girl w/Piglets, #4572...................................$310.00
Girl's Head, #2041 ....$415.00
Goya Lady, #5125...$200.00
Happy Anniversary, #6475, MIB..................$255.00
Hebrew Student, #4684, 11½" $750.00
Hindu Children on Elephant, #5352, MIB.................$260.00
I Love You Truly, #1528, 14", MIB.............$410.00

Innocence in Bloom, #7644, MIB..................$235.00
It Wasn't Me, #7672, MIB.............................$245.00
Jazz Drums, #5929, 8", MIB.........................$370.00
Julia, #1361, MIB..$230.00
King's Guard, #5642, 14¼".............................$550.00
Kiyoko, #1450..$340.00
Litter of Love, #1441, MIB...........................$425.00
Little Traveler, #7602, MIB, from $800 to.................$900.00
Mile of Style, #6507 ....$285.00
Mother & Child, #4701, M...........................$165.00
Mozart, #5915..$610.00
Muneco Cowboy, #4969, M (G box)............$240.00
My Little Treasure, #6503 ....$265.00
Naughty Girl w/Hat, #5006..........................$235.00
Ocean Beauty, #5785, MIB...........................$430.00
Othello & Desdemona, #1145 ....$3,500.00
Peace Offering, #13559, MIB $515.00
Petals of Peace, #6579, MIB.........................$240.00
Pocket Full of Wishes, #7650, MIB..............$245.00
Poetry, #1839, MIB $460.00
Puppet Painter, #5396, 9½"..........................$530.00
Rabbit, peeking over log, #4773..................$75.00
Shelley, #1357, MIB......................................$230.00
Sheriff Puppet, #4969 ....$330.00
Sitting Pekinese, #4641................................$475.00
Snow Man, #5713, MIB.................................$250.00
Spring Bouquet, #7603, MIB........................$350.00
Summer on the Farm, #5285, MIB $260.00
Sunday in the Park, #5365, 6x8x9", MIB.................$360.00
Ten & Growing, #7635, MIB.........................$290.00
Torso in White, #4512 ....$265.00
Try This One, #5361, MIB.............................$300.00
Trying on the Hat, #5011G...........................$230.00
Walking the Dogs, #6760, MIB $300.00

Longaberger Baskets

In the early 1900s in the small Ohio town of Dresden, John Wendell 'J.W.' Longaberger developed a love for hand-woven baskets. In 1973 J.W. and his fifth child, Dave, began to teach others how to weave baskets. J.W. passed away during that year, but the quality and attention to detail found in his baskets were kept alive by Dave through the Longaberger Company®.

Each basket is hand woven, using hardwood maple splints. Since 1978 each basket has been dated and signed by the weaver upon completion. In 1982 the practice of burning the Longaberger name and logo into the bottom of each basket began, guaranteeing its authenticity as a Longaberger Basket®.

New baskets can be obtained only through sales consultants, usually at a basket home party. Collector and speciality baskets are available only for a limited time throughout the year. For example, the 1992 Christmas Collection Basket was offered only from September through December 1992. After this, the basket was no longer available from Longaberger®. Once an item is discontinued or retired, it can only be obtained on the secondary market.

This information is from *The Tenth Edition Bentley Collection Guide*, published in June 2002. See the Directory for ordering information or call 1-800-837-4394.

Advisor: Jill S. Rindfuss (See Directory, Longaberger Baskets)

Baskets

Note: Values are for baskets only, unless accessories such as liners and protectors are mentioned in the description. Sizes may vary as much as one-half inch. All dimensions are given in (length) x (width) x (height).

1979-93, Retired Mini Cradle™ (basket only), sm, rectangular, no color trim or weave, no handles, wood rockers, from $60 to..**$160.00**

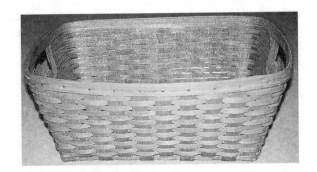

1979 – 1998, Retired Small Laundry™ (basket only), no color trim or weave, cut-out handles, produced with dark stain from 1979 to 1985, changed to 'classic' lighter stain 1986 – 1998, 10x24x17", from $127.00 to $250.00. (From the collection of Nancy McDaniels)

1983, JW Medium Market® (basket only), rectangular, blue weave & trim, 1 stationary handle, brass tag: Longaberger — JW Medium Market, from $1,257 to............**$1,777.00**
1984-90, Booking/Promo Candle™ (basket only), rectangular, no color trim or weave, 1 stationary handle, ⅜" weave, from $41 to **$65.00**
1987, Easter Signature Single Pie™ (basket only), sq, red, blue & green weave, 1 stationary handle; all have Dave Longaberger's signature, from $193 to ..**$300.00**
1988, Holiday Hostess Large Market™ (basket only), rectangular, red & green weave w/red or green trim, 1 stationary handle, from $119 to................................**$135.00**
1990-01, Heartland Bakery™ (basket only), rectangular, Hartland Blue shoestring weave, 2 leather ears, Heartland logo burned on bottom of basket, from $42 to **$55.00**
1990-92, Hostess Collection Remembrance™ (basket only), rectangular, no color trim or weave, 2 swinging handles, woven attached lid, from $125 to **$175.00**
1991, JW Corn® (basket only), round, blue trim & accent weave, 2 leather handles, brass tag: Longaberger - JW Corn, from $272 to **$450.00**

1991, Mother's Day Medium Purse™ (basket only), rectangular, pink trim & accent weave, 1 swinging handle, from $56 to...**$119.00**
1992, All-American Small Market™ (basket only), rectangular, red trim w/red & blue accent weave, 2 swinging handles, from $97 to..**$100.00**
1992, Father's Day Paper™ (basket only), rectangular, higher in the back than in the front, Dresden blue & burgundy trim, no handles, from $70 to **$95.00**
1993, All-Star Trio™ (w/liner & protector), rectangular, red & blue weave & trim, 2 leather ears, from $48 to ...**$80.00**
1993, Christmas Bayberry™ (basket only), sq, red or green trim & accent weave, 2 swinging handles, ⅜" weave, from $64 to..**$90.00**
1994, Bee Basket™ (basket only), rectangular, rose pink & purple weave, 1 swinging handle, brass tag: Celebrate Your Success - 1994 - Bee Basket, from $155 to..**$200.00**
1994, Boo™ (basket only), rectangular, orange & black weave & trim, 1 swinging handle, from $93 to..............**$135.00**
1994, Holiday Hostess Sleigh Bell™ (basket only), round top, rectangular bottom, red or green trim w/red & green accent weave, 2 swinging handles, from $182 to.........**$250.00**
1994, Shades of Autumn Recipe™ (basket only), rectangular w/higher back, green rust & deep blue weave w/rust trim, Woodcrafts lid, set of recipe cards included, from $66 to **$75.00**
1995, Horizon of Hope™ (basket only), rectangular, no color weave or trim, 1 stationary handle, American Cancer Society logo on bottom, from $75 to **$95.00**
1995, Sweetheart Sentiments™ (basket only), sq, red trim & shoestring accent weave, 1 swinging handle, from $46 to..**$70.00**
1995-97, Woven Traditions Spring® (basket only), sq, red, blue & green shoestring weave, 1 stationary handle, from $51 to...**$65.00**
1996, Employee Christmas Cracker™ (basket only), rectangular, red & green shoestring weave, no handles, from $65 to..**$95.00**
1997, Incentive $500 Million Celebration™ (basket only), rectangular, red & stained double trim, red accent weave, 2 swinging handles, brass tag, from $230 to................**$275.00**
1997, 20th Century - First Edition™ (basket only), rectangular, natural w/flag design, 1 swinging handle, brass tag: First Edition, from $64 to **$105.00**
1998, Collector's Club Harbor™ (basket only), rectangular, blue & green double trim & accent weave, 2 swinging handles from $98 to **$110.00**
1999, Lots of Luck™ (basket only), round, green chain link weave & trim,⅜" weave, 1 stationary handle, no tag, special burned-in logo, from $90 to............**$130.00**
1999, May Series Daisy™ (basket only), round, blue weave & trim, 1 swinging handle, ⅜" weave, board bottom, from $67 to...**$85.00**
1999, Traditions Generosity™ (basket only), oval, green trim & accent weave, 2 swinging handles, no box, brass tag, from $112 to...**$170.00**

2000, Autumn Reflections Small Harvest Blessings™ (basket only), rectangular, sage, brown & burgundy accent weave, 2 leather ears, from $56 to **$64.00**

2000, Cheers™ (basket only), oval, stained, periwinkle & purple double trim, 1 stationary handle, board bottom w/burned in logo, commemorative silver tag, from $61 to **$71.00**

2000, Feature October Fields™ (basket only), tall, round, no color trim or weave, 1 swinging handle, from $66 to **$90.00**

2001, Collectors Club Whistle Stop™ (basket only), tall, rectangular, blue trim, red shoestring weave, star-shaped tacks 1 swinging handle, w/box, commemorative tag, Collectors Club logo burned on bottom, from $100 to..........**$130.00**

2001, Special Events Inaugural™ (basket only), rectangular, blue trim w/pewter star studs, red shoestring accent weave, 1 swinging handle, from $44 to................**$50.00**

Miscellaneous

1990, Father Christmas Cookie Mold™ First Casting, brown pottery, inscription on back: Longaberger Pottery — First Casting - Christmas 1990, w/box, from $40 to ...**$60.00**

1990-91, Roseville Grandma Bonnie's Apple Pie Plate,™ pottery, blue accents, embossing on bottom: Roseville, Ohio, w/box, from $50 to **$65.00**

1992-95, Booking/Promo Potpourri Sachet™, Herbal Garden™ or Garden Splendor™ fabrics, from $13 to...............**$20.00**

1999, Fruit Medley Pottery - Pitcher,™ Vitrified China, hand-painted fruit designs, logo on bottom, w/box, from $99 to..**$175.00**

1999-01, Pottery Candy Corn Crock™, vitrified china, round, candy corn design, Longaberger Pottery emblem on bottom, w/box, from $22 to.................................**$36.00**

2002, Pottery Falling Leaves Vase™, vitrified china, round opening, butternut color w/sage lip, Longaberger Pottery emblem, w/box, from $45 to...............................**$80.00**

Lu Ray Pastels

This was one of Taylor, Smith, and Taylor's most popular lines of dinnerware. It was made from the late 1930s until sometime in the early 1950s in five pastel colors: Windsor Blue, Persian Cream, Sharon Pink, Surf Green, and Chatham Gray.

If you'd like more information, we recommend *Collector's Guide to Lu Ray Pastels* by Kathy and Bill Meehan (Collector Books).

Baker, vegetable; gray, oval, 9½" **$30.00**
Baker, vegetable; oval, 9½" **$20.00**
Bowl, '30s oatmeal..**$60.00**
Bowl, coupe soup; flat **$18.00**
Bowl, cream soup..**$70.00**
Bowl, fruit; Chatham Gray, 5"..**$16.00**
Bowl, fruit; 5" **$5.00**

Bowl, lug soup; tab handled **$24.00**
Bowl, mixing; 5½"..**$125.00**
Bowl, mixing; 10¼"...**$150.00**
Butter dish, gray, w/lid **$90.00**
Butter dish, w/lid **$50.00**
Cake plate **$70.00**
Calendar plates, 8", 9", 10", ea.....................................**$40.00**
Casserole, w/lid **$125.00**
Chocolate cup, AD; straight sides................................**$80.00**
Chocolate pot, AD; straight sides **$400.00**
Coaster/nut dish...**$65.00**
Coffee cup, AD **$20.00**
Coffeepot, AD..**$200.00**
Creamer, AD..**$40.00**
Creamer, individual (goes w/chocolate pot) **$92.00**
Cup/bowl, cream soup..**$70.00**
Egg cup, double; any color other than Chatham gray ...**$24.00**
Egg cup, double; gray **$30.00**
Epergne **$125.00**
Jug, water; footed **$125.00**
Muffin cover..**$125.00**
Muffin cover w/underplate **$145.00**
Nappy, vegetable; round, 8½"..**$20.00**
Pickle tray...**$28.00**
Pitcher, juice...**$200.00**
Pitcher, water; flat bottom, other than yellow...........**$125.00**
Pitcher, water; yellow, flat bottom **$95.00**
Plate, Chatham Gray, 9" **$16.00**
Plate, 6"...**$3.00**
Plate, 7"...**$12.00**
Plate, 8"...**$20.00**
Plate, 9"...**$10.00**
Plate, 10"..**$20.00**
Platter, 11½" **$20.00**
Platter, 13" **$24.00**
Relish dish, 4-part **$95.00**
Salt & pepper shakers, pr **$18.00**
Sauce boat **$28.00**
Sauce/gravy boat, w/fixed stand, any color but yellow .**$35.00**
Sauce/gravy boat, w/fixed stand, yellow....................**$22.50**
Saucer, AD coffee **$8.50**

Sugar bowl with lid, $15.00; creamer, from $8.00 to $10.00.

Saucer, chocolate $30.00
Saucer, cream soup............$28.00
Sugar bowl, AD; individual, w/lid (goes w/chocolate pot)..$92.00
Teacup $8.00
Teapot, curved spout............$125.00
Teapot, flat spout............$160.00
Tumbler, fruit juice $50.00
Tumbler, water............$80.00
Vase, bud............$400.00

Lunch Boxes

Character lunch boxes made of metal have been very collectible for several years, but now even those made of plastic and vinyl are coming into their own.

The first lunch box of this type ever produced featured Hopalong Cassidy. Made by the Aladdin company, it was constructed of steel and decorated with decals. But the first fully lithographed steel lunch box and matching thermos bottle was made a few years later (in 1953) by American Thermos. Roy Rogers was its featured character.

Since then hundreds have been made, and just as is true in other areas of character-related collectibles, the more desirable lunch boxes are those with easily recognizable, well-known subjects — western heroes; TV, Disney, and cartoon characters; and famous entertainers like the Bee Gees and the Beatles.

Values hinge on condition. Learn to grade your lunch boxes carefully. A grade of 'excellent' for metal boxes means that you will notice only very minor defects and less than normal wear. Plastic boxes may have a few scratches and some minor wear on the sides, but the graphics must be completely undamaged. Vinyls must retain their original shape; brass parts may be tarnished, and the hinge may show signs of beginning splits. If the box you're trying to evaluate is in any worse condition than we've described, to be realistic, you must cut these prices drastically. Values are given for boxes without matching thermoses, unless one is mentioned in the line. If you'd like to learn more, we recommend *Collector's Guide to Lunch Boxes* by Carole Bess White and L.M. White, and *Schroeder's Collectible Toys, Antique to Modern*, both published by Collector Books.

Note: Watch for reproductions marked 'China.'

Metal

Adam-12, 1972, VG............$35.00
Addams Family, 1974, EX $50.00
America on Parade, 1975, VG............$20.00
Annie, 1981, EX+ $28.00
Astronauts, 1969, VG+............$50.00
Back in '76, 1975, EX $45.00
Batman & Robin, 1966, w/thermos, NM............$200.00
Battlestar Galactica, 1978, w/thermos, EX $45.00
Bonanza, 1963, VG $85.00
Brady Bunch, 1970, w/thermos, EX............$125.00

Buccaneer, 1961, EX, $185.00.

Buck Rogers, 1979, EX............$35.00
Cable Car, 1962, dome top, NM $125.00
Cartoon Zoo Lunch Chest, 1962, EX............$175.00
Chitty-Chitty Bang-Bang, 1968, VG+............$75.00
Clash of the Titans, 1980, VG $20.00
Cracker Jack, 1979, EX $50.00
Davy Crockett, 1955, green rim, VG $75.00
Disney Express, 1979, EX............$20.00
Dr Dolittle, 1967, w/thermos, EX $95.00
Duchess, 1960, w/thermos, NM............$125.00
Dudley Do-Right, 1962, blue trim, NM............$1,000.00
Fall Guy, 1981, w/thermos, NM............$35.00
Family Affair, 1969, w/thermos, EX............$135.00
Flying Nun, 1968, EX............$60.00
Ghostland, 1977, EX............$50.00
Gremlins, 1984, w/thermos, M $40.00
Gun Smoke, 1959, EX............$150.00
Guns of Will Sonnett, 1968, EX............$100.00
Hair Bear Bunch, 1971, EX............$60.00
Happy Days, 1976, VG............$35.00
Hogan's Heroes, 1966, dome top, w/thermos, EX....$200.00
HR Pufnstuf, 1970, w/thermos, NM............$185.00
Jetsons, 1963, dome top, EX............$350.00
Land of the Giants, 1968, VG $75.00
Lawman, 1961, EX+............$100.00
Lidsville, 1971, w/thermos, from $100 to $125.00
Little House on the Prairie, 1978, w/thermos, NM....$100.00
Lone Ranger, 1954, VG............$100.00
Lone Ranger, 1980, VG............$20.00
Magic Kingdom, 1979, EX............$25.00
Marvel Super Heroes, 1976, EX............$45.00
Mod Tulip, 1962, dome top, EX............$100.00
Mork & Mindy, 1979, VG+............$30.00
Mr Merlin, 1981, VG $25.00
Muppet Babies, 1985, EX............$10.00
Paladin, 1960, w/thermos, NM $425.00
Partridge Family, 1971, w/thermos, EX............$50.00
Peanuts, 1973, EX............$25.00
Pete's Dragon, 1978, EX............$45.00
Play Ball, 1969, w/thermos, EX+............$35.00
Raggedy Ann & Andy, 1973, w/thermos, EX............$40.00
Road Runner, 1970, EX............$75.00
Ronald McDonald, 1982, w/thermos, M $40.00
Roy Rogers & Dale Evans Double R Bar Ranch, 1954, woodgrain rim, w/thermos, NM............$175.00

Scooby Doo, 1973, w/thermos, NM $175.00
Six Million Dollar Man, 1974, w/thermos, EX $55.00
Space: 1999, 1974, G $25.00
Sport Goofy, 1983, VG $20.00
Star Trek: The Motion Picture, 1979, EX+ $75.00
Strawberry Shortcake, 1980, w/thermos, EX...............$25.00
Super Friends, 1976, w/thermos, EX $50.00
Superman, 1978, w/thermos, EX $35.00
Tarzan, 1966, w/thermos, NM $150.00
Thundercats, 1985, w/thermos, EX............................$25.00
UFO, 1973, VG..$35.00
Voyage to the Bottom of the Sea, 1967, w/thermos,
    NM **$400.00**
Wagon Train, 1964, VG $60.00
Wild Bill Hickok & Jingles, NM................................$160.00
Woody Woodpecker, 1972, w/thermos, NM.............$200.00
Yankee Doodles, 1975, w/thermos, G $20.00

Plastic

Astrokids, 1988, w/thermos, M $25.00
Benji, 1974, EX...$15.00
Cabbage Patch Kids, 1983, yellow, w/thermos, EX $12.00
Dick Tracy, 1990, w/thermos, M $13.00
Disney School Bus, 1990, M $15.00
Dr Seuss, 1996, EX...$15.00
Hammerman, 1991, w/thermos, NM $30.00
Holly Hobbie, 1989, w/thermos, M $25.00
Hulk Hogan, 1989, EX...$10.00
Kermit the Frog, 1981, dome top, EX $25.00
Looney Tunes, 1988, purple, w/thermos, VG $10.00
Mickey Mouse & Donald Duck, 1984, w/thermos, EX ...$10.00
Mr T, 1984, orange, w/thermos, EX $20.00
Muppet Babies, 1986, w/thermos, EX......................$15.00
Pee Wee Herman, EX $15.00
Pink Panther (And Sons), 1984, EX.........................$10.00
Popeye & Sons, 1987, yellow, 3-D, M $35.00
Robot Man, 1984, EX..$15.00
Smurfs 1983, dome top, w/thermos, EX $20.00
Superman, 1986, dome top, EX..............................$25.00
Teenage Mutant Ninja Turtles, 1990, purple, w/thermos,
    M $10.00
Voltron, 1984, w/thermos, NM................................$15.00

Vinyl

Airport Control Tower, 1972, EX $150.00
Annie, 1981, EX $45.00
Barbarino, 1977, brunch bag, NM $125.00
Barbie & Francie, 1965, w/thermos, NM $200.00
Barbie & Midge, 1965, w/thermos, NM $200.00
California Raisins, 1988, EX..................................$20.00
Dawn, 1970, w/thermos, EX..................................$175.00
Donny & Marie, 1977, w/thermos, EX......................$110.00
Dudley Do-Right, 1972, railroad scene, w/thermos, NM...$475.00
Fess Parker Kaboodle Kit from the Daniel Boone TV Show,
    1964, NM $165.00

Jr Deb, 1960, EX...$100.00
Mardis Gras, 1971, floral, w/thermos, EX $60.00
Mary Poppins, 1973, VG $50.00
Peanuts, Snoopy at Mailbox, 1969, red, EX...............$60.00
Pepsi-Cola, 1980, yellow, EX $50.00
Psychedelic Blue, 1970, EX $75.00
Pussycats, 1968, w/thermos, NM............................$125.00
Ronald McDonald, 1988, lunch bag, EX $20.00
Roy Rogers, cream, w/thermos, NM $350.00
Sesame Street, yellow gingham, EX $25.00
Snoopy, 1977, brunch bag, w/bottle, EX...................$75.00
Soupy Sales, 1965, w/thermos, NM..........................$300.00
Strawberry Shortcake, 1980, checked design, VG.......$35.00
The Sophisticate, 1970, brunch bag, w/bottle, EX....$100.00
Tropicana Swim Club, 1980, EX $85.00
Twiggy, 1967, w/thermos, EX $175.00
Wizard in the Van, 1978, orange, VG+ $100.00
Wonder Woman, 1977, yellow, w/thermos, EX..........$85.00
World of Dr Seuss, 1970, w/thermos, NM $200.00
World Traveler, 1961, brunch bag, w/bottle, M $150.00

Alvin and the Chipmunks, 1963, with thermos, EX, $125.00. (Photo courtesy Joe Hilton and Greg Moore)

Thermoses

Values are given for thermoses made of metal unless noted otherwise.

ABC Wild World of Sports, 1976, 13", EX...................$35.00
Boating, 1959, EX $75.00
Campbell's Soups, 1968, EX $85.00
Casey Jones, 1960, EX..$100.00
Casper the Friendly Ghost, 1966, EX $95.00
CB'er, 1976, plastic, 12", M...................................$35.00
Davy Crockett, 1955, unused, M (EX box)...............$200.00
Dukes of Hazzard, 1980, plastic, VG+ $10.00
Fireball XL-5, EX...$50.00
Flintstones, 1964, EX $50.00
Fonz, 1976, NM+...$50.00
Greyhound, 1970, plastic/glass, EX $35.00
Hopalong Cassidy, 1950, EX+...............................$55.00
Jonathan Livingston Seagull, plastic, 1973, EX $15.00

Jr Miss, 1966, EX..$35.00
Kewtie Pie, 1964, M...$60.00
King Kong, 1977, plastic, EX+ $20.00
Lassie & Black Beauty (Pets & Pals), 1961, EX $25.00
Major League Baseball, 1968, M $50.00
NFL Quarterback, 1964, EX.............................$60.00
Osmonds, 1973, plastic, M $60.00
Outdoor Sports, 1960, EX................................$45.00
Peanuts, 1966, EX..$25.00
Peter Pan, 1976, plastic, EX $25.00
Play Ball, 1969, NM+ $75.00
Punky Brewster, 1985, plastic, EX $15.00
Satellite, 1958, EX $40.00
Secret Agent T, 1968, EX.................................$35.00
Spalding Tennis Balls, 1960s, 13", EX $45.00
Spider-Man/Incredible Hulk, 1983, plastic, EX...........$20.00
Street Hawk, 1984, plastic, EX.........................$35.00
Super Friends, 1976, plastic, EX $20.00
Superman, 1967, EX $75.00
Transformers, 1986, plastic, M $15.00
US Mail, 1969, for dome box, EX......................$25.00
Wild Bill Hickok & Jingles, 1955, EX................$50.00
Wonder Woman, 1977, plastic, EX.....................$35.00
Ziggy, 1979, plastic, EX....................................$35.00
Zorro, 1958, EX...$150.00

Maddux of California

Founded in Los Angeles in 1938, Maddux not only produced ceramics but imported and distributed them as well. They supplied chain stores nationwide with well-designed figural planters, TV lamps, novelty and giftware items, and during the mid-1960s their merchandise was listed in every major stamp catalog. Because of an increasing amount of foreign imports and an economic slowdown in our own country, the company was forced to sell out in 1976. Under the new management, manufacturing was abandoned, and the company was converted solely to distribution. Collectors have only recently discovered this line, and prices right now are affordable though increasing.

Ashtray, gunmetal gray, triangular, #731, 10½" $12.00
Bowl, console; oval free-form, 2x13x6¼", w/spread-wing 6" flamingo standing to 1 side................$70.00
Bowl, console; white oblong shell form, silver sticker, 3x14½".......................................$18.00
Bowl, vegetable; turquoise & white w/embossed swirls, w/lid, #3066B, 4½x7¾" $20.00
Bowl, white w/embossed sqs & circles of different sizes along rim, #3093, 2x5½"..........$16.00
Candy/nut bowl, green to blue, center ring handle, #3251S USA, 1½x6¼" $8.00
Figurine, flamingo, head down, wings spread, 1940s, 8"................................$75.00
Figurine, flamingo, neck curled, #305, copyright 1959, 9½"..................................$65.00

Figurine, flamingo, wings up, 13¼" $95.00
Planter, brown striped look, 4½x6½"................$6.00
Planter, gazelle, #0542, 9¾"...........................$35.00
Planter, gold-plated metal around sides, rectangular, #506 ..$7.50
Planter, spread-wing flamingo over grassy receptacle, #358, rare, 11" $225.00
Planter, stag jumping log (planter), contains flower frog, EX details to legs & horns, #518 ....$60.00
Planter, swan ea side, taupe, 4x9½x3¾" $25.00

TV lamp, basset hound, $140.00.
(Photo Lee Garmon)

TV lamp, couple dancing, #8008..................$75.00
TV lamp, doe & fawn running, 11x10¼".........$55.00
TV lamp, ducks, #0835, 8½x10" $65.00
TV lamp, gold-tone metal center w/black planter ea side, #0107W...............................$35.00
TV lamp, horse, #0858, 13x11x6½"..................$70.00
TV lamp, orange w/red panel, #8019, 9x9½".............$30.00
TV lamp, Prairie Schooner (covered wagon), #0844, 11"..$30.00
TV lamp, quail (3), #8016, 11½x9½" $70.00
TV lamp, Siamese cat, original Underwriters label, 12½"................................$125.00
TV lamp, swan planter, white porcelain, #0828, 12½"....$45.00
TV lamp, swans (2), #0825, 10x11½"..........$45.00
Vase, deer heads decor, pink, #0226..........$22.00
Vase/planter, flamingos back-to-back figural, ca 1950, 5" .$60.00
Wall pocket, bird in metal holder (resembles cage), 7x7" cage.......................................$35.00

Magazines

There are numerous magazines around today, but unless they're in fine condition (clean, no missing or clipped pages, and very little other damage); have interesting features (cover illustrations, good advertising, or special-interest stories); or deal with sports greats, famous entertainers, or world-renowned personalities, they're worth very little. Issues printed prior to 1950 generally have value, and pre-1900 examples are now considered antique paper. Address labels on the fronts are acceptable, but if your magazine has one, follow these guidelines. Subtract 5% to 10% when the label is not intruding on the face of the cover. Deduct 20% if the label is on the face of an important cover and 30% to 40% if on the face of an important illustrator cover, thus ruining framing quality. If you find a magazine with no label, it will be worth about 25% more than one in about the same condition but having a label. For further information see *The Masters Price & Identification Guide to Old Magazines* (5th edition now available); *Life Magazines, 1898 to 1994; Saturday Evening Post, 1899 – 1965;* and several other up-to-the-minute guides covering specific magazine titles — all by our advisor Denis C. Jackson. See also TV Guides.

Advisors: Denis C. Jackson; Don Smith, Rare National Geographics (See Directory, Magazines)

Newsletter: *The Illustrator Collector's New*
(Sample issue: $3.50; Subscription $18.00 per year in U.S.)
Denis C. Jackson, Editor
P.O. Box 1958
Sequim, WA 98382
www.olypen.com/ticn; e-mail: ticn@olypen.com

American Blacksmith, 1917, January, VG.....................$28.00
American Home, 1946, June, VG.....................$20.00
American Nudist Leader, 1956, June, EX.....................$25.00
Arizona Highways, 1980, December, VG.....................$3.00
Avant Garde, 1968, January, VG+.....................$100.00
Avant Garde, 1969, January, EX.....................$30.00
Breeder's Gazette, 1915, February 15, Shorthorn Cow named Buttercup 64th, VG+.....................$14.00
Cabaret, 1956, August, Jane Mansfield, VG+ $55.00
Case & Comment, 1987, January/February-November/ December, VG, ea.....................$5.00
Collier's, 1943, March 13, The Navy of the Future, EX...$40.00
Commentator, 1938, January, VG+ $25.00
Coronet, 1945, August, VG+ $18.00
Cosmopolitan, 1916, July, On Summer Seas cover by Harrison Fisher, VG+.....................$120.00
Cosmopolitan, 1924, July, G $60.00
Cosmopolitan, 1977, August, Arnold Schwarzenegger nude center fold, EX $35.00
Cosmopolitan, 1990, May, Madonna, EX $25.00
Creem, 1970, May, Ted Nugent, VG.....................$80.00
Cue, 1956, August, Walt Kelly & Pogo, VG $80.00
Datebook, 1959, September, Tab Hunter, VG $50.00
Ebony, 1952, March, VG.....................$55.00
Elle, 1996, July, Meg Ryan, EX $22.00
Esquire, 1944, February, VG $50.00
Farmer's Almanac, 1913, VG.....................$9.00
Field & Stream, 1910, January, VG.....................$60.00
Forest & Stream, 1918, May, VG.....................$30.00
Fortune, 1930, December, VG+ $60.00
Fortune, 1930, February, 1st issue, EX.....................$75.00
Fortune, 1930, September, Skyscrapers, EX.............$68.00
Fortune, 1931, April, VG+ $60.00
Fortune, 1937, February, VG.....................$33.00

Fortune, 1937, May, VG+ $15.00
Fortune, 1938, January, VG+.....................$16.00
Glamour, 1961, November, Anne deZagheb, EX........$30.00
Glamour, 1972, November, Liz O'Brien, EX $35.00
Golf, 1959, April, 1st issue, M.....................$180.00
Hardware Ages, 1925, October 22, VG.....................$18.00
Harper's Magazine, 1951, May, VG+ $9.00
Hobbies, 1957, September, Mechanical Banks, VG+ ..$12.00
Hollywood, 1941, December, Clarke Gable, VG+.......$60.00
Hollywood, 1941, May, Hedy Lamarr, VG+.....................$55.00
Hop Up, 1952, May, Custom Ford, VG $10.00
Hot Rod, 1949, April, VG $52.00
Hot Rod, 1949, July, VG.....................$50.00
Hot Rod, 1950, January, VG.....................$80.00
House Beautiful, 1911, June, VG+.....................$15.00
Hunting & Fishing, 1927, January, bull elk on cover, VG+ ..$20.00
Hunting & Fishing, 1928, May, EX.....................$15.00
Hunting & Fishing, 1931, July, EX.....................$18.00
Judge Magazine, 1920, September 4, humor, VG........$14.00
Junior Home, 1930, April, G $18.00
Kirkeby Hotels, 1949, June, EX $22.00
Ladies' Magazine, 1830, October, VG+ $100.00
Life, 1937, January 18, Henry & Edsel Ford, EX $20.00
Life, 1937, May 3, Jean Harlow, EX.....................$40.00
Life, 1937, November 22, VG.....................$18.00
Life, 1938, February 7, Gary Cooper, VG+ $20.00
Life, 1939, November 13, Claudette Colbert, EX........$18.00
Life, 1940, September 2, Dionne's Communion, VG ..$20.00
Life, 1940, September 30, Wendell Willkie, VG..........$20.00
Life, 1942, April 17, Nelson Rockefeller, VG $18.00
Life, 1942, July 4, United We Stand, EX.....................$28.00
Life, 1942, June 22, War Stamp Bride, VG.....................$15.00
Life, 1943, July 12, Roy Rogers & Trigger, VG.............$50.00
Life, 1945, December 17, Paulette Goddard, VG $20.00
Life, 1946, April 8, Barnum & Bailey Circus, VG $20.00
Life, 1946, December 28, Metropolitan Opera Ballet, EX..$40.00
Life, 1946, February 18, Dorothy McQuire, VG.....................$20.00
Life, 1946, January 21, Cardinal Spellman, VG.....................$20.00
Life, 1947, March 31, Spring Hat in Color, EX.....................$25.00
Life, 1952, September 1, Ernest Hemingway, VG........$35.00
Life, 1953, April 20, Marlon Brando as Antony in Julius Caesar, VG $30.00
Life, 1953, December 7, Audrey Heburn, EX $30.00
Life, 1953, November 30, Creatures of the Sea, EX $25.00
Life, 1954, November 1, Dorothy Dandridge, VG.......$75.00
Life, 1955, April 11, Grace Kelly, EX.....................$50.00
Life, 1955, August 8, Ben Hogan Tells His Secret, VG..$150.00
Life, 1955, January 10, The Great Garbo, VG.............$30.00
Life, 1956, August 27, Adlai Stevenson & Mrs Roosevelt, VG $50.00
Life, 1956, June 25, The Remarkable Mickey Mantle, VG $150.00
Life, 1956, March 26, Julie Andrews, EX.....................$25.00
Life, 1957, March 11, Senator Kennedy, VG.............$40.00
Life, 1958, April 7, Sugar Ray Beats Bisilio, VG $30.00
Life, 1959, April 20, Marilyn Monroe, VG $75.00
Life, 1961, September 1, Jackie Kennedy, EX.............$18.00

Life, 1965, (Mickey) Mantle's Misery, EX, $55.00.

Life, 1971, September 10, First 25 Years of Television, VG+ $9.00

Life, 1972, December 29, Special Double Issue, The Year in Pictures, VG...$16.00

Life, 1988, Spring, Special Issue, The Dream Then & Now, Martin Luther King, VG+ $9.00

Literary Digest, 1021, October 1, VG $20.00

Look, 1939, July 18, Vivien Leigh on cover, G............$40.00

Look, 1941, January 14, President Roosevelt, VG+ $20.00

Look, 1946, October, Ted Williams on cover, G..............$40.00

Look, 1950, August 29, Hopalong Cassidy on cover, G .$40.00

Look, 1952, April 9, Marilyn Monroe on cover, G $35.00

Look, 1952, March 25, VG...$9.00

Look, 1955, March 31, Kim Novak on cover, VG..........$9.00

Look, 1956, February 7, G...$9.00

Look, 1961, March 14, Ingrid Bergman on cover, VG ...$7.00

Look, 1961, October 10, Perry Mason on cover, VG ..$10.00

Look, 1967, November 28, Vietnam article by Robert F Kennedy $12.00

Look, 1968, December 9, John Lennon cover by Avedon, pull-out portfolio of all 4 Beatles, EX $50.00

Look, 1969, December 16, Princess Grace at 40 on cover, G...$47.00

Los Angeles, 1977, April, Farrah Faucett, EX..............$55.00

Low Rider, 1980, March, NM.......................................$55.00

Low Rider, 1981, October, NM....................................$60.00

Mad Magazine, 1956, July, VG...................................$105.00

Mad Magazine, 1957, October, #35, VG......................$45.00

Mad Magazine, 1960, October, NM $25.00

Mad Magazine, 1971, July, Buy It...or Leave It!, EX....$22.00

Mad Magazine, 1974, September, EX $23.00

Mad Magazine, 1976, July, Arbor Day Special, Alfred E Neuman cover, EX...$22.00

Mademoiselle, 1950, May, VG+.................................$50.00

McCall's Needlework & Crafts, 1971, Spring/Summer, VG..$9.00

Mechanix Illustrated, 1941, May, EX $25.00

Motor Age, 1926, January, G..$70.00

Motor Boating magazine, 1921, February, VG.............$90.00

Movie Thrills, 1950, July, Hopalong Cassidy, EX $60.00

National Geographic, 1905, August, VG $68.00

National Geographic, 1908, November, VG.................$50.00

National Geographic, 1915-16, ea $15.00

National Geographic, 1917-24, ea $9.00

National Geographic, 1925-29, ea $8.00

National Geographic, 1930-45, ea $7.00

National Geographic, 1946-55, ea $6.00

National Geographic, 1956-67, ea $5.50

National Geographic, 1968-89, ea $4.50

National Geographic, 1990-present, ea $2.00

New Yorker, 1932, January 2, G.................................$105.00

New Yorker, 1934, December 15, VG+ $60.00

New Yorker, 1934, June 2, EX......................................$80.00

New Yorker, 1942, June 13, VG....................................$60.00

New Yorker, 1948, March 20, VG $85.00

People Magazine, 1978, August 21, The Elvis Legend, EX..$18.00

People Magazine, 1986, September 29, Bobby Is Back, And Here's How Dallas Did It!, EX $9.00

PIC, 1942, April 28, Veronica Lake, VG $60.00

Playboy, 1955, September, VG+ $55.00

Playboy, 1957, March, Sandra Edwards, EX $175.00

Playboy, 1957, November, Betty Blue, EX................$150.00

Playboy, 2956, December, Third Anniversary Issue, Lisa Winters, VG..$55.00

Police Gazette, 1947, December, Ester Williams, EX ..$18.00

Police Gazette, 1963, July, Judy Garland/Castro cover, EX.$18.00

Popular Mechanics, 1947, April, G+ $20.00

Radio News, 1942, November, Special US Army Signal Corps Issue, EX...$16.00

Radio News, 1943, June, VG..$20.00

Radio News, 1944, November, VG $13.00

Rolling Stone, 1967, November 9, 1st issue, John Lennon, VG...$110.00

Rolling Stone, 1968, April, Beatles, VG+.....................$68.00

Rolling Stone, 1968, May 25, Johnny Cash, VG+ $80.00

Rolling Stone, 1987, November, 20th Anniversary, EX...$20.00

Rolling Stone, 1994, June 2, Kurt Cobain, EX $30.00

Rolling Stones, 1984, June 7, Dennis Wilson, EX........$25.00

Saturday Evening Post, 1940, January 2, Robert E Lee cover, VG...$20.00

Saturday Evening Post, 1943, July 3, flags on cover, EX..$20.00

Saturday Evening Post, 1947, November 1, John Falter cover of football game, VG...$20.00

Screen Album, 1944, Fall, Betty Grable, VG+..............$65.00

See, 1955, July, Marilyn Monroe, EX...........................$60.00

Seventeen, 1955, March, VG $55.00

Son of Mad (Magazine), 1964, March, VG...................$20.00

Sport, 1960, August, Mickey Mantle, EX $65.00

Sports Car Magazine, 1983, November, Road America Cup Review, VG+...$8.00

Sports Illustrated, 1954, August 10, Girl in the Surf, EX .$30.00

Sports Illustrated, 1957, March 18, Ted Linsey & Gordie Howe, VG+ $50.00

Sports Illustrated, 1997, April 27, Tiger Woods, EX $12.00

Stage, 1938, February, Grumpy (Snow White) on cover, EX..$60.00

Suffragist, 1917, January 31, New York Pickets at the White House Gate, VG **$95.00**

Sunshine & Health, 1950, December, NM **$25.00**

Teen Screen, 1966, August, EX **$12.00**

Thrasher, 1989, November, Vol 9, #11, EX **$35.00**

Time, 1968, September 13, Beatles, VG+ **$60.00**

Time, 1973, June 11, Super Horse Secretariat, VG **$90.00**

Time, 1975, October, Bruce Springsteen, VG+ **$60.00**

Time, 1987, April, U2, NM **$70.00**

True Crime, 1941, November 1, G **$18.00**

Trump, 1957, January, VG **$65.00**

TV Stage, 1956, October, Honeymooners, EX **$55.00**

Vette Magazine, 1985, May, EX **$40.00**

Vogue, 1947, April 1, VG **$50.00**

Vogue, 1981, November, EX **$35.00**

Vogue, 1990, August, Claudia Schiffer, EX **$25.00**

Western Trucking, 1954, October, VG **$65.00**

Woman's Day, 1964, August, 12-page Bonus Book on Victorian Art Glass, EX **$15.00**

Youth's Companion, 1890, May 22, VG **$12.00**

Pulp Magazines

As early as the turn of the century, pulp magazines were beginning to appear, but by the 1930s, their popularity had literally exploded. Called pulps because of the cheap wood-pulp paper they were printed on, crime and detective stories, westerns, adventure tales, and mysteries were the order of the day. Crime pulps sold for as little as 10¢; some of the westerns were 15¢. Plots were imaginative and spicy, if not downright risque. The top three publishers were Street and Smith, Popular, and the Thrilling Group. Some of the more familiar pulp-magazine authors were Agatha Christy, Clarence E. Mulford, Erle Stanley Gardner, Ellery Queen, Edgar Rice Burroughs, Louis L'Amour, and Max Brand. Until the 1950s when slick-paper magazines signed their death warrant, they were published by the thousands. Because of the poor quality of their paper, many have not survived. Those that have are seldom rated better than very good. A near-mint to mint example will bring a premium price, since it is almost impossible to locate one so well preserved. Except for a few very rare editions, many are in the average price range suggested below — some much lower.

Amazing Stories, 1926, September, VG **$75.00**

Amazing Stories, 1929, January, EX **$325.00**

Amazing Stories, 1929, May, VG+ **$125.00**

Amazing Stories, 1938, November, VG **$30.00**

Amazing Stories, 1949, January, VG **$25.00**

Astounding Science-Fiction, 1934, May, VG **$25.00**

Astounding Stories, 1940, July, VG+ **$30.00**

Dime Mystery, 1935, March, VG **$195.00**

Dime Mystery, 1937, April, VG+ **$80.00**

Dime Mystery, 1940, October, G **$45.00**

Doc Savage, 1938, December, VG+ **$63.00**

Famous Fantastic Mysteries, 1940, December, VG **$20.00**

Famous Fantastic Mysteries, 1948, July, VG+ **$25.00**

Fantastic Adventures, 1950, May, VG **$25.00**

Fantastic Novels, 1948, September, EX **$25.00**

Fantastic Story, 1950, Spring, EX **$25.00**

Fortune, 1940, October, VG+ **$63.00**

Future Science Fiction, 1953, November, VG+ **$25.00**

Home & Field, 1933, September, VG+ **$20.00**

Horror Stories, 1936, February, VG **$125.00**

Marvel Science Stories, 1938, August, Vol 1, #1, VG ...**$85.00**

Planet Stories, 1952, July, VG **$35.00**

Science Fiction Quarterly, 1954, May, VG **$35.00**

Shadow, 1938, December, EX **$100.00**

Shadow, 1940, December 15, EX **$125.00**

Shadow, 1940, January 1, EX **$200.00**

Spicy Adventure Stories, 1936, July, VG **$400.00**

Spicy Stories, 1933, July, VG **$60.00**

Startling Stories, 1939, September, VG+ **$50.00**

Startling Stories, 1946, Winter, VG- **$25.00**

Startling Stories, 1950, January, Schomburg robot, VG **$100.00**

Super Science Novels, 1949, July, VG **$30.00**

Thrilling Wonder Stories, 1937, October, VG **$25.00**

Thrilling Wonder Stories, 1951, December, VG **$25.00**

Unknown, 1939, December, VG **$50.00**

Weird Tales, 1928, June, G **$80.00**

Weird Tales, 1943, September, EX **$45.00**

Weird Wales, 1950, September, VG+ **$25.00**

Wonder Stories, 1935, September, G+ **$20.00**

Marbles

There are three broad categories of collectible marbles, the antique variety, machine-made, and contemporary. Under those broad divisions are many classifications. Everett Grist delves into all three categories in his books called *Big Book of Marbles, Antique and Collectible Marbles,* and *Machine Made and Contemporary Marbles* (Collector Books).

Sulfide marbles have figures (generally animals or birds) encased in the center. The glass is nearly always clear; a common example in excellent condition may run as low as $100.00, while those with an unusual subject or made of colored glass may go for more than $1,000.00. Many machine-made marbles are very reasonable, but if the colors are especially well placed and selected, good examples sell in excess of $50.00. Peltier comic character marbles often bring prices of $100.00 and up with Betty Boop, Moon Mullins, and Kayo being the rarest and most valuable (in that order). (They'll sell for $250.00 to $350.00 each.) Watch for reproductions. New comic character marbles have the design printed on a large area of plain white glass with color swirled through the back and sides.

No matter where your interests lie, remember that condition is extremely important. From the nature of their use, mint-condition marbles are very rare and may be worth as much as three to five times more than one that is near-mint. Chipped and cracked marbles may be worth half or less, and some will be worthless. Polishing detracts considerably.

When no size is given, assume our values are for average-size marbles from ½" to 1" in excellent condition.

See also Akro Agate.

Blue oxblood **$175.00**
Christensen Agate, blue slag.....................**$25.00**
Christensen Agate, flame, from $175 to.....**$250.00**
Christensen Agate, green slag, sm..........**$20.00**
Christensen Agate, guinea, from $275 to.........**$350.00**
Christensen Agate, hurricane, from $175 to **$225.00**

Christensen Agate, slags, MIB, $1,250.00. (Photo courtesy Everett Grist/Brian Estepp)

Christensen Agate, striped opaque, from $275 to.....**$300.00**
Clay, common type, ⅝".................................**$.50**
Diaper folds, black, orange & brown opaque swirls, ¾".**$150.00**
Iridescent glass (aka carnival glass), ea ....**$.05**
Limeade corkscrew.....................................**$30.00**
Master Made, sunburst................................**$10.00**
Moss agate, sm...**$1.50**
Mustard & Ketchup, yellow & white & red swirls, sm.**$100.00**
Orange peel, black opaque w/orange & yellow triangular patch, ⅝".......................................**$250.00**
Peltier, Bimbo **$100.00**
Peltier, Kayo...**$350.00**
Peltier, Liberty, red, white & blue **$80.00**
Peltier, Skeezix...**$100.00**
Rocket, translucent black & orange swirl, ¹¹⁄₁₆".........**$200.00**
Slag, orange & white, ⅝"............................**$60.00**
Slag, red & white on crystal base, ⅝".........**$30.00**
Solid color, sm, used for Chinese Checker game, ea......**$.05**
Submarine, cobalt, white & brown swirls.........**$175.00**
Sulfide, bear, 1¾"......................................**$175.00**
Sulfide, pig, 1¾" **$175.00**
Sulfide, pony, 1¾" **$200.00**
Sulfide, rabbit, EX detail, 1¾"....................**$250.00**
Superman (watch for reproductions), sm.........**$225.00**

Match Safes

Match safes or vesta boxes, as they are known in England, evolved to keep matches dry and to protect an individual from unintentional ignition. These containers were produced in enormous quantities over a 75-year period from various materials including silver, brass, aluminum, and gold. Their shapes and designs were limitless and resulted in a wide variety of popular and whimsical styles. They have become very sought-after collectibles and can usually be recognized by a small, rough striking surface, usually on the bottom edge. Collectors should be cautious of numerous sterling reproductions currently on the market. Prices are for examples in excellent condition.

Advisor: George Sparacio (See Directory, Match Safes)

Club: International Match Safe Association
PO Bo x791
Malaga, NJ 08328
Website: www.matchsafe.org
e-mail: imsaoc@aol.com @aol.com

Anheuser-Busch refrigerated rail car, '20,000 car loads,' nickel-plated brass, 3x1½" **$275.00**
Banded agate, orange/red color, rounded end, flat top, brass trim, 2¾x1⅛".....................................**$75.00**
Burt Machine Co, celluloid wrapped, black & white graphics, nickel-plated ends, Whitehead & Hoag, 2⅞x1½".**$175.00**
Cawston Ostrich Farm, multicolor celluloid wrap, nickel-plated brass ends, Whitehead & Hoag, 2¾x1½"......**$225.00**
Cherubs, 9 faces along edge, sterling w/gold wash inside, Unger Bros, catalog #7568, 2¾x1¾" **$375.00**
Cigars, bunch of 10, nickel-plated brass figural, 2¾x1½" ...**$195.00**
Clown, seated, lg nose, single hair curl on head, brass figural, 2½x1⅜" **$400.00**
Coffeepot shape, brass, 1⅞x1¾" **$150.00**
Columbian World's Fair, Columbus & Jefferson, Chicago World's Fair 1893 on disk, oval cross section, nickel-plated brass **$110.00**
Erotica, couple in intimate embrace, automata type, nickel plated, 2½x1½".....................................**$3,500.00**
Fish motif, sterling, Gorham Mfg Co, catalog #340, 2¾x1½"...**$350.00**
Fishing motif, fishermen catching trout, insert type, August Goertz Co, 2¾x1½"...............................**$585.00**
Frog w/bulging eyes, brass figural, Japanese, 2¾x1¾"..**$395.00**
Hobo shoe shape, advertising on sole, aluminum, Western Aluminum Co, 3x1⅜"...............................**$75.00**
Home Insurance/3-horse fire engine, sterling, William Kerr, 2½x1⅜" **$550.00**
Hunting dog w/duck in mouth, silver plate, Pairpoint Mfg, catalog #5006 ....**$115.00**
Karlsbad souvenir, steel w/inlaid stone top, 2⅛x¾x¾" ..**$150.00**
Kidney shaped w/sea life motif, sterling, Whiting Mfg, catalog #2337, 2¾x1⅜" **$375.00**
King George V & Queen Mary commemorative, book shape, vulcanite, Hamburg Rubber Co, 2x1½"................**$75.00**
Knight in armor/castle motif, sterling, 2½x1⅜" **$195.00**
Lady of the Light, Palace of Machinery, 1904 World's Fair, brass, 2¾x1½"...**$165.00**
Leg w/leather wrap, figural, brass-plated ends, Goliasch & Co, 2¼x1⅛"...**$140.00**
Morgan Tires, gutta percha, slip top lid, 2¾x1⅜".......**$55.00**
Mr Punch, brass figural, hand holding vesta socket, 2⅜x1½"...**$165.00**

Owl on branch, brass figural, 2¼x1¼" **$175.00**

Pillar postal box w/bone vesta socket on top, Bryant & May, Victoria Regina postal rates, litho tin, 2⅝x1¾".....**$65.00**

Quincy Rock Mine, Copper Country Souvenir, copper, 2⅝x1½" **$165.00**

Risque motif on lid & inside lid, enamel on brass, French, 1⅞x1½" **$375.00**

Saddle, polo mallet & bridle motif, silver plate, 2½x1½" ..**$275.00**

Security Rod Co, Uncle Sam, celluloid wrapped, brown graphics, Whitehead & Hoag, 2¾x1½" **$225.00**

Serpent w/red glass eye wrapped around body of safe, sterling, Carter, Gough & Co, 2⅝x1½" **$395.00**

Shoe w/cigar cutter attached to lid, nickel-plated brass figural, 2¾x¾" **$95.00**

Shriners of North America motif, star set w/garnet, sterling, Fairchild, 2⅜x1⅝" **$175.00**

Sorrento ware, wood w/inlaid decoration of lady, 2¾x1½" **$95.00**

Suitcase, nickel-plated brass figural, 1⅜x1⅞" **$175.00**

Swimmers in wave, sterling, Kerr, catalog #941, 2¾x1⅞" ..**$450.00**

Temptation of St Anthony, sterling, Wm Kerr Co, 3x1¾" ..**$795.00**

Three of a Kind w/2 donkeys, hidden dice compartment, nickel-plated brass, 1⅜x2⅞" **$120.00**

Wild boar head/whistle combo, brass figural, 3¾x1½" ...**$495.00**

Max, Peter

Born in Germany in 1937, Peter Max came to the United States in 1953 where he later studied art in New York City. His work is colorful and his genre psychedelic. He is a prolific artist, best known for his designs from the '60s and '70s that typified the 'hippie' movement. In addition to his artwork, he has also designed housewares, clothing, toys, linens, etc. In the 1970s, commissioned by Iroquois China, he developed several lines of dinnerware in his own distinctive style. Today, many of those who were the youth of the hippie generation are active collectors of his work.

Alarm clock, yellow Clock on orange, General Electric, 1960s, 7x5½x4½", NM.......................................**$60.00**

Ashtray, brown butterfly-like graphics, ceramic, 10" dia, EX...**$50.00**

Belt, button-chain; bright pink stars on silver botton linked by silver ring, 14 1¾" litho-tin buttons, 31" overall, ...**$300.00**

Book, memories; flowers w/sun above Memories graphics, 1960, 8¼x10½", NM...**$18.00**

Book, Paper Airplane, 33 designs to cut out & fold, 1971, EX...**$18.00**

Book, Peter Max Paints America, hardback, padded covers, 11x8½", EX...**$150.00**

Book, Peter Max Retrospektive 1963-93, soft cover, 131 pages, M **$85.00**

Bowl, green checkerboard w/red & blue border, 1¾x7" **$35.00**

Bowl, white w/green butterfly-like graphics, Iroquois, 7" **$35.00**

Calendar print, Hula Festival, Scott Converting Paper, 14x8½", EX...**$30.00**

Catalog, Girl Scout Equipment, Fall 1970, 24 pages ..**$28.00**

Mug, white w/blue butterfly-like graphics, Iroquois, 4½" **$40.00**

Patch, multicolored graphics, 1972, MIP.....................**$30.00**

Pillow, Hello & smiling teeth on gray, inflatable, 1960s, 16x16" **$35.00**

Pillow, profile of 2 faces against black & white stars & stripes, vinyl blow-up, 16x16", NM **$35.00**

Pillowcase, Love w/head above V, 1970s, 42x36", EX...**$45.00**

Pin-back, postage stamp replica, 1¼x1⅝" **$12.00**

Pin-back, Statue of Liberty graphics, 1981, 3x2" **$80.00**

Plaque, Brown Lady, porcelain, framed, 13x16" **$135.00**

Plate, purple & white checkerboard w/yellow, blue & red border, Iroquois, 10"..**$35.00**

Postcard, John Lennon, from Beatle's Yellow Submarine movie, 1968, 14x10¼" **$310.00**

Poster, Outer Space, 36x22⅞", NM+ **$165.00**

Print, Cosmic Windows, #22/75, original, 26x36", minimum value **$640.00**

Program, 1995 Grammys, NM.....................................**$50.00**

Puzzle, jigsaw; Better World, person standing w/umbrella, 550 pcs, MIB **$14.00**

Replica, Dale Earnhardt's #3 Goodwrench Service Plus Pit Wagon, 1/16 scale, Action, MIB **$110.00**

Stationery, multicolored cloud-like balloons on light pink, sun w/rainbow-colored rays on box, 20 pcs, 1970s, MIB..**$38.00**

Teakettle, gray w/4 graphic flower-like oval panels, graniteware, 8½", EX...**$100.00**

Tie, purple & white stars on light blue, Italian, B Forman Co import, silk, M...**$110.00**

Tray, Mechanical Man, 13" dia, EX w/original paper label ..**$55.00**

Tray, serving; metal, 13", NM, from $50.00 to $65.00.

Wristwatch, clouds w/sun & rays, multicolored, Save the Rain Forest on band, 1988, EX....................................**$70.00**

McCoy Pottery

This is probably the best known of all American potteries, due to the wide variety of goods they produced from 1910 until the pottery finally closed only a few years ago.

They were located in Roseville, Ohio, the pottery center of the United States. They're most famous for their cookie jars, of which were made several hundred styles and variations. (For a listing of these, see the section entitled Cookie Jars.) McCoy is also well known for their figural planters, novelty kitchenware, and dinnerware.

They used a variety of marks over the years, but with little consistency, since it was a common practice to discontinue an item for awhile and then bring it out again decorated in a manner that would be in sync with current tastes. All of McCoy's marks were 'in the mold.' None were ink stamped, so very often the in-mold mark remained as it was when the mold was originally created. Most marks contain the McCoy name, though some of the early pieces were simply signed 'NM' for Nelson McCoy (Sanitary and Stoneware Company, the company's original title). Early stoneware pieces were sometimes impressed with a shield containing a number. If you have a piece with the Lancaster Colony Company mark (three curved lines — the left one beginning as a vertical and terminating as a horizontal, the other two formed as 'C's contained in the curve of the first), you'll know that your piece was made after the mid-'70s when McCoy was owned by that group. Today even these later pieces are becoming collectible.

If you'd like to learn more about this company, we recommend *The Collector's Encyclopedia of McCoy Pottery* and *The Collector's Encyclopedia of Brush-McCoy Pottery*, both by Sharon and Bob Huxford; and *McCoy Pottery, Collector's Reference & Value Guide, Volumes 1, 2 & 3,* by Bob and Margaret Hanson and Craig Nissen. All are published by Collector Books.

A note regarding cookie jars: Beware of *new* cookie jars marked McCoy. It seems that the original McCoy pottery never registered their trademark, and for several years it was legally used by a small company in Rockwood, Tennessee. Not only did they use the original mark, but they reproduced some of the original jars as well. If you're not an experienced collector, you may have trouble distinguishing the new from the old. Some (but not all) are dated #93, the '#' one last attempt to fool the novice, but there are differences to watch for. The new ones are slightly smaller in size, and the finish is often flawed. He has also used the McCoy mark on jars never produced by the original company, such as Little Red Riding Hood and the Luzianne mammy. Eventually it became known that the last owners of the McCoy pottery actually did register the trademark; so, having to drop McCoy, he has since worked his way through two other marks: Brush-McCoy and (currently) BJ Hull.

See Also Cookie Jars.

Advisor: Bob Hanson

Newsletter: *NM Xpress*
Carol Seman, Editor
8934 Brecksville Rd., #406, Brecksville, OH 44141
440-526-2094 (voice and fax)
e-mail: McCjs@aol.com; http://members.aol.com/nmXpress

Basket, embossed foliage on white matt, 3 holes at rim for hanging, unmarked, 1930s, 5", from $40 to.........**$60.00**
Bookends, horse, white w/gold trim, unmarked, 8", pr, from $125 to................**$150.00**
Bookends, Lily, green w/decor, 1948, 5½x5", from $125 to................**$150.00**
Candy dish, gondola, Sunburst Gold, marked, 3½x11½", from $50 to................**$60.00**
Cornucopia planter, made in a variety of colors, marked, 1940s, 4", from $30 to................**$35.00**
Dog dish, Dog embossed on green or maroon, marked, 5", from $70 to................**$90.00**
Ferner, Hobnail, pastel, NM mark, 8¼", from $30 to..**$40.00**
Figurine, donkey, glossy, unmarked, 1940s, 7", from $25 to................**$30.00**
Flower bowl ornament, peacock, creamy white, unmarked, 4¾", from $100 to................**$125.00**
Flower holder, cornucopia, Sunburst Gold, NM mark, from $35 to................**$50.00**
Flower holder, frog, green, NM mark, 1940s, 3⅛", from $500 to................**$600.00**
Flower holder, pigeon figural, yellow or rose, 4x3½", from $100 to................**$125.00**
Flowerpot, Hobnail, made in a variety of colors, NM mark, 4", from $50 to................**$65.00**
Flowerpot & saucer, embossed geometric decor on green, yellow, white or pink, marked, 1954, 6", from $20 to..**$25.00**
Jardiniere, Butterfly, coral, NM mark, 3½", from $50 to .**$60.00**
Jardiniere, embossed acorn decor, matt colors, unmarked, 4½", from $35 to................**$50.00**
Jardiniere, embossed foliage on green to brown matt, 1930s, 7", from $70 to................**$95.00**
Jardiniere, Hobnail, pastel matt, unmarked, 1940s, 6", from $90 to................**$110.00**
Jardiniere, Holly, onyx, unmarked, 1930s, 10½", from $100 to................**$150.00**
Jardiniere, Spring Wood, pink, white or mint green, marked, 1960, 10½", from $30 to................**$45.00**
Jardiniere, Swallows, made in several glazes, 7", ea from $90 to................**$150.00**
Jardiniere & pedestal, Basketweave, green or white, 8½", 12½", from $275 to................**$350.00**
Lamp, Wagon Wheel, green or black, unmarked, 1954, 8", from $60 to................**$75.00**
Lazy susan, 2 divided pcs form circle, marked, 1966, 12" dia, from #35 to................**$45.00**
Oil jar, streaky green, NM, 12", from $125 to...........**$200.00**
Pitcher, ball jug, glossy red, unmarked, 7½", from $50 to................**$60.00**
Pitcher/vase, parrot figural, green or brown spray decorated, marked, 1952, 7", from $150 to **$200.00**

Planter, baby crib, blue or pink, unmarked, 1954, 4x6½",
from $60 to..**$75.00**

Planter, Basketweave, yellow, pink or lime, marked, 1956,
7½" L, from $15 to..**$20.00**

Planter, bird dog w/game in mouth, green & brown, marked,
1954, 8½x12½", from $250 to.........................**$300.00**

Planter, Bird of Paradise, gold trim, marked, 1946, 4½x12½",
from $65 to...**$80.00**

Planter, doe & fawn, pastel blue or green, NM mark, 7", from
$50 to...**$60.00**

Planter, Floraline, bear figural, brown, 3½x5", from $18 to..**$25.00**

Planter, frog, green or yellow, unmarked, 1951, 3x5", from
$25 to...**$30.00**

Planter, hand, pastel, NM mark, 1940s, 7¾", from $50 to ..**$60.00**

Planter, kitten (beside basket), pink, NM mark, 6", from $50
to...**$65.00**

Planter, Mary Ann shoe, pink, yellow or blue, NM mark,
1940s, 5" L, from $25 to **$40.00**

Planter, shoe, brown, unmarked, 1970s, 5", from $30 to ..**$40.00**

Planter, squirrel figural, brown or gray decorated, marked,
1955, 4½x5", from $25 to **$35.00**

Planter, Wild Rose, lavender, yellow, blue or pink, marked,
1952, 3½x8", from $50 to **$60.00**

Planter bowl, Brocade, green, marked, 1956, 4x5½", from
$15 to...**$20.00**

Platter, fish figural, white, brown or rose, USA Ovenproof,
1973, 8¼x18", from $40 to **$55.00**

Pretzel jar, unmarked, Nelson McCoy Sanitary Stoneware, 1926, from $110.00 to $135.00.

Stein, German scenes, Hand Decorated USA, 1978, 8¾", from
$40 to...**$60.00**

Stretch animal, hound (dachshund), pastel, unmarked, 1940s,
5x8¼", from $175 to.......................................**$225.00**

Stretch animal, lion, pastel color, unmarked, 1940s, 5¼x4",
from $150 to...**$175.00**

Vase, Butterfly, yellow or blue, handles, USA mark, 10", from
$150 to...**$200.00**

Vase, embossed leaves & berries on blue to green matt,
1930s, 5", from $50 to......................................**$70.00**

Vase, embossed water lilies on white, lizard handles, 9", from
$350 to...**$500.00**

Vase, green matt, embossed ribs, sm handles, flared foot,
1930s, 9", from $80 to **$110.00**

Vase, hand, blue matt, NM mark, 1943, 7", from $100 to **$150.00**

Vase, Ivy, hand decorated, marked, 1953, 9", from $100 to .**$150.00**

Vase, parrot perched before vase, made in a variety of colors, marked, 1940s, 7½", from $45 to **$60.00**

Vase, swan form, pastel, 6", from $35 to **$45.00**

Vase, triple lily, white or yellow, marked, 1950, 8½", from
$50 to...**$70.00**

Wall pocket, flower, turquoise, yellow or white, unmarked,
6", from $40 to...**$50.00**

Wall pocket, lily bud, pastel matt, NM mark, 1940s, 8", from
$200 to...**$250.00**

Wall pocket, Mexican embossed on yellow, 7½", from $50
to...**$60.00**

Brown Drip Dinnerware

One of McCoy's dinnerware lines that was introduced
in the 1960s is beginning to attract a following. It's a
glossy brown stoneware-type pattern with frothy white
decoration around the rims. Similar lines of brown
stoneware were made by many other companies, Hull
and Pfaltzgraff among them. McCoy simply called their
line 'Brown Drip.'

Baker, oval, 10½"..**$10.00**
Baker, oval, 12½"..**$15.00**
Bean pot, individual, 12-oz....................................**$4.00**
Bean pot, 1½-qt, from $15 to.................................**$20.00**
Bean pot, 3-qt, from $25 to....................................**$30.00**
Bowl, cereal; 6"..**$4.00**
Bowl, chili; #7016, 2x5¼".......................................**$6.00**
Bowl, lug soup; 12-oz...**$8.00**
Bowl, onion soup; #7054.......................................**$7.00**
Bowl, spaghetti or salad; 12½"...............................**$20.00**
Bowl, vegetable; divided......................................**$12.00**
Bowl, 1½x6½"...**$4.00**
Butter dish, ¼-lb...**$15.00**
Candle holders, pr, from $18 to..............................**$22.00**
Canister, coffee..**$30.00**
Casserole, 2-qt...**$15.00**
Casserole, 3½-qt...**$18.00**
Casserole, 3-qt, w/hen-on-nest lid, from $45 to..........**$50.00**
Cookie jar, 8½"...**$45.00**
Corn tray, individual, from $8 to.............................**$15.00**
Creamer..**$5.00**
Crock, Bicentennial, USA mark, 9"...........................**$10.00**
Cruet, oil & vinegar; ea from $12 to.........................**$15.00**
Cup, 8-oz..**$5.00**
Custard cup, 6-oz..**$4.00**
Gravy boat, from $12 to..**$15.00**
Mug, pedestal base, 12-oz.....................................**$7.50**
Mug, 8-oz..**$5.00**
Pie plate, 9", from $12 to......................................**$15.00**
Pitcher, jug style, 32-oz..**$20.00**
Plate, dinner; 10"..**$7.00**
Plate, salad; 7"...**$4.00**
Plate, soup & sandwich; w/lg cup ring.....................**$10.00**
Platter, fish form, 18"...**$32.00**
Platter, oval, 14"...**$15.00**

Salt & pepper shakers, pr, from $6 to......................**$8.00**
Snack server, 5-compartment, #906, 12½" **$25.00**
Souffle dish, 2-qt...**$9.50**
Sugar bowl, w/lid, 4¼"..**$8.00**
Teapot, 6-cup, from $18 to **$22.00**
Trivet, concentric circles, round................................**$9.00**
Tureen, soup; #0121, w/lid, 8x8" **$24.00**

Melmac Dinnerware

The postwar era gave way to many new technologies in manufacturing. With the discovery that thermoplastics could be formed by the interaction of melamine and formaldehyde, Melmac was born. This colorful and decorative product found an eager market due to its style and affordability. Another attractive feature was its resistance to breakage. Who doesn't recall the sound it made as it bounced off the floor when you'd accidentally drop a piece!

Popularity began to wane: the dinnerware was found to fade with repeated washings, the edges could chip, and the surfaces could be scratched, stained, or burned. Melmac fell from favor in the late '60s and early '70s. At that time, it was restyled to imitate china that had become popular due to increased imports.

As always, demand and availability determine price. Our values are for items in mint condition only; pieces with scratches, chips, or stains have no value. Lines of similar value are grouped together. As there are many more manufacturers other than those listed, for a more thorough study of the subject we recommend *Melmac Dinnerware* by Gregory R. Zimmer and Alvin Daigle Jr.

See also Russel Wright.

Advisor: Gregory R. Zimmer (See Directory, Melmac)

Internet Information: Melmac Dinnerware Discussion List: www.egroups.com; search for MelmacDinnerware

Aztec, Debonaire, Flite-Lane, Mar-Crest, Restraware, Rivieraware, Stetson, Westinghouse

Bowl, cereal; from $2 to..**$3.00**
Bowl, fruit; from $1 to..**$2.00**
Bowl, serving; from $4 to...**$5.00**
Bowl, soup; from $3 to..**$4.00**
Butter dish, from $5 to..**$7.00**
Creamer, from $1 to...**$2.00**
Cup & saucer, from $2 to...**$3.00**
Gravy boat, from $5 to...**$6.00**
Plate, bread; from $1 to...**$2.00**
Plate, dinner; from $2 to **$3.00**
Plate, salad; from $2 to..**$3.00**
Salt & pepper shakers, pr, from $4 to.........................**$5.00**
Sugar bowl, w/lid, from $3 to **$4.00**
Tumbler, 6-oz, from $6 to..**$7.00**
Tumbler, 10-oz, from $7 to **$8.00**

Boontoon, Branchell, Brookpark, Harmony House, Prolon, Watertown Lifetime Ware

Bowl, cereal; from $4 to...**$5.00**
Bowl, fruit; from $3 to...**$4.00**
Bowl, serving; from $8 to...**$10.00**
Bowl, soup; w/lid, from $5 to.....................................**$6.00**
Bowl, vegetable; divided, from $8 to..........................**$10.00**
Bread tray, from $8 to..**$10.00**
Butter dish, from $8 to...**$10.00**
Casserole, w/lid, from $20 to.....................................**$25.00**
Creamer, from $5 to...**$6.00**
Cup & saucer, from $3 to...**$4.00**
Gravy boat, from $6 to...**$8.00**
Jug, w/lid, from $20 to...**$25.00**
Plate, bread; from $2 to...**$3.00**
Plate, compartment; from $10 to **$12.00**
Plate, dinner; from $4 to..**$5.00**
Plate, salad; from $4 to..**$5.00**
Platter, from $8 to..**$10.00**
Salad tongs, from $12 to **$15.00**
Salt & pepper shakers, pr, from $6 to.........................**$8.00**
Sugar bowl, from $6 to...**$8.00**
Tray, tidbit; 2-tier, from $12 to..................................**$15.00**
Tray, tidbit; 3-tier, from $15 to..................................**$18.00**
Tumbler, 6-oz, from $10 to...**$12.00**
Tumbler, 10-oz, from $12 to **$15.00**

Fostoria, Lucent

Bowl, cereal; from $7 to...**$9.00**
Bowl, serving; from $15 to **$18.00**
Butter dish, from $15 to...**$18.00**
Creamer, from $8 to...**$10.00**
Cup & saucer, from $8 to...**$12.00**
Plate, bread; from $3 to...**$4.00**
Plate, dinner; from $6 to **$8.00**
Platter, from $12 to..**$15.00**
Relish tray, from $15 to **$18.00**
Sugar bowl, w/lid, from $12 to **$15.00**

Metlox Pottery

Founded in the late 1920s in Manhattan Beach, California, this company initially produced tile and commercial advertising signs. By the early '30s, their business in these areas had dwindled, and they began to concentrate their efforts on the manufacture of dinnerware, artware, and kitchenware. Carl Gibbs has authored *Collector's Encyclopedia of Metlox Potteries*, published by Collector Books, which we recommend for more information.

Carl Romanelli was the designer responsible for modeling many of the figural pieces they made during the late '30s and early '40s. These items are usually imprinted with his signature and are very collectible today. Coming on strong is their line of 'Poppets,' made from the mid-'60s through the mid-'70s. There were eighty-eight in all, whimsical, comical, sometimes grotesque. They represented characters ranging from the seven-piece Salvation Army Group to royalty, religious figures, policemen, and professionals. Many came with a name tag, some had paper labels, others backstamps. If you question a piece whose label is missing, a good clue to look for is pierced facial features.

Poppytrail and Vernonware were the trade names for their dinnerware lines. Among their more popular patterns were California Ivy, California Provincial, Red Rooster, Homestead Provincial, and the later embossed patterns, Sculptured Grape, Sculptured Zinnia, and Sculptured Daisy.

Some of their lines can be confusing. There are two 'rooster' lines, Red Rooster (red, orange, and brown) and California Provincial (this one is in dark green and burgundy), and three 'homestead' lines, Colonial Homestead (red, orange, and brown like the Red Rooster line) Homestead Provincial (dark green and burgundy like California Provincial), and Provincial Blue. See also Cookie Jars.

Advisor: Carl Gibbs, Jr. (See Directory, Metlox)

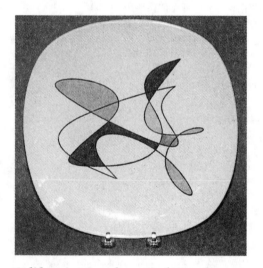

California Freeform, plate, dinner; from $32.00 to $35.00.

California Ivy, bowl, divided vegetable; oval, 11", from $45 to **$50.00**
California Ivy, bowl, soup; 6¾", from $20 to **$22.00**
California Ivy, coaster, 3¾", from $22 to **$25.00**
California Ivy, cup & saucer, from $16 to...................**$18.00**
California Ivy, platter, oval, 13", from $45 to..............**$50.00**
California Ivy, salt & pepper shakers, sm, pr, from $28 to..**$30.00**
California Ivy, teapot, 6-cup, from $115 to................**$125.00**
California Provincial, bowl, salad; 11⅛", from $100 to....**$110.00**
California Provincial, cruet, oil; w/lid, 7-oz, from $42 to ..**$45.00**
California Provincial, gravy boat, 1-pt, from $45 to....**$50.00**
California Provincial, plate, luncheon; 9", from $28 to...**$30.00**
California Provincial, salt & pepper shakers, pr, from $30 to...**$32.00**
California Provincial, sugar bowl, w/lid, 8-oz, from $35 to **$38.00**

California Provincial, turkey platter, 22½", from $300 to..**$325.00**
California Tempo, butter dish, from $45 to **$50.00**
California Tempo, plate, barbecue; 12", from $35 to..**$40.00**
California Tempo, sauce boat, 1-pt, from $25 to **$28.00**
Colonial Heritage, bowl, cereal; from $14 to **$16.00**
Colonial Heritage, bowl, salad; from $75 to...............**$80.00**
Colonial Heritage, buffet server, round, from $65 to..**$70.00**
Colonial Heritage, mug, no lid, lg, from $30 to.........**$32.00**
Colorstax, bowl, mixing; 16-oz, from $30 to **$35.00**
Colorstax, cup & saucer, demitasse; from $28 to........**$32.00**
Colorstax, plate, salad; 7¾", from $11 to...................**$12.00**
Homestead Provincial, bowl, cereal; 7¼", from $20 to .**$22.00**
Homestead Provincial, bowl, fruit; 6", from $16 to.....**$18.00**
Homestead Provincial, bowl, vegetable; round, 10", from $55 to **$60.00**
Homestead Provincial, bread server, 9½", from $75 to...**$80.00**
Homestead Provincial, candle holder, from $55 to.....**$60.00**
Homestead Provincial, casserole, chicken lid, 1-qt 10-oz, from $185 to...**$200.00**
Homestead Provincial, plate, salad; 7½", from $14 to ..**$15.00**
Homestead Provincial, soup tureen ladle, from $60 to...**$65.00**
Homestead Provincial, tumbler, 11-oz, from $45 to....**$50.00**
Lotus, coffeepot, 6-cup, from $125 to......................**$135.00**
Lotus, cup & saucer, demitasse; from $26 to..............**$30.00**
Lotus, gravy, from $38 to **$40.00**
Navajo, pitcher, milk; 1-qt, from $50 to.....................**$55.00**
Navajo, plate, dinner; 10½", from $14 to...................**$15.00**
Navajo, salt & pepper mills, pr, from $67 to **$75.00**
Provincial Blue, butter dish, from $75 to...................**$80.00**
Provincial Blue, egg cup, from $40 to **$45.00**
Provincial Blue, mug, cocoa; 8-oz, from $30 to.........**$32.00**
Provincial Blue, pitcher, milk; 1-qt, from $75 to........**$85.00**
Provincial Blue, plate, bread & butter; 6⅜", from $10 to ..**$11.00**
Provincial Blue, salt shaker/mill & pepper mill, from $105 to **$115.00**
Red Rooster, bowl, vegetable; 7⅛", from $35 to.........**$40.00**
Red Rooster, canister, coffee; from $65 to **$70.00**
Red Rooster, coffeepot, 6-cup, from $115 to.............**$125.00**
Red Rooster, cruet set, 2-pc, complete, from $110 to...**$120.00**
Red Rooster, gravy boat, 1-pt, from $35 to.................**$40.00**
Red Rooster, mug, no lid, lg, 1-pt, from $35 to **$38.00**
Red Rooster, pitcher, sm, 1½-pt, from $40 to..............**$50.00**
Red Rooster, plate, dinner; 10", from $13 to **$15.00**
Red Rooster, platter, oval, 13½", from $45 to..............**$50.00**
Sculptured Daisy, bowl, fruit; 6½", from $12 to.........**$14.00**
Sculptured Daisy, bowl, vegetable; round, sm, 7", from $32 to **$35.00**
Sculptured Daisy, cup & saucer, from $12 to.............**$14.00**
Sculptured Daisy, oval baker, 11", from $45 to..........**$50.00**
Sculptured Daisy, pitcher, sm, 1½-pt, from $45 to **$50.00**
Sculptured Grape, bowl, divided vegetable; round, 9½", from $50 to **$55.00**
Sculptured Grape, plate, bread & butter; 6⅜", from $10 to **$11.00**
Sculptured Grape, plate, dinner; 10½", from $16 to...**$18.00**
Sculptured Grape, salad fork & spoon, from $65 to...**$70.00**
Sculptured Grape, sauce boat, 1-pt, from $45 to........**$50.00**

Tickled Pink, mug, 12-oz, from $20 to **$22.00**
Tickled Pink, relish, 3-section, 12¾", from $40 to **$45.00**
Tickled Pink, tumbler, 14-oz, from $25 to **$28.00**
Woodland Gold, creamer, 10-oz, from $25 to **$28.00**
Woodland Gold, plate, salad; 8", from $9 to **$10.00**

Miscellaneous

Bowl, console; Yorkshire, vertical ribs, from $45 to ...**$50.00**
California Ivy Artware, Dutch shoe planter, lg, from $35
 to...**$38.00**
California Ivy Artware, planter box, sm, from $28 to .**$30.00**
Disney figurine, Dumbo, miniature, 1¾", from $175 to ..**$200.00**
Disney figurine, Pinocchio, from $400 to **$450.00**
Disney figurine, Sleepy (or any dwarf from Snow White fig-
 ures), from $200 to **$250.00**
Disney figurine, White Rabbit or Mad Hatter, ea, from $250
 to...**$275.00**
Miniature, aardvark, from $125 to **$175.00**
Miniature, duck, laughing, head skyward, 3", from $35
 to **$50.00**
Miniature, Jack/donkey, standing or sitting, 3", ea, from $50
 to...**$80.00**
Miniature, lizard, 9½", from $180 to **$240.00**
Modern Masterpiece, Flower Holder (Cornucopia Maid), Carl
 Romanelli, 8¾", from $225 to **$250.00**
Modern Masterpiece, Sail Fish vase, Carl Romanelli, 9", from
 $140 to...**$160.00**
Modern Masterpiece, Two-Fish vase, Carl Romanelli, 14",
 from $275 to...**$325.00**
Nostalgia Line, Dobbin, American Royal Horses, 11x9", from
 $150 to...**$160.00**
Nostalgia Line, Old Ford, from $75 to **$85.00**
Nostalgia Line, powder horn w/strap, from $45 to.....**$50.00**

**Nostalgia, Victorian carriage, #625, 11x5½x5", from
$90.00 to $100.00; large hackney horse, #644, 8¾x 8¾",
from $180.00 to $190.00; coachman, mama, papa, or
Mary Jane, from $65.00 to $70.00 each.**

Poppet, Emma the Cook, 8", from $45 to....................**$55.00**
Poppet, Melinda, tennis girl w/4" bowl, from $60 to .**$70.00**

Poppet, Ralph, bather man, 11¾", from $45 to...........**$55.00**
Toppet, Anne, girl w/flowers, from $70 to..................**$80.00**
Toppet, Arthur, knight, from $70 to **$80.00**
Vase, bud; cowboy boot, 5¼", from $30 to................**$35.00**

Milk Bottles

Between the turn of the century and the 1950s, milk was bought and sold in glass bottles. Until the '20s, the name and location of the dairy was embossed in the glass. After that it became commonplace to pyro-glaze (paint and fire) the lettering onto the surface. Farmers sometimes added a cow or some other graphic that represented the product or related to the name of the dairy.

Because so many of these glass bottles were destroyed when paper and plastic cartons became popular, they've become a scarce commodity, and today's collectors have begun to take notice of them. It's fun to see just how many you can find from your home state — or try getting one from every state in the union!

What makes for a good milk bottle? Collectors normally find the pyro-glaze decorations more desirable, since they're more visual. Bottles from dairies in their home state hold more interest for them, so naturally New Jersey bottles sell better there than they would in California, for instance. Green glass examples are unusual and often go for a premium; so do those with the embossed baby faces. (Watch for reproductions here!) Those with a 'Buy War Bonds' slogan or a patriotic message are always popular, and cream-tops are good as well.

Some collectors enjoy adding 'go-alongs' to enhance their collections, so the paper pull tops, advertising items that feature dairy bottles, and those old cream-top spoons will also interest them. The spoons usually sell for about $10.00 to $18.00 each.

Advisor: John Shaw (See Directory, Milk Bottles)

Newsletter: *The Milk Route*
National Association of Milk Bottle Collectors, Inc.
The Milk Route
PO Box 105, Blooming Grove, NY 10914

Newsletter: *Creamers*
Lloyd Bindscheattle
P.O. Box 11, Lake Villa, IL 60046-0011
Subscription: $5 for 4 issues

Anderson Bros & Trojan warrior, blue pyro, round, 10-oz....**$8.00**
Barlow Dairy, Sugar Grove PA, green pyro, sq ½-pt..**$12.00**
Benewah Creamery, Spokane WA, green pyro, squat qt .**$22.50**
Borden's & Elsie, red pyro, sq ½-pt............................**$16.00**
Cloverleaf Blue Ribbon Farms, Stockton CA (spelled in full), red
 pyro, Mordentop (cream-top variation), round qt......**$25.00**
Cloverleaf Blue Ribbon Farms, Stockton CA (spelled in full),
 red pyro, round qt...**$22.00**

Hunt's Dairy, Skowhegan ME (state not shown), red pyro, round ½-pt **$12.50**

Indian Hill Farm, orange pyro, tall round qt..............**$24.00**

Martin Farms, Rochester VT, orange pyro, round ½-pt .**$15.00**

MH Williams Ayrshire Dairy & Ayrshire cows, maroon pyro, tall round qt **$28.00**

MH Williams Jr, Fort Edward NY Hilltop Farms, Ayrshire cows, maroon pyro, sq qt.......................................**$12.00**

Morgan Bros Creameries, black & orange pyro, round ½-pt.**$18.00**

Mullen's Dairy, red pyro, round 2-qt **$20.00**

New Ulm Dairy, New Ulm MN, 50th Anniversary of Pearl Harbor, red & blue pyro, sq qt.............................**$12.00**

O.H. Hoffmire & Son Dairy, Trumansburg, NY, red pyro, Scottie dog and boy, from $75.00 to $85.00. (Photo courtesy Candace Sten Davis and Patricia J. Baugh)

Party Tonight/You Never...Cream Top, green & yellow pyro, no city or state shown, cream-top, sq qt **$14.00**

Pine Grove Dairy, Skaneateles NY, green & orange pyro, tall round qt, lt wear...**$22.50**

Reservoir Dairy, Woonsocket RI, maroon pyro, sq qt....**$12.00**

Royale Dairy, Keyser WV, yellow pyro on amber, sq qt...**$12.00**

Scooby, multicolor, Warner Brothers series, 1999, sq qt ...**$15.00**

Smith's Dairy, Erie PA, maroon pyro, round ½-pt **$14.00**

Smith's Dairy Farm, Erie PA, maroon pyro, sq qt **$22.50**

Sylvester, multicolor, Warner Brothers series, 1999, qt....**$15.00**

Vincent Farms Dairy, Marshall MI, orange & black pyro, squat qt...**$15.00**

Waldron's Dairy, Califon NJ, red pyro, round pt.........**$15.00**

Miller Studios

Imported chalkware items began appearing in local variety stores in the early '50s. Cheerfully painted hot pad holders, thermometers, wall plaques, and many other items offered a lot of decorator appeal. While not all examples will be marked Miller Studios, good indications of that manufacturer are the holes on the back where stapled-on cardboard packaging has been torn away — thus leaving small holes. There should also be a looped wire hanger on the back, although a missing hanger does not seem to affect price. Copyright dates

are often found on the sides. Miller Studios, located in New Philadelphia, Pennsylvania, is the only existing American firm that makes hand-finished wall plaques yet today. Although they had over three hundred employees during the 1960s and 1970s, they presently have approximately seventy-five.

Animals, cows, mother & 2 calves, 6" & 3", set of 3 ..**$10.00**

Animals, deer, brown, 12½", pr..................................**$18.00**

Animals, horses, brown, 12½", 10½", pr.....................**$20.00**

Bathometer, w/swans, 1981, 6¾x6¾" **$23.00**

Birds, bluebirds, blue & yellow, 1970, 4x3", set of 3..**$23.00**

Fish, wall plaques, mama & 3 baby fish, 1960s, 9x6", 3x3" **$20.00**

Hot pad holder, recipe box w/vegetables & wooden spoon, 1981, 6½x6"..**$13.00**

Hot pad holders, apple & pear faces, 1970, 5x5½", pr...**$15.00**

Planter, flamingos on ea side, 5x6½" **$30.00**

Planter, horse head on turquoise, 9½x4x4".................**$25.00**

Plaque, kitchen stove, A Kitchen Is the Heart of the Home, 6½x7" **$13.00**

Plaque, water well, One Today Is Worth Two Tomorrows, copper colored, 1979, 5½", MIP **$8.00**

Plaque/hot pad holder, sunflower face, holds banner w/saying at bottom, 1973, 7¾", pr.................................**$12.00**

Plaques, poodles, boy (blue) & girl (pink), 1972, 5½" dia, pr..**$15.00**

Thermometer, poodle in bathtub, 1973, from $9.00 to $12.00.

Model Kits

By far the majority of model kits were vehicular, and though worth collecting, especially when you can find them still mint in the box, the really big news are the figure kits. Most were made by Aurora during the 1960s. Especially hot are the movie monsters, though TV and comic strip character kits are popular with collectors too. As a rule of thumb, assembled kits are valued at about half as much as conservatively priced mint-in-box kits. The condition of the box is just as important as the contents, and top collectors will usually pay an additional 15% (sometimes even more) for a box that retains the factory plastic wrap still intact. For more information, we recommend *Aurora History and Price Guide* by Bill Bruegman (Cap'n Penny Productions). *Schroeder's Toys, Antique to Modern,* contains prices and descriptions of hundreds of models by a variety of manufacturers.

Adams, Chuck Wagon, 1958, MIB $40.00

Addar, General Aldo, 1973 – 1974, MIB, from $50.00 to $75.00.

Addar, Planet of the Apes, Cornelius, MIB (sealed)....$90.00
Addar, Planet of the Apes, Dr Zira, 1974, MIB (sealed)...$80.00
AEF, Aliens, Bishop, 1980s, MIB..............................$35.00
Airfix, Apollo Saturn V, MIB (sealed)........................$30.00
Airfix, Saturn 1B, 1991, MIB (sealed)........................$75.00
AMT, BJ & the Bear, KW Aerodyne & Trailer, 1982, MIB (sealed) $35.00
AMT, Munster Koach, 1964, MIB...............................$150.00
AMT, Star Trek, Mr Spock, 1967, MIB.......................$135.00
AMT/Ertl, Batmobile, 1989, MIB (sealed) $20.00
AMT/Ertl, Star Trek: Deep Space Nine, Defiant, 1996, MIB...$15.00
Arii, Macross, Quilted-Queleual Ship, MIB $30.00
Arii, Southern Cross, ATAC-Bowie Emerson, MIB.......$25.00
Aurora, Alfred E Neuman, 1969, assembled, EX.......$125.00
Aurora, Batman, 1966, MIB......................................$285.00
Aurora, Bloodthirsty Pirates, Captain Kidd, 1965, MIB ..$80.00
Aurora, Castle Creatures, Frog, 1966, MIB.................$250.00
Aurora, Comic Scenes, Incredible Hulk, 1974, MIB..$100.00
Aurora, Comic Scenes, Lone Ranger, 1974, MIB $50.00
Aurora, Dick Tracy, 1967, MIB $150.00
Aurora, Dracula's Dragster, assembled, M $100.00
Aurora, Famous Fighters, US Air Force Pilot, 1958, MIB...$300.00
Aurora, Frightening Lightning, Dracula, MIB.............$350.00
Aurora, Godzilla, 1969, glow-in-the-dark, MIB.........$200.00

Aurora, Incredible Hulk, 1966, MIB $250.00
Aurora, King Kong, 1964, assembled, EX...................$75.00
Aurora, Mod Squad Station Wagon, 1969, MIB (sealed)......$150.00
Aurora, Monster Scenes, Dr Deadly's Daughter, 1971, MIB ..$65.00
Aurora, Mummy, 1972, glow-in-the-dark, MIB (sealed).......$135.00
Aurora, Prehistoric Scenes, Cave Bear, 1972, MIB (sealed) ...$65.00
Aurora, Prehistoric Scenes, Sail Back Reptile, 1975, MIB......$90.00
Aurora, Robin the Boy Wonder, 1966, MIB (sealed).$100.00
Aurora, Salem Witch, 1965, assembled, EX $65.00
Aurora, Tonto, 1974, MIB (sealed) $50.00
Aurora, Zorro, 1965, assembled, EX..........................$125.00
Aurora, 2001: A Space Oddyssey, Space Shuttle Orian, 1975, MIB (sealed)..$170.00
Bandai, Gundam, Mobile Suit #11, 1980, green, MIB.$20.00
Bandai, Prehistoric Animal Series, Stegosaurus, 1973, MIB ..$65.00
Bandai, Thunderbird, 1984, MIB $40.00
Billiken, Frankenstein, MIB.....................................$125.00
Billiken, King Kong, MIB $95.00
Billiken, Ultra Zone, Peguila, 1989, vinyl, MIB $90.00
Dark Horse, Mummy, 1995, MIB...............................$150.00
Dark Horse, Ray Harryhausen's King Kong, MIB $95.00
Halcyon, Alien Warrior w/Egg & Base, MIB...............$50.00
Hawk, Indian Totem Poles, Grave of Ske-Dans Totem, 1966, MIB $45.00
Hawk, Weird-Ohs, Huey's Hut Rod, 1969, MIB $50.00
Horizon, Creature From the Black Lagoon, 1988, MIB..$110.00
Horizon, Dracula, 1988, MIB $50.00
Horizon, Marvel Universe, Cable, 1994, MIB..............$40.00
Horizon, Mummy, 1988, MIB....................................$60.00
Horizon, Phantom of the Opera, 1988, MIB...............$50.00
Horizon, Robocop, Robocop #10, 1989, MIB $60.00
Horizon, Wolf-Man, MIB $60.00
Hubley, 1932, Chevy Coupe, MIB $50.00
Imai, Orguss, Dr Doom, 1991, MIB...........................$40.00
Imai, Orguss, Thor, 1993, MIB.................................$50.00
ITC, Wire Haired Terrier, 1959, MIB.........................$30.00
Life-Like, Neanderthal Man, MIB (sealed)..................$50.00
Life-Like, Tyrannosaurus, MIB (sealed)......................$35.00
Lindberg, Lucky Loser, 1965, MIB $20.00
Lindberg, Wells Fargo Overland Stagecoach, 1960s, MIB....$50.00
Monogram, Backdraft (movie), Fire Chief Car, 1991, MIB ..$20.00
Monogram, Battlestar Galactica, Cylon Basestar, 1978, MIB ..$75.00
Monogram, Buck Rogers, Starfighter, 1979, MIB.........$70.00
Monogram, Elvira Macabremobile, MIB (sealed) $35.00
Monogram, Ford Tri-Motor Anarctic, 1950s, MIB $50.00
Monogram, Fred Flypogger as Speed Shift!, 1965, MIB ..$175.00
Monogram, Godzilla, 1978, MIB (sealed) $125.00
Monogram, Green Hornet Dragster, 1960s, MIB $55.00
Monogram, Luminators, Dracula, MIB (sealed)...........$15.00
Monogram, Luminators, King Kong, MIB $40.00
Monogram, Luminators, Mummy, MIB........................$20.00
Monogram, Snoopy Is Joe Cool, 1970, MIB $135.00
Monogram, Tiajuana Taxi, 1960s, MIB.......................$85.00
Monogram, Wolf-Man, 1983, MIB (sealed) $60.00
MPC, '71 Road Runner, NMIB....................................$50.00
MPC, Alien, 1979, MIB $70.00
MPC, Beatle's Yellow Submarine, 1968, MIB (sealed) ..$300.00

MPC, Bionic Woman, Bionic Repair, MIB (sealed)............**$32.00**
MPC, Dark Shadows, Werewolf, MIB......................**$200.00**
MPC, Dukes of Hazzard, Daisy's Jeep, 1980, MIB **$50.00**
MPC, Night Crawler, 1975, assembled, EX..................**$50.00**
MPC, Star Wars, R2-D2, 1978, MIB **$50.00**
MPC, 1970 Jeepster Safari Wagon, EXIB **$40.00**
Palmer, Brontosaurus Skeleton, 1950s, MIB **$60.00**
Palmer, Happy Days Burger Buggy, 1974, MIB, from $50
   to **$75.00**

Precision, Cap'n Kidd The Pirate, 1959, MIB, $70.00. (Photo courtesy Rick Polizzi)

Pyro, Classic Auburn Speedster, MIB **$85.00**
Pyro, Gladiator Show Cycle, 1970, MIB.....................**$50.00**
Pyro, Indian Medicine Man, 1960s, MIB **$70.00**
Pyro, Peacemaker 45, 1960, MIB (sealed) **$100.00**
Pyro, Rawhide Cowpuncher, 1958, MIB **$60.00**
Pyro, Surf's Up! Surf Trailer Bicycle, 1970, MIB **$40.00**
Revell, Aerobee Hi Research Rocket, 1958, MIB.........**$90.00**
Revell, Charlie's Angels Mobile Unit Van, 1977, MIB..**$45.00**
Revell, Coast Guard Cutter Campbell, 1956, EXIB **$50.00**
Revell, Dr Seuss Zoo, Norvel the Bashful Blinket, 1952,
   MIB...**$85.00**
Revell, Evil Eye, 1980, glow-in-the-dark, MIB **$35.00**
Revell, F-89D Scorpion USAF Jet, 1950s, MIB **$75.00**
Revell, Happy Days '29 Model Pickup, 1982, MIB......**$30.00**
Revell, Lockheed F-104 USAF Starfighter, 1950s, MIB...**$75.00**
Revell, Search Patrol 2-in-1 Kit, 1984, MIB **$24.00**
Revell, Teddy the Koala Bear, MIB **$40.00**
Revell, VF-1A Fighter, 1985, MIB (sealed) **$40.00**
Screamin', Air Assault Martian, 1995, MIB **$50.00**
Screamin', London After Midnight Vampire, MIB........**$75.00**
Screamin', Werewolf, MIB.......................................**$50.00**
Screamin' Star Wars, C-3PO, 1993, MIB **$45.00**
Strombecker, Walt Disney's Rocket to the Moon, 1956,
   MIB..**$225.00**
Superior, Seeing Eye, 1959, MIB................................**$35.00**
Testors, Top Gun, A-4 Aggressor, 1987, MIB..............**$10.00**
Testors, Weird-Ohs, Beach Bunny Catching Rays, 1994, MIB
   (sealed) **$30.00**
Tomy, Lensmen, Galactic Fighter Striker I, MIB.........**$40.00**
Toy Biz, Ghost Rider, 1996, MIB **$30.00**

Tsukuda, Ghostbusters, Stay Puft Man (sm), 1984, MIB...**$40.00**
Tsukuda, Metaluna Mutant, MIB................................**$75.00**

Modern Mechanical Banks

The most popular (and expensive) type of bank with today's collectors are the mechanicals, so called because of the antics they perfrom when a coin is deposited. Over three hundred models were produced between the Civil War period and the first World War. On some, arms wave, legs kick, or mouths open to swallow up the coin — amusing nonsense intended by the inventor to encourage and reward thriftiness. Some of these original banks have been known to sell for as much as $20,000.00 — well out of the price range most of us can afford! So many opt for some of the modern mechanicals that are available on the collectibles market, including Book of Knowledge and James D. Capron, which are reproductions marked to indicate that they are indeed replicas. But beware — unmarked modern reproductions are common.

Reynolds Toys have been producing banks from their own original designs since 1971; some of Mr. Reynolds's banks are in the White House and the Smithsonian.

Advisor: Dan Iiannotti (See Directory, Banks)

'96 Political Wish, Reynolds, 1996, edition of 50 ......**$900.00**
Artillery Bank, Book of Knowledge, NM...................**$295.00**
Bad Accident, James Capron, M..............................**$795.00**
Bobby Riggs & Billy Jean King, John Wright Limited edition
   of 250, scarce, M..**$795.00**
Butting Buffalo, Book of Knowledge, NM.................**$325.00**
Cat & Mouse, Book of Knowledge, NM **$325.00**
Clown on Globe, James Capron, M **$775.00**
Console TV, litho tin, EX...**$100.00**
Dentist Bank, Book of Knowledge, EX **$175.00**
Drive-In, Reynolds, 1971, edition of 10, M **$1,000.00**
Eagle & Eaglets, Book of Knowledge, M...................**$450.00**
Elephant, James Capron, M **$250.00**
Foxy Grandpa, Reynolds, 1974, edition of 10, M......**$975.00**

Frog Bank (Two Frogs), James Capron, NM, $625.00. (Photo courtesy Dan Iannotti)

Humpty Dumpty, Book of Knowledge, M **$325.00**
John Deer Anvil, diecast, MIB **$125.00**
Leap Frog, Book of Knowledge, NM **$335.00**
Lion & Monkeys, James Capron, M........................**$875.00**
Magician, Book of Knowledge, MIB **$325.00**
Man w/Mustache & Top Hat, litho tin, NM.............**$275.00**
Milking Cow, Book of Knowledge, NM....................**$295.00**
Monkey w/Tray, litho tin, EX **$200.00**
Mule Entering Barn, James Capron, NM...................**$495.00**
Paddy & the Pig, Book of Knowledge, NM **$375.00**
Penny Pineapple, Richards/Wilton, commemorates Hawaii
    50th state, NM..**$450.00**
Professor Pug Frog, James Capron, M **$850.00**
Race Course, James Capron, NM............................**$575.00**
Reynolds Foundry, Reynolds, 1974, edition of 15 .**$3,400.00**
Suitcase, Reynolds, 1979, edition of 22.....................**$825.00**
Tammany, Book of Knowledge, NMIB....................**$325.00**
Trick Dog, James Capron, NM.................................**$400.00**
Trick Pony, Book of Knowledge, NM......................**$350.00**
Uncle Bugs, Warner Bros, M **$195.00**
Uncle Sam, Richards/Wilton, rear trap, scarce, NM.....**$450.00**
William Tell, Book of Knowledge, NM.....................**$325.00**

Mood Indigo by Inarco

This line of Japan-made ceramics probably came out in the 1960s, and enough of it was produced that a considerable amount has reached the secondary market. Because of the interest today's collectors are exhibiting in items from the '60s and '70s, it's beginning to show up in malls and co-ops, and the displays are surprisingly attractive. The color of the glaze is an electric blue, and each piece is modeled as though it were built from stacks of various fruits. It was imported by Inarco (Cleveland, Ohio) and often bears that company's foil label.

Collectors are sticklers for condition (damaged items are worth very little, even if they are rare) and prefer pieces with a deep, rich blue color and dark numbers on the bottom that are very legible. All pieces carry a number, and most collectors use these to keep track of their acquisitions. In addition to the items described and evaluated below, here is a partial listing of other known pieces.

E-2374 — Covered Candy Dish, 9"
E-2375 — Covered Dish, 6"
E-2376 — Oval Dish, 8¼"
E-3145 — Pitcher, 6"
E-3267 — Oil Lamp
E-3445 — Plate, 9½"
E-3462 — Pedestal Cake Plate, 9½"
E-2719 — Relish Tray, 7½"
E-2920 — Gravy Boat, with saucer, 8"
E-3095 — Fluted Vase, 7¾"

E-3096 — Vase, 8"
E-3100 — Cigarette Lighter
E-2429 — Pitcher, 6"
E-2431 — Coffee Cup, 4"
E-2432 — Hanging Plate,
    with fruit, 10"
E-3563 Candle Holder, 5"
E-4011 — Butter Dish,
    with lid, 7½"

These pieces can be bought for as little as $5.00 to as much as $30.00. Prices vary widely, and bargains can still be had at many flea markets and garage sales.

Advisors: David and Debbie Crouse (See Directory, Mood Indigo)

Bell, 5", from $5 to **$15.00**
Candle holder, goblet shape, 4½", pr **$28.00**
Centerpiece, stacked-up fruit on ribbed incurvate base,
    12x6"...**$15.00**
Cookie jar/canister, E-2374, 8"...............................**$18.00**
Creamer & sugar bowl, w/lid, from $10 to **$12.00**
Cruet **$17.50**
Gravy boat, E-2373, 6½" **$15.00**
Jar, cylindrical, w/lid, 6½"...**$15.00**
Ladle, 9¾"..**$25.00**
Pitcher, E-2853, footed, 6"...**$15.00**
Salt & pepper shakers, E-2371, 3½", pr **$12.00**

Teapot, E-2430, 8", $15.00.

Tray, 8½x5¾" **$28.00**
Trivet, 6" dia...**$10.00**

Moon and Star

Moon and Star (originally called Palace) was first produced in the 1880s by John Adams & Company of Pittsburgh. But because the glassware was so heavy to transport, it was made for only a few years. In the 1960s, Joseph Weishar of Wheeling, West Virginia, owner of Island Mould & Machine Company, reproduced some of the original molds and incorporated the pattern into approximately forty new and different items. Two of the largest distributors of this line were L.E. Smith of Mt. Pleasant, Pennsylvania, who pressed their own glass, and L.G. Wright of New Martinsville, West Virginia, who had theirs pressed by Fostoria and Fenton. Both companies carried a large and varied assortment of shapes and colors. Several other companies were involved in its manufacture as well, especially of the smaller items. All in all, there may be as many as one hundred different pieces, plenty to keep you involved and excited as you do your searching.

The glassware is already collectible, even though it is still being made on a limited basis. Colors you'll see most often are amberina (yellow shading to orange-red), green, amber, crystal, light blue, and ruby. Pieces in ruby and light blue are more popular and harder to find than the other colors, which seem to be abundant. Purple, pink, cobalt, amethyst, tan slag, and light green and blue opalescent were made, too, but on a lesser scale.

Current L.E. Smith catalogs contain a dozen or so pieces that are still available in crystal, pink, cobalt (lighter than the old shade), and these colors with an iridized finish. A new color was introduced in 1992, teal green, and water set in sapphire blue opalescent was pressed in 1993 by Weishar Enterprises. They are now producing limited editions in various colors and shapes, but they are marking their glassware 'Weishar,' to distinguish it from the old line. Cranberry Ice (light transparent pink) was introduced in 1994.

Unless another color is specified, our values are given for ruby and light blue. For amberina, green, and amber, deduct at least 30%. These colors are less in demand, and unless your prices are reasonable, you may find them harder to sell. Values peaked very quickly a few years ago, and for now, at least, they've dropped off considerably, probably due to the fact that they rose so rapidly in the first place. But the glass is of good quality, the line is extensive (therefore fun to hunt for), and we predict there will always be a market for the better examples.

Ashtray, allover pattern, moons form scallops along rim, 4 rests, 8" dia **$20.00**
Ashtray, moons at rim, star in base, 6-sided, 5½".......**$14.00**
Ashtray, moons at rim, star in base, 6-sided, 8½".......**$20.00**
Banana boat, allover pattern, moons form scallops along rim, 9" **$28.00**
Banana boat, allover pattern, moons form scallops along rim, 12" **$40.00**
Basket, allover pattern, moons form scallops along rim, footed, incurvate upright handles, 4", from $15 to.....**$22.00**
Basket, allover pattern, moons form scallops along rim, solid handle, 9", from $50 to...................................**$60.00**
Basket, allover pattern, moons form scallops along rim, solid handle, 6" **$35.00**
Bell, pattern along sides, plain rim & handle **$35.00**
Bowl, allover pattern, footed, crimped rim, 7½" **$25.00**
Bowl, allover pattern, footed, scalloped rim, 12x5"....**$40.00**
Butter dish, allover pattern, scalloped foot, patterned lid & finial, 6x5½" dia **$45.00**
Butter dish, allover pattern, stars form scallops along rim of base, star finial, oval, ¼-lb, 8½" **$50.00**
Butter/cheese dish, patterned lid, plain base, 7" dia, from $50 to **$55.00**
Cake plate, allover pattern, low collared base, 13" dia, from $50 to **$60.00**
Cake salver, allover pattern w/scalloped rim, raised foot w/scalloped edge, 5x12" dia, from $50 to............**$60.00**

Cake stand, allover pattern, plate removes from standard, 2-pc, 11" dia **$75.00**
Candle bowl, allover pattern, footed, 8", from $25 to ..**$30.00**
Candle holder, allover pattern, bowl style w/ring handle, 2x5½", ea..**$14.00**
Candle holders, allover pattern, flared & scalloped foot, 6", pr...**$40.00**
Candle holders, allover pattern, flared base, 4½", pr....**$25.00**
Candle lamp, patterned shade, clear base, 2-pc, 7½", from $20 to..**$25.00**

Candy dish, allover pattern on base and lid, footed ball shape, 6", $20.00.

Canister, allover pattern, 1-lb or 2-lb **$12.00**
Canister, allover pattern, 3½-lb or 5-lb **$18.00**
Chandelier, dome shape, 14" dia, w/font, amber **$175.00**
Chandelier, ruffled dome shape w/allover pattern, amber, 10" **$65.00**
Cheese dish, patterned base, clear plain lid, 9½" **$60.00**
Compote, allover pattern, footed, flared crimped rim, 5"...**$15.00**
Compote, allover pattern, raised foot, patterned lid & finial, 7½x6" **$30.00**
Compote, allover pattern, raised foot on stem, patterned lid & finial, 10x6"...**$50.00**
Compote, allover pattern, raised foot on stem, patterned lid & finial, 12x8"...**$60.00**
Compote, allover pattern, scalloped foot on stem, patterned lid & finial, 8x4"..**$35.00**
Compote, allover pattern, scalloped rim, footed, 5½x8"..**$28.00**
Compote, allover pattern, scalloped rim, footed, 5x6½"..**$15.00**
Compote, allover pattern, scalloped rim, footed, 7x10"....**$35.00**
Console bowl, allover pattern, scalloped rim, flared foot w/flat edge, 8"..**$20.00**
Creamer, allover pattern, raised foot w/scalloped edge, 5¾x3"..**$30.00**
Creamer & sugar bowl (open), disk foot, sm.............**$25.00**
Cruet, vinegar; 6¾"...**$65.00**
Decanter, bulbous w/allover pattern, plain neck, foot ring, original patterned stopper, 32-oz, 12" **$75.00**
Epergne, allover pattern, 1-lily, flared bowl, scalloped foot, minimum value **$95.00**
Epergne, allover pattern, 2-pc, 9", minimum value **$65.00**
Fairy lamp, cylindrical dome-top shade, 6" **$25.00**

Goblet, water; plain rim & foot, 5¾" **$12.00**
Goblet, wine; plain rim & foot, 4½", from $10 to.........**$9.00**
Jardiniere, allover pattern, patterned lid & finial, 9¾", minimum value..**$85.00**
Jardiniere/cracker jar, allover pattern, patterned lid & finial, 7¼", minimum value **$65.00**
Jardiniere/tobacco jar, allover pattern, patterned lid & finial, 6", minimum value..**$45.00**
Jelly dish, allover pattern, patterned lid & finial, stemmed foot, 10½", from $55 to **$60.00**
Jelly dish, patterned body w/plain flat rim & disk foot, patterned lid & finial, 6¾x3½"....................................**$30.00**
Lamp, miniature; amber, from $115 to.......................**$125.00**
Lamp, miniature; blue, from $165 to..........................**$190.00**
Lamp, miniature; green **$135.00**
Lamp, miniature; milk glass, from $200 to **$225.00**
Lamp, miniature; red, from $175 to **$200.00**
Lamp, oil or electric; allover pattern, all original, amber, 24"...**$175.00**
Lamp, oil or electric; allover pattern, all original, red or light blue, 24", minimum value......................................**$275.00**
Lamp, oil; allover pattern, all original, common, 12", from $50 to...**$65.00**
Lighter, allover patterned body, metal fittings, from $40 to..**$50.00**
Nappy, allover pattern, crimped rim, 2¾x6", from $12 to..**$15.00**
Pitcher, water; patterned body, ice lip, straight sides, plain disk foot, 1-qt, 7½", from $65 to **$75.00**
Plate, patterned body & center, smooth rim, 8"..........**$30.00**
Relish bowl, 6 lg scallops form allover pattern, 1½x8"..**$30.00**
Relish dish, allover pattern, 1 plain handle, 2x8" dia .**$35.00**
Relish tray, patterned moons form scalloped rim, star in base, rectangular, 8" **$35.00**
Salt & pepper shakers, allover pattern, metal tops, 4x2", pr...**$25.00**
Salt cellar, allover pattern, scalloped rim, sm flat foot..**$6.00**
Sherbet, patterned body & foot w/plain rim & stem, 4¼x3¾"...**$25.00**
Soap dish, allover pattern, oval, 2x6"............................**$9.00**
Spooner, allover pattern, straight sides, scalloped rim, raised foot, 5¼x4"...**$45.00**
Sugar bowl, allover pattern, patterned lid & finial, sm flat foot, 5¼x4"...**$35.00**
Sugar bowl, allover pattern, straight sides, patterned lid & finial, scalloped foot, 8x4½" **$35.00**
Sugar shaker, allover pattern, metal top, 4½x3½" **$45.00**
Syrup pitcher, allover pattern, metal lid, 4½x3½".......**$65.00**
Toothpick holder, allover pattern, scalloped rim, sm flat foot..**$9.00**
Tumbler, iced tea; no pattern at flat rim or on disk foot, 11-oz, 5"...**$18.00**
Tumbler, juice; no pattern at rim, short pedestal foot, 4½"..**$18.00**
Tumbler, juice; no pattern at rim or on disk foot, 5-oz, 3½"..**$12.00**
Tumbler, no pattern at rim or on disk foot, 6½" **$25.00**

Tumbler, no pattern at rim or on disk foot, 7-oz, 4¼" .**$12.00**
Vase, 6", from $22 to **$30.00**

Mortens Studios

During the 1940s, a Swedish sculptor by the name of Oscar Mortens left his native country and moved to the United States, settling in Arizona. Along with his partner, Gunnar Thelin, they founded the Mortens Studios, a firm that specialized in the manufacture of animal figurines. Though he preferred dogs of all breeds, horses, cats, and wild animals were made, too, but on a much smaller scale.

The material he used was a plaster-like composition molded over a wire framework for support and reinforcement. Crazing is common, and our values reflect pieces with a moderate amount, but be sure to check for more serious damage before you buy. Most pieces are marked with either an ink stamp or a paper label.

Airedale terrier, w/sticker: I am an Airedale, 4¾x6", NM..**$80.00**
Boston bull terrier, black & white, 3½x7", from $75 to...**$100.00**
Boxer, standing, 7"..**$75.00**
Boxer pup, 4" L, from $90 to......................................**$110.00**
Chihuahua, Show Dog series, 1½x2" **$70.00**
Cocker spaniel, 2¼"..**$60.00**

Cocker spaniel, #763, 5¼", from $65.00 to $75.00.

Collie, Royal Design, recumbent, original sticker, NM, from $65 to...**$75.00**
Collie, standing, w/sticker, 6x7", NM, from $90 to ...**$120.00**
Dachshund, red, 4¼x9¼", NM, from $65 to...............**$80.00**
Doberman Pinscher, 7", from $80 to.........................**$110.00**
English setter, Show Dog series, NM, from $150 to..**$185.00**
German shepherd pup, 3½" **$40.00**
Horse, Royal Design, 6½x8", from $90 to **$110.00**
Irish setter, Show Dog series **$90.00**
Pekingese, #740, 3½", EX...**$65.00**
Pomeranian, Show Dog series, 2¼x1¾", from $70 to...**$85.00**
St Bernard, 6½"...**$75.00**

Morton Pottery

Six different potteries operated in Morton, Illinois, during a period of ninety-nine years. The first pottery, established by six Rapp brothers who had immigrated from Germany in the mid-1870s, was named Morton Pottery Works. It was in operation from 1877 to 1915 when it was reorganized and renamed Morton Earthenware Company. Its operation, 1915 – 1917, was curtailed by World War I. Cliftwood Art Potteries, Inc. was the second pottery to be established. It operated from 1920 until 1940 when it was sold and renamed Midwest Potteries, Inc. In March 1944 the pottery burned and was never rebuilt. Morton Pottery Company was the longest running of Morton's potteries. It was in operation from 1922 until 1976. The last pottery to open was the American Art Potteries. It was in production from 1947 until 1961.

All of Morton's potteries were spin-offs from the original Rapp brothers. Second, third, and fourth generation Rapps followed the tradition of their ancestors to produce a wide variety of pottery. Rockingham and yellow ware to Art Deco, giftwares, and novelties were produced by Morton's potteries.

To learn more about these companies, we recommend *Morton Potteries: 99 Years, Vol. II,* by Doris and Burdell Hall.

Advisors: Doris and Burdell Hall (See Directory, Morton Pottery)

Morton Pottery Works — Morten Earthenware Company, 1877 – 1917

Baker, deep, yellow ware, 8" dia	**$50.00**
Bank, acorn shape, green, Acorn Stoves, 3¼"	**$75.00**
Chamber pot, yellow ware, miniature	**$70.00**
Jardiniere, brown, Rockingham, 7"	**$40.00**
Jug, brown, Rockingham, miniature	**$45.00**
Marble, cobalt, 4¼"	**$45.00**
Milk boiler, brown Rockingham, 1½-pt	**$45.00**
Teapot, brown, restaurant, nesting set of 2, individual	**$50.00**
Teapot, standard shape, yellow ware, 1-cup	**$50.00**

Cliftwood Art Potteries, Inc., 1920 – 1940

Bowl, shallow, flower; cobalt, 10"	**$40.00**
Bowl, sq, green/yellow drip over white, w/lid, 6"	**$50.00**
Figurine, cat, brown drip, reclining, 8½"	**$55.00**
Figurine, geese (attached pr), white/yellow, 4x2¾"	**$30.00**
Figurine, tiger, yellow w/brown stripes, miniature, 4x1½"	**$55.00**
Flower frog, disc, cobalt, 3"	**$14.00**
Flower frog, lily pad, blue, 4"	**$24.00**
Miniature, hen & rooster, blue/yellow drip, 2¼x¾", pr	**$20.00**
Planter, broken eggshell on tripod, 14k gold, 3¾"	**$25.00**
Salt shakers, stove top, yellow/green drip over white, 5", pr	**$30.00**

Midwest Potteries, Inc., 1940 – 1944

Figurine, dancing lady, white w/gold decor, 8½"	**$50.00**
Figurine, pony, yellow w/gold decor, 12"	**$45.00**

Miniature, camel, brown, 2½"	**$18.00**

Morton Pottery Company, 1922 – 1976

Ashtray, hexagon, red, Nixon, 3¾"	**$40.00**
Ashtray, teardrop, Rival Crock Pot, 6"	**$12.00**
Bank, kitten, recumbent, yellow/white spray	**$30.00**
Bowl, plain nappy, Sears Roebuck, Vincent Price, blue spongeware	**$45.00**
Employee service pin, bronze w/emerald, 15 years	**$35.00**
Figurine, fawn, brown spray, 7x5x2"	**$15.00**
Grass grower, Jolly Jim	**$24.00**
Stein, beer; leaf design, brown Rockingham, 5"	**$18.00**
TV lamp, horse head, brown	**$60.00**

American Art Potteries, 1947 – 1963

Candlestick, free-form, green, #141, w/3 cups, 8x9"	**$40.00**
Figurine, deer w/antlers, brown/green/white spray, leaping, #502, 11½"	**$55.00**
Figurine, Poland China hog, white w/gray spots, green base, 5½x7½"	**$50.00**
Figurine, wild horse, brown spray, 3504, 11½"	**$40.00**
Planter, deer reclining by stump, green w/brown spray	**$24.00**
Planter, lamb, white & pink, #456, 8½"	**$25.00**
TV lamp, conch shell, brown/green spray, 6½"	**$30.00**
Vase, conch shell, green/yellow spray, #131, 6"	**$25.00**
Vase, ruffled tulip form, brown/yellow/pink spray, 9"	**$24.00**

Moss Rose

Though a Moss Rose pattern has been produced by Staffordshire and American pottery companies alike since the mid-1800s, the ware we're dealing with here has a much different appearance. The pattern consists of a pink briar rose with dark green mossy leaves on stark white glaze. Very often it is trimmed in gold. In addition to dinnerware, many accessories and novelties were also made. It was a popular product of Japanese manufacturers from the 1950s on, and even today giftware catalogs show a few Moss Rose items.

Refer to *Schroeder's Antiques Price Guide* (Collector Books) for information on the early Moss Rose pattern.

Ashtray, sm	**$6.00**
Bell	**$10.00**
Bowl, Japan, 1950s, 4x7"	**$20.00**
Bowl, sauce	**$6.00**
Bowl, vegetable; Ucagco, 10"	**$35.00**
Bud vase, 3½"	**$15.00**
Butter dish, w/lid, 2½x3½x7¼"	**$45.00**
Candle holders, cornucopia style, gold trim, 4", pr	**$35.00**
Candle holders, Japan, 3", pr	**$15.00**
Candy dish, fluted, w/lid	**$22.00**
Chocolate pot	**$23.00**
Cigarette lighter, gold trim, lg	**$15.00**
Cottage cheese dish	**$15.00**

Creamer, lg $15.00
Creamer, sm...$9.00
Cup, demitasse; gold trim, footed, 2" $12.00
Cup & saucer, Japan, 2½", 5½"...............................$10.00
Cup & saucer, Ucagco, footed $10.00
Dinnerware set, Japan, 1960s, child size, 38-pc, MIB ..$165.00
Dresser box, gold trim, 3x4½x2½"...........................$20.00
Dresser box, ruffled edge, gold trim, w/lid, round, footed,
    6¼x3½" $35.00
Egg boiler, electric, NM $55.00
Egg cup...$9.00
Incense burner, gold trim, 3-footed, w/domed lid, 3¼" ..$15.00
Lamp, Aladdin; gold trim, 5¾".................................$18.00
Lamp, oil; 2-handled, Japan, 7½" $30.00
Mirror, on stand $15.00
Nut dish w/4 nut cups $35.00
Pin tray, butterfly shape $15.00
Plate, dinner; Mikasa, gold trim, 10" $15.00
Plate, salad..$6.50
Platter, Ucagco, rare, 12", from $65 to $85.00
Port wine stopper $10.00
Ring holder, molded as a lady's hand, 8" $30.00
Salt & pepper shakers, pr $18.00
Smoke set, flat tray w/4 ashtrays & lighter..............$40.00
Snack set, shell-shaped plate w/cup ring, matching cup, ser-
    vice for 4 ....$40.00
Sugar bowl, gold trim, w/lid, 4x5½" $13.00
Sugar bowl, Ucagco, open, lg..................................$15.00
Tea set, child's, 17-pc $75.00
Tea set, stacking; creamer & sugar bowl set atop teapot..$30.00
Teapot, musical, plays Tea For Two $55.00
Teapot, regular...$30.00
Teapot, whistling, electric, Japan, 6" $15.00
Tidbit, 2-tier, Japan $20.00
Toothbrush holder, holds 4 upright, #2646 ....$28.00
Trays, butterfly shaped, stacking set of 4 ....$15.00

Motion Clocks (Electric)

Novelty clocks with some type of motion or animation were popular in spring-powered or wind-up form for hundreds of years. Today they bring thousands of dollars when sold. Electric-powered or motor-driven clocks first appeared in the late 1930s and were produced until quartz clocks became the standard, with the 1950s being the era during which they reached the height of their production.

Four companies led their field. They were Mastercrafters, United, Haddon, and Spartus in order of productivity. Mastercrafters was the earliest and longest-lived, making clocks from the late '40s until the late '80s. (They did, however, drop out of business several times during this long period.) United began making clocks in the early '50s and continued until the early '60s. Haddon followed in the same time frame, and Spartus was in production from the late '50s until the mid-'60s.

These clocks are well represented in the listings that follow; prices are for examples in excellent condition and working.

With an average age of forty years, many now need repair. Dried-out grease and dirt easily cause movements and motions not to function. The other nemesis of many motion clocks is deterioration of the fiber gears. Originally intended to keep the clocks quiet, fiber gears have not held up like their metal counterparts. For fully restored clocks, add $50.00 to $75.00 to our values. (Full restoration includes complete cleaning of motor and movement, repair of same; cleaning and polishing face and bezel; cleaning and polishing case and repairing if necessary; and installing new line cord, plug, and light bulb if needed.) Brown is the most common case color for plastic clocks. Add 10% to 20% or more for cases in onyx (mint green) or any light shade. If any parts noted below are missing, value can drop one-third to one-half. We must stress that 'as is' clocks will not bring these prices. Deteriorated, nonworking clocks may be worth less that half of these values.

This is one of many areas of collecting that has been greatly affected by Internet trading. Dealers report that the selling price of many motion clocks is much lower than a few years ago, and right now, at least the market is very volatile. We have tried to be realistic with our suggested values but concede that to a large extent they are fluctuating.

Note: When original names are not known, names have been assigned.

Advisors: Sam and Anna Samuelian (See Directory, Motion Clocks)

Haddon

Based in Chicago, Illinois, Haddon produced an attractive line of clocks. They used composition cases that were hand painted, and sturdy Hansen movements and motions. This is the only clock line for which new replacement motors are still available.

Home Sweet Home, grandma in rocker, brown, 7½x12"...$125.00
Rancho, cabin, cowboy & bucking bronco, scene lights up,
    7x12", EX, from $150 to $200.00
Teeter Totter, children on seesaw, from $125 to.......$175.00

Mastercrafters

Based in Chicago, Illinois, this company produced many of the most appealing and popular collectible motion clocks on today's market. Cases were made of plastic, with earlier examples being a sturdy urea plastic that imparted quality, depth, and shine to their finishes. Clock movements were relatively simple and often supplied by Sessions Clock Company, who also made many of their own clocks.

Airplane, Bakelite & chrome, from $175 to...............$225.00
Blacksmith, plastic, from $75 to $100.00
Carousel, plastic, carousel front, from $175 to.........$225.00
Church or Bell Ringer, plastic, man inside pulls cord to ring
    bell, 12" $100.00
Fireplace, marbleized plastic, drum inside causes fire anima-
    tion, from $60 to..$90.00

Swinging Bird, plastic, w/cage front, from $125 to ..**$150.00**
Swinging Girl, onyx-colored plastic, girl swings in lighted area below clock, 1950s, 11", from $100 to........**$125.00**

Swinging Playmates, plastic, from $100.00 to $125.00.

Waterfall w/Pines, brown plastic w/silver face, flowing water & fire flickering animation, 11".........................**$100.00**

Spartus

This company made clocks well into the '80s, but most later clocks were not animated. Cases were usually plastic, and most clocks featured animals.

Cat, black & white, eyes go up & down, tail moves side to side, 1963-64, 20", from $25 to **$40.00**
Panda Bear, eyes move back & forth, from $25 to.....**$40.00**
Water Wheel (L style), plastic, from $20 to **$30.00**
Waterfall & Wheel, plastic, from $50 to **$75.00**

United

Based in Brooklyn, New York, United made mostly cast-metal cases finished in gold or bronze. Their movements were somewhat more complex than Mastercrafters'. Some of their clocks contained musical movements, which while pleasing can be annoying when continuously run.

Ballerina, wooden, from $75 to.................................**$125.00**
Bobbing Chicks, metal frame, various colors, 12x11", from $35 to...**$50.00**
Bobbing Chicks, wooden house, green & red, from $40 to..**$60.00**
Cowboy w/Rope, metal, wooden base, from $100 to ...**$150.00**
Fireplace, gold metal case, flickering fire animation, 8½x12", from $50 to...**$75.00**
Hula Girl, moves her hips as boy beats drum, 1950s, from $200 to...**$250.00**
Majorette, metal case w/gold paint, baton spins, 1950s, from $75 to...**$125.00**

Owl, wood & metal, eyes move back & forth, 11", from $75 to...**$100.00**
Windmill, pink plastic w/metal feet, scene in base, windmill-arms revolve, from $75 to.................................**$125.00**

Motorcycle Collectibles

At some point in nearly everyone's life, they've experienced at least a brief love affair with a motorcycle. What could be more exhilarating than the open road — the wind in your hair, the sun on your back, and no thought for the cares of today or what tomorrow might bring. For some, the passion never diminished. For most of us, it's a fond memory. Regardless of which description best fits you personally, you will probably enjoy the old advertising and sales literature, books and magazines, posters, photographs, banners, etc., showing the old Harleys and Indians, and the club pins, dealership jewelry and clothing, and scores of other items of memorabilia such as collectors are now beginning to show considerable interest in. For more information and a lot of color photographs, we recommend *Motorcycle Collectibles With Values* by Leila Dunbar (Schiffer). See also License Plates.

Advisor: Bob 'Sprocket' Eckardt (See Directory, Motorcycles)

Ad, Harley-Davidson 5-35, Popular Mechanics 1912, 9¾x6¾", EX...**$25.00**
Ad, Indian Scout, Prince & Chief, 1926, w/original mailer, 10⅛x7", EX..**$30.00**
Ashtray, 1952 Dealers Conference w/logo, aluminum, 4½x4½", EX..**$60.00**
Bank, Harley-Davidson, gas tank shape w/pig face, tail & feet, red-edged white lettering on black, 8x11"..............**$190.00**
Battery checker, Harley-Davidson, glass tube w/plastic bulb & syphon, 1950s, EXIB...**$85.00**
Bolo tie, old brass motorcycle on red & white braided tie, 1950s, EX..**$70.00**
Booklet, 1916 Indian Motorcycle Instruction Book..., 40 pages, EX...**$170.00**
Brochure, Cleveland Motorcycle, America's Finest Four, 1929, EX...**$55.00**
Brochure, Van Veen OCR 1000, German built, 1970s, EX...**$55.00**
Can, Triumph Cycle Bath Motorcycle Engine Degreaser, blue on white, 15-oz, 1970s, EX **$45.00**
Clock, Cushman Motor Skooter, name on oblong light-up panel above round clock, metal, glass & plastic, 18x26x5", EX **$850.00**
Clock, Harley-Davisdon Motorcyles, neon w/polished aluminum case, 1990s, 20 " dia, NM+.....................**$750.00**
Earrings, Harley-Davidson, red, white & blue #1, AMF era, pr..**$30.00**
Handbook, owner's; Velocette Viper 350, Venom MSS500, Clubman Endurance, Thruxton 500, 1966, 88 pages, 4x6½", VG **$23.00**
Helmet, red, white & blue flag theme, World Famous Brand, 1974, EX...**$80.00**

Manual, Motorcycling Electrical; Bernal Osborn, hardback w/dust jacket, 128 pages, 1953, EX.....................**$40.00**

Manual, Triumph, For Speed Twin, Tiger 100 & 111, Thunderbird, Trophy & 3T Deluxe Model, 1945-55, 212 pages, VG+.....................**$20.00**

Oil can, Chain Saver, Fluid Chain Lubricant, gold can w/white shield w/black letters, logo, ca 1964, EX..............**$135.00**

Oil can, Harley-Davidson, black gold & white, logo in center, 1-qt, EX.....................**$175.00**

Oil can, Harley-Davidson, Power Blend Motorcycle Oil, black & white on gray, 1-qt, EX.....................**$35.00**

Oil can, Harley-Davidson Pre-Luxe Premium Deluxe, black & white w/black, white & yellow letters, 1-qt, EX ..**$65.00**

Oiler can, Indian Chain-Oil, round w/yellow paper label, screw lid w/screw-on spout, 4½", G+ **$275.00**

Patch, Harley-Davidson, eagle w/claws in logo, 1970s, 10½x8", EX.....................**$42.00**

Pin, Harley-Davidson, metal grooved w/letters w/black paint, gas tank shape, 1x1½", EX.....................**$70.00**

Pin, Harley-Davidson, motorcycle figural, gold-tone metal, 2½", EX.....................**$28.00**

Pin, Harley-Davidson, Sex, Drugs & Rock & Roll, white on black w/logo in center, 1970s, ⅞" dia, EX...........**$15.00**

Pin, Indian Motorcycles, Indian head w/wings at side w/Indian Motorcycle engraving, 2" W, EX...........**$40.00**

Pin, Indian Motorcycles, round cast image of Indian in full headdress on red background, 1½" dia, NM......**$160.00**

Pin, Indian Motorcycles, winged Indian head in full headdress, 2-pc stamped design, safety-pin mount, ¾x2", EX+ **$400.00**

Pin, laughing Indian head, figural, feather in hair, marked Indian Motorcycles & Baston Bros on back, EX ..**$50.00**

Pin, motorcycle figural, chopper-style, silver-tone metal w/black highlights, 1⅛x3", EX.....................**$25.00**

Pin, old motorcycle above banner w/Harley-Davidson, stamped metal, clasp-style back, ¾" W, EX..........**$60.00**

Pin, Triumph, leaping tiger over Triumph in black, 1950s, 1x½", EX.....................**$65.00**

Postcard, 1941 Indian '45'/Featuring The New 'Double Action' Spring Frame, color image of cycle in landscape, unused, M.....................**$100.00**

Poster, Vintage Motorcycle Ralley, man on BMW motorcycle w/map asking policeman for directions, 31x19", EX **$85.00**

Salt & pepper shakers, Harley-Davidson, Stamina for War or Peace, can shape, metal w/Bakelite bottoms, 2", EX, pr.....................**$28.00**

Sign, Cushman Motor Scooter Sales-Service, painted tin w/wooden frame, red-edged white lettering on green, 17x72", VG **$265.00**

Sign, Harley-Davidson Motorcycles & motorcycle in 3-D, painted wood, 17x24", EX.....................**$45.00**

Sign, Harley-Davidson Motorcycles Sales & Service/ Authorized Dealer, embossed tin, white, Scioto Sign Co, 24x30", EX+.....................**$1,800.00**

Sign, Indian Motorcycles, brown border & letters on yellow, 12x18", NM **$20.00**

Sign, Indian Motorcycles, red glass neon w/black base, Art Deco chrome stripes, Neon Products, 1930s, 16x20", NM **$3,900.00**

Sign, Raleigh/The Record Breaker, porcelain, shows colorful front half of speeding cyclist, 20x16", EX+......**$3,800.00**

Spark plug, Genuine Harley-Davidson, 2½", EXIB.....**$75.00**

Thermometer, Harley-Davidson Motorcycles in red on yellow, old motorcycles graphic, 1980s, M................**$28.00**

Trophy, Alton Dragway, metal motorcycle & rider above winged lady, wood base, 1962, 14" **$35.00**

Trophy, heavy cast metal motorcycle on wooden column wooden base, marked First 1960, 14", EX...........**$25.00**

Watch fob, Indian Motorcycles, gold and black on metal, EX, $100.00.

Watch fob, Indian Motorcycles, Indian head form in full headdress w/6-color cloisonne, 1¾", EX+..........**$350.00**

Wrench, combination; ¾" & ½", marked Indian Motorcycles, came w/motorcycles, ⅛x6", EX **$25.00**

Movie Posters and Lobby Cards

Although many sizes of movie posters were made and all are collectible, the preferred size today is still the one-sheet, 27" wide and 41" long. Movie-memorabilia collecting is as diverse as films themselves. Popular areas include specific films such as *Gone With the Wind, Wizard of Oz*, and others; specific stars — from the greats to character actors; directors such as Hitchcock, Ford, Speilberg, and others; specific film types such as B-Westerns, all-Black casts, sports related, Noir, '50s teen, '60s beach, musicals, crime, silent, radio characters, cartoons, and serials; specific characters such as Tarzan, Superman, Ellery Queen, Blondie, Ma and Pa Kettle, Whistler, and Nancy Drew; specific artists like Rockwell, Davis, Frazetta, Flagg, and others; specific art themes, for instance, policeman, firemen, horses, attorneys, doctors, or nurses (this list is endless). And some collectors just collect posters they like. In the past twenty years, movie memorabilia has steadily increased in value, and in the last few years the top price paid for a movie poster has reached $453,500.00. Movie memorabilia is a new field for collectors.

In the past, only a few people knew where to find posters. Recently, auctions on the East and West coasts have created much publicity, attracting scores of new collectors. Many posters are still moderately priced, and the market is expanding, allowing even new collectors to see the value of their collections increase.

Advisors: Cleophas and Lou Ann Wooley, Movie Poster Service (See Directory, Movie Posters)

An Affair To Remember, 1957, Cary Grant & Deborah Kerr, window card, 22x14", VG $65.00

Around the World in Eighty Days, 1957, David Niven & all-star cast, souvenir book, EX $25.00

Auntie Mame, 1958, Rosalind Russell, window card, 22x14", EX..$35.00

Bad Seed, 1956, Patty McCormack, lobby card set, EX ..$50.00

Bambi, 1966 reissue, Disney animation, 6-sheet, 81x81", EX..$65.00

Bang the Drum Slowly, 1973, Robert DeNiro, ½-sheet & insert, rolled, VG..$25.00

Barbarella, 1966, Jane Fonda, rolled, 60x40", VG $65.00

Baron of Arizona, 1950, Vincent Price, 1-sheet, 41x27", EX..$45.00

Battle Beyond the Sun, 1962, Francis Ford Coppola film, ½-sheet (28x22") & lobby card set, EX $50.00

Battle of the Drag Racers, 1966, Road Runner & Speedy Gonzales cartoon artwork, 1-sheet, 41x27", EX....$65.00

Beneath the Planet of the Apes, 1970, window card, 22x14", M $25.00

Birdman of Alcatraz, 1962, Burt Lancaster, insert, 36x14", EX..$50.00

Boys Town, 1957 reissue, Spencer Tracy & Mickey Rooney, ½-sheet, 28x22", EX..$40.00

Captain Caution, 1948 reissue, Victor Mature, ½-sheet, rolled, 22", EX $35.00

Carousel, 1956, Shirley Jones & Gordon MacRae, window card, 22x14", EX..$50.00

Cat on a Hot Tin Roof, Elizabeth Taylor, 1958, 41x27", from $150.00 to $200.00.

Cheyenne Autumn, 1964, Richard Widmark & James Stewart, lobby card set, EX $50.00

Clambake, 1967, Elvis, 1-sheet, 41x27", EX.................$50.00

Cool Hand Luke, 1967, Paul Newman, 1-sheet, 41x27", EX+ $100.00

Country Girl, 1954, Grace Kelly, Bing Crosby, William Holden, insert, 14x36", EX $50.00

Daddy Long Legs, 1955, Fred Astaire & Leslie Caron, window card, 22x14", VG $35.00

Dangerous When Wet, 1953, Esther Williams & Fernando Lamas w/Tom & Jerry animation, insert, 36x14", EX..........$85.00

David & Bathsheba, 1951, Gregory Peck & Susan Hayward, window card, 22x14", EX..............................$35.00

David Copperfield, 1962 reissue, Freddie Barthalomew & WC Fields, lobby card set, EX $400.00

Death of a Salesman, 1962, Fredrich March, insert, 14x36", EX..$50.00

Desiree, 1954, Marlon Brando, Jean Simmons, Merle Oberon, window card, 22x14", EX..............................$50.00

Dirty Harry, 1971, Clint Eastwood, 1971, 21x14", EX...$65.00

Dr Strangelove, 1963, Peter Sellers & George C Scott, lobby card set, EX..$125.00

Farmer Takes a Wife, 1953, Betty Grable, 3-sheet, 41x81", EX..$85.00

Farmer's Daughter, 1947, Loretta Young & Joseph Cotton, 1-sheet, 41x27", VG+...$65.00

For Your Eyes Only, 1981, Roger Moore, 1-sheet, 41x27", EX..$35.00

Funny Face, 1957, Audrey Hepburn & Fred Astaire, window card, 22x14", EX..$65.00

Gaslight, 1944, Ingrid Bergman & Joseph Cotton, ½-sheet, 28x22", EX..$325.00

GI Blues, 1960, Elvis, 3-sheet, 81x41", VG $150.00

Gigi, 1958, Leslie Caron & Louis Jourdan, lobby card set, EX..$75.00

Glenn Miller Story, 1954, Jimmy Stewart, window card, repaired, 22x14" $50.00

Goldfinger, 1964, Sean Connery, 1-sheet, 41x27", EX...$285.00

Great White Hope, 1970, James Earl Jones, 1-sheet, 41x27", EX..$35.00

Greatest Story Ever Told, 1965, Max Von Sydow, ½-sheet, 41x27", VG..$35.00

Gunfight at the OK Corral, 1957, Kirk Douglas & Burt Lancaster, lobby card set, EX $50.00

Guys & Dolls, 1955, Marlon Brando, Jean Simmons, Frank Sinatra, lobby card set, glossy, 14x11", EX...........$75.00

Hills of Home, 1948, Lassie film w/Edmund Gwenn, Donald Crisp, Janet Leigh, insert, 36x14", EX $50.00

I Want To Live, 1958, Susan Hayward, window card, 22x14", VG $25.00

If Winter Comes, 1948, Walter Pidgeon & Deborah Kerr, 1-sheet, 41x27", EX $50.00

Incredible Shrinking Man, 1957, Grant Williams, 1-sheet, 41x27", VG $225.00

Iron Curtain, 1948, Dana Andrews & Gene Tierney, ½-sheet, 28x22", EX..$75.00

Jaws, 1977, shark & boat scene, 1-sheet, 41x27", EX .$85.00

Jim Thorpe All American, Burt Lancaster, insert, 36x14", EX..$65.00

Johnny Guitar, 1954, Joan Crawford, window card, 22x14", EX..**$65.00**

Last Time I Saw Paris, 1954, Elizabeth Taylor & Van Johnson, 6-sheet, 81x81", EX.........................**$150.00**

Lawrence of Arabia, 1971 reissue, Peter O'Toole, window card, 22x14", EX......................................**$35.00**

Lion in Winter, 1968, Peter O'Toole & Katharine Hepburn, ½-sheet, 28x22", VG...........................**$35.00**

Longest Yard, 1974, Burt Reynolds, lobby card set, EX..**$20.00**

Lost World, 1960, Claude Rains, window card, 22x14", EX **$35.00**

Malcom X, 1972, documentary, 1-sheet, 41x27", EX...**$40.00**

Man for All Seasons, 1967, Paul Scofield, window card, 22x14", EX **$25.00**

Master of the World, 1961, Vincent Price & Peter Lorre, lobby card set, EX **$45.00**

Meet Me in Las Vegas, 1956, Cyd Charisse, 6-sheet, 81x81", unused, M...**$100.00**

Miracle Worker, 1962, Patty Duke & Anne Bancroft, ½-sheet, 28x22", EX **$50.00**

Mr Robinson Crusoe, 1953 reissue, Douglas Fairbanks Sr, 1-sheet, 41x27", EX...**$35.00**

Mr 880, 1950, Burt Lancaster, Edmond Gwen, Dorothy McGuire, lobby card set, EX **$50.00**

Munster Go Home, 1966, cartoon artwork of cast, 3-sheet, 81x41", EX..**$150.00**

Murder on the Orient Express, 1974, Amsel artwork of all-star cast, 1-sheet, 41x27", EX **$45.00**

On Our Merry Way, 1948, James Stewart, Henry Fonda, Paulette Goddard, 3-sheet, 81x41", EX **$125.00**

On the Waterfront, 1954, Marlon Brando, lobby card, 14x11", VG **$25.00**

Paris When It Sizzles, 1964, Audrey Hepburn & William Holden, 1-sheet, 41x27", EX **$50.00**

Patton, 1970, George C Scott, 1-sheet, 41x27", EX......**$50.00**

Please Don't Eat the Daisies, 1960, Doris Day & David Niven, insert, 36x14", EX...**$35.00**

Poseidon Adventure, 1972, disaster image, 1-sheet, 41x27", EX...**$50.00**

Quicksand, 1950, Mickey Rooney, James Cagney, Peter Lorre, stone litho, 3-sheet, 81x41", EX **$85.00**

Raiders of the Lost Ark, 1982, Harrison Ford w/whip above other characters, 1-sheet, rare, 41x27", EX **$65.00**

Rally 'Round the Flag Boys, 1959, Paul Newman, Joanne Woodward, Joan Collins, lobby card set, VG **$35.00**

Rear Window, 1954, James Stewart & Grace Kelly, window card, 22x14", EX...**$125.00**

Rob Roy, 1953, Richard Todd, 3-sheet, 81x41", EX.....**$60.00**

Sandpiper, 1965, Elizabeth Taylor & Richard Burton, ½-sheet, 28x22", EX **$65.00**

Searchers, 1956, John Wayne & Natalie Wood, ½-sheet, 28x22", EX **$400.00**

Shampoo, 1975, Warren Beatty, ½-sheet, rolled, 28x22", VG+ **$35.00**

Shane, 1959 reissue, Alan Ladd, 1-sheet, 41x27", EX..**$65.00**

Singin' in the Rain, 1952, Gene Kelly, Debbie Reynolds, Donald O'Connor, window card, 22x14", EX.....**$200.00**

Slattery's Hurricane, 1949, Veronica Lake, Richard Widmark, Linda Darnell, ½-sheet, 28x22", VG **$50.00**

Snows of Kilmanjaro, 1952, Susan Hayward, Gregory Peck, Ava Gardner, lobby card set, EX **$65.00**

Song of the South, 1956 reissue, Disney, insert, 36x14", EX...**$45.00**

South Pacific, 1959, Mitzi Gaynor, title card, VG **$20.00**

Stagecoach, 1966, Norman Rockwell art featuring Bing Crosby, Ann-Margaret & all-star cast, rolled, 60x40", EX...**$100.00**

State Fair, 1945, Dana Andrews, Jeanne Crain, Vivian Blaine, 1-sheet, 41x27", EX...**$150.00**

The Champ, 1962 reissue, Wallace Berry & Jackie Cooper, 1-sheet, 41x27", EX...**$25.00**

The Entertainer, 1960, Laurence Olivier & Joan Plowright, lobby card set, EX **$40.00**

The Greatest, 1977, Muhammad Ali as himself, 1-sheet, rolled, 41x27" **$50.00**

Three Stooges Meet Hercules, 1961, insert, 36x14", EX..**$50.00**

Time Machine, 1960, Rod Taylor, French stone litho, 63x47", EX...**$400.00**

Train Robbers, 1973, John Wayne & Ann-Margaret, ½-sheet, rolled, 28x22", EX..**$50.00**

Tropic Zone, 1953, Ronald Reagan & Rhonda Fleming, insert, 36x14", EX...**$50.00**

Twist Around the Clock, 1961, Chubby Checker, 1-sheet, 41x27", EX...**$75.00**

Two Lost Worlds, 1950, James Arness w/artwork of the monsters, insert, 36x14", EX..................................**$85.00**

Untamed, 1955, Tyrone Power & Susan Hayward, ½-sheet, 28x22", EX **$50.00**

Voodoo Tiger, 1952, Johnny Weissmuller, 1-sheet, 41x27", EX...**$45.00**

War & Peace, 1956, Audrey Hepburn & Henry Fonda, lobby card set, EX **$50.00**

West Side Story, United Artists, 1961, one-sheet, EX, $350.00.

White Christmas, 1954, Bing Crosby, Danny Kaye, Rosemary Clooney, Vera-Ellen, window card, 22x14", EX....**$65.00**

Wild Bunch, 1969, William Holden, 60x40", VG.........**$50.00**

Wild River, 1960, Montgomery Clift & Lee Remick, ½-sheet, rolled, 28x22", VG...**$30.00**

World of Abbott & Costello, 1965, 1-sheet, 41x27", EX ..**$35.00**
Zorba the Greek, 1965, Anthony Quinn, window card, 22x14", EX **$25.00**
2001: A Space Odyssey, 1968, Stanley Kubrick film, window card, 22x14", unused, M...**$75.00**

Napkin Dolls

Cocktail, luncheon, or dinner..., paper, cotton, or damask..., solid, patterned, or plaid — regardless of size, color, or material, there's always been a place for napkins. In the late 1940s and early 1950s, buffet-style meals were gaining popularity. One accessory common to many of these buffets is now one of today's hot collectibles — the napkin doll. While most of the ceramic and wooden examples found today date from this period, many homemade napkin dolls were produced in ceramic classes of the 1960s and 1970s.

For information on napkin dolls as well as egg timers, string holders, children's whistle cups, baby feeder dishes, razor blade banks, pie birds, laundry sprinkler bottles, and other unique collectibles from the same era, we recommend *Collectibles for the Kitchen, Bath and Beyond*; for ordering information see our advisor's listing in the Directory.

Advisor: Bobbie Zucker Bryson (See Directory, Napkin Dolls)

Holland Mold's Dottie (mold #H-446), ca 1955, 6½", from $75.00 to $95.00. (Photo courtesy Bobbie Zucker Bryson)

Betson's yellow Colonial lady, bell clapper, marked Hand Painted, 9", from $75 to **$90.00**
Byron Molds, pink & white lady w/arms crossed holding a bouquet, bow on top of head, 8½", from $65 to.**$85.00**
California Ceramic mold, yellow & purple lady w/candle holder in top of hat, 12½", from $65 to...............**$85.00**
California Originals, Miss Versatility Cocktail Girl, 13", from $75 to...**$95.00**
California Originals, pink & white, Spanish dancer, slits in back only, foil label, 15", from $110 to **$150.00**
Can Can, ceramic figure of blue & gold girl holding skirt open to expose legs, 9½", from $125 to **$150.00**

Enesco, Genie at Your Service, holding lantern, paper label, 8", from $100 to...**$135.00**
German, metal silhouette of Deco woman, black & gold w/wire bottom, marked E Kosta DBGM 1744970, 8⅞", from $115 to...**$135.00**
Goebel, half doll holding a rose on wire frame, marked Goebel, W Germany, ca 1957, 8¼", from $225 to...............**$250.00**
Hachiya Bros, lady holding yoke w/bucket salt & pepper shakers, hat conceals candle holder, from $125 to.........**$150.00**
Holland Mold, Daisy, No 514, 7¼", from $75 to.........**$95.00**
Holland Mold, Rebecca No H-265, wearing white dress w/2 tiers of napkin slits, 10½", from $150 to.............**$195.00**
Holland Mold, Rosie, No H-132, 10⅞", from $60 to...**$75.00**
Holt Howard, yellow Sunbonnet Miss, marked Holt Howard, 1958, 5", from $125 to.......................................**$150.00**
Japan, angel, pink, holding flowers, slits in shoulders so napkins form wings, 5⅜", from $100 to **$115.00**
Japan, lady in blue w/pink umbrella, bell clapper, unmarked, 9", from $70 to...**$85.00**
Japan, lady in pink dress w/blue shawl & yellow hat, 8½", from $65 to...**$85.00**
Japan, Santa, marked Chess, 1957, 6¾", from $95 to ..**$150.00**
Kreiss & Co, angel, candle holder in halo, holding a Christmas tree, 11", from $90 to **$110.00**
Kreiss & Co, green doll w/gold trim holding muff, jeweled eyes, candle holder in hat, marked, 10¼", from $95 to..**$110.00**
Kreiss & Co, green doll w/poodle, jeweled eyes, necklace & ring, candle holder behind hat, marked, 10¾", from $100 to..**$125.00**
Kreiss & Co, yellow lady w/fan, candle holder behind fan, marked, 10½", from $75 to **$95.00**
Mallory Ceramics Studio, Christine, blue dress w/purple flower trim, blonde hair, 9", from $135 to.........**$150.00**
Marcia of California, woman w/molded apron, 1 hand holding bowl on her head, blue iridescent finish, 13", from $95 to..**$150.00**
Marybelle, mold P71, Southern lady holding hat, 9¾", from $150 to..**$195.00**
Rooster, black w/red & yellow trim, slits in sides for napkins, w/matching salt & pepper shakers, from $55 to..**$65.00**
Servy Etta, wood, gray w/marble base, marked USD Patent No 159,005, 11½" from $35 to.............................**$45.00**
Swedish doll, wooden, marked Patent No 113861, 10", from $25 to..**$35.00**
Viking Japan, man (bartender), green & white, holding tray w/candle holder, 8¾", from $85 to.....................**$100.00**
Willoughby Studio, golden yellow lady w/brown applied trim holding a tilted pitcher, 12", from $100 to..**$125.00**
Wooden Jamaican lady, movable arms, papel label: Ave 13 Nov 743, A Sinfonia, Tel 2350 Petropolis, 6", from $65 to..**$85.00**
Wooden pink & blue doll w/red strawberry toothpick holder on head, 8", from $60 to **$75.00**
Wooden umbrella, marked Reg Prop No 382.649, Reproduction Prohibited, Industria Argentina, 8⅜", from $25 to..**$45.00**

NASCAR Collectibles

Over the past decade, interest in NASCAR racing has increased to the point that the related collectibles industry has mushroomed into a multi-billion dollar business. Posters, magazines, soda pop bottles, model kits, and scores of other items are only a few examples of items produced with the sole intention of attracting racing fans. Also included as a part of this field of collecting are items such as race-worn apparel — even parts from the racing cars themselves — and these, though not devised as such, are the collectibles that command the highest prices! If you're a racing fan, you'll want to read *Racing Collectibles* by the editors of *Racing Collector's Price Guide* (Collector Books).

Activity center, plastic stationary car w/rotating fabric seat, activities for baby, Nascar Safety 1st, MIB **$80.00**

Bank, Dale Earnhardt 1996 Atlanta Olympics, dark windows, yellow tires, 1/24 scale, M **$110.00**

Bedspread, racing advertising on Perma-Prest, Sears, full size, 1970s, 90x106", M **$60.00**

Binoculars, Nikon Nascar series, 8x25, slim design to fit in shirt pocket, diopter control, MIB **$70.00**

Bobbin' head doll, Dale Jarret, Legends of the Track, MIB **$25.00**

Bowling ball, Jeff Gordon, Viz-a Ball, undrilled, 8-lb, M **$100.00**

Cake mold set, Race Car Cake Baking Kit, Official Nascar License, MIB...**$30.00**

Cap, Dale Jarrett #88, Coca-Cola logo, cloth w/bill front, M **$15.00**

Car seat/booster, Dale Earnhardt, 5-point harness, A-lock adjustment, EX **$85.00**

Car set, Nascar 50th Anniversary, 29 diecast replicas w/collector card & display stand, MIB **$60.00**

Clock, neon; Dale Earnhardt Jr, black acrylic frame, 20x18" **$145.00**

Clock, Ricky Rudd #28, neon in black acrylic frame, 20x18" **$125.00**

Comic book, Racing Pettys, 1980, art by Bob Kane, $75.00. (Photo courtesy Racing Collectibles)

Fan, ceiling; NASCAR & colored stripes on ea of 4 blades, w/light kit, MIB................**$100.00**

Figurine, Jeff Gordon Rookie, Sports Image, hand signed autograph, 1994, limited edition, M w/certificate.**$75.00**

Jacket, suede, Dale Earnhardt Jr, JH Design Chase, black satin lining, inner zip pocket, EX.................................**$150.00**

Jacket, 50th Anniversary, Jeff Hamilton Collection, black leather, M..**$125.00**

License plate attachment, America's #1 Motorsport w/American & checkered flags & eagle, plastic, 6x12" **$10.00**

Mirror, Budweiser, Brickyard 400 Inaugural, Indianapolis Motor Speedway, 1994, 34x26", NM...................**$120.00**

Necklace, Dale Earnhardt #3, gold-tone metal, Made in USA, M in original packaging **$10.00**

Pedal car, Jeff Gordon, Pepsi, stick brake, molded plastic w/tube steel frame, 17x48x22", M......................**$215.00**

Photograph, Dale Earnhardt, color, autographed, 8x10", w/certificate of authenticity, M **$55.00**

Pocketknife, Geoff Bodine, Daytona 500, canoe style, bone handle, Case limited edition, MIB **$225.00**

Pocketknife, Neil Bonnett, Alabama, dark red bone trapper style w/etched blade, Case, 1991, MIB...............**$125.00**

Pocketknives, Dale Earnhart, Snap-On Tools, Frost Cutlery #7536, models 105SS & 152SS, NRFB.................**$110.00**

Postcard, Bobby Allison, Camaro, 1974, 6x9", EX.......**$60.00**

Poster, Jeff Gordon, Du Pont advertising, paper, 35x23", M **$12.50**

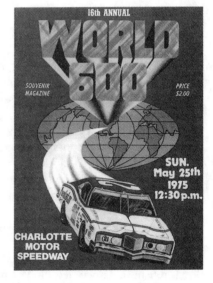

Poster, 16th Annual World 600, Charlotte Motor Speedway, 1975, Dale Ernhardt's first Winston Cup race, $120.00. (Photo courtesy Racing Collectibles)

Ratchet, Snap-On, Earnhard's signature on blue handle, ⅜", M **$50.00**

Ring, #3 Dale Earnhardt, black onyx & mother-of-pearl checkerboard cabochon in 10k yellow gold **$55.00**

Shirt, crew; Jasper Engines & Transmissions, etc, short sleeves, M...**$85.00**

Sign, Coca-Cola Racing Family, Earnhardt, Rudd, Burton, Labonte & 2 others, head shape, 33x26", M.......**$100.00**

Silver coin, Jeff Gordon champion racer 1 side & #24 on reverse, 1-troy oz, 3½" dia, MIB...........................**$75.00**

Standup, Bill Elliot, Coca-Cola, 72x36", folds in half ..**$195.00**
Sticker, Robby Gordon #31, Action Sports, 3" dia, M ...**$3.50**
Sunglasses, Gatorz Nascar edition, wraparound polished aluminum radiator frame w/chrome lenses, M in case..**$70.00**
Tap handle, Dale Earnhardt Jr #8, Budweiser, MIB **$80.00**
Umbrella, Miller Beer, vinyl, 77" dia w/72" pole, promo item, M **$80.00**
Wrenches, combination; Snap-On Signature series, Childress, Earnhardt & McReynolds, 3-pc, M in tin car case **$80.00**

New Martinsville

Located in a West Virginia town by the same name, the New Martinsville Glass Company was founded in 1901 and until it was purchased by Viking in 1944 produced quality tableware in various patterns and colors that collectors admire today. They also made a line of glass animals which Viking continued to produce until they closed in 1986. In 1987 the factory was bought by Mr. Kenneth Dalzell who reopened the company under the title Dalzell-Viking. He used the old molds to reissue his own line of animals, which he marked 'Dalzell' with an acid stamp. These are usually priced in the $50.00 to $60.00 range. Examples marked 'V' were made by Viking for another company, Mirror Images. They're valued at $15.00 to $35.00, with colors sometimes higher.

Advisor: Roselle Schleifman (See Directory, Elegant Glass)

Ashtray, Moondrops, blue or red **$30.00**
Basket, Janice, crystal, 11"................................**$75.00**
Bonbon, Prelude, handled, 6"................................**$18.00**
Bonbon, Radiance, ice blue or red, 6" **$35.00**
Bowl, celery; Radiance, ice blue or red, 10" **$45.00**
Bowl, console; Moondrops, colors other than blue or red, round, 3-footed, 12"................................**$37.50**
Bowl, fruit; Janice, crystal, ruffled top, 12"................**$50.00**
Bowl, Janice, crystal, cupped, 3-toed, 10½"................**$45.00**
Bowl, Janice, crystal, 2-handled, crimped, 6"............**$20.00**
Bowl, Meadow Wreath, crystal, crimped, #4220/26 ....**$35.00**
Bowl, Meadow Wreath, crystal, crimped, footed, #4266/26, 11"................................**$40.00**
Bowl, Moondrops, blue or red, footed, concave top, 8⅜"..**$50.00**
Bowl, Prelude, crystal, shallow, 13" **$45.00**
Bowl, punch; Meadow Wreath, crystal, #4221/26, 5-qt.**$125.00**
Bowl, relish; Radiance, ice blue or red, 2-part, 7" **$35.00**
Candlestick, Addie, black, cobalt, Jade or red, 3½"....**$30.00**
Candlestick, Radiance, ice blue or red, ruffled, 6", pr ..**$175.00**
Candlesticks, Moondrops, colors other than blue or red, ruffled, 5", pr **$25.00**
Candy jar, Radiance, ice blue or red, flat, w/lid **$100.00**
Celery, Prelude, crystal, 10½"................................**$30.00**
Comport, cracker; Janice, crystal, for cheese plate **$15.00**
Comport, Moondrops, blue or red, 4"................**$32.50**
Creamer, Radiance, amber **$12.00**
Cup, punch; Meadow Wreath, crystal, tab handled, 4-oz....**$7.50**
Cup, punch; Radiance, amber................................**$7.00**

Goblet, Moondrops, blue or red, 5-oz, 4¾" **$24.00**
Goblet, Moondrops, colors other than blue or red, 8-oz, 5¾"................................**$20.00**
Ice pail, Janice, crystal, handled, 10" **$65.00**
Jam jar, Janice, blue or red, w/lid, 6"................**$50.00**
Ladle, Radiance, amber, for punch bowl................**$100.00**
Mayonnaise, Prelude, crystal, 3-pc **$35.00**
Mug, Moondrops, colors other than blue or red, 12-oz, 5⅛"................................**$24.00**
Pitcher, berry cream; Janice, blue or red, 15-oz........**$125.00**
Plate, blue or red, 2-handled, 12"................................**$55.00**
Plate, cake; Prelude, crystal, 3-footed, 11"................**$35.00**
Plate, lunch; Addie, pink................................**$7.00**
Plate, Meadow Wreath, crystal, 11" **$35.00**
Plate, Prelude, crystal, handled, 6½"................**$12.50**
Plate, sherbet; Moondrops, blue or red, 6⅛"................**$8.00**
Platter, Janice, blue or red, oval, 13"................**$90.00**
Platter, Moondrops, blue or red, oval, 12"................**$47.00**
Relish, Prelude, crystal, 5-part, 13"................**$35.00**

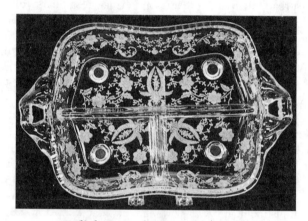

Relish tray, three-part, $55.00.

Salt & pepper shakers, Radiance, amber, pr...............**$50.00**
Stem, wine; Prelude, crystal, 3-oz **$22.00**
Sugar bowl, Prelude, crystal, 4-footed **$15.00**
Tray, Janice, blue or red, 2-handled, oval, for creamer & sugar bowl................................**$30.00**
Tumbler, Radiance, amber, 9-oz **$20.00**
Tumbler, shot; Moondrops, colors other than blue or red, 2-oz, 2¾"................................**$9.00**
Vase, ball; Janice, blue or red, 9" **$145.00**
Vase, bud; Prelude, crystal, 10"................................**$30.00**
Vase, Meadow Wreath, crystal, flared, #42/26 ....**$50.00**
Vase, Moondrops, colors other than blue or red, rocket style, 9¼"................................**$150.00**

Nichols, Betty Lou

This California artist/potter is probably best known for her head vases, which display her talents and strict attention to detail to full advantage. Many of her ladies were dressed in stylish clothing and hats that were often decorated with applied lace, ruffles, and bows; the signature long eyelashes are apparent on nearly every model she made. Because these applications are delicate and susceptible to damage, mint-condition examples are rare and very valuable. Most of her head vases and figurines carry not only her name but the name of the subject as well.

Figure vase, Margot, open baskets on ea side may be used as planters, 10½", NM, from $100 to **$145.00**
Figure vase, white dress w/lavender polka dots & lavender yoke, holding black & lavender hat, label, 8x5½", EX **$60.00**
Figurine, Holly, standing girl w/song book, 6½"........**$40.00**
Figurine, Santa & Mrs Claus, standing, 9", 9½", M, pr ..**$250.00**
Head vase, blonde in white blouse w/gold edge at neck, green jumper w/flowers, white hat w/blue trim, 3", NM...**$50.00**
Head vase, Ermintrude, green dress w/white stripes, black & white ermine tips on shoulder, matching hat, 8½", M..**$350.00**

Head vase, Louisa, 6", EX/NM, $185.00.
(Photo courtesy Treasure Farm)

Head vase, Mary Lou, black dress w/ruffled white yoke & 2 black buttons, white hat w/black rim, 6", NM, from $200 to..**$275.00**
Head vase, Nancy, lavender dress w/pale lavender ruffles, black hat w/black & white ribbon, blonde w/curls, 6½", EX **$235.00**
Head vase, Nellie, blue w/white polka-dot dress w/ruffles, 5", M **$225.00**
Head vase, Nellie, pink dress w/white polka dots & ruffles, matching hat, 9x6½", M **$385.00**
Head vase, Vicky, black hair, rose-colored dress w/white polka dots, white ribbon at neckline & matching hat, 7", EX **$245.00**
Head vase, young lady in white dress w/lavender & black flowers, black hair, white hat, 3½", M **$80.00**
Planter, crawling baby, 4x5", M...................................**$85.00**

Niloak Pottery

The Niloak Pottery company was the continuation of a quarter-century-old family business in Benton, Arkansas. Known as the Eagle Pottery in the early twentieth century, its owner was Charles Dean Hyten who continued in his father's footsteps making utilitarian wares for local and state markets. In 1909 Arthur Dovey, an experienced potter formerly from the Rookwood Pottery of Ohio and the Arkansas-Missouri based Ouachita Pottery companies, came to Benton and created America's most unusual art pottery. Introduced in 1910 as Niloak (kaolin spelled backwards), Dovey and Hyten produced art pottery pieces from swirling clays with a wide range of artificially created colors including red, blue, cream, brown, gray, and later green. Connected to the Arts & Crafts Movement by 1913, the pottery was labeled as Missionware (probably due to its seeming simplicity in the making). Missionware (or swirl) production continued alongside utilitarian ware manufacturing until the 1930s when economic factors led to the making of another type of art pottery and later to (molded) industrial castware. In 1931 Niloak Pottery introduced Hywood Art Pottery (marked as such), consisting of regular glaze techniques including overspray, mottling, and drips of two colors on vases and bowls that were primarily hand thrown. It was short-lived and soon replaced with the Hywood by Niloak (or Hywood) line to increase marketing potential through the use of the well-recognized Niloak name. Experienced potters, designers, and ceramists were involved at Niloak; among them were Frank Long, Paul Cox, Stoin M. Stoin, Howard Lewis, and Rudy Ganz. Many local families with long ties to the pottery included the McNeills, Rowlands, and Alleys. Experiencing tremendous financial woes by the mid-1930s, Niloak came under new management which was led by Hardy L. Winburn of Little Rock. To maximize efficiency and stay competetive, they focused primarily on industrial castware such as vases, bowls, figurines, animals, and planters. Niloak survived into the late 1940s when it became known as the Winburn Tile Company of North Little Rock; it still exists today.

Virtually all of Niloak Missionware/swirl pottery is marked with die stamps. The exceptions are generally fan vases, wall pockets, lamp bases, and whiskey jugs. Be careful when you buy unmarked swirl pottery — it is usually Evans pottery (made in Missouri) which generally has either no interior glaze or is chocolate brown inside. Moreover, Evans made swirl wall pockets, lamp bases, and even hanging baskets that find their way on to today's market and are sold as Niloak. Niloak stickers are often placed on these unmarked Evans pieces — closely examine the condition of the sticker to determine if it is damaged or mutilated from the transfer process.

For more information, we recommend *The Collector's Encyclopedia of Niloak Pottery* (Collector Books) by our advisor David Edwin Gifford, a historian of Arkansas pottery.

Advisor: David Edwin Gifford (See Directory, Niloak)

Ashtray, Arkansas w/Pegasus & recessed diamond, Ozark Blue, Niloak in low relief, 4¼x3½", from $75 to .**$100.00**

Ball jug, Delft Blue, castware, Hywood by Niloak incised mark), 5½", from $125 to.................................**$175.00**

Bowl, Mission, incurvate rim, marked Patent Pend'g, 4¼", from $125 to.................................**$175.00**

Candlestick, Mission, 1st art mark, 10", from $175 to ..**$225.00**

Candlestick, Mission, 3-color swirl, 2nd art mark, 7", from $125 to.................................**$175.00**

Cigarette jar, cylindrical, 1st art mark, 4¾x3¼", from $275 to.................................**$325.00**

Creamer, Fox Red, marked Niloak in low relief, 4¾", from $10 to.................................**$15.00**

Figurine, elephant, Ozark Blue, hollow, unmarked, 2¼", from $50 to.................................**$75.00**

Figurine, Razorback hog, maroon, unmarked, 3¾", from $100 to.................................**$200.00**

Figurine, Southern Bell, Ozark Dawn II, Peterson design, marked Niloak in low relief, 7¼", from $100 to ..**$125.00**

Figurine, swan, Ozark Blue, hollow, Potteries sticker, 2¾", from $50 to.................................**$100.00**

Flower frog, duck, Ozark Dawn II, unmarked, 6", from $45 to.................................**$65.00**

Pitcher, Fox Red, hand thrown, 2nd art mark, 3¼", from $15 to.................................**$20.00**

Pitcher, Peacock Blue II, petal design, unmarked Hywood, 8¾", from $100 to.................................**$125.00**

Pitcher, water; Ozark Dawn II, w/ice guard, Niloak mark in block letters, 7¾", from $75 to.................................**$100.00**

Planter, bear figural, brown, $35.00.

Planter, Circus Elephant, Stars of the Big top design, white, incised mark, 7", from $35 to.................................**$45.00**

Planter, Mission, 1st art mark, 4½", from $175 to **$225.00**

Shakers, geese, Ozark Dawn II, Alley design, Potteries sticker, 2", pr, from $35 to.................................**$45.00**

Tumbler, Peacock Blue II, unmarked Hywood, 5", from $35 to.................................**$55.00**

Vase, castware, 4-ruffle rim, Hywood by Niloak mark, Potteries sticker, 9", from $200 to.................................**$250.00**

Vase, Delft Blue, hand thrown, Hywood by Niloak mark & EZ ink stamp, 4½", from $75 to.................................**$100.00**

Vase, Green & Tan Bright, applied rim-to-hip handles, Hywood Art Pottery, 6½", from $250 to.................................**$350.00**

Vase, Mission, bulbous, sm rim, 2nd art mark, 5¼", from $125 to.................................**$150.00**

Vase, Mission, can neck, die-stamped Benton Ark mark, 6¼", from $225 to.................................**$275.00**

Vase, Mission, cylinder w/slight flare at base, 1st art mark, 8¼", from $275 to.................................**$325.00**

Vase, Mission, inverted cone w/disk foot, 1st art mark, 9½", from $325 to.................................**$375.00**

Vase, Mission, shouldered, 1st art mark, 8", from $200 to..**$250.00**

Vase, Mission, unmarked, 2", from $175 to **$200.00**

Vase, Ozark Blue, slightly bulbous, unmarked, 6¾", from $75 to.................................**$100.00**

Vase, Ozark Dawn I, handles, unmarked, 6", from $150 to.................................**$200.00**

Vase, Winged Victory, ivory, Joe Alley design, marked Niloak in low relief, 7¼", from $25 to.................................**$35.00**

Noritake

Before the government restricted the use of the Nippon mark in 1921, all porcelain exported from Japan (even that made by the Noritake Company) carried the Nippon mark. The company that became Noritake had its beginning in 1904 and over the years experienced several changes in name and organization. Until 1941 (at the onset of WWII) they continued to import large amounts of their products to America. (During the occupation, when chinaware production was resumed, all imports were to have been marked 'Occupied Japan,' though because of the natural resentment on the part of the Japanese, much of it was not.)

Many variations will be found in their marks, but nearly all contain the Noritake name. Reproductions abound; be very careful. If you'd like to learn more about this subject, we recommend *The Collector's Encyclopedia of Noritake* by Joan Van Patten, and *The Collector's Encyclopedia of Early Noritake* by Aimee Neff Alden. All are published by Collector Books.

Newsletter: *Noritake News*
David H. Spain
1237 Federal Ave. E, Seattle, WA 98102; 206-323-8102

Ashtray, bird applied to 3-lobed tray w/tree scenic in center, red mark, 3½", from $100 to.................................**$140.00**

Ashtray, flowers on shaded cream, 4 rests, M-in-wreath mark, 5¾".................................**$50.00**

Ashtray, horses molded in relief inside, red body w/4 green rests, green M-in-wreath mark, 5½" dia, from $200 to......**$275.00**

Ashtray, lady figural, skirt forms tray, green M-in-wreath mark, 5¼" dia, from $350 to.................................**$400.00**

Basket vase, red w/flower decor inside, simple gold handle, red M-in-wreath mark, 5½", from $125 to..........**$140.00**

Bowl, nut; squirrel & nuts molded in relief, green M-in-wreath mark, 6½" L, from $135 to.....................**$160.00**

Bowl, river scenic, 8-sided, red M-in-wreath mark, 6½"..**$35.00**

Cake plate, multicolor flowers on white, sm pierced handles, red M-in-wreath mark, 11", from $50 to **$65.00**

Celery tray, pastel roses on white to ivory w/gold trim, pierced handles, green M-in-wreath mark, 11" L, from $45 to **$65.00**

Chamberstick, Egyptian decor & orange lustre, black handles, green mark, 6½", from $220 to **$260.00**

Cheese dish, yellow band w/Deco flowers on white, slant lid, M-in-wreath mark, 8" L **$100.00**

Cigarette box, classical figures in reserve on lid, red mark, 5½" L, from $150 to...................................... **$180.00**

Compote, swans in river scenic, handles, M-in-wreath mark, 9" L... **$80.00**

Flower holder, bird on stump figural, multicolor lustre, green mark, 4¾", from $160 to **$200.00**

Game plate, game bird scene (variety of scenes found), fruit baskets & swags on border, red mark, 8½", from $85 to.. **$120.00**

Humidor, simple Deco-style flower on yellow band over white, gold trim, green M-in-wreath mark, sq sides, 5¾"... **$185.00**

Jam jar, strawberries on yellow, rose finial, slot for spoon in lid, attached tray, green M-in-wreath mark, green mark **$90.00**

Lemon dish, lemon on orange lustre, applied lemon bud at side, red mark, 6¾" L, from $75 to **$95.00**

Lemon dish, lemons in white w/orange lustre rim, sm handle, red M-in-wreath mark, 5¾" dia, from $30 to.......... **$40.00**

Napkin ring, multicolor roses, M-in-wreath mark, 2¼" L **$35.00**

Plaque, lady seated on sofa, silhouette scene on ivory, green M-in-wreath mark, 8½", from $275 to................. **$325.00**

Plaque, ship, marked, 10" dia, from $185 to.................. **$225.00**

Plate, windmill & river landscape, bright colors, M-in-wreath mark, 7½"... **$65.00**

Powder puff box, dancing lady in red & black, green M-in-wreath mark, 4" dia, from $275 to **$325.00**

Relish dish, orange lustre w/applied bird at center divide, green mark, 8" L, from $120 to **$150.00**

Salt shaker, river scenic in earth tones, green M-in-wreath mark, 2½", from $5 to **$8.00**

Syrup, trees, river & red-roofed cottage scene, M-in-wreath mark, 4½", +undertray............................... **$85.00**

Tea caddy, oriental scenes on lustre ware, rose finial, red M-in-wreath mark, 3¾", from $235 to **$275.00**

Tray, river scenic, blue & brown tones, blue backstamp, 12" L, from $65 to **$80.00**

Tulip vase, flower form, purple & green, red M-in-wreath mark, 5½", from $200 to **$250.00**

Vase, jack-in-the-pulpit; river scenic, M-in-wreath mark, 7¾"... **$180.00**

Vase, man on camel scene, squatty, backstamp, 2½", from $125 to.. **$160.00**

Vase, river scenic, gold scroll handles, red M-in-wreath mark, 7", from #100 to.. **$140.00**

Wall pocket, swan scenic band above orange lustre, flared top, red mark, 8" L, from $100 to........................ **$140.00**

Azalea

The Azalea pattern was produced exclusively for the Larkin Company, who offered it to their customers as premiums from 1916 until the 1930s. It met with much success, and even today locating pieces to fill in your collection is not at all difficult. The earlier pieces carry the Noritake M-in-wreath mark. Later the ware was marked Noritake, Azalea, Hand Painted, Japan.

Bowl, #12, 10".. **$42.50**
Bowl, deep, #310... **$68.00**
Bowl, vegetable; divided, #439, 9½"........................... **$295.00**
Butter chip, #312, 3¼"... **$120.00**
Candy jar, w/lid, #313 .... **$750.00**

Cheese/butter dish, #314, $135.00.

Compote, #170.. **$98.00**
Creamer & sugar bowl, gold finial, #410............... **$155.00**
Creamer & sugar shaker, #122.................................. **$125.00**
Cup & saucer, #2 .... **$20.00**
Egg cup, #120 .... **$40.00**
Mustard jar, #191, 3-pc... **$50.00**
Plate, breakfast; #98.. **$28.00**
Plate, dinner; #13, 9¾" **$22.00**
Platter, #17, 14".. **$60.00**
Platter, #56, 12".. **$58.00**
Relish, oval, #18, 8½".. **$20.00**
Salt & pepper shakers, bell form, #11, pr.................. **$30.00**
Spoon holder, #189, 8".. **$115.00**
Teapot, #15.. **$110.00**
Vase, bulbous, #452.. **$1,150.00**

Tree in the Meadow

Made by the Noritake China Company during the 1920s and 1930s, this pattern of dinnerware is beginning to show up more and more at the larger flea markets and antique malls. It's easy to spot; the pattern is hand painted, so there are variations, but the color scheme is always browns, gold-yellows, and orange-rust, and the design features a large dark tree in the foreground, growing near a lake. There is usually a cottage in the distance.

Bowl, cream soup; 2-handle **$35.00**
Bowl, oval, 9½" **$28.00**
Bowl, vegetable; 9" **$35.00**
Cake plate, open handles **$35.00**
Cheese dish **$75.00**
Condiment set, 5 pcs **$45.00**
Cup & saucer, breakfast **$18.00**
Gravy boat **$50.00**
Plate, dinner; 9¾" **$95.00**
Platter, 10" **$135.00**
Relish, divided **$35.00**
Tea set, 3 pcs **$135.00**

Various Dinnerware Patterns, ca 1933 to Presett

So many lines of dinnerware have been produced by the Noritake company that to list them all would require a volume in itself. In fact, just such a book is available — *The Collector's Encyclopedia of Early Noritake* by Aimee Neff Alden (Collector Books). And while many patterns had specific names, others did not, so you'll probably need the photographs this book contains to help you identify your pattern. Contained herein is only a general guide for the more common pieces and patterns. It can be used to roughly evaluate lines from about 1933 until the mid-1960s.

Bowl, berry; from $12 to **$14.00**
Bowl, soup; from $12 to **$15.00**
Creamer, from $25 to **$30.00**
Cup & saucer, demitasse; from $18 to **$25.00**
Gravy boat, from $45 to **$60.00**
Plate, dinner; from $18 to **$30.00**
Platter, 13½" to 14" in length, from $60 to ...**$75.00**
Platter, 16" or more in length, from $75 to ...**$100.00**
Salt & pepper shakers, pr, from $30 to **$50.00**
Tea & toast set (sm cup w/tray), from $15 to ...**$35.00**
Vegetable bowl/tureen, w/lid, from $70 to ...**$120.00**

Novelty Radios

Novelty radios come in an unimaginable variety of shapes and sizes from advertising and product shapes to character forms, vehicles, and anything else the manufacturer might dream up. For information on these new, fun collectibles read *Collector's Guide to Novelty Radios* by Marty Bunis and Robert Breed, and *Schroeder's Collectible Toys, Antique to Modern* (Collector Books).

Archie, jukebox form, Vanity Fair/Archie Co, 1977, 6", M..**$50.00**
Ballentine's Scotch, bottle shape, made in Hong Kong, 9", EX...**$25.00**
Boxing Kangaroo, cloth figure, official product of American Cup Defense in 1987, Korea, 11", NM **$100.00**
Bubble Tape Bubble Gum Dispenser, adjustable necklace & belt clip, China, 3" dia, NM, from $15 to **$25.00**
Bullwinkle, 1969, 12", NM **$150.00**

Bumper car, Playtime Concepts, 14", NM, from $100 to ..**$125.00**
Cherry 7-Up, Popworks jukebox, M, from $50 to **$75.00**
Cool Sounds, cooler bag w/AM-FM radio, distributed by Sunhill, 8x13", NM **$25.00**
Evil Knievel, tire shape, Montgomery Ward, 1974, battery-op, EX **$35.00**
Fonzie, plastic figure, Sutton, 1974, M **$65.00**
Girl w/Bird, girl holds bird in hand that moves as station pointer, Japan, 7½x7", NM **$40.00**
Harley-Davidson Motorcycle, w/cassette player & headphones, China, 15", from $50 to **$75.00**
Heileman's Old Style Beer, can shape, NM **$65.00**
Hershey's Syrup, bottle shape, battery-op, 8", MIB **$40.00**
Kendall Dual Action Heavy Duty Motor Oil, sm profile can, NM **$35.00**
Maxwell House Instant Coffee Powder Can, Hong Kong, 4x2½" dia, NM, from $75 to **$100.00**
MCI, Make Our Customers See Stars, Friends & Family, Isis model 39, NM **$30.00**
Mr T, figure flexing muscles, belt clip on back, battery-op, 1983, 5", NM **$30.00**
National Adhesives, oil-drum shape, made by PRI/HKA of Hong Kong, NM **$65.00**
Nestle Nesquik Milk Shake Mix, NM, from $35 to **$50.00**
Old Spice Can, Isis model 105, 7", NM, from $75 to ..**$100.00**
Oreo Cookies/Dairy Queen Blizzard, Isis model 39, NM, from $25 to **$35.00**
Pepsi, shirt-pocket style...**$25.00**
Pink Panther, stuffed cloth, 12", NM, from $25 to **$35.00**
Poweready Batteries, battery shape, from $50 to........**$75.00**
Radio Shack, round battery shape, AM, 4½x2½" dia, NM .**$20.00**
Scooby-Doo, figure w/green collar & red tongue hanging out of mouth, NM **$28.00**

Sears Easy Living Paint Can, Hong Kong, NM, from $35.00 to $50.00. (Photo courtesy Marty Bunis and Robert Breed)

Smurf, stereo series, w/speakers, Peyo, 1964, NM, from $50 to **$75.00**

Snoopy Doghouse, Determined, plastic, 1970s, 6x4", NMIB, from $50 to...**$60.00**

Snoopy Spaceship, AM, plastic, Concept 2000/Determind, 1970s, 6x8", MIB, from $125 to **$175.00**

Sosnick Hot Mustard, Russian Style, AM-FM, made in China, 3x4", NM...**$75.00**

Sunkist Orange Soda, AM/FM, NM.....................**$40.00**

Tune-A-Fish, shower radio, AM-FM, Spectra, MIP **$20.00**

Watkins Baking Powder, can shape, battery-op, 5½", NMIB **$35.00**

Novelty Telephones

Novelty telephones modeled after products or advertising items are popular with collectors — so are those that are character related. For further information we recommend *Schroeder's Collectible Toys, Antique to Modern* (Collector Books).

Bart Simpson, Columbia Tel-Com, 1990s, MIB............**$35.00**

Cabbage Patch Girl, 1980s, EX, from $65 to...............**$75.00**

Care Bears, purple, intercom system only, 1983, MIB ...**$50.00**

Coca-Cola, Coke can w/receiver on side, rotary dial, contour wave design on red, 13", EX **$375.00**

Dale Earnhardt #3 Goodwrench Car, MIB **$60.00**

Darth Vader, 1983, MIB **$200.00**

Flintstones, gray w/red horn-shaped handset, 5-hole dial, early 1960s, EX..**$80.00**

Ghostbusters, white ghost inside red circle, receiver across center, Remco, 1987, EX..............................**$20.00**

Gumball machine, MIB **$135.00**

John Force's Castrol GTX Funny Car, Columbia Tel-Com, EX **$35.00**

Keebler Elf, NM **$100.00**

Kemit the Frog, candlestick-type, MIB.......................**$80.00**

Mickey Mouse, Western Electric, 1976, EX **$175.00**

Power Rangers, NM **$25.00**

Raggedy Ann Talking Telephone, Copyright Bobbs-Merrill, 1980, 9", EX **$25.00**

Raid Bug, from $90 to...**$100.00**

R2-D2 (Satr Wars), 12", EX.......................................**$35.00**

Spider-Man, REC Sound, 1994, MIB **$30.00**

Spider-Man climbing down chimney, The Amazing Spider-Man on receiver, NM, from $165 to **$200.00**

Star Trek Enterprise, 1993, NM **$25.00**

Winnie the Pooh, sq base, M, from $225 to.............**$250.00**

Occupied Japan Collectibles

Some items produced in Japan during the period from the end of WWII until the occupation ended in 1952 were marked Occupied Japan. No doubt much of the ware from this era was marked simply Japan, since obviously the 'Occupied' term caused considerable resentment among the Japanese people, and they were understandably reluctant to use the mark. So even though you may find identical items marked simply Japan or Made in Japan, only those with the more limited Occupied Japan mark are evaluated here.

Assume that the items described below are ceramic unless another material is mentioned. For more information, we recommend *Occupied Japan Collectibles* by Gene Florence (Collector Books).

Newsletter: *The Upside Down World of an O.J. Collector*
The Occupied Japan Club
c/o Florence Archambault
29 Freeborn St., Newport, RI 02840-1821
Published bimonthly. Information requires SASE.

Ashtray, alligator form w/tail curled up & mouth open .**$15.00**

Ashtray, baseball glove, metal, embossed mark..........**$15.00**

Ashtray, Indian in canoe form, 2¼x4½" **$22.50**

Ashtray, peacock decor in center, metal.......................**$7.50**

Ashtray, Statue of Liberty embossed on metal, NY City souvenir...**$12.50**

Bell, chef w/rolling pin, 3"..**$35.00**

Bookends, masted ships support 2 books on bases, wood, pr...**$75.00**

Box, dragon (ornate) decor, metal, w/lid, crown mark, 4x7"..**$27.50**

Bracelet, rhinestones in stretch metal band, Lady Patricia ..**$35.00**

Butter dish, basketweave pattern, T-in-circle mark, ¼-lb....**$20.00**

Candy dish, metal, 3-part, embossed T in chicken-shaped emblem...**$20.00**

Cigarette lighter, metal, horse head, embossed mark .**$30.00**

Clock, wooden owl form, eyes move, 6" **$250.00**

Coasters, papier-mache, floral decor, 8-pc set w/box...**$25.00**

Condiment set, jar, shakers & tray, white w/multicolor Colonial scene, gold trim **$35.00**

Creamer, collie's head form, Ugaco, 4½"....................**$25.00**

Creamer, cow figural, brown & white, 3⅜x5¼".........**$30.00**

Crumb butler, metal, Washington DC souvenir..........**$10.00**

Cup & saucer, demitasse; lg embossed dragon, gold trim, blue mark **$20.00**

Cup & saucer, demitasse; multicolor flowers w/gold, porcelain **$20.00**

Cup & saucer, thatch house river scene, MIOJ mark..**$17.50**

Figurine, Balinese lady dancer, gold trim, 8¾" **$38.00**

Figurine, bird on branch, 7⅞" **$40.00**

Figurine, Black fiddler, dressed in red & blue, 6".......**$35.00**

Figurine, boy & girl w/dogs, she w/closed umbrella, sq bases, 8", pr...**$90.00**

Figurine, boy sitting on fence w/cat below, 4" **$15.00**

Figurine, boy w/umbrella, 6x4" **$32.00**

Figurine, bride & groom, bisque, 6"............................**$45.00**

Figurine, collie, porcelain, 5"......................................**$27.50**

Figurine, Colonial man, blue coat, tricorner hat, 10½" ..**$65.00**

Figurine, couple fishing, shelf sitter, bisque, 4"..........**$20.00**

Figurine, courting couple w/lambs, 8¼x9¼" **$250.00**

Figurine, Dutch boy & girl w/detachable buckets, blue, 4¼", pr...**$35.00**

Figurine, Dutch lady at well, 4½"...............................**$12.50**

Figurine, elk, celluloid, silver spray, 7x7½"................**$20.00**

Figurine, girl w/basket, Hummel type, 6¼" **$35.00**
Figurine, horse & sulky, metal, embossed camel mark ..**$30.00**
Figurine, Indian chief w/tomahawk, 6"......................**$38.00**
Figurine, lady w/feathers in hair, fancy gown, 10½" ..**$45.00**
Figurine, Little White Riding Hood, 4⅛" **$15.00**
Figurine, man w/lady in rickshaw, celluloid, wood base, 2"..**$20.00**
Figurine, mermaid w/orange tail on rocks **$30.00**
Figurine, Mexican man on donkey, white base w/gold trim, 8¼" **$40.00**
Figurine, monkey in brown suit, red circle w/cross mark, 3½" **$35.00**
Figurine, Oriental dancer w/green headdress, holds fan, 6¼" **$22.00**
Figurine, Oriental lady in skirt w/basket on head, gold trim, 8" **$30.00**
Figurine, Scottish lass in blue & red, bisque, 4½" **$25.00**
Figurine, yellow coach led by 2 white horses, 3".......**$10.00**
Incense burner, elephant w/howdah lid, gold trim, Ucago **$35.00**
Incense burner, footed pot w/embossed dragon, gold trim..**$25.00**
Incense burner, Mexican man, seated, 4" **$30.00**

Lamps, blue bonnet motif, 12" socket height, $100.00 for the pair. (Photo courtesy Florence Archambault)

Mug, elephant figural, trunk forms handle, 4¾" **$20.00**
Pitcher, chicken form, white w/red, black & yellow trim, red mark..**$25.00**
Planter, Cupid on sled, bisque, paper label, 5"..........**$45.00**
Planter, heart w/angel playing accordion, 3⅝" **$15.00**
Planter, mallard duck (multicolor) next to sq white stone pot...**$15.00**
Planter, shoe house, red roof, blue shoestring, 4½x5" .**$15.00**
Plate, German Shepherd portrait, 4" **$25.00**
Plate, Hibiscus, oepn lace edge, 8¾"........................**$22.50**
Plate, lacquerware, pagoda scene, sq w/canted corners, Maruni..**$40.00**
Powder jar, applied gold flower on white, 4x4½"......**$40.00**

Salt & pepper shakers, bees on white honeycomb domes w/handled tray, 3-pc...........................**$20.00**
Salt & pepper shakers, cabbage form, 3¼x4⅛", pr **$17.50**
Salt & pepper shakers, chef & stove, 5", pr **$45.00**
Salt & pepper shakers, metal, cowboy boots w/spurs, marked in heel, pr..**$20.00**
Salt & pepper shakers, metal, penguin figural, pr **$22.50**
Salt & pepper shakers, red birds, 3¼", pr **$20.00**
Snack set, plate w/fluted edge, white w/pink floral & gold trim..**$20.00**
Tape measure, celluloid, pig form **$50.00**
Teapot, floral on brown, sm **$20.00**
Toby mug, devil bust, 2"...**$47.50**
Tray, sailfish decor, shell shaped, 3" dia....................**$10.00**
Vase, ballerina figure beside urn on footed base, gold trim, 8¼"...**$60.00**
Vase, lacquerware, Maruni, 13" **$150.00**
Wall figure, Dutch boy w/flower baskets, chalkware, Yomaka, 7½"..**$22.50**
Wall pocket, ballerina embossed on wreath form, white w/gold accents, UCAGO, 4¾" **$25.00**
Wall pocket, conical form w/blossom & leaves on swirl design, pink & yellow on glossy brown, 7" **$25.00**
Wall pocket, iris form, multicolor...............................**$25.00**
Wall pocket, teapot form w/flower decor, 6x8" **$25.00**

Old MacDonald's Farm

This is a wonderful line of novelty kitchenware items fashioned as the family and the animals that live on Old MacDonald's Farm. It's been popular with collectors for quite some time, and prices are astronomical, though they seem to have stabilized, at least for now.

These things were made by the Regal China Company, who also made some of the Little Red Riding Hood items that are so collectible, as well as figural cookie jars, 'hugger' salt and pepper shakers, and decanters. The Roerigs devote a chapter to Regal in their book *The Collector's Encyclopedia of Cookie Jars* and, in fact, show the entire Old MacDonald's Farm line.

Advisor: Rick Spencer (See Directory, Regal China)

Butter dish, cow's head...**$220.00**
Canister, flour; cereal; or coffee; med, ea from $225 to..**$275.00**
Canister, pretzels; peanuts; popcorn; chips; or tidbits; lg, ea from $325 to...**$375.00**
Canister, salt, sugar, or tea; med, ea from $225 to .**$275.00**
Canister, soap; or cookies; lg, ea from $350 to........**$425.00**
Cookie jar, barn, from $295 to **$325.00**
Creamer, rooster, from $110 to...............................**$125.00**
Grease jar, pig, from $200 to **$250.00**
Pitcher, milk; from $425 to **$450.00**
Salt & pepper shakers, boy & girl, pr **$80.00**
Salt & pepper shakers, churn, gold trim, pr...............**$95.00**
Salt & pepper shakers, feed sacks w/sheep, pr........**$195.00**

Spice jar, assorted lids, sm, ea from $125 to **$150.00**
Sugar bowl, hen...**$135.00**
Teapot, duck's head, from $295 to............................**$325.00**

Paper Dolls

One of the earliest producers of paper dolls was Raphael Tuck of England, who distributed many of their dolls in the United States in the late 1800s. Advertising companies used them to promote their products, and some were often included in the pages of leading ladies' magazines.

But over the years, the most common paper dolls have been those printed on the covers of a book containing their clothes on the inside pages. These were initiated during the 1920s and because they were inexpensive retained their popularity even during the Depression years. They peaked in the 1940s, but with the advent of television in the 1950s, children began to loose interest. Be sure to check old boxes and trunks in your attic; you just may find some!

But what's really exciting right now are those from more recent years — celebrity dolls from television shows like 'The Brady Bunch' or 'The Waltons,' the skinny English model Twiggy, and movie stars like Rock Hudson and Debbie Reynolds. Our values are for paper dolls in mint, uncut, original condition. Just remember that cut sets (even if all original components are still there) are worth only about half as much. Damaged sets or those with missing pieces should be priced accordingly.

If you'd like to learn more about them, we recommend *Price Guide to Lowe & Whitman Paper Dolls* and *Price Guide to Saalfield and Merrill Paper Dolls* by Mary Young, and *Schroeder's Collectible Toys, Antique to Modern.*

Advisor: Mary Young (See Directory, Paper Dolls)

Newsletter: *Paper Dolls News*
Ema Terry
P.O. Box 807
Vivian, LA 71082; Subscription: $12 per year for 4 issues; want lists, sale items and trades listed

Airline Stewardess, Lowe #4913, 1957 ....**$35.00**
Annette, Whitman #2083, 1958....................................**$75.00**
Annie Oakley, Whitman #2056, 1955 ....**$75.00**
Archie Girls/Betty & Veronica, Lowe #2764, 1964 ......**$50.00**
Archies, Whitman #1987, 1969, from $45 to...............**$50.00**
Betty Grable, Merrill #1558, 1951, 8-page version, from $175 to..**$250.00**
Beverly Hillbillies, Whitman #1955, 1964....................**$85.00**
Blondie, Whitman #1174, 1953..................................**$185.00**
Blue Bonnet, Merrill #3444, 1942, from $90 to **$125.00**
Brenda Lee, Lowe #2785, 1961, from $50 to...............**$75.00**
Bride & Groom, Lowe #2493, 1959 ....**$35.00**
Carol Lynley, Whitman #2089, 1960 ....**$60.00**
Cyd Charisse, Whitman #2084, 1956 ....**$115.00**
Debbie Reynolds, Whitman #1178, 1953 ....**$125.00**
Donna Reed, Saalfield #4412, 1959, from $75 to **$100.00**

Dude Ranch Turnabouts, Lowe #1026, 1943..............**$40.00**
Evelyn Rudie, Saalfield #4446, 1958, from $40 to.......**$60.00**
Flintstones, Whitman #4796, 1962 ....**$60.00**
Gloria Jean, Saafield #1666, 1941 ....**$125.00**
Gloria's Make-Up, Lowe #2585, 1952..........................**$50.00**
Gretchen, Whitman #4613, 1966.................................**$15.00**
Heidi & Peter, Saalfield #4424, 1961 ....**$25.00**
Hollywood Personalities, Lowe #1049, 1941 ....**$400.00**
It's a Date, Whitman #1976, 1956, from $35 to...........**$50.00**
Jane Russell, Saalfield #4328, 1955.........................**$100.00**
Jane Withers, Whitman #986, 1941...........................**$138.00**
Joanne Woodward, Saalfield #4436, 1958, from $75 to..**$125.00**
Julia, Saalfield #6055, 1969, from $50 to.....................**$75.00**
Laugh-In Party, Saalfield #6045, 1969, boxed, from $40 to ..**$65.00**
Little Women, Saalfield #1345, 1963 ....**$35.00**
Magic Stay-On Doll, Whitman #4618, 1963 ....**$20.00**
Mary Martin, Saafield #368, 1944...............................**$60.00**
Mommy & Me, Whitman #2093, 1960 ....**$40.00**
Mother & Daughter, Saalfield, #1330, 1962................**$35.00**
Mouseketeers, Whitman #1974, 1963 ....**$60.00**
Mrs Beasley, Whitman #1993, 1972, EX......................**$25.00**
National Velvet, Whitman #1958, 1961........................**$50.00**
One Hundred & One Dalmatians, Whitman #1993, 1960..**$60.00**
Pat Crowley, Whitman #2050, 1955.............................**$75.00**
Patty Duke, Whitman #1991, from $40 to....................**$50.00**
Pee-Wee Cut-Outs, Whitman #1965, 1967...................**$35.00**
Raggedy Ann & Andy, Saalfield #2739, 1961, authorized edition, from $35 to...**$45.00**
Rock Hudson, Whitman #2087, 1957 ....**$65.00**
Sally, Sue & Sherry, Lowe #2785, 1969 ....**$10.00**
Shirley Temple, Saafield #2425, 1942.......................**$135.00**
Sleeping Beauty, Whitman #4723, 1958......................**$65.00**
Square Dance, Lowe #968, 1950..................................**$25.00**
Susan Dey as Laurie, Saalfield #6024, 1971-72...........**$50.00**
Tabetha, Magic Wand #115, 1966..............................**$100.00**
Tender Love 'N Kisses, Whitman #1944-1, 1978..........**$15.00**
That Girl, Saafiled #1379, 1967 ....**$55.00**
TV Tap Stars, Lowe #990, 1952 ....**$30.00**
Umbrella Girls, Merrill #2562, 1956.............................**$65.00**
Vera Miles, Whitman #2986, 1957, from $80 to.........**$125.00**
Virginia Weilder, Whitman #1016, 1942, from $60 to..**$80.00**
Ziegfield Girls, Merrill, #3466, 1941 ....**$400.00**

Pencil Sharpeners

The whittling process of sharpening pencils with pocketknives was replaced by mechanical means in the 1880s. By the turn of the century, many ingenious desk-type sharpeners had been developed. Small pencil sharpeners designed for the purse or pocket were produced in the 1890s. The typical design consisted of a small steel tube containing a cutting blade which could be adjusted by screws. Mass-produced novelty pencil sharpeners became popular in the late 1920s. The most detailed figurals were made in Germany. These German sharpeners that originally sold for less than a dollar are now considered highly collectible!

Disney and other character pencil sharpeners have been produced in Catalin, plastic, ceramic, and rubber. Novelty battery-operated pencil sharpeners can also be found. For over fifty years pencil sharpeners have been used as advertising giveaways — from Baker's Chocolates and Coca-Cola's metal figurals to the plastic 'Marshmallow Man' distributed by McDonald's. As long as we have pencils, new pencil sharpeners will be produced, much to the delight of collectors.

Advisors: Phil Helley; Martha Hughes (See Directory, Pencil Sharpeners)

Bakelite, airplane, yellow w/red marbling, Keep 'Em Flying in white letters, star logo, 2¾x2½", EX.................$45.00
Bakelite, Bambi, Walt Disney Productions, round, 1".$50.00
Bakelite, Br'er Fox, round & fluted, 1⅜" $55.00
Bakelite, Donald Duck, waving w/house & tree, bottle-cap shape, 1½"..$60.00
Bakelite, elephant head, 2" $20.00
Bakelite, Hep Cats, WDP, decal on metal, bottle cap-shape, 1¼"..$40.00
Bakelite, Joe Carrioca, tortoise shell w/decal, 6-sided, WDP, 1¾x⅜", EX...$60.00
Bakelite, mantel clock, Germany, 2" $65.00
Bakelite, Panchito, Walt Disney Productions, round, 1"...$42.00
Bakelite, pig, 1⅜" $25.00
Bakelite, Pinocchio, silhouette-cut w/decal, WDP, 1¾x1⅛x¾", VG+...$55.00
Bakelite, Popeye, silhouette-cut w/decal, 1930s $80.00
Bakelite, Scottie dog, black & orange swirl figural, carved collar & eyes, Souvenir Hot Springs, 1½", EX......$50.00
Bakelite, Scottie dog, orange, 1½" $30.00

Bakelite, Snow White figural, Disney, $95.00.

Bakelite, US Army Plane, red w/white letters & logo, from $70 to..$90.00
Bakelite, US Army Tank, olive green w/white letters & logo, 1x1¾x⅜", from $70 to...$90.00
Bakelite, Walt Disney's train, figural, 1¾"..................$90.00
Bakelite, 1939 NY World's Fair...................................$80.00

Celluloid, pelican, Japan, 3"......................................$125.00
Metal, airplane, removable motor & prop winds sharpener, marked Anco, 2¼", EX...$115.00
Metal, Atlas holding globe, painted, 3" $45.00
Metal, camera figural, EMB Marti Co, Spain, EXIB $23.00
Metal, Charlie Chaplin, Germany, 2¼".....................$150.00
Metal, Cinderella's coach w/horse, wheels turn, marked Hong Kong, EX..$10.00
Metal, cuckoo clock, Germany, 2¼" $120.00
Metal, Great Dane, Germany, 2"................................$90.00
Metal, horse on platform, copper-tone finish, 3¼x2¾" .$12.00
Metal, John F Kennedy 35th President 1917-1963 (bust), embossed, bronzed, 3"...$15.00
Metal, Olympic Swimmer on round platform, figural, die-cast, EX...$45.00
Metal, penguin on platform, Japan, 2", EX.................$42.00
Metal, seltzer bottle, Germany, 2-pc, 2½", VG.........$120.00
Metal, stop-&-go light, 2¼".......................................$75.00
Metal, touring car, 2-pc, Germany, 1¾" $40.00
Metal, US Columbia, spacecraft figural, wheels turn, silver w/black letters, 3¼", EX.....................................$12.00
Metal, 1905 Rolls Royce, bronze, 3⅛x1⅜", EX...........$13.00
Occupied Japan, Black Uncle Sam w/bow tie $150.00
Occupied Japan, clown w/bow tie $75.00
Occupied Japan, smiling pig w/hat.............................$80.00
Plastic, Batman, Alco, 1981, MIP $12.00
Plastic, fireman, red outfit w/black belt & shoes, Fire in white on hat, hands at sides, unmarked, 2½", EX.........$10.00
Plastic, Flash Gordon Rocket Ship, red & green, Kum West Germany, 3"..$27.00
Plastic, penguin figural, Japan, 2½" $25.00
Plastic, Ronald McDonald, 2"....................................$12.00
Plastic, sewing machine figural, movable wheel & needle, Made in Germany, 1970s, 2x2", EX.....................$20.00
Plastic, Sunbeam Bread, 1" $15.00
Plastic, Superman bust figural, Alco, 1977, MIP.........$23.00
Plastic, Tony the Tiger head, 1973, 4"........................$18.00
Plastic, Topo Gigio, mouse on base, marked Copyright by Maria Perego, 1964, Empire Made, 3" $18.00
Plastic, 2 basketball players act out shooting ball in hoop, marked Wiggle TV Kohner #601, 1960s, EX.........$10.00
Pottery, bird, white w/yellow & brown features, gold trim, Holt Howard, 1958, EX $20.00
Wood, Mallard duck, Made in Hong Kong, 1970s, 3¼x1¾", EX...$12.00

Pennsbury Pottery

From the 1950s throughout the 1960s, this pottery was sold in gift stores and souvenir shops along the Pennsylvania Turnpike. It was produced in Morrisville, Pennsylvania, by Henry and Lee Below. Much of the ware was hand painted in multiple colors on caramel backgrounds, though some pieces were made in blue and white. Most of the time, themes centered around Amish people, barber shop singers, roosters, hex signs, and folksy mottos.

Much of the ware is marked, and if you're in the Pennsylvania/New Jersey area, you'll find a lot of it. It's fairly prevalent in the Midwest as well and can still sometimes be found at bargain prices.

Advisor: Shirley Graff (See Directory, Pennsbury)

Ashtray, Amish, 5" dia **$25.00**
Ashtray, Summerset 1804-1954, 5"..................**$30.00**
Bank, Hershey Kiss, brown, 4"..........................**$20.00**
Bank, pig w/Stuff Me, 7"....................................**$200.00**
Basket, desk; Two Women Under Tree, 5"..........**$50.00**
Bell, Mother's Day, Mother Comforting Child, 1977 ...**$40.00**
Bowl, Dutch Talk, 9" dia....................................**$90.00**
Bowl, pretzel; Red Barn, 12x8" **$150.00**
Bowl, Toleware, 9"...**$40.00**
Butter dish, Hex, w/lid, 5x4" **$45.00**
Candle holder, holly, 5 /2".................................**$45.00**
Candle holders, roosters, 4", pr **$85.00**
Charger, St George Slaying Dragon, 13½" **$225.00**
Coaster, Doylestown Trust Co 1896-1958, 5".....**$25.00**
Coaster, Quartet, 5"...**$30.00**

Cruets, Amish man and lady's head as stoppers, 7", $150.00 for the pair.

Cruets, oil & vinegar; Black Rooster, pr....................**$150.00**
Figurine, Barn Swallow, #123, 6¼" **$375.00**
Figurine, Blue Bird, #103, 4"......................................**$200.00**
Figurine, Blue Jay, #108, 10½" **$400.00**
Figurine, Gold Finch, #102 ....**$150.00**
Figurine, Marsh Wren, #106, 6½" **$120.00**
Mug, beer; eagle, 5"..**$35.00**
Mug, beverage; Red Barn, 5".......................................**$50.00**
Mug, coffee; Amish, 3¼"..**$30.00**
Mug, coffee; Gay Ninety, 3¼".....................................**$40.00**
Mug, coffee; Hex **$22.00**
Pie pan, Mother Serving Pie, 9"..................................**$90.00**
Pitcher, Folkart, mini, 2½"...**$30.00**
Pitcher, white w/running horses decal, gold trim, 1-qt..**$80.00**
Plaque, Eagle, #P214, 22"...**$175.00**

Plaque, Flying Cloud 1851, 9½x7" **$110.00**
Plaque, Iron Horse Ramble, Reading Railroad 1960, 7¼x5¼"..**$60.00**
Plaque, Making Pie, 6" **$60.00**
Plaque, Mercury Dime, 8" **$65.00**
Plaque, Neshaminy Woods, rare, 7½x5½" **$85.00**
Plaque, Pea Hen, 6" dia **$40.00**
Plaque, Pennsbury Manor, 8".......................................**$70.00**
Plaque, Stourbridge Lion 1829, 11x8" **$55.00**
Plaque, Toleware, brown, 5x7".....................................**$40.00**
Plate, Boy & Girl, w/primary colors, 11" **$95.00**
Plate, bread; Give Us This Day Our Daily Bread, 9x6" ..**$40.00**
Plate, Christmas; Treetops, 1961 ....**$45.00**
Plate, eagle, 8" **$50.00**
Plate, Family, 11" dia...**$110.00**
Plate, Green Rooster, rare **$80.00**
Plate, Mother's Day, Mother w/Child, 1972, marked Glen View **$40.00**
Plate, turkey hunt, 11"..**$85.00**
Platter, Red Rooster, oval, 11".....................................**$45.00**
Relish tray, tulip pattern, 3-part, 14½x11½" **$95.00**
Salt & pepper shakers, Amish heads, pr......................**$60.00**
Salt & pepper shakers, Amish man & woman, pr.......**$45.00**
Sugar bowl, Green Rooster, w/lid **$40.00**
Teapot, Red Rooster, 4-cup **$60.00**
Tray, horses, octagonal, 5x3".......................................**$30.00**
Tray, novelty; Colt 31 Caliber, 7½x5"..........................**$45.00**
Wall pocket, bellows shape w/eagle in high relief, 10"..**$65.00**
Wall pocket, floral w/blue border, 6½".........................**$65.00**
Warming plate, Picking Apples, electrified, 6x6".........**$75.00**

Pepsi-Cola

People have been enjoying Pepsi-Cola since before the turn of the century. Various logos have been registered over the years; the familiar oval was first used in the early 1940s. At about the same time, the two 'dots' between the words Pepsi and Cola became one, though more recent items may carry the double-dot logo as well, especially when they're designed to be reminiscent of the old ones. The bottle cap logo came along in 1943 and with variations was used through the early 1960s.

Though there are expensive rarities, most items are still reasonable, since collectors are just now beginning to discover how fascinating this line of advertising memorabilia can be. There are three books in the series called *Pepsi-Cola Collectibles*, written by Bill Vehling and Michael Hunt, which we highly recommend. Another good reference is *Introduction to Pepsi Collecting* by Bob Stoddard. For still more information we recommend *Antique and Collectible Advertising Memorabilia* by B.J. Summers (Collector Books).

Note: In the descriptions that follow, P-C was used as an abbreviation for Pepsi-Cola; the double-dot logo is represented by the equal sign.

Advisor: Craig Stifter (See Directory, Pepsi-Cola)

Newsletter: *Pepsi-Cola Collectors Club Express*
Bob Stoddard, Editor
P.O. Box 817
Claremont, CA 91711; Send SASE for information

Ashtray, ceramic, round w/mini Pepsi bottle & lamp shade in center, embossed Bill's Novelties on bottom, EX+..**$275.00**

Ashtray, smoked glass w/enameled bottle cap opposite chrome cigarette rest, 1950s, 3½" dia, NM **$75.00**

Ballpark vendor carrier, wood w/red-on-white Drink P-C oval logo on blue & white stripes, w/strap, 1950s, 6x19", VG...**$175.00**

Blotter, Drink...Delicious Healthful, black on brown, G ..**$70.00**

Blotter, Pepsi & Pete The Pepsi-Cola Cops, 1939, EX+ ...**$80.00**

Bottle carrier, 6-pack, aluminum, side bands angled upward w/Drink P-C oval on blue & white stripes, curved handle, VG **$50.00**

Bottle carrier, 6-pack, cardboard, P=C Bigger/Better 25¢ logo, red, white & blue, NM+ **$30.00**

Bottle carrier, 6-pack, wood w/wood grip on wire handle, EX **$100.00**

Bottle display, chalkware, sexy lady in red gown next to bottle, bottle cap & Sparkling Quality on base, 1940s, 11", EX+ **$3,400.00**

Calendar, 1941, full paper pad, NM, $250.00.

Calendar, 1943, Famous American Paintings, complete, 23x17", VG...**$50.00**

Calendar, 1944, Our America, 22x17", EX....................**$30.00**

Calendar, 1960, P-C Bottling Co, art by Lawson Wood, complete, EX+...**$110.00**

Change mat, rubber oval w/Pepsi logo & Thank You, 1960s, 9x11", EX..**$100.00**

Charm, gold-tone, P=C on shamrock w/horseshoe on chain, NM **$60.00**

Clock, bottle cap next to clock face on yellow box on ribbed gold-tone back base, plastic/metal light-up, 1950s, 13x17"...**$250.00**

Clock, Say Pepsi Please, numbers on gold perforated frame, 16x16", EX...**$125.00**

Dispenser, plastic box w/stainless steel parts, Pepsi/P-C bottle cap logos, red, white & blue, VG+................**$250.00**

Display rack, metal, 3-tiered w/P=C logo, dark blue, 1940s, 43x18x12", EX+ **$475.00**

Door push bar, porcelain, Enjoy P-C Iced, yellow & white stripes, 3x30", EX...**$175.00**

Fan, cardboard w/wooden handle, Drink P=C/12 Ounce Bottle 5¢, Pepsi cop on reverse, 1940, 12", NM+ **$125.00**

Game, Big League Baseball, 1950s-60s, EX..............**$125.00**

Menu board, tin, Drink P=C/Bigger Better, blackboard w/wood-look frame & red rope border, 1940s, 30x20", NM+.**$375.00**

Menu board, tin, Have a Pepsi & bottle cap on yellow, blackboard bottom, yellow raised rim, 30x20", NM.....**$85.00**

Menu board, wood, P=C sign w/ribbon trailing above double row of slots, 1940s, 20x25", EX....................**$125.00**

Miniature 6-pack, cardboard carrier w/6 swirl bottles, slanted bottle cap & P-C on stripes, 2½", EX...................**$70.00**

Money clip, brass & chrome dollar sign, 1950s, 2", NM+ ..**$65.00**

Paperweight, glass, rectangular w/rounded corners, P=C logo, VG **$50.00**

Pocket mirror, rectangular w/P=C & The Light Refreshment on oval center showing birthstones, EX+ **$100.00**

Radio, fountain dispenser form, Say Pepsi Please, red, white & blue w/leather strap, 1950s, EX+....................**$295.00**

Recipe booklet, Hospitality Recipes, shows tilted bottle on wavy band, 1940, NM..**$25.00**

Salt & pepper shakers, early bottles w/P=C oval labels, EXIB, pr **$165.00**

Sign, cardboard, Certified Quality, lady lounging on floor w/Pepsi, cap logo lower left, self-framed, 1940s, 22x28", EX+ **$725.00**

Sign, cardboard, The Light Refreshment, girl in lounge chair w/bottle, yellow background, 1957, 11x25", EX+ ..**$100.00**

Sign, celluloid button, Ice Cold P=C Sold Here, blue/white/blue wavy logo, 1930s-40s, 9" dia, VG+ **$110.00**

Sign, celluloid button, P=C bottle cap w/More Bounce to the Ounce ribbon tag on metallic gold, 1960s, 9" dia, EX+ **$220.00**

Sign, celluloid button hanger, Ice Cold P=C Sold Here, red, white & blue, 1930s-40s, 9" dia, NM...................**$450.00**

Sign, flange, litho tin panel w/rounded corners, Ice Cold P=C Sold Here, blue/white/blue wavy logo, 1940s, 10x15", EX **$350.00**

Sign, flanged bottle cap, masonite w/metal flange, P=C logo w/3-quarters of crimping showing, 2-sided, 1940s, 11x13", NM...**$425.00**

Sign, light-up, molded plastic stand-up Santa waving, Pepsi bottle in toy bag, 1960s, EX+...............................**$150.00**

Sign, paper, Listen to Country-Spy/Pepsi's Radio Thriller!..., P=C bottle cap, red & blue on white, 8x19", NM+.........**$85.00**

Sign, plastic, figural cowboy kid roping box of popcorn & cup of Pepsi, 14x18", EX+...................................**$60.00**

Sign, porcelain, Drink/P=C bottle cap/Iced on yellow, rounded corners, 1950s, 12x29", NM+ **$500.00**

Sign, tin, Enjoy Pepsi Five Cents, P=C bottle cap in center, blue w/white line trim, canted corners, 1940s, 10x26", EX **$400.00**

Sign, tin, More Bounce to the Ounce ribbon tag & P-C bottle cap on white, self-framed border, 33x57", G......**$150.00**

Sign, tin diecut bottle, P=C hexagonal label w/lg 5¢ circle above, 1930s, 45x12", EX+ **$625.00**

Sign, tin triangular screen brace w/Say Pepsi & bottle cap on blue w/red, white & blue ribbon, 1930s-40s, 10", EX........**$400.00**

Stick pin, bottle shape, 1940s, M...............................**$70.00**

Syrup can, 1-gal, red, white & blue bands w/P-C bottle caps on center band, 1951, EX.......................................**$55.00**

Tape measure, chrome Zippo lighter-type case w/gray plastic bottom, EX **$50.00**

Thermometer, tin, Have a Pepsi/The Light Refreshment, 3-quarter bottle cap logo below, yellow & white, 1956, 27", EX **$175.00**

Thermometer, tin, Have a Pepsi/The Light Refreshment & bottle cap on white & yellow, 1950s, 27", EX....**$150.00**

Thermometer, tin, More Bounce to the Ounce ribbon tag at bottom, P-C bottle cap at top, curved stepped ends, 27x8", VG **$250.00**

Thermometer, tin, Pepsi logo top & bottom on white, sq corners, beveled edge, 28x7", EX **$50.00**

Tip tray, P=C in red on white milk glass, serrated edges, NM+ **$200.00**

Toy dispenser/bank, litho tin, battery-op, Linemar, 1950s, 10x7x5", EXIB **$350.00**

Trash can, shaped like Pepsi can, 1970s, 16", EX.......**$20.00**

Tray, Coast to Coast/Bigger & Better, slanted bottle superimposed over US map, 1930s, 11x14", EX+............**$350.00**

Tray, Enjoy P=C/Hits the Spot, red, white & blue, 10½x14", VG **$90.00**

Whistle, plastic double bottle shape, 3", EX...............**$80.00**

Perfume Bottles

Here's an area of bottle collecting that has come into its own. Commercial bottles, as you can see from our listings, are very popular. Their values are based on several factors. For instance, when you assess a bottle, you'll need to note: is it sealed or full, does it have its original label, and is the original package or box present.

Figural bottles are interesting as well, especially the ceramic ones with tiny regal crowns as their stoppers.

Advisor: Monsen & Baer (See Directory, Perfume Bottles)

Club: International Perfume Bottle Association (IPBA)
Susan Arthurt, Membership Secretary
295 E. Sweedsford Rd. PMB 185
Wayne, PA 19087
e-mail:jcabbott@verizon.net; www.perfume bottles.org
Membership: $45 USA or $50 Canada

A de Markoff, Tiara, frosted flask, M in coral moire box..**$80.00**

Artfield Creations, Forward March, clear w/gold eagle top, 2½" w/figural hand stand......................................**$55.00**

Avon, Quaintance, clear w/red rose cap, 2½", M in green velvet book-form box, Avon's 63rd Anniversary ..**$55.00**

Baccarat/D'orsay, Milord, portrait on clear, #793, 1944, 2¼"...**$55.00**

Blown, Harrison's Columbian Perfumery, smooth base, flared mouth, 5⅛", EX...**$35.00**

Caron, Muguet de Bonheur, clear replica of standard model w/sm label, 3½", MIB...**$55.00**

Caron, Tabac Blond, clear flat oval, molded stopper, 3¼", MIB...**$110.00**

Ciro, Bel Horizon, clear w/gold cap, black & yellow label, 2½", MIB...**$60.00**

Ciro, Surrender, faceted gemstone shape, labels, 4", MIB ..**$100.00**

Corday, jet Parfumè, fountain-shaped bottle, aqua stopper, ca 1924, near full, very rare, 5¾" **$3,575.00**

Da Valois, Chypre, vertical ribs, amber stopper, 4", MIB **$70.00**

Dulaurier, Lily of the Valley, clear w/cork stopper, 2⅜", rests in turquoise opaque glass shoe **$55.00**

Duvelle, Le Gui, green teardrop w/metallic labels, 3¼", MIB...**$16.50**

Elizabeth Arden, Cyclamen, white & clear fan shape, gold enamel sides, empty, 5", in rare triangular box w/Lucite window **$3,575.00**

Estèe Lauder, Cinnabar, Foo dog, solid perfume, 1¾", empty...**$275.00**

Estèe Lauder, Pink Slipper, silver metal covered in pink rhinestones, 2½" L, in pink pouch **$200.00**

Evening in Paris foil label on cobalt, silver-colored top, 5½"...**$22.00**

Guerlain, Shalimar, clear shouldered form w/gold label, cobalt top, 4x3", MIB...**$55.00**

Helena Rubenstein, Apple Blossom, clear w/pink cap, empty, 1 dram, in gold box w/celluloid window..............**$35.00**

Helena Rubenstein, Heaven Sent, bottle held by sm Harlequin in blue & pink suit, 2¾", MIB..............**$35.00**

Helena Rubenstein, Heaven Sent, solid perfume, gold oval w/red stone centered on lid, 1½" L, MIB **$35.00**

Houbigant, Violette, clear flask w/gold lozenge stopper, violet label, w/contents (some evaporation), 3¼", MIB.....**$35.00**

Jacqueline Cochran, Shining Hour, cologne & perfume, 3⅛", 2¼", in flocked clocktower box **$175.00**

L Lelong, Impromptu, clear/frosted tower, no label, 6½" .**$145.00**

Lancome, Nativitè, frosted sq bottle, winged angel against rays of gold molded across both bottle & stopper, 1945, 4"..**$2,310.00**

Lanvin, My Sin, clear w/black & silver label, black stopper, 1¼", MIB...**$30.00**

Lazell, Bocadia, black enamel, gold label, 1920s, 4", MIB...**$80.00**

Lenthèric, Adam's Rib, clear w/gold cap, gold name, replica miniature, 2", NMIB **$75.00**

Lenthèric, Tweed, gold metal compact for solid perfume, green & white cameo on lid, 1¾", MIB................**$55.00**

Lucretia Vanderbilt, Concentrated Extract, cobalt w/silver butterfly, 2¼", in signed leather pouch **$200.00**

Matchabelli, Added Attraction, red & gold crown w/gold screw-on cap, gold label, 1½", MIB (presentation) **$200.00**

Max Factor, Hypnotique, cream perfume compact, blue & white cameo of lady & dog on lid, 1¼x1⅜", MIB..............**$45.00**

Ota, Bouquet, set of 10 pearl-shaped iridescent glass bottles, ea 1", in presentation box designed for 10 pearls **$4,125.00**

Renoir, Chi-Chi, clear & frosted miniature w/Bakelite top, 2", M in red & white box w/lady in plumes.............**$90.00**

Richard Hudnut, Le Dèbut Noir, black octagon w/gilded glass stopper, 1¾"...**$90.00**

Richard Hudnut, Sweet Orchid, frosted rectangle, 3", MIB **$175.00**

Schiaparelli, Shocking, cream perfume, metal heart w/intertwined ribbons & rhinestones, 1½", MIB...........**$255.00**

Stuart Products, Barette by Karoff: Chypre, Gardenia & Orchid, clear bottles w/brass caps, tallest 3⅜", MIB..............**$75.00**

Vigny, Echo Troublant, Heur Intime, Guili-Guili, clear bottles w/frosted stoppers, 3¼", set of 3, MIB...............**$200.00**

Vivadoux, Mai d'Or, clear finial w/gold tip, glass dropper, front label, empty, 3¼", in red box......................**$50.00**

Wm H Brown, Pearls of Violets & Pearls of Lilies, clear w/corks toppers, 2½", pr, NM in woven-basket box..............**$35.00**

Ybry, Femme de Paris, clear cased in green, sq, gold label, empty, 2½", in green leather case w/glass cupid medallion **$2,000.00**

Pez Candy Dispensers

Though Pez candy has been around since the late 1920s, the dispensers that we all remember as children weren't introduced until the 1950s. Each had the head of a certain character — a Mexican, a doctor, Santa Claus, an animal, or perhaps a comic book hero. It's hard to determine the age of some of these, but if yours have tabs or 'feet' on the bottom so they can stand up, they were made in the last ten years. Though early on, collectors focused on this feature to evaluate their finds, now it's simply the character's head that's important to them. Some have variations in color and design, both of which can greatly affect value.

Condition is important; watch out for broken or missing parts. If a Pez is not in mint condition, most are worthless. Original packaging can add to the value, particularly if it is one that came out on a blister card. If the card has special graphics or information, this is especially true. Early figures were sometimes sold in boxes, but these are hard to find. Nowadays you'll see them offered 'mint in package,' sometimes at premium prices. But most intense Pez collectors say that those cellophane bags add very little if any to the value.

For more information, refer to *A Pictorial Guide to Plastic Candy Dispensers Featuring Pez* by David Welch; *Schroeder's Collectible Toys, Antique to Modern* (Collector Books); and *Collecting Toys #6* by Richard O'Brien.

Advisor: Richard Belyski (See Directory, Pez)

Newsletter: *Pez Collector's News*
Richard Belyski, Editor
P.O. Box 14956
Surfside Beach, SC 29587; e-mail: peznews@juno.com
www.pezcollectorsnews.com; Subscription: $19 for 6 issues
5th Annual Northeast PEZ Collectors Gathering, April 3 – 5, 2003

Aardvark, w/feet **$5.00**
Arlene, w/feet, pink, from $3 to..............................**$5.00**
Asterix Line, any character, ea from $4 to **$6.00**
Bambi, no feet **$50.00**
Baseball Glove, no feet......................................**$175.00**
Batgirl, no feet, soft head **$125.00**
Betsy Ross, no feet **$150.00**
Bouncer Beagle, w/feet...**$6.00**
Bugs Bunny, no feet **$15.00**
Captain America, no feet **$100.00**
Captain Hook, no feet **$85.00**
Chick in Egg, no feet...**$25.00**
Chick in Egg, no feet, w/hair...............................**$125.00**
Chip, w/feet **$80.00**
Cool Cat, w/feet...**$65.00**
Dino, w/feet, purple, from $1 to **$3.00**
Donald Duck's Nephew, no feet...............................**$30.00**
Droopy Dog (A), no feet, plastic swivel ears.............**$25.00**
Droopy Dog (B), w/feet, painted ears, MIP **$6.00**
Duck Tales, any character, w/feet, ea **$6.00**
Eerie Spectres, Air Spirit, Diabolic or Zombie (no feet), ea ..**$200.00**
Fat-Ears Rabbit, no feet, pink head..........................**$20.00**
Fat-Ears Rabbit, no feet, yellow head **$15.00**
Frog, w/feet, whistle head **$40.00**
Garfield, w/feet, teeth, from $1 to.............................**$3.00**
Goofy, no feet, ea **$10.00**
Gorilla, no feet, black head **$80.00**
Henry Hawk, no feet...**$65.00**
Indian Brave, no feet, reddish...............................**$150.00**
Inspector Clouseau, w/feet......................................**$5.00**
Jerry Mouse, w/feet, painted face.............................**$6.00**
Jerry Mouse, w/feet, plastic face **$15.00**
Jungle Mission, interactive dispenser **$10.00**
Koala, w/feet, whistle head....................................**$40.00**
Li'l Bad Wolf, w/feet...**$20.00**
Merlin Mouse, w/feet...**$20.00**
Miss Piggy, w/feet, eyelashes.................................**$15.00**
Mowgli, w/feet..**$15.00**
Nintendo, any character, ea from $4 to **$6.00**
Odie, w/feet..**$5.00**
Olive Oyl, no feet...**$200.00**
Panda, w/feet, whistle head.....................................**$6.00**
Penguin, w/feet, whistle head **$6.00**
Peter Pez (A), no feet...**$65.00**
Practical Pig (B), no feet......................................**$30.00**
Road Runner, no feet..**$20.00**
Road Runner, w/feet...**$15.00**
Sheik, no feet **$55.00**
Speedy Gonzales (A), w/feet....................................**$15.00**
Speedy Gonzales (B), no feet, from $1 to....................**$3.00**
Spider-Man, no feet, from $10 to **$15.00**
Spider-Man, w/feet, from $1 to.................................**$3.00**
Spike, w/feet...**$6.00**
Star Wars, any character, ea from $1 to **$3.00**
Thor, no feet **$300.00**
Tiger, w/feet, whistle head.....................................**$6.00**
Tom (Tom & Jerry), no feet.....................................**$35.00**

Tom (Tom & Jerry), w/feet, painted face $6.00
Tom (Tom & Jerry), w/feet, plastic face $15.00
Wile E Coyote, w/feet $60.00
Yappy Dog, no feet, green or orange, ea $65.00

Pfaltzgraff Pottery

Pfaltzgraff has operated in Pennsylvania since the early 1800s making redware at first; then stoneware crocks and jugs, yellow ware, and spongeware in the '20s; artware and kitchenware in the '30s; and stoneware kitchen items through the hard years of the '40s. In 1950 they developed their first line of dinnerware, called Gourmet Royale (known in later years as simply Gourmet). It was a high-gloss line of solid color accented at the rims with a band of frothy white, similar to lines made later by McCoy, Hull, Harker, and many other companies. Although it also came in pink, it was the dark brown that became so popular. Today these brown stoneware lines have captured the interest of young collectors as well as the more seasoned, and they all contain more than enough unusual items to make the hunt a bit of a challenge and loads of fun.

The success of Gourmet was just the inspiration that was needed to initiate the production of the many dinnerware lines that have become the backbone of the Pfaltzgraff company.

A giftware line called Muggsy was designed in the late 1940s. It consisted of items such as comic character mugs, ashtrays, bottle stoppers, children's dishes, a pretzel jar, a cookie jar, etc. All of the characters were given names. It was very successful and continued in production until 1960. The older versions have protruding features, while the later ones were simply painted on.

Village, an almond-glazed line with a folksy, brown stenciled tulip decoration, is now discontinued. It's a varied line with many wonderful, useful pieces, and besides the dinnerware itself, the company catalogs carried illustrations of matching glassware, metal items, copper accessories, and linens.

Several dinnerware lines are featured in our listings. To calculate the values of Yorktowne, Heritage, and Folk Art items not listed below, use Village prices.

For further information, we recommend *Pfaltzgraff, America's Potter,* by David A. Walsh and Polly Stetler, published in conjunction with the Historical Society of York County, York, Pennsylvania.

Note: Pfaltzgraff dinnerware prices have been tremendously affected by eBay. Because it is still so readily available on the secondary market, eBay always has hundreds of items up for auction, and many times they are sold at no reserve. This plus the fact that the dinnerware is heavy and shipping charges can mount up fast has caused values to decline, though interest is still evident.

Christmas Heritage, bowl, soup/cereal, #009, 5½", from $2 to $3.50
Christmas Heritage, cheese tray, #533, 10½x7½", from $5 to $7.00

Christmas Heritage, pedestal mug, #290, 10-oz............$3.00
Christmas Heritage, plate, dinner; #004, 10", from $3 to ..$5.00
Gourmet Royale, ashtray, #AT32, skillet shape, 9", from $10 to $12.00
Gourmet Royale, ashtray, #321, 7¾", from $9 to $12.00
Gourmet Royale, ashtray, 12", from $12 to..................$14.00
Gourmet Royale, baker, #321, oval, 7½", from $8 to .$10.00
Gourmet Royale, baker, #323, 9½", from $10 to.........$12.00
Gourmet Royale, bean pot, #11-1, 1-qt, from $10 to..$12.00
Gourmet Royale, bean pot, #11-2, 2-qt, from $15 to..$20.00
Gourmet Royale, bean pot, #11-3, 3-qt....................$25.00
Gourmet Royale, bean pot, #11-4, 4-qt....................$35.00
Gourmet Royale, bean pot, #30, w/lip, lg, from $30 to .$40.00
Gourmet Royale, bean pot warming stand..................$10.00
Gourmet Royale, bowl, #241, oval, 7x10", from $10 to..$12.00
Gourmet Royale, bowl, cereal; #934SR, 5½" $3.50
Gourmet Royale, bowl, mixing; 6", from $8 to $10.00
Gourmet Royale, bowl, mixing; 8", from $10 to $12.00
Gourmet Royale, bowl, salad; tapered sides, 10", from $10 to $14.00
Gourmet Royale, bowl, soup; 2¼x7¼", from $4 to $6.00
Gourmet Royale, bowl, spaghetti; #219, shallow, 14", from $15 to $20.00
Gourmet Royale, bowl, vegetable; #341, divided $10.00
Gourmet Royale, butter dish, #394, ¼-lb stick type, from $9 to $12.00
Gourmet Royale, butter warmer, #301, stick handle, double spout, 9-oz, w/stand, from $12 to $14.00
Gourmet Royale, candle holders, tall, w/finger ring, 6", pr, from $25 to $35.00
Gourmet Royale, canister set, 4-pc............................$60.00
Gourmet Royale, casserole, hen on nest, 2-qt, from $65 to .$75.00
Gourmet Royale, casserole, individual, #399, stick handle, 12-oz, from $7 to $8.50
Gourmet Royale, casserole, stick handle, 1-qt, from $9 to $12.00
Gourmet Royale, casserole, stick handle, 3-qt, from $15 to ...$20.00
Gourmet Royale, casserole, stick handle, 4-qt, from $25 to..$35.00
Gourmet Royale, casserole-warming stand....................$7.00
Gourmet Royale, chafing dish, w/handles, lid & stand, 8x9", from $25 to $30.00
Gourmet Royale, cheese shaker, bulbous, 5¾", from $12 to..$15.00
Gourmet Royale, chip 'n dip, #306, 2-pc set, w/stand, from $22 to $25.00
Gourmet Royale, chip 'n dip, #311, molded in 1 pc, 12", from $14 to $18.00
Gourmet Royale, coffee server, from $20 to $25.00
Gourmet Royale, creamer, #382, from $4 to..................$5.00
Gourmet Royale, cruet, coffeepot shape, fill through spout, 4", from $17 to $20.00
Gourmet Royale, cup & saucer, demitasse $18.00
Gourmet Royale, cup & saucer, from $4.50 to $6.00
Gourmet Royale, egg/relish tray, 15" L, from $18 to ..$22.00
Gourmet Royale, gravy boat, #426, 2-spout, lg, +underplate, from $9 to..$14.00
Gourmet Royale, gravy boat, w/stick handle, 2-spout, from $8 to $12.00

Gourmet Royale, jug, #384, 32-oz, from $20 to **$28.00**

Gourmet Royale, jug, #386, ice lip, from $25 to **$32.00**

Gourmet Royale, ladle, sm, from $12 to....................**$15.00**

Gourmet Royale, ladle, 3½" dia bowl, w/11" handle, from $18 to **$20.00**

Gourmet Royale, Lazy Susan, #220, 5-part, molded in 1 pc, 11", from $15 to **$20.00**

Gourmet Royale, Lazy Susan, #308, 3 sections w/center bowl, 14", from $22 to **$25.00**

Gourmet Royale, mug, #391, 12-oz, from $5 to **$7.00**

Gourmet Royale, mug, #392, 16-oz, from $9 to **$12.00**

Gourmet Royale, pie plate, #7016, 9½", from $10 to .**$12.00**

Gourmet Royale, plate, dinner; #88R, from $5 to **$7.00**

Gourmet Royale, plate, egg; holds 12 halves, 7¾x12½", from $15 to **$20.00**

Gourmet Royale, plate, grill; #87, 3-section, 11", from $9 to..**$12.00**

Gourmet Royale, plate, salad; 6¾", from $1 to **$2.00**

Gourmet Royale, plate, steak; 12", from $9 to **$12.00**

Gourmet Royale, platter, #320, 14", from $12 to........**$15.00**

Gourmet Royale, platter, #337, 16", from $18 to........**$20.00**

Gourmet Royale, rarebit, #330, w/lug handles, oval, 11"...**$9.00**

Gourmet Royale, relish dish, #265, 5x10" **$9.00**

Gourmet Royale, roaster, #325, oval, 14", from $15 to ...**$20.00**

Gourmet Royale, roaster, #326, oval, 16", from $20 to ...**$28.00**

Gourmet Royale, salt & pepper shakers, #317/#318, 4½", pr...**$9.00**

Gourmet Royale, salt & pepper shakers, bell shape, pr from $15 to **$20.00**

Gourmet Royale, scoop, any size, from $8 to.............**$12.00**

Gourmet Royale, shirred egg dish, #360, 6", from $7 to..**$10.00**

Gourmet Royale, souffle dish, #393, 5-qt, +underplate, from $50 to **$60.00**

Gourmet Royale, sugar bowl, from $4 to **$6.00**

Gourmet Royale, teapot, #381, 6-cup, from $12 to.....**$18.00**

Gourmet Royale, tray, serving; round, 4-section, center handle, from $15 to **$20.00**

Gourmet Royale, tray, tidbit; 2-tier, from $10 to **$14.00**

Gourmet Royale, tray, 3-part, 15½" L....................**$25.00**

Gourmet Royale, trivet, from $9.00 to $12.00.

Heritage, butter dish, #002-028.................................**$6.00**

Heritage, cake/serving plate, #002-529, 11¼" dia **$9.00**

Heritage, cup & saucer, #002-002, 9-oz......................**$3.00**

Heritage, soup tureen, #002-160, 3½-qt.....................**$30.00**

Muggsy, ashtray **$125.00**

Muggsy, bottle stopper, head, ball shape **$85.00**

Muggsy, canape holder, Carrie, lift-off head pierced for toothpicks, from $125 to..**$150.00**

Muggsy, cigarette server...**$125.00**

Muggsy, clothes sprinkler bottle, Myrtle, Black, from $275 to...**$375.00**

Muggsy, clothes sprinkler bottle, Myrtle, white, from $250 to...**$350.00**

Muggsy, cookie jar, character face, minimum value ...**$250.00**

Muggsy, mug, action figure (golfer, fisherman, etc), any, from $65 to **$85.00**

Muggsy, mug, Black action figure.............................**$125.00**

Muggsy, mug, character face, ea from $35 to **$38.00**

Muggsy, shot mug, character face, ea from $40 to **$50.00**

Muggsy, tumbler **$60.00**

Muggsy, utility jar, Handy Harry, hat w/short bill as flat lid, from $175 to..**$200.00**

Planter, donkey, brown drip, common, 10", from $15 to...**$20.00**

Planter, elephant, brown drip, scarce, from $90 to ..**$100.00**

Village, baker, #236, rectangular, tab handles, 2-qt, from $10 to..**$12.00**

Village, baker, #237, sq, tab handles, 9", from $9 to ..**$12.00**

Village, baker, #24, oval, 10¼", from $7 to...................**$9.00**

Village, baker, #240, oval, 7¾", from $6 to...................**$8.00**

Village, bean pot, 2½-qt, from $22 to.........................**$28.00**

Village, beverage server, #490, from $18 to...............**$22.00**

Village, bowl, butter; w/spout & handle, 8", from $22 to..**$28.00**

Village, bowl, fruit; #008, 5"......................................**$3.00**

Village, bowl, mixing; #453, 1-qt, 2-qt & 3-qt, 3-pc set, from $45 to..**$50.00**

Village, bowl, rim soup; #012, 8½" **$6.00**

Village, bowl, serving; #010, 7", from $8 to **$12.00**

Village, bowl, soup/cereal; #009, 6"............................**$4.00**

Village, bowl, vegetable; #011, 8¾" **$12.00**

Village, bread tray, 12" **$15.00**

Village, butter dish, #028..**$8.00**

Village, canisters, #520, 4-pc set, from $50 to **$55.00**

Village, casserole, w/lid, #315, 2-qt, from $18 to........**$22.00**

Village, coffee mug, #89F, 10-oz, from $5 to................**$7.00**

Village, coffeepot, lighthouse shape, 48-oz, from $20 to..**$25.00**

Village, cookie jar, #540, 3-qt, from $15 to.................**$20.00**

Village, creamer & sugar bowl, #020, from $9 to **$12.00**

Village, cup & saucer, #001 & #002.............................**$3.50**

Village, flowerpot, 4½", from $12 to **$15.00**

Village, gravy boat, #443, w/saucer, 16-oz, from $10 to ..**$12.00**

Village, measuring cups, ceramic, 4 on hanging rack....**$45.00**

Village, measuring cups, copper, 4 on wooden rack w/pierced copper insert, EX **$40.00**

Village, onion soup crock, #295, stick handle, sm, from $5 to...**$7.00**

Village, pedestal mug, #90F, 10-oz **$3.50**

Village, pitcher, #416, 2-qt, from $20 to.....................**$25.00**

Village, plate, dinner; #004, 10¼", from $3 to **$4.00**
Village, platter, #016, 14", from $12 to **$18.00**
Village, quiche, 9" **$16.00**
Village, soup tureen, #160, w/lid & ladle, 3½-qt, from $40
   to **$45.00**
Village, table light, #620, clear glass chimney on candle hold-
   er base, from $12 to **$14.00**

Pie Birds

Pie birds are hollow, china or ceramic kitchen utensils. They date to the 1800s in England, where they were known as pie vents or pie funnels. They are designed to support the upper crust and keep it flaky. They also serve as a steam vent to prevent spill over.

Most have arches on the base and they have one, and *only* one, vent hole on or near the top. There are many new pie birds on both the US and British markets. These are hand painted rather than airbrushed like the older ones.

The Pearl China Co. of East Liverpool, Ohio, first gave pie birds their 'wings.' Prior to the introduction in the late 1920s of an S-neck rooster shape, pie vents were non-figural. They resembled inverted funnels. Funnels which contain certain advertising are the most sought after.

The first bird-shaped pie vent produced in England was designed in 1933 by Clarice Cliff, a blackbird with an orange beak on a white base. The front of the base is imprinted with registry numbers. The bird later carried the name Newport Pottery; more recently it has been marked Midwinter Pottery.

Advisor: Linda Fields (See Directory, Pie Birds)

Newsletter: Pie Birds Unlimited
For subscription information, contact:
Linda Fields
158 Bagsby Hill Lane
Dover, TN 37058

Bluebird with babies on nest, © stamp, 1950, 5", $400.00 to $500.00.

Bear, howling, brown & cream w/pink features, 4" ...**$55.00**
Benny the Baker, w/2 utensils, 5½" **$165.00**
Bird, multicolored, Mortone, from $45 to **$65.00**
Bird, white w/blue features, Royal Winchester, 3½" ..**$85.00**
Black chef, blue clothes, 4⅜" **$160.00**
Black crow, 3¾" **$55.00**
Black fireman, blue uniform w/yellow hat, holding axe,
   marked England, 3¾" **$50.00**
Blackbird, 2-headed, black w/yellow beaks, marked
   England, 7¼", from $65 to **$75.00**
Bluebird, black speckles, heavy pottery, US, 1950s....**$60.00**
Boy Scout, yellow uniform w/brown hat, marked England,
   3½" **$65.00**
Canary, yellow w/pink lips..**$40.00**
Chick, yellow, Josef Original, 3¼" **$75.00**
Chicken in chef's hat, Made in England, 3¾" **$65.00**
Clown, in blue w/white collar, standing on drum, Made in
   England, 5" **$70.00**
Cutie Pie, Josef Original (or A Lorrie Design), hen wearing
   bonnet..**$75.00**
Dalmatian, seated, 1980s...**$40.00**
Dragon head, green, marked England, 4¼" **$75.00**
Duck, long neck, rose w/black wings, 5" **$115.00**
Dutch girl, blonde w/white dress & green apron & hat,
   4½" **$300.00**
Eagle, burnt orange, 4¾" **$50.00**
Elephant, clear glass, embossed Scotland, 4¾" **$50.00**
Elephant, raised trunk, white, marked Nutbrown Pie Funnel,
   Made in England, 1940s, 3½" **$185.00**
Elf, white & red, Made in England, 3½" **$75.00**
Funnel, marked Grimwade Perfection **$110.00**
Funnel, plain aluminum, from $10 to **$15.00**
Funnel, yellow ware, marked Mason Cash (paper label),
   new, from $15 to **$18.00**
Goose, white, Made in England, 7½" **$135.00**
Loch Ness Monster, clear glass, embossed Scotland, 4"...**$50.00**
Mrs Badger, green striped dress, bonnet, flowered apron,
   marked England, 3½" **$50.00**
Mrs Mouse, blue dress, white apron w/green trim, Made in
   England, 3½" **$50.00**
Mushroom, white w/orange, brown & green, marked Crown
   Runnymede England, 2½" **$50.00**
Owl, marked England, 6" **$50.00**
Rooster, S-neck, burgundy & blue on white, Pearl China Co,
   from $150 to..**$175.00**
Rooster on chimney peak, 6"......................................**$50.00**
Welsh lady, marked Cymru, from $95 to..................**$125.00**
Witch, black outfit w/white stars, holding broom in front,
   marked England, 6½" **$50.00**
Wizard, black outfit w/white stars, long white beard, marked
   England, 7½" **$50.00**

Pierce, Howard

Howard Pierce studied at the Chicago Art Institute, California's Pomona College, and the University of Illinois. He married Ellen Van Voorhis of National City, California, who was also to become his business partner. Howard worked alongside William Manker for a short time, and today it is sometimes difficult to tell one artist's work from the other's without first looking at the marks. This is especially true with some of their vases, nut cups, trays, and cups and saucers.

Howard was creative with his designs and selective with his materials. While working as a draftsman at Douglas in Long Beach, California, during World War II, Howard kept his artistic spirit alive by working on weekends in the medium of pewter. The pewter lapel pins he created are considered very desirable by today's collectors and usually sell in the $200.00 to $300.00 range. He dabbled in polyurethane for only a short time as he found he was allergic to it. Today these polyurethane pieces — made nearly exclusively for his immediate family — are scarce and costly. They are extremly lightweight, usually figures of birds on bases. They were hand painted, and many of them have a powdery feel. Howard made a few pieces from aluminum and bronze. Bisque, cement, and porcelain (some with Mount St. Helen's ash) were also used for a limited number of items. (Be cautious not to confuse Howard's 'textured' items with the Mount St. Helen's ash pieces.) Howard's creativity extended itself to include paper as a workable medium as well, as he often made their own Christmas cards. His love for wildlife was constant throughout his career, and he found porcelain to be the best material to use for wildlife models.

Howard's earliest mark was probably 'Howard Pierce' in block letters. This was used on metalware (especially the lapel pins), but also can be found on a few very small ceramic animals. After the Pierces moved to Claremont, California, they used this mark: 'Claremont Calif. Howard Pierce,' usually with a stock number. A rubber stamp 'Howard Pierce Porcelains' was used later. Eventually 'Porcelains' was omitted. Not all pieces are marked, especially when part of a two- or three-piece set. As a rule, only the largest item of the set is marked.

In 1992 due to Howard's poor health, he and Ellen destroyed all the molds they had ever created. Later, with his health somewhat improved, he was able to work a few hours a week, creating miniatures of some of his original models and designing new ones as well. These miniatures are marked simply 'Pierce.' Howard Pierce passed away in February 1994. For further information see *Collector's Encyclopedia of Howard Pierce Porcelain* by Darlene Hurst Dommel.

Advisor: Darlene Hurst Dommel (See Directory, Pierce, Howard)

Ashtray, ebony black or brown on white, unmarked, 2x4", ea **$35.00**
Bank, pig, high gloss brownish gray, 4x7"................**$175.00**
Bowl, black sprayed w/contrasting blue, marked Pierce 1991, 4x6½" **$125.00**
Dish, sea green mottled interior w/brown exterior, marked Pierce 1981, 12", minimum value **$150.00**
Figurine, black songbird w/etched feathers, 4", minimum value **$250.00**

Figurine, cat, slant-eyed, black, 8x3"....................**$75.00**
Figurine, coyote, howling, light brown, stamped & signed, 6" **$85.00**
Figurine, dachshund, dark brown matt, 9½" L..........**$120.00**
Figurine, deer, recumbent, glossy brown, 5½"...........**$70.00**
Figurine, dolphin riding wave, 9½" L, NM **$125.00**
Figurine, elephant, trunk up, glossy gray w/some brown, 4½"...**$125.00**
Figurine, gazelle, brown high gloss, on base, #100P, 11¼x4" **$125.00**
Figurine, goose, gray high gloss, 7x6¼" **$35.00**
Figurine, Madonna w/Child, gold leaf, unmarked, 13½" ..**$85.00**
Figurine, monkey, matt gray flecked w/black highlights, 6¼x3"...**$85.00**
Figurine, mountain sheep ram, white w/brown horns, 7¼x3"..**$100.00**
Figurine, owl, brown matt, 8¼"...............................**$95.00**
Figurine, owl, white, 5" **$55.00**
Figurine, panther, black high gloss, 2x12", minimum value ..**$200.00**
Figurine, pigeon, black w/speckled chest, 7¼x5½" ...**$65.00**
Figurine, porcupine, black ink stamp, 4½x6" **$100.00**
Figurine, quail (2) in tree, rough gray matt, marked, 9x3¼"..**$100.00**
Figurine, raccoon, brown w/dark rings on tail, 8½" L..**$115.00**
Figurine, red bird on black rock, 6x4"........................**$85.00**
Figurine, roadrunner, brown matt, 9"..........................**$95.00**
Figurine, robin, orange breast, black ink stamp, 4½x3½", from $60.00 ....**$75.00**
Figurine, rooster, glossy brown, 3251P, 9¼x6"............**$80.00**
Figurine, woman w/basket, bubbly volcanic glaze, 8" ..**$125.00**

Figurine/vase, squirrels on stump, 11½x7", from $250.00 to $275.00. (Photo courtesy Darlene Hurst Dommel)

Figurines, chipmunks, gray gloss w/dark brown stripe down back, 5", 3", pr **$90.00**
Figurines, dogs w/long droopy ears, brown matt, 8¼", 6", pr **$160.00**
Figurines, duck mother & 2 ducklings, brown, mother: 6½" L, set of 3..**$80.00**
Figurines, geese, solid black, 7½", 8½", pr **$60.00**

Figurines, giraffe family, brown matt, 11½", 9½", 5½", set of 3 ....**$195.00**
Figurines, girl feeding goose, 6½", 3½", pr **$80.00**
Figurines, llamas, mother & baby, dark blue, 8½x6", 5½x3½", pr **$200.00**
Figurines, native couple, brown & white matt, 7¼x2¼", 7¾x3", pr **$190.00**
Figurines, owls, glossy gray w/brown markings, 5", 3", pr ..**$90.00**
Figurines, seals, mother & pup, black high gloss, 5¼x6", 2½x3¼", pr...**$125.00**
Flower holder, girl holding bowl, 9¼"....................**$75.00**
Flower holder, owls (2) in tree, brown matt, holes in back for flowers, 7½" **$95.00**
Magnet, coyote, on base, unmarked, 5½" **$75.00**
Magnet, rabbit, brown, 3½" **$75.00**
Vase, owl & foliage motif, cream w/black motif, 5x4"....**$75.00**

Pin-Back Buttons

Literally hundreds of thousands of pin-back buttons are available; pick a category and have fun! Most fall into one of three fields — advertising, political, and personality related, but within these three broad areas are many more specialized groups. Just make sure you buy only those that are undamaged, are still bright and unfaded, and have well-centered designs and properly aligned printing. The older buttons (those from before the 1920s) may be made of celluloid with the paper backing printed with the name of a company or a product.

See also Political.

Advisor: Michael McQuillen (See Directory, Pin-Back Buttons)

A&P Best Wishes of the Season, red, white & green, celluloid, 1¾", VG **$22.00**
AMOCO, Join the American Party, man wearing hat, tin litho, G **$25.00**
Anoka Halloween Capitol of the World, football player before pumpkin, black & orange, ca 1950s, 1½", NM...**$22.00**
Apollo II Moon Landing, Armstrong, Collins & Aldrin pictured, red, white & blue, July 20, 1969, ¾", NM w/ribbon..**$10.00**
Benicia State Capitol Building, 1958, 2", EX.................**$2.00**
Bond Bread, First Flight Paris to New York, black & white, celluloid, Bastian Bros, EX......................**$38.00**
Bye-Lo Baby Reg US Pat Off Patent Applied for K & Kay, blue & white, Whitehead & Hoag, c 1922, ⅞", EX.........**$45.00**
Cedar Point Ohio 1937, Lake Shore Pioneer Chapter, green & white, celluloid, EX.................................**$10.00**
Chevrolet, New Chevrolet Six, Queen of the Shows, lady's portrait on blue, ca 1929, NM.....................**$65.00**
Cincinnati Redleg Booster, red & white, ca 1946, NM..**$10.00**
High Admiral Cigarettes, It's Naughty - But It's Nice, lady showing frilly slip, celluloid, Whitehead & Hoag, EX.........**$48.00**
High Admiral Cigarettes on globe, celluloid w/metal stud, Whitehead & Hoag Pat Pend, EX **$28.00**

I Support Ronald McDonald House, Mfg by MAS Novelties LTD Toronto, 2¼", M..............................**$2.00**
Los Angeles County Good Roads Association, multicolor, celluloid, Whitehead & Hoag, 1920s, ⅞", NM..........**$30.00**
Masonic symbol, Chinese flags & symbols, marked Brunt Co on back, EX....................................**$8.00**
Ozark Airlines, red, white & black, used for child identification w/space for name & destination city, M.......**$11.00**
Paige the Most Beautiful Car in America, eagle & map, Whitehead & Hoag, 1920s, 1", EX....................**$60.00**
Peppy Flame, I'll Work My Blazing Little Head Off for You, celluloid front, metal back, Nipsco, 1960, 1¾", NM.....**$45.00**
Quaker Rolled White Oats, Try Me 30 Days, celluloid, 1¼", G...**$20.00**
Santa w/pack, Meet Me at Gray's, celluloid, Whitehead & Hoag, 1¼", NM **$75.00**
Uncle Remus Syrup, Black figure on white, multicolor, EX..**$16.00**
University of Michigan, w/original ribbons & football charm, 1940s era, NM..**$20.00**
Zamora Circus, shriner's red hat on white w/green lettering, 1940s, 1¾", EX..**$7.00**
Zorro, 7-Up, red, white & black, Walt Disney Productions, ca 1957, 1¼", M..**$15.00**
4 H Club Member, green & white, 1933, ⅝", EX........**$10.00**

Kellogg's Pep Pins

Chances are if you're over fifty, you remember them — one in each box of PEP (Kellogg's wheat-flake cereal that was among the first to be vitamin fortified). There were eighty-six in all, each carrying the full-color image of a character from one of the popular cartoon strips of the day — Maggie and Jiggs, the Winkles, Dagwood and Blondie, Superman, Dick Tracy, and many others. Very few of these cartoons are still in print.

The pins were issued in five sets, the first in 1945, three in 1946, and the last in 1947. They were made in Connecticut by the Crown Bottle Cap Company, and they're marked PEP on the back. You could wear them on your cap, shirt, coat, or the official PEP pin beanie, an orange and white cloth cap made for just that purpose. The Superman pin — he was the only D.C. Comics Inc. character in the group — was included in each set.

Values are given for pins in near mint condition; prices should be sharply reduced when foxing or fading is present. Any unlisted pins are worth from $10.00 to $15.00.

Bo Plenty, NM...**$30.00**
Corky, NM...**$16.00**
Dagwood, NM..**$30.00**
Dick Tracy, NM..**$30.00**
Early Bird, NM...**$6.00**
Fat Stuff, NM...**$15.00**
Felix the Cat, NM...**$65.00**
Flash Gordon, NM..**$30.00**
Flat Top, NM..**$25.00**

Goofy, NM...$10.00
Gravel Girtie, NM...$15.00
Harold Teen, NM...$15.00
Inspector, NM..$12.50
Jiggs, NM..$20.00
Judy, NM...$10.00
Kayo, NM...$20.00
Little King, NM..$15.00
Little Moose, NM...$15.00
Maggie, NM...$25.00
Mama De Stross, NM..$30.00
Mama Katzenjammer, NM....................................$25.00
Mamie, NM..$14.00

Moon Mullins, NM, $10.00. (Photo courtesy Doug Dezso)

Navy Patrol, NM..$6.00
Olive Oyle, NM..$30.00
Orphan Annie, NM..$25.00
Pat Patton, NM...$10.00
Perry Winkle, NM..$15.00
Phantom, NM..$60.00
Pop Jenks, NM..$15.00
Popeye, NM...$30.00
Rip Winkle, NM..$20.00
Skeezix, NM..$15.00
Superman, NM..$35.00
Toots, NM..$15.00
Uncle Walt, NM..$15.00
Uncle Willie, NM..$12.50
Winkles Twins, NM...$45.00
Winnie Winkle, NM..$15.00

Pinup Art

Some of the more well-known artists in this field are Vargas, Petty, DeVorss, Elvgren, Moran, Ballantyne, Armstrong, and Phillips, and some enthusiasts pick a favorite and concentrate their collections on only his work. From the mid-thirties until well into the fifties, pinup art was extremely popular. As the adage goes, 'Sex sells.' And well it did. You'll find calendars, playing cards, magazines, advertising, and merchandise of all types that depict these unrealistically perfect ladies. Though not all items will be signed, most of these artists have a distinctive, easily identifiable style that you'll soon be able to recognize.

Unless noted otherwise, values listed below are for items in at least near-mint condition.

Advisor: Denis Jackson (See Directory, Pinup Art)

Newsletter: *The Illustrator Collector's News*
Denis Jackson, Editor
P.O. Box 1958
Sequim, WA 98382; 360-452-3810
ww.olypen.com/ticn
e-mail: ticn@olypen.com

Arcade card, Catchy Number, blond in pink tuning radio, 5¼x3¼", VG..$70.00
Arcade card, Cover-All Beauty, girl in pink undies & hard hat, 5¼x3¼"...$37.50
Arcade card, Let's Make Up, girl & dog, Deckard, 5¼x3¼"...$37.50
Book, Bettie Page the Life of a Pin-Up Legend, Essex & Swanson, hardcover, 1996, w/dust jacket.............$50.00
Book, Elvgren His Life & Art, Collins & Elvgren, hardcover, 200 pages...$45.00
Book, Flip #1, 3 flip-book movies w/Marilyn, Lili St Cyr and Jane Russell, Hillman Publications, 1955, EX.......$37.50
Bottle opener, girl showing off her backside, heavy gold-tone metal w/red & black enameling, 5½"..................$25.00
Calendar, Alluring, girl in white gown w/corsage, Zoe Mozert, full pad, 1960, 45x22", EX.......................$85.00
Calendar, different Petty girl ea page (12 complete), Esquire, 1955...$50.00
Calendar, I'm For You, girl in blue & white swimsuit & red pumps, Al Buell, 1960, partial pad, 23x11", EX...$55.00
Calendar, Metcaf, 1952, US Royal Tires, Brown & Bigelow, complete, 33x16", EX...................................$60.00
Calendar print, Figures Don't Lie, lady in undies on scale, Elvgren, 1940s, 9½x7⅜".................................$15.00
Calendar print, Out on a Limb, semi-nude on flowering branch, Ruth Decard, image: 16x11½"................$30.00
Calendar print, Stop sign, lady at wheel in short skirt, del Masters, 6x5"..$7.50
Calendar print, Switch Hitch, cowgirl w/foot resting on saddle, Elvgren, 6x5"...$6.50
Calendar top, woman in sheer lingerie w/red bow at waist carries candle, 12x9⅛" image on 14⅜x12" stock.$24.00
Calendar/note pad, I've Been Spotted, girl in windblown red dress, Elvgren, 1958-1959, 7x3¼", NM................$12.50
Calendar/notepad, A Nice Crip, girl on ladder picking apples, Elvgren, advertising for OH company, 1960, 6x3¼", EX...$12.50
Lighter, blond & brunette portraits in swimsuits on metal, Empress Japan, miniature, 1", NM...................$25.00
Lithograph, Honey-Moon, nude stretched across crescent moon in starry sky, C Moss, 1939, 7¾x5¾".........$25.00
Lithograph, lady w/bouquet, gauzy pink top w/flowered straps, Erbit, 1940s, 10x8"................................$15.00
Lithograph, Needing a Lift, lady hitchhiker raising skirt, Elvgren, Litho USA, 8¼x4"................................$10.00
Magazine, Tab, August 1960, 2-page spread of Jayne Mansfield as brunette, EX......................................$20.00

Magazine page, Jane Russell in low-cut black dress, running fingers through hair, Esquire, 1954, 19x13" **$7.50**

Magazine page, Janis Paige, scanty attire & fur coat, Esquire, 1954, 19x13" **$7.50**

Magazine page, Jeanmaire, in leotard, Esquire, 1954, 19x13" **$7.50**

Oil on canvas, blond in thigh-high hose & stiletto pumps, Willis, 12x9" **$50.00**

Photo, Barbara Nichols, black lacy outfit, reclining in chaise lounge, black & white glossy, 8x10" **$32.50**

Photo, Marilyn Monroe, close-up portrait in white fur & pearls, black & white glossy, 8x10" **$7.00**

Photo, Marilyn standing w/blown skirt, black & white glossy, 8x10" **$7.50**

Playing cards, blond in black lingerie plays w/ribbon & kitten, Elvgren, Brown & Bigelow, complete deck, NM **$32.50**

Playing cards, The Forces, pinup girl on face of ea card, David Wright, Carlo Mundi, WWII era, MIB.........**$60.00**

Postcard, Coquette, brunette in yellow swimsuit, Curt Teich & Co, ca 1948, 5½x3½", EX...................................**$15.00**

Postcard, Jean Arthur in skimpy cowgirl outfit, black & white photo, EX **$20.00**

Postcard, Joan Collins, dressed in leotard & white shirt, black & white photo, 1950s era, EX....................**$22.50**

Postcard, Miss Lead, lady in red at piano, Meet the Misses series #4, Cropp, 3½x5½", EX **$10.00**

Postcard, She Can't Get My Point of View, comic risque scene on linen, Curt Teich & Co, 3½x5½" **$7.50**

Postcard, Shirley Eaton photo, 1940s, EX **$32.50**

Postcard, Vera Ellen in swimsuit, real photo, simulated signature, NM...**$25.00**

Poster, Bettie Page, lacy undies & black gloves, on tiger skin, 34x24", EX **$12.50**

Poster, Bettie Page, reclining in chair w/legs up, black & white, 35x23", EX...**$12.50**

Poster, Diana, beauty w/bow walks w/2 whippets, Vargas, 36x24" **$40.00**

Poster, Marilyn in gold-lame gown, hands on hips, 36x24"...**$17.50**

Poster, Temptation, reclining brunette, Alberto Vargas, 24x36" **$40.00**

Poster book, Best of Elvgren, softcover, 16 prints, 10x14" ..**$30.00**

Print, A Complete Bust, lady holding bra straps, Bradley, 1945, 11¼x9¼", EX...**$22.50**

Print, Beauty on the Beach, lady in red bathing suit & purple pumps, Munson, 7x9¼", NM **$15.00**

Print, blond in black strapless gown (resembles Marilyn), D'Ancona, Litho in USA, 8x6" **$25.00**

Print, Blossom Time, lady in wide-brimmed hat w/flowers, Boynton, dated 1939, 9½x7½"............................**$15.00**

Print, brunette in strapless gown w/roses in lap, signed Frahm, 1950s, 8x6"..**$22.50**

Print, lady rolling garter up her leg, Billy DeVorss, 1940s, image: 16⅝x11⅝", EX.......................................**$17.50**

Print, Orchid Lady, nude before mirror reaching out toward orchids, Erbit, 1940s, 10x8" **$24.00**

Print, Stars, nude's backside, brunette w/flower over right ear, 1940s, image: 10x8" **$28.00**

Tie, hand-painted sexy girl, glued-on sunglasses on red silk, 1950s...**$42.50**

Playing Cards

Here is another collectible that is inexpensive, easy to display (especially single cards), and very diversified. Among the endless variations are backs that are printed with reproductions of famous paintings and pinup art, carry advertising of all types, and picture tourist attractions and world's fair scenes. Early decks are scarce, but those from the '40s on are usually more attractive anyway, so pick an area that interests you most and have fun! Though they're usually not dated, you may find some clues that will help you to determine an approximate date. Telephone numbers, zip codes, advertising slogans, and patriotic messages are always helpful.

See also Pinup Art.

Club/Newsletter: American Antique Deck Collectors; 52 Plus Joker Club
Clear the Decks, quarterly publication
Larry Herold, Auctioneer
300 E. 34th St., Apt. 6E
New York, NY 10016; e-mail: herojr@banet.net

American Airlines, AA & eagle logo on white, 52+J, MIB **$12.50**

American Red Cross, pre-zip code address, NMIB **$10.00**

Braniff International, white block letters on red, 1960s, MIB...**$14.00**

Brewick Hunt #1855, foxhunt scene, pinochle, 48 cards, NMIB..**$20.00**

Brunette w/dogs, Congress, double deck, ea 52+2 Jokers, EXIB w/original instructions **$28.00**

Calico Kitten, Congress, 52+2 Jokers, used, VG.........**$10.00**

Card suits form border on red & blue backs, double deck, felt-covered box marked Tiffany & Co, MIB (worn box)...**$12.50**

Cats by Gladys Emerson Cook, US Playing Cards, double deck, 1940s-50s, complete, EXIB........................**$50.00**

Century of Progress, Chicago, fair logo backs, 1934, MIB (EX box) **$50.00**

Delta Air Lines, Miami, cityscape & sailboats, MIB, sealed...**$14.00**

Delta Airlines, New York, Statue of Liberty backs, MIB, sealed...**$14.00**

Delta Airlines, 50 years of Delta Service, blue & gold, 1979, MIP (sealed) **$12.50**

Double Kitten, double deck, 1951, MIB (gold-tone, unopened) w/original instructions for canasta.....**$45.00**

Fighting cocks on backs, Duratone, double deck, ea 52+Joker, MIB..**$28.00**

Firestone Tires, blue & white F in shield logo, Firestone, The People Tire People, MIB.......................................**$10.00**

Flying geese, Congress, 52 (no jokers), G.................**$10.00**

Foxhunt scene on red, Haddon Hall Pinochle Playing Cards, EE Fairchild Corporation on red, white & blue box, MIB **$35.00**

Henry Wadsworth Longfellow & Ralph Waldo Emerson homes, double deck, ea 52+Jokers, NMIB...........**$22.00**

Hunting Dogs, Congress, double deck, ea 52+Jokers+advertising cards, VG...**$22.00**

Independent Safety Match, Independence Hall pictured, red, white & blue backs, 51+1 Joker, VG+...................**$50.00**

Kem Cards, statue backs, narrow, double deck, 1935, VGIB **$12.50**

Kentucky Derby, Churchill Downs, race scene backs, 1960s, complete, M, unused..**$12.50**

Luden's Cough Drops, cough drop box shapes, 52+2 Jokers, NMIB...**$27.50**

Mickey Mouse as King w/Goofy as Joker, Donald as Jack, Minnie as Queen, Walt Disney Productions, MIB (plastic box) **$15.00**

Ming vase & Sevres vase backs, Congress, double deck w/cellutone finish, NMIB **$12.50**

RG Dun Cigars, Duargone, green backs, MIB (sealed)..**$16.50**

Schering Medical II, Coricidin, non-standard courts, 1966, 52+2 Jokers+booklet, NM.....................................**$20.00**

Shaw Savill Line, flag & ship's protrait backs, double deck, EXIB (map inside lid & gold embossed label on box front)...**$30.00**

Southern Pacific Rail Lines, Sunset, Overland, Golden State & Shasta Routes pictures on face, train backs, 1943, EXIB...**$42.50**

Spring, Norman Rockwell, 54 (2 trump cards) complete, EX...**$6.00**

Steamboat #99, pattern backs, wide, 1930s, 52+steamboat Joker, NMIB..**$55.00**

Virgo, blue & white Zodiac backs, 52+Joker+Virgo extra card, EXIB...**$12.50**

Western Aces, western film stars, 1960, postcard size, 52+12 aces, EX+..**$50.00**

Western Airlines, red & white logos form grid, MIB (sealed)..**$10.00**

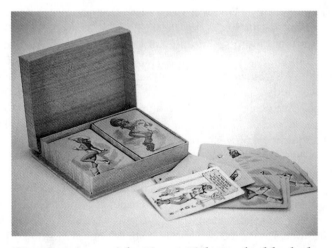

Western pinup girls, Lipsey Fish Co, double deck, 1947, MIB, from $35.00 to $45.00.

Political Memorabilia

Political collecting is one of today's fastest-growing hobbies. Between campaign buttons, glassware, paper, and other items, collectors are scrambling to acquire these little pieces of history. Before the turn of the century and the advent of the modern political button, candidates produced ribbons, ferrotypes, stickpins, banners, and many household items to promote their cause. In 1896 the first celluloid (or cello) buttons were used. Cello refers to a process where a paper disc carrying a design is crimped under a piece of celluloid (now acetate) and fastened to a metal button back. In the 1920s the use of lithographed (or litho) buttons was introduced.

Campaigns of the 1930s through the 1990s have used both types of buttons. In today's media-hyped world, it is amazing that in addition to TV and radio commercials, candidates still use some of their funding to produce buttons. Bumper stickers, flyers, and novelty items also still abound. Reproductions are sometimes encountered by collectors. Practice and experience are the best tools in order to be aware.

One important factor to remember when pricing buttons is that condition is everything. Buttons with any cracks, stains, or other damage will only sell for a fraction of our suggested values. Listed below are some of the items one is likely to find when scrutinizing today's sales.

For more information about this hobby, we recommend you read Michael McQuillen's monthly column 'Political Parade' in *Antique Week* newspaper.

Advisor: Michael McQuillen (See Directory, Political)

Club: A.P.I.C. (American Political Items Collectors) of Indiana
Michael McQuillen
P.O. Box 50022
Indianapolis, IN 46250-0022
e-mail: michael@politicalparade.com or Website: www.politicalparade.com; National organization serving needs of political enthusiasts; send SASE for more information

Badge, Delegate, 1952 Republican National Convention, blue ribbon & brass medallion w/Lincoln bust, Crafts Inc, EX **$50.00**

Badge, Honorary Assistant Sergant at Arms, 1960 Republican National Convention, brass, Crafters Inc, EX........**$50.00**

Bank, JFK Bust w/John F Kennedy 1917-1963, copper-colored metal, 5½", EX...**$35.00**

Book, My Hope for America, Lyndon B Johnson, 121 pages, 1964, signed inside front cover, EX.....................**$250.00**

Booklet, The Roden Doctrine, promoting George Roden for president 1976, 20 pages, EX................................**$15.00**

Bottle stopper, LBJ head w/cork bottom, 4¼", NMIB.**$55.00**

Campaign Cookie Cutter, tin w/band hand, 2x3", NM in original blue box w/red letters & white elephant **$25.00**

Can, tin; Johnson Juice, A Drink for Health Care, silver donkey on blue, VG **$45.00**

Creamer, white w/President & Mrs John F Kennedy, gold trim, EX...**$25.00**

Cup, toasting; 1983 Summit of Industrialized Nations, Ronald Reagan faux signature, Pewter Silversmiths, 1¾", EX...**$75.00**

Dish, Inaugural Luncheon 1965 engraved in bottom, silver w/raised edges, fancy rim, marked Gorham Sterling, 3" dia, EX...**$55.00**

Dish, Republican Senator Inner Circle frosted on clear, winged eagle on lid, sq, 2¾", EX.........................**$50.00**

Doll, LBJ, w/button, plastic, Remco, 1964, 6", NM **$35.00**

Figurine, elephant waving hat w/'80' sits on crate w/draped US flag, pewter, Hallmark, 1980, 2"......................**$45.00**

Game, Meet the Presidents, quiz game, profiles of presidents on tokens, Selchow & Righter, 1965, VG (w/box)..**$35.00**

Glass, Congress Hotel, image of Republican elephant & hotel logo fired-on **$20.00**

Hat pin, Lyndon B Johnson, 10-gal hat shape, brass, EX...**$35.00**

License attachment, 1953 Ike/Nixon Inauguration, NM, $150.00. (Photo courtesy Michael McQuillen)

License plate, All the Way With LBJ, red on white w/red border, 1964, 12x6", EX..**$30.00**

Medal, eagle w/banner, Assistant Sergant at Arms for 1928 Republican National Convention, Whitehead & Hoag, 5", EX..**$55.00**

Medal, 1932 Chicago Republican National Convention Telegraph Operators, Bastian Bros, EX (original card)................**$75.00**

Pennant, 1964 Democratic Convention Atlantic City, w/Johnson image in shield, red & blue on white felt, 29", EX...**$35.00**

Periscope, inaugural; Souvenir of Washington DC Inaugural, 4" image of LBJ & White House Dome, 20x4¾x3", EX **$75.00**

Pin-back, America Needs Ted, blue on white Lineart profile of T Kennedy, 1976, 1¾", EX **$15.00**

Pin-back, For Experienced Leadership, Kennedy & Johnson, red, white & blue, 3½", EX......................................**$35.00**

Pin-back, For President Adlai E Stevenson, black & white picture on white w/black rim, 1¼", EX **$30.00**

Pin-back, I'm a Democrat, peanut w/wide mouth open eating bug-eyed elephant on red, tin, EX.................**$20.00**

Pin-back, I'm a Democrat for Willkie, red, white & blue w/star at bottom, ⅞", EX..**$15.00**

Pin-back, JFK profile, flicker style, 3", EX **$25.00**

Pin-back, Johnson/Kennedy, red, white & blue rim, picture button, 1¼"...**$55.00**

Pin-back, Our Next President Taft in '48, red & blue on white, 1¾", EX **$15.00**

Pin-back, Peace & Prosperity, Vote LBJ in '64, blue letters w/red bars behind image on white, 6", EX.........**$30.00**

Pin-back, President Nixon, Now More Than Ever, red, white & blue, 1¼", EX **$5.00**

Pin-back, Rockefeller for President, photo in center, red & blue on white, 1⅛", EX...**$5.00**

Pin-back, Souvenir of President Harding's Pacific Coast Tour, brown-tone, oval, 1¼", EX **$1,000.00**

Pin-back, Taft for President, black w/white rim, 1½", EX ..**$100.00**

Pin-back, Truman Fights for Human Rights, blue on white, ⅞", EX..**$500.00**

Pin-back, Vote Democrat, Johnson/Humphrey, pictures on gold-outlined shield, 3½", EX **$20.00**

Pin-back, Vote For Tennessee's Carter Delegates May 25, white on green, 3", EX...**$40.00**

Pin-back, 50th Anniversary...Republican Party, side-by-side profiles of Lincoln 1854 & T Roosevelt 1904, ⅞", EX..**$130.00**

Plate, FDR, International Pewter, #250 of 7,500 made, 9¼", EX..**$75.00**

Plate, For President Benjamin Harrison, laurel leaves on white porcelain, Imperial China, 8", EX...............**$80.00**

Plate, JFK & family, color photo w/white border, 7¼", EX..**$25.00**

Plate, sepia-tone of Truman w/faux signature, green border w/gold rim & scrolls, Pickard China, 10⅝", EX....**$50.00**

Plate, W Wilson portrait, End of First World War 1919, French, EX..**$110.00**

Poster, LBJ for the USA, 1964 Presidential Campaign, portrait, 11x16", EX **$35.00**

Program, Hamiltonian & Republican National Convention, Chicago June 1912, VG+ **$150.00**

Program, Official Inaugural; Truman 1949, VG+.........**$85.00**

Program, souvenir; 1964 Democratic National Convention, EX..**$40.00**

Pull-toy, Republican National Convention New Orleans '88, wood w/rope tail, leather ears, 10x11", EX..........**$50.00**

Salt & pepper shakers, ceramic w/colored photo of Truman 1894-1972, EX..**$20.00**

Sign, No Parking; Presidental Inauguration, midnight 1-19 to midnight 1-20 1965, heavy tin, VG+......................**$70.00**

Spoon, Lyndon B Johnson, name & image engraved on handle, Apollo 8 in bowl, Wm Rogers, EX................**$20.00**

Watch, From Peanuts to President, Jimmy Carter photo in center, Unique Time Co, M..................................**$75.00**

Porcelier China

The Porcelier Manufacturing Company was founded in East Liverpool, Ohio, in 1926. They moved to Greensburg, Pennsylvania, in 1930, where they continued to operate until closing in 1954. They're best known for their extensive line of vitrified china kitchenware, but it should also be noted that they made innumerable lighting fixtures.

The company used many different methods of marking their ware. Each mark included the name Porcelier, usually written in script. The mark can be an ink stamp in black, blue, brown, or green; engraved into the metal bottom plate (as on electrical pieces); on a paper label (as found on lighting fixtures); incised block letters; or raised block letters. With the exception of sugar bowls and creamers, most pieces are marked.

Our advisor for this category, Susan Grindberg, has written the *Collector's Guide to Porcelier China, Identification and Values* (Collector Books).

Advisor: Susan Grindberg (See Directory, Porcelier)

Ball jug, Mexican	$80.00
Boiler, Oriental Deco, 6-cup	$45.00
Creamer, Dutch Boy & Girl	$8.00
Creamer, Pink Flower Platinum set	$8.00
Creamer, Silhouette Hostess set	$12.00
Decanter, Quilted Floral Cameo	$40.00
Percolator, electric: Flower Pot Hostess set	$75.00
Pitcher, disc; Hearth	$70.00
Pitcher, Leaf Band, 2-cup	$25.00
Pitcher, Ribbed band, 2-cup	$25.00
Pot, Autumn Leaves, ribbed, 4-cup	$25.00
Pot, Basketweave Cameo, 4-cup	$30.00
Pot, Dainty Rose, 4-cup	$40.00
Pot, Double Floral, 2-cup	$35.00
Pot, Flamingo, 4-cup	$40.00
Pot, Goldfinches, 8-cup	$30.00
Pot, Magnolia, 6-cup	$35.00
Pot, Nautical, 6-xup	$30.00
Pot, Pears, 2-cup	$30.00
Pot, Ribbed Cameo Flower Basket, 6-cup	$30.00
Pot, Rose & Wheat, 4-cup	$25.00
Pot, tankard; Solid, 6-cup	$30.00
Pot, Tree Trunk, 2-cup	$40.00
Pot, 1939 New York World's Fair, 8-cup	$250.00
Pretzel jar, Serv-All Line, platinum	$75.00
Sugar bowl, Medallion	$10.00
Sugar bowl, Orange Poppy Hostess set	$12.00
Sugar bowl, Rope Bow	$12.00
Urn, electric; Field Flowers Hostess set	$95.00
Waffle iron, Barock-Colonial, gold, #461	$225.00

Powder Jars

Ceramic

With figural ceramics becoming increasingly popular, powder jars have become desired collectibles. Found in various subjects and having great eye appeal, they make interesting collections. For more information we recommend *Collector's Guide to Made in Japan Ceramics* (there are four in series) by Carole Bess White (Collector Books).

Advisor: Carole Bess White (See Directory, Japan Ceramics)

Bamboo w/flower motif, black & white on orange, Japan, 3½" dia, from $15 to	$20.00
Colonial lady, blue hoop skirt, ¾-figure lid, Japan, 7", from $30 to	$40.00
Colonial lady w/rose in right hand, bouquet in other arm, Japan, 7", from $125 to	$165.00
Dog pr, white w/black ears etc, atop basketweave lid (w/fruit decal) & bowl, Japan, 4", from $25 to	$45.00

Flapper, orange coat with white trim, blue and yellow hat, Japan, 4", from $65.00 to $85.00. (Photo courtesy Carole Bess White)

Flowers in relief (red, blue & green) over entire dome lid, yellow bowl, Japan, 3¾" dia	$20.00
Garden scene on white background w/blue border, solid blue jar w/gold trim, Noritake, 4¾" dia	$65.00
Heart shape, Oriental lady w/fan in center of lid, Noritake, 3", from $300 to	$400.00
Lady, hoop skirt as lid & bowl, gold & multicolored lustre, Goldcastle, 4", from $65 to	$85.00
Lady, ½-figure in pink dress w/hands folded, floral decor on pink jar, Noritake, 5", from $295 to	$355.00
Landscape, fall scene in earth tones, green Noritake mark #27, 3½" dia	$75.00
Oriental lady w/parasol in orange dress atop purple lustre scalloped lid & jar, Noritake, from $295 to	$355.00
Pierrot, yellow costume w/multicolored trim, Goldcastle, 4¼", from $75 to	$100.00
Rabbit, ear cocked, on hexagonal lid & bowl, yellow w/multicolored trim, Japan, 5¼", from $45 to	$65.00

Glass

Glassware items such as powder jars, trays, lamps, vanity sets, towel bars, and soap dishes were produced in large quantities during the Depression era by many glasshouses who were simply trying to stay afloat. They used many of the same colors as they had in the making of their colored Depression glass dinnerware that has been so popular with collectors for more than thirty years.

Some of their most imaginative work went into designing powder jars. Subjects ranging from birds and animals to Deco nudes and Cinderella's coach can be found today, and this diversity coupled with the fact that many were made in several colors provides collectors with more than enough variations to keep them interested and challenged.

Advisor: Sharon Thoerner (See Directory, Powder Jars)

Amethyst glass, very plain, New Martinsville, 4½" dia...**$35.00**
Annabella, pink transparent..**$175.00**
Annette, pink frost...**$200.00**
Annette w/2 dogs, crystal **$75.00**
Ballerina, pink frost...**$185.00**
Bambi, marigold iridescent, Jeannette........................**$32.00**
Blue carnival w/smocking design, Indiana Glass Co, 6½x6" **$25.00**
Carrie, black, draped nude figural stem, painted flowers .**$195.00**
Cleopatra II, crystal, shallow base, deep lid, 4¾".......**$95.00**
Colonial Lady, light blue opaque, Akro Agate **$100.00**
Crinoline Girl, crystal, off-the-shoulder gown, flowers in right hand, embossed bows on skirt..........................**$40.00**
Crinoline Girl, green frost, off-the-shoulder gown, flowers in right hand, embossed bows on skirt...................**$165.00**
Curtsy, pink frost **$140.00**
Dancing Girl, green frost, feminine features, rope trim at top of base...**$120.00**
Dolly Sisters, green frost **$225.00**
Elephant (trunk down), green frost, lg **$85.00**
Elephant w/carousel base, pink frost........................**$125.00**
Elephants battling, pink frost......................................**$125.00**
Gretchen, green transparent **$195.00**
Horse & coach, pink frost, round **$350.00**
Jackie, green frost...**$120.00**
Jackie, pink frost...**$160.00**
Judy, green, New Martinsville.....................................**$75.00**
Lillian VII, pink frost, cone-shaped base **$195.00**
Martha Washington, crystal, Colonial lady between boy & girl...**$100.00**
Minstrel, crystal..**$50.00**
Minstrel, pink frost...**$95.00**
Modernistic, pink satin, New Martinsville, original sticker label **$115.00**
Obelisk, green frost, flat, no feet................................**$85.00**
Pagoda, blue frost w/Frances Mandel label...............**$40.00**
Parakeets, crystal frost...**$155.00**
Poodle, iridescent, Jeannette......................................**$50.00**
Roxana, green frost...**$135.00**
Royal Coach, pink frost w/white & gold overspray, black lid..**$225.00**
Scottie, light blue opaque, Akro Agate **$150.00**
Scottie, pink transparent, Jeannette...........................**$70.00**
Southern Belle, green frost **$195.00**
Sphinx, pink frost...**$110.00**
Terrier (sm, standing), pink frost...............................**$125.00**
Three Birds, green or pink frost, ea..........................**$125.00**
Twins, green frost...**$155.00**
Vamp, green frost, flapper's head forms finial **$155.00**
Vamp, pink frost, flapper's head forms finial...........**$120.00**
Wendy, fully painted **$145.00**

Precious Moments

Precious Moments is a line consisting of figurines, picture frames, dolls, plates, and other items, all with inspirational messages. They were created by Samuel J. Butcher and are produced by Enesco Inc. in the Far East. You'll find these in almost every gift store in the country, and some of the earlier, discontinued figurines are becoming very collectible. For more information, we recommend *Collector's Value Guide to Precious Moments by Enesco* (CheckerBee Publishing).

Our values are for examples in mint condition and retaining their original box.

Faith Is the Victory, #521396, introduced Spring 1989, retired, MIB **$145.00**
Fruit of the Spirit Is Love, #521213, introduced Spring 1993, retired, MIB **$35.00**
God Is Love Dear Valentine, #523518, introduced Spring 1989, retired, MIB **$32.00**
God's Speed, #E3112, Fish mark, introduced Spring 1979, retired, MIB **$65.00**
Hand That Rocks the Future, #E3108, Fish mark, introduced Spring 1979, suspended, MIB **$67.50**
I Believe in Miracles, #E7156, Hourglass mark, introduced Spring 1981, suspended, MIB **$75.00**
Jesus Is the Only Way, #520756, introduced Spring 1988, suspended, MIB...**$60.00**
Let Love Reign, #E9273, introduced Spring 1983, retired, MIB **$60.00**
Light of the World Is Jesus, #521507, introduced Spring 1989, retired, MIB **$75.00**

The Lord Bless You and Keep You, E3114, 1979, Fish mark, MIB, $50.00.

Love Is From Above, #521841, introduced Spring 1989, suspended, MIB...**$55.00**
Love Is Sharing (boy), #E3110B, Fish mark, introduced Spring 1979, retired, MIB **$75.00**

Make a Joyful Noise - 1993 Easter Egg, various marks after 1983, introduced Spring 1993, MIB **$30.00**

Merry Christmas Deer, #522317, introduced Spring 1989, retired, MIB **$80.00**

Mother Sew Dear (frame), #E7241, Fish mark, introduced Spring 1981, suspended, MIB **$56.00**

Nobody's Perfect, #E9268, Fish mark, introduced Spring 1982, retired, MIB **$85.00**

Our Club Is Soda-Licious, #PM962, various marks after 1983, introduced Spring 1996, MIB **$55.00**

Perfect Grandpa, #E7160, Fish mark, introduced Spring 1981, suspended, MIB **$75.00**

Praise the Lord Anyhow, #E9254, Cross production mark (decal), introduced Spring 1983, retired, MIB **$150.00**

Seek Ye the Lord, #E9261, Fish mark, introduced Spring 1982, suspended, MIB **$45.00**

Sun Is Always Shining Somewhere, #163775, introduced Spring 1995, retired, MIB **$40.00**

There Is Joy in Serving Jesus, #E7157, Fish mark, introduced Spring 1982, retired, MIB **$50.00**

Tubby's First Christmas, #525278, introduced Spring 1992, retired, MIB **$12.00**

We Three Kings, musical, #E0520, introduced Spring 1993, suspended, MIB **$140.00**

Wishing You a Comfy Christmas, #527750, introduced Spring 1992, retired, MIB **$32.00**

Wishing You a Cozy Season, #521949, introduced Spring 1989, suspended, MIB **$48.00**

Wishing You a Happy Bear Hug, #520659, introduced Spring 1994, suspended, MIB **$30.00**

Wishing You a Season Filled w/Joy, #E2805, Fish mark, introduced Spring 1980, retired, MIB **$75.00**

Princess House Company

The home party plan of Princess House was started in Massachusetts in 1963 by Charlie Collis. His idea was to give women an opportunity to have their own business by being a princess in their house, thus the name for this company. The founder wanted every woman to be able to afford fine glassware. Originally the company purchased glass from other manufacturers; but as they grew, the need developed to make their own. In 1972 they bought the Louis Glass Company of West Virginia.

In 1987 Collis sold his company to Colgate-Palmolive. It became a division of that company but was still allowed to operate under its own name. In 1994 a group of investors bought Princess House from Colgate-Polmolive; they own the company yet today. In order to better focus on the home party plan which had been its primary goal, the company sold the glassmaking division to Glass Works WV in 2000. This company will continue to make glass for Princess House but will also allow the facility to develop a new and greater glass market.

Most Princess House pieces are not marked in the glass — they carry a paper label. The original line of Pets also carries the Princess House label, but animals from the Wonders of the Wild and Crystal Treasures lines are all marked with a PH embossed on the glass itself. This new PH mark will make it easy to identify these pieces on the secondary market.

Heritage is a crystal cut floral pattern. It was introduced not long after the company started in business. Fantasia is a crystal pressed floral pattern, introduced about 1980. Both lines continue today; new pieces are being added, and old items are continually discontinued.

Advisors: Debbie and Randy Coe (See Directory, Cape Cod)

Animals, Birds, and Fish

Bear, Bernie, crystal, #813, 3½x2¼" **$29.50**

Bear, Brewster, crystal, #928, 2½" L **$25.00**

Bird, crystal, #458, 7¾" L **$12.00**

Cat, crystal, #811, 3½x2½" **$29.50**

Cow, Chloe, crystal, #817, 2½x4" **$28.00**

Dog, Puppy, crystal, #812, 1½x4½" **$29.50**

Pig, Penelope, crystal, #883, 3x3¾" **$28.00**

Sea Lion, crystal, #873, 5¼x3¼" **$35.00**

Fantasia

Bowl, cereal; #513, 5½-oz, 5½" **$5.00**

Bowl, salad dressing; #3323, 3 bowls in silver-plated holder **$23.50**

Bowl, salad; #521, 50-oz, 8¾" **$16.00**

Butter dish, #527, ¼-lb, 8" L **$18.00**

Casserole, #596, lg oval roaster w/lid **$29.50**

Creamer, #532, 10½-oz, 4" **$5.00**

Cup & saucer, #514 & #515, 6-oz **$6.50**

Deviled egg plate, #591, 10" **$20.00**

Goblet, water; #500, 8-oz, 6¼" **$8.00**

Mug, coffee or chocolate; #516, 9-oz, 4" **$6.00**

Napkin holder, #518, 3½x6" **$14.00**

Pitcher, #546, 55-oz, 8½" **$24.50**

Plate, bread & butter; #512, 6" **$2.50**

Plate, dinner; #511, 10" **$12.00**

Plate, salad; #437, 8" **$5.00**

Plate, torte; #509, 13" **$18.00**

Relish, #534, 3-part, tab handles, oblong, 7x12½" **$14.00**

Salt & pepper shakers, #528, 3¼", pr **$12.00**

Sugar bowl, #532, w/lid, 10-oz, 5" **$7.50**

Tray, 2-tiered serving; #533, w/center handle **$19.50**

Tumbler, #545, flat, 12½-oz, 5" **$7.00**

Heritage

Bell, #495, 6" **$8.00**

Bowl, centerpiece; #470, 11¾" **$35.00**

Bowl, cereal; #667, 5½" **$5.00**

Butter dish, #461, round w/dome lid, 4¾x4½" **$17.50**

Candy jar, #443, 3-bowl stack w/lid, 9½" **$22.00**

Carafe, wine; #493, 32-oz, 8½" **$14.50**

Decanter, #440, 46½-oz, 15" **$28.00**

Goblet, water; #418, 11-oz **$7.00**

Ice server, #863, 52-oz...**$18.00**
Icer, #816, w/liner, 8½-oz **$12.00**
Mayonaise set, #429, bowl, liner & spoon....................**$9.50**
Mug, #50, footed, 10-oz, 5½".....................................**$5.00**
Pitcher, beverage; #459, 75-oz, 10".........................**$24.00**
Pitcher, juice; #402, 22-oz, 6½"...............................**$14.00**
Plate, dinner; #648, 10"...**$8.00**
Plate, lunch; #547, 8"..**$6.00**
Salt & pepper shakers, #471, 4", pr...........................**$12.00**
Tumbler, #460, flat, 11½-oz, 5"...................................**$6.00**
Tumbler, cooler; #462, flat, 23-oz, 6¾" **$9.00**
Vase, #411, 4¼"...**$8.00**
Vase, bud; #409, crimped top, 10"..............................**$12.50**

Purinton Pottery

The Purinton Pottery Company moved from Ohio to Shippenville, Pennsylvania, in 1941 and began producing several lines of dinnerware and kitchen items hand painted with fruits, ivy vines, and floral designs in bold brush strokes of color on a creamy white background. The company closed in 1959 due to economic reasons.

Purinton has a style that's popular today with collectors who like the country look. It isn't always marked, but you'll soon recognize its distinct appearance. Some of the rarer designs are Palm Tree, Peasant Garden, and Pennsylvania Dutch, and examples of these lines are considerably higher than the more common ones. You'll see more Apple and Fruit pieces than any, and in more diversified shapes.

Advisor: Joe McManus (See Directory, Dinnerware)

Club/Newsletter: Purinton News & Views
c/o Joe McManus
PO Box 153, Connellsville, PA 15425

Apple, bowl, fruit; plain border, 12" **$35.00**
Apple, bowl, range; w/lid, 5½" **$65.00**
Apple, butter dish, open, 6½" L **$65.00**
Apple, coffeepot, w/drip filter, 8-cup, 11"................**$110.00**
Apple, cruets, oil & vinegar; sq, 5", pr.......................**$75.00**
Apple, dish, w/lid, 9" L **$65.00**
Apple, grill platter, 12" **$45.00**
Apple, pitcher, beverage; 2-pt, 6¼".............................**$65.00**
Apple, pitcher, Rubel mold, 5"....................................**$75.00**
Apple, platter, meat; 12"...**$40.00**
Chartreuse, coffeepot, 8 cup, 8".................................**$75.00**
Chartreuse, cruets, oil & vinegar; 1-pt, tall, 9½", pr ...**$75.00**
Chartreuse, platter, grill; 12".......................................**$30.00**
Chartreuse, saucer, 5½"..**$3.00**
Chartreuse, wall pocket, 3½"..**$35.00**
Crescent Flower, jar, 3½"...**$45.00**
Crescent Flower, jug, Dutch; 2-pt, 5¾" **$75.00**
Crescent Flower, salt & pepper shakers, round, 2¾", pr .**$65.00**
Crescent Flower, vase, 2-handled, 7½".....................**$125.00**

Desert Flower, sea horse cocktail dish, 11¾"..............**$55.00**
Desert Scene, plate, 8½" **$75.00**
Fruit, bottle, vinegar; cobalt trim, 1-pt, 9½" **$35.00**
Fruit, cookie jar, oval, red trim, 9" **$60.00**
Fruit, cup, 2½"...**$10.00**
Fruit, jug, Kent; 1-pt, 4½"..**$30.00**
Fruit, plate, chop; 12"...**$35.00**
Fruit, plate, dinner; 9¾"...**$20.00**
Fruit, salt & pepper shakers, jug style, 2½", pr..........**$20.00**
Fruit, salt & pepper shakers, red trim, range style, 4", pr...**$40.00**
Fruit, teapot, 4-cup, 5"...**$55.00**
Fruit, tumbler, 12-oz, 5"...**$20.00**
Grapes, bowl, range; w/lid, 5½" **$45.00**
Heather Plaid, creamer, 3"...**$20.00**
Heather Plaid, grease jar, w/lid, 5½".............................**$60.00**
Heather Plaid, mug, handled, 8-oz, 4"..........................**$25.00**
Heather Plaid, plate, chop; 12".......................................**$25.00**
Intaglio, bean pot, 3¾"..**$50.00**
Intaglio, bowl, vegetable; divided, 10½" **$30.00**
Intaglio, butter dish, side handle, open, 6½" **$55.00**
Intaglio, decanter, miniature, 5"....................................**$35.00**
Intaglio, jug, 5-pt, 8"...**$75.00**
Intaglio, plate, chop; 12"...**$25.00**

Intaglio, plate, from $10.00 to $15.00; mug jug, eight-ounce, 4¾", $40.00.

Intaglio, platter, meat, 12"..**$30.00**
Intaglio, relish tray, pottery handle, 3-section, 10" dia....**$45.00**
Intaglio, sugar bowl, w/lid, 5" **$30.00**
Ivy-Red Blossom, coffeepot, 8".....................................**$65.00**
Ivy-Red Blossom, pitcher, beverage; 2-pt, 6¼"............**$55.00**
Ivy-Red Blossom, teapot, w/drip filter, 9"....................**$75.00**
Ivy-Yellow Blossom, creamer, 3½".................................**$15.00**
Ivy-Yellow Blossom, teapot, 6-cup, 6" **$45.00**
Maywood, baker, 7"..**$15.00**
Maywood, bowl, salad; 11"..**$25.00**
Maywood, bowl, vegetable; open, 8½" **$15.00**
Maywood, plate, chop; 12"...**$20.00**
Maywood, plate, salad; 11"..**$25.00**
Maywood, teapot, 6-cup, 6½"..**$45.00**

Ming Tree, cup, 2½"..$15.00
Ming Tree, planter, 5"...$35.00
Ming Tree, plate, dinner; 9¾"..................................$20.00
Ming Tree, platter, meat; 12"...................................$40.00
Morning Glory, jug, honey; 6¼".............................$50.00
Mountain Rose, bean pot, 3¾".................................$65.00
Mountain Rose, creamer & sugar bowl, miniature, open, 2"..$50.00
Mountain Rose, marmalade jar, w/lid, 4½"...............$65.00
Normandy Plaid, bowl, fruit; 12".............................$35.00
Normandy Plaid, cookie jar, oval, w/lid, 9½".............$60.00
Normandy Plaid, jug, 5-pt, 8"...................................$75.00
Normandy Plaid, pitcher, beverage; 2-pt, 6¼".............$55.00
Normandy Plaid, platter, meat; 12"...........................$30.00
Normandy Plaid, roll tray, 11".................................$35.00
Palm Tree, basket planter, 6¼"..............................$100.00
Palm Tree, plate, dinner; 9¾"................................$125.00
Peaasant Leady, candle holder, signed, minimum value..$500.00
Peasant Garden, pitcher, Rubel mold, 4"..................$125.00
Peasant Garden, plate, breakfast; 8½".....................$100.00
Peasant Garden, tea cup, 2½"...................................$35.00
Pennsylvania Dutch, bowl, vegetable; divided, 10½"..$50.00
Pennsylvania Dutch, cookie jar, slant top w/wooden lid, 7x7"..$125.00
Pennsylvania Dutch, jug, honey; 6¼".........................$85.00
Pennsylvania Dutch, plate, dinner; 9¾".....................$25.00
Pennsylvania Dutch, platter, meat; 12".......................$50.00
Pennsylvania Dutch, salt & pepper shakers, stacking, 2¼", pr..$50.00
Pennsylvania Dutch, tumbler, 12-oz, 5".....................$35.00
Pennsylvania Dutch, wall pocket, 3½".......................$65.00
Petals, coffeepot, 8-cup, 8"......................................$75.00
Petals, cup, 2½"...$15.00
Petals, mug, juice; 6-oz, 2½".....................................$15.00
Petals, plate, dinner; 9¾"...$20.00
Petals, teapot, 2-cup, 4"...$45.00
Pineapple, pickle dish, unusual sponge edge, 6".......$35.00
Provincial Fruit, bowl, fruit; 12"..............................$40.00
Provincial Fruit, tumbler, 12-oz, 5"..........................$20.00
Ribbon Flower, bowl, fruit; 12".................................$50.00
Saraband, candle holder, 2x6"..................................$20.00
Saraband, canister, tea, sugar, w/lid, sq, 5½", ea......$25.00
Saraband, cookie jar, w/lid, oval, 9½".......................$30.00
Saraband, plate, chop; 12".......................................$15.00
Saraband, salt & pepper shakers, stacking, 2¼", pr....$10.00
Seaform, bowl, dessert; 4".......................................$20.00
Seaform, plate, dinner; 10".......................................$25.00
Seaform, saucer, 5½"..$8.00
Sunflower, jug, oasis; 9½x9½", minimum value.......$500.00
Sunflower, tumbler, 12-oz, 5"...................................$30.00
Sunny, wall pocket, 3½"..$40.00
Tea Rose, plate, breakfast; 8½".................................$25.00
Tea Rose, platter, meat; 11".......................................$45.00
Tea Rose, platter, meat; 12".......................................$50.00
Tea Rose, saucer, 5½"..$8.00
Turquoise, baker, 7" dia $30.00
Turquoise, bowl, vegetable; divided, 10½"................$35.00
Turquoise, plate, soup & salad; Rubel mold, w/cup ..$55.00
Windflower, jug, honey; 6¼".....................................$40.00

Purses

By definition a purse is a small bag or pouch for carrying money or personal articles, but collectors know that a lady's purse is so much more! Created in a myriad of wonderful materials reflecting different lifestyles and personalities, purses have become popular collectibles. Lucite examples and those decorated with rhinestones from the 1940s and 1950s are 'hot' items. So are the beautifully jeweled Enid Collins bags of the 1950s and 1960s. Tooled leather is a wonderful look as well as straw, silk, and suede. Look for fine craftsmanship and designer names. For further information, we recommend *Antique Purses* by Richard Holiner.

Beaded, earth-tones w/dark gray threads, beaded arm strap, concealed zipper, vinyl lining, 6¼x12", EX $75.00
Beaded clutch, chocolate hand-beaded body w/gold-tone frame, fold-over clutch, satin lining, 1940s, 4¼x8¼", EX...$55.00
Beth Collection, black leather in soft weave, shoulder strap, fabric lining, zippered pocket, 14x12", EX $75.00
Bienen-Davis, rhinestones on white silk, strap handle, 1950s, 6½x4½", EX $195.00
Bottega Veneta, rust-brown leather w/tassel snap clasp, shoudler strap, leather lined, metal name plate, EX...............$350.00
Coach, black leather w/shoulder strap, zippered pocket, brass turn closure, 1970s, 5½x9", EX $55.00
Cord fabric (black) w/Lucite clasp, matching arm strap, pocket w/mirror, 1950s, 5x9½", EX.............................$45.00
Cotton houndstooth fabric w/bamboo handle & frame, vinyl lining, Made in Italy, 1960s, 9½x16x4", EX $250.00
Dooney & Bourke, black & cordovan leather, 2 pockets (1 w/zipper), brass button & loop closure, shoulder strap, 6x8", EX..$75.00
Enid Collins, Aquarius waterbearer amid flowers, leather handles, wooden bottom, 10½x8½x4", NM $245.00
Enid Collins, jeweled flowers on white w/black trim, zippered & open pockets inside, 10x12x4", NM.....$115.00
Enid Collins, pineapple, watermelon & lemons, mirror inside lid, 5½x11¼", EX..$215.00
Fabric, red plaid w/red faux grain leather flap, 2 pockets, snap closure, 1950s, EX...$30.00
Garay, black & white plaid flannel, zippered pocket, black leather trim, 1950s, 15x11", M............................$165.00
Garay, floral print, handle will hide to transform into a clutch, 1950s, 6½x13", M $125.00
Gucci, brown suede clutch, leather trim, gold-plated frame, 6x7¾x2¾", EX...$200.00
Jacques Loumels, snakeskin, ecru leather accordion sides, strap handle, buckle front, snap closure, 1960s, 6x8x4", EX $165.00
JR Florida, red burlap, gold-plated frame w/snap closure, red vinyl liner, built-in change purse, 1970s, 10x7", EX.$45.00

Judith Leiber, gray snakeskin w/jeweled gold-tone frame, w/storage bag & coin purse, leather strap, 7x11", EX **$225.00**

Judith Leiber, Sleeping Cat, gold cat figural w/rhinestone bow, 1980, 3x5", M..**$350.00**

Leather, white & camel w/velour lining, zippered pocket, 2 reversed RSs on flap, shoulder strap, 9x11", EX ..**$75.00**

Leather w/painted brocade-look floral decor, wooden rings attach to strap, outside & inside pockets, 1970s, 13x12", EX **$125.00**

Lennox, black faux alligator w/gold-tone frame, 2 inside pockets, cloth lining, shoulder strap, 8x9¾", EX .**$95.00**

Lewis, floral print w/gold silk lining, gold-tone frame w/snap closure, strap handle, 1950s, 6½x11½", M **$145.00**

Louis Vuitton, Coach, bright orange w/original cardboard shaper, 1970s, 8x5½" w/chain handle, M...........**$170.00**

Lucite, black basket form, shines like patent leather, brass clasp, Lucite handle, 1950s, 3½x8½", EX **$110.00**

Lucite, clear carved diamond pattern, rectangular w/4 clear round feet, 3-ball clasp, 4x10x4" w/9" handles..**$235.00**

Lucite, laminated travel stickers & swirling gold threads on white basket form, 1950s, 4x9x6", NM................**$395.00**

Lucite, tortoise shell, Ranhill Corp, 5½x4½", $75.00.

Margaret Smith, navy floral material, strap handle, pink lining, 1960s, 7½x11x4", M **$75.00**

Margaret Smith Gardner Maine, mod flower print, metal closure, snap handle, 1960s, 9x11x4", EX **$115.00**

Morris Moskowitz, plaid pony hair w/leather trim & lining, adjustable strap, 1950s, 7x10x4", EX **$295.00**

Nettie Rosenstein, red Persian lamb w/ornate gold handle & clasp (resembles jewelry), 1950s, 4x8½x3"..........**$395.00**

Nicholas Reich, snakeskin leather w/embossed color, brass handle, leather lining, 1960s, 7x8½x3", EX **$265.00**

Pheasant feathers on brown wool felt, silver-tone frame, fabric lined, 1940s, 8x9½", M.....................................**$195.00**

Plastic, brown 1" sqs form body, brown cloth lining w/2 pockets, zipper closure w/tassel, 1950s, 8x14", EX..........**$95.00**

Rabbit fur w/leopard print, black leather-like frame & handle, cloth lined, zippered pocket, 1940s, 8x10", EX.....**$195.00**

Rex, metal & plastic gold- and silver-tone basketweave basket shape, pearl gray w/clear handle, 1950s, 8"..............**$150.00**

Saks Fifth Avenue, black leather w/pocketwatch on chain that fits in sm front pocket, 1940s, 7x8½x5", EX.........**$250.00**

Silk clutch, multicolor & gold threads, peach silk lining, inside pocket, snap closure, 1940s, 5x7", EX **$65.00**

Stylecraft Miami, plastic hot-pink beads, fold-over flap closure, fabric liner, Made in Italy 1950s, 6½x7", EX **$50.00**

Suede, blue w/faux crocodile leather trim, black faille lining, snap closure, faux leather handle, 1960s, 6½x13", EX........**$145.00**

Tooled leather, brown w/hand-painted flowers & tan leather stitching, rustic clasp, strap handle, 1970s, 11x10x4", EX **$145.00**

Vittadini, faux alligator taupe-colored leather, chain ornament, inside pockets, double straps, snap closure, 14x11", M...**$150.00**

Wicker, elephant figural, natural finish, howdah forms lid, Hong Kong, ca 1960s?, 13½x15", M...................**$200.00**

Puzzles

The first children's puzzle was actually developed as a learning aid by an English map maker, trying to encourage the study of geography. Most nineteenth-century puzzles were made of wood, rather boring, and very expensive. But by the Victorian era, nursery rhymes and other light-hearted themes became popular. The industrial revolution and the inception of color lithography combined to produce a stunning variety of themes ranging from technical advancements, historical scenarios, and fairy tales. Power saws made production more cost effective, and wood was replaced with less expensive cardboard.

As early as the '20s and '30s, American manufacturers began to favor character-related puzzles, the market already influenced by radio and the movies. Some of these were advertising premiums. Die-cutters had replaced jigsaws, cardboard became thinner, and now everyone could afford puzzles. During the Depression they were a cheap form of entertainment, and no family get-together was complete without a puzzle spread out on the card table for all to enjoy.

Television and movies caused a lull in puzzle making during the '50s, but advancements in printing and improvements in quality brought them back strongly in the '60s. Unusual shapes, the use of fine art prints, and more challenging designs caused sales to increase.

If you're going to collect puzzles, you'll need to remember that unless all the pieces are there, they're not of much value, especially those from the twentieth century. The condition of the box is important as well. Right now there's a lot of interest in puzzles from the '50s through the '70s that feature popular TV shows and characters from that era. Remember, though a frame-tray puzzle still sealed in its original wrapping may be worth $10.00 or more, depending on the subject matter and its age, a well used example may well be worthless as a collectible.

To learn more about the subject, we recommend *Schroeder's Toys, Antique to Modern* (Collector Books). *Toys of the Sixties, A Pictorial Guide*, by Bill Bruegman (Cap'n Penny Productions) is another good source of information.

Newsletter: *Piece by Piece*
P.O. Box 12823
Kansas City, KS 66112-9998; Subscription: $8 per year

Alvin & the Chipmunks, jigsaw, APC, 1984, 125 pcs, MIB..**$10.00**
Banana Splits, frame-tray, Whitman, 1969, set of 4, MIB.....**$50.00**
Barney Google & Snuffy Smith, frame-tray, Jaymar, 1940s-50s, NM...**$40.00**
Batman, jigsaw, Whitman, 1966, 150 pcs, 14x18", NMIB..**$30.00**
Battlestar Galactica, jigsaw, Parker Bros, 1978, 140 pcs, MIB (sealed)..**$15.00**
Beatles, jigsaw, Meanies Invade Pepperland, 650 pcs, EXIB, from $100 to..**$150.00**
Bee Gees, jigsaw, APC, 1979, MIB.................................**$35.00**
Bionic Woman, frame-tray, APC, 1976, MIP, from $35 to..**$45.00**
Bullwinkle, jigsaw, Whitman, 1960, EXIB...................**$25.00**
Buzz Lightyear & Woody, jigsaw, 60 pcs, MIB.............**$8.00**
Cisco Kid, frame-tray, Saalfield, NM.............................**$40.00**
Cloud Strife, jigsaw, Final Fantasy 7, 7x10", MIB (sealed).**$35.00**
Daniel Boone Wilderness Scout, frame-tray, Jaymar, EX..**$20.00**
David Cassidy, jigsaw, APC, 1972, 500 pcs, MIB, from $35 to...**$45.00**
Davy Crockett, frame-tray, Jaymar, 1950s, EX.............**$75.00**
Dimwit, frame-tray, lg or sm, EX, ea.............................**$10.00**
Disney World, jigsaw, Whitman/Western, 1970s, depicts Donald, Huey, Dewey & Louie in 20,000 Leagues Under the Sea, MIB...**$45.00**
Donald Duck, jigsaw, Whitman, 1965, 100 pcs, 8½x11", MIB (sealed)..**$40.00**
Dr Seuss' Cat in the Hat, frame-tray, 1980s, EX..........**$20.00**
Dr Strange, jigsaw, Third Eye, 1971, 500 pcs, MIB...**$100.00**
Dukes of Hazzard, jigsaw, 1981, 200 pcs, EXIB..........**$10.00**
Elvis, jigsaw, 1977, MIB...**$35.00**
Family Affair, frame-tray, Whitman, 1971, MIP...........**$35.00**
Flintstones, frame-tray, Whitman, 1964, NM................**$45.00**
Fox & the Hound, frame-tray, Jaymar, EX.....................**$6.00**
Frankenstein, jigsaw, American Publishing, 1974, EX (EX canister)..**$15.00**
Gay Purr-ee, frame-tray, Whitman, 1962, NM.............**$15.00**
Goldfinger, jigsaw, Milton Bradley, 1965, VG (VG box)..**$35.00**
Grizzly Adams, jigsaw, House of Games, 1978, 100 pcs, MIB...**$15.00**
Gunsmoke, frame-tray, Whitman, 1958, EX.................**$30.00**
Gunsmoke, jigsaw, Whitman, 1969, 100 pcs, NM (EX box)..**$45.00**
Hot Wheels, frame-tray, 1986, EX................................**$5.00**
Howdy Doody, frame-tray, Whitman, 1954, Howdy's One-Man Band, EX...**$50.00**
Impossibles, frame-tray, Whitman, 1967, EX...............**$25.00**
Incredible Hulk, jigsaw, Whitman, 1979, 100 pcs, MIB.**$25.00**
Jetsons, frame-tray, Whitman, 1960s, NM, from $35 to.**$45.00**
Jinks, frame-tray, Whitman, 1960s, NM, from $20 to..**$30.00**
Josie & the Pussycats, jigsaw, Hope, 1972, NM (NM canister)...**$35.00**
Kermit the Frog, frame-tray, Fisher-Price, 1981-82, M...**$5.00**
Lady & the Tramp, frame-tray, Whitman, 1964, EX....**$10.00**
Lassie, frame-tray, Milton Bradley, 1959, w/puppies, 14x10", EX..**$25.00**

Lassie, frame-tray, Whitman, 1966, NM......................**$20.00**
Lassie, frame-tray, Wrather, 1966, w/Forest Ranger, 8x10", EX..**$15.00**
Lassie & Timmy, frame-tray, Whitman, EX..................**$25.00**
Lone Ranger, jigsaw, Milton Bradley, 1980, 250 pcs, MIB..**$65.00**
Mary Poppins, frame-tray, Whitman #4436, 1964, 11½x14½", VG..**$18.00**
Michael Jackson, jigsaw, Colorforms, 1984, 500 pcs, MIB..**$10.00**
Mighty Heroes, frame-tray, Whitman, 1967, M...........**$50.00**
Mighty Mouse, jigsaw, Whitman, 1967, 100 pcs, NMIB..**$15.00**
Mighty Mouse Playhouse, jigsaw, Fairchild, 1956, MIB..**$20.00**
Miss Piggy, frame-tray, Fisher-Price, 1981-82, M........**$15.00**
Muppets, frame-tray, Fisher-Price, 1981-82, M............**$15.00**
Nancy & Sluggo, jigsaw, Whitman, 1973, NMIB.........**$15.00**
New Kids on the Block, jigsaw, Milton Bradley, 1990, 100 pcs, MIB, from $10 to...............................**$15.00**

Patty Duke Jr. Jigsaw Puzzle, Whitman, 1963, 100 pieces, MIB, from $35.00 to $45.00. (Photo courtesy Greg Davis and Bill Morgan)

Peanuts, jigsaw, Charles Schultz, 1960s, EXIB.............**$75.00**
Pinocchio, frame-tray, 1980s, EX..................................**$6.00**
Pinocchio, jigsaw, Jaymar, 300 pcs, 14x22", VG (G box)..**$38.00**
Planet of the Apes, jigsaw, HG Toys, 1967, EX (EX canister)...**$40.00**
Popeye's Comic Picture Puzzle, jigsaw, Parker Bros, set of 4, EXIB...**$100.00**
Quick Draw McGraw, frame-tray, Whitman, 1960, EX.**$25.00**
Raggedy Ann & Andy, jigsaw, Milton Bradley, 1989, 60 pcs, MIB...**$15.00**
Road Runner, frame-tray, 1966, NM............................**$20.00**
Rod Stewart, jigsaw, 1973, MIB...................................**$40.00**
Roger Ramjet, frame-tray, Whitman, 1966, M.............**$75.00**
Rookies, jigsaw, American Publishing, 1975, EX (EX container)...**$40.00**
Shazam, jigsaw, Whitman Big Little Book series, 1960, NMIB.**$50.00**
Silver Surfer, jigsaw, Third Eye, 1971, 500 pcs, MIB.**$100.00**
Six Million Dollar Man, jigsaw, APC #1536, from $8 to..**$12.00**
Sleeping Beauty, jigsaw, Jaymar, 1960s, NMIB...........**$20.00**
Snoopy, jigsaw, Milton Bradley, 1989, Snoopy & Gang playing baseball, 1,000 pcs, 27x20", EXIB.................**$10.00**
Space Ghost, frame-tray, Whitman, 1967, NM.............**$50.00**

Space: 1999, jigsaw, Hope (England), 80 pcs, 9x12", EX (G box) **$32.00**

Spider-Man, frame-tray, Playskil, 1981, EX **$18.00**

Spider-Man & Thor, jigsaw, 4-G Toys, 1974, 75 pcs, MIB ..**$50.00**

Star Trek, frame-tray, Whitman, 1978, M **$15.00**

Steve Canyon in China, jigsaw, Jaymar, 1950s, EX (EX box)..**$20.00**

Storybook Kiddles, frame-tray, Whitman, 1968, set of 4, MIB, from $50 to...**$65.00**

Superman Springs Into Action, jigsaw, Saalfield, 1940, 500 pcs, EXIB...**$300.00**

Tarzan, jigsaw, Whitman, 1968, EXIB **$25.00**

Three Stooges, jigsaw, Colorforms, Hold Your Fire, EXIB.**$475.00**

Thunderbirds, jigsaw, Whitman, 1968, EXIB **$25.00**

Top Cat, frame-tray, Whitman, 1960s, MIP, from $20 to ..**$25.00**

Uncle Scrooge, jigsaw, Western, 100 lg pcs, 14x18", MIB (sealed)...**$40.00**

Voyage to the Bottom of the Sea, jigsaw, Milton Bradley, 1966, NMIB..**$85.00**

Welcome Back Kotter, frame-tray, Whitman, 1977, MIP .**$12.50**

Wild Bill Hickok, jigsaw, Built Rite, 1956, 100 pcs, EXIB...**$25.00**

Woody Woodpecker, jigsaw, Whitman Big Little Book series, 1960s, NMIB **$50.00**

Yogi Bear, frame-tray, Whitman, 1960s, NM...............**$35.00**

ZZ Top, jigsaw, 1980s, NM (NM canister) **$35.00**

Pyrex

Though the history of this heat-proof glassware goes back to the early years of the twentieth century, the Pyrex that we tend to remember best is more than likely those mixing bowl sets, casseroles, pie plates, and baking dishes that were so popular in kitchens all across America from the late 1940s right on through the 1960s. Patterned Pyrex became commonplace by the late '50s; if you were a new bride, you could be assured that your bridal shower would produce at least one of the 'Cinderella' bowl sets or an 'Oven, Refrigerator, Freezer' set in whatever pattern happened to be the most popular that year. Among the most recognizable patterns you'll see today are Gooseberry, Snowflake, Daisy, and Butter-Print (roosters, the farmer and his wife, and wheat sheaves). There was also a line with various solid colors on the exteriors. You'll seldom if ever find a piece that doesn't carry the familiar logo somewhere. To learn more about Pyrex, we recommend *Kitchen Glassware of the Depression Years* by Gene Florence (Collector Books).

Bowl, blue, sq base, 12", from $35 to.........................**$38.00**

Bowl, cereal; blue, 5¾" **$3.50**

Bowl, mixing; American Heritage, 6½", from $8 to....**$10.00**

Bowl, mixing; American Heritage, 8½", from $12.50 to..**$15.00**

Bowl, mixing; blue, 8½", from $10 to.........................**$12.50**

Bowl, mixing; blue fired-on color, 6½", from $8 to....**$10.00**

Bowl, mixing; Butter-Print Cinderella, 6¾", from $8 to ..**$10.00**

Bowl, mixing; Cinderella, 8¼", from $8 to..................**$10.00**

Bowl, mixing; Gooseberry, 8¼", from $8 to...............**$10.00**

Bowl, mixing; green fired-on color, 8½", from $10 to..**$12.50**

Bowl, mixing; mixed fired-on colors, set of 4, from $30 to...**$38.00**

Bowl, mixing; red fired-on color, 7½", from $10 to ...**$12.50**

Bowl, mixing; yellow fired-on color, 9½", from $12.50 to..**$15.00**

Bowl, vegetable; blue, 9" **$8.00**

Casserole, Cinderella, fired-on color, clear lid, from $15 to...**$20.00**

Creamer, blue **$4.50**

Cup & saucer, demitasse; blue **$20.00**

Divided dish, blue, from $30 to..................................**$35.00**

Measuring cup, crystal, 1-cup, from $8 to..................**$10.00**

Measuring cup, crystal, 2-spout, from $22 to **$25.00**

Measuring cup, red, 16-oz, from $100 to...................**$125.00**

Pie plate, blue, 10", from $30 to.................................**$35.00**

Plate, dinner; blue, 9¾"..**$4.50**

Plate, sandwich; blue, 11½"..**$5.50**

Refrigerator container, blue & white, 4¼x6¾", from $10 to...**$12.00**

Refrigerator container, red fired-on color, 3½x4¾", from $5 to...**$6.00**

Refrigerator dish, blue fired-on color, 4¼x6¾", from $8 to...**$10.00**

Refrigerator dish, Butter-Print Cinderella, 6¼x6¾", from $12.50 to...**$15.00**

Refrigerator dish, Gooseberry, 3½x4¾", from $6 to **$8.00**

Refrigerator dish, yellow fired-on color, 3½x4¾", from $7 to...**$8.00**

Refrigerator dish, yellow fired-on color, 7x9", from $12.50 to...**$15.00**

Railroadiana

It is estimated that almost two hundred different railway companies once operated in this country, so to try to collect just one item representative of each would be a challenge. Supply and demand is the rule governing all pricing, so naturally an item with a marking from a long-defunct, less prominent railroad generally carries the higher price tag.

Railroadiana is basically divided into two main categories, paper and hardware, with both having many subdivisions. Some collectors tend to specialize in only one area — locks, lanterns, ticket punches, dinnerware, or timetables, for example. Many times estate sales and garage sales are good sources for finding these items, since retired railroad employees often kept such memorabilia as keepsakes. Because many of these items are very unique, you need to get to know as much as possible about railroad artifacts in order to be able to recognize and evaluate a good piece. For more information we recommend *Railroad Collectibles, Revised 4th Edition,* by Stanley L. Baker (Collector Books).

Advisors: Lila Shrader; John White, Grandpa's Depot (See Directory Railroadiana)

Dinnerware

Ashtray, C&O, Chessie, 4 rests, no back stamp, 4"..... **$33.00**
Ashtray, KCS, Roxbury, 4 rests, no back stamp, 4"....... **$25.00**
Bowl, berry; B&O, Centenary, full back stamp, 5¼"..**$65.00**
Bowl, berry; GN, Glory of the West, bottom stamp, 5¼"..**$76.00**
Bowl, chili; Fred Harvey, Southwest, side logo, no back stamp, 5"........ **$83.00**
Bowl, master salad; SP, Prairie-Mountains-Wildflower, no back stamp, 3½x9½"........ **$248.00**
Bowl, oatmeal; NYNH&H, Platinum Blue, bottom stamp, 6¼"........ **$90.00**
Bowl, rim soup; IC, Louisane, top logo, no back stamp, 9¼"........ **$143.00**
Butter pat, ATSF, California Poppy, back stamp, 3½", from $135 to........ **$185.00**
Butter pat, ATSF, Mimbreno, no back stamp, 3⅛"...... **$48.00**
Butter pat, CB&Q, Violets & Daisies, bottom stamped, 3½"........ **$70.00**
Butter pat, Fred Harvey, Webster, no back stamp, 3"...**$20.00**
Butter pat, NYC, Hudson (Haviland), bottom stamp, 3" sq..**$200.00**
Butter pat, UP, Blue & Gold, no back stamp, 3½", from $8 to........ **$15.00**
Chamber pot, CP, Caledonia Springs Hotel, side logo, no back stamp, 8¼" dia........ **$225.00**
Chocolate pot, ATSF, California Poppy, no back stamp, 5½"........ **$135.00**
Chocolate pot, B&O, Centenary, Shenango, full back stamp, 5¼"........ **$98.00**
Compote, B&O, Capitol, pedestal foot, top logo, rich gold, 2¾x5¾"........ **$170.00**
Compote, Uintah, Mesa, pedestal foot, top mark, no back stamp, 4x7"........ **$1,275.00**
Creamer, Inter-State News Service, handle, Inter-State, side logo, individual, 3"........ **$105.00**
Creamer, L&N, Regent, no back stamp, 3¼"........ **$78.00**
Creamer, Pullman, Indian Tree, handle, side logo, no back stamp, 2¾"........ **$90.00**
Creamer, SP, Sunset, side logo, no back stamp, 4"...**$178.00**
Cup, bouillon; CN, Truro, handles, Shenango, side logo, no back stamp........ **$56.00**
Cup, bouillon; MK&T, Katy Ornaments, handles, no back stamp........ **$20.00**
Cup & saucer, C&O, Chessie, side logo, no back stamp..**$115.00**
Cup & saucer, demitasse; Erie, Starucca, cup: side logo, saucer: top logo........ **$192.00**
Cup & saucer, demitasse; PRR, Broadway Limited, cup: no back stamp, saucer: full back stamp........ **$125.00**
Cup & saucer, MP, Eagle, cup: side mark, no back stamp, saucer: top mark, bottom stamp........ **$115.00**
Cup & saucer, UP, Harriman Blue, tall cup, both w/full back stamps........ **$157.00**
Egg cup, MP, Eagle, pedestal foot, side logo, 2⅜"...**$228.00**
Egg cup, UP, Blue & Gold, pedestal foot, no back stamp, 2½"........ **$67.00**
Gravy boat, ATSF Mimbreno, bottom stamp, 8"........ **$300.00**
Gravy boat, UP, Historical, side mark, no back stamp, 6"..**$585.00**
Hot food cover, NYNH&H, Platinum Blue, side mark, bottom stamp, 6"........ **$155.00**
Hot water pot, NP, Verde Green, w/lid, side logo w/YPL logo........ **$255.00**
Mustard pot, ATSF, Mimbreno, bottom stamp, 2"..... **$450.00**
Plate, ATSF, Mimbreno, full back stamp, 9¾"........ **$180.00**
Plate, B&O, Centenary, Lamberton, full shield back stamp, 10½"........ **$55.00**
Plate, D&H, Adirondack, top mark, no back stamp, 5½"...**$250.00**
Plate, GN, Mountains & Flowers, full back stamp, 10"..... **$400.00**
Plate, IC, Pirate, no back stamp, 10"........ **$125.00**
Plate, PRR, Allegheny, EX gold, back stamped, 6"...**$400.00**
Plate, service; C&O, Homestead, top mark, no back stamp, 11½"........ **$22.00**
Plate, SP, Prairie-Mountain-Wildflowers, oval, divided, full back stamp, 12x8"........ **$200.00**
Plate, UP, Desert Flower, bottom stamp, 10½"........ **$40.00**
Platter, B&O, Centenary, Scammell, full back stamp, 14"..**$415.00**
Platter, D&RGW, Prospector, top mark, no back stamp, 11½x9¼"........ **$128.00**
Platter, UP, Historical, top mark, 5¾x8"........ **$225.00**
Relish dish, Buffalo, Rochester & Pittsburgh, top mark, no back stamp, 5½x11"........ **$415.00**
Relish dish, NYC, Dewitt Clinton, top logo, bottom stamp, 9¾x4¾"........ **$75.00**
Relish dish, Reading, Stotesbury, no back stamp, 10¼x4½"..**$245.00**
Sherbet, PRR, Purple Laurel, pedestal foot, full back stamp, 2¾"........ **$65.00**
Teapot, ATSF, California Poppy, no back stamp, 5".**$128.00**
Teapot, FEC, Mistic, no back stamp, 5¼"........ **$165.00**
Teapot, L&N, Regent, 5½"........ **$130.00**

Glassware

Ashtray, PRR, enamel Keystone logo, 6" sq........ **$17.00**
Bottle, milk; Fred Harvey embossed, ½-pt........ **$33.00**
Bottle, tobasco; MP w/original label & buzz saw logo, 1¾"........ **$14.00**
Champagne, CMStP&P, Olympian box logo, 4½"....... **$77.00**
Champagne, DL&W, w/Phoebie Snow in white enameled side logo, 4½"........ **$26.00**
Cordial, B&O, Capitol Dome logo & B&O, 3⅞"........ **$65.00**
Goblet, GN, frosted Rocky encircled logo, footed, 5½"..**$46.00**
Old fashioned, CB&Q w/Burlington Route logo & 1" frosted band, 3¼"........ **$18.00**
Paperweight, GN w/Rocky silhouette, red & blue on white, domed, 3" dia........ **$57.00**
Roly-poly, IC, enameled Panama Limited train w/diamond logo, 2¾"........ **$10.00**
Swizzle stick, B&O on blue glass, 5"........ **$13.00**
Tumbler, juice; ATSF, Santa Fe enamel & script, 3¾".**$13.00**
Tumbler, NYC, 50th Anniversary 20th Century Limited, 5¼"........ **$22.00**

Linens and Uniforms

Blanket, Pullman, wool, salmon color, 56x84"........ **$88.00**

Coat, GM&O conductor's, black wool, brass buttons, service star & bar..**$55.00**

Hat, NYO&W station agent's, badge, no buttons......**$150.00**

Headrest cover, Wabash, Follow the Flag logo, colorful, 15x21"...**$36.00**

Jacket, SRR waiter's, 1" cloth logos on collar, white...**$48.00**

Napkin, CB&Q, white-on-white rectangular logo, 16x22"..**$26.00**

Napkin, GN, white-on-white sheaf of wheat w/Greek key border, 18" sq...**$42.00**

Napkin, PRR, white-on-white script on corners, 21" sq **$32.00**

Shop cloth, Wabash, Work Safely, Wipe Out Accidents, 12x15"...**$24.00**

Tablecloth, CP, white-on-white belt logo w/wheat sheaves, 52x54"...**$32.00**

Tablecloth, Pullman, white on white, 36x44"..............**$30.00**

Towel, hand; New Haven, white w/blue center stripe, 12x15"...**$20.00**

Uniform, UP conductor's, coat, pants & vest, includes all buttons, 1950s...**$125.00**

Silver Plate

Chocolate pot, CM&O, hinged lid, bottom stamp, 5".**$88.00**

Coffeepot, UP, hinged lid, International, bottom stamp, individual, 5⅜"..**$56.00**

Corn holders, Michigan Central, Keystone logo top mark, 3", pr...**$75.00**

Fork, cocktail; CMStP&P, Broadway, International, bottom stamp **$22.00**

Fork, cocktail; N&W, Troy, Gorham, top mark, 7½"....**$170.00**

Fork, dinner; SAL, Cromwell, International, top mark, 7½"..**$28.00**

Knife, dinner; Pullman, Roosevelt, top mark, 8½"......**$47.00**

Knife, luncheon; Central RR of NJ, Cromwell, Meriden, 7⅜"..**$38.00**

Spoon, bar; CP, Windsor, Rogers, top logo, 8"............**$35.00**

Spoon, condiment; CP, Windsor, Elkington, top mark w/belt logo...**$34.00**

Spoon, condiment; NYC, Century, International, top mark, 4¼"..**$36.00**

Spoon, soup; GN, Hutton, round bowl, International, top logo, 6"..**$43.00**

Spoon, soup; MStP&SStM, Empire, Rogers, bottom mark w/SOO, 7⅛"...**$32.00**

Sugar bowl, D&RGW, handles, w/lid, Reed & Barton, bottom stamp, 9-oz...**$132.00**

Sugar bowl, MP, International, buzz saw side logo, bottom stamp, 12-oz..**$88.00**

Sugar tongs, CP, Kings, Elkington, side logo, 4⅜"....**$135.00**

Sugar tongs, SP, Grecian, International, interior mark, 4"..**$63.00**

Syrup, D&H, attached underplate, hinged lid, side logo, Reed & Barton, 5½"...**$125.00**

Tablespoon, CRI&P, Belmont, top mark: RI, bottom mark: Rock Island Lines...**$24.00**

Teapot, Michigan Central, hinged lid, bottom stamp, 16-oz, 5¼"...**$145.00**

Teaspoon, PRR, Kings, Adams, bottom mark, 6"........**$26.00**

Tray, T&P, Eagle, rectangular, International, top logo, bottom stamp, 7x10½"..**$115.00**

Miscellaneous

Mask, Great Northern Railroad, logo goat, heavy paper with junior menu on back, ca 1940s, 14x10", from $15.00 to $18.00. (Photo courtesy Buffalo Bay)

Badge, breast; Omaha, NE & Council Bluffs IA, trainman's ..**$42.00**

Badge, breast; Penn Central conductor's, 2¼x2½" **$45.00**

Badge, hat; CRI&P brakeman's, Rock Island in black enamel on silver...**$77.00**

Baggage check, Boston & Maine, brass w/leather strap, 1¼x2¾"...**$44.00**

Book, Alaska RR, Rules & General Instructions, 95-page, 1947 ....**$22.00**

Book, History of the Wabash, 320-page, 1984, 9x11".**$25.00**

Book, Moody's Transportation Manual, hardcover, 1,818-page, 1976 ....**$50.00**

Book, shop; D&H-issue, locomotive diagrams, 20 pages of diagrams, 1966, 13x20"...**$125.00**

Booklet, GN Dining Car Secrets, 1940s, 32-page **$11.00**

Brochure, ATSF, interior scenes of Super Chief accommodations, 1940s, 24-page...**$40.00**

Button, Pacific Electric Interurban, gold color, ⅞"......**$22.00**

Buttons, NYC, gold color, ½" & ⅞", set of 5..............**$11.00**

Buttons, Rutland RR, silver color, ½" & ⅞", set of 8 ..**$18.00**

Calendar, ATSF, Indian scenes, 13 sheets bound in metal strip, 1957, 14x24"..**$38.00**

Calendar, Bangor & Aroostook, GM passenger locomotive, plastic, 1952, pocket size **$22.00**

Calendar, GN, plastic, 1950, pocket size......................**$21.00**

Calendar, GN, Streamlined Empire Builder, plastic, 1948, pocket size **$100.00**

Calendar, NYC, 12 attached 10x12" sheets on 18x27" sheet w/NY view, 1949...**$48.00**

Chisel, NYC, side marked: NYCRR, 11½" **$23.00**

Cigarette case, PRR, silver-colored metal w/enamel Keystone logo, 4½x2½"...**$44.00**

First-aid kit, C&NW, metal w/unopened supplies, wall mount, top mark, 9x6x3" **$32.00**

Insulator, Canadian Pacific, stamped CPR, white porcelain, 4"...**$10.00**

Insulator, Hudson Bay Railway, marked HBR, aqua, 3⅞"..**$16.00**

Kerosene can, GN, bail, caps, nickel-plated, side mark, 12" **$48.00**

Menu, ATSF, Aboard the Chief, Blanket Weaver cover, 1951, opens to 9½x14" **$16.00**

Menu, California Zephyr, luncheon, single card, 1969, 8½x11" **$20.00**

Menu, CRI&P, celebrating 1852 to 1952, The Rocket, 5x10" .. **$82.00**

Menu, UP, child's breakfast, winking bear cover, 1940s, 5x7" unfolded **$14.00**

Napkin, PRR, Pennsy freight diesel over Keystone logo, paper, opens to 10" sq **$28.00**

Oil can, NYC, seamed galvanized metal, long spout, side mark, 7" **$56.00**

Pen, ballpoint; Monon, The Monon Line, black & yellow .. **$12.50**

Pencil, mechanical; Minneapolis & St Louis, black & red train logo, 5½" **$55.00**

Pencil, mechanical; Southern Railroad, pearlized, 5¼" .. **$30.00**

Pin, service; 25 years, blue enamel & gold-fill w/ruby, silver plate, ½" **$25.00**

Pin, service; 25 years, Long Bell Lumber Co RR, ½" .. **$18.00**

Playing cards, C&NW, girl waving & logo, 1952, 52+2, w/case **$68.00**

Playing cards, N&W w/logo on cards & case, double deck, unopened **$30.00**

Playing cards, PRR w/Keystone logo, pinochle deck, slip-case **$10.00**

Playing cards, Wabash Bluebird at bend Forest Park, St Louis, 1951, w/case **$40.00**

Property marker, L&N, brass, 8x4½", 5/16" thick **$40.00**

Ruler, C&NW, streamliners on reverse side, metal guide, 15" **$10.00**

Stationery, ATSF, ream (500 sheets) of onionskin, letterhead, 8½x11" **$25.00**

Stool, MP, rubber pads on feet, side mark, 10x13x15½" .. **$340.00**

Tie carrier, PRR, Keystone logo top mark, Hubbard manu-facturing, 14" from handle to handle **$40.00**

Timetable, employee; Marquette Railway, Detroit-Grand Rapids Division, September 1946 .... **$40.00**

Timetable, public, Wabash system, October 1956 .... **$17.50**

Token, UP, 1940 NY World's Fair, aluminum, 15/16" dia **$3.00**

Razor Blade Banks

Razor blade banks are receptacles designed to safely store used razor blades. While the double-edged disposable razor blades date back to as early as 1904, ceramic and fig-ural razor blade safes most likely were not produced until the early 1940s. The development of the electric razor and the later disposable razors did away with the need for these items, and their production ended in the 1960s.

Shapes include barber chairs, barbers, animals, and bar-ber poles, which were very popular. Listerine produced a white donkey and elephant in 1936 with political overtones. They also made a white ceramic frog. These were used as promotional items for shaving cream. Suggested values are based on availability and apply to items in near-mint to excellent condition. Note that regional pricing could vary.

Advisor: Debbie Gillham (See Directory, Razor Blade Banks)

Barber, wood w/Gay Blade bottom, unscrews, Woodcraft, 1950, 6", from $65 to **$75.00**

Barber, wood w/key & metal holders for razor & brush, 9", from $60 to **$80.00**

Barber bust w/handlebar mustache, coat & tie, from $50 to **$70.00**

Barber chair, sm, from $100 to **$125.00**

Barber head, different colors on collar, Cleminson, from $25 to **$35.00**

Barber holding pole, Occupied Japan, marked Blades on back, 4", from $65 to **$75.00**

Barber holding pole, Occupied Japan, 4", from $50 to . **$60.00**

Barber pole, red & white, w/ or w/out attachments & vari-ous titles, from $20 to **$25.00**

Barber pole w/barber head & derby hat, white, from $40 to **$60.00**

Barber pole w/face, red & white, from $30 to **$40.00**

Barber standing in blue coat & stroking chin, from $65 to **$85.00**

Barber w/buggy eyes, pudgy full body, Gleason look-alike, from $65 to **$75.00**

Barbershop quartet, 4 singing barber heads, from $95 to .. **$125.00**

Box w/policeman holding up hand, metal, marked Used Blades, from $75 to **$100.00**

Dandy Dans, plastic w/brush holders, from $25 to **$35.00**

Friar Tuck, Razor Blade Holder (on back), Goebel .. **$300.00**

Frog, green, marked For Used Blades, from $60 to **$70.00**

Grinding stone, For Dull Ones, from $80 to **$100.00**

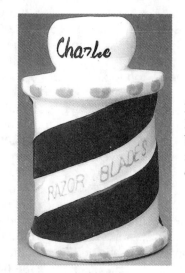

Half barber pole, hangs on wall, may be personalized with name, $60.00. (Photo courtesy Debbie Gillham)

Half shaving cup, hangs on wall, marked Gay Blades w/flo-ral design, from $75 to **$100.00**

Half shaving cup, hangs on wall, marked Gay Old Blade w/quartet, from $65 to **$75.00**

Indian head, porcelain, marked Japan, 4" **$25.00**

Listerine donkey, from $20 to **$30.00**

Listerine elephant, from $25 to **$35.00**

Listerine frog, from $15 to **$25.00**

Looie, right- or left-hand version, from $85 to..........**$110.00**

Man shaving, mushroom shape, Cleminson, from $25 to..**$35.00**

Man shaving, mushroom shape, Cleminson, personalized, from $45 to **$55.00**

Outhouse, white ceramic, Specialist in Used Blades on bottom, from $75 to **$90.00**

Razor Bum, from $85 to...**$100.00**

Safe, green, marked Blade Safe on front, from $40 to...**$60.00**

Shaving brush, ceramic, wide style w/decal, from $45 to..**$65.00**

Souvenir, wood-burned outhouse, For Gay Old Blades, by Crosby, found w/names of several states, from $35 to **$45.00**

Tony the Barber, Ceramic Arts Studio, from $85 to **$95.00**

Reamers

Reamers were a European invention of the late 1700s, devised as a tool for extracting liquid from citrus fruits, which was often used as a medicinal remedy. Eventually the concept of freshly squeezed juice worked its way across the oceans. Many early U.S. patents (mostly for wood reamers) were filed in the mid-1880s, and thanks to the 1916 Sunkist 'Drink An Orange' advertising campaign, the reamer soon became a permanent fixture in the well-equipped American kitchen. Most of the major U.S. glass companies and pottery manufacturers included juicers as part of their kitchenware lines. However, some of the most beautiful and unique reamers are ceramic figures and hand-painted, elegant china and porcelain examples. The invention of frozen and bottled citrus juice relegated many a reamer to the kitchen shelf. However, the current trend for a healthier diet has garnered renewed interest for the manual juice squeezer.

Most of the German and English reamers listed here can be attributed to the 1920s and 1930s. Most of the Japanese imports are from the 1940s.

Advisor: Bobbie Zucker Bryson (See Directory, Reamers)

Newsletter: *National Reamer Collectors Association*
Debbie Gillham
301-977-5727 e-mail: reamers@erols.com or
www.reamers.org

Ceramics

Camel, kneeling, beige lustre w/light green top, 4¼", from $200 to...**$250.00**

Child's, orange lustre w/red, blue & yellow flowers, 5-sided, 2-pc, Japan, from $150 to **$200.00**

Citrus face on teapot shape, pink sponged look w/multicolor details, Napco Japan, 5¼" **$210.00**

Clown, white w/red heart buttons, black & white hat & orange hair, Japan, Sigma, 6½", from $75 to.....**$100.00**

Clown head in saucer, green & white, Germany, Goebel, 5" dia, from $200 to **$250.00**

Clown head in saucer, Sourpuss, 4¾", from $115 to ..**$125.00**

Clown's face, wide smiling red mouth & nose, blue eyes, multicolor on white, Japan, 2-pc, 4¼", from $60 to......**$75.00**

Duck figural, multicolor lustreware, reamer sits on back, Made in Japan, 1940s, 3½", from $45 to..............**$65.00**

Duck figural, orange & green on white pearlized body ..**$110.00**

Floral, red & black, Japan, 2-pc, 5½"........................**$70.00**

Lemon, yellow w/green leaves, white top, Germany, 2-pc, 3¼"...**$70.00**

Pear, yellow lustreware w/gold trim, leaves, Made in Japan, 3-pc, 4½", from $45 to **$55.00**

Plaid design, green & white, Japan, 2-pc, 2¼"............**$80.00**

Puddinhead, 2-pc, 6¼" **$250.00**

Swan figural, cream w/rose flowers & green base, Japan, 2-pc, 4¼", from $65 to...**$85.00**

Teapot, white w/yellow & maroon flowers, Nippon, 2-pc, 3¼"..**$90.00**

Teapot, yellow, tan & white, England/Shelley, 2-pc, 3½" ..**$125.00**

White w/rust leaves & dark blue trim, boat-shaped, 3½", from $55 to...**$75.00**

Yellow & white spatter design, 2-pc, Stangl, 6¼", from $50 to...**$65.00**

Glassware

Amber, handle & spout opposite, Indiana Glass, from $300 to...**$325.00**

Amber, panelled, loop handle, from $25 to **$28.00**

Apple Green, Sunkist, from $50 to..............................**$55.00**

Canary (vaseline), straight sides, Fry, from $65 to......**$75.00**

Chalaine Blue (dark), Sunkist, from $125 to **$155.00**

Clambroth, boat shape, from $200 to **$225.00**

Cornflower Blue, from $100 to...................................**$125.00**

Crystal, Crisscross, tab handle, Hazel-Atlas, from $18 to..**$22.00**

Crystal, elephant decorated base, Fenton, 2-pc, from $110 to...**$125.00**

Crystal, embossed ASCO, Good Morning Orange Juice, from $25 to **$30.00**

Crystal, embossed Sunkist Oranges & Lemons, from $30 to **$35.00**

Crystal, embossed Tcheco-Slovaquie on handle, from $30 to **$35.00**

Crystal, embossed thumbprint design, 2-pc, from $45 to..**$50.00**

Crystal, footed, Cambridge, sm, from $22 to..............**$25.00**

Crystal, Glasbake, McKee on handle, from $65 to......**$75.00**

Crystal, Jenkins, 2-pc, from $50 to **$55.00**

Crystal, loop handle, lg, from $20 to **$25.00**

Crystal, sq, marked Italy, from $20 to........................**$25.00**

Crystal, tab handle, Hazel-Atlas, lg, from $15 to........**$18.00**

Dark green opaque, McKee Glass, marked Sunkist Pat 68764 Made in USA, from $40 to **$55.00**

Emerald green, straight sides, Fry, from $35 to..........**$38.00**

Gray, Sunkist, from $175 to **$185.00**

Green, embossed Valencia, from $225 to **$275.00**

Green, handle & spout opposite, from $40 to **$45.00**

Green, Hex Optic, bucket type, from $40 to..............**$45.00**

Green, log handle, from $100 to **$125.00**

Green, marked Argentina, from $125 to **$150.00**

Green, Orange Juice Extractor, from $55 to $65.00
Green, pointed cone, Federal, from $25 to $28.00
Green, ribbed, seed dam, tab handle, Federal, from $25 to $28.00
Green, tab handle, Hazel-Atlas, from $25 to $28.00
Green, 2-cup pitcher w/sunflower in bottom, 2-pc, from $130 to..$150.00
Green, 4-cup pitcher & reamer set, marked A&J, Hazel-Atlas, from $45 to...$50.00
Green, 4-cup pitcher & reamer set, US Glass, from $140 to...$150.00
Green, 6-sided cone, vertical handle, Indiana Glass, from $85 to...$95.00
Jadite, embossed McK, 6", from $50 to $55.00
Milk glass, embossed Fleur-de-Lis, from $75 to $85.00
Milk glass, embossed McK, from $25 to $30.00
Milk glass, embossed Thatcher Mfg Co, from $25 to..$30.00
Milk glass, embossed Valencia, from $120 to............$150.00
Pearl (white opalescent), straight sides, Fry, from $35 to...$40.00
Pink, Jennyware, from $125 to $135.00
Pink, ribbed, loop handle, Federal, from $40 to.........$45.00
Pink, tab handle, Hazel-Atlas, lg, from $40 to............$45.00
Pink, Westmoreland, 2-pc, from $200 to $225.00
Pink, 6-sided cone, vertical handle, from $175 to $195.00
Pink (light), Cambridge, from $200 to $225.00
Skokie Green, pointed cone, 5¼", from $65 to $75.00
Ultramarine, Jennyware, from $125 to $135.00
Yellow, 2-cup pitcher & reamer set, Hazel-Atlas, from $350 to...$375.00

Metal

Silver plate, bird form, marked Muss Bach, 4½" L, from $20 to..$30.00
Silver plate, 2-pc, marked Meriden SP Co International S Co, 5⅛", from $115 to...$135.00

Records

Records are still plentiful at flea markets and some antique malls, but albums (rock, jazz, and country) from the '50s and '60s are harder to find in collectible condition (very good or better). Garage sales are sometimes a great place to buy old records, since most of what you'll find there have been stored more carefully by their original owners.

There are two schools of thought concerning what makes a record collectible. While some collectors prefer the rarities — those made in limited quantities by an unknown who later became famous, or those aimed at a specific segment of music lovers — others like the vintage Top-10 recordings. Now that they're so often being replaced with CDs, we realize that even though we take them for granted, the possibility of their becoming a thing of the past may be reality tomorrow.

Whatever the slant your collection takes, learn to visually inspect records before you buy them. Condition is one of the most important factors to consider when assessing value. To be judged as mint, a record may have been played but must have no visual or audible deterioration — no loss of gloss to the finish, no stickers or writing on the label, no holes, no skips when it is played. If any of these are apparent, at best it is considered to be excellent, and its value is up to 90% lower than a mint example. Many of the records you'll find that seem to you to be in wonderful shape would be judged only very good, excellent at the most, by a knowledgeable dealer. Sleeves with no tape, stickers, tears, or obvious damage at best would be excellent; mint condition sleeves are impossible to find unless you've found old store stock.

LPs must be in their jackets, which must be in at least excellent condition. Be on the lookout for colored vinyl or picture discs, as some of these command higher prices; in fact, older Vogue picture discs commonly sell in the $25.00 to $75.00 range, some even higher. It's not too uncommon to find old radio station discards. These records will say either 'Not for Sale' or 'Audition Copy.' These 'DJ copies' may be worth more than their commercial counterparts, especially where records of 'hot' artists such as the Beatles, Elvis Presley, and the Beach Boys are involved.

If you'd like more information, we recommend *American Premium Record Guide* by L.R. Docks.

Advisor: L.R. Docks (See Directory, Records)

45 rpm

Condition codes reflect the state of the jacket as well as the the condition of the record itself; without the jacket many 45s are of no value.

Adventurers, Rock & Roll Uprising, Columbia 42227, EX ..$10.00
Allman Brothers, Black Hearted Woman, Capricorn 8803, NM .$5.00
Archies, Jingle Jangle, Kirshner 5002, M $5.00
Atkins, Chet; String Along, RCA 1236, EX...................$30.00
Avalon, Frankie; Where Are You/Tuxedo Junction, Chancellor C-1052, NM..$15.00
Bachelors, Delores, Earl 101, EX $30.00
Banana Splits, The Tra La La Song, NM....................$25.00
Beatles, I Want To Hold Your Hand, VG+..................$45.00
Beatles, Twist & Shout, Tollie 9001, yellow label w/green print, NM $75.00
Bee Gees, You Should Be Dancing (1-sided), RSO 853, NM $10.00
Belmonts, Walk On By, Sabina 517, EX.....................$15.00
Benton, Brook; The Ties That Bind, Mercury 71566, NM..$20.00
Billy & Lilly, La Dee Dah, Casino 105, EX...................$8.00
Buckinghams, Mercy Mercy Mercy, Columbia 44182, NM $10.00
Cadillacs, Speedo, Josie 785, EX..................................$8.00
Campbell, Glen; Turn Around Look at Me, Crest 1087, EX $10.00
Capitols, Day By Day, Getaway 721, EX $20.00
Cascades, A Little Like Lovin', RCA Victor 47-8206, NM..$30.00
Cupids, The Answer to Your Prayer, Decca 30279, EX..$12.00
Del Vikings, True Love, Fee Bee 902, EX...................$20.00

Domino, Fats; Little School Girl, Imperial 5272, EX....**$15.00**
Donovan, Mellow Yellow, Epic 10098, NM.................**$15.00**
Duprees, You Belong to Me, Coed 569, EX **$8.00**
Everly Brothers, All I Have To Do Is Dream, Cadence 1348,
   M **$15.00**
Fiestas, Broken Heart, 1122, EX **$10.00**
Five Satins, Our Love Is Forever, Ember 1014, EX......**$10.00**
Fuller, Jerry; A Certain Smile, LIN 5015, EX...............**$12.00**
Fuller, Johnny; Johnny Ace's Last Letter, Aladdin 3278,
   EX...**$20.00**
Gallahads, Keeper of Dreams, Starla 15, EX...............**$12.00**
Gilley, Mickey; Susie-Q, Astro 104, EX **$20.00**
Goldsboro, Bobby; See the Funny Little Clown, United Artist
   672, 1963, NM **$10.00**
Haley, Bill; & the Comets, Rock Around the Clock, Decca
   29124, black label, EX **$10.00**
Hodges, Eddie; I'm Gonna Knock on Your Door, Cadence
   1397, 1961, NM **$25.00**
Hooker, John Lee; Blue Monday, De Luxe 6004, EX..**$30.00**
Jackson, Michael; Rockin' Robin, Motown 1197, M **$5.00**
Jan & Dean, There's a Girl, Dore 531, EX...................**$12.00**
Kenny G, Songbird, Artista 9588, M **$2.00**
Little Jr Jesse, Funky Stuff, Metro-Dome 1003, NM...**$150.00**
Mathis, Johnny; It's Not for Me To Say, Columbia 40851,
   M **$6.00**
Motley Crue, Smokin' in the Boys Room, Elektra 69625,
   M **$2.00**
Nelson, Ricky; Travelin' Man/Hello Mary Lou, Imperial 5741,
   1961, NM **$30.00**
Neville, Aaron; Show Me the Way, Minit 618, EX.......**$10.00**
Paper Lace, The Night Chicago Died, Mercury 73492, M ..**$5.00**
Parton, Dolly; Here You Come Again, RCA 11123, M ..**$5.00**
Penguins, Will You Be Mine, Mercury 71033, EX **$15.00**
Peter & Gordon, Nobody I Know, Capitol 5211, NM ...**$15.00**
Platters, My Prayer, Mercury 70893, maroon label, EX.**$10.00**
Presley, Elvis; Money Honey, RCA Victor 6641, EX....**$20.00**
Queen, We Are the Champions/We Will Rock You, Elektra
   45441, M **$10.00**
Rascals, People Got To Be Free, Atlantic 2537, M **$5.00**
Rolling Stones, Time Is on My Side, London 9708, M ..**$10.00**
Royal, Billy Joe; Down in the Boondocks, Columbia 43305,
   2965, red vinyl, NM **$40.00**
Spanky & Our Gang, Sunday Will Never Be the Same,
   Mercury 72679, M **$5.00**
Turner, Ike & Tina; I Wanna Jump, Minit 32077, NM.**$25.00**
Valli, Frankie; Can't Take My Eyes Off You, Philips 40446,
   M **$5.00**
Vinton, Bobbie; Roses Are Red, Epic 9509, M.............**$8.00**

78 rpm

Armstrong, Louis; Are You My Lucky Star, Decca 580,
   NM **$10.00**
Astaire, Fred; Cheek to Cheek, Brunswick 7486, EX..**$10.00**
Auburn, Frank; & His Orchestra, My Ideal, Harmony 1240, EX.**$12.00**
Badgers, It All Depends on You, Broadway 1058, EX.**$10.00**
Baker, Buddy; Box Car Blues, Victor 21549, EX **$15.00**

Berry, Chuck; Maybelline, Chess 1604, EX.................**$15.00**
Billy & Lilly, La Dee Dah, Swan 4002, EX.................**$20.00**
Billy James' Dance Orchestra, Sweet Child, Oriole 565,
   EX...**$20.00**
Boots & His Buddies, Ain't Misbehavin', Bluebird 7241,
   EX...**$10.00**
Campus Cut-Ups, Ballin' the Jack, Edison 52616, EX .**$100.00**
Carter Family, Keep on the Sunny Side, Bluebird 5006,
   NM **$10.00**
Cash, Johnny; Luther Played the Boogie, Sun 316, EX...**$60.00**
Four Tunes, I Understand Just How You Feel, Jubilee 5132,
   EX...**$25.00**
Garland, Judy; You Can't Have Everything, Decca 1463,
   EX...**$10.00**
Harmonians, What a Night for Spooning, Harmony 716-H,
   EX...**$10.00**
Holiday, Billie; & Her Orchestra, Solitude, Okeh 6270, EX..**$10.00**
Imperial Dance Orchestra, Can't We Be Friends, Banner
   0505, EX...**$10.00**
Jolson, Al; April Showers, Brunswick 6502, EX...........**$30.00**
Ku, Sam Jr; Farewell Blues, Gennett 6190, EX...........**$75.00**
Marlow, Earl; & His Orchestra, Wabash Moon, Parlophone
   PNY-34179, EX **$25.00**
Martin, Dean; One Foot in Heaven, Embassy 124, EX.**$35.00**
Mills Brothers, Diga Diga Doo, Brunswick 6519, EX..**$14.00**
New Orleans Jazz Band, Tin Roof Blues, Banner 1318,
   EX...**$15.00**
Porter's Blue Devils, Steamboat Sal, Gennett 5249, EX...**$15.00**
Prairie Ramblers, Jesus Hold My Hand, Vocalion 03115,
   EX...**$15.00**
Presley, Elvis; Blue Moon, RCA Victor 20-6640, EX....**$50.00**
Richman, Harry; No Hot Water, Banner 1510, EX.......**$20.00**
Rodgers, Jimmy; My Good Gal's Gone, Bluebird 5942,
   EX...**$40.00**
Rounders, Broadway Melody, Regal 8744, EX..............**$8.00**
Six Black Diamonds, Long Lost Mama, Banner 1217, EX ...**$8.00**
Tampa Blue Jazz Band, Get Hot, Okeh 4397, EX.......**$10.00**
Texas Rhythm Boys, Benzedrine Blues, Royalty 600, EX...**$50.00**
Vallee, Rudy; & His Connecticut Yankees, Honeymoon Hotel,
   Bluebird 5171, EX **$15.00**
Varsity Eight, Fallin' Down, Cameo 782, EX................**$10.00**
Wanderers, Tiger Rag, Bluebird 5887, EX.................**$15.00**

LP Albums

Archies Greatest Hits, Kirshner, EX **$15.00**
Beatles, Rock 'N Roll Music, Capitol SKBO-1137, set of 2,
   EX...**$35.00**
Benton, Brook; & the Sandmen, Endlessly, Mercury 20464,
   EX...**$30.00**
Cannon, Freddie; Palisades Park, Swan 507, EX.........**$50.00**
Christie, Lou; Lightnin' Strikes, MCA 4360, NM...........**$25.00**
Coasters, One by One, Atco 123, EX **$35.00**
Cochran, Eddie; Never To Be Forgotten, Liberty 3220,
   EX...**$60.00**
Darren, James; Sings the Movies, Colpix 418, EX.......**$20.00**
Del Vikings, They Sing They Swing, Mercury 20314, EX..**$75.00**

Diamonds, The Diamonds, Mercury 20309, EX..........**$75.00**

Domino, Fats; Rockin' & Rollin' With Fats Domino, Imperial 9004, EX..**$40.00**

Five Satins, Five Satins Encore, Ember 401, EX **$125.00**

Hooker, John Lee; Plays & Sings the Blues, Chess 1438, black label, EX **$75.00**

Horton, Johnny; Johnny Horton, Dot 3221, EX..........**$40.00**

Jefferson Airplane, Takes Off, RCA 3584, VG+ **$25.00**

Jones, George; Salutes Hank Williams, Mercury 20596, EX..**$30.00**

Led Zeppelin, Houses of the Holy, Atlantic, EX............**$7.00**

Monkees, Meet the Monkees, Colgems 101, EX.........**$20.00**

Oliver, Good Morning Starshine, Crewe Records, EX...**$8.00**

Partridge Family, A Partridge Christmas Card, NM (w/original cellophane)...**$35.00**

Patsy Cline, Patsy Cline, Coral 8611, EX.....................**$30.00**

Presley, Elvis; Frankie & Johnny, RCA Victor 3558, EX ..**$20.00**

Presley, Elvis; Loving You, RCA 1515, EX...................**$30.00**

Ricky Nelson, Ricky Nelson, Imperial 9050, EX.........**$40.00**

Righteous Brothers, Just Once in My Life, Phillies Records PHLP 4008, NM...**$25.00**

Rogers, Roy; Souvenir Album, RCA Victor 3041, EX...**$20.00**

Snow, Hank; Sings Your Favorite Country Hits, RCA 3317, EX...**$40.00**

Who, Happy Jack, Decca, VG+ **$6.00**

Young, Neil; Harvest, Reprise 2032, NM.....................**$20.00**

Red Wing

For almost a century, Red Wing, Minnesota, was the center of a great pottery industry. In the early 1900s several local companies merged to form the Red Wing Stoneware Company. Until they introduced their dinnerware lines in 1935, most of their production centered around stoneware jugs, crocks, flowerpots, and other utilitarian items. To reflect the changes made in 1935, the name was changed to Red Wing Potteries Inc. In addition to scores of lovely dinnerware lines, they also made vases, planters, flowerpots, etc., some with exceptional shapes and decoration.

Some of their more recognizable lines of dinnerware and those you'll most often find are Bob White (decorated in blue and brown brush strokes with quail), Tampico (featuring a collage of fruit including watermelon), Random Harvest (simple pink and brown leaves and flowers), and Village Green (or Brown, solid-color pieces introduced in the '50s). Often you'll find complete or nearly complete sets, and when you do, the lot price is usually a real bargain.

If you'd like to learn more about the subject, we recommend *Red Wing Stoneware, An Identification and Value Guide,* and *Red Wing Collectibles,* both by Dan and Gail DePasquale and Larry Peterson. B.L. Dollen has written *Red Wing Art Pottery, Books I* and *II.* All are published by Collector Books.

Advisors: Wendy and Leo Frese, Artware (See Directory, Red Wing); and B.L. and R.L. Dollen, Dinnerware (See Directory, Red Wing)

Club/Newsletter: *Red Wing Collectors Newsletter*
Red Wing Collectors Society, Inc.
Doug Podpeskar, membership information
624 Jones St., Eveleth, MN 55734-1631
218-744-4854; www.redwingcollectors.org. Please include SASE when requesting information.

Art Ware

Ashtray, gold/brown, sq w/sm sq cigarette rest in center, #M3005, 11"...**$35.00**

Ashtray, Pretty Red Wing (Indian maiden) embossed in well, from $200.00 to $250.00. (Photo courtesy B.L. and R.L. Dollen)

Ashtray, red, wing shaped, marked Red Wing Potteries USA **$60.00**

Bowl, brown w/orange interior, flat, #414, 7"............**$38.00**

Bowl, Compote, flecked Nile Blue w/Colonial Buff interior, gold wing label, #5022, 7".....................................**$55.00**

Bowl, flecked Zephyr Pink, curled edge, #M1463, 12"...**$45.00**

Bowl, maroon w/white crackle interior, contoured, #1272, 11"...**$45.00**

Bowl, shell; flecked Nile Blue, #M1567, 9"................**$50.00**

Butter dish, brown, boat shaped, Butter Boat embossed on side..**$12.00**

Candle holders, gray w/coral interior, petal shaped, #B1411, 4", pr..**$35.00**

Candle holder, Hyacinth, tapered, #678, 6" **$30.00**

Candle holders, salmon colored, scalloped edge, #1619, 4½", pr...**$35.00**

Compote, white, pedestal, brass handles, #M1598, 8" ..**$55.00**

Cornucopia, flecked Nile Blue w/Colonial Buff interior, #442, 15"...**$75.00**

Dish, marmalade; aqua, pear shaped, 4½"..................**$18.00**

Figurine, swans, white, side-by-side facing opposite, flecked green, #B2506, 9"..**$150.00**

Jardiniere, flecked pink, scalloped top, #M1610, 6"....**$22.00**

Jardiniere, flecked yellow, scalloped top, brass handles, #M1610, 10"...**$55.00**

Juicer, yellow, pedestal, #256 ....**$150.00**
Planter, gray w/coral interior, embossed leaf, #677, 8½"..**$32.00**
Planter, gray w/coral interior, sq, #1378, 5½".....**$40.00**
Planter, shoe; white w/light green interior, silver wing label, #651, 6" **$75.00**
Planter, yellow w/brown interior, basketweave design, #431, 10" **$28.00**
Teapot, yellow, chicken shaped, #257.....................**$125.00**
Vase, gloss blue w/coral interior, contoured, #1202, 5½".....**$40.00**
Vase, gloss fleck orchid (semi-matt), fluted top, #505, 7½"..**$55.00**
Vase, gloss gray w/coral interior, #B1397, 7"..............**$35.00**
Vase, gloss maroon w/gray interior, trophy style, #871, 7½" **$55.00**
Vase, pitcher; gloss fleck Nile Green w/Colonial Buff interior, fish handles, #220, 10" **$120.00**
Vase, semi-matt white w/green interior, leaf foot, #M1439, 6" **$50.00**
Vase, swirl; #1590, gloss yellow, 10" **$50.00**
Wall pocket, Cypress Green, funnel shaped, #M1630, 10"..**$90.00**

Dinnerware

Capistrano, bowl, cereal............................**$14.00**
Capistrano, butter dish, w/lid **$25.00**
Capistrano, cup & saucer, tea **$12.00**
Capistrano, dish, vegetable; divided............**$20.00**
Capistrano, nappy **$18.00**
Capistrano, plate, 10½" **$16.00**
Capistrano, soup tureen, w/lid **$35.00**
Capistrano, teapot, w/lid **$70.00**
Capistrano, trivet..**$28.00**
Desert Sun, bean pot, w/lid, 1½-qt **$40.00**
Desert Sun, beverage server, w/lid **$75.00**
Desert Sun, bowl, fruit **$10.00**
Desert Sun, bowl, salad; 10" **$40.00**
Desert Sun, bowl, vegetable; divided...............**$22.00**
Desert Sun, bread tray..**$50.00**
Desert Sun, cup & saucer; AD **$18.00**
Desert Sun, gravy boat, w/lid **$35.00**
Desert Sun, pitcher, water; 1½-qt..........................**$55.00**
Desert Sun, platter, 13"..**$24.00**
Desert Sun, salt & pepper shakers, pr **$20.00**
Lexington, beverage server, w/lid **$50.00**
Lexington, bowl, cereal **$8.00**
Lexington, coffee cup **$10.00**
Lexington, dish, vegetable; divided..........................**$18.00**
Lexington, nappy **$14.00**
Lexington, plate, 7½" **$10.00**
Lexington, relish dish **$16.00**
Lexington, salt & pepper skakers, pr **$12.00**
Lexington, supper tray..**$14.00**
Lexington, teapot, w/lid **$55.00**
Lotus, bowl, rim soup **$10.00**
Lotus, creamer..**$10.00**
Lotus, cup & saucer, tea..**$10.00**
Lotus, dish, sauce/fruit **$6.00**
Lotus, gravy boat, w/tray **$20.00**

Lotus, pitcher, water..**$35.00**
Lotus, plate, chop **$30.00**
Lotus, spoon rest..**$15.00**
Lute Song, bowl, salad; lg **$25.00**
Lute Song, bowl, vegetable **$22.00**
Lute Song, bread tray **$25.00**
Lute Song, casserole, w/lid **$40.00**
Lute Song, celery dish **$18.00**
Lute Song, creamer **$12.00**
Lute Song, platter, sm **$24.00**
Lute Song, relish dish, 6-pc **$65.00**
Lute Song, salt & pepper shakers, pr..........................**$16.00**
Lute Song, teapot, w/lid..**$65.00**
Magnolia, beverage server, w/lid..........................**$50.00**
Magnolia, bowl, cereal **$8.00**
Magnolia, casserole, w/lid..**$30.00**
Magnolia, celery dish..**$16.00**
Magnolia, coffee cup **$12.00**
Magnolia, dish, vegetable; divided..........................**$18.00**
Magnolia, salt & pepper shakers, pr **$12.00**
Magnolia, supper tray..**$14.00**
Plum Blossom, beverage server, w/lid..........................**$55.00**
Plum Blossom, bowl, cereal **$12.00**
Plum Blossom, creamer & sugar bowl w/lid...........**$45.00**
Plum Blossom, cup & saucer, tea..........................**$12.00**
Plum Blossom, dish, fruit **$12.00**
Plum Blossom, dish, vegetable; open **$18.00**
Plum Blossom, pitcher, water; 20-oz..........................**$45.00**
Plum Blossom, plate, 6½"..**$8.00**
Plum Blossom, teapot, w/lid, 4-cup..........................**$50.00**
Tampico, bowl, rim soup..**$18.00**
Tampico, dish, vegetable; divided..........................**$28.00**
Tampico, gravy boat, w/tray..**$40.00**
Tampico, mug, coffee..**$22.00**
Tampico, nappy..**$22.00**
Tampico, pitcher, water; 2-qt..**$80.00**
Tampico, plate, 8½"..**$14.00**
Tampico, salt & pepper shakers, pr **$25.00**
Tampico, teapot, w/lid..**$65.00**

Regal China

Perhaps best known for their Beam whiskey decanters, the Regal China company (of Antioch, Illinois) also produced some exceptionally well-modeled ceramic novelties, among them their 'hugger' salt and pepper shakers, designed by artist Ruth Van Tellingen Bendel. Facing pairs made to 'lock' together arm-in-arm, some huggies are signed Bendel while others bear the Van Tellingen mark. (Of all pieces about 15% are Bendel and 85% are Van Tellingen.) Another popular design is her Peek-a-Boo Bunny line, depicting the coy little bunny in the red and white 'jammies' who's just about to pop his buttons. (The cookie jar has been reproduced.)

See also Cookie Jars; Old MacDonald's Farm.

Bank, Monkey c C Miller, from $110 to....................**$120.00**

Creamer, rooster figural, marked Pat Pending 383 ...**$140.00**

Ice bucket, Jim Beam, birds in branches on white, cork insert **$100.00**

Jug, water; Ovaltine 1904-1979, special edition, 6x4½" dia **$15.00**

Salt & pepper shakers, A Nod to Abe, 3-pc nodder.**$300.00**

Salt & pepper shakers, Bendel, bears, white & pink w/brown trim, pr, from $125 to **$150.00**

Salt & pepper shakers, Bendel, bunnies, white w/black & pink trim, pr, from $125 to **$150.00**

Salt & pepper shakers, Bendel, kissing pigs, gray w/pink trim, lg, pr, from $350 to....................................**$375.00**

Salt & pepper shakers, Bendel, love bugs, burgundy, lg, pr, from $150 to..**$185.00**

Salt & pepper shakers, Bendel, love bugs, green, sm, pr ...**$65.00**

Salt & pepper shakers, cat, sitting w/eyes closed, white w/hat & gold bow, pr...................................**$225.00**

Salt & pepper shakers, clown, pr............................**$350.00**

Salt & pepper shakers, Dutch girl, pr **$275.00**

Salt & pepper shakers, Fifi, pr................................**$450.00**

Salt & pepper shakers, fish, marked C Miller, 1-pc.....**$55.00**

Salt & pepper shakers, French chef, white w/gold trim, pr, from $250 to..**$350.00**

Salt & pepper shakers, Goldilocks, 4⅜", pr **$230.00**

Salt & pepper shakers, Humpty Dumpty, pr.............**$140.00**

Salt & pepper shakers, Peek-a-Boo, red dots, lg (has been reproduced), pr, from $450 to **$500.00**

Salt & pepper shakers, pig, marked C Miller, 1-pc **$95.00**

Salt & pepper shakers, Snuggle-Hug Bears, Copr 1958 R Bendel, from $150 to..**$170.00**

Salt & pepper shakers, Snuggle-Hug Bunnies, Copr 1958 R Bendel, from $150 ....**$175.00**

Salt & pepper shakers, tulip, pr................................**$50.00**

Salt & pepper shakers, Van Tellingen, bears, brown, pr from $25 to..**$28.00**

Salt & pepper shakers, Van Tellingen, Black boy & dog, pr...**$125.00**

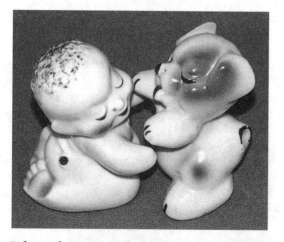

Salt and Pepper shakers, Van Tellingen, boy and dog, white, $75.00 for the pair.

Salt & pepper shakers, Van Tellingen, bunnies, solid colors, pr, from $28 to **$32.00**

Salt & pepper shakers, Van Tellingen, ducks, pr **$38.00**

Salt & pepper shakers, Van Tellingen, Dutch boy & girl, from $45 to...**$50.00**

Salt & pepper shakers, Van Tellingen, Mary & lamb, pr ...**$60.00**

Salt & pepper shakers, Van Tellingen, Peek-a-Boo, red dots, sm, pr, from $250 to..**$275.00**

Salt & pepper shakers, Van Tellingen, Peek-a-Boo, white solid, sm, pr **$200.00**

Salt & pepper shakers, Van Tellingen, sailor & mermaid, pr, from $225 to.......................................**$260.00**

San Joaquin Snack Jar, James B Beam Distilling Co Genuine Regal China 1977, 12", from $100 to..................**$125.00**

Restaurant China

Restaurant china, also commonly called cafe ware, diner china, institutional china, hotelware, or commercial china, is specifically designed for use in commercial food service. In addition to restaurants, it is used on board airplanes, ships, and trains, as well as in the dining areas of hotels, railroad stations, airports, government offices, military facilities, corporations, schools, hospitals, department and drug stores, amusement and sports parks, churches, clubs, and the like. Though most hotelware produced in America before 1900 has a heavy gauge nonvitrified body, vitrified commercial china made post-1910 includes some of the finest quality ware ever produced, far surpassing that of nonvitrified household products. A break- and chip-resistant rolled or welted edge is characteristic of American ware produced from the 1920s through the 1970s and is still frequently used, though no longer a concern on the very durable high alumina content bodies introduced in the 1960s. In addition, commercial tableware is also made of porcelain, glass-ceramic, glass laminate, glass, melamine, pewter-like metal, and silver plate. Airlines use fine gauge china in first class, due to space and weight factors. And beginning in the late 1970s, fine gauge porcelain and bone china became a popular choice of upscale restaurants, hotels, and country clubs. To reduce loss from wear, most decoration is applied to bisque, then glazed and glaze fired (i.e. underglaze) or to glaze-fired ware, then fired into the glaze (i.e. in-glaze). Until the 1970s many restaurants regularly ordered custom-decorated white, deep tan, blue, or pink-bodied patterns. However, it is estimated that more than 90% of today's commercial ware is plain or embossed white. For decades collectors have searched for railroad and ship china. Interest in airline china is on the rise. Attractive standard (stock) patterns are now also sought by many. Western motifs and stencil airbrushed designs are especially treasured. The popularity of high quality American-made Oriental designs has increased. Most prefer traditional medium-heavy gauge American vitrified china, though fine china collectors no doubt favor the commercial china products of Pickard or Royal Doulton. While some find it difficult to pass up any dining concern or transportation system top-marked piece, others seek ware that is decorated with a military logo or department store, casino, or amusement park name. Some collect only creamers, others butters or teapots. Some look for ware made by a particular manufacturer (e.g. Tepco), others specific patterns such as Willow or Indian Tree, or pink, blue, or tan body colors. It is currently considered fashionable to serve home-cooked meals on mismatched top-marked hotelware. Reminiscent of days gone by, pre-1960s restaurant or railroad china brings to mind pre-freeway cross-country vacations by car or rail when dining out was an event, unlike the quick stops at today's fast-food and family-style restaurants. For a more through study of the subject, we recommend *Restaurant China, Identification & Value Guide for Restaurant, Airline, Ship & Railroad Dinnerware, Volume 1* and *Volume 2,* by Barbara Conroy (Collector Books); her website with a list of contents and details of her books along with many pages of additional restaurant china information is listed in the Directory.

In the lines below, TM indicates top-marked or side-marked with name or logo. Please note: Commercial food service china is neither advertising nor souvenir china, since it is not meant to be removed from the restaurant premises.

Advisor: Barbara Conroy (See Directory, Dinnerware)

Restaurant and Transportation China Online Forums: www.cabinclass.com/ (click links for forum and china pattern archive)
http://restaurantwarecollectors.com/

Restaurant, Hotel, Department and Drug Store, Casino, and Company Cafeteria China

Ah Fong's compote, Oriental symbols TM, red rim, Jackson, 1970s **$27.00**
Blue Willow 8" plate, Jackson, 1940s........................**$18.00**
Cafè Beaux Arts 7½" TM coffeepot, Steelite, 1980s **$25.00**
Carriage House 10½" TM plate, Tepco, 1950s-60s......**$22.00**
Colonel Lee's Mongolian Bar-B-Que 7" TM chop suey, blue on white, unmarked **$15.00**
Conti-Hansa Hotel ashtray, Hutschenreuther, 1950s-60s ..**$10.00**
Copper Penny Restaurants TM mug, Shenango, 1970 date code **$20.00**
Crab Pot TM bouillon, Wallace, late 1950s **$15.00**
Deauville Hotel 9½" TM plate, Laughlin, 1968 date code **$18.00**
Dick's Dragon Restaurant 7½" TM plate, Oriental lettering in center, Wallace, 1950s......................................**$16.00**
El San Juan Hotel & Casino TM ashtray, blue & gold on white, Abco Trading, late 1980s **$12.00**
Fireman's Fund Insurance Company (company cafeteria) 9" TM plate, Walker, 1956 date code **$25.00**
Giants (San Francisco Giants' stadium restaurant) 6½" TM plate, Jackson, 1981..**$85.00**
Hacienda Hotel & Casino TM creamer (man on rearing horse), McNichol, late 1950s.............................**$70.00**
Highlands Inn TM cup & saucer, Jackson, 1977 & 1978 date codes..**$20.00**

Hotel Richmond 9¾" TM service plate, green transfer, gold band, John Maddock & Sons, 1910s.....................**$40.00**
Humbolt County Fairgrounds 5" TM fruit, Wallace, 1950s .**$18.00**
Hyatt Hotels TM cup, brown logo & band, Villeroy & Boch, 1980s..**$9.00**
Keith's Model T Truck Stop TM cup & saucer (casino), Shenango, 1971 & 1973 date codes **$110.00**
Maxim's Restaurant 12" TM plate, Rego, 1980s **$25.00**
Miami Beach Athletic Club 10½" TM service plate, Syracuse, 1950s..**$35.00**
Moustache Cafè TM mug, Inter American, late 1980s-early 1990s **$18.00**
Plaza Hotel 11" TM service plate, hotel decal center, scenic border, Lamberton, 1920s.................................**$75.00**
President Hotel TM ashtray, Noritake, 1970s...............**$10.00**
Qwikee Donut Shop TM mug, Shenango, 1969 date code **$80.00**
Safeway (company dining) 7¼" TM plate, Homer Laughlin, 1972 date code..**$18.00**
Sears Restaurants mug, Syracuse, 1973 date code **$20.00**
Showboat Hotel & Casino TM bouillon, Tepco, 1950s-early 1960s..**$40.00**
Silver's TM cup & saucer, AD; Trenton, 1920s **$40.00**
Sonnabend Hotels (hotel backstamp), 10¼" plate, Coach & Four pattern, Mayer, 1950s.................................**$25.00**
Surfside Hotel 10¾" TM service plate, Iroquois, 1930s..**$35.00**
Sushi Sam's TM tumbler, cobalt on light blue, Sai Japan, 1980s **$12.50**
Walgreens TM mug, Shenango, 1975 date code **$25.00**
Wardman Park Inn TM teapot, Warwick, 1920s **$50.00**
Washington Hotel (The) TM match stand, Mayer, 1930s...**$30.00**
Western Sizzlin' Steak House 6¼" TM plate, comic red & black cows on white, Homer Laughlin, ca 1988 ..**$20.00**
White Mountain View House 9¾" TM service plate, Syracuse, 1953 date code..**$35.00**
White Tower TM mug, Sterling, ca 1936-50s **$45.00**

Transportation and Military China

Air Canada 6" Gold Scallops pattern airline backstamp plate, Royal Stafford, 1964-70s **$15.00**
Alaska Airlines Gold Coast TM cup & saucer, racket & airline backstamp, 1980s...**$22.00**
Amtrak National pattern blue teapot, Hall...................**$24.00**
Baltimore Mail Line 7¼" TM plate, Schammell, 1930s ...**$45.00**
Bowater Steamship Co 8" TM plate, Maddock (England), 1940s..**$35.00**
Canadian Pacific Railway coffeepot, Cobalt Floral pattern, Shenango, dated 1913, RY backstamp **$150.00**
Canadian Pacific Railway crescent salad, Foliage pattern, Ridgway, late 1950s, RY backstamp **$40.00**
Chicago, Rock Island & Pacific Railroad TM coffeepot, La Salle pattern, Buffalo......................................**$450.00**
Colonial Line 12½" TM platter, Warwick, 1920s..........**$75.00**
CP Air 4½" metallic gold logo TM teapot, ca 1968-88 ...**$70.00**
Delta Air Lines 6¾" L casserole, Delta White pattern, Pfaltzgraff...**$2.00**

Denver & Rio Grand Western Railroad souvenir TM mug, peach lustre, Fire-King, 1960s................**$12.50**

Holland America Cruises 8¼" TM souvenir plate, Bing & Grondahl, dated 1981...................**$25.00**

Iberia Airlines TM butter pat, Spanish Globe pattern, Alvarez, 1970s................................**$25.00**

Kuwait Airways 7½" TM plate, East-West pattern, Hutchenreuther, 1980s+, airline backstamp.........**$15.00**

NYK Line rice bowl, Nitta Maru pattern, Mino & NYK backstamp......................................**$30.00**

Philippine Airlines 'Philippines' pattern 6¾" long casserole, mid-1980s, $15.00. (Photo courtesy Barbara Conroy)

Royal Air Maroc TM butter pat, Morocco pattern, Bernardaud, 1980s, airline backstamp...................**$30.00**

Royal Cruise Line TM mug, Crown Odyssey pattern, Porsgrund, 1982 date code **$15.00**

Royal Viking TM peanut holder, Royal Viking Sun pattern, Porsgrund backstamp, 1980s..................**$14.00**

Singapore Airlines 6½" TM plate, gold logo, Narumi, 1990s, airline backstamp.....................**$16.00**

Sun Line 6¼" TM plate, Stella Solaris pattern, Richard-Ginori, 1980s......................................**$25.00**

Trans World Airlines 6" TM plate, Michaud, ca 1975-84, airline backstamp.......................**$8.00**

Trans-Europe Express TM ashtray, Inverted TEE pattern, Langenthal, dated 1976.....................**$25.00**

Treasure Island Naval Station TM mug, Crestor Inc, 1970s ..**$20.00**

US Navy Captain's mess 6½" flag TM plate, Buffalo, early 1940s......................................**$18.00**

US Navy Wardroom Officer's mess 9" anchor TM plate, Shenango 1978 date code **$16.00**

Rock 'n Roll Memorabilia

Ticket stubs and souvenirs issued at rock concerts, posters of artists that have reached celebrity status, and merchandise such as dolls, games, clothing, etc., that was sold through retail stores during the heights of their careers are just the things that interest collectors of rock 'n roll memorabilia. Some original, one-of-a-kind examples — for instance, their instruments, concert costumes, and personal items — often sell at the large auction galleries in the East where they've realized very high-dollar prices. For more information we recommend *Rock-N-Roll Treasures* by Joe Hilton and Greg Moore (Collector Books). Greg has also written *A Price Guide to Rock and Roll Collectibles* which is distributed by L-W Book Sales. *Collector's Guide to TV Toys & Memorabilia* by Greg Davis and Bill Morgan contains additional information and photos (it is also published by Collector Books).

Note: Most posters sell in the range of $5.00 to $10.00; those listed below are the higher-end examples in excellent or better condition.

See also Beatles Collectibles; Elvis Presley Memorabilia; Magazines; Movie Posters; Pin-Back Buttons; Records.

Advisor: Bojo/Bob Gottuso (See Directory, Character and Personality Collectibles)

Aerosmith, poster, promotional for Bootleg album, 1970s, 42x44", EX **$85.00**

Alice Cooper, application for membership & letter from club president, 1972, unfilled, NM................**$60.00**

Alice Cooper, belt buckle, enameled face, 1978, 3x2¼" ..**$30.00**

Alice Cooper, doll, real hair, imitation leather pants, plays Welcome to My Nightmare, Art Asylum, 18", NM ...**$30.00**

Alice Cooper, pillow, Million Dollar Babies, 1973, 13x13", NM **$200.00**

Alice Cooper, program magazine, Billion Dollar Babies, 58+ pages, EX..............................**$75.00**

Animals/Eric Burdon, poster, Fillmore Auditorium, 1967, M **$100.00**

Bee Gees, book, The Legend, Illustrated Story of the Bee Gees, 1979, M **$45.00**

Bee Gees, poster, all 3 members in white, One Stop Posters, #530, 42x58", EX **$35.00**

Bee Gees, puzzle, jigsaw; dressed in white, complete, 1979, 11x17", NMIB **$20.00**

Bee Gees, record player, sing-along microphone & strobe light, Vanity Fair, 1979, NM.................**$110.00**

Black Sabbath, concert handbill, Warehouse New Orleans, 3/27/71, w/Seatrain & Melting Pot, 8½x11", EX....**$105.00**

Black Sabbath, tour program, 1975, Black Sabbath in white on black w/lightning bolt, EX................**$25.00**

Bobby Sherman, sheet music, La La La (If I Had You), EX...**$12.00**

Bobby Vinton, box, silver plate w/blue velvet inside, card: BV & Blue Velvet Theatre...Merry Cristmas 1993, 5½x2", EX................................**$25.00**

Bobby Vinton, concert program, 1970s, 16 pages, VG+ ..**$40.00**

Boby Vinton, poster, in green shirt against block wall, 1978, 23x35", NM.............................**$12.00**

Brenda Lee, book, Brenda Lee, 1956-62, photos, stories & discography, 84 pages, Paul Kinsbury, hardbound, EX.........**$15.00**

Brenda Lee, magazine, The Journal April 1999, Lee on cover, 16 pages, NM **$15.00**

Brenda Lee, press kit, Warner Bros, 1991, 7 pages w/8x10" photo, EX **$15.00**

Brenda Lee, promotional ad, Billboard 9/11/71, 11x14", EX $10.00

Brenda Lee/Gene Vincent, 1962 England tour program, The King & Queen of Rock, VG+ $35.00

Buddy Holly, book, His Life & Music, John Goldrosen, 1975, hardback w/dustcover, VG..................................$15.00

Buddy Holly, sheet music, Everyday, 9x12", EX.......$120.00

Buddy Holly, song & music book, Best of Buddy Holly, 1978, EX $25.00

Dave Clark 5, sheet music, Glad All Over, 1963, EX ..$15.00

Dave Clark 5, tour program, 1966, 24 pages, VG $25.00

David Cassidy, magazine, Tiger Beat September 1971, on cover, 4 panel poster inside, EX..........................$25.00

David Cassidy, poster, Artko, 1972, 11x17", EX $18.00

David Cassidy, press kit, 13 pages photos & info, Enigma Entertainment, 1990, EX..................................$100.00

David Cassidy, sheet music, Lyin' to Myself, 8 pages, 1990, M..$20.00

David Cassidy, song book, Rock Me Baby album, lyrics, guitar & piano music, 64 pages, EX $50.00

Davis Cassidy, puzzle, jigsaw; Witman #7492, 224 pcs, EXIB..$42.00

Everly Brothers, sheet music, Wake Up, Little Susie, 1957, EX $16.00

Everly Brothers, song book, Song Folio #1, Acuff-Rose Studios, 48 pages, 1959, 9x12", EX........................$12.00

Greadful Dead, gunnie sack, featuring Electric Sam, EX $15.00

Greatful Dead, poster, Oakland Coliseum 1993-94, New Years Eve, 13x19", EX................................$80.00

Jerry Garcia, doll, made by Gund for Liquid Blue, w/guitar, MIB $20.00

John Lee Hooker, concert handbill, w/Norman Greenbaum, Matrix, November 1970, 5¼x8½", M....................$32.00

John Lee Hooker, poster, w/Booker T, Alvin Youngblood & his Garage Band, Fillmore, San Fransisco, 1977, 13x19", EX $55.00

KISS, Army Kit, complete, 1st edition, 1975, M $200.00

KISS, belt buckle, brass w/logo, 1976..........................$35.00

KISS, belt buckle, chrome letters KISS, NM..............$210.00

KISS, belt buckle, Rock & Roll Over, enameled, Pacifica, 1977, NM $100.00

KISS, doll, Gene Simmons, Mego, 1978, 14", EX+ $95.00

KISS, earrings, letters spell Paul out vertically, 1980s, NM, pr..$100.00

KISS, ink pen, Peter, 1970s, MOC $200.00

KISS, key chains, faces, 1 of ea member, set of 4, M.$800.00

KISS, model, Custom Chevy Van, AMT, 1970s, MIB (sealed)..$125.00

KISS, patch, silver KISS on black, 1970s, 4x2", M.......$12.00

KISS, pool cue, logo & faux signatures, 1997, MIP ..$150.00

KISS, poster, 4-scene composite, 1970s, 24x35", M.....$20.00

KISS, poster calender, 1975, 18x36", NM $150.00

KISS, puzzle, Peter Criss (drummer) w/2 black panthers, 200 pcs, Milton Bradley, M (sealed box) $65.00

KISS, tour book, Destroyer Tour, 1976, EX $120.00

KISS, tour program, 10th Anniversary, EX................$140.00

KISS, transistor radio, color logo & group photo, 1977, MIB..$175.00

KISS, trash can, black w/logo & group photo, metal, Aucoin Management, 1978, 19½", EX................$125.00

KISS, Your Face Makeup Kit, missing 1 brush, 1970s, VG+..$275.00

Monkees, toy guitar, turn crank to produce music, paper face, 15", EX, from $110.00 to $135.00. (Photo courtesy Bojo)

Moody Blues, Long Distance Voyager tour program, 1987, from $15.00 to $20.00. (Photo courtesy Greg Davis and Bill Morgan)

Rolling Stones, banner, red w/blue print, 1975 tour, 68x42", VG+..$50.00

Rolling Stones, book, Voodoo Lounge, w/interactive floppy disk, 1995, MIP..$50.00

Rolling Stones, guest pass, No Security Tour, 1999, laminated, M..$50.00

Rolling Stones, lithograph, album cover of Voodoo Lounge, 25x27", NM..$50.00

Rolling Stones, movie flyer, Gimme Shelter, 1970, 5½x7½", EX..$80.00

Rolling Stones, poster, multicolored artwork, Candlestick Park, 9/17-18/1981, 30x20", NM $50.00

Rolling Stones, press kit, Rolling Stones at the Max (IMAX), 1990, complete, EX................................$30.00

Rolling Stones, program, 1965, 20 pages, 11x11", EX.$55.00

Rolling Stones, sheet music, Get Off of My Cloud, Gideon, 1965, 9x11", EX $25.00

Rolling Stones, stand-up, for Some Girls album, cardboard, 1978, 19x11", EX................................$60.00

Rolling Stones, T-shirt, Tatoo You, 1989 North American Tour, NM................................$30.00

Rolling Stones, ticket, War Memorial Auditorium, Rochester NY, 11/1/65, unused, NM................................$65.00

Rolling Stones, tour program, 1978, EX $20.00

Rolling Stones, 9" balloons, 1983, MIP........................$55.00

Rookwood

Although this company was established in 1879, it continued to produce commercial artware until it closed in 1967. Located in Cincinnati, Ohio, Rookwood is recognized today as the largest producer of high-quality art pottery ever to operate in the United States.

Most of the pieces listed here are from the later years of production, but we've included some early pieces as well. With few exceptions, all early Ohio art pottery companies produced an artist-decorated brown-glaze line — Rookwood's was called Standard. Among their other early lines were Sea Green, Iris, Jewel Porcelain, Wax Matt, and Vellum.

Virtually all of Rookwood's pieces are marked. The most familiar mark is the 'reverse R'-P monogram. It was first used in 1886, and until 1900 a flame point was added above it to represent each passing year. After the turn of the century, a Roman numeral below the monogram was used to indicate the current year. In addition to the dating mark, a die-stamped number was used to identify the shape.

The Cincinnati Art Galleries routinely hold large and important cataloged auctions. The full-color catalogs occasionally contain company history and listings of artists and designers with their monograms (as well as company codes and trademarks). Collectors now regard them as an excellent source for information and study. *Rookwood Pottery* by Nick and Marilyn Nicholson and Tim Thomas is another fine reference (Collector Books).

Ashtray, #1317, 1922, owl, maroon matt, 5¾"............$80.00

Ashtray, #1646, 1928, green on pink, 6⅜" dia $100.00

Ashtray, #2647, 1930, fox, rust matt, 6¾" dia, NM....$150.00

Bookends, #2185, 1919, Elizabethan ladies, 5½", NM, pr .$200.00

Bookends, #2275, 1943, rooks, ivory matt, 5", pr $325.00

Bookends, #2275, 1949, crows, celadon green high glaze, signed McDonald, 5", pr, NM $130.00

Bookends, #2446, 1927, girl on bench, green on pink, 5½", pr $450.00

Bookends, #2829, 1937, birds, blue matt, 5", EX......$160.00

Bookends, #2836, 1927, cactus flowers, gray on pink, 3¾", pr $200.00

Bookends, #6124, 1937, elephants, ivory matt, 7", pr..$500.00

Bookends, #2634, Spanish galleons, green matt with rust highlights, 1941, 5", $375.00 for the pair. (Photo courtesy Cincinnati Art Gallery)

Bowl, #2153, 1930, leaves & berries at rim, pink matt, 7½"..$150.00

Bowl, #6132, 1946, broad leaf form, blue high glaze, 6½"......$50.00

Bowl, #6313, 1932, molded lobed form w/yellow drip over pink high glaze, 8" $130.00

Candlesticks, #1193, 1921, molded leaves, brown matt, 7", pr $350.00

Covered dish, #2459, 1927, ram's head handles, mottled blue matt, 5" $160.00

Figurine, #2457, 1944, grotesque face, ivory matt, 3½"..$250.00

Figurine, #6843, 1944, cockatoo, yellow, ivory & green high glaze, 9" $375.00

Figurine, #6907, 1951, Colonial lady, yellow high glaze, 7¾" $150.00

Paperweight, #6383, 1946, canary, ivory matt, 3⅝", NM ...$130.00

Paperweight, #6937, 1951, lady, yellow high glaze, 7½" .$375.00

Paperweight, 36490, 1946, elephant seated, green high glaze, 3¾" $170.00

Trivet, #1212, 1922, incised swirling decoration, blue & green high glaze, 6" sq $250.00

Trivet, #2351, 1943, embossed sea gulls, 5⅞" $325.00

Vase, #1840, 1922, mottled blue & tan matt, 3" $160.00

Vase, #2089, 1935, Arts & Crafts design, mustard matt, 3½" $260.00

Vase, #2097, 1919, swan, burgundy & aqua mottled matt, 3½" $325.00

Vase, #2123, 1941, molded flowers, pink matt, 5½" .$110.00

Vase, #2135, 1930, Greek Key design, green on pink, 5¾" $160.00

Vase, #2139, 1922, molded berries, turquoise matt, 4½"...$170.00

Vase, #2141, 1937, Arts & Crafts design, mottled turquoise, 6½" $325.00

Vase, #2284, 1932, molded geometric decoration, green & pink matt, 5" $110.00

Vase, #2768, 1930, molded form, mottled pink & green matt, 7½" $180.00

Vase, #5318F, 1932, mottled burgundy & brown high glaze, 3" $120.00

Vase, #6108, 1930, molded floral decoration, blue matt, 5",
NM **$60.00**
Vase, #6109, 1935, hexagonal, pink matt, 6" **$140.00**
Vase, #6214, 1937, Deco-style deer & foliage, 4¼"...**$250.00**
Vase, #6214, 1937, molded deer & geometric design, ivory
matt, 5" **$90.00**
Vase, #6440, 1942, geometric design, celadon green, 5"..**$90.00**

**Vase, #6471, green and blue matt, 1936, Xd but
mint, 9", $325.00; Vase, multitone blue matt,
1922, 7", $260.00.**

Vase, #6478, 1935, raised design, ivory high glaze w/green
crystalline interior, 6"...**$140.00**
Vase, #6503, 1936, tan & green crystalline high glaze over
ribbed body, 4¼"..**$150.00**
Vase, #6510, 1936, vertical stylized leaves, mottled blue &
green crystalline matt, 5¼"...................................**$230.00**
Vase, #6511, 1937, molded floral decoration, ivory matt,
6" **$100.00**
Vase, #6545, 1935, molded leaf & berry decoration, tan matt,
3" **$225.00**
Vase, #6644, 1950, yellow drip over green high glaze,
7"...**$230.00**
Vase, #6722, 1938, village scene, blue high glaze, original
paper label, 10½" **$150.00**
Vase, #6830, 1946, green crystalline lily form, 6" **$230.00**
Vase, #6833, 1949, molded water lily design, red high glaze,
6" **$200.00**
Vase, #6871, 1946, wisteria, light blue micro-crystalline, 13⅞",
NM **$350.00**
Vase, #6893, 1946, molded flowers, ivory matt, 9" ...**$300.00**
Vase, bud; #5163, 1930, draped female figures, tan matt,
9⅛" **$400.00**
Wall pocket, #2008, 1921, blue matt, 7⅜" **$275.00**
Wall pocket, #6975, 1947, lady, tan high glaze, Clotilda
Zanetta, 8½" **$170.00**

Rooster and Roses

Back in the 1940s, newlyweds might conceivably have received some of this imported Japanese-made kitchenware as a housewarming gift. They'd no doubt be stunned to see the prices it's now bringing! Rooster and Roses (Ucagco called it Early Provincial) is one of those lines of novelty ceramics from the '40s and '50s that are among today's hottest collectibles. Ucagco was only one of several importers whose label you'll find on this pattern; among other are Py, ACSON, Norcrest, and Lefton. The design is easy to spot. There's the rooster yellow breast with black crosshatching, brown head, and of course, the red crest and waddle; large full-blown roses with green leaves and vines; and a trimming of yellow borders punctuated by groups of brown lines. (You'll find another line having blue flowers among the roses, and one with a rooster with a green head and a green borders. These are not considered Rooster and Roses by purist collectors, though there is a market for them as well.) The line is fun to collect, since shapes are so diversified. Even though there has been relatively little networking among collectors, more than one hundred items have been reported and no doubt more will surface.

Advisor: Jacki Elliott (See Directory, Rooster and Roses)

Candy dish, flat chicken-shaped tray with three-dimensional chicken head, made in three sizes, from $75.00 to $100.00 each. (Photo courtesy Jacki Elliott)

Ashtray, rectangular, part of set, 3x2".............................**$9.50**
Ashtray, round or sq, sm, from $15 to......................**$25.00**
Ashtray, sq, lg, from $35 to..**$40.00**
Basket, flared sides, 6", from $45 to **$65.00**
Bell, from $55 to...**$95.00**
Bell, rooster & chicken on opposing sides, rare, from $95
to **$125.00**
Biscuit jar, w/wicker handle, from $65 to...................**$95.00**
Bonbon dish, pedestal base, minimum value **$55.00**
Bowl, cereal; from $14 to..**$25.00**
Bowl, rice; on saucer, from $25 to **$35.00**
Bowl, 8", from $45 to **$55.00**
Box, trinket; w/lid, round, from $25 to **$35.00**
Box, 4½x3½", from $25 to...**$35.00**

Bread plate, from $15 to **$25.00**

Butter dish, ¼-lb, from $20 to **$25.00**

Candle warmer (for tea & coffeepots), from $25 to ...**$45.00**

Candy dish, w/3-dimensional leaf handle, from $25 to...**$45.00**

Canister set, round, 4-pc, from $150 to **$175.00**

Canister set, sq, 4-pc, from $100 to **$150.00**

Canister set, stacking, rare, minimum value.............**$150.00**

Carafe, no handle, w/stopper lid, 8", from $65 to......**$85.00**

Carafe, w/handle & stopper lid, 8", from $85 to.......**$125.00**

Casserole dish, w/lid, from $65 to **$85.00**

Castor set in revolving wire rack, 2 cruets, mustard jar & salt & pepper shakers, rare, from $125 to.................**$150.00**

Chamberstick, saucer base, ring handle, from $25 to.**$35.00**

Cheese dish, slant lid, from $40 to **$55.00**

Cigarette box w/2 trays, hard to find, from $65 to.....**$75.00**

Coaster, ceramic disk embedded in round wood tray, rare, minimum value...**$45.00**

Coffee grinder, rare, minimum value **$150.00**

Coffeepot, 'Coffee' on neck band, w/creamer & sugar bowl, both w/appropriately lettered neck bands, 3 pcs, from $75 to...**$85.00**

Condiment set, 2 cruets, salt & pepper shakers w/mustard jar on tray, miniature, from $50 to.............................**$75.00**

Condiment set, 2 cruets, salt & pepper shakers w/mustard jar atop wire & wood holder, 4 spice canisters below, minimum...**$125.00**

Cookie jar, ceramic handles, from $85 to **$100.00**

Creamer & sugar bowl, w/lid, lg...................................**$25.00**

Creamer & sugar bowl on rectangular tray, from $65 to..**$75.00**

Cruets, cojoined w/twisted necks, sm..........................**$45.00**

Cruets, oil & vinegar, flared bases, pr..........................**$45.00**

Cruets, oil & vinegar, sq, lg, pr, from $30 to..............**$35.00**

Cruets, oil & vinegar, w/salt & pepper shakers in shadow box, from $55 to...**$75.00**

Cup & saucer **$25.00**

Demitasse pot, w/4 cups & saucer, minimum value...**$150.00**

Demitasse pot, w/6 cups & saucers, minimum value...**$175.00**

Egg cup, from $20 to..**$25.00**

Egg cup on tray, from $35 to **$45.00**

Egg plate, from $55 to **$65.00**

Flowerpot, buttress handles, 5", from $35 to..............**$45.00**

Hamburger press, wood w/embedded ceramic tray, round, minimum value **$24.00**

Instant coffee jar, no attached spoon holder on side, minimum value...**$35.00**

Instant coffee jar, spoon-holder tube on side, rare.....**$45.00**

Jam & jelly containers, cojoined, w/lids & spoons, from $35 to..**$45.00**

Jam & jelly containers, cojoined, w/lids & spoons, w/loop handles & lids, very rare **$85.00**

Jam jar, attached underplate, from $35 to...................**$45.00**

Ketchup or mustard jar, flared cylinder w/lettered label, ea, from $25 to..**$30.00**

Lamp, pinup, made from either a match holder or a salt box, ea, from $75 to **$100.00**

Lazy Susan on wood pedestal, round covered box at center, 4 sections around outside (2 w/lids), from $150 to ..**$250.00**

Marmalade, round base w/tab handles, w/lid & spoon, minimum value, from $35 to...**$55.00**

Match holder, wall mount, from $65 to **$85.00**

Measuring cup set, 4-pc w/matching ceramic rack, from $45 to..**$65.00**

Measuring spoons on 8" ceramic spoon-shaped rack, from $40 to..**$55.00**

Mug, rounded bottom, med, from $20 to.....................**$25.00**

Mug, straight upright bar handle, lg, from $20 to.......**$35.00**

Napkin holder, from $30 to **$40.00**

Pipe holder/ashtray, from $30 to..................................**$50.00**

Pitcher, bulbous, 5", from $25 to..................................**$30.00**

Pitcher, 'Milk' on neck band, from $22.50 to **$35.00**

Pitcher, 3½", from $15 to...**$20.00**

Planter, rolling pin shape, rare, minimum value.........**$50.00**

Plate, dinner; from $25 to **$35.00**

Plate, luncheon; from $15 to **$25.00**

Plate, side salad; crescent shape, hard to find, from $50 to..**$60.00**

Platter, 12", from $55 to...**$80.00**

Recipe box, part of shadow box set, from $25 to **$35.00**

Relish tray, 2 round wells w/center handle, 12", from $35 to..**$40.00**

Relish tray, 3 wells w/center handle, from $55 to **$65.00**

Rolling pin, minimum value **$50.00**

Salad fork, spoon & salt & pepper shakers w/wooden handles, on ceramic wall rack, minimum value.........**$55.00**

Salad fork & spoon w/wooden handles on ceramic wall-mount rack, from $45 to **$65.00**

Salt & pepper shakers, drum shape w/long horizontal ceramic handle, lg, pr, from $30 to...............................**$40.00**

Salt & pepper shakers, w/applied rose, sq, pr............**$23.00**

Salt & pepper shakers, w/handle, pr, from $15 to......**$20.00**

Salt & pepper shakers, w/lettered neck band, pr **$25.00**

Salt & pepper shakers, 4", pr, from $15 to **$20.00**

Salt box, wooden lid..**$60.00**

Salt box, wooden lid, from $45 to **$55.00**

Shaker, cheese or sugar, 7", from $20 to **$30.00**

Skillet, 4"...**$18.00**

Slipper, 3-dimensional rose on toe, rare, from $85 to ..**$125.00**

Snack tray w/cup, oval, 2-pc, minimum value............**$45.00**

Snack tray w/cup, rectangular, 2-pc, from $50 to.......**$60.00**

Spice rack, 3 rows of 2 curved-front containers, together forming half-cylinder shape w/flat back..............**$85.00**

Spice set, 9 sq containers in wood frame w/pull-out ceramic tray in base, from $75 to.......................................**$95.00**

Spoon holder, w/lg salt shaker in well on side extension, from $20 to..**$25.00**

Stacking tea set, teapot, creamer & sugar bowl, from $70 to..**$90.00**

Syrup pitcher, w/2 sm graduated pitchers on tray, minimum value...**$60.00**

Tazza (footed tray), 3x6" dia..**$45.00**

Teapot, from $55 to...**$65.00**

Toast holder, minimum value **$75.00**

Tray, closed tab handles ea end, 11", from $25 to **$30.00**
Tray, round w/chamberstick-type handle on 1 side, 5½", from $15 to. **$20.00**
Tumbler, from $15 to..**$20.00**
Vase, round w/flat sides, 6", from $20 to **$30.00**
Wall hanger, teapot shape, pr.....................................**$90.00**

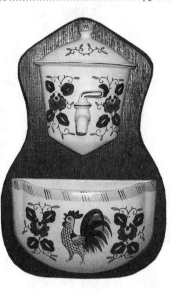

Wall pocket, lavabo, two-piece, mounted on board, from $85.00 to $125.00.

Wall pocket, scalloped top, bulbous bottom, from $55 to **$65.00**
Wall pocket, teapots, facing ea other, pr, minimum value **$90.00**
Watering can, from $30 to..**$45.00**

Roselane Sparklers

Beginning as a husband and wife operation in the late 1930s, the Roselane Pottery Company of Pasadena, California, expanded their inventory from the figurines they originally sold to local florists to include a complete line of decorative items that eventually were shipped to Alaska, South America, and all parts of the United States.

One of their lines was the Roselane Sparklers. Popular in the '50s, these small animal and bird figures were airbrush decorated and had rhinestone eyes. They're fun to look for, and though prices are rising steadily, they're still not terribly expensive.

If you'd like to learn more, there's a chapter on Roselane in *The Collector's Encyclopedia of California Pottery, Second Edition,* by Jack Chipman.

Advisor: Lee Garmon (See Directory, Advertising, Reddy Kilowatt)

Angelfish, 4½", from $20 to **$25.00**
Basset hound, sitting, 4", from $15 to **$18.00**
Basset hound pup, 2", from $12 to **$15.00**
Bulldog, fierce expression, looking right, 2", from $12 to..**$15.00**
Bulldog, fierce expression, looking up & right, jeweled collar, lg, from $22 to **$25.00**

Bulldog, sitting, slender body, looking right, 6"..........**$25.00**
Cat, recumbent, head turned right, tail & paws tucked under body, from $20 to..**$25.00**
Cat, Siamese, looking straight ahead, no collar, 5" **$45.00**
Cat, Siamese, sitting, looking straight ahead, jeweled collar, 7", from $40 to **$50.00**
Cat, sitting, head turned right, tail out behind, from $25 to **$28.00**
Cat, standing, head turned right, tail arched over back, jeweled collar, 5½", from $25 to **$30.00**

Cat with two kittens, rare, from $40.00 to $45.00. (Photo courtesy Lee Garmon)

Chihuahua, sitting, left paw raised, looking straight ahead, 7"..**$28.00**
Cocker spaniel, 4½" from $15 to................................**$20.00**
Deer, standing, head turned right, looking downward, 5½"..**$25.00**
Deer w/antlers, standing jeweled collar, 4½", from $22 to **$28.00**
Elephant, sitting on hind quarters, 6"........................**$28.00**
Elephant, trunk raised, striding, jeweled headpiece, 6"...**$28.00**
Fawn, legs folded under body, 4x3½"........................**$25.00**
Fawn, upturned head, 4x3½" **$20.00**
Fawn, 4½x1½"..**$20.00**
Kangaroo, mama holding babies, 4½", from $40 to ...**$45.00**
Kitten, sitting, 1¾" **$12.00**
Owl, very stylized, lg round eyes, teardrop-shaped body, lg **$25.00**
Owl, 3½" **$15.00**
Owl, 5¼" **$25.00**
Owl, 7"...**$30.00**
Owl baby, 2¼", from $12 to **$15.00**
Pheasants, 1 (pink, 3¾"), 1 (blue, 5"), looking back, pr, from $30 to **$35.00**
Pig, lg...**$25.00**
Pouter pigeon, 3½"...**$20.00**
Raccoon, standing, 4½", from $20 to **$25.00**
Whippet, sitting, 7½", from $25 to **$28.00**

Rosemeade

The Wahpeton Pottery Company of Wahpeton, North Dakota, chose the trade name Rosemeade for a line of bird and animal figurines, novelty salt and pepper shakers, bells, and many other items which were sold from the 1940s to the 1960s through gift stores and souvenir shops in that part of the country. They were marked with either a paper label or an ink stamp; the name Prairie Rose was also used. See *Collector's Encyclopedia of Rosemeade Pottery* by Darlene Hurst Dommel (Collector Books) for more information.

Advisor: Bryce Farnsworth (See Directory, Rosemeade)

Club: North Dakota Pottery Collectors Society
Sandy Short
Box 14, Beach, ND 58621
701-872-3236; www.ndpcs.org
Annual dues: $15; sponsors annual convention and includes 4 newsletters

Candle holder, cloverleaf-shaped wax bowl, blue, w/sticker, 1⅝x3¾"...**$65.00**
Creamer & sugar bowl, blue tulips, 2", pr..................**$90.00**
Creamer & sugar bowl, light blue, miniature...........**$105.00**
Cup, man w/mustache on side of cup, black, 3½".....**$80.00**
Figurine, buffalo, 6¼"...**$200.00**
Figurine, cock pheasant, 14½x9", minimum value ...**$350.00**
Figurine, elephant, rare teal green, w/sticker, 5x6" **$75.00**
Figurine, goat, w/original label, 2⅛x2⅜" **$170.00**
Figurine, kitty, tail in air, white, w/sticker, 2x2"..........**$45.00**
Figurines, elephants, gray, w/original stickers, 1½x1½", pr...**$90.00**
Figurines, Russian Wolfhounds, w/Prairie Rose sticker, 6½x7", pr...**$210.00**
Novelty, Indian moccasin, 1½x3½"..............................**$50.00**
Pin tray, lily pad shape, blue-green w/white flower w/yellow center, 5" dia **$140.00**
Planter, swan, blue w/mauve, w/sticker, 5¼" **$55.00**
Plaque, horse head, bronze colored, 4½x6" **$320.00**
Salt & pepper shakers, beavers, brown, 3", pr...........**$50.00**
Salt & pepper shakers, brown bears, seated, 2¾", pr.**$50.00**
Salt & pepper shakers, buffalo, brown, w/sticker, pr ..**$135.00**
Salt & pepper shakers, cactus, w/stickers, 1⅜", pr.....**$65.00**
Salt & pepper shakers, Chihuahua heads, pr...........**$420.00**
Salt & pepper shakers, cow & bull, 2", pr.................**$160.00**
Salt & pepper shakers, deer, leeping, pr **$70.00**
Salt & pepper shakers, ear of corn shape, 2¼", pr, w/tray ..**$80.00**
Salt & pepper shakers, elephants, gray, w/stickers, 2½x2½", pr...**$60.00**
Salt & pepper shakers, mice, white, 1¾", 2", pr **$100.00**
Salt & pepper shakers, oxen heads, brown w/ivory-colored horns, w/stickers, pr...**$60.00**
Salt & pepper shakers, parrots, w/original stickers, 3", pr ..**$100.00**
Salt & pepper shakers, raccoons, 1 begging, 1 on all fours, pr **$170.00**
Salt & pepper shakers, Siamese cats, 3", pr.................**$60.00**

Salt & pepper shakers, skunks, 3x3¾", pr...................**$75.00**

Salt and pepper shakers, standing pigs, 3¾", from $125.00 to $150.00 for the pair. (Photo courtesy Darlene Hurst Dommel)

Toothpick holder, cock pheasant, w/sticker, 4" **$75.00**
Toothpick holder, ear of corn, 1½"..............................**$75.00**
Vase, deer stands beside vase, blue & mauve, 4x8" ...**$70.00**
Vase, yellow, 5½x4¼" dia...**$40.00**
Vase, Yellow Fleck, w/sticker, 6"..................................**$80.00**
Wall hanging, shape of North Dakota, glossy wine, marked Old Four-Eyes, Medora N Dak **$210.00**
Wall pocket, deer lying in leaves, off-white to pink, 5"..**$45.00**

Roseville Pottery

This company took its name from the city in Ohio where they operated for a few years before moving to Zanesville in the late 1890s. They're recognized as one of the giants in the industry, having produced many lines of the finest in art pottery from the beginning to the end of their operations. Even when machinery took over many of the procedures once carefully done by hand, the pottery they produced continued to reflect the artistic merit and high standards of quality the company had always insisted upon.

Several marks were used over the years as well as some paper labels. The very early art lines often carried an applied ceramic seal with the name of the line (Royal, Egypto, Mongol, Mara, or Woodland) under a circle containing the words Rozane Ware. From 1910 until 1928 an Rv mark was used, the 'v' being contained in the upper loop of the 'R.' Paper labels were common from 1914 until 1937. From 1932 until they closed in 1952, the mark was Roseville in script, or R USA. Pieces marked RRP Co Roseville, Ohio, were not made by the Roseville Pottery but by Robinson Ransbottom of Roseville, Ohio. Don't be confused. There are many jardinieres and pedestals in a brown and green blended glaze that are being sold at flea markets and antique malls as Roseville that were actually made by Robinson Ransbottom as late as the 1970s and 1980s. That isn't to say they don't have some worth of their own, but don't buy them for old Roseville.

Most of the listings here are for items produced from the 1930s on — things you'll be more likely to encounter today. If you'd like to learn more about the subject, we recommend *The Collector's Encyclopedia of Roseville Pottery, Vols 1* and *2* (revised editions, 2001 pricing by Mike Nickel) by Sharon and Bob Huxford (Collector Books); *A Price Guide to Roseville Pottery by the Numbers* by John Humphries (L&W Book Sales); *Roseville in All Its Splendor* by Jack and Nancy Bomm (L&W Book Sales); and *Collector's Compendium of Roseville Pottery, Vols 1* and *2*, by R.B. Monsen (Monsen & Baer).

Advisor: Mike Nickel (See the Directory, Roseville)

Newsletter: *Rosevilles of the Past*
Nancy Bomm, Editor
P.O. Box 656
Clarcona, FL 32710-0656; Subscription: $19.95 per year for 6 to 12 newsletters

Apple Blossom, bowl, #326-6, green or pink, 2½x6½", from $150 to **$175.00**
Apple Blossom, bowl vase, #342-6, blue, 6", from $325 to **$375.00**
Apple Blossom, vase, #388-10, blue, 10", from $350 to ..**$450.00**
Artwood, planter, #1054, 6½x8½", from $85 to **$95.00**
Artwood, planter set, center section (#1051-6") & 2 side sections (#1050-4"), from $110 to **$125.00**
Baneda, center bowl, #233, green, 3½x10", from $600 to..**$700.00**
Baneda, vase, #592, green, 7", from $725 to.............**$800.00**
Baneda, vase, #596, green, 9", from $1,500 to.......**$1,750.00**

Baneda, vases, #599, green, 12", from $2,700.00 to $3,250.00; #596, pink, 9", from $1,250.00 to $1,500.00.

Bittersweet, basket, #809-8, 8½", from $200 to.........**$250.00**
Bittersweet, double vase, #858, 4", from $150 to......**$175.00**
Blackberry, basket, from $1,100 to **$1,300.00**
Blackberry, vase, 6", from $550 to **$600.00**
Bleeding Heart, hanging basket, #362, blue, 8" dia, from $375 to...**$425.00**
Bleeding Heart, vase, #976-15, green or pink, 15", from $750 to...**$850.00**

Bushberry, center bowl, #385-10, green, 13", from $150 to **$175.00**
Bushberry, double cornucopia, #155-8, orange, 6", from $150 to **$175.00**
Bushberry, window box, #383-6, blue, 6½", from $150 to..**$175.00**
Cameo II, double bud vase, 4x7½", from $350 to....**$400.00**
Cameo II, hanging basket, 4½x7", from $350 to.......**$450.00**
Capri, ashtray, #598-9, 9", from $40 to.........................**$50.00**
Capri, bowl, #529-9, 9", from $20 to.............................**$30.00**
Capri, shell dish, #C-1120, 13½", from $50 to.............**$60.00**
Capri, window box, #569-10, 3x10", from $45 to **$55.00**
Carnelian I, flower frog, 4½", from $75 to **$85.00**
Carnelian I, vase, no handles, 6", from $70 to............**$80.00**
Carnelian II, basket, 4x10", from $200 to **$250.00**
Carnelian II, ewer, 12½", from $600 to......................**$700.00**
Clemana, vase, #280, tan, 6½", from $300 to...........**$350.00**
Clemana, vase, #750, blue, 7½", from $250 to...........**$275.00**
Clematis, center bowl, #458-10, blue, 14", from $200 to..**$250.00**
Clematis, center bowl, #458-10, brown or green, 14", from $175 to...**$200.00**
Clematis, vase, #103-6, brown or green, 6", from $90 to ..**$110.00**
Columbine, candlesticks, #1146-4½", pink, 5", pr, from $225 to...**$250.00**
Columbine, vase, #151-8, pink, 8", from $275 to......**$325.00**
Corinthian, footed bowl, 4½", from $100 to..............**$125.00**
Corinthian, wall pocket, 8", from $275 to..................**$325.00**
Cosmos, flower frog, #39, tan, 3½", from $150 to....**$175.00**
Cosmos, hanging basket, #361, blue, 7", from $400 to..**$425.00**
Cremona, vase, 8", from $200 to **$250.00**
Cremona, vase, 12", from $350 to **$400.00**
Dahlrose, bowl vase, #420, 4", from $150 to............**$175.00**
Dahlrose, candlesticks, #1069, 3½", pr, from $175 to..**$225.00**
Dawn, ewer, #834-16, 16", pink or yellow, from $800 to...**$900.00**
Dawn, vase, #833-12, green, 12", from $500 to **$600.00**
Dogwood I, vase, 14½", from $550 to......................**$650.00**
Dogwood I, window box w/liner, 5½x13½", from $350 to..**$400.00**
Dogwood II, jardiniere, 6", from $150 to **$175.00**
Dogwood II, vase, 7", from $200 to..........................**$250.00**
Donatello, compote, 5", from $125 to........................**$175.00**
Donatello, powder jar, 2x5", from $450 to **$550.00**
Donatello, vase, 12", from $350 to............................**$400.00**
Earlam, candlesticks, #1080, 4", pr, from $600 to **$650.00**
Earlam, planter, #89, 5½x10½", from $400 to **$450.00**
Falline, candle holders, #1092, tan, 4", pr, from $800 to.**$1,000.00**
Falline, vase, #646, blue, 8", from $1,200 to **$1,400.00**
Florane, basket, 8½", from $300 to **$350.00**
Florane, bowl, 5", from $125 to.................................**$150.00**
Florane (late line), bowl, 10", from $30 to **$35.00**
Florane (late line), planter box, 6", from $25 to **$30.00**
Florentine, candlestick, 10½", from $150 to **$175.00**
Florentine, double bud vase, 4½", from $100 to **$125.00**
Foxglove, cornucopia, #166-6, blue, 6", from $175 to ..**$200.00**
Foxglove, vase, #47-8, green/pink, 8½", from $275 to.**$325.00**
Freesia, basket, #390-7, tangerine, 7", from $225 to.**$250.00**
Freesia, candlesticks, #1160-2, green, 2", pr, from $140 to **$160.00**

Freesia, center bowl, #464-6, blue, 8½", from $125 to .**$150.00**

Fuchsia, center bowl, #353-14, blue, 4x15½", from $375 to **$425.00**

Fuchsia, vase, #891-6, green, 6", from $200 to.........**$225.00**

Futura, center bowl, #188, 4", from $700 to.............**$800.00**

Futura, frog for center bowl, #188, from $75 to **$100.00**

Futura, pillow vase, #81, 5x6", from $450 to............**$550.00**

Futura, vase, #382, 7", from $375 to **$450.00**

Futura, vase, #409, aka football urn, 9", from $1,250.00 to $1,500.00.

Gardenia, hanging basket, #661, 6", from $300 to....**$350.00**

Gardenia, window box, #658-8, 3x8½", from $100 to ...**$125.00**

Imperial I, basket, #7, 9", from $200 to **$250.00**

Imperial I, compote, 6½", from $175 to **$225.00**

Imperial II, bowl, 4½", from $400 to **$450.00**

Imperial II, hanging basket, 7", from $75 to **$100.00**

Imperial II, vase, tapered, 5", from $350 to.............**$400.00**

Iris, basket, #355-10, blue, 9½", from $475 to..........**$550.00**

Iris, center bowl, #362-10, pink or tan, 3½x12½", from $200 to **$225.00**

Iris, vase, #924-9, blue, 10", from $450 to **$475.00**

Ivory II, vase, #274-6, 6½", from $75 to **$95.00**

Ixia, center bowl, #330-7, 3½x10½", from $150 to...**$175.00**

Ixia, double candlestick, #1127, 3", from $150 to.....**$175.00**

Jonquil, #541, 7", from $400 to...............................**$475.00**

Jonquil, candlesticks, #1982, 4", pr, from $450 to.....**$550.00**

La Rose, jardiniere, 6½", from $150 to.....................**$175.00**

La Rose, vase, 4", from $125 to **$150.00**

Laurel, bowl, #252, green, 3½", from $500 to...........**$550.00**

Laurel, vase, #674, russet, 9½", from $600 to............**$700.00**

Lotus, bowl, #L6-9, 3x9", from $150 to **$175.00**

Luffa, jardiniere, #631, 7", from $350 to..................**$400.00**

Luffa, vase, #689, 8", from $650 to...........................**$750.00**

Magnolia, candlesticks, #1157-4½, 5", pr, from $120 to ..**$150.00**

Magnolia, cornucopia, #184-6, 6", from $85 to **$95.00**

Magnolia, ewer, #14-10, 10", from $175 to **$200.00**

Magnolia, planter, #183-6, 6", from $90 to................**$110.00**

Mayfair, flowerpot, #71-4, 4½", from $70 to...............**$85.00**

Mayfair, pitcher, #1101-5 or #1102-5, 5", ea, from $75 to ..**$85.00**

Mayfair, vase, #1106-12, 12½", from $90 to............**$100.00**

Ming Tree, conch shell, #563, 8½", from $90 to.....**$110.00**

Ming Tree, hanging basket, 6", from $225 to **$250.00**

Mock Orange, pillow vase, #930-8, 7", from $150 to..**$175.00**

Mock Orange, window box, #956-8, 8½x4½", from $100 to **$125.00**

Moderne, triple candle holder, #1112, 6", from $275 to..**$350.00**

Moderne, vase, #787, 6½", from $175 to **$225.00**

Montacello, vase, tan, 5", from $350 to **$400.00**

Montacello, basket, 6½", blue, from $1,200 to.......**$1,400.00**

Morning Glory, basket, #340, green, 10½", from $1,200 to..**$1,300.00**

Morning Glory, center bowl, #1102, 5", pr, from $750 to...**$850.00**

Moss, bowl vase, #290, pink/green or orange/green, 6", ea from $350 to...**$400.00**

Moss, triple candlesticks, #1108, blue, 7", from $600 to..**$700.00**

Mostique, bowl, 7", from $150 to.............................**$175.00**

Mostique, compote, 7", from $300 to.......................**$350.00**

Orian, center bowl, #275, yellow, 5x12", from $300 to...**$325.00**

Orian, vase, red, #733, 6", from $225 to...................**$250.00**

Peony, basket, #379-12, 11", from $250 to **$275.00**

Peony, conch shell, #436, 9½", from $110 to............**$135.00**

Peony, pitcher, #1326, 7½", from $275 to **$325.00**

Pine Cone, candlesticks, #112, brown, 2½", pr, from $150 to...**$175.00**

Pine Cone, center bowl, blue, 11", from $400 to......**$450.00**

Pine Cone, mug, #960-4, green, 4", from $300 to.....**$350.00**

Pine Cone, pitcher, #485-10, green, 10½", from $550 to...**$650.00**

Pine Cone, planter, #124, blue, 5", from $250 to......**$300.00**

Poppy, bowl, #642-3, gray-green, 3½", from $100 to ...**$125.00**

Poppy, ewer, #880-18, pink, 18½", from $1,000 to...**$1,100.00**

Primrose, vase, #761-6, blue or pink, 6½", from $175 to...**$200.00**

Raymor, gravy boat, #190, 9½", from $30 to **$35.00**

Raymor, shirred egg, #200, 10", from $40 to **$45.00**

Raymor, water pitcher, #189, 10", from, $100 to **$150.00**

Rosecraft Blended, bud vase, #36-6, from $90 to **$110.00**

Rosecraft Blended, jardiniere, 4", from $90 to...........**$100.00**

Rosecraft Hexagon, candlestick, blue, 8", from $550 to..**$600.00**

Rosecraft Hexagon, vase, brown, 4", from $175 to...**$225.00**

Rosecraft Panel, bowl vase, brown, 4", from $150 to ...**$175.00**

Rosecraft Panel, covered jar, green, from $600 to **$700.00**

Rosecraft Vintage, bowl, 3", from $125 to **$150.00**

Rosecraft Vintage, vase, 12", from $550 to **$650.00**

Rozane 1917, bowl, green background, 3", from $100 to..**$125.00**

Rozane 1917, urn, 6½", from $175 to **$200.00**

Russco, vase, heavy crystals, 7", from $200 to **$225.00**

Russco, vase, 9½", from $150 to **$175.00**

Savona, console bowl, 4x10", from $125 to **$150.00**

Savona, flowerpot & saucer, 6", from $250 to...........**$300.00**

Silhouette, double planter, #757-9, 5½", from $125 to..**$150.00**

Silhouette, ewer, #716-6, 6½", from $100 to.............**$125.00**

Snowberry, center bowl, #1BL-8, green, 11", from $125 to...**$150.00**

Snowberry, ewer, #1TK-15, blue or pink, 16", from $600 to..**$700.00**
Snowberry, pillow vase, #1FH-6, blue or pink, 6½", from $150 to..**$175.00**
Sunflower, center bowl, 3x12½", from $900 to......**$1,000.00**

**Sunflower, vase, #493, 10",
from $1,500.00 to $1,700.00.**

Sunflower, window box, 3½x11", from $900 to **$1,000.00**
Teasel, vase, #881-6, light blue or tan, 6", from $175 to .**$200.00**
Teasel, vase, #887-10, dark blue or rust, 10", from $450 to...**$500.00**
Thorn Apple, bowl vase, #305-6, 6½", from $200 to ..**$250.00**
Thorn Apple, double bud vase, #1119, 5½", from $175 to **$225.00**
Topeo, center bowl, blue, 13", from $400 to **$450.00**
Topeo, vase, red, 14", from $900 to.......................**$1,000.00**
Tourmaline, bowl, 8", from $75 to **$100.00**
Tourmaline, pillow vase, 6", from $100 to **$125.00**
Tuscany, vase, gray/light blue, 12", from $225 to.....**$250.00**
Tuscany, vase, pink, 4", from $100 to........................**$125.00**
Velmoss, vase, #718, 8", red, from $350 to...............**$400.00**
Velmoss, vase, #722, green, 14½", from $600 to.......**$650.00**
Velmoss, vase, 8", from $200 to................................**$250.00**
Velmoss Scroll, vase, 5", from $150 to **$175.00**
Volpato, vase, 12", from $250 to...............................**$300.00**
Water Lily, hanging basket, #468/USA, blue, 9", from $350 to...**$375.00**
Water Lily, vase, #78-9, rose w/green, 9", from $350 to..**$400.00**
White Rose, candlesticks, #1142, 4½", pr, from $125 to..**$150.00**
White Rose, double bud vase, #148, 4½", from $85 to.....**$95.00**
Wincraft, bookends, #259, 6½", pr, from $175 to **$225.00**
Wincraft, cornucopia, #221-8, 9x5", from $150 to.....**$175.00**
Windsor, center bowl, blue, 3½x10½", from $450 to ..**$550.00**
Windsor, vase, #546, rust, from $300 to....................**$350.00**
Zephyr Lily, candlesticks, #1162-2, blue, 2", pr, from $150 to...**$175.00**
Zephyr Lily, fan vase, #205-6, green, 6½", from $125 to..**$150.00**
Zephyr Lily, hanging basket, 7½", from $300 to.......**$350.00**

Royal China

The dinnerware and kitchenware lines made by Royal China of Sebring, Ohio (1934 – 1986), have become very collectible, those cataloged here in particular. The most sought after today have as their origins supermarket and gas station promotions; some were given away, and others distributed by stamp companies. They were also retailed through major outlet stores such as Montgomery Ward, Sears Roebuck, and W.T. Grant.

The Royal China Company is credited with revolutionizing the dinnerware industry through the introduction of Kenneth Doyle's stamping machine in 1948. Prior to this innovative technique, decals were laboriously applied by hand.

Veteran collectors find that the number of shapes and patterns produced by Royal seems almost endless, and many can turn up in unexpected colors. For example, Currier & Ives is not restricted to blue but on rare occasions can be found in pink, yellow, green, black, and even multiple colorations. To simplify pattern identification, focus on the pattern's border which will nearly always be consistent. Memory Lane features a border of oak leaves and acorns. Bucks County, an exclusive of W.T. Grant, sports a gold Pennsylvania Dutch tulip-motif garland. Fair Oaks has magnolia blossoms surrounded by periwinkle edging. The Willows (Blue Willow, Pink Willow, Yellow, etc.) speak for themselves. Colonial Homestead and Old Curiosity Shop are typically found in green and are often mistaken one for the other. Here's how to tell the difference: Old Curiosity Shop's border depicts metal hinges and pulls, while Colonial Homestead's features wooden boards with pegged joints. Most Currier & Ives dinnerware pieces regardless of color will have the famous scroll border designed by art director Gordon Parker.

Be on the lookout for matching accessories by a variety of manufacturers. These were done in all sorts of media including paper, plastic, glass, and metal. A wide variety of coordinating items can be found including clocks, lamps, placemats, and bakeware that match a number of Royal patterns. These items are disappearing fast but none quicker than the matching glassware, most notably Gay Fad. From three-ounce juice tumblers to fourteen-ounce Zombie glasses, these items were produced in several treatments and styles in clear, frosted, and milk glass.

Our advisor is happy to answer any questions on American clay products from figurines to dinnerware via e-mail. For further reading on this subject with an emphasis on Currier & Ives, we highly recommend *A Collector's Guide for Currier & Ives Dinnerware by the Royal China Company* by Elden R. Aupperle (with 2001 Price Guide, 112 pages, soft cover) as well as the newsletter and clubs listed below.

Advisor: BA Wellman (See Directory, Dinnerware)

Club/Newsletter: *Currier and Ives China by Royal*
c/o Jack and Treva Hamlin
145 Township Rd. 1088, Proctorville, OH 45669; 740-886-7644

Club: C&I Dinnerware Collectors
E.R. Aupperle, Treasurer
29470 Saxon Road
Toulon, IL 61483
309-896-3331, fax: 309-856-6005, www.royalchinaclub.com

Blue Heaven, bowl, fruit nappy; 5½" **$3.00**
Blue Heaven, bowl, vegetable; 10" **$20.00**
Blue Heaven, creamer **$5.00**
Blue Heaven, cup & saucer **$5.00**
Blue Heaven, gravy boat...**$15.00**
Blue Heaven, plate, dinner; 10"..................................**$6.00**
Blue Heaven, platter, tab handles, 10½".....................**$20.00**
Blue Heaven, sugar bowl...**$8.00**
Blue Willow, ashtray, 5½"..**$12.00**
Blue Willow, bowl, cereal; 6¼"....................................**$15.00**
Blue Willow, bowl, fruit nappy; 5½" **$6.50**
Blue Willow, bowl, soup; 8¼".......................................**$15.00**
Blue Willow, bowl, vegetable; 10" **$22.00**
Blue Willow, butter dish, ¼-lb **$45.00**
Blue Willow, casserole, w/lid.......................................**$95.00**
Blue Willow, creamer...**$6.00**
Blue Willow, cup & saucer **$6.00**
Blue Willow, gravy boat, double spout **$22.00**
Blue Willow, pie plate, 10"...**$30.00**
Blue Willow, plate, bread & butter; 6¼".......................**$3.00**
Blue Willow, plate, dinner; 10".....................................**$8.00**
Blue Willow, plate, salad; rare, 7¼".............................**$7.00**
Blue Willow, platter, oval, 13" **$32.00**
Blue Willow, platter, serving; tab handles, 10½" **$20.00**
Blue Willow, salt & pepper shakers, pr.......................**$25.00**
Blue Willow, sugar bowl, w/lid.....................................**$15.00**
Blue Willow, teapot..**$125.00**
Blue Willow, tray, tidbit; 2-tier **$75.00**
Buck's County, ashtray, 5½"...**$15.00**
Buck's County, bowl, soup; 8½"....................................**$18.00**
Buck's County, bowl, vegetable; 10"............................**$28.00**
Buck's County, casserole, w/lid **$125.00**
Buck's County, creamer...**$8.00**
Buck's County, cup & saucer.......................................**$8.00**
Buck's County, gravy boat, double spout....................**$28.00**
Buck's County, plate, bread & butter; 6¼" **$4.00**
Buck's County, plate, dinner; 10"................................**$12.00**
Buck's County, platter, oval, 13"..................................**$45.00**
Buck's County, platter, serving; tab handles, 10½".....**$25.00**
Buck's County, salt & pepper shakers, pr **$25.00**
Buck's County, sugar bowl, w/lid **$18.00**
Buck's County, teapot **$145.00**
Colonial Homestead, bowl, cereal; 6¼" **$15.00**
Colonial Homestead, bowl, fruit nappy; 5½" **$4.00**
Colonial Homestead, bowl, soup; 8¼".........................**$12.00**
Colonial Homestead, bowl, vegetable; 10" **$20.00**
Colonial Homestead, casserole, angle handles, w/lid.**$75.00**
Colonial Homestead, chop plate, 12"..........................**$18.00**
Colonial Homestead, creamer.....................................**$5.00**
Colonial Homestead, cup & saucer **$5.00**
Colonial Homestead, gravy boat, double spout..........**$15.00**

Colonial Homestead, pie plate **$25.00**
Colonial Homestead, plate, bread & butter; 6".............**$2.00**
Colonial Homestead, plate, dinner; 10".......................**$5.00**
Colonial Homestead, plate, salad; rare, 7¼" **$7.00**
Colonial Homestead, platter, oval, 13" **$24.00**
Colonial Homestead, platter, serving; tab handles, 10½" ..**$15.00**
Colonial Homestead, salt & pepper shakers, pr..........**$18.00**
Colonial Homestead, sugar bowl, w/lid........................**$15.00**
Colonial Homestead, teapot...**$95.00**

Currier & Ives

Note that our prices are for items in the blue pattern. This line was made on a very limited basis in pink as well. To evaluate that color, you'll have to double our values.

Currier & Ives, ashtray, 5½", from $15 to **$18.00**
Currier & Ives, bowl, cereal; round (various sizes made) ..**$15.00**
Currier & Ives, bowl, fruit nappy; 5½"...........................**$5.00**
Currier & Ives, bowl, salad/cereal; tab handle, 6¼" ...**$35.00**
Currier & Ives, bowl, soup; 8½"....................................**$14.00**
Currier & Ives, bowl, vegetable; deep, 10", from $30 to..**$35.00**
Currier & Ives, bowl, vegetable; 9" **$25.00**
Currier & Ives, butter dish, Fashionable, ¼-lb, from $40 to .**$55.00**
Currier & Ives, casserole, angle handles, w/lid.........**$115.00**
Currier & Ives, casserole, tab handles, w/lid.............**$250.00**
Currier & Ives, clock plate, blue numbers, 2 decals, from $150 to...**$200.00**
Currier & Ives, clock plate, non-factory.....................**$50.00**
Currier & Ives, creamer, angle handle........................**$8.00**

Currier & Ives, sugar bowl, flared top, no handle, $48.00; candle lamp, from $250.00 to $300.00; creamer, tall, round handle, $48.00. (This rare creamer and sugar bowl was restyled in the 1960s for Montgomery Ward.) (Photo courtesy Jack and Treva Hamlin)

Currier & Ives, cup & saucer **$6.00**

Currier & Ives, gravy boat, double spout, from $20 to..**$25.00**

Currier & Ives, gravy boat, tab handles, w/liner (like 7" plate), from $100 to......................................**$135.00**

Currier & Ives, gravy ladle, 3 styles, ea from $35 to ..**$50.00**

Currier & Ives, pie baker, 10", (depending on picture) from $30 to......................................**$90.00**

Currier & Ives, plate, bread & butter; 6⅜", from $3 to..**$5.00**

Currier & Ives, plate, calendar; ca 1969-86, ea from $25 to **$75.00**

Currier & Ives, plate, chop; Getting Ice, 11½", from $35 to **$45.00**

Currier & Ives, plate, chop; Getting Ice, 12¼" **$38.00**

Currier & Ives, plate, chop; Rocky Mountains, 11½"..**$65.00**

Currier & Ives, plate, dinner; 10"......................................**$7.00**

Currier & Ives, plate, luncheon; very rare, 9"..............**$25.00**

Currier & Ives, plate, salad; rare, 7" **$15.00**

Currier & Ives, platter, oval, 13"......................................**$35.00**

Currier & Ives, platter, tab handles, 10½" dia, from $20 to......................................**$30.00**

Currier & Ives, salt & pepper shakers, pr, from $30 to......................................**$35.00**

Currier & Ives, sugar bowl, angle handles **$18.00**

Currier & Ives, sugar bowl, no handles, w/lid............**$35.00**

Currier & Ives, teapot, many different styles & stampings, from $110 to......................................**$150.00**

Currier & Ives, tidbit tray, 2- or 3-tier, abundant, from $50 to......................................**$125.00**

Currier & Ives, tumbler, iced tea; glass, 12-oz, 5½"....**$18.00**

Currier & Ives, tumbler, juice; glass, 5-oz, 3½", from $8 to..**$12.00**

Currier & Ives, tumbler, old-fashioned; glass, 3¼", from $8 to......................................**$15.00**

Currier & Ives, tumbler, water; glass, 4¾" **$15.00**

Fair Oaks, bowl, divided vegetable..............................**$45.00**

Fair Oaks, bowl, soup......................................**$15.00**

Fair Oaks, bowl, vegetable; 9"......................................**$30.00**

Fair Oaks, butter dish......................................**$45.00**

Fair Oaks, casserole, w/lid......................................**$135.00**

Fair Oaks, creamer......................................**$12.00**

Fair Oaks, cup & saucer......................................**$8.00**

Fair Oaks, plate, bread & butter **$3.00**

Fair Oaks, plate, dinner; 10"......................................**$12.00**

Fair Oaks, platter, tab handles, 10½" **$22.00**

Fair Oaks, salt & pepper shakers, pr **$25.00**

Fair Oaks, sugar bowl, w/lid **$18.00**

Fair Oaks, teapot **$125.00**

Memory Lane, bowl, cereal; 6¼"......................................**$15.00**

Memory Lane, bowl, fruit nappy; 5½" **$5.00**

Memory Lane, bowl, soup; 8½"......................................**$12.00**

Memory Lane, bowl, vegetable; 10" **$25.00**

Memory Lane, butter dish, ¼-lb **$35.00**

Memory Lane, creamer......................................**$6.00**

Memory Lane, gravy boat, double spout **$18.00**

Memory Lane, gravy boat liner, from $12 to **$15.00**

Memory Lane, gravy ladle, plain, white, for all sets, from $45 to......................................**$65.00**

Memory Lane, plate, bread & butter; 6⅜"....................**$3.00**

Memory Lane, plate, chop; 12"......................................**$25.00**

Memory Lane, plate, chop; 13"......................................**$35.00**

Memory Lane, plate, dinner......................................**$8.00**

Memory Lane, plate, luncheon; rare, 9¼"....................**$15.00**

Memory Lane, plate, salad; rare, 7"..............................**$10.00**

Memory Lane, platter, oval, 13"......................................**$35.00**

Memory Lane, platter, tab handles, 10½"....................**$15.00**

Memory Lane, salt & pepper shakers, pr....................**$25.00**

Memory Lane, sugar bowl, w/lid..................................**$15.00**

Memory Lane, tumbler, iced tea; glass......................**$18.00**

Memory Lane, tumbler, juice; glass **$9.00**

Old Curiosity Shop, bowl, fruit nappy; 5½" **$5.00**

Old Curiosity Shop, bowl, soup/cereal; 6½" **$15.00**

Old Curiosity Shop, bowl, vegetable; 9"......................**$22.00**

Old Curiosity Shop, bowl, vegetable; 10"....................**$25.00**

Old Curiosity Shop, casserole, w/lid............................**$90.00**

Old Curiosity Shop, creamer......................................**$6.00**

Old Curiosity Shop, cup & saucer **$5.00**

Old Curiosity Shop, plate, bread & butter; 6⅜" **$3.00**

Old Curiosity Shop, plate, dinner; 10" **$6.00**

Old Curiosity Shop, platter, tab handles, 10½" **$15.00**

Old Curiosity Shop, salt & pepper shakers, pr............**$20.00**

Old Curiosity Shop, sugar bowl, w/lid **$12.00**

Old Curiosity Shop, teapot **$115.00**

Royal Copley

This is a line of planters, wall pockets, vases, and other novelty items, most of which are modeled as appealing animals, birds, or human figures. They were made by the Spaulding China Company of Sebring, Ohio, from 1942 until 1957. The decoration is underglazed and airbrushed, and some pieces are trimmed in gold (which can add 25% to 50% to their values). Not every piece is marked, but they all have a style that is distinctive. Some items are ink stamped; others have (or have had) labels.

Royal Copley is really not hard to find, and unmarked items may sometimes be had at bargain prices. The more common pieces seem to have stabilized, but the rare and hard-to-find examples are showing a steady increase. Your collection can go in several directions; for instance, some people choose a particular animal to collect. If you're a cat lover, they were made in an extensive assortment of styles and sizes. Teddy bears are also popular; you'll find them licking a lollipop, playing a mandolin, or modeled as a bank, and they come in various colors as well. Wildlife lovers can collect deer, pheasants, fish, and gazelles, and there's also a wide array of songbirds.

If you'd like more information, we recommend *Collector's Guide to Royal Copley Plus Royal Windsor & Spaulding, Books I* and *II,* by Joe Devine.

Advisor: Joe Devine (See Directory, Royal Copley)

Ashtray, butterfly shape, USA on bottom, paper label, 5x9" **$25.00**

Bank, Farmer Pig, paper label, flat unglazed bottom w/2 holes, 5½"......................................**$80.00**

Bank, teddy bear, black & white w/red bow at neck, pink sucker held vertically, paper label, 8".................**$175.00**

Candle holder/planter, star & angel, yellow & white, 3 runners, paper label, 6¾" **$30.00**

Candy dish, leaf shape, impressed USA on bottom....**$25.00**

Coaster, antique auto center, 4⅝"................................**$40.00**

Coaster, Dutch painting w/man & woman in garden, 4⅝".**$40.00**

Creamer, leaf handle, 3" **$35.00**

Dogwood plaque planter, Home Is Where the Heart Is, #69, 4½"...**$30.00**

Figurine, Blackamoor, 8½", from $24.00 to $26.00.

Figurine, cat, black w/red bow at neck, paper label, 8"..**$90.00**

Figurine, nuthatch, paper label, hand-painted mask, 4½"....**$18.00**

Figurine, rooster, black & white on green base, paper label, 8" **$110.00**

Figurine, sea gull, white w/gold trim, 8" **$55.00**

Figurine, spaniel, seated, paper label, 6¼"..................**$25.00**

Figurine, wren, paper label, 3½".................................**$32.00**

Lamp, birds in the bower, paper label, 8" **$60.00**

Lamp, pig, flat unglazed bottom, 6½".........................**$100.00**

Lamp Oriental boy or girl, paper label, 7½", ea **$85.00**

Pitcher, Floral Beauty, 8"...**$50.00**

Planter, Bamboo, oval, 3 runners, paper label, 5¾" ...**$15.00**

Planter, barefooted boy, tan hat, paper label, 7½" **$45.00**

Planter, Big Blossoms, green stamp, 3".......................**$12.00**

Planter, black & white dog at mailbox, paper label, 8½", from $100 to...**$125.00**

Planter, boy w/bucket, black trousers w/blue jacket & hat, paper label, 6¼"..**$35.00**

Planter, cat, black, red bow at neck, paper label, 8"..**$50.00**

Planter, cat, white w/pink eyes & black bow at neck, resting, 5¾"x7½"..**$150.00**

Planter, clown, 2 runners, paper label, 8¼" **$85.00**

Planter, cockatiel, bird on kidney-shaped planter, paper label, 8½" **$60.00**

Planter, deer & fawn, 2 runners, paper label, 8¼" **$35.00**

Planter, dog, Stuffed Animal Series, paper label, 5½" ...**$50.00**

Planter, dog in picnic basket, paper label, 7¾" **$75.00**

Planter, fish decor, oval, paper label, 3¾"..................**$30.00**

Planter, Flower Arrangment, green stamp, 3½"...........**$12.00**

Planter, Linley decal, gold stamp on bottom, 4" **$15.00**

Planter, Oriental girl beside a bale of bamboo, 3 runners, paper label, 7¾"...**$65.00**

Planter, Playful Norma in Basket, pink or blue scarves, paper label, 8"...**$85.00**

Planter, poodle, white, sitting beside planter, 7⅛"x5½"..**$50.00**

Planter, Three Tracks, 2 runners, paper label, 4½".....**$18.00**

Razor blade receptacle, barber pole, outlined in gold, paper label, BLADE in black, 6¼"............................**$75.00**

Sugar bowl, rose & yellow w/green leaf-shaped handles, raised letters on bottom, 3"...................................**$35.00**

Tidbit, triangular w/brass center handle, molded rooster design at corners w/tracks between, 7⅞"............**$30.00**

Vase, Blue Beauty, gold stamp on bottom, outlined in gold, paper label, 6¾"..**$14.00**

Vase, fish, yellow & black w/brown stripe, paper label, 6" **$60.00**

Vase, Floral Elegance, raised letters on bottom, 8" **$25.00**

Vase, Lord's Prayer, cylindrical, decal, #339, green, 8"..**$45.00**

Vases, white with ivy, gold trimmed, from $25.00 to $35.00 each.

Royal Haeger

Many generations of the Haeger family have been associated with the ceramic industry. Starting out as a brickyard in 1871, the Haeger Company (Dundee, Illinois) progressed to include artware in their production as early as 1914. That was only the beginning. In the '30s they began to make a line of commercial artware so successful that as a result a plant was built in Macomb, Illinois, devoted exclusively to its production.

Royal Haeger was their premium line. Its chief designer in the 1940s was Royal Arden Hickman, a talented artist and sculptor who also worked in mediums other than pottery. For Haeger he designed a line of wonderfully stylized animals and birds, high-style vases, and human figures and masks with extremely fine details.

Paper labels were used extensively before the mid-'30s. Royal Haeger ware has an in-mold script mark, and their Flower Ware line (1954 – 1963) is marked 'RG' (Royal Garden).

Collectors need to be aware that certain glazes can bring two to three times more than others. For those wanting to learn more about this pottery, we recommend *Haeger Potteries Through the Years* by David D. Dilley (L-W Book Sales).

Advisor: David D. Dilley (See Directory, Royal Haeger)

Club: Haeger Pottery Collectors of America
Lanette Clarke
5021 Toyon Way
Antioch, CA 94509, 925-776-7784; Monthly newsletter available

Ashtray, foot shape w/footprint design, green w/olive green specks, Royal Haeger USA #175, 11½x6¼x1½" ...**$15.00**

Ashtray, oblong w/convex sides, cream drip glaze over Pumpkin, Royal Haeger #1016-S USA (also w/H foil label), 18x4½" **$20.00**

Ashtray, palm leaf form, Green Agate, Royal Haeger #134 USA, 19x4 14x2¼" **$15.00**

Ashtray, rectangular, Briar Agate, Royal Haeger c #R-125 USA, 4½x8"..**$8.00**

Ashtray, sq acorn leaf shape w/applied acorns, green, Haegar c 1976 #2145, 9¾x9¾" **$10.00**

Ashtray, sq w/deep round bowl, corners turned up, Gold Tweed, Royal Haeger #109-S USA, 7x7x2¼" **$10.00**

Bookend/planter, ball form, Chartreuse, Genuine Haeger on foil label, 7x5x4¾", pr.................................**$35.00**

Bookend/planter, panthers on bases, glossy Ebony, Royal Haeger #R-638 USA, 1950s, 7¾" & 7½", pr **$150.00**

Bookend/planter, stallion head, Chartreuse, #R-641 (unmarked), 8¾x5½x3½"...................................**$50.00**

Bowl, incurvate rim, brown & dark purple, #106 (unmarked), ca 1930, 3x8" dia..................................**$30.00**

Bowl, leaf form, Ebony & Chartreuse, Royal Haeger #R-877 USA, ca 1951, 7½x3¾x2¼" **$20.00**

Bowl, ring-shaped w/embossed daisies, Chartreuse, Royal Haeger USA, #R-224 (unmarked), 2x11¾" dia......**$40.00**

Bowl, white w/orange, yellow & reddish brown streaks on rough bisque, Royal Haeger USA..., #3177 (unmarked), 11" dia..**$25.00**

Bowl/planter, octagonal w/tapered sides, embossed rope pattern, Peasant Red, white interior, Haeger #834 USA, 8½" dia..**$8.00**

Candle holder, cornucopia, Green Briar, #R-312 (unmarked), ca 1949, 5½x5x2¾".......................................**$10.00**

Candle holder, double tier block form w/rounded corners & top, #R-579 (unmarked), 2½x2x2"......................**$20.00**

Candle holder, triple plum, Mauve Agate, #R-433 (unmarked), 5x11"...**$25.00**

Candle holders, oval bowl w/4 fluted corners, Blue Crackle, Haeger #3004 c, 1⅜x5¾x3¼", pr **$15.00**

Candle holders, oval bowl w/4 fluted corners, Peacock, Haeger #3004 c, 1⅜x5¾x3¼", pr **$25.00**

Candy dish, triple shell form w/fish finial, blue, USA, #R-459 (unmarked), ca 1946, 3x8½".........................**$50.00**

Candy dish, 4 leaves w/center metal handle, Mandarin Orange, Haeger c #8044-H, 6½x8¾x8¾"..............**$15.00**

Cigarette box, 3 horse heads form finial on flat lid on rectangular box, Green Agate, Royal Haeger #R-685 USA, 6¾x4x5"..**$75.00**

Cigarette lighter, ball form, blue w/black streaks, #8167 (unmarked), 3½x3" dia...................................**$15.00**

Cigarette lighter, ribbed cylinder, Mandarin Orange, Haeger in H on foil label, #899, 1950s-60s, 5x3" dia **$15.00**

Cigarette lighter, vertical fish form, Jade Crackle, #812-H, 1960s, 10x4" dia base **$30.00**

Compote, hexagonal, Lilac, Royal Haeger c #342 USA, 6x7"..**$15.00**

Compote, oval, Cotton White & Turquoise, Haeger c #3003 USA & Haeger in H design foil label, 4½x12" **$15.00**

Dish, oval w/deep fluting, peach & cream w/blue & green, Royal Haeger by Royal Hickman/USA #309, 15x8x3"..........**$30.00**

Dish, pheasant shape, Gold Tweed, Royal Haeger c #329-H USA, 21¼x7¼x5½"..................................**$40.00**

Dish, shell form, Chartreuse & Silver Spray, Royal Haeger #R-97 USA, 14x7½x2¾" **$30.00**

Dish, spiral plume shape, Peach Agate, Royal Haeger by Royal Hickman Made in USA #R-277, ca 1942, 1x7" **$20.00**

Dish, sq w/pointed upturned corners, blue w/black specks, Haeger #3961 USA, ca 1967-68, 8x8x2½" **$8.00**

Dish, water lily form, yellow-orange w/dark tips, Royal Haeger c #364-H USA, Handcrafted Haeger foil label, 16x9x2"..**$30.00**

Figurine, cocker spaniel, lying on belly w/legs spread out, brown w/black tail, #R-777 (unmarked), 1950s, 5½" L **$40.00**

Figurine, cocker spaniel mother, $50.00. (Photo courtesy David Dilley)

Figurine, duck, head looking up w/mouth open, white, #F-3 (unmarked), ca 1941, 5"..**$10.00**

Figurine, Egyptian cat, sitting upright winking (1 glass eye), Mandarin Orange, Royal Haeger c #616 USA, 1950s, 15½"..**$60.00**

Figurine, elephant trumpeting, Chartreuse & Honey, Royal-Haeger - Dundee Illinois on crown foil label, #R-784, 8½"..**$40.00**

Figurine, gypsy girl w/2 baskets, brown & green, #R-1224 (unmarked), 16½"..**$75.00**

Figurine, hen pheasant, Mauve Agate, #R-424 (unmarked), 5¼x15"..**$50.00**

Figurine, morning dove, wings down or up, brown or white, #650 or #649, ca 1973, 10" L, ea..........................**$15.00**

Figurine, rooster, brown w/white drip glaze, #R-1762, ca 1973, 20"...**$150.00**

Figurine, rooster, red w/green & black or Burnt Sienna, Royal Haeger #612 USA, 11", ea **$50.00**

Flower frog, birds (2) on domed base, Cloudy Blue, #R-359 (unmarked), 1940s, 8¾x5" dia base **$150.00**

Flower frog, frog looking over back, Chartreuse, Royal Haeger - Dundee Illinois on foil label, #R-838, 3¾x4½"....**$75.00**

Flower frog, nude astride fish, #R-363, yellow, 10", $125.00. (Photo courtesy David Dilley)

Lamp, petal louvre reflector, Walnut & Ebony, #5353 (unmarked), ca 1954, 11¼".................................**$50.00**

Lamp base, bucking bronco w/cactus finial, browns, caramel & green, #5190 (unmarked), 26" **$250.00**

Lamp base, fish riding wave, yellow, unmarked, 10½" base **$125.00**

Planter, colonial girl w/basket planter in crook of arm, Chartreuse, #3318 (unmarked), 9" **$20.00**

Planter, donkey cart, blue, #3296 (unmarked), ca 1943, 3x5" **$15.00**

Planter, owls (2) on planter, stylized, Green Marigold, Copyrighted The Haeger Potteries Inc Macomb Ill..., #H-72, 9"...**$30.00**

Planter, ring shaped on pedestal base, light green to dark green shading, Haeger c USA, #3819 (unmarked), 7½x10" dia...**$10.00**

Planter, tapered pot w/scrolled design between ribbed top & bottom bands, Roman Bronze, Haeger/Sascha B, #8172, 8¾"...**$75.00**

Vase, ball-shaped w/long skinny neck, Amethyst, Haeger — USA & Haeger in H - Craftsmen For A Century, #R-1919, 10⅜"..**$20.00**

Vase, goblet, metallic gold w/white interior, Haeger USA c, ##928, ca 1962-69, 9⅜"......................................**$15.00**

Vase, octagonal panels w/trumpet neck, Peasant Orange, Royal-Haeger-USA c, #4165 (unmarked), 11⅜" **$20.00**

Vase, pitcher w/long neck & squatty bulbous bottom, glossy & matt brown w/tan, Royal-Haeger-USA, #8183-X (unmarked), 12" **$15.00**

Vase, shell form on sq wave pedestal base, Chartreuse w/white interior, Royal Haeger - USA #321, 7¾".**$25.00**

Vase, 4-sided w/embossed vertical leaf design, Chartreuse & Silver Spray, Royal Haeger - #R-527 USA, 7¼".....**$25.00**

RumRill

RumRill-marked pottery was actually made by other companies who simply provided the merchandise that George Rumrill marketed from 1933 until his death in 1942. Rumrill designed his own lines, and the potteries who filled the orders were the Red Wing Stoneware Company, Red Wing Potteries, Shawnee (but they were involved for only a few months), Florence, and Gonder. Many of the designs were produced by more than one company. Examples may be marked RumRill or with the name of the specific pottery.

For more information we recommend *Collector's Encyclopedia of Red Wing Art Pottery* and *Red Wing Art Pottery* by B.L. and R.L. Dollen (Collector Books).

Advisors: Wendy and Leo Frese, Three Rivers Collectibles (See Directory, Rum Rill)

Bowl, console; #?13, ivory, 4¾x12x3" **$30.00**

Candle holders, Manhattan Group, #554, seafoam green, 2⅞x3¾", pr..**$28.00**

Figurine, seal w/glass bowl on nose, #330, black, 8", +bowl **$135.00**

Jug, #50, bright yellow, 5½" **$65.00**

Pitcher, Gypsy Orange, #50, 8", no lid, $40.00, with lid, $75.00. (Photo courtesy B.L. and R.L. Dollen)

Vase, #320, embossed ribs, handles, green matt, 5¾"...**$40.00**

Vase, #504, dark yellow, trumpet neck, upturned handles, 7⅝x6"..**$40.00**

Vase, #638, ivory w/soft green interior, flared rim, handles, 5⅜"...**$45.00**

Vase, Grecian, #506, ivory, handles, 7¼"....................$45.00
Vase, H-4, pink speckles on white, 9x5½"..................$35.00
Vase, Miscellaneous Group, #504, light green opalescent matt, 7½"...........................$40.00
Vase, Novelty, no number, pale green, original sticker; RumRill made in USA, 4¼"...................$40.00
Vase, Swan Group, blended green, 3 swan handles, 1930s, 4½x7½"...................$150.00

Russel Wright Designs

One of the country's foremost industrial designers, Russel Wright, was also responsible for several lines of dinnerware, glassware, and spun aluminum that have become very collectible. American Modern, produced by the Steubenville Pottery Company (1939 – 1959) is his best known dinnerware and the most popular today. It had simple, sweeping lines that appealed to tastes of that period, and it was made in a variety of solid colors. Iroquois China made his Casual line, and because it was so serviceable, it's relatively easy to find today. It will be marked with both Wright's signature and 'China by Iroquois.' His spun aluminum is highly valued as well, even though it wasn't so eagerly accepted in its day, due to the fact that it was so easily damaged.

If you'd like to learn more about the subject, we recommend *The Collector's Encyclopedia of Russel Wright, Third Edition,* by Ann Kerr (Collector Books).

Note: Values are given for solid color dinnerware unless a pattern is specifically mentioned.

American Modern

The most desirable colors are Canteloupe, Glacier Blue, Bean Brown, and White; add 50% to our values for these colors. Chartreuse is represented by the low end of our range; Cedar, Black Chutney, and Seafoam by the high end; and Coral and Gray near the middle. To evaluate patterned items, deduct 25%.

Bowl, vegetable; divided; from $135 to.....................$150.00
Butter dish, from $200 to..........................$250.00
Ice box jar, from $250 to...........................$275.00
Plate, bread & butter; 6", from $6 to...........................$8.00
Plate, child's, from $60 to............................$80.00
Plate, dinner; 10", from $18 to.................................$20.00
Platter, from $45 to.......................................$50.00
Saucer, demitasse; from $25 to............................$30.00
Sugar bowl, redesigned, from $25 to.....................$30.00

Highlight

Bowl, soup/cereal; made in 2 sizes, ea from $30 to ..$35.00
Bowl, vegetable; oval, from $65 to.............................$75.00
Creamer, from $40 to....................................$55.00
Plate, dinner; from $35 to............................$40.00
Platter, oval, sm, from $50 to........................$75.00
Sugar bowl, from $65 to.................................$75.00

Iroquois Casual

To price Brick Red, Aqua, and Cantaloupe Casual, double our values; for Avocado, use the low end of the range. Oyster, White, and Charcoal are at the high end.

Bowl, cereal; 5", from $12 to.........................$15.00
Bowl, fruit; redesigned, 5¾", from $14 to $16.00
Butter dish, ½-lb, from $75 to.........................$125.00
Creamer, redesigned, from $25 to $30.00
Gravy stand, from $15 to..................................$20.00
Mug, restyled, from $70 to...............................$85.00
Plate, dinner; 10", from $12 to........................$15.00
Platter, oval, 14½", from $45 to...................$55.00
Sugar bowl, stacking, from $20 to............................$25.00

Knowles

The high end of the range should be used to evaluate solid-color examples.

Bowl, vegetable; divided, from $55 to........................$75.00
Creamer, from $35 to.................................$45.00
Cup & saucer, from $12 to..........................$16.00

Esquire, Snowflower pattern, creamer, $14.00; sugar bowl, $25.00.

Plate, dinner; 10¾", from $15 to.............................$18.00
Platter, oval, 13", from $45 to $55.00
Salt & pepper shakers, pr, from $30 to......................$40.00
Sauce boat, from $40 to...............................$50.00

Plastic

These values apply to Home Decorator, Residential, and Flair (which is at the high end of the range). Copper Penny and Black Velvet items command 50% more. Meladur items are all hard to find in good condition, and values can be basically computed using the following guidelines (except for the fruit bowl, which in Meladur is valued at $7.00 to $8.00).

Bowl, covered onion soup; #716, ea pc, from $18 to ..**$20.00**
Bowl, lug soup; #706, from $10 to..............................**$12.00**
Bowl, vegetable; #709, oval, deep, from $15 to..........**$18.00**
Bowl, vegetable; #714, divided, from $20 to..............**$25.00**
Creamer, #711, from $10 to....................................**$12.00**
Cup, #701, from $6 to..**$8.00**
Plate, dinner; #703, from $8 to **$10.00**
Saucer, #702, from $3 to..**$5.00**

Spun Aluminum

Bowl, from $75 to...**$95.00**
Casserole, from $150 to...**$200.00**
Cheese knife, from $75 to......................................**$100.00**
Gravy boat, from $150 to.......................................**$200.00**
Muddler, from $75 to..**$100.00**
Relish rosette, sm...**$75.00**
Sandwich humidor, from $150 to **$175.00**
Sherry pitcher, from $250 to **$275.00**
Vase, sm, from $75 to..**$125.00**
Waste basket, from $125 to.....................................**$150.00**

Sterling

Values are given for undecorated examples.

Bowl, bouillon; 7-oz, from $18 to **$20.00**
Celery, 11¼", from $28 to **$36.00**
Cup, demitasse; 3½-oz, from $65 to **$100.00**
Pitcher, water; 2-qt, from $125 to.............................**$150.00**
Plate, dinner; 10¼", from $10 to................................**$15.00**
Platter, oval, 10½", from $18 to **$20.00**
Sauce boat, 9-oz, from $25 to....................................**$27.00**
Sugar bowl, w/lid, 10-oz, from $22 to **$25.00**

White Clover (for Harker)

Bowl, vegetable; open, 7½", from $65 to...................**$75.00**
Bowl, vegetable; w/lid, 8¼", from $75 to.................**$100.00**
Clock, General Electric, from $75 to **$85.00**
Creamer, clover decor, from $25 to............................**$35.00**
Pitcher, clover decor, w/lid, 2-qt, from $100 to **$150.00**
Plate, barbecue; color only, 11", from $25 to.............**$35.00**
Plate, chop; clover decor, 11", from $40 to **$50.00**
Plate, dinner; clover decor, 9¼", from $18 to.............**$20.00**
Salt & pepper shakers, either size, pr, from $30 to **$35.00**
Sugar bowl, w/lid (individual ramekin), from $30 to .**$35.00**

Salt Shakers

Probably the most common type of souvenir shop merchandise from the '20 through the '60s, salt and pepper shakers can be spotted at any antique mall or flea market today by the dozens. Most were made in Japan and imported by various companies, though American manufacturers made their fair share as well. When even new shakers retail for $10.00 and up, don't be surprised to see dealers tagging the better vintage varieties with some hefty prices.

Miniature shakers are hard to find, and their prices have risen faster than any others'. They were all made by Arcadia Ceramics (probably an American company). They're under 1½" tall, some so small they had no space to accommodate a cork. Instead they came with instructions to 'use Scotch tape to cover the hole.'

Advertising sets and premiums are always good, since they appeal to a cross section of collectors. If you have a chance to buy them on the primary market, do so. Many of these are listed in the Advertising Character Collectibles section of this guide.

Recent sales have shown a rise in price for some low-line shakers that are being purchased not by salt shaker collectors but people with a connection to the theme or topic they represent. (Doctors will buy doctor-related shakers, etc.) Fishing shakers are on the rise, especially breed fish. High-end shakers are getting soft. Many of the vintage rare sets are being reproduced and redesigned so collectors can own a set at a more reasonable cost.

There are several good books which we highly recommend to help you stay informed: *Florence's Big Book of Salt & Pepper Shakers* by Gene Florence; *Salt and Pepper Shakers, Vols I, II, III,* and *IV,* by Helene Guarnaccia; and *The Collector's Encyclopedia of Salt and Pepper Shakers, Figural and Novelty, First* and *Second Series,* by Melva Davern. All are published by Collector Books.

See also Advertising Character Collectibles; Breweriana; Holt Howard; Occupied Japan; Regal China; Rosemeade; Shawnee; Vandor; and other specific companies.

Advisor: Judy Posner (See Directory, Salt and Pepper Shakers)

Club: Novelty Salt and Pepper Club
c/o Irene Thornburg, Membership Coordinator
581 Joy Rd.
Battle Creek, MI 49017
Publishes quarterly newsletter and annual roster. Annual dues: $20 in USA, Canada, and Mexico; $25 for all other countries

Advertising

Ballantine Ale Beer packs, cardboard w/metal lids, 2⅜",
　pr **$20.00**
Budweiser Budman, ceramic, Ceramarte Brazil, 1991, 3⅝",
　MIB **$45.00**
Cigarette pack & matches, Yenems Cigarette pack, ceramic,
　unmarked, 3¾", 2⅞", pr...**$24.00**
Cobalt Harvestore Silos, ceramic, marked S & P, 4¾", pr...**$55.00**
Conoco gas pumps, plastic w/decals, 2¾", MIB.........**$95.00**
Coors beer barrels, ceramic, Adolph Coors Golden Colorado,
　2", NM, pr...**$35.00**
Flour Fred, hard plastic figural, Spiller's Homepride Flour,
　3⅛", pr..**$55.00**
Goetz Country Club beer bottle, glass w/metal lids, applied
　decals, 4½", pr **$35.00**

Golden Guernsey Dairy milk bottles, glass w/metal lids, 1930s, 3⅜", pr $65.00

Kellogg's Snap & Pop, porcelain, multicolor details, Japan mark, 2½" $50.00

Magic Chef Range, milk glass w/image of Magic Chef on front, red plastic lids, 3½", pr $65.00

Nugget Sam, Nugget Casino, ceramic, Japan, 4", pr ...$75.00

Old Cliff House Restaurant, ceramic, seals on rock, flat unglazed bottoms, 3¾", pr $25.00

Old Dooley & Schultz Utica Beer steins, ceramic, marked Webco, taller: 4⅜", pr $125.00

Old Erie Beverage soda bottles, green glass w/heavy metal screw-off lids, 6", pr $35.00

Old Gunther Beer bottle, glass w/metal tops, foil labels, 4", pr $28.00

Old Life Soda bottles, glass w/decal labels & metal lids, 4½", EX, pr $75.00

Old Strasburg Railroad men, ceramic conductor & engineer, unmarked Japan, 4¼", pr $32.00

Peerless Beer Men, plastic figural, gnome-like characters, 1950s, 5", pr $95.00

Pep-Up Soda bottles, glass w/metal screw-off lids, 5¾", pr $55.00

Philips 66, plastic, $30.00 for the pair.

Pure Oil Company gas pumps, plastic, white w/red & white w/blue, 2¾", pr $135.00

Quaker Oats Co building, ceramic, white w/blue lettering, Japan mark, 3⅛", pr $35.00

Quaker State Motor Oil cans, heavy cardboard, 1940s-50s,½", EX, pr $40.00

Schlitz Beer bottles, glass w/metal lids, 4" bottles on wooden stand, 3-pc set..................................$22.00

Tuborg & Carlsberg Beer bottles, glass w/decals & metal lids, 2½" on original wooden stand, 3-pc set...............$30.00

Animals, Birds, and Fish

Baseball player elephant & bear, ceramic, bright colors, unmarked Japan, 1940s-50s, 4", pr $125.00

Bear artist & easel, ceramic, bear holds palette & has 1 eye closed, multicolor, unmarked, 3¼", pr $32.00

Bear driving car, ceramic, bright colors, car is 2nd shaker, Japan mark, 3½" overall, pr $35.00

Bees on hives, ceramic, S&P on wing handles, illegible mark, 3½", pr $22.00

Bird in hand, ceramic, multicolor, unmarked, 2½x3⅞", pr $35.00

Bluebirds, ceramic, multicolor w/rhinestone eyes, Japan sticker, Copyright #239, 3", pr $24.00

Cat & mouse, ceramic, realistic, flat unglazed bottoms, cat: 1¾x3¼", pr $28.00

Circus elephants w/hats, ceramic, realistic, multicolor cold paint, unmarked Japan, 4½", pr $24.00

Cow, ceramic, 1-pc, stamped B542, 10" L $26.00

Cow mother holding baby, ceramic, hand painted under the glaze, Made in Japan mark, 1950s, nesting pr $25.00

Dachshund, ceramic, gold trim, 1950s, 1-pc, 10" L.....$35.00

Dinosaurs, ceramic, green, resembles Dino, Made in Japan, 3¼", pr $35.00

Dogs w/hats smoking cigars, ceramic, multicolor, Japan mark, 1959, 3¼", pr $22.00

Elephant, ceramic, 1 w/umbrella, 2nd w/walking stick, black Japan mark, 1950s, 3½", pr $26.00

Frog on mushroom, bone china, foil label: Bone China Japan, 2", pr $14.00

Moose heads, ceramic, realistic looking, Victoria Ceramics Japan label, 1950s, 3", pr...................$28.00

Owls, bone china, white w/painted details, plastic corks, 2⅜", pr $14.00

Polar bears, ceramic, realistic, unmarked Japan, 1950s, 2¾x4⅜", pr $24.00

Purple cow on wire frame, ceramic shakers hang from frame, Japan, 4x5", 3-pc set..............................$30.00

Rabbit & cabbage, ceramic, multicolor, Parkcraft, 4", pr $25.00

Rabbits, ceramic, 1 w/umbrella, 2nd w/suitcase, Japan mark, 1950s, 3¼", pr $22.00

Rooster & hen, ceramic, realistic details, shiny multicolors, unmarked, 1950s era, 3¾", pr $22.00

Rooster & hen, ceramic, white w/red details & gold trim, Japan mark, 1950s, 2½", pr $20.00

Rooster & hen, clear glass w/gold metal heads, Czechoslovakia, 3", pr $30.00

Roosters, pink bisque, white w/blue & gold trim, Japan label, 1950s, 3½", pr $25.00

Scottie dogs, porcelain, red & blue, marked Germany, 1930s-40s, 2½", pr $28.00

Skunk & cent, ceramic, play on words: skunk & scent, 1950s, 2¾", pr $22.00

Spaniels, ceramic, realistic, Japan mark, 1950s, taller: 3", pr $24.00

Teddy bears play piggy back, ceramic, dressed, stacking, red Japan mark, 4¼", pr $18.00

Turtle, ceramic, poised on 3 feet, stacking shell is 2nd shaker, 1950s, 3⅝", 2-pc set $22.00

Black Americana

Chef busts, ceramic, 1 black w/yellow accents, 2nd yellow w/brown, unmarked, 1940s, 5⅜", pr **$40.00**

Chieftains, ceramic, from $35.00 to $45.00 for the pair. (Photo courtesy Helene Guarnaccia)

Clown-face teapots, red clay, bright cold paint, lid is yellow hat, wire bale handle, Japan paper label, 4", pr .. **$25.00**

Heads, red clay w/black glaze, he in chef's hat, she w/bandanna tied into a bow on top, embossed Japan mark, 2¾", pr **$35.00**

Mammy & chef, ceramic, hand painted under glaze, unmarked, Canada souvenir indicated on Mammy's apron, fat, 3¼", pr **$135.00**

Mammy & Pappy, ceramic, yellow attire, hands in pockets, Occupied Japan, pr **$50.00**

Mammy w/broom, ceramic, multicolor w/gold trim, Norcrest Fine China Japan labels, #H424, rare, 4¼", pr ... **$395.00**

Man w/bottles, ceramic, bottle shakers rest in his pockets, Germany, #8195, 6⅜", 3-pc set **$110.00**

Native boy leans into alligator's mouth, ceramic, unmarked Japan, 1950s, alligator: 5" L, pr **$65.00**

Native boy riding hippo, ceramic, boy plays banjo, hand-painted details, stacking, Japan, 1940s-50s, pr ... **$195.00**

Native couple, ceramic, she watches as he eats watermelon slice, unmarked Japan, 1950s, 4½", pr **$90.00**

Native graduates, ceramic, hand painted, red Japan stamp, 1950s, 3½", pr **$165.00**

Native ladies, ceramic, exaggerated ethnic caricatures, wearing only grass skirts, red Japan mark, 1950s, 3½", pr ... **$60.00**

Character

Aladdin & lamp, ceramic, maroon & white, flat unglazed bottoms, unmarked, 1950s, 2x3½", pr **$24.00**

Babar the elephant & girlfriend, ceramic, bright colors, unmarked, 3½", pr **$55.00**

Billy Sykes & Capt Cuttle, ceramic, made in England, 2½", pr **$40.00**

Bimbo (Betty Boop's dog), ceramic, cold-painted details, marked USA, 1930s, 2½", pr **$125.00**

Daisy Duck & grocery bag, ceramic, Walt Disney, The Good Company a Division of Applause, 3¼", pr **$40.00**

David the Gnome, ceramic, copyright 1979 Uleboek BV, 5", pr **$60.00**

Doc & Bashful dwarfs, ceramic, marked Foreign, 1930s, 2⅞", pr **$95.00**

Ferdinand the Bull, ceramic, Disney, black Japan mark, late 1930s, 2¾", pr **$90.00**

Goose & golden egg, ceramic, Vallona Starr, 5½", pr. **$45.00**

Goose & golden egg, ceramic, white w/gold trim, unmarked American, 1950s, goose: 3", pr **$30.00**

Heckle & Jeckle, ceramic, shiny multicolor, marked Japan & Miyao, 4¼", pr **$85.00**

Humpty Dumpty busts, ceramic, hand painted, unglazed bottoms, unmarked California pottery, 1½", pr **$26.00**

Jerry Colonna pushing cart w/suitcases (shakers), ceramic, Made in Japan label, 5", 3-pc set **$65.00**

Jock & Tramp, ceramic dogs, unmarked Japan, 1590s, Jock: 3x3", pr **$55.00**

Mammy & Pappy Yokum on sadiron shape, ceramic, 1968 Dogpatch USA, unmarked Japan import, pr **$60.00**

Mary w/lamb & schoolhouse, ceramic, flat unglazed bottoms, unmarked, ca 1950s, 3¼", pr **$30.00**

Miss Muffet & spider, ceramic, Poinsettia Studio, she: 2½", pr **$85.00**

Moon Mullins, glass w/hard plastic hats, cold-painted features, Japan label, 1930s, 3", pr **$55.00**

Old King Cole & throne, ceramic, stacking, marked Japan, foil label: Hand Painted Royal Japan, 1940s-50s, 4¼", pr **$55.00**

Old Mother Hubbard & dog, ceramic, gold trim, Poinsettia Studio, she: 3½", pr **$95.00**

Oswald & Homer, ceramic, Napco Japan #1C3635, copyright 1958 Walter Lantz Productions, 4", pr **$175.00**

Paul Bunyan & tree stump, porcelain, shiny multicolor, Made in Japan label, Paul: 4½", pr **$28.00**

Pebbles & Bamm-Bamm, ceramic, Harry James, Hanna-Barbera, 4", pr **$50.00**

Pinocchio, porcelain, multicolor, Made in Japan, 5", pr. **$165.00**

Pixie & Dixie, ceramic, mice dressed as cowboy & Indian, Made in Japan label, 3¼", pr **$55.00**

Pixie baseball players, ceramic, red clothes, Japan mark, 3½", pr **$75.00**

Pixie heads, multicolor ceramic, Japan #6981, 3¼", pr.. **$29.00**

Pixies riding rocket ships, ceramic, multicolor on white w/gold details, unmarked, 1950s, 2¾x3½", pr **$60.00**

Pluto, ceramic, cold paint, Walt Disney Productions, 1940s, 3¼", pr **$40.00**

Pluto & doghouse, ceramic, Disney, The Good Company a Division of Applause, 3¼", pr **$40.00**

Preacher & Dandy Crows, ceramic, Disney, Japan foil label, 1940s-50s, 4", pr **$90.00**

Raggedy Ann, ceramic, unmarked vintage import, 4", pr .. **$40.00**

Rockabye Baby & cradle, ceramic, stacking, Japan, 1950s, 3½x3⅝", pr **$40.00**

Rudolph the Red Nose Reindeer busts, ceramic, #4370, 3", pr **$28.00**

Sam Weller & Sairey Gamp, ceramic, Made in England, 3", pr **$40.00**

Si & Am, ceramic Siamese cats, Japan paper label, 3½", pr..**$90.00**

Tom Sawyer & fence, ceramic, multicolor, flat unglazed bottoms, unmarked Parkcraft, 3", pr.........................**$45.00**

Woody Woodpecker & Winnie, ceramic, W Lantz 1990 label, pr..**$49.00**

Yosemite Sam, ceramic, Lego paper label, 1960s, pr..**$125.00**

Ziggy & dog, ceramic, Universal Press Syndicates, 1979, Ziggy: 3¼", NM, pr....................................**$35.00**

Fruit, Vegetables, and Other Food

Anthropomorphic pear & orange people, ceramic, Japan (unmarked), crude paint, 2½", pr.........................**$20.00**

Carrots in upright bunch tied w/string, & similar celery, ceramic, Made in Japan label, 4⅛", pr.................**$12.00**

Corn in shuck, ceramic, Japan, pr.....................**$10.00**

Eggplant, ceramic, upright naturalistic depictions, no mark, 3¼"..**$10.00**

Fruit bowl, plastic, pineapple & orange form shakers, bowl is for sugar, 1950s, 4-pc set...................**$20.00**

Ice cream cones, glass w/metal dome lids, in metal stand, no mark, 5", pr..**$18.00**

Ladybug w/carrot & leaf, ceramic, 2⅞", pr.................**$12.00**

Lima beans, ceramic, naturalistic depictions, Japan, 3⅛", pr..**$10.00**

Oranges, ceramic, 1 whole, 1 half, Japan, 2¼", pr.......**$5.00**

Pears, ceramic, on center-handled leaf try, Japan, 2¾", pr..**$10.00**

Peppers, 1 green banana type, 1 red, plastic, in wicker-look basket, Hong Kong, 5⅜" L, pr....................**$15.00**

Pineapples, ceramic, natural colors, no mark, 3", pr....**$7.00**

Pineapples, ceramic, on tray w/hula dancer in center, no mark, 3"...**$12.00**

Red peppers, ceramic, Occupied Japan, 1⅜", pr........**$12.00**

Spice tins, metal, Radford Spices, Made in England, 3¼", pr..**$5.00**

Strawberry people, ceramic, Japan, 3", pr.................**$15.00**

Strawerries, ceramic, red w/green stem loop handles, 3", pr...**$8.00**

Watermelon halves, ceramic, Japan, 2¾", pr.................**$8.00**

Tomatoes, ceramic, in green basket, from $15.00 to $18.00 for the pair.

Holidays and Special Occasions

Christmas, Gingerbread man & lady, ceramic, embossed Japan, 4½", pr..**$20.00**

Christmas, Santa & Mrs Claus heads on tray, ceramic, Chap Stick Co, Hong Kong, #81604, pr.........................**$18.00**

Christmas, Santa & Mrs Claus in rockers, ceramic, unmarked Japan, 3⅞", pr..**$20.00**

Christmas, Santa & Mrs Claus sitting in rockers, ceramic, Napco AX 9/20/0, 3⅝", pr.............................**$25.00**

Christmas, Santa against trees, ceramic bell/shaker combination, 1950 Napco Cleve Ohio, Made in Japan label, pr...**$26.00**

Christmas, Santa faces, ceramic, cold paint, Japan paper label, pr..**$18.00**

Christmas, skunks in Santa hats, ceramic, Kriess, 3¾", pr..**$25.00**

Christmas, snowman & tree, ceramic, 2½", pr...........**$15.00**

Halloween, cat & skull on pile of books, ceramic, red Japan mark, 2⅜", pr..**$50.00**

Thanksgiving, John Alden & Priscilla, ceramic, Hallmark Cards Inc, 3¼", pr...**$15.00**

Thanksgiving, pilgrim & turkey, ceramic, Japan paper label, #29932, 5¼", pr....................................**$15.00**

Thanksgiving, turkeys, ceramic, National Potteries, Cleveland OH, Napco, 3¾", pr..................................**$15.00**

Household Items

Candlesticks, ceramic, black base, yellow cup, red candle, 3¾", pr..**$8.00**

Clocks, rough wood, Walking Glen NY, 3¼", pr.........**$10.00**

Coffee mills, ceramic, brown glaze, embossed Japan, 4", pr...**$10.00**

Dryers, plastic, Laundromat, 3", pr.....................**$15.00**

Irons, ceramic, 1 red, 1 white, gold trim, no mark, 3¼", pr...**$12.00**

Lamp, plastic shades on double iron frame, USA, 4¾", pr...**$10.00**

Light bulbs, amber glass, Taiwan, Republic of China, 3½", pr...**$5.00**

Mixer, plastic, Pat Pend, 4½"........................**$15.00**

Mugs, ceramic w/berry decals, Knotts Berry Farm, embossed Japan, 4½", pr..**$12.00**

Potbellied stoves, ceramic, black w/gold, no mark, 3⅞", pr...**$10.00**

Rolling pins, cedar wood, souvenir, 3½" L, pr.............**$5.00**

Skillets, chrome w/black handles & knobs, Pat Pend, 4⅝", pr...**$5.00**

Spinning wheels, ceramic w/brown drip glaze, Made in Japan paper label, 3¾", pr..................................**$15.00**

Steins, ceramic, white w/embossed tavern scene on brown band, no mark, 4⅞", pr.....................................**$12.00**

Telephone people, ceramic, Japan paper label, 2⅞", pr...**$55.00**

Toaster, chrome, Star Lite, Japan, 3¾".................**$15.00**

Toaster, plastic, in 2 parts, Carvanite, Los Angeles, USA, 4¼"..**$18.00**

Toaster & toast, plastic, toast pieces are shakers, pop-up action, 1950s, 3x4¼", MIB..................**$22.00**

TV, plastic, no mark, shakers inside, 3" **$18.00**

Miniatures

Bible & oil lamp, ceramic, lamp: 1½", NM, pr............**$20.00**

Bride & groom, ceramic, painted details, Japan marks, 2½", pr...**$26.00**

Candlesticks, ceramic, Arcadia, 1½", pr **$24.00**

Coal scuttle & bellows, ceramic, Arcadia, bellows: 1⅜", pr **$20.00**

Gift packages, ceramic, white w/fancy bows, 1950s, unmarked, pr..**$18.00**

Pipe & slippers, ceramic, unmarked, pipe, 2⅜", slippers: 2¼" L, pr...**$22.00**

Rainbow & pot of gold, ceramic, Arcadia, pot: ½", EX, pr....**$38.00**

Roller skates, ceramic, gold wheels, Arcadia, 1½", pr ..**$45.00**

Thimble & gold thread, No Silver Threads Among the Gold on top of spool, ceramic, Arcadia, 1¼", pr..................**$18.00**

People

Baseball batter & catcher, ceramic, cold painted (EX), black Japan marks, 1940s-50s, pr **$85.00**

Baseball umpire & batter, ceramic, multicolor, Japan paper labels, 5", pr **$75.00**

Boxing men, ceramic, painted details, corks in bottom of trunks, unmarked, 1940s-50s, 3½", pr..................**$50.00**

Boys in space suits, ceramic, white w/multicolor details, power packs on backs, Japan mark, 1590s, 3¾", pr............**$45.00**

Clowns, ceramic, bright hand-painted colors, Japan labels, 4½", pr..**$60.00**

Clowns, ceramic, seated w/legs & arms straight out, bright colors, Tilso Japan label, 1950s, 2¾x9¼", pr........**$60.00**

Clowns, ceramic, 1 seated, 2nd stands on head, red & white polka-dot suits, ZOG CA, 1940s-50s, tallest: 4½", pr..**$85.00**

Clowns, ceramic, 1 w/banjo, 2nd w/horn, multicolor, orange Japan mark, 1390s, 3½", pr......................................**$30.00**

Couple smile/frown turnabouts, ceramic, multicolor, Japan mark, 5", pr **$25.00**

Dutch girl & windmill, ceramic, multicolor, red Japan mark, 4¼", pr...**$34.00**

Hillbilly & jug, ceramic, multicolor, man dozing on pig 'pillow,' Japan label, 1950s, 1¾x4½", pr..................**$23.00**

Hula girls, ceramic, bright colors, EX details, marked Miko BES Copyright 1966, 6", pr **$135.00**

Hunter & rabbit, ceramic, brown & black w/white bunny, 1950s, hunter: 3½", pr **$22.00**

Lady praying & man under bed, ceramic, pastels, 1950s, lady: 3¼", pr...**$26.00**

Man & woman plug-in set, ceramic, multicolor, Japan, #7395, 5", pr..**$175.00**

Man about to flush himself down toilet, Good-Bye Cruel world, ceramic, Japan label, 1950s, pr..................**$40.00**

Martians, ceramic, I Just Arrived From Mars & Hi Ho I'm a Li Li Lo, Japan stickers, 3½", pr.....................................**$40.00**

Nude bather in tub, pottery, flat unglazed bottoms, unmarked (attributed to USA), 1950s, 2½x3¼", pr..................**$60.00**

Nude boy, Bruxelles on base, ceramic, 3⅝", pr..........**$28.00**

Nude girls leaning at sides of barrels, ceramic, unmarked, 1950s, pr...**$24.00**

Nude woman, ceramic, headless figure w/bust forming shakers, Japan label, 6½" long, 3-pc set.......................**$35.00**

Rabbis, rare subject matter, from $150.00 to $200.00 for the pair. (Photo courtesy Judy Posner)

Shoemaker & elf, ceramic, resembles majolica, multicolor, green Japan mark, 4", pr..**$32.00**

Skulls, ceramic, white w/brown detailing, Japan paper label, 3¼", pr...**$25.00**

Souvenir

Alamo, metal building replicas, bronze colors, original corks, Japan mark, 1¾x2½", pr **$50.00**

Alcatraz prison inmate busts, ceramic, multicolor, Japan import, 4½", pr..**$45.00**

Alcatraz prison inmates, ceramic, standing figures in striped clothes, Sonsco foil label (Japan import), 4½", pr......**$45.00**

Bahama policemen, ceramic, black & white uniforms, 1950s, 4⅜", pr..**$32.00**

Baseball players, Copalis Beach WA, ceramic, flat unglazed bottoms, unmarked, 1950s, 3½", pr **$85.00**

Bowling ball & pin, ABC 1951 & St Paul MN (bowling conference), ceramic, gold & ivory, pr **$22.00**

Canadian Soldier (Beefeater) Boys, ceramic, Ernsdale Canada foil stickers on backs, Made in Toronto, 4", pr....**$22.00**

Cigar & book w/Havana & products & sights, ceramic, Parkcraft, pr..**$40.00**

Eiffel Tower & book w/Paris City of Light..., ceramic, Parkcraft, tower: 4", pr **$35.00**

Grandfather clocks, House of David Benton Harbor MI, plastic, 4⅜", pr..**$26.00**

Jugs, Coney Island Ohio Amusement Park, ceramic, Made in USA Hand Crafted 22k gold, 1950s, 3½", pr **$14.50**

Miss America & New Jersey, ceramic, marked Parkcraft, Miss America 2⅞", pr **$50.00**

Movieland Wax Museum, metal cars on gold-tone metal tray, Made in Japan, 3-pc set...**$28.00**

Oranges cluster w/San Francisco Chinatown & symbol on fruit, ceramic, Japan mark, 1-pc **$20.00**

Oriental couple, Korea 67-68, carved stone (heavy), 4⅜", pr......................**$60.00**

Pagoda & book w/Tokyo & products, ceramic, Parkcraft, 2¾", pr......................**$40.00**

Potty & window, Arizona, ceramic, 1950s, window: 2¾", pr **$24.00**

Seashell, Fisherman's Wharf San Francisco decal, ceramic, flat unglazed bottom, 2½", pr......................**$10.00**

Shamrock & book w/Killarny & products, ceramic, Parkcraft, 2⅛", pr......................**$40.00**

Sheaf of wheat & book w/Kansas, ceramic, Parkcraft, pr..**$50.00**

Singing Tower, Lake Wales FL, silver-tone metal, 3½", pr..**$45.00**

Space Needle, ceramic, painted details, dated 1962, 4⅞", pr **$24.00**

Space shuttle, 8th Annual Novelty Salt & Pepper Convention, 1993, limited production, 5½"......................**$95.00**

Spouting Geyser Saratoga Springs New York, ceramic, Staffordshire Royal Winton Jonroth England, 2½", pr..**$24.00**

St Lawrence Seaway Ship, ceramic, stacks form shakers, Eisenhower Lock on side, 1950s, 2x6½", 3-pc set ..**$39.00**

Wrigley Building & book w/Chicago & products, ceramic, Parkcraft, 3½", NM, pr......................**$35.00**

1973 National Scout Jamboree, ceramic, gold trim on top, 2⅜x3", pr......................**$15.00**

Miscellaneous

Anthropomorphic comical train, ceramic, red Japan mark, 4-pc, 2½x9" L......................**$35.00**

Anthropomorphic spoon & fork people, ceramic, green Japan mark, 5⅛", pr......................**$30.00**

Barrels, wooden, Italy, 3½", pr......................**$10.00**

Battleship, red & white plastic, shakers as smokestacks, 4½"......................**$10.00**

Boots, ceramic, red w/flowers, Japan, 2½", pr..............**$7.00**

Bowling pins, ceramic, black w/red & white neck bands, no mark, 5", pr......................**$10.00**

Cigar in ashtray, ceramic, brown, white & yellow, unmarked, 1950s, 1½x2¼"......................**$20.00**

Covered wagons pulled by horses, chrome, Japan, 1⅞", pr......................**$8.00**

Feet, ceramic, red nails, no mark, 3¼", pr **$10.00**

Flying saucer, ceramic, Coventry China, 1950s, 1¼x2½x3", pr......................**$45.00**

Golf bag & ball, ceramic, unglazed bottoms, unmarked, 1950s, bag: 3¼", pr......................**$20.00**

Golf ball & club, ceramic, Japan paper label, 3⅛", pr..**$18.00**

Hands, 2 fit together as if shaking, ceramic, CC Co, 3", pr..**$12.00**

Helmet & ball, ceramic, no mark, 2", pr......................**$18.00**

Ice cream sodas, plastic, 1 strawberry & 1 chocolate, 1950s, 3½", pr......................**$17.00**

Jugs, ceramic, 3⅝", pr **$10.00**

Jugs, wooden, cork stoppers, 2¾", pr......................**$5.00**

Kachina dolls, ceramic, 4½", pr......................**$12.00**

Lighthouses, ceramic, pink brick, GH 95, 4¼", pr......**$15.00**

Mill & matching shaker, wooden, 4⅜", pr..................**$10.00**

Old-fashioned open auto w/man & woman (shakers) passengers, plastic, Pat Pending, USA, 5⅞" **$15.00**

Pipe on pipe holder, ceramic, brown, black & green, Trevewood, 1950s, 2x3¾", pr **$20.00**

Rocket (Buck Rogers type), ceramic, white w/gold trim, unmarked, 1950s, 4¾", pr......................**$45.00**

Schoolhouse & desk, ceramic, red & brown, flat unglazed bottoms, unmarked, 1950s, schoolhouse: 3", pr...**$22.00**

Slot machines, ceramic, 3", pr......................**$8.00**

Totem poles, ceramic, 4½", pr......................**$15.00**

Tugboats, ceramic, no mark, 2¼", pr......................**$10.00**

Urn shapes, sterling, Duchin Creation, weighted, 4⅝", pr ..**$10.00**

Violin & case, ceramic, white & brown, unmarked, 1950s, violin: 3½", pr......................**$20.00**

Windmills, wooden, 2⅜", pr......................**$8.00**

Schoop, Hedi

One of the most successful California ceramic studios was founded in Hollywood by Hedi Schoop, who had been educated in the arts in Berlin and Germany. She had studied not only painting but sculpture, architecture, and fashion design as well. Fleeing Nazi Germany with her husband, the famous composer Frederick Holander, Hedi settled in California in 1933 and only a few years later became involved in producing novelty giftware items so popular that they were soon widely copied by other California companies. She designed many animated human figures, some in matched pairs, some that doubled as flower containers. All were hand painted and many were decorated with applied ribbons, sgraffito work, and gold trim. To a lesser extent, she modeled animal figures as well. Until fire leveled the plant in 1958, the business was very productive. Nearly everything she made was marked.

If you'd like to learn more about her work, we recommend *The Collector's Encyclopedia of California Pottery, Second Edition,* by Jack Chipman (Collector Books).

Ashtray, ballerina doing splits on back rim, turquoise over white w/gold, 8½x7¾x4"......................**$125.00**

Bowl, shell form, ivory & gold w/black interior, 1940s, 12"......................**$45.00**

Candlestick, double; twisted, branch-like **$50.00**

Dish, leaf shape w/nude cherub kneeling, 6x12"......**$125.00**

Dresser box, Deco lady, base is half of her long full skirt, hands together under chin, 7"......................**$85.00**

Figurine, Oriental man in brown & white shirt w/matching hat & white pants, 12½"......................**$60.00**

Figurine, rooster, multicolored, 13" **$85.00**

Figurines, Oriental couple, both carrying a pot, 12", 12½", pr......................**$125.00**

Flower holder, girl holding flowers, purple vase at side, 9¼"......................**$85.00**

Flower holder, Maguerita, basket on head, dress held out to side, 12", EX......................**$110.00**

Flower holder, Tyrolean girl holding skirt out as planter, 11" **$90.00**

Flower holders, Balinese dancers in gray w/gold trim, 12", pr **$210.00**

Flower holders, French peasants in green w/red striped shirts, both carrying basket, 13", 12½", pr..........**$180.00**

Flower holders, Harlequin dancers, white w/spattered gold, black face masks, fiddle-shaped planters in back, 13", pr **$200.00**

Planter, horse, white w/green bows & saddle, must be signed, 7", from $65 to.....................................**$75.00**

Soap dish, lady in pink & brown dress holds dish overhead, 10½", from $90 to..**$110.00**

Tray, butterfly form, orange w/gold & white, ca 1942 .**$45.00**

Scouting Collectibles

Collecting scouting memorabilia has long been a popular pastime for many. Through the years, millions of boys and girls have been a part of this worthy organization founded in England in 1907 by retired Major-General Lord Robert Baden-Powell. Scouting has served to establish goals in young people and help them to develop leadership skills, physical strength, and mental alertness. Through scouting, they learn basic fundamentals of survival. The scouting movement came to the United States in 1910, and the first World Scout Jamboree was held in 1911 in England. If you would like to learn more, we recommend *A Guide to Scouting Collectibles With Values* by R.J. Sayers (ordering information is given in the Directory).

Advisor: R.J. Sayers (See Directory, Scouting Collectibles)

Boy Scouts

Award, Silver Beaver; blue & white ribbon w/solid beaver charm, 1938-1950s, w/original presentation box, EX.............**$125.00**

Badge, shows Scout salute in green enameled circle, marked Silver on back, original box, EX.........................**$200.00**

Belt buckle, owl w/Wood Badge below, pewter, currently available..**$25.00**

Book, Boy Scouts Motor-Cycles, Ralph Victor, 1911, VG+..**$55.00**

Book, Boy Scouts Yearbook, hardcover, blue w/gold lettering, edited by Frank K Matthews, 1932, 8x10", EX.........**$24.00**

Book, Manual of Drills for Boy Scouts, Jas Brown & Co, Glasgow 1916, 98 pages, VG+.............................**$40.00**

Book, The Sea Scout Manual, 505 pages, 5th edition & reprint, 1929, VG+ **$20.00**

Bookends, Be Prepared on logo, copper-tone cast metal, pr..**$65.00**

Box, wooden w/lid, engraved w/scout & master & scout laws, 1930s, 5x3½", EX...**$40.00**

Bugle, Rexcraft Official; BSA trademark, scout logo, brass, w/mouthpiece, EX...**$60.00**

Bulletin, The Boy Scout Scheme, #5, March 1, 1911, 29 pages, EX...**$75.00**

Camera, Boy Scout Kodak, olive drab green, w/matching case, ca 1929, EX...**$175.00**

Cap, Sea Scout, white over navy, logo on front, EX ..**$40.00**

Compact, image of California w/cities & places of interest, covered wagon w/BSA National Jamboree Irvine CA, 1953, EX..**$25.00**

Compass, Taylor International Co #1075, 1949-52, 2", EXIB...**$25.00**

First aid kit, complete in metal can, Bauer & Black, 1932, EX+...**$40.00**

Game, Ten Pins, Milton Bradley, 1920s, VG+ **$250.00**

Handbook, Boy Scouts of America, Doubleday, Page & Co, 1911, VG...**$375.00**

Handbook, BSA Handbook for Boys, 1 scout w/signal flag & 1 w/binoculars, 512 pages, 1927, VG+ **$60.00**

Hat, Ranger; Official BSA, tan, EX................................**$35.00**

Kit, Rocks & Minerals, #2143, complete, 1930s, EXIB...**$25.00**

Magazine, Boy's Life, The Boy Scout; Remington Schuyler cover of scout w/2 deer, February 1923, 56 pages, 11x14", EX..**$40.00**

Match safe, metal, cylindrical, Marbles Gladstone Mich USA Pat'd 1900, NM (EX box) **$105.00**

Paint book, scouts in action, left page shows color illustration & right is for coloring, 50 pages, hardback, 1912, VG...**$40.00**

Patch, Assistant Scoutmaster, yellow outlined eagle on green background, 1930s, from $50.00 to $75.00. (Photo courtesy Manion's International Auction House Inc.)

Patch, Nat'l Jamboree Irvine Ranch, Calif, 2-horse drawn covered wagon, for jacket, 1953, 5⅝", M **$175.00**

Patch, Order of the Arrow WWW, Miquin Lodge, 1933-58, 25th Anniversary, 3" dia, EX+ **$125.00**

Pillow case, scout scenes, 1957 National Jamboree, unused, 18" sq +fringe, NM...**$35.00**

Pin, collar; Explorers Advisor, enameled silver, marked silver on back, 1940s, ⅞", EX...**$140.00**

Pin, United States Treasury War Service Award, bronze, blue ribbon, 1919, 1⅝x½", EX.......................................**$60.00**

Pocket signal disk, for Morse code & signal flags, 1914, EX..**$30.00**

Pocketknife, mother-of-pearl handle w/Be Prepared on shield, knife, screwdriver, can & bottle opener, 1940s, EX..**$70.00**

Pocketknife, Remington RS3333, bone handle, nickel silver bolsters, bail, round scout shield, etching, 3¾", EX **$150.00**

Poster, Get in the Scrap To Slap the Japs, Boy Scout Scrap Iron & Steel Drive, WWII era, 8½x14", EX.........**$210.00**

Poster, Scout pouring milk on bowl of Kellogg's cereal, 1944, 30x25", VG+ **$350.00**

Stamp/decal, On to Washington, scout w/eagle background, August 21-30, 1935, 1¾x2¾", EX..........................**$60.00**

Tableware, knife, spoon & fork, leather case w/logo, Schrade, EX **$40.00**

Whistle, metal w/compass mounted on tube, marked Acme Boy Scout England, 3¼x½", EX **$60.00**

Girl Scouts

Barrette, gold-tone, ca 1950s, 2¼" long, $9.00.
(Photo courtesy John Shuman)

Book, The Girl Scouts Director, hardbound w/dust jacket, Edith Lovell, 253 pages, 1925, VG+........................**$65.00**

Bracelet, cuff; brass w/green enameled logos, 1950s, EX..**$60.00**

Bracelet, cuff; images of scouts hiking, biking, skiing, etc w/ emblem in center, silver-plated brass, ¾" wide, EX......**$65.00**

Catalog, Girl Scout Equipment, Fall 1940, 39 pages, EX..**$20.00**

Catalog, Girl Scout Equipment, Fall 1951, EX **$25.00**

Charm bracelet, 12 enameled charms, 1960s, M (original GSA box) **$110.00**

Compass, metal, Taylor, 2" dia, EX (original box) **$40.00**

Figurine, saluting girl scout on base w/emblem, pottery, 1940s, 7½", EX **$60.00**

Knife, sheath; Remington RH251, w/original green leather sheath, 4" blade, 7¾" overall, EX **$180.00**

Lunch box, brown w/white images of scouts in action, 2 handles, metal, 7¾x4¼x5½", EX **$65.00**

Pin, Mariner; anchor & chain, #9-115 Midshipmate Guard, 1950s, MOC...**$75.00**

Pin, Outstanding Volunteer; red w/white lettering, ¾" dia..**$80.00**

Pin, world on winged GS emblem, silver plated, marked R on back, 1⅜x½", EX+ **$165.00**

Plaque, GS emblem, Syrocco, 6½x6½", EX...............**$120.00**

Sebastians

These tiny figures were first made in 1938 by Preston W. Baston and sold through gift stores, primarily in the New England area. When he retired in 1976, the Lance Corporation chose one hundred designs which they continued to produce under Baston's supervision. Since then, the discontinued figures have become very collectible.

Baston died in 1984, but his son, P.W. Baston, Jr., continues the tradition.

The figures are marked with an imprinted signature and a paper label. Early labels (before 1977) were green and silver foil shaped like an artist's palette; these are referred to as 'Marblehead' labels (Marblehead, Massachusetts, being the location of the factory) and figures that carry one of these are becoming hard to find and are highly valued by collectors.

Ben Franklin...**$65.00**
Betsy Ross **$100.00**
Cow Jumped Over the Moon **$250.00**
Diedrich Knickerbocker, MIB....................................**$60.00**
Eagle Boy Scout..**$110.00**
Family Sing, MIB..**$45.00**

Farmer, 3", $35.00; Wife, 2¼", $28.00.

Howard Johnson Pieman **$200.00**
Huckleberry Finn **$50.00**
John Hancock **$85.00**
Jordan March Observer, Marblehead era **$55.00**
Juliet..**$35.00**
Lobsterman, Marblehead era......................................**$45.00**
Mark Twain **$95.00**
Mr Obocell **$135.00**
Mrs Beacon Hill, Marblehead era, MIB.....................**$50.00**
Paul Bunyan...**$110.00**
Pheobe From the House of Seven Gables, Marblehead era, MIB **$45.00**
Plymouth Plantation **$125.00**
Robert E Lee **$95.00**
Shoemaker...**$70.00**
Swan Boat **$50.00**
The Nativity...**$70.00**
Twain's Home..**$550.00**
William & Hannah Penn **$200.00**
Williamsburg Couple, MIB **$50.00**

Shawnee Pottery

In 1937 a company was formed in Zanesville, Ohio, on the suspected site of a Shawnee Indian village. They took the tribe's name to represent their company, recognizing the Indians to be the first to use the rich clay from the banks of the Muskingum River to make pottery there. Their venture was very successful, and until they closed in 1961, they produced many lines of kitchenware, planters, vases, lamps, and cookie jars that are very collectible today.

They specialized in figural items. There were 'Winnie' and 'Smiley' pig cookie jars and salt and pepper shakers; 'Bo Peep,' 'Puss 'n Boots,' 'Boy Blue,' and 'Charlie Chicken' pitchers; Dutch children; lobsters; and two lines of dinnerware modeled as ears of corn.

Values sometimes hinge on the extent of an item's decoration. Most items will increase by 100% to 200% when heavily decorated with decals and gold trimmed.

Not all of their ware was marked Shawnee; many pieces were simply marked U.S.A. (If periods are not present, it is not Shawnee) with a three- or four-digit mold number. If you'd like to learn more about this subject, we recommend *Shawnee Pottery, The Full Encyclopedia,* by Pam Curran; *The Collector's Guide to Shawnee Pottery* by Duane and Janice Vanderbilt; and *Shawnee Pottery, Identification & Value Guide,* by Jim and Bev Mangus.

See Also Cookie Jars.

Advisors: Jim and Beverly Mangus (See Directory, Shawnee)

Club: Shawnee Pottery Collectors' Club
P.O. Box 713
New Smyrna Beach, FL 32170-0713; Monthly nationwide newsletter. SASE (c/o Pamela Curran) required when requesting information. Optional: $3 for sample of current newsletter

Ashtray, panther paw, black & white, marked USA ...**$27.00**
Ashtray, shell, green, pink or white, marked Shawnee USA 204 ....**$25.00**
Bank, Howdy Doody, marked Bob Smith USA, 6½"..**$550.00**
Candle holder, Aladdin, white, turquoise, yellow or flax blue, marked USA, 2¼"...**$12.00**

Creamer, elephant, marked Pat USA, from $35.00 to $38.00. (Photo courtesy Duane Vanderbilt)

Creamer, elephant, white w/gold trim, marked Pat USA ..**$210.00**
Creamer, Puss 'n Boots, cream, marked Pat Puss 'n Boots.**$55.00**
Creamer, Puss 'n Boots, gold trim, marked Shawnee USA #85 ....**$60.00**
Creamer, Snowflake, marked USA...........................**$20.00**
Creamer, tilt; yellow, marked USA 10 ....**$50.00**
Figurine, donkey w/basket, marked USA **$22.00**
Figurine, tumbling bear, unmarked.........................**$75.00**
Flower frog, dolphin, low base, unmarked, 3½" **$45.00**
Grease jar, cottage, marked, USA 8........................**$375.00**
Hanging basket, marked USA 685, 3" **$60.00**
Lamp, boy w/mandolin, unmarked..........................**$35.00**
Lamp, harvest queen, unmarked **$55.00**
Pitcher, Bo Peep, marked USA Pat Bo Peep, 40-oz....**$90.00**
Pitcher, Chanticleer, plain, marked Pat Chanticleer **$90.00**
Planter, baby shoes on base, marked USA **$12.00**
Planter, baby skunk, marked Shawnee 512..............**$35.00**
Planter, basket, embossed flower, marked USA 640 ...**$35.00**
Planter, bird, marked USA 508................................**$14.00**
Planter, blow fish, marked USA...............................**$10.00**
Planter, box car, marked USA 552...........................**$55.00**
Planter, boy at gate, unmarked................................**$12.00**
Planter, butterfly, gold, marked Shawnee USA 524 ....**$25.00**
Planter, canopy bed, marked Shawnee 734..............**$80.00**
Planter, cat, marked USA..**$15.00**
Planter, Chinese boy & vase, gold, marked USA 702 .**$16.00**
Planter, clown w/pot, marked USA 619....................**$15.00**
Planter, deer, marked USA **$10.00**
Planter, dog & jug, marked USA 610 ....**$10.00**
Planter, dog in a boat, marked Shawnee 736............**$35.00**
Planter, elephant, marked USA................................**$20.00**
Planter, elf & shoe, marked Shawnee 765................**$14.00**
Planter, fawn, unmarked, 9"....................................**$10.00**
Planter, girl & mandolin, marked USA 576..............**$24.00**
Planter, high heels, marked USA **$12.00**
Planter, kitten, marked USA 723.............................**$35.00**
Planter, lovebirds, marked USA **$12.00**
Planter, madonna, marked USA **$30.00**
Planter, panda & cradle, marked Shawnee USA 2031 ...**$32.00**
Planter, penguin, marked USA.................................**$8.00**
Planter, pony, marked Kenwood 1509......................**$65.00**
Planter, rabbit, marked USA....................................**$16.00**
Planter, rocking horse, marked USA 526 ....**$24.00**
Planter, shell, gold, marked USA 665......................**$16.00**
Planter, southern girl, marked USA, 8½" **$12.00**
Planter, swan & elf, marked Kenwood 2030 ....**$50.00**
Planter, three pigs, marked USA..............................**$14.00**
Planter, top hat, marked USA **$12.00**
Planter, tractor & trailer, marked 680 & 681, pr **$70.00**
Planter, train engine, marked USA 550 ....**$55.00**
Planter, wheelbarrow, marked USA..........................**$10.00**
Planting dish, marked Shawnee USA 2004, 7" **$10.00**
Salt & pepper shakers, Bo Peep & Sailor Boy, gold trim, sm, pr...**$95.00**
Salt & pepper shakers, Chanticleer, lg, pr **$50.00**
Salt & pepper shakers, duck, sm, pr.........................**$35.00**
Salt & pepper shakers, Flower & Fern, sq, lg, pr **$30.00**

Salt & pepper shakers, Muggsy, decals, gold trim, pr, minimum value **$400.00**

Salt & pepper shakers, owl, green eyes, sm, pr..........**$35.00**

Salt & pepper shakers, Smiley, blue bib, decals, gold trim, lg, pr **$295.00**

Salt & pepper shakers, Smiley, peach bib, sm, pr **$50.00**

Salt & pepper shakers, sunflower, sm, pr....................**$35.00**

Salt & pepper shakers, Winnie & Smiley, clover bud, sm, pr...**$75.00**

Salt & pepper shakers, Winnie & Smiley, hearts, lg, pr ..**$180.00**

Teapot, blue & red flowers w/gold, marked USA.......**$75.00**

Teapot, fern, embossed, peach, yellow, blue or green, 8-cup, marked USA **$60.00**

Teapot, Granny Ann, green apron, marked Pat Granny Ann **$130.00**

Teapot, Pennsylvania Dutch, 14-oz, marked USA.......**$70.00**

Teapot, Tom Tom, marked Tom the Piper's Son Pat USA...**$120.00**

Vase, burlap, marked USA, 4"....................................**$12.00**

Vase, geometric, marked USA, 5" **$14.00**

Vase, hand, marked USA, 7" **$14.00**

Vase, wheat, marked USA 1266, 6" **$22.00**

Wall pocket, Little Bo Peep, marked USA 586 ....**$40.00**

Wall pocket, red feather, unmarked............................**$45.00**

Corn Ware

Bowl, fruit; King or Queen, marked Shawnee 94.......**$48.00**

Bowl, mixing; King or Queen, marked Shawnee 8, from $35 to...**$45.00**

Butter dish, Queen, w/lid, marked Shawnee 72 ....**$55.00**

Casserole, Queen, marked Shawnee 74, from $50 to.**$55.00**

Cookie jar, King or Queen, marked Shawnee 66 .....**$350.00**

Creamer, King, gold trim, marked Shawnee 70, from $95 to...**$110.00**

Creamer, King, marked Shawnee 70 ....**$32.00**

Mug, King or Queen, marked Shawnee 69, 8-oz........**$50.00**

Pitcher, #71, from $65.00 to $75.00; creamer, #70, $32.00. (Photo courtesy Duane Vanderbilt)

Plate, Queen, marked Shawnee 689, 10"....................**$40.00**

Popcorn set, Queen..**$200.00**

Relish tray, King, marked Shawnee 79, from $40 to...**$45.00**

Salt & pepper shakers, King or Queen, lg, pr............**$40.00**

Salt & pepper shakers, King or Queen, sm, pr..........**$28.00**

Sugar bowl, King or Queen, marked Shawnee 78, w/lid ...**$35.00**

Teapot, King or Queen, marked Shawnee 65, 10-oz..**$175.00**

Lobster Ware

Baker, open, marked 915, 5" **$40.00**

Butter dish, w/lid, marked Kenwood USA 927.........**$110.00**

Casserole, French; marked 902, 16-oz **$25.00**

Hors d'oeuvre holder, marked USA, 7¼"..................**$275.00**

Mug, marked Kenwood USA 911, 8-oz.......................**$85.00**

Plate, compartment; marked Kenwood USA 912......**$100.00**

Relish, w/lid, marked Kenwood USA 926, 5½"...........**$50.00**

Snack jar, marked Kenwood USA 925, 40-oz............**$775.00**

Spoon holder, double, marked USA 935, 8½", $250.00. (Photo courtesy Jim and Bev Mangus)

Valencia

Teapot, regular, eight-cup, no mark, $65.00. (Photo courtesy Jim and Bev Mangus)

Ashtray...**$24.00**

Bowl, fruit; unmarked, 5"..**$20.00**

Candle holders, bulbous, pr **$35.00**

Carafe, w/lid..$50.00
Coaster...$15.00
Coffepot, regular, no lid, unmarked..........................$40.00
Cookie jar...$85.00
Egg cup..$18.00
Fork..$35.00
Marmite, 4½"...$24.00
Nappy, unmarked, 8½"...$20.00
Pie server...$55.00
Pitcher, ice lip, marked USA.....................................$40.00
Plate, chop; 13"..$25.00
Plate, 9¾"...$14.00
Relish tray, compartments.......................................$135.00
Sugar bowl, w/lid..$22.00
Utility tray...$18.00
Vase, bud...$14.00
Waffle set, 5 pcs...$100.00

Sheet Music

Flea markets are a good source for buying old sheet music, and prices are usually very reasonable. Most examples can be bought for less than $5.00. More often than not, it is collected for reasons other than content. Some of the cover art was done by well-known illustrators like Rockwell, Christy, Barbelle, and Starmer, and some collectors like to zero in on their particular favorite, often framing some of the more attractive examples. Black Americana collectors can find many good examples with Black entertainers featured on the covers and the music reflecting an ethnic theme.

You may want to concentrate on music by a particularly renowned composer, for instance George M. Cohan or Irving Berlin. Or you may find you enjoy covers featuring famous entertainers and movie stars from the '40s through the '60s, for instance. At any rate, be critical of condition when you buy or sell sheet music. As is true with any item of paper, tears, dog ears, or soil will greatly reduce its value.

If you'd like a more thorough listing of sheet music and prices, we recommend *The Sheet Music Reference and Price Guide* by Anna Marie Guiheen and Marie-Reine A. Pafik (Collector Books), and *The Collector's Guide to Sheet Music* by Debbie Dillon.

After All Is Said & Done, Dave Ringle, 1931.................$6.00
All I Want for Christmas Is My Two Front Teeth, Don Gardner, 1946...$8.00
America First, John Philip Sousa, 1916.......................$25.00
And Russia Is Her Name, EY Harburg & Jerome Kern, 1943...$10.00
Around the World in 80 Days, Harold Adamson & Victor Young, Movie: Around the World in 80 Days, 1956.................$5.00
Autumn Serenade, Sammy Gallop & Peter DeRose, 1945.$5.00
Bananas, Marvin Hamlisch, Movie: Bananas, Photo cover: Woody Allen & Louise Lasser, 1971.......................$6.00

Because of You, Hammerstein & Wilkinson, Movie: Because of You, Photo cover: Loretta Young & Jeff Chandler, 1940...$8.00
Bible Tells Me So, Dale Evans, Photo cover: Roy Rogers & Dale Evans, 1945..$16.00
Blue Skirt Waltz, Mitchell Parish & Vaclav Blaha, 1944...$5.00
Brigadoon, Alan J Lerner & Fredrick K Loewe, Movie: Brigadoon, 1947...$5.00
By a Wishing Well, Mack Gordon & Harry Revel, Movie: My Lucky Star, Photo cover: Sonja Henie & Richard Greene, 1938...$5.00
Careless Hands, Bob Hilliard & Carl Sigman, Photo cover: John Laurenz, 1949..$3.00
Carlotta, Cole Porter, Movie: Can Can, 1943................$5.00
Cherries, Marois & Dartmouth, Photo cover: Doris Day, 1952..$3.00

Cocktails for Two, Arthur Johnson and Sam Cowlow, 1934, $10.00. (Photo courtesy Guiheen & Pafik)

Cold Cold Heart, Hank Williams, 1951........................$4.00
Cool, Stephen Sondheim & Leonard Bernstein, Movie: West Side Story, 1957...$5.00
Cynthia's in Love, Jack Owens, Earl Gish & Billy White, Photo cover: Perry Como, Cover artist: Barbelle, 1942............$5.00
Dashing Cavaliers, ET Paull, Cover artist: ET Paull, 1938..$35.00
Dig Down Deep, Walter Hirsch, Sano Marco & Gerald Marks, War Bond Song WWII, 1942...............................$20.00
Don't Drink the Water, Williams & Gordon, Movie: Don't Drink the Water, Photo cover: Jackie Gleason, 1969...........$6.00
Down in the Glens, Harry Gordon & Tommie Connor, 1947...$3.00
Dreamy Old New England Moon, Marty Berk, Frank Capano & Max C Freedman, Photo cover: Vaughn Monroe, 1948..$5.00
Enchanted Sea, Frank Metis & Randy Starr, 1959.........$5.00
Eyes of Blue, Stone & Young, Movie: Shane, Photo cover: Alan Ladd, Jean Arthur & Van Heflin, 1953............$5.00
Five Minutes With Mr Thornhill, Claude Thornhill, 1942..$5.00
Forever Darling, Cahn & Kaper, Movie: Forever Darling, Photo cover: Lucille Ball, Desi Arnaz & James Mason, 1955...$8.00

From This Day Forward, Mort Greene & Leigh Harline, Movie: From This Day Forward, Photo cover: Joan Fontaine, 1946 ....**$5.00**

Girl on the Police Gazette, Irving Berlin, Movie: On the Avenue, Photo cover: Dick Powell & Alice Faye, 1937 ....**$15.00**

Goldfinger, Bricusse, Newley & Barry, Movie: Goldfinger, Photo cover: Sean Connery & Honor Blackman, 1964 ....**$8.00**

Goodnight, Sleep Tight, Sylvia Fine, Movie: Five Pennies, Photo cover: Danny Kaye & Louis Armstrong, 1959 ....**$6.00**

Guitar Boogie, Arthur Smith, Photo cover: Arthur Smith, 1946..**$5.00**

Have I Told You Lately That I Love You, Scott Wiseman, Photo cover: Bing Crosby & Andrews Sisters, 1946............**$10.00**

He's in Love, Robert Wright & Chet Forrest, Musical: Kismet, 1953 ....**$6.00**

Heigh-Ho, Larry Morey & Frank Churchill, Movie: Snow White, Disney, 1938..**$16.00**

Holiday for Strings, David Rose, 1943....................**$5.00**

How Do You Do?, Robert McGimsey, Movie: Song of the South, Disney, 1946..**$10.00**

I Beg of You, Elvis Presley, 1957 ....**$20.00**

I Don't Want To Be Hurt Anymore, McCarthy, Photo cover: Nat King Cole, 1962 ....**$3.00**

I Hear the Music Now, Seelen & Fain, Movie: The Jazz Singer, Photo cover: Danny Thomas & Peggy Lee, 1953 ...**$8.00**

I Married an Angel, Lorenz Hart & Richard Rodgers, Movie: I Married an Angel, Cover artist: Sorokin, 1938 ....**$8.00**

I Still Get Jealous, Sammy Cahn & Jule Styne, Musical: High Button Shoes, 1948 ....**$5.00**

I Went to Your Wedding, Jessie Mae Robinson, Photo cover: Patti Page, 1952 ....**$8.00**

I'd Give a Million Tomorrows, Milton Berle & Jerry Livingston, Photo cover: Arthur Godfrey, 1948 ......**$6.00**

I'll Know, Jo Swerling, Abe Burrows & Frank Loesser, Musical: Guys & Dolls, 1950 ....**$5.00**

I'm All Right, Loggins, Movie: Caddyshack, Photo cover: Bill Murray, Rodney Dangerfield & Chevy Chase, 1980 .**$3.00**

I'm Gonna Live Till I Die, Al Hoffman, Walter Kent & Mann Curtis, Photo cover: Danny Scholl, 1950.................**$6.00**

I'm Not Your Stepping Stone, Monkees, 1966...............**$5.00**

I've Got the Sun in the Morning, Irving Berlin, Movie: Annie Get Your Guns, 1946 ....**$10.00**

If I Only Had a Brain, Ray Bolger & EY Harburg, Movie: Wizard of Oz, Signed by EY Harburg, 1939.........**$25.00**

Ike for Four More Years, Irving Berlin, 1956.............**$25.00**

In My Arms, Frank Loesser & Ted Grouya, 1943 ....**$3.00**

In the Middle of an Island, Nick Aquaviva & Ted Varneck, 1957...**$3.00**

Irish Soldier Boy, Bill Lanyon & Pat DeWitt, Photo cover: Connie Foley, 1950 ....**$3.00**

It Was Written in the Stars, Leo Robin & Harold Arlen, Movie: Casbah, 1948 ....**$6.00**

It's So Peaceful in the Country, Alec Wilder, Photo cover: Mildred Bailey, 1942 ....**$3.00**

Jiminy Cricket, Leigh Harline & Ned Washington, Movie: Pinocchio, Disney, 1940 ....**$10.00**

Just a Prayer, Charles Tobias & David Kapp, Photo cover: Kate Smith, 1944 ....**$6.00**

Keep It a Secret, Jessie Mae Robinson, 1952...............**$3.00**

Lady Bird, Cha Cha Cha, Cover artist: Norman Rockwell, 1968 ....**$25.00**

Leaving on a Jet Plane, John Denver, Photo cover: Peter, Paul & Mary, 1969 ....**$5.00**

Let's Take an Old Fashioned Walk, Irving Berlin, Musical: Miss Liberty, 1948 ....**$10.00**

Little April Shower, Frank Churchill & Larry Morey, Movie: Bambi, Disney, 1942..**$12.00**

Little Toot, Allie Wrubel, Movie: Melody Time, Disney, 1948 ....**$10.00**

Lot of Livin' To Do, Lee Adams & Charles Strouse, Movie: Bye Bye Birdie, 1960 ....**$6.00**

Love Star, Al Lewis, Larry Stock & Vincent Rose, 1945.**$3.00**

Make It With You, David Gates, 1970.....................**$3.00**

March of the Cards, Bob Hilliard & Sammy Fain, Movie: Alice in Wonderland, Disney, 1951 ....**$12.00**

May You Always, Larry Markes & Dick Charles, Photo cover: McQuire Sisters, 1958 ....**$5.00**

Mexico, Charles Wolcott & Ray Gilbert, Movie: Three Cabelleros, Disney, 1945 ....**$15.00**

Misty, Johnny Burke & Erroll Garner, 1955 ....**$3.00**

Most Expensive Statue in the World, Irving Berlin, Musical: Miss Liberty, 1949 ....**$12.00**

My Brooklyn Love Song, Tibbles & Idriss, Movie: If You Knew Susie, Photo cover: Eddie Cantor, 1947........**$8.00**

My Heart Cries for You, Carl Sigman & Percy Faith, Photo cover: Dinah Shore, 1950 ....**$5.00**

My Mother Would Love You, Cole Porter, Movie: Panama Hattie, 1942..**$5.00**

My Ten Ton Baby & Me, Wilson, Transportation, 1942..**$5.00**

Nice To Be Around, Williams & Williams, Movie: Cinderella Liberty, Photo cover: James Caan & Marsha Mason, 1973 ....**$4.00**

Nobody's heart, Lorenz Hart & Richard Rodgers, Movie: All's Fair, 1942 ....**$5.00**

Nuttin' for Christmas, Sid Tepper & Roy C Bennett, Photo cover: Stan Freberg, 1955 ....**$3.00**

Old Lamp-Lighter, Charles Tobias & Nat Simon, Photo cover: Sammy Kaye, 1941 ....**$4.00**

On the Street Where You Live, Lerner & Lowe, Movie: My Fair Lady, 1956 ....**$5.00**

Only One, Anne Croswell & Lee Pochriss, Musical: Tovarich, 1963...**$3.00**

Painting the Roses Red, Bob Hilliard & Sammy Fain, Movie: Alice in Wonderland, Disney, 1951 ....**$20.00**

Pernambuco, Frank Loesser, Movie: Where's Charley, Caricature: Ray Bolger, 1948 ....**$6.00**

Please Remember, Bobby Troup & Walter Gross, Photo cover: Four Freshman, 1953..**$3.00**

Promises, Al Hoffman, Milton Drake & Jerry Livingston, Photo cover: Guy Lombardo, Cover artist: J Geyler, 1945...**$3.00**

Rainbow, Russ Hamilton, 1957 ....**$5.00**

Right Into Your Arms, Charles Lynes, 1945 ....**$3.00**

Rose With a Broken Stem, Tolchard Evans, 1937 ....**$4.00**

Sailor Boys Have To Talk to Me in English, Bob Hilliard & Milton DeLugg, 1955.......................................**$5.00**

Sealed With a Kiss, Peter Udell & Gary Geld, Photo cover: Bobby Vinton, 1960 ....**$2.00**

Silver in the Moon, HA Pooley, 1945 ....**$3.00**

Sky Anchors, Waring, Transportation, 1942 ....**$10.00**

So Far, Richard Rodgers & Oscar Hammerstein II, Musical: Allegro, 1951 ....**$3.00**

Someone Who Cares, Harvey, Movie: Fools, Photo cover: Jason Robards & Katherine Ross, 1971 ....**$4.00**

Song of the South, Sam Coslow & Arthur Johnston, Movie: Song of the South, Disney, 1946 ....**$12.00**

Star Eyes, Don Raye & Gene DePaul, Movie: I Dood It, Photo cover: Red Skelton & Eleanor Powell, 1943 ....**$5.00**

Strip Polka, Johnny Mercer, Photo cover: Andrew Sisters, 1942...**$3.00**

Sweet Eloise, Mack David & Russ Morgan, Photo cover: Buddy Franklyn, Cover artist: Sig-Ch, 1942 ....**$4.00**

Take Care, When You Say Te Quiero, Henry Prichard, 1946..**$5.00**

Tell Me Why, Al Alberts & Marty Gold, Photo cover: Four Aces, 1951...**$5.00**

There Is a Tavern in Town, Harry Henneman, 1942 ....**$5.00**

Thirsty for Your Kisses, Lee Morris & Bill Ficks, Photo cover: Ames Brothers, Cover artist: BJH, 1950.................**$3.00**

This Is the First Time, Wally Peterson, 1949.................**$2.00**

Three Coins in the Fountain, Sammy Cahn and Jule Styne, 1954, $5.00. (Photo courtesy Guiheen & Pafik)

Tom Dooley, Ed Jackson, 1958......................................**$3.00**

Tulips & Heather, Milton Carson, Photo cover: Perry Como, 1950..**$3.00**

Under the Bridges of Paris, Dorcas Cochran & Vincent Scotto, 1953..**$3.00**

Volare, Mitchell Parish & Domenico Modugno, Photo cover: McGuire Sisters, 1958...**$3.00**

Warm All Over, Frank Loesser, Musical: Most Happy Fella, 1956..**$6.00**

Watermelon Weather, Paul Francis & Hoagy Carmichael, Photo cover: Perry Como & Eddie Fisher, 1952.....**$5.00**

What Do I Have To Do To Get My Picture in the Papers, Irving Berlin, Musical: Miss Liberty, 1949 ....**$10.00**

What Have They Done to My Song, Ma, Melanie Safka, Photo cover: Melanie, 1970...**$2.00**

When Love Beckoned, Cole Porter, Movie: DuBarry Was a Lady, 1943...**$6.00**

When You're Gone, Goldsmith & Goldsmith, Movie: Babes, Photo cover: Susan Clark, 1975 ....**$2.00**

Windshield Wiper, Joseph J Lilley & Dick Peterson, 1948 ..**$5.00**

With a Kiss, Myrow, Blane & Wells, Movie: French Line, Photo cover; Jane Russell, 1953.............................**$3.00**

Wonder Why, Sammy Cahn and Nicholas Brodsky, 1951, $10.00. (Photo courtesy Guiheen & Pafik)

Woody Woodpecker, George Tibbles & Ramsey Idriss, 1947...**$5.00**

Shell Pink Glassware

This beautiful soft pink, opaque glassware was made for only a short time in the late 1950s by the Jeannette Glass Company. Though a few pieces are commanding prices of more than $200.00 (the Anniversary cake plate, the cigarette box with the butterfly finial, and the Lazy Susan tray), most pieces carry modest price tags, and the ware, though not as easy to find as it was a few years ago, is still available for the collector who is willing to do some searching. Refer to *Collectible Glassware from the 40s, 50s, and 60s,* by Gene Florence (Collector Books) for photos and more information.

Ashtray, butterfly shape..**$28.00**

Base, for Lazy Susan, w/ball bearings **$160.00**

Bowl, Florentine, footed, 10"...**$30.00**

Bowl, Gondola, 17½"..**$40.00**

Bowl, Holiday, footed, 10½"...**$45.00**

Bowl, Lombardi, design in center, 4-footed, 11"........**$42.00**

Bowl, Napco #2250, w/berry design, footed..............**$15.00**

Bowl, Pheasant, footed, 8"	$37.50
Bowl, Wedding, w/lid, 6½"	$22.50
Cake plate, Anniversary	$225.00
Cake stand, Harp, 10"	$45.00
Candle holders, Eagle, 3-footed, pr	$85.00
Candle holders, 2-light, pr	$45.00
Candy dish, Floragold, 4-footed, 5¼"	$20.00
Candy dish, sq, w/lid, 6½"	$30.00
Candy jar, Grapes, 4-footed, w/lid, 5½"	$20.00
Candy jar bottom, National	$10.00
Celery/relish, 3-part, 12½"	$45.00
Cigarette box, butterfly finial	$235.00
Comport, Napco #2256, sq	$12.50
Compote, Windsor, 6"	$20.00
Cookie jar, w/lid, 6½"	$100.00
Creamer, Baltimore Pear	$15.00
Cup, punch; 5-oz	$6.00
Honey jar, beehive shape, notched lid	$40.00
Pitcher, Thumbprint, footed, 24-oz	$27.50
Pot, Napco #2249, crosshatch design	$15.00
Powder jar, w/lid, 4¾"	$45.00
Punch base, 3½"	$35.00
Punch bowl, 7½-qt	$60.00
Punch ladle, pink plastic	$20.00
Relish, Vineyard, octagonal, 4-part, 12"	$42.00
Stem, sherbet; Thumbprint, 5-oz	$12.50
Stem, water goblet; Thumbprint, 8-oz	$17.50
Sugar bowl, Baltimore Pear, footed, w/lid	$11.00
Tray, Harp, 2-handled, 12½x9¾"	$60.00
Tray, Lazy Susan, 5-part, 13½"	$55.00
Tray, snack; w/cup indent, 7¾x10"	$9.00
Tray, Venetian, 6-part, 16½"	$40.00
Tray, 5-part, 2-handle, 15¾"	$85.00
Tumbler, juice; Thumbprint, footed, 5-oz	$8.00
Vase, cornucopia, 5"	$15.00

Vase, 'heavy bottom,' National, 9", $135.00. (Photo courtesy Gene Florence)

Vase, 7"	$30.00

Shirley Temple

Born April 23, 1928, Shirley Jane Temple danced and smiled her way into the hearts of America in the movie *Stand Up and Cheer*. Many successful roles followed and by the time Shirley was eight years old, she was #1 at box offices around the country. Her picture appeared in publications almost daily, and any news about her was news indeed. Mothers dressed their little daughters in clothing copied after hers and coiffed them with Shirley hairdos.

The extent of her success was mirrored in the unbelievable assortment of merchandise that saturated the retail market. Dolls, coloring books, children's clothing and jewelry, fountain pens, paper dolls, stationery, and playing cards are just a few examples of the hundreds of items that were available. Shirley's face was a common sight on the covers of magazines as well as in the advertisements they contained, and she was the focus of scores of magazine articles.

Though she had been retired from the movies for nearly a decade, she had two successful TV series in the late '50s, *The Shirley Temple Story-Book* and *The Shirley Temple Show*. Her reappearance caused new interest in some of the items that had been so popular during her childhood, and many were reissued.

Always interested in charity and community service, Shirley became actively involved in a political career in the late '60s, serving at both the state and national levels.

If you're interested in learning more about her, we recommend *Shirley Temple Dolls and Collectibles* by Patricia R. Smith and *Shirley in the Magazines* by Gen Jones.

The lower range of our doll prices represents a played-with doll in good condition, while the higher figure is applicable for an example in at least excellent or near-mint condition. Note: As you can see, it is very important to learn how to access the condition of your doll in order to arrive at an accurate evaluation.

Newsletter: *Lollipop News*
P.O. Box 6203
Oxnard, CA 93031; Dues: $14 per year

Newsletter: *The Shirley Temple Collectors News*
8811 Colonial Rd.
Brooklyn, NY 11209; Dues: $20 per year; checks payable to Rita Dubas

Book, Captain January/The Little Colonel, Random House, 1950s, w/dust jacket, EX	$30.00
Book, Shirley Temple in Heidi, Saafield, 1937, EX	$55.00
Book, Shirley Temple in Stowaway, Saafield #1767, EX	$80.00
Book, Shirley Temple's Autobiography, signed & leather bound, #41 of 5,000 copies, Easton Press, NM	$215.00
Book, The Littlest Rebel, 1939, VG+	$40.00
Bowl, cereal; white portrait on cobalt glass, 1930s, original only	$60.00
Doll, bisque, 6", unlicensed Japanese, from $65 to	$250.00
Doll, composition, 11", Ideal, from $400 to	$975.00

Doll, composition, 13", Ideal, from $350 to **$750.00**
Doll, composition, 16", Ideal, from $400 to **$800.00**
Doll, composition, 20", Ideal, from $300 to **$1,100.00**
Doll, composition, 22", Ideal, from $375 to **$1,200.00**
Doll, composition, 27", Ideal, from $450 to **$1,750.00**

Doll, composition head, Ideal, open mouth with six upper teeth, original mohair wig, five-piece composition body, original Scottie dress, replaced undies, shoes, and socks, 18", EX, $650.00. (Photo courtesy McMasters Doll Auctions)

Doll, vinyl, 12", all original, 1957, NM......................**$275.00**
Doll, vinyl, 15", marked ST//15, all original, 1958-61, from $100 to...**$375.00**
Doll, vinyl, 17", Montgomery Wards reissue, 1972, all original, from $50 to...**$200.00**
Doll, vinyl, 36", marked Doll Dreams & Love, Hank Garfinkle, all original, from $75 to......................**$250.00**
Doll clothes, for 12" doll, ca 1950s, complete, w/tag, from $75 to...**$125.00**

Handkerchiefs, ca 1930s, boxed set of three, from $140.00 to $150.00. (Photo courtesy Pat Smith/Rita Dubas; photography by John DeLuca)

Handkerchiefs, images in oval of movie characters, silk, set of 12, EX..**$270.00**
Pin, The World's Darling, Genuine Shirley Temple Doll, came on composition dolls, M **$130.00**
Pitcher, white protrait on cobalt glass, 11-oz, 4⅜", EX.**$45.00**
Playset, Shirley Temple's Magnetic TV Theater, 1958, MIB **$235.00**
Record set, Shirley Temple w/...Walt Disney's Dumbo, 3-record set w/book, 1940s, EX.................................**$55.00**

Shoes, oilcloth, center snap, fits 17" or 18" doll, pr....**$80.00**
String holder, chalk, 1940s-50s, 6¾x6¼", EX **$400.00**

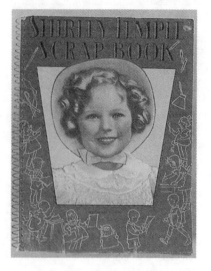

Scrapbook, 1936, EX, $45.00.

Shot Glasses

Shot glasses are small articles of glass that generally hold an ounce or two of liquid; they measure about 2" to 4" in height. They've been around since the 1830s have been made in nearly every conceivable type of glass.

Shot glass collectors are usually quantity collectors often boasting of hundreds or even a thousand glasses! The most desirable to collectors are whiskey sample or advertising glasses from the Pre-Prohibition era. Most carry etched white lettering that comprises messages relating to a distiller, company, proprietor, or other alcohol-related advertising. Shot glasses like these sell for around $75.00 to $100.00, but recently many rare examples have been auctioned off at prices in excess of $300.00.

These values are only estimates and should be used as a general guide. Many one-of-a-kind items or oddities are a bit harder to classify, especially sample glasses. Often this may depend on the elaborateness of the design as opposed to simple lettering. For more information, we recommend *Shot Glasses: An American Tradition,* and *The Shot Glass Encyclopedia*, both by Mark Pickvet.

Note: Values for shot glasses in good condition are represented by the low end of our ranges, while the high end reflects estimated values for examples in mint condition.

Advisor: Mark Pickvet (See Directory, Shot Glasses)

Barrel shaped, from $5 to **$7.50**
Black porcelain replica, from $3.50 to **$5.00**
Carnival colors, plain or fluted, from $100 to **$150.00**

Carnival colors, w/patterns, from $125 to $175.00
Colored glass tourist, from $4 to $6.00
Culver 22k gold, from $6 to..$8.00

Depression, colors, from $10.00 to $12.50. (Photo courtesy Mark Pickvet)

Depression, colors w/patterns or etching, from $17.50 to ..$25.00
Depression, tall, general designs, from $10 to $12.50
Depression, tall, tourist, from $5 to................................$7.50
Frosted w/gold designs, from $6 to $8.00
General, advertising, from $4 to......................................$5.00
General, etched designs, from $5 to $7.50
General, porcelain, from $4 to...$6.00
General, w/enameled design, from $3 to $4.00
General, w/frosted designs, from $3.50 to....................$5.00
General, w/gold designs, from $6 to $8.00
General tourist, from $3 to...$5.00
Inside eyes, from $6 to...$8.00
Iridized silver, from $5 to...$7.50
Mary Gregory or Anchor Hocking Ships, from $150 to ..$200.00
Nudes, from $25 to..$35.00
Plain, w/or w/out flutes, from 50¢ to..............................$.75
Planet Hollywood/Hard Rock Cafe, from $10 to $12.50
Pop or soda advertising, from $12.50 to......................$15.00
Porcelain tourist, from $3.50 to......................................$5.00
Rounded European designs w/gold rims, from $4 to...$6.00
Ruby flashed, from $35 to...$50.00
Sayings & toasts (1940s & 1950s), from $5 to $7.50
Sports (Professional Teams), from $5 to $7.50
Square, general, from $6 to...$8.00
Square, w/etching, from $10 to $12.50
Square, w/pewter, from $12.50 to $15.00
Square, w/2-tone bronze & pewter, from $15 to $17.50
Standard glass w/pewter, from $12.50 to.....................$15.00
Steuben crystal, from $150 to $200.00
Taiwan tourist, from $2 to...$3.00
Tiffany, Galle or fancy art, from $600 to $8.00
Turquoise & gold tourist, from $6 to $8.00
Whiskey or beer advertising, modern, from $5 to $7.50
Whiskey sample glass, M, from $75 to $350.00
Whiskey sample glasses, good condition, from $50 to..$100.00
19th-century cut patterns, from $35 to.........................$50.00

Silhouette Pictures

These novelty pictures are familiar to everyone. Even today a good number of them are still around, and you'll often see them at flea markets and co-ops. They were very popular in their day and never expensive, and because they were made for so many years (the '20s through the '50s), many variations are available. Though the glass in some is flat, in others it is curved. Backgrounds may be foil, a scenic print, hand tinted, or plain. Sometimes dried flowers were added as accents. But the characteristic common to them all is that the subject matter is reverse painted on the glass. People (even complicated groups), scenes, ships, and animals were popular themes. Though quite often the silhouette was done in solid black to create a look similar to the nineteenth-century cut silhouettes, colors were sometimes used as well.

In the '20s, making tinsel art pictures became a popular pastime. Ladies would paint the outline of their subjects on the back of the glass and use crumpled tinfoil as a background. Sometimes they would tint certain areas of the glass, making the foil appear to be colored. This type is popular with with collectors of folk art.

If you'd like to learn more about this subject, we recommend *The Encyclopedia of Silhouette Collectibles on Glass, 1996 – 97 Price Guide for Encyclopedia of Silhouette Collectibles on Glass,* and *Vintage Silhouettes on Glass and Reverse Paintings* (copyright 2000, all new items pictured) by Shirley Mace. These books show examples of Benton Glass pictures with frames made of metal, wood, plaster, and plastic. The metal frames with the stripes are most favored by collectors as long as they are in good condition. Wood frames were actually considered deluxe when silhouettes were originally sold. Recently some convex glass silhouettes from Canada have been found, nearly identical to the ones made by Benton Glass except for their brown tape frames. Backgrounds seem to be slightly different as well. Among the flat glass silhouettes, the ones signed by Diefenbach are the most expensive. The wildflower pictures, especially ones with fine lines and good detail, are becoming popular with collectors.

Advisor: Shirley Mace (See Directory, Silhouette Pictures)

Convex Glass

Boy stands beside girl in pumpkin, BG 45-233, Benton Glass $50.00
Boy w/fishing pole walks w/dog, BG 810-223, Benton Glass..$40.00
Couple at piano, BG 45-252, Benton Glass.................$35.00
Couple dancing in interior scene, she in ruffled gown, BG 68-264, Benton Glass......................................$40.00
Couple in landscape, colorful background (lithographic print), BG 68-305, Benton Glass............................$45.00
Couple kissing at fence, pastel floral background, BG 45-377, Benton glass...$35.00
Couple taking ride in 1-horse sleigh, BG 68-260, Benton Glass $45.00

Couple wave good-bye to sailing ship, simple colored background (lithographic print), BG 45-363, Benton Glass $45.00

Courting couple dancing in outoor scene, BG 45-245, Benton Glass $35.00

Fence & tree, courting couple airbrushed background, Sandre, BG 68-407, Benton Glass.......................$30.00

Indian maiden w/bow, colorful rocky western scenic background (lithographic print), BG 68-347, Benton Glass $65.00

Lacy curtain & kitten w/yarn, baby & teddy nursery print, Charlotte Becker, BG 68-425, Benton Glass $60.00

Lady admiring young boy's catch, Benton Glass #45-109, $45.00. (Photo courtesy Shirley and Ray Mace)

Lady seated at piano, rose over white moirè, BG-278, Benton Glass $70.00

Sailing ship scene, BG 45-241, Benton Glass..............$35.00

Shepherdess blowing horn, colorful background (lithographic print), BG 68-332, Benton Glass.......................$40.00

Venetian gondola, colorful street scene background (lithographic print), BG 68-313, Benton Glass $45.00

Flat Glass

Boy & girl feeding ducks, AP 3½ 5-204, Art Publishing Co $40.00

Children dance around maypole, GG 56-6, Gleam o' Gold label, PF Volland.....................................$50.00

Girl feeding swans, c HS 1930 on front, H 68-11, Henry Henriksen $25.00

Goldilocks & the Three Bears, RE 711-3, Reliance Picture Frame Co $75.00

Happy Bride, lady adjust veil for bride, BB 46-50, Buckbee-Brehm $40.00

Lady w/bow of dress being pulled by Scottie dog, DE 810-14, Deltrex Products Co $45.00

Little Jack Horner Sat in a Corner, boy w/pie, dog watching, BB 46-33, Buckbee-Brehm...................................$40.00

My Mother, lady rocking, California wild flowers make up background, FI 68-22, Fisher Studios....................$55.00

Nude about to dive into water, LM 58-3, Lee Mero....$50.00

Profile bust of man in top hat, printed on paper, AP 57-198, Art Publishing Co................................$25.00

Sprite-like figure resting on flower, rainbow backbround, RI 45-794, C&A Richards Co $240.00

Thermometer, 1940 calendar, Newton #45-21, $40.00. (Photo courtesy Shirley and Ray Mace)

Silverplated and Sterling Flatware

The secondary market is being tapped more and more as the only source for those replacement pieces needed to augment family heirloom sets, and there are many collectors who admire the vintage flatware simply because they appreciate its beauty, quality, and affordability. Several factors influence pricing. For instance, a popular pattern though plentiful may be more expensive than a scarce one that might be passed over because it very likely would be difficult to collect. When you buy silverplate, condition is very important, since replating can be expensive.

Pieces with no monograms are preferred; in fact, newer monogrammed sterling is very hard to sell. Monograms seem to be better accepted on pieces over one hundred years old. To evaluate monogrammed items, deduct 20% from fancy or rare examples; 30% from common, plain items; and 50% to 70% if they are worn.

Interest in silverplated flatware from the 1950s and 1960s is on the increase as the older patterns are becoming harder to find in excellent condition. As a result, prices are climbing.

Dinner knives range in size from 9⅜" to 10"; dinner forks from 7⅜" to 7¾". Luncheon knives are approximately 8½" to 8¾", while luncheon forks are about 6¾" to 7". Place knives measure 8⅞" to 9¼", and place forks 7⅛" to 7¼".

Our values are given for flatware in excellent condition. Matching services often advertise in various trade papers and can be very helpful in helping you locate the items you're looking for.

If you'd like to learn more about the subject, we recommend *The Standard Encyclopedia of American Silverplate* by Frances M. Bones and Lee Roy Fisher, and *Silverplated Flatware* by Tere Hagan (Collector Books).

Advisor: Rick Spencer (See Directory, Regal)

Silverplate

Adoration, 1939, berry spoon, 1847 Rogers.................**$30.00**
Adoration, 1939, dinner fork, 1847 Rogers **$7.00**
Adoration, 1939, grapefruit spoon, 1847 Rogers **$9.00**
Adoration, 1939, teaspoon, 1847 Rogers.....................**$4.00**
Caprice, 1937, cocktail/seafood fork, Nobility.............**$7.00**
Caprice, 1937, gravy ladle, Nobility...........................**$24.00**
Caprice, 1937, iced tea spoon, Nobility **$8.00**
Caprice, 1937, salad fork, Nobility.............................**$7.00**
Coronation, 1936, dessert spoon, Community **$7.50**
Coronation, 1936, dinner knife, French blade, Community ..**$9.00**
Coronation, 1936, jelly server, Community **$16.00**
Coronation, 1936, luncheon fork, Community **$7.00**
Coronation, 1936, relish spoon, Community **$16.00**
Daffodil, 1950, butter spreader, flat handled, individual, 1847 Rogers.................**$8.00**
Daffodil, 1950, carving knife, 1847 Rogers **$40.00**
Daffodil, 1950, viande-grille fork, 1847 Rogers **$7.00**
Danish Princess, 1938, luncheon fork, Holmes & Edwards ..**$7.00**
Danish Princess, 1938, pickle fork, Holmes & Edwards .**$14.00**
Danish Princess, 1938, soup spoon, oval, Holmes & Edwards **$8.00**
Danish Princess, 1938, tomato/flat server, Holmes & Edwards **$60.00**
Danish Princess, 1938, viande-grille knife, modern blade, Holmes & Edwards **$7.00**
Danish Princess, 1938, 5 o'clock coffee spoon, Holmes & Edwards **$7.00**
Eternally Yours, 1941, cold meat fork, 1847 Rogers ...**$38.00**
Eternally Yours, 1941, demitasse spoon, 1847 Rogers ..**$12.00**
Eternally Yours, 1941, dinner fork, 1847 Rogers **$8.00**
Eternally Yours, 1941, punch ladle, hollow handled, 1847 Rogers.................**$225.00**
Eternally Yours, 1941, tablespoon, pierced, 1847 Rogers..**$35.00**
Evening Star, 1950, carving set, steak size, 2-pc, Community ..**$65.00**
Evening Star, 1950, cocktail/seafood fork, Community.**$8.00**
Evening Star, 1950, pie server, flat handled, Community ..**$35.00**
Evening Star, 1950, place setting, viande-grille size, modern blade, 4-pc, Community **$27.00**
Evening Star, 1950, salad fork, Community **$7.00**
Exquisite, 1940, butter spreader, flat handled, individual, Rogers & Bros **$7.00**
Exquisite, 1940, dinner fork, Rogers & Bros...............**$7.00**
Exquisite, 1940, gravy ladle, Rogers & Bros **$25.00**
Exquisite, 1940, master butter knife, Rogers & Bros....**$5.00**
Exquisite, 1940, sugar spoon, Rogers & Bros **$5.00**
First Love, 1937, dessert fork, engraved tines, 1847 Rogers **$18.00**
First Love, 1937, pie server, flat handled, pierced floral design, 1847 Rogers.................**$65.00**
First Love, 1937, soup spoon, 1847 Rogers **$8.00**
First Love, 1937, sugar tongs, 1847 Rogers.................**$48.00**
First Love, 1937, teaspoon, 1847 Rogers.....................**$4.00**
Grenoble, 1938, cold meat fork, Prestige Plate **$25.00**
Grenoble, 1938, cream soup spoon, Prestige Plate.......**$8.00**
Grenoble, 1938, jelly server, Prestige Plate.................**$15.00**

Grenoble, 1938, tablespoon, pierced, Prestige Plate...**$16.00**
Grenoble, 1938, viande-grille knife, modern blade, Prestige Plate **$7.00**
Heritage, 1953, berry spoon, 1847 Rogers...................**$27.00**
Heritage, 1953, bonbon/candy nut spoon, pierced, w/teeth, 1847 Rogers **$18.00**
Heritage, 1953, pickle fork, 1847 Rogers **$15.00**
Heritage, 1953, salad fork, 1847 Rogers......................**$7.00**
Heritage, 1953, tomato/flat server, 1847 Rogers.........**$35.00**
Lady Hamilton, 1932, dinner knife, French blade, Community **$7.00**
Lady Hamilton, 1932, iced tea spoon, Community **$8.00**
Lady Hamilton, 1932, jelly server, Community **$15.00**
Lady Hamilton, 1932, sugar spoon, Community...........**$5.00**
Leilani, 1961, cocktail/seafood spoon, 1847 Rogers....**$7.00**
Leilani, 1961, master butter knife, flat, 1847 Rogers.....**$5.00**
Leilani, 1961, relish spoon, 1847 Rogers.....................**$12.00**
Leilani, 1961, teaspoon, 1847 Rogers **$4.00**
Lovelace, 1936, sugar tongs, 1847 Rogers...................**$30.00**
Lovely Lady, 1937, berry spoon, Holmes & Edwards .**$28.00**
Lovely Lady, 1937, butter spreader, flat handled, individual, Holmes & Edwards **$7.00**
Lovely Lady, 1937, dinner fork, Holmes & Edwards.....**$7.00**
Lovely Lady, 1937, tablespoon, pierced, Holmes & Edwards **$20.00**
Milady, 1940, jelly server, Community **$16.00**
Milady, 1940, soup spoon, round bowl, Community....**$8.00**
Milady, 1940, viande-grille fork, Community **$7.00**
Morning Rose, 1960, gravy ladle, Community.............**$18.00**
Morning Rose, 1960, place setting, dinner size, modern blade, 4-pc, Community **$25.00**
Morning Rose, 1960, 5 o'clock coffee spoon, Community..**$5.00**
Morning Star, 1948, cocktail/seafood fork, Community..**$10.00**
Morning Star, 1948, cold meat fork, Community........**$20.00**
Morning Star, 1948, demitasse spoon, Community **$10.00**
Morning Star, 1948, luncheon fork, Community..........**$8.00**
Morning Star, 1948, tablespoon, Community..............**$12.00**
Proposal, 1954, dinner fork, 1881 Rogers **$7.00**
Proposal, 1954, pie server, flat handled, 1881 Rogers...**$18.00**
Queen Bess II, 1946, berry spoon, Tudor Plate..........**$18.00**
Queen Bess II, 1946, iced tea spoon, Tudor Plate........**$7.00**
Queen Bess II, 1946, salad fork, Tudor Plate...............**$6.00**
Queen Bess II, 1946, sugar tongs, Tudor Plate...........**$24.00**
Reflection, 1959, grapefruit spoon, 1847 Rogers **$10.00**
Reflection, 1959, master butter knife, flat, 1847 Rogers ..**$5.00**
Reflection, 1959, pie server, flat handled, 1847 Rogers ..**$38.00**
Reflection, 1959, relish spoon, 1847 Rogers **$14.00**
Rememberance, 1948, carving set, steak size, 2-pc, 1847 Rogers **$75.00**
Rememberance, 1948, cream soup spoon, 1847 Rogers..**$10.00**
Rememberance, 1948, soup ladle, hollow handled, 1847 Rogers.................**$145.00**
Rememberance, 1948, tea strainer, 1847 Rogers **$100.00**
Royal Rose, 1939, cold meat fork, Nobility **$16.00**
Royal Rose, 1939, dessert spoon, oval, Nobility...........**$8.00**
Royal Rose, 1939, dinner knife, modern blade, Nobility .**$8.00**
Royal Rose, 1939, gravy ladle, Nobility.......................**$20.00**

Royal Rose, 1939, salad serving set, melamine plastic top, Nobility **$35.00**
South Seas, 1955, demitasse spoon, Community...........**$7.00**
South Seas, 1955, gravy ladle, Community **$20.00**
South Seas, 1955, soup spoon, oval, Community **$7.00**
South Seas, 1955, tablespoon, pierced, Community ...**$18.00**
Spring Garden, 1949, iced tea spoon, Holmes & Edwards ..**$8.00**
Spring Garden, 1949, jelly server, Holmes & Edwards..**$15.00**
Spring Garden, 1949, salad serving spoon, Holmes & Edwards **$30.00**
Spring Garden, 1949, teaspoon, Holmes & Edwards **$4.00**
Springtime, 1957, berry spoon, 1847 Rogers **$18.00**
Springtime, 1957, dinner fork, 1847 Rogers..................**$7.00**
Springtime, 1957, relish spoon, 1847 Rogers **$8.00**
Springtime, 1957, sugar tongs, 1847 Rogers **$18.00**

White Orchid, 1953, dinner knife and fork, Community, from $7.00 to $9.00 each.

White Orchid, 1953, cream soup spoon, Community...**$8.00**
White Orchid, 1953, pickle fork, Community..............**$15.00**
White Orchid, 1953, soup ladle, hollow handled, Community **$195.00**
White Orchid, 1953, soup spoon, oval, Community.....**$8.00**
Youth, 1940, gravy ladle, Holmes & Edwards **$20.00**
Youth, 1940, jelly server, Holmes & Edwards.............**$15.00**
Youth, 1940, teaspoon, Holmes & Edwards **$4.00**

Sterling

Afterglo, 1956, gravy ladle, Oneida **$50.00**
Afterglo, 1956, salad fork, Oneida **$25.00**
Alexandra, 1961, bonbon/nut spoon, Lunt, 6¼" **$40.00**
Alexandra, 1961, pickle fork, Lunt, 5⅞".......................**$32.00**
Alexandra, 1961, soup spoon, oval, Lunt, 6¾"............**$40.00**
Alexandra, 1961, tablespoon, pierced, Lunt, 8⅜".......**$90.00**
Angelique, 1959, cold meat fork, International, 9⅛" ..**$70.00**
Angelique, 1959, salad fork, International, 6½" **$28.00**
Angelique, 1959, tablespoon, International, 8½"........**$60.00**
Blossomtime, 1950, cream soup spoon, International, 6½"..**$28.00**
Blossomtime, 1950, lemon fork, International, 4⅝" **$20.00**
Blossomtime, 1950, sugar spoon, International, 6" **$28.00**
Brocade, 1950, butter spreader, flat handled, individual, International, 5⅝" **$25.00**
Brocade, 1950, jelly server, International, 6½" **$40.00**
Brocade, 1950, teaspoon, International, 6" **$20.00**
Cameo, 1959, cheese server, Reed & Barton, 7⅝" **$40.00**
Cameo, 1959, tablespoon, pierced, Reed & Barton, 8½" ..**$80.00**
Camillia, 1942, luncheon fork, Gorham, 7¼" **$28.00**
Camillia, 1942, sugar spoon, Gorham, 6" **$25.00**

Celeste, 1956, cold meat fork, Gorham, 8½"...............**$55.00**
Celeste, 1956, teaspoon, Gorham, 5⅞" **$25.00**
Chateau Rose, 1940, cream soup spoon, Alvin, 6¼" ..**$28.00**
Chateau Rose, 1940, gravy ladle, Alvin, 6⅛" **$80.00**
Classic Bouquet, 1972, sugar spoon, Gorham, 6¼" **$40.00**
Classic Rose, 1954, butter spreader, paddle blade, hollow handled, individual, Reed & Barton, 6¼" **$25.00**
Classic Rose, 1954, cream ladle, Reed & Barton, 5½"...**$37.00**
Classic Rose, 1954, lemon fork, Reed & Barton, 4⅞"..**$28.00**
Classique, 1961, bonbon/candy nut spoon, Gorham, 4¾"..**$37.00**
Classique, 1961, tomato/flat server, Gorham, 8⅝" **$100.00**
Contessina, 1965, cocktail/seafood fork, Towle, 5⅞".**$20.00**
Contessina, 1965, pickle fork, Towle, 5¾"...................**$20.00**
Contour, 1950, tablespoon, Towle, 8¾".......................**$65.00**
Contour, 1950, teaspoon, Towle, 6⅜" **$25.00**
Damask Rose, 1946, baby spoon, Oneida **$25.00**
Damask Rose, 1946, carving knife, Oneida, 11¼" **$50.00**
Damask Rose, 1946, jelly server, Oneida, 6⅜" **$28.00**
Damask Rose, 1946, salad fork, Oneida, 6½"..............**$26.00**
Dancing Flowers, 1950, cheese server, Reed & Barton, 6⅝"...**$32.00**
Dancing Flowers, 1950, teaspoon, Reed & Barton, 6" ..**$20.00**
Debussy, 1959, gravy ladle, Towle, 6⅝" **$90.00**
Debussy, 1959, lemon fork, Towle, 5⅜" **$37.00**
Diamond, 1958, berry spoon, Reed & Barton, 9½" ..**$135.00**
Diamond, 1958, sugar tongs, Reed & Barton, 4½" **$38.00**
Eloquence, 1953, soup spoon, oval, Lunt, 6⅝" **$38.00**
Eloquence, 1953, sugar spoon, Lunt, 6"......................**$50.00**
English Gadroon, 1939, cake breaker, Gorham, 11⅛"..**$48.00**
English Gadroon, 1939, pickle fork, Gorham, 5⅞" **$30.00**
English Provincial, 1965, gravy ladle, Reed & Barton, 6¾" ..**$55.00**
English Provincial, 1965, lemon fork, Reed & Barton, 5⅛" ..**$22.00**
Florentine Lace, 1951, master butter knife, flat, Reed & Barton, 7⅜" **$60.00**
Florentine Lace, 1951, salad fork, Reed & Barton, 6½" **$40.00**
Florentine Lace, 1951, sugar spoon, Reed & Barton, 6⅛" ..**$40.00**
French Provincial, 1948, cheese server, Towle, 5⅜"..**$40.00**
French Provincial, 1948, teaspoon, Towle, 5⅞" **$20.00**
Grandeur, 1960, cold meat fork, Oneida, 8⅜" **$50.00**
John & Priscilla, 1940, cream soup spoon, Westmoreland, 6⅛" **$25.00**
John & Priscilla, 1940, gravy ladle, Westmoreland, 6¼"..**$40.00**
Lyric, 1940, berry spoon, Gorham, 8⅞" **$125.00**
Lyric, 1940, sugar tongs, Gorham, 4" **$48.00**
Milburn Rose, 1940, cocktail/seafood fork, Westmoreland, 5½" **$25.00**
Milburn Rose, 1940, gravy ladle, Westmoreland, 6"....**$45.00**
Old Master, 1942, lemon fork, Towle, 5⅜" **$28.00**
Old Master, 1942, salad fork, Towle, 6¼" **$30.00**
Old Mirror, 1940, cream soup spoon, Towle, 6⅜" **$37.00**
Queen's Lace, 1949, tomato/flat server, International, 8" ..**$125.00**
Richelieu, 1935, berry spoon, International, 8¾" **$200.00**
Rose Tiara, 1963, lemon fork, Gorham, 4⅜" **$22.00**
Silver Melody, 1955, dessert spoon, oval, International, 6¾" **$32.00**
Silver Melody, 1955, lemon fork, International, 5⅜"...**$28.00**
Silver Sculpture, 1954, pickle fork, Reed & Barton, 5¾"..**$27.00**
Silver Wheat, 1952, gravy ladle, Reed & Barton, 6⅝".**$65.00**

Silver Wheat, 1952, cheese server, hollow handle, Reed & Barton **$28.00**
Silver Wheat, 1952, luncheon fork, Reed & Barton, 7⅜" .. **$28.00**
South Wind, 1952, tablespoon, Towle, 8¾" **$70.00**
Spring Glory, 1942, jelly server, International, 6½" **$37.00**
Spring Glory, 1942, sugar spoon, International, 5⅞" **$28.00**
Tapestry, 1964, bonbon/candy nut spoon, Reed & Barton .. **$40.00**
Tapestry, 1964, salad fork, Reed & Barton, 7" **$38.00**
Tara, 1955, pickle fork, Reed & Barton, 5¾" **$32.00**
Valencia, 1965, soup spoon, oval, International, 7¼" . **$32.00**
Virginian, 1942, cold meat fork, Oneida, 8" **$70.00**
Wild Rose, 1948, jelly server, International, 6⅜" **$32.00**
Wild Rose, 1948, teaspoon, International, 5¾" **$17.00**
Wild Rose, 1962, demitasse spoon, Wallace, 4" **$18.00**
Young Love, 1958, relish spoon, Oneida, 5¼" **$28.00**

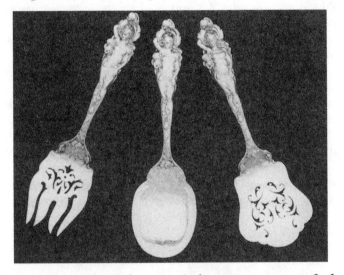

Love Disarmed, early twentieth century, meat fork, large serving spoon, pierced flat server, Reed and Barton, 21 troy ounces, $1,500.00. (Currently being produced; bearing new mark: $1,000.00.)

Skookum Indian Dolls

The Skookums Apple Packers Association of Wenatchee, Washington, had a doll made from their trademark. Skookum figures were designed and registered by a Montana woman, Mary McAboy, in 1917. Although she always made note of the Skookum's name, she also used the 'Bully Good' trademark along with other information to inform the buyer that 'Bully Good' translated is 'Skookums.' McAboy had an article published in the March 1920 issue of *Playthings* magazine explaining the history of Skookum dolls. Anyone interested can obtain this information on microfilm from any large library.

In 1920 the Arrow Novelty Company held the contract to make the dolls, but by 1929 the H.H. Tammen Company had taken over their production. Skookums were designed with life-like facial characteristics. The dried apple heads of the earliest dolls did not last, and they were soon replaced with heads made of a composition material. Wool blankets formed the bodies that

were then stuffed with dried twigs, leaves, and grass. The remainder of the body was cloth and felt.

Skookum dolls with wooden legs and felt-covered wooden feet were made between 1917 and 1949. After 1949 the legs and feet were made of plastic. The newest dolls have plastic heads. A 'Skookums Bully Good Indians' paper label was placed on one foot of each early doll. Exact dating of a Skookum is very difficult. McAboy designed many different tribes of dolls simply by using different blanket styles, beading, and backboards (for carrying the papoose). The store display dolls, 36" and larger, are the most valuable of the Skookums. Prices range from $2,000.00 to $2,500.00 per doll or $4,500.00 to $5,000.00 for the pair.

Advisor: Jo Ann Palmieri (See Directory Skookum Dolls)

Child, plastic legs, 6" to 8", from $35 to **$50.00**
Child, plastic legs, 8" to 10", from $50 to **$75.00**
Child, wooden legs, 6½", from $35 to **$50.00**
Female, wooden legs, 13½" **$400.00**
Female, wooden legs, 16" **$600.00**
Female w/papoose, wooden legs, 8" to 10", from $75 to .. **$150.00**
Female w/papoose, wooden legs, 10" to 12", from $150 to **$250.00**
Female w/papoose, wooden legs, 14" to 16", from $250 to **$300.00**
Male, wooden legs, 8" to 10", from $125 to **$175.00**

Male, wooden legs, 10" to 12", from $175.00 to $250.00.

Male, wooden legs, 12" to 14", from $200 to **$275.00**
Male, wooden legs, 14" to 16", from $300 to **$400.00**

Smiley Face

The Smiley Face was designed in 1963 by Harvey Ball, a commercial artist that had been commissioned by an insurance company to design a 'happy' logo to use on office supplies and pin-back buttons — seems spirits were low due to unpopular company policies, and the office manager was looking for something that would cheer up her employees. 'Operation Smile' was a huge success. Who would have thought that such a simple concept — tiny eyes with a curving line to represent a big smile in black on a bright yellow background — would have become the enduring icon that it did. Mr. Young was paid a mere $45.00 for his efforts, and no one even bothered to obtain a trademark for Smiley! Over the year, many companies have designed scores of products featuring the happy face. The McCoy Pottery Comany was one of them; they made a line of cookie jars, mugs, banks, and planters. No matter if you collect Smiley or McCoy, you'll want to watch for those!

The Smiley face is enjoying renewed popularity today — you'll find many 'new' examples in those specialty catalogs we all get so many of. But if you buy the vintage Smileys, expect to pay several times their original retail price. Right now, these are hot!

Bank, McCoy...**$40.00**

Bank, Treasure Craft Made in USA, 6", from $65.00 to $70.00. (Photo courtesy Jim and Beverly Mangus)

Bank, yellow w/black face & white legs, Play Pals Plastics, 1971 ....**$30.00**
Clock, wall; plastic, flower petal edges, battery-op, 10" dia, M **$25.00**
Cookie jar, McCoy, 12", from $60 to **$75.00**
Diary, multicolored panel w/Smiley Face, spiral, Colorbok, 5¾x4¼x1", M **$8.00**
Frisbee, yellow face, Wham-O, 1980s, 10" dia **$12.00**
Ice bucket, yellow w/black face on 1 side, yellow face on other side, Have a Nice Day on lid, brass handle .**$75.00**
Martini shaker, glass, 24-oz, 9½" **$35.00**
Mug, ivory w/red face, McCoy **$20.00**
Mug, yellow w/black face, McCoy **$30.00**
Necklace, sm black & yellow beads w/lg yellow Smiley Face beads, 2 strands, M **$25.00**
Pez candy dispenser, Wal-Mart, MOC **$6.00**
Pin, hot pink w/black face, ½" dia **$10.00**
Planter, w/attached underplate, marked McCoy #03, 4½"..**$35.00**

Salt & pepper shakers, yellow w/black face, marked Japan, 3" dia, EX, pr...**$10.00**
Teapot, ceramic, yellow ball shape w/Smiley Face, black handle & spout, from $15 to.............................**$18.00**
Telephone, yellow w/black features, receiver in top, 1996, EX..**$55.00**
Tumbler, red face w/black smile on white, 5" **$7.00**
Vase, yellow w/black face, single holder on top, Enesco, 6" dia, MIB **$10.00**
Watch, yellow face w/Smile along bottom of crystal, black plastic band, Fada Inc, Japanese movement, VG+ **$25.00**

Snow Domes

Snow dome collectors buy them all, old and new. The older ones (from the '30s and '40s) are made in two pieces, the round glass globe that sits on a separate base. They were made here as well as in Italy, and today this type is being imported from Austria and the Orient.

During the '50s, plastic snow domes made in West Germany were popular as souvenirs and Christmas toys. Some were half-domes with blue backs; others were made in bottle shapes or simple geometric forms.

There were two styles produced in the '70s. Both were made of plastic. The first were designed as large domes with a plastic figure of an animal, a mermaid, or some other character draped over the top. In the other style, the snow dome itself was made in an unusual shape.

Commemorative, Nautilus, glass, $50.00; War Between the States, plastic, $15.00. (Photo courtesy Nancy McMichael)

Angel w/gift, Happy Birthday on white porcelain base, Josef, 5¾x4" dia **$35.00**
Betty Boop in long black car, MIB..........................**$24.00**
Christmas, nativity scene, lighted by battery, Made in Hong Kong, 3"..**$18.00**
Christmas, Santa w/dome in tummy, sm Santa w/pack inside dome, plastic, 1960s, 5½"..........................**$30.00**
Christmas, Santa w/gift in his arms, belly is snow dome, hard plastic, 1960s, 5½" **$14.00**

Christmas, snowman & trees, Hong Kong, #833, 2¼" ...**$10.00**

Christmas, snowman w/carrot nose, Santa w/bag of toys & trees in tummy dome, plastic, Made in Hong Kong, 5¾" ..**$20.00**

Jemima Puddle Duck (Beatrix Potter character), New England Collectors Society, 1992, 4" **$32.50**

Jeremy Fisher (Beatrix Potter character), New England Collectors Society, 1992 1st limited edition, 4" **$40.00**

Jiminy Cricket, Disney, 1st limited edition, 4x3⅛" **$20.00**

Musical, carousel horse, San Francisco Music Box Co, 5¾".**$15.00**

Musical, Lion King, plays Circle of Life, Disney, 7x6", NM...**$35.00**

Musical, Santa & sleigh w/Ronald McDonald & other McDonald characters, plays Winter Wonderland, MIB **$30.00**

Musical, Tara from Gone w/the Wind, lights up, w/certificate of authenticity **$20.00**

Pendulum clock w/angel resting on crescent moon in mini globe, painted polyresin, battery-powered clock, 14", MIB **$32.50**

Pez dispenser bride & groom, Pez on black plastic base, retired, MIB **$35.00**

Royal Canadian Mounted Police on horseback, plastic w/white base, Made in Hong Kong **$18.00**

Santa, scene in tummy of 2 children building snowman, plastic, Made in Hong Kong, 5½" **$20.00**

Santa & Reindeer, plastic, Made in Hong Kong, #833, 3¾x2¾" **$10.00**

Snoopy WWI Flying Ace, w/Woodstock & friends along body of plane base, 5", MIB **$35.00**

Souvenir, alligator holding globe, Florida on front, plastic, Hong Kong stamped on bottom, 4¾" **$15.00**

Souvenir, Crystal Cave, PA, plastic w/white base, 2¼" ..**$14.00**

Souvenir, elephant atop dome w/2 elephants inside, plastic, Zoological Park NC, Made in Hong Kong, 5" **$35.00**

Souvenir, Hearst Castle, San Simeon CA, plastic w/yellowed base, 2⅛" **$25.00**

Souvenir, Oakland Tribune, Oakland A's, plastic, green & white snow, 3x3⅝x2" **$20.00**

Souvenir, Paris Bulldogs, Parisian street scene, plastic, Made in France, 2¼x3" **$25.00**

Souvenir, Radio City Rockettes, 4 dancers, hard plastic, 3¼x3¼" **$55.00**

Souvenir, South Carolina surfers, plastic, Hong Kong, #352, 2¼" **$36.00**

Souvenir, Wildwood by the Sea, NJ, plastic w/white base, 2½x3" **$22.00**

Souvenir, 1982 World's Fair, plastic, Made in Hong Kong, #806, 3⅜" **$28.00**

Tinker Belle, Disney, Made in England, 3⅞" **$42.50**

Soda-Pop Memorabilia

A specialty area of the advertising field, soft-drink memorabilia is a favorite of many collectors. Now that vintage Coca-Cola items have become rather expensive, interest is expanding to include some of the less widely exploited sodas — Grapette, Hires Root Beer, and Dr. Pepper, for instance. See also Coca-Cola; Pepsi-Cola.

Advisor: Craig Stifter (See Directory, Soda-Pop Memorabilia)

Newsletter: National Pop Can Collectors
Bruce Mobley, Director
PO Box 163, Macon, MO 63552-0163
www.one-mans-junk.com/N PCC

A-Treat Beverages, calendar, 1959, complete, EX **$85.00**

Altpeter's Beverages, bottle topper, cardboard, Keep Cool With..., baseball players confronting umpire, NM..**$25.00**

B-1 Lemon Lime Soda, thermometer, tin, More Zip in Every Sip!, exclamation mark gauge on blue & white stripes, 15", NM **$65.00**

B-1 Lemon-Lime Soda, display, cardboard, automated w/star lights flashing behind screen, More Zip..., 1960, 16x13x4", EX **$100.00**

Barq's, sign, cardboard, Drink...It's Good, red & white lettering at left of bottle on red dot, blue ground, 11x28", NM **$85.00**

Birchola, fan, cardboard w/stick handle, reverse shows couple in each other's gaze at table, EX....................**$75.00**

Bireley's, light scounces, orange-painted bottle shapes w/embossed name, silver-painted spiral brackets, 12", EX, pr..**$800.00**

Bireley's, sign, tin, Got a Minute? Enjoy a Cool Refreshing Bireley's, shows fruit & bottles, 1950s, 13x20", NM .**$250.00**

Bireley's, thermometer, tin, Drink...Non-Carbonated Beverages, bottle next to gauge, yellow, 26x10", EX..................**$200.00**

Bubble Up, Sign, celluloid, Just Pure Pleasure! above bubble logo on green background, 9x13", NM, $135.00. (Photo courtesy Gary Metz)

Bubble Up, sign, tin, Bubble Up ...Has Pa-Zazz!, lg bottle cap on blue ground w/bubbles, beveled edge, 12x28", NM..**$125.00**

Canada Dry, clock, round w/glass front, metal frame, Enjoy..., black numbers & dots w/crown & shield logo, 1962, 15", EX......................................**$500.00**

Canada Dry, door plate, porcelain, Drink Canada Dry/Take Home a Carton, shows bottle, yellow ground, 1950s, 14", EX+ **$150.00**

Canada Dry, sign, porcelain, Drink (green script) Canada Dry (red block) Beverages (green script) on white, 12x35", EX **$175.00**

Cliquot Club Beverages, thermometer, tin, curved corners, Quality Since..., arched above oval image of Cliquot boy, NM **$75.00**

Cliquot Club Ginger Ale, sign, cardboard diecut stand-up, ...50 Years the Favorite, lady & boy w/lg bottle, 39", EX **$130.00**

Dad's Root Beer, sign, tin, straight-sided bottle on blue tray, yellow ground, red border, 1940s-50s, 29x13", EX+ **$280.00**

Donald Duck Beverages, sign, tin, curved corners, shows Donald's head, blue & white w/blue border, 20x28", EX+ **$365.00**

Donald Duck Cola, sign, cardboard diecut stand-up, Tops for Flavour, bottle cap/hand-held bottle in ice, 1950s, 26", NM+ **$150.00**

Donald Duck Cola, sign, diecut paper on cardboard easel back, 22x26", EX, $85.00. (Photo courtesy Buffalo Bay)

Double Cola, menu board, tin, logo above blackboard, red, white & blue, 28x20", NM+ **$95.00**

Double Cola, radio, can shape, EX **$35.00**

Dr Pepper, bottle opener, diecut metal lion's head w/etched design & lettering, 3", EX.......................................**$85.00**

Dr Pepper, calendar, 1951, complete, EX+ **$100.00**

Dr Pepper, decal, Try a Frosty Pep.../Dr Pepper/And Ice Cream, hand pouring bottle over ice cream, 1950, 13x9", NM **$50.00**

Dr Pepper, match holder, tin, 1940s-50s, 6", NMIB ..**$200.00**

Dr Pepper, sign, flange, bottle cap atop Sold Here panel, red & black on white, yellow flange, 1950s-60s, 18x22", NM...**$1,100.00**

Dr Pepper, sign, tin, red oval above gold V on white, embossed, curved corners, raised rim, 1960s, 12x28", EX **$125.00**

Dr Pepper, thermometer, tin, curved top, Hot or Cold Enjoy...Pepper Upper, oval logo, red & white, 1950s, 16", EX **$175.00**

Dr Pepper, thermometer, tin, When Hungry, Thirsty or Tired Drink..., yellow, 1940s, 26", EX **$400.00**

Frostie Root Beer, clock, bottle cap form, 18" dia, VG ..**$100.00**

Frostie Root Beer, dial type, 12" dia, M **$125.00**

Frostie Root Beer, menu board, tin, A Real Taste Treat..., mascot holding bottle flanked by slots, 1950, 12x36", NM+ **$500.00**

Grapette, clock, round light-up w/metal frame, lg bottle in center, 1940s, NM+ **$450.00**

Grapette, sign, porcelain oval, Grapette Soda, white on blue w/white & red border, 10x17", EX **$300.00**

Grapette, thermometer, tin, Remember To Buy..., bottle next to gauge, 15", EX...**$100.00**

Green River, sign, celluloid oval, A Quality Drink for a Quick Pick-Up on red border of moonlit river scene, 7", VG+ **$40.00**

Hires, dispenser, metal box w/flat lift-off lid, Hires R-J Root Beer logos, 1940s, 22x12x16", VG+ **$300.00**

Hires, menu board, 30x16", EX, $170.00. (Photo courtesy Buffalo Bay)

Hires, menu board, tin, Drink...In Bottles, blackboard center w/light blue & white striped bottom, 28x20", NM ..**$125.00**

Hires, recipe book, EX **$65.00**

Hires, sign, cardboard diecut, With Lunch 5¢, open bottle & full glass, 1940s, 11x10", NM+ **$95.00**

Hires, sign, tin, Hires Refreshes Right! Since 1876, tilted bottle, light blue, 1940s, 42x13", NM.....................**$300.00**

Hires, sign, tin, Hires to You!, slanted lettering & bottle against cloud on blue, 1940s-50s, 42x14", EX+ ..**$375.00**

Hires, sign, tin, round embossed R-J logo, red, white & blue, 24" dia, EX..**$125.00**

Hires, sign, tin bottle shape, 1950s, 22", M **$175.00**

Hires, thermometer, tin bottle shape w/Since 1879 label, 29", NM **$250.00**

Hires, tin w/cardboard back, Got a Minute/Have a Hires/Your Invitation To Refresh on white 'invitation,' 1950s, 9x6", NM **$175.00**

Kist Beverages, calendar, 1946, Get Kist for a Nickel!, garden girl admiring orange poppies, 26x14", NM+.......**$175.00**

Kist Beverages, clock, round light-up, glass front w/metal frame, Enjoy..., Telechron, 15", EX+...................**$175.00**

Kist Beverages, door pull, advertising on backplate w/black handle, EX+...**$115.00**

Kist Beverages, sign, tin bottle shape, orange, 1940s-50s, 48", NM+ **$425.00**

Mission Beverages, bottle topper, cardboard, Try This Delicious New Beverage, hand squeezing fresh orange juice, M **$60.00**

Mission Beverages, menu board, cardboard, Mission of California/Today's Specials, slots flank bottle & fruit, 13x32", NM **$125.00**

Mission Beverages, thermometer, tin w/stepped sides, bottle on white, 1950s, 17", NM **$165.00**

Moxie, ashtray, ceramic, white round dish w/3 rests, Moxie Man in center, EX+ **$70.00**

Moxie, bottle carrier w/bottles, cardboard, 6-pack, Moxie & Man & Moxie symbol on red & yellow stripes, EX+ **$100.00**

Moxie, clock, plastic sq w/gold embossed frame, Roman numerals, Since 1884/Old Fashioned Moxie on orange, 16x16", EX **$200.00**

Moxie, sign, carboard diecut, He's Got Moxie 5¢, bust of boy in baseball cap holding up bottle, 1940s, 16x12", M **$250.00**

Moxie, sign, tin flange, octagonal, Drink Moxie 100%, red, green & white, 8x8", VG+ **$325.00**

Moxie, thermometer, tin, Drink Moxie/It's Always a Pleasure To Serve You, Moxie man next to gauge, red, 1953, 25", EX+ **$700.00**

Nehi, clock, round w/glass front, metal frame, Drink Nehi Orange & Other Flavors on yellow dot, blue numbers, 15", NM **$375.00**

Nehi, sign, flange, Drink Nehi Ice Cold next to diecut bottle on yellow panel, red trim, 1940s, 13x18", NM ...**$525.00**

Nehi, sign, tin, Nehi Quality Beverages lettered below lg bottle on white, embossed, 1940s, 20x6", EX **$100.00**

Nesbitt's, distance chart, cardboard w/steel frame, shows distance from central point to other cities, 1955, 31x7", EX+ **$40.00**

Nesbitt's, sign, cardboard, family barbecue scene w/advertising disk in upper right corner, 1940s, 24x36", EX+ **$250.00**

Nesbitt's, sign, porcelain, Nesbitt's Orange on geometric background, orange white & black, 1950s, 12x25", NM **$375.00**

NuGrape, blotter, image of bottle, unused, EX+ **$30.00**

NuGrape, bottle topper, cardboard, Hits the Spot... on oval w/man in shirt & tie holding bottle, EX **$60.00**

NuGrape, clock, round light-up, name on yellow oval over tilted bottle, Telechron, 15" dia, EX **$275.00**

NuGrape, tray, A Flavor You Can't Forget, oval image of hand-held bottle, 13x11", VG..**$60.00**

Orange-Crush, bottle display, cardboard, At Ease!/Always in the Krinkly Bottle!, 2 serviceman, w/bottle, 1940s, VG **$700.00**

Orange-Crush, calendar, 1946, 31x16", complete, VG ..**$125.00**

Orange-Crush, dispenser, clear glass beveled bowl on clamp base, white diamond logo, top spigot, 1930s-40s, NM..**$375.00**

Orange-Crush, menu board, metal, Drink Orange-Crush Frosty Cold next to Crushy logo, blackboard bottom, 1954, 28x19", EX..**$275.00**

Orange-Crush, reverse-painted glass, round, Fresh!/Drink O-C, shows Crushy w/bottle, white & orange, 9½" dia, VG+..**$200.00**

Orange-Crush, sign, tin, Ask for a.../Natural Flavor! Natural Color, yellow & white on orange, 1970s, 12x24", NM+..**$85.00**

Orange-Crush, thermometer, tin w/curved top & bottom, bottle cap above gauge, turquoise, 1950s, 15x6", NM......**$130.00**

Orange-Crush, toy truck, diecast wind-up, London Toy/Canada, scarce, 6", VG **$100.00**

Orange-Kist, sign, cardboard diecut stand-up, ...And Other Kist Flavors, Rolf Armstrong girl bending over, 12x9", VG+..**$250.00**

Orange-Kist, sign, tin, Drink... & Other Flavors, orange & black on orange, 6x13", NM **$60.00**

Royal Crown Cola, bottle topper & bottle, cardboard, Santa in wreath w/bottle, EX **$18.00**

Royal Crown Cola, clock, round, blue numbers (12-3-6-9) w/blue crowns on white, red & white diamond logos, EX **$130.00**

Royal Crown Cola, neon clock, metal and plastic, orange light tubes, 34x37", VG, $1,950.00.

Royal Crown Cola, sign, cardboard, RC Mad Mad Cola in multicolored lettering w/girl & bottle on white, 22x34", NM **$60.00**

Royal Crown Cola, sign, tin, bottle on white, raised border, vertical, 36x16", NM..**$475.00**

Royal Crown Cola, sign, tin, Drink Royal Crown Cola/Best By Taste Test, bottles flank lettering on red, 18x58", NM+ **$400.00**

Royal Crown Cola, sign, tin bottle shape, 1952, 60", NM..**$400.00**

Royal Crown Cola, thermometer, tin, blue, bottle next to gauge, 1960s, 17", NM..**$230.00**

Royal Crown Cola, thermometer, tin, red w/gauge on yellow arrow pointing up, Best By Taste-Test, 1960s, 26", NM **$275.00**

Seven-Up, ashtray, cardboard, sq w/scalloped corners, Put Your Ashes Here & Save Our Table, logo in center, EX+ **$35.00**

Seven-Up, bill hook, celluloid button, I'd Hang for a Chilled 7-Up, EX+ **$35.00**

Seven-Up, calendar, 1943, General McArthur, complete, VG+ $35.00

Seven-Up, clock, rectangular, First Against Thirst/logo, vertical w/bowed sides, EX $75.00

Seven-Up, display, glass, bottle embedded in 'iceberg,' 1940s-50s, 9x7x8", NM $425.00

Seven-Up, door push bar, 'Fresh Up' With Seven-Up! in green 'firecracker' letters on white flanked by red logos, 32", NM $50.00

Seven-Up, mechanical pencil, bottle in liquid end, EX+..$40.00

Seven-Up, money clip, enameled dollar symbol w/logo, M $30.00

Seven-Up, music box, can shape, plays theme to Love Story, NM $50.00

Seven-Up, sign, cardboard, The All-Family Drink!, baby in highchair, gold self-frame, 1956, 13x23", NM+...$100.00

Seven-Up, sign, porcelain, tilted logo next to phrase on white, green bottom band & border, curved corners, 20x28", NM $475.00

Seven-Up, sign, school crossing, metal w/diecut cartoon cop holding sign atop 7-Up logo on round base, 1950s, 60", G $800.00

Seven-Up, thermometer, dial-type, glass w/metal frame, round logo in center, 10" or 12", NM, from $150 to .$200.00

Seven-Up, tin bottle shape, 2-sided, wet-look, 44x13", EX..$275.00

Squeeze, sign, cardboard diecut stand-up, Drink.../Delightfully Refreshing/Always Welcome, kids at fridge, 1940s-50s, EX $225.00

Squeeze, sign, tin, orange keyhole symbol w/kids on bench & bottle on white, embossed, 20x28", NM $350.00

Squirt, calendar, 1948, 4 different girls, 24x14", complete, NM $120.00

Squirt, display figure, Squirt boy next to bottle on base marked Just Call Me Squirt, chalkware, 1947, 13x8", EX+ $725.00

Squirt, doll, Squirt boy, squeeze vinyl, 1961, very rare, 6", M $450.00

Squirt, tin flange oval, Switch to Squirt/Never an After-Thirst, yellow ground, 13x18", NM $200.00

Squirt, tray, tin oval, Squirt The Drink w/the Happy Taste, boy & lg bottle in center, decorative border, 15x12", G $250.00

Sun Crest, calendar, 1949, complete, EX+ $140.00

Sun Crest, sign, cardboard, Have a Party...Get Tingle-Ated w/Sun Crest, girl w/starry eyes & party platter, 17x22", VG $25.00

Sun Crest, thermometer, dial type, Get Tingle-Ated With.../All Weather Refresher, shows bottle, glass w/metal frame, EX $200.00

Sun Crest, thermometer, tin bottle shape, 17", EX+..$225.00

Sun Crest, tin bottle cap shape, Get Tingle-Ated Drink..., yellow & orange, 1950s, 36", NM $165.00

Sun Drop Cola, sign, tin diecut bottle, 60", EX........$500.00

Sun Spot, sign, tin, Drink America's Favorite..., image of 3 bottles & round logo on black, 1940s, 15x12", EX......$75.00

Triple AAA Root Beer, sign, tin bottle shape, 45x12", NM+ $100.00

Tru Ade, sign, tin, Drink a Better Beverage, lg bottle on red, yellow border, 1940s-50s, 54x18", VG+ $300.00

Vernor's, sign, tin oval, Drink...Deliciously Different, blue lettering on yellow, 1965, 32x48", EX+ $140.00

Vernor's, thermometer, dial type w/green & yellow divided ground, 12" dia, EX $150.00

Whistle, cooler, metal picnic chest w/round decals on sides, wire clasp, 2 wire swing handles, Progress, 12x18x8", VG $160.00

Whistle, display, cardboard, 3 elves waving banners & pushing real 7-oz bottle on cart, 1948, NM+ $450.00

Whistle, pocket mirror, rectangular, 2 elves holding trademark sign, Golden Orange Refreshment, 1940s, 2x3", NM $150.00

Whistle, sign, cardboard, Golden Orange Goodness, 3-quarter view of girl in neck scarf, beveled border, 20x15", NM+ $125.00

Soda Bottles With Painted Labels

The earliest type of soda bottles were made by soda producers and sold in the immediate vicinity of the bottling company. Many had pontil scars, left by a rod that was used to manipulate the bottle as it was blown. They had a flat bottom rather than a 'kick-up,' so for transport, they were laid on their side and arranged in layers. This served to keep the cork moist, which kept it expanded, tight, and in place. Upright the cork would dry out, shrink, and expel itself with a 'pop,' hence the name 'soda pop.'

Until the '30s, the name of the product or the bottler was embossed in the glass or printed on a paper label (sometimes pasted over reused returnable bottles). Though a few paper labels were used as late as the '60s, nearly all bottles produced from the mid-'30s on had painted-on (pyro-glazed) lettering, and logos and pictures were often added. Imaginations ran rampant. Bottlers waged a fierce competition to make their soda logos eye catching and sales inspiring. Anything went! Girls, airplanes, patriotic designs, slogans proclaiming amazing health benefits, even cowboys and Indians became popular advertising ploys. This is the type you'll encounter most often today, and collector interest is on the increase. Look for interesting, multicolored labels, rare examples from small-town bottlers, and those made from glass in colors other than clear or green.

A&W Root Beer, clear glass, 10-oz $10.00

Adams, clear glass, 1-qt $25.00

Ayer's, clear glass, 10-oz $10.00

Big Boy, clear glass, 1-qt $25.00

Buffalo Rock Ginger Ale, clear glass, 7-oz $15.00

Canfield's, clear glass, 9-oz $10.00

Cardinal, clear glass, 12-oz $20.00

Choc-ola, clear glass, 9-oz $10.00

Clicquot Club Quality Flavors, green glass, 12-oz $10.00

Dr Nut, clear glass, 7-oz $10.00

Dr Swett's Original Root Beer, clear glass, 12-oz $15.00

Dybala, green glass, 1-qt $15.00

Flagship, clear glass, 10-oz **$10.00**
Fresca, green glass, 1-pt, 12-oz......................**$15.00**
Glengarry, clear glass, 7½-oz..........................**$15.00**
Gold Dot, clear glass, 12-oz **$10.00**
Golden Gate, clear glass, 1-qt **$20.00**
Hillbilly, green glass, 10-oz............................**$10.00**
Icy, clear glass, 10-oz....................................**$15.00**
Independence, clear glass, 7-oz **$15.00**
Jack Frost, clear glass, 1-qt............................**$15.00**
Liberty, clear glass, 8-oz.................................**$25.00**
Like, green glass, throwaway, 10-oz **$10.00**
Long's, clear glass, 10-oz................................**$15.00**
Maui, clear glass, 7-oz....................................**$20.00**
Miscoe Orange Dry, amber glass, 7½-oz.......**$15.00**
Nectar Sparkling Beverages, green glass, 7-oz...........**$10.00**
Orange Ball, clear glass, 12-oz **$15.00**
Orange-Crush, clear glass, 10-oz **$10.00**
Playboy, green glass, 1-qt **$25.00**
Polar, clear glass, 7-oz....................................**$15.00**
Purity's Ginger Ale, green glass, 1-qt..............**$15.00**
Red Arrow, clear glass, 7-oz............................**$10.00**
Royal Palm, clear glass, 6-oz...........................**$15.00**
Set Up, green glass, 7-oz.................................**$45.00**
Smile, clear glass, 16-oz..................................**$20.00**
Squeeze, clear glass, 7-oz or 8-oz...................**$10.00**
Squirt (Low Calorie), green glass, 10-oz **$10.00**
Sun Crest, clear glass, 12-oz...........................**$10.00**
Topflight, clear glass, 10-oz **$15.00**
Vincent's, green glass, 7-oz.............................**$15.00**
Vino Punch, amber glass, 7-oz........................**$25.00**
Walsh's, green glass, 7-oz................................**$10.00**
Yacht Club, green glass, 7½-oz........................**$15.00**
Yoo Hoo Chocolate, clear glass, 8-oz.............**$10.00**
Zee, clear glass, 7-oz......................................**$25.00**

Sporting Goods

Catalogs and various ephemera distributed by sporting good manufacturers, ammunition boxes, and just about any other item used for hunting and fishing purposes are collectible. In fact, there are auctions devoted entirely to collectors with these interests.

One of the best known companies specializing in merchandise of this kind was the gun manufacturer, The Winchester Repeating Arms Company. After 1931, their mark was changed from Winchester Trademark USA to Winchester-Western. Remington, Ithaca, Peters, and Dupont are other manufacturers whose goods are especially sought after.

Advisor: Kevin R. Bowman (See Directory, Sports Collectibles)

Booklet, Remington UMC, 1911 Game Laws of the United States & Canada, 1911, 100 pages, VG+ **$40.00**
Booklet, Winchester Gun Salesman's Sample, shows model #12, 1950s, EX...**$35.00**

Box, ammunition; Peters HV Blue Bill sixteen-gallon, two-piece, empty, VG, $135.00; Western twenty-gallon Field one-piece with quail, EX, $250.00. (Photo courtesy Dixie Sporting Goods)

Box, buckshot; Winchester, '0000 Buck Lead, 1-lb, 32 caliber, 2¾x1¾x1⅛", VG...**$40.00**
Box, cartridge; Remington Nitro Club X7D6, 12-gauge, VG- **$35.00**
Box, cartridge; Winchester Blank, Winchester Repeating Arms Co, red letters on cardboard, empty, 1x1¼x¾", VG+ **$9.00**
Box, cartridge; Winchester Supplement Chambers, .32 caliber, w/6 in original wrappers, VG+ **$250.00**
Box, shotshell; Peters High Velocity Smokeless Shotgun Shells, 2½" 410 gauge, EX **$270.00**
Box, shotshell; Peters Paper Shot Shells, League, 12-guage, 2-pc, faded, VG+..**$210.00**
Box, shotshell; Remington Express Extra Long Range, New Remington Crimp, 12 gauge, empty, VG+ **$12.00**
Brochure, Winchester Model 63 Semi-Automatic Rifle, Speed King, 1930s, 12x10" folds to 6¼x3¼", EX.............**$30.00**
Call, goose; Noah Schenider, 1940s, EX......................**$80.00**
Call, turkey; Henry Gibson, gobbler pictured, cedar, Pat 1/5/1897, 9⅞x1⅛", EX+...**$4,500.00**
Call, turkey; ML Lynch 101 Foolproof, 1965, EX.......**$220.00**
Can, Berdahl Sportsmen's Oil, hunting & fishing graphics, EX...**$80.00**
Can, Winchester Gun Oil, green, oval, EX **$205.00**
Can, Winchester Gun Oil, red w/white & black letters over yellow w/black letters on bottom, 1950s, EX.......**$50.00**
Catalog, Marlin Firearms, 200 pages, 1899, 4½x7", VG+.**$330.00**
Catalog, VL&A's Just for Sport Fall & Winter Catalog #81, bear pictured on cover, 96 pages, 1930s, EX.............**$115.00**
Fly rod, Heddon #8457, med action, walnut w/cork handle, 8½-foot, w/original label, EX................................**$85.00**
Fly rod, HL Leonard, bamboo, brass cap, 9½-foot, EX..**$520.00**
Fly rod, Pflueger, marked Progress #80, wooden crank handle, EX...**$50.00**
Fly rod, Southbend #77, bamboo, 4-pc, w/original cloth bag, EX...**$70.00**
Fly rod, Winchester #5090, retractable, 9-foot, dated 1923, EX...**$65.00**
Fly rod & reel, Californian, WR Murphy Mfg Co, 1950s, EX **$55.00**
Grease tube, Winchester Gun Grease, 2-oz, EX (VG box) **$25.00**
Hand trap, Winchester Standard, gun-blued metal w/wooden handle, 1920s, EX+ **$180.00**
Mailing envelope, Remington Guns & Rifles, lady holding rifle, postmarked 1902, VG **$45.00**
Paddle, The Winchester Store, w/logo & man holding fish, 20⅛", NM..**$35.00**

Patch, Ithaca above eagle w/Heritage, Craftsmanship & Pride below, 1970s, M.................................**$12.00**

Patch, 1955 Remington Shooting Star, red letters on gray shield shape w/yellow star & border, 3½x3", EX+............**$20.00**

Playing cards, Winchester Western, red letters on blue w/flying goose in center, M (sealed) **$17.50**

Print, Lynn Bogue Hunt, flying ducks, Dupont Powder Co, 1917, 14½x13½", EX..................................**$32.50**

Scabbard, Winchester, soft leather w/name, holds 40" gun, NM **$100.00**

Screwdriver, Smith & Wesson, blued steel, checkered steel handle, came w/new gun, EX **$80.00**

Sight, Lyman Improved Combination Rear; for Winchester Repeating Rifles Model 1890 & Model 1906, EX (VG box) **$80.00**

Sign, Your Sporting Firearms & Ammunition Headquarters featuring Remington, peel-off window sticker, 10¼x8", NM **$25.00**

Target, NRA Standard B-4; For Small-Bore Rifle Shooting Outdoors, Remington, cardboard, 1920s, 18½" sq, EX.................**$13.00**

Tin, Dupont Superfine Gunpowder, dated 1925, M....**$50.00**

Sports Cards

Collecting memorabilia from all kinds of sports events has been a popular hobby for years. Baseball has long been known as the 'national pastime' with literally millions of fans who avidly follow the sport at every level from 'sand lot' to the major leagues. So it only follows that many collectors find sports trading cards a worthwhile investment. Hundreds have been printed and many are worth less than 20¢ apiece, but some of the better cards bring staggering prices, as you'll see in our listings.

If you're totally unfamiliar with these cards, you'll need to know how to determine the various manufacturers. 1) Bowman: All are copyrighted Bowman of B.G.H.L.I. except a few from the fifties that are marked '...in the series of Baseball Picture Cards.' 2) Donruss: All are marked with the Donruss logo on the front. 3) Fleer: From 1981 to 1984, the Fleer name is on the backs of the cards; after 1985 it was also on the front. 4) Score & Sportflics: Score written on the front, Sportflics on back of each year. 5) Topps: 1951 cards are baseball game pieces with red or blue backs (no other identification). After that, either Topps or T.G.C. appears somewhere on the card. 6) Upper Deck: market front and back with Upper Deck logo and hologram.

Learn to judge the condition of your card, since its condition is a very important factor when it comes to making an accurate evaluation. Superstars' and Hall of Famers' cards are most likely to appreciate, and the colored photo cards from the '30s are good investments as well. Buy modern cards by the set while they're inexpensive. Who knows what they may be worth in years to come. Any of today's rookies may be the next Babe Ruth!

Though many of these cards have cooled off considerably from their heyday of few years ago, many are holding their values well. We've listed some of the better cards and the prices they've recently realized at auction.

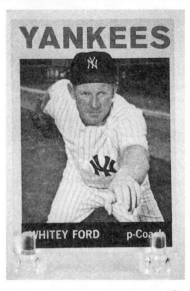

Whitey Ford, Topps, #380, NM, $15.00.

Barry Bonds, Fleer, #604, 1987, M **$530.00**
Bill Russell, Fleer, #62, 1961, VG+.............................**$95.00**
Bob Feller, Bowman, #6, 1950, VG+ **$60.00**
Bob Friend, Topps, #28, 1964, NM+ **$200.00**
Bobby Lane, Bowman, #53, 1954, EX+........................**$80.00**
Brooks Robinson, Topps, #20, 1968, EX.....................**$25.00**
Cal Ripken, Topps, #21, 1982, M................................**$315.00**
Don Drysdale, Fleer, #41, 1963, NM+ **$100.00**
Don Meredith, Fleer, #41, 1961, NM+ **$80.00**
Duke Snider, Topps, #210, 1955, NM+ **$180.00**
Dusty Rhodes, Topps, #1, 1955, NM+ **$725.00**
Eddie Matthews, Bowman, #64, 1954, VG+.................**$60.00**
Ernie Banks, Bowman, #242, 1955, EX........................**$70.00**
Frank Gifford, Bowman, #16, 1953, NM **$65.00**
Jackie Robinson, Topps, #50, 1955, EX **$220.00**
Jerry West, Fleer, #43, 1961, VG **$85.00**
Jim Brown, Fleer, #11, 1961, NM+ **$250.00**
Joe Montana, Topps, #216, 1981, M...........................**$765.00**
Joe Namath, Topps, #122, 1965, EX...........................**$245.00**
Joe Sakic, Topps, #113, 1989, NM+ **$215.00**
John Elway, Topps, #63, 1984, NM **$335.00**
Karl Malone, Fleer, #68, 1986, NM+ **$225.00**
Keith Thomas, Topps, #129, 1953, NM......................**$345.00**
Ken Raffensberger, Topps, #118, 1952, NM...............**$190.00**
Kobe Bryant, Fleer, #203, 1996, M **$205.00**
Lance Alworth, Fleer, #72, 1963, EX...........................**$80.00**
Larry Doby, Bowman, #115, 1952, EX **$65.00**
Lawrence Taylor, Topps, #434, 1982, NM+...............**$120.00**
Lew Alcindor, Topps, #25, 1969, EX **$260.00**
Lou Gehrig, Fleer, #31, 1961, NM...............................**$90.00**
Lynn Swann, Topps, #282, 1975, NM+......................**$180.00**
Marcus Allen, Topps, #294, 1983, NM+......................**$75.00**
Mark McGuire, Topps, #401, signed, 1985, NM **$80.00**
Michael Jordan, Fleer, #57, 1986, NM+...................**$2,400.00**
Mickey Mantle, Topps, #150, 1958, VG+ **$190.00**
Miguel Tejado, Bowman, #411, 1997, M...................**$120.00**
Monte Irvin, Topps, #194, 1956, M **$2,400.00**

Nellie Fox, Bowman, #232, 1951, EX...........................$70.00
Nolan Ryan, Topps, #712, 1970, EX+.....................$270.00
Pat Summerall, Bowman, #52, 1955, NM.................$105.00
Pee Wee Reese, Bowman, #58, 1954, EX+ $90.00
Phil Rizzuto, Bowman, #52, 1952, EX+.....................$100.00
Reggie White, Toppps, #58, 1984, NM+.......................$85.00
Roberto Clemente, Topps, #478, 1959, NM $2,900.00
Roger Clemens, Fleer, Update series, #U-27, 1984, NM+ ..$310.00
Ron Hunt, Topps, #6, 1964, M.................................$225.00
Ron Kline, Topps, #175, 1953, EX+............................$265.00
Ronnie Lott, Topps, #486, 1982, NM+.......................$200.00
Sammy Sosa, Bowman, #312, 1990, NM+...............$2,150.00
Stan Musial, Bowman, #24, 1949, EX+.......................$75.00
Ted Williams, Fleer, #63, 1959, NM+.......................$400.00
Ted Williams, Topps, #5, 1956, VG+.......................$400.00
Tony Gwynn, Fleer, #360, 1983, M $300.00
Warren Spahn, Bowman, #99, 1953, NM+ $105.00
Wayne Gretzky, Topps, #18, 1979, EX+....................$215.00
Willie Mays, Bowman, #89, 1954, NM $125.00
Willie Mays, Topps, #300, 1963, EX+ $70.00
Yogi Beera, Bowman, #60, 1949, VG+......................$110.00

Sports Collectibles

When the baseball card craze began sweeping the country well over a decade ago, memorabilia relating to many types of sports began to interest sports fans. Today ticket stubs, autographed baseballs, sports magazines, and game-used bats and uniforms are prized by baseball fans, and some items, depending on their age or the notoriety of the player or team they represent, may be very valuable. Baseball and golfing seem to be the two sports most collectors prefer, but hockey and auto racing are gaining ground. Game-used equipment is sought out by collectors, and where once they preferred only items used by professionals, now the sports market has expanded, and collectors have taken great interest in the youth equipment endorsed by many star players now enshrined in their respective Hall of Fame. Some youth equipment was given away as advertising premiums and bear that company's name or logo. Such items are now very desirable.

See also Autographs; Indianapolis 500 Memorabilia; Magazines; Motorcycle Memorabilia; NASCAR Collectibles; Pin-Back Buttons; Puzzles.

Advisors: Don and Anne Kier (See Directory, Sports Collectibles)

Base mitt, Denkert Double-Buckle; soft black leather w/dark green trim, backstrap buckle, NM.......................$475.00
Baseball, Sandy Koufax signature, Official National League Williams White ball, NM $165.00
Bat, 1939 Centennial Mini-Bat, 1839-1939-100th-1939 burned into bat, EX+ $80.00
Book, America's National Game, AG Spaulding, history, Uncle Sam in uniform on cover, 1911, EX $360.00
Book, Story of the Brooklyn Dodgers, Pee Wee Reese on cover, first edition, VG+ $50.00

Booklet, Mickey Mantle's Batting Tips, Mantle on cover, Alvarn Co, 1962, EX...$25.00
Box, D&M Hockey Gloves, maroon w/Lucky Dog logo & hockey player, rare, VG $140.00

Calendar, 1943, advertising Old Judge Coffee, picturing members of 1942 World Champion Cardinals, first advertising piece to show rookie Stan Musial, VG, $375.00.

Catalog, 1917 Reach Equipment, Zimmerman Hardware, baseball-tennis-golf, EX+.......................................$65.00
Catalog, 1962 Rawlings Sports Equipment, Stan Musial & Ken Boyer on cover, EX...................................$60.00
Catchers mask, spider style, wired-on pads, unmarked, early, EX...$50.00
Football, Commemorating Opening Game at Heinz Field, Steelers vs Browns (canceled due to 9/11), #279 out of 550 made, M $160.00
Game, Superstar Wrestling, Deluxe Edition, 1984, NM..$280.00
Jersey, Dodgers Duke Snider, white w/blue Dodgers & red #4, signed, EX (in 30x30" frame).......................$185.00
Jersey, 1993 Colorado Rockies, inaugural year, Wedge #22 on back, Russell Athletics, EX...................................$250.00
Magazine, 1947 Dodgers Baseballs Beloved Bums, team photo, history, EX.......................................$60.00
Media guide, 1952 Detroit Tigers, history of 1951 team, EX $110.00
Media guide, 1956 Cardinals Sketchbook, EX.............$50.00
Pennant, New York American League Champions, 1940s, 26", EX+ $95.00
Pennant, Red Sox, Elway Park, 29", VG+ $45.00
Pennant, Yale, football, w/pin, ca 1910, EX.............$160.00
Pennant, 1947 All-Star, red w/white border, 27", VG..$295.00
Pennant, 1952 Brooklyn Dodgers World Series Champs, blue & white, 30", NM $320.00
Pennant, 1955 Brooklyn Dodgers National League Champions, 29", VG+ $390.00
Pennant, 1968 Yankees, picture pennant w/Mickey Mantle, 1940s, 29", EX $115.00
Photo, Hugh Jennings, wire photo, dated 5/07, VG..$85.00
Photo, 1940 Brooklyn Dodgers, wire photo by Acme News Pictures, 7x9", EX..$60.00

Photographs, 1943 Chicago Cubs, 6x8", set of 24, $50.00. (Photo courtesy Ernie Reed)

Pin, lapel; USAC Race Car Owner 1957, 2 crossed flags behind emblem w/cloisonne detail on gold-tone, ½x¾", NM+ **$50.00**

Pin, Ted Williams, photo w/bat on shoulders, union stamp on reverse, 1" dia, EX..**$70.00**

Player roster, 1952 Dodgers, review of 1951 season & 1952 Spring Training schedule, EX.................................**$95.00**

Postcard, Dizzy Dean Gold Medal, ca 1934, EX **$50.00**

Press guide, 1956 Yankee's, Mickey Mantle's Triple Crown season, EX **$90.00**

Press guide, 1960 Milwaukee Braves, EX **$40.00**

Press guide, 1968 World Series, Detroit Tigers edition, EX ..**$60.00**

Press kit, 1970 Baltimore Orioles World Series, EX **$30.00**

Press pin, World Series Dodgers, 1988, M **$75.00**

Program, 1924 Tournament of Roses, multicolored cover, VG **$100.00**

Program, 1950 Whiz Kids World Series, scored in pencil, VG+...**$125.00**

Program, 1952 Yankees vs Browns, Mickey Mantle in line-up, EX..**$35.00**

Program, 1955 World Series, Yankees vs Dodgers, Game #7, NM+ **$160.00**

Program, 1958 World Series, Yankees vs Braves, Braves edition, unscored, EX **$60.00**

Program, 1964 World Series, Yankee Stadium, unscored, EX+ **$70.00**

Program, 1964 World Series, Yankees vs Cardinals, Cardinals edition, NM...**$40.00**

Schedule, New York Yankees, Brooklyn Dodgers & New York Giants, 1955, The Seaman's Bank, EX **$125.00**

Schedule, 1960 Dodgers, LA Times, pocket size, EX..**$55.00**

Scorecard, 1950 Phillies vs St Louis, w/St Louis autographs, unscored, EX...**$65.00**

Spring training roster, 1951 Yankees, Joe DiMaggio's last season, EX..**$85.00**

Stick pin, football player kicking ball, unmarked, 3¼", EX..**$85.00**

Tag, Hartland Statue, Don Drysdale, 1960, VG+.......**$140.00**

Tag, Hartland Statue, Ernie Banks, 1960, VG+..........**$150.00**

Ticket, Muhammed Ali vs Floyd Patterson, full, framed, EX...**$440.00**

Yearbook, 1956 Brooklyn Dodgers, cartoon drawing on front cover of hobo, EX **$100.00**

Yearbook, 1957 Brooklyn Dodgers Ebbetts Field, 50¢ copy, 50 pages photos, information, EX **$105.00**

St. Clair Glass

Since 1941, the St. Clair family has operated a small glasshouse in Elwood, Indiana. They're most famous for their lamps, though they've also produced many styles of toothpick holders, paperweights, and various miniatures as well. Though the paperweights are usually stamped and dated, smaller items may not be marked at all. In addition to various colors of iridescent glass, they've also made many articles in slag glass (both caramel and pink) and custard.

At the present, rose weights are in demand, especially the rare pedestal roses; so are sulphides, in particular those with etching or windows. Pieces signed by Ed and Paul are rare, as these brothers signed only items they made during their breaks or lunch time. For more information, we recommend *St. Clair Glass Collector's Book, Vol II,* by our advisor, Ted Pruitt.

Advisor: Ted Pruitt (See Directory, St. Clair)

Bell, flowers, from $75 to **$100.00**

Bell, 10th Annual Convention, from $75 to...............**$100.00**

Bird, lg, from $75 to..**$100.00**

Bird, sm, from $35 to...**$40.00**

Bowl, fluted & scalloped rim, from $225 to.............**$250.00**

Bowl, sauce; Paneled Grape, from $35 to...................**$40.00**

Covered dish, dolphin, from $100 to **$125.00**

Covered dish, horse, from $125 to............................**$150.00**

Doorstop, apple form, lg, from $375 to....................**$400.00**

Doorstop, duck, from $600 to **$625.00**

Figurine, buffalo, amber & chocolate, from $50 to.....**$57.00**

Figurine, Scottie dog, any color except black, from $150 to **$200.00**

Fruit, apple, from $95 to **$100.00**

Fruit, pear, carnival, from $95 to **$100.00**

Fruit, strawberry, carnival, from $140 to...................**$150.00**

Goblet, Rose in Snow, from $40 to.............................**$50.00**

Goblet, Thistle, from $40 to...**$50.00**

Lamp, 3-ball base w/leaded shade, from $975 to..**$1,000.00**

Marble, sulfide baseball player, Ed St Clair, from $125 to .. **$150.00**
Novelty, piano, from $115 to......................................**$125.00**
Paperweight, cameo, dove, from $175 to.................**$200.00**
Paperweight, crimped, sm, from $40 to......................**$50.00**
Paperweight, flowers, sm, from $40 to **$50.00**
Paperweight, rose, red or pink, from $800 to........**$1,200.00**
Paperweight, speckled glass, from $90 to **$100.00**
Paperweight, sulfide, Betsy Ross, from $325 to........**$350.00**
Paperweight, sulfide, John Tyler, from $125 to........**$150.00**
Paperweight, sulfide, Kennedy, windowed, Paul St Clair,
    miniature, from $300 to......................................**$350.00**
Paperweight, sulfide, Washington, Ed St Clair, from $300
    to **$400.00**
Pitcher, Hollyband, from $75 to **$85.00**
Plate, Kewpie, from $450 to **$500.00**
Plate, Mt St Helens, from $25 to....................................**$30.00**
Plate, Reagan - Bush, from $25 to..................................**$30.00**
Ring bowl, center post, from $100 to **$125.00**
Ring post, from $55 to...**$65.00**
Salt cellar, oblong, from $45 to......................................**$50.00**
Salt cellar, swan, red, from $125 to...........................**$150.00**
Salt cellar, wheelbarrow, from $30 to **$35.00**
Sugar bowl, from $90 to **$100.00**
Toothpick holder, Indian, from $25 to.........................**$30.00**
Toothpick holder, Kingfisher, from $25 to..................**$30.00**
Toothpick holder, S Repeat, from $25 to....................**$30.00**

Toothpick holder, Three-Face: Indian head, Liberty Bell, and Washington bust, cobalt with gold, made in 1974 for 1976 Bicentennial celebration, 2½", $50.00. (This mold belonged to Maude and Bob St. Clair but was pressed by Joe St. Clair.)

Tumbler, Fleur-de-Lis, from $40 to.............................**$50.00**
Tumbler, Grape & Cable, from $40 to **$50.00**
TV lamp, unsigned, from $975 to **$1,000.00**
Vase, floral paperweight base, ruffled rim, from $80 to..**$85.00**
Wine glass, Paneled Grape, from $35 to **$45.00**
Wine glass, Pinwheel, from $35 to **$45.00**

Stanford Corn

Teapots, cookie jars, salt and pepper shakers, and other kitchen and dinnerware items modeled as ears of yellow corn with green shucks were made by the Stanford company, who marked most of their ware. The Shawnee company made two very similar corn lines; just check the marks to verify the manufacturer.

Butter dish..**$60.00**

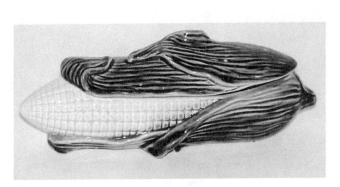

Casserole, 8½", $50.00.

Cookie jar..**$100.00**
Creamer & sugar bowl **$60.00**
Cup **$20.00**
Pitcher, 7½"..**$65.00**
Plate, 9" L **$35.00**
Relish tray..**$45.00**
Salt & pepper shakers, sm, pr **$30.00**
Salt & pepper shakers, 4", pr..**$35.00**
Spoon rest **$30.00**
Teapot...**$75.00**
Tumbler **$35.00**

Stangl Birds

The Stangl Pottery Company of Flemington and Trenton, New Jersey, made a line of ceramic birds which they introduced in 1940 to fulfill the needs of a market no longer able to access foreign imports, due to the onset of WWII. These bird figures immediately attracted a great deal of attention. At the height of their productivity, sixty decorators were employed to hand paint the birds at the plant, and the overflow was contracted out and decorated in private homes. After WWII inexpensive imported figurines once again saturated the market, and for the most part, Stangl curtailed their own production, though the birds were made on a very limited basis until as late as 1978.

Nearly all the birds were marked. A four-digit number was used to identify the species, and most pieces were signed by the decorator. An 'F' indicates a bird that was decorated at the Flemington plant.

For more information see *Collector's Encyclopedia of Stangl Artware, Lamps, and Birds* by Robert Runge, Jr. (Collector Books).

Advisors: Popkorn Antiques (See Directory, Stangl)

Club: Stangl/Fulper Collectors Club
P.O. Box 538
Flemington, NJ 08822; www.stanglfulper.com
Yearly membership: $25 (includes quarterly newsletter)

Wren, #3401, old version, $300.00; wrens, 3401D, old version, $600.00.

Audubon Warbler, #3755, w/pink flower, 4½" $445.00
Bird of Paradise, #3408, 5⅛" $125.00
Bluebirds, #3276D, 2 on branch, 8x4⅜" $225.00
Bobolink, #3595, 4¾" $160.00
Brewer's Blackbird, #3591, 3⅜" $175.00
Broadbill Hummingbird, #3629, 4⅞" $150.00
Broadtail Hummingbird, #3626S, 6⅛" $150.00
Cardinal, #3444, red matt, 7x7" $130.00
Chestnut-Sided Warbler, #3812, 4" $135.00
Cock Pheasant, #3492, 6⅛" $175.00
Cockatoo, #3584, 12¼" $265.00
Drinking Duck, #3250E, 1½" $95.00
European Finch, #3922, 4¾" $1,200.00
Evening Grosbeak, #3813 ....$150.00
Golden-Crowned Kinglet, #3848, 4⅛" $100.00
Hen Chicken, #3446, 7½" $165.00
Hen Pheasant, #3491, 6⅝" $175.00
Indigo Bunting, #3589, 3¼" $75.00
Kentucky Warbler, #3598, 3⅝" $50.00
Kingfisher, #3406S, green, 3⅝" $85.00
Lovebird, #3400, old style, 4¼" $125.00
Nuthatch, #3593, 2⅝" $65.00
Oriole, #3402, 3¼" $50.00
Parula Warbler, #3583, 4¼" $55.00

Penguin, #3274, 5½" **$500.00**
Quacking Duck, #3250F, 3¾" **$90.00**
Red-Headed Woodpecker, #3751S, red matt, 6¼".....**$500.00**
Riefers Hummingbird, #3628, 4⅞"..........................**$150.00**
Rivoli Hummingbird, #3627 ....**$150.00**
Scarlet Tanager, #3749S, 4½" **$445.00**
Standing Duck, #3250A, 3¼" **$90.00**
Titmouse, #3592, 3⅜" **$60.00**
Turkey, #3275, 3⅜" **$400.00**
White-Crowned Pigeon, #3518D, 7⅞x12½" **$1,250.00**

Stangl Dinnerware

The Stangl Company of Trenton, New Jersey, grew out of the Fulper company that had been established in Flemington early in the 1800s. Martin Stangl, president of the company, introduced a line of dinnerware in the 1920s. By 1954, 90% of their production centered around their dinnerware lines. Until 1942 the clay they used was white. Although most of the dinnerware they made until WWII had solid-color glazes, they also did many hand-painted (but not carved) patterns in the 1930s and early 1940s. In 1942, however, the first of the red-clay lines that have become synonymous with the Stangl name was created. Designs were hand carved into the greenware, then hand painted. More than one hundred different patterns have been cataloged. From 1974 until 1978, a few lines previously discontinued on the red clay were reintroduced with a white clay body. Soon after '78, the factory closed.

If you'd like more information on the subject, read *The Collector's Encyclopedia of Stangl Dinnerware* by Robert C. Runge, Jr. (Collector Books) and *Stangl Pottery* by Harvey Duke.

Advisors: Popkorn Antiques (See Directory, Stangl)

Amber Glo, coffee server, 10½", $75.00.

Amber-Glo, ashtray, #3914, 1954, sq $40.00
Amber-Glo, creamer, 1954, casual $20.00
Americana, ashtray, 1935, 4" $20.00
Americana, creamer, 1935 ....$10.00
Americana, sugar bowl, 1935, individual $20.00
Apple Delight, casserole, skillet shape, 1965, 8" $30.00
Apple Delight, plate, 1965, 10" $30.00
Bella Rosa, coffee mug, 1960, 1-cup $25.00
Bella Rosa, gravy boat, 1960..$20.00
Bittersweet, bowl, lug soup; 1962 ....$12.00
Bittersweet, mug, 1962, 2-cup $40.00
Bittersweet, teapot, 1962 ....$65.00
Blue Tulip, bowl, salad; 1942, 11" $100.00
Blue Tulip, egg cup, 1942..$25.00
Blue Tulip, teapot, 1942...$125.00
Blueberry, cruet, 1947, w/stopper $60.00
Blueberry, cup, 1947 ....$10.00
Blueberry, sugar bowl, 1947 ....$25.00
Carnival, butter dish, 1954 ....$30.00
Carnival, gravy underplate, 1954 ....$8.00
Caughley, casserole, blue, 1964, oval, 4½-pt $75.00
Caughley, coffeepot, blue, 1964, 8-cup $125.00
Caughley, flowerpot, yellow, pink or green, 1964, 7" ...$35.00
Caughley, plate, brown or dark green, 1964, 6" $8.00
Caughley, tray, yellow, pink or green, 1964, oval, 8¼" ..$15.00
Colonial, butter chip, 1931 ....$20.00
Colonial, gravy boat, 1931 ....$35.00
Colonial, plate, grill; 1931, 11" $30.00
Country Garden, bowl, salad; 1956, 12" $100.00
Country Garden, pitcher, 1956, 6-oz $25.00
Country Garden, relish dish, 1956 ....$25.00
Cranberry, bowl, cereal; 1973 ....$25.00
Cranberry, salt shaker, 1973 ....$10.00
Festival, cigarette box, 1961..$125.00
Festival, pitcher, 1961, ½-pt $30.00
Flora, bowl, fruit; 1947 ....$10.00
Flora, pitcher, 1947, 1-qt $50.00
Florette, bowl, vegetable; 1961, 8" $25.00
Florette, pickle dish, 1961 ....$15.00
Florette, warmer, 1961, ...$20.00
Fruit & Flowers, ashtray, leaf form, not carved, 1958.$35.00
Fruit & Flowers, creamer, 1958....................................$25.00
Fruit & Flowers, plate, picnic; 1958, 10" $6.00
Fruit & Flowers, sugar bowl, 1958 ....$25.00
Garland, butter dish, 1959..$65.00
Garland, plate, 1958, 8" $20.00
Golden Blossom, pitcher, 1964, 1-qt $30.00
Golden Blossom, teapot, 1964......................................$45.00
Golden Harvest, casserole, 1953, individual, 4" $15.00
Golden Harvest, salt shaker, 1953, wood lid...............$55.00
Magnolia, ashtray, 1952, rectangular $25.00
Magnolia, coffee carafe, 1952, shape #2000 ....$175.00
Magnolia, plate, 1952, 8" $12.00
Magnolia, teapot, 1952 ....$65.00
Mediterranean, bowl, lug soup; 1966..........................$20.00
Mediterranean, pitcher, 1966, 1-pt..............................$45.00
Paisley, bowl, coupe soup; 1963 ....$15.00

Paisley, pitcher, 1963, 6-oz...$15.00

Pink Dogwood, cup, from $10.00 to $12.00. (Photo courtesy Robert C. Runge, Jr.)

Pink Lily, bread tray, 1953 ....$45.00
Pink Lily, plate, 1953, 11"...$20.00
Prelude, creamer, 1947 ....$15.00
Prelude, plate, 1947, 9" $15.00
Provincial, teapot, 1957 ....$85.00
Provincial, warmer, 1957...$25.00
Star Flower, gravy boat underplate, 1952 ....$10.00
Star Flower, plate, 1952, 10" $20.00
Thistle, bread tray, 1950+..$55.00
Thistle, coffee server, 1950, casual............................$200.00
Thistle, pitcher, 1950, 1-pt $40.00
Thistle, plate, grill; 1950, 9" $55.00
Thistle, saucer, 1950, from $5 to..................................$6.00
Tiger Lily, bowl, cereal; 1957......................................$25.00
Tiger Lily, coffee mug, 1957+......................................$35.00
Town & Country, bowl, salad; blue, 1974, 12" $125.00
Town & Country, cup, blue, 1974...............................$25.00
Town & Country, flowerpot, brown, green, honey or yellow, 1964, 5" $25.00
Town & Country, napkin ring, blue, 1964..................$20.00
Town & Country, saucer, black or crimson, 1964.......$10.00
Town & Country, sugar bowl, brown, green, honey or yellow, 1964 ....$25.00
Vineyard, bowl, cereal; 1947.......................................$25.00
Vineyard, plate, chop; 1947, 14½" $150.00
Wild Rose, butter dish, 1955.......................................$45.00
Wild Rose, coffeepot, 1955, 4-cup $125.00
Wild Rose, plate, 1955, 9" $20.00
Yellow Tulip, cup, 1942 ....$12.00
Yellow Tulip, mug, 1942, 2-cup $50.00
Yellow Tulip, tidbit, 1942...$15.00

Star Wars

In the late '70s, the movie 'Star Wars' became a box office hit, most notably for its fantastic special effects and its ever-popular theme of space adventure. Two more movies followed, 'The Empire Strikes Back' in 1980 and 'Return of the Jedi' in 1983. After the first movie, an enormous amount of related merchandise was released. A large percentage of these items was action figures, made by the Kenner company who used the logo of the 20th Century Fox studios (under whom they were licensed) on everything they made until 1980. Just before the second movie, Star Wars creator, George Lucas, regained control of the merchandising rights, and items inspired by the last two films can be identified by his own Lucasfilm logo. Since 1987, Lucasfilm Ltd. has operated shops in conjunction with the Star Tours at Disneyland theme parks.

What to collect? First and foremost, buy what you yourself enjoy. But remember that condition is all-important. Look for items still mint in the box. Using that as a basis, if the box is missing, deduct at least half from its mint-in-box value. If a major accessory or part is gone, the item is basically worthless. Learn to recognize the most desirable, most valuable items. There are Star Wars bargains yet to be had!

Original packaging helps date a toy, since the package or card design was updated as each new movie was released. Naturally, items representing the older movies are more valuable than later issues. For more coverage of this subject, refer to *Schroeder's Collectible Toys, Antique to Modern,* and *Star Wars Super Collector's Wish Book* by Geoffery T. Carlton (both are published by Collector Books).

Note: Though the market was inundated with scores of 'collectors' items promoting *Episode 1* and *Episode 2: Attack of the Clones,* the latest movies in the series, very few have attracted enough interest to cause significant trading on the secondary level.

Bank, Chewbacca (kneeling), Sigma, M **$75.00**
Bop bag, Darth Vader, MIB..................**$125.00**
Card game, Return of the Jedi, Parker Bros, 1983, MIB (sealed) **$10.00**
Display, any character, diecut cardboard stand-ups, life-size, EX, ea **$30.00**
Doll, Paploo, plush, MIB..................**$135.00**
Doll, R2-D2, stuffed cloth, w/speaker, Kenner, 1978-79, 10", EX..................**$25.00**
Figture, Return of the Jedi, M (NM card)..................**$75.00**
Figure, A-Wing Pilot, Tri-logo, M (NM card)..................**$120.00**
Figure, Amanaman, Power of the Force, M (EX card)..**$250.00**
Figure, Anakin Skywalker, Tri-logo, M (EX card) **$110.00**
Figure, AT-AT Commander, Empire Strikes Back, M (NM card)..................**$10.00**
Figure, AT-ST Driver, Return of the Jedi, complete, NM, from $10 to..................**$15.00**
Figure, B-Wing Pilot, Return of the Jedi, M (NM card)...**$40.00**
Figure, Barada, Power of the Force, M (NM card) ...**$125.00**
Figure, Ben Obi-Wan Kenobi, Power of the Force, 1995-present, long saber, MOC (red)..................**$25.00**
Figure, Ben Obi-Wan Kenobi, Return of the Jedi, M (NM card)..................**$100.00**
Figure, Ben Obi-Wan Kenobi, Star Wars, w/saber tip, NM, from $14 to..................**$18.00**

Figure, Bespin Security Guard (Black), Empire Strikes Back, complete, NM..................**$12.00**
Figure, Bespin Security Guard (Black), Empire Strikes Back, M (NM card)..................**$60.00**
Figure, Boba Fett, Power of the Force, 1995-present, 12", MIB..................**$75.00**
Figure, Boba Fett, Return of the Jedi, desert scene, M (EX card)..................**$325.00**
Figure, Boba Fett, Star Wars, complete, NM..................**$75.00**
Figure, Bossk, Empire Strikes Back, M (NM card)...**$140.00**
Figure, C-3-PO, Star Wars, M (VG card) (12-back)...**$175.00**
Figure, C-3PO, Power of the Force, M (EX card)..................**$70.00**
Figure, Captain Tarpuls, Episode 1/Wave 4, MOC..................**$15.00**
Figure, Chancellor Valcrum, Episode I/Wave 3, MOC..**$10.00**
Figure, Chewbacca, Empire Strikes Back, M (VG card)...**$55.00**
Figure, Chewbacca, Star Wars, M (NM card) (12-back)..**$360.00**
Figure, Chewbacca, Tri-logo, M (EX+ card)..................**$90.00**
Figure, Chief Chirpa, Tri-logo, M (NM+ card)..................**$65.00**
Figure, Cloud Car Pilot, Empire Strikes Back, M (EX card), from $65 to..................**$75.00**
Figure, Darth Vader, Empire Strikes Back, M (EX+ card)..**$175.00**
Figure, Darth Vader, Power of the Force, M (EX card)..................**$125.00**
Figure, Darth Vader, Power of the Force, 1995-present, 12", MIB..................**$45.00**
Figure, Death Squad Commander, Star Wars, M (NM card) (20/21-back)..................**$160.00**
Figure, Death Star Droid, Empire Strikes Back, M (EX+ card)..................**$120.00**
Figure, Death Star Monster, Power of the Force, complete, NM..................**$30.00**
Figure, Destroyer Droid, Episode I/Wave 9, MOC..................**$15.00**
Figure, Emperor, Tri-logo, M (EX+ card)..................**$50.00**
Figure, EV-9D9, Power of the Force, complete, NM...**$85.00**
Figure, FX-7, Empire Strikes Back, MOC..................**$100.00**
Figure, Gammorrean Guard, Return of the Jedi, M (NM card)..................**$40.00**
Figure, General Madine, Return of the Jedi, M (NM card)..**$70.00**
Figure, Greedo, Power of the Force, 1995-present, 12", MOC..................**$35.00**
Figure, Hammerhead, Empire Strikes Back, M (NM+ card)..................**$150.00**
Figure, Han Solo, Empire Strikes Back, M (NM card)...**$260.00**
Figure, Han Solo, Return of the Jedi, trench coat, NM (NM card)..................**$65.00**
Figure, Han Solo, Tri-logo, Hoth gear, M (VG+ card)...**$50.00**
Figure, IG-88, Empire Strikes Back, M (NM card)....**$200.00**
Figure, Imperial Commander, Return of the Jedi, M (EX card)..................**$40.00**
Figure, Imperial Dignitary, Tri-logo, M (EX+ card).....**$80.00**
Figure, Imperial Gunner, Power of the Force, M (EX+ card)..................**$120.00**
Figure, Jawa, Empire Strikes Back, M (VG+ back).....**$60.00**
Figure, Klaatu, Return of the Jedi, M (NM card)..................**$35.00**
Figure, Lando Calrissian, Tri-logo, M (EX+ card)......**$100.00**
Figure, Lobot, Return of the Jedi, M (G card)..................**$20.00**
Figure, Luke Skywalker, Empire Strikes Back, Bespin outfit, complete, NM..................**$20.00**

Figure, Luke Skywalker, Power of the Force, 1995-present, 12", MIBN **$25.00**

Figure, Luke Skywalker, Return of the Jedi, X-Wing Pilot outfit, M (EX+ card) **$60.00**

Figure, Lumat, Return of the Jedi, M (EX card).......... **$50.00**

Figure, Paploo, Return of the Jedi, NM (NM card) **$60.00**

Figure, Power Droid, Star Wars, complete, NM.......... **$10.00**

Figure, Princess Leia Organa, Empire Strikes Back, Hoth gear, M (NM+ card) **$180.00**

Figure, Princess Leia Organa, Star Wars, 12", MIB (sealed)...**$325.00**

Figure, Qui-Gon Jinn, Episode I/Wave 6, MOC **$15.00**

Figure, Rebel Commander, Tri-logo, M (NM card) ...**$100.00**

Figure, Rebel Soldier, Empire Strikes Back, M (NM card)..**$75.00**

Figure, R2-D2, Empire Strikes Back, M (NM card) ...**$125.00**

Figure, R2-D2, Star Wars, complete, EX **$12.00**

Figure, Sio Bibble, Episode I/Wave 9, MOC.............. **$20.00**

Figure, Snagglepuss, Empire Strikes Back, M (NM card) ..**$130.00**

Figure, Star Destroyer Commander, Return of the Jedi, M (EX card) **$35.00**

Figure, Stormtrooper, Empire Strikes Back, M (NM card) .**$140.00**

Figure, Teebo, Power of the Force, M (EX card)......**$135.00**

Figure, TIE Fighter, Empire Strikes Back, M (NM box) **$500.00**

Figure, TIE Fighter Pilot, Return of the Jedi, M (EX card)..**$55.00**

Figure, Tusken Raider, Return of the Jedi, M (G card).......**$80.00**

Figure, Ugnaught, Empire Strikes Back, M (NM card)..**$90.00**

Figure, Warok, Power of the Force, complete, NM **$60.00**

Figure, Wicket W Warrick, Return of the Jedi, complete, NM .**$20.00**

Figure, Yak Face, Power of the Force, 1995-present, MOC, (green) **$8.00**

Figure, Yoda, Empire Strikes Back, orange snake, M (EX+ card).. **$175.00**

Figure, Zuckuss, Power of the Force, 1995-present, MOC (green w/slide)... **$25.00**

Figure, 2-1B, Empire Strikes Back, complete, NM **$10.00**

Figure, 4-Lom, Power of the Force, 1995-present, MOC (green) **$10.00**

Figure, 8D8, Return of the Jedi, M (NM card)............. **$40.00**

Figure, 8D8, Tri-logo, M (NM+ card) **$125.00**

Hand puppet, Yoda, Empire Strikes Back, MIB **$75.00**

Ice skates, Darth Vader & Royal Guards, Return of the Jedi, MIB **$45.00**

Magnets, Return of the Jedi, set of 4, MOC................. **$25.00**

Mask, Darth Vader, hard plastic, Don Post, EX........... **$65.00**

Paint kit, Luke Skywalker or Han Solo, Craftmaster, MOC, ea **$15.00**

Pillow, Jabba the Hut, plush, M **$50.00**

Playset, Bespin Control Room, Micro Collection, MIB..**$75.00**

Playset, Bespin World, Micro Collection, M (EX box)...**$150.00**

Playset, Cloud City, Empire Strikes Back, M (EX box)...**$275.00**

Playset, Creature Cantina, EXIB................................ **$100.00**

Playset, Death Star Compactor, Star Wars, Micro Collection, M (EX box)... **$150.00**

Playset, Death Star Space Station, Star Wars, M (EX sealed box) **$475.00**

Playset, Droid Factory, MIB **$100.00**

Playset, Ewok Assult Catapult, Return of the Jedi, MIB (sealed) **$50.00**

Playset, Ewok Family Hut, MIB **$50.00**

Playset, Ewok Fire Cart, M (NM box) **$40.00**

Playset, Hoth Generator Attack, Micro Collection, MIB (sealed) **$100.00**

Playset, Hoth Rescue, Power of the Force, MIB **$250.00**

Playset, Hoth Wampa Cave, Micro Collection, M (EX box)...**$60.00**

Playset, Jabba the Hutt Dungeon, Return of the Jedi, MIB (sealed) **$250.00**

Playset, Patrol Dewback, MIB (sealed) **$125.00**

Playset, Sy Snootles & the Rebo Band, Tri-logo, M (EX box)... **$140.00**

Presto Magix Transfer Set, Wicket, set of 120, MIB **$30.00**

Radio Watch, R2-D2 & C-3PO on face, Lucasfilm/Bradley, 1982, MIB **$50.00**

Sew 'N Show Cards, Wicket & Friends, MIB.............. **$18.00**

Speaker phone, Darth Vader, MIB............................. **$150.00**

Vehicle, AT-AT, Empire Strikes Back, MIB................ **$300.00**

Vehicle, ATL Interceptor, MIB **$135.00**

Vehicle, Boba Fett's Slave I, Power of the Force, 1995-present, MIB (green or purple).................................. **$35.00**

Vehicle, Darth Vader's TIE Fighter, Star Wars, MIB...**$125.00**

Vehicle, Desert Sail Skiff, Return of the Jedi, MIB **$40.00**

Vehicle, Ewok Battle Wagon, Power of the Force, MIB **$235.00**

Vehicle, Imperial Cruiser, Empire Strikes Back, M (EX box)...**$100.00**

Vehicle, Imperial Tie Fighter, Star Wars, diecast, MOC, from $75.00 to $100.00.

Vehicle, Jawa Sandcrawler, Star Wars, complete, NM .**$350.00**

Vehicle, Millennium Falcon, Power of the Force, 1995-present, MIB **$40.00**

Vehicle, Rebel Transport, M (EX box)....................... **$175.00**

Vehicle, Scout Walker, Tri-logo, MIB........................ **$100.00**

Vehicle, Slave I, Empire Strikes Back, M (NM sealed box).**$250.00**

Vehicle, Speeder Bike, Tri-logo, MIB **$75.00**

Vehicle, Y-Wing Fighter, Star Wars, diecast, M (EX box)..**$200.00**

Stauffer, Erich

From a distance, these child-like figures closely resemble Hummel figurines. They're marked 'Designed by Erich Stauffer' in blue script, often with a pair of crossed arrows or a crown. They always carry a number, sometimes with the letter S or U before it. As an added bonus, you may find a paper label bearing the title of the featured subject. Arnart Imports Inc imported Erich Stauffer figurines from Japan from the late 1950s through the 1980s. Some of these pieces may be found with original Arnart blue and gold stickers.

Figurines range in size from 4½" up to 12½" tall. The most common is the single figure, but some may have two or three children on a single base. The most interesting are those that include accessories or animals to complete their theme. Note that Arnart Imports also made a similar line, but those pieces are smaller and not of the same quality. As a rule, figures marked Erich Stauffer and/or Arnart Imports would be valued at $4.00 to $5.00 per inch in height, sometimes a bit more if the accessories are unique and if stickers and tags are present.

Note: The majority of the listings that follow were gleaned from Internet auction sales. They indicate not only the winning bid but also include postage, insurance, and occasionally handling charges as well, since those costs must be added to the winning bid to arrive at an accurate reflection of the final costs.

Advisor: Joan Oates (See Directory, Erich Stauffer Figurines)

#S8442, Music Folies (sic), girl, standing, playing harp/zither, 1 goose by her feet, 8¾"......................................**$35.00**
#S8446, bluejay on nest w/flowers on branch, 4½"....**$13.50**
#S8520, planter, 2-section, boy standing w/1 hand pointing to bandaged leg, other hand saluting, 5¼"...............**$20.00**
#U8561, Sore Thumb, boy w/hammer in 1 hand, bandaged thumb on other hand, 7¼" **$15.00**
#U8588, Kindergarten News, boy sitting, reading open newspaper, 6" **$22.00**
#44/173, Play Time, boy, standing, holding baseball bat, 5¾"..**$15.00**
#44/94, girl, standing, playing harp/zither, 1 goose, 4½"..**$15.00**
#8343, boy sitting under open umbrella, ball in hand for his dog, 5" **$23.00**
#8343, Rainy Days, boy sitting under umbrella, 1 goose, 5" **$20.00**
#8344, Winter Time, angel holding lantern & snow shovel, 5" **$30.00**
#8395, By the Old Apple Tree, boy sitting under tree playing his fiddle, 1 goose, 5"..**$25.00**
#8399, wall plaque, boy in cowboy outfit standing against stone wall playing fiddle while dog watches.......**$30.00**
#8399, wall plaque, girl standing against stone wall, holding flowers, handled basket at her feet, 6" **$25.00**
#8684, Little Deb, girl in full, Southern-style pink dress holding a green box/present in 1 hand, 5"...................**$28.00**

Steiff Animals

These stuffed animals originated in Germany around the turn of the century. They were created by Margaret Steiff, whose company continues to operate to the present day. They are identified by the button inside the ear and the identification tag (which often carries the name of the animal) on their chest. Over the years, variations in tags and buttons help collectors determine approximate dates of manufacture.

Teddy bear collectors regard Steiff bears as some of the most valuable on the market. When assessing the worth of a bear, they use some general guidelines as a starting basis, though other features can come into play as well. For instance, bears made prior to 1912 that have long gold mohair fur start at a minimum of $75.00 per inch. If the bear has dark brown or curly white mohair fur instead, that figure may go as high as $135.00. From the 1920 to 1930 era, the rule of thumb would be about $50.00 minimum per inch. A bear (or any other animal) on cast-iron or wooden wheels starts at $75.00 per inch; but if the tires are hard rubber, the value is much lower, more like $27.00 per inch.

It's a fascinating study which is well covered in *Teddy Bears and Steiff Animals, First, Second,* and *Third Series,* by Margaret Fox Mandel (Collector Books). Also see Cynthia Powell's *Collector's Guide to Miniature Teddy Bears.*

Newsletter/Club: *Collector's Life*
The World's Foremost Publication for Steiff Enthusiasts
Beth Savino
P.O. Box 798
Holland, OH 43528; 1-800-862-TOYS; fax: 419-473-3947

Original Teddy, caramel mohair, glass eyes, original button and tag, 38", M, from $1,000.00 to $2,000.00.

Baby Chick, spotted Dralon w/felt comb, plastic feet & beak, all ID, 1971, 4", NM **$85.00**

Basset Hound, mohair, swivel head, original green collar, chest tag, 1950s, 4½", NM..................................**$165.00**

Bazi Dog, mohair, plastic eyes, original blue collar, chest tag, 1960s, 4", NM **$110.00**

Bear, Margaret Strong, cinnamon mohair, brass button & cloth, stock tag, 1982-90, 9", NM..................**$125.00**

Bear, white mohair, clear glass eyes, FF underscored button & US Zone tag, w/growler, 1947, 17", EX.......**$1,800.00**

Bendy Bear, dark brown, all ID, 1984, 3½", M...........**$45.00**

Bengal Tiger, mohair, glass eyes, raised script button & chest tag, 1959-61, rare, 5½", M...**$450.00**

Bessy Cow, mohair w/felt horns & udders, glass eyes, original collar & bell, no ID, 1950s, 9", NM..............**$150.00**

Boar, black w/brown face, all ID, 1950s, 11", M **$175.00**

Boxer Dog, mohair w/velvet chin, glass eyes, original blue leather collar, all ID, 1954, 4", NM **$165.00**

Cat, black velvet w/mohair tail, original ribbon, US Zone tag, 1948, 3", M...**$165.00**

Cocker Spaniel, black & white w/freckles, glass eyes, jointed head, no ID, 1930s, 13", EX...............................**$200.00**

Collie, lying down, all ID, 1960, 9", M.....................**$225.00**

Cosy Kamel, Dralon, all ID, 1968, 10½", M..............**$125.00**

Dally Dog, mohair, glass eyes, swivel head, original red collar, raised script button, 6½", NM.....................**$150.00**

Diggy Badger, mohair w/glass eyes, 6", EX **$100.00**

Dormy Dormouse, mohair & Dralon, all ID, 1968, 7½", M...**$125.00**

Electola Fox Dog, velvety Dralon w/mohair ears, original red leather collar, chest tag, 1968, rare, 4½", NM.....**$900.00**

Eric Bat, mohair, w/tag, 1960s, rare, minimum value ...**$675.00**

Floppy Kitty, sleeping, tan w/black stripes, original ribbon & chest tag, 8", EX..**$100.00**

Floppy Panther, brass button & stock tag, 1972, 17", NM..**$185.00**

Fox, standing, mohair, glass eyes, raised script button, 5", EX...**$80.00**

Foxy Dog, original ribbon & chest tag, 1950, 3", EX...**$110.00**

Gogo Chinchilla, Dralon & felt, all ID, 5½", M.........**$200.00**

Goldy Hamster, mohair, glass eyes, all ID, 4", NM...**$100.00**

Hide-A-Gift Cocker Spaniel, black & white, all ID, 1950, 5½", NM...**$185.00**

Jocko Monkey, long curly mohair, glass eyes, fully jointed, raised script button, 1950s, 18", NM....................**$300.00**

Jolanthe Pig, mohair w/felt ears, incised button, 1960, 5", NM **$125.00**

Koala Bear, fully jointed, all ID, 1955-58, 9", M........**$700.00**

Lam Llama, cream mohair w/black & brown detail, glass eyes, raised script button & chest tag, 1957, rare, 17½", M **$600.00**

Lizzy Lizzard, velvet, glass eyes, no ID, 1959-61, 12", EX ..**$385.00**

Mallard Drake, airbrushed Dralon, black plastic eyes, yellow felt bill, 10½", EX...**$150.00**

Molly Dog, white mohair w/red-brown tipping, glass eyes, original ribbon & bell, all ID, 1950s, 7", M........**$225.00**

Nagy Beaver, mohair w/felt hands & feet, glass eyes, all ID, 1958, 3¾", M...**$100.00**

Nagy Beaver, mohair w/felt hands & feet, glass eyes, all ID, 1958, 7", M..**$165.00**

Neander Caveman, felt mohair suit, rubber face, original tooth on string, all ID, 1968, 8", M.....................**$485.00**

Original Teddy, caramel mohair, all ID, 1950s, 6", M ...**$400.00**

Original Teddy, tan mohair, all ID, 1968, 9", M........**$175.00**

Original Teddy, tan mohair, all ID, 1968, 13", M.....**$225.00**

Peky Dog, mohair, glass eyes, swivel head, all ID, 1950s, 8", M...**$200.00**

Pony, mohair w/felt ears, all ID, FAO Schwarz Exclusive, 1967-68, rare, 6½", EX...**$350.00**

Rabbit, puppet, mohair, glass eyes, original blue ribbon, US Zone tag, 1948, 9", EX...**$100.00**

Scottie Dog, original collar, raised script button, 1950-57, 4", rare, NM..**$300.00**

Siamy Cat, white mohair w/brown tipping, glass eyes, no ID, 1950s, rare, 5", NM..**$300.00**

Snaky Snake, puppet, mohair, raised script button, 1966-67, rare, 13", EX...**$450.00**

Snobby Poodle, puppet, original ribbon, all ID, 1955-58, 9", NM..**$100.00**

Susi Cat, mohair, plastic eyes, original pink ribbon, all ID, 1960s, 5", NM...**$200.00**

Tucky Turkey, mohair w/felt wings & tail, velvet face, glass eyes, all ID, 1952, 4", M.....................................**$365.00**

Unicorn, mohair & Dralon, all ID, 1983, 7", NM.......**$165.00**

Woolie Baby Duck, metal feet, raised script button & stock tag, 1950s, 1½", M..**$55.00**

Woolie Cat, gray & white, original ribbon, raised script button & stock tag, 1970-74, 2½", M **$85.00**

Woolie Fish, green & yellow, raised script button & stock tag, 1968, 1½", NM...**$35.00**

Yes/No Jumbo Elephant, ear button & chest tag, 1970s, 10", EX...**$200.00**

Yuku Gazelle, all ID, 1962-63, rare, 7½", M...............**$325.00**

Zicky Goat, mohair, glass eyes, wood horns, original ribbon & bell, chest tag, 6", EX **$100.00**

Zotty Bear, caramel mohair, plastic eyes, original ribbon, chest tag, 6½", M..**$250.00**

String Holders

Today we admire string holders for their decorative nature. They are much sought after by collectors. However, in the 1800s, they were strictly utilitarian, serving as dispensers of string used to wrap food and packages. The earliest were made of cast iron. Later, advertising string holders appeared in general stores. They were made of tin or cast iron and were provided by companies pedaling such products as shoes, laundry supplies, and food. These advertising string holders command the highest prices.

These days we take cellophane tape for granted. Before it was invented, string was used to tie up packages. String holders became a staple item in the home kitchen. To add a whimsical touch, in the late 1920s and 1930s, many string holders were presented as human shapes, faces, animals, and fruits. Most of these novelty string holders were made of chalkware (plaster of Paris), ceramics, or wood fiber. If you were lucky, you might have won a plaster of Paris 'Super

Hero' or comic character string holder at your local carnival. These prizes were known as 'carnival chalkware.' The Indian string holder was a popular giveaway, so was Betty Boop and Superman.

Our values reflect string holders in excellent condition.

Advisor: Larry G. Pogue (See Directory, String Holders)

Aunt Jemima, chalkware, head & neck only, white head wrap w/pink, 1940-50s, 7¾"...............................**$395.00**

Bananas, chalkware, 1890s, 5¾", $85.00. (Photo courtesy Larry G. Pogue)

Bird atop gourd, ceramic, blue bird w/black features on orange gourd, 7"...**$90.00**

Black boy eating watermelon in bathtub, chalkware, 'wooden' tub, marked ATCO, 7½x6½" **$645.00**

Black boy riding alligator, chalkware, string hole in mouth, dated 1948, 9" **$345.00**

Black porter, ceramic, black face w/red hat & lips, string hole in white teeth, marked Fredericksburg, 6½" **$425.00**

Bonzo, chalkware, blue w/pink belly, 6½"..............**$185.00**

Bride, ceramic, puffy white gown w/green floral decor, white hat, bouquet in hands, Japan, 6¼", from $130 to..**$145.00**

Buddha, ceramic, cream gloss, incised Japan mark, 1940s, 5¾"..**$145.00**

Cat, ceramic, face only, white w/pink bow w/black dots, scissors holder, Japan sticker, 5⅜" **$145.00**

Cat, chalkware, face w/blue bow, red rose between ears, string hole in mouth, 7".......................................**$165.00**

Cat on ball of twine, ceramic, brown, string hole in mouth, 5¾"...**$75.00**

Cat w/ball of string, white, sits on counter top, made in Japan for Fitz & Floyd, 2-pc **$87.50**

Cat w/ball of string & bow, chalkware, EX original paint, 6½"..**$98.00**

Cat w/ball of twine, bow around neck, chalkware, original paint, 6½", EX...**$97.50**

Chef, ceramic, face only, white w/pink cheeks, brown hat, string hole in mouth, Japan, 6"..........................**$145.00**

Chef, ceramic, head only, white face shades to brown, bushy eyebrows, white hat, string hole in mouth, Japan, 1940s, 6"..**$165.00**

Chipmunk, ceramic, white w/black whiskers, black & white striped bow, scissors holder, brown hat, 5⅛" **$135.00**

Coca-Cola Kid, chalkware, face only, bottle cap hat, string hole in mouth, 8"..**$545.00**

Corn, chalkware, yellow ears w/green leaves, string hole in bottom, 5½"...**$175.00**

Dog w/collar, ceramic, white face w/black features, red collar, scissors holder, Arthur Wood, England, 4½".........**$155.00**

Drunk man, ceramic, head only, white hat & face w/rosy cheeks, 1 eye closed, Elsa incised on back, 5½"..**$210.00**

Elsie the Cow, chalkware, bust w/yellow daisies on collar, string hole in mouth, 6¾" **$525.00**

Felix the Cat, chalkware, face only, black & white, string hole in mouth..**$295.00**

Goldie the Goldfish, chalkware, yellow lady fish, string hole in mouth, 1950s, 6¾"...**$87.50**

Gourd, chalkware, original green paint, string hole in bottom, 7½"..**$135.00**

Heart, ceramic, String Along w/Me in black on white, black flowers w/green leaves, 5½" **$125.00**

Hippo, ceramic, knitting blue & white plaid cloth, scissors in nose for glasses, countertop, unmarked, 6"..........**$75.00**

Little Boy Blue, chalkware, seated on yellow hay, blue pants, string hole in red horn, 6½" **$395.00**

Little Chef (aka Rice Krispy Guy), chalkware, original paint, 7", EX...**$185.00**

Little Red Riding Hood, chalkware, head only, red hood w/white decor, Universal Statuary Co, 1941, 9½"..**$275.00**

Mammy, ceramic, white dress w/black zigzag trim & pink dots, 6½", from $225 to......................................**$250.00**

Mammy, ceramic, white dress w/brown & green plaid lines, Made in Japan, 6½", from $195 to **$235.00**

Mammy, ceramic, yellow top, blue skirt, rose-colored bow in hair, scissors holder, 6½"......................................**$385.00**

Monkey on ball of twine, chalkware, brown monkey, red ball, 7½" **$245.00**

Old Indian Man, chalkware, red headband w/black & white stripes, string hole in mouth, 10¼" **$285.00**

Pear, chalkware, red-brown to yellow, green leaves, string hole in bottom, 5½"...**$90.00**

Pear w/plums, chalkware, orange pear w/dark blue plums, green leaves, string hole in bottom, 7¾"..............**$85.00**

Pumpkin face, chalkware, orange pumpkin w/white face, winking, string hole in mouth, 5" **$185.00**

Rose, chalkware, orange-pink w/silvery-green leaves, 8"..**$175.00**

Rosie the Riveter (aka Sailor Girl), chalkware, green scarf in hair, Bello, Universal Statuary Co, 1941, 8x7" **$295.00**

Scottie dog, chalkware, face only, gray w/dark shaded features, 7" **$155.00**

Senor, chalkware, head only, black & green sombrero w/white underside, red earring, 8¼" **$95.00**

Senora, chalkware, head only, silver headpiece w/colored faux stones, string hole in mouth, 8"..................$275.00

Shirley Temple, chalkware, face w/curly brown hair, string hole in mouth, ca 1940s-50s, 6¾x6¼"................$395.00

Strawberry, chalkware, red w/green leaves, bite taken out of side, 6½"..$115.00

Willy the Worm on apple, chalkware, yellow worm on red apple w/black door & window, green leaves, 6½"............$110.00

Winnie the Pooh, chalkware, seated, yellow w/red shirt, gold honey in blue barrel & on 1 hand, 8½".............$325.00

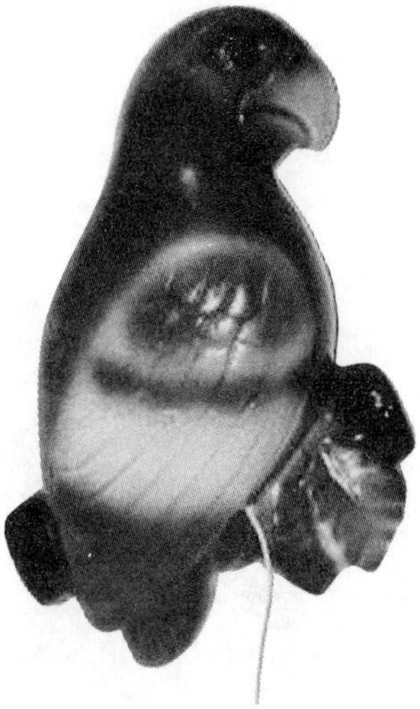

Parrot, chalkware, 9½", $185.00. (Photo courtesy Larry G. Pogue)

Swanky Swigs

These glasses, ranging in size from 3⅛" to 5⅝", were originally distributed by the Kraft company who filled them with their cheese spread. They were introduced in the 1930s and can still be found in the supermarket today in a clear small glass with indented designs. There are approximately 223 different variations of colors and patterns ranging from sailboats, bands, animals, dots, stars, checkers, etc.

In 1999 a few Kraft Australian Swanky Swigs started turning up. We now have American, Canadian, and Australian Kraft Swanky Swigs. They have been verified as Kraft Australian swigs because of the Kraft ads in magazines.

Here is a listing of some of the harder-to-find examples: In the small (Canadian) size (about 3¹⁄₁₆ to 3¼") look for Band No. 5 (two red and two black bands); Galleon (two ships on each example, made in five colors — black, blue, green, red, and yellow); Checkers (made in four color combinations — black and red, black and yellow, black and orange, and black and white, all having a top row of black checks); and Fleur-De-Lis (black fleur-de-lis with a bright red filigree motif).

In the regular size (about 3⅜" to 3⅞") look for Dots Forming Diamonds (diamonds made up of small red dots); Lattice and Vine (white lattice with flowers in these combinations — white and blue, white and green, and white and red); Texas Centennial (a cowboy and horse in these colors — black, blue, green, and red); three special issues with dates of 1936, 1938, and 1942; and Tulip No.2 (available in black, blue, green, and red).

In the large (Canadian) size (about 4³⁄₁₆" to 5⅝" you'll find Circles and Dot (circles with a small dot in the middle, in black, blue, green, and red); Star No. 1 (small scattered stars, made in black, blue, green, and red); Cornflower No. 2 (in dark blue, light blue, red, and yellow); Provincial Cress (made only in red/burgundy with maple leaves); and blue.

Even the lids are collectible and are valued at a minimum of $3.00, depending on condition and the advertising message they convey.

For more information we recommend *Swanky Swigs* by Ian Warner; *Collectible Glassware of the 40s, 50s, and 60s* and *The Collector's Encyclopedia of Depression Glass*, both by Gene Florence.

Note: All are American issue unless noted Canadian.

Advisor: Joyce Jackson (See Directory, Swanky Swigs)

Antique #1, black, blue, brown, green, orange or red, Canadian, 3¼", ea....................................$8.00

Antique #1, black, blue, brown, green, orange or red, Canadian, 1954, 4¾", ea.........................$20.00

Antique #1, black, blue, brown, green, orange or red, 1954, 3¾", ea..$4.00

Antique #2, lime green, deep red, orange, blue or black, Canadian, 1974, 4⅝", ea.........................$20.00

Bachelor Button, red, green & white, 1955, 3¾".........$3.00

Bachelor Button, red, white & green, Canadian, 1955, 3¼"...$6.00

Bachelor Button, red, white & green, Canadian, 1955, 4¾"...$15.00

Band #1, red & black, 1933, 3⅜".................................$3.00

Band #2, black & red, Canadian, 1933, 4¾"..............$20.00

Band #2, black & red, 1933, 3⅜"................................$3.00

Band #3, white & blue, 1933, 3⅜" $3.00

Band #4, blue, 1933, 3⅜"..$3.00

Bicentennial Tulip, green, red or yellow, 1975, 3¾", ea..$15.00

Blue Tulips, 1937, 4¼"...$20.00

Bustlin' Betty, blue, brown, green, orange, red or yellow, Canadian, 1953, 3¼", ea.............................$8.00

Bustlin' Betty, blue, brown, green, orange, red or yellow, Canadian, 1953, 4¾", ea...........................$20.00

Bustlin' Betty, blue, brown, green, orange, red or yellow, 1953, 3¾", ea......................................$4.00

Carnival, blue, green, red or yellow, 1939, 3½", ea......$9.00

Checkerboard, white w/blue, green or red, Canadian, 1936, 4¾", ea...$20.00

Checkerboard, white w/blue, green or red, 1936, 3½", ea ..$20.00

Circles & Dot, any color, 1934, 3½", ea........................$7.00

Circles & Dot, black, blue, green or red, Canadian, 1934, 4¾", ea...$20.00

Coin, clear & plain w/indented coin decor around base, Canadian, 1968, 3⅛" or 3¼", ea $2.00

Coin, clear & plain w/indented coin decor around base, 1968, 3¾"..$1.00

451

Colonial, clear w/indented waffle design around middle & base, 1976, 3¾", ea ....**$.50**

Colonial, clear w/indented waffle design around middle & base, 1976, 4⅜", ea **$1.00**

Cornflower #1, light blue & green, Canadian, 1941, 4⅝", ea ..**$20.00**

Cornflower #1, light blue & green, Canadian, 3¼", ea .**$8.00**

Cornflower #1, light blue & green, 1941, 3½", ea **$4.00**

Cornflower #2, dark blue, light blue, red or yellow, Canadian, 1947, 3¼", ea **$8.00**

Cornflower #2, dark blue, light blue, red or yellow, Canadian, 1947, 4¼", ea **$30.00**

Cornflower #2, dark blue, light blue, red or yellow, 1947, 3½", ea **$4.00**

Crystal Petal, clear & plain w/fluted base, 1951, 3½", ea ...**$2.00**

Dots Forming Diamonds, any color, 1935, 3½", ea **$50.00**

Ethnic Series, lime green, royal blue, burgundy, poppy red or yellow, Canadian, 1974, 4⅝", ea **$20.00**

Forget-Me-Not, dark blue, light blue, red or yellow, Canadian, 3¼", ea **$8.00**

Forget-Me-Not, dark blue, light blue, red or yellow, 1948, 3½", ea **$4.00**

Galleon, black, blue, green, red or yellow, Canadian, 1936, 3⅛", ea **$30.00**

Hostess, clear & plain w/indented groove base, Canadian, 1960, 3⅛" or 3¼", ea **$2.00**

Hostess, clear & plain w/indented groove base, Canadian, 1960, 5⅝", ea **$5.00**

Hostess, clear & plain w/indented groove base, 1960, 3¾", ea **$1.00**

Jonquil (Posy Pattern), yellow & green, Canadian, 1941, 3¼" **$8.00**

Jonquil (Posy Pattern), yellow & green, Canadian, 1941, 4⅝", ea **$20.00**

Jonquil (Posy Pattern), yellow & green, 1941, 3½", ea.**$4.00**

Kiddie Kup, black, blue, brown, green, orange or red, Canadian, 1956, 3¼", ea **$6.00**

Kiddie Kup, black, blue, brown, green, orange or red, Canadian, 1956, 4¾", ea **$20.00**

Kiddie Kup, black, blue, brown, green, orange or red, 1956, 3¾", ea **$3.00**

Lattice & Vine, white w/blue, green or red, 1936, 3½", ea **$100.00**

Petal Star, clear, 50th Anniversary of Kraft Cheese Spreads, 1933-1983, ca 1983, 3¾", ea **$2.00**

Petal Star, clear w/indented star base, Canadian, 1978, 3¼", ea **$2.00**

Petal Star, clear w/indented star base, 1978, 3¾", ea ......**$.50**

Plain, clear, like Tulip #1 w/out design, 1940, 3½", ea .**$4.00**

Plain, clear, like Tulip #3 w/out design, 1951, 3⅞", ea .**$5.00**

Provencial Crest, red & burgundy, Canadian, 1974, 4⅝", ea **$25.00**

Sailboat #1, blue, 1936, 3½", ea **$12.00**

Sailboat #2, blue, green, light green or red, 1936, 3½", ea.**$12.00**

Special Issue, Cornflower #1, light blue flowers/green leaves, Greetings From Kraft, etc, 1941, 3½" **$410.00**

Special Issue, Lewis-Pacific Dairyman's Assoc, Kraft Foods, Sept 13, 1947, Chehalis WA, 3½"........................**$100.00**

Special Issue, Posy Pattern Tulip, red tulip w/green leaves, Greetings From Kraft, CA Retail Assoc, etc, 1940, 3½" **$350.00**

Special Issue, Posy Pattern Violet, Greetings From Kraft, CA Retail Assoc, Grocers Merchants, Del Monte, 1942, 3½" **$350.00**

Special Issue, Sailboat #1, blue, Greetings From Kraft, CA Retail Assoc, Grocers Merchants, Del Monte, 1936, 3½" **$350.00**

Special Issue, Tulip #1, red, Greetings From Kraft, CA Retail Assoc, Grocers Merchants, Del Monte, 1938, 3½"..:...**$350.00**

Special Issue, 4-H Club, clear glass w/3 green parallel lines top/bottom, 2 clovers, Farewell Luncheon, 27th National 4-H Club Congress, Guest of JL Kraft, Dec 2, 1948 ....**$300.00**

Sportsmen Series, 1976, Canadian, 4⅝": Forest Green Soccer, Poppy Red Baseball; Royal Blue Skiing; Deep Red Football, $20.00 each. (Photo courtesy Joyce Jackson)

Stars #1, black, blue, green, red or yellow, Canadian, 1934, 4¾", ea **$20.00**

Stars #1, black, blue, green or red, 1935, 3½", ea **$7.00**

Stars #1, yellow, 1935, 3½", ea **$25.00**

Stars #2, clear w/orange stars, Canadian, 1971, 4⅝", ea ...**$5.00**

Texas Centennial, black, blue, green or red, 1936, 3½", ea **$30.00**

Tulip (Posy Pattern), red & green, Canadian, 1941, 3¼", ea **$8.00**

Tulip (Posy Pattern), red & green, Canadian, 1941, 4⅝", ea **$20.00**

Tulip (Posy Pattern), red & green, 1941, 3½", ea **$4.00**

Tulip #1, black, blue, green, red or yellow, Canadian, 3¼", ea **$8.00**

Tulip #1, black, blue, green, red or yellow, 1937, 3½", ea **$4.00**

Tulip #1, black, blue, green or red, Canadian, 1937, 4⅝", ea **$20.00**

Tulip #2, black, blue, green or red, 1938, 3½", ea **$25.00**

Tulip #3, dark blue, light blue, red or yellow, Canadian, 1950, 4¾", ea...**$20.00**

Tulip #3, dark blue, light blue, red or yellow, Canadian, 3¼", ea..**$8.00**

Tulip #3, dark blue, light blue, red or yellow, 1950, 3⅞", ea..**$4.00**

Violet (Posy Pattern), 1941, blue and green: Canadian, 4⅝", $20.00; 3½", $4.00; Canadian, 3¼", $8.00. (Photo courtesy Gene Florence)

Wildlife Series, black bear, Canadian goose, moose or red fox, Canadian, 1975, 4⅝", ea $20.00

Syroco

Syroco Inc. originated in New York in 1890 when a group of European wood carvers banded together to produce original hand carvings for fashionable homes of the area. Their products were also used in public buildings throughout upstate New York, including the state capitol. Demand for those products led to the development of the original Syroco reproduction process that allowed them to copy original carvings with no loss of detail. They later developed exclusive hand-applied color finishes to further enhance the product, which they continued to improve and refine over ninety years.

Syroco's master carvers use tools and skills handed down from father to son through many generations. Woods used, depending on the effect called for, include Swiss pear wood, oak, mahogany, and wormy chestnut. When a design is completed, it is transformed into a metal cast through their molding and tooling process. A compression mold system using wood fiber was employed from the early 1940s to the 1960s. Since 1962 a process has been in use in which pellets of resin are injected into a press, heated to the melting point, and then injected into the mold. Because the resin is liquid, it fills every crevice, thus producing an exact copy of the carver's art. It is then cooled, cleaned, and finished.

Other companies have produced similar items, among them are Multi Products, now of Erie, Pennsylvania. It was incorporated in Chicago in 1941 but in 1976 was purchased by John Hronas. Multi Products hired a staff of artists, made some wood originals and developed a tooling process for forms. They used a styrene-based material, heavily loaded with talc or calcium carbonate. A hydraulic press was used to remove excess material from the forms. Shapes were dried in kilns for seventy-two hours, then finished and, if the design required it, trimmed in gold. Their products included bears, memo pads, thermometers, brush holders, trays, plaques, nut bowls, napkin holders, etc., which were sold mainly as souvenirs. The large clocks and mirrors were made before the 1940s and may sell for as much as $100.00 and more, depending on condition. Syroco used gold trim, but any other painted decoration you might encounter was very likely done by an outside firm. Some collectors prefer the painted examples and tend to pay a little more to get them. You may also find similar products stamped 'Ornawood,' 'Decor-A-Wood,' and 'Swank'; these are collectible as well.

See also Motion Clocks.

Ashtray, double, glass bowls, cigarette compartment in center, from $10 to $20.00
Ashtray, florals at sides, rectangular receptacle, from 2 to 4 rests, Syroco, 4x6", from $6 to $10.00
Ashtray, florals at sq sides, round receptacle, from 2 to 4 rests, Syroco, 5½x5½", from $7 to $10.00
Ashtray, raised acorns & oak leaves around edges w/squirrel in center, glass ashtray insert, 5" dia $35.00
Ashtray, steer & building on sides, marked Alamo TX, from $5 to..$10.00
Barometer, ship's captain at wheel, round mechanism at wheel's center, from $10 to.................................$15.00
Bookends, Diana the Huntress w/hound, pr, from $10 to..$15.00
Bookends, End of the Trail, pr, from $10 to $15.00
Bookends, horse head inside horseshoe, 6¾x4¾", pr...$30.00
Bookends, lg wild rose, pr, from $10 to......................$15.00
Bookends, Mount Rushmore, pr, from $10 to.............$15.00
Bookends, Scottie dog w/front legs on bench, 6½x4½", pr $30.00
Bookends, stagecoach, 3 men, rooster & Ye Old Inn sign, 1940s, pr...$40.00
Box, bear, waterfall & trees on lid, marked Yellowstone National Park, 3½x4½", from $5 to.........................$7.00
Box, cowboy boots & saddle on lid, w/paper label...$12.50
Box, deer & trees, 4½x6", from $4 to $6.00
Box, floral design at sides & on lid, Syroco, 5½x5½", from $5 to $10.00
Box, rope design on lid, velvet lining, Syroco, 6x6", from $10 to $15.00
Box, standing dog on lid, 4x6", from $5 to.................$10.00
Box, swirl design, 5½x7", from $8 to..........................$10.00
Brush holder, ship w/white triple mainsails, 4½", from $7 to $12.00
Brush holder, 2 drunks w/keg, 5", from $5 to $10.00
Brush holder, 4 puppies in basket, from $8 to $10.00
Brush holder, 4 puppies in basket, wall hanging, w/brush...$20.00

Cigarette box/ashtray, Scottie dog on lid, marked, 8" long, from $20.00 to $24.00. (Photo courtesy Candace Sten Davis and Patricia J. Baugh)

Clock, cuckoo; blue bird cuckoo, key wound, 4½x4"...$55.00
Clock, white & gold scroll design, 8-day wind-up, 26"..$40.00

Coat racks, Raggedy Ann & Andy, Andy (#7510) sits on fence, Ann (#7509) leans on fence, 9x12", pr **$20.00**

Corkscrew, bartender shaking drink w/towel over arm, ca 1930, 8", EX...**$100.00**

Figure, musician, painted, from $10 to **$15.00**

Figure, seated Indian, from $6 to **$10.00**

Figurine, buffalo, red nostrils & black eyes, 3¼x2¼x1½"..**$35.00**

Figurine, bullfighter, 1968, 20x34½".........................**$30.00**

Figurine, Cape Cod fisherman & woman, painted, pr, from $6 to...**$15.00**

Figurine, Pinocchio, fingers crossed behind back, name on base, marked Walt Disney Prod Multi Products Chicago, 5".**$48.00**

Figurines, peacocks on dogwood branch, gold, 8¼", 12½", pr...**$20.00**

Figurines, 1 cherub w/horn, 1 w/harp, 15", 17", pr....**$30.00**

Mirror, oval w/gold scrollwork border, #2369, made by Dart Industries for Syroco, 24½x16½".........................**$28.00**

Picture frame, 3x2½"...**$6.00**

Picture frame, 8x5½", from $6 to **$12.00**

Pin holder, baby shoe shape, green velvet for pins, 3x2½"..**$15.00**

Pipe holder, 2 horses at gate, 3 rests, from $12 to **$15.00**

Plaque, cat on hind legs playing violin, 5½x3½"........**$70.00**

Plaque, Washington DC, brown, 9⅛x6½".....................**$12.50**

Plaque, 10-point buck embossed on shield, 3-D effect, 10½"...**$15.00**

Plaques, geisha girls in frame, 23x6½", pr..................**$25.00**

Plate, barn & silo pastoral scene at center, fruits & vegetables at rim, 8", from $2 to..**$5.00**

Plate, pine cones & leaves, 4", from $2 to....................**$5.00**

Thermometer, bear w/thermometer in side, 4½x2½".**$25.00**

Thermometer, Black figure, marked Multi Prod 1949, 5½"...**$50.00**

Thermometer, captain at ship's wheel, painted, marked Copyright Thad Co, 4".......................................**$15.00**

Thermometer, man w/umbrella stands beside thermometer, 6"...**$20.00**

Thermometer, Scottie dogs at sides, magnet at bottom, 4", from $5 to..**$10.00**

Tie rack, bartender behind bar w/bottles, painted, 6x9½", from $10 to...**$20.00**

Tie rack, Boy Scout insignia in center w/tents on sides, 10¼" L..**$35.00**

Tie rack, leaping bass on waves, 8 wire hangers, 8¾x5"..**$20.00**

Tie rack, pointer dog at top, metal hangers, 7x12", from $10 to..**$20.00**

Toothpick holder, Scottie dog figural, 4½x1½x3¼", EX...**$35.00**

Tray, flowers, marked Multi Products, 11" L, from $8 to .**$14.00**

Wall hanging, Aquarius sign (Zodiac), #7042, 1½" **$10.00**

Wall plaque, crucifix, white, 8", from $5 to.................**$10.00**

Wall plaque, eagle on top of mirror, 1960, 29x17½" ..**$35.00**

Wall plaque, Our Mother of Perpetual Help, 4x5", from $5 to..**$10.00**

Wall plaque, Scottie dog, repainted, 6", from $2 to **$8.00**

Wall shelf, floral w/acanthus leaf, bead trim at top edge, Multi Products, 9x7", pr, from $7 to **$12.00**

Wall shelves, lg rose design, 6½" shelf on 9½" rose, EX........**$50.00**

Taylor, Smith and Taylor

Though this company is most famous for their pastel dinnerware line, Lu Ray, they made many other patterns, and some of them are very collectible in their own right. They were located in the East Liverpool area of West Virginia, the 'dinnerware capitol' of the world. Their answer to HLC's very successful Fiesta line was Vistosa. It was made in four primary colors, and though quite attractive, the line was never developed to include any more than twenty items. Other lines/shapes that collectors especially look for are Taverne (also called Silhouette — similar to a line made by Hall), Conversation (a shape designed by Walter Dorwin Teague, 1950 to 1954), and Pebbleford (a textured, pastel line on the Versatile shape, made from 1952 to 1960).

For more information we recommend *Collector's Guide to LuRay Pastels* by Bill and Kathy Meehan (Collector Books), which covers several dinnerware lines in addition to LuRay.

Note: To evaluate King O'Dell, add 15% to the values we list for Conversation. For Boutonniere, add 15% to our Ever Yours values; and for Dwarf Pine, add the same amount to the values suggested for Versatile. Any of the rooster lines are priced in the same range as Ever Yours.

See also LuRay Pastels.

Autumn Harvest, dinner plate, on Ever Yours shape, $2.00. (Photo courtesy Bill and Kathy Meehan)

Castle, cake plate...**$25.00**

Castle, casserole...**$45.00**

Castle, cup & saucer...**$10.00**

Castle, plate, dinner; 10"..**$15.00**

Castle, sauce boat...**$22.00**

Castle, sugar bowl, w/lid...**$15.00**

Castle, teapot..**$60.00**

Conversation, casserole...**$30.00**

Conversation, plate, dinner...**$3.00**

Conversation, salt & pepper shakers, pr......................**$6.00**

Conversation, sauce boat...**$9.00**

Conversation, sugar bowl, w/lid.....................$6.00

Ever Yours, cake server, $18.00; carafe, $18.00, and warming stand, $6.00. (Photo courtesy Bill and Kathy Meehan)

Ever Yours, cup & saucer.............................$3.75
Ever Yours, platter, round $7.00
Ever Yours, sugar bowl $5.00
Ever Yours, water jug $18.00
Laurel, bowl, vegetable; round $7.00
Laurel, cup & saucer...................................$4.50
Laurel, plate, hard to find, 8".....................$11.00
Laurel, plate, 9"...$5.00
Laurel, platter, 11½".....................................$7.00
Pastoral, bowl, cereal...................................$4.50
Pastoral, cup & saucer..................................$6.00
Pebbleford, coffee server $30.00
Pebbleford, cup & saucer................................$6.50
Pebbleford, egg cup, double $12.00
Pebbleford, platter, 11"..................................$7.50
Pebbleford, salt & pepper shakers, pr $10.00
Pebbleford, sauce boat...................................$10.00
Silhouette/Taverne, bowl, vegetable; oval..................$35.00
Silhouette/Taverne, butter dish........................$175.00
Silhouette/Taverne, casserole..........................$90.00
Silhouette/Taverne, cup & saucer......................$15.00
Silhouette/Taverne, plate, dinner; 10".........$30.00
Silhouette/Taverne, platter, 13½"....................$35.00
Silhouette/Taverne, sugar bowl, w/lid $25.00
Taylorstone, coffee server $12.00
Taylorstone, creamer $2.50
Taylorton, casserole.....................................$27.00
Taylorton, coffee server.................................$25.00
Taylorton, cup & saucer.................................$3.50
Taylorton, sauce boat....................................$5.00
Versatile, bowl, vegetable; round $5.00
Versatile, plate, dinner.................................$2.50
Versatile, platter, 13"..................................$7.00
Versatile, water jug......................................$18.00

Vistosa, bowl, cream soup; from $20 to $25.00
Vistosa, bowl, salad; footed, 12", from $175 to.........$200.00
Vistosa, creamer...$20.00

Vistosa, plate, 9", from $15.00 to $20.00; plate, 7", from $12.00 to $18.00; plate, 6", from $10.00 to $15.00; after-dinner coffee cup and saucer, from $45.00 to $55.00. (Photo courtesy Bill and Kathy Meehan)

Vistosa, plate, 10", from $50 to $60.00
Vistosa, platter, 13", from $40 to.................$50.00
Vistosa, sauce boat, from $150 to $175.00
Vistosa, teapot, 6-cup, from $150 to $175.00

Tiara Exclusives

Tiara Exclusives was the dream of a determined man named Roger Jewett. With much hard work and planning and the involvement of Jim Hooffstetter of Indiana Glass, Tiara home party plan operations were initialized in July of 1970. Tiara Exclusives was a subsidiary of Indiana Glass, which is a division of Lancaster Colony. Tiara did not manufacture the glassware it sold. Several companies were involved in producing the glassware, among them Indiana Glass, Fenton, Fostoria, Dalzell Viking, and L.E. Smith. The Tiara Exclusives direct selling organization closed in 1998.

In 1999 and 2000, Home Interiors offered a small selection of Tiara Sandwich Glass dinnerware in an attractive transparent purple color called Plum. They have also marketed Tiara's square honey box and children's dish set.

Advisor: Mandi Birkinbine (See Directory, Tiara)

Crown Dinnerware

In the mid-1980s Tiara made Crown Dinnerware in Imperial Blue. This is the pattern most collectors know as King's Crown Thumbprint. The color is a rich medium blue, brighter than cobalt.

Bowl, 2⅛x4¼", from $7 to..............................**$9.00**
Bowl, 4x9¼"...**$17.00**
Cup **$3.00**
Goblet, stemmed, 8-oz, from $3 to **$5.00**
Pitcher, 8¾", from $25 to **$30.00**
Plate, bread; 8" **$5.00**
Plate, dinner; 10"..**$7.00**
Saucer **$2.00**

Honey Boxes

One of Tiara's more popular items was the honey box or honey dish. It is square with tiny tab feet and an embossed allover pattern of bees and hives. The dish measures 6" tall with the lid and was made in many different colors, ranging in value from $15.00 up to $50.00, depending on the color.

Amber, from $15 to **$25.00**
Black, from $25 to **$35.00**
Chantilly (pale) Green, from $35 to **$45.00**
Clear, from $35 to **$45.00**
Light blue, from $25 to.................................**$50.00**
Peach, from $35 to **$40.00**
Spruce (pale) Green, from $20 to **$35.00**

Sandwich Pattern

Among the many lovely glass patterns sold by Tiara, the Sandwich pattern was the most popular. Tiara's Sandwich line reintroduced Indiana Glass and Duncan & Miller Glass designs from the 1920s and 1930s alongside items designed specifically for Tiara. Tiara Sandwich Glass has been made in Crystal, Amber, Ruby, Chantilly (light green), Spruce (teal), Peach, and other colors in limited quantities. The dark blue color named Bicentennial Blue was introduced in 1976 in observance of America's Bicentennial. According to the Tiara brochure, Bicentennial Blue Sandwich glass (sometimes also called Anniversary or Midnight Blue by collectors) was approved for a production of 15,000 sets. We've listed a few pieces of Tiara's Sandwich below, and though the market is unstable and tends to vary from region to region, our estimates will serve to offer an indication of current asking prices. Because this glass is not rare and is relatively new, collectors tend to purchase only items in perfect condition. Chips or scratches will decrease value significantly.

With most items, the quickest way to tell Anchor Hocking's Sandwich from Tiara and Indiana Sandwich is by looking at the flower in the pattern. The Tiara/Indiana flower is outlined with a single line and has convex petals. Anchor Hocking's flower is made with double lines, so has a more complex appearance, and the convex area in each petal is tiny. Tiara's Chantilly Green Sandwich is a pale green color that resembles the light green glass made by Indiana Glass during the Depression era. Use of a black light can help determine the age of pale green Sandwich Glass. The green Sandwich made by Indiana Glass during the Depression will fluoresce yellow-green under a black light. Tiara's Chantilly

Green reflects the purple color of the black light bulb, but does not fluoresce yellow-green. To learn more about the two lines, we recommend *Collectible Glassware from the 40s, 50s, and 60s,* by Gene Florence (Collector Books). Also available are *Collecting Tiara Amber Sandwich Glass, Collecting Tiara Bicentennial Blue Sandwich Glass, Collecting Tiara Chantilly Green Sandwich Glass, Collecting Tiara Sandwich Glass in Peach and Spruce,* all by our advisor, Mandi Birkinbine (See the Directory for ordering information).

Ashtray, Amber, 1¼x7½".............................**$15.00**
Basket, Amber, tall & slender, 10¾x4¾".....**$50.00**

Basket, Ruby, 10¾x4¾", from $50.00 to $80.00. (Photo courtesy Mandi Birkinbine)

Bowl, Amber, slant slides, 1¾x4¾" **$5.50**
Bowl, Amber, 6-sided, 1¼x6¼" **$12.00**
Bowl, console; Amber, footed, flared rim, 3⅞x11".....**$40.00**
Bowl, salad; Amber, crimped, 4¾x10", from $15 to ...**$18.00**
Bowl, salad; Amber, slant-sided, 3x8⅜".....................**$20.00**
Bowl, salad; Chantilly Green, slant-sided, 3x8⅜", from $15 to **$25.00**
Butter dish, Amber, domed lid, 6" H, from $20 to......**$25.00**
Butter dish, Bicentennial Blue, domed lid, 6" H, from $25 to..**$35.00**
Butter dish, Chantilly Green, domed lid, 6" H **$35.00**
Butter dish, dark Teal Green, domed lid, 6", from $30 to...**$40.00**
Cake plate, Chantilly Green, footed, 4x10", from $55 to .**$70.00**
Candle holders, Amber, flared foot, 3¾", pr..............**$18.00**
Candle holders, Amber, scalloped rim, footed, 3¼x5½", pr **$25.00**
Candle holders, Chantilly Green, 8½", pr...................**$45.00**
Candy box, Amber, w/lid, 7½", from $65 to **$80.00**
Canister, Amber, 26-oz, 5⅝", from $12 to...................**$20.00**
Canister, Amber, 38-oz, 7½", from $12 to...................**$20.00**
Canister, Amber, 52-oz, 8⅞", from $18 to...................**$26.00**
Celery tray/oblong relish, Bicentennial Blue, 10⅜x4⅜"..**$18.50**
Clock, Amber, wall hanging, 12" dia, from $20 to......**$25.00**
Clock, Amber, wall hanging, 16" dia, from $45 to......**$55.00**
Clock, Peach, wall hanging, 12" dia, from $18 to.......**$20.00**
Clock, Spruce, wall hanging, 12" dia, from $18 to......**$20.00**

Compote, Amber, 8" $25.00
Creamer & sugar bowl, Bicentennial Blue, round, flat, pr, from $20 to..$25.00
Cup, coffee; Amber, 9-oz $4.00
Cup, punch; & saucer, crystal, 2⅝x3⅜" $6.00
Cup, snack; Amber $4.00
Dish, club, heart, diamond or spade shape, Amber, 4", ea from $3 to...$5.00
Dish, club, heart, diamond or spade shape, clear, 4", ea...$3.00
Egg tray, Amber, 12", from $12 to $18.00
Egg tray, Chantilly Green, from $15 to $22.00
Egg tray, Spruce Green, 12"..$15.00
Fairy lamp, Amber, egg shape, pedestal foot, 2-pc, 5¾", from $14 to...$18.00
Fairy lamp, Chantilly Green, from $18 to $26.00
Fairy Lamp, Regal Blue, 2-pc, 5¾"..............................$25.00
Goblet, table wine; Amber, 8½-oz, 5½"........................$7.50
Goblet, water; Amber, 8-oz, 5¼", from $6 to $8.00
Goblet, water; Bicentennial Blue, 8-oz, 5¼", from $8 to ..$12.00
Goblet, water; clear, 5¼", from $6 to...........................$9.00
Goblet, water; Spruce Green, 8-oz, 5¼", from $4 to $5.50
Gravy boat, Amber, 3⅛x7⅜", from $45 to..................$60.00
Mug, Amber, footed, 5½"..$8.00
Napkin holder, Amber, footed fan shape, 4x7½", from $15 to..$20.00
Pitcher, Amber, 8¼", from $35 to $50.00
Pitcher, Peach, 8½", from $20 to $30.00
Plate, dinner; Amber, 10", from $9.50 to.....................$12.50
Plate, dinner; Chantilly Green, from $8 to..................$12.00
Plate, salad; Amber, 8"...$7.00
Plate, salad; Chantilly Green, 8¼", from $4 to $8.00
Platter, Amber, sawtooth rim, 12", from $8.50 to $12.00
Puff box, Horizon Blue, 2x3¾" dia $18.00
Salt & pepper shakers, Amber, 4¾", pr from $18 to...$25.00
Sherbet, Amber, 3x3⅝"..$5.00
Tray, Amber, divided relish, 4-compartment, 10", from $25 to..$30.00
Tray, Amber, footed, 1¾x12¾"...................................$35.00
Tray, Chantilly Green, 3-part, 12"................................$19.00
Tray, egg; Amber, 12", from $15 to $20.00
Tray, egg; Peach, 12", from $20 to $35.00
Tray, egg; Spruce, 12", from $15 to.............................$18.00
Tray, tidbit; Horizon Blue, center silver-colored metal handle, 8¼" dia $17.50
Tumbler, Amber, juice, 8-oz, 4", from $12 to $14.00
Tumbler, Amber, water; 10-oz, 6½"...............................$8.00
Vase, Amber, ruffled, footed, 3¼x6½" $16.00
Vase, bud; Amber, 3⅝", from $15 to $25.00
Wine set, Amber, decanter, tray & 8 goblets..............$55.00

Tire Ashtrays

Manufacturers of tires issued miniature versions containing ashtray inserts that they usually embossed with advertising messages. Others were used as souvenirs from world's fairs. The earlier styles were made of glass or glass and metal, but by the early 1920s, they were replaced by the more familiar rubber-tired variety. The inserts were often made of clear glass, but colors were also used, and once in awhile you'll find a tin one. The tires themselves were usually black; other colors are rarely found. Hundreds have been produced over the years; in fact, the larger tire companies still issue them occasionally, but you no longer see the details or colors that are evident in the pre-WWII ashtrays. Although the common ones bring modest prices, rare examples sometimes sell for up to several hundred dollars. For ladies or non-smokers, some miniature tires were called pin trays.

For more information we recommend *Tire Ashtray Collector's Guide* by Jeff McVey.

Advisor: Jeff McVey (See Directory, Tire Ashtrays)

Goodyear Vector, clear insert with manufacturer's imprint, 6" tire, $17.50. **(Photo courtesy Jeff McVey)**

Armstrong Rhino-Flex, Miracle SD, name in gold, glass insert w/rhino & name, 6"...$25.00
Bridgestone, D-Lug, Tubeless, clear glass insert w/logo name in center, 3x8¾"...$30.00
Firestone, Champion, Safety-Lock Cord, gum dipped, clear insert w/embossed 'f' & pledge, 6" $45.00
Firestone, Cushion Traction Mileage on solid brass insert, marked Firestone Made in USA 40x12, 4½x2", EX .$140.00
Firestone, High Speed, amber glass insert, Century of Progress Chicago 1934, 5¾"..................................$85.00
Firestone, red & black plastic insert w/3 extended rests, 6"...$10.00
Firestone, Steel Belted Radial 721, glass insert w/red & white logo, 6" $15.00
Firestone, Steel Radial 500, clear glass insert, Spirit of '76 white decal, 5¾" $25.00
General, Steelex Radial, glass insert, black letters: 'goes a long way to make friends,' 6½"............................$17.50
General, Streamline Jumbo, green glass insert w/'goes a long way to make friends,' 5" $65.00

Gislaved Steel Belted Radial, blue glass insert w/'G,' 6" ...**$85.00**

Goodrich Silvertown, Golden Ply 600-16 4 ply, amber glass insert, 6⅛" **$45.00**

Goodrich Silvertown, Lifesaver Radial HR-70-15, clear glass insert, 6"..**$20.00**

Goodyear, Air Wheel Made w/Supertwist Cord, all weather, 5.50-16, green glass insert, 5⅝" **$45.00**

Goodyear, American Eagle Radial, Flexten, clear insert, white decal w/name & eagle, 5¾"............................**$15.00**

Goodyear, Hi-Miler Cross Rib, nylon, clear glass insert w/blue logo, 6¼"..**$20.00**

Hood Arrow, paper label in glass insert w/man in uniform holding sign w/address, 6½" **$110.00**

Kelly Springfield, Voyager, Aramid Belted Radial, clear insert w/green decal, 6"..**$20.00**

Miller, Miller Delux, Long Safe Mileage, Geared to the Road, clear insert, 7" **$80.00**

Mohawk, Akron O, glass insert w/yellow bottom & local Urbana IL ad, 1930s, 5⅜" **$35.00**

Pennsylvania Tires, pink glass insert, 5¼" **$40.00**

Pennsylvania Vaccum Cup 33x5 (reproduction in cobalt, sea mist green & other 'modern' colors) **$20.00**

Pennsylvania Vacuum Cup 34x4, 1-pc, all glass **$150.00**

Seiberling, Patrician De Lux 4 ply, green glass insert, cream decal, local ad, 3½" **$45.00**

Seiberling, Sealed-Aire, 760-15, clear glass insert, 5⅞"...**$20.00**

Vogue Tyres, white tire w/glass insert w/Vogue Tyres logo in red, real rubber w/tread, 6" dia.........................**$80.00**

Tobacco Collectibles

Until lately, the tobacco industry spent staggering sums advertising their products, and scores of retail companies turned out many types of smoking accessories such as pipes, humidors, lighters, and ashtrays. Even though the smoking habit isn't particularly popular nowadays, collecting tobacco-related memorabilia is!

See also Advertising Character Collectibles, Joe Camel; Cigarette Lighters.

Club/Newsletter: *Tobacco Jar*
Society of Tobacco Jar Collectors
1705 Chanticleer Drive
Cherry Hill, NJ 08003
www.tobaccojarsociety.com

Ashtay, Player Navy Mixture, copper w/embossed sailor in center, 5½" dia, EX...**$35.00**

Ashtray, RJ Reynolds, leaf shape, bronze, 8¾", EX.....**$20.00**

Bank, Old Honesty 5¢ Cigars, Indian stands on base, cast iron, 13", EX...**$25.00**

Box, Fame, Globe Tobacco Co, wood w/winged lady playing horn paper lithograph, 10x3½x2", VG+ **$50.00**

Cigarette box, Red Kamel, tax stamp 1909, EX.........**$130.00**

Counter display, Squadron Leader 10¢, single-engine biplane, EX...**$30.00**

Display box, Honest Weight Tobacco, Waymen & Bros, 24 unopened foil pouches, 11x6½", EX...................**$240.00**

Doorstop, Virgin Tobacco Cigars, baseball player figural, cast-iron, 12", EX..**$35.00**

Fan, Lucky Strike, die-cut cardboard, Frank Sinatra image, EX+, $250.00.

Humidor, Austrian porcelain, hand-painted gentleman with pipe, 7x7", EX, $125.00. (Photo courtesy Buffalo Bay)

Lunch pail, Brotherhood Tobacco, VG+ **$55.00**

Lunch pail, Cuban Star Tobacco, flag graphic, tin, 7x5¼"..**$55.00**

Lunch pail, Union Leader Cut Plug, red w/gold letters, hinged lid, wire handle, 4¼x7¾x5¼", VG+ **$50.00**

Mug, Mail Pouch Chewing Tobacco, For Bloth Bros West Virginia, porcelain, 1982, M **$15.00**

Pin-back button, Santa w/Always Bring Chesterfields, 2¼" dia, EX **$40.00**

Plug cutter, Superior, table mount, cast-iron, 18", EX.**$50.00**

Pocket mirror, Mascot Crushed Cut Tobacco, dog graphics on white w/red border, VG+.............................**$22.50**

Pocket tin, Edgworth Ready-Rubbed, America's Finest Pipe Tobacco, blue w/white vertical stripes, flat top, 4½", EX **$180.00**

Pocket tin, Hi-Plane, rare 2 engine variation, vertical, flat top, EX **$105.00**

Pocket tin, Lucky Strike Genuine Roll Cut, sample size, hinged flat top, 3¼x2½", EX **$110.00**

Pocket tin, Union Leader Redi-Cut Tobacco, Uncle Sam graphics, vertical, flat top, 4½", EX.....................**$75.00**

Poster, Always Smoke Chesterfield, Bob Hope photo, 1940s, 60x30", EX......................................**$150.00**

Price list, RJ Reynolds, 1946, 23 pages, picture of plant in Winston-Salem NC, EX......................................**$18.00**

Rolling kit, Bugler Thrift Kit, rolling machine, papers, instructions, Brown & Williamson Tobacco Corp, VG+......................................**$22.00**

Rolling papers, Union Leader Cut Plug, gold letters on red, VG+......................................**$20.00**

Sign, Buy Chesterfields Here, metal w/embossed pack of cigarettes, 17¾x11¾", EX......................................**$60.00**

Sign, Chesterfield Cigarettes, 1941 Miss America Rosemary La Planche as Statue of Liberty, heavy cardboard, 11x21", VG+......................................**$65.00**

Sign, For Cigarettes Jockey Cigarette Tobacco 5¢, pack graphics, cardboard, 21x11", EX......................................**$35.00**

Sign, Red Man Land, Home of America's Best Chew, Indian Chief graphics, tin, 16x6", EX+......................................**$190.00**

Sign, Smoke Model Tobacco, Did You Say 10¢?, heavy paper, 62x17½", EX......................................**$25.00**

Sign, Union Leader Smoking Tobacco, lithographed tin, 15½x10½", EX......................................**$35.00**

Store bin, Sweet Miss Chewing Tobacco, can shape, holds 48 packs, 11x8¼" dia, VG+......................................**$225.00**

Store display, Ogden's Special Mixture, tobacco pack design, 3½x2½", EX......................................**$32.50**

Store display, Rod & Gun Smoking Mixture, w/12 individual packs, 10x6x4", EX......................................**$30.00**

Store display, She Prefers Bond Street Aromatic Pipe Tobacco..., cardboard, 17x15", EX......................................**$35.00**

Store display, Yankee Girl Chewing Tobacco, girl w/flag in shield w/red & white checked ground, cardboard, 11¾x8", EX......................................**$20.00**

Thermometer, Camels, Have a Real Cigarette, open pack graphics on red, 15½x6", EX......................................**$40.00**

Thermometer, Chew Silver Cut Tobacco, die-cut tin, 38½x8", EX......................................**$80.00**

Thermometer, Treat Yourself to Cash Value Chewing Tobacco..., tin, 9" dia, EX......................................**$80.00**

Thermometer, Treat Yourself to the Best, Chew Mail Pouch Tobacco, porcelain, 39x8", EX......................................**$170.00**

Thermometer, Union Worker Chewing Tobacco, blue on white, glass front on aluminum, round, EX......................................**$70.00**

Tin, Camel Cigarettes, R.J. Reynolds, Winston-Salem, North Carolina, 1950, 3¼x3½" diameter, EX+, $30.00.

Tin, Charm of the West, Ginna, Victorian woman w/dog beside horse, 3¾x2½x¾", VG+......................................**$320.00**

Tin, City Club Crushed Cubes, Burley Tobacco Co, 6x4¼" dia, VG+......................................**$260.00**

Tin, Continental Cubes, Revolution-era man reading paper, concave, VG......................................**$225.00**

Tin, Dan Patch Fine Cut, horse w/man on sulky, paper label on tin, EX......................................**$150.00**

Tin, Hindoo Granulated Plug Smoking Tobacco Strater Brothers, Hindu man seated smoking, 3½x3½x1", VG+......................................**$350.00**

Tin, Honeymoon Rum-Flavored Tobacco 10¢, red w/man sitting on crescent moon, EX......................................**$300.00**

Tin, McClelland Tobacco Company Navy Cavendish, 1995, 3½-oz, unopened, NM......................................**$25.00**

Tin, Model Smoking Tobacco, white, EX......................................**$310.00**

Tin, Plow Boy Tobacco, store display, shows man w/plow, holds 48 packages, 10½x9½x7½", VG+......................................**$265.00**

Tin, pocket; Half & Half Buckingham Bright Cut Plug Smoking Tobacco, 3½x3", VG, $20.00.

Tin, Ridgeway Pipe Tobacco, red & white, 2-oz can, 1970s, unopened, EX......................................**$50.00**

Tin, Sunset Trails 5¢ Cigars, man & woman on horses, EX..**$390.00**

Tobacco bag, Snug Harbor Cut Plug, Larus Bros, drawstring type, 4½x7½", VG......................................**$25.00**

Tobacco can, Home Comfort Tobacco, Smoke & Chew, red & white, 6x5" dia, EX......................................**$22.00**

Tobacco can, Sign, Copenhagen Snuff, It Satisfies, tin, 16½x23", EX......................................**$20.00**

Tobacco decanter, Heroes of '76, drummer/flute player/flag carrier/eagle w/E Pluribus Unum all embossed, Imari, 6x5½"......................................**$30.00**

Tobacco pack, Days of Work Chewing Tobacco, w/6 sealed (cellophane) cuts, EX......................................**$60.00**

Tobacco pouch, Bowl of Roses Pipe Mixture, man sits in chair w/flowers in vase on table, EX......................................**$20.00**

Tobacco pouch, Ripple Cigarette Tobacco, papers inside, unopened, ¾-oz, 3x4½", EX......................................**$20.00**

Tobacco tag, Jack Rabbit, picture of rabbit in black on white, ⅝" dia, VG......................................**$55.00**

Toothbrush Holders

Novelty toothbrush holders have been modeled as animals of all types, in human forms, and in the likenesses of many storybook personalities. Today all are very collectible, especially those representing popular Disney characters. Most of these are made of bisque and are decorated over the glaze. Condition of the paint is an important consideration when trying to arrive at an evaluation.

For more information, refer to *Pictorial Guide to Toothbrush Holders* by Marilyn Cooper.

Advisor: Marilyn Cooper (See Directory, Toothbrush Holders)

Baby Bunting, shaker top, child in brown bunny suit w/blue bow at neck, Germany, 6¾", from $350 to........**$400.00**

Bear, paws hold 1 brush, hangs, tray at feet holds toothpaste, Japan (Goldcastle), 6", from $85 to......................**$95.00**

Bonzo, lustreware, 2 holes, hangs, feet hold toothpaste, Japan, 5¾", from $80 to **$95.00**

Boy w/top hat, dog at side, 2 holes, hangs, tray at feet holds toothpaste, Japan, 5½", from $65 to......................**$75.00**

Carousel, 4 holes, hangs, no tray, Crown mark, 5", from $100 to...**$120.00**

Cat howling, 1 hole, free-standing, no tray, Red Wing, 5", from $85 to...**$100.00**

Cat standing on front paws, 1 hole, hangs, no tray, Japan, 5⅜", from $90 to...**$100.00**

Children in auto, 2 holes, hangs, green tray below car tires holds toothpaste, Japan, 5", from $70 to **$85.00**

Clown w/bug on nose, 3 holes, hangs, tray holds toothpaste, 5⅛", from $150 to................................**$175.00**

Dachshund, 2 holes, hangs, feet form holder for toothpaste, 5¼", from $70 to...**$80.00**

Dog begging, lustre, 2 holes, hangs, no tray, 3¾", from $90 to...**$100.00**

Donkey w/mane, loop in mane holds 1 brush, 2 holders, hangs, tray at feet holds toothpaste, Japan, 5¾", from $90 to...**$110.00**

Dutch boy & girl kissing, 2 holes, hangs, tray at feet holds toothpaste, Japan, 6¼", from $55 to......................**$65.00**

Dutch boy & girl sitting on mantel, 3 holes, free-standing, w/tray, Japan (Goldcastle), 4¼", from $95 to.....**$105.00**

Dwarf (Happy), bisque, 1 hole, free-standing, no tray, Japan, 3½", from $600 to...**$625.00**

Elephant w/tusk, lustreware, 1 hole, tray at feet holds toothpaste, Japan, 5½", from $80 to **$100.00**

Girl washing boy's face, 2 holes, hangs, tray at feet holds toothpaste, 5", from $80 to......................................**$90.00**

Indian chief, 2 holes, hangs, tray at base holds toothpaste, 4½", from $250 to...**$300.00**

Lone Ranger, chalk, 1 hole, free-standing, no tray, 4", from $70 to...**$80.00**

Pinocchio & Figaro, 1 hole, free-standing, no tray, Shafford, 5¼", from $450 to...**$475.00**

Pirate w/sash, 2 holes, hangs, tray at feet holds toothpaste, Japan, 6", from $80 to **$90.00**

Skeezix, metal, 2 holes, hangs, no tray, K-USA, 6", from $150 to..**$175.00**

Soldier w/sash, 2 holes, hangs, feet form tray to hold toothpaste, Japan, 6", from $80 to **$90.00**

Three Little Pigs, 3 holes, free-standing, w/tray, Japan (Goldcastle), 4", from $90 to............................**$110.00**

Uncle Willie, 2 holes, hangs, feet form tray to hold toothpaste, Japan, 5⅛", from $85 to **$95.00**

Toys

Toy collecting has long been an area of very strong activity, but over the past decade it has literally exploded. Many of the larger auction galleries have cataloged toy auctions, and it isn't uncommon for scarce nineteenth-century toys in good condition go for $5,000.00 to $10,000.00 and up. Toy shows are popular, and there are clubs, newsletters, and magazines that cater only to the needs and wants of toy collectors. Though once buyers ignored toys less than thirty years old, in more recent years, even some toys from the '80s are sought after.

Condition has more bearing on the value of a toy than any other factor. A used toy in good condition with no major flaws will still be worth only about half (in some cases much less) as much as one in mint (like new) condition. Those mint and in their original boxes will be worth considerably more than the same toy without its box.

There are many good toy guides on the market today including: *Modern Toys, American Toys, 1930 to 1980,* by Linda Baker; *Collecting Toys* and *Collecting Toy Trains* by Richard O'Brien; *Schroeder's Collectible Toys, Antique to Modern; Elmer's Price Guide to Toys* by Elmer Duellman; *Toys of the Sixties, A Pictorial Guide,* by Bill Bruegman; *Occupied Japan Toys With Prices* by David C. Gould and Donna Crevar-Donaldson; and *Cartoon Toys and Collectibles* by David Longest. More books are listed in the subcategory narratives that follow. With the exception of O'Brien's (Books Americana) and Bruegman's (Cap't Penny Productions), all the books we've referred to are published by Collector Books.

See also Advertising Character Collectibles; Breyer Horses; Bubble Bath Containers; Character Collectibles; Disney Collectibles; Dolls; Fast-Food Collectibles; Fisher-Price; Halloween; Hartland Plastics Inc.; Model Kits; Paper Dolls; Games; Puzzles; Star Wars; Steiff Animals.

Action Figures and Accessories

Back in 1964, Barbie dolls were taking the feminine side of the toy market by storm. Hasbro took a risky step in an attempt to capture the interest of the male segment of the population. Their answer to the Barbie doll craze was GI Joe. Since no self-respecting boy would admit to playing with dolls, Hasbro called their boy dolls 'action figures,' and to the surprise of many, they were phenomenally successful. Today action figures generate just as much enthusiasm among toy collectors as they ever did among little boys.

Action figures are simply dolls with poseable bodies. Some — the original GI Joes, for instance, were 12" tall, while others were 6" to 9" in height. In recent years, the 3¾" figure has been favored. GI Joe was introduced in the 3¾" size in the '80s and proved to be unprecedented in action figure sales. (See also GI Joe.)

In addition to the figures themselves, each company added a full line of accessories such as clothing, vehicles, play sets, weapons, etc. — all are avidly collected. Be aware of condition! Original packaging is extremely important. In fact, when it comes to the recent issues, loose, played-with examples are seldom worth more than a few dollars.

For more information, refer to *Collectible Action Figures* by Paris and Susan Manos (Collector Books).

Club: The Mego Adventurers Club
Old Forest Press, Inc.
PMB 195, 223 Wall St.
Huntington, NY 11743
Membership: $18.95 per year ($30 foreign); Includes 6 issues of *Mego Head,* the official club newsletter

Adventures of Indiana Jones, accessory, Map Room, Kenner, MIB (sealed)............**$110.00**
Adventures of Indiana Jones, figure, Cairo Swordsman, Kenner, 3¾", MOC............**$30.00**
Adventures of Indiana Jones, figure, Indiana Jones, Kenner, 3¾", MOC............**$200.00**
Battlestar Galactica, figure, Colonial Scarab, Mattel, 12", MIB (sealed)............**$45.00**
Battlestar Galactica, figure set, Cylon Centurian & Colonial Warrior, Mattel, 12", MIB............**$125.00**
Best of the West, accessory, Circle X Ranch, Marx, MIB, from $135 to............**$160.00**
Best of the West, accessory, Jeep & Horse Trailer, Marx, MIB............**$150.00**
Best of the West, accessory, Travel Case, Marx, NM ..**$30.00**
Best of the West, figure, Chief Cherokee, Marx, complete, NM (NM box)............**$160.00**
Best of the West, figure, General Custer, Marx, complete, NM (VG Fort Apache Fighters box)............**$65.00**
Best of the West, figure, Jaimie West, Marx, complete, NM (EX box)............**$75.00**
Best of the West, figure, Janice West, Marx, complete, NM (EX box)............**$45.00**
Best of the West, figure, Princess Wildflower, Marx, complete, NMIB............**$135.00**
Best of the West, figure, Sam Cobra, Marx, later version w/quick-draw grip, MIB............**$40.00**
Best of the West, figure, Sheriff Garrett, Marx, complete, NM (VG box)............**$175.00**
Best of the West, horse, Thunderbolt, cream, Marx, complete, EXIB............**$45.00**
Big Jim, accessory, Jungle Truck, Mattel, M............**$45.00**
Big Jim, accessory, Rescue Rig, Mattel, complete, M..**$35.00**
Big Jim, figure, any character, Mattel, complete, EX, ea from $20 to............**$25.00**

Black Hole, figure, Dan Holland, 1979, 8", MIB............**$22.00**
Black Hole, figure, Old Bob, Mego, rare, MOC............**$215.00**
Blackstar, accessory, Battle Set, MIP............**$50.00**
Blackstar, figure, White Knight, MOC............**$30.00**
Bonanza, figure, Ben, Little Joe, Hoss or Outlaw, American Character, 8", ea from $180 to............**$225.00**
Buck Rogers, figure, any character, Mego, 3¾", MOC, ea...**$20.00**
Captain Action, accessory, Action Cave, Ideal, M.....**$100.00**
Captain Action, accessory, Anti-Gravitational Power Pack, Ideal, complete, MIB............**$180.00**
Captain Action, accessory, Aquaman outfit, Ideal, complete, MIB, from $450 to............**$550.00**
Captain Action, accessory, Inter-Galactic Jet Mortar, Ideal, complete, MIB............**$180.00**
Captain Action, accessory, Parachute Pack, Ideal, complete, NM............**$65.00**
Captain Action, figure, Captain America, Ideal, 1967, complete, NMIB............**$250.00**
Captain Action, figure, Mera, Ideal, complete, rare, MIB...**$400.00**
Captain Action, figure, Robin, Ideal, complete, 8½", M.....**$225.00**
Captain Action, figure, Steve Canyon, Ideal, 12", MIB.......**$215.00**
Dragon Heart, figure set, Draco w/Bowen or Evil Griffin Dragon w/King, MIB (sealed), ea............**$15.00**
Dukes of Hazzard, figure, any character, Mego, 8", MOC, ea from $30 to............**$35.00**
Dungeons & Dragons, figure, Strongheart, Warduke or Zarak, MOC, ea............**$20.00**
Lone Ranger Rides Again, accessory, Prairie Wagon, Gabriel, MIB............**$40.00**
Lone Ranger Rides Again, figure, any character, Gabriel, 9", MIB, ea............**$50.00**
M*A*S*H, accessory, Jeep w/Hawkeye figure, TriStar, 1981, MIB............**$30.00**
M*A*S*H, figure, any character, TriStar, 1981, 3¾", MOC, ea............**$20.00**
Major Matt Mason, accessory, Astro Trac, Mattel, 1966, MIB............**$100.00**
Major Matt Mason, accessory, Satellite Locker, Mattel, 1967, EX............**$30.00**
Major Matt Mason, accessory, Space Station, Mattel, 1966, MIB............**$200.00**
Major Matt Mason, figure, Callisto, Mattel, 1968, 6", MOC............**$200.00**
Man From UNCLE, figure, Illya Kuryakin, Gilbert, 12", MIB............**$100.00**
Micronauts, accessory, Astro Station, Mego, EXIB......**$50.00**
Micronauts, figure, Baron Karaza, Mego, MIB............**$75.00**
Micronauts, figure, Blizzard, Mego, MIB............**$60.00**
Micronauts, figure, Megas, Mego, NRFB............**$60.00**
Official Scout High Adventure, accessory, camping set, Kenner, complete, M............**$25.00**
Official Scout High Adventure, figure, Bob Scout, Kenner, MIB............**$30.00**
Official Scout High Adventure, figure, Dave Cub Scout, Kenner, MIB............**$30.00**
Official World's Greatest Super Heroes, accessory, Amazing Spider Car, MIB............**$50.00**

Official World's Greatest Super Heroes, figure, Batman, Bend 'n Flex, Mego, 5", NMOC **$50.00**

Official World's Greatest Super Heroes, figure, Captain America, Mego, 8", EX.............................**$50.00**

Official World's Greatest Super Heroes, figure, Green Goblin, Mego, 8", EX **$125.00**

Official World's Greatest Super Heroes, figure, Joker, Mego, complete, 8", M **$55.00**

Official World's Greatest Super Heroes, figure, Riddler, First Fighting, 8", M **$150.00**

Official World's Greatest Super Heroes, figure, Spider-Man, Bend'n Flex, Mego, MOC **$75.00**

Official World's Greatest Super Heroes, figure, Supergirl, Bend'n Flex, Mego, MOC (sealed) **$150.00**

Planet of the Apes, accessory, Forbidden Zone Trap, Mego, MIB (sealed)...........................**$265.00**

Planet of the Apes, figure, Alan Verdon, Mego, 8", MOC ..**$130.00**

Planet of the Apes, figure, Cornelius, Mego, complete, 8", M...**$50.00**

Planet of the Apes, figure, Dr Zaius, Mego, complete, 8", M....**$50.00**

Planet of the Apes, figure, Peter Burke, Mego, 8", MOC....**$110.00**

Power Lords, figure, any character, MOC, ea from $20 to ..**$30.00**

Robotech, accessory, Bioroid Hovercraft, MIB............**$15.00**

Robotech, figure, Lisa Hayes, Matchbox, MOC **$15.00**

Robotech, figure, Rick Hunter, Matchbox, MOC **$18.00**

Ronin Warriors, figure, any character, MOC, ea from $10 to...........................**$15.00**

Space: 1999, figures, Dr Russell or Professor Bergman, Mattel, 1975, MOC, ea...........................**$20.00**

Starriors, figure, Backfire, MIB (sealed) **$20.00**

Starriors, figure, Vulture, MIB **$25.00**

Starsky & Hutch, figures, Starsky or Hutch, 1st issue or 2nd issue, Mego, 1975-76, MOC, ea from $25 to........**$35.00**

Super Heroes, Robin, Mego, 8", M (on French card), $75.00. (Photo courtesy June Moon)

Super Pirates, figure, Black Beard, Mego, complete, 8", M...........................**$35.00**

Super Powers, figure, Batman, Kenner, MOC, from $40 to **$50.00**

Super Powers, figure, Darkseid, Kenner, MOC **$15.00**

Super Powers, figure, Firestorm, Green Arrow or Hawkman, Kenner, MOC, ea **$25.00**

Super Powers, figure, Lex Luther, Kenner, MOC.........**$15.00**

Super Powers, figure, Mantis, w/ID card & comic book, Kenner, NM **$20.00**

Super Powers, figure, Orion, Kenner, MOC (unpunched) ..**$30.00**

Super Powers, figure, Red Tornado, Kenner, MOC **$45.00**

Super Powers, figure, Riddler, Kenner, MOC (unpunched Mexican Super Amigos) **$110.00**

Thundercats, figures, any character other than Driller or Stinger, LJN, MOC, ea from $20 to **$30.00**

Thundercats, figures, Driller or Stinger, LJN, MOC, ea from $25 to...........................**$35.00**

Waltons, figure set, Johnboy & Mary Ellen, Mom & Pop or Grandma & Grandpa, Mego, 1974, 8", MIB, ea set..**$35.00**

Wizard of Oz, accessory, Wizard of Oz & His Emerald City, Mego, complete, MIB **$250.00**

Wizard of Oz, figure, any character except Scarecrow or Wicked Witch, Mego, 8", MOC, ea **$35.00**

Wizard of Oz, figure, Scarecrow or Wicked Witch, Mego, 8", MOC, ea...........................**$45.00**

Wonder Woman, figure, Nubia, Mego, 1976, 12", MIB, from $75 to...........................**$100.00**

Wonder Woman, figure, Steve Trevor, Mego, 1976, 12", EXIB...........................**$75.00**

Wonder Woman, figure, Wonder Woman, Mego, 1976, 12", MIB, from $100 to **$125.00**

World Wrestling Federation, figure, British Bulldog, Hasbro, MOC, from $10 to...........................**$12.00**

World Wrestling Federation, figure, Hulk Hogan, white shirt, LJN, MOC...........................**$30.00**

World Wrestling Federation, figure, Rick Martel, Hasbro, MOC...........................**$20.00**

World Wrestling Federation, figure, Rick Rude, Hasbro, MOC...........................**$25.00**

World Wrestling Federation, figure, Vince McMan, LJN, MOC...........................**$25.00**

Battery Operated

It is estimated that approximately 95% of the battery-operated toys that were so popular from the '40s through the '60s came from Japan. The remaining 5% were made in the United States by other companies. To market these toys in America, many distributorships were organized. Some of the largest were Cragstan, Linemar, and Rosko. But even American toy makers such as Marx, Ideal, Hubley, and Daisy sold them under their own names, so the trademarks you'll find on Japanese battery-operated toys are not necessarily that of the manufacturer, and it's sometimes just about impossible to determine the specific company that actually did make them. After peaking in the '60s, the Japanese toy industry began to decline, bowing out to competition from the cheaper diecast and plastic toy makers.

Remember that it is rare to find one of these complex toys that has survived in good, collectible condition.

Batteries caused corrosion, lubricants dried out, cycles were interrupted and mechanisms ruined, rubber hoses and bellows aged and cracked, so the mortality rate was extremely high. A toy rated good, that is showing signs of wear but well taken care of, is generally worth about half as much as the same toy in mint (like new) condition. Besides condition, battery-operated toys are rated on scarcity, desirability, and the number of 'actions' they preform. A 'major' toy is one that has three or more actions, while one that has only one or two is considered 'minor.' The latter, of course, are worth much less.

In addition to the books we referenced in the beginning narrative to the toy category, you'll find more information in *Collecting Battery Toys* by Don Hultzman (Books Americana) and *Collector's Guide to Battery Toys* by Don Hultzman (Collector Books).

Alps, Accordion Player Hobo w/Monkey, MIB, from $500 to **$575.00**
Alps, Antique Gooney Car, 1960s, 9", EX **$120.00**
Alps, Balloon Blowing Monkey, 1950s, 11½", NM ...**$125.00**
Alps, Big Top Champ Circus Clown, 1960s, 15", NMIB, from $120 to...**$150.00**
Alps, Cappy the Happy Baggage Porter, 1960s, 12", MIB, from $300 to...**$375.00**
Alps, Charlie the Funny Clown, 9", NMIB, from $300 to ..**$350.00**
Alps, Flexie the Pocket Monkey, 1960s, 12", EX......**$115.00**
Alps, Mary's Little Lamb, 1950s, 10½", EX................**$150.00**
Alps, Pipie the Whale, 1950s, rare, 12", EX.............**$225.00**
Alps, Talking Trixie, 1950s, 6½", EX........................**$65.00**
Bandai, Musical Ice Cream Truck, 1960s, 10½", EX .**$225.00**
Bandai, Sea Bear #7, 1950s, 10", EX **$100.00**
Bandai, Wonderland Locomotive, 1960s, 9", EX.........**$65.00**
Cragstan, Chimp & Pup Rail Car, rare, 9", EX..........**$140.00**
Cragstan, Periscope Firing Range, MIB **$190.00**
Cragstan, Radar Jeep, 11", NMIB **$100.00**
Gakken, Musical Showboat, 1960s, 13", EX **$190.00**
Gakken, Playland Train, 1970s, 7½" dia, NM **$40.00**
Haji, Peppermint Twist, 1950s, 12", NM **$225.00**
Hasbro, Mentor Wizard, MIB, from $120 to **$150.00**

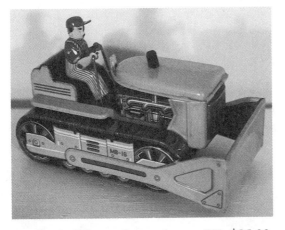

Japan, Bulldozer, bump 'n go, EX, $85.00.
(Photo courtesy June Moon)

K, Zoom Boat F-570, 1950s, 10", EXIB **$170.00**
KKS, Water Spouting Whale w/Flopping Tail, 1950s, 13", EX...**$150.00**
Linemar, Army Radio Jeep, 1950s, 7", EX **$150.00**
Linemar, Calypso Joe, 10", EX **$340.00**
Linemar, Switchboard Operator, 1950s, rare, 7½", NM .**$525.00**
Marusan, Smoky (sic) Bear, EXIB.............................**$225.00**
Marx, Alley the Roaring Stalking Alligator, 1960s, 17½", EXIB **$450.00**
Marx, Barking Boxer Dog, 1950s, 7", EX **$100.00**
Marx, Barnyard Rooster, 1950s, 10", EX **$125.00**
Marx, Big Parade, 1963, 15" L, NMIB......................**$200.00**
Marx, Great Garloo, 1960s, 23", EX **$400.00**
Marx, Marx-A-Copter, 1961, NMIB **$250.00**
Marx, Mighty Kong, 1950s, 11", EX **$300.00**
Marx, Penny the Poodle, 1960, NM (EX box)...........**$125.00**
Marx, Squawky the Parrot, NMIB.............................**$575.00**
Masudaya, Overland Express Locomotive, EXIB.......**$140.00**
Masudaya, Western Choo Choo, EX (G box) **$60.00**
MT, Airport Saucer, 1960s, 8" dia, NM **$140.00**
MT, B-Z Rabbit, 1950s, 7" L, EX **$100.00**
MT, Big Ring Circus, NM..**$175.00**
MT, Hungry Sheep, 1950s, 9", EX **$150.00**
MT, Lucky Cement Mixer, 1960s, 12", from $265 to .**$325.00**
MT, Mickey Mouse Flying Saucer, MIB, from $200 to...**$250.00**
MT, Puzzled Puppy, 1950s, 5", EX **$150.00**
MT, Rambling Ladybug, 1960s, 8", EX **$100.00**
NGS, Pat the Dog, 1950s, 9½", MIB, from $140 to...**$175.00**
Plaything Toys, Sam the Shaving Man, 1960s, 11½", EXIB..**$265.00**
Remco, Batman Flying Batplane, 1966, 12", EXIB **$125.00**
Rosko, Dozo the Steaming Clown, 1960s, 10", MIB, from $500 to..**$575.00**
S&E, Dentist Bear, 1950s, 9", NM, from $400 to........**$475.00**
S&E, Rabbits & the Carriage, 1950s, rare, 8" L, EX ...**$225.00**
SH, Dip-ie the Whale, 1950s, 13", EX **$190.00**
Technofix, Big Dipper, 1960s, 21" L, EX...................**$150.00**
TN, Aerial Ropeway, 1950s, 5", EXIB, from $125 to.**$165.00**
TN, Bartender, 1960s, 11½", MIB **$65.00**
TN, Bingo the Clown, 1950s, rare, 13", NM, from $400 to ..**$475.00**
TN, Electro Toy Fire Engine, 1950s, MIB, from $145 to..**$175.00**
TN, Fire Command Car, 1950s, EX...........................**$260.00**
TN, Pee Pee Puppy, 1960s, 9", NMIB **$150.00**
TN, Pilot Electro Boat, 11", NMIB **$170.00**
TN, Slalom Game, 11" base, EXIB...........................**$150.00**
Tomiyama, Cindy the Meowing Cat, 1950s, 12", EX **$75.00**
Tomiyama, Winston the Barking Bulldog, 1950s, 10", NM **$120.00**
Wen-Mac, Walt Disney's Tomorrowland Rocket Ride, 1960, rare, 29", EX **$300.00**
Y, Captain Blushwell, 1960s, 11", VG........................**$65.00**
Y, Drinking Dog w/Lighted Eyes, 1950s, 9", EX **$140.00**
Y, Hungry Baby Bear (mama feeds baby), 1950s, 9½", EXIB...**$140.00**
Y, Pat the Roaring Elephant, 1950s, 9", EX...............**$225.00**
Y, Puffy Morris, 1960s, 10", MIB.............................**$285.00**

Guns

One of the bestselling kinds of toys ever made, toy guns were first patented in the late 1850s. Until WWII most were made of cast iron, though other materials were used on a lesser scale. After the war, cast iron became cost prohibitive, and steel and diecast zinc were used. By 1950 most were made of either diecast material or plastic. Hundreds of names can be found embossed on these little guns, a custom which continues to the present time. Because of their tremendous popularity and durability, today's collectors can find a diversity of models and styles, and prices are still fairly affordable. See also Cowboy Character Collectibles.

Newsletter: *Toy Gun Collectors of America*
Jim Buskirk, Editor and Publisher
3009 Oleander Ave., San Marcos, CA 92069; 760-559-1054.
Published quarterly, covers both toy and BB guns. Dues: $17 per year

Actoy Lone Ranger Pistol, antique bronze finish, 10", VG ..**$125.00**
Actoy Wyatt Earp Buntline Special, 11", M.............**$150.00**
Daisy Buck Rogers Pop Gun, silver plastic, 10", VG ..**$100.00**
Daisy Model A BB Gun, break action, wood stock, EX ..**$350.00**
Daisy Model H BB Gun, lever action, wood stock, EX ...**$125.00**
Daisy No 107 Buck Jones Special BB Gun, pump action, wood stock, EX................**$150.00**
Daisy Red Ryder Gun & Holster Set, MIB **$250.00**
George Schmidt Dale Evans Pistol, jeweled, rare, 10¼", VG **$300.00**
Hamilton Specialties Secret Agent Hideaway Pistol, diecast w/nickel-plated finish, blue plastic grips, VG (G box) **$45.00**
Hubley Cowboy Cap Pistol No 275, 1950s, diecast w/nickel-plated finish, white plastic steer grips, 12", G **$100.00**
Hubley Scout Rifle, 1960, lever action, nickel-plated, EX ..**$125.00**
Hubley Tiny Tommy Machine Gun, plastic, 10", NMIB.**$50.00**
Kenton Bull's-Eye Cap Gun, engraved cast iron, 1940, 6½", M **$125.00**
Kenton Gene Autry Repeating Cap Pistol, cast iron w/facsimile signature on red plastic grips, 8", EXIB **$20.00**
Kenton Law Maker Repeating Cap Pistol, nickel-plated finish, white plastic grips, 9", M (VG box) **$250.00**
Kilgore American Cap Gun, cast iron, revolving cyclinder, 1940s, 9½", EX................**$350.00**
Kilgore Wyatt Earp Cap Pistol, diecast w/nickel-plated finish, white plastic horse-head grips, 9", NM **$150.00**
King Model 5536 BB Gun, lever action, wood stock, EX ..**$35.00**
King No 22 BB Gun, lever action, wood stock, EX....**$70.00**
KO Super Space Gun, litho tin w/plastic barrel, 9½", NMIB **$100.00**
Leslie-Henry Annie Oakley Pistol, gold-tone finish, rare, 9", EX **$400.00**
Leslie-Henry Gene Autry Pistol, diecast w/nickel-plated finish, 8", NM (EX box) **$200.00**
Leslie-Henry Ranger Rider Two-Gun & Holster Set, complete w/bullets, 1950s, M (EX box) **$350.00**

Leslie-Henry Roy Rogers Pistol, gold-tone finish, EX..**$225.00**
Lone Star Cisco Kid 100 Shot Repeater, diecast w/silver finish, brown plastic grips, 1960s, 9", NMIB...........**$100.00**
Mac No 100 Machine Gun, pressed steel w/McDowal decal, 13", EX................**$125.00**
Maco USA Machine Gun, plastic w/yellow cardboard barrel, complete w/plastic tripod & bullets, 1950s, 12", MIB........**$175.00**
Marx Blast Away Cap Gun, plastic, 8", EXIB..............**$75.00**
Marx Bullet Shooting Colt .45 Peacemaker Pistol, blue w/plastic simulated wood grips, 1960s, M...........**$65.00**
Marx G-Man Machine Gun, sparks & makes machine gun sound, wood stock handle, 24", EX...................**$325.00**
Marx Popeye Pirate Pistol, litho tin, 1935, 8", MIB...**$250.00**
Mattel Agent Zero-M Camera Gun, 1960s, 15", NM ..**$100.00**
Mattel Agent Zero-W Fanner 50 Cap Pistol, diecast w/black-painted finish, brown simulated wood grips, 11", NM................**$100.00**
Mattel Power-Jet Squad Gun, brown & black plastic w/diecast works, 1965, 30½", EX **$85.00**
Nichols Model 61, chrome finish, revolving cylinder, rare, M **$350.00**
Ohio Art Astro Ray Signal Dart Gun, red plastic w/white trim, 1960s, EXIB................**$250.00**
Stevens Pawnee Bill Cap Gun, 1940, cast iron, 7½", VG ..**$175.00**
Tigrett Hopalong Cassidy Zoomerang Gun, red plastic, 1950, 9", NMIB................**$175.00**
TN Space Control Gun, litho tin, friction, 1960, 4", VG..........**$50.00**
Tops Plastics Dick Tracy Sub-Machine Water Gun, EXIB..**$1,250.00**
Wesco Lugar Automatic, hard plastic, complete w/10 pellets, 1950s, 7", NMIB **$100.00**
Wyandotte Hopalong Cassidy Pistol, nickel-plated, 9", VG ..**$175.00**
Wyandotte Red Ranger Clicker Pistol, tin w/cattle head on grip, 6½", NM (G box) **$100.00**

Ramp Walkers

Though ramp-walking figures were made as early as the 1870s, ours date from about 1935 on. They were made in Czechoslovakia from the '20s through the '40s and in this country during the '50s and '60s by Marx, who made theirs of plastic. John Wilson of Watsontown, Pennsylvania, sold his worldwide. They were known as 'Wilson Walkies' and stood about 4½" high. But the majority has been imported from Hong Kong.

Advisor: Randy Welch (See Directory, Toys)

Ankylosaurus w/Clown, Marx.................**$40.00**
Baby Walk-A-Way, plastic, lg.................**$40.00**
Bear, plastic.................**$20.00**
Big Bad Wolf & Three Little Pigs, Disney.................**$150.00**
Brontosaurus w/Monkey, Marx **$40.00**
Bunnies Carrying Carrot, plastic **$35.00**
Chicks Carrying Easter Egg, plastic **$35.00**
Chilly Willy Penguin on Sled Pulled by Parent, Marx/Walter Lanz.................**$25.00**
Choo-Choo Cherry, Funny Face drink mix, w/plastic coin weight.................**$60.00**

Cowboy on Horse, plastic w/metal legs, sm..............$30.00
Donald's Trio (Nephews), Disney/France, NMOC....$150.00
Double Walking Doll (boy behind girl) plastic, lg......$60.00
Dutch Boy & Girl, plastic.....................................$40.00
Eskimo, Wilson $100.00
Flash Turtle, Long John Silver's, w/plastic coin weight, 1989..$15.00
Fred Flintstone on Dino, Marx/Hanna-Barbera $75.00
Goofy Riding Hippo, Disney...................................$45.00
Hap & Hop Soldiers, Marx...................................$25.00
Horse, plastic, lg..$30.00
Lion w/Clown, Marx..$40.00
Mama Duck w/3 Ducklings, plastic $35.00
Man w/Carved Wood Hat, Czechoslovakian $45.00
Mickey Mouse & Donald Duck Riding Alligator, Disney ..$40.00
Mickey Mouse & Minnie, plastic w/metal legs, Disney, sm...$40.00
Milking Cow, plastic, lg......................................$40.00
Minnie Mouse Pushing Baby Stroller, Disney..............$35.00
Monkey, Czechoslovakian....................................$45.00
Nurse, Wilson..$30.00
Pebbles on Dino, Hanna-Barbera/Marx....................$75.00
Penguin, Wilson..$25.00
Pig, Czechoslovakian...$30.00
Pluto, plastic w/metal legs, sm, Disney $35.00
Popeye, Wilson...$200.00
Popeye & Wimpy, Marx.......................................$85.00
Quinn Penguin, Long John Silver's, w/plastic coin weight, ...$15.00
Rabbit, Wilson..$75.00
Root'n Toot'n Raspberry, Funny Face drink mix, w/plastic coin weight...$60.00
Santa & Mrs Claus (faces on both sides), Marx..........$50.00
Santa Claus, Wilson...$90.00
Sheriff Facing Outlaw, plastic $65.00
Spark Plug, Marx...$200.00
Top Cat & Benny, Marx.......................................$65.00
Wimpy, Wilson..$175.00
Wiz Walker Milking Cow, Charmore, plastic, lg..........$40.00

Rings

Toy rings are a fairly new interest in the collecting world. Earlier radio and TV mail-order premiums have been popular for some time but have increased in value considerably over the past few years. Now there is a growing interest in other types of rings as well — those from gumball machines, World's Fairs souvenirs, movie and TV show promotions, and any depicting celebrities. They may be metal or plastic; most have adjustable shanks. New rings are already being sought out as future collectibles.

Note: Unless noted otherwise, all rings listed here are considered to be in fine to very fine condition. Wear, damage, and missing parts will devalue them considerably.

Advisors: Bruce and Jan Thalberg (See Directory, Toys)

Agent 007, Seal, 1960s, from $35 to...........................$50.00

Bazooka Joe, initial, 1950s, EX, from $175 to...........$225.00
Buck Rogers, Ring of Saturn, M, from $475 to.........$600.00
Buffalo Bill, 1950s, VG.......................................$35.00
Captain Midnight, Flight Commander, EX, from $425 to..$500.00
Davy Crockett, TV Flicker, M................................$110.00
Green Hornet, flicker, plastic, 1960s, 12 in set, ea from $15 to...$25.00
Lone Ranger, Flashlight, 1947, NM (VG mailer), from $165 to..$225.00
Radio Orphan Annie, Post Cereal, MIP....................$30.00
Roy Rogers, Microscope, EX, from $125 to..............$160.00
Space Patrol, Hydrogen Ray Gun, glow-in-the-dark, 1950s, NM, from $350 to $450.00
Tom Mix, Magnet, NM, from $110 to.....................$145.00
Zorro, Logo, lg Z, 1960s, M, from $50 to $75.00

Don Winslow membership ring, 1932, gold-colored metal, EX, from $400.00 to $650.00. Superman Pep airplane, 1940s, spring-loaded plane on gold-colored metal band, NM, from $150.00 to $250.00.

Robots and Space Toys

Japanese toy manufacturers introduced their robots and space toys as early as 1948. Some of the best examples were made in the '50s, during the 'golden age' of battery-operated toys. They became more and more complex, and today some of these in excellent condition may bring well over $1,000.00. By the '60s, more and more plastic was used in their production, and the toys became inferior.

Action Robot, wind-up, litho tin w/plastic helmet, 8½", EX..$450.00
Apollo 11 Space Robot, TN, 1960s, battery-op, tin & plastic, 14", EX...$165.00
Atomic Spaceship XX-2, Japan, friction, litho tin, 14", EX $165.00
Cragstan Satellite, 1950s, battery-op, litho tin, 8" dia..$185.00
Dino-Robot, Horikawa, battery-op, tin & plastic, 11", NMIB $1,500.00
Excavator Robot, SH, 1960s, battery-op, plastic, 10", EX..$200.00
Fighting Robot, Horikawa, battery-op, tin w/plastic chest gears, 9", EXIB $375.00
Gear Robot, SH, battery-op, litho tin, rare, 11½", NMIB......$725.00
Lavender Robot, MT, battery-op, litho tin, rare, 15", NM $3,500.00

Lunar Bulldozer, TN, battery-op, litho tin & plastic, 9½", NMIB...**$375.00**

Mars King, SH, battery-op, litho tin, 9", VG.............**$150.00**

Moon Rocket, Masudaya, battery-op, litho tin, 10", NMIB..**$250.00**

Mr Sandman the Robot, Wolverine, battery-op, litho tin, 11½", NM..**$500.00**

New Sky Robot, SH, 1960s, battery-op, mostly plastic, 9", EX...**$125.00**

Planet Y Space Station, TN, 1960s, battery-op, litho tin, EX...**$275.00**

Ratchet Robot, Nomura, wind-up, 8", NMIB..........**$1,500.00**

Robot 2500, Durham, 1970s, battery-op, plastic, 10½", EX...**$125.00**

Sky Patrol Flying Saucer, KO, 1950s, battery-op, litho tin, 7½" dia, EX..**$200.00**

Space Beetle No 2, Y, 1970s, battery-op, mostly plastic, 9", EX...**$100.00**

Space Patrol Rocket Lite, Ray-O-Vac, 1950s, battery-op, 12", NMIB..**$475.00**

Sparky Robot, Linemar, wind-up, 8", EXIB...............**$475.00**

Television Spaceman, Alps, battery-op, tin & plastic, 14", NMIB..**$925.00**

Turbo Jet Car, Ideal, 1950s, wind-up, litho tin & plastic, NMIB..**$165.00**

USA-NASA Apollo, MT, 1960s, battery-op, litho tin, EXIB ...**$350.00**

Video Robot, SH, 1960s, battery-op, litho tin, 10", EX..**$175.00**

Slot Car Racers

Slot cars first became popular in the early 1960s. Electric raceways set up in storefront windows were commonplace. Huge commercial tracks with eight and ten lanes were located in hobby stores and raceways throughout the United States. Large corporations such as Aurora, Revell, Monogram, and Cox, many of which were already manufacturing toys and hobby items, jumped on the bandwagon to produce slot cars and race sets. By the end of the early 1970s, people were losing interest in slot racing, and its popularity diminished. Today the same baby boomers that raced slot cars in earlier days are revitalizing the sport. Vintage slot cars have made a comeback as one of the hottest automobile collectibles in recent years. Want ads for slot cars frequently appear in newspapers and publications geared toward the collector. As you would expect, slot cars were generally well used, so finding vintage cars and race sets in like-new or mint condition is difficult. Slot cars replicating the 'muscle' cars from the '60s and '70s are extremely sought after, and clubs and organizations devoted to these collectibles are becoming more and more commonplace. Large toy companies such as Tomy and Tyco still produce some slots today, but not in the quality, quantity, or variety of years past.

Advisor: Gary Pollastro (See Directory, Toys)

Accessory, AMT, Service Parts Kit #2000, VG...........**$100.00**

Accessory, Aurora Model Motoring, 1969, color, EX...**$30.00**

Accessory, Aurora Thunderjet Transformer, VG..........**$20.00**

Accessory, Eldon Curve Track, MOC.........................**$10.00**

Accessory, Strombecker Lap Counter, MIB................**$25.00**

Accessory, Tyco Stick Shift 4-Speed Controller, EX....**$10.00**

Acessory, Aurora AFX, Pit Kit, G.............................**$15.00**

Aurora AFX, Aztec Dragster, #1963, red, EX.............**$20.00**

Aurora AFX, Ultra 5, complete, EXIB.......................**$75.00**

Aurora G-Plus, Corvette, #1954, orange, red & silver, EX..**$12.00**

Car, Aurora, Javelin, red, white & blue, NM..............**$30.00**

Car, Aurora AFX, Chevy Chevelle #29, red, white & blue, EX...**$30.00**

Car, Aurora AFX, Dodge Challenger, #1773, lime & blue, NM...**$35.00**

Car, Aurora AFX, Dodge Street Van, orange & red, MIB...**$40.00**

Car, Aurora AFX, Matador Taxi, white, EX................**$20.00**

Car, Aurora AFX, Shadow Cam Racer, black, EX........**$20.00**

Car, Aurora G-Plus, Amrac Can Am, yellow & black w/white stripe, EX..**$15.00**

Car, Aurora G-Plus, Rallye Ford Escort, #1737, green & blue, EX...**$15.00**

Car, Aurora Thunderjet, '63 Corvette, #1356, yellow, EX..**$50.00**

Car, Aurora Thunderjet, '73 Duster, EX....................**$30.00**

Car, Aurora Thunderjet, Cougar, #1389, white, EX.....**$40.00**

Car, TCR, Maintenance Van, red & white, EX............**$15.00**

Car, Tyco, Bandit Pickup, black & red, EX................**$12.00**

Car, Tyco, Camaro Funny Car, silver, green & black, EX....**$40.00**

Car, Tyco, Funny Mustang, orange w/yellow flames, EX....**$25.00**

Car, Tyco, GM Aerocoupe #43, blue & flourescent red, EX....**$65.00**

Car, Tyco, Lamborghini, silver, EX...........................**$20.00**

Car, Tyco, Military Police #45, white & blue, EX........**$30.00**

Car, Tyco, Turbo Firebird, black & gold, NM........**$1,200.00**

Car, Tyco, Volvo 850 #3, white & blue, EX...............**$20.00**

Set, Aurora, Home Raceway by Sears, #79N9513C, VG....**$200.00**

Set, Aurora AFX, Jackie Stewart Challenger Raceway, NMIB...**$75.00**

Set, Cox, Ontario 8, #3070, w/Eagle & McLaren, G (G box)..**$75.00**

Set, Gilbert Race Set #19041, VG (VG box)................**$95.00**

Set, Iseal, Alcan Highway Torture Track, 1968, MIB...**$50.00**

Set, Remco, Mighty Mike Action Track, NMIB...........**$75.00**

Set, Strombecker, Road Race Set, from $125 to........**$150.00**

Tomy, Thunderbird #11 (Bill Elliot sign), red & white, EX...**$25.00**

Vehicles

These are the types of toys that are intensely dear to the heart of many a collector. Having a beautiful car is part of the American dream, and over the past eighty years, just about as many models, makes, and variations have been made as toys for children as the real vehicles for adults. Novices and advanced collectors alike are easily able to find something to suit their tastes as well as their budgets.

One area that is especially volatile includes those '50s and '60s tin scale-model autos by foreign manufacturers — Japanese, U.S. Zone German, and English toy makers. Since these are relatively modern, you'll still be able to find some at yard sales and flea markets at reasonable prices.

There are several good references for these toys: *Collecting Toy Cars and Trucks* by Richard O'Brien; *Hot Wheels, A Collector's Guide,* by Bob Parker; *Collector's Guide to Tootsietoys* by David Richter; *Collector's Guide to Tonka Trucks, 1947 – 1963,* by Don and Barb deSalle; *Matchbox Toys, 1948 to 1993, Collector's Guide to Diecast Toys and Scale Models,* and *Toy Car Collector's Guide* by Dana Johnson; and *Hot Wheels, The Ultimate Red Line Guide,* by Jack Clark and Robert P. Wicher.

Newsletter: *The Replica*
Bridget Shine, Editor
Highways 136 and 20, Dyersville, IA 52040; 319-875-2000

Newsletter: *Matchbox USA*
Charles Mack
62 Saw Mill Rd., Durham, CT 06422
e-mail: MTCHBOXUSA@aol.com;
www.charliemackonline.com; 203-349-1655

Bandai, Cadillac Sedan, tin, friction, 1964, 17", NMIB **$900.00**
Bandai, Ford Thunderbird, tin, friction, 1959, 8", NM+ **$150.00**
Buddy L, Army Supply Truck w/Cannon, pressed steel, green w/canvas cover, 1950s, 22", NMIB **$225.00**
Buddy L, Ranch Truck, pressed steel, tan w/brown horse head decals on doors, white-wall tires, 1950s, 12½", VG......**$75.00**
Corgi, #153, Bluebird Record Car, MIB.................**$125.00**
Corgi, #162, Tyrell P34 Racer, MIB.......................**$40.00**
Corgi, #202, Renault R16, MIB............................**$40.00**
Corgi, #205, Riley Pathfinder, red, MIB.................**$130.00**
Corgi, #215, Ford Thunderbird Sport, MIB...............**$125.00**
Corgi, #234, Ford Consul Classic, MIB...................**$85.00**
Corgi, #241, Chrysler Ghia, MIB..........................**$80.00**
Corgi, #263, Rambler Marlin, MIB **$75.00**
Corgi, #266, Chitty-Chitty Bang-Bang, replica, MIB ..**$125.00**
Corgi, #312, Jaguar E Type, MIB..........................**$100.00**
Corgi, #342, Lamborghini P400 GT Miura, MIB..........**$60.00**
Corgi, #384, Renault 11 GTL, cream, MIB.................**$20.00**
Corgi, #405, Bedford Utilicon Fire Dept, red, MIB ...**$200.00**
Corgi, #482, Chevrolet Fire Chief Car, MIB.............**$100.00**
Corgi, #500, US Army Rover, MIB **$400.00**
Corgi, #805, Hardy Boy's Rolls Royce, MIB..............**$300.00**
Cragstan, Beach Jeep, litho tin, friction, 7", NMIB....**$100.00**
Dinky, #101, Sunbeam Alpine, MIB.......................**$175.00**
Dinky, #110, Aston Martin DB5, MIB......................**$100.00**
Dinky, #137, Plymouth Fury, MIB.........................**$130.00**
Dinky, #155, Ford Angila, MIB **$120.00**
Dinky, #169, Fire Corsair, MIB **$100.00**
Dinky, #188, Ford Berth Caravan, MIB....................**$60.00**
Dinky, #201, Plymouth Stock Car, MIB....................**$75.00**
Dinky, #370, Dragster Set, MIB...........................**$70.00**
Dinky, #475, Ford Model T, MIB...........................**$100.00**
Dinky, #538, Buick Roadmaster, MIB......................**$300.00**
Dinky, #612, Commando Jeep, MIB.........................**$50.00**
Dinky, #673, Scout Car, MIB..............................**$50.00**
Hot Wheels, Alive 55, red-line tires, chrome, hood opens, 1976, M..**$85.00**

Hot Wheels, Beatnik Bandit, red-line tires, blue w/white interior, 1968, NM+ **$35.00**
Hot Wheels, Brabham Repco F1, red-line tires, aqua or blue, 1969, NM+...**$30.00**
Hot Wheels, Bye Focal, red-line tires, 1971, light green, M **$265.00**
Hot Wheels, Camaro Z-28, black-wall tires, metal-flake red, 1984, MIP..**$12.50**
Hot Wheels, Chevy Stocker, metal-flake red, MIP **$12.00**
Hot Wheels, Classic '36 Ford Coupe, red-line tires, aqua, 1969, NM+...**$50.00**
Hot Wheels, Cockney Cab, red-line tires, 1971, NM+..**$75.00**
Hot Wheels, Custom Eldorado, red-line tires, yellow w/white interior, 1968, NM+ **$70.00**
Hot Wheels, Demon, red-line tires, blue, 1970, NM+ .**$34.00**
Hot Wheels, Dune Daddy, red-line tires, light green, 1973, NM+ **$75.00**
Hot Wheels, Gun Slinger, red-line tires, light olive, 1975, M **$55.00**
Hot Wheels, Hot Heap, red-line tires, orange, 1968, NM+ **$40.00**
Hot Wheels, Inferno, red-line tires, 1976, M **$55.00**
Hot Wheels, Large Charge Mexican, black-wall tires, orange, 1985, M **$40.00**
Hot Wheels, Paramedic, black-wall tires, yellow, 1977, NM+ **$20.00**
Hot Wheels, Porsche 917, red-line tires, yellow, NM+...**$50.00**
Hot Wheels, Road Torch, black-wall tires, red, 1987, MIP **$20.00**
Hot Wheels, Street Beast, black-wall tires, red, 1988, MIP **$10.00**
Ichiko, Ford Thunderbird, tin, friction, 1969, 10½", EXIB..**$300.00**
Ichiko, Highway Patrol Car, litho tin, friction, 8", EXIB..**$125.00**
Joustra, Porsche Sedan, tin, friction, 8", EXIB **$100.00**
KKK, Airport Limousine, litho tin, friction, 1960s, 6", NMIB..**$100.00**
Marx, Deluxe Auto Transport, pressed steel, 1940s, 22", VG..**$200.00**
Marx, US Army Truck & Searchlight, pressed steel, w/canvas cover, 1950s, 30", EX..................................**$200.00**
Matchbox, #K02-B, 1964, MIP, from $25 to **$40.00**
Matchbox, AMX Javelin, #9-E, 1971, lime w/silver hood scoop, doors open, MIP **$12.00**
Matchbox, Camaro IROC Z, #51-J, 1985, green, MIP, from $6 to **$8.00**
Matchbox, Caterpillar Bulldozer, #64-F, 1979, yellow w/black blade, tan canopy, MIP, from $8 to **$10.00**
Matchbox, DAF Tipper Container Truck, #47-C, 1968, blue w/yellow container, gray container cover, MIP, from $25 to.**$30.00**
Matchbox, Dodge Caravan, #68-F, burgundy w/black stripes, 1984, MIP, from $16 to **$20.00**
Matchbox, Dodge Stake Truck, #4-D, 1967, blue-green stakes, MIB, from $60 to **$75.00**
Matchbox, Ford Model A Truck, #38-H, 1982, blue w/Kellogg's labels, MIP, from $8 to................**$10.00**

Matchbox, Ford Perfect Sedan, #30-A, 1956, light blue, MIP, fom $35 to $50.00

Matchbox, Ford Skip Truck, #70-G (Preschool series), blue w/red metal skip, 1988, MIP, from $6 to................$8.00

Matchbox, GMC Cement Mixer, #K-6-C, 1971, MIP $15.00

Matchbox, Harley-Davidson Motorcycle, #50-G, 1980, from $4 to $6.00

Matchbox, Javelin AMX, #K-54-A, burgundy or red, 1975, MIP, ea $15.00

Matchbox, Land Rover Fire Truck, #57-D (Super-Fast), 1970, MIB, from $25 to $40.00

Matchbox, Matra Rancho Rescue Set, #K-104-A, 1983, MIP, from $15 to $20.00

Matchbox, Mercury Parkline Police Car, #55-D, 1968, blue dome light, M $10.00

Matchbox, Pickford Removal Van, #46-B, 1960, dark blue w/gray plastic wheels, MIP, from $60 to..............$75.00

Matchbox, Prince Henry Vauxhall (1914), #Y-2-C, blue w/white seats, 1970, MIP, from $20 to $25.00

Matchbox, Team Matchbox Formula 1 Racer, #24-E, 1973, metallic blue w/white driver, #1 label, MIP, from $275 to $325.00

Matchbox, Volkswagen 1500 Saloon, #15-D, 1968, off-white w/137 decals on doors, M, from $10 to..............$12.00

Sanyo, Taxi Cab, litho tin, friction, 1960s, 6", NMIB.$100.00

Schuco, Mercedes 220 S, tin, wind-up, 5", EXIB.......$100.00

Smith-Miller, Dump Truck, pressed steel, rubber tires, 1954, 12", NM $450.00

Smith-Miller, Emergency Towing Service, #802, pressed steel, 1940s-50s, EX $675.00

Smith-Miller, MIC Aerial Ladder Truck, marked LAFD, pressed steel, 1950s, 23½", NM $900.00

TN, Livestock Truck, litho tin, friction, 1950s, 10", NMIB..$125.00

TN, Mercedes Benz 230 SL Convertible, tin, friction, 9½", NMIB..$150.00

TN, Sports Car, tin w/see-through green plastic top, friction, 1950s, 8", NM (EX box)..$200.00

Tonk, Steel Carrier, 24", EX..$150.00

Tonka, Allied Van Lines Truck, #1089, 1962, 16", NMIB..$150.00

Tonka, Fire Jeep, #425, 1963-64, M.........................$300.00

Tonka, Jet Delivery Truck, 1962, NM.........................$265.00

Tonka, Wrecker, #250, 1953, EX.................................$250.00

Tootsietoy, Boat Transport Tractor-Trailer w/Boats, maroon cab w/yellow trailer, white & blue boats (2), 1969, MIP $70.00

Tootsietoy, Safari Hunt, #1463, 1968, MIB.................$95.00

Tootsietoy, Township School Bus, HO series, 1960s, scarce, NM $40.00

Wyandotte, Construction Engineering Dump Truck, working side-action dump bed, 1940s, 20", EX+ $225.00

Wyandotte, Express Truck, w/baggage cart, 1940s, 22", G..$250.00

Y, Avenue Coach Bus, litho tin, friction, 1950s, 15", NM.....$185.00

Wind-Ups

Wind-up toys, especially comic character or personality related, are greatly in demand by collectors today. Though most were made through the years of the '30s through the '50s, they carry their own weight against much earlier toys and are considered very worthwhile investments. Mechanisms vary; some are key wound while others depended on lever action to tighten the mainspring and release the action of the toy. Tin and celluloid were used in their manufacture, and although it is sometimes possible to repair a tin windup, experts advise against putting your money into a celluloid toy whose mechanism is not working, since the material may be too fragile to tolerate the repair.

AAA, Pinky Racer, litho tin, 5½", EXIB.....................$125.00

Alps, Chico the Cha Cha Monkey, 9", MIB..............$100.00

Alps, Reading Bunny, tin & plush w/cloth outfit, 7", MIB...$175.00

Alps, Trick Seal, celluloid, 6", MIB...........................$100.00

Arnold, Bee & Flower Sparkler, litho tin, 4½", NM ..$175.00

Arnold, Howdy Doody Acrobat, litho tin w/cloth clothes, 15", VG $250.00

Asahi Toy, Jumpy Rudolph, cable action, 1950s, 6", EX ..$150.00

Aviva, Snoopy All-American Express, wood, 1975, MIB, from $125 to $150.00

Borgfeldt, Pinocchio, composition, 10½", NM..........$450.00

Chein, Big Top Tent, tin w/plastic dome, 1961, 10", EXIB $200.00

Chein, Fish, litho tin, advances as tail fin moves, 1940s, NM $125.00

CK, King Merry, celluloid, 12", EXIB $200.00

Emporium Specialties, Monkey Shines, litho tin, 18", EXIB..$250.00

G&K, Clown on Cart, litho tin, 4½", VG $400.00

Haji, Animal Scooter w/Rabbit, litho tin, NM (VG box)..$125.00

Haji, Circus Clown Cycle, litho tin w/vinyl-headed figure, friction, 5", EXIB $150.00

Irwin, Dancing Cinderella & Prince, plastic, 1950, 5", M (EX box)..$200.00

Irwin, Racing Car, plastic, 1950s, scarce, 12½", MIB..$200.00

Japan, Lazy Bones the Sleepy Pup, plush & tin, 1960s, 11", NMIB..$125.00

Japan, Mr Tortoise, litho tin, 1960s, NMIB..................$75.00

K, Brave Indian, litho tin horse & rider, rare, 5", NM (EX box)..$225.00

KO, Mystery Police Car, litho tin, friction, 6", NMIB..$450.00

Kohler, Duck, litho tin, quacks & flaps wings, 1950s, NM $75.00

Linemar, Babes in Toyland Soldier, litho tin, 1961, 6", EX $260.00

Linemar, Banjo Player, litho tin, 5", NM....................$200.00

Linemar, Calypso Joe the Drummer, litho tin, 6", NM (EX box) $300.00

Linemar, Clarabelle the Clown, litho tin, 5", EX........$300.00

Linemar, Clown Juggler, 8½", NM, from $450 to $550.00

Linemar, Donald Duck on Motorcycle, litho tin, friction, 1960s, 3", NM $450.00

Linemar, Fifer Pig (Three Little Pigs), litho tin, 4½", NM..$175.00

Linemar, Fred Flintstone on Dino (Flintstone Pals on Dino), litho tin, 8", EXIB..$500.00

Linemar, Mickey's Delivery Cycle, litho tin & celluloid, friction, NM..$600.00

Linemar, Pluto Pulling Cart, litho tin, friction, 1960s, NM .**$450.00**

Linemar, Popeye Tricycle, litho tin w/cloth pants, 6½", VG **$500.00**

Linemar, Superman Turnover Tank, litho tin, 4", NM ..**$400.00**

Lionel, Mickey Mouse Handcar, tin w/composition Mickey & Minnie figures, 9", G **$500.00**

Marx, Careful Johnny, tin w/plastic bobbing head, 6½", NMIB...**$250.00**

Marx, Cowboy Rider, 1941, NMIB.................**$375.00**

Marx, Disney Turnover Tank, litho tin, 1950s, rare, 4", EXIB...**$1,000.00**

Marx, Donald Duck Duet, litho tin, 1946, 10½", EX (G box), from $800 to.................................**$950.00**

Marx, Flintstone Log Car, plastic, friction, 1977, 5", MIB..**$200.00**

Marx, Mickey Mouse Scooter, plastic, friction, 1959, 4", EXIB...**$225.00**

Marx, Tumbling Monkey, 1942, EX, $175.00.

Mattel, Music Box Carousel, litho tin & plastic, 1953, 9", NMIB...**$150.00**

MT, Little Miss Automatic Ironer, litho tin, 1950s, 4", NMIB **$75.00**

Occupied Japan, Black Porter, celluloid, 3½", NM, from $150 to...**$200.00**

Occupied Japan, Donkey w/Rider, celluloid, 5", NMIB ..**$200.00**

Occupied Japan, Luck Sledge, celluloid, rare, 5", M (G box)...**$300.00**

Occupied Japan, Monkey Playing Banjo, celluloid, 7½", VG **$175.00**

Ohio Art, Airport, litho tin, 1950s, 9", NM (EX box).**$250.00**

Schuco, Curvo 1000 Motorcycle w/Driver, litho tin, 5", NMIB...**$550.00**

Schuco, Motorcycle w/Driver, litho tin, 5", VG **$200.00**

TN, Grasshopper, litho tin, 6", MIB..........................**$100.00**

TPS, Bozo the Clown, litho tin, 6", EX (VG box) **$400.00**

TPS, Comical Clara, litho tin, 1950s, 5½", NMIB, from $300 to...**$375.00**

TPS, Magic Circus, litho tin & plastic, 6", EXIB, from $150 to...**$180.00**

Unique Art, Capitol Hill Racer, litho tin, 17", EX (G box)...**$175.00**

Unique Art, GI Joe & His Jouncing Jeep, litho tin, 1941, 7", NM **$250.00**

Unique Art, Hobo Train, litho tin, 8", EX **$350.00**

Unique Art, Rodeo Joe, litho tin, 9", EX **$225.00**

Unique Art, Sail Away Carousel, litho tin, 1940s, 9½", EX **$200.00**

Wolverine, Action Jumper, litho tin, 26" ramp, MIB .**$350.00**

Wolverine, Dandy Andy Rooster, tin, 10", NMIB.......**$600.00**

Wolverine No. 31 Merry-Go-Round, 1950s, MIB, $450.00. (Photo courtesy June Moon)

Wyandotte, Easter Bunny Motorcycle, litho tin, 9½", G..**$200.00**

Wyandotte, Hoky & Poky, litho tin, 6", NM (EX box) ...**$400.00**

Wyandotte, Man on Flying Trapeze, litho tin, 9", NM (EX box) **$250.00**

Yonezawa, Groolies Car, litho tin, 4½", NM (EX box)...**$175.00**

Transistor Radios

Introduced during the Christmas shopping season of 1954, transistor radios were at the cutting edge of futuristic design and miniaturization. Among the most desirable is the 1954 four-transistor Regency TR-1 which is valued at a minimum of $750.00 in jade green. Black may go for as much as $300.00, other colors from $350.00 to $400.00. The TR-1 'Mike Todd' version in the 'Around the World in Eighty Days' leather book-look presentation case goes for $4,000.00 and up! Some of the early Toshiba models sell for $250.00 to $350.00, some of the Sonys even higher — their TR-33 books at a minimum of $1,000.00, their TR-55 at $1,500.00 and up! Certain pre-1960 models by Hoffman and Admiral represented the earliest practical use of solar technology and are also highly valued. Early collectible transistor radios all have civil defense triangle markings at 640 and 1240 on the frequency dial and nine or fewer transistors. Very few desirable sets were made after 1963.

Values in our listings are for radios in at least very good condition — not necessarily working, but complete and requiring very little effort to restore them to working order. Cases may show minor wear. All radios are battery-operated unless noted otherwise. For more information we recommend *Collector's Guide to Transistor Radios* (there are two editions), by Marty and Sue Bunis (Collector Books).

Advisors: Marty and Sue Bunis (See Directory, Radios)

Admiral, #909, All World, 1960, horizontal, 9 transistors, battery, fold-down front, telescoping antenna, w/handle **$75.00**

Admiral, Airline, #GEN-1254A, horizontal, 7 transistors, AM, battery, center Montgomery Wards logo, 1965.....**$50.00**

Admiral, CH-620, Tops All, horizontal, 6 transistors, AM, battery, 1961 ....**$30.00**

Admiral, YK212GP Caprice, vertical, plastic, 10 transistors, thumbwheel tuning, lattice grill, crown logo, battery, AM **$15.00**

Admiral, Y2067 Super 7, 1960, vertical, 7 transistors, window dial, lattice grill, crown logo, AM **$25.00**

Admiral, Y2226 Golden Eagle, vertical, 1962, plastic, 6 transistors, window dial, perforated grill, crown logo, AM **$30.00**

Admiral, Y2301GPS, 1963, vertical, black plastic, 6 transistors, round dial, perforated grill, crown logo, battery, AM .**$30.00**

Admiral, Y2433 Little Jewel, 1963, horizontal, white plastic, 6 transistors, round dial knob, handle, crown logo, AM **$15.00**

Admiral, Y701R, vertical, 6 transistors, circular window dial, vertical grill bars, crown logo, AM **$20.00**

Airline, GEN-1202B, 1963, horizontal, oval dial w/side thumbwheel tuning, M/W logo on grill, battery, AM.............**$35.00**

Alaron, B-666 Deluxe Hi-Fi, 1963, vertical, 6 transistors, thumbwheel tuning, perforated grill, battery, AM..............**$20.00**

Aristotone, HT-1244, vertical 12 transistors, plastic w/metal perforated grill, battery, Japan, AM **$30.00**

Arvin, #62R19, 1962, vertical, black plastic w/textured grill w/crown logo, battery, AM **$15.00**

Arvin, #7595, 1959, horizontal, 4 transistors, lattice grill, swing handle, battery, AM **$35.00**

Benida, PR-1161, vertical, 6 transistor, plastic w/metal grill w/logo, Japan, battery, AM **$35.00**

Bulova, #685, 1962, vertical, 4 transistors, round dial, grill w/oval-shaped cutouts, battery, AM.....................**$35.00**

Capehart, T6-202 Incomparable, 1961, vertical, 6 transistors, ½-circle window dial, slotted grill, crown logo, AM ...**$125.00**

Channel Master, #6518A, horizontal, slide rule dial, metal perforated grill, 2 antennas, Japan, battery, AM/FM.....**$30.00**

Columbia, #600G, 1960, vertical, 6 transistors, green plastic w/round metal grill, Japan, battery, AM **$35.00**

Continental, TR-716, 1965, 7 transistors, perforated grill w/logo, battery, AM..**$40.00**

Coronado, STP-502, pen holder/radio, 1962, 2 transistors, grill w/vertical bars, Japan, AM **$35.00**

Crown, TRF-1700, 1965, horizontal, 14 transistors, 3-band slide rule dial, telescoping antenna, battery, AM/FM/SW..**$20.00**

Elgin, R-1200, 1964, horizontal, 10 transistors, front horizintal dial, perforated, grill, battery, AM **$15.00**

Emerson, #888 Titan, 1963, vertical, plastic, 8 transistors, oval dial, perforated grill, AC/battery, AM **$80.00**

General Electric, C2419A Mickey Mouse, clock/radio/alarm, 3-D Mickey head pointer dial, other Disney characters, AC, AM **$75.00**

General Electric, P1791E, vertical, plastic, round 2-band dial, 9 transistors, handle, battery, AM **$15.00**

General Electric, P795B, 1958, horizontal, leather, dial knob, plastic lattice grill, leather handle, battery, AM **$20.00**

General Electric, P825A, 1961, vertical, round dial, circular cutouts on grill, metal fold-out stand, battery, AM........**$30.00**

General Electric, P930, 1964, horizontal, 8 transistors, 3-band slide rule, telescoping antenna, battery, AM/2 SW.**$20.00**

Graetz, #41F Grazia, 1966, horizontal, 9 transistors, 2-band slide rule dial, West Germany, battery, AM/FM....**$30.00**

Grundig, Micro-Boy 400, vertical, slide rule dial, perforated grill, battery **$30.00**

Heathkit, GR-151A, leather, 2-tone blue plastic, 6 transistors, horizontal bars on grill, pull-out handle, battery, AM......**$20.00**

Hitachi, TH-667, 1960, horizontal, plastic, 6 transistors, checkered grill w/logo, Japan, battery, AM **$80.00**

Hoffman, #729, 1964, horizontal, 2-band slide rule dial, 2 telescoping antennas, battery, AM/FM **$15.00**

Jade, #171, vertical, plastic, 7 transistors, window dial w/thumbwheel tuning, side strap, battery, AM **$10.00**

Juliette, CLA-1020, lamp/radio, plastic, 5 transistors, slide rule dial, AC, AM **$25.00**

Lafayette, FS-200, 1960, horizintal, window dial w/thumbwheel tuning, perforated grill, battery, AM **$110.00**

Linmark, TR-4016, 1963, 10 transistors, 4-band slide rule dial, telescoping antenna, battery, AM/2 SW/LW **$25.00**

Magnavox, AM-82 Envoy, 1964, horizontal, leather, 8 transistors, slide rule dial, logo on grill, battery, AM **$15.00**

Masterwork, M2815, 1964, horizontal, 10 transistors, 2 round dials, telescoping antenna, battery, AM/FM.........**$20.00**

Masterwork, M2815, 1964, horizontal, 10 transistors, 2 round dials (1 AM, 1 FM), battery **$20.00**

Mitchell, 1102, 1955, vertical, simulated leather, 4 transistors, round dial, hinged back, battery, AM **$450.00**

Monacor, RE-606, 1964, vertical, 6 transistors, window dial, vertical grill bars, side strap, battery, AM..............**$10.00**

Motorola, X11B, 1959, vertical, 6 transistors, oval window dial, metal perforated grill w/'M' logo, battery, AM **$45.00**

Motorola, X27W, 1961, horizontal, white plastic, 7 transistors, window dial, metal grill, side strap, battery, AM .**$35.00**

Motorola, X50E, 1962, horizontal, black leather, 6 transistors, round dial, handle, battery/AC, AM **$20.00**

Nordmende, Mambo, 1961, horizontal, 7 transistors, round 2-band dial, wedge-shaped lattice grill, battery, AM/LW **$40.00**

Norwood, MN-1000, 1965, horizontal, 10 transistors, 2-band rule dial, telescoping antenna, battery, AM/FM **$15.00**

Panasonic, R-103, 1964, horizontal, 6 transistors, round dial, lower grill w/logo, battery, AM **$15.00**

Panasonic, T-745, 1964, horizontal/table, wooden, 12 transistors, 4-band slide rule dial, battery, AM/FM/2 SW .**$30.00**

Penncrest, #1896, 1963, horizontal, leather, 12 transistors, 2 round dials (1 AM, 1 FM), logo on grill, battery, AM/FM **$25.00**

Philco, T-905-124, 1962, horizontal, 9 transistors, 2-band dial over checkered grill, battery, AM/FM (pushbuttons) **$30.00**

Philco, T5-124 '500', horizontal, plastic, window dial, battery, AM...**$35.00**

Plata, 9TA-370, 1962, horizontal, 10 transistors, 4-band slide rule dial, telescoping antenna, battery, AM/2 SW/LW **$35.00**

RCA, T-1EH Rio, 1959, vertical, plastic, 1959, 6 transistors, round dial, swing handle, battery, AM..................**$25.00**

RCA, 1-T-4J, Hawaii, 1959, vertical, plastic, 8 transistors, swing handle, battery, AM **$35.00**

Realtone, TR-1948, 1964, 9 transistors, window dial, lg grill w/horizontal bars, battery, AM **$15.00**

Ross, RE-66, 1965, horizontal, 6 transistors, logo on grill, strap, battery, AM...**$25.00**

Sharp, FW-503, 1964, horizontal, 4-band slide rule, knob & logo on grill, telescoping antenna, battery, AM/FM/SW/Marine **$35.00**

Silvertone, 1202, 1961, vertical, plastic, 6 transistors, thumbwheel dial knob, metal grill, battery, AM **$30.00**

Silvertone, 5220, 1964, horizontal, leather, 8 transistors, lattice, grill, leather handle, battery, AM **$15.00**

Sony, ICR-100, 1966, horizontal, world's first integrated curcuit radio, plug-in recharger unit, battery, AM...**$200.00**

Sony, TR-881, horizontal, 8 transistors, 2 horizontal dials, metal grill, telescoping antenna, battery, AM/Marine........**$40.00**

Star-Lite, T-603, vertical, plastic, 6 transistors, window dial, metal perforated grill, battery, AM **$90.00**

Sylvania, 7P13, 1960, horizontal, leather, 7 transistors, dial knob, logo on grill, leather handle, battery, AM..**$20.00**

Tempest, AF-1200, vertical, plastic, 2-band slide rule, metal perforated grill, telescoping antenna, battery, AM/FM..**$15.00**

Toshiba, 8TH-428R, 1963, horizontal/table, 8 transistors, 3 slide rule dial scales, checkered grill, battery, AM/2SW **$35.00**

Trancel, TR 80, vertical, plastic, 8 transistors, see-through panel w/dial, metal perforated grill w/logo, battery, AM...**$125.00**

Universal, RE-64 Deluxe, 1964, vertical, 6 transistors, window dial, lattice grill, made in Taiwan, battery, AM.....**$15.00**

Vista, NTR-966, 1964, vertical, window dial, round perforated grill, battery, AM...**$50.00**

Westinghouse, H-903P8GP, 1964, vertical, dial knob, metal perforated grill, battery, AM....................................**$20.00**

Westinghouse, H611P5, 1957, horizontal, 5 transistors, round dial, checkered grill, battery, AM..........................**$85.00**

Westinghouse, H769P7, 1960, horizontal, 7 transistors, round dial, checkered grill, leather handle, battery, AM...**$15.00**

Zenith, Royal 13, vertical, plastic, window dial over vertical grill bars, made in Hong Kong, battery, AM **$20.00**

Toshiba, made for J.C. Penney, six-transistor, complete with cases for radio and earphones, $20.00.

TV Guides

This publication goes back to the early 1950s, and granted, those early issues are very rare. But what an interesting, very visual way to chronicle the history of TV programming!

Values in our listings are for examples in fine to mint condition; be sure to reduce them significantly when damage of any type is present. For insight into *TV Guide* collecting, we recommend *The TV Guide Catalog* by Jeff Kadet, the *TV Guide* Specialist.

Advisor: Jeff Kadet (See Directory, *TV Guides*)

1953, April 10, Jack Webb..**$88.00**
1953, August 14, Patti Page...**$34.00**
1953, June 5, Martin & Lewis......................................**$117.00**
1954, February 26, Libarace **$28.00**
1954, July 17, Roy Rogers..**$350.00**
1954, October 9, Lucille Ball...**$150.00**
1955, January 1, Loretta Young.....................................**$81.00**
1955, July 2, Lassie & Rin-Tin-Tin **$98.00**
1955, October 1, Mickey Mouse & His Club.............**$150.00**
1956, December 15, Dinah Shore..................................**$22.00**
1956, July 7, Lassie **$84.00**
1956, May 19, Phil Silvers as Sgt Bilko **$89.00**
1956, September 8, Elvis Presley.................................**$525.00**
1957, January 19, Jerry Lewis..**$48.00**
1957, July 13, Gale Davis as Annie Oakley **$68.00**
1957, May 11, James Arness of Gunsmoke...................**$71.00**
1958, January 18, John Payne of The Restless Gun **$70.00**
1958, May 24, Dick Clark of American Bandstand......**$78.00**

1958, October 25, George Burns.................................$68.00	1978, December 16, cast of Eight Is Enough..............$19.00
1959, December 12, Danny Thomas $31.00	1978, January 7, cast of Happy Days $27.00
1959, May 30, Steve McQueen $150.00	1978, October 28, cast of Mork & Mindy..................$35.00
1959, November 21, Clint Walker as Cheyenne $66.00	1979, February 24, James Arness..............................$33.00
1960, August 13, Nick Adams as The Rebel..............$66.00	1979, July 7, cast of Barney Miller...........................$14.00
1960, February 6, Richard Boone as Palladin.............$66.00	1979, November 10, The Bee Gees...........................$19.00
1960, June 25, cast of Bonanza $125.00	1980, December 27, Tom Selleck of Magnum PI.......$21.00
1961, April 22, Garry Moore $75.00	1980, February 2, cast of Different Strokes................$15.00
1961, July 22, Maharis & Milner of Route 66.............$128.00	1980, July 19, cast of Love Boat $13.00
1961, May 4, Raymond Burr as Perry Mason.............$68.00	1981, February, cast of WKRP in Cincinnati...............$16.00
1962, August 4, Cast of Dennis the Menace $62.00	1981, July 25, Prince Charles & Lady Diana Spencer..$19.00
1962, November 10, cast of Beverly Hillbillies...........$95.00	1981, June 13, cast of Trapper John MD $16.00
1963, March 16, Richard Chamberlain.......................$37.00	1982, March 13, cast of Three's Company...................$24.00
1963, May 11, Ronny Howard & Don Knotts............$150.00	1982, May 8, Goldie Hawn $6.00
1963, October 19, Judy Garland $45.00	1982, October 2, Genie Francis $10.00
1964, February, Danny Kaye.....................................$30.00	1983, April 9, Elvis Presley.......................................$13.00
1964, May 30, cast of McHale's Navy.......................$50.00	1983, December 31, Farrah Fawcett $21.00
1964, September 19, Special Fall Preview $150.00	1983, February 12, final M*A*S*H episode.................$33.00
1965, April 24, Andy Griffith....................................$82.00	1984, August, cast of Simon & Simon $23.00
1965, May 8, Bob Denver as Gilligan $128.00	1984, May 19, Morgan Fairchild................................$17.00
1965, October 30, Addams Family.............................$86.00	1984, October 6, cast of Paper Dolls $12.00
1966, April 2, Dean Martin.......................................$77.00	1985, December 21, cast of Highway to Heaven.........$24.00
1966, May 26, Sally Field of Gidget...........................$25.00	1985, May 11, Cheryl Ladd.......................................$15.00
1966, November 26, Ron Ely as Tarzan.....................$58.00	1985, October 19, cast of Golden Girls.....................$13.00
1967, January 28, cast of The Monkees $125.00	1986, January 11, cast of Scarecrow & Mrs King $19.00
1967, May 20, Andy Griffith & Anita Corsaut.............$52.00	1986, May 10, cast of Cheers $13.00
1967, November 18, Shatner & Nemoy of Star Trek...$95.00	1986, May 31, Anderson of MacGyver........................$37.00
1968, January 6, Bob Conrad of Wild Wild West........$91.00	1987, August 15, Alf..$10.00
1968, May 11, cast of Daniel Boone $20.00	1987, January 3, Angela Lansbury $15.00
1968, October 5, cast of My Three Sons....................$24.00	1987, November 14, Danson & Alley of Cheers..........$15.00
1969, February 1, Men of High Chaparral $50.00	1988, April 9, Harry Hamlin......................................$10.00
1969, July 5, McCord & Milner of Adam 12...............$40.00	1988, January, cast of Falcon Crest $13.00
1969, September 27, cast of Marcus Welby MB..........$21.00	1988, July 2, cast of Designing Women $15.00
1970, April 4, cast of Brady Bunch $125.00	1989, March 25, Oscars $10.00
1970, July 25, cast of Mayberry RFD.........................$20.00	1989, May 13, Tracy Scoggins of Dynasty..................$8.00
1970, October 31, Mike Conners of Mannix...............$37.00	1989, September 30, Liz Taylor & Mark Harmon........$11.00
1971, February 6, cast of The Odd Couple $36.00	1990, March 10, cast of LA Law................................$10.00
1971, June 19, cast of Eddie's Father $26.00	1990, November 17, Muppets $7.00
1971, September 4, Jack Lord of Hawaii Five-O $58.00	1990, September 8, Women of Twin Peaks.................$24.00
1972, August 26, Olympics $10.00	1991, January 26, Cybill Shepherd.............................$15.00
1972, March 18, Sonny & Cher.................................$28.00	1991, May 4, Larry Hagman: Adios Dallas...................$15.00
1972, November 4, John Wayne $21.00	1991, November 23, Madonna $17.00
1973, June 16, cast of Maude...................................$28.00	1992, January 25, Superbowl XXVI $15.00
1973, March 24, Ann-Margret...................................$26.00	1992, May 23, Seinfield $17.00
1973, Nov 17, Frank Sinatra.....................................$26.00	1992, November 14, Michael Jackson $15.00
1974, August 17, Police Story $10.00	1993, January 9, Bill & Hillary Clinton.......................$20.00
1974, December 7, Michael Landon of Little House ...$35.00	1993, November 20, Waltons Come Home Again........$25.00
1974, February 9, cast of M*A*S*H...........................$15.00	1993, September 25, Raymond Burr...........................$44.00
1975, August 16, cast of Emergency..........................$95.00	1994, April 30, Garth Brooks $12.00
1975, May 31, cast of The Bob Newhart Show $19.00	1994, August 20, Barbara Streisand by Hirschfield $22.00
1975, November 15, Soul & Glaser of Starsky & Hutch.$33.00	1994, January 1, Tim Allen.......................................$16.00
1976, March 13, cast of Chico & the Man..................$18.00	1995, July 15, Kes & Neelix of Voyager.....................$15.00
1976, May 8, Lindsay Wagner of The Bionic Woman.$21.00	1995, May 13, The Judds..$10.00
1976, September 11, Bob Dylan $28.00	1995, November 25, Jane Seymour $10.00
1977, January 1, John Travolta..................................$24.00	1996, April 13, Steve Yzerman of the Redwings.........$36.00
1977, March 19, last Mary Tyler Moore Show $31.00	1996, January 27, Troy Aikman of the Cowboys.........$50.00
1977, November 26, cast of Soap..............................$21.00	1996, June 15, Teri Hatcher $12.00

1997, February 15, NASCAR'S Dale Earnhardt............**$35.00**
1997, June 17, Farrah at 50 ....**$21.00**
1997, May 3, Kentucky Derby Special (S Sellers)........**$50.00**
1998, August 22, The Rat Pack **$35.00**
1998, February 14, David Pearson & Jeff Gordon.......**$35.00**
1998, May 16, Julia Roberts................................**$10.00**
1999, April 19, Lucy Lawless & Jeri Ryan **$10.00**
1999, July 17, NASCAR'S Tony Stewart **$25.00**
1999, November 13, Pierce Brosnan **$18.00**

Twin Winton

The genius behind the designs at Twin Winton was sculptor Don Winton. He and his twin, Ross, started the company while sill in high school in the mid-1930s. In 1952 older brother Bruce Winton bought the company from his two younger brothers and directed its development nationwide. They produced animal figures, cookie jars, and matching kitchenware and household items during this time. It is important to note that Bruce was an extremely shrewd business man, and if an order came in for a nonstandard color, he would generally accommodate the buyer — for an additional charge, of course. As a result, you may find a Mopsy (Raggedy Ann) cookie jar, for instance, in a wood stain finish or some other unusual color, even though Mopsy was only offered in the Collector Series in the catalogs. This California company was active until it sold in 1976 to Roger Bowermeister, who continued to use the Twin Winton name. He experimented with different finishes. One of the most common is a light tan with a high gloss glaze. He owned the company only one year until it went bankrupt and was sold at auction. Al Levin of Treasure Craft bought the molds and used some of them in his line. Eventually, the molds were destroyed.

One of Twin Winton's most successful concepts was their Hillbilly line — mugs, pitchers, bowls, lamps, ashtrays, decanters, and novelty items molded after the mountain boys in Paul Webb's cartoon series. Don Winton was the company's only designer, though he free-lanced as well. He designed for Disney, Brush-McCoy, Revell Toys, The Grammy Awards, American Country Music Awards, Ronald Reagan Foundation, and numerous other companies and foundations.

Twin Winton has been revived by Don and Norma Winton (the original Don Winton and his wife). They are currently selling new designs as well as some of his original artwork through the Twin Winton Collector Club on the Internet at twinwinton.com. Some of Don's more prominent pieces of art are currently registered with the Smithsonian in Washington, D.C.

If you would like more information, read *A Collector's Guide to Don Winton Designs*, written by our advisor Mike Ellis. Other sources of information are *The Collector's Encyclopedia of Cookie Jars* (three in the series) by Joyce and Fred Roerig. (All are published by Collector Books.)

Note: color codes in the listings below are as follows: A — avocado green; CS — Collectors Series, fully painted; G — gray; I — ivory; O — orange; P — pineapple yellow; R — red; and W — wood stain with hand-painted detail. Values are based on actual sales as well as dealers' asking prices.

See also Cookie Jars.

Advisor: Mike Ellis (See Directory, Twin Winton)

Club: Twin Winton Collector Club
Also Don Winton Designs (other than Twin Winton)
266 Rose Lane
Costa Mesa, CA 92627; 714-646-7112 or fax: 7414-645-4919
twinwinton.com; e-mail: ellis5@pacbell.net

Ashtray, elf, W, F, 8x8" **$100.00**
Bank, dobbin, W, I, G, A, P, O, R, 8"..........................**$40.00**
Bank, Dutch girl, W, I, G, A, P, O, R, 8".....................**$50.00**

Bank, elephant, wood stain with hand-painted details, $50.00. (Photo courtesy Mike Ellis)

Bank, Foo Dog, W, I, G, A, P, O, R, 8"......................**$125.00**
Bank, Gunfighter Rabbit, W, I, G, A, P, O, R, 8".........**$50.00**
Bank, kitten, W, I, G, A, P, O, R, 8".............................**$50.00**
Bank, lamb, W, I, G, A, P, O, R, 8" **$40.00**
Bank, Pirate Fox, W, I, G, A, P, O, R, 8"....................**$65.00**
Bank, shack, W, I, G, A, P, O, R, 8".............................**$50.00**
Bank, shoe, W, I, G, A, P, O, R, 8"............................**$85.00**
Bank, teddy bear, W, I, G, A, P, O, R, 8"....................**$40.00**
Candle holder, Aladdin, W, I, G, A, P, O, R, 9½x6½"..**$45.00**
Candle holder, El Greco, W, I, G, A, P, O, R, short, 4½x6"..**$12.00**
Candle holder, Ravel, W, I, G, A, P, O, R, long, 5x9"..**$18.00**
Candy jar, nut w/squirrel finial, W, I, G, A, P, O, R, 8x9"...**$75.00**
Candy jar, Pot 'o Candy, W, I, G, A, P, O, R, 8x10"....**$65.00**
Candy jar, Ranger Bear, W, I, G, A, P, O, R, 8x10½"..**$85.00**
Candy jar, shoe, W, I, G, A, P, O, R, 10x10"................**$75.00**
Canister, Bucket Canisters, Coffee Bucket, wood finish, 5x6" **$30.00**
Canister, Bucket Canisters, Flour Bucket, wood finish, 7x8" **$50.00**
Canister, Canister Farm, Cookie Barn, W, I, G, A, P, O, R, 8x12" **$80.00**

Canister, Canister Farm, Sugar Dairy, W, I, G, A, P, O, R, 4x8" **$55.00**
Canister, Canisterville, house, flour, wood finish, 7x11" .**$125.00**
Canister, Canisterville, house, sugar, wood finish, 5x9" **$95.00**
Canister, Pot 'o Tea, W, I, G, A, P, O, R, 4x5" **$20.00**
Cocktail napkin holder, elephant, W, I, G, A, P, O, R, 6x4" .**$150.00**
Cocktail napkin holder, horse, W, I, G, A, P, O, R, 6x4" ..**$150.00**
Creamer & sugar bowl, hen & rooster, W, G, I, 5x6" .**$200.00**
Expanimals, additional dividers, W, ea **$15.00**
Expanimals, chipmunk, W, 7½" **$125.00**
Figuirine, squirrel looking sideways, 2½x4" **$30.00**
Figurine, beaver lying down, #315, 1x2½" **$8.00**
Figurine, blind mouse, #208, ¾" **$6.00**
Figurine, cow, #450, brown, 2" **$11.00**
Figurine, female cat, W, I, G & hand painted, 9½" **$75.00**
Figurine, shaggy dog, W, I, G & hand painted, 8" **$65.00**
Figurine, skunk w/head turned, #309, ¾" **$7.00**
Figurine, Yogi Bear sitting on a stump, 5" **$150.00**
Figurines, cocker spaniel, W, I, G & hand painted, 7" ...**$50.00**
Lamp, cat & fiddle, W, 11" **$175.00**
Lamp, monkey, W, 13" **$175.00**
Lamp, seal, W, 12" **$175.00**
Lamp, squirrel on tree truck, W, 12" **$175.00**
Mug, bear, W, I, G, A, P, O, R, 3¾" **$85.00**
Mug, kitten, W, I, G, A, P, O, R, 3¼" **$85.00**
Napkin holder, Bambi, W, I, G, A, P, O, R, 6x7" **$85.00**
Napkin holder, dobbin, W, I, G, A, P, O, R, 7x5" **$65.00**
Napkin holder, Dutch girl, W, I, G, A, P, O, R, 8½x5½" ..**$75.00**
Napkin holder, elf, W, I, G, A, P, O, R, 8x5" **$85.00**
Napkin holder, lamp, W, I, G, A, P, O, R, 7x5" **$75.00**
Napkin holder, Ranger Bear, W, I, G, A, P, O, R, 9x4" ...**$75.00**
Napkin holder, shack, W, I, G, A, P, O, R, 7x7" **$65.00**
Planter, cat w/boat, W, 8" **$50.00**
Planter, dog, W, 8" **$50.00**
Planter, rabbit crouching beside basket, 5x8" **$85.00**
Planter, rabbit w/eggshell, 6x8" **$85.00**
Planter, Ranger Bear by stump, W, 8" **$50.00**
Salt & pepper shakers, barrel, W, I, G, A, P, O, R, pr...**$30.00**
Salt & pepper shakers, bull, W, I, G, A, P, O, R, pr...**$40.00**
Salt & pepper shakers, chipmunk, W, I, G, A, P, O, R, pr ..**$40.00**
Salt & pepper shakers, cookie pot, W, I, G, A, P, O, R, pr ..**$30.00**
Salt & pepper shakers, cop, W, I, G, A, P, O, R, pr....**$40.00**
Salt & pepper shakers, cow, W, I, G, A, P, O, R, pr...**$50.00**
Salt & pepper shakers, donkey, W, I, G, A, P, O, R, pr...**$40.00**
Salt & pepper shakers, Dutch girl, W, I, G, A, P, O, R, pr...**$35.00**
Salt & pepper shakers, elf, W, I, G, A, P, O, R, pr......**$40.00**
Salt & pepper shakers, Foo Dog, W, I, G, A, P, O, R, pr..**$125.00**
Salt & pepper shakers, frog, W, I, G, A, P, O, R, pr.**$125.00**
Salt & pepper shakers, Gunfighter Rabbit, W, I, G, A, P, O, R, pr...**$45.00**
Salt & pepper shakers, hen, W, I, G, A, P, O, R, pr....**$50.00**
Salt & pepper shakers, Hotei, W, I, G, A, P, O, R, pr.**$30.00**
Salt & pepper shakers, Indian (Chief), W, I, G, A, P, O, R, pr...**$75.00**
Salt & pepper shakers, jack in the box, W, I, G, A, P, O, R, pr **$125.00**
Salt & pepper shakers, kangaroo, W, I, G, A, P, O, R, pr ..**$85.00**

Salt & pepper shakers, kitten (Persian), W, I, G, A, P, O, R, pr...**$40.00**
Salt & pepper shakers, lamb, W, I, G, A, P, O, R, pr..**$30.00**
Salt & pepper shakers, monk or Friar Tuck, W, I, G, A, P, O, R, pr **$35.00**
Salt & pepper shakers, Mother Goose, W, I, G, A, P, O, R, pr.**$45.00**
Salt & pepper shakers, mouse, W, I, G, A, P, O, R, pr ..**$40.00**
Salt & pepper shakers, owl, W, I, G, A, P, O, R, pr....**$30.00**
Salt & pepper shakers, pear, W, I, G, A, P, O, R, pr..**$75.00**
Salt & pepper shakers, poodle, W, I, G, A, P, O, R, pr...**$50.00**
Salt & pepper shakers, raccoon, W, I, G, A, P, O, R, pr.**$45.00**
Salt & pepper shakers, Ranger Bear, W, I, G, A, P, O, R, pr.**$40.00**
Salt & pepper shakers, Sailor Elephant, W, I, G, A, P, O, R, pr...**$35.00**
Salt & pepper shakers, shack, W, I, G, A, P, O, R, pr....**$40.00**
Salt & pepper shakers, shoe, W, I, G, A, P, O, R, pr..**$50.00**
Salt & pepper shakers, snail, W, I, G, A, P, O, R, pr..**$125.00**
Salt & pepper shakers, squirrel, W, I, G, A, P, O, R, pr..**$40.00**
Salt & pepper shakers, teddy bear, W, I, G, A, P, O, R, pr..**$50.00**
Spoon rest, lamb, W, I, G, A, P, O, R, 5x10" **$40.00**
Spoon rest, owl, W, I, G, A, P, O, R, 5x10" **$40.00**
Spoon rest, pig, W, I, G, A, P, O, R, 5x10" **$40.00**
Spoon rest, Ranger Bear, W, I, G, A, P, O, R, 5x10" ...**$40.00**
Sppon rest, Dutch girl, W, I, G, A, P, O, R, 5x10" **$40.00**
Talking picture, Hotei, W, I, G, A, P, O, R, 11x7" .**$110.00**
Talking picture, shoe, W, I, G, A, P, O, R, 10x11" **$110.00**
Talking picture, teddy bear, W, I, G, A, P, O, R, 11x7" **$110.00**
Wall planter, bear head, W, 5½" **$100.00**
Wall planter, rabbit head, W, 5½" **$100.00**

Hillbilly Line

Ladies of the Mountains, stein, 8" **$70.00**
Men of the Mountains, ashtray, sm, 4½x4½" **$20.00**
Men of the Mountains, bank, Mountain Dew Loot, 7"..**$75.00**

Men of the Mountains, barrel mug with Hillbilly handle, 4", $30.00. (Photo courtesy Mike Ellis)

Men of the Mountains, bowl, bathing hillbilly, 6x6"...**$40.00**
Men of the Mountains, figurine, Ezra or Zeke, 5½", ea.**$40.00**

Men of the Mountains, ice bucket, #TW-30 Suspenders, 14x7½"......**$250.00**

Men of the Mountains, ice bucket, #TW-31 Bathing, 16x7½"......**$450.00**

Men of the Mountains, mustache mug, 3"......**$50.00**

Men of the Mountains, pitcher, #H101, 7½"......**$85.00**

Men of the Mountains, pouring spout, #H-104, 6½"..**$25.00**

Men of the Mountains, pretzel bowl, #H-105, 4½"....**$40.00**

Men of the Mountains, punch cup, #111, 3"......**$15.00**

Men of the Mountains, tankard, 1-gal, 15"......**$250.00**

Universal Dinnerware

This pottery incorporated in Cambridge, Ohio, in 1934, the outgrowth of several smaller companies in the area. They produced many lines of dinnerware and kitchenware items, most of which were marked. They're best known for their Ballerina dinnerware (simple modern shapes in a variety of solid colors) and Cat-Tail (see Cat-Tail Dinnerware). The company closed in 1960.

Baby's Breath, bowl, soup; lug handles, 6⅞", from $9 to..**$12.00**

Baby's Breath, plate, bread & butter; from $3 to..........**$6.00**

Baby's Breath, plate, dinner; from $12 to......**$15.00**

Baby's Breath, sugar bowl, w/lid, from $12 to..........**$15.00**

Ballerina, cake plate......**$30.00**

Ballerina, egg cup, from $20 to......**$22.00**

Ballerina, gravy boat, from $15 to......**$18.00**

Ballerina, plate, dinner......**$10.00**

Ballerina, salt & pepper shakers, pr, from $12 to......**$15.00**

Ballerina, sugar bowl, w/lid, from $14 to......**$16.00**

Ballerina Mist, bowl, serving; 7½"......**$14.00**

Ballerina Mist, bowl, vegetable; open, round..........**$25.00**

Ballerina Mist, creamer, open......**$12.00**

Ballerina Mist, cup & saucer......**$12.00**

Ballerina Mist, plate, chop; tab handles......**$18.00**

Ballerina Mist, plate, dinner; from $8 to......**$10.00**

Ballerina Mist, platter, round, from $10 to......**$14.00**

Ballerina Mist, salt & pepper shakers, pr, from $12 to...**$15.00**

Ballerina Mist, sugar bowl, w/lid, from $15 to..........**$18.00**

Calico Fruit, bowl, fruit; 5", from $7 to......**$9.00**

Calico Fruit, bowl, 4", w/lid, from $12 to......**$18.00**

Calico Fruit, custard cup, 5-oz, from $6 to......**$7.50**

Calico Fruit, pie plate, 10", from $30 to......**$35.00**

Calico Fruit, pitcher, utility; 6⅜"......**$35.00**

Calico Fruit, pitcher, w/hinged lid, 3-qt, from $40 to.**$50.00**

Calico Fruit, plate, bread & butter......**$6.00**

Calico Fruit, plate, utility; 11½", from $25 to......**$28.00**

Calico Fruit, platter, 13½"......**$28.00**

Calico Fruit, salt & pepper shakers, pr, from $20 to...**$25.00**

Cherry Blossom, sauce boat......**$15.00**

Harvest, bowl, mixing; gold trim, lg......**$22.00**

Harvest, cup & saucer, from $15 to......**$15.00**

Harvest, pie plate, gold trim......**$20.00**

Harvest, pitcher, milk; 1-qt, w/gold trim......**$25.00**

Highland, gravy boat, no underplate......**$20.00**

Highland, sugar bowl, w/lid......**$14.00**

Laurella, plate, luncheon; 9⅜"......**$20.00**

Mixed Fruit, refrigerator jar, with lid, 4", $12.00 to $18.00.

Oriental Flower, platter, lug handles, 12", from $10 to..**$12.00**

Oriental Flower, platter, lug handles, 13", from $12 to..**$14.00**

Rambler Rose, bowl, fruit; from $8 to......**$10.00**

Rambler Rose, creamer, open, from $18 to......**$22.00**

Rambler Rose, cup & saucer, from $15 to......**$18.00**

Rambler Rose, plate, dinner; from $15 to......**$18.00**

Rambler Rose, plate, luncheon; sq, 7¼", from $12 to...**$15.00**

Red & White, casserole, w/lid......**$20.00**

Vogue, creamer, light blue, open......**$12.00**

Woodvine, bowl, oval, from $12 to......**$15.00**

Woodvine, bowl, serving; 3½x9¾", from $15 to........**$18.00**

Woodvine, creamer, from $12 to......**$15.00**

Woodvine, cup & saucer, from $8 to......**$10.00**

Woodvine, gravy boat, from $15 to......**$18.00**

Woodvine, plate, salad; from $4 to......**$5.00**

Woodvine, plate, 6", from $3 to......**$4.00**

Woodvine, relish dish, from $12 to......**$15.00**

Woodvine, salt & pepper shakers, pr, from $12 to.....**$18.00**

Woodvine, sugar bowl, w/lid, from $15 to......**$20.00**

Woodvine, utility jar, w/lid, 26-oz, from $20 to..........**$25.00**

Valentines

If you are a new collector of antique valentines, you'll be able to get your collection off and running for very little cash. But as in any field, the more knowledgeable collector who is seeking to enhance an already well rounded collection will find that those extra special cards are more pricey. Until your knowledge reaches that level, however, you can always be a visionary and start out with the school valentines of today, i.e., Harry Potter, Britney Spears, 'N Sync, Monster, Inc. These are the collectibles of tomorrow.

Topical valentines are always good — transportation, ethnic, pedigree dogs, cats, comic characters, sports themes, etc. Just remember to keep these seven factors in mind when investing in cards for your collection: category, age, condition, size, manufacturer, artist signature, and scarcity.

For more information we recommend *Valentines With Values, Valentines for the Eclectic Collector,* and *100 Years of Valentines,* all by Katherine Kreider (available from the author).

Values are for cards in excellent condition.

Advisor: Katherine Kreider (See Directory, Valentines)

Newsletter: *National Valentine Collectors Bulletin*
Evalene Pulati
P.O. Box 1404
Santa Ana, CA 92702; 714-547-1355;

Dimensional, big-eyed kid w/castle in background, 1920s, 6x3½x2½"..**$20.00**

Dimensional, bluebirds & lily of the valley, ca 1930s, printed in Germany, 7¼x4x2½"...**$25.00**

Dimensional, boy in garden, early 1900s, made in Germany, 4x4½x3½"..**$10.00**

Dimensional, cannon, accented w/scraps, early 1900s, printed in Germany, 5x6x3"..................................**$45.00**

Dimensional, cat sitting on tennis racket, early 1900s, printed in Germany, 7½x5x1"......................................**$25.00**

Dimensional, cherub, early 1900s, printed in Germany, 2x1x1"..**$3.00**

Dimensional, collie in front of doghouse w/original chain, 1920s, printed in Germany, 6x5x1".....................**$15.00**

Dimensional, heart-shaped w/flower die-cut scraps, 1915, 5x3x3"..**$15.00**

Dimensional, holding hands w/forget-me-nots, early 1920s, 8x4x3½"..**$30.00**

Dimensional, hot air balloon in the ocean, 1920s, made in Germany, hold-to-light, 10x5x2"..........................**$45.00**

Dimensional, Victorian couple (center motif), w/red roses, early 1900s, printed in Germany, 8½x4x3"...........**$30.00**

Dimensional, Victorian horse-drawn carriage, w/honeycomb paper puff, 9x10x5"...................................**$45.00**

Flat, boy in tuxedo, easel back, early 1900s, printed in Germany, 2½x1"..**$2.00**

Flat, car (sedan), early 1900s, printed in Germany, 9½x8"..**$15.00**

Flat, children under umbrella, 1920s, Gibson, JG Scott, 3½x2"...**$3.00**

Flat, Flintstones, 1960s, 4½x3"...............................**$6.00**

Flat, girl playing tambourine, 1920s, 3½x4"................**$2.00**

Flat, ice cream soda, 1940s, 4x3".............................**$2.00**

Flat, ironing, 1930s, Carrington Co, 4½x5½"................**$4.00**

Flat, Pink Panther, 1960s, 4½x3"..............................**$6.00**

Flat, poodle (flocked), 1950s, 7x3½"..........................**$6.00**

Flat, Raggedy Ann & Andy, 1930s, by Volland, 6x6"..**$45.00**

Flat, Raggedy Ann & Andy, 1970s, Hallmark, 5x4".......**$8.00**

Flat, Rosie the Riveter, 1940s, USA, 4x3½"................**$10.00**

Flat, Victorian girl holding tulips, early 1900s, signed Clapsaddle, 4x2½"..**$6.00**

Flat, West Highland white terrier, 1930s, 4x5".............**$6.00**

Folded-Flat, chef w/rolling pin, 1940s, 4x3".............**$2.00**

Folded-Flat, roller coaster, 1940s, 3½x4"......................**$2.00**

Folded-flat, roller coaster, 1940s, USA, 4x6", EX, $3.00. (Photo courtesy Katherine Kreider)

Folded-Flat, stilts w/children, 1940s, 3½x3"................**$2.00**

Greeting card, All My Love, satin motif, hand-rolled crepe-paper roses, 1950s, by Paramount, 12x10"...........**$10.00**

Greeting card, angel sitting on throne, early 1900s, no maker, 5½x3½"...**$5.00**

Greeting card, Baby's First Valentine, 1950s, 4x4"........**$2.00**

Greeting card, Donald Duck, 1946, Hallmark, 4x3½".**$10.00**

Greeting card, German beer stein, 1950s, Hallmark, 9½x4¼"...**$5.00**

Greeting card, Kewpie, 1910-1920s, signed Rose O'Neill, 6½x4"...**$50.00**

Greeting card, pearlized fan, hand colored, 1930s, USA, Rust Craft, 6x8½"..**$6.00**

Greeting card, white embossed kitten, early 1900s, 5x3¾".**$5.00**

Greeting card, Whitney Bathing Beauty, 1940s, USA, 3x3½"...**$3.00**

Greeting card, Whitney flower series, 1940s, USA, 3x3½"...**$3.00**

Honeycomb paper puff, basket, 1920s, Beistle, 5x4"....**$6.00**

Honeycomb paper puff, cherubs netting hearts, early 1900s, printed in Germany, 5½x4¼x4¼".....................**$20.00**

Honeycomb paper puff, pedestal w/cherubs, 1920s, Beistle, 8x5x5"...**$6.00**

Honeycomb paper puff, sailboat, 1920s, 9x6x4"........**$25.00**

Mechanical-Flat, African American farm boy, ca 1940s, 4x2"...**$6.00**

Mechanical-Flat, big-eyed kids on scale, w/side easels, printed in Germany, 7½x12".......................................**$40.00**

Mechanical-Flat, Boy Scout & native American, 1930s, printed in Germany, 3¾x5½"......................................**$10.00**

Mechanical-Flat, Cleo the Fish, Disney, 1938, USA, 4½x2".**$15.00**

Mechanical-Flat, Felix the Cat, 1930s, 5x3½"..............**$15.00**

Mechanical-Flat, Girl Scout on horse, 1920s, printed in Germany, 4x2½"..**$10.00**

Mechanical-Flat, ice cream cone girl, 1950s, made in USA, 6½x4¾"...**$8.00**

Mechanical-Flat, Mexican man in desert, 1940s, USA, 6x5"...**$5.00**

Mechanical-Flat, miniature fairy, 1920s, Germany, 4x3"...**$6.00**

Mechanical-Flat, monkey w/harmonica, 1920s, printed in Germany, 8x4"..**$8.00**

Mechanical-Flat, pedal car, early 1930s, printed in Germany, 6x6"..**$15.00**

Mechanical-Flat, polar bear w/Eskimo, 1920s, printed in Germany, 4x3½"..**$5.00**

Mechanical-Flat, Red Cross nurse, 1940s, trademark 'G,' printed in Germany, 7x5"..**$10.00**

Mechanical-Flat, roadster & motorcycle, early 1920s, printed in Germany, 4½x6½"..**$15.00**

Mechanical-Flat, Snow White, Disney, 1938, USA, 6x2½" ..**$25.00**

Novelty, Avon scratch-off cards, 1977, USA, 4x4" **$5.00**

Novelty, Chiclets Gum w/original boxes attached to card, Art Deco, 1920s, USA, 10x5" **$15.00**

Novelty, Dutch Boy w/gum, 1920s, JG Scott, Gibson, 6½x3½"..**$15.00**

Novelty, Jack in the Beanstalk booklet, 1940s, USA, 6½x3½"..**$10.00**

Novelty, lollipop card w/policeman, USA, Rosen, 6x5"...**$6.00**

Novelty, Lov-o-gram, Charles Twelvetrees, 4½x6" closed..**$8.00**

Novelty, plastic sailboat w/lollipop, USA, 5½x6x1¼".**$10.00**

Novelty, puzzle, 1930s-40s, no maker, 5½x5½".........**$10.00**

Penny Dreadful, barber, 1930s, USA, 8x6" **$3.00**

Penny Dreadful, doctor, 1930s, USA, 8x6" **$3.00**

Penny Dreadful, motorcycle cop, 1930s, USA, 8x6".......**$3.00**

Vallona Starr

Triangle Studios opened in the 1930s, primarily as a gift shop that sold the work of various California potteries and artists such as Brad Keeler, Beth Barton, Cleminson, Josef Originals, and many others. As the business grew, Leona and Valeria, talented artists in their own right, began developing their own ceramic designs. In 1939 the company became known as Vallona Starr, a derivation of the three partners' names — (Val)eria Dopyera de Marsa, and Le(ona) and Everett (Starr) Frost. They made several popular ceramic lines including Winkies, Corn Design, Up Family, Flower Fairies, and the Fairy Tale Characters salt and pepper shakers. There were many others. Vallona Starr made only three cookie jars: Winkie (beware of any jars made in colors other than pink or yellow); Peter, Peter, Pumpkin Eater (used as a TV prize-show giveaway); and Squirrel on Stump (from the Woodland line). For more information we recommend *Vallona Starr Ceramics* by Bernice Stamper.

See also Cookie Jars.

Advisor: Bernice Stamper (See Directory, Vallona Starr)

Bowl, cereal; corn design, single green ear along rim on yellow, from $20 to **$25.00**

Bowl, Humpty Dumpty, white & pink on red brick pedestal, & cup, white, pink & green, set, minimum value.....**$125.00**

Buffet dish, divided, corn design divides the dish into 2 parts, green & yellow, from $35 to............................**$40.00**

Butter dish, ear of corn shape, #47, 1950s, w/lid, 6½x2¾x1¾", from $40 to............................**$50.00**

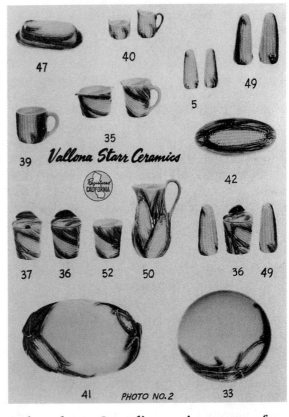

Catalog sheet, Corn line, prices range from $18.00 for the tumbler to $60.00 for the large platter. (Photo courtesy Bernice Stamper)

Cigarette box, man in doghouse, multicolored, minimum value **$65.00**

Creamer & sugar bowl, corn design, ear tab handles on sugar, green & yellow, 4½", pr, from $30 to........**$40.00**

Creamer & sugar bowl, pink w/gold trim, green leaves on base, Cosmos Line **$35.00**

Creamer & sugar bowl, tulip form, pink w/gold trim, from $15 to..**$20.00**

Marmalade, corn design, green & yellow, w/lid, from $25 to..**$30.00**

Pitcher, corn design, yellow & green, 1-qt **$55.00**

Pitcher, Winkie, pink & yellow w/blush, minimum value .**$100.00**

Plate, dinner; corn design, green & yellow, single ear at rim, 10", from $25 to..**$30.00**

Platter, 3-D corn in center, #30, 13x8¼" **$60.00**

Salt & pepper shakers, Aladdin-style fortune teller, seated w/legs crossed, 4½", pr..**$30.00**

Salt & pepper shakers, bears eating (adapted from fairy tale), pr, from $35 to..**$40.00**

Salt & pepper shakers, brown toadstool & green frog, souvenir of Catalina Island (sticker), pr, from $10 to ..**$15.00**

Salt & pepper shakers, Drip & Drop, marked w/name, pr, from $25 to..**$30.00**

Salt & pepper shakers, flying saucer, silver w/red pilot, pr, minimum value **$300.00**

Salt & pepper shakers, Gingham Dog & Calico Cat, pr, from $45 to..**$50.00**

Salt & pepper shakers, kitten & milk bottle, yellow w/black trim, white bottle, pr, from $25 to........................**$30.00**

Salt & pepper shakers, kittens, 1 sitting, 1 lying down, white w/gold trim, ca 1956, 1¼x3¾", pr, from $25 to...**$35.00**

Salt & pepper shakers, Mad Wife & Husband in Doghouse, pr **$125.00**

Salt & pepper shakers, prospector & jug, multicolor miner w/silver pan & gold nuggets, jug marked XXX, pr, minimum value..**$95.00**

Salt & pepper shakers, World War II block wardens, lg bodies w/wide black belt, shoes & hat, pr, minimum value **$125.00**

Spoon rest, corn design, green & yellow, single ear on oval form, from $20 to................................**$25.00**

Tumbler, ear of corn, 3½".............................**$18.00**

Vandor

For more than thirty-five years, Vandor has operated out of Salt Lake City, Utah. They're not actually manufacturers but distributors of novelty ceramic items made overseas. Some pieces will be marked 'Made in Korea,' while others are marked 'Sri Lanka,' 'Taiwan,' or 'Japan.' Many of their best things have been made in the last few years, and already collectors are finding them appealing — anyone would. They have a line of kitchenware designed around 'Cowmen Mooranda' (an obvious take off on Carmen), another called 'Crocagator' (a darling crocodile modeled as a teapot, a bank, salt and pepper shakers, etc.), character-related items (Betty Boop and Howdy Doody, among others), and some really wonderful cookie jars reminiscent of '50s radios and jukeboxes.

For more information, we recommend *The Collector's Encyclopedia of Cookie Jars, Vol II,* by Joyce and Fred Roerig (Collector Books).

See also Cat Collectibles and Elvis Presley Memorabilia.

Advisor: Lois Wildman (See Directory, Vandor)

Beatles, box, guitar shape, MIB....................................**$25.00**

Betty Boop, bank, Betty sits on top of white bank, 7½"..**$45.00**

Betty Boop, bath set, soap dish, toothbrush holder & cup, MIB **$45.00**

Betty Boop, cookie jar, in Corvette Convertible, MIB.**$60.00**

Betty Boop, cookie jar, in full white dress w/red vertical stripes, MIB **$70.00**

Betty Boop, cookie jar, w/her dog Pudgy on Empire State Building, MIB **$50.00**

Betty Boop, figurine, arms raised, 6", MIB.................**$25.00**

Betty Boop, ink box, MIB..**$30.00**

Betty Boop, music box, as cowgirl, 8", MIB.............**$50.00**

Betty Boop, salt & pepper shakers, as chef holding shakers on tray, 3 pcs, M.....................................**$45.00**

Betty Boop, salt & pepper shakers, as shopper w/packages, MIB **$25.00**

Betty Boop, salt & pepper shakers, on motorcycle w/dog, MIB **$20.00**

Betty Boop, tea set, pot, tray & 2 cups & saucers, MIB ..**$40.00**

Betty Boop, teapot, in bi-plane, MIB.........................**$30.00**

Curious George, cookie jar, George hangs onto side of rock-etship, 13", MIB...**$70.00**

Curious George, mug, George hangs onto handle, MIB..**$25.00**

Flintstones, bank, Pebbles & Dino, 1980, 6½x6".........**$48.00**

Flintstones, bank, standing Fred figural, 9" **$65.00**

Fred or Wilma Flintstone, mug, from $15.00 to $20.00 each; standing Fred, C 1989, from $125.00 to $150.00. (Photo courtesy Joyce and Fred Roerig)

Grateful Dead/Dancing Bear, mirror, MIB...................**$25.00**

Harley-Davidson, cookie jar, engine shape, MIB........**$30.00**

Howdy Doody, cookie jar, head, 1988, 10"..............**$390.00**

Howdy Doody/Pink Cadillac, salt & pepper shakers, pr ..**$80.00**

I Love Lucy, cookie jar, Lucy in lg tub smashing grapes for wine, M..**$115.00**

Mona Lisa, bank, 1992, from $25.00 to $35.00; salt and pepper shakers, 1992, from $20.00 to $25.00 for the pair; teapot, 1992, from $35.00 to $40.00. (Photo courtesy Joyce and Fred Roerig)

Pink Flamingo, cookie jar, radio shape, MIB **$30.00**

Pink Panther, salt & pepper shakers, Pink Panther head on loafers, pr **$20.00**

Scooby Doo Surfing/Mystery Machine, table lamp, 18", MIB **$50.00**

Vernon Kilns

Founded in Vernon, California, in 1931, this company produced many lines of dinnerware, souvenir plates, decorative pottery, and figurines. They employed several well-known artists whose designs no doubt contributed substantially to their success. Among them were Rockwell Kent, Royal Hickman, Don Blanding, and Walt Disney, all of whom were responsible for creating several of the lines most popular with collectors today.

In 1940 they signed a contract with Walt Disney to produce a line of figurines, vases, bowls, and several dinnerware patterns that were inspired by Disney's film *Fantasia*. The Disney items were made for a short time only and are now expensive.

The company closed in 1958, but Metlox purchased some of the molds and continued to produce some of their bestselling dinnerware lines through a specially established 'Vernonware' division.

Most of the ware is marked in some form or another with the company name and in some cases the name of the dinnerware pattern.

If you'd like to learn more, we recommend *Collectible Vernon Kilns, Second Edition,* by Maxine Feek Nelson (Collector Books).

Advisor: Maxine Nelson (See Directory, Dinnerware)

Newsletter: *Vernon Views*
P.O. Box 24234
Tempe, AZ 85285; Published quarterly beginning with the spring issue; $10 per year, includes free ads to subscribers

Anytime Shape

Patterns you will find on this shape include Tickled Pink, Heavenly Days, Anytime, Imperial, Sherwood, Frolic, Young in Heart, Rose-A-Day, and Dis 'N Dot.

Bowl, chowder; from $5 to...$10.00
Bowl, vegetable; divided, 9", from $10 to $15.00
Butter pat, individual, 2½", from $15 to $18.00
Casserole, w/lid, 8" dia, from $20 to..........................$30.00
Creamer, from $6 to...$10.00
Gravy boat, from $10 to...$15.00
Pitcher, 1-pt, from $15 to $20.00
Plate, bread & butter; 6", from $2 to............................$4.00
Plate, chop; 13", from $12 to.......................................$20.00
Plate, snack; indented for tumbler, rare, 8x12", from $35 to..$40.00
Platter, 11", from $12 to...$18.00
Relish dish, 3-section, from $15 to $25.00
Sugar bowl, w/lid, from $8 to $12.00
Tumbler, 14-oz, from $12 to $22.00

Chatelaine Shape

This designer pattern by Sharon Merrill was made in four color combinations: Topaz, Bronze, Platinum, and Jade.

Bowl, salad; Topaz & Bronze, 12", from $35 to..........$50.00
Bowl, serving; Topaz & Bronze, 9", from $20 to........$30.00
Plate, bread & butter; decorated Platinum & Jade, 6½", from $6 to..$8.00
Plate, chop; decorated Platinum & Jade, 14", from $45 to..$65.00
Platter, Topaz & Bronze, 16", from $35 to...................$50.00
Salt & pepper shakers, decorated Platinum & Jade, pr, from $20 to..$30.00

Lotus and Pan American Lei Shape

Patterns on this shape include Lotus, Chinling, and Vintage. Pan American Lei was a variation with flatware from the San Marino line. To evaluate Lotus, use the low end of our range as the minimum value; the high end of values apply to Pan American Lei.

Bowl, coupe soup; Pan American Lei only, 8½" $25.00
Bowl, mixing; Pan American Lei only, 5" $30.00
Bowl, mixing; Pan American Lei only, 9" $50.00
Bowl, salad; Pan American Lei only, 10½".................$75.00
Butter dish, w/lid, oblong, from $20 to $35.00
Creamer, from $12 to...$15.00
Mug, 9-oz, from $12 to..$25.00
Plate, coupe chop; Pan American Lei only, 13" $60.00
Plate, coupe; Pan American Lei only, 6"....................$12.00
Plate, offset; Lotus only, 7½", from $7 to $9.00
Sauce boat, from $15 to..$35.00
Sugar bowl, Pan American Lei only, w/lid.................$35.00
Sugar bowl, w/lid, from $15 to $18.00

Melinda Shape

Patterns found on this shape are Arcadia, Beverly, Blossom Time, Chintz, Cosmos, Dolores, Fruitdale, Hawaii (Lei Lani on Melinda is priced at two times to three times base value), May Flower, Monterey, Native California, Philodendron. The more elaborate the pattern, the higher the value.

Bowl, fruit; 5½", from $5 to..$8.00
Bowl, serving; oval, 10", from $15 to..........................$25.00
Casserole, w/lid, 8" inside dia, from $35 to................$65.00
Jam jar, w/lid, from $45 to...$50.00
Plate, chop; 14", from $25 to.......................................$50.00
Plate, luncheon; sq, 8½", from $12 to.........................$18.00
Platter, 16", from $30 to...$50.00
Relish, leaf shape, 2-part, 11", from $25 to................$35.00
Sauce boat, from $18 to..$25.00
Teacup, from $8 to $25.00
Teapot, w/lid, 6-cup, from $45 to $65.00

Montecito Shape (and Coronado)

This was one of the company's more utilized shapes — well over two hundred patterns have been documented. Among the most popular are the solid colors, plaids, the florals, westernware, and the Bird and Turnbull series. Bird,

Turnbull, and Winchester 73 (Frontier Days) are two to four times base values. Disney hollow ware is seven to eight times base values. Plaids (except Calico), solid colors, and Brown-eyed Susan are represented by the lower range.

Ashtray, round, 5½", from $12 to.................................**$15.00**
Bowl, lug chowder; round, open, tab handles, 6", from $8 to...**$15.00**
Bowl, mixing; 6", from $19 to **$25.00**
Bowl, mixing; 8", from $25 to **$35.00**
Bowl, rim soup; 1½x8¼", from $12 to **$15.00**
Bowl, salad; angular, 15", from $45 to **$65.00**
Bowl, salad; round, 13", from $40 to **$65.00**
Bowl, serving, angular, 9", from $15 to **$20.00**
Bowl, serving, oval, 10", from $18 to.......................**$22.00**
Bowl serving; round, 2½x8⅞", from $15 to **$20.00**
Carafe, w/stopper, angular or round, 10-cup, from $30 to **$40.00**
Casserole, chicken pie; stick handled, w/lid, 4", from $18 to **$25.00**
Casserole, 2-handled, w/lid, angular, 7½", from $25 to ...**$45.00**
Coaster, ridged, 3¾", from $15 to **$20.00**
Comport, footed, early, scarce, 9½" dia, from $45 to.**$65.00**
Custard cup, scarce, 3", from $20 to **$25.00**
Egg cup, double, cupped or straight sides, from $15 to..**$20.00**
Jam jar, notched lid, 5", from $50 to **$65.00**
Jug, bulbous bottom, 1-pt, from $20 to **$35.00**
Lemon server, center brass handle, 6", from $20 to....**$25.00**
Mug, bulbous bottom, applied handle, 8-oz, 3¾", fom $15 to **$25.00**
Pitcher, streamlined, 2-qt, 11", from $35 to **$45.00**
Pitcher, syrup; drip-cut top, from $45 to **$75.00**
Plate, bread & butter; 6½", from $4 to.......................**$8.00**
Plate, chop; 12", from $12 to **$30.00**
Plate, chop; 17", from $35 to **$75.00**
Plate, luncheon; 8½", from $8 to...............................**$12.00**
Platter, 14", from $25 to...**$40.00**
Salt & pepper shakers, lg, pr, from $25 to **$40.00**
Sugar bowl, open, individual, angular, from $10 to ...**$15.00**
Tidbit, 3-tier, wooden fixture, from $20 to **$35.00**
Trio buffet server, from $45 to **$65.00**
Tumbler, #5, straight sides, 5", 14-oz, from $18 to......**$25.00**

San Fernando Shape

Known patterns for this shape are Desert Bloom, Early Days, Hibiscus, R.F.D, Vernon's 1860, and Vernon Rose.

Bowl, fruit; 5½", from $6 to......................................**$8.00**
Bowl, mixing; RFD pattern only, 6", from $19 to **$22.00**
Bowl, rim soup; 8", from $12 to................................**$20.00**
Butter dish, w/lid, mail box shape, RFD pattern only, from $35 to...**$45.00**
Coaster, ridged, RFD pattern only, 3¾", from $12 to .**$18.00**
Olive dish, oval, 10", from $18 to **$30.00**
Plate, chop; 14", from $25 to **$45.00**
Plate, salad; 7½", from $7 to....................................**$12.00**

Platter, 12", from $18 to..**$25.00**
Salt & pepper shakers, figural mail box shape, pr, from $20 to..**$25.00**
Teacup, from $8 to **$12.00**
Teapot, w/lid, 6-cup, from $45 to **$65.00**

San Marino Shape

Known patterns for this shape are Barkwood, Bel Air, California Originals, Casual California, Gayety, Hawaiian Coral, Heyday, Lei Lani (two to three times base values), Mexicana, Pan American Lei (two to three times base values), Raffia, Shadow Leaf, Shantung, Sun Garden, and Trade Winds.

Bowl, coupe soup; 8½", from $8 to...........................**$12.00**
Bowl, mixing; 5", from $12 to **$15.00**
Bowl, mixing; 9", from $28 to **$35.00**
Bowl, salad; individual, 5½", from $8 to **$12.00**
Butter dish, w/lid, oblong, from $20 to.....................**$35.00**
Creamer, from $7 to...**$10.00**
Cup & saucer, jumbo; from $15 to **$20.00**
Flowerpot, 3", w/saucer, from $23 to.......................**$32.00**
Mug, 9-oz, from $12 to..**$20.00**
Pitcher, 1-pt, from $18 to **$22.00**
Plate, bread & butter; 6", from $3 to **$6.00**
Plate, chop; 13", from $15 to **$25.00**
Platter, 13", from $15 to..**$25.00**
Sugar bowl, w/lid, from $10 to **$12.00**
Tumbler, style #5, 14-oz, from $12 to **$20.00**

Ultra Shape

More than fifty patterns were issued on this shape. Nearly all the artist-designed lines (Rockwell Kent, Don Blanding, and Disney) utilized Ultra. The shape was developed by Gale Turnbull, and many of the elaborate flower and fruit patterns can be credited to him as well; use the high end of our range as a minimum value for his work. For Frederick Lunning, use the mid range. For other artist patterns, use these formulas based on the high end: Blanding — 2X (Aquarium 3X); Disney, 5 – 7X; Kent — Moby Dick, 2½X, Our America, 3½X, and Salamina, 5 – 7X.

Bowl, chowder; 6", from $8 to **$15.00**
Bowl, coupe soup; 7½", from $10 to.........................**$18.00**
Bowl, mixing; 5", from $15 to **$20.00**
Bowl, mixing; 7", from $25 to **$30.00**
Bowl, 1-pt, from $15 to **$25.00**
Casserole, w/lid, 8" dia, from $35 to........................**$55.00**
Creamer, open, regular, short or tall, from $12 to **$18.00**
Mug, 8-oz, 3½", from $15 to.....................................**$30.00**
Pitcher, open, 1-pt, jug style, 4½", from $18 to **$32.00**
Plate, chop; 12", from $15 to **$35.00**
Plate, salad; 7½", from $7 to....................................**$12.00**
Salt & pepper shakers, pr, from $15 to......................**$25.00**
Teacup, from $10 to **$18.00**

Year 'Round Shape

Patterns on this shape include Blueberry Hill, Country Cousin, and Lollipop Tree.

Bowl, fruit; 5½", from $4 to..................................**$6.00**
Bowl, vegetable; 9" dia, from $10 to...................**$14.00**
Casserole, w/lid, 8", from $20 to.....................**$30.00**
Creamer, from $6 to..**$10.00**
Pitcher, 1-qt, from $15 to..................................**$20.00**
Platter, 11", from $10 to....................................**$18.00**
Teapot, w/lid, from $25 to.................................**$35.00**

Fantasia

Bowl, goldfish, #121..**$400.00**
Figurine, Baby Weems, from The Reluctant Dragon, #37 ..**$350.00**
Figurine, black unicorn, #13, from $250 to **$400.00**
Figurine, gray baby Pegasus, #19, from $300 to **$450.00**
Figurine, Hop Low, #35 or #36, ea, from $95 to **$125.00**
Figurine, Nubian Centaurette, #23, from $900 to...**$1,100.00**
Figurine, ostrich, #29, from $800 to.......................**$1,200.00**
Figurine, Pegasus, #21, from $300 to **$400.00**
Figurine, rearing unicorn, #15, from $300 to............**$500.00**

Vietnam War Collectibles

In 1949 the French had military control over Vietnam. This was true until they suffered a sound defeat at Dienbienphu in 1954. This action resulted in the formation of the Geneva Peace Conference which allowed the French to make peace and withdraw but left Vietnam divided into North Vietnam and South Vietnam. The agreement was to reunite the country in 1956 when the general elections took place. But this didn't happen because of South Vietnam's political objections. The strife continued and slowly America was drawn into the conflict from the time of the Eisenhower administration until the Paris Peace Agreement in 1973. The war itself lingered on until 1975 when communist forces invaded Saigon and crushed the South Vietnamese government there.

Items relating to this conflict from the 1960s and early 1970s are becoming collectible. Most reflect the unpopularity of this war. College marches and political unrest headlined the newspapers of those years. Posters, pinback buttons, political cartoons, and many books from that period reflect the anti-war philosophy of the day and are reminders of turbulent times and political policies that cost the lives of many brave young men.

Book, The First Team, war recounts of 1st Calvary Division, Viet Nam, 1965-96, EX..............................**$32.50**
Book, Viet Nam in Flames, war photos, Kwok Hing Printing Press, 1969, 221 pages, w/dust jacket, 11x13½", EX **$85.00**

Canteen, Viet Cong, green painted aluminum w/khaki-color straps, made in China, M **$25.00**
Cap, field; olive-drab cotton, short bill, star badge pin, EX...**$15.00**
Flight jacket, Alpha Industries w/Scovill zipper, Army Ground Forces patch, Alamo Flight Patch, Warrant officer insignia **$60.00**
Flight jacket, leather, Martin Lane & Co, brass Scovill zipper, NM, unused.......................................**$215.00**
Flight jacket, N-3B, fur collar, drawstrings at hood & waist, NM **$150.00**
Flight suit, sage green cotton twill, Type K-2B, issued 1959, M, unused..**$15.00**
Hat, jungle; cotton khaki or olive drab, w/star badge pin, EX...**$18.00**
Hat, USMC drill instructor's, w/chin strap, EX............**$27.50**
Helmet, pith/sun; wood pulp body w/olive drab cotton cover, adjustable webbing, star badge assembly, M unused **$30.00**
Infrared (IR) 8598 Image Tube, goggles type, ca 1960-70s, EX in original packaging.................................**$35.00**
Knife, survival; Camillus, early 6" blade, EX w/original sheath **$185.00**
Knife, throwing; Olsen OK HC, brown-fiber handle, 7¼" blade, 11¼" overall, 1960s-60s, w/sheath, EX **$65.00**
Lighter, Zippo, hand engraved USN Never Again & name, 1971 ....**$75.00**
Patch, 1st Recon BN, Swift, Silent, Deadly, skull & crossbones on green diamond, 5½x4", NM **$15.00**

Poster, Rich Man's War, black and white newspaper collage with soldier, 1970, 22x17", VG+, $80.00 at auction.

Poster, The Vietnam War Continues, August 1969: 43,925 American Soldiers Are Dead, other statistics, 22x17", VG **$28.00**
Scarf, Viet Cong award, black & white checkered weave .**$25.00**
Watch, Benrus, dark face w/hands that glow in dark, brown cloth band, dated Feb 1969, EX **$60.00**
Water test kit, US Army Marine AN-M2, complete w/booklet, NM **$30.00**

View-Master Reels and Packets

William Gruber was the inventor who introduced the View-Master to the public at the New York World's Fair and the Golden Gate Exposition held in California in 1939. Thousands of reels and packets have been made since that time on every aspect of animal life, places of interest, and entertainment.

Over the years the company has changed ownership five times. It was originally Sawyer's View-Master, G.A.F (in the mid-sixties), View-Master International (1981), Ideal Toy and, most recently, Tyco Toy Company. The latter three companies produced them strictly as toys and issued only cartoons, making the earlier non-cartoon reels and the three-reel packets very collectible.

Sawyer made two cameras so that the public could take their own photo reels in 3-D. They made a projector as well, so that the homemade reels could be viewed on a large screen. 'Personal' or 'Mark II' cameras with their cases usually range in value from $100.00 to $200.00; rare viewers such as the blue 'Model B' start at about $100.00, and the 'Stereo-Matic 500' projector is worth $175.00 to $200.00. Most single reels range from $1.00 to $5.00, but some early Sawyer's and G.A.F's may bring as much as $35.00 each, character-related reels sometimes even more.

Club: View-Master Reel Collector
Roger Nazeley
4921 Castor Ave.
Philadelphia, PA 19124
215-743-8999; e-mail: vmreelguy2@aol.com

ABC Circus, #B-411, 3-reel set, MIP $18.00
Bambi, B-400, 3 reel set, MIP $14.00
Buffalo Bill Jr, #965b, single reel, MIP $5.00
Casper the Friendly Ghost, B-533, 3-reel set, MIP (sealed) $20.00
Cinderella, B-318, 3-reel set, MIP $12.00

Dr. Shrinker and Wonderbug, GAF, MIP, $18.00.

Godzilla, J-23, 3-reel set, MIP (sealed).........................$23.00
Goldilocks & the Three Bears, FT-6, single reel, w/book, MIP...$5.00
Jack & the Beanstalk, FT-3, single reel, MIP $4.00
Kiss, #002305, single reel, MIP...................................$8.00
Little Black Sambo, FT-8, single reel, w/book, MIP....$12.00
Mary Poppins, B-3762, single reel, MIP $3.00
Muppet Movie, K-27, 3-reel set, MIP (sealed) $24.00
Peanuts, B-536, 3-reel set, MIP $15.00
Puss-in-Boots, B-320, 3-reel set, MIP.........................$12.00
Roy Rogers — The Holdup, #946, single reel, MIP $5.00
Shaggy DA, B-368, 3-reel set, MIP (sealed).................$20.00
Snow White & the Seven Dwarfs, FT-4, single reel, w/book, MIP...$5.00
Spider-Man vs Dr Octopus, K-31, 3-reel set, MIP $12.00
Tarzan Rescues Cheetah, #975, single reel, w/book, MIP..$7.00
Welcome Back Kotter, #002056, single reel, MIP $4.00

Viking Glass

Located in the famous glassmaking area of West Virginia, this company has been in business since the 1950s; they're most famous for their glass animals and birds. Their Epic Line (1950s and 1960s) was innovative in design and vibrant in color. Rich tomato-red, amberina, brilliant blues, strong greens, black, amber, and deep amethyst were among the rainbow hues in production at that time. During the 1980s the company's ownership changed hands, and the firm became known as Dalzell-Viking. Viking closed their doors in 1998.

Some of the Epic Line animals were reissued in crystal, crystal frosted, and black.

Advisor: Mary Lou Bohl (See Directory, Viking)

Ashtray, fish shape, amber, 5x4" $25.00
Ashtray, ruby red, ball shape, 4" $25.00
Basket, light blue, 8x8"..$30.00
Bell, red, honeycomb design, 5¾" $20.00
Bookends, owl, green, 7", pr.......................................$30.00
Bowl, light purple, Hobnail, 3-footed, 3½" $38.00
Bowl, ruby red, rounded sides, 1960s, 3x3"................$25.00
Candlesticks, ruby red, dolphin, tail up, on 6-sided base, Dalzell-Viking, 19", pr......................................$55.00
Candy dish, Teardrop, lime green, w/lid, 8x5" $25.00
Cookie jar, pineapple shape, amberina, 8x17"...........$60.00
Decanter, deep orange w/clear pointed stopper, 1960s, 19½x5¼"..$60.00
Figurine, bird, long tail, clear on frosted base, rare, 9½", from $80 to...$100.00
Figurine, bunny, light green, 6¼".............................$30.00
Figurine, duck, fighting; green, head bent down, 6"..$50.00
Figurine, eagle, clear, Dalzell-Viking, 7½" $50.00
Figurine, egret, ruby red, stylized w/long slender neck, beak upright, on dome base, rare, 11½", from $75 to..$95.00
Figurine, fish, amber, 7x7x2¼" $40.00

Figurine, hound dog, ruby red, seated, 8½", from $50 to..**$65.00**

Figurine, pig, black w/glossy finish, head resting on ground, marked Dalzell w/acid stamp, 4"............................**$70.00**

Figurine, seal, 9¾" long, $15.00. (Photo courtesy Lee Garmon/Dick Spencer)

Figurine, turtle, ruby red, 1¾x5" **$50.00**

Lamp, fairy; Diamond Point, light green, footed, 7" ...**$35.00**

Lamp, fairy; owl, blue **$35.00**

Nappy, apple shape, pigeon blood, 2¼x4½" **$30.00**

Novelty, mushroom, dark blue, 4x6¼" (across top) ...**$45.00**

Paperweight, pear shape, ruby red, 6", minimum value..**$75.00**

Paperweight, pumpkin, orange, Epic Line, 4¼" **$45.00**

Paperweight, raccoons, crystal, flat-sided w/3 molded raccoon heads, Viking label on back, 3½x6" **$50.00**

Paperweight, strawberry, deep red w/green stem, 3½", minimum value...**$45.00**

Patio light, light pink, 5" **$55.00**

Pitcher, ruby red, 7½x9", w/4 tumblers, 4x3" **$125.00**

Tumblers, ruby red, Honeycomb, 8-oz, 5½", set of 4 ....**$65.00**

Wade Porcelain

If you've attended many flea markets, you're already very familiar with the tiny Wade figures, most of which are 2" and under. Wade made several lines of these miniatures, but the most common were made as premiums for the Red Rose Tea Company. Most of these sell for $3.50 to $7.00 or so, with a few exceptions such as the Gingerbread man. Wade also made a great number of larger figurines as well as tableware and advertising items.

The Wade Potteries began life in 1867 as Wade and Myatt when George Wade and a partner named Myatt opened a pottery in Burslem — the center for potteries in England. In 1882 George Wade bought out his partner, and the name of the pottery was changed to Wade and Sons. In 1919 the pottery underwent yet another change in name to George Wade & Son Ltd. 1891 saw the establishment of another Wade Pottery — J & W Wade & Co., which in turn changed its name to A.J. Wade & Co. in 1927. At this time (1927) Wade Heath & Co. Ltd. was also formed.

These three potteries plus a new Irish pottery named Wade (Ireland) Ltd. were incorporated into one company in 1958 and given the name The Wade Group of Potteries. In 1990 the group was taken over by Beauford plc. and given the name Wade Ceramics Ltd., remaining so until the present time. In early 1999, Wade Ceramics Ltd. was bought out from Beauford plc. by the Wade management.

If you'd like to learn more, we recommend *The World of Wade, The World of Wade Book 2,* and *Wade Price Trends — First Edition,* by Ian Warner and Mike Posgay.

Advisor: Ian Warner (See Directory, Wade)

Newsletters: *The Wade Watch, Ltd.*
8199 Pierson Ct.
Arvada, CO 80005; 303-421-9655 or 303-424-4401 or fax: 303-421-0317; e-mail: idwarner@home.com

Club: The Official International Wade Collector's Club
The Official Wade Club Magazine
Wade Ceramics Ltd.
Royal Works, Westport Rd., Burslem, Stoke-on-Trent, Staffordshire, ST6 4AP, England, UK; e-mail: club@wade.co.uk; http:www.wade.co.uk/wade

Disney, Big Mama, 1981-87, 1¾"x1¾" **$68.00**

Disney Blow-Up, Scamp, Wade Porcelain Copyright Walt Disney Productions Made in England, 4⅛" **$235.00**

Dogs & Puppies Series, Corgi (adult), 1979, 2¼"........**$45.00**

Dumbo, 1958-65, 1⅜x1⅝"...**$90.00**

Happy Family, Pig (parent), 1⅛x1⅛"...........................**$25.00**

Happy Family, Rabbit, baby, 1⅛"..................................**$18.00**

Nursery Favourite, Polly Kettle, 1973, 2⅞" **$55.00**

Nursery Favourite, Puss-in-Boots, 1976, 2⅞x1⅛"........**$55.00**

Red Rose Tea (USA), Koala Bear, 1985, 1⅜" **$6.00**

Red Rose Tea (USA), Rhino, 1985,⅞"............................**$6.00**

Safari Set, Langur, 1976-77, 1⅜"..................................**$6.00**

Safari Set, Orangutan, 1976-77, 1¼" **$5.00**

Survival Set, Armadillo, 1984-85, 1"............................**$18.00**

Survival Set, Harp Seal, 1984-85, 1½" **$18.00**

Tom & Jerry Series, Tom, 1973-79, 3⅝x2⅛"................**$85.00**

TV Pet Series, Percy, 1½x1¼".....................................**$110.00**

Whimsie, 1953, Leaping Fawn, 1⅞x1½" **$48.00**

Whimsie, 1956, Husky, unmarked, 1¼".......................**$50.00**

Whimsie, 1956, Italian Goat, 1⅜" **$77.00**

Whimsie, Land Series, Retriever, 1½x1⅝"....................**$16.00**

Whoppas, Bobcat, 1½"...**$30.00**

Whoppas, Polar Bear, 1976, 1½" **$26.00**

Wall Pockets

A few years ago there were only a handful of avid wall pocket collectors, but today many are finding them intriguing. They were popular well before the turn of the century. Roseville and Weller included at least one and sometimes several in many of their successful lines of art pottery, and other American potteries made them as well. Many were imported from Germany, Czechoslovakia, China, and Japan. By the 1950s, they were passè.

Some of the most popular today are the figurals. Look for the more imaginative and buy the ones you especially like. If you're buying to resell, look for those designed as animals, large exotic birds, children, luscious fruits, or those that are particularly eye catching. Appeal is everything. Examples with a potter's mark are usually more pricey (for instance Roseville, McCoy, Hull, etc.), because of the crossover interest in collecting their products. For more information refer to *Made in Japan Ceramics* (there are four in the series) by Carole Bess White, and *Collector's Guide to Wall Pockets, Affordable and Others,* by Marvin and Joy Gibson.

Advisor: Carole Bess White (See Directory, Japan Ceramics)

Baby seated in crook of swan's neck, lustre finish on cream, painted features on baby, Bradley Exclusives/Japan..**$22.00**

Basket, embossed floral design in yellow, green & blue lustre w/bold black trim, Japan, 7½", from $25 to ...**$40.00**

Basket w/flowers & butterfly, multicolored lustre, Japan, 6½"..**$25.00**

Bird on basketweave hanging nest, w/embossed floral branch, multicolors on cream, Japan, 8"...............**$12.00**

Bird on flowerpot, multicolored lustre finish, Made in Japan, 6½"...**$40.00**

Birds (3) on a branch, black angled pocket w/dark orange blossoms, blue & green birds w/white breasts, Japan, 7¼"...**$25.00**

Bluebird on basket, ceramic, unmarked, 8¼", from $20.00 to $25.00. (Photo courtesy Fredda Perkins)

Bottle, bulbous ribbed body w/tapered neck, 2-tone glossy finish, Japan, 4¼"......................................**$10.00**

Carrots, 3 glossy orange carrots w/green tops, 5½", from $20 to **$35.00**

Cat (winking) climbing wall, w/neck bow, color accents on white, 7"...**$10.00**

Cat playing mandolin on conical form, multicolored lustre, Japan, 6", from $35 to **$45.00**

Cherub between 2 columns, flesh tones & light browns on white, Japan, 4½"...............................**$14.00**

Chicken & egg w/wrap-around branch, yellow & brown, Japan, 4¼", from $20 to **$300.00**

Colonial lady w/fan, glossy multicolored finish w/gold trim around neckline, Japan, 5¾", from $35 to...........**$50.00**

Conical form (3-sided) w/painted butterfly & blossoms, red & gold w/gold diamond design on black, 8¼"...**$25.00**

Conical form w/bell flowers & butterfly, multicolored lustre, Japan, 8½", from $40 to **$60.00**

Conical form w/embossed oriental man on basketweave, blue, green & black on cream, black rim, Made in Japan, 6"...**$15.00**

Conical form w/flared rim, vertical floral & stripe design w/leaf bottom, glossy multicolors on white, Italy, 9¾" **$22.00**

Conical form w/swirl design, dark green, European, 10"...**$12.00**

Conical form w/vertical corn-row weave, embossed & painted floral decor, twisted rope-type rim, Japan, 5½", $25 to...**$40.00**

Conical leaf form w/embossed butterflies (2), blue & orange on black w/gold veining & trim, Made in Japan, 6".......**$18.00**

Cornucopia w/lady, incised Germany 8922, 7¼".........**$50.00**

Cowboy boot, side view, plain glossy brown, Japan, 3½"..**$7.00**

Cuckoo clock, bird on top & 1 in window, leaf trim, blue, rose & yellow on white, Japan, 5" **$15.00**

Daffodills, 2 in bloom & 2 buds, yellow on green, Japan, stamped #994, 4"...**$12.00**

Duck in flight, horizontal w/wings down, green, white & deep rose w/white ring around neck, 8¼"...........**$20.00**

Duck in flight on crescent moon, painted embossed grass & flowers, Japan, 6¼"..**$15.00**

Dutch boy w/basket & goose against stone wall, multicolored, Made in Japan, 6"..**$18.00**

Fish, arched body (as if jumping out of water), white w/round black eye, 10"...**$25.00**

Fish, round body w/brown airbrushing, glossy finish, Japan, 4"...**$15.00**

Flower w/ruffled edges, yellow w/green stem, Jamy Ceramic Fashions, 6½"...**$25.00**

Frame w/painted bear scene, inscribed Hungry as a Bear, gold-painted filigree trim on white, Japan, 3¾" sq.........**$12.00**

Girl's head w/ponytail, profile, eyes closed, flowers in hair & holding bouquet, UCAGO Ceramics/Japan, 4½"..**$22.00**

Goat & palm trees, greens, browns & black, Made in Japan, 5½x7"...**$20.00**

Horse head, white stylized form w/brown line trim, Made in Japan Pat 64211, 6"...**$15.00**

Horse head in horseshoe, glossy brown, Made in Japan, 8½"...**$25.00**

Indian head form in full headdress, facing forward, multicolored lustre & shiny finish, Japan, 7¼", from $45 to..........**$75.00**

Indian head form in full headdress, profile, med tan skin w/blue & tan airbrushing on white, 6" **$20.00**

Lady dancing, head tilted back & holding out cape, blue w/white flowers, Made in Japan, 8½"..................**$55.00**

Mask on leaf vase, red mask on 3 2-tone green leaves w/flared top, black trim, stamped Wreath w/Blossom, 5¼"...**$15.00**

Pears (2 upside down) & leafy branch, yellow, green & brown glossy finish, Made in Japan, 4½"..............**$12.00**

Pitcher w/painted bird motif, outlined bird w/hash-mark trim, Made in Japan, 6¾"...................**$14.00**

Polar bear, white embossed figure against blue background, penguin's head peeks out between legs, Japan, 5½".......**$30.00**

Pot w/openwork ivy, Walter Wilson, 5"....................**$12.00**

Sailboat, metallic gold & blue lustre, Brown China, 5¾"..**$20.00**

Sailboat, multicolored lustre & shiny finish, Japan, 5¼", from $30 to................**$45.00**

Telephone, wall type w/2 bells, receiver & hand crank on sides, white w/painted floral design, L&F Ceramics, 7"..................**$22.00**

Umbrella, pointing downward w/bow on curved upright handle, painted apple branch on white, Orion sticker, 6½"................**$12.00**

Vase, cream w/brown handles, marked Brown China, 5½"................**$15.00**

Violin w/applied pansy motif, purple, yellow & green on white w/gold accents, 6½".................**$12.00**

Watering can w/painted rooster design, multicolors on white, Halsey Import Co/Japan, 1953, 5"..................**$12.00**

Wallace China

This company operated in California from 1931 until 1964, producing many lines of dinnerware, the most popular of which today are those included in their Westward Ho assortment, Boots and Saddles, Rodeo, and Pioneer Trails. All of these lines were designed by artist Till Goodan, whose signature appears in the design. All are very heavy, their backgrounds are tan, and the designs are done in dark brown. The Rodeo pattern has accents of rust, green, and yellow. When dinnerware with a western theme became so popular a few years ago, Rodeo was reproduced, but the new trademark includes neither 'California' or 'Wallace China.'

Advisor: Marv Fogleman (See Directory, Dinnerware)

Ashtray, Boots & Saddle, 5½", from $45 to.................**$60.00**

Ashtray, Chi Chi Club Palms Springs, 5½", minimum value.................**$50.00**

Bowl, Chuck Wagon, 1955, 6¾".................**$35.00**

Bowl, Festival, 1x4¾" dia.................**$30.00**

Bowl, Shadowleaf, 6½".................**$35.00**

Bowl, vegetable; Rodeo, oval, 12".................**$250.00**

Butter pat, Hibiscus, from $40 to.................**$45.00**

Creamer, Rodeo, 3½", from $100 to.................**$120.00**

Creamer, Shadowleaf, individual, 3x1½" dia, from $25 to.**$45.00**

Cup, roses, white on pink.................**$22.50**

Cup & saucer, Rodeo, lg.................**$75.00**

Mug, coffee; Chuck Wagon.................**$80.00**

Pitcher, water; Bird of Paradise, w/ice lip.................**$150.00**

Pitcher, water; Rodeo, 72-oz.................**$315.00**

Pitcher, water; Shadowleaf, w/ice lip.................**$150.00**

Plate, Apache Land Village Globe, 9½", minimum value..**$100.00**

Plate, Boots & Saddle, 7".................**$70.00**

Plate, Boots & Saddle, 9", from $95 to.................**$125.00**

Plate, Boots & Saddle, 10½", from $95 to.................**$115.00**

Plate, Little Buckaroo, 9", from $125 to.................**$150.00**

Plate, Rodeo, 7¼", from $55 to.................**$65.00**

Plate, Rodeo, 10¾", from $100 to.................**$125.00**

Plate, Surfer Girl, 10½".................**$50.00**

Plate, 49er, 6¼".................**$22.50**

Salt & pepper shakers, Rodeo, 3½", pr.................**$125.00**

Saucer, Chuck Wagon.................**$20.00**

Sugar bowl, Rodeo, w/lid, from $125 to.................**$150.00**

Watt Pottery

The Watt Pottery Company operated in Crooksville, Ohio, from 1922 until sometime in 1935. It appeals to collectors of country antiques, since the body is yellow ware and its decoration rather quaint.

Several patterns were made: Apple, Autumn Foliage, Cherry, Dutch Tulip, Morning-Glory, Pansy, Rooster, Tear Drop, Starflower, and Tulip among them. All were executed in bold brush strokes of primary colors. Some items you'll find will also carry a stenciled advertising message, made for retail companies as premiums for their customers.

For further study, we recommend *Watt Pottery, An Identification and Price Guide,* by Sue and Dave Morris, published by Collector Books.

Advisor: Sue Morris (See Directory, Dinnerware)

Club/Newsletter:
Watt Collectors Association
1431 4th St. SW
PMB 221, Mason City, IA 50401

Apple, baking dish, unmarked, 2¼x5¼x10"..........**$1,500.00**

Apple, bean pot, 2-handled, #76, 6½x7½".................**$175.00**

Apple, bowl, #106, 3½x10¾".................**$350.00**

Apple, bowl, cereal/salad; #52, 2¼x6½".................**$50.00**

Apple, bowl, mixing; #5, 2¾x5".................**$65.00**

Apple, bowl, mixing; #9, 5x9".................**$85.00**

Apple, bowl, mixing; #64, 5x7½".................**$60.00**

Apple, bowl, mixing; ribbed, #602, 1¾x4¾".................**$125.00**

Apple, bowl, spaghetti; individual, #44, 1½x8".................**$400.00**

Apple, bowl, w/lid, #67, 6½x8½".................**$125.00**

Apple, canister, w/lid, #72, 9½x7".................**$500.00**

Apple, casserole, French handled, individual, #18, 4x8"..**$225.00**

Apple, casserole, tab handled, #18, 4x5".................**$225.00**

Apple, coffeepot, w/lid, #115, 9¾x7".................**$3,000.00**

Apple, cookie jar, #503, 8¼x8¼".................**$450.00**

Apple, creamer, #62, 4¼x4½".................**$90.00**

Apple, cruets, oil & vinegar; w/lids, marked w/V or O on front, 7", pr.................**$1,800.00**

Apple, fondue pot, w/out lid, 3x9".................**$900.00**

Apple, mug, #61, 3x3¼".................**$500.00**

Apple, mug, #121.................**$185.00**

Apple, pie plate, #33, 1½x9" $150.00
Apple, pitcher, #15, 5½x5¾" $75.00
Apple, plate, dinner; #101, 10" $600.00
Apple, plate, dinner; no mark on bottom, 9½".......$450.00
Apple, platter, #31, 15" dia $350.00
Apple, salt & pepper shakers, barrel shape, 4x2", pr ...$600.00
Apple, salt & pepper shakers, hourglass shape, raised letters on front, 4½x2½", pr.....................................$275.00
Apple, sugar bowl, w/lid, #98, 4½x5" $400.00
Apple, tumbler, #56, 4½x4" **$1,000.00**
Apple (Double), bowl, #73, 4x9" **$125.00**
Apple (Double), bowl, mixing; #06, 3x6" $75.00
Apple (Double), creamer, #62, 4½x4½" **$400.00**
Autumn Foliage, creamer, #62, 4¼x4½" $200.00
Autumn Foliage, cruets, oil & vinegar; w/lids, #126, 7", pr **$550.00**
Autumn Foliage, pie plate, #33, 1½x9" $125.00
Autumn Foliage, platter, #31, 15" dia $110.00
Autumn Foliage, sugar bowl, w/lid, #98, 4½x5".......$300.00
Autumn Foliage, teapot, #505, 5¾x9" **$1,600.00**
Banded (Blue & White), casserole, w/lid, 4½x8¾" $45.00
Banded (Green & White), bowl, #9, 5x9" $25.00
Banded (White), pitcher, 7x7¾" $85.00
Basketweave, mug, cream, #806, made for Heirloom Stoneware Co, 5¼x3¼" $15.00
Brown-Banded, mug, #121, 3¾x3".....................$125.00
Butterfly, bowl, #7, 4x7" $275.00
Cherry, bowl, mixing; #8, 4x8" $45.00
Cherry, casserole, w/lid, #3/19, 5x9" $175.00
Cherry, pitcher, salesman's sample, #15 ....$200.00
Cherry, pitcher, w/advertising, #15, 5½x5¾".......$175.00
Cherry, planter, #31, 15" dia $145.00
Cut-Leaf Pansy, creamer & sugar bowl, pr.............$175.00

Cut-Leaf Pansy, cup and saucer, $90.00.

Cut-Leaf Pansy, Dutch oven, w/lid, 7x10½".............$175.00
Cut-Leaf Pansy, platter, 15" dia.................................$110.00
Cut-Leaf Pansy, saucer, bull's eye pattern w/swirl, 6½"...$20.00
Dutch Tulip, bean pot, 2-handled, #76, 6½x7½"......$350.00
Dutch Tulip, bowl, w/lid, #05, 4x5" $250.00
Dutch Tulip, pitcher, refrigerator; #69, 8x8½"..........$600.00
Dutch Tulip, plate, divided; unmarked, 10½" dia.....$800.00
Eagle, bowl, cereal; #74, 2x5½".................................$85.00
Eagle, pitcher, w/ice lip, unmarked, 8x8½" $450.00

Esmond, platter, 15"...$175.00
Goodies, jar, #72, 9½x7½"................................$350.00
Kitch-N-Queen, bowl, mixing; plain sides, #14, 7x14"...$60.00
Kitch-N-Queen, bowl, mixing; ribbed, #5, 2¾x5"......$60.00
Kitch-N-Queen, bowl, mixing; ribbed, #9, 5x9" $55.00
Kitch-N-Queen, cookie jar, w/lid, #503, 8¼x8¼" $225.00
Kla Ham'rd, bowl, 4½x6½".................................$25.00
Morning Glory, cookie jar, w/lid, #95, 10¾x7½"......$400.00
Morning Glory, creamer, #97, 4¼x4½".............$500.00
Morning Glory, pitcher, w/ice lip, #96, 8x8½"..........$375.00
Morning Glory, sugar bowl, #98, 4¼x5".............$250.00
Old Pansy, bowl, spaghetti; #39, no black band, 3x13" ..$80.00
Old Pansy, casserole, #2/48, 4¼x7½"..................$75.00
Old Pansy, pitcher, cross-hatch pansy pattern, 7x7¾"..$275.00
Old Pansy, platter, #49, 12" dia $85.00
Peedeeco, casserole, stick handled, individual, 3¾x7½"...$25.00
Raised Pansy, casserole, French handled, individual, 3¾x7½"...$90.00
Raised Pansy, pitcher, 7x7¾"............................$225.00
Rooster, bowl, w/lid, #05, 4x5" $190.00
Rooster, ice bucket, unmarked, 7¼x7½"............$275.00
Rooster, pitcher, refrigerator; sq shape, #69, 8x8½"..$550.00
Rooster, salt & pepper shakers, hourglass shape, holes in top depict S or P, 4½x2½", pr..................$40.00
Rooster, sugar bowl, w/lid, #98, 4½x5"............$500.00
Shaded Brown, cookie jar, 7½x7".......................$35.00
Shaded Brown, mug, unmarked, 3x3¾".............$10.00
Speckled Watt Ware, bowl, #120, part of chip 'n dip set, 2x5"...$10.00
Starflower, bean pot, 2-handled, #76, 6½x7½" $175.00
Starflower, bowl, berry; 1½x5¾".......................$35.00
Starflower, cookie jar, w/lid, #21, 7½x7" $185.00
Starflower, creamer, #62, 4¼x4½" $250.00
Starflower, grease jar, w/lid, #47, 5x4½"...........$250.00
Starflower, ice bucket, w/lid, 7¼x7½" $185.00
Starflower, mug, #121, 3¾x3"............................$275.00
Starflower, pie plate, #33, 1½x9".......................$200.00
Starflower, pitcher, refrigerator; sq shape, #69, 8x8½" 2"..$700.00
Starflower, pitcher, w/ice lip, #17, 8x8½".................$175.00
Starflower, platter, #31, 15" $110.00
Starflower, salt & pepper shakers, hourglass shape, raised letters on front, 4½x2½", pr..........................$275.00
Starflower, salt & pepper shakers, red & green bands, barrel shape, 4x2½", pr..$375.00
Starflower, tumbler, round-sided, #56, 4x3½" $275.00
Starflower, tumbler, slant-sided, #56, 4½x4"............$325.00
Starflower (Green on Brown), bowl, mixing; #5, 2¾x5"..$35.00
Starflower (Green on Brown), tumbler, #56, 4½x4"..$175.00
Starflower (Pink on Black), casserole, w/lid, 4½x8¾".$125.00
Starflower (Pink on Green), cup & saucer $65.00
Starflower (Pink on Green), plate, bread; 6½" dia $35.00
Starflower (White on Blue), bowl, spaghetti; #39, 3x13".$250.00
Starflower (White on Green), bowl, #39, 3x13" $100.00
Starflower (White on Red), mug, #121, 3¾x3"..........$400.00
Tear Drop, bean server, #75, individual, 2¼x3½".......$30.00
Tear Drop, bowl, #66, 3x7"...................................$45.00
Tear Drop, bowl, #73, 4x9½" $130.00

Tear Drop, casserole, sq shape, w/lid, 6x8" **$850.00**
Tear Drop, cheese crock, #80, 8x8¼" **$375.00**
Tear Drop, creamer, #62, 4¼x4½" **$275.00**
Tear Drop, salt & pepper shakers, barrel shape, 4x2½", pr..**$350.00**
Tulip, bowl, nesting; #602, 4¾" dia **$275.00**
Tulip, creamer, #62, 4¼x4½" **$225.00**
Tulip, pitcher, #15, 5½x5¾" **$550.00**
White Daisy, plate, salad; marked Watt USA, 8½" dia ..**$65.00**
Woodgrain, bowl, chip 'n dip; #61, 2¾x11¼" **$75.00**
Woodgrain, cookie jar, #617W, 11x8" **$90.00**

Weeping Gold

In the mid- to late 1950s, many American pottery companies produced lines of 'Weeping Gold.' Such items have a distinctive appearance; most appear to be covered with irregular droplets of lustrous gold, sometimes heavy, sometimes fine. On others the gold is in random swirls, or there may be a definite pattern developed on the surface. In fact, real gold was used; however, there is no known successful way of separating the gold from the pottery. You'll see similar pottery covered in 'Weeping Silver.' Very often, ceramic whiskey decanters made for Beam, McCormick, etc., will be trimmed in 'Weeping Gold.' Among the marks you'll find on these wares are 'McCoy,' 'Kingwood Ceramics,' and 'USA,' but most items are simply stamped '22k (or 24k) gold.'

Pitcher, Jim Beam, from $25.00 to $40.00.

Ashtray, hands, 3-footed, Hand Painted 22k Gold USA Weeping-Bright Gold, 1½x5x3¾" **$25.00**
Bowl, centerpc; marked Hand Decorated Weeping Bright Gold, w/handles, 10x5¾" **$18.50**
Candy dish, ruffled edge, marked Hand Decorated 22k Gold USA Weeping Bright Gold, 5x8" **$20.00**
Candy dish, w/star-shape lid, marked Elynor China...**$25.00**
Cup & saucer, demi; marked Hand Decorated 22k Gold USA Weeping Bright Gold....................................**$25.00**

Ewer, marked Holly Ross Distinguished China 22k gold, 11⅜"..**$30.00**
Figurine, panther, 6x11" **$35.00**
Figurine, peacock, tail down, 7x9¾x3"....................**$35.00**
Flower holder, swan, Sunburst, McCoy, 3½x4"...........**$40.00**
Lamp, black enameling at base, 2 handles, 12" to top of socket..**$45.00**
Nut dish, shell shape, #55, marked Hand Decorated Weeping Gold 22k, 5x4½x1½" **$22.50**
Pitcher, marked Elynor China Made in USA, 11½" **$25.00**
Planter, swan form, Hand Decorated Weeping Bright Gold USA, 5x8x3½"....................................**$22.50**
Vase, bud; stick neck, unmarked, 8" **$25.00**
Vase, slim cylinder w/softly rounded shoulder, 11x5" ..**$40.00**
Wall pocket, fan shape, Sunburst, McCoy, 8x8½".......**$75.00**

Weil Ware

Though the Weil company made dinnerware and some kitchenware, their figural pieces are attracting the most collector interest. They were in business from the 1940s until the mid-1950s, another of the small but very successful California companies whose work has become so popular today. They dressed their 'girls' in beautiful gowns of vivid rose, light dusty pink, turquoise blue, and other lovely colors enhanced with enameled 'lace work' and flowers, sgraffito, sometimes even with tiny applied blossoms. Both paper labels and ink stamps were used to mark them, but as you study their features, you'll soon learn to recognize even those that have lost their labels over the years. Four-number codes and decorators' initials are usually written on their bases.

If you want to learn more, we recommend *The Collector's Encyclopedia of California Pottery, Second Edition,* by Jack Chipman.

Bowl, fruit; pink outside & green inside, #726, 14¾x7¾x3½"..**$18.00**
Bowl, vegetable; Yellow Rose, sq, divided, 10½x6¾" ..**$30.00**
Box, Ming Tree, #955, w/lid, 5x5"............................**$45.00**
Butter dish, Malay Bamboo, w/lid................................**$20.00**
Casserole, Malay Bamboo, w/lid & handles, 8x5x3½"..**$60.00**
Coffeepot, Bamboo, pink, w/lid, 7½" **$75.00**
Creamer, Malay Blossom................................**$18.00**
Cup & saucer, Malay Blossom, sq, 2⅜", 5⅞"...............**$15.00**
Figurine, lady in long dress w/hands in muff, wearing hat, 10" **$65.00**
Flower holder, girl in long pink dress carries 2 white cone-shaped baskets, kerchief on head, 9½" **$60.00**
Flower holder, lady in green dress w/flowers sits between short & tall vases, #4039, 9½x6½"....................**$60.00**
Flower holder, lady in long dress, left hand securing lg picture hat, no mark, 10" **$48.00**
Flower holder, lady in long pink dress w/hand-painted flowers stands, rests hands on sq open columns, #4027, lg **$80.00**

Flower holder, lady in long white dress w/rose-colored apron, blue scarf, carrying blue pot in front, #1676, 11"......$65.00

Flower holder, lady in white dress w/flowers pushing cart, #4001, 8¼"......$40.00

Flower holder, lady in white w/blue trim & flowers holds 2 baskets, #4051, 11¼"......$45.00

Flower holder, lady in blue dress w/blue scarf around neck sits between 2 planters, 8½"......$45.00

Gravy boat w/underplate, Yellow Rose, 1-pc, 4" H....$30.00

Pitcher, water; Malay Bamboo, w/ice lip, 8½"......$30.00

Plate, bread & butter; Malay Blossom, sq, 6"......$8.00

Plate, dinner; Malay Blossom, sq, 9¾"......$15.00

Platter, Yellow Rose, sq, 13"......$15.00

Relish tray, Malay Blossom, 3-section, 6x9"......$25.00

Saucer, Malay Blossom, sq......$8.00

Snack plate, Malay Blossom, w/cup indentation, 12¼" sq, w/matching sq cup......$20.00

Spoon holder, Yellow Rose, 4¼x8"......$65.00

Sugar bowl, Malay Blossom, w/lid......$25.00

Vase, Ming Tree, slanted top, #915, 11"......$25.00

Vase, Ming Tree, sq, 8½x4½"......$15.00

Vase, seashell, #720, 6x9"......$30.00

Wall pocket, boy sits between 2 pots on shelf, #4046, 10"..$45.00

Weller

Though the Weller Pottery has been closed since 1948, they were so prolific that you'll be sure to see several pieces anytime you're 'antiquing.' They were one of the largest of the art pottery giants that located in the Zanesville, Ohio, area, using locally dug clays to produce their wares. In the early years, they made hand-decorated vases, jardinieres, lamps, and other useful and decorative items for the home, many of which were signed by notable artists such as Fredrick Rhead, John Lessell, Virginia Adams, Anthony Dunlavy, Dorothy England, Albert Haubrich, Hester Pillsbury, E.L. Pickens, and Jacques Sicard, to name only a few. Some of their early lines were First and Second Dickens, Eocean, Sicardo, Etna, Louwelsa, Turada, and Aurelian. Portraits of Indians, animals of all types, lady golfers, nudes, and scenes of Dickens stories were popular themes, and some items were overlaid with silver filigree. These lines are rather hard to find at this point in time, and prices are generally high; but there's plenty of their later production still around, and some pieces are relatively inexpensive.

If you'd like to learn more, we recommend *The Collector's Encyclopedia of Weller Pottery* by Sharon and Bob Huxford.

Arcadia, bud vase, leaf formed on round base, 7½", from $25 to......$30.00

Arcadia, fan vase, leaf form, 8x15", from $90 to......$100.00

Atlas, candle holders, 5-point star shape, #C-12, pr, from $95 to......$110.00

Atlas, covered dish, 5-point star shape, #C-2, from $125 to......$175.00

Barcelona, candle holder, painted flower design on round flat base w/integral cup, 2x5" dia, from $75 to..$100.00

Barcelona, vase, handles from ruffled rim to hip, painted flower medallion on horizontal ribbing, 8", from $200 to......$250.00

Blossom, basket, ball shape w/scrolled handle, blossom decor, 6", from $75 to......$85.00

Blossom, cornucopia, embossed floral decor, 8½", from $60 to......$70.00

Blossom, double vase, branch handle connects 2 vases w/ruffled rims, flared base, blossom decor, #G-12, 12½", from $125 to......$175.00

Blossom, vase, 9½", from $75.00 to $85.00.

Blue Drapery, bowl, roses on drapery-type ground, 3", from $55 to......$65.00

Blue Drapery, jardiniere, straight tapered sides, roses on drapery-type ground, 5", from $100 to......$125.00

Bonito, bowl, painted flower w/leaf band around rim, artist initialed CF, 3½", from $100 to......$135.00

Bonito, vase, flared, painted flower on leafy stem w/blue band, 5", from $100 to......$135.00

Bouquet, bowl vase, 3-footed, #B-3, 4½", from $35 to..$40.00

Bouquet, vase, cylindrical w/slightly flared rim & round base, embossed floral decor, #B-7, from $75 to......$85.00

Bouquet, vase, round pot w/straight upright rim, embossed floral design, #B-6, from $35 to......$40.00

Bouquet, vase, sm loop handles at wavy rim on urn tapering to flat bottom, dogwood branch decor, #B-15, 5", from $45 to......$50.00

Cactus, frog, 4", from $100 to......$125.00

Cactus, Pan w/lily, 5", from $100 to......$125.00

Cactus, planter, dachshund, 4½x8½", from $100 to.$125.00

Cameo, hanging basket, tulip-shaped bowl w/scalloped rim, white embossed flowers on pastel, 5", from $85 to......$110.00

Cameo, planter, oblong w/incurvate sides, plain rim, embossed white flowers on pastel, 4", from $65 to......$75.00

Cameo, vase, sq w/flat bottom, embossed white flowers on pastel, 8½", from $65 to......$75.00

Chengtu, ginger jar, tapered, footed, Chinese Red, 12", from $225 to......$275.00

Chengtu, vase, 4-sided w/flared rim & base, Chinese Red, 9", from $100 to................................**$125.00**

Clarmont, candlestick, ribbed column w/grape design on cup & round base, 10", from $100 to................**$150.00**

Classic, wall pocket, wide fan shape w/cut-out scallops & embossed flowers forming rim, 6", from $125 to .**$150.00**

Classic, window box, oblong w/fan-shaped cut-out scallops & embossed flowers forming rim, 4", from $75 to......**$85.00**

Coppertone, candle holder, water lily form, 2", from $75 to................................**$85.00**

Coppertone, pitcher, fish handle, 7½", from $900 to..**$1,100.00**

Coppertone, vase, flared scalloped rim, 6½", from $150 to................................**$200.00**

Cornish, bowl, ball-shaped w/sm scrolled handles, berry & leaf design over ribbed band, 4", from $55 to **$65.00**

Cornish, vase, tapered w/plain wide rim, sm scrolled handles, berry & leaf design over ribbed band, 6", from $65 to................................**$75.00**

Creamware, bowl, footed w/blue cameo & open pattern, handled, 2½", from $50 to................................**$60.00**

Creamware, Decorated; mug, painted floral design, 5", from $100 to................................**$125.00**

Creamware, Decorated; vase, shouldered w/plain rim, tapered, painted grape & geometric design, 11½", from $300 to................................**$400.00**

Creamware, planter, footed sq form w/sq handles, blue & brown geometric & open pattern, 3", from $55 to .**$65.00**

Darsie, vase, bulbous w/plain flared rim, tasseled rope swag design, 5½", from $45 to................................**$55.00**

Darsie, vase, cylindrical w/flared scalloped rim, tasseled rope swag design, 7½", from $50 to................................**$60.00**

Delsa, basket, footed tulip shape w/embossed pansy decor on textured ground, 7", from $85 to................**$95.00**

Delsa, vase, cylindrical w/wide flared scalloped rim, tapers to footed base, embossed floral decor, 6", from $40 to................................**$50.00**

Elberta, bowl w/frog, round w/6-pointed rim, green & brown shading, 10", from $150 to................................**$200.00**

Elberta, cornucopia vase, shaded browns, 8", from $85 to..**$95.00**

Elberta, nut dish, irregular pinched rim, brown & green shading, 3", from $55 to................................**$65.00**

Fleron, batter pitcher, ribbed, 11½", from $200 to....**$250.00**

Fleron, ribbed w/ruffled rim, flared base, 9", from $125 to................................**$175.00**

Fleron, vase, ribbed w/ruffled rim, contoured sides, 8½", from $125 to................................**$175.00**

Floral, console bowl, boat shape w/upturned ends, rose & swag decor, #F-9, 4½x10", from $50 to................**$60.00**

Florenzo, fan vase, fluted w/flower & berries on swagged branch, 5½", from $55 to................................**$65.00**

Florenzo, planter, sq fluted & 4-footed pot w/roses & branch design, 3½", from $55 to................................**$65.00**

Florenzo, window box, fluted oblong shape w/flower & berry swag design, 3", from $55 to................................**$70.00**

Forest, basket, woodland scene, 8½", from $250 to.**$300.00**

Forest, pitcher, woodland scene, glossy, 5", from $200 to...**$250.00**

Forest, vase, woodland scene, 12", from $250 to **$350.00**

Gloria, bowl, sq w/pinched rim, stemmed flower & leaf design, #G-15, from $50 to................................**$60.00**

Gloria, double vase, 2 lg cups w/ruffled rims, stemmed flower & leaf design, 4½", from $50 to................**$60.00**

Gloria, ewer, bulbous w/handle from rim to shoulder, stemmed flower & leaf design, #G-12, from $85 to................**$100.00**

Goldenglow, ginger jar, handled, blossom & leaf design, 8", from $225 to................................**$275.00**

Goldenglow, triple candle holder, fluted cups on scrolled base, 7½", from $150 to................................**$175.00**

Greenbriar, ewer, ribbed w/double-loop handles from rim to shoulder, drip glazes, 11½", from $250 to..........**$300.00**

Greenbriar, smooth bulbous form w/rolled rim, drip glazes, 8½", from $175 to................................**$225.00**

Greora, strawberry vase, textured mottling over brown shading, 5", from $125 to................................**$150.00**

Greora, vase, 3-sided & 3-footed, textured mottling over shading, 4½", from $75 to................................**$85.00**

Ivoris, basket, footed, serrated rim, floral decor, 5", from $85 to................................**$95.00**

Ivoris, powder box, w/lid, 4", from $40 to................**$50.00**

Lido, basket, swirled bowl w/ruffled rim forming handle, 8½", from $85 to................................**$95.00**

Lido, ewer, swirled, 10½", from $95 to................**$115.00**

Lido, planter, leaf form w/scrolled stem, 2x9", from $25 to................................**$30.00**

Loru, bowl, incurvate sides, scalloped rim, embossed leafy design, 2½x8", from $40 to................................**$45.00**

Loru, cornucopia, scalloped rim, 4", from $25 to **$35.00**

Loru, vase, cylindrical w/vertical panels & slightly flared scalloped rim, embossed leafy decor, 8½", from $70 to................................**$80.00**

Loru, vase, 11", from $75.00 to $85.00.

Louella, basket, painted flower decor on drapery-type ground, 6½", from $100 to................................**$130.00**

Louella, vase, bulbous w/ruffled rim, integral loop handles, painted flower on drapery-type ground, 8", from $100 to................................**$130.00**

Malverne, console bowl & frog, irregular shape w/flower-shaped tab handles, flower-shaped frog, 2x14½", from $225 to..**$275.00**

Malverne, wall pocket, conical form w/bud & leaf design, 11", from $200 to..**$250.00**

Manhattan, vase, tapered w/wide flared rim, flowers & lattice work around base, 5½", from $35 to....................**$40.00**

Marvo, double bud vase, gate type w/leafy design between 2 tree trunks, 5", from $85 to................................**$95.00**

Marvo, hanging basket, bowl w/allover flower & leaf design, 5", from $125 to................................**$150.00**

Melrose, basket, grape branch & blossom decor, branch handle, 10", from $200 to................................**$250.00**

Melrose, console bowl, footed w/ruffled rim & upturned handles, rose branch decor, 5x8½", from $125 to................................**$150.00**

Mi-Flo, bowl, round w/upturned tab handles, rolled rim, embossed flowers & fluted design, 4", from $50 to..**$60.00**

Noval, candlestick, column w/blossoms around black-trimmed cup & handles, apples at trimmed base, 9½", from $125 to................................**$150.00**

Noval, compote, black trim on cream w/applied apple handles & finial on lid, 9½", from $200 to................**$250.00**

Novelty Line, frog & lotus blossom, 4", from $85 to..**$95.00**

Novelty Line, kangaroo w/open pouch, 5½", from $100 to................................**$125.00**

Oak Leaf, basket, ball shape w/branch handle, embossed oak leaf design, #G-1, 7½", from $85 to............**$110.00**

Oak Leaf, bowl, boat shape w/irregular rim, embossed oak leaf design, 3½", from $60 to................................**$70.00**

Oak Leaf, wall pocket, conical form w/embossed oak leaf design, 8½", from $125 to................................**$150.00**

Panella, bowl, 3-footed, incurvate rim, pansy decor, 3½", from $40 to................................**$45.00**

Panella, cornucopia, scalloped rim, pansy decor, 5½", from $45 to................................**$55.00**

Panella, ginger jar, tapers to tall round flared base, ear-shaped handles, pansy decor, 6½", from $100 to............**$125.00**

Paragon, candle holders, straight-sided cups on round bases, 2", pr, from $125 to................................**$150.00**

Pastel, planter, swirled heart form, #P-10, 6", from $50 to................................**$60.00**

Pastel, vase, 4-sided & 4-footed flared shape, #P-17, 6", from $30 to................................**$35.00**

Patra, nut dish, textured w/pinched rim, single handle, #2, 3", from $75 to................................**$85.00**

Patra, vase, textured w/stylized floral design at pinched rim, 3-footed, 5", from $125 to................................**$150.00**

Patricia, planter, duck form, 2¼", from $45 to............**$50.00**

Patricia, squatty urn w/bottle neck, 2 swan-head handles, 4", from $75 to................................**$85.00**

Pearl, bowl, embossed pearl swags w/sq flowers, 3", from $115 to................................**$140.00**

Pearl, wall vase, pearls draped over rose band at rim, 7", from $175 to................................**$225.00**

Pierre, pitcher, embossed basketweave pattern, 7½", from $75 to................................**$100.00**

Pierre, sugar bowl, embossed basketweave pattern, open, 2", from $10 to................................**$15.00**

Pierre, teapot, embossed basketweave pattern, 8½", from $100 to................................**$150.00**

Raydance, vase, bulbous w/wide rim, scrolled handles, leaf design, 7½", from $40 to................................**$45.00**

Roba, vase, bulbous V-shaped ruffled rim, flowers & branch form handles, flared base, textured, #R-2, 9", from $100 to................................**$125.00**

Roba, vase, handles from flared scalloped rim to top of shoulder, tapers to flared base, floral decor, #R-2, 9", $100 to................................**$125.00**

Roba, wall pocket, cornucopia form w/embossed floral branch decor, 10", from $175 to................................**$225.00**

Rosemont, jardiniere, bluebird on floral branch on black, integral handles, 6½", from $300 to................**$350.00**

Rosemont, jardiniere, vase, waisted w/bluebird on branch on black, 10", from $350 to................................**$400.00**

Rudlor, console bowl, boat shape w/4 bead handle at ea end, floral branch decor, 4½x17½", from $100 to......**$125.00**

Rudlor, vase, slightly bulbous footed cylinder w/upside down ear-shaped handles, blossom & branch decor, 9", $40 to................................**$50.00**

Sabrinian, window box, oblong w/shell motif, 3½x9", from $175 to................................**$225.00**

Scandia, bowl, black incised leaf design on tan band around rim on black, 3", from $65 to................................**$75.00**

Senic, planter, footed bowl w/irregular ruffled rim, palm tree design, #S-17, 5½", from $85 to................................**$95.00**

Senic, vase, tapered bucket shape w/scalloped rim, 2 sm tab handles, embossed landscape scene, #S-9, 8", from $100 to................................**$125.00**

Senic, vase, 3-footed ball form w/flared ruffled rim, embossed scene, #S-1, 5", from $50 to................**$60.00**

Silvertone, basket, fan shape w/grape motif, branch handle, 13", from $400 to................................**$450.00**

Softone, candle holder, cup w/swag design on flat round base, 2½", from $20 to................................**$25.00**

Softone, double bud vase, center handle connects 2 cylinders, 9", from $30 to................................**$35.00**

Stellar, vase, bulbous, star design over matt finish, 5½", from $400 to................................**$500.00**

Sydonia, cornucopia vase, slender form, mottled texture, 8", from $70 to................................**$80.00**

Sydonia, fan vase, 2-tone mottled texture, 6½", from $85 to................................**$95.00**

Turkis, vase, angled bowl w/angled handles from rolled rim to hip, drip glaze over dark plum, 5½", from $125 to................................**$150.00**

Turkis, vase, ruffled rim, flared base, drip glaze over dark plum, 8", from $150 to................................**$175.00**

Tutone, vase, cylindrical w/irregular rim & flared flat base, blossom & leaf design, 12½", from $200 to.......**$250.00**

Tutone, vase/candle holder, crescent shape w/flower & berry decor, 7", from $110 to................................**$135.00**

Tutone, wall pocket, angled conical form w/leaf design, 10½", from $250 to................................**$275.00**

Utility Ware, flowerpot/jar, tapers to flat bottom, painted plaid design, 3½", from $25 to **$30.00**

Utility Ware, pitcher, straight-sided w/embossed ribbing, 5½", from $40 to...**$50.00**

Utility Ware, teapot, pineapple form, 6½", from $150 to...**$200.00**

Vase, tapered on round base, plain wide rim, vertical leaf design, 9", from $85 to...**$95.00**

Velva, vase, footed bulbous form w/upturned handles, leafy floral branch down front, 9", from $100 to **$125.00**

Velva, vase, footed shouldered form w/upturned handles, leafy floral branch panel down front, 7½", from $65 to..**$75.00**

Warwick, planter, 3-footed irregular shape w/single branch handle, 3½", from $95 to **$120.00**

Warwick, vase, textured tree trunk w/blossom & leafy branch design, 9½", from $125 to.....................................**$150.00**

Wild Rose, console bowl, boat shape w/flared ends, oval base, rose & leaves on branch design, 6½", from $25 to..**$30.00**

Wild Rose, triple candle holder, 3 horn-shaped holders on single base, rose design, 6", from $75 to............**$100.00**

Wild Rose, vase, curved V-shaped rim, handles curved from middle to top of flared base, rose design, 8½", from $45 to..**$55.00**

Woodcraft, ashtray, tree stump form w/oak leaf, 3", from $125 to..**$150.00**

Woodcraft, bud vase, tree trunk form w/apple branch handles, 6½", from $55 to...**$65.00**

Woodcraft, hanging basket, conical form w/flared scalloped rim, apple branch decor, 6", from $125 to **$150.00**

Woodcraft, vase, owl in knothole, 13", from $800.00 to $1,000.00; tankard, foxes in den, 12", from $1,100.00 to $1,250.00.

Woodrose, vase, straight-sided wooden bucket form w/rose motif, 7", from $75 to **$85.00**

Woodrose, wall pocket, flared wooden bucket form w/rose motif, 6", from $100 to **$125.00**

Zona, pitcher, apple branch on cream, branch handle, 6", from $100 to...**$125.00**

Zona, pitcher, cream; duck motif on white, brown trim, 3½", from $90 to...**$100.00**

Zona, platter, apple branch & berries on cream, 12", from $60 to..**$85.00**

Zona, teapot, apple branch on cream, branch handle, 5", from $100 to...**$125.00**

West Coast Pottery

This was a small company operating in the 1940s and 1950s in Burbank, California. The founders were Lee and Bonnie Wollard; they produced decorative pottery such as is listed here. For more information on this company as well as many others, we recommend *The Collector's Encyclopedia of California Pottery* by Jack Chipman (Collector Books).

Figurine, bird, pink & green, #343, 9¾" **$13.50**

Flowerpot, ribbed sides w/incurvate top edge, #416, 4¼x7"...**$12.50**

Planter, conch shell w/lg opening, green, #842, 7¼" .**$20.00**

Planter, shell shape, turquoise blue, #613, 14x4x6" **$30.00**

Planter/vase, seashell on base, burgundy, #850, 6x9½" **$15.00**

Vase, embossed parrot, yellow, #463, 10"...................**$40.00**

Vase, hand-painted bird and flowers, designed by Ken Wheeler/#602, $65.00. (Photo courtesy Jack Chipman)

Wall pocket, feather-like w/scrolled ends, burgundy/gray, #305, 6x8½", pr...**$20.00**

Western Collectibles

Although the Wild West era ended over one hundred years ago, today cowboy gear is a hot area of collecting. These historic collectibles are not just found out West. Some of the most exceptional pieces have come from the East

Coast states and the Midwest. But that should come as no surprise when you consider that the largest manufacturer of bits and spurs was the August Buemann Co. of Newark, New Jersey (1868 – 1926).

For more information refer to *Old West Cowboy Collectibles Auction Update & Price Guide*, which lists auction-realized prices of more than 650 lots, with complete descriptions and numerous photos. You can obtain a copy from our advisor, Dan Hutchins.

Advisor: Dan Hutchins (See Directory, Western Collectibles)

Bit, engraved silver & copper broken heart, 7 silver spots & sm silver heart, EX...................**$80.00**
Bit & bridle, leather w/silver studs, VG....................**$140.00**
Boots, black leather w/white flowers & butterflies stitched in red & yellow, sq toe, 1940s, EX.........................**$300.00**
Boots, leather, black w/tan uppers w/butterfly design, 1940s, EX..**$265.00**
Bowie knife, bone handle wrapped in brass, 19th C, 11" blade, 15½" overall, EX....................................**$1,750.00**
Branding iron, saddlebag style, EX............................**$60.00**
Cowboy boots, marked Kirkendall's Bench Made, w/original spurs, 1930s, EX...**$380.00**
Cuffs, snakeskin w/elk hide liner, w/fringe, EX, pr....**$90.00**
Fence tool, hammer head & nail puller, fits on saddle horn, cast iron, marked Atomic Glaskin Mfg, EX.........**$110.00**

Hat, brown Stetson 7X Beaver, ca 1950, MIB, $110.00.

Holsters, FA Meanea Co, leather, double loop, matched pr, EX **$375.00**
Saddle, cowboy; wooden stirrups, tooled images, JC Higgins, 1950s, EX...**$160.00**
Spurs, hand-crafted wrought iron w/silver overlay w/floral pattern, EX **$300.00**
Spurs, wrought iron w/card suits in silver overlay, pr..**$275.00**

Westmoreland Glass

The Westmoreland Specialty Company was founded in 1889 in Grapeville, Pennsylvania. Their mainstay was a line of opalware (later called milk glass) which included such pieces as cream and sugar sets and novel tea jars (i.e., Teddy Roosevelt Bear Jar, Oriental Tea Jars, and Dutch Tea Jar), as well as a number of covered animal dishes such as hens and roosters on nests. All of these pieces were made as condiment containers and originally held baking soda and Westmoreland's own mustard recipe. By 1900 they had introduced a large vari-

ety of pressed tablewares in clear glass and opal, although their condiment containers were still very popular. By 1910 they were making a large line of opal souvenir novelties with hand-painted decorations of palm trees, Dutch scenes, etc. They also made a variety of decorative vases painted in the fashion of Rookwood Pottery, plus sprayed finishes with decorations of flowers, fruits, animals, and Indians. Westmoreland gained great popularity with their line of painted, hand-decorated wares. They also made many fancy-cut items.

These lines continued in production until 1939, when the Brainard family became full owners of the factory. The Brainards discontinued the majority of patterns made previously under the West management and introduced dinnerware lines, made primarily of milk glass, with limited production of black glass and blue milk glass. Colored glass was not put back into full production until 1964 when Westmoreland introduced Golden Sunset, Avocado, Brandywine Blue, and Ruby.

The company made only limited quantities of carnival glass in the early 1900s and then re-introduced it in 1972 when most of their carnival glass was made in limited editions for the Levay Distributing Company. J.H. Brainard, president of Westmoreland, sold the factory to Dave Grossman in 1981, and he, in turn, closed the factory in 1984. Westmoreland first used the stamped W over G logo in 1949 and continued using it until Dave Grossman bought the factory. Mr. Grossman changed the logo to a W with the word Westmoreland forming a circle around the W.

Milk glass was always Westmoreland's main line of production. In the 1950s they became famous for their milk glass tableware in the #1881 Paneled Grape pattern. It was designed by Jess Billups, the company's mold maker. The first piece he made was the water goblet. Items were gradually added until a complete dinner service was available. It became their most successful dinnerware line, and today it is highly collectible, primarily because of the excellence of the milk glass itself. No other company has been able to match Westmoreland's milk glass in color, texture, quality, or execution of design and pattern.

Advisor: Cheryl Schafer (See Directory, Westmoreland)

Covered Animal Dishes

Camel, Green or Yellow Mist, ea **$125.00**
Cat on rectangular lacy base, caramel, green or purple marbled, ea...**$250.00**
Cat on rectangular lacy base, milk glass....................**$125.00**
Cat on vertical rib base, milk glass, 5½"......................**$40.00**
Cat on vertical rib base, purple marbled, 5½" **$75.00**
Chick on oval 2-handled basket, Antique Blue...........**$65.00**
Chick on oval 2-handled basket, milk glass, 4" **$30.00**
Chick on oval 2-handled basket, milk glass w/22k gold or red accents, Apricot Mist......................................**$50.00**
Chick on pile of eggs, milk glass, no details (+) **$35.00**
Chick on pile of eggs, milk glass w/hand-painted details (+) **$65.00**

Dove & hand on rectangular lacy base, milk glass ..**$175.00**
Duck on wavy base, any marbled color, 8x6" **$100.00**
Duck on wavy base, crystal, Dark or Light Blue Mist, 8x6", ea **$50.00**
Duck on wavy base, milk glass or Milk Glass Mist, ea .**$60.00**
Duck on wavy base, purple marbled carnival, Levey, 8"..**$150.00**
Fox on diamond or lacy base, chocolate or Electric Blue carnival, ea **$200.00**
Fox on diamond or lacy base, milk glass w/hand-painted realistic fur, ea....................**$300.00**
Fox on diamond or lacy base, purple marbled, purple marbled carnival, ruby or green marbled, ea **$275.00**
Fox on lacy base, milk glass....................**$255.00**
Hen on basketweave base, Antique Blue, Golden Sunset or any Mists, 3½", ea....................**$30.00**
Hen on basketweave base, black milk glass, 3½" **$40.00**
Hen on basketweave base, milk glass, 3½" **$20.00**
Hen on basketweave base, milk glass w/hand-painted accents, 3½" **$25.00**
Hen on diamond base, Antique Blue, Bermuda Blue or Brandywine Blue, 5½", ea **$60.00**
Hen on diamond base, chocolate, 7½"....................**$195.00**
Hen on diamond base, milk glass, 7½" **$40.00**
Hen on diamond base, milk glass or Olive Green, 5½", ea....................**$30.00**
Hen on diamond base, purple, green or ruby marbled, 7½", ea **$200.00**
Hen on diamond base, ruby or purple marbled (noniridized), 5½", ea....................**$85.00**
Hen on diamond base, ruby or purple marbled carnival, 5½", ea....................**$100.00**
Hen on lacy base, milk glass, 7½" **$60.00**
Lamb on picket fence base, Antique Blue, 5½"..........**$60.00**
Lamb on picket fence base, caramel or purple slag carnival, 5½", ea **$125.00**
Lamb on picket fence base, milk glass, 5½" **$40.00**
Lion on diamond base, Electric Blue carnival (500 made), turquoise or emerald green carnival, 8", ea **$225.00**
Lion on diamond base, milk glass, 8"....................**$150.00**
Lion on diamond base, purple marbled, 8"....................**$200.00**
Lion on lacy base, milk glass, 8"....................**$175.00**
Lion on picket fence base, milk glass w/blue head, 5½"..**$125.00**
Lovebirds on base, black milk glass, 6½"....................**$75.00**
Lovebirds on base, black or pink carnival, 6½", ea .**$100.00**
Lovebirds on base, Crystal Mist, Moss Green or Olive Green, 6½", ea....................**$45.00**
Lovebirds on base, Dark or Light Blue, Green, Pink or Yellow Mist, 6½", ea....................**$55.00**
Lovebirds on base, Golden Sunset, Bermuda Blue or Brandywine Blue, 6½", ea **$55.00**
Lovebirds on base, milk glass or milk glass carnival, 6½", ea **$50.00**
Mother eagle & babies on basketweave, milk glass, 8" ..**$130.00**
Mother eagle & babies on basketweave, milk glass w/hand painted accents **$150.00**
Mother eagle & babies on basketweave base, Crystal Mist top on Brown Mist base, 8"....................**$65.00**

Mother eagle & babies on basketweave base, purple marbled carnival (160 made), 8" **$250.00**
Mother eagle & babies on basketweave base, purple or ruby marbled, 8", ea....................**$200.00**
Mother eagle & babies on basketweave base, turquoise carnival (limited edition) or chocolate, 8", ea **$225.00**
Rabbit (mule-earred) on picket-fence base, caramel or purple marbled, 5½", ea....................**$100.00**
Rabbit (mule-earred) on picket-fence base, hand-painted milk glass or pink opaque top on milk glass base, 5½", ea **$60.00**
Rabbit (mule-earred) on picket-fence base, white carnival (1,500 made) or caramel marbled carnival, 5½", ea **$130.00**

Rabbit with eggs on diamond base, Electric Blue carnival, 1/500, ca 1978, $200.00. (Photo courtesy Frank Grizel)

Rabbit w/eggs on diamond or lacy base, chocolate, ruby or purple marbled, 8", ea....................**$200.00**
Rabbit w/eggs on diamond or lacy base, milk glass, 8", ea....................**$150.00**
Rabbit w/eggs on diamond or lacy base, milk glass w/hand-painted accents **$160.00**
Rabbit w/eggs on diamond or lacy base, purple slag carnival (150 made), 8", ea **$250.00**
Rabbit w/eggs on diamond or lacy base, white carnival (1,500 made), 8", ea....................**$200.00**
Robin on twig nest base, Almond, Mint Green or Antique Blue, ea....................**$80.00**
Robin on twig nest base, any Mist color, 6¼", ea.......**$60.00**
Robin on twig nest base, caramel, vaseline, purple marbled or turquoise carnival, 6¼", ea....................**$150.00**
Robin on twig nest base, milk glass, Olive Green or pink, 6¼", ea....................**$50.00**
Robin on twig nest base, pink, black (experimental) or ruby, 6¼", ea....................**$150.00**
Rooster on diamond base, chocolate, 7½"....................**$175.00**
Rooster on diamond base, milk glass, 7½"....................**$70.00**
Rooster on diamond base, milk glass w/Minorca decoration (hand-painted realistic feathers), 7½" **$125.00**

Rooster on diamond base, ruby, purple marbled or purple marbled carnival, 7½", ea $200.00

Rooster on diamond base, Ruby, 7½" $100.00

Rooster on ribbed base, milk glass or milk glass w/hand-painted accents, 5½"...$35.00

Rooster on ribbed base, purple marbled, 5½" $85.00

Rooster on ribbed base, ruby carnival, 5½" $60.00

Rooster standing, black milk glass, 8½"......................$85.00

Rooster standing, milk glass or crystal, 8½" $35.00

Rooster standing, milk glass w/Minorca decoration, hand-painted, 8½" $75.00

Swan (closed neck) on diamond base, milk glass or blue opaque, ea...$95.00

Swan (raised wing) on lacy base, black milk glass, 6x9½"..$275.00

Swan (raised wing) on lacy base, emerald green, purple marbled, pink or cobalt carnival, 6x9½", ea.............$225.00

Swan (raised wing) on lacy base, Ice Blue or turquoise carnival, 6x9½", ea...$200.00

Swan (raised wing) on lacy base, milk glass, milk glass Mother of Pearl, Light Blue or Pink Mist, 6x9½", ea..........$175.00

Toy chick on basketweave base, Brandywine Blue, Dark Blue Mist or Moss Green, 2", ea.............................$20.00

Toy chick on basketweave base, milk glass or milk glass w/red accents, 2", ea...$15.00

Toy chick on basketweave base, milk glass w/any fired-on color, 2", ea...$20.00

Figurals and Novelties

Bird, ashtray or pipe holder, marbled (any color), ea ..$35.00

Bird, ashtray or pipe holder, Mist (any color), ea.......$25.00

Bulldog, Crystal Mist, painted collar, rhinestone eyes, 2½"...$35.00

Butterfly, Almond, Mint Green, Mint Green Mist or milk glass, 2½", ea...$25.00

Butterfly, Almond, Mint Green, Vaseline or Antique Blue, lg, ea..$40.00

Butterfly, any Mist colors, lg, ea..................................$40.00

Butterfly, Mist colors other than Mint Green Mist, 2½", ea..$20.00

Butterfly, purple, caramel or green marbled, lg, ea....$50.00

Butterfly, purple carnival, 1977 limited edition, lg......$55.00

Butterfly, ruby or rubina, 2½", ea $25.00

Cardinal, crystal, solid $20.00

Cardinal, purple marbled, solid...................................$35.00

Cardinal, ruby carnival, solid......................................$30.00

Cardinal, ruby or any Mist color, solid, ea..................$25.00

Cat in boot, Green, Dark Blue or Yellow Mist, hollow, ea...$35.00

Duck, salt cellar, crystal carnival (1,500 made)..........$35.00

Duck, salt cellar, milk glass, Apricot or Green Mist, ea ..$25.00

Egg, trinket box, Mist (any color), w/lid $15.00

Egg, trinket box, Mist (any color), w/white daisy, w/lid...$25.00

Egg on gold stand, Almond w/any decal or Crystal Mist w/floral spray, blown, hollow, ea $50.00

Egg on gold stand, Almond w/any hand-painted decor, blown, hollow, ea...$60.00

Egg on gold stand, black glass (plain, blown, hollow) ..$40.00

Egg on gold stand, black glass w/Oriental Poppy, blown, hollow..$60.00

Grandma's slipper, Antique Blue, Antique Blue Mist, Almond, or Mint Green, ea $30.00

Grandma's slipper, any Mist color, ea $25.00

Grandma's slipper, any Mist color w/hand painting...$30.00

Grandma's slipper, black glass or milk glass Mother of Pearl, ea..$35.00

Grandma's slipper, Honey, Ice Blue carnival or cobalt blue carnival, ea...$40.00

Mantel clock, candy container, Brandywine Blue, hollow, no markings..$35.00

Mantel clock, candy container, milk glass w/hand-painted clock face, hollow, no markings $45.00

Mantel clock, milk glass or Moss Green, hollow, not marked, ea...$30.00

Napkin ring, Brown, Light Blue or Pink Mist w/flower, 6-sided, ea..$35.00

Napkin ring, milk glass w/holly decor, 6-sided...........$50.00

Napkin ring, milk glass w/pink flower, 6-sided..........$35.00

Owl on 2 stacked books, Almond, Mint Green, Antique Blue or black, 3½", ea...$30.00

Owl on 2 stacked books, any Mist color, 3½", ea $25.00

Owl on 2 stacked books, blue, pink, yellow opaque or Brandywine Blue, 3½", ea $25.00

Owl on 2 stacked books, milk glass, 3½" $20.00

Owl on 2 stacked books, purple marbled, 3½" $40.00

Owl standing on tree stump, Almond Mist, Antique Blue or Antique Blue Mist, not marked, 5½", ea...............$40.00

Owl standing on tree stump, Crystal, Dark Blue or Yellow Mist, not marked, 5½", ea......................................$35.00

Owl standing on tree stump, crystal carnival, ruby or milk glass w/22k gold-rubbed feathers, 5½", ea $45.00

Owl standing on tree stump, milk glass or milk glass Mother of Pearl, not marked, 5½", ea................................$30.00

Owl standing on tree stump, purple marbled or ruby carnival, 5½", ea..$55.00

Owl toothpick holder, aqua, milk glass, Moss Green or pink, 3", ea...$20.00

Owl toothpick holder, crystal, 3"................................$15.00

Owl toothpick holder, green, ruby or purple marbled, 3", ea...$30.00

Penguin on ice floe, blue or Blue Mist, ea...............$100.00

Penguin on ice floe, Crystal Mist or milk glass, ea.....$80.00

Porky pig, cobalt carnival, 3"......................................$40.00

Porky pig, Crystal Mist w/hand-painted decor, yellow opaque, milk glass, crystal, Dark Blue Mist or Mint Green, 3", ea $30.00

Porky pig, milk glass or Mint Green w/hand-painted decor, 3", ea...$35.00

Pouter pigeon, Apricot, Dark or Light Blue, Green or Pink Mist, ea..$35.00

Pouter pigeon, Lilac Mist...$40.00

Revolver, black glass or crystal w/black hand-painted grips, solid, ea...$90.00

Revolver, crystal, solid..$70.00
Robin, Almond, Antique Blue, Antique Blue Mist or ruby, solid, 3¼", ea $30.00
Robin, crystal, solid, 3¼"......................................$20.00
Robin, crystal, solid, 5¼"......................................$20.00
Robin, Dark Blue, Green or Pink Mist, solid, 3¼", ea ...$25.00
Robin, ruby or any Mist colors, solid, 5¼", ea............$25.00
Robin, Smoke, 5⅛"..$24.00
Swallow, Almond, Antique Blue or Mint Green, solid, ea ..$30.00
Swallow, Green or Yellow Mist, solid $25.00
Turtle, paperweight, Dark Blue, Green or Lilac Mist, no holes, ea $50.00
Turtle, paperweight, milk glass, no holes....................$75.00
Wren, Almond, Almond Mist or any opaque color, solid .$35.00
Wren, milk glass or any other color Mist, solid, ea $30.00
Wren, pink or Smoke, 2½".......................................$20.00
Wren on sq-base perch, any color combination, solid, ea ..$55.00

Lamps

Boudoir, English Hobnail/#555, milk glass, stick type w/flat base..$45.00
Candle, Almond, Mint Green or ruby w/hand-painted decor, w/shade, mini $45.00
Candle, Cameo, any color w/Beaded Bouquet, w/shade, mini $50.00
Candle, Cameo, Crystal Mist w/Roses & Bows, w/shade, mini $55.00
Candle, Crystal Mist w/any decal, w/shade, mini $30.00
Candle, milk glass w/roses & bows, w/shade, mini .$135.00
Electric, any child's decor, w/shade, wood base, mini ..$80.00
Electric, any color w/Mary Gregory-style decor, w/shade, brass base w/scroll work, 8½" $100.00
Electric, any color w/Roses & Bows, w/shade, brass base w/scroll work, 8½" $125.00
Electric, Colonial; any color or decor, brass base w/scroll work, glass shade $125.00
Electric, Dolphin; crystal $125.00
Electric, Dolphin; green or pink, ea..........................$175.00
Electric, English Hobnail, amber or crystal, 9½", ea...$55.00
Electric, 1049 Dolphin, Roselin, from $80 to.............$175.00
Electric, 1707 Spiral, Roselin, w/cutting, 8", from $35 to...$55.00
Electric, 1915 Vanity, aquamarine, w/cutting, 12", from $60 to...$80.00
Fairy, Irish Waterford, any Mist w/hand-painted flowers, low foot, 2-pc $50.00
Fairy, Irish Waterford, crystal w/ruby stain, low foot, 2-pc..$70.00
Fairy, Thousand Eye, crystal, footed $20.00
Fairy, Thousand Eye, ruby, flat or footed, ea.............$50.00

Modern Giftware

Ashtray, Beaded Grape/#1884, milk glass w/Roses & Bows, 6½x6½"...$45.00
Ashtray, English Hobnail, milk glass, sq, 8" $20.00

Basket, English Hobnail/#555, crystal or milk glass, 9", ea $30.00
Basket, Paneled Grape/#1881, milk glass, Brandywine Blue or Golden Sunset, 8", ea $150.00
Basket, Paneled Grape/#1881, red carnival, limited editon of 500, 8"...$200.00
Basket, Pansy/#757, purple or green slag, split handle, ea $35.00
Bell, Cameo/#754, w/Beaded Bouquet trim, any color ..$35.00
Bell, Cameo/#754, w/hand-painted Cameo, any color ...$30.00
Bonbon, Waterford/#1932, ruby on crystal, metal w/handle..$38.00
Bottle, toilet; Paneled Grape/#1881, milk glass, 5-oz .$65.00
Bowl, centerpiece; star shape, green or purple marbled, ea..$50.00
Bowl, English Hobnail, milk glass or crystal, oval, 10", ea...$22.50
Bowl, Lotus/#1921, black, round, lg $50.00
Bowl, Lotus/#1921, milk glass, oval $30.00
Bowl, Maple Leaf/#1928, milk glass, 6-point, 6" H.....$35.00
Bowl, purple or green slag, leaf form, #300, ea $45.00
Bowl, Ring & Petal/#1875, milk glass or Moss Green, cupped & footed, 10", ea..$25.00
Bowl, wedding; milk glass, #1874, 10" $40.00
Bowl, wedding; milk glass w/any hand-painted decoration...$75.00
Bowl, wedding; milk glass w/Roses & Bows, 10" $100.00
Bowl (Grandfather), Sawtooth/#556, Almond, Antique Green or Mint Green, ea $145.00
Box, heart shape, Chocolate, Dark Blue or Green Mist $55.00
Box, heart shape, Chocolate or Crystal Mist w/any anniversary...$65.00
Box, trinket; any Mist color, 4-footed, sq, #1902 ....$25.00
Box, trinket; Crystal Mist w/Roses & Bows, 4-footed, sq..$35.00
Box, trinket; heart shape, any Mist color w/daisy design .$35.00
Box, trinket; heart shape, milk glass or milk glass w/Mother of Pearl, w/Roses & Bows, ea $40.00
Candle holders, dolphin, milk glass, hexagonal base, 9", pr...$80.00
Candle holders, Paneled Grape/#1881, milk glass, 4", pr...$25.00
Candle holders, Waterford, ruby on crystal, 6", pr......$65.00
Candy dish, Beaded Bouquet/#1700, Colonial pattern, milk glass $35.00
Candy dish, Beaded Grape/#1884, Brandywine Blue, w/lid, 3½"..$35.00
Candy dish, Beaded Grape/#1884, milk glass w/Roses & Bows, low foot, w/lid, 5"................................$47.50
Candy dish, Paneled Grape/#1881, Dark Blue Mist, crimped, 3-footed, 7½"...$35.00
Compote, Brandywine Blue Opalescent, crimped & ruffled, footed, 6½"..$45.00
Dresser set, Blue, Yellow or Green Mist, w/daisy desgin, 4-pc..$50.00
Dresser set, Paneled Grape/#1881, 4-pc....................$325.00
Grandma's slipper, hand-painted Christmas decor, #1900 ..$40.00
Grandma's slipper, no painting..................................$20.00
Pin tray, Heart/#1820, Blue Mist...............................$30.00
Soap dish, Paneled Grape/#1881, milk glass.............$110.00

Urn, ruby on crystal, footed, #1943, w/lid..................**$95.00**

Plates

Beaded Edge/#22, milk glass w/birds, florals or poultry, 7", ea **$20.00**

Bicentennial decoration, Paneled Grape/#1881, limited edition, 14½"...**$225.00**

Forget-me-not/#2, black, Mary Gregory style, 8" **$55.00**

Forget-me-not/#2, Blue or Brown Mist, Mary Gregory style, 8", ea...**$60.00**

Hearts, heart shape/#HP-1, Almond or Mint Green w/dogwood decal, 8", ea **$30.00**

Hearts, heart shape/#HP-1, any color w/daisy decal, 8"....**$25.00**

Lattice Edge/#1890, Dark Blue Mist, Mary Gregory style, 11"...**$65.00**

Luncheon, Paneled Grape/#1881, milk glass w/hand-painted decor, 8½" **$40.00**

Plain, dinner/#PL-8; black glass w/Christmas nativity decor, 8½"...**$80.00**

Wicket border, milk glass w/Revolutionary War scenes, 9"..**$60.00**

Tableware

Plate, dinner; Old Quilt, milk glass, $70.00; plate, salad; $35.00; plate, bread and butter; $25.00; cup and saucer (rare), $32.00. (Photo courtesy Frank Grizel)

Bowl, banana; Doric, milk glass, footed, 11" **$30.00**

Bowl, banana; Old Quilt/#500, milk glass, footed, 11"...**$150.00**

Bowl, banana; Paneled Grape/#1881, milk glass, 12"....**$150.00**

Bowl, Old Quilt/#500, milk glass, round, 10¼" **$120.00**

Bowl, Paneled Grape/#1881, milk glass, belled or lipped, footed, oval, 11", ea..**$75.00**

Bowl, Paneled Grape/#1881, milk glass, cupped, 8"..**$45.00**

Bowl, Paneled Grape/#1881, milk glass, round, 10½"..**$120.00**

Bowl, Paneled Grape/#1881, milk glass, shallow, skirted foot, 6x9"...**$60.00**

Bowl, relish; Old Quilt/#500, milk glass, round, 3-part ...**$35.00**

Bowl, relish/appetizer; Paneled Grape, milk glass, 3-pc set..**$65.00**

Box, chocolate; Paneled Grape/#1881, milk glass, w/lid, 6½" dia **$45.00**

Butter dish, Paneled Grape/#1881, Golden Sunset or Crystal Mist, ea...**$30.00**

Butter dish, Paneled Grape/#1881, milk glass, w/lid, ¼-lb...**$25.00**

Butter/cheese dish, Old Quilt/#500, milk glass, w/lid, round **$45.00**

Butter/cheese dish, Old Quilt/#500, purple marbled, w/lid, round **$125.00**

Butter/cheese dish, Old Quilt/#500, purple marbled carnival, w/lid, round..**$125.00**

Butter/cheese dish, Paneled Grape/#1881, milk glass, w/lid, round, 7"..**$35.00**

Butter/cheese dish, Paneled Grape/#1881, purple marbled, w/lid, round, 7"..**$75.00**

Cake plate, Irish Waterford/#1932, ruby on crystal, low foot 12"...**$95.00**

Cake salver, Beaded Grape/#1884, milk glass, sq, footed, 11"...**$95.00**

Cake salver, Doric, milk glass, footed, 11" **$30.00**

Cake salver, Old Quilt/#500, milk glass, skirted, bell foot, 12"...**$125.00**

Cake salver, Paneled Grape/#1881, milk glass, design underneath **$90.00**

Cake salver, Paneled Grape/#1881, milk glass, skirted, 11"...**$65.00**

Canape set, Paneled Grape/#1881, milk glass, 3-pc, 12½" tray, 3½" cocktail & ladle..................................**$120.00**

Candelabra, Lotus/#1921, any Mist color, 3-light, pr...**$70.00**

Candelabra, Lotus/#1921, milk glass, 3-light, pr..........**$60.00**

Candelabra, Paneled Grape/#1881, milk glass, 3-light, pr..**$400.00**

Candle holder, Paneled Grape/#1881, milk glass, arc shape, 2-light, 8", ea..**$45.00**

Canister, Crystal Mist w/any decal, w/lid, 62-oz, 9"....**$35.00**

Canister, Paneled Grape/#1881, milk glass, footed, w/lid, 7½x4½" **$300.00**

Canister, Paneled Grape/#1881, milk glass, footed, w/lid, 10x5¾"...**$500.00**

Canister, Paneled Grape/#1881, milk glass, footed, w/lid, 11½x6¾"..**$400.00**

Compote, Paneled Grape/#1881, milk glass, lipped or crimped, 9", ea..**$65.00**

Cup & saucer, Paneled Grape/#1881, milk glass.........**$21.00**

Decanter, Paneled Grape/#1811, milk glass, w/stopper..**$150.00**

Decanter, Swirl & Ball, crystal **$80.00**

Egg tray, Paneled Grape/#1881, milk glass, w/center handle, 10" **$75.00**

Egg tray, Paneled Grape/#1881, milk glass, w/center handle, 12" **$90.00**

Epergne, Paneled Grape/#1881, Almond or Mint Green, flared, 3-pc set, 14", ea..**$300.00**

Epergne, Paneled Grape/#1881, milk glass, flared, 3-pc set, 14"...**$250.00**

Epergne, Paneled Grape/#1881, milk glass, lipped, 2-pc set (no base), 9"...**$150.00**

Epergne, Paneled Grape/#1881, milk glass, lipped, 3-pc set, 12"...**$250.00**

Goblet, water; Della Robbia, crystal w/ruby stain, 8-oz, 6" $25.00

Goblet, water; Old Quilt/#500, Brandywine Blue, Golden Sunset or milk glass, footed, 8-oz, ea **$15.00**

Goblet, water; Paneled Grape/#1881, milk glass, footed, 8-oz **$15.00**

Goblet, wine; Paneled Grape/#1881, milk glass, footed, 2-oz **$22.00**

Pitcher, syrup; Old Quilt/#500, milk glass, 3-oz, 3½".**$40.00**

Plate, dinner; Beaded Grape/#1884, milk glass...........**$55.00**

Plate, dinner; Paneled Grape/#1881, milk glass, 10½"..**$45.00**

Plate, salad; Della Robbia, crystal............................**$15.00**

Plate, salad; Paneled Grape/#1881, milk glass, 8½"....**$22.00**

Plate, salad; Princess Feather, Golden Sunset, 8" **$25.00**

Plate, Waterford, clear w/ruby stain, 10" **$65.00**

Punch bowl set, Old Quilt/#500, milk glass, bowl, base, ladle & 12 cups **$960.00**

Punch bowl set, Paneled Grape/#1881, milk glass, bowl, base, ladle & 12 cups **$575.00**

Punch bowl set, Princess Feather/#201, crystal, bowl, base, ladle & 12 cups..**$250.00**

Toothpick, Paneled Grape/#1881, milk glass **$30.00**

Tray, tidbit; Beaded Grape/#1884, milk glass, 2-tier...**$95.00**

Tray, tidbit; Dolphin, any color other than Crystal Mist, center handle **$45.00**

Tray, tidbit; Dolphin, Crystal Mist, center handle........**$35.00**

Tray, tidbit; Octagon, Crystal Mist w/any decal, w/center handle **$30.00**

Tray, tidbit; Paneled Grape/#1881, any Mist color w/daisy design **$35.00**

Tray, tidbit; Paneled Grape/#1881, milk glass, 2-tier, 8½" & 10½" plates **$80.00**

Tray, tidbit; Paneled Grape/#1881, milk glass, 2-tier, 8½" & 10½" plates w/poinsettia decor **$100.00**

Tumbler, iced tea; Paneled Grape/#1881, milk glass, 12-oz **$22.50**

Tumbler, iced tea; Waterford, clear w/ruby stain, 12-oz ...**$25.00**

Tumbler, juice; Old Quilt/#500, milk glass, flat, 5-oz .**$25.00**

Tumbler, old-fashioned; Paneled Grape/#1881, milk glass, flat, 6-oz..**$35.00**

Water set, Swirl & Ball, purple carnival, 3-pt pitcher & 6 8-oz tumblers..**$265.00**

Wexford

Wexford is a diverse line of glassware that Anchor Hocking has made since 1967. At one time, it was quite extensive, and a few pieces remain in production yet today. It's very likely you'll see it at any flea market you visit, and it's common to see a piece now and then on your garage sale rounds. It's not only very attractive but serviceable — nothing fragile about this heavy-gauge glassware! Right now, it's not only plentiful but inexpensive, so if you like its looks, now's a good time to begin your collection. Gene Florence lists seventy-seven pieces in his book *Anchor Hocking's Fire-King and More* and

says others will no doubt be reported as collectors become more familiar with the market.

Ashtray, 8½" $6.00

Bowl, salad; footed, 10" $10.00

Bowl, salad; 5¼" $3.50

Butter dish, ¼-lb $3.00

Cake stand $15.00

Candle holder, 5", pr $35.00

Candy dish, footed, w/lid, 6¾x7¾"..........................$12.00

Creamer, 8-oz $2.50

Cruet, w/stopper, 5½-oz $3.00

Cup, punch/snack; 7-oz $2.00

Goblet, cordial, 3½-oz $2.50

Goblet, footed, 10-oz..$3.50

Ice bucket, w/lid $15.00

Jar, storage; 34-oz..$4.00

Jar, w/lid, 96-oz $12.50

Pitcher, footed, 18-oz $10.00

Plate, dinner; scalloped edge, 9½" $18.00

Platter, serving; 14" dia $5.00

Punch bowl, 11-qt $10.00

Punch bowl base (salad), 9¾" $10.00

Relish, 3-part, 8½"..$4.00

Relish tray, 11" $4.00

Relish tray, 5⅛x9⅞" $4.00

Salt & pepepr shakers, 2-oz, pr $3.00

Sherbet, stemmed, 7-oz $2.00

Tidbit, 2-tier, 6" & 11" plates..................................$10.00

Tidbit tray, 9½" $5.00

Tumbler, on-the-rocks, 10-oz $2.50

Wheaton

The Wheaton Company of Millville, New Jersey, has produced several series of bottles and flasks which are very collectible today. One of the most popular features portraits of our country's presidents. There was also a series of twenty-one Christmas bottles produced from 1971 through 1991, and because fewer were produced during the last few years, the newer ones can be hard to find and often bring good prices. Apollo bottles, those that feature movie stars, ink bottles, and bitters bottles are among the other interesting examples. Many colors of glass have been used, including iridescents.

Andrew Jackson, green iridescent $15.00

Apollo XII, ruby red, 8"..$15.00

Ball & Claw Bitters, violet amethyst, 9½" **$18.00**

Ball & Claw Bitters, World's Best Remedy, Indian Drug Specialty Co, purple, 9" $30.00

Berring's Bitters, amber, apples on 3 sides, sq, 9x3"..**$15.00**

Carter's Ink, ruby, octagonal w/Gothic-style cathedral arches, 2¾", from $20 to $30.00

Fiddle, blue, 9"..$23.50

First National Bank, ruby red, 6¼"............................$300.00

Fisch's Bitters, fish shape, blue, 3"..............................$25.00

Fruit pattern, blue, 6"...$40.00

Indian Chief, bank, blue, 6".....................................$35.00

James Madison, green, 7¾", MIB..............................$20.00

Jenny Lind, cobalt blue, Swedish Nightingale on back, 5½"..$80.00

John Adams, green carnival, EXIB $25.00

Liberty Bell, amber, 7½"..$20.00

Pocahontas, cobalt blue, 5".....................................$40.00

Poison, skull & crossbones on 1 side, w/RIP on other, coffin shape, royal blue, 3"....................................$45.00

Poison, skull & crossbones on 1 side w/RIP on other, amethyst, 5"..$28.00

Poison, skull shape, green, 5"..................................$55.00

Presidential set, blue, green & brown carnival, miniatures, EXIB..$50.00

Robert E Lee, green iridescent, MIB...........................$15.00

Thomas Edison, blue carnival, 8½"...........................$13.00

Tuckahoe Country School 1891, green, miniature $22.50

Uncle Sam, green, 6"..$35.00

Wheaton Glass Factory, bank, clear, 6".....................$30.00

William McKinley, green iridescent............................$12.00

Will-George

This is a California-based company that began operations in the 1930. It was headed by two brothers, William and George Climes, both of whom had extensive training in pottery science. They're most famous today for their lovely figurines of animals and birds, though they produced many human figures as well. For more information on this company as well as many others, we recommend *The Collector's Encyclopedia of California Pottery* by Jack Chipman (Collector Books).

Candle holders, petal shape, green outside w/pink inside, 6½", pr...$125.00

Condiment set, Spanish onions, salt & pepper shakers, sugar bowl w/lid..$65.00

Figurine, artist holding palette, multicolored, 8".........$95.00

Figurine, blue jay on perch, 10"..............................$110.00

Figurine, cardinal, on tree branch, 12½" $150.00

Figurine, cardinal on branch, 10" $75.00

Figurine, dachshund, 6½x9".....................................$200.00

Figurine, flamingo, head down, 6¼"..........................$85.00

Figurine, flamingo, head up, 9½"..............................$185.00

Figurine, flamingo, preening, 10" $210.00

Figurine, flamingo, wings up, 7½", from $200 to $250.00

Figurine, giraffe, 14½"..$150.00

Figurine, monk, brown bisque, 4½"...........................$50.00

Figurine, pheasant, 6x14", from $200 to $250.00

Figurine, robin, 3"..$45.00

Flower holder, bird in tree w/holes in branches for flowers, 7"...$40.00

Pitcher, rooster figural, multicolored, 8¾".................$130.00

Planter, pink interior, green exterior w/embossed leaves, 10x3½x3"..$70.00

Tumbler, chicken figural, multicolored, 4½" $50.00

Wilton Pans

You've probably seen several of these as you make your garage sale rounds, but did you know that some are quite collectible? Especially good are the pans that depict cartoon, story book, or movie characters. And, of course, condition is vital — examples with the insert, instructions, and accessory pieces bring the highest prices.

Wilton started mass merchandising the shaped pans in the early 1960s, and the company has been careful to keep up with trends in pop culture since then. Thus, many of the pans are of limited production which adds to the collectible factor. The company also makes all the items needed for cake decorating, including food dyes, frosting tips, and parchment triangles for making the frosting tubes. In addition, they train instructors in the Wilton Method and support the classes in the Wilton Method taught at craft stores such as Joann's and Michael's for people who want to learn to decorate. Most of the character and other shaped pans require simple decorating techniques which appeals to amateurs, while the simpler pans (for instance, the heart tiers or the grand piano) can call more more complex decorations, calling for those with professional-level decorating skills.

Who knows if there will be a market for Teletubby pans fifteen years from now? As with any collectible, future demand is impossible to predict. But since many Wilton pans can be found at garage sales and in thrift stores for $3 or less, right now it doesn't take a lot of money to start a collection.

Advisor: Cheryl Moody (See Directory, Wilton Cake Pans)

Boba Fett from Star Wars, LucasFilm, LTD 1983, 13¾x12¼", M w/insert & instructions.....................................$65.00

Bowling a Strike, ball & 3 pins, w/insert, 1990, M $35.00

Butterfly, 1987, 11x13x2", NM..................................$25.00

Charlie Brown, holding baseball glove, w/original plastic face, United Features Syndicate, 1950, EX............$25.00

Christmas tree, 2 pcs form tree w/3rd acting as heat conducting core, 3-pc set forms 3-D tree, clips missing, NM...$35.00

C3PO from Star Wars, LucasFilm Ltd 1983, 13¼x12¼", NM...$62.50

Darth Vader from Star Wars, LucasFilms, unused w/instructions, M, from $15 to.....................................$35.00

Dumbo, 1976 Walt Disney Productions, 8½x6", EX....$20.00

Fire truck, w/insert & instructions, 1991, M $10.00

Flag, sm (uses 1 mix), 1974, EX.................................$10.00

Football player, 1987, 13½", EX................................$15.00

Goofy, Disney Enterprises, #2105-344, folded insert, NM ..$38.00

Grand piano, complete set w/15 pcs, includes bench, keyboard/etc, ca 1969, M, from $65 to.......................$75.00

Guitar, complete w/accessories, 1977, 19x10"............$12.00

Haunted House, #502-2464, 1983, EX.........................$10.00

Heart, 8-tier, largest: 15", smallest: 7", set of 8, M.......$45.00

Herbie the Love Bug, 1976, 14½x10", EX...................$24.00

Kitty Cat, complete w/instructions, 9x15", EX, from $10 to..**$15.00**

Little Mermaid, w/original plastic face, w/instructions, M, from $25 to.................................**$50.00**

Lone-Star State (Texas), w/insert, 1987, M.................**$40.00**

Mystical Dragon, w/instructions, 10x14½", M **$40.00**

Parisian Classic Cookie Mold, makes 18 cookies, 1984, w/recipes & instructions, M **$42.50**

Pinocchio, Walt Disney, #515-701, EX.......................**$24.00**

Raggedy Ann w/jump rope, w/insert & booklet, 1981, M, from $15 to...**$25.00**

Rudolph the Red-Nosed Reindeer, with instructions, unused, M, $20.00.

Sailboat, w/insert, 1984, NM **$35.00**

Snoopy (as Red Baron or typist), unused, w/original instructions, dated 1965, M, from $25 to **$40.00**

Stork & Bundle of Joy, 1983, NM, from $15 to **$20.00**

Wonder Woman, w/original plastic face, 1978, 17x9½", EX, from $15 to..**$30.00**

Winfield

The Winfield pottery first began operations in the late 1920s in Pasadena, California. In 1946 their entire line of artware and giftware items was licensed to the American Ceramic Products Company, who continued to mark their semiporcelain dinnerware with the Winfield name. The original Winfield company changed their trademark to 'Gabriel.' Both companies closed during the early 1960s. For more information, see *The Collector's Encyclopedia of California Pottery* by Jack Chipman (Collector Books).

Ashtray, Bamboo, lg, 10"...**$12.00**

Ashtray, Dragon Flower, 6¾"...**$8.00**

Ashtray, Passion Flower, 3¾"..**$3.00**

Bowl, cereal; Dragon Flower, 5¾"..................................**$7.50**

Bowl, cereal; Passion Flower, 6"....................................**$8.50**

Bowl, divided vegetable; Bamboo **$22.00**

Bowl, fruit; Bamboo, 5"...**$8.50**

Bowl, fruit; Desert Dawn, 5"...**$7.50**

Bowl, rice; Passion Flower, 4½"...................................**$11.00**

Bowl, vegetable; Blue Pacific, 9".................................**$27.50**

Bowl, vegetable; Dragon Flower, sq, 9".......................**$42.00**

Bowl, vegetable; Dragon Flower, 9"..............................**$25.00**

Casserole, Blue Pacific, w/lid, 1½-qt, 6½" dia **$38.00**

Casserole, Dragon Flower, 3-qt....................................**$55.00**

Chop plate, Dragon Flower, 11"....................................**$37.50**

Coffeepot, Desert Dawn..**$42.00**

Coffeepot, Passion Flower, w/lid..................................**$45.00**

Creamer, Bamboo...**$17.50**

Creamer, Blue Pacific...**$15.00**

Creamer, Dragon Flower **$12.00**

Creamer, Passion Flower **$12.00**

Cup & saucer, Bamboo **$9.50**

Cup & saucer, Blue Pacific...**$10.00**

Cup & saucer, Dragon Flower.......................................**$10.00**

Egg cup, Dragon Flower, double, 3½"..........................**$18.50**

Gravy boat, Dragon Flower **$28.00**

Mug, Dragon Flower, 3½"..**$12.00**

Plate, bread & butter; Dragon Flower, 5¾" **$3.50**

Plate, Coronation, 10"...**$14.00**

Plate, dinner; Desert Dawn, 10"...................................**$15.00**

Plate, dinner; Passion Flower, 10".................................**$12.00**

Platter, Desert Dawn, 12"...**$27.50**

Platter, Dragon Flower, 12"...**$32.00**

Platter, Passion Flower, rectangular, 14".......................**$30.00**

Relish dish, Bird of Paradise, rectangular, 11½x7½x1½" .**$20.00**

Relish dish, Tiger Lily, leaf shaped, 3-part, handled...**$35.00**

Relish tray, Dragon Flower, 3-part, w/handle, 16"......**$32.50**

Salt & pepper shakers, Bamboo, pr **$16.00**

Salt & pepper shakers, Desert Dawn, pr **$12.00**

Salt & pepper shakers, Passion Flower, pr **$14.00**

Sugar bowl, Bamboo, open **$15.00**

Sugar bowl, Blue Pacific, w/lid....................................**$24.00**

Sugar bowl, Desert Dawn, w/lid...................................**$24.00**

Sugar bowl, Dragon Flower, w/lid................................**$17.50**

World's Fairs and Expositions

Souvenir items have been issued since the mid-1800s for every world's fair and exposition. Few fairgoers have left the grounds without purchasing at least one. Some of the older items were often manufactured right on the fairgrounds by glass or pottery companies who erected working kilns and furnaces just for the duration of the fair. Of course, the older items are usually more valuable, but even souvenirs from the past fifty years are worth hanging on to.

Advisor: Herbert Rolfes (See Directory, World's Fairs and Expositions)

Newsletter: *Fair News*
World's Fair Collectors' Society, Inc.
Michael R. Pender, Editor
P.O. Box 20806-3806
Sarasota, FL 34276
941-923-2590, e-mail: wfcs@aol.com;
members.aol.com/Bbqprod/wfcs.html Dues: $20 (6 issues) per year in USA; $25 in Canada; $30 for overseas members

Chicago, 1933

Ashtray, Chicago Fair, The American Way of Life, white w/red letters, Vernon Kilns, 5¾" dia, EX **$15.00**

Booklet, How Firestone High Speed Tires Are Made, 32 pages, 5x8", VG+ **$15.00**

Bottle opener, fair logo in blue on white, slides open, 2½" closed, EX....................................**$15.00**

Bottle opener, nude handle w/Fort Dearborn & Century of Progress, EX **$25.00**

Box, keepsake; metal w/Fort Dearborn & Chicago skyline, cedar lined, 3½x4", EX....................**$18.50**

Bracelet, copper, Chicago World's Fair 1933 w/fair scenes, EX **$40.00**

Brochure, Messmore's & Damon's World a Million Years Ago, T-rex & Statue of Liberty, 8 pages, 4½x6¼", NM **$30.00**

Butler set, fair scene in poor silver plate, dustpan, 6x6", scoop, 6x2", VG- **$15.00**

Cane, hard wood w/silver band reads Prosperity Cane, metal tip, 34", EX **$160.00**

Card, 400 Outstanding Women of the World, 5½x3½", EX **$10.00**

Charm bracelet, 7 charms w/different buildings, 7" L, VG+, from $20 to....................**$30.00**

Cigarette lighter, Hall of Science logo on side of green & nickle-plated silver, EX+....................**$115.00**

Coin, Good Luck, logo on back, 1¼" dia, EX.............**$10.00**

Compact, logo on chrome w/white paint background, 1¾x2⅛", VG, from $50 to....................**$100.00**

Corkscrew, key shape, Chicago, Century of Progress on handle, 1933 as teeth to key, 6", EX **$50.00**

Dish, Buckingham Fountain in center, fair buildings in round vignettes at rim, brass, 4¾" dia, EX....................**$15.00**

Doll cradle, marked Selected by 1933 Chicago World's Fair, Lullabye, wooden, 20x13½x9", EX....................**$135.00**

Guide book, Official World's Fair 1934, w/map, 192 pages, EX..**$30.00**

Jewelry box, keg shape w/4 brass bands & metal logo, 5¾x4", VG+ **$25.00**

Lamp, brass w/applied scene & words on glass, electric, 4½x3¼" dia, VG+ **$65.00**

Letter opener, wood w/1933 carved on handle, Wood Art Products, 10", EX **$18.00**

Menu, Mayflower Doughnut & Maxwell House Coffee, EX, from $25 to....................**$30.00**

Mug, Travel Building on front, logo on back, copper, marked Solid Copper WB, 3½", VG **$15.00**

Penknife, yellow plastic w/red Drink Coca-Cola in Bottles 5¢, Colonial Prov USA on blade, 3¾", EX **$30.00**

Pennant, Travel Building, 25x8½", EX **$45.00**

Photograph, orotone; Travel & Transport Building, 4x5" image in frame, EX **$55.00**

Pillow cover, Chicago buildings w/searchlights, rope border, 16x16", EX **$70.00**

Pin, Century of Progress & logo in gold on blue, Green Duck, ⅝x½", NM (EX card) **$15.00**

Pitcher, swan body embossed into pitcher w/neck & head as handle, Hall of Science decal, Made in Czechoslovakia, 5", EX....................**$85.00**

Plate, Federal Building in green on white, Pickard, sq, 7½"...**$25.00**

Playing cards, picture on back, logo on jokers & aces, unused, MIB....................**$60.00**

Playing cards, Sky Ride, orange in blue box, VG+ (w/box) **$12.50**

Print, World Fair Chicago 1933, Frasier, 36x24", EX....**$30.00**

Program, Wings of a Century, Romance of Transportation, EX..**$20.00**

Ring, hammered sterling w/logo on front, EX **$60.00**

Sombrero, black felt w/gold trim & gold balls hanging from cord border, Old Mexico Souvenir, 7½" dia, VG+..**$35.00**

Spoon, Chicago Century...Progress logo on handle w/Hall of Science on back of handle, Science Court in bowl, Onieda, EX..**$10.00**

Spoon, gold w/engaving on handle, Green Duck, EX ..**$10.00**

Stein, embossed scene w/nude handle, green, pottery, 6½", EX..**$45.00**

Table runner, depicts Fort Dearborn, 264x13½", VG+G+ .**$200.00**

Tapestry, Court of States Building, 18x18", EX...........**$20.00**

Ticket, general admission, full w/stub, EX **$30.00**

Tie bar, Travel & Transportation Buildings, tin, 3", EX ..**$20.00**

Vase, bud; girl stands beside vase w/fair logo, Made in Japan, 4¼", EX..**$20.00**

Viewer, 40 Views of History of Chicago, 1833-1933, Century of Progress, 5¾x3x2", VG (EX box)....................**$100.00**

New York, 1939

Ashtray, Trylon & Perisphere w/2 arches behind (bowl), copper, slight oxidation, 5⅛x3⅝", VG+ **$40.00**

Book, Views of NYWF, Trylon & Perisphere in metallic silver on blue & orange, Art Deco style, 48 pages, 11½x11", EX..**$75.00**

Coasters, plastic, red, blue, light green & yellow (2 ea), 3", in Deco-style holder, EX....................**$75.00**

Flag, orange & blue w/Trylon & Perisphere in white, 5½x4" on 11" pole, EX....................**$50.00**

License plate, blue, orange & cream, Officially Approved souvenir, NG Slater Corp, 11½x4½", EX.............**$165.00**

Menu, Ballantine Beer 3 Ring Inn, map of fair on cover, 2½ pages inside, VG **$40.00**

Mirror, hand; Trylon & Perisphere on back, Souvenir of NYWF 1939, 12x4", VG+ **$50.00**

Photograph, aerial view, Underwood, 13x9½", EX.....**$25.00**

Pin, gilded-metal plane w/World's Fair USA Flight 1939 NX 18973 on wings, blue & orange flag w/Trylon & Perisphere, EX..**$35.00**

Plate, Trylon & Perisphere in blue, Tiffany & Co, Adams, England, NM, from $75 to....................**$100.00**

Plate, Trylon & Perisphere in center w/fair buildings on border, J&G Meakin, NM, from $75 to **$100.00**

Salt & pepper shakers, Trylon & Perisphere, silver plated, 4", pr..**$50.00**

Scarf, fair buildings & scenes, blue, rust, green, yellow & white, silk, 20x20", EX..............................**$50.00**

Snow globe, Trylon & Perisphere, black base w/NYWF 1939 in orange, 3½"..**$100.00**

Tea set, white w/orange & green peacocks, Hand Painted Herend, 1940, pot, creamer & sugar bowl, 4 cups & saucers...**$250.00**

Teapot, Trylon & Perisphere, blues & greens on cream, Porcelier, 54-oz, 8x4½" dia, EX, minimum value ...**$100.00**

Tie holder, w/6 pegs, 4x2" caddy, Syrocco, EX..........**$45.00**

Yo-yo, Trylon & Perisphere & NYWF 1939, 2¼" dia, M, from $150 to...**$200.00**

Seattle, 1962

Bank, Seattle Colosseum replica, plastic, EX..............**$60.00**

Bowl, Monorail, Space Needle & Century 21 symbol on black, plastic, 8" dia, M.......................................**$15.00**

Lighter, Century Exposition 21 symbol w/Seattle World's Fair 1962, Penguin Superlative Automatic Lighter, Japan, VG...**$60.00**

Plate, Space Needle & fair buildings on blue, marked Japan Century Souvenir Inc, 7" dia, EX.....................**$10.00**

Postcard, Monorail Entrance, color, VG **$3.00**

Shoehorn, medallion w/Space Needle, Monorail & Century 21 symbol w/rhinestone crown on top, 5½", EX.**$10.00**

Tie, Oxford gray silk w/Century 21 symbol, Space Needle & Monorail overall, 2x55", VG+...............................**$25.00**

Tumblers, fair buildings on colored frosted glass, Century Exposition 21 symbol, 6¾x2¾" dia, set of 6, EX.**$60.00**

Whiskey bottle, Space Needle shape, 4 scenes on 4 sides, Jim Beam paper label, Regal China, 13", EX..............**$18.50**

New York, 1964

Ashtray, fair buildings, gold border & cigarette rests (3), 4" dia, EX **$18.00**

Bank, Unisphere, blue, MIB.......................................**$70.00**

Booklet, Vatican Pavillion, 8-page fold-out w/floor plan, EX...**$8.00**

Bookmark, Peace Through Understanding, white w/red & blue, M (in original cellophane)............................**$40.00**

Bowl, Unisphere, Monorail & other buildings, US Steel, 11½x10¼", EX...**$45.00**

Brochure, Trailways Visit World's Fair, Trailways Bus Co, EX..**$15.00**

Charm, globe w/World's Fair 1964-1965, sterling, ½" dia, NM...**$25.00**

Dime, Neutron Irradiated; 1946 Eisenhauer dime, Atomic Energy Commission, 2" dia, EX **$25.00**

Dime bank, Unisphere, daily register, on original cardboard holder, EX, minimum value **$125.00**

Flag, blue & orange w/white globe, miniature, EX **$15.00**

Guide, Official NYWF, 1964 edition, EX......................**$18.00**

License plate, NY World's Fair 64, navy & gold, EX...**$22.50**

Magazine, Persistence of Vision, Disney History, Walt's Involvement of NYWF, 144 pages, 8½x11", M.....**$25.00**

Matchbook, Coca-Cola Pavillion, NM..........................**$20.00**

Nodders, World's Fair Twins, magnetic kissing boy & girl, 5", MIB..**$100.00**

Pennant, Unisphere, felt, 11", EX................................**$15.00**

Plate, General Cigar Building, smoky glass w/gold image & lettering, oval, 8½", EX.......................................**$50.00**

Program, Hawaii Exhibit, 96 pages, EX **$15.00**

Puzzle, Greyhound Bus Station, MIB (sealed)............**$22.50**

Rain bonnet, MIP...**$18.00**

Scarf, Philippine Pavillion, multicolored, 15" sq, NM .**$45.00**

Ticket, Lincoln Bus; to fair, w/envelope, EX..............**$15.00**

Tray, Unisphere w/NY skyline in background, blue enamel on copper, marked US Steel Made in Japan, EX..**$50.00**

Yona

Yona Lippin was a California ceramist who worked for Hedi Schoop in the early 1940s and later opened her own studio. Much of her work is similar to Schoop's. She signed her work with her first name. You'll also find items marked Yona that carry a 'Shafford Made in Japan' label, suggesting a later affiliation with that importing company. For more information, see *The Collector's Encyclopedia of California Pottery* by Jack Chipman (Collector Books).

Coffee set, red & white vertical stripes, pot, creamer & sugar bowl (w/lid), 2 cups & saucers **$50.00**

Figurine, angel in blue nightgown, gold hat & wings, sits on white cloud w/Speak No Evil, 1958, Made in Japan, 4½"...**$25.00**

Figurine, Dutch girl in blue dress, #29, 5"..................**$25.00**

Figurine, lady in green skirt, #25, 9½"........................**$45.00**

Figurine, lady in rose dress w/blue & white apron, bucket on shoulder, blue hat, #19, 9¼" **$45.00**

Figurines, Male Alter Ego, tall man w/'So I Told the Boss,' short man w/'Have You Found a New Job Yet?,' 5", 3", pr **$40.00**

FIgurines, Oriental couple in red w/bowls on head, 9", pr **$30.00**

Flower holder, lady in white dress w/rose trim, green hat, #47, 7¼"..**$35.00**

Ice bucket, red & white vertical stripes, Ice in black, 6½", EX..**$60.00**

Letter holder, Our Mail, Merry Christmas, Santa & holly, wall mount, 6⅝x8¾x2"..**$35.00**

Salt & pepper shakers, clowns w/feet in the air, 1957, pr ..**$35.00**

Salt & pepper shakers, Dutch children, green & white costumes, 4", pr...**$35.00**

Auction Houses

Many of the auction galleries we've listed here have appraisal services. Some, though not all, are free of charge. We suggest you contact them first by phone to discuss fees and requirements.

American Social History and Social
Movements
P.O. Box 203
Tucker, GA 30085
www.ashsm.com; admin@ashsm.com;
678-937-1835; fax: 678-937-1837

Aston Macek Auctions
2825 Country Club Rd.
Endwell, NY 13760-3349
Phone or fax: 607-785-6598
Specializing in and appraisers of
Americana, folk art, other primitives,
furniture, fine glassware, and china

Bill Bertoia Auctions
2141 DeMarco Dr.
Vineland, NJ 08360
856-692-1881; fax: 856-692-8697
bill@bertoiaauctions.com
www: Bertoiaauctions.com
Online Auctions: Bertoiaonline.com
Specializing in antique toys and collectibles

Cincinnati Art Gallery
225 E. Sixth St.
Cincinnati, OH 45202
513-381-2128; fax: 513-381-7527
www.cincinnatiartgalleries.com
Specializing in American art pottery,
American and European fine paintings,
watercolors

Collectors Auction Services
RD 2, Box 431
Oil City, PA 16301
814-677-6070
www.caswel.com
Specializing in advertising, oil and gas,
toys, rare museum and investment-
quality antiques

David Rago
Auction hall: 333 N. Main St.
Lambertville, NJ 08530
609-397-7330; fax: 609-397-6790

rago@ragoarts.com
Gallery: 17 S Main St.
Lambertville, NJ 08530
Specializing in American art pottery
and Arts & Crafts

Early Auction Co.
123 Main St.
Milford, OH 45150
513-831-4833; fax: 513-831-4833
www.EarlyAuctionCo.com;
info@earlyaucitonco.com
Specializing in fine art glass, antique
furniture, and collectibles

Flying Deuce
1224 Yellowstone
Pocatello, ID 83201
208-237-2002; fax: 208-237-4544
www.flying2.com; flying2@nicoh.com
Specializing in vintage denim apparel; catalogs $10.00 for upcoming auctions; con-
tact for details on consigning items

Garth's Auctions, Inc.
2690 Stratford Rd.
Box 369,
Delaware, OH 43015
740-362-4771; fax: 740-363-0164
www.garth's.com; info@garths.com

Jackson's Auctioneers & Appraisers of
Fine Art & Antiques
2229 Lincoln Street
Cedar Falls, IA 50613
319-277-2256
jacksons@jacksonsauction.com;
www.jacksonsauctions.com
Specializing in American and European
art pottery and art glass, American and
European paintings, decorative arts,
toys, and jewelry

James D. Julia
P.O. Box 830, Rt. 201
Showhegan Rd.
Fairfield, ME 04937

207-453-7125; fax: 207-453-2502
www.juliaauctions.com;
jjulia@juliaauctions.com

Kerry and Judy's Toys
1414 S. Twelfth St.
Murray, KY 42071
502-759-3456
kjtoys@apex.com
Specializing in 1920s through 1960s toys;
consignments always welcomed

L.R. 'Les' Docks
Box 691035
San Antonio, TX 78269-1035
www.docks.home.texas.net
Providing occasional mail-order record
auctions, rarely consigned (the only consignments considered are exceptionally
scarce and unusual records)

Lloyd Ralston Gallery, Inc.
109 Glover Ave.
Norwalk, CT 06850
www.lloydralstontoys.com;
lrt@lloydralstontoys.com

Manion's International Auction House, Inc.
P.O. Box 12214
Kansas City, KS 66112
913-299-6692; fax: 913-299-6792
www.manions.com;
collecting@manions.com

Michael John Verlangieri
Calpots.com
PO Box 844, Cambria, CA 93428
805-927-4428.
www.calpots.com; michael1@calpots.com
Specializing in fine California pottery; cataloged auctions (video tapes available)

Monson & Baer, Annual Perfume Bottle
Auction
Monsen, Randall; and Baer, Rod
Box 529
Vienna, VA 22183

703-938-2129; fax: 703-242-1357
Cataloged auctions of perfume bottles;
will purchase, sell, and accept consign-
ments; specializing in commercial,
Czechoslovakian, Lalique, Baccarat,
Victorian, crown top, factices, miniatures

Noel Barrett Antiques & Auctions
P.O. Box 300
Carversville, PA 18913
215-297-5109; fax: 215-297-0457
www.noelbarrett.com

Richard Opfer Auctioneering, Inc.
1919 Greenspring Dr.
Timonium, MD 21093
410-252-5863
www.opferauction.com

Smith House
P.O. Box 336
Eliot, ME, 03903
207-439-4614; fax: 207-439-8554
smithtoys@aol.com;
www.smithousetoys.com
Specializing in toys

Toy Scouts Inc.
137 Casterton Ave.
Akron, OH 44303
330-836-0668; fax: 330-869-8668
toyscouts@toyscouts.com
www.toyscouts.com
Specializing in baby-boom era collectibles

Treadway Gallery Inc.
2029 Madison Rd.
Cincinnati, OH 45208
513-321-6742; fax: 513-871-7722
www.treadwaygallery.com
Member: National Antique Dealers
Association, American Art Pottery
Association, International Society of
Appraisers, and American Ceramic Arts
Society

Clubs and Newsletters

There are hundreds of clubs and newsletters mentioned throughout this book in their respective categories. There are many more available to collectors today; some are generalized and cover the entire realm of antiques and collectibles, while others are devoted to a specific interest such as toys, coin-operated machines, char-acter collectibles, or railroadiana. We've listed several below. You can obtain a copy of most newsletters simply by requesting one. If you'd like to try placing a 'for-sale' ad or a mail bid in one of them, see the introduction for suggestions on how your ad should be composed.

Akro Agate Collectors Club., Inc.
Clarksburg Crow (The Crow) newsletter
Roger and Claudia Hardy
10 Bailey Street, Clarksburg, WV 26301-2524;
rhardy0424@aol.com
Dues: $25.00; Canadian or Foreign, $35.00.
US checks or money orders only

America's Most Wanted To Buy
P.O. Box 171707, Little Rock, AR 72222
501-660-4030; fax 501-614-8810
AMWCI@aol.com
http://kaleden.com/publications/1.html

American Matchcover Collecting Club
(AMCC)
PO Box 18481
Asheville, NC 28814
828-254-4487; fax: 828-254-1066;
bill@matchcovers.com
www.matchcovers.com

Dues $10 yearly +$3 registration fee for
first year, includes *Front Striker Bulletin*.
Also available: *Matchcover Collector's
Price Guide*, 2nd edition, $25.20+$3.25
shipping and handling

Antique Advertising Association of
America (AAAA)
PO Box 1121
Morton Grove, IL 60053
708-446-0904
Also *Past Times* newsletter for collec-
tors of popular and antique advertis-
ing. Subscription: $35 per year

Antique and Collectors Reproduction News
Mark Chervenka, Editor
PO Box 12130
Des Moines, IA 50312-9403
800-227-5531 (subscriptions only)
fax: 501-614-8810, acrn@repronews.com

Monthly newsletter showing differences between old originals and new
reproductions. Subscription: $32 per
year

Antique Journal
Michael F. Shores, Publisher
Jeffery Hill Editor/General Manager
2329 Santa Clara Ave. #207
Alameda, CA 94501
800-791-8592

The Antique Trader Weekly
P.O. Box 1050 CB
Dubuque, IA 52003-1050
563-588-2073; fax: 800-531-0880
www.collect.com
Subscription: $38 (52 issues) per year

Antique Week
P.O. Box 90, 27 N. Jefferson

Knightstown, IN 46148
800-876-5133 or 765-345-5133;
fax: 800-695-8153; login@tias.com
www.tias.com/mags/antiqueweek
Weekly newspaper for auctions, antique
shows, antiques, collectibles and flea
markets. Subscription: $37.75 per year

The Bicycle Trader Newsletter
858 Stanyan St.
San Francisco, CA 94117
415-876-4545; fax: 415-876-4507
info@bicycletrader.com
www.bicycletrader.com

The Carnival Pump
International Carnival Glass Assoc., Inc.
Carl Booker
944 West Pine St.,
Griffith, IN 46319

Cast Iron Marketplace
P.O. Box 16466
St. Paul, MN 55116
Subscription $30 per year, includes free ads up to 200 words per issue

Coin-Op Newsletter
Ken Durham, Publisher
909 26th St., NW; Suite 502
Washington, DC 20037
www.GameRoom.Antiques.com
Free e-mail newsletter available; send your e-mail address to durham@GameRoomAntiques.com

Compact Collectors Club
Roselyn Gerson
PO Box 40, Lynbrook, NY 11563; 516-593-8746; fax: 516-593-0610; compactlady@aol.com. Publishes *Powder Puff* Newsletter, which contains articles covering all aspects of compact collecting, restoration, vintage ads, patents, history, and articles by members and prominent guest writers; Seeker and sellers column offered free to members

Dorothy Kamm's Porcelain Collector's Companion
P.O. Box 7460
Port St. Lucie, FL 34985-7460
561-465-4008; fax: 561-460-9050; dorothy.kamm@usa.net
Published bimonthly, Subscription: $30 per year

Dragonware Club
c/o Suzi Hibbard
849 Vintage Ave.
Fairfield, CA 94585
Dragon_Ware@hotmail.com
www.Dragonware.com
Information requires long SASE

Early Typewriter Collectors Association
ETCetera Newsletter
Chuck Dilts/Rich Cincotta
PO Box 286
Southboro, MA 01772
etcetera@writeme.com
http://typewriter.rydia.net/etcetera.htm
Subscription: $25 in USA (4 issues)

Grandpa's Depot
John Grandpa White
6720 E. Mississippi Ave., Unit B,
Denver, CO 80224
303-758-8540; fax: 303-321-2889
Publishes catalogs on railroad-related collectibles

International Golliwog Collector Club
Beth Savino
PO Box 798
Holland, OH 43528
1-800-862-TOYS; fax: 419-473-3947
toystore.net

International Ivory Society
11109 Nicholas Dr.
Wheaton, MD 20902
301-649-4002
Membership is free

International Match Safe Association
PO Box 791
Malaga, NJ 08328
856-694-4167
email: IMSAoc@aol.com;
www.matchsafe.org
Quarterly newsletter and annual convention

National Bicycle History Archive
Box 28242
Santa Ana, CA 92799
714-647-1949
Oldbicycle@aol.com
www.members.aol.com/oldbicycle
Resource for vintage and classic cycles from 1920 to 1970. Collection of over 1,000 classic bicycles. Over 30,000 original catalogs, books, photos. Also over 100 original old bicycle films 1930s – 70s. Restoration and purchase

Newspaper Collectors Society of America
517-887-1255
info@historybuff.com;
www.historybuff.com
Publishes booklet with current values and pertinent information

Nutcracker Collectors' Club
Susan Otto, Editor
11204 Fox Run Dr.

Chesterland, OH 44026; $15.00 annual dues, quarterly newsletters sent to members, free classifieds

Old Stuff
Donna and Ron Miller, Publishers
P.O. Box 1084
McMinnville, OR 97128
www.oldstuffnews.com
Published 6 times annually; Copies by mail: $3.50 each; Annual subscription: $20

Paper Collectors' Marketplace
470 Main St.
P.O. Box 128
Scandinavia, WI 54977-0128
715-467-2379; fax: 715-467-2243
pcmpaper.com
Subscription: $19.95 (12 issues) per year in USA; Canada and Mexico add $15 per year

Paperweight Collectors Association, Inc.
PMB 130
274 Eastchester Dr. #117
High Point, NC 27262

Paper Pile Quarterly
P.O. Box 337
San Anselmo, CA 94979-0337
415-454-5552;
www.paperpilecollectibles.com
Subscription: $20 per year in USA and Canada

Southern Oregon Antiques and Collectibles Club
P.O. Box 508
Talent, OR 97540
Meets 1st Wednesday of the month; Promotes 2 shows a year in Medford, OR
www.soacc.com; contact@soacc.com

Stanley Tool Collector News
c/o The Old Tool Shop
208 Front St.
Marietta, OH 45750
Features articles of interest, auction results, price trends, classified ads, etc.; Subscription: $20 per year; Sample: $6.95
www.stanleytoolcollector.com

Statue of Liberty Collectors' Club
Iris November

P.O. Box 535
Chautauqua, NY 14722
216-831-2646

Table Toppers
1340 West Irving Park Rd.
P.O. Box 161
Chicago, IL 60614
312-769-3184
Membership $19 (single) per year, includes *Table Topic*, a bimonthly newsletter for those interested in table-top collectibles

Thimble Collectors International
Kay Conners, membership chairperson
3230 E. Upper Haden Lake Rd.
Hayden, ID 83835
Membership: $25 U.S. ($30 international)
www.thimblecollectors.com

Three Rivers Depression Era Glass Society
Meetings held 1st Monday of each month at DeMartino's Restaurant, Carnegie, PA
For more information call:
D. Hennen
3725 Sylvan Rd.
Bethel Park, PA 15102
412-835-1903; leasure@pulsenet.com
412-831-2702

Tiffin Glass Collectors
P.O. Box 554
Tiffin, OH 44883
Meetings at Seneca Cty. Museum on 2nd Tuesday of each month
www.tiffinglass.org

The Trick or Treat Trader
P.O. Box 499, Winchester, NH 03470
4 issues: $15 (USA) or $20 (International)

The Wheelmen
Magazine: *Wheelmen Magazine*
63 Stonebridge Road
Allen Park, NJ 07042-1631
609-587-6487; hochne@aol.com
www.thewheelmen.org
A club with about 800 members dedicated to the enjoyment and preservation of our bicycle heritage

Special Interests

In this section of the book we have listed hundreds of dealers/collectors who specialize in many of the fields this price guide covers. Many of them have sent information, photographs, or advised us concerning current values and trends. This is a courtesy listing, and they are under no obligation to field questions from our readers, though some may be willing to do so. If you do write to any of them, don't expect a response unless you include an SASE (stamped self-addressed envelope) with your letter. If you have items to offer them for sale or are seeking information, describe the piece in question thoroughly and mention any marks. You can sometimes do a pencil rubbing to duplicate the mark exactly. Photographs are still worth a 'thousand words,' and photocopies are especially good for paper goods, patterned dinnerware, or even smaller three-dimensional items.

It's a good idea to include your phone number if you write, since many people would rather respond with a call than a letter. And suggesting that they call back collect might very well be the courtesy that results in a successful transaction. If you're trying to reach someone by phone, always stop to consider the local time on the other end of your call. Even the most cordial person when dragged out of bed in the middle of the night will very likely *not* be receptive to you.

With the exception of the Advertising, Books, Bottles, Character Collectibles, and Toys sections which we've alphabetized by character or type, buyers are listed alphabetically under bold topics. A line in italics indicates only the specialized interests of the particular buyer whose name immediately follows it. Recommended reference guides not available from Collector Books may be purchased directly from the authors whose addresses are given in this section.

Abingdon Pottery
Louise Dumont
318 Palo Verde Dr.
Leesburg, FL 34748-8811 (Summer: 103 Arnolds Neck Dr., Warwick, RI 02886)

Advertising
Aunt Jemima
Judy Posner
P.O. Box 2194 SC
Englewood, FL 34295
www.judyposner.com

941-475-1725
judyposner@yahoo.com

Big Boy
Steve Soelberg
29126 Laro Dr.
Agoura Hills, CA 91301
818-889-9909

Campbell's Soup
Author of book
Dave Young

414 Country Ln. Ct.
Wauconda, IL 60084
847-487-4917

Cereal boxes and premiums
Dan Goodsell
P.O. Box 48021
Los Angeles, CA 90048
323-930-0763

Jewel Tea products and tins
Bill and Judy Vroman

739 Eastern Ave.
Fostoria, OH 44830
419-435-5443

Mr. Peanut
Judith and Robert Walthall
P.O. Box 4465
Huntsville, AL 35815
256-881-9198
Also Old Crow memorabilia

Watches
Editor of newsletter: The Premium
Watch Watch©
Sharon Iranpour
24 San Rafel Dr.
Rochester, NY 14618-3702
585-381-9467; fax: 585-383-9248
watcher1@rochester.rr.com

Airline Memorabilia
Richard Wallin
P.O. Box 1784
Springfield, IL 62705
217-498-9279: RRWALLIN@aol.com

Akro Agate
Author of book
Claudia and Roger Hardy
West End Antiques
97 Milford St.
Clarksburg, WV 26301-2524
304-624-7600
Closed Mondays; specializing in furniture, glass & Akro
Order from the authors: *Complete Line of Akro Agate* (with prices), 1992. Pictures all pieces, $20.00 plus $3.50 priority mail. *Akro Agate Price Guide*, revised 2nd edition, price updates 1998 (corresponds with first book), $10.00 plus $3.50 priority, or both books $30.00 plus $3.95 priority mail

Aluminum
Author of book
Dannie Woodard
P.O. Box 1346
Weatherford, TX 76086

Animal Dishes
Author of book
Everett Grist
P.O. Box 91375
Chattanooga, TN 37412-3955
423-510-8052
Has authored books on aluminum, advertising playing cards, letter openers, and marbles

Appliances
Jim Barker
Toaster Master General
P.O. Box 746
Allentown, PA 18105

Aprons
Darrell Thomas
PO Box 7131
Appleton, WI 54912-7068

Ashtrays
Author of book
Nancy Wanvig
Nancy's Collectibles
P.O. Box 12
Thiensville, WI 53092

Autographs
Don and Anne Kier
2022 Marengo St.
Toledo, OH 43614
419-385-8211; d.a.k.@worldnet.att.net

Automobilia
Leonard Needham
118 Warwick Dr. #48
Benicia, CA 94510
www.tias.com/stores/macadams;
707-748-4286

Tire ashtrays
Author of book ($12.95 postpaid)
Jeff McVey
1810 W State St., #427
Boise, ID 83702

Autumn Leaf
Gwynneth Harrison
P.O. Box 1
Mira Loma, CA 91752-0001
909-685-5434; morgan99@pe.net

Avon Collectibles
Author of book
Bud Hastin
P.O. Box 11530
Ft. Lauderdale, FL 33339

Banks
Modern mechanical banks
Dan Iannotti
212 W Hickory Grove Rd.
Bloomfield Hills, MI 48302-1127S
248-335-5042;
modernbanks@ameritech.net

Barware
Especially cocktail shakers
Arlene Lederman Antiques
150 Main St.
Nyack, NY 10960

Specializing in vintage cocktail
shakers
Author of book
Stephen Visakay
P.O. Box 1517
W Caldwell, NJ 07707-1517

Bauer
Co-authors of Collector's Compass:
20th Centry Dinnerware
(Martingale Press)
Michele and Frank Miele
Home Grown Antiques
7 First Ave. E. #9
Kalispell, MT 59901
406-756-7259
info@homegrownantiques.com
Specializing in American dinnerware, glassware, and pottery, with special emphasis on California dinnerware. Selling on the Internet since 1997 at www.homegrownantiques.com

Beanie Babies
Amy Sullivan
c/o Collector Books
P.O. Box 3009
Paducah, KY 42002-3009

Beatnik and Hippie Collectibles
Richard M. Synchef
208 Summit Dr.
Corte Madera, CA 94925
415-927-8844
Also Peter Max

Bicycles and Tricycles
Consultant, collector, dealer
Lorne Shields
Box 211
Chagrin Falls, OH 44022-0211
440-247-5632; fax: 905-886-7748
vintage@globalserve.net
Alternate address: P.O. Box 87588
300 John St. Post Office
Thornhill, Ontario, Canada L3T 7R3

Black Americana
Buy, sell and trade
Judy Posner
P.O. Box 2194 SC
Englewood, FL 43295
www.tias.com/stores/jpc
judyposner@yahoo.com
Also toys, Disney, salt and pepper shakers, general line

Black Glass
Author of book
Marlena Toohey
703 S Pratt Pky.
Longmont, CO 80501
303-678-9726

Bobbin' Heads by Hartland
Author of guide; newsletter
Tim Hunter
4301 W. Hidden Valley Dr.
Reno, NV 89502
702-626-5029

Bookends
Author of book
Louis Kuritzky
4510 NW 17th Pl.
Gainesville, FL 32605
352-377-3193

Books
Big Little Books
Ron and Donna Donnelly
6302 Championship Dr.
Tuscaloosa, AL 35405

Bottle Openers
Charlie Reynolds
2836 Monroe St.
Falls Church, VA 22042
703-533-1322
reynoldstoys@erols.com

Bottles
Dairy and Milk
John Shaw
2201 Scenic Ridge Court
Mt. Flora, FL 32757 (Nov-May)
352-735-3831
43 Ridgecrest Dr.
Wilton, ME 04294 (June-Oct)
207-645-2442

Breyer
Felicia Browell
123 Hooks Lane
Cannonsburg, PA 15317
fbrowell@nauticom.net

British Royal Commemoratives
Author of book, Catalogs issued monthly,
$5 each
Audrey Zeder
1320 SW 10th St
North Bend, WA 98045
Specializing in British Royalty Commemoratives from Queen Victoria's reign through current royalty events

Brush-McCoy Pottery
Authors of book
Steve and Martha Sanford
230 Harrison Ave.
Campbell, CA 95008
408-978-8408

Bubble Bath Containers
Matt and Lisa Adams
8155 Brooks Dr.

Jacksonville, FL 32244
904-772-6911
beatles@bellsouth.net

Cake Toppers
Jeannie Greenfield
310 Parker Rd.
Stoneboro, PA 16153-2810
724-376-2584

Calculators
Author of book
Guy Ball
14561 Livingston St.
Tustin, CA 92780
www.mrcalc@usa.net

California Perfume Company
Not common; especially items marked
Goetting Co.
Dick Pardini
3107 N El Dorado St., Dept. G
Stockton, CA 95204-3412
Also Savoi Et Cie, Hinze Ambrosia, Gertrude Recordon, Marvel Electric Silver Cleaner, and Easy Day Automatic Clothes Washer

Specializing in California pottery and
porcelain; Orientalia
Marty Webster
6943 Suncrest Drive
Saline, Michigan 48176
313-944-1188

Editor of newsletter: The California
Pottery Trader
Michael John Verlangieri Gallery
Calpots.com
P.O. Box 844
W Cambria, CA 93428-0844
805-927-4428. Specializing in fine California pottery; cataloged auctions (video tapes available); www.calpots.com

Camark
Tony Freyaldenhoven
P.O. Box 1295
Conway, AR 72033

Cameras
Classic, collectible, and usable
C.E. Cataldo
Gene's Cameras
4726 Panorama Dr. SE
Huntsville, Alabama 35801
256-536-6843; MtSano@aol.com

Wooden, detective, and stereo
John A. Hess
P.O. Box 3062
Andover, MA 01810
Also old brass lenses

Candy Containers
Glass
Jeff Bradfield
90 Main St.
Dayton, VA 22821
540-879-9961
Also advertising, cast-iron and tin toys, postcards and Coca-Cola

Author of book
Doug Dezso
864 Paterson Ave.
Maywood, NJ 07607
Other interests: Tonka Toys, Shafford black cats, German bisque comic character nodders, Royal Bayreuth creamers, and Pep pins

Cape Cod by Avon
Debbie and Randy Coe
2459 SE TV Hwy PMB #321
Hillsboro, OR 97123-7919
Also Elegant and Depression glass,
art pottery, Fenton, Golden Foliage
by Libbey Glass Company, and
Liberty Blue dinnerware
Authors of *Elegant Glass; Liberty Blue*
Dinnerware; Glass Animals and
Figurines; Avon's Cape Cod

Carnival Chalkware
Author of book
Thomas G. Morris
P.O. Box 8307
Medford, OR 97504-0307
chalkman@cdsnet.net

Cast Iron
Door knockers, sprinklers, figural
paperweights and marked cook-
ware
Craig Dinner
P.O. Box 4399
Sunnyside, NY 11104
718-729-3850
ferrouswheel123@aol.com

Cat Collectibles
Karen Shanks
P.O. Box 150784
Nashville, TN 37215
615-297-7403 or
www.catcollectors.com
musiccitykitty@yahoo.com

Ceramic Arts Studio
BA Wellman
P.O. Box 673
Westminster, MA 01473
ba@dishinitout.com
Also most areas of American clay
products

Character and Personality
Collectibles
Author of books
Dealers, publishers, and appraisers of
collectible memorabilia from the
'50s through today
Bill Bruegman
Toy Scouts, Inc.
137 Casterton Ave.
Akron, OH 44303
330-836-0668; fax: 330-869-8668
toyscouts@toyscouts.com
www.toyscouts.com

Any and all
Terri Ivers
Terri's Toys
114 Whitworth Ave.
Ponca City, OK 74601
580-762-8697 or 580-762-5174
toylady@cableone.net

Batman, Gumby, and Marilyn Monroe
Colleen Garmon Barnes
114 E Locust
Chatham, IL 62629

Beatles
Bojo
Bob Gottuso
P.O. Box 1403
Cranberry Twp., PA 16066-0403
Phone or fax: 724-776-0621
www.bojoonline.com;
bojo@zbzoom.net; we do Rock 'n
Roll pricing for all of Schroeder's

guides; specializing in Beatles, KISS,
Monkees, and Elvis original licensed
memorabilia. Beatles sale catalog
available 4X a year, send $3 for
copy

California Raisins
Ken Clee
Box 11412
Philadelphia, PA 1911
215-722-1979

California Raisins
Larry De Angelo
516 King Arthur Dr.
Virginia Beach, VA 23464
757-424-1691

Disney, Western heroes, Gone With
the Wind, character watches ca
1930s to mid-1950s, premiums,
and games
Ron and Donna Donnelly
6302 Championship Dr.
Tuscaloosa, AL 35405

Disney
Buy, sell, and trade
Judy Posner
P.O. Box 2194 SC
Englewood, FL 34295
judyposner@yahoo.com

Elvis Presley
Author of book
Rosalind Cranor
P.O. Box 859
Blacksburg, VA 24063

Elvis Presley
Lee Garmon
1529 Whittier St.
Springfield, IL 62704

Character and Promotional
Drinking Glasses
Authors of book; editors of Collector
Glass News
Mark Chase and Michael Kelly
P.O. Box 308
Slippery Rock, PA 16057
412-946-2838; fax: 724-946-9012
cgn@glassnews.com
www.glassnews.com

Character Clocks and Watches
Bill Campbell
1221 Littlebrook Ln.
Birmingham, AL 35235
205-853-8227; fax: 405-658-6986
Also Character Collectibles,
Advertising Premiums

Character Nodders
Matt and Lisa Adams
8155 Brooks Dr.
Jacksonville, FL 32244
904-772-6911
beatles@bellsouth.net

Chintz
Mary Jane Hastings
310 West 1st South
Mt. Olive, IL 62069
Phone or fax: 217-999-1222

Author of book
Joan Welsh
7015 Partridge Pl.
Hyattsville, MD 20782
301-779-6181

Christmas Collectibles
Especially from before 1920 and
decorations made in Germany
J.W. 'Bill' and Treva Courter
3935 Kelley Rd.
Kevil, KY 42053
Phone: 270-488-2116; fax: 270-488-2055

Clocks
All types
Bruce A. Austin
1 Hardwood Hill Rd.
Pittsford, NY 14534
716-387-9820

Clothes Sprinkler Bottles
Ellen Bercovici
5118 Hampden Ln.
Bethesda, MD 20814
301-652-1140

Clothing and Accessories
Ken Weber
11744 Coral Hills Place
Dallas TX 75229
cecilimose@aol.com;
www.vintagemartini.com

Flying Deuce
1224 Yellowstone
Pocatello, ID 83201
208-237-2002; fax: 208-237-4544
flying2@nicoh.com; www.flying2.com

Coca-Cola
Also Pepsi-Cola and other brands
of soda
Craig Stifter
218 S. Adams St.
Hinsdale, IL 60521
630-789-5780
cstifter@ameritech.net

Coin-Operated Vending Machines
Ken and Jackie Durham
909 26th St., NW
Washington, D.C. 20037

Compacts
Unusual shapes, also vanities and
accessories
Author of book
Roselyn Gerson
P.O. Box 40
Lynbrook, NY 11563

Cookbooks
Author of book
Bob Allen
P.O. Box 56
St. James, MO 65559
Also advertising leaflets

Cookie Jars
Joe Devine
1411 3rd St.
Council Bluffs, IA 51503
712-323-5233 or 712-328-7305
Also Black Americana, salt and pepper shakers

Buy, sell, and trade
Judy Posner
P.O. Box 2194 SC
Englewood, FL 34295
judyposner@yahoo.com

Corkscrews
Author of books
Donald A. Bull
P.O. Box 596

Wirtz, VA 24184
540-721-1128;
www.corkscrewmuseum.com
corkscrew@bullworks.net

Cow Creamers
Shirley Green
1550 E. Kamm Ave. #116
Kingsburg, CA 93631
209-897-7125
granas@psnw.com

Cracker Jack Items
Phil Helley
Old Kilbourn Antiques
629 Indiana Ave.
Wisconsin Dells, WI 53965
Also sand pails, dexterity games, and
Cracker Jack

Wes Johnson, Sr.
106 Bauer Ave.
Louisville, KY 40207

Author of books
Larry White
108 Central St.
Rowley, MA 01969-1317
978-948-8187; larrydw@erols.com

Crackle Glass
Authors of book
Stan and Arlene Weitman
101 Cypress St.
Massapequa Park, NY 11758
516-799-2619; fax: 516-797-3039
Also specializing in Overshot

Cuff Links
National Cuff Link Society
Eugene R. Klompus
P.O. Box 5700
Vernon Hills, IL 60061
Phone or fax: 847-816-0035;
genek@cufflink.com
Also related items

Cups and Saucers
Authors of books
Jim and Susan Harran
208 Hemlock Dr.
Neptune, NJ 07753
www.tias.com/stores/amit

Dakins
Jim Rash
135 Alder Ave.
Egg Harbor Township, NJ 08234

Decanters
Homestead Collectibles
Art and Judy Turner
R.D. 2, Rte. 150
P.O. Box 173
Mill Hall, PA 17751
570-726-3597; fax: 717-726-4488

deLee
Authors of book
Joanne and Ralph Schaefer
3182 Williams Rd.
Oroville, CA 95965-8300
530-893-2902 or 530-894-6263
jschaefer@sunset.net

Dinnerware
Blair
Joe McManus
P.O. Box 153
Connelsville, PA 15425
jmcmanus@hhs.net

Blue Danube
Lori Simnioniw
Auburn Main St. Antiques
120 E. Main St.
Auburn, WA 98002
253-804-8041
Specializing in glassware, china, jewelry, and furniture

Blue Ridge
Author of several books
Bill and Betty Newbound
2206 Nob Hill Dr.
Sanford, NC 27330
Also milk glass, wall pockets, figural planters, collectible china and glass.

Cat-Tail
Ken and Barbara Brooks
4121 Gladstone Ln.
Charlotte, NC 28205

Currier & Ives Dinnerware
Author of book
Eldon R. Bud Aupperle
29470 Saxon Road
Toulon, IL 61483
309-896-3331; fax: 309-856-6005

Fiesta, Franciscan, Bauer, Harlequin, Riviera, Lu Ray, Metlox, and Homer Laughlin
Fiesta Plus
Mick and Lorna Chase
380 Hawkins Crawford Rd.
Cookeville, TN 38501
931-372-8333
fiestaplus@yahoo.com
www.fiestaplus.com

Homer Laughlin China
Author of book
Darlene Nossaman
5419 Lake Charles
Waco, TX 76710

Johnson Brothers
Author of book
Mary Finegan, Marfine Antiques
P.O. Box 3618
Boone, NC 28607
828-262-3441

Liberty Blue
Gary Beegle
92 River St.
Montgomery, NY 12549
914-457-3623
Also most lines of collectible modern American dinnerware as well as character glasses

Purinton Pottery
Joe McManus
P.O. Box 153
Connellsville, PA 15425
724-628-4409; jmcmanus@hhs.net
Also Blair

Author of book
Susan Morris
P.O. Box 158
Manchester, WA 98353
360-871-7376
d.s.morris@charter.net

Restaurant China
Author of books (Volume 1 and Volume 2)
Barbara J. Conroy
restaurantchina@attbi.com

http://members.attbi.com/
~restaurantchina/home.htm
(Lists contents and details of books and links to restaurant china sites)

Royal China
BA Wellman
P.O. Box 673
Westminster, MA 01473-0673
ba@dishinitout.com
Also Ceramic Arts Studio

Russel Wright, Eva Zeisel, Homer Laughlin
Charles Alexander
221 E 34th St.
Indianapolis, IN 46205
317-924-9665

Vernon Kilns
Author of book, Collectible Vernon Kilns, Second Edition
Maxine Nelson
7657 E. Hazelwood St.
Scottsdale, AZ 85251

Wallace China
Marv Fogleman
Marv's Memories
73 Waterman
Irvine, CA 92602
Specializing in American, English, and Western dinnerware

Watt Pottery
Author of book
Susan Morris
P.O. Box 158
Manchester, WA 98353
360-871-7376
d.s.morris@charter.net

Dollhouse Furniture and Accessories
Renwal, Ideal, Marx, etc.
Judith A. Mosholder
186 Pine Springs Camp Rd.
Boswell, PA 15531
814-629-9277; jlytwins@floodcity.net

Dolls
Annalee Mobilitee Dolls
Jane's Collectibles
Jane Holt
P.O. Box 115
Derry, NH 03038

Betsy McCall and friends
Marci Van Ausdall, Editor
P.O. Box 946
Quincy, CA 95971-0946
530-283-2770

Chatty Cathy and Mattel talkers
Authors of books
Don and Kathy Lewis
Whirlwind Unlimited
187 N Marcello Ave.
Thousand Oaks, CA 91360
805-499-8101
chatty@ix.netcom.com

Dolls from the 1960s – 70s, including Liddle Kiddles, Barbie, Tammy, Tressy, etc.
Co-author of book on Tammy, author of Collector's Guide to Dolls of the 1960s & 1970s
Cindy Sabulis
P.O. Box 642
Shelton, CT 06484
203-926-0176

Dolls from the 1960s – 70s, including Liddle Kiddles, Dolly Darlings, Petal People, Tiny Teens, etc.
Author of book on Liddle Kiddles; must send SASE for info
Paris Langford
415 Dodge Ave.
Jefferson, LA 70121
504-733-0676

Editor of newsletter: The Holly Hobbie Collectors Gazette
Donna Stultz
1455 Otterdale Mill Rd.
Taneytown, MD 21787-3032
410-775-2570
hhgazette@netscape.net

Liddle Kiddles and other small dolls from the late'60s and early '70s
Dawn Diaz
20460 Samual Dr.
Saugus, CA 91530-3812
661-263-TOYS

Door Knockers
Craig Dinner
Box 4399
Sunnyside, NY 11104
718-729-3850

Egg Cups
Author of book
Brenda Blake
Box 555
York Harbor, ME 03911
207-363-6566
eggcentric@aol.com

Egg Timers
Ellen Bercovici
5118 Hampden Ln.
Bethesda, MD 20814
301-652-1140

Jeannie Greenfield
310 Parker Rd.
Stoneboro, PA 16153-2810
724-376-2584

Roselle Schleifman
16 Vincent Rd.
Spring Valley, NY 10977

Erich Stauffer Figurines
Joan Oates
685 S. Washington
Constantine, MI 49042
269-435-8353
koates120@earthlink.net
Also Phoenix Bird china

Ertl Banks
Homestead Collectibles
P.O. Box 173
Mill Hall, PA 17751
Also decanters

Eyewinker
Sophia Talbert
921 Union St.
Covington, IN 47932
765-793-3256

Fast Food Collectibles
Author of book
Ken Clee
Box 1142
Philadelphia, PA 19111
215-722-1979

Authors of several books
Joyce and Terry Losonsky
7506 Summer Leave Lane
Columbia, MD 21046-2455
McDonald's® Collector's Guide to Happy Meal® Boxes, Premiums and Promotions ($9 plus $2 postage). *McDonald's ® Happy Meal® Toys in the USA* and *McDonald's® Happy Meal® Toys Around the World* (both full color, $24.95 each plus $3 postage), and *Illustrated Collector's Guide to McDonald's ® McCAPS®* ($4 plus $2 postage) are available from authors

Bill and Pat Poe
220 Dominica Cir. E
Niceville, FL 32578-4085
850-897-4163; fax: 850-897-2606
BPOE@cox.net
Also older McDonald's collectibles, Pez, Smurfs, and California Raisins

Fisher-Price
Author of book
Brad Cassity
2391 Hunters Trail
Myrtle Beach, SC 29579
843-236-8697

Fishing Collectibles
Publishes fixed-price catalog
Dave Hoover
1023 Skyview Dr.
New Albany, IN 47150
Also miniature boats and motors

Flashlights
Editor of newsletter
Bill Utley
P.O. Box 4095
Tustin, CA 92781
714-730-1252; fax: 714-505-4067

Florence Ceramics
Jerry Kline
Florence Showcase
P.O. Box 468
Bennington, VT 05201
802-442-3336; fax: 802-442-7354
Website: www.sweetpea.net;
sweetpea@sweetpea.net
Shop: 1265 South Route 7,
Bennington (2 miles south of downtown on US Rte 7), daily 10–5

John and Peggy Scott
4640 S Leroy
Springfield, MO 65810

Flower Frogs
Author of book
Bonnie Bull
Flower Frog Gazette Online
www.flowerfrog.com

Frankoma
Authors of book
Phyllis and Tom Bess
14535 E 13th St.
Tulsa, OK 74108

Fruit Jars
Especially old, odd or colored jars
John Hathaway
3 Mills Rd.
Bryant Pond, ME 04219
Also old jar lids and closures

Games
Paul Fink's Fun and Games
P.O. Box 488
59 S Kent Rd.
Kent, CT 06757
203-927-4001;
gamesandpuzzles@mohawk.net
www.gamesandpuzzles.com

Gas Station Collectibles
Scott Benjamin
Oil Co. Collectibles Inc.
Petroleum Collectibles Monthly Magazine
P.O. Box 556
LaGrange, OH 44050-0556
440-355-6608
Specializing in gas globes, signs, and
magazines

Gay Fad Glassware
Donna S. McGrady
P.O. Box 14, 301 E. Walnut St.
Waynetown, IN 47990
765-234-2187; dmcg@tctc.com

Geisha Girl China
Author of book
Elyce Litts
P.O. Box 394
Morris Plains, NJ 07950
happy-memories@worldnet.att.net
Also ladies' compacts

Glass Animals
Author of book
Lee Garmon
1529 Whittier St.
Springfield, IL 62704

Glass Shoes
Author of book
The Shoe Lady
Libby Yalom
P.O. Box 7146
Adelphi, MD 20783

Granite Ware
Author of books
Helen Greguire
864-457-7340
Also carnival glass and toasters

Griswold
Grant Windsor
P.O. Box 72606
Richmond, VA 23235-8017
804-320-0386

Guardian Service Cookware
Dennis S. McAdams
3110 E. Lancaster Rd.
Hayden Lake, ID 83835
HAYDENMAC4@aol.com

Guardian Service Cookware
2110 Harmony Woods Road
Owings Mills, MD 21117-1649
410-560-0777;
http://members.aol.com/vettelvr93/

Hagen-Renaker
Gayle Roller
P.O. Box 222
San Marcos, CA 92079-0222

Hallmark
The Baggage Car
3100 Justin Dr., Ste. B
Des Moines, IA 50322
515-270-9080

Halloween
*Author of books; autographed copies
available from the author*
Pamela E. Apkarian-Russell
Chris Russell & The Halloween
Queen Antiques
P.O. Box 499
Winchester, NH 03470
halloweenqueen@cheshire.net
adam.net/~halloweenqueen/home.html
Also other holidays, postcards, and
Joe Camel

Hartland Plastics, Inc.
Author of book
Gail Fitch
1733 N Cambridge Ave. #109
Milwaukee, WI 53202

*Specializing in Western Hartlands
Buy and sell; hold consignment
auctions specializing in vintage toys*
Kerry and Judy Irvin
Kerry and Judy's Toys
1414 S. Twelfth St.
Murray, KY 42071
270-759-3456; kjtoys@apex.net

Specializing in sports figures
James Watson
25 Gilmore St.
Whitehall, NY 12887

Head Vases
Larry G. Pogue
L&J Antiques & Collectibles
8142 Ivan Court
Terrell, TX 75161
972-551-0221; TIAS.com member
Also antique and estate jewelry

Horton Ceramics
Darlene Nossaman
5419 Lake Charles
Waco, TX 76710

Hull
Author of several books on Hull
Brenda Roberts
906 S. Ann Dr.
Marshall, MO 65340

Imperial Glass
Kathy Doub
5359 Iron Pen Place
Columbia, MD 21044
410-995-1254

Indiana Glass
Donna Adler
502 E. Birch St.
Shelton, WA 98584
360-426-5303
Donna's Place on the web:
http://dr54eagle.rubylane.com
Also Wedgwood, Mosser, Depression,
and more

Indy 500 Memorabilia
Eric Jungnickel
P.O. Box 4674
Naperville, IL 60567-4674
630-983-8339

Insulators
Jacqueline Linscott
3557 Nicklaus Dr.
Tutusville, FL 32780

Japan Ceramics
Author of books

Carole Bess White
P.O. Box 819
Portland, OR 97207

Jewel Tea
Products or boxes only; no dishes
Bill and Judy Vroman
739 Eastern Ave.
Fostoria, OH 44830
419-435-5443

Jewelry
Author of books
Marcia Brown (Sparkles)
P.O. Box 2314
White City, OR 97503
541-826-3039; fax: 541-830-5385
Author of *Unsigned Beauties of
Costume Jewelry* and *Signed Beauties
of Costume Jewelry*; co-author and
host of seven *Hidden Treasure* book-
on-tape videos; Antique shows:
Robby/Don Miller Appraisal Clinics,
Palmer Wirf Shows, Calender Shows

*Men's accessories and cuff links only;
edits newsletter*
The National Cuff Link Society
Eugene R. Klompus
P.O. Box 5700
Vernon Hills, IL 60061
Phone or fax: 847-816-0035

Josef Originals
Authors of books
Jim and Kaye Whitaker
Eclectic Antiques
P.O. Box 475, Dept. GS
Lynnwood, WA 98046

Kay Finch
*Co-Authors of book, available from
authors*
Mike Nickel and Cynthia Horvath
P.O. Box 456
Portland, MI 48875
517-647-7646
Also fine Ohio art pottery

Kentucky Derby and Horse Racing
Betty L. Hornback
707 Sunrise Ln.
Elizabethtown, KY 42701
betty'santiques@KVNET.org
Inquiries require a SASE with fee
expected for appraisals and/or identification of glasses. Booklet picturing
Kentucky Derby, Preakness, Belmont
and other racing glasses available for
$15 ppd.

Kitchen Prayer Ladies
*Issues price guide ($6.96 plus $1
postage and handling)*
April and Larry Tvorak
P.O. Box 493401
Leesburg, FL 34749-3401
Also interested in Enesco, Pyrex, and
figural ceramics

Lamps
Aladdin
Author of books
J.W. Courter
3935 Kelley Rd.
Kevil, KY 42053
502-488-2116

Motion lamps
Eclectic Antiques
Jim and Kaye Whitaker

P.O. Box 475, Dept. GS
Lynwood, WA 98046

Authors of book
Sam and Anna Samuelian
P.O. Box 504
Edgemont, PA 19028-0504
610-566-7248
Also motion clocks, transistor and
novelty radios

Lefton
Author of books
Loretta DeLozier
P.O. Box 50201
Knoxville, TN 37950-0201

Letter Openers
Author of book
Everett Grist
P.O. Box 91375
Chattanooga, TN 37412-3955
423-510-8052

License Plates
Richard Diehl
5965 W Colgate Pl.
Denver, CO 80227

Longaberger Baskets
*The **only** reference tool for
Consultants, Collectors, and
Enthusiasts of Longaberger Baskets®*
Jill S. Rindfuss, Editor
The Bentley Collection Guide ®
5870 Zarley Street, Suite C
New Albany, OH 43054
Monday through Friday, 9:00 a.m. —
5:00 p.m. (EST)
1-800-837-4394
www.bentleyguide.com;
info@bentlyguide.com
The most accurate and reliable reference
tool available for evaluating Longaberger
Products®. Full color with individual photographs of most baskets and products
produced since 1979. Published once a
year in June with a free six-month update
being sent in January to keep the guide
current for the entire year.

Holds exclusive auctions
Greg Michael
Craft & Michael Auction/Realty Inc.
P.O. Box 7
Camden, IN 46917
219-686-2615 or 219-967-4442
fax: 219-686-9100;
gpmmgtco@netusal1.net.

Lunch Boxes
Norman's Ole and New Store
Philip Norman
126 W Main St.
Washington, NC 27889-4944
252-946-3448

Terri's Toys and Nostalgia
Terri Ivers
206 E. Grand
Ponca City, OK 74601
580-762-8697 or 580-762-5174
fax: 405-765-2657;
toylady@poncacity.net

Magazines
*Issues price guides to illustrators, pin
ups, and old magazines of all kinds*
Denis C. Jackson
Illustrator Collector's News
P.O. Box 1958

Sequim, WA 98382
ticn@olypen.com
National Geographic
Author of guide
Don Smith's National Geographic
Magazines
3930 Rankin St.
Louisville, KY 40214
502-366-7504

Marbles
Author of books
Everett Grist
P.O. Box 91375
Chattanooga, TN 37412-3955
423-510-8052

Block's Box is the longest continuously
running absentee marble auction
service in the country; catalogs issued
Stanley A. & Robert S. Block
P.O. Box 51
Trumbull, CT 06611
203-261-3223 or 203-926-8448
bblock@well.com
pages.prodigy.com/marbles/mcc.html
Prodigy: BWVR62A

Match Safes
George Sparacio
P.O. Box 791
Malaga, NJ 08328
856-694-4167; fax:856-694-4536
mrvesta1@aol.com

McCoy Pottery
Author of books
Robert Hanson
16517 121 Ave. NE
Bothell, WA 98011

Melmac Dinnerware
Co-author of book
Gregg Zimmer
4017 16th Ave. S
Minneapolis, MN 55407

Metlox
Author of book; available from author
Carl Gibbs, Jr.
P.O. Box 131584
Houston, TX 77219-1584
www.ccdinnerware.com

Milk Bottles
John Shaw
2201 Scenic Ridge Court (Nov – May)
Mt. Flora, FL 32757
352-735-3831
43 Ridgecrest Dr.
Wilton, ME 04294 (June – Oct)
207-645-2442

Mood Indigo
David and Debbie Crouse
2140 Capitol Ave.
Des Moines, Iowa 50317
515-265-4880
Watch for website listing Mood
Indigo with numbers and pictures:
www.crouse.ws/inarco

Morton Pottery
Authors of books
Doris and Burdell Hall
B&B Antiques
210 W Sassafras Dr.
Morton, IL 61550-1245

Motion Clocks
Electric; buy, sell, trade and restore

Sam and Anna Samuelian
P.O. Box 504
Edgemont, PA 19028-0504
610-566-7248
Also motion lamps, transistor and
novelty radios

Motorcycles and Motorcycle
Memorabilia
Bob 'Sprocket' Eckardt
P.O. Box 172
Saratoga Springs, NY 12866
518-584-2405; sprocketBE@aol.com
Buying and trading; Also Literature,
posters, toys, trophies, medals, FOB's,
pennants, FAM - AMA & Gypsy Tour
items, programs, photos, jerseys,
clocks, advertising items, signs, show-
room items, motorcycles, and parts

Bruce Kiper
Ancient Age Motors
2205 Sunset Ln.
Lutz, FL 33549
813-949-9660
Also related items and clothing

Movie Posters
Movie Poster Service
Cleophas and Lou Ann Wooley
Box 517
Canton, OK 73724-0517
580-886-2248; fax: 580-886-2249
mpsposters@pldi.net
In business full time since 1972;
own/operate mail-order firm with
world's largest movie poster inventory

Napkin Dolls
Co-Author of book
Bobbie Zucker Bryson
1 St. Eleanoras Ln.
Tuckahoe, NY 10707
914-779-1405; napkindoll@aol.com
www.reamers.org
To order a copy of the second edition of *Collectibles for the Kitchen,
Bath & Beyond* (featuring 500+ new
items & updated pricing on napkin
dolls, egg timers, string holders, children's whistle cups and baby feeder
dishes, razor blade banks, pie birds,
laundry sprinkler bottles, and other
unique collectibles from the same
era), contact Krause Publications, PO
Box 5009, Iola, WI 54945-5009; 1-800-
258-0929

Orientalia and Dragonware
Suzi Hibbard
849 Vintage Ave.
Fairfield, CA 94585

Paper Dolls
Author of books
Mary Young
P.O. Box 9244
Wright Bros. Branch
Dayton, OH 45409

Pencil Sharpeners
Phil Helley
629 Indiana Ave.
Wisconsin Dells, WI 53965
608-254-8659

Advertising and figural
Martha Hughes
4128 Ingalls St.
San Diego, CA 92103
619-296-1866

Pennsbury
Joe Devine
1411 3rd St.
Council Bluffs, IA 51503
712-323-5322 or 712-328-7305

Shirley Graff
4515 Graff Rd.
Brunswick, OH 44212

Pepsi-Cola
Craig Stifter
218 S. Adams St.
Hinsdale, IL 60521
630-789-5780; cstifter@ameritech.net
Other soda-pop memorablia as well

Perfume Bottles
*Especially commercial, Czechoslovakian,
Lalique, Baccarat, Victorian, crown
top, factices, miniatures. Buy, sell,
and accept consignments for auctions*
Monsen and Baer
Box 529
Vienna, VA 22183
703-938-2129

Pez
Richard Belyski
P.O. Box 124
Sea Cliff, NY 11579
516-676-1183
peznews@juno.com

Pie Birds
Linda Fields
158 Bagsby Hill Lane
Dover, TN 37058
931-232-5099; Fpiebird@compu.net.
Organizer of Piebird Collector's
Convention and author of *Four &
Twenty Blackbirds;* Specializing in pie
birds, pie funnels, and pie vents

Pierce, Howard
Author of books
Darlene Dommel
P.O. Box 22493
Minneapolis, MN 55422-0493
763-374-9645
Specializing in Howard Pierce and
Dakota potteries

Pin-Back Buttons
Michael and Polly McQuillen
McQuillen's Collectibles
P.O. Box 50022
Indianapolis, IN 46250
317-845-1721;
michael@politicalparade.com
www.politicalparade.com

Pinup Art
*Issues price guides to pinups,
illustrations, and old magazines*
Denis C. Jackson
Illustrator Collector's News
P.O. Box 1958
Sequim, WA 98382
360-452-3810; fax: 360-683-9807
ticn@olypen.com

Pocket Calculators
Author of book
International Assn. of Calculator
Collectors
Guy D. Ball
P.O. Box 345
Tustin, CA 92781-0345
Phone or fax: 714-730-6140
mrcalc@usa.net

Political
Michael and Polly McQuillen
McQuillen's Collectibles
P.O. Box 50022
Indianapolis, IN 46250
317-845-1721;
mmcquillen@politicalparade.com
www.politicalparade.com

Before 1960
Michael Engel
29 Groveland St.
Easthampton, MA 01027

Pins, banners, ribbons, etc.
Paul Longo Americana
Box 5510
Magnolia, MA 01930
978-525-2290

Poodle Collectibles
Author of book
Elaine Butler
233 S Kingston Ave.
Rockwood, TN 37854

Porcelier
Jim Barker
Toaster Master General
P.O. Box 746
Allentown, PA 10106

Author of book
Susan Grindberg
1412 Pathfinder Rd.
Henderson, NV 89014
702-898-7535
porcelier@anv.net or
sue@porcelierconnection.com
www.porcelierconnection.com

Postcards
Pamela E. Apkarian-Russell
Chris Russell and the Halloween
Queen Antiques
P.O. Box 499
Winchester, NH 03470
halloweenqueen@cheshire.net;
adam.net/~halloweenqueen/home.html
Also Halloween and other holidays

Sharon Thoerner
15549 Ryon Ave.
Bellflower, CA 90706
562-866-1555
rthoerner@juno.com
Also slag glass

Puzzles
Wooden jigsaw type from before 1950
Bob Armstrong
15 Monadnock Rd.
Worcester, MA 01609

Radio Premiums
Bill Campbell
1221 Littlebrook Ln.
Birmingham, AL 35235
205-853-8227; fax: 405-658-6986

Radios
Author of book
Harry Poster
P.O. Box 1883
S Hackensack, NJ 07606
201-410-7525
Also televisions, related advertising
items, old tubes, cameras, 3-D view-
ers and projectors, View-Master and
Tru-View reels and accessories

Railroadiana
*Also steamship and other
transportation memorabilia*
Lila Shrader
Shrader Antiques
2025 Hwy. 199
Crescent City, CA 95531
707-458-3525
Also Buffalo, Shelley, Niloak, and
Hummels

Any item; especially china and silver
Catalogs available
John White, 'Grandpa'
Grandpa's Depot
6720 E. Mississippi Ave., Unit B
Denver, CO 80224-1850
303-300-3984; fax: 303-758-8540
Also related items

Razor Blade Banks
Debbie Gillham
47 Midline Ct.
Gaithersburg, MD 20878
301-977-5727

Reamers
*Co-author of book, ordering info
under Napkin Dolls*
Bobbie Zucker Bryson
1 St. Eleanoras Ln.
Tuckahoe, NY 10707
914-779-1405
napkindoll@aol.com
www.reamers.org

Records
Picture and 78 rpm kiddie records
Peter Muldavin
173 W 78th St. Apt 5-F
New York, NY 10024
212-362-9606
kiddie78s@aol.com

Especially 78 rpms, author of book
L.R. 'Les' Docks
Box 691035
San Antonio, TX 78269-1035
docks@texas.net; Write for want list

Red Wing
Authors of books
B.L. and R.L. Dollen
Dollen Books & Antiques
P.O. Box 386
Aboca, IA 51521-0386
Collector Book authors specializing in
Red Wing Art Pottery and Dinnerware

Red Wing Artware
Hold cataloged auctions
Wendy and Leo Frese
Three Rivers Collectibles
P.O. Box 551542
Dallas, TX 75355
214-341-5165
rumrill@ix.netcom.com

Regal China
Rick Spencer
Salt Lake City, UT
801-973-0805

Rooster and Roses
Jacki Elliott
9790 Twin Cities Rd.
Galt, CA 95632
209-745-3860

Rosemeade
NDSU research specialist

Bryce Farnsworth
1334 14½ St. S
Fargo, ND 58103
701-237-3597

Roseville
Mike Nickel
P.O. Box 456
Portland, MI, 48875
517-647-7646
Also Kay Finch, other Ohio art pot-
tery

Royal Bayreuth
Don and Anne Kier
2022 Marengo St.
Toledo, OH 43614
419-385-8211; d.a.k@worldnet.att.net

Royal Copley
Author of books
Joe Devine
1411 3rd St.
Council Bluffs, IA 51503
712-323-5233 or 712-328-7305
Buy, sell, or trade; Also pie birds

Royal Haeger
Author of book
David D. Dilley
Indianapolis, IN
317-251-0575
glazebears@aol.com or
bearpots@aol.com

RumRill
Hold cataloged auctions
Wendy and Leo Frese
Three Rivers Collectibles
P.O. Box 551542
Dallas, TX 75355
214-341-5165
rumrill@ix.netcom.com

Ruby Glass
Author of book
Naomi L. Over
8909 Sharon Ln.
Arvada, CO 80002
303-424-5922

Salt and Pepper Shakers
Figural or novelty
Buy, sell, and trade
Judy Posner
P.O. Box 2194 SC
Englewood, FL 34295
judyposner@yahoo.com

Sascha Brastoff
Lonnie Wells
Things From the Past
PO Box 2182
Rocklin, CA 95677
1997 Hunter Dr.
Rocklin, CA 95765
916-415-0454
thingsfromthepast@tias.com

Scouting Collectibles
*Author of book: A Guide to Scouting
by Collectibles With Values;
available sending $30.95
(includes postage)*
R.J. Sayers
P.O. Box 629
Brevard, NC 28712
Certified antiques appraiser; owner of
Southeastern Antiques & Collectibles,
305 N. Main St., Hendersonville, NC
28792

Sebastians
Jim Waite
112 N Main St.
Farmer City, IL 61842
800-842-2593

Sewing Machines
Toy only
Authors of book
Darryl and Roxana Matter
P.O. Box 65
Portis, KS 67474-0065

Shawnee
Authors of books
Beverly and Jim Mangus
5147 Broadway NE
Louisville, OH 44641

Rick Spencer
Salt Lake City, UT
801-973-0805

Shot Glasses
Author of book
Mark Pickvet
Shot Glass Club of America
5071 Watson Dr.
Flint, MI 48506

Silhouette Pictures (20th Century)
Author of book
Shirley Mace
Shadow Enterprises
P.O. Box 1602
Mesilla Park, NM 88047
505-524-6717; fax: 505-523-0940
shadow-ent@zianet.com
www.geocities.com/MadisonAvenue/
Boardroom/1631/

Silverplated and Sterling Flatware
Rick Spencer
Salt Lake City, UT
801-973-0805
Appraisals available at small cost

Skookum Indian Dolls
Jo Ann Palmieri
27 Pepper Rd.
Towaco, NJ 07082-1357

Soda Fountain Collectibles
Harold and Joyce Screen
2804 Munster Rd.
Baltimore, MD 21234
410-661-6765
hscreen@home.com

Soda-Pop Memorabilia
Craig Stifter
217 S. Adams St.
Hinsdale, IL 60521
630-789-5780 cstifter@ameritech.net

Sports Collectibles
Sporting goods
Kevin R. Bowman
P.O. Box 4500
Joplin, MO 64803
417-781-6418 (Mon through Fri after 5
pm CST, Sat and Sun after 10 am
CST); showmequail@joplin.com

Equipment and player-used items
Don and Anne Kier
2022 Marengo St.
Toledo, OH 43614
419-385-8211; d.a.k.@worldnet.att.net

Bobbin' head sports figures
Tim Hunter
4301 W Hidden Valley Dr.
Reno, NV 89502
702-856-4357; fax: 702-856-4354
thunter885@aol.com

Golf collectibles
Pat Romano
32 Sterling Dr.
Lake Grove, NY 11202-0017

St. Clair Glass
Ted Pruitt
3350 W 700 N
Anderson, IN 46011
Book available ($25)

Stangl
Birds, dinnerware, artware
Popkorn Antiques
Bob and Nancy Perzel
P.O. Box 1057
Flemington, NJ 08822
908-782-9631; popcorn@blast.net

Statue of Liberty
Mike Brooks
7335 Skyline
Oakland, CA 94611

String Holders
Larry G. Pogue
L&J Antiques & Collectibles
Terrell, TX 75161
972-551-0221; TIAS.com member

Swanky Swigs
Joyce Jackson
900 Jenkins Rd.
Aledo, TX 76008-2410
817-441-8864
jjpick3@earthlink.net

Teapots and Tea-Related Items
Author of book
Tina Carter
882 S Mollison
El Cajon, CA 92020

Tiara Exclusives
Author of Books
Mandi Birkinbine
P.O. Box 121
Meridian, ID 83680-0121
www.shop4antiques.com
tiara@shop4antiques.com
*Collecting Tiara Amber Sandwich
Glass, $15.95; Collecting Tiara
Bicentennial Blue Sandwich Glass,
$12.95; Collecting Tiara Chantilly
Green Sandwich Glass, $15.95; and
Collecting Tiara Sandwich Glass in
Peach and Spruce, $15.95a are all
available from author at above
address. Please allow four to six
weeks for delivery. Postage not
included.*

Tire Ashtrays
Author of book ($12.95 postpaid)
Jeff McVey
1810 W State St., #427
Boise, ID 83702-3955

Toothbrush Holders
Author of book
Marilyn Cooper
8408 Lofland Dr.
Houston, TX 77055-4811

Special Interests

Toys

Any and all
June Moon
1486 Miner Street
Des Plaines, IL 60016
847-294-0018
junmoonstr@aol.com;
www.junemooncollectibles.com

Aurora model kits, and especially toys from 1948 – 1972
Author of books; dealers, publishers and appraisers of collectible memorabilia from the '50s through today
Bill Bruegman
137 Casterton Dr.
Akron, OH 44303
330-836-0668; fax: 330-869-8668
www.toyscouts.com

Diecast vehicles
Mark Giles
P.O. Box 821
Ogallala, NE 69153-0821
308-284-4360

Fisher-Price pull toys and playsets up to 1986
Author of book; available from the author
Brad Cassity
2391 Hunters Trail
Myrtle Beach, SC 29579
843-236-8697

Hot Wheels
D.W. (Steve) Stephenson
11117 NE 164th Pl.
Bothell, WA 98011-4003

Model kits other than Aurora
Gordy Dutt
Box 201
Sharon Center, OH 42274-0201

Puppets and marionettes
Steven Meltzer
1255 2nd St.
Santa Monica, CA 90401
310-656-0483

Rings, character, celebrity, and souvenir
Bruce and Jan Thalberg
23 Mountain View Dr.
Weston, CT 06883-1317
203-227-8175

Sand toys
Authors of book
Carole and Richard Smyth
Carole Smyth Antiques
P.O. Box 2068
Huntington, NY 11743

Slot race cars from 1960s – 70s
Gary T. Pollastro
5047 84th Ave. SE
Mercer Island, WA 98040

Tin litho, paper on wood, comic character, penny toys and Schoenhut
Wes Johnson, Sr.
3606 Glenview Ave.
Glenville, KY 40025

Tops and spinning toys
Bruce Middleton
5 Lloyd Rd.
Newburgh, NY 12550
914-564-2556

Toy soldiers, figures, and playsets
The Phoenix Toy Soldier Co.
Bob Wilson
8912 E. Pinnacle Peak Rd.
PMB 552
Scotsdale, AZ 85225
480-699-5005 or toll free: 1-877-269-6074
fax: 480-699-7628
bob@phoenixtoysoldier.com
www.phoenixtoysoldier.com

Transformers and robots
David Kolodny-Nagy
Toy Hell
P.O. Box 75271
Los Angeles, CA 90075
toyhell@yahoo.com
www.angelfire.com/ca2/redpear

Walkers, ramp-walkers, and windups
Randy Welch
Raven'tiques
27965 Peach Orchard Rd.
Easton, MD 21601-8203
410-822-5441

Trolls
Author of book
Pat Peterson
1105 6th Ave. SE
Hampton, IA 50441-2657
SASE for information

TV Guides
Giant illustrated 1948-1999 TV Guide Catalog, $3.00; 2000+ catalog, $2.00
TV Guide Specialists
Jeff Kadet
P.O. Box 20
Macomb, IL 61455

Twin Winton
Author of book; now out of print
Mike Ellis
266 Rose Ln.
Costa Mesa, CA 92627
949-646-7112; fax: 949-645-4919
TwinWinton.com

Valentines
Author of books, available from author; fee charged for appraisal
Katherine Kreider
Kingsbury Antiques
P.O. Box 7957
Lancaster, PA 17604-7957
717-892-3001
Kingsbry@aol.com

Vallona Starr
Author of book
Bernice Stamper
7516 Eloy Ave.
Bakersfield, CA 93308-7701
805-393-2900

Vandor
Lois Wildman
175 E. Chick Rd.
Camano Island, WA 98282

Viking
Mary Lou Bohl
1156 Apple Blossom Dr.
Neenah, WI 54956

Wade
Author of book
Ian Warner
P.O. Box 93022
Brampton, Ontario
Canada L6Y 4V8
idwarner@home.com

Western Collectibles
Author of book
Warren R. Anderson
American West Archives
P.O. Box 100
Cedar City, UT 84721

435-586-9497
Also documents, autographs, stocks and bonds, and other ephemera

Author of books
Dan Hutchins
Hutchins Publishing Co.
P.O. Box 25040
Colorado Springs, CO 80936
719-572-1331
Also makers of horse-drawn vehicles;
Author of *Old Cowboy Saddles & Spurs*, Volumes 1, 2, 3, 4, 5, and 6;
and *Cowboy Collectilbes, Auction Update & Price Guide*

Western Heroes
Author of books, ardent researcher, and guest columnist
Robert W. Phillips
Phillips Archives of Western Memorabilia
1703 N Aster Pl.
Broken Arrow, OK 74012-1308
918-254-8205; fax: 918-252-9363

Westmoreland
Cheryl Schafer
RR 2, Box 37
Lancaster, MO 63548
660-457-3510; cschafer@atlantic.net
Winter address (November 1 – May 1)
P.O. Box 1443
Webster, FL 33597
352-568-7383

Wilton Pans
Cheryl Moody
Hoosier Collectibles
607 N. Lafayette Blvd.
South Bend, IN 46601
www.hoosiercollectibles.com

World's Fairs and Expositions
Herbert Rolfes
Yesterday's World
P.O. Box 398
Mount Dora, FL 32756
352-735-3947
NY1939@aol.com

Index

Index